CHILDREN

CHILDREN

JOHN W. SANTROCK
University of Texas at Dallas

wcb
WM. C. BROWN PUBLISHERS
DUBUQUE, IOWA

Book Team

Editor *James M. McNeil*
Developmental Editor *Sandra E. Schmidt*
Production Editor *Vickie Putman Caughron*
Designer *David C. Lansdon*
Permissions Editor *Mavis M. Oeth*
Photo Research Editor *Michelle Oberhoffer*
Visuals Processor *Joyce Watters*

wcb group

Chairman of the Board *Wm. C. Brown*
President and Chief Executive Officer *Mark C. Falb*

wcb

Wm. C. Brown Publishers, College Division

Executive Vice-President, General Manager *G. Franklin Lewis*
Editor in Chief *George Wm. Bergquist*
Director of Production *Beverly Kolz*
National Sales Manager *Bob McLaughlin*
Marketing Research Manager *Craig S. Marty*
Production Editorial Manager *Colleen A. Yonda*
Manager of Design *Marilyn A. Phelps*
Photo Research Manager *Faye M. Schilling*

Cover photo courtesy of Northern Telecom. Photographer JoAnn Carney.

The credits section for this book begins on page 673 and is considered an extension of the copyright page.

Library of Congress Catalog Card Number: 87–70073

ISBN 0–697–01220–4

Printed in the United States of America by Wm. C. Brown Publishers
2460 Kerper Boulevard, Dubuque, IA 52001

10 9 8 7 6 5 4 3 2 1

BRIEF CONTENTS

SECTION 1 THE SCIENCE OF CHILD DEVELOPMENT

CHAPTER 1   HISTORY, ISSUES, AND METHODS 4

CHAPTER 2   THEORIES 38

SECTION 2 BIOLOGICAL FOUNDATIONS AND INFANCY

CHAPTER 3   THE EVOLUTIONARY PERSPECTIVE, GENETICS, PRENATAL DEVELOPMENT, AND THE BIRTH PROCESS 82

CHAPTER 4   PHYSICAL AND PERCEPTUAL MOTOR DEVELOPMENT OF INFANTS 122

CHAPTER 5   LEARNING, COGNITION, AND LANGUAGE IN INFANCY 158

CHAPTER 6   SOCIAL AND PERSONALITY FOUNDATIONS AND DEVELOPMENT IN INFANCY 204

SECTION 3 EARLY CHILDHOOD

CHAPTER 7   PHYSICAL AND COGNITIVE
                 DEVELOPMENT IN EARLY
                 CHILDHOOD 254

CHAPTER 8   SOCIAL AND PERSONALITY
                 DEVELOPMENT IN EARLY
                 CHILDHOOD 298

SECTION 4 MIDDLE AND LATE CHILDHOOD

CHAPTER 9   PHYSICAL AND COGNITIVE
                 DEVELOPMENT IN MIDDLE AND
                 LATE CHILDHOOD 346

CHAPTER 10   INTELLIGENCE AND
                 ACHIEVEMENT 386

CHAPTER 11   SOCIAL AND PERSONALITY
                 DEVELOPMENT IN MIDDLE AND
                 LATE CHILDHOOD 438

SECTION 5 ADOLESCENCE

CHAPTER 12   PHYSICAL AND COGNITIVE
                 DEVELOPMENT IN ADOLESCENCE
                 500

CHAPTER 13   SOCIAL DEVELOPMENT IN
                 ADOLESCENCE 542

CHAPTER 14   PERSONALITY DEVELOPMENT IN
                 ADOLESCENCE 580

CONTENTS

CHILD DEVELOPMENT CONCEPT TABLES xxiii
FOCUS ON CHILD DEVELOPMENT BOXES xxv
PREFACE xxix

SECTION 1 THE SCIENCE OF CHILD DEVELOPMENT

CHAPTER 1 HISTORY, ISSUES, AND METHODS 4

IMAGINE . . . YOU ARE A CHILD PSYCHOLOGIST OBSERVING AN
  11-MONTH-OLD GIRL, LISTENING TO A 3-YEAR-OLD BOY, AND
  INTERVIEWING A 12-YEAR-OLD GIRL AND HER PARENTS 6
PREVIEW 7
CHILD DEVELOPMENT IN CONTEMPORARY SOCIETY 7
Divorce, Working Mothers, and Latchkey Children 7
Computers and Children 8
Hurried Children, Type A Behavior Pattern, and Children's Health 8

CHILD DEVELOPMENT AND HISTORY 9
Historical Accounts of Childhood 9
    Ancient Greece and Rome 10
    The Middle Ages 10
    The Renaissance 11
The Scientific Beginnings of Child Development 11
    Late 19th-Century Research 11
    Twentieth-Century Research 11
    Sociopolitical Influences on the Study of Child Development 13
Contemporary Child Development Research 13

PERIODS AND PROCESSES OF CHILD DEVELOPMENT 15
Periods of Development 15
Processes of Development 17
What Is Development? 19

ISSUES IN CHILD DEVELOPMENT 19
Qualitative Change 19
Stages of Development 19
Continuity-Discontinuity in Development 20
Individual Differences 20
Genetic/Biological and Environmental/Social Influences on Development 22

METHODS 23
Ways of Collecting Information About Children 23
    Systematic Observation 25
    Interviews and Surveys/Questionnaires 27
    Standardized Tests 27

Strategies of Research Design 30
   Experimental Strategy 30
   Quasi-Experimental Strategy 31
   Correlational Strategy 32
The Time Span of Inquiry 32
   Cross-Sectional Designs 33
   Longitudinal Designs 33
   Sequential Designs 33
Ethical Considerations in Studying Children 34

THINKING BACK, LOOKING AHEAD 34
SUMMARY 35
KEY TERMS 36
SUGGESTED READINGS 37

CHAPTER 2   THEORIES   38

IMAGINE . . . YOU ARE 10 YEARS OLD AND HAVE JUST WRITTEN AN
  ESSAY ON THE RARE ALBINO SPARROW 40
PREVIEW 42
PSYCHOANALYTIC THEORY 42
Sigmund Freud's Classical Psychoanalytic Theory 42
   The Structure of Personality 42
   Defense Mechanisms 44
   Freud's Psychosexual Stages of Personality Development 45
   Freud's Theory Today 50
Contemporary Psychoanalytic Theorists and Erikson's Life-Cycle View 50
Strengths and Weaknesses of Psychoanalytic Theory 52

COGNITIVE THEORIES OF DEVELOPMENT 53
Cognitive Developmental Theory 53
   Stages of Cognitive Development 55
   Processes Responsible for Developmental Changes 57
The Information Processing Perspective 60
   The Computer Metaphor—Old and New Models 60
   Questions Raised About Children's Cognition by the Information Processing Perspective
   62
Strengths and Weaknesses of the Cognitive Theories 63

BEHAVIORAL/SOCIAL LEARNING THEORIES 65
Skinner's Behaviorism 65
Social Learning Theory 66
Strengths and Weaknesses of Behavioral/Social Learning Theories 68

ETHOLOGICAL THEORY 70
Classical Ethological Theory and the European Zoologists 70
The Neo-Ethological View of Robert Hinde 71
   Three Questions Ethologists Ask About Children's Development 71
   Selected Issues of Interest to Ethologists 72
Strengths and Weaknesses of Ethological Theory 73

AN ECLECTIC THEORETICAL ORIENTATION 74
THINKING BACK, LOOKING AHEAD 76
SUMMARY 77
KEY TERMS 78
SUGGESTED READINGS 79

SECTION 2   BIOLOGICAL FOUNDATIONS AND
                     INFANCY

CHAPTER 3   THE EVOLUTIONARY PERSPECTIVE,
                       GENETICS, PRENATAL DEVELOPMENT,
                       AND THE BIRTH PROCESS   82

IMAGINE . . . THAT YOU ARE MARRIED AND THAT YOU AND YOUR
   SPOUSE HAVE JUST GONE TO SEE A GENETIC COUNSELOR 84
PREVIEW 85
THE EVOLUTIONARY PERSPECTIVE AND GENETICS: HUMANS
   ARRIVED LATE IN DECEMBER 85
Natural Selection—Bacteria to Blue Whales With Lots of Beetles in Between 85
Genes and the Nature of Genetic-Environmental Interaction 86
   What Are Genes? 86
   Some Genetic Principles 87
   Methods Used by Behavior Geneticists 89
   Genetic-Environmental Interaction and Its Effect on Development 91

THE COURSE OF PRENATAL DEVELOPMENT 92
Conception and the Zygote 92
   Standard Conception and the Zygote 92
   New Methods of Conception 94
The Germinal Period 95
The Embryonic Period 96
   Three Layers and Support Systems 96
   Further Embryonic Developments 96
The Fetal Period 97

TERATOLOGY AND HAZARDS TO PRENATAL DEVELOPMENT 100
Teratology and the Effects of Teratogens 100
Maternal Diseases and Conditions 100
   Maternal Diseases and Infections 102
   The Mother's Age 102
   Nutrition 103
   Emotional State and Stress 103
Drugs 104
   The Thalidomide Tragedy 104
   Alcohol 104
   Cigarette Smoking 106

THE BIRTH PROCESS 106
Childbirth Strategies 106
    Standard Childbirth 106
    The Leboyer Method 108
    The Lamaze Method 108
Stages of Birth and Delivery Complications 108
The Use of Drugs During Childbirth 111
Preterm Infants and Age-Weight Considerations 111
    Birth Date and Weight 111
    Measures of Neonatal Health and Responsiveness 114
    Conclusions About Preterm Infants 114
Bonding 115

THINKING BACK, LOOKING AHEAD 117
SUMMARY 118
KEY TERMS 120
SUGGESTED READINGS 121

CHAPTER 4   PHYSICAL AND PERCEPTUAL MOTOR DEVELOPMENT OF INFANTS   122

IMAGINE . . . YOU ARE FROM OUTER SPACE AND HAVE COME UPON
  A CREATURE THAT SEEMS HELPLESS 124
PREVIEW 125
PHYSICAL DEVELOPMENT 125
Reflexes, States, and Activities 125
    Reflexes 125
    States 128
    Eating Behavior 131
Physical Growth and Motor Development 133
    The First Year 133
    The Second Year 135
    Rhythmic Motor Behavior 137
    The Brain 139
SENSORY AND PERCEPTUAL DEVELOPMENT 141
What Are Sensation and Perception? 141
Visual Perception 141
    Visual Preferences 144
    Visual Acuity and Accommodation 144
    Perception of Color 145
    Perception of Objects and Faces 145
    Perception of Depth 146
    Perception of Spatial Relations 148
Other Senses 149
    Hearing 149
    Smell 152
    Taste 152
    Touch 152
    Pain 153
The Relatedness of Different Sensory Dimensions 153

THINKING BACK, LOOKING AHEAD 155
SUMMARY 155
KEY TERMS 157
SUGGESTED READINGS 157

CHAPTER 5   LEARNING, COGNITION, AND LANGUAGE IN INFANCY   158

IMAGINE . . . YOUR SON IS ONE YEAR OLD AND IS LEARNING
  MATH AND A FOREIGN LANGUAGE 160
PREVIEW 161
LEARNING 161
What Is Learning? 161
Classical Conditioning 161
    The Basic Classical Conditioning Experiment and Its Elements 161
    Why Does Classical Conditioning Work? 163
    Classical Conditioning in Infancy 164
    Evaluation of Classical Conditioning 164
Operant Conditioning 165
Imitation 166
Evaluation of the Learning Approaches 168

PIAGET'S THEORY OF INFANT DEVELOPMENT 168
An Overview of Piaget's View of Development 168
The Stage of Sensorimotor Development 168
    Simple Reflexes (Birth to One Month of Age) 170
    First Habits and Primary Circular Reactions (One to Four Months of Age) 170
    Secondary Circular Reactions (Four to Eight Months of Age) 170
    Coordination of Secondary Circular Reactions (8 to 12 Months of Age) 170
    Tertiary Circular Reactions, Novelty, and Curiosity (12 to 18 Months of Age) 171
    Internalization of Schemes (18 Months to 2 Years of Age) 171
Object Permanence 172

ATTENTION AND MEMORY 174
Attention 174
    The Orienting Response 174
    Scanning Visual Patterns 174
Memory 175
    Conjugate Reinforcement 176
    Conscious Memory 176

INDIVIDUAL DIFFERENCES, DEVELOPMENTAL SCALES, AND THE
  MEASUREMENT OF INFANT INTELLIGENCE 177
History of Interest in Infant Testing 179
The Bayley Scales of Infant Development 179
Other Developmental Scales 180
Conclusions About Infant Testing of Intelligence and Continuity in Mental Development 181

LANGUAGE DEVELOPMENT 183
The Nature of Language 183
The Rule Systems of Language 184
    Phonology 184
    Morphology 184
    Syntax 184
    Semantics 185
    Pragmatics 185

Theoretical Views of Language Acquisition 185
  The Behavioral View 185
  Nativist Theory 187
  Cognitive Theory 191
  Conclusions About Theories of Language 193
Environmental Influences on Language 193
Milestones in Language Development During Infancy 195
  Preverbal Developments 195
  One-Word Utterances 197
  Two-Word Utterances 200

THINKING BACK, LOOKING AHEAD 200
SUMMARY 200
KEY TERMS 203
SUGGESTED READINGS 203

CHAPTER 6   SOCIAL AND PERSONALITY FOUNDATIONS AND DEVELOPMENT IN INFANCY 204

IMAGINE . . . YOU ARE FACED WITH CHOOSING A DAY-CARE CENTER FOR YOUR ONE-YEAR-OLD CHILD 206
PREVIEW 207
THE ROLE OF BIOLOGY AND CULTURE IN UNDERSTANDING SOCIAL AND PERSONALITY DEVELOPMENT IN INFANCY 207
Biological Influences 207
Sociocultural Influences 208

FAMILY PROCESSES 210
The Beginnings of Parenthood 210
Reciprocal Socialization and Mutual Regulation 211
The Family as a System 212
The Construction of Relationships 214

ATTACHMENT 214
What Is Attachment? 214
Theories of Attachment 215
  Ethological Theory 215
  Psychoanalytic Theory 216
  Social Learning Theory 216
  Cognitive Developmental Theory 217
  Evaluation of Attachment Theories 218
The Developmental Course of Attachment, Individual Differences, and Situational Influences 218
  The Developmental Course of Attachment 218
  Individual Differences and Situational Influences 219
Attachment and the Construction of Relationships 221
Attachment and Temperament 224
Infant-Father Attachment and Involvement 226
  The Father's Role and Involvement With the Child 226
  Father Attachment 227
Attachment and Other Social Influences on Development 229

SIBLING AND PEER INFLUENCES DURING INFANCY 231
Sibling Influences 231
Peer Influences 232

DAY CARE DURING INFANCY 232
The Scope and Nature of Day Care 232
The Effects of Day Care on the Infant's Development 233
Some Conclusions About Day Care 234

EMOTIONAL AND PERSONALITY DEVELOPMENT DURING INFANCY 235
The Functions of Emotions in Infancy 235
Communication of Emotions in Preverbal Infants 235
    Display of Emotions 236
    Recognition of Emotions 236
Further Developments in Emotions During Infancy 236
Personality Development in Infancy 237
    Trust 237
    The Developing Sense of Self and Independence 237
    Self-Control 241

PROBLEMS AND DISTURBANCES IN INFANCY 243
Genetics and Early Experience Revisited 243
Early Experience 244
Child Abuse 245
Autism 246

THINKING BACK, LOOKING AHEAD 248
SUMMARY 248
KEY TERMS 251
SUGGESTED READINGS 251

SECTION 3   EARLY CHILDHOOD

CHAPTER 7   PHYSICAL AND COGNITIVE DEVELOPMENT IN EARLY CHILDHOOD 254

IMAGINE . . . YOU ARE FOUR YEARS OLD AND ATTENDING A
    MONTESSORI PRESCHOOL 256
PREVIEW 258
PHYSICAL DEVELOPMENT IN EARLY CHILDHOOD 258
Height, Weight, Fat, Muscle, and Other Bodily Parts 258
Individual Variation in Physical Development 259
Motor and Perceptual Development 259
Nutrition, Health, and Exercise 261
    Nutrition 262
    Health and Illness 263
    Exercise 267

COGNITIVE DEVELOPMENT IN EARLY CHILDHOOD 269
Preoperational Thought 269
    The General Nature of Preoperational Thought 269
    The Symbolic Function Substage 270
    The Substage of Intuitive Thought 275
    Some Criticisms of Piaget's Ideas on Preschool Thought 276
Information Processing 277
    Attention 277
    Memory 279
    Task Dimensions and Analyses 280

LANGUAGE DEVELOPMENT IN EARLY CHILDHOOD 281
The Mean Length of Utterance 281
Further Development in the Basic Properties of Language 283
    Phonology 284
    Morphology 284
    Syntax 284
    Semantics 286
    Pragmatics 286

EARLY CHILDHOOD EDUCATION 289
The Nature and Effects of Early Childhood Education 289
Compensatory Education 290
Project Follow Through 290
The Long-Term Effects of Project Head Start and Preschool Education with Low-Income
Children 293

THINKING BACK, LOOKING AHEAD 293
SUMMARY 294
KEY TERMS 296
SUGGESTED READINGS 296

CHAPTER 8   SOCIAL AND PERSONALITY
              DEVELOPMENT IN EARLY
              CHILDHOOD 298

IMAGINE . . . TWO FOUR-YEAR OLDS ARE PLAYING AND ONE SAYS
  TO THE OTHER: "YOU STAY HERE WITH THE BABY WHILE I GO
  FISHING." 300
PREVIEW 301
FAMILIES 301
Parenting Styles 301
Sibling Relationships 303
    Sibling and Parent-Child Relationships 303
    Birth Order 305
    Siblings as Models and Teachers 305
The Changing Family in a Changing Society 306
    Working Mothers 306
    Effects of Divorce on Children 307

PEER RELATIONS AND PLAY IN EARLY CHILDHOOD 310
The Nature of Peer Relations 310
    The Meaning of the Term *Peers* 310
    Peers and Competent Social Development 310
    Cross-Cultural Comparisons of Peer Relations 311
    Peer Relations and Perspective Taking 311
The Development of Peer Relations 311
The Distinct but Coordinated Worlds of Parents and Peers 312
Play 314
    Functions of Play 314
    Types of Play 315
    Pretend Play 317
    New Directions in Research on Children's Play 319

TELEVISION 320
Functions of Television 321
Children's Exposure to Television 322

The Role of Television as a Social Agent 323
   Aggression 323
   Prosocial Behavior 324
   The Social Context of Viewing Television 324
Commercials 324
Formal Features of Television 324
THE SELF, SEX ROLES, AND MORAL DEVELOPMENT IN EARLY
  CHILDHOOD 327
The Self 327
   "I" and "Me" 327
Sex Roles 329
   Biological Influences 329
   Cognitive Factors 330
   Environmental Influences 331
   The Development of Sex Roles 335
Moral Development 336
   Piaget's View of Moral Reasoning 336
   Moral Behavior 338
   Moral Feelings and Guilt 339
   Altruism 339
THINKING BACK, LOOKING AHEAD 340
SUMMARY 340
KEY TERMS 343
SUGGESTED READINGS 343

SECTION 4 MIDDLE AND LATE CHILDHOOD

CHAPTER 9   PHYSICAL AND COGNITIVE
               DEVELOPMENT IN MIDDLE AND
               LATE CHILDHOOD 346

IMAGINE . . . YOU ARE NINE YEARS OLD AND ARE HAVING A
  "CONVERSATION" WITH YOUR COMPUTER 348
PREVIEW 349
PHYSICAL DEVELOPMENT IN MIDDLE AND LATE CHILDHOOD 349
Basic Physical Attributes 349
Health and Fitness 350
Handicapped Children 351
   The Prevalence of Handicapped Children 351
   Issues in the Special Education of the Handicapped 353
   Learning Disabilities 355
   Hyperactive Children 357
PIAGET'S THEORY AND COGNITIVE DEVELOPMENTAL CHANGE IN
  MIDDLE AND LATE CHILDHOOD 358
Concrete Operational Thought 359
   The Beaker Task—Studying the Conservation of Liquid 359
   Reversibility and the Nature of a Concrete Operation 359
   Classification 360
   Constraints on Concrete Operational Thought 360
Piaget and Education 360
Piaget's Contributions and the Neo-Piagetian Critiques 361

INFORMATION PROCESSING 364
Memory 364
    Control Processes 365
    Characteristics of the Learner 366
Drawing Inferences 370
    Schemata and Scripts 371
    The Development of Scripts in Children 371
An Information Processing Conception of Intelligence 372
Knowledge Versus Process Views of Intelligence 376
Information Processing and Education 377

THINKING BACK, LOOKING AHEAD 382
SUMMARY 382
KEY TERMS 384
SUGGESTED READINGS 385

CHAPTER 10   INTELLIGENCE AND ACHIEVEMENT 386

IMAGINE . . . YOU MUST DETERMINE WHETHER OR NOT A CHILD IS
  MENTALLY RETARDED 388
PREVIEW 389
INTELLIGENCE 389
Theories, Definition, and Measurement 389
    Binet and the Concept of Intelligence 389
    The Wechsler Scales 391
    The Many Faces of Intelligence 393
Alternatives and Supplements to Standardized Intelligence Tests 394
    Culture-Fair Tests 395
    Social Intelligence 396
Stability and Change in Intelligence 397
Genetic-Environmental Influences on Intelligence 398
    Genetic Influences on Intelligence 399
    Environmental Influences on Intelligence 399
    The Complex Interaction of Genetic-Environmental Influences on Intelligence 402
Mental Retardation, Giftedness, and Creativity 402
    Mental Retardation 402
    Gifted Children 403
    Creativity 404

THE 3 RS AND BILINGUALISM 407
Writing and Reading 407
    Writing Systems 407
    Techniques for Teaching Reading 409
Bilingualism 412
    Simultaneous Acquisition of Two Languages 412
    Successive Acquisition of Two Languages 412
Mathematics 414
    Educational Goals for Children's Mathematics 414
    Cross-Cultural Comparisons of Achievement in Mathematics 414
MOTIVATION AND ACHIEVEMENT 418
Motivation and Its Importance in Children's Development 418

Theories of Achievement Motivation and Achievement-Related Factors 419
    The Achievement Motivation Views of McClelland and Atkinson 419
    Attribution Theory 422
    Delay of Gratification 423
Sociocultural Influences 424
    Cultural Standards of Achievement 427
    Parental and Peer Influences 428
    School/Teacher Influences 428
THINKING BACK, LOOKING AHEAD 434
SUMMARY 434
KEY TERMS 437
SUGGESTED READINGS 437

CHAPTER 11   SOCIAL AND PERSONALITY
                  DEVELOPMENT IN MIDDLE AND
                  LATE CHILDHOOD   438

IMAGINE . . . YOU ARE TEACHING A FOURTH-GRADE CLASS AND A
  BOY YELLS, "YOU JERK!" 440
PREVIEW 441
FAMILY PROCESSES AND RELATIONSHIPS IN MIDDLE AND LATE
  CHILDHOOD 441
Amount of Parent-Child Interaction 441
Parent-Child Issues 441
Discipline Techniques 442
Changes in Control Processes 442
Mutual Cognitions 442
Changes in Parental Maturation 443
Societal Changes in the Types of Families 443
    Stepfamilies 443
    Latchkey Children 444
PEER RELATIONS IN MIDDLE AND LATE CHILDHOOD 444
Amount and Form of Peer Interaction 445
Popular, Rejected, and Neglected Children 445
Social Cognition 446
    Social Information Processing 446
    Social Knowledge 446
Friendships 449
    The Incidence of Friendship and Cognitive Factors 449
    Intimacy and Similarity in Friendships 450
    Shared Support and Knowledge 451
    Conversational Skills 451
Children's Groups 452
SCHOOLS 452
The Impact of Schooling and the Elementary School Setting 452
Open Versus Traditional Classrooms and Schools 453
Teachers 454
    Teaching Styles and Traits 454
    Erikson's Criteria for a Good Teacher 455
Aptitude-Treatment Interaction 455

Social Class and Ethnicity 457
  Social Class 457
  Ethnicity 457
THE SELF, SEX ROLES, AND MORAL DEVELOPMENT IN MIDDLE AND
  LATE CHILDHOOD 460
The Self 460
  Selman's Ideas on the Self and Perspective Taking 461
  Self-Esteem 462
  Measuring Self-Concept 462
  Social Competence 464
Sex Roles 466
  Masculinity, Femininity, and Androgyny 466
  Sex-Role Stereotypes and Sex Differences 469
Moral Development 475
  Kohlberg's Stages of Moral Development 476
  Research on Kohlberg's Stages and Influences on the Stages 477
  Critics of Kohlberg 479
  Social Conventional Reasoning 484
  Moral Education 484

PROBLEMS AND DISTURBANCES IN MIDDLE AND LATE CHILDHOOD
  485
The Wide Spectrum of Problems and Disturbances 485
Childhood Depression 488
School-Related Problems 489
Resilient Children 492

THINKING BACK, LOOKING AHEAD 492
SUMMARY 493
KEY TERMS 496
SUGGESTED READINGS 496

SECTION 5   ADOLESCENCE

CHAPTER 12   PHYSICAL AND COGNITIVE
DEVELOPMENT IN ADOLESCENCE
500

IMAGINE . . . A 14-YEAR-OLD GIRL THINKING, "GET PREGNANT?
  IT WON'T HAPPEN TO ME!" 502
PREVIEW 503
HISTORICAL BACKGROUND, BIOLOGY/CULTURE, AND
  CONTINUITY/DISCONTINUITY 503
Historical Background 503
  G. Stanley Hall—The Storm and Stress View 503
  The Inventionist View of Adolescence 504
  Stereotyping Adolescents 505
Biology/Culture and Continuity/Discontinuity 505
  Biology/Culture 505
  Continuity/Discontinuity in Development 506
PHYSICAL DEVELOPMENT IN ADOLESCENCE 506
The Nature of the Pubertal Process 506

The Endocrine System 508
Physical Changes 511
    Height and Weight 511
    Sexual Maturation and Behavior 513
Psychological Accompaniment of Physical Changes 516
    Body Image 516
    Early and Late Maturation 517
    On-Time/Off-Time in Pubertal Development 518
COGNITIVE DEVELOPMENT IN ADOLESCENCE 522
Formal Operational Thought 522
    The Characteristics of Formal Operational Thought 522
    Early and Late Formal Operational Thought 528
    Individual Variation in Formal Operational Thought 529
Social Cognition 529
    Egocentrism 529
    Implicit Personality Theory 532
    Social Monitoring 533
Career Orientation and Work 534
    Exploration and Cognitive Factors in Career Development 534
    Work 534

THINKING BACK, LOOKING AHEAD 538
SUMMARY 538
KEY TERMS 540
SUGGESTED READINGS 541

CHAPTER 13   SOCIAL DEVELOPMENT IN
                        ADOLESCENCE   542

IMAGINE . . . YOU ARE OBSERVING AN EIGHTH-GRADE CLASS AND
    THE TEACHER SAYS, "I DON'T WANT ANY MORE 'WHAT IF'
    QUESTIONS." 544
PREVIEW 546
FAMILIES AND ADOLESCENT DEVELOPMENT 546
Autonomy and Attachment-Connectedness 546
    The Multidimensionality of Autonomy 546
    Parenting Strategies for Promoting Healthy Autonomy 547
    Attachment, the Coordinated Worlds of Parents and Peers, and Connectedness 548
Parenting Strategies and Parent-Adolescent Conflict 551
    Parenting Strategies With Adolescents 551
    Parent-Adolescent Conflict 551
The Maturation of the Adolescent and the Maturation of Parents 553
    The Maturation of the Adolescent 553
    The Maturation of Parents 556
The Effects of Divorce on Adolescents 557
    Wallerstein and Kelly: Carrying Forward the Divorce Experience 557
    Hetherington: Effects of Divorce on the Heterosexual Behavior of Adolescent Girls 557

PEERS AND ADOLESCENT DEVELOPMENT 560
Peer Pressure and Conformity 560
Peer Modeling and Social Comparison 561

Cliques and Crowds 562
   Distinguishing Cliques and Crowds 562
   Coleman's Study of Leading Adolescent Groups 562
   Cliques, Crowds, and Self-Esteem 563
   Children and Adolescent Groups 564
Dating 565
   The Functions of Dating 566
   Incidence of Dating and Age Trends 566
   Sex Differences and Similarities in Dating 566
   The Construction of Dating Relationships: Family and Peer Factors 567

SCHOOLS 568
The Controversy Surrounding the Function of Secondary Schools 568
Effective Schools 570
School Organization 571
   The Organization of Secondary Schools 571
   The Transition to Middle or Junior High School 573
After-School Needs of Adolescents 575

THINKING BACK, LOOKING AHEAD 576
SUMMARY 577
KEY TERMS 579
SUGGESTED READINGS 579

CHAPTER 14   PERSONALITY DEVELOPMENT IN ADOLESCENCE   580

IMAGINE . . . YOU ARE GROUCHO MARX DEVELOPING AN IDENTITY 582
PREVIEW 584
IDENTITY 584
Erikson's Ideas on Identity 584
   Personality and Role Experimentation 586
   The Complexity of Erikson's Theory 589
   A Contemporary View of Identity Development 590
The Four Statuses of Identity 590
Developmental Changes in Identity 591
Sex Differences and Similarities in Identity 592
Family Influences on the Adolescent's Identity 593
The Measurement of Identity 593
Identity and Intimacy 596
   Erikson's Views of Identity and Intimacy 596
   The Five Statuses of Intimacy 597
   Research on Intimacy 597
   Complexity of Identity-Intimacy Pathways 598
PROBLEMS AND DISTURBANCES 600
Drugs 600
   Actual Drug Use by Adolescents 600
   Alcohol 602
   Marijuana 604
   Preventive Health Efforts 605
Delinquency 606
   What Is Juvenile Delinquency? 606
   What Causes Delinquency? 606
   Sociocultural Influences on Delinquency 608

Suicide 609
 Incidence of Suicide 609
 Causes of Suicide 612
 Prevention of Suicide 612
Eating Disorders 613
 Incidence of Eating Disorders 613
 Anorexia Nervosa 613
 Bulimia 613
 Obesity 615
Adolescent Problems Versus Childhood Problems 616
THE TRANSITION FROM ADOLESCENCE TO ADULTHOOD 617
THINKING BACK, LOOKING AHEAD 618
SUMMARY 618
KEY TERMS 621
SUGGESTED READINGS 621

SUGGESTED READINGS 621
GLOSSARY 623
REFERENCES 638
CREDITS 673
NAME INDEX 679
SUBJECT INDEX 691

CHILD DEVELOPMENT CONCEPT TABLES

1.1 Child Development and History 14

1.2 Periods, Processes, and Issues in Development 24

1.3 Measures Used to Obtain Information About Children's Development 30

2.1 Psychoanalytic Theory 54

2.2 Cognitive Theories 64

2.3 Behavioral/Social Learning Theories 69

2.4 Ethological Theory 74

3.1 The Evolutionary Perspective and Genetics 93

3.2 The Course of Prenatal Development 99

3.3 Teratology and Hazards to Prenatal Development 107

3.4 Childbirth Strategies, Stages of Birth and Delivery Complications, and the Use of Drugs 113

4.1 Reflexes, States, and Activities 132

4.2 Physical Growth and Motor Development 140

4.3 The Nature of Sensation and Perception, Theories of Perceptual Development, Visual Perception, and Auditory Perception 151

5.1 Learning 169

5.2 Piaget's Theory, Attention and Memory, and Infant Intelligence Tests 182

5.3 The Nature of Language, Rule Systems of Language, Theoretical Views of Language Acquisition, and Environmental Influences on Language 196

6.1 Biology, Culture, and Family Processes 215

6.2 Attachment 230

6.3 Siblings and Peers, Day Care, Emotional Development, and Personality Development 242

7.1 Physical Development in Early Childhood 268

7.2 Cognitive Development in Early Childhood 288

8.1 Parenting Styles, Sibling Relationships, and the Changing Family 309

8.2 Peers, Play, and Television 326

8.3 The Self and Sex-Role Development 337

9.1   Physical Development in Middle and Late Childhood 358
9.2   Piaget's Theory and Cognitive Developmental Change in Middle and Late Childhood 364
9.3   Information Processing 378
10.1 The Psychometric Approach to Intelligence 408
10.2 The 3 Rs and Bilingualism 418
10.3 Motivation, Achievement Motivation, and Achievement-Related Factors 427
11.1 Families, Peers, and Schools in Middle and Late Childhood 459
11.2 The Self, Sex Roles, and Moral Development 486
12.1 Historical Background, Biology/Culture, and Continuity/Discontinuity 507
12.2 Physical Development in Adolescence 521
12.3 Cognitive Development in Adolescence 535
13.1 Families and Adolescent Development 559
13.2 Peers and Adolescent Development 569
14.1 Identity 598
14.2 Drugs and Delinquency 611

1.1 Infant and Maternal Diets in Guatemala and San Diego 21

1.2 The Neighborhood Walk 28

2.1 Relationships, Development, and Defense Mechanisms 46

2.2 Dreams, Freud, and Piaget—From Bird-Headed Creatures to Bathtubs 58

3.1 AA Scores at Mid-Pregnancy, Neonatal Arousal and Preschool Vigilance 105

3.2 A Father in the Delivery Room: "It Was Out of This World!" 109

3.3 Anesthesia, Oxytocin, and Infant States 112

3.4 Preemies Are Different 116

4.1 Rattles, Bells, Pinpricks, and Cuddles 130

4.2 "Slices" of Space and "Eyes" in the Back of Your Head 142

4.3 Yellow Kangaroos, Gray Donkeys, Thumps, Gongs, and Four-Month-Old Infants 150

4.4 The Three-Day-Old Male Infant and the Circumstraint Board 154

5.1 Smiles, Frowns, and Surprises 166

5.2 Fathoming the Permanence of Things in the World 173

5.3 Infantile Amnesia, A Sibling's Birth, and Rats 178

5.4 The Curious Case of Genie 188

5.5 Baby Talk 194

6.1 Attachment Bonds, Peer Relations, Depression, and Schizoid Behavior 222

6.2 Intense Mothers and Avoidant Babies—The Importance of Temperament 225

6.3 A Child Called Noah 247

7.1 "Feet Not Cold Now" 265

7.2 Where Pelicans Kiss Seals, Cars Float on Clouds, and Humans Are Tadpoles 271

7.3 Merds That Laugh Don't Like Mushrooms 282

7.4 Foots, Feets, and Wugs 285

FOCUS
ON CHILD
DEVELOPMENT
BOXES

7.5   Variations in Early Education With Impoverished Children 291

8.1   Nose Punchers, Pinchers, and Isolates 313

8.2   The Symbolic World of Children's Play 318

8.3   How Good Are Girls at Wudgemaking If the Wudgemaker Is a "He"? 332

9.1   Type A Children, Illness, Stress, and Achievement 352

9.2   10 + 12 = ?: The Importance of Short-Term Memory and Automatization 362

9.3   Metamemory—Predicting Memory Span and Knowing How Much to Study 368

9.4   Scripts for Sandboxes, Snacks, and Spelling 373

9.5   Information Processing, Education, and the Information Age 379

10.1   Bird to Beethoven—Seven Frames of Mind 395

10.2   Doran, Dr. Graham, and the Repository for Germinal Choice 400

10.3   Novel Thinking, Insight, and Automatization in the Gifted and the Retarded 405

10.4   Achievement in Math Requires Time and Practice— Comparisons of Children in the United States and Japan 415

10.5   Pretzels and Marshmallows—Delay of Gratification in Childhood and Adjustment in Adolescence 425

10.6   Revisiting the Internal-External Dimension of Achievement 432

11.1   Destroying a Block Tower While Cleaning Up a Room— Intention-Cue Detection Skills in Children 447

11.2   Bright Girls, Learned Helplessness, and Expectation 473

11.3   Not Just Any Peer Communication Will Do—The Role of Transactive Discussion 480

11.4   Amy Says They Should Just Talk It Out and Find Some Other Way to Make Money 483

11.5   Elizabeth and Her Depression—Why Does Such Sadness Develop in Children? 490

12.1   Gonadotropins, Sex Steroids, Adrenal Androgens, and the Adolescent   510

12.2   Physical Attractiveness, Pubertal Change, and Self-Esteem in Adolescent Girls   519

12.3   Jay and His Haircut—The Development of Sarcasm   527

12.4   Imaginary Audiences   530

13.1   Mothers, Daughters, and Girlfriends   550

13.2   Monitoring the Lives of Adolescents After School   552

13.3   Jocks, Populars, Normals, Druggies/Toughs, Independents and Nobodies   563

13.4   Beyond the Zoo   572

13.5   Facilitating the Transition to Junior High School   574

14.1   Sawyer, Hitler, Luther, and Gandhi   587

14.2   Individuation and Connectedness in Families   594

14.3   Agent, Environment, and Host   607

14.4   Delinquency and Family Processes—Cause, Correlate, or Consequence?   610

14.5   Jane, A 16-Year-Old Anorexic   614

The task of presenting the wealth of classic and contemporary research information on child development in an interesting, teachable, learnable fashion is not a simple one. Research has blossomed in many domains of human development, ranging across the biological, cognitive, and social realms. And the gains in knowledge in these important areas have occurred in all age periods of the child's life, from prenatal development through adolescence. The 1980s have witnessed an explosion of research on child development—thousands of researchers are searching for clues to explain why children develop the way they do.

My goals in writing this book were to provide a chronologically organized, comprehensive, and contemporary overview of the research process at every stage of child development; to do so in an exciting and enthusiastic manner; and to accomplish this task in such a way that comprehension is organized and facilitated. Frequent examples and applications point out the relevance of these research findings to real children.

PREFACE

TO THE INSTRUCTOR

Organization and Coverage

Children is organized chronologically, with 5 sections and 14 chapters. Section 1 introduces students to the science of child development. It is followed by sections on biological foundations and infancy, early childhood, middle and late childhood, and adolescence. Material is presented topically within the chronological framework. Because different processes of development are more significant at different stages of development, topic emphasis varies among sections. For example, there is a separate chapter devoted to physical development in infancy and a separate chapter on social development in adolescence; for other stages, these topics are treated in combination with other topics, such as cognitive or personality development.

The research base of child development is expanding so rapidly that material was added in each section of the book right up to the time the book went to press. Thus, the very latest ideas in the field of child development are examined in the text.

A brief sampling of some of the highlights in each chapter should provide a sense of the contemporary flavor of research discussed:

Chapter 1, "History, Issues, and Methods," includes a description of the Neighborhood Walk, a naturalistic interview conducted while walking through the child's neighborhood. Chapter 2, "Theories," discusses the ethological and information processing perspectives as important theories of children's development.

In Section 2 on biological foundations and infancy, Chapter 3, "The Evolutionary Perspective, Genetics, Prenatal Development, and the Birth Process," provides information about the chorionic villus test to assess birth defects, new methods of conception, and the effects of maternal drug exposure on prenatal and postnatal development. Chapter 4, "Physical and Perceptual Motor Development of Infants," presents the results of an intriguing investigation of circumcision that provides new information about the newborn's methods of coping with stress. Chapter 5, "Learning, Cognition, and Language in Infancy," describes recent research on the prediction of intelligence in childhood based on measurements of attention in the young infant. Chapter 6, "Social and Personality Foundations and Development in Infancy," discusses temperament characteristics of the mother and the infant that are involved in the nature of attachment.

In Section 3 on early childhood, Chapter 7, "Physical and Cognitive Development in Early Childhood," shows the role of health in the preschool child's social and cognitive development, and Chapter 8, "Social and Personality Development in Early Childhood," describes new directions in play research.

In Section 4 on middle and late childhood, Chapter 9, "Physical and Cognitive Development in Middle and Late Childhood," includes a discussion of Type A children, illness, stress, and achievement. Chapter 10, "Intelligence and Achievement," includes a comparison of math achievement among children in the United States and Japan. Bright girls, expectation, and learned helplessness are discussed in Chapter 11, "Social and Personality Development in Middle and Late Childhood."

In Section 5 on adolescence, the link between hormonal changes and adjustment in early adolescence is discussed in Chapter 12, "Physical and Cognitive Development in Adolescence." The relationships of early adolescent girls with their mothers and their girlfriends are featured in Chapter 13, "Social Development in Adolescence," and the role of individuation and connectedness in the families of adolescents and adolescent identity development are presented in Chapter 14, "Personality Development in Adolescence."

This brief glimpse at some of the contemporary research described in *Children* is only the beginning of an exciting journey through the child's development. Let's look further at how this excitement is captured.

TO THE STUDENT

As I wrote *Children,* I imagined myself telling you about research on children and describing their lives by talking with you. It is my hope that the conversational style of the writing helps to make the book flow more smoothly and provides a more personal encounter between us than found in many texts.

Writing style is one way to communicate excitement and enthusiasm. Another way is the choice of research discussed. Because of the level of sophistication reached in child development research, you will have to work to understand many concepts. Nonetheless, I think you will be pleasantly surprised by the frequent inclusion of truly innovative and creative moments in research and the lively manner in which they are presented.

Given that you are provided with a wealth of detailed information that is on the cutting edge of the field of child development and that this information is presented in an enthusiastic and exciting way, there is still a third task an author must accomplish—to organize the material in such a way that you can learn it easily.

The Learning System

On the one hand, I want to challenge the reader with the latest, most comprehensive research knowledge in the field of child development. But I also want to help you in your task of learning. The learning system used in *Children* should help you to close the last page of this textbook with a better understanding of children's development.

An extensive amount of organization and integration is built into *Children.* Each chapter begins with a detailed **Chapter Outline** and **"Preview"** of major topics. A very special, innovative feature of *Children* is the **"Child Development Concept Table,"** which appears two or three times in each chapter. It is an organizational device that activates your memory of key topics that have been discussed in the chapter and shows how they are related to each other. The concept tables also enhance your comprehension of complex concepts and ideas, allowing you to get a "handle" on such information before you reach the end of the chapter. The child development concept tables are a way to allow complete coverage of the field of child development without overwhelming you. Then, at the end of each chapter, you are provided with a functional **"Summary"** outline that helps you to see the pieces of the chapter together.

Too often, students do not get a sense from their textbooks of how the individual chapters fit together. Special attention was given to this problem in *Children*. At the end of each chapter, just before the "Summary," you will read a section called **"Thinking Back, Looking Ahead."** This section is a prose description that integrates some of the most important points in the chapter or section.

The extensive organization just described is a key feature in the learning system of *Children*. However, there are many other learning aids as well. Each chapter begins with an **"Imagine"** section, an easy-to-read prologue of an aspect of children's development related to some chapter topic. In addition, each chapter has a number of boxes called **"Focus on Child Development,"** which provide you with other points of view, applications, or an in-depth look at an interesting research study. A number of the boxes have been written to show you how the research process in child development actually works. **Key Terms** are boldfaced in the text, listed at the end of the chapter, and defined in a page-referenced **"Glossary"** at the end of the book. **"Suggested Readings"** also appear at the end of each chapter.

INSTRUCTIONAL AND LEARNING AIDS

Melvyn B. King, State University of New York-Cortland, and Debra E. Clark, The Neurological Institute-Cortland, have provided a helpful *Instructor's Manual* for use with *Children* that will save time in preparing for this course. For each chapter, the manual includes a Chapter Summary, Learning Objectives, List of Key Terms (referenced to learning objectives and text page), Research Project (with complete instructions and data collection forms), Classroom Activities, Essay Questions, and Lecture Suggestions. A comprehensive Test Item File is also included in the *Instructor's Manual*. It contains multiple-choice, true-false, and fill-in-the-blank questions, each referenced to text page and learning objective and identified as factual, conceptual, or applied. The *Instructor's Manual* also contains a brief essay on "Ethics, Human Subjects, and Informed Consent."

The *Student Study Guide,* also written by Melvyn B. King and Debra E. Clark, contains the following elements for each chapter: Learning Objectives, Chapter Overview, Guided Review, Key Terms Matching Exercises, Student Self-Tests (two 20-question practice tests), Thought Questions, and a Student Research Project (with complete instructions and data collection forms). A brief essay on "Ethics, Human Subjects, and Informed Consent" is also included to familiarize the students with the research process. Each item in the Guided Review, Key Terms Matching Exercises, and Student Self-Tests is referenced to the appropriate text page and learning objective.

All test questions are available on **ωcb** TestPak, a free, computerized testing service available to adopters of *Children.* The call-in/mail-in service offers a test master, a student answer sheet, and an answer key within two working days of receipt of the instructor's request.

TestPak is also available for instructors who want to use their Apple® IIe, Apple® IIc, or IBM PC microcomputer system to create their own tests. Upon adoption of *Children* and upon request, the instructor will receive the Test Item File, program diskettes, and user's guide. With these, the instructor can create tests, answer sheets, and answer keys. The program allows for adding, deleting, or modifying test questions. No programming experience is necessary.

ACKNOWLEDGMENTS

Children came about through the efforts of many people. James McNeil, Psychology Editor, and Sandy Schmidt, Senior Developmental Editor, were special contributors. They orchestrated the development of the book and provided direction as well as enthusiasm for the project. Vickie Putman Caughron, Senior Production Editor, provided excellent support in monitoring the production of *Children.* Mary Monner deserves mention for her copyediting, making my words more sensible. Jeanne Rhomberg, Design Editor, provided creative touches to make *Children* more attractive. Michelle Oberhoffer selected and tracked down many photographs. Mavis Oeth spent many hours obtaining permissions.

James Bartlett, University of Texas at Dallas, and Steven Yussen, the University of Wisconsin, provided valuable material for various sections of the book. Special thanks go to Melvyn B. King and Debra E. Clark, of SUNY-Cortland and The Neurological Institute-Cortland, who prepared an excellent *Instructor's Manual* and *Student Study Guide.* Thanks also go to Elizabeth LeClair, who prepared the glossary.

A very special note of appreciation goes to my family. My wife, Mary Jo, was very understanding during this project, and my children, Tracy and Jennifer, continue to be sources of pleasure and examples.

Finally, the experienced teachers and researchers who reviewed *Children* at each stage of its development provided many valuable insights and constructive criticism that made the book a much better text than would otherwise have been possible. I am deeply indebted to the following individuals for their assistance:

Harry H. Avis—Sierra College

Ruth Brinkman—St. Louis Community College, Florissant Valley

Dr. Alice S. Honig—Syracuse University

Diane Carlson Jones—Texas A&M University

Ellen Junn—Indiana University

Claire B. Kopp—UCLA

Karla Miley—Black Hawk College

Jane A. Rysberg—California State University, Chico

Ross A. Thompson—University of Nebraska, Lincoln

Dorothy A. Wedge—Fairmont State College

William H. Zachry—University of Tennessee, Martin

John W. Santrock

CHILDREN

The first cry of a newborn baby in Chicago or
Zamboanga, in Amsterdam or Rangoon, has the same
pitch and key, each saying, "I am! I have come through!
I belong! I am a member of the Family." . . .
babies arriving, suckling, growing into youths restless
and questioning.

Carl Sandburg

HISTORY, ISSUES AND METHODS

IMAGINE . . . YOU ARE A CHILD PSYCHOLOGIST OBSERVING AN 11-MONTH-OLD GIRL, LISTENING TO A 3-YEAR-OLD BOY, AND INTERVIEWING A 12-YEAR-OLD GIRL AND HER PARENTS

PREVIEW

CHILD DEVELOPMENT IN CONTEMPORARY SOCIETY

Divorce, Working Mothers, and Latchkey Children
Computers and Children
Hurried Children, Type A Behavior Pattern, and Children's Health

CHILD DEVELOPMENT AND HISTORY

Historical Accounts of Childhood
Ancient Greece and Rome
The Middle Ages
The Renaissance
The Scientific Beginnings of Child Development
Late 19th-Century Research
Twentieth-Century Research
Sociopolitical Influences on the Study of Child Development
Contemporary Child Development Research

CHILD DEVELOPMENT CONCEPT TABLE 1.1: CHILD DEVELOPMENT AND HISTORY

PERIODS AND PROCESSES OF CHILD DEVELOPMENT

Periods of Development
Processes of Development
What Is Development?

ISSUES IN CHILD DEVELOPMENT

Qualitative Change
Stages of Development
Continuity-Discontinuity in Development

FOCUS ON CHILD DEVELOPMENT 1.1: INFANT AND MATERNAL DIETS IN GUATEMALA AND SAN DIEGO

Individual Differences
Genetic/Biological and Environmental/ Social Influences on Development

CHILD DEVELOPMENT CONCEPT TABLE 1.2: PERIODS, PROCESSES, AND ISSUES IN DEVELOPMENT

METHODS

Ways of Collecting Information About Children
Systematic Observation
Interviews and Surveys/Questionnaires

FOCUS ON CHILD DEVELOPMENT 1.2: THE NEIGHBORHOOD WALK
Standardized Tests

CHILD DEVELOPMENT CONCEPT TABLE 1.3: MEASURES USED TO OBTAIN INFORMATION ABOUT CHILDREN'S DEVELOPMENT

Strategies of Research Design
Experimental Strategy
Quasi-Experimental Strategy
Correlational Strategy
The Time Span of Inquiry
Cross-Sectional Designs
Longitudinal Designs
Sequential Designs
Ethical Considerations in Studying Children

THINKING BACK, LOOKING AHEAD

SUMMARY

KEY TERMS

SUGGESTED READINGS

CHAPTER 1

IMAGINE . . . YOU ARE A CHILD
PSYCHOLOGIST OBSERVING AN 11-
MONTH-OLD GIRL, LISTENING TO A 3-
YEAR-OLD BOY, AND INTERVIEWING A
12-YEAR-OLD GIRL AND HER PARENTS

A small curly-haired girl named Danielle, age 11 months, is beginning to whimper. After a few seconds, she begins to wail. The psychologist observing Danielle is conducting a research study on the nature of attachment between infants and their mothers. The psychologist is watching Danielle's behavior in a university laboratory room filled with dolls, teddy bears, and jigsaw puzzles. The walls of the room are emblazoned with blue, yellow, and red rainbows. Along one of the walls runs a ten-foot-long two-way mirror so that the psychologist can observe children like Danielle unobtrusively and record their activities on videotape.

In Danielle's case, the observation session begins with Danielle seated on her mother's lap for several minutes. Then the mother places Danielle down and leaves the room. At this point, the whimpering described earlier begins, followed by a loud cry. Subsequently, the mother reenters the room, and Danielle's crying ceases. Quickly, Danielle crawls over to where her mother is seated and reaches out to be held. This scenario is but one of a number of ways in which research psychologists study the nature of attachment during infancy. If the psychologist perceives the baby's distress to be too intense, the session is shortened or even terminated. Later in the chapter, we consider such ethical considerations in the study of children.

A quizzical, serious look spreads across the face of Zachary, age three. Zachary is sitting across the table from a child psychologist. On the table between them sits a Snoopy doll. The child psychologist asks Zachary to close or cover both of his eyes, and Zachary complies. The child psychologist tells Zachary that, while Zachary's eyes are closed, "My eyes are open." Then he asks Zachary several questions, such as "Do I see you? Do I see Snoopy?" Zachary says that the psychologist cannot see him but that he can see Snoopy. The psychologist is interested in determining whether Zachary understands that he has a private, thinking self not directly visible to others, so the psychologist asks Zachary where he does his thinking and knowing. Zachary points to his head and says, "In here." Then the psychologist asks, "Can I see you thinking in there?" Zachary says no, responding that he does not have any big holes that the psychologist can see through to observe his thinking and knowing (Flavell, Shipstead, & Croft, 1978). Through questioning sessions such as the one between three-year-old Zachary and the child psychologist, inferences are made about the nature of children's thinking. In the case of Zachary, it appears that he has a rudimentary sense of a private, thinking self that is not accessible to others in any direct, observable fashion.

Jennifer is a slender, striking, blonde-haired girl, sitting on an examining table with a sheet draped over her body at the clinical center of a hospital. Jennifer, a twelve-year-old, has just been examined by the pediatric nurse and an endocrinologist to determine her pubertal stage, height, and weight. Now the nurse pricks her arm and obtains a blood sample from a vein. The blood sample is placed on ice so that it can be analyzed later for the concentrations of different hormones present. The research study in which Jennifer is participating also requires information about her psychological and social adjustment. On a separate day, Jennifer responds to a series of questionnaires and is interviewed in a homelike setting at the research laboratory. Her parents also are interviewed there. One hundred seven other boys and girls, ages 9 to 15, have gone through exactly the same procedures as Jennifer and her parents. The researchers studying Jennifer and her late childhood and early adolescent compatriots are trying to determine whether there is a relation between levels of various hormones and the social/psychological adjustment of boys and girls. In this particular study, there seems to be a stronger link between the hormone levels of boys and their psychological adjustment than is true for girls (Nottelmann et al., 1985).

PREVIEW

Danielle, Zachary, and Jennifer are three of many thousands of infants, children, and adolescents who participate every year in a myriad of fascinating research studies seeking to learn more about how and why children develop. Watching infants like Danielle through a two-way mirror as they respond to systematic changes in their mother's behavior, listening to and observing Zachary's comments about Snoopy and his own private thoughts, and searching for the complex story about hormones and psychological adjustment are only three examples of the exciting study of child development. Research with children is anything but dull—watching children, listening to children, and then trying to solve the mystery of how and why they are who they are is among the most rewarding enterprises in science.

Throughout history, there have been diverse and contradictory answers to some of the most fundamental questions of interest to child psychologists: What is a child's mind like? Why do children behave the way they do? How can we help children with their problems? What are the contributions of biology and experience, of genes and environment, to the psychological makeup of children? Today's child psychologists are able to answer these questions about children's minds and behaviors more certainly because of a tradition of careful thinking, observing, and experimenting. As expressed by Carl Sagan (1979) in the introduction to his fascinating book *Broca's Brain,* we live in an extraordinary time in history, a time of an explosion in knowledge about ourselves and our children's lives:

In all of the 4-million-year history of the human family, there is only one generation privileged to live through that unique transitional moment (the time when we pass from ignorance to knowledge on fundamental issues; the age where we begin in wonder and end in understanding): that generation is ours. (p. xiv)

CHILD DEVELOPMENT IN CONTEMPORARY SOCIETY

Wherever you turn in the world today, the development and well-being of children capture the public's attention, the interest of scientists, and the concern of policymakers. Common topics of interest covered in newspapers and magazines include test-tube babies, genetic engineering, child abuse, parenting strategies to raise a genius child, effects of divorce on children, Type A behavior patterns, working mothers and latchkey children, the effects of television on children, and the use of computers to teach children. What child development researchers are discovering in each of these areas has significant consequences for understanding children. Let's look at several of these topics more closely.

Divorce, Working Mothers, and Latchkey Children

The contemporary family faces many pressures. The divorce rate has increased exponentially in our lifetime—huge numbers of children are being reared in single-parent families, and many of these same children subsequently are spending at least part of their childhood in stepfamilies. What are the effects of divorce on children? Does divorce affect children differently than it affects adolescents? Does it matter whether a child is growing up in a single-parent family in which the father has custody as opposed to a single-parent family in which the mother has custody? Is there more stress in some kinds of divorce circumstances than in others? Is it important that the divorced mother has adequate support systems available? Does divorce affect girls and boys differently? These are among the many questions child development researchers ask and attempt to answer as they explore the social and psychological worlds of children from divorced families.

Not only are children today more likely to grow up in divorced families and in stepfamilies than in the past, but they also are much more likely to live in a family in which the mother has a full-time career. Many mothers have less time to spend with their children. Who cares for young children while the mother works and how day care influences children have become important issues. Researchers are interested in finding out whether children growing up in families with working mothers differ from children growing up in families where the mother plays the traditional homemaker role. They also want to know how day care affects infants and children—in particular, what constitutes quality day care and how day care influences children's development.

How will computers influence our children in the future?

Along with the increased number of divorced and working-mother families has come a significant trend for more children to live a portion of their day unmonitored by adults. These so-called "latchkey" children (because some carry the key to their house on a string around their neck) come home after elementary or secondary school to a world with no adult supervision because their parents are working. What effect does this lack of monitoring have on children's and adolescents' lives? Does it make them more autonomous and competent, or does it increase their fears, insecurity, and frequency of getting into trouble? Such questions are among those being studied by child development researchers who are interested in family processes.

Computers and Children

We have moved from an industrial society to a postindustrial society, one that has been called the information age (Santrock & Yussen, 1987). Our lives and the economy are increasingly married to the quality, speed, and availability of information. Advances in computer science have been particularly involved in this explosion of information. Computers, which once were available only to large businesses and government, now are in the hands of four- and five-year-olds in their home or at school. How will such changes in information and computers influence learning and development? Are there sex differences in computer skills and capabilities—that is, do boys find computer use easier than girls? Does the introduction of the computer into the home change the nature of family interaction? Does the computer become a companion, babysitter, or mentor for the child? Can the computer help the child to think in more organized, logical ways? These are among the questions being addressed by child researchers as they explore the world of children, information, and computers.

Hurried Children, Type A Behavior Pattern, and Children's Health

It is difficult to document whether we experience more stress than our grandparents did when they were growing up, but it seems that we do. We live in a fast-paced world, one that increasingly has become more achievement oriented, with standards of society signalling to parents and children that they should achieve as much as possible as soon as possible in their lives. Such rising standards in our American society led David Elkind (1981) to write the book *The Hurried Child,* in which he spelled out some of the dangers children face as they are pushed into stressful circumstances, in some cases too early in their development. In particular, Elkind is worried about children whose parents have very high standards for them but who are unwilling to invest the time and energy necessary to provide a warm, emotional support system that will help the children to cope with such stress.

Psychologists have documented the presence of a Type A behavior pattern in adults—one characterized by extreme competitiveness, impatience, quickness to anger, and easily aroused hostility—that seems to reflect the stress we encounter in our world. This behavior pattern has been linked to the incidence of cardiovascular disease in adults (e.g., Friedman & Rosenman, 1974). Can such a behavioral pattern be detected in children, and, if so, is it linked to cardiovascular problems in childhood and later in adulthood? Is the Type A behavior pattern associated with the way parents rear their children? Do genes play a role in the Type A behavior pattern of children? Researchers are beginning to investigate these questions to determine the nature of stress in childhood and the ways in which stress can be reduced.

While health psychology is only a recently developed area of psychology (e.g., Stone, Cohen, & Adler, 1979), there is tremendous interest in understanding the origin, course, treatment, and maintenance of health (Stone, 1983). Increasingly, a developmental perspective is being applied to health psychology as interest in early prevention and intervention increases (Maddux, Roberts, Sledden, & Wright, 1986). Questions and issues beginning to be addressed by researchers in the health psychology field include: How does the child's cognitive development influence health behavior, such as his or her understanding of the link between illness and health? When and how do children form attitudes about smoking, diet, exercise, and hygiene? What are the most effective ways to increase a child's responsibility for health?

Now that we have surveyed some of the pressing contemporary concerns in the field of child development, we turn back the clock and seek to understand the historical unfolding of interest in child development.

CHILD DEVELOPMENT AND HISTORY

At first, the infant,
Mewling and puking in the nurse's arms,
Then the whining schoolboy, with his satchel
And shining morning face, creeping
like snail. . . .   Shakespeare

While Shakespeare was a man for all seasons and ages in many respects, he often defined children in terms of such qualities as foolishness, emotionality, innocence, impotence, and need for discipline from adults (Borstelmann, 1983). But as we shall see, the history of interest in childhood goes much further back in time than Shakespeare.

Historical Accounts of Childhood

Childhood is such a distinct period that it is hard to imagine that it wasn't always thought to be that way. Philip Aries's (1962) book on the historical interest in childhood has served as a guide for many years in efforts to understand how children were viewed and treated at different historical points. Aries's samples of art and publications of different eras indicate that most societies divided development into infancy, which lasted for many years, and adulthood, which extended somewhere from what we now call middle childhood to postadolescence. Aries concluded that the child was often portrayed as a miniature adult (Figure 1.1).

While the conception of childhood as a miniature adulthood has persisted for many years, there has been a lively reawakening of interest in the study of childhood from a historical perspective during the last decade (Borstelmann, 1983; Cairns, 1983; Kessen, 1979). This renewed study has cast some doubt on Aries's conclusions, which likely were overdrawn, reflecting artistic style, aristocratic subjects and artists, and an idealization of society at the time. For example, as we see next, even the societies of ancient Rome and Greece held rich conceptions of children.

FIGURE 1.1   Painting portraying the child as a miniature adult. Aries used paintings such as this one to conclude that, historically, children often have been viewed and treated like miniature adults. More recent analyses suggest his conclusions were somewhat overdrawn.

Ancient Greece and Rome

Accounts of the societies of ancient Greece and Rome have generally indicated that children in these societies were treated poorly. Abandoned infants, sexually abused children, and murdered newborns (infanticide) have been described. In general, the societies of ancient Greece and Rome were much more brutal than our contemporary world. However, writings also suggest that ancient societies sometimes treated children with special attention and rules. For example, ancient Greek society was interested in how children were related to deities and specified laws and customs for how children should be educated and reared (Borstelmann, 1983).

The Middle Ages

As the Roman Empire declined during the second and third centuries A.D., the medieval period of history began and extended for about 1,000 years. Just as the way in which the ancient Greeks and Romans treated children has been oversimplified, so has a stereotype appeared about the way children were viewed and treated during the Middle Ages. For the most part, this stereotype suggests that there was little growth in understanding children and that the religious nature of the child's existence was all that mattered.

During the Middle Ages, the goal of child rearing was salvation; that is, parenting was designed to remove the sin from children's lives. For example, the Catholics and the Puritans believed that it was more important to rear a child who had been saved than a child who was happy. This concept of children, sometimes called the **original sin view,** reflected the philosophical perspective that children basically were bad and that only through the constraints of societal upbringing and/or salvation could they become mature, competent adults.

Indeed, Christianity during the Middle Ages pervasively influenced children's lives. It preached ideas about the soul, developed competing notions about the pureness and innocence of each soul born into the world on the one hand and original sin on the other, and took a strong view on the religious rearing of children. As part of Christianity, medieval medicine flourished and was characterized in large part by philosophy, faith, and common sense.

In spite of this strong religious influence, however, a number of ideas about the special treatment of infant health appeared, and legal systems, such as the Magna Carta in England, were generated. While the Roman legal system had dealt with children strictly as property, the Magna Carta gave children more rights, including inheritance rights and the right to special treatment (such as housing and custodial care in the case of mental disturbance) if they had major disabilities.

The Renaissance

The time period from the 14th to the 17th centuries is usually referred to as the Renaissance, an era of rejuvenation and advances in art, music, philosophy, literature, and science. Changes in economic matters, political policies, and religious denominations infiltrated families and produced a great deal of change. As kinship ties began to weaken somewhat in the face of such upheaval, it is not surprising that the Church continued to exert a strong role in children's lives. The experiences of Renaissance children, as at all points in history, depended on the socioeconomic circumstances they grew up in. Schooling became more available to children during the Renaissance, and the field of pediatric medicine emerged.

Renaissance philosophers began to speculate about the nature of the developing child and how he or she should be reared. While such interest also was evident as early as the Greek society of Plato and Aristotle, it was not nearly as great as the interest sparked during the Renaissance.

We have already seen how the original sin view of the child prevailed during the Middle Ages. Two contrasting views about the nature of the child emerged during the Renaissance—the **tabula rasa** and **innate goodness views.** Near the end of the 17th century, John Locke argued that children are not innately evil, but instead are like a blank tablet, a *tabula rasa* as he called it. Locke believed that childhood experiences were important in determining adult characteristics. Thus, he advised parents to spend time with their children and to help them learn to become contributing members of society. During the 18th century, Jean-Jacques Rousseau agreed with Locke that children are not basically evil. However, Rousseau stressed that, rather than being like a blank slate (that is, neither good nor bad), children are innately good. Because of their innate goodness, Rousseau reasoned that children should be permitted to grow naturally with little parental monitoring or constraint.

The original sin, *tabula rasa,* and innate goodness views of children initiated the nature-nurture debate in development. The original sin and innate goodness views place a premium on the importance of nature in development, while the *tabula rasa* perspective emphasizes the significance of nurture. We discuss the nature-nurture argument again later in the chapter, but for now, let's move on to the scientific beginnings of child development.

The Scientific Beginnings of Child Development

As psychology became a science and its ties with philosophy lessened, more scientific approaches to studying and understanding children developed in the late 19th century and the early part of the 20th century.

Late 19th-Century Research

By the end of the 19th century, psychology was firmly established as a science, although the scientific study of children, for the most part, was not a factor. The biologist Charles Darwin made the scientific study of children a respectable effort when he developed a baby journal for recording systematic observations of a child's behavior. Developmental psychologists describe Darwin's baby journal as the first systematic strategy for obtaining data about child development (Kessen, 1965).

Darwin's biological, evolutionary perspective was very much a part of the theory of child development proposed by G. Stanley Hall (1904). Hall believed that child development follows a natural evolutionary course that is revealed by child study. He also theorized that child development unfolds in a stagelike fashion, with motives and capabilities distinct at each stage. Hall had much to say about adolescence, believing that it was full of "storm and stress." He believed that education in such matters as scientific thinking and morality should begin only after the age of 15 because of the inevitable conflict in the adolescent years. Later in this book, when we discuss adolescent development, we will see that Hall's "storm and stress" view of adolescence was inappropriate. Hall, like Darwin, also believed that child development required a systematic method of study (White, 1985). He tried to develop such a method with various questionnaires, but they were weak and unconvincing.

Twentieth-Century Research

Sigmund Freud's psychoanalytic theory was prominent in the early part of the 20th century. Although his theory had a strong child development component, it never was set forth in a form that would generate a great deal of research. His ideas about child development were compatible with Hall's ideas; that is, he emphasized conflict and strong biological influences on development.

FIGURE 1.2 Gesell's photographic dome. Gesell is the man inside the dome with the infant. Cameras rode on metal tracks at the top of the dome and were moved as needed to record the child's activities. Others, such as the female in this photo, could observe from outside the dome without being seen by the child.

During the late 1920s and 1930s, John Watson's theory of behaviorism profoundly influenced thinking about children. Watson proposed a view of children very different from Freud, arguing that children can be shaped into whatever society wishes by examining and changing the environment. One element of Watson's view, and behaviorism in general, was a strong belief in the scientific study of children's behavior. It was argued that, if children are to be studied scientifically, their behavior has to be observed in a highly empirical, systematic way.

In addition to psychoanalytic theory and behaviorism, another view that was influential in promoting the study of children in the 1920s through the 1940s was that of Arnold Gesell (1928; Gesell et al., 1934; Gesell & Ilg, 1949). With his photographic dome, Gesell could systematically observe children's behavior without interrupting them (Figure 1.2). In addition to his methodological contributions, Gesell developed a theoretical perspective that was heavily biological in nature. He called his theory maturational to describe how child development unfolds according to physical changes. Gesell tried to be precise in charting what a child is like at a specific age. He believed that certain characteristics simply "bloomed with age" because of a biological, maturational blueprint.

While Watson's behavioral view also stressed observation, the behavioral view was very different from the biological, maturational perspective of Gesell. Watson believed that the environment could be changed to make the child behave in a particular fashion, while Gesell argued that a genetic blueprint provided a maturational unfolding in which the environment was merely the setting for development, not the cause of it.

In addition to the generation of these theories, another occurrence helped to promote the scientific study of child development. Child Welfare Research Stations, supported by money from the Laura Spelman Rockefeller Foundation, were established at the University of California, Berkeley; Columbia University; the University of Iowa; the University of Minnesota; and Yale University. By the 1930s, researchers at these locations were systematically conducting a number of inquiries about the nature of child development. At Iowa, an effort was being made to determine whether nursery school had an impact on intelligence test scores. At Minnesota, Mildred Parten was observing children's play and developing norms for children of different ages. And at Berkeley, Jean MacFarlane was beginning the California Guidance Study, which eventually led to a longitudinal investigation that has charted the unfolding of development over many decades of the life cycle.

Next we see that, in addition to the development of theories and research within the field of child development, there have been sociopolitical influences that have motivated research on children's development (White, 1985).

Sociopolitical Influences on the Study of Child Development

At the turn of this century, national movements that produced the first White House Conference on Children and the founding of the Children's Bureau also fostered G. Stanley Hall's child research. The New Deal initiatives of the Roosevelt era also had an impact on the founding of the child development research movement in the 1930s and 1940s. Developmental psychology seems to have flourished at historical points when there has been substantial national activity on behalf of children and families.

While developmental psychology waned to some degree during the 1950s, it came to life again in the 1960s. In addition to discovering the cognitive developmental view of Jean Piaget, developmental psychologists also were influenced by the poverty programs of the Great Society. The War on Poverty led to the formation of Project Head Start, an early preschool program designed to give impoverished children an early start in education, as well as to research projects on the nature of child development in families from low-income neighborhoods.

Now, in the 1980s, we find considerable research interest in studying the effects of divorce on children, the role of the working mother in the child's development, and sex role development in females—all research efforts that have been influenced by the changing sociopolitical nature of society.

Contemporary Child Development Research

Childhood is now considered a highly eventful and unique period of life that lays the foundation for the adult years and is highly differentiated from them. We value child development as a special time for growth, and we invest great resources in caring for and educating children. We protect children from the excesses of adult work through stringent child labor laws; we treat children's crimes against society under a special system of juvenile justice; and we have governmental provisions for helping children when regular family support systems fail or when families seriously interfere with a child's well-being.

The research effort aimed at understanding how and why children develop is flourishing. In the 1930s, there was only a handful of child development research institutes and only several competing theories. Today there are huge numbers of researchers studying many domains of child development, and a multitude of theories about child development are available to guide the direction of that research.

Child Development Concept Table 1.1 summarizes the main ideas of our discussion of history and child development. Now we turn our attention to the nature of the periods and processes of child development.

Child Development Concept Table 1.1   Child Development and History

Concept	Processes/Related Ideas	Characteristics/Description
Child development in contemporary society	Divorce, working mothers, and latchkey children	Contemporary child development researchers are interested in understanding the nature of family processes, particularly such changing circumstances as the increased number of children from divorced, working-mother, and latchkey families.
	Computers and children	We now live in the information age, an age that involves extensive computer usage. Child developmentalists are fascinated by the role computers may play in the child's development.
	Hurried children, Type A behavior pattern, and children's health	Elkind argued that children are growing up too fast. Psychologists are beginning to explore the early appearance of Type A behavior patterns in children. Strong interest has been generated in the origin, development, and maintenance of children's health.
Child development and history	Historical accounts of childhood	Aries's historical accounts of children suggested little concern about children's developmental status apart from adults, except for the infancy period. The recent revival of historical interest in childhood indicates that Aries's view likely was overdrawn and that greater concern for children's status was present than previously thought.
	Ancient Greece and Rome	The children of antiquity usually are described as being subjected to considerable abuse. However, there is evidence that children did have a special place in ancient societies.
	The Middle Ages	Christianity had a profound impact on how children were viewed in the Middle Ages. The original sin view of children reflected the philosophical perspective that children basically were bad.
	The Renaissance	During the Renaissance, a number of cultural and scientific advances were made. Two philosophical views of the child that became prominent were the *tabula rasa* view and the innate goodness view.
The scientific beginnings of child development	Late 19th-century research	Darwin's evolutionary view strongly influenced thinking about child development. G. Stanley Hall developed a biological view of children's development. Darwin is credited with the first systematic method of studying children—the baby journal. Hall developed some questionnaires to study children, but they were weak.
	Twentieth-century research	By the 1930s, competing theories about the nature of child development existed, such as Freud's psychoanalytic/biological view and Watson's behavioral perspective. The behavioral view served an important function in developing empirical research strategies. Gesell set forth a maturational view of development and also conducted detailed observations of children at different ages. Child research stations were formed through funding by the Laura Spelman Rockefeller Foundation.
	Sociopolitical influences on the study of child development	At different points in the 20th century, sociopolitical occurrences have stimulated the study of children. One such example is the Great Society in the 1960s, during which research on children in poverty was promoted.
	Contemporary child development research	Today, theory and research about child development flourish, with many competing views and large numbers of researchers seeking to understand how and why children develop. Societal happenings continue to influence the study of children, as exemplified by the current interest in the study of sex role development in females.

PERIODS AND PROCESSES
OF CHILD DEVELOPMENT

In studying the nature of children's development, we often refer to certain periods of development, as well as to particular processes.

Periods of Development

Periods are time frames that characterize a particular segment of development. The **prenatal period** extends from conception to birth. It is a time of awesome physical change that begins with genetic transmission and continues through a number of cellular and structural changes. While the development of the embryo and fetus are genetically preprogrammed, there are many environmental influences on prenatal development. In Chapter 3, we outline the periods of development within the prenatal time frame and describe some of the possible environmental hazards to prenatal development.

Infancy begins at birth and extends through the 18th to 24th month. Infancy is a time of extensive dependency on adults. It is the beginning of many physical and psychological activities, such as language, symbolic thought, sensorimotor coordination, and social learning. This period usually ends as the child develops competencies that reflect his or her independence from parents, such as walking long distances from the caregiver or talking in short phrases. Infant development is described in Section 2 of this book.

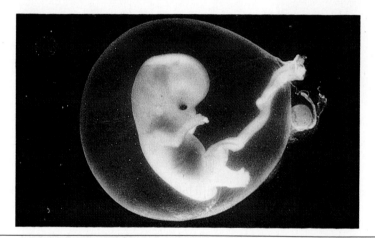

What is the prenatal period like?

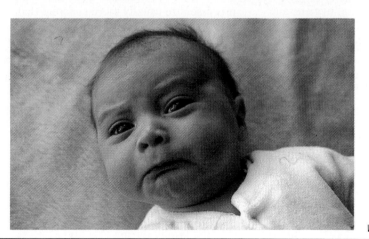

What characterizes infant development?

What distinguishes the preschool years from other periods of development?

How can we define middle and late childhood?

Early childhood, or the preschool years, extends from the end of infancy to about five or six years of age, roughly corresponding to the period when the child prepares for formal schooling. Among the tasks mastered are the ability to care for oneself (personal hygiene and dressing oneself), self-sufficiency (self-initiated play), and the development of school-readiness skills (following instructions, using writing implements, and identifying letters, numbers, and sounds). Peer relations also become more predominant during this time. First grade usually marks the end of this period. Early childhood is discussed in Section 3 of this book.

Middle and late childhood extends from about 6 to 11 years of age and is sometimes called the elementary school years. Middle childhood refers to the 6-to-8-year age range, and late childhood refers to the 9-to-11-year age range. Fundamental skills such as reading, writing, and arithmetic are mastered, and conceptual reasoning becomes more advanced. During this period, the child is formally introduced to the larger world and its culture through the study of history, civics, business and government, art and music, and contemporary social problems. Physical growth slows substantially, and thought processes are usually more concrete than in the next period. Peer relations are more time consuming than in earlier development. Middle and late childhood is evaluated in Section 4 of this book.

Adolescence is a period of transition from childhood to early adulthood, beginning approximately at 11 to 13 years of age and ending at 18 to 21 years of age. Adolescence begins with rapid physical change—dramatic gains in height and weight, change in body contour, and development of secondary sex characteristics, such as enlargement of breasts, development of pubic and facial hair, and deepening of voice. Logical and abstract thought processes increase, as does concern about identity and independence. More and more time is spent outside the family during this period. Researchers tend to

How can we best describe adolescence?

distinguish the early from the late phases of adolescent development. **Early adolescence** corresponds to the junior high school years, roughly from 10 to 15 years of age. This period also roughly corresponds to puberty, the time of rapid change to maturation. **Late adolescence** includes the late teenage years and early twenties, roughly from 16 to 21 years of age. The fascinating world of adolescents is portrayed in Section 5 of this book.

While the sections of this book are organized mainly around periods of development, individual chapters are process-oriented. Let's now see what we mean by processes of development.

Processes of Development

Focus on yourself for a moment. You are a unique person. Your thoughts, feelings, and behaviors are unlike anyone else's; yet you are like many other people your age. You have the same biological equipment—a brain, eyes, a heart. You, like everyone else, have a mind that thinks, reasons, and remembers. And you have some social experiences that are common to others as well. Virtually all of us grew up in a family and had relationships with peers and friends, and most of us spent many years in elementary and secondary schools.

How have you become simultaneously unique yet similar to others of your generation? What processes contributed to this outcome? These are the questions posed by developmental psychologists who attempt to understand the processes of change that contribute to commonality and distinctiveness in children. **Processes** are the explanations that child developmentalists use to explain the nature of development. Some of these processes are biological and physical in nature, others are cognitive, and still others are social and/or personality related.

Biological processes that influence development focus on evolution, ethology, and genetics. Darwin's theory of evolution rests on the principle of natural selection and emphasizes considerable genetic diversity in a species. Because of this diversity, some organisms have more beneficial characteristics that help them to adapt to their environment and that are likely to be perpetuated. Ethology is a modified instinctual view of the organism that stresses the release of unlearned patterns of behavior under certain environmental circumstances. Ethologists carefully observe the organism in its natural habitat. The field of genetics emphasizes genes as the basic building blocks of living organisms.

"Well, whatever it is we change into, it can't come soon enough for me."

Drawing by D. Reilly; © 1973 The New Yorker Magazine, Inc.

The emphasis on evolution, ethology, and genetics in child development reveals its strong ties to biology. Child developmentalists turn to biological processes to explain physical growth and development, as well as cognitive development. Some have also looked to biology as the basis of children's social behavior.

Physical development involves detectable changes in physical and anatomical features. Weight gain, overall height changes, growth of head and limbs, gross and fine motor development, and pubertal changes are all part of these physical changes. Throughout the discussion of physical growth and development in this book, we address the biological foundations of these changes, as well as the experiences that might modify these biological forces.

In addition to biological and physical processes that account for developmental change is a second set of processes that are cognitive in nature. **Cognitive processes** refer to mental activities—thought, perception, memory, attention, problem solving, language, and the like. These processes, like physical growth processes, have strong biological ties. Jean Piaget's cognitive-developmental theory of development—a giant theory from the 1960s on—stresses the biological underpinnings of cognitive stages in children. These cognitive activities are seen as strong, often causal, influences on how children behave in various life circumstances. Cognitive theorists stress that it is not so much what children experience in life as

how children use their cognitive activities to modify and understand their experiences.

An unresolved question in child development involves the degree to which development is based on unlearned, biological processes, as Gesell believed, and the degree to which it is due to experience and social processes, as Watson argued. This intriguing issue, which is known as the nature-nurture or genetic-environmental question, is explored in detail in Chapter 3. Historically, most developmental theories emphasizing social development have been environmentally oriented. However, cognitive and biological influences on social development are also now being studied. In this book, we refer to **social processes** as those pertaining to the child's interactions with people. Two four-year-old peers playing with each other, a mother reasoning with her child about his behavior, and a child arguing with her sibling are all examples of social processes.

Personality processes traditionally have referred more to a property of the child than to social interactions. Yet, it is difficult to meaningfully portray aspects of personality, such as the self, moral development, and sex-role development, without referring to the child's social world. Thus, the discussions of children's social and personality development often overlap. For example, when children's sex roles are described, we discuss the social contributions of families and peers. And when we describe peer relations, information about personality characteristics that contribute to peer popularity are outlined.

When studying the different processes of children's development in this book, keep in mind that the child is an integrated person with only one mind and one body. Biological/physical, cognitive, and social/personality processes are inextricably interwoven. In many chapters, you will learn how social experiences constrain or enhance cognitive development, how cognitive processes influence social development, and how cognitive processes are tied to biological development. Now that we have seen how development consists of a number of different periods and processes, we turn our attention to an overall description of what development is.

What Is Development?

The central concept of this book is **development.** What does it mean when we say that a child has "developed" in some respect? Developmentalists use the term *development* to refer to a pattern of movement or change that begins at conception and continues throughout the entire life span. The pattern of change involves growth (as in infancy) and also decay (as in death). The pattern of movement is complex because it often is the product of interrelated biological/physical, cognitive, and social/personality processes.

Now that we have discussed the periods and processes that characterize children's development and considered what development is, we focus on some of the main issues generated when scientists try to understand how and why children develop.

ISSUES IN CHILD DEVELOPMENT

A developmental perspective on children raises certain important questions that often guide child development research. These issues involve qualitative change during childhood, stages of child development, continuity and discontinuity in development, the nature of individual differences, and genetic/biological and environmental/social influences on development.

Qualitative Change

Jean Piaget, a great pioneer of developmental psychology, made many important claims about the development of intellectual functioning in children. Among these claims, perhaps none is more provocative than his claim of **qualitative change** in intelligence; that is, that a child's intelligence is not simply less than an adult's but that it is intelligence of a qualitatively different kind. For example, Piaget argued that very young children (five-months old) lack a fully developed object concept (Flavell, 1985) in that they do not conceive of objects as existing independently of themselves. According to Piaget, this object concept is something that must develop over the first two years of life and represents an outstanding intellectual achievement of this period. Before the object concept is fully developed, the child may not realize that an object continues to exist when the child's back is turned or when the object itself has disappeared behind another object. Such inferences of object permanence appear intuitive and transparently obvious to adults and, indeed, to three-year-old children. Thus, it is clearly arguable that a shift from one type of thinking to another, not simply an accumulation of mental power, occurs. The development of the object concept represents a prototype of what qualitative change in development can mean.

Does development involve qualitative changes of the sort Piaget claimed? The answer is not obvious, but a developmental perspective suggests that qualitative changes are possible. For example, there may be qualitative changes in personality, although not necessarily for all children, and not necessarily for intellectual or biological processes. These are empirical issues that can be resolved on the basis of intensive research efforts in particular problem areas of development. The developmental perspective on children simply raises the question of qualitative change—it does not answer the question.

Stages of Development

In addition to his claim of qualitative change in intelligence, Piaget also proposed that there are identifiable stages of intellectual development in childhood. The notion of stages is a controversial one within psychology; researchers disagree about the existence of developmental stages and also about the characteristics of such stages.

Any conceptualization of developmental **stages** must incorporate the notion of qualitative change. Beyond this, the stages of development concept implies that qualitative changes must occur in certain sequences (Stage 2 must be preceded by Stage 1 and not vice versa). Many developmental psychologists (Flavell, 1985) would go still further and claim that the idea of stages implies (1) a certain degree of abruptness of transition from one stage to another and (2) concurrence in the appearance of behaviors or competencies that characterize a given stage. That is, if an entire set of organized behaviors appears rather suddenly in the course of development and does so for most, if not all, individuals at a certain point in the life span, there is clear evidence for a developmental stage of some sort. Unfortunately, evidence for such occurrences is rare and unconvincing, leading some investigators to doubt the stage concept (Flavell, 1985) and others to redefine the concept (Wohlwill, 1973). Despite these problems, the concept of stages has an enduring appeal for developmental psychologists, and we will return to this concept repeatedly throughout this text.

Continuity-Discontinuity in Development

To what extent is an older child's development based on experiences that occurred a number of years earlier? The issue of **continuity-discontinuity** primarily focuses on the extent to which early dimensions of the child and his or her life are related to what the child or adolescent is like at a later point in development.

For many years, it was believed that early experience, particularly within the family during the first five years of life, was the primary determinant of development later in life, even during the adult years. This view initially was proposed by Freudian psychoanalytic theorists and had an important impact on developmental thinking for many years. Such a view represents a strong form of the continuity argument.

In recent years, psychologists have begun to question whether early experience is the sole or even the primary determinant of later development. While it is agreed that early experiences represent important prototypical models for how later experiences are handled, many developmental psychologists argue that early experiences do not have irreversible effects. These psychologists take

a discontinuity stance in the sense that they emphasize the individual's capacity for change throughout the life cycle, rather than later development being determined by early experiences alone. Thus, from this perspective, while infant experiences have important ramifications for development in later childhood and adolescence, experiences during later childhood and adolescence also contribute to the nature of the older child and adolescent's development.

Arguments about the relative importance of early experience and the degree to which development is continuous or discontinuous are still very much alive in the study of child development. Focus on Child Development 1.1 describes an example of continuity in development between infancy and middle childhood.

So far, we have examined some characteristics that developmental psychologists use to describe all children, but as we see next, it is also important to remember how individualized children's lives are.

Individual Differences

Something you already know but that bears repeating is that, in some ways, one child is like all other children in the world, yet in other ways, the child is different. Every child has a brain and some way of communicating with others, for example. But the particular brain and particular way in which the child communicates may somehow be different from all other children.

Scientists who study children have tended to search for the general principles that characterize development more than for children's individual variations. For example, when researchers investigate the effects of divorce on children, they may report that children from divorced families show more self-control problems than those from intact (never divorced) families. Yet, if we actually looked at the data the researcher collected, we likely would find that not every child from a divorced family shows self-control problems. We might find that 50 of the 75 children from divorced families experienced self-control problems, while only 25 of the 75 children from intact families showed such difficulties. In this example, then, 25 of the children from divorced families did not reveal self-control problems. A fascinating aspect of child development research is trying to determine why such individual differences among children occur.

FOCUS ON CHILD DEVELOPMENT 1.1

INFANT AND MATERNAL DIETS IN GUATEMALA AND SAN DIEGO

David Barrett, Marian Radke-Yarrow, and Robert Klein (1982) have conducted investigations that suggest that an infant's diet may be linked with the child's emotional characteristics at the time he or she enters elementary school. The first investigation, a five-year longitudinal study, focused on 148 boys and girls in three rural Guatemalan villages. The second study was a survey of 65 six- to eight-year-old children from low-income families in San Diego.

In the Guatemalan study, researchers studied children who had received supplemental high-calorie drinks in addition to their regular diets from birth to age four, and whose mothers had received supplements during pregnancy. The average child in the villages studied was not grossly underfed; for example, a typical four-year-old weighing 35 pounds was estimated to be living on about 1,300 calories a day, while standards established by the World Health Organization call for such a child to receive about 1,600 calories. To study the effects of the increased nutrition on the emotional characteristics of the children, researchers administered a battery of psychological tests and observed the children during various play, competitive, and problem-solving situations.

Research results showed that children who had better nutritional supplements prenatally and for the first two years after birth were consistently more active, involved, and helpful than their peers and less anxious; they also were more likely to express happy or sad emotions than were others in the group, who often appeared withdrawn or uninterested. Whether children received food supplements from ages two to four years, however, did not seem to influence their behavior when they were six- to eight-year-olds.

In the research study conducted with low-income families in San Diego, children whose mothers were undernourished during pregnancy and whose weight was low at birth were compared with children whose mothers had better diets. The undernourished group interacted less with their school-age peers, were more dependent on adults, and appeared sadder and more unfriendly.

According to the researchers, these results suggest a cycle in which subtle alterations of the central nervous system and lack of energy often combine with a poor home environment to stunt the child's emotional growth. The result may be withdrawal on the part of the child and neglect or rejection on the part of the caregiver. It seems that the child attempts to adapt to the physiological stress of nutritional deficit by developing behaviors that remove him or her from the environment and inhibit the later development of appropriate patterns of social interaction. The researchers believe that nutrition may be critical in the first years of life because it is during infancy that the child is beginning to develop patterns of dealing with the world and responding to others.

How might early nutritional patterns be related to later emotional development?

For example, in trying to understand why some children from divorced families have self-control problems and others do not, the researcher might probe for information about the nature of postdivorce family functioning, examining such factors as the economic situation, the availability of support systems, and the continuing relationship of the ex-spouse to the custodial parent and the child.

Consider also an investigation of children's reasoning. An investigator presents a problem to a group of fourth-grade children. Half of the children are given an organized strategy for solving the problem, while the other half are not. The results of the study might show that the children who were given the organized strategy were more likely to solve the problem than those who were not given the strategy. However, closer inspection of the results might show that while group differences in the children's problem solving favor the organized strategy group, some of the children who were not given the organized strategy also solved the problem. Again, as in the divorce example, this might lead researchers to question why these individual differences occurred. Genetic differences in intelligence between the children might account for some of the variation, as could the children's different environmental experiences. For example, some of the children may have experienced superior teachers who provided efficient and organized ways to solve problems, while other children may not have been as fortunate.

The issue of individual differences also raises the question of what children bring to a situation when they are being studied by child development researchers. Thus, the individual differences a child from a divorced family may bring to a situation in which self-control is being studied may have been influenced by factors such as support systems and the relationship of the ex-spouse to the custodial parent and child. And the individual differences a child may bring to the problem-solving situation likely are influenced by such factors as genetic background and schooling experiences.

As you read about many different research studies in this book, keep in mind that group differences in children usually are being reported but that there is also individual variation among the children in the study. Individual variation often leads to intriguing questions that can be the focus of further research.

In explaining the nature of individual differences in problem solving, it was mentioned that both genetic and environmental factors might be producing the differences among the children being studied. Genetic and environmental factors are also key ingredients for understanding why continuity and discontinuity occur in development. And the issue of qualitative change and stages of development also raises the question of the degree to which such change or the presence of stages is due to genetic and environmental influences. Let's explore this important issue of genetic and environmental influences on development further.

Genetic/Biological and Environmental/ Social Influences on Development

A child is both a biological being and a social being, influenced by genetic inheritance from both parents as well as by countless hours of interaction with people in his or her environment. Virtually all contemporary views of child development recognize the importance of both genetic/biological factors and environmental/social influences on the child's development. But child developmentalists often disagree about the relative influence of these factors. Recall how Gesell argued so strongly for biological determination of development, while Watson stressed environmental determinism during the 1920s and 1930s. It is rare today to find someone as devoted to the biological view as Gesell or as wedded to the environmental view as Watson.

Newborn birds come into the world ready to sing the song of their species. They only have to listen to their parents sing the song a few times to get it right and then they know the song for the rest of their lives. Today, many developmental psychologists believe that human children are biologically predisposed to learn the language of *Homo sapiens* in a similar manner. But aren't the experiences we have in the culture in which we live important in our development as well?

For about 2,000 years, the Ik of Uganda lived as nomadic hunters. But some 50 years ago, their livelihood was destroyed when the government of Uganda turned their hunting ground into a national park. Because hunting was forbidden in the park, the Ik were forced to try to farm the steep, barren mountain areas of the park.

Colin Turnbull lived among the Ik for 1½ years and described the disastrous results for the displaced Ik in his book *The Mountain People* (1972). Famine, crowding, and drought led to tremendous upheavals in family orientation and moral values. Children were sent out on their own with no life supports supplied by parents. The children often banded together in pairs and triplets to fend off adults and other youth who vied with them for food and water. Boys and girls learned that, to exist in their world, they had to look out for themselves and show little respect or concern for others. Interestingly, when they had children of their own, they, in turn, put them out on their own at a very early age, even as young as three years.

The principle of individual survival became far and away the most important motive in the life of the Ik. Turnbull described the Ik as having no love at all. What we regard as positive virtues, such as kindness, affection, and consideration for others, simply did not exist in the Ik. Imagine yourself on a barren mountainside away from civilization in the country of Uganda. Your way of life has been disrupted. You no longer have food. Would you act as the members of the Ik culture did?

So while we biologically are predisposed to sing the song of our species, experiences with our environment modify what the song is like. A consistent theme in this book is that children's development is due to an interaction of genetic/biological and environmental/social factors.

Child Development Concept Table 1.2 summarizes the main ideas of our discussion of different periods and processes of development as well as several important issues in child development. Attempts to understand the periods and processes of development and to generate more valid conclusions about issues, such as those we just discussed, have led to an increased scientific orientation in the study of children's development. Next, we see that an extensive number of methods have been developed to further this scientific orientation.

METHODS

How can we obtain scientific information about children's development? The "Imagine" section at the beginning of the chapter showed that researchers have conducted systematic observations of infant attachment, developed questions and interview strategies to determine children's understanding of thinking, and analyzed blood samples and used multiple measures, such as interviews, observations, and tests, to learn more about the relation of hormones and psychological adjustment. In this section, we look at the kinds of measures child psychologists use to obtain information about children, chart the strategies used in designing research studies, consider the time span of the inquiry, and finally, evaluate ethical considerations in studying children.

Ways of Collecting Information About Children

Many types of measures can be used to obtain information about children. Researchers can observe the behavior of infants and children in a laboratory or in natural settings, such as at home or school or while at play, put questions to children in the form of interviews or questionnaires/surveys, or develop and administer standardized tests.

Child Development Concept Table 1.2 Periods, Processes, and Issues in Development		
Concept	**Processes/Related Ideas**	**Characteristics/Description**
Periods of development	Prenatal	The prenatal period extends from conception to birth and is a time of dramatic physical change.
	Infancy	Infancy extends from birth through the 18th to 24th month and is a time of considerable dependence on adults. It also marks the emergence of many abilities, such as language.
	Early childhood	Early childhood extends from approximately age two to age five and is also called the preschool period. Self-sufficiency increases, as do school-readiness skills.
	Middle and late childhood	Middle and late childhood extends from about 6 to 11 years of age and is also called the elementary school years. Academic skills are mastered, and there is formal exposure to the larger world.
	Adolescence	Adolescence lasts from about 11 to 13 years of age to 18 to 21 years of age. Early adolescence, a time of rapid maturation, is distinguished from late adolescence. Identity and independence are important characteristics.
Processes of development	Biological/physical	Biological and physical processes include evolution, ethology, and genetic influences, as well as physical growth.
	Cognitive	Cognitive processes focus on such mental activities as perception, memory, thinking, problem solving, and language.
	Social/personality	Social processes pertain to interactions with people, while personality processes are related more to the properties of the person. However, these processes often are interrelated.
	Interrelation of processes of development	These processes are often linked together, such that cognitive processes influence social development and social processes affect cognitive development. Keep in mind that the child is an integrated human being with only one mind and body.
What is development?	Biological/physical, cognitive, and social/personality processes	Development is a pattern of movement or change, beginning at conception and continuing throughout the life span.
Issues in child development	Qualitative change	The issue of qualitative change focuses on whether development is different from one point to another, rather than simply being more or less. Qualitative changes are difficult to document.
	Stages of development	The issue of stages of development emphasizes whether qualitative changes occur in certain sequences. This controversial issue has endured in child development.
	Continuity-discontinuity in development	The most widely debated aspect of this issue is the extent to which later development is dependent on earlier experiences/development.
	Individual differences	In some ways, one child is like all other children, but in other ways he or she is different. Scientists have tended to study group differences among children rather than individual variation. Research studies, while usually reporting such group differences, also reveal considerable individual variation among children. The individual variation often stimulates further research to explain the variation.
	Genetic/biological and environmental/social influences	The child is both a biological and a social being. His or her behavior is influenced by both genetic and environmental interaction.

How do child psychologists use systematic observation to study children?

Systematic Observation

The importance of observation was captured by George Sand (1877), who said, "The whole secret of the study of nature lies in learning how to use one's eyes." Another astute observer, Ralph Waldo Emerson, noted: "God hides things by putting them near us." And as Sherlock Holmes said to Watson, "You see, but you do not observe."

We look at things all of the time, but this usually does not constitute scientific observation or research. If we are not trained as an observer and do not practice our skills on a regular basis, we are not quite sure what to look for, may not remember what we have seen, may change what we look for from one moment to the next, and may communicate our observations ineffectively.

For observations to be effective, we have to know what we are looking for, whom we are going to observe, when and where we are going to observe, how the observations are going to be made, and in what form the observations are going to be recorded—this is the process of **systematic observation.** Systematic observation has helped to advance many different disciplines—biology, physics, anthropology, and, of course, child development.

The most common way of recording what is seen when watching children is to write down observations, using shorthand or symbols. Tape recorders, cameras, special coding sheets, and two-way mirrors also make observations of children more efficient. Initially, an observer may not have specific categories to code, but rather needs to get a feel or sense of what is happening. Extensive observation may lead to the development of specific categories of children's behavior that can be coded. To ensure the reliability of observations, a second observer often watches a portion of the children in a research study to confirm what the first observer is seeing. If the two observers agree consistently on what they are seeing, then the observations are described as having good reliability. If the two observers do not agree, then much less faith is placed in the quality of the observations. To improve reliability of observers, child psychologists often spend considerable time training the observers to look for certain things, discuss beforehand what will be coded in one category rather than another, and so forth.

The observations child psychologists make can be classified in terms of the location or setting in which the observations are made. Much of the research conducted in child psychology is carried out in a **laboratory,** a controlled setting in which much of the "real world" with its complex factors has been removed. Laboratory settings are useful when it is necessary to control for certain factors that influence development but that are not the focus of the particular research inquiry. However, there are costs involved when conducting laboratory research with children. First, it is virtually impossible to do laboratory research without the participants knowing that they are in a research study. Second, the laboratory setting may be "unnatural" and cause "unnatural" behavior on the part of the participants. For example, if a father knows he is being watched in a scientific laboratory, is he likely to engage in less intensive, less power-oriented discipline in interacting with his son? Third, there are some aspects of development that are difficult, if not impossible (and unethical), to investigate in the laboratory. Consider matters pertaining to how marital conflict and physical punishment affect children's development—they would not be viable candidates for laboratory observation.

While laboratories remain an extremely valuable setting for conducting research inquiries, naturalistic observations or field studies are becoming increasingly popular. **Naturalistic observations** (or **field studies**) refer to research conducted in children's real-world settings, such as homes, schools, playgrounds, neighborhoods, shopping malls, and day-care centers. Piaget's observations of his children at home were naturalistic observations. Jane Goodall (1972) spent months living with chimps in Africa to observe their behavior in a natural setting. Roger Barker wrote *One Boy's Day* after he had followed a young boy around for an entire day and observed his behavior in a variety of natural settings (Barker & Wright, 1951).

Though often presented as a dichotomy, laboratory and naturalistic research actually can be viewed as two points on a continuum that is labeled "naturalism" or "control." For example, researchers can conduct laboratory studies with a decidedly "natural" character. For example, the description of the infant attachment study in the "Imagine" section that opened this chapter revealed how the laboratory room was filled with toys to make it more like a home setting. A naturalistic study of children's memory might involve their recollection of autobiographical events, rather than of some unknown combination of letters like "isz," or "bkd." Naturalistic studies also can be conducted under controlled conditions. For example, researchers might observe the school behavior of children who have been exposed to two decidedly different teaching styles, one a high degree of verbal interaction and question asking, the other a low incidence of verbal interaction and question asking.

While systematic observation is important in studying children's development, some research is conducted more efficiently by asking questions.

Interviews and Surveys/Questionnaires

An **interview** is a set of questions put to someone and the responses the person makes. The interview can range from very structured to very unstructured. For example, a very unstructured interview might include questions like, "Tell me about some of the things you do with your friends," or "Tell me about yourself," while a very structured interview might question whether the child highly approves, moderately approves, moderately disapproves, or highly disapproves of his or her friends cheating on tests at school.

Interviews can be conducted in different kinds of settings, just as observations. An interview might take place at a university nursery school, in the child's home, or in an unfamiliar room. Too little attention has focused on how such settings might influence the kind of information obtained from interviews with children. One interview strategy, called the Neighborhood Walk, involves the interviewer talking with the child as they walk through the child's neighborhood (see Focus on Child Development 1.2).

Researchers also question children through surveys or questionnaires. A **survey/questionnaire** is similar to a highly structured interview except that the child reads the question and marks his or her answer on a sheet of paper rather than verbally responding to the interviewer. One major advantage of surveys and questionnaires is that they can be given to large numbers of people, sometimes as many as 10,000 children and their parents. For example, the National Survey of Children (Zill, 1977) sampled the views of thousands of children from various parts of the United States on a variety of topics by using a questionnaire. In such surveys, the more personal and concrete the subject matter, the more consistent the children's responses (Vaillancourt, 1973).

In the National Survey on Children (Zill, 1977), a subsample of children were selected for interviews. This was done because structured interviews conducted by an experienced psychologist can produce more detailed responses than are possible in a questionnaire and can help to eliminate careless responses. A good interviewer can encourage the child to open up as well.

Interviews and surveys/questionnaires, though, are not without their problems. Perhaps the most critical of these problems is the response set known as **social desirability.** A socially desirable response is one given by the child because he or she thinks it is more socially acceptable than how he or she truly thinks or feels. When asked about how well the child gets along with peers or about how many friends he or she has, the socially isolated child may not want to report peer and friendship difficulties and consequently may give a socially desirable response of getting along well with peers and having a number of friends. Skilled interviewing techniques and built-in questions designed to eliminate such defenses are critical in obtaining accurate information from interviews and surveys/questionnaires.

Standardized Tests

Remember those standardized achievement tests you used to take in elementary and secondary school with a large group of your classmates in the auditorium, gym, or library? And possibly you individually were given an intelligence or personality test that was standardized as well. **Standardized tests** can be questionnaires, structured interviews, or behavioral in nature. Their distinctive feature is that they are developed to identify a child's characteristics or abilities, relative to those of a large group of similar children. The use of standardized tests usually involves giving the child a percentile score, such as saying that the child scored in the 92nd percentile on the Stanford Binet Intelligence Test. The percentile score indicates how much higher or lower the child scored than the large group of children who initially took the test (those on whom the test was standardized). The most widely used standardized tests are those involving assessment of children's intelligence, such as the Stanford Binet Intelligence Test just mentioned. However, standardized tests, such as the Harter Perceived Competence Scale for Children (Harter, 1982), also are used to assess aspects of children's social development, such as social competence.

FOCUS ON CHILD DEVELOPMENT 1.2

THE NEIGHBORHOOD WALK

When you go someplace you have been before, you often remember something you otherwise would not have thought about. For example, if you took a walk through the neighborhood you grew up in, you likely would remember such things as, "Over there in that field is where a bunch of my friends and I used to play," or "The old man who lived in that house was scary—we never went near his place." As you turn down another street, you might remember, "The school was a warm and friendly place—I really felt good when I was there."

In an effort to determine children's sources of support for their social development during the middle and late childhood years, Brenda Bryant developed a technique called the Neighborhood Walk, which involved an interviewer accompanying a child on a walk through the child's neighborhood. Bryant believed that the walk through the neighborhood provided concrete cues of neighborhood settings relevant to questions being asked the child. Thus, when asking the child about specific neighbors, the interviewer pointed to the neighbors' homes and asked the questions. Children were asked such questions as whether neighbors talked with them, if they knew the names of the neighbors, and when they last talked with the neighbors.

One hundred and sixty-eight children participated in this project—72 had just finished the first grade, and 96 had just completed the fourth grade. The emphasis in the interview was on the child's reported experience of involvement with personal, home, and community resources. The children took the interviewers down manicured streets, through favorite orchards, and to empty lots and favorite hiding places. Following the Neighborhood Walk, the children were given a number of measures to determine their social development, such as their self-concept, how much they felt in control of their lives, how much they were able to take the perspective of others, how cooperative and competitive they were, their individualized work orientation, and their level of empathy.

An analysis of the children's responses to many different questions during the Neighborhood Walk revealed that three types of resources were reported by the children: (1) others

as resources (primarily interpersonal sources of support, such as peers and parents); (2) intrapersonal resources, such as hobbies and fantasies; and (3) environmental resources, such as places to join others (see the table).

The results connecting support systems and the child's social development showed that the first-grade children had much less developed and integrated social networks than the fourth-grade children. And the findings confirmed that extended family and neighborhood resources were linked with the child's social development. For example, as shown in the table, relationships with grandparents, intimate talks with pets, informal meeting places, and involvement in formally sponsored organizations were related to various aspects of the child's social development.

As can be seen, modifications of standard interviews, such as the Neighborhood Walk, can be invaluable in discovering important influences on the child's development.

How might peers function as important resources for children?

Categories Representing Sources of Support Derived From the Neighborhood Walk With Children

I. Others as resources (primarily interpersonal sources of support)
  A. Peer generation
    1. Know and interact with peers
    2. Intimate talks with peers
    3. Peer generation among the 10 most important individuals
  B. Pet "generation"
    1. Pets as special friends
    2. Intimate talks with pets
    3. Pet "generation" among the 10 most important individuals
  C. Parent generation
    1. Know and interact with adult generation
    2. Special talks with adults
    3. Intimate talks with parent generation
    4. Parent generation among the 10 most important individuals
    5. Involvement in father's work
    6. Involvement in mother's work
  D. Grandparent generation
    1. Know and interact with grandparent generation
    2. Intimate talks with grandparent generation
    3. Grandparent generation among the 10 most important individuals
  E. Spiritual support
II. Intrapersonal sources of support
  A. Hobbies
  B. Fantasies
    1. Structured
    2. Unstructured
  C. Access to skill development and public display of skills
III. Environmental sources of support
  A. Access to independence (places to get off to by self)
  B. Places to join others

Source: From "The Neighborhood Walk: Sources of Support in Middle Childhood" by B. K. Bryant, 1985, *Monographs of the Society for Research in Children, 50* (3, Serial No. 210), 35.

Neighborhood/Community and Family Influences on Children's Social Development

Support Factor	Social-Emotional Functioning
More knowing and interacting with adults	Empathic
More intimate talks with grandparent generation	Empathic
More grandparent generation in top 10	Internal locus of control
More intimate talks with pets	Competitive
More places to get off to by self	Accepting of individual differences
More informal, unsponsored meeting places	Accepting of individual differences
More involvement in formally sponsored organizations (involving both structured and unstructured activities)	Individualistic

Source: From "The Neighborhood Walk: Sources of Support in Middle Childhood" by B. K. Bryant, 1985, *Monographs of the Society for Research in Children, 50* (3, Serial No. 210), 48.

Child Development Concept Table 1.3		Measures Used to Obtain Information About Children's Development	
Method	**Main Characteristics**	**Advantages**	**Disadvantages**
Systematic observation	Systematic observation involves careful watching of behavior under controlled conditions in a laboratory or naturalistic setting.	Systematic observation allows precise control over what is being studied.	In a laboratory setting, subject awareness and unnatural aspects are disadvantages; in a natural setting, less control is a disadvantage.
Interviews and surveys/ questionnaires	Interviews and surveys/ questionnaires involve questions put to someone and the responses he or she makes. Interviews range from structured to unstructured and involve verbal responses to the interviewer. Surveys/ questionnaires involve paper-and-pencil responses.	Interviews and surveys/ questionnaires allow a person's perceptions to be assessed, which may give important information beyond observed behavior. Surveys/ questionnaires can be given to very large samples.	Interviews and surveys/ questionnaires assess a person's perceptions, which may not tell much about his or her behavior. Social desirability responses are another disadvantage.
Standardized tests	Standardized tests involve questionnaires, structured interviews, or behavior designed to identify an individual's characteristics relative to those of a large group of similar individuals.	Standardized tests provide a comparison of one individual's score with large numbers of other people's scores.	Standardized tests are based on the belief that behavior is stable; yet, behavior may be different outside of the test situation.

The main advantage of standardized tests is their ability to provide a comparison of one child's score with large numbers of other children's scores. That is, they provide information about individual differences among children. However, information on standardized tests does not always predict behavior in nontest situations accurately. Standardized tests are based on the belief that a child's thoughts and behaviors are consistent and stable, varying little from one context to another. But while intelligence and personality, two primary targets of standardized tests, have some stability, they sometimes vary depending on the situation in which the child is evaluated. Thus, a child may perform poorly on a standardized intelligence test, but when observed in a less anxious context, such as the natural surroundings of his or her home or neighborhood, the child may perform much better. This problem is especially relevant to minority group children, some of whom have been inappropriately classified as mentally retarded on the basis of intelligence test scores.

Child Development Concept Table 1.3 summarizes our discussion of systematic observation, interviews and surveys/questionnaires, and standardized tests—prominent measures used to discover information about children. In addition to considering what measures to use when studying children, however, researchers must also decide on the strategy for the investigation.

Strategies of Research Design

A research study can be designed using experimental strategy, quasi-experimental strategy, or correlational strategy.

Experimental Strategy

In many instances, researchers want their child development studies to be conducted in an experimental way because, more than other strategies, experimental strategy allows the precise determination of whether something is causing a child to act, feel, or think in a particular way. An **experiment** is a carefully controlled context in which the factors that are believed to influence the mind or behavior are controlled. The experimenter manipulates the "influential" factors, called **independent variables,** and measures the **dependent variables,** which are the measures/behaviors examined for any change due to the influence of the independent variables. The following hypothetical experiment should help to clarify experimental strategy and the importance of the experiment in the study of children:

Suppose we want to investigate how aerobic activity by pregnant women affects the development of the infant. First, to clearly define our independent variable, we decide that the nature and frequency of the aerobic activity of the pregnant women should be four times per week (one hour per session) under the direction of a trained instructor. We also need a control group of pregnant women who do not engage in the aerobic activity. We randomly assign the subjects to the two conditions: the pregnant women in one group exercise and the pregnant women in the other group do not. The group that gets the exercise is called the **experimental group,** while the group that gets zero level of the independent variable (in this case, aerobic activity) is referred to as the **control group.** The control group is the comparison or baseline group in our study. We also give careful consideration to our dependent variables. We choose two measures— breathing and sleeping patterns—to assess in the infants. The two sets of offspring are tested during the first week of life on these dependent variables. Our results indicate that the experimental group infants have more regular breathing and sleeping patterns than their control group counterparts. We conclude that aerobic exercise by pregnant women promotes more regular breathing and sleeping patterns in newborn children.

A final comment needs to be made about the random assignment of the subjects to the experimental and control groups. By randomly assigning the pregnant women to the two conditions, we greatly reduced the likelihood that the two groups differed on some relevant variable, such as the woman's exercise history, health problems, or intelligence. Why? Because every subject with any particular degree of a specific characteristic was equally likely to end up in either the experimental group or the control group. Such random assignment can be accomplished by consulting a table of random numbers in a statistics book, but flipping a coin is basically the same concept.

Quasi-Experimental Strategy

Often, researchers use a technique that resembles experimental strategy in all important respects except one—the degree of prior control exercised over the independent variable. In such a pseudoexperiment, sometimes called a **quasi experiment,** researchers cannot randomly assign subjects to experiences or conditions. In such investigations, people's experiences determine which group they will be in. For example, researchers might study the self-esteem of working women versus homemakers, the coping skills of divorced women versus married women, and the social skills of children attending day-care centers versus those living with their mothers at home. Thus, quasi experiments are useful for obtaining information about social matters that create tricky problems for exercising tight experimental control. They are not true experiments, however, since researchers cannot randomly assign the participants. Therefore, causation cannot be inferred from quasi experiments. Indeed, many developmental psychologists (e.g., Schaie, 1977) simply like to categorize quasi experiments as correlational studies, which are discussed in the next section.

Let's evaluate our aerobic activity and pregnant women example in a quasi-experimental manner. In our quasi-experimental study, we decide to study the aerobic exercisers as they actually exist in society, rather than randomly assigning them to conditions of exercise and no exercise. We might decide that, to be included in the aerobic group, women must have said that they exercised aerobically on a regular basis, defined as three or more 45-minute aerobic classes per week, during their pregnancy. It is also important to have a control group of nonexercisers. Since we have not randomly assigned women to these two groups, the two groups must be matched on certain characteristics (Cook & Campbell, 1979), such as age and social class (e.g., education and occupation). Our goal is still to discover the relation of aerobic activity by pregnant women to their offsprings' breathing and sleeping patterns. The results of our quasi experiment indicate no differences between the infants whose mothers are aerobic exercisers and those whose mothers are nonexercisers. Our results may reflect a failure to match the two groups on such relevant variables as intelligence and health. Or the aerobic exercisers may not have exercised as regularly as they said they did, while the nonexercisers may have exercised more than they indicated.

We described three different research strategies. How might these strategies be used to study aerobic exercise by pregnant women and its effect on their offspring?

Correlational Strategy

It is often interesting to know how one measured characteristic is associated with another—height with weight, intelligence with motivation, self-esteem with social class, drug use with parental upbringing, and so forth. The most common measure of such association is called **correlation** and is represented statistically by the **correlation coefficient.**

The correlation coefficient ranges from −1.00 to +1.00. A negative number indicates an inverse relation. For example, a frequent finding is that individuals with high IQs are reasonably rapid learners, which indicates a high positive correlation. By contrast, there is usually a negative correlation between permissive parenting and a child's self-control. The higher the number in the index (whether positive or negative), the stronger the association between the variables. An index of zero indicates that there is no association between the variables.

A correlation alone cannot be used to support the argument that one event causes another. We can't argue, for example, that because height and weight are positively correlated, we grow tall because we gain weight (or vice versa). It is always possible that some unnoticed third factor is the causal agent that links these two events together. Figure 1.3 gives an example of the subtle but critical distinction between correlation and causation.

To further understand the principle of correlation, let's consider another example related to aerobic activity. In this case, we are interested in the correlation between the aerobic activity of adolescents and whether their parents and/or best friends exercise aerobically. We find a positive correlation between the frequency of adolescents' aerobic activity and that displayed by both their parents and their friends. We cannot conclude, however, that the aerobic activity of parents and friends *caused* the adolescents' aerobic activity.

We have examined the methods and the strategies that child psychologists can use to obtain information about children. Another important consideration is the time span of the inquiry.

The Time Span of Inquiry

When studies of children's development are conducted, the time span of the inquiry becomes an important issue. Development occurs over time, so it makes sense that child developmentalists are concerned about the time span of their investigations. Some developmental investigations are conducted over very short periods of time, while others follow children for years. Here we examine three possible research designs that reflect different time spans: cross-sectional designs, longitudinal designs, and sequential designs.

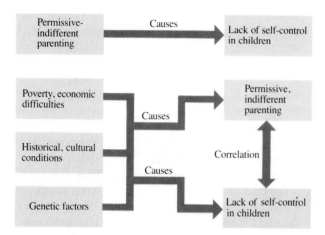

FIGURE 1.3 Evaluating the correlation between parenting and children's behavior. One variable may increase as another increases (or may decrease as another decreases), but this does not necessarily mean the first causes the second. For instance, if we find that as parents use more permissive-indifferent ways to deal with their children, the children's self-control decreases, it does not necessarily mean that the parenting style caused the children's behavior. Rather, the link between these variables could be attributed to other factors, such as genetic background, poverty, and sociohistorical conditions.

	Cohort		
	1982	1984	1986
Time of testing 1986	4 years old	2 years old	Newborn
1988	6 years old	4 years old	2 years old
1990	8 years old	6 years old	4 years old

FIGURE 1.4 Example of a sequential design. This design includes three cohorts (born in 1982, 1984, and 1986) tested at three different times (1986, 1988, and 1990) plus new independent samples of cohorts.

Cross-Sectional Designs

When researchers do not study children across time but rather sample their thoughts and behaviors at one point in time, the study is said to be **cross-sectional** in nature. For example, if researchers were interested in studying children's problem-solving ability, they might select three groups of children of different ages, say 5-, 8-, and 11-year-olds, and administer one or more problem-solving tests to them. All of this could be accomplished in a very brief period of time—even a large study can often be completed in a month or so. By far the majority of studies of children's development are cross-sectional, undoubtedly because of the brief period of time they require. Let's now look at designs that last for much longer periods of time.

Longitudinal Designs

Some child developmentalists believe that, if they truly are going to study the nature of developmental changes in children, the children have to be studied as they develop through time. If researchers wanted to study children's problem-solving abilities longitudinally in the age span previously described, they might select a sample of 5-year-old children and test the children on several occasions as they aged, possibly at 8 years of age and then again at 11 years of age. **Longitudinal designs** are particularly helpful in controlling for individual variation in the course of development. For example, in the cross-sectional comparison of 5-, 8-, and 11-year-olds, even though the three age groups of children probably would match on some variables, such as social class, other factors, such as health and personality, might vary across the children of different ages. However, in longitudinal studies, children serve as their own controls with regard to individual variation. While there are few longitudinal studies of children in comparison to cross-sectional studies, these investigations have made substantial contributions to the understanding of child development. Throughout the text, you will discover frequent references to longitudinal designs.

Sequential Designs

In recent years, developmental psychologists have constructed **sequential designs** (e.g., Baltes, 1973; Baltes, Reese, & Lipsitt, 1980; Schaie, 1965). These designs combine the cross-sectional and longitudinal designs and allow researchers to see whether the same pattern of development is revealed by the different time span strategies. Figure 1.4 shows a sequential research design involving children of three different ages, tested at three different times, and born at three different points in history.

The testing of children born at different points in history has become a particularly important issue in the study of development. A cohort is a population of people born at a particular point in history. **Cohort effects** refer to effects due to a child's time of birth or generation but not actually to his or her age. Cohorts of children can differ on such dimensions as years of education, child-rearing practices, health, attitudes on topics like sex and religion, exposure to the media, economic hardships or boom, and so forth.

We have described a number of different measures that can be used to obtain information about children, discussed different strategies for designing research, and focused on the dimension of time in data collection. But there is another important concern that any competent child development researcher has when he or she conducts an investigation of children—the well-being of the children. Remember from the "Imagine" section at the beginning of the chapter that, if a child appears to become too distressed during a research session, the session is stopped. Such concern for the welfare of the child is an important part of the research enterprise. Next we look more closely at some of the ethical standards of child psychologists when they conduct research with children.

Ethical Considerations in Studying Children

Child psychologists subscribe to the code of ethics of the American Psychological Association and the Society for Research in Child Development. Most training programs require their graduate students to learn these codes. To be licensed to practice psychology in most states, prospective psychologists must pass a formal test on ethical standards. Among the most important concepts in working with children are the following ethical imperatives:

1. Psychologists must always obtain informed consent from parents or legal guardians if children are to be tested in any way or are to be the objects of research. Parents have the right to a complete and accurate description of what will be done with their children and may refuse to let their charges participate.
2. Children have rights, too. The psychologist is obliged to explain precisely what the child will experience. Children may refuse to participate, even after parental permission has been given. If so, the investigator must not test the child. Similarly, if a child becomes upset during some professional interaction, it is the psychologist's obligation to calm the youngster. If the psychologist fails to do so, the activity must be discontinued.
3. The psychologist must always weigh the potential for harming children against the prospects of contributing some clear benefits to them. If there is the chance of any harm—such as when drugs are to be used, social deception is to take place, or the child is to be treated aversively (e.g., punished or reprimanded)—the psychologist must be able to convince a group of impartial peers that the benefits of the experience for the child clearly outweigh any chance of harm.
4. The psychologist must always adhere to accepted standards of practice, using techniques and procedures that treat children courteously and respectfully. Since children are in a vulnerable position and lack power and control when facing an adult, the psychologist should always strive to make the professional encounter a positive and supportive experience.

THINKING BACK, LOOKING AHEAD

Child development is an exciting field of inquiry, one with historical glimpses of blank slates, miniature adults, and whining schoolboys. As science has progressed, more objective efforts aimed at understanding children's development have appeared. Now in the 20th century, observations of Danielle's attachment to her mother, Zachary's access to his private, thinking self, and Jennifer's hormonal changes reflect how the scientific enterprise spans different ages and periods of development. Contemporary child development researchers truly are privileged to be living at a time when we are rapidly progressing from ignorance to knowledge. But while the increase in knowledge of children's development has been substantial, it is important to keep in mind the thoughts of Bertrand Russell, who captured not only the curiosity of science but its skepticism as well, when he said, "What is wanted is not the will to believe, but the wish to find out, which is the exact opposite."

Many frontiers have yet to be crossed in the scientific exploration of children's development, but as researchers continue to explore those frontiers, it is imperative that they retain an emphatic concern about the well-being of children. Child development research should not only provide information about general rules of development but should also generate ideas about how the lives of children can be improved.

In this first chapter, we only briefly touched on theoretical ideas about children's development, such as those of Freud, Watson, and Gesell. Such theories go together with methods and research issues to form the core of the scientific study of child development. In the next chapter, we devote full attention to the major theories of how children develop.

SUMMARY

I. Child development has received considerable attention in contemporary society. Among the topics of interest are those pertaining to divorce, working mothers, and latchkey children; computers and children; and hurried children, Type A behavior pattern, and children's health.

II. Among the features of child development and history are historical accounts of childhood, discussion of the scientific approaches to child development that arose in the late 19th as well as the 20th century, and the status of contemporary child development research.

A. Aries's historical accounts of children suggested little concern about children's developmental status apart from adults, except for the infancy period. The recent revival of historical interest in childhood indicates that Aries's view likely was overdrawn and that greater concern for children's status was present than previously thought.

1. The children of ancient Greece and Rome usually are described as being subjected to considerable abuse. However, there is evidence that children did have a special place in these societies.

2. Christianity had a profound effect on how children were viewed during the Middle Ages. Here, also, too many stereotypes have been generated about the nature of children and how they were viewed. The prevailing philosophical concept of children during the Middle Ages was called the original sin view.

3. During the Renaissance, tremendous cultural and scientific advances were made. Two contrasting philosophical views about the nature of the child became prominent—the *tabula rasa* and innate goodness views.

B. The late 19th century and the 20th century saw the scientific beginnings of child development.

1. Darwin's evolutionary view strongly influenced thinking about child development. G. Stanley Hall developed a biological view of children's development. Darwin is credited with the first systematic method of studying children—the baby journal. Hall developed some questionnaires to study children, but they were weak.

2. By the 1930s, competing theories about the nature of child development existed, such as Freud's psychoanalytical/biological view and Watson's behavioral perspective. The behavioral view served an important function in developing empirical research strategies. Gesell set forth a maturational view of development and also conducted detailed observations of children at different ages. Child research stations were formed through funding by the Laura Spelman Rockefeller Foundation.

3. At different points in the 20th century, sociopolitical occurrences have stimulated the study of children. One such example is the Great Society in the 1960s, during which time research on children in poverty was promoted.

C. Today, theory and research about child development flourish, with many competing views and large numbers of researchers conducting intriguing studies to discover how and why children develop. Societal happenings continue to influence the nature of child development research, as exemplified by the current interest in the study of sex role development in females.

III. In studying child development, it is important to learn about the periods of development, the processes of development, and what development is.

A. The periods of development are the prenatal, infancy, early childhood, middle and late childhood, and adolescence periods.

B. The processes of development encompass biological/physical processes, cognitive processes, and social/personality processes. It is important to consider the interrelation of these processes because the child should be viewed as an integrated being.

C. Development is a pattern of movement or change that begins at conception and continues throughout the entire life span. In the case of child development, development usually involves growth, but it can also involve decay, as in death.

IV. Five important issues in child development are (1) qualitative change, (2) stages of development, (3) continuity-discontinuity in development, (4) individual differences, and (5) genetic/biological and environmental/social influences on development.

V. To understand the nature of methods used to study children's development, it is important to consider measures, research designs and strategies, the time span of the inquiry, and ethical issues.

A. Among the most important measures used to study children's development are systematic observation, interviews and surveys/questionnaires, and standardized tests.

B. Important considerations in research design and strategy are whether the study will be conducted in an experimental, quasi-experimental, or correlational manner.

C. Child developmentalists are particularly interested in the time span of inquiry because development unfolds over time. Three research strategies involving time span considerations are cross-sectional, longitudinal, and sequential designs. Cohort effects—those pertaining to time of birth and generation—are important to consider when evaluating the time span of inquiry.

D. When children are studied, it is important to abide by a code of ethics and to consider the ethical issues involved in conducting research with children.

KEY TERMS

adolescence 16
biological processes 17
cognitive processes 18
cohort effects 34
continuity-discontinuity 20
control group 31
correlation 32
correlation coefficient 32
cross-sectional designs 33
dependent variables 30
development 19
early adolescence 17
early childhood 16
experiment 30
experimental group 31
independent variables 30
infancy 15
innate goodness view 11
interview 27
laboratory 26
late adolescence 17

longitudinal designs 33
middle and late childhood 16
naturalistic observations (field studies) 26
original sin view 10
periods 15
personality processes 18
physical development 18
prenatal period 15
processes 17
qualitative change 19
quasi experiment 31
sequential designs 33
social desirability 27
social processes 18
stages 20
standardized tests 27
survey/questionnaire 27
systematic observation 25
tabula rasa view 11

SUGGESTED READINGS

Appelbaum, M. I., & McCall, R. B. (1983). Design and analysis in developmental psychology. In P. H. Mussen (Ed.), *Handbook of child psychology* (4th ed.), Vol. 1. New York: Wiley.
A comprehensive and authoritative treatment of methodology, techniques for designing developmental research, and approaches to special research problems, such as social interaction and field research. An excellent reference source.

Borstelmann, L. J. (1983). Children before psychology: Ideas about children from antiquity to the late 1800s. In P. H. Mussen (Ed.), *Handbook of child psychology* (4th ed.), Vol. 1. New York: Wiley.
A comprehensive treatment of the historical conception of children from ancient times until the 18th century. An excellent portrait of many different historical societies and influential philosophers who wrote about children.

Child Development and *Developmental Psychology* 214.
These two research journals are highly respected outlets for scientific information about children's development. Leafing through the last several years of these journals will give you a sense of what researchers in child development are interested in.

Kessen, W. (1979). The American child and other cultural inventions. *American Psychologist, 34,* 815–820.
An intriguing essay describing how childhood has come to be understood and viewed in contemporary America. Contrasts this conception with conceptions of children at other times in history.

THEORIES

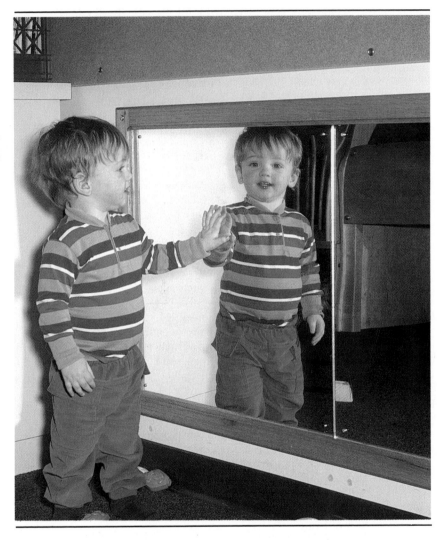

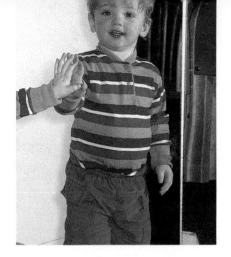

IMAGINE . . . YOU ARE 10 YEARS OLD AND HAVE JUST WRITTEN AN ESSAY ON THE RARE ALBINO SPARROW

PREVIEW

PSYCHOANALYTIC THEORY

Sigmund Freud's Classical Psychoanalytic Theory

The Structure of Personality
Defense Mechanisms

FOCUS ON CHILD DEVELOPMENT 2.1: RELATIONSHIPS, DEVELOPMENT, AND DEFENSE MECHANISMS

Freud's Psychosexual Stages of Personality Development
Freud's Theory Today

Contemporary Psychoanalytic Theorists and Erikson's Life-Cycle View

Strengths and Weaknesses of Psychoanalytic Theory

CHILD DEVELOPMENT CONCEPT TABLE 2.1: PSYCHOANALYTIC THEORY

COGNITIVE THEORIES OF DEVELOPMENT

Cognitive Developmental Theory

Stages of Cognitive Development
Processes Responsible for Developmental Changes

FOCUS ON CHILD DEVELOPMENT 2.2: DREAMS, FREUD, AND PIAGET—FROM BIRD-HEADED CREATURES TO BATHTUBS

The Information Processing Perspective

The Computer Metaphor—Old and New Models
Questions Raised About Children's Cognition by the Information Processing Perspective

Strengths and Weaknesses of the Cognitive Theories

CHILD DEVELOPMENT CONCEPT TABLE 2.2: COGNITIVE THEORIES

BEHAVIORAL/SOCIAL LEARNING THEORIES

Skinner's Behaviorism
Social Learning Theory
Strengths and Weaknesses of Behavioral/Social Learning Theories

CHILD DEVELOPMENT CONCEPT TABLE 2.3: BEHAVIORAL/SOCIAL LEARNING THEORIES

ETHOLOGICAL THEORY

Classical Ethological Theory and the European Zoologists
The Neo-Ethological View of Robert Hinde

Three Questions Ethologists Ask About Children's Development
Selected Issues of Interest to Ethologists

Strengths and Weaknesses of Ethological Theory

CHILD DEVELOPMENT CONCEPT TABLE 2.4: ETHOLOGICAL THEORY

AN ECLECTIC THEORETICAL ORIENTATION

THINKING BACK, LOOKING AHEAD

SUMMARY

KEY TERMS

SUGGESTED READINGS

CHAPTER 2

IMAGINE . . . YOU ARE 10 YEARS OLD AND HAVE JUST WRITTEN AN ESSAY ON THE RARE ALBINO SPARROW

An amazing thing happened when Jean was only 10 years old. He wrote an article about the rare albino sparrow, which was published in the *Journal of the Natural History of Neuchâtel.* The article was so brilliant that the curators of the Geneva Museum of Natural History, who had no idea that the article had been written by a 10-year-old, offered the preadolescent boy a job as curator of the museum. The offer was quickly withdrawn when the heads of the museum realized that Jean was only a child. Jean Piaget, born August 9, 1896 in Neuchâtel, Switzerland, later became one of the most influential forces in child development research in the 20th century.

What would influence someone like Piaget, or even yourself, to develop a theory of how and why children develop? The individual interested in developing such a theory usually goes through a long university training program that likely culminates in a doctoral degree. As part of the training, the individual is exposed to many ideas about a particular topic, such as personality, child development, adolescence, or clinical psychology. But another factor that undoubtedly influences an individual to develop a particular theory focuses on the kind of life experiences the theorist had during his or her childhood years. Let's look further now at some of the growing-up experiences of two important theorists discussed in this chapter—Piaget and Erik Erikson.

Jean Piaget

Piaget's interest in zoology continued through his adolescent years and culminated in his doctoral dissertation on the behavior of mollusks in 1918 at the University of Neuchâtel. During his adolescence, though, Piaget was not just interested in zoology. Philosophy and psychology books filled his room, and he spent much of his spare time reading Kant, Durkheim, and James (philosopher, sociologist, and psychologist, respectively).

While his studies had taken him in the direction of biology and other intellectual pursuits, the deteriorating health of Piaget's mother had an important impact on the first job that he accepted after he completed his doctorate degree. In 1918, Piaget took a position at Bleuler's psychiatric clinic in Zurich, where he learned about clinical techniques for interviewing children. Then, still at the young age of 22, he went to work in the psychology laboratory at the University of Zurich, where he was exposed to the insights of Alfred Binet, who developed the first intelligence test. By the time Piaget was 25, his experience in varied disciplines had helped him to see important links between philosophy, psychology, and biology.

In his autobiography, Piaget (1952) detailed why he chose to pursue the study of cognitive development rather than emotional development:

I started to forego playing for serious work very early. Indeed, I have always dètested any departure from reality, an attitude which I relate to . . . my mother's poor mental health. It was this disturbing factor which at the beginning of my studies in psychology made me keenly interested in psychoanalytic and pathological psychology. Though this interest helped me to achieve independence and to widen my cultural background, I have never since felt any desire to involve myself deeper in that particular direction, always much preferring the study of normalcy and of the workings of the intellect to that of the tricks of the unconscious. (p. 238)

Erik Erikson

Erik Homberger Erikson was born June 15, 1902, near Frankfurt, Germany, to Danish parents. Before Erik was born, his parents separated, and his mother left Denmark to live in Germany, where she had some friends. At age three, Erik became ill, and his mother took him to see a pediatrician named Homberger. Young Erik's mother fell in love with the pediatrician, married him, and gave Erik the middle name of his new stepfather.

Erik attended primary school between the ages of 6 and 10 and then the gymnasium (high school) from the ages of 11 to 18. He studied art and a number of languages rather than scientific courses like biology and chemistry. Erik did not like the formal atmosphere of his school, and this was reflected in his grades. At age 18, rather than going to college, the adolescent Erikson wandered through the continent, keeping notes about his experiences in a personal diary. After a year of travel through Europe, he returned to Germany and enrolled in an art school, became dissatisfied, and enrolled in another. Then he began to give up his sketching and eventually traveled to Florence, Italy. Robert Coles vividly describes Erikson at this time:

To the Italians he was not an unfamiliar sight: the young, tall, thin Nordic expatriate with long, blond hair. He wore a corduroy suit and was seen by his family and friends as not odd or "sick" but as a wandering artist who was trying to come to grips with himself, a not unnatural or unusual struggle—particularly in Germany. (Coles, 1970, p. 15)

PREVIEW

Piaget and Erikson were giants in developmental psychology. Piaget's intellectual curiosity and precocity were well reflected in his belief that the most important aspects of development are those that are cognitive in nature. And Erikson's wandering through Europe and his distaste for formal schooling undoubtedly found their way into his theory of development, particularly his view that adolescence is a time of life when we search for clues as to who we are and what we are all about.

Piaget and Erikson developed major theories of child development, as have other theorists you will read about in this chapter. A theory is a set of assumptions to explain something. Theories not only are crafted out of the experiences individuals have in their lives, but also after a considerable amount of reflective thought. The following passage, which refers to Sir Isaac Newton, who developed the theory of gravity, stimulates images of the kind of thinking required to develop a theory:

Where the statue stood of Newton,
With his prism and silent face,
The index of a mind for
Ever voyaging through the
Strange Seas of Thought, alone.   Wordsworth

PSYCHOANALYTIC THEORY

When we hear the term *psychoanalysis* and the name Sigmund Freud, we often think of a bearded man pensively listening to a client who is lying on a couch and recounting his or her early childhood experiences. The stereotype is not completely farfetched—the traditional psychoanalysis practiced by Freud did have the client lying on the couch, with no eye contact between the client and Freud. (One commentary indicated that Freud was shy and did not like having people staring at him all day.) However, there also were conceptual reasons for not having eye contact—Freud believed that the therapist should be an opaque mirror in which the client could see himself or herself, and the unobtrusive presence of the therapist was believed to facilitate this.

Psychoanalytic theory is a view of personality that emphasizes the private, unconscious aspects of the mind. It also emphasizes biological forces and the symbolic transformation of experience. As we discuss Freud's theory, the strong role of biological instincts will become apparent, but so too will the belief shared by all psychoanalytic theorists that how children use symbols, many of which are beyond their conscious awareness, to represent experience is important as well.

Sigmund Freud's Classical Psychoanalytic Theory

There are many details to Freud's theory, and his ideas have filled many volumes. We begin by touching on the nature of the man.

Sigmund Freud was loved and hated, looked up to and looked down on. To many people, he was a master; to others, he was clearly wrong in his views on personality. Regardless of whether he is viewed as right or wrong in his assumptions about personality, Freud clearly must be regarded as one of the most influential thinkers of the 20th century.

Freud was a medical doctor who specialized in neurology. He developed his ideas about psychoanalysis from his work with patients who had mental problems. He was born in 1856 in Austria and died in London at the age of 83. He spent most of his life as a physician in Vienna, Austria. He finally became convinced that he needed to leave Vienna toward the end of his life because of the anti-Semitism of the Nazis.

Freud was the firstborn child in his Jewish family. His mother saw him as very special, and his brothers and sisters treated him as a genius. One of Freud's main conceptions is that of the **Oedipus complex,** which consists of a child feeling a great deal of anxiety over sexual attraction to the parent of the opposite sex. It is very possible that this view arose from Freud's own romantic attachment to his mother, who was young and beautiful.

Freud spent a great deal of time trying to understand how the unconscious mind works, and as we see next, it is to this aspect of our mind that he attributed the greatest control.

The Structure of Personality

Freud believed that personality is like an iceberg, with the conscious aspects of the mind being the tip of the iceberg above the water and the unconscious aspects representing the bulk of the iceberg beneath the water

Sigmund Freud (1856–1939)

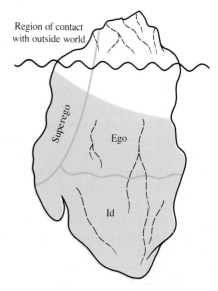

Conscious and unconscious processes. This rather odd-looking diagram illustrates Freud's belief that most of the important personality processes occur below the level of conscious awareness. People's conscious thoughts and behaviors reflect the ego and the superego to some degree. But, whereas the ego and superego are partly conscious and partly unconscious, the primitive id is the unconscious, totally submerged part of the "iceberg."

(Figure 2.1). One of the best-known aspects of Freud's theory is his division of personality into three structures: id, ego, and superego (Freud, 1924). According to Freud, at birth, the mind houses only one personality structure—the id. Freud viewed the **id** as a bundle of sexual and aggressive instincts or drives that are primarily unconscious. From the time we are born, Freud believed, sexual and aggressive instincts dominate our life, always having to be kept in check. But because these instincts are primarily unconscious, said Freud, we are not aware of the underlying motivation of much of our behavior. By describing the newborn as a bundle of sexual and aggressive instincts, Freud was taking a philosophical stance that suggests that people are born into the world as basically evil or bad. Therefore, it is up to society to transform the bundle of evil into a socially acceptable creature. Freud was somewhat pessimistic about society being able to accomplish this task. The reasons for his pessimism can probably be traced to two factors. First, the biological determinism of instinct theory was predominant at the time Freud was developing his views; second, Freud had experienced the horrors of World War I.

Freud believed not only that a dark, evil side of personality is within each of us, but that it is the controlling force in our lives. According to Freud, this id works according to the **pleasure principle,** always seeking pleasure and avoiding pain, regardless of what impact such pleasure seeking and pain avoiding will have on our life in the real world. The thinking of the id was referred to

by Freud as **primary process thinking,** which involves the effort on the part of the id to satisfy its wants and needs by simply forming a mental image of the object it desires. Thus, Freud believed that children dream about sex, about food, and about how they would like to beat up the bully who keeps making them look bad. In some ways, then, the needs of the id can be satisfied through wish-fulfilling mental images, as well as through actual behavior.

Clearly, it would be a chaotic and dangerous world if the child's personality was all id. However, according to Freud, in early childhood, other aspects of personality develop.

As a child, you learned that you could not always get what you wanted. You couldn't eat 26 popsicles, and sometimes you weren't even allowed to eat 1. Sometimes, you had to gulp down spinach or peas, and you had to learn to use the potty rather than your diaper.

According to Freud, a new part of your personality was being formed—the **ego,** which is the side of personality that considers the demands of reality. Just as the id obeys the pleasure principle, the ego abides by the **reality principle.** This principle suggests that, as we were growing up, we found ways to satisfy the wants and needs of the id within the boundaries of reality. We began to adhere to the admonishments of our parents and to realize that we had to consider our peers and the fact that our world was not one in which sexual and aggressive impulses could go unrestrained. The ego helped us to test reality—to see how far we could go without getting into trouble or hurting ourselves.

The ego houses the child's higher mental functions, such as reasoning, problem solving, and decision making, and for that reason, it is sometimes referred to as the executive branch of personality. However, according to Freud, the ego develops out of the id and is forever wedded to it. Thus, although Freud recognized the importance of cognitive functions, such as problem-solving capabilities, he nonetheless believed that these always come into conflict with the wishes of the id, and in Freud's view, the ego usually is the loser.

According to Freud, the id and the ego are void of any morality; they do not take into account whether something is right or wrong. This is left to the third branch, sometimes called the moral branch, of personality: the **superego.** It is mainly through interactions with parents that the superego develops. By rewarding prosocial conduct and punishing antisocial behavior, parents teach children certain moral principles. Freud believed that the superego has two compartments—a **conscience,** which reflects children's moral inhibitions that are the product of their parents' punishments, and an **ego ideal,** which indicates children's standards of perfection that are the result of their parents' reward of good behavior. Freud believed that children's feelings or emotions are an important aspect of the superego. Guilt is a feeling that inhibits children's immoral behavior, and pride is an emotion that encourages moral behavior. In Freud's view, moral development is primarily a result of feelings of guilt that are instilled by punitive parents, and such guilt is responsible for keeping id impulses in check. Figure 2.2 shows a representation of the development of the id, ego, and superego.

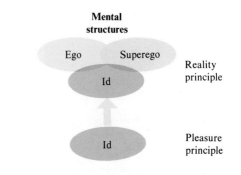

FIGURE 2.2   The development of personality structures according to Freud's theory.

At times, the three different components of personality work in opposition to one another. The child's id may want to steal something, while his or her ego reasons that this is not an intelligent thing to do and his or her superego says that it is morally wrong to steal. For the most part, though, the three components of personality work together. However, even in working together, Freud always saw the id as a producer of conflict for the ego and the superego. Regardless of how well the child has adapted to reality and how well he or she has worked out an advanced moral system to live by, Freud believed that the impulses of the id will cause conflict. Indeed, Freud's view of the child is one in which conflict is always a dominant characteristic.

Now we turn our attention to one of the most useful concepts in psychoanalytic theory—defense mechanisms. As you will see, these mechanisms help children to adapt to the reality of the world.

Defense Mechanisms

The ego has a tendency to distort perceptions of reality in favor of the fantasy-oriented desires of the id. One way of reducing the conflict between the id and the ego is to express the desires of the id in a disguised manner. This is accomplished by means of defense mechanisms. **Defense mechanisms** are a powerful part of the symbolic transformation of experience. For example, a child may have a very strong aggressive drive, but it may not be safe for him or her to express such desires of the id. Consequently, the child may develop a defense mechanism that channels his or her aggressive impulses into socially

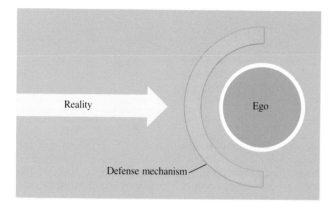

FIGURE 2.3 The function of an ego defense mechanism. Like a shield, the defense mechanism protects the ego from the harsher aspects of reality.

acceptable activities like playing sports (see Figure 2.3). Now we turn our attention to four specific defense mechanisms: repression, reaction formation, regression, and projection.

Freud believed that the most powerful and pervasive defense mechanism is **repression,** a tendency of the ego to push anxiety-producing information into the unconscious mind. For example, he thought that the Oedipus complex is solved through repression. As another example, a child may actually harbor the motive to brutally harm someone but repress the wish into the unconscious aspect of the mind because he or she knows that it will lead to harmful consequences.

Reaction formation refers to the process by which repressed thoughts appear in the conscious part of the child's mind as mirror opposites of the repressed thoughts. When I was in elementary school, I was asked whether I liked a particular girl. My response was, "Are you kidding? I hate her!" In truth, I was embarrassed about the fact that I really liked her and had gotten to the point where I had repressed my puppy love for her. The repressed feeling of love had come out in its mirror opposite—hate.

The defense mechanism of **regression** is the tendency to return to an earlier stage of development. Under stress, children or adults may have a tendency to go back to patterns of behavior that brought reward and security at an earlier age. Thus, some children may eat a lot of food when they get frustrated. By eating a lot, they satisfy

their oral need, a regression to the satisfying feelings of their infant years. Similarly, some children may cry when they get frustrated and can't seem to cope with their current problems. Such crying often represents a regression to infancy, according to Freudian theory. In recent years, other researchers have elaborated on Freud's ideas about defense mechanisms and regression. As we see in Focus on Child Development 2.1, Peter Blos and Anna Freud persuasively argue that changes in adolescence probably are more important than Sigmund Freud thought and, further, that defense mechanisms, particularly regression, are a key ingredient in interpreting development.

Projection occurs when children perceive their external world in terms of their personal conflicts. All children have characteristics that they are not proud of and that are distasteful to their ego. One way they cope with these undesirable traits is to project them onto someone else. For example, the child who is not considerate of others may label other children as selfish and uncaring about the feelings of others.

As we see next, in addition to having strong views on the structure of personality and defense mechanisms, Freud also believed that the personality unfolded in a developmental fashion.

Freud's Psychosexual Stages of Personality Development

Another important aspect of Freud's theory is that it is a stage theory. Freud argued that development involves distinct, qualitative changes—changes that he called the stages of development. These stages, according to Freud, occur in a universal fashion and in a fixed sequence; the fact that they are qualitative means that they are dramatic changes that significantly alter a child's life from one period of development to the next. Freud's is one of the most widely discussed stage theories in developmental psychology, as well as one of the most prominent theories of personality.

According to Freud, as the id, ego, and superego develop, we go through five clearly distinguishable stages. Each one can be defined in terms of an overriding theme that guides our life at that particular point in development. Freud's theory is said to be psychosexual because personality development is intertwined with the development of the sexual drive. Freud's five psychosexual stages are: oral, anal, phallic, latency, and genital.

FOCUS ON CHILD DEVELOPMENT 2.1

RELATIONSHIPS, DEVELOPMENT, AND DEFENSE MECHANISMS

For Peter Blos (1962), one of the most well-accepted contemporary psychoanalytic theorists who studies adolescents, regression during adolescence is not defensive at all, but rather is an integral part of puberty. Such regression, according to Blos, is inevitable and universal. The nature of this regression may vary from one adolescent to the next. It may involve childhood autonomy, compliance, and cleanliness, or it may involve a sudden return to the passiveness that characterized the adolescent's behavior during infancy or early childhood. Blos believes that intrafamilial struggles during adolescence reflect the presence of unresolved conflicts from childhood.

An excellent example of how the psychoanalytic theorist works in tying together adolescent feelings with childhood experiences rests in the work of Joseph Adelson and Margery Doehrman (1980). When their patient, John, was 16, he entered a group therapy session with other adolescents. At this time, he was recovering from severe depression following the breakup of a serious relationship with a girlfriend. The girl's mother actually referred John to the clinic, sensing that John's depression was severe, just as she had earlier detected that his dependency on her daughter was acute. John was a handsome, intelligent, articulate adolescent and a leader at school, hardly the type of person you would think might be deeply and severely depressed.

After a series of sessions with John, it became apparent that he kept most girls at a distance, particularly when they seemed to want to get seriously involved or to "mother" him. On the other hand, he was attracted to girls who were either aloof or tomboyish. It gradually became clear that John's relationships with girls were characterized by a wish to reestablish a union with his mother and that he had an intense fear of that wish. He was attracted to girls who were standoffish, but once he established a relationship with one of them, he would sink into an uncontrollable dependency upon her, to the point of being enthralled by such dependency.

To some degree, then, John's attachments to girls represented a wish to become reunited with his mother. What was John's relationship with his mother like in adolescence?

He was often abusive toward her; he complained that she nagged at him all the time; but in truth he was frightened by his regressive feelings toward her, according to Adelson. The regressive feelings came out clearly in group therapy when his intelligent participation would be replaced by sarcasm and then scorn whenever he seemed to be drawn to the "maternal" females in the group. This was particularly true with the woman therapist, who was seen as the group's "mother."

Although some psychoanalytic writers, like Blos, consider regression a normal part of adolescent development, for individuals like John, the reappearance of unresolved conflicts from early childhood requires therapy. For most individuals, however, the conflicts are not so serious that therapy is warranted. Thus, the intensity and persistence of the regression determine whether it is a healthy or unhealthy part of adolescent development.

Anna Freud (1958, 1966) has developed the idea that defense mechanisms are the key to understanding adolescent adjustment. She believes that the problems of adolescence are not to be unlocked by understanding the id, or instinctual forces, but instead are to be discovered in the existence of "love objects" in the adolescent's past, both Oedipal and pre-Oedipal. She argues that the attachment to these love objects, usually parents, is carried forward from the infant years and merely toned down or inhibited during the latency years. During adolescence, these pregenital urges may be reawakened, or worse, newly acquired genital (adolescent) urges may combine with the urges that developed in early childhood.

Anna Freud goes on to describe how adolescent defense mechanisms are used to ward off these infantile intrusions. Youth may withdraw from their attachment and identification with their parents and suddenly transfer their love to others—to parent substitutes, to leaders who represent ideals, or to peers. Or, rather than transferring the attachment to someone else, adolescents may reverse their feelings toward the attachment figure—replacing love with hate or dependence with rebellion. Finally, the instinctual fears may even generate unhealthy defensive solutions—for example, the adolescent may withdraw within himself or herself, which could lead to grandiose ideas of triumph or persecution; or regression could occur. Thus, from Anna Freud's perspective, a number of defense mechanisms are essential to the adolescent's handling of conflicts.

During the first 12 to 18 months of life, the activities of the infant that bring the greatest amount of pleasure center around the mouth; hence, the infant is in the **oral stage** of development. The activities of chewing, sucking, and biting are the infant's chief sources of pleasure and also reduce tension.

The period lasting from about 18 months of age to three years of life is called the **anal stage** in Freud's theory because the child's greatest pleasure surrounds the anus, or the eliminative functions associated with it. The shift to the anal stage is brought about by the maturation of the sphincter muscles and the child's ability to hold back or expel waste material at will. It is assumed that the exercise of the anal muscles reduces tension. This period is not easily forgotten by parents who typically experience considerable concern over their initially unsuccessful efforts at toilet training.

During Freud's **phallic stage,** which lasts from about the third to the sixth year of life, the focus is on the child's genitals. It is during this period, according to Freud, that boys and girls become acutely aware of their sexual anatomy and the anatomical differences between the sexes. This awareness sets up a number of complex psychological problems. Working through these highly stressful conflicts about sexual matters may take a number of years and is said to form the basis for the mature adult's sexual identity.

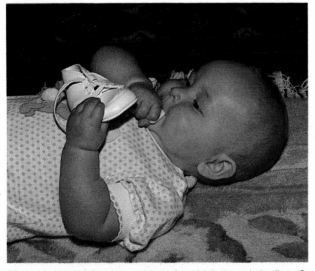

The oral stage of development lasts from birth through the first 12 to 18 months of life. What characterizes the oral stage?

The phallic stage lasts from about three through five years of age. How does a child's relation to his parents change during this stage?

The anal stage lasts from about 18 months to three years of age. How does it fit into Freud's theory?

During these early years, the development of identification with parents is a central theme in Freud's view. The identification process proceeds differently for boys and girls. All children initially identify with their mother. However, during the phallic stage, boys switch this identification to their father. This is a time when considerable conflict and psychosexual desires for the opposite-sexed parent need to be resolved. As noted earlier, a boy's sexual desire for the mother and rivalrous feelings toward the father are called the Oedipus complex. A girl's desire for her father and rivalrous feelings toward her mother are called the **Electra complex.** Freud actually pictured identification as a defense mechanism in which the child resolves inner conflict and sexual desires for the opposite-sexed parent by patterning himself or herself after the parent of the same sex.

But the child does not completely resolve the sexual conflicts experienced during the preschool years. Instead, the troublesome feelings are repressed, driven from

The latency stage lasts from about six years of age until puberty. How might this stage influence peer relations?

consciousness and locked away in the unconscious id. This repression marks the onset of Freud's **latency stage,** the long period of middle and late childhood that lasts from about age 6 to age 11 or 12. During the latency stage, the child represses all interest in sexual matters, instead showing more intellectual interest and a desire to learn about the world. This activity channels much of the child's energy into emotionally safe areas and aids the child in forgetting the highly stressful problems of the previous stage. However, the latency stage is like the lull before the storm.

Freud's **genital stage** begins with the onset of puberty and lasts throughout the adult years. At the beginning of the genital stage, sexual interest is reawakened. Freud believed that during the adolescent years, the individual feels strong sexual desires for someone other than his or her parents. Freud believed, however, that Oedipal sexual feelings may reemerge as the individual seeks a love object outside the family. Figure 2.4 reveals the fluctuations in sexual drive that Freud believed underlie personality development, as well as the development of the psychosexual stages.

The genital stage begins with puberty and lasts through the remainder of our adult lives. How do the effects of this stage affect adolescent friendships with the opposite sex?

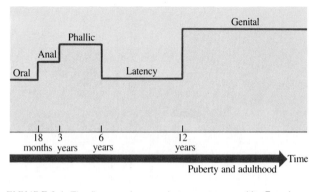

FIGURE 2.4 The five psychosexual stages proposed by Freud.

Before we go on to other psychoanalytic views, let's briefly evaluate the status of Freud's theory today, noting in particular the pervasive influence it has had on our pursuit of understanding the mind and behavior.

Freud's Theory Today

Few psychologists accept all of Freud's major theses today. His belief that virtually all of our behavior is motivated by unconscious desire seems too sweeping a statement. Many of the things that bother us are very well known to us. And sexual tension does not undergird all of our efforts to be competent in our world. Thus, each concept in Freud's theory should be evaluated for the broad insights it provides and not for its literal accuracy.

Freud's ideas opened up many doors in psychology that had previously been ignored or considered too controversial for exploration. Current inquiries about sex roles, parent–child and parent–adolescent conflict, and aggression can all be traced to Freud's inquiries about development. Next, however, we see that Freud's theory has its dissenters as well.

Contemporary Psychoanalytic Theorists and Erikson's Life-Cycle View

Freud had many followers—several of them outstanding thinkers in their own right—who proposed revisions of his theory. Because Freud was exploring so many new and uncharted regions of personality development, it is not surprising that a number of people believed that his theory needed modifications.

Many contemporary psychoanalytic theorists still stress the developmental unfolding of personality, the way in which adult characteristics are heavily determined by childhood experiences, and the importance of unconscious thought processes. However, they tend to downplay the importance of sexual instincts in a child's development, instead placing more emphasis on rational thought processes and cultural influences. Many contemporary psychoanalytic theorists are called **neo-psychoanalytic theorists** because, while they accept a number of Freudian ideas, they believe that Freud was wrong about one or more main issues. One such theorist is Erik Erikson.

Like Freud, Erikson (1950, 1968) stresses the importance of early family experiences and unconscious thought. However, he believes that Freud shortchanged the importance of culture in determining personality. For example, both Freud and Erikson describe changes that take place during adolescence. For Freud, these changes are primarily sexual in nature, but for Erikson, they involve the development of an identity. Erikson believes that it is during adolescence that individuals begin a thorough search for who they are, what they are all about, and where they are going in life. As part of this search for an identity, the adolescent often experiments with a variety of roles, some sexual, others ideological, and still others vocational.

While Freud described changes in development only through the adolescent years, Erikson presents a true life-cycle perspective in that his view covers eight stages of development from birth through the late adulthood years. Each stage of development (age) centers around a salient and distinct emotional concern stemming from biological pressures from within and sociocultural expectations from outside the person (see Figure 2.5). These emotional concerns or conflicts may be resolved in a positive and healthy manner or in a pessimistic and unhealthy way (Erikson, 1968). Each conflict has a unique time period during which it ascends and overshadows all the others. For the stages to proceed smoothly, each earlier conflict should be resolved satisfactorily.

Erikson's first stage, **trust versus mistrust,** corresponds to the oral stage in Freudian theory. An infant is almost entirely dependent upon his or her mother for food, sustenance, and comfort. The mother is the pri-

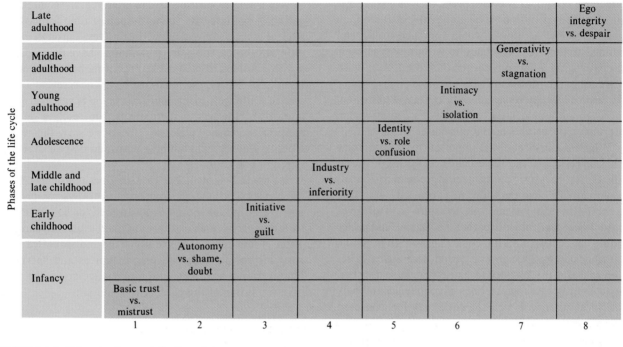

Phases of the life cycle	1	2	3	4	5	6	7	8
Late adulthood								Ego integrity vs. despair
Middle adulthood							Generativity vs. stagnation	
Young adulthood						Intimacy vs. isolation		
Adolescence					Identity vs. role confusion			
Middle and late childhood				Industry vs. inferiority				
Early childhood			Initiative vs. guilt					
Infancy		Autonomy vs. shame, doubt						
Infancy	Basic trust vs. mistrust							

FIGURE 2.5   Erikson's stages of development.

mary representative of society to the child. If she discharges her infant-related duties with warmth, regularity, and affection, the infant develops a feeling of trust toward the world. The infant's trust is a comfortable feeling that someone will always be around to care for his or her needs even though the mother occasionally disappears. Alternatively, a sense of mistrust or fearful uncertainty can develop if the mother fails to provide these needs in the caretaking setting. According to Erikson, she is setting up a distrusting attitude that will follow the child through life.

Autonomy versus shame and doubt is Erikson's second stage and corresponds to the anal stage in Freudian theory. The infant begins to gain control over the bowels and bladder. Parents begin imposing demands on the child to conform to socially acceptable forms and occasions for eliminating wastes. The child may develop the healthy attitude of being capable of independent or autonomous control of his or her own actions, or may develop the unhealthy attitude of shame or doubt because he or she is incapable of control.

Erikson's **initiative versus guilt** stage corresponds to the phallic period in Freudian theory. The child is caught in the midst of the Oedipal or Electra conflict, with its alternating love-hate feelings for the parent of the opposite sex and with fear of fulfilling the sexual fantasies that abound. The child may discover ways to overcome feelings of powerlessness by engaging in various activities. If this is done, then the basic healthy attitude of being the initiator of action will result. Alternatively, the child may fail to discover such outlets and feel guilt at being dominated by the environment.

Erikson's **industry versus inferiority** stage coincides with the Freudian period of latency and covers the years of middle childhood, when the child is involved in expansive absorption of knowledge and the development of intellectual and physical skills. As the child is drawn into the social culture of peers, he or she evaluates accomplishments by self-comparison with others. If the child views himself or herself as basically competent, feelings of productiveness and industriousness result. On the other hand, if the child sees himself or herself as incompetent, particularly in comparison with peers, then he or she feels unproductive and inferior. This unhealthy attitude may negatively color the child's whole approach to life and learning, producing a tendency to withdraw from new and challenging situations rather than meet them with confidence and enthusiasm.

Erikson's **identity versus identity confusion (diffusion)** stage is roughly associated with Freud's genital stage, centering on the establishment of a stable personal identity. Whereas, for Freud, the important part of identity formation resides in the adolescent's resolution of sexual conflicts, for Erikson, the central ingredient is the establishment of a clear path toward a vocation—selection of a job or an occupational role to aspire to. This gives the adolescent an objective that he or she and other members of society simultaneously acknowledge. If the adolescent comes through this period with a clearly selected role and the knowledge that others in society can clearly identify this role, feelings of confidence and purposefulness emerge. If not, the child may feel confused and troubled.

Erikson's first post-Freudian stage is called **intimacy versus isolation.** Early adulthood brings with it a job and the opportunity to form an intimate relationship with a member of the opposite sex. If the young adult forms friendships with others and a significant, intimate relationship with one individual in particular, then a basic feeling of closeness with others will result. A feeling of isolation may result from an inability to form friendships and an intimate relationship.

A chief concern of adults is to assist the younger generation in developing and leading useful lives. Erikson's **generativity versus stagnation** stage centers on successful rearing of children. Childless adults often need to find substitute young people through adoption, guardianship, or a close relationship with the children of friends and relatives. Generativity, or the feeling of helping to shape the next generation, is the positive outcome that may emerge. Stagnation, or the feeling of having done nothing for the next generation, is the unhealthy outcome.

According to Erikson, in the later years, we enter the period of **ego integrity versus despair,** a time for looking back at what we have done with our lives. Through many different routes, the older person may have developed a positive outlook in each of the preceding periods of emotional crises. If so, the retrospective glances reveal a picture of a life well spent, and the person is satisfied (ego integrity). However, if the older person resolved one or more of the earlier crises in a negative way, the retrospective glances yield doubt, gloom, and despair over the worth of one's life.

It should be noted that Erikson does not believe that the proper solution to a stage crisis is always completely positive in nature. Some exposure and/or commitment to the negative end of the individual's bipolar conflict often is inevitable (for example, the individual cannot trust all people under all circumstances and survive). However, in a healthy solution to a stage crisis, the positive resolution of the conflict is dominant.

Strengths and Weaknesses of Psychoanalytic Theory

Like most grand theories of development, psychoanalytic theory has its strengths and weaknesses. The strengths of psychoanalytic theory are:

1. The role of the past. Today, we assume that past experiences influence our current thought and behavior. The psychoanalytic emphasis on early experience in influencing thought and behavior later in development is an important part of developmental psychology.
2. The developmental course of personality. Viewing personality from a developmental stance continues to be another important theme in the field.
3. Mental representation of the environment. The psychoanalytic belief that environmental experiences are mentally transformed and represented in the mind continues to receive attention by psychologists.
4. Role of the unconscious mind. Psychoanalytic theorists forced psychologists to recognize that the mind contains both conscious and unconscious thoughts.

5. Conflict emphasis. Psychoanalytic theory has promoted the belief that conflict is an important ingredient of psychological problems and adjustment.
6. Influence on developmental psychology as a discipline. Psychoanalytic theory forced developmental psychologists to study personality and adjustment in addition to experimentally oriented topics, such as sensation, perception, and learning.

Psychoanalytic theory is not without its flaws. In fact, some of its strengths may be its weaknesses as well, often because orientations were stated in such an extreme manner.

Another weakness of psychoanalytic theory is that the theory's main concepts have been very difficult to test scientifically. Researchers have tried to investigate these concepts, such as repression, in the laboratory, but their efforts generally have failed. Much of the data used to support psychoanalytic theory are from patient reconstructions of the past, often the distant past (for example, an adult's recollection of his or her early childhood experiences), and thus the accuracy of these memories is questionable. Other data supporting psychoanalytic theory come from the subjective evaluation of clinicians. However, clinicians may see what they expect to see because of their theoretical framework.

Other flaws of psychoanalytic theory are that Freud and many other psychoanalytic theorists (excluding Erikson) overemphasized the importance of sexuality in development. They also placed too much faith in the power of the unconscious mind to control behavior, often ignoring the role of conscious thought processes.

Overall, the psychoanalytic view provides a perspective that is too negative and pessimistic. We clearly are not born with a bundle of evil instincts and drives. Psychoanalytic theory often overstates the importance of the first five years of life as determinants of subsequent development. Personality development continues throughout the human life cycle and is influenced by past, present, and anticipated future circumstances, a point accurately espoused by Erikson. In many instances, later experiences may be just as important as early experiences in determining development.

Child Development Concept Table 2.1 summarizes our discussion of the many different aspects of psychoanalytic theory. While psychoanalytic theory argues that the unconscious aspects of the child's mind hold the key to understanding development, the next perspective argues that the most important features of children's development are conscious thoughts.

COGNITIVE THEORIES OF DEVELOPMENT

We are in the midst of a cognitive revolution in psychology. Psychology no longer is defined as the scientific study of behavior, but rather the scientific study of mind and behavior (Santrock, 1986), a definition that emphasizes such cognitive processes as thinking, memory, attention, language, reasoning, problem solving, perception, and the like, in addition to behavior. This cognitive revolution has infiltrated the study of child development as well, due to the fact that, during the 1960s and 1970s, child developmentalists became enamored with the fascinating insights of Swiss psychologist Jean Piaget. Rather than focusing on the role of environmental experiences, or on unconscious thought as psychoanalytic theorists had, Piaget stresses that the key ingredient of child development is an understanding of the unfolding of *conscious* thought.

Cognitive Developmental Theory

Because Piaget's theory is described in the chapters ahead as we move through the infant, early childhood, middle and late childhood, and adolescent years, we highlight only some of the main features of the perspective here.

Cognitive developmental theory focuses on the rational thinking of the developing individual. It also stresses that cognitive development unfolds in a stage-like sequence, which is ordered and uniform for all individuals. The leading figure in cognitive developmental theory is Jean Piaget. Another is Lawrence Kohlberg, whose views on moral development appear later in this book.

Child Development Concept Table 2.1   Psychoanalytic Theory

Concept	Processes/Related Ideas	Characteristics/Description
What is psychoanalytic theory?	Unconscious thought, biological processes, and symbolic thought	Psychoanalytic theory is a view of personality development that emphasizes that the child's mind is primarily unconscious, that biological processes represent an important foundation for development, and that symbolic thought processes are an important ingredient of development.
Sigmund Freud's classical psychoanalytic theory	The man	While there are mixed feelings about Freud, he was one of the great contributors to child development theory in the 20th century. Freud was a medical doctor from Vienna, Austria.
	The structure of personality	According to Freud, the id is the instinctual, biological aspect of personality—the pleasure principle and primary process thinking lie here. The ego is the rational part of personality—the reality principle is here. The superego is the moral branch of personality—it is made up of the conscience and an ego ideal.
	Defense mechanisms	Defense mechanisms help to reduce conflict between the id and the ego by means of disguise—they include repression, reaction formation, regression, and projection. Peter Blos and Anna Freud believe that defense mechanisms, particularly regression, are very important in linking childhood experiences and adolescent development.
	Freud's psychosexual stages of personality development	Freud believed that personality develops in five psychosexual stages: (1) the oral stage centers pleasure on the mouth in the first year of life; (2) the anal stage focuses on the anus in the second and third years of life; (3) the phallic stage focuses on the child's genitals during the preschool years; (4) the latency stage occurs during the elementary school years and involves reduced sexual motivation; and (5) the genital stage begins with adolescence and continues through adulthood—it is the time of sexual reawakening and interest.
	Freud's theory today	Few psychologists accept all of Freud's major theses today, although his ideas have opened up many doors in understanding child development.
Contemporary psychoanalytic theorists and Erikson's life-cycle theory	Contemporary psychoanalytic theory	Many contemporary psychoanalytic theorists play down sexual instincts, often placing more emphasis on rational thought processes and cultural influences. Many contemporary psychoanalytic theorists are neo-psychoanalytic in their orientation; that is, they accept some basic Freudian ideas but disagree on one or more major points.
	Erikson's life-cycle psychoanalytic theory	Erikson argues that development unfolds in psychosocial—not psychosexual—stages. He believes that stages occur through a combination of biology and culture, and he emphasizes culture more than Freud. Erikson proposes eight stages, ranging from infancy (trust versus mistrust) through late adulthood (ego integrity versus despair). One of his most famous stages—identity versus identity confusion—corresponds to adolescent development.
Strengths and weaknesses of psychoanalytic theory	Strengths	Strengths include concern about the past, developmental emphasis, mental representation of the social world, the role of the unconscious mind, emphasis on conflict, and the influence on child development as a discipline.
	Weaknesses	Weaknesses include concepts that are difficult to test, the lack of an empirical data base, too much emphasis on the unconscious mind, too much stress on sexual motivation, a pessimistic view of development, and too much emphasis on very early development.

Piaget's (1952, 1967) ideas form one of the most complete theoretical statements about intelligence available in psychology. Piaget believed that the core of development is rationality—that is, logical thinking—and that intelligence develops from the interaction of hereditary and environmental forces, although he tended to place a stronger premium on the importance of biological adaptation than on environmental factors. Piaget was more interested in *how* children think than in *what* they think. For example, it was important to Piaget that a young child could order a set of primary colors from lightest to darkest, but unimportant that the young child knew the names of the colors. Piaget also was interested in the general nature of thought, rather than how children at the same stage of thought differ from one another. Let's look more closely at Piaget's cognitive developmental stages and how they represent qualitatively different ways of thinking.

Stages of Cognitive Development

A brief outline of Piaget's stages of thought follows (Piaget, 1967). As is the case with all such theories, the time periods designated for various stages are only approximate. An individual child may move out of a stage sooner or remain in a stage longer than is indicated by the ages given. The more significant claim is that a child moves through the given stages in the established sequence and that no child violates this sequence.

Piaget's **sensorimotor stage** lasts from birth to about two years of age, corresponding to the period known as infancy. During this time, the infant develops the ability to organize and coordinate his or her sensations and perceptions with his or her physical movements and actions. This coordination of sensation with action is the source of the term *sensorimotor*. The stage begins with the newborn, who has little more than reflexes to coordinate his or her senses with actions. The stage ends with the two-year-old, who has complex sensorimotor patterns and is beginning to develop a primitive symbol system. For example, the two-year-old can imagine looking at a toy and manipulating it with his or her hands before he or she actually does so. The child can also use simple sentences—for example, "Mommy, jump"—to represent a sensorimotor event that has just occurred.

The sensorimotor stage of development lasts from birth to approximately two years of age. How would you describe the sensorimotor stage to a friend?

Piaget's **preoperational stage** lasts from two to seven years of age, cutting across the preschool and early middle school years. During this time, the child's symbol system expands. The use of language and perceptual images moves well beyond the capabilities of a child at the end of the sensorimotor period. The child tends to see things from his or her own perspective and to confuse this perspective with that of others. The child has difficulty manipulating the images and representations of events and is therefore likely to get stuck (centered) in static states and to be unable to reverse situations mentally. For example, if liquid is poured from a short, fat container into a tall, thin one, the child may notice only that the height of the water has changed (centering). If asked to imagine what would happen if the water were returned to the original container, the child has a tough time visualizing the reversal (irreversibility).

The preoperational stage lasts from approximately two to seven years of age. What are children's thoughts like in the preoperational stage?

The concrete operational stage lasts from approximately seven to eleven years of age. What is meant by concrete operational thought?

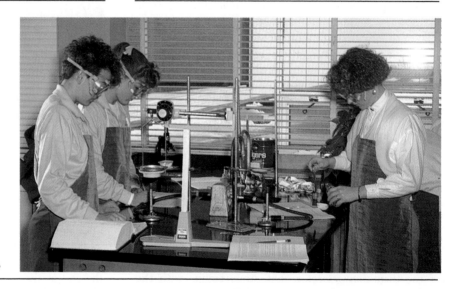

The formal operational stage appears between the ages of 11 to 15. What did Piaget mean by formal operational thought?

Piaget's **concrete operational stage** lasts from 7 to 11 years of age, cutting across the major portion of the middle school years. During this time, the child's thinking crystallizes into more of a system. The shift to a more perfect system of thinking is brought about by several changes. One of these is the shift from egocentrism to relativism. Relativism is the ability to think about something from different perspectives and to think simultaneously about two or more aspects of a problem. Another change is the child's ability to pose and operate mentally in a series of actions. Performing mental arithmetic, imagining a game of table tennis, and thinking about how to tie a knot are all examples of this change. Children in the sensorimotor and preoperational stages, by contrast, are unable to perform these mental operations.

One limitation of concrete thinking is that the child has to rely on concrete events in order to think in this way. He or she needs to be able to perceive the objects and events that he or she will think about.

Piaget's final stage is the **formal operational stage,** which appears between the ages of 11 and 15 years. Piaget believed that individuals enter the most advanced form of thought during early adolescence. The most important aspect of this stage is the ability to move beyond a world of actual, concrete experiences and to think in abstract and more logical terms. In developing a more abstract system of thought, the adolescent often thinks about ideal circumstances, rather than what is concrete and real. He or she may begin to think about what the ideal parent is like and to compare his or her parents to that standard. He or she usually begins to entertain many possibilities for his or her future and is more fascinated with what he or she can become than with what he or she is right now. The adolescent begins to think in a more systematic way in solving problems, developing hypotheses about why something is happening the way it is. Subsequently, he or she may test these hypotheses in a deductive fashion.

Piaget's stages of cognitive development are summarized in Table 2.1. Next, we see that Piaget was intrigued by what causes developmental change.

Processes Responsible for Developmental Changes

Piaget believed that several interrelated processes are responsible for changes in children's thought: adaptation, organization, and equilibration. The adaptation that Piaget emphasized is subdivided into **assimilation** and **accommodation,** which usually occur together. In assimilation, we try to incorporate new features of the environment into already existing ways of thinking about it. In accommodation, we try to incorporate new features of the environment into our thinking by slightly modifying existing modes of thought. An example may help to clarify these concepts. A young girl is given a hammer and nails to hang a picture on the wall. She has never used a hammer before. From experience and observation, though, she realizes that a hammer is an object to be held, that it is swung by the handle to hit the nail, and that it is usually swung a number of times. Realizing each of these things, she incorporates her behavior into a conceptual framework that already exists (assimilation). However, the hammer is heavy, so she has to hold

Table 2.1   Piaget's Stages of Cognitive Development

Stage	General Description	Age Level
Sensorimotor stage	The child progresses from instinctual reflexive action at birth, to symbolic activities, to the ability to separate self from object in the environment. He or she develops limited capabilities for anticipating the consequences of actions.	0–2 years
Preoperational stage	The child's ability to think becomes refined during this period. First, he or she develops what Piaget called preconceptual thinking, in which he or she deals with each thing individually but is not able to group objects. The child is able to use symbols, such as words, to deal with problems. During the latter half of this period, the child develops better reasoning abilities but is still bound to the here-and-now.	2–7 years
Concrete operational stage	At this stage, the child develops the ability to perform intellectual operations—such as reversibility, conservation, and ordering of things by number, size, or class, etc. His or her ability to relate time and space also matures during this period.	7–11 years
Formal operational stage	This is the period in which the person learns hypothetical reasoning. He or she is able to function purely on a symbolic, abstract level. His or her conceptualization capacities mature.	11–15 years

FOCUS ON CHILD DEVELOPMENT 2.2

DREAMS, FREUD, AND PIAGET— FROM BIRD-HEADED CREATURES TO BATHTUBS

Many of us dismiss the nightly excursion into the world of dreams as a second-rate mental activity not worthy of our rational selves. In focusing on the less mysterious waking world, we deny ourselves the opportunity of chance encounters with distant friends, remote places, dead relatives, gods and demons, and reworked childhood experiences. Aren't you curious about this remarkable ability of our minds and the minds of children to escape the limits of time and space?

If you are a male, do you dream about pits, caves, bottles, apples, and airplanes? If you are a female, do you dream about reptiles, serpents, umbrellas, and poles? If so, psychoanalytic theorists would argue that your dreams have a strong sexual symbolic content. They believe that dreams conceal but that they can be made to reveal the dreamer's conception of the world.

Freud viewed dreaming as completely unconscious and thought it reflected sexual and aggressive impulses that could not be expressed during waking hours. These impulses are always pressing for activation, he said, and dreams are an important way in which such tensions can be relieved. Freud argued that, in its final form, the dream is a distorted and symbolic version of the impulses that triggered it and that the raw materials for dreams are traces of past perceptual experiences, including both recent and distant encounters. He believed that dreams were highly unorganized with often bizarre patterns of elements. (See figure below for a pictorial representation of one of Freud's own boyhood dreams.)

However, not all psychologists believe that dreams are a clash between sexual and aggressive instincts and the constraints of reality. Increasingly, psychologists describe both sleep and dreams as being closer to conscious thought than had been believed in the past. For example, David Foulkes (1982) followed 42 children longitudinally from the time they were 3 years old until they were 15. Each child spent nine

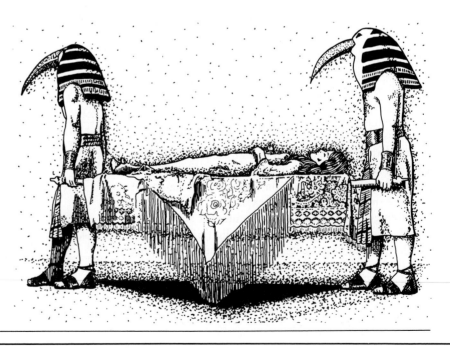

Freud traced the bizarre birdlike creatures who carried his mother in this dream to illustrations in a bible that his father had given him when he was a child.

nights per year in Foulkes's sleep laboratory, where dream reports were obtained. Foulkes's findings about the nature of dreams at different ages in childhood closely parallel Piaget's ideas about stages of conscious cognitive development. A sample of the simple, egocentric dream of a preoperational child was, "I was asleep in the bathtub." There was no evidence of fantastic characters in the young children's dreams. The five-, six-, and seven-year-olds began to tell more concrete stories when reporting their dreams, and the adolescents' dreams were much more abstract, reflecting the formal operational quality of such mental excursions during the night.

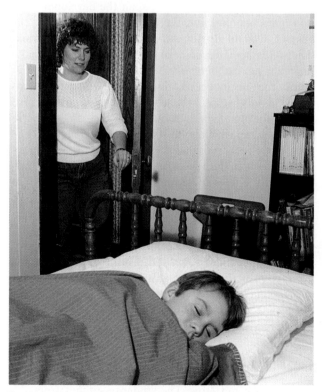

Psychologists now recognize that dreaming is much closer to conscious thought than once was assumed.

it near the top. Because she swings too hard, the nail bends, so she has to adjust the pressure of her strikes. These adjustments reveal her ability to alter the concept slightly (accommodation) (Yussen & Santrock, 1981).

Piaget believed that the other two properties of thought—organization and equilibration—are also important. Every level of thought from sensorimotor to formal operational is organized in some manner. Continual refinement of this **organization** is a part of development. Another important aspect of thought focuses on the development of a more lasting balance. This goal is achieved as thought becomes more logical and abstract. But before a new stage of thought can be attained, we must face the inadequacy of our current one. We must experience cognitive conflict or uncertainty. The mechanism by which we resolve cognitive conflict and reach a balance of thought is called **equilibration.** If a child believes that the amount of liquid is changed simply because we pour it into a container of a different shape, he or she might be puzzled by such issues as where the "extra" liquid came from and whether there actually is more liquid to drink. These puzzles eventually are solved as the child's thought process moves to a higher stage. The child is faced with many such inconsistencies and counterexamples every day.

Piaget's lasting contributions to the field of child development are that he identified a broad spectrum of abilities that develop in childhood, he invented many clever tasks that are still used to gauge intellectual change, and he offered many intriguing hypotheses that have been pursued by others in the field.

Piaget emphasized describing how changes in children's conscious thought occur, while Freud believed that major developmental changes are unconscious in nature. In particular, Freud was intrigued by the nature of dreams and saw them as completely unconscious in nature. Recently, researchers have considered the fascinating possibility that dreams are closer to conscious thinking than had been assumed in the past. Focus on Child Development 2.2 discusses Freud's views on dreaming and some recent Piagetian-inspired research on children's dreams.

At about the same time that Piaget's theory was becoming a fixture in child development, another cognitive approach was gaining favor among American psychologists, one referred to as the information processing perspective.

The Information Processing Perspective

The **information processing perspective** is concerned with how people process information about their world—how they attend to information, code and retrieve the information, how they reason about the information, and so forth. The information processing approach shares with behaviorism the belief that careful experimentation is central to advancing knowledge about development. Although cognitive psychologists are dealing with unobservable processes, like memories and plans, they have been very precise in controlling conditions and developing ingenious experiments to reveal how mental processes work.

Computer science has had an important influence on the information processing approach (Siegler, 1983). Computers are essentially high-speed information processing systems that can be programmed. It was thought that computers could provide a logical and concrete, though perhaps oversimplified, version of how information is processed in a child's mind (Hunt, 1982). We now explore in more detail how development of the computer has played an important role in the information processing perspective.

The Computer Metaphor—
Old and New Models

The information processing approach focuses on the elementary processes of cognition and relies on a computer metaphor—the human mind is viewed as a type of computational device in some ways similar to computers (Figure 2.6). Because information processing psychologists view the mind as a computational device, their theories and models are often pictured in the form of computer programs or "flowcharts."

So far, we have been making frequent reference to the computer analogy of a child's mind. But aren't there some things that a computer can do that a child's mind cannot, and conversely, aren't there some things a child's mind can do that a computer cannot?

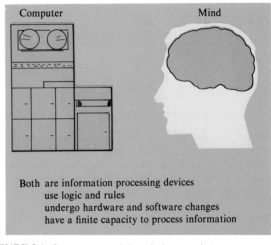

FIGURE 2.6 Computers and the mind: an analogy.

Two models of information processing—one rather old and the other quite new—span the development of information processing theory from the 1950s to the present. Donald Broadbent's (1958) model of information processing (with some of the terms modified to make his model more understandable) is pictured in Figure 2.7. Notice that his model has three memory "stores," a sensory memory store, which holds sensory features of stimuli for very short periods of time, a short-term memory store, which holds stimuli in consciousness once they have been recognized, and a long-term memory store, which is the repository of all permanent knowledge. At the level of sensory memory, the system can engage in **parallel processing** of information—that is, several different messages can be processed and remembered at once. But at the level of short-term memory, there is a type of "bottleneck." The limited capacity of short-term memory makes it difficult for more than one message to be handled at any one time. A filter serves the function of selective attention—it protects short-term memory from becoming "overloaded."

Although you may not realize it, you have probably had experiences that support Broadbent's model. Consider the experience of an elementary schoolchild in the classroom. The teacher is talking and so are two classmates in the next row. The student switches from the teacher's lecture to the conversation going on around her.

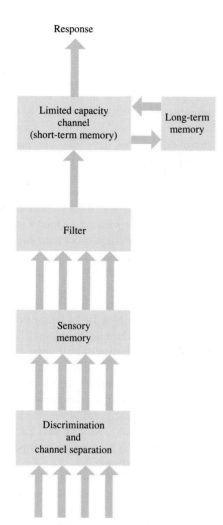

FIGURE 2.7 Broadbent's information processing model, developed in the 1950s (Wingfield and Sandoval, 1980).

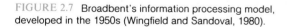

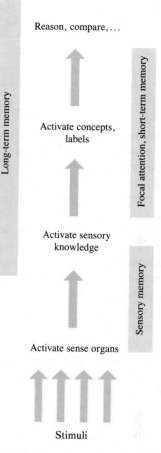

FIGURE 2.8 Klatzky's information processing model, developed in the 1980s (Klatzky, 1984).

This is easy to do—without moving her head or using her eyes, she can "tune in" one conversation, then "switch" to another, then move to a third, and so on. It is almost like changing channels on the radio. But when she switches from the teacher's lecture to the student conversation, what exactly happens? Does she actually stop hearing the teacher? Not really. She still is aware of the sounds being made. What happens is that she stops "following" the content of the teacher's lecture and begins following the content of the student conversation.

This is consistent with the idea of a filter between sensory memory (which holds only sensory features such as sounds) and short-term memory (which holds the recognized content of what you have attended to).

Broadbent's model of information processing was very influential, but today our conceptions of information processing have become more complex and flexible. This is illustrated by Roberta Klatzky's (1984) model in Figure 2.8. Comparing this model to Broadbent's earlier effort, we note a major change in emphasis: Whereas Broadbent's model stressed the importance of memory stores (sensory, short-term, and long-term), Klatzky's model emphasizes processes. Instead of information being "transferred" from one store to the next, information is processed along a continuum of levels—there is "shallow" sensory analysis of stimuli ("activate sensory knowledge"), "deeper" processes of categorization and naming of stimuli ("activate concepts, labels"), and still "deeper" processes of thinking and making inferences about stimuli ("reason, compare"). For example, in reading a word, your system might first process the visual features—its letters—then recognize the word and "look up" its meaning, and finally relate this word to other words you have read in order to understand a whole sentence.

Of course, memories are not absent from Klatzky's model. It is just that their functions have been changed to an extent. Long-term memory is not something reached only at the end of processing—it is involved in processing virtually from the start. Sensory analysis, categorization, naming and thinking, and inferencing all involve communication with appropriate types of long-term memory knowledge. For example, the child's ability to read depends on long-term memory codes that allow recognition of individual letters and words, as well as on codes that support understanding. Further, all types of analysis can leave new memory records in long-term memory. Thus, the child can remember what he or she has done. However, in most situations, the "deeper" sorts of analysis support better long-term memory.

In sum, the information processing perspective has spawned models of how information flows through the child's mind. As we see next, the information processing perspective also raises questions about the nature of children's cognition.

Questions Raised About Children's Cognition by the Information Processing Perspective

The information processing approach raises important questions about the nature of children's cognition. One of these questions is: Does processing speed increase as children grow older? The idea that speed is an important factor is implicit in information processing models. First, many cognitive tasks—both in the laboratory and in real life—are performed under time pressure. For example, as children move into the more formal setting of school, they have a limited amount of time to write letters, add and subtract numbers, and complete their homework.

Second, speed is an advantage even in tasks without time pressure. Consider memorizing a foreign language vocabulary: Although the child might have all semester to learn a set of words, obviously, it is preferable if he or she is able to learn the words quickly. A good deal of evidence indicates that processing speed is slower in younger children than in older children, although the causes of these differences have not yet been determined. While the causes might be biological in origin, they might in some cases reflect differences in knowledge about and/or practice on a task.

A second question that the information processing approach raises is: Does processing capacity increase as children grow older? Information processing capacity can be viewed as a type of "mental energy" needed to perform mental work. The difficulty children have in dividing their attention between two things at once is attributed to limits on capacity. So also is the trouble they have performing complex tasks (such as mentally working complicated arithmetic problems). Although capacity is thought to be limited at all ages, there is no generally accepted measure of a child's capacity, and thus findings are ambiguous. For example, it is possible that capacity does not change with age but that young children must spend more capacity on lower-level processes (such as identifying stimuli), leaving less capacity for higher-level processes (such as dividing attention or performing complex computations).

A third question is: What is the role of knowledge in accounting for developments in cognitive processing? If a child has knowledge that is relevant to a task, information processing is generally more efficient. It is known, for example, that "masters" at chess are much better than novices at remembering the details of chessboard displays (Chase & Simon, 1973). Older children obviously know more than younger children. Could it be that age differences in information processing are entirely attributable to age differences in knowledge? This seems unlikely, but the role of knowledge in cognitive development is currently a research focus (Flavell, 1985).

Finally, the information processing approach raises the question of whether there are differences in development pertaining to "controlled" versus "automatic" processes. The essential differences between these two processes are twofold: First, **controlled processes** are assumed to draw heavily on information processing capacity—this is why they are called "effortful." **Automatic processes** draw minimally on such capacity. Second, controlled processes are intentional, that is, "done on purpose." Automatic processes are more difficult to control—once initiated, they tend to "run off" on their own. Many findings suggest that age differences in cognition frequently involve controlled processes. In contrast, at least some automatic processes appear to be "age-invariant." This pattern fits well with the hypothesis that amount of capacity is relatively low in early childhood. Unfortunately, researchers disagree on how best to define controlled and automatic processes (Shiffrin & Schneider, 1977; Hasher & Zacks, 1979). Another complication is that a process that is controlled at one age might be automatic at another.

Now that we have considered both the cognitive developmental and information processing perspectives, we examine the strengths and weaknesses of the cognitive theories.

Strengths and Weaknesses of the Cognitive Theories

Among the strengths of the cognitive developmental and information processing perspectives are:

1. Piaget's theory was "a breath of fresh air" in developmental psychology. It came when thought was viewed as unconscious (psychoanalytic theory), not as an important influence on behavior (behaviorism), or highly varied across individuals (psychometric theory). Piaget's was the first theory to provide a rich description of children's thought processes.
2. Piaget's theory directed research toward uncovering how children's thought unfolds maturationally, and it revealed the importance of biological adaptation in development.
3. The information processing perspective provided a very strong research-oriented atmosphere for the study of children's cognition.
4. The information processing perspective demonstrated a precision in conceptualizing children's thought. This approach has produced detailed examination of children's memory processes.

The weaknesses of the cognitive developmental and information processing perspectives include:

1. There is skepticism about the pureness of the Piagetian stages.
2. Piaget's concepts are somewhat loosely defined.
3. The information processing model has not yet produced an overall perspective on development.
4. Both the Piagetian and information processing views may have underestimated the importance of environmental experiences, particularly those involving families, and the unconscious mind in determining behavior.

Both the cognitive developmental and information processing perspectives continue to contribute in important ways to our knowledge about children's development. Today, there is considerable enthusiasm in evaluating the accuracy of Piaget's provocative theory, with the result that some of his ideas remain unscathed while others are requiring considerable modification. And the information processing perspective has opened up many avenues of research on children's cognition, provided detailed descriptions of the way the child's mind works, and offered numerous sophisticated methodological advances for investigating the nature of children's thoughts. These two perspectives have given cognition its now recognized important place as one of the key strands of development. Because of the input from the cognitive perspectives, the child is no longer viewed as having only primarily unconscious thoughts, as the early psychoanalytic theorists stressed, or as displaying only overt behavior and as being only influenced by environmental experiences, as the behaviorists argued. The cognitive approaches have provided an optimistic view of children's development, ascribing to children the ability and motivation to know their world and to cope with it in constructive ways.

The chapters on cognitive development in this book are filled with research studies that have been conducted in the theoretical spirit of cognitive developmental and information processing perspectives. From the Piagetian perspective, you will encounter a number of ideas about the infant's development of object permanence in Chapter 5, the preschool child's preoperational thought, particularly the nature of egocentrism, in Chapter 7, the

Child Development Concept Table 2.2 Cognitive Theories		
Concept	**Processes/Related Ideas**	**Characteristics/Description**
Cognitive developmental theory	What is cognitive developmental theory?	Cognitive developmental theory focuses on the development of rational thought in the child and stresses that cognition unfolds in a sequence of stages. The leading figure in cognitive developmental theory is Swiss psychologist Jean Piaget.
	Stages of cognitive development	Piaget argued that children move through a sequence of four stages of development: (1) the sensorimotor stage involves the coordination of action and sensation, (2) the preoperational stage is when the child's symbol system expands, (3) the concrete operational stage is when thinking becomes more systematic and relativistic but still is concrete, and (4) the formal operational stage involves abstract, logical thought.
	Processes responsible for developmental changes	Piaget believed that adaptation (which can be subdivided into assimilation and accommodation), organization, and equilibration are responsible for changes in cognitive development.
Information processing perspective	What is the information processing perspective?	The information processing perspective is concerned with how people process information about their world—their attentional, memory, and reasoning processes, among others.
	The computer metaphor—old and new models	The information processing approach emphasizes a computer metaphor—comparing a child's mind to a computer. Broadbent's model of information processing stressed the importance of memory stores, while Klatzky's model emphasizes processes.
	Questions raised about children's cognition by the information processing perspective	Four important questions raised by the information processing perspective involve: (1) processing speed, (2) capacity, (3) the role of knowledge, and (4) controlled versus automatic processes.
Strengths and weaknesses of cognitive theories	Strengths	Among the strengths of cognitive theories are Piaget's rich description of children's thought, his emphasis on biological maturation and adaptation, the strong research orientation of the information processing approach, and the precision with which the workings of the child's mind can be described by the information processing view.
	Weaknesses	Among the weaknesses of cognitive theories are the skepticism about Piaget's stages, Piaget's rather loose definitions, no overall developmental perspective in the information processing approach, and an underestimation of environmental and unconscious thought influences on development.

elementary schoolchild's concrete operational thought and neo-Piagetian critiques in Chapter 9, and the adolescent's formal operational thought, as well as social cognition, in Chapter 12. From the information processing perspective, you will learn about many different aspects of attention, memory, problem solving, and thinking in Chapters 5, 7, 9, and 12.

A summary of the main concepts of our discussion of the cognitive developmental and information processing perspectives is presented in Child Development Concept Table 2.2. So far, we have discussed a perspective that emphasizes the importance of unconscious thought (psychoanalytic theory) and one that stresses the significance of conscious thought (the cognitive theories). Next, we study a perspective that proposes that the key to understanding children's development rests not in the mind, but in enviroment-behavior connections.

BEHAVIORAL/SOCIAL LEARNING THEORIES

The behavioral point of view often is discussed as a unified perspective on development, but like most theoretical perspectives, it contains more than one viewpoint. The two main forms of the behavioral view are represented by the traditional, stronger version of behaviorism, reflected in the ideas of B. F. Skinner, and Albert Bandura and Walter Mischel's modified behavioral view, known as social learning theory. Before we talk about these two prominent variations of the behavioral view, let's look at some common features of the behavioral perspective.

First, the behavioral perspective emphasizes the influence of the environment on the behavior of the child. Second, the child's behavior is viewed as learned. Third, a strong methodological orientation that stresses the fine-grained, meticulous observation of the child's behavior is followed. Fourth, the child's mental events or cognitive processes either are viewed as outside the realm of scientific study or as mediators of environmental experience on behavior, rather than causes of behavior.

Now let's look more closely at Skinner's behaviorism, Bandura and Mischel's social learning theory, and finally, the behavioral perspective's strengths and weaknesses.

Skinner's Behaviorism

During World War II, B. F. Skinner put together a rather strange-sounding project—he constructed a pigeon-guided missile. The missile had a pigeon in the warhead, and the pigeon operated the flaps on the missile and guided it home by pecking at an image of a target. The pigeons actually did their job quite well in nonwar trial runs, but the Navy just could not bring itself to have pigeons piloting its missiles during war. Skinner, however, congratulated himself on the degree of control he was able to exercise over the pigeons. Following the pigeon experiment, he wrote a novel, *Walden Two* (1948), presenting his ideas about building a scientifically managed society. Skinner believed that existing societies are

B. F. Skinner

very poorly managed because people believe in myths like free will. Skinner said that humans are no more free than pigeons. In the long run, he argued, we would be much happier if we recognized that our lives would be more prosperous under the control of positive reinforcement.

Skinner also has argued that the mysteries of child development can be solved by observing the behavior of children. According to Skinner, looking for the internal determinants of the child's behavior inhibits the search for the true causes of the child's behavior that reside in the external environment. Some child developmentalists would say that Skinner is arguing that children are empty organisms, but Skinner (1953) says that he objects to looking for these determinants not because they do not exist but because they are irrelevant to the relation between stimuli (observable characteristics of the environment) and responses (overt behaviors of the child).

According to Skinner, one of the major ways in which stimuli and responses are linked together is through the principle of **operant conditioning** (sometimes referred to as **instrumental conditioning**). In this type of learning, the individual operates on the environment; that is, the individual does something, and, in turn, something happens to him or her. Another way of saying this is that the individual's behavior is instrumental in causing some effect in the environment. The lives of individuals are full of operant conditioning situations. For example, consider the following conversation:

John Hey, where did you get that new notebook?
Bob My mother bought it for me.
John Oh, yeah? Why?
Bob Because I got mad about something and started yelling at her.
John You mean if you get mad and throw a fit, your mom buys you a notebook?
Bob I guess that's the way it works!

At the heart of such occurrences is this principle: Behavior is determined by its consequences. According to this principle, behavior followed by a positive stimulus is likely to recur, while behavior followed by a negative stimulus is not as likely to recur. The positive experience is referred to as **reinforcement,** and the negative experience is labeled **punishment.**

Think for a moment about the last two weeks in your life, focusing on the positive and negative consequences of your actions. Perhaps a man frowned at you when you smiled at him, or a friend told you what a nice person you were for buying her a book. Perhaps a teacher wrote a note on the bottom of your paper, complimenting your writing skills, or your basketball coach made you run 50 extra laps around the gym for being late to practice. At any rate, the lives of infants, children, and adolescents are full of situations in which behavior is followed by positive or negative consequences. These consequences have significant effects on an individual's future behavior.

One area of development in which the principle of operant conditioning has been applied liberally is **behavior modification.** This approach to changing behavior is widely practiced by clinicians, counselors, and teachers in an effort to resolve problems. Sometimes, even parents are trained to more effectively manage problems by following the principles of operant conditioning (e.g., Becker, 1971). Basically, the procedure of behavior modification involves substituting acceptable patterns of behavior for unacceptable ones. Contingencies are established to ensure that acceptable responses are acquired or learned; this learning is facilitated by

reinforcement. Behavior modification experts argue that most of the emotional problems of children occur because their environment is arranged with the wrong set of contingencies—meaning that unacceptable behaviors are inadvertently reinforced. Hence, the adolescent who frequently engages in delinquent behavior may be doing so because he or she is rewarded for such behavior, either through the material rewards of the objects stolen or the social attention received from peers.

Skinner's ideas have been used extensively in restructuring the learning environments of children. Many psychologists, though, reject Skinner's notion that the cognitive determinants of children's behavior cannot be studied and are not important to understanding the linkage between stimuli and responses. Even some of Skinner's fellow behaviorists feel this way; while they give ballpark approval to Skinner's ideas about reinforcement contingencies, observable behavior, and careful experimental methodology, they nonetheless believe that he is wrong to ignore the cognitive determinants of children's behavior.

Skinner is the name most associated with behaviorism. But as we see next, another view, one that is more flexible about some aspects of development, such as the role of cognition, also has some important things to say about environment-behavior connections.

Social Learning Theory

The social learning theorist shares the behaviorist's concern for studying linkages between environmental conditions and the child's behavior and for the use of meticulous observation, but the social learning theorist argues that traditional behaviorists like Skinner have missed some of the richness of development by paying too little attention to the child's social world and his or her cognitive interpretation of behavior and the environment. According to the social learning theorist, cognitive processes mediate the relation between the environment and the child's behavior. Thus, today's social learning appropriately is called **cognitive social learning theory.** Let's now explore some of the ways in which cognitive social learning theory has moved away from the traditional behavioral view of Skinner by discussing Albert Bandura and Walter Mischel's views.

Albert Bandura

To learn more about Bandura's social learning theory, we focus on the consequences of behavior, the concept of reciprocal determinism, and the importance of observational learning, and describe further the role of cognition in mediating the child's behavior and environmental conditions.

Bandura (1977) believes that behavior is determined by self-produced consequences of the child's actions as well as by consequences from the external environment, such as rewards or punishments from others. In other words, self-reinforcement is just as important in determining the child's behavior as is external reinforcement. Children congratulate and condemn themselves, and social learning theorists view such self-congratulations and self-criticisms as important determinants of children's behavior. Consider the achievement behavior of a 10-year-old boy. Although he works hard in school because it will likely lead to a good grade, his own need for excellence will just as likely motivate him to work hard. Substandard performance, on the other hand, might lead to self-criticism. In this sense, the boy's achievement behavior is as much a function of his reaction to himself as reactions to others and to external determinants. This idea of self-produced consequences for one's behavior differs from Skinner's ideas, which describe behavior as determined only by external consequences.

The existence of self-produced consequences and personal performance standards suggests that using reinforcement to control someone else's behavior will not always be successful. As Bandura (1977) has pointed out, if external reinforcement were always effective, we would behave like weather vanes—in the presence of a John Bircher, we would act like a John Bircher, while in the presence of a Communist, we would behave like a Communist. Instead, behavior develops through the process of reciprocal control. Consider the following conversation between a 17-year-old boy and girl:

Bob Oh, come on, Nancy, let's go to the drive-in tonight.
Nancy (Looks away as if she doesn't hear him)
Bob Look, Nancy, I'm talking to you! Don't ignore me.
Nancy What, Bob?
Bob I said, let's go to the drive-in tonight.
Nancy Bob, I know what you want to do—you just want to make out.
Bob (Yelling) Don't make me look like a fool! You make me feel so stupid when you embarrass me like that.
Nancy Well, maybe we can go in a couple of weeks.
Bob Well, all right.

What has been learned in this interchange? Nancy has learned that she can control Bob's advances with vague promises. Bob has learned that, if he gets upset and amplifies his feelings, he can at least get Nancy to make some kind of promise. This type of interchange occurs all the time in relationships throughout the life span. It is a coercive process in which two people attempt to control each other's behavior. Indeed, whenever one person is trying to control another, the second person is usually resisting control or attempting to control in return. In this sense, Bandura (1971) asserts that the manipulation and control of people suggested by Skinner in *Walden Two* could never evolve.

Bandura (1977) refers to this concept of behavior as **reciprocal determinism.** According to Bandura, the child is not completely driven by inner forces or manipulated helplessly by environmental factors; rather, the child's psychological makeup is best understood by analyzing the continuous reciprocal interaction between behavior and its controlling conditions. In other words, the child's behavior partly constructs the environment, and the resulting environment, in turn, affects the child's behavior.

Bandura (1971, 1977) also believes that children learn extensively by example. Much of what children learn involves observing the behavior of parents, peers, teachers, and others. This form of social learning is called **observational learning.** For example, the 10-year-old who watches the teacher smile at her friend for turning in her work on time may be motivated to do likewise.

Bandura believes that, if learning proceeded in the trial-and-error fashion advocated by Skinner, it would be very laborious and even hazardous. For example, putting a 15-year-old girl in an automobile, having her drive down the road, and rewarding the positive responses she makes would be senseless. Instead, many of the complex educational and cultural practices of children are learned through their exposure to competent models who display appropriate ways to solve problems and cope with the world.

We mentioned earlier that Bandura's view is best labeled a cognitive social learning theory. However, it was not Bandura, but Walter Mischel (1973) who coined the label cognitive social learning theory. Adding the labels *cognitive* and *social* to learning theory changes the character of the view considerably, moving it further away from the strictly environment-behavior version offered by Skinner. Indeed, cognitive social learning is not too far removed conceptually from the ideas of the information processing perspective discussed under cognitive theories of children's development. Cognitive social learning theorists indeed are very interested in how children process information about themselves and their social world. In studying observational learning, Bandura (1977) focuses on such information processing components as attention and memory, and in investigating social behavior, Mischel (1973) is interested in such cognitive matters as expectancies and plans.

Now that we have considered Skinner's traditional behavioral view and also the social learning perspective, we discuss the strengths and weaknesses of the behavioral/social learning tradition.

Strengths and Weaknesses of Behavioral/ Social Learning Theories

Among the strengths of the behavioral/social learning theories are:

1. The behavioral/social learning approaches have shown that specific behaviors and environmental stimuli are important determinants of development.
2. Both views have demonstrated the contribution of the observational method in learning about development.
3. The rigorous experimental approach of these views has fostered a climate of scientific investigation in the field of development.
4. The social learning perspective has highlighted the tremendous importance of information processing in mediating the relation between behavior and environmental stimuli.
5. The social learning perspective has sensitized us to the importance of adapting to changing environmental circumstances, and both the behavioral and social learning perspectives have stressed how development may vary from one context to another, depending upon the nature of the context.

Among the weaknesses of the behavioral/social learning perspectives are:

1. The behavioral view has been heavily criticized for its belief that cognitive processes are irrelevant to understanding development. This criticism does not apply to cognitive social learning theory.
2. Both the behavioral and social learning views are nonchronological in that the processes determining children's development are essentially the same at all ages.
3. The behavioral and social learning approaches have paid too little attention to the biological foundations of development.
4. Both the behavioral and social learning perspectives reduce development to very fine-grained elements, possibly missing the gestalt of development, which is realized by looking at more global dimensions as well.

Child Development Concept Table 2.3 Behavioral/Social Learning Theories		
Concept	**Processes/Related Ideas**	**Characteristics/Description**
The behavioral perspective	Overriding principles	The behavioral perspective emphasizes environment and behavior; learned behavior; and strong methodology, including meticulous observation; and views cognitive processes as either not important or as mediators of environmental-behavior connections.
Skinner's behaviorism	External control	Skinner believes that the child's behavior can be manipulated by controlling the environment in which the child lives.
	Operant conditioning (instrumental conditioning)	According to Skinner, as the child operates on the environment, consequences for his or her actions occur. These consequences, which can be rewarding or punishing, either increase or decrease his or her behavior.
	Behavior modification	Behavior modification, which rests on behavioral principles, is a widely used approach to helping children with problems.
Social learning theory	Basic ideas	Social learning theory shares with traditional behaviorism a belief in the importance of the environment and its connections to the child's behavior and also a belief in the use of meticulous observation. However, social learning theorists also argue that traditional behaviorism misses some of the richness of development by paying too little attention to the child's social world and his or her cognitive interpretation of behavior and the environment.
	Bandura and Mischel's social learning theory	Bandura emphasizes the importance of self-produced consequences for one's behavior, reciprocal determinism, observational learning, and the role of cognition in mediating environmental-behavior relations. Walter Mischel actually coined the label *cognitive social learning theory*, the current popular version of social learning theory.
Strengths and weaknesses of the behavioral/social learning theories	Strengths	Among the strengths of the behavioral/social learning views are: the belief that specific behaviors and environmental stimuli are important determinants of development, the use of meticulous observation, a rigorous experimental approach, the social learning emphasis on cognition as a mediator of environmental-behavior relations, and emphasis on adaptation to a changing social world and the importance of context in development.
	Weaknesses	Among the weaknesses of the behavioral/social learning views are: the failure to recognize the causative role of cognition, the nonchronological perspective, too little attention paid to biological processes, too reductionistic, and too mechanical.

5. Critics have said that the behavioral and the social learning views are too mechanical. However, this perhaps is not a fair charge against Bandura's contemporary cognitive social learning theory. His ideas on social interaction are at least partly consistent with a contextual world view.

While the behavioral and psychoanalytic views dominated thinking about children's development (along with some strong biological, descriptive research by Gesell and others) for much of the first half of the 20th century, most child psychologists believe that Skinner's strong behavioral view does not recognize some of the important ingredients of children's lives. Nonetheless, some

behavioral processes are important in describing and explaining the complexity of the child's world—reinforcement, punishment, and imitation clearly are involved in how experiences influence the child's development. The cognitive social learning view is recognized by many child psychologists today as making an important contribution to our understanding of how the child interacts with his or her social world and interprets that world.

Child Development Concept Table 2.3 summarizes a number of important aspects of the behavioral/social learning views. Now we turn our attention to a view that has received considerable attention recently in the field of child development—ethological theory.

ETHOLOGICAL THEORY

To learn about the biological emphasis of ethology, we initially focus on the work of the European zoologists Konrad Lorenz and Niko Tinbergen and then move on to the more recent neo-ethological view of Robert Hinde.

Classical Ethological Theory and the European Zoologists

Ethology emerged as an important viewpoint because of the work of two European zoologists—Konrad Lorenz and Niko Tinbergen. Basically, their **classical ethological theory** is tied to the belief that behavior is biologically determined. In particular, the ethologists stress that the key to the biological determination of behavior is the role evolution plays. The ethologists believe that we can only fully appreciate the nature of the child's behavior if we recognize that many patterns of the child's behavior are transmitted by means of evolution. Lorenz (1935), in particular, reminded biologists and psychologists of the importance early experience plays in development and its potential irreversibility. In the 1930s, when Lorenz's ideas were first set forth, he was particularly interested in demonstrating that the behaviorists were wrong in their view that behavior is learned and due to environmental experience alone (Cairns, 1983).

Working mostly with graylag geese, Lorenz (1965) studied a behavior pattern that was considered to be programmed within the genes of the animals. A newly hatched gosling seemed to be born with the instinct for following its mother. Observations showed that the gosling was capable of such behavior as soon as it was hatched from the egg. Lorenz proved that it was incorrect to assume that such behavior was programmed in the animal.

In a remarkable series of experiments, Lorenz separated the eggs laid by one female goose into two groups. One group he returned to the female goose to be hatched by her; the other group was hatched in an incubator. The goslings in the first group performed as predicted; they followed their mother as soon as they were hatched. But those in the second group, who saw Lorenz when they were first hatched, followed him everywhere, just as though he were their mother. Lorenz marked the goslings and then placed both groups under a box. Mother

goose and "mother" Lorenz stood aside as the box was lifted. Each group of goslings went directly to its "mother" (see Figure 2.9). Lorenz called this process **imprinting**—rapid, innate learning within a limited critical period of time and involving attachment to the first moving object seen.

While Lorenz was busy observing and conducting experiments with graylag geese, Tinbergen (1951, 1969) was observing the behavior of stickleback fish, a small fish that lives in North European fresh waters. Early in the spring, both sexes are ready to mate. Through an intricate system, each member of the pair engages in certain behaviors that serve as a stimulus for the behavior of the other member. First, the male stickleback marks off a territory and forms a nest at the bottom of the water. Then his belly changes color, becoming bright red. The bright red color signals the female stickleback that he is ready to mate. At some point, a female stickleback swims into his territory with her abdomen swollen by the presence of eggs and her head in an upward position. Her abdomen and posture signal the male's next behavior, an impressive zigzag dance. The dance stimulates the female to approach the male. As she does so, the male turns and swims toward the nest. The female follows, and the male puts his head in the nest opening. He subsequently withdraws his head indicating to the female that she should now place her entire body in the nest. Once the female is in the nest, the male begins shaking and taps her in a rhythmic manner at the base of her tail. This tapping signals her to lay the eggs, after which she abruptly leaves the nest. Then the male enters the nest and deposits his sperm, thus fertilizing the eggs.

Tinbergen's work with the stickleback fish illustrated an important idea in ethology—the fixed-action pattern, which means nearly the same thing as instinct, being defined as unlearned behavior that is universal in a species. The unlearned behavior is triggered by naturally occurring stimuli, referred to as **sign stimuli.**

The ethological views of Lorenz and Tinbergen forced American developmental psychologists to recognize the importance of the biological basis of behavior. But the research and theorizing of ethology still seemed to lack some important ingredients that would elevate it to the ranks of the other perspectives discussed so far in this chapter. In particular, there was little or nothing in the classical ethological view about the nature of social re-

FIGURE 2.9 Konrad Lorenz, a pioneering student of animal behavior, is followed through the water by three imprinted graylag geese.

lationships in children's lives, something that certainly any major theory of child development must deal with. And the concept of the **critical period**—a fixed time period very early in development that exists for the emergence of a behavior—seemed to be at least to some degree overdrawn. Further, classical ethological theory had been weak in stimulating studies with human children. By far the majority of the research focused on lower animals. As we see next, recent expansion of the perspective is now having an important impact on the scientific study of children's lives.

The Neo-Ethological View of Robert Hinde

Ethologist Robert Hinde (1983) has presented a provocative view of development, one that goes beyond the classical ethological theory of the early European zoologists, by emphasizing the importance of social relationships, describing sensitive periods of development rather than critical periods, and presenting a framework that is beginning to stimulate research with human children. Insight into the **neo-ethological view** appears in Hinde's description of three questions ethologists ask about children and discussion of selected issues of interest to ethologists.

Three Questions Ethologists Ask About Children's Development

In considering any social behavior, an ethologist is likely to ask three questions: (1) Why did the child behave in this way? (2) How does the child's behavior change over time and why? and (3) What is the evolutionary origin of the child's behavior?

With regard to the first question about why the child behaved in a particular way, the ethologist believes that it is essential to conduct an elaborate description and classification of behavioral events and antecedent conditions. For example, if an observer discovers a particular behavior is less likely to be elicited by a stranger than by familiar individuals, the observer infers that experience likely plays a role in determining the behavior.

The second question the ethologist wants to answer involves delving further into the past. As an organism develops, its behavior changes. The course of such development requires analysis and explanation. After the ethologist asks the basic question, "How does the behavior change?" then he or she wants to know the extent to which such changes are due to environmental influences, as well as how such influences produced their effects. For example, the ethologist studying delinquent behavior in adolescents would be interested in knowing not only the immediate contextual influences on the behavior but the developmental course that preceded the behavior as well. Thus, from this perspective, delinquent behavior in adolescents might depend on propensities acquired in childhood that are carried forward to adolescence, as well as on such possible immediate determinants as recent frustrations (a long hot summer in a ghetto) and peer modeling.

The third question focuses on the evolutionary origin of the behavior under investigation. The ethologist finds that comparisons between closely related species provide information about the possible evolutionary course of a particular behavior. For example, John Bowlby's theory of attachment, which is described in Chapter 6, was built on the belief that a young primate depends on its mother for protection and food and therefore is biologically predisposed with a repertoire of behaviors for maintaining proximity to the mother.

Selected Issues of Interest to Ethologists

Among the many issues of children's development, the following are of interest to ethologists: the role of observation, functional considerations, dichotomies in development and organismic-environmental interaction, sensitive periods, and relationships and personality.

Like behaviorists, ethologists emphasize the importance of careful observation as a key to understanding development. Ethologists, however, place much more emphasis on observing behavior in its natural surroundings. For example, Tinbergen observed the stickleback fish in the brushes of a marsh rather than in an aquarium. Ethologists believe that behavioral laboratories are not good settings for observing children's behavior—rather, they believe that the child's behavior should be meticulously observed in the natural surroundings of home, playground, neighborhood, school, and so forth. Thus, ethologists have been a strong force in the trend toward observing children's development in naturalistic surroundings.

A second issue ethologists address concerns functional considerations of behavior. They point out that child development is studied by adults, who see the end point of development being mature adulthood, but that the behavior of the infant should be considered in terms of its natural selection. The behavior likely was not shaped because the child is a miniature adult but so that the infant can succeed at that particular point in development. For example, caterpillars are excellent leaf eaters, but they do not pretend to be butterflies. Ethologists argue that the word *development* too often diverts attention from viewing each stage of development in its own right.

A third issue of interest to ethologists such as Hinde focuses on the dichotomy that often is proposed between innate and learned behavior. Put succinctly, the ethologist argues that such a dichotomy is not very accurate. We go into this issue in greater detail in Chapter 3 when we discuss the contributions of heredity and environment to children's development. The ethologist believes that trying to tease apart hereditary and environmental contributions to development leads to a false dichotomy. However, ethologists do stress that there has been too little consideration of the extent to which the child is predisposed to learn something. And they point out that what an individual learns and the situations in which the individual learns vary among species.

A fourth issue ethologists emphasize focuses on sensitive periods. Hinde makes a distinction between critical periods and sensitive periods. Classical ethologists, such as Lorenz, argued for the importance of critical periods and imprinting, noting how an irreversible critical period exists in the attachment of geese. Ethologists now recognize that the critical period concept may have been too rigid. The more recently developed concept of **sensitive period** implies that a given effect can be produced more readily during one period than earlier or later. However, according to Hinde, it does not imply that the period is necessarily closely tied to chronological age or that the same effects could not be obtained (although perhaps with more difficulty) later. Viewed in this manner, the concept of the sensitive period is more flexible than that of the critical period. For example, with human children, there may be some long, reasonably flexible sensitive periods for such important processes as language, vision, and attachment.

A fifth issue believed to be important by ethologists emphasizes the child's relationships and personality. Here, as with the sensitive period concept, there is a considerable expansion and reworking of the classical ethological view in the neo-ethological perspective of

Hinde. His perspective on children's social development argues that relationships with other people form one of the most, if not the most, important aspects of the environment and that if children's development is to be fully understood, the properties and dynamics of relationships must be charted. Hinde (1983) argues that certain properties of relationships, such as synchrony and competitiveness, are not descriptive of the behavior of individuals in isolation. He also believes that relationships can have properties that emerge from the frequency and patterning of interactions over time. For example, if the relationship of the mother and infant is studied at one point in time, researchers may not be able to describe the relationship as rejecting, controlling, or permissive. But through detailed observations over a prolonged period of time, researchers may become more confident and accurate about such categorization. Hinde (1983) also believes that researchers must pay attention to how participants' personalities influence relationships, as well as how relationships affect participants' personalities.

Now that we have considered a number of ideas about ethological theory, we focus on the strengths and weaknesses of the theory.

Strengths and Weaknesses of Ethological Theory

Among the strengths of ethological theory are:

1. The theory emphasizes the biological and evolutionary basis of behavior, providing an important perspective and giving biology an appropriate, prominent role in determining children's development.
2. Ethologists use careful observations in naturalistic surroundings to obtain information about children's development.
3. Ethologists believe that children's development involves some rather long sensitive periods of development.
4. The theory emphasizes the functional importance of behavior, such that behavior needs to be looked at in terms of its adaptiveness in a particular period of development.
5. Hinde emphasizes the properties of relationships and the belief that relationships are the most important environmental influence on children's development.

However, like the other theories we have discussed, ethology has its critics as well:

1. At times, even the emphasis on sensitive periods seems too rigid, and the classical ethological view of critical periods has not proven very satisfactory.
2. The emphasis in most ethological theories still slants more strongly toward a biological-evolutionary explanation of behavior rather than a biological-environmental mix.
3. The theory has been slow in generating testable ideas with human children.
4. Some of the major beliefs in the theory may not be testable, such as the strong emphasis on the evolutionary basis of behavior.
5. The theory often seems to provide a better explanation of behavior retrospectively than prospectively—that is, ethology is better at explaining what happened to cause a child's behavior after it already has occurred than in predicting the occurrence of the behavior in the future.

Many developmental psychologists have been slow to accept the significance of ethological views, for among other reasons, the fact that much ethological research was with lower animals rather than human children. Thus, while in the 1960s and 1970s, the works of Lorenz and Tinbergen were often discussed by child developmentalists, only a handful of researchers viewed the ethological perspective as highly influential. Now the ethological perspective is having a strong impact on the way psychologists think about children's development. In particular, the perspective has spawned an extensive research effort aimed at understanding the nature of the infant's attachment, which is described in detail in Chapter 6. The perspective also has forced many child psychologists to consider the use of naturalistic observations, rather than controlled, laboratory observations, in their effort to collect valid information about children.

Child Development Concept Table 2.4 summarizes the main points of our discussion of ethological theory. While we have studied four different major theoretical perspectives on children's development and several versions of each theory, as we see next, no particular theory has a complete answer to the complex development of children.

Child Development Concept Table 2.4	Ethological Theory	
Concept	**Processes/Related Ideas**	**Characteristics/Description**
Classical ethological theory and the European zoologists	Emphasis on biology, evolution, critical periods, animal research, naturalistic observations	European zoologists, led by Lorenz and Tinbergen, objected to the strong environmentalism of American behaviorism. They argued that the biological basis of behavior is important and that it has an evolutionary tie. They also demonstrated early critical periods, at which time a characteristic has an optimal time of emergence, and conducted naturalistic observations of animals.
The neo-ethological view of Robert Hinde	Characteristics of Hinde's view	Hinde emphasizes sensitive, rather than critical, periods, arguing that the critical period concept is too rigid. He still places a premium on the importance of naturalistic observation and biological/evolutionary ties but has expanded the ethological view to include the importance of social relationships. Hinde also believes that it is very important to take into account the developmental history of the child.
	Three questions ethologists always ask about children's behavior	The three questions are: (1) Why did the child behave in this way? (2) How does the child's behavior change over time and why? and (3) What is the evolutionary origin of the child's behavior?
	Selected issues of interest to ethologists	Issues of interest to ethologists are: the role of observation, functional considerations, organismic-environmental interaction, sensitive periods, and relationships and personality.
Strengths and weaknesses of ethological theory	Strengths	Among the strengths of the ethological view are an emphasis on the biological/evolutionary basis of behavior, use of naturalistic observation, sensitive periods, functional importance of behavior, and Hinde's emphasis on the properties of relationships.
	Weaknesses	Among the weaknesses of the theory are the somewhat rigid nature of the critical, sensitive period hypothesis; too little attention to environmental contributions; slowness in generating research with human children; difficulty in testing some of the beliefs; and inability to predict future behavior as well as explain past behavior.

AN ECLECTIC THEORETICAL ORIENTATION

No single indomitable theory is capable of explaining the rich complexity of children's development. Each of the theories described in this chapter has made important contributions to our understanding of children's development, but none provides a complete description and explanation. Psychoanalytic theory best describes the child's unconscious mind, while Erikson's life-cycle view and Piaget's cognitive developmental theory seem to do the best job of revealing how children's later stages are tied to earlier stages of development. Piaget's theory is the most complete description of the unfolding of children's cognitive development, and the information processing perspective is the most accurate view in charting the precision of the child's cognitive processes. The behavioral/social learning theories have been the most adept at examining the important role of environment in the child's development. And the ethological view has

sensitized developmental psychologists to the significance of biological influences on children's development. It is important to recognize that, while theories are helpful guides in understanding children's development, relying on a single theory to explain children's development likely is a mistake.

An attempt was made in this chapter to present four theoretical perspectives objectively. The same **eclectic orientation** will be maintained throughout this book. In this way, you can view the study of children's development as it actually exists—with different theorists making different assumptions about children's development, stressing different empirical problems, and using different strategies to discover information about children.

These theoretical perspectives, along with the research issues and methods described in Chapter 1, provide a sense of the scientific nature of child development. Table 2.2 compares the four main theoretical approaches emphasized in this chapter—psychoanalytic,

Table 2.2   Theoretical Comparisons and Issues in Child Development

Issues	Theories			
	Psychoanalytic Theory	Cognitive Theory	Behavioral/Social Learning Theory	Ethological Theory
Qualitative change and stages of development	Strong emphasis— Freud stressed psychosexual stages; Erikson stressed psychosocial stages.	Strong emphasis by Piaget; not emphasized in information processing perspective.	Deemphasized.	Stages are deemphasized, but qualitative change is stressed.
Continuity-discontinuity in development	Discontinuity between stages emphasized, but continuity between early development and later development is stressed; later changes in development more likely in Erikson's view.	For Piaget, discontinuity between stages stressed, but continuity between early and later development emphasized. Continuity-discontinuity has not been an important issue to information processing psychologists.	Continuity emphasized in the sense that development is viewed as smooth, and void of abrupt stage change. Continuity comes in the form of consistent environmental experiences and discontinuity in the form of inconsistent, new environmental experiences.	Discontinuity comes in the form of critical or sensitive periods. Continuity occurs in the sense that early experiences are thought to be important predictors of later development and in the emphasis in the neo-ethological view on studying the history of the child's experiences. Continuity between child and lower animals also stressed.
Individual differences	Not emphasized, although child's individual experiences with family thought to be important.	Not emphasized traditionally, but recent studies starting to be concerned with individual variation.	Not emphasized in behavioral approach, but social learning approach emphasizes person-environment interaction.	Not emphasized.
Genetic/biological and environmental/social factors	Freud stressed biological determination interacting with child's familial experiences in first five years; Erikson provides a more balanced biological-cultural interaction perspective on development.	Piagetian perspective places high degree of importance on biological factors. Environment provides the setting for cognitive structures to unfold. Peer experiences and role-taking opportunities are very important in Piaget's view. Information processing approach is not overly concerned with this issue, but hardware-software computer metaphor implies biological-environmental interaction.	Environment viewed as cause of behavior in both behavioral and cognitive social learning views.	Strong biological view, although neo-ethological approach is giving more attention to biological-environmental interaction, particularly child's experiences in close relationships.

(continued on following page)

Table 2.2 Continued				
	Theories			
Issues	**Psychoanalytic Theory**	**Cognitive Theory**	**Behavioral/Social Learning Theory**	**Ethological Theory**
Importance of cognition	Cognition is emphasized, but in the form of unconscious, rather than conscious, thought.	Cognition is viewed as a primary determinant of behavior.	Cognition is strongly deemphasized in the behavioral view but plays an important mediating role between the environment and the child's behavior in the cognitive social learning view.	Cognition is not emphasized.
Research methods	Clinical interviews, unstructured personality tests, and psychohistorical analyses of lives are stressed.	Interviews and observations are emphasized.	The behavioral/social learning view emphasizes a fine-grained approach through the use of detailed observations, often in controlled settings.	Observation in naturalistic settings is the main way ethologists collect data.

cognitive, behavioral/social learning, and ethological—in terms of how they view each of the issues raised in Chapter 1: qualitative change and stages of development, continuity-discontinuity in development, individual differences, and genetic/biological and environmental/social factors. The theories also are compared in terms of research methods and the degree to which they emphasize cognition in development. By studying Table 2.2, you should be able to integrate some of the most important ideas about issues and methods described in Chapter 1 with the main theories described in Chapter 2.

THINKING BACK, LOOKING AHEAD

You now know something about the 11-year-old Swiss boy who wrote a precocious essay on the rare albino sparrow and who later became a giant in developmental psychology by showing how conscious thoughts are important in development. You've read about the tall, blond-haired youth who wandered around Europe at the age of 18 and who later identified eight stages of the human life cycle, one of which—the search for identity—characterized the youth of the wanderer. You know something about a famous behaviorist who was delighted when he was able to control the behavior of pigeons to the point where the pigeons could pilot missiles. Later, this same person applied such ideas to humans, believing that their lives would be more enjoyable if they recognized how positive reinforcement could be used to control behavior. You've read about a man who became a "mother" to a group of hatched goslings, revealing the importance of biology and sensitive periods in development. And finally, you've learned that each theoretical perspective often has variations represented by different theorists—Freud is not all there is to psychoanalytic theory—Erikson and others are important too; Piaget is not the only cognitive theorist—the computer revolution ushered in another perspective as well; Skinner is not the only representative of the behavioral tradition—others with a behavioral orientation have greatly expanded and revised such views; and there is more to ethology than the goslings of Lorenz—neo-ethologists are now even theorizing about the properties of social relationships.

In Section 2, we focus in greater detail on an aspect of development so important that it already has been addressed on a number of occasions in Chapters 1 and 2. Section 2 is called "Biological Foundations and Infancy." It includes four chapters, emphasizing the evolutionary perspective, genetics, prenatal development, and the birth process (Chapter 3); physical and perceptual development (Chapter 4); learning, cognition, and language (Chapter 5); and social and personality development (Chapter 6). Before we leave this chapter, think for a moment about the following words that stimulate images of some of the themes raised by theorists, such as the nature of unconscious and conscious thought, as well as the nature of development itself:

> Time past and time future
> Allow but a little consciousness,
> To be conscious is not to be in time
> But only in time can the moment in the rose-garden,
> The moment in the arbour where the rain beat,
> The moment in the draughty church at smokefall
> Be remembered; involved with past and future,
> Only through time is time conquered.   T. S. Eliot

SUMMARY

I. Psychoanalytic theory is a view of personality development emphasizing the unconscious nature of the child's mind, the biological foundations of development, and the importance of symbolic thought. Freud's classical psychoanalytic theory and Erikson's life-cycle view are discussed.
  A. Freud's classical psychoanalytic theory presented Freud's ideas on the structure of personality, defense mechanisms, and psychosexual stages of personality development.
  B. Many contemporary psychoanalytic theorists play down sexual instincts, often placing more importance on rational thought processes and cultural influences. A number of contemporary psychoanalytic theorists are classified as neo-psychoanalytic; that is, they accept some basic Freudian ideas but disagree on one or more major points.
  C. Erikson's life-cycle view emphasizes eight stages of psychosocial development from birth through the late adulthood years. Erikson believes that stages occur through a combination of biology and culture.

II. Cognitive theories of development stress that the key ingredient of child development is an understanding of the unfolding of conscious thought. Cognitive developmental theory and the information processing perspective are discussed.
  A. Cognitive developmental theory focuses on the development of rational thought in the child and stresses that cognition unfolds in a sequence of stages. The leading figure in cognitive developmental theory is Swiss psychologist Jean Piaget. Piaget argued that children move through four stages of development—sensorimotor, preoperational, concrete operational, and formal operational. He also believed that adaptation (assimilation, accommodation), organization, and equilibration are the processes responsible for changes in cognitive development.
  B. The information processing perspective focuses on how people process information about their world—their attentional, memory, and reasoning processes, among others. The approach emphasizes a computer metaphor—comparing a child's mind to a computer, Broadbent's model of information processing stressed the importance of memory stores, while Klatzky's model emphasizes processes. Questions raised by the information processing approach involve processing speed, capacity, the role of knowledge, and controlled versus automatic processes.

III. The behavioral perspective emphasizes environment and behavior, learned behavior, and strong methodology (including careful observation). It also views cognitive processes as either unimportant or as mediators of environmental-behavior linkages. Skinner's behaviorism and Bandura and Mischel's social learning theory are discussed.
  A. Skinner's behaviorism emphasizes external control of the child's behavior, operant conditioning, and widespread use of behavior modification.
  B. Social learning theory shares with traditional behaviorism a belief in the importance of the environment and its connections with behavior and also a belief in the use of meticulous observation. However, social learning theorists also argue that traditional behaviorism misses much of the richness of development by paying too little attention to the child's social world and cognitive processes. Bandura's social learning theory stresses the importance of self-produced consequences for one's behavior, reciprocal determinism, observational learning, and the role of cognition in mediating environmental-behavior relations. Mischel's cognitive social learning theory has made an important contribution to understanding children's personality development.

IV. The ethological perspective is now having a strong impact on the way psychologists think about child development. Classical ethological theory and the neo-ethological view of Robert Hinde are discussed.
   A. Classical ethological theorists, led by European zoologists Lorenz and Tinbergen, objected to the strong environmentalism of American behaviorism. They argued that the biological basis of behavior is important and that it has an evolutionary tie. They also demonstrated early critical periods, at which time a characteristic has an optimal time of emergence, and conducted naturalistic observations.
   B. The neo-ethological view of Robert Hinde emphasizes sensitive, rather than critical, periods. Hinde still places a premium on the importance of naturalistic observation and biological/evolutionary ties but has expanded the ethological view to include the importance of social relationships. Hinde also believes that it is very important to know about the developmental history of the child. Three questions that neo-ethologists ask about the child's behavior are: (1) Why did the child behave in this way? (2) How does the child's behavior change over time and why? and (3) What is the evolutionary origin of the child's behavior? Neo-ethologists are interested in the role of observation, functional considerations, organismic-environmental interaction, sensitive periods, and relationships and personality.
V. No single theory can explain the rich, awesome complexity of the child's development. Each of the theories presented has made a different contribution, and it probably is a wise strategy to adopt an eclectic theoretical perspective as we attempt to understand the nature of the child's development.

KEY TERMS

accommodation 57
anal stage 47
assimilation 57
automatic processes 63
autonomy versus shame and doubt 51
behavior modification 66
classical ethological theory 70
cognitive developmental theory 53
cognitive social learning theory 66
concrete operational stage 56
conscience 44
controlled processes 62
critical period 71
defense mechanisms 44
eclectic orientation 74
ego 44
ego ideal 44
ego integrity versus despair 52
Electra complex 48
equilibration 59
formal operational stage 57
generativity versus stagnation 52
genital stage 49
id 43
identity versus identity confusion (diffusion) 52
imprinting 70

industry versus inferiority 51
information processing perspective 60
initiative versus guilt 51
intimacy versus isolation 52
latency stage 45
neo-ethological view 71
neo-psychoanalytic theorists 50
observational learning 68
Oedipus complex 42
operant conditioning (instrumental conditioning) 65
oral stage 47
organization 59
parallel processing 60
phallic stage 47
pleasure principle 43
preoperational stage 55
primary process thinking 43
projection 45
psychoanalytic theory 42
punishment 66
reaction formation 45
reality principle 44
reciprocal determinism 67
regression 45
reinforcement 66
repression 45
sensitive period 72
sensorimotor stage 55
sign stimuli 70
superego 44
trust versus mistrust 50

SUGGESTED READINGS

Bandura, A. (1977). *Social learning theory*. Englewood
  Cliffs, NJ: Prentice-Hall.
  Provides extensive information about Bandura's social
  learning theory. Includes ideas about imitation and
  many other important learning processes.
Cowan, P. (1978). *Piaget with feeling*. New York: Holt,
  Rinehart, & Winston.
  Provides a well-written overview of Piaget's theory and
  draws implications of the theory for understanding
  children's emotional development.
Erikson, E. H. (1968). *Identity: Youth and crisis*. New York:
  Norton.
  Must reading for anyone interested in developmental
  psychology. Erikson outlines his eight stages and talks
  extensively about identity development.
Hinde, R. (1983). Ethology and child development. In P. H.
  Mussen (Ed.), *Handbook of child psychology* (4th ed.),
  Vol. 2. New York: Wiley.
  Hinde's views are having a significant impact on the
  study of children's socialization. Here he outlines the
  questions ethologists ask and the research issues that
  interest ethologists.
Hunt, M. (1982). *The universe within*. New York: Simon
  and Schuster.
  Hunt traveled to many universities and talked with top
  scholars in the cognitive area. This book provides
  considerable insight into the importance of the
  information processing perspective. Written in an
  interesting way.
Salkind, N. (1981). *Theories of human development*. New
  York: Van Nostrand.
  Focuses on many different theories of development,
  including those of Freud, Erikson, Piaget, Skinner, and
  Bandura, as well as Gesell's maturational view, which
  we described in Chapter 1. Also includes a chapter on
  the dialectical nature of development.

As nine months go to the shaping of an infant ripe for his birth.
So many a million of ages have gone to the making of man.

Tennyson

THE EVOLUTIONARY PERSPECTIVE, GENETICS, PRENATAL DEVELOPMENT, AND THE BIRTH PROCESS

IMAGINE . . . THAT YOU ARE
MARRIED AND THAT YOU AND
YOUR SPOUSE HAVE JUST GONE
TO SEE A GENETIC COUNSELOR

PREVIEW

THE EVOLUTIONARY
PERSPECTIVE AND GENETICS:
HUMANS ARRIVED LATE IN
DECEMBER

Natural Selection—Bacteria to Blue
Whales With Lots of Beetles in Between
Genes and the Nature of Genetic-
Environmental Interaction
What Are Genes?
Some Genetic Principles
Methods Used by Behavior Geneticists
*Genetic-Environmental Interaction and Its
Effect on Development*

**CHILD DEVELOPMENT CONCEPT
TABLE 3.1: THE EVOLUTIONARY
PERSPECTIVE AND GENETICS**

THE COURSE OF PRENATAL
DEVELOPMENT

Conception and the Zygote
Standard Conception and the Zygote
New Methods of Conception

The Germinal Period
The Embryonic Period
Three Layers and Support Systems
Further Embryonic Developments

The Fetal Period

**CHILD DEVELOPMENT CONCEPT
TABLE 3.2: THE COURSE OF
PRENATAL DEVELOPMENT**

TERATOLOGY AND HAZARDS TO
PRENATAL DEVELOPMENT

Teratology and the Effects of Teratogens
Maternal Diseases and Conditions
Maternal Diseases and Infections
The Mother's Age
Nutrition
Emotional State and Stress

Drugs
The Thalidomide Tragedy
Alcohol

**FOCUS ON CHILD
DEVELOPMENT 3.1: AA SCORES AT
MID-PREGNANCY, NEONATAL
AROUSAL, AND PRESCHOOL
VIGILANCE**
Cigarette Smoking

**CHILD DEVELOPMENT CONCEPT
TABLE 3.3: TERATOLOGY AND
HAZARDS TO PRENATAL
DEVELOPMENT**

THE BIRTH PROCESS

Childbirth Strategies
Standard Childbirth
The Leboyer Method
The Lamaze Method

**FOCUS ON CHILD
DEVELOPMENT 3.2: A FATHER IN
THE DELIVERY ROOM: "IT WAS
OUT OF THIS WORLD!"**

Stages of Birth and Delivery
Complications
The Use of Drugs During Childbirth

**FOCUS ON CHILD
DEVELOPMENT 3.3: ANESTHESIA,
OXYTOCIN, AND INFANT STATES**

**CHILD DEVELOPMENT CONCEPT
TABLE 3.4: CHILDBIRTH
STRATEGIES, STAGES OF BIRTH
AND DELIVERY COMPLICATIONS,
AND THE USE OF DRUGS**

Preterm Infants and Age-Weight
Considerations
Birth Date and Weight
*Measures of Neonatal Health and
Responsiveness*
Conclusions About Preterm Infants

**FOCUS ON CHILD
DEVELOPMENT 3.4:
PREEMIES ARE DIFFERENT**

Bonding

THINKING BACK, LOOKING
AHEAD

SUMMARY

KEY TERMS

SUGGESTED READINGS

CHAPTER 3

IMAGINE . . . THAT YOU ARE MARRIED AND THAT YOU AND YOUR SPOUSE HAVE JUST GONE TO SEE A GENETIC COUNSELOR

You have been married for several years. You would like to start a family, but you are frightened. The newspapers and popular magazines are full of stories about infants born prematurely who do not survive, infants with debilitating physical defects, and cases of genetically caused mental retardation. You feel that such a child would create a social, economic, and psychological strain on your marriage and on society in general.

You turn to a genetic counselor for help. Genetic counselors are usually physicians or biologists who are familiar with the kinds of problems that can be inherited, the odds for encountering them, and helpful measures for offsetting some of the effects. You tell the counselor that there has been a history of mental retardation in your family. Your younger sister was born with Down's syndrome, a form of mental retardation. Your spouse's older brother has hemophilia, a condition in which bleeding is difficult to stop. You wonder what the chances are that a child of yours might also be retarded or have hemophilia and what measures might be taken to reduce the child's chances of having these problems.

The counselor probes more deeply because she understands that these facts in isolation do not give her the complete picture. She learns that no other relatives in your family are retarded and that your mother was in her late 40s when your younger sister was born. She concludes that the retardation was due to the age of your mother, not to some general tendency of your family members to inherit retardation. It is well known that women over 40 have a much higher probability of giving birth to retarded children than do younger women. Apparently, the ova (egg cells) are not as healthy in older women as in women under the age of 40. (However, in 25 percent of Down's syndrome cases, the genetic cause has been traced to the father. If the father is 55 years or older, the

incidence of Down's Syndrome in offspring increases (Stene, Mikkelson, & Peterson, 1977; Magenis, Overton, Chamberline, Brady, & Lovrien, et al., 1977). The counselor then determines that there is a small but clear possibility that your spouse may be a carrier of hemophilia and transmit the condition to a son. The counselor can find no other evidence from the family history that indicates genetic problems.

The decision, then, is up to you. In this case, the genetic problem does not seem likely, so the choice would probably be to go ahead with trying to have a child. But what should parents do if they face the strong possibility of having a child with a major birth defect? Ultimately, the decision rests on the couple's ethnic and religious beliefs. They must decide how to balance these against the quality of their child's life.

The moral dilemma is even more acute, of course, once a pregnancy has begun. **Amniocentesis,** a test that can detect Down's syndrome and more than a hundred other birth defects, can be performed about the 14th to 16th week of pregnancy. This test has been particularly helpful to older mothers. A long, thin needle is inserted into the abdomen to extract a sample of amniotic fluid, the liquid that cushions the fetus. Fetal cells in the fluid are grown in the laboratory for two to four weeks and can then be studied for chromosomal and some metabolic disorders. The later that amniocentesis is performed, the better the diagnostic potential. However, the earlier it is performed, the more useful it can be in deciding whether a pregnancy will be terminated.

Scientists are continuing to search for more accurate, safe assessments of high-risk situations where hereditary information suggests that difficulties might be present. A measure called the **chorionic villus test** has been available since the mid-1980s. A small sample of the placenta is removed during the first trimester, between the ninth and tenth weeks, with the diagnostic results usually requiring two to three weeks. The potential advantage of the chorionic villus test is one of time. For example, if the diagnosis provided by amniocentesis suggests severe birth defects, a decision about a possible abortion cannot be made until some point in the second trimester, a point when an abortion is less simple, less safe, and more traumatic than in the first trimester. The chorionic villus test, by contrast, allows an abortion decision to be made by close to the end of the first trimester.

PREVIEW

As we look at the woman, we only see someone who is pregnant. From the outside, we do not know if the fetus is a boy or a girl, blond or brunette. At one time, you, too, floated around in darkness in a sea of fluid inside your mother's womb. From the moment you were conceived to the moment you were born, some astonishing things were going on. This chapter relates the story of those masterful developments.

In the early 19th century, Samuel Taylor Coleridge had the vision to foresee how important the prenatal period is in the child's development:

Yes, the history of man for the nine months preceding his birth would, probably, be far more interesting, and contain events of greater moment, than all three score and ten years that follow it.

THE EVOLUTIONARY PERSPECTIVE AND GENETICS: HUMANS ARRIVED LATE IN DECEMBER

In evolutionary terms, human beings are relative newcomers to earth. Yet, in a short time, we have established ourselves as the most successful and dominant species. As Carl Sagan (1980) pointed out, humans arrived late in December if we consider evolutionary time in terms of a calendar year. As our earliest ancestors left the forest to feed in the savannas, and finally to form hunting societies on the open plains, their minds and behaviors changed. How did this evolution come about? The answer lies in the principle of natural selection.

Natural Selection—Bacteria to Blue Whales With Lots of Beetles in Between

After completing an around-the-world voyage on the HMS *Beagle,* observing the life and surrounding conditions of many different species, Charles Darwin published *On the Origin of Species* in 1859. He concluded that organisms reproduce at rates that could lead to enormous increases in population sizes of most species.

Yet, the size of populations remains almost the same from one year to the next. Darwin reasoned that there must be an intense, constant struggle for food, water, and resources among the many young born every generation, such that many of the young do not survive until they are mature enough to reproduce. Those that do survive pass their genes on to the next generation. And, as Darwin believed, the ones that make it long enough to reproduce likely are superior in a number of ways to those who do not. That is, the survivors are better adapted to their world than the nonsurvivors. According to Darwin's theory, gradually, over the course of many generations, the organisms with the favorable characteristics make up more of the population, and over very, very long time periods, the reproductive advantage produces a gradual modification of the whole population. On the other hand, if environmental conditions change, new sets of characteristics might be favored and the whole process could move in a different direction. For Darwin, and many scientists today, the principle of **natural selection** guides the evolutionary process (Campbell, 1985).

More than a million species have been described, from bacteria to blue whales, with lots of beetles in between. The concept of natural selection is to be found in the disappearing acts of moths, the quills of porcupines, and the deceptive markings of butterflies (see Figure 3.1). Evolution is also evidenced in the technological advances, feeding behavior, intelligence, and longer parental care of human beings.

For the most part, as mentioned earlier, evolution proceeds at a very slow pace. The evolutionary paths of human beings and the great apes began to diverge about 14 million years ago! Modern man—*Homo sapiens*—came into existence only about 50,000 years ago. And the beginning of civilization as we know it began about 10,000 years ago. In the ensuing 10,000 years, there have been no sweeping evolutionary changes in humans: Our brain is not 10 times as big, we do not have a third eye in the back of our head, and we cannot fly. This is not surprising because we only have existed for about 50,000 years, and it takes much longer for a mammalian species to develop.

FIGURE 3.1   A black and white noctuid moth. How is natural selection at work in the disappearing act of moths?

The nature of evolution is still debated by scientists, however. Two such debates focus on the pace of evolution and its adaptive nature. Some contemporary thinkers, such as Steven Jay Gould (1983), believe that there are times when evolution occurs in spurts and lags, rather than being gradual. And other scientists today emphasize that not all evolution is adaptive (Merrill, 1986).

Genes and the Nature of Genetic-Environmental Interaction

The story of human development begins at conception, when a single male sperm fertilizes a female ovum and a biological process begins that will lead to the development of a fully formed infant. To learn more about genetic influences on the child's development, we discuss what genes are, some basic genetic principles, and the methods of behavior geneticists, and then we draw some conclusions about the nature of genetic-environmental interaction.

What Are Genes?

Each child carries the genetic code he or she inherited from his or her parents. Physically, this code is carried by biochemical agents called genes and chromosomes, which are located within the cells of the child's body. The genes and chromosomes that all children inherit are alike in one important respect: They all contain human genetic codes. A fertilized human egg cannot develop into a dog, a cat, or an elephant.

Each child begins life as a single cell weighing about one twenty-millionth of an ounce! This tiny piece of matter houses a child's entire complement of genes and chromosomes. Encoded in the genes and chromosomes is a blueprint or set of instructions that orchestrates development from a single cell into a child made of trillions of cells that each contain a perfect replica of the original genes and chromosomes.

Each human cell consists of 46 chromosomes and 50,000 or more genes located at various places on the chromosomes. **Chromosomes** are threadlike structures that come in structurally similar pairs (23 pairs in humans). The chromosomes are composed of the remarkable substance **DNA** (deoxyribonucleic acid), the double-stranded molecule that looks like a long ladder twisted into a helix (see Figures 3.2 and 3.3). A **gene** is a short segment of the DNA ladder, distinguished by its unique sequences of "rungs," called bases. The genes act as a blueprint that the cells use to reproduce themselves and to manufacture the proteins that maintain life-sustaining processes.

Genes are transmitted from parents to offspring by means of **gametes,** or sex cells, which are created in the testes of males and in the ovaries of females. Gametes are formed by the splitting of cells; this process is called **meiosis.** In meiosis, each pair of chromosomes in the cell separates, and one member of each pair goes into each gamete, or daughter cell. Thus, each human gamete has 23 unpaired chromosomes. **Reproduction** takes place

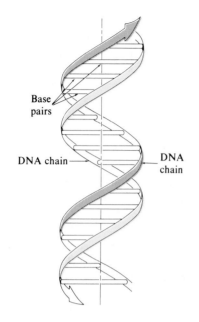

FIGURE 3.2   The double helix: the DNA molecule.

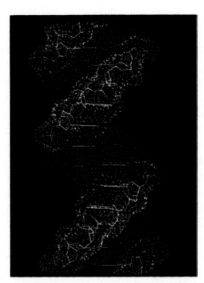

FIGURE 3.3   A DNA molecule. The horizontal bars are the important bases or "rungs" of the DNA ladder. The sequence of these bases plays a key role in scientists' efforts to locate the identity of a gene.

when a female gamete (ovum) is fertilized by a male gamete (sperm) to create a single-celled **zygote.** In the zygote, two sets of unpaired chromosomes combine to form one set of paired chromosomes, one member of each pair being from the mother and the other member from the father. In this manner, each parent contributes 50 percent of his or her heredity to the offspring.

No one possesses all the characteristics that our genetic structure makes possible. The actual combination of genes produces what is known as the **genotype.** However, not all of this genetic material is apparent in our observed and measurable characteristics. These observed and measurable characteristics, called **phenotypes,** include physical traits, such as height, weight, eye color, and skin pigmentation, and psychological characteristics, such as intelligence, creativity, personality, and social tendencies.

Some Genetic Principles

Genetic determination is a highly complex affair, and much is unknown about how genes work. However, a number of genetic principles have been discovered, including dominant-recessive genes, sex-linked genes, polygenically inherited characteristics, reaction range, and canalization.

Dominant-Recessive Genes   The important principle of **dominant-recessive genes** was worked out with such simple forms of life as peas by Gregor Mendel. Mendel found that, when he combined round pea plants with wrinkled pea plants, the next generation of pea plants consistently came out round. The gene for round pea plants was *dominant,* and the one for wrinkled plants was *recessive* (tending to go backward or recede).

What is the color of your parents' hair? If they both have brown hair, you probably have brown hair. If one of your parents has brown hair and the other has blond hair, you still are likely to have brown hair because brown hair is controlled by a dominant gene. Blond hair, by contrast, is based on a recessive gene. However, if both of your parents have blond hair, then you are likely to have blond hair because there is no dominant gene to interfere with the appearance of blond hair. Examples of other dominant gene-linked traits include brown eyes, farsightedness, and dimples; examples of recessive gene-linked traits are blue eyes, normal vision, and freckles.

Sex-Linked Genes   A second important genetic principle refers to **sex-linked genes.** Some characteristics are determined by genes carried on the 23rd chromosome pair—the one that determines the sex of the offspring—with the result that these characteristics are more or less likely to appear in members of one sex. The sex-linked chromosomes are referred to as X and Y. The female has two X chromosomes, whereas the male has one X and one Y chromosome. Females, then, always contribute an X chromosome to the offspring, so it is the male who determines the sex of the offspring because he contributes either an X (it will be a girl) or a Y (it will be a boy). (Figure 3.4 illustrates the genetic makeup of a male and a female.)

Let's look at one sex-linked human characteristic—color blindness. The gene for color blindness is recessive and appears only on the X chromosome. Most females with this recessive gene also have a dominant gene for normal vision on their second X chromosome. For a female to be color-blind, she has to have a recessive gene on both her X chromosomes. By contrast, because males have only one X chromosome, when the recessive gene for color blindness shows up there, the male will be color-blind because he does not have a second X chromosome to cancel out the recessive gene. In other words, if a female inherits the recessive gene, it may not show up, but if a male inherits it, the trait will appear.

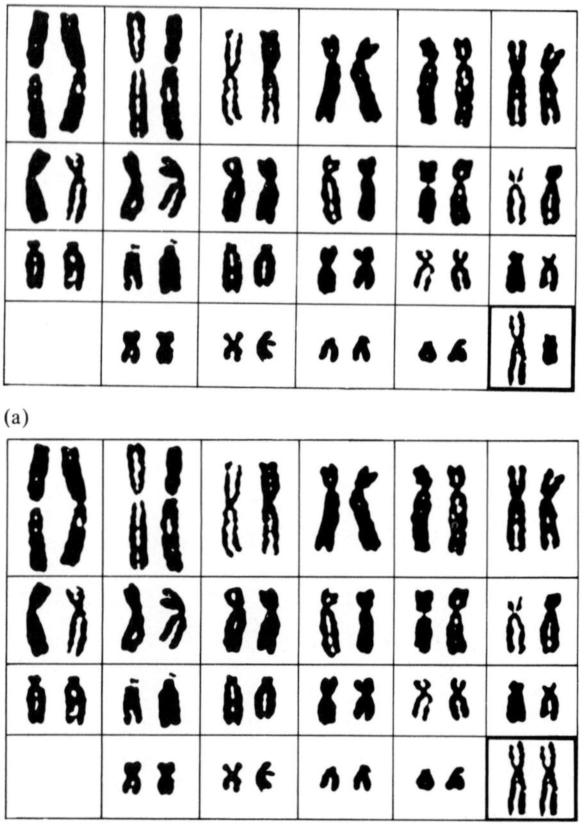

Polygenic Inheritance   Another very important genetic principle is **polygenic inheritance.** Genetic transmission is usually more complex than the rather simple examples we have just examined. Few psychological characteristics are the result of the actions of single gene pairs. Most are actually determined by the interaction of many different genes (remember that there are as many as 50,000 or more of these in the chromosomes). Traits produced by the mixing of genes are said to be polygenically determined.

Reaction Range   For each genotype, there is a range of phenotypes that can be expressed (see Figure 3.5). Imagine that we could identify all the genetic loci that would make a child introverted or extraverted. Would

(a)

(b)

FIGURE 3.4 The 23 chromosome pairs of humans. At the top (a), the 23rd pair contain one X and one Y chromosome (it is a male). At the bottom (b), the 23rd pair contain two X chromosomes (it is a female).

measured introversion-extraversion in childhood be predictable from knowledge of the specific genetic loci? That is, would we know how introverted or extraverted the child would be? The answer is no, because even if our genetic model was adequate, introversion-extraversion is a characteristic shaped by experience throughout life. For example, parents may push an introverted young child into social situations and encourage the child to become more gregarious.

To understand characteristics such as intelligence and introversion-extraversion, think about a series of genetic codes that predispose the child to develop in a particular way and imagine environments that, to a certain degree,

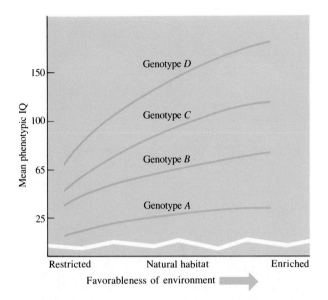

FIGURE 3.5 Reaction range. This figure plots a hypothetical set of reaction ranges of intellectual development for several genotypes under environmental conditions that range from poor to good. Although each genotype responds favorably to improved environments, some are more responsive than others to environmental deprivation and enrichment.

are responsive or unresponsive to this development. For instance, there may be individuals whose genotype predisposes them to be introverted in an environment that promotes a turning inward of personality, yet in an environment that encourages social interaction and outgoingness, these individuals may become at least reasonably extraverted. However, it would be unlikely, under this argument, for the person with the introverted genotype to become a strong extravert. This concept of **reaction range** suggests a range of phenotypes for each genotype, with a limit on how much environment can change characteristics, such as personality and intelligence.

Sandra Scarr (1984) explains reaction range this way: Each of us has a range of potential. For example, a person with "medium-tall" genes for height who grows up in a poor environment may be shorter than average. But in an excellent nutritional environment, the person may grow up taller than average. However, no matter how well fed the person is, an individual with "short" genes will never be taller than average. Scarr believes that intelligence works in the same manner. That is, there is a range within which environment can modify intelligence, but intelligence is not completely malleable. Reaction range gives us an estimate of how modifiable intelligence is. The idea of reaction range is compatible with the view that intelligence is influenced by genetic-environmental interaction.

Canalization   Some scientists argue that genotypes, in addition to producing many phenotypes, also show just the opposite track for many characteristics. They argue that some characteristics are somewhat immune to extensive changes in the environment. These characteristics seem to stay on track or on a particular developmental course regardless of the environmental assaults on them (Waddington, 1957). **Canalization** is the term chosen to describe the narrow path or developmental course that certain characteristics take. Apparently, there are preservative forces that help to protect or buffer an individual from environmental extremes. For example, Jerome Kagan (1984) points to his research on Guatemalan infants who had experienced extreme malnutrition as infants, yet showed normal social and cognitive development later in childhood. And some abused children do not grow up to become child abusers themselves.

Methods Used by Behavior Geneticists

A field of inquiry that has connected the fields of biology and psychology in recent years is called **behavior genetics.** Behavior genetics is concerned with the degree and nature of the hereditary basis of behavior. Researchers in this field assume that behaviors are jointly determined by the interaction of hereditary and environmental factors. While there have been studies of selective breeding and inbreeding with lower animals, we focus on those methods behavior geneticists use to study genetic influences in human children—the twin study, the family-of-twins design, the kinship study, and the adoption study.

These strategies focus on the genetic relationship of an individual to members of his or her family. In the twin study and family-of-twins design, the focus is on the genetic relationship between twins. In the **twin study,** the comparison is between identical twins (**monozygotic,** meaning that they come from the same egg) and fraternal twins (**dizygotic,** meaning that they come from two different eggs and are therefore genetically more distant than identical twins). (See Figure 3.6 for two identical twins.) In the **family-of-twins design,** monozygotic twins, siblings, half-siblings, and parent and offspring are compared. **Kinship studies** of the role of heredity in behavior include other family members as well, such as uncles, cousins, grandparents, and so forth, who vary systematically in their genetic relatedness. **Adoption studies** concentrate on individuals who are genetically more similar or more dissimilar from each other. For example, an adopted child is genetically closer to his or her biological parents than to the adoptive parents. Investigators look to see if the child's characteristics are more similar to the biological parents or the adoptive parents. Three large-scale adoption studies currently being conducted include a Minnesota study (Scarr & Weinberg, 1983), the Texas Adoption Project (Horn, 1983), and the Colorado Adoption Project (Plomin & DeFries, 1983).

The concept of **heritability** also is often used in studies of behavioral genetics. Heritability is a mathematical estimate, often computed with a standard heritability quotient. Similarity is measured by use of the correlation coefficient *r*. The highest degree of heritability is 1.00. For example, a heritability quotient of .80 for intelligence suggests a strong genetic influence, one of .50 a moderate genetic influence, and one of .20 a much weaker, but nonetheless perceptible, genetic influence.

Although heritability values may vary considerably from one study to the next, it is often possible to determine the average magnitude of the quotient for a particular characteristic. For some kinds of physical characteristics and mental retardation, the heritability quotient approaches 1.00. That is, the environment makes almost no contribution to variation in the characteristic. This is not the same as saying that the environment has no influence; the characteristic could not be expressed without the environment.

FIGURE 3.6 Identical twins. How might these identical twins be studied to reveal information about genetic influences on development?

However, the heritability index is not a flawless measure of genetic factors in development. It is only as good as the information fed into it and the assumptions made about genetic-environmental interaction. For example, Sandra Scarr and Kenneth Kidd (1983) suggested three limitations on the heritability index. First, how varied are the environments being sampled? The narrower the range of environments, the higher the heritability index; the broader the range of environments, the lower the heritability index. Second, how reliable and valid are the measures used in the investigation? That is, what is the quality of the intelligence measures? The personality assessments? The weaker the measure, the less confidence

Drawing by Ziegler; © 1985 The New Yorker Magazine, Inc.

researchers have in the heritability index. And, third, the heritability index assumes that genetics and environment can be separated and that information can be quantitatively added together to come up with a discrete amount of influence for each. In reality, as we have stressed throughout our discussion of genetics, these two factors interact, and their interaction is often lost when the heritability index is formulated.

Genetic-Environmental Interaction and Its Effect on Development

Both genes and an environment are necessary for an organism to exist. Sandra Scarr and Richard Weinberg (1980), in an article entitled "Calling All Camps! The War Is Over," summarized this often-repeated point: One cannot assess the relative impact of heredity and environment on intelligence *per se* because everyone must have both a viable gene complement and an environment in which the genes can be expressed over development. No genes, no organism; no environment, no organism.

What do we know and what do we need to know about the role of genetic-environmental interaction in development? According to Scarr and Kidd (1983), we already know the following:

1. There are literally hundreds of disorders that appear because of miscodings in such genetic material as DNA. Normal development clearly is inhibited by these defects in genetic material.
2. Abnormalities in chromosome number adversely influence the development of physical, intellectual, and behavioral features of individuals, usually in a severe manner.
3. There is no one-to-one relation between genotype and phenotype.
4. It is very difficult to distinguish between genetic and cultural transmission. There usually is a familial concentration of a particular behavioral disorder, but most familial patterns are considerably different than what would be precisely predicted from simple modes of inheritance.
5. When we consider the normal range of variation, the stronger the genetic resemblance, the stronger the behavioral resemblance. This holds more strongly for intelligence than personality or interests. The influence of genes on intelligence is present in early child development and continues through the late adulthood years.
6. Being raised in the same family accounts for some portion of intellectual differences among individuals, but common rearing accounts for little of the variation in personality or interests. One reason for this discrepancy may be that families place similar pressures on their children for intellectual development in the sense that the push is clearly toward a higher level, while they do not direct their children toward similar personalities or interests, in which extremes are not particularly desirable. That is, virtually all parents would like their children to have above-average intellect, but there is much less agreement about whether a child should be encouraged to be highly extraverted.

In response to the question, "What do we still need to know about the role of genetic-environmental interaction in development?", Scarr and Kidd (1983) commented that it is very beneficial to know the pathways by which genetic abnormalities influence development. The PKU success story is but one such example. Scientists discovered the genetic linkage of the disorder and subsequently how the environment could be changed to reduce the damage to development. PKU (phenylketonuria) is a form of mental retardation due to a recessive gene that causes enzyme malfunctioning. Mental functioning deteriorates rapidly if the enzyme deficiency is not treated shortly after birth. If detected early, the absence of the enzyme can be treated by diet.

Understanding variation in the normal range of development is much more complicated in most instances than revealing the genetic path of a specific disorder. For example, an understanding of the differences between two brothers—one with an IQ of 95 and the other with an IQ of 125—requires a polygenic perspective. Models of cultural and genetic inheritance, and their complex interactions, are more likely to explain behavioral variation than more molecular models of gene pathways, at least in the foreseeable future.

Developmental models of genetic influence across the entire life cycle are critical to understanding development. While developmental psychologists are very familiar with the species-specific patterns of development described by Piaget and Erikson, few of them attribute these patterns to evolutionary, genetic factors. Rather, developmental psychologists have tended to search for the proximal, immediate causes of these patterns. However, there may be some more distal reasons for such patterns of development, namely causes that have evolved over the course of millions of years. For instance, puberty is not an environmentally produced accident of development—it is heavily influenced by evolutionary and genetic programming. While puberty can be affected by such environmental factors as nutrition, health, and the like, the basic evolutionary and genetic program is wired into the species. It cannot be eliminated; nor should it be ignored. Such an evolutionary perspective is becoming an important facet of developmental psychology and is directing attention to new forms of analysis, raising new questions, and providing a more complete account of the nature of development.

Child Development Concept Table 3.1 summarizes our discussion of the many different aspects of the evolutionary perspective and genetics. Now we turn our attention to the incredible story of conception itself and the months of prenatal development.

THE COURSE OF PRENATAL DEVELOPMENT

You developed from the union of one of thousands of eggs with one of millions of sperm. Had the union of the sperm and egg come a day or even an hour earlier or later, you may have been very different—maybe even a different sex, with a different hair color, and a different side to your personality. Let's explore this fascinating beginning of our lives in more detail.

Conception and the Zygote

Discussions of conception used to be rather straightforward, but now there are many ways in which conception can take place. First, though, let's study standard conception.

Standard Conception and the Zygote

Life processes begin when a single sperm cell from the male unites with the ovum (egg) in the female's fallopian tube in a process called fertilization or **conception** (Figure 3.7). The ovum is produced in the female's ovaries at about midpoint in the female's menstrual cycle. Fertilization occurs within several days after the ovum begins its journey from the ovaries through the fallopian tubes to the uterus. If the ovum travels to the uterus without being fertilized, it disintegrates within several days, making conception impossible until the next menstrual cycle.

Child Development Concept Table 3.1   The Evolutionary Perspective and Genetics

Concept	Processes/Related Ideas	Characteristics/Description
The evolutionary perspective	Natural selection	Charles Darwin proposed his theory of evolution after traveling around the world and observing the adaptation of a variety of species to their natural habitats. The principle of natural selection emphasizes the existence of genetic diversity in a species. Because of this diversity, some organisms have beneficial characteristics that help them to adapt to their environment. These beneficial characteristics are likely to be perpetuated. Most scientists today believe that natural selection provides the best explanation of evolution and that evolution occurs at a slow pace.
Genetics	What are genes?	Each human cell contains 46 chromosomes and 50,000 or more genes. Chromosomes come in pairs (23 pairs in humans) and are made up of DNA, which has a double helix shape. A gene is a short segment of the DNA ladder and is distinguished by its unique sequences of "rungs," called bases. Genes are transmitted from parents to offspring by gametes, or sex cells. Gametes are formed by the splitting of cells, a process called meiosis. Reproduction takes place when a female gamete (ovum) is fertilized by a male gamete (sperm) to create a single-celled zygote. The actual combination of genes produces what is known as the genotype, while observed and measurable characteristics, such as behaviors, are called phenotypes.
Some genetic principles	Dominant-recessive genes	A dominant gene exerts its full effect, regardless of its genetic partner. A recessive gene's code is masked by a dominant gene and is only expressed when the recessive gene is paired with another recessive gene.
	Sex-linked genes	Some characteristics are determined by genes located on the 23rd chromosome pair, the one determining the sex of the offspring. The result is that these characteristics are more or less likely to appear in members of one sex.
	Polygenic inheritance	Few psychological characteristics are the result of the actions of single gene pairs. Traits produced by the mixing of genes are said to be polygenically determined.
	Reaction range	Given any individual genotype, there is a range of phenotypes that can be expressed.
	Canalization	Canalization describes the narrow path or developmental course that certain characteristics take.
Methods used by behavior geneticists	Twin study, family-of-twins design, kinship study, and adoption study	Since selective breeding and inbreeding cannot be used with humans, behavior geneticists rely on the twin study, the family-of-twins design, the kinship study, and the adoption study to study the effects of genes on children's development. Currently, a number of twin and adoption studies are being conducted.
	Heritability	Heritability refers to a mathematical estimate of the degree to which a characteristic is inherited. It is by no means flawless, and unfortunately, the nature of genetic-environmental interaction gets lost in heritability computation.
Genetic-environmental interaction	Its nature	Conclusions about the nature of heredity and environment suggest that the heredity versus environment issue is somewhat misleading since both genes and environment are necessary even for a child to exist. However, we do know that genes set some limitations on development and that the genes of a particular species increase the likelihood that some forms of behavior will emerge at some points rather than other points.

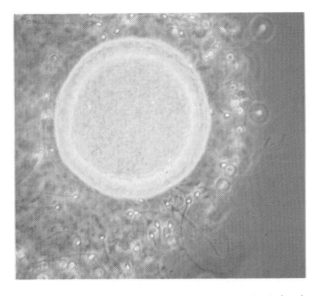

FIGURE 3.7 An ovum ready for release has been extracted and placed into a nutritive solution together with a drop of specially treated seminal fluid. The sperm eagerly work their way toward the ovum. Notice the difference in size.

Recall from earlier in the chapter that the sex cells are called gametes and that reproduction takes place when a female gamete (ovum) is fertilized by a male gamete (sperm). This process creates a single-celled zygote whose chromosomes come 50 percent from the father and 50 percent from the mother. By the time the zygote ends its three- to four-day journey through the fallopian tubes and reaches the uterus, it has divided into approximately 12 to 16 cells. These early cell divisions are referred to as **cleavage divisions** and result in the formation of embryonic cell masses. Conception, cleavage divisions, the journey of the zygote to the uterus, and the development of embryonic cell masses are collectively called the **zygote period.** The zygote period begins at conception and lasts for three to four days after conception.

As we see next, conception can now occur in many different ways.

New Methods of Conception

The year is 1978, and one of the most dazzling occurrences of the 1970s is about to unfold. Mrs. Brown is

FIGURE 3.8 Louise Brown and her parents. Louise and other test-tube babies like her seem to have no problems associated with the in-vitro fertilization procedure.

infertile, but her physician informs her of a new procedure that could enable her to have a baby. The procedure involves removing the mother's ovum surgically, fertilizing it in a laboratory medium with live sperm cells obtained from the father or male donor, storing the fertilized egg in a laboratory solution that substitutes for the uterine environment, and finally implanting the egg in the mother's uterus. The procedure is called **in-vitro fertilization.** In the case of Mrs. Brown, the procedure was successful, and nine months later, her daughter Louise was born (see Figure 3.8).

Nature's way of reproduction

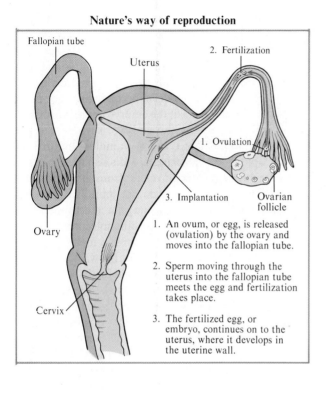

1. An ovum, or egg, is released (ovulation) by the ovary and moves into the fallopian tube.

2. Sperm moving through the uterus into the fallopian tube meets the egg and fertilization takes place.

3. The fertilized egg, or embryo, continues on to the uterus, where it develops in the uterine wall.

New ways of creating babies

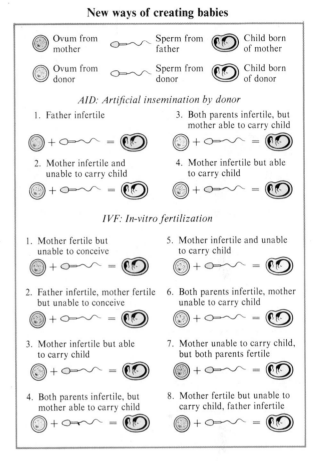

FIGURE 3.9   Methods of fertilization.

Since the first in-vitro fertilization in the 1970s, a number of variations have brought hope to childless couples. A woman's egg can be fertilized with the husband's sperm, or the husband and wife may contribute their sperm and egg with the resulting embryo being carried by a third party, who essentially is donating her womb. A summary of nature's way of reproduction and new ways of creating babies is presented in Figure 3.9.

Now that we have considered the zygote period and alternative methods of conception, let's move further along in the prenatal period.

The Germinal Period

The period from conception until about 12 to 14 days later is called the **germinal period.** The germinal period includes the zygote period discussed earlier. It also in-volves continued cell division and the attachment of the zygote to the uterine wall.

Approximately one week after conception, when the zygote is composed of approximately 100 to 150 cells, it is called the **blastula.** Differentiation of cells already has commenced in the blastula as an inner and outer layer are formed. The inner layer of the blastula, called the **blastocyst,** later develops into the embryo. The outer layer, called the **trophoblast,** subsequently provides nutrition and support for the embryo. During the second week after conception, a major milestone involves the firm attachment of the zygote to the uterine wall in a process called **implantation** (the mass of cells is technically called the zygote until the time of implantation). Implantation usually occurs about 10 days after conception.

The Embryonic Period

During the **embryonic period,** the embryo differentiates into three layers and support systems develop, in addition to further embryonic development.

Three Layers and Support Systems

While the zygote becomes attached to the uterine wall, the cells of the zygote are forming two layers. It is at this time that the mass of cells changes names from zygote to embryo. This development marks the beginning of the embryonic period, which lasts until about eight weeks after conception. The inner layer of cells is called the **endoderm** and subsequently will develop into the digestive and respiratory systems. The outer layer of cells divides into two parts. The outermost layer—the **ectoderm**—will become the nervous system, sensory receptors (such as ear, nose, and eyes), and skin parts (such as hair and nails). The middle layer—the **mesoderm**—

9-22

Ketcham

"MY MOM SAYS I COME FROM HEAVEN. MY DAD SAYS HE CAN'T REMEMBER AN' MR. WILSON IS POSITIVE I CAME FROM MARS!"

DENNIS THE MENACE® used by permission of Hank Ketcham and © by News America Syndicate

will become the circulatory system, bones, muscle, excretory system, and reproductive system. Every bodily part eventually develops from these three layers, with the endoderm for the most part producing internal bodily parts, the mesoderm generating parts surrounding the internal areas, and the ectoderm becoming surface parts.

While the three layers of the embryo are being formed, life support systems for the embryo, such as the placenta, the umbilical cord, and the amnion, mature and develop rapidly. The **placenta** is a disk-shaped group of tissues in which small blood vessels from the mother and the offspring intertwine but do not join. The **umbilical cord** houses two arteries and one vein and connects the baby to the placenta. Very small molecules, such as oxygen, water, salt, and food from the mother's blood, as well as carbon dioxide and digestive wastes from the embryo's blood, can pass back and forth between the mother and infant. The large molecules that cannot pass through the placental wall are red blood cells and a number of harmful substances, such as most bacteria, maternal wastes, and hormones. The mechanisms that govern transfer of substances across the placental barrier are very complex and still not entirely understood (Rosenblith & Sims-Knight, 1985). Another important structure in the life support system of the embryo is the **amnion,** a sort of bag or envelope of clear fluid in which the developing embryo floats. The amnion serves as a buffer for the embryo. The membranes of the amnion actually begin to develop as early as the second week after conception.

Further Embryonic Developments

Before most women even know that they are pregnant, there are some very important embryonic developments. In the third week, the neural tube that eventually becomes the spinal cord is forming. At about 21 days, eyes begin to appear, and by 24 days, the cells for the heart begin to differentiate.

During the fourth week, the first appearance of the urogenital system is apparent, and arm and leg buds emerge. Four chambers of the heart begin to take shape, and blood vessels begin to surface. (Figure 3.10 shows a four-week-old embryo.)

From the fifth to eighth weeks after conception, arms and legs become even more differentiated, and the face starts to form but still is not very recognizable. The intestinal tract develops, facial structures fuse, and at about eight weeks, the developing organism weighs about 1/30 of an ounce and is just over 1 inch long.

The first eight weeks of development are very important ones. Many bodily systems are being formed at this time. When such systems are in the formation process, they are particularly vulnerable to environmental changes. The first two months of prenatal development have been called **organogenesis** because it is during this time that organ systems are being formed and may be adversely influenced by environmental events. Later in the chapter, we explore these hazards in some detail.

The Fetal Period

The **fetal period** of prenatal development begins two months after conception and lasts for seven months on the average. Growth and development continue their dramatic course during this time. (Figure 3.11 shows a fetus at eight weeks after conception.) By three months after conception, the fetus is about 3 inches long and weighs approximately 1 ounce. It has become active,

moving its arms and legs, opening and closing its mouth, and moving its head. A number of physical and anatomical features become differentiated as well. The face, forehead, eyelids, nose, and chin are distinguishable, as are the upper arms, lower arms, hands, and lower limbs. The genitals can be identified as male or female.

By the end of the fourth month, the fetus is about 6 inches long and weighs about 4 to 7 ounces. While a great deal of growth already has occurred in the head and facial structures, there now is a growth spurt in the lower parts of the body. A number of prenatal reflexes (automatic responses involving one part of the body), such as arm and leg movements, become stronger and can be felt by the mother for the first time. (Figure 3.12 shows the fetus at 4½ months—notice the sucking reflex.)

By the end of the fifth month, the fetus is about 12 inches long and weighs close to a pound. Structures of the skin have formed—there are toenails and fingernails. The fetus also is more active, showing a preference for a particular position in the womb.

By the end of the sixth month, the fetus is about 14 inches long and has gained another pound. The eyes and eyelids are completely formed. A fine layer of hair covers

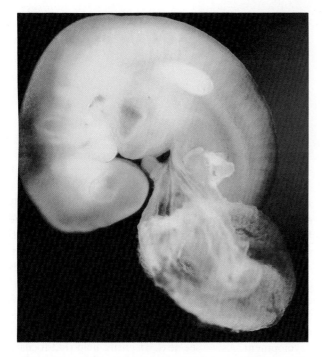

FIGURE 3.10 At four weeks, the embryo is about .2 inches long, and the head, eyes, and ears begin to show. The head and neck are half the body length; the shoulders will be located where the whitish arm buds are attached.

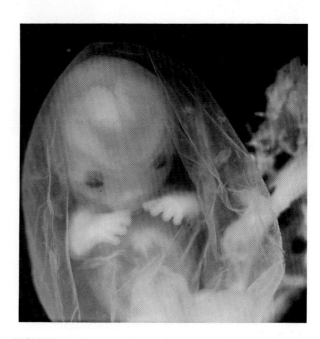

FIGURE 3.11 Fetus at eight weeks.

FIGURE 3.12   At four-and-one-half months, the fetus has grown to a length of about 18 centimeters (just over 7 inches). When the thumb comes close to the mouth, the head may turn. The lips and tongue will begin their sucking motions—a survival reflex.

the head. A grasping reflex is present, and there is evidence of irregular breathing movements.

By the end of the seventh month, the fetus is about 16 inches long and has gained another pound, now weighing approximately 3 pounds. At this time, the chances of survival are very good if the fetus is born prematurely. If born prematurely, however, the infant is very sensitive to infection and must be cared for in the well-regulated environment of an incubator. We discuss premature birth in more detail later in the chapter.

During the eighth and ninth months, the fetus grows longer and gains substantial weight—about 4 pounds.

At birth, the average American baby weighs 7 pounds and is 20 inches long. During these last two months, the fatty tissues develop, and the functioning of various organ systems (for example, heart and kidneys) is stepped up.

Child Development Concept Table 3.2 summarizes our discussion of the course of fetal development. As scientists have become more accurate in charting the course of prenatal development, they have also become fascinated by how environmental experiences can modify such development. As we see next, an entire field that focuses on hazards to prenatal development has emerged.

Child Development Concept Table 3.2   The Course of Prenatal Development

Concept	Processes/Related Ideas	Characteristics/Description
Conception and the zygote	Standard conception and the zygote	Standard conception occurs when a single sperm cell unites with the ovum in the female's fallopian tube, a process called fertilization. The single-celled zygote created by this process has 50 percent of its chromosomes from the mother and 50 percent from the father. Early cell divisions are called cleavage divisions. The first three to four days after conception is called the zygote period.
	New methods of conception	Since the first in-vitro fertilization in the 1970s, a variety of procedures have been developed to allow otherwise infertile couples to have a child.
The germinal period	Defined as the period from conception until about 10 to 14 days later	Cell division continues, and a cell mass of about 100 to 150 cells is formed at about one week after conception. This cell mass is called the blastula. The blastula differentiates into inner (blastocyst) and outer (trophoblast) layers. At about 10 to 14 days after conception, the zygote attaches to the uterine wall.
The embryonic period	Defined as the period that lasts from approximately two weeks to eight weeks after conception	During the embryonic period, the embryo differentiates into three layers, life support systems develop, and organ systems form (organogenesis).
	Three layers and support systems	At two to three weeks after conception, the outer layer of the embryo differentiates into the ectoderm and mesoderm, and the inner layer of the embryo differentiates into the endoderm. The placenta matures, and the umbilical cord is forming.
	Further embryonic developments	At three to four weeks after conception, the neural tube is forming, eyes are appearing, the heart is being differentiated, arm and leg buds emerge, and heart chambers take shape. At five to eight weeks after conception, the arms and legs are more differentiated, the face starts to form, the intestinal tract develops, and the facial structures fuse. At eight weeks, the organism weighs about 1/30 of an ounce and is just over 1 inch long.
The fetal period	The fetal period lasts from about two months after conception until nine months or when the infant is born	Growth and development continue their dramatic course, and organ systems mature to the point where life can be sustained outside the womb.
	Three months after conception	The fetus is about 3 inches long and weighs approximately 1 ounce. It has become active, and some facial features are noticeable.
	Four months after conception	The fetus is about 6 inches long and weighs 4 to 7 ounces. There is increased growth in the lower parts of the body. Prenatal reflexes are becoming apparent, and the mother feels movement for the first time.
	Five months after conception	The fetus is about 12 inches long and weighs about 1 pound. Structures of the skin have formed, and the fetus becomes more active.
	Six months after conception	The fetus is about 14 inches long and weighs 2 pounds. The eyes and eyelids now are completely formed, a fine layer of hair covers the head, the grasping reflex appears, and irregular breathing emerges.
	Seven months after conception	The fetus is 16 inches long and weighs 3 pounds. The chances of survival from this point on are excellent.
	Eight to nine months after conception	The fetus grows longer and gains considerable weight. Fatty tissues develop, and the functioning of various organ systems is stepped up. The average American baby weighs 7 pounds and is 20 inches long.

TERATOLOGY AND HAZARDS TO PRENATAL DEVELOPMENT

Some expectant mothers tiptoe about in the belief that everything they do and feel has a direct effect on their unborn child. Others behave casually, assuming that their experiences have little impact on the unborn child. The truth lies somewhere between these two extremes. Although living in a protected, comfortable environment, the fetus is not totally immune to the larger environment surrounding the mother. The environment can affect the child in a number of well-documented ways. Thousands of babies are born deformed or mentally retarded every year or suffer from other congenital defects that are sometimes a result of events as early as one or two months prior to conception.

Scientists are finding that many environmental situations during prenatal development are associated with birth characteristics. The environmental influences range from drugs the mother has taken, diseases she might have encountered, her age, her eating habits, and the degree of emotional stress she experiences. In this section, we explore many such environmental influences on prenatal development.

Teratology and the Effects of Teratogens

The field of study that investigates the causes of congenital (birth) defects is called **teratology.** Any agent that causes birth defects is referred to as a **teratogen** (from the Greek word *tera,* meaning "monster"). In most instances, there is no consistent link between a specific teratogen (such as a drug) and a specific birth defect (such as malformation of the legs). There are so many different teratogens that virtually every fetus is exposed to at least several of them. Thus, it often is very difficult to determine which teratogen causes a particular birth defect. In addition, it sometimes takes a long time for the effects of some teratogens to show up—only about half are present at birth.

Despite the many unknowns about teratology, scientists have been able to discover the identity of some teratogens and the particular point of fetal development at which they do their greatest damage (see Figure 3.13). As Figure 3.13 shows, sensitivity to teratogens occurs about three weeks after conception. Early in the embryonic period, the likelihood of a structural defect is greatest, since this is when organs are being formed. After organogenesis is complete, teratogens are less likely to cause anatomical defects. Exposure during the later fetal period is more likely to stunt growth or to create problems in the way the organs function. The preciseness of organogenesis is evident when teratologists point out that vulnerability of the brain is greatest at 15 to 25 days after conception, the eye at 24 to 40 days, the heart at 20 to 40 days, and the legs at 24 to 36 days (Tuchmann-Duplessis, 1975).

In the following sections, we explore how certain environmental agents influence prenatal development. That is, we examine how maternal diseases and conditions as well as drugs influence the embryo or fetus. While we have chosen this way to present information about teratogens, keep in mind that another way to understand the effects of teratogens on prenatal development is in terms of the mechanisms that may cause the problem (Rosenblith & Sims-Knight, 1985): (1) environmental agents may function at a genetic level, causing chromosomal or gene damage that can alter the instructional map for development; (2) environmental agents may damage organ systems at the time they are being formed (organogenesis) and differentiated; and (3) environmental agents may decrease or retard normal growth and development after organogenesis is complete. For example, with regard to the brain, damage could occur because of any of these three mechanisms. Now let's turn our attention to the environmental agents themselves.

Maternal Diseases and Conditions

In this section, we look at maternal diseases and infections, the mother's age, malnutrition, and the mother's emotional state and stress to learn how they influence prenatal development.

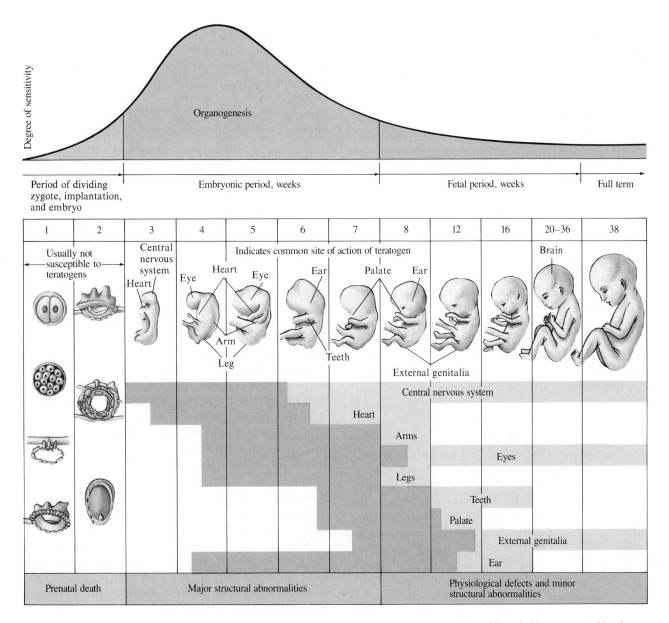

FIGURE 3.13 Teratogens and the timing of their effects on prenatal development. The danger of structural defects caused by teratogens is greatest early in embryonic development. This is the period of organogenesis and it lasts for several months. Damage caused by teratogens during this period is represented by the dark-colored bars. Later assaults by teratogens typically occur during the fetal period and, instead of structural damage, are more likely to stunt growth or cause problems of organ function.

Maternal Diseases and Infections

Maternal diseases or infections can produce defects by crossing the placental barrier, or they can cause damage during the birth process itself.

Rubella and Syphilis

Rubella (German measles) and syphilis (a venereal disease) are two maternal diseases that can have damaging effects on prenatal development. A rubella outbreak in 1964–1965 produced 30,000 prenatal and neonatal (newborn) deaths, and more than 20,000 infants were born with congenital malformations, ranging from mental retardation, to blindness and deafness, to heart malformations. The greatest damage seems to occur when mothers contract rubella in the third and fourth weeks of pregnancy, although infection during the second month is also damaging in a number of cases. Elaborate efforts have been made to ensure that rubella will never again have the same disastrous effects as it did in the mid-1960s. A vaccine that prevents German measles is routinely administered to children, and mothers who plan to have children should have a blood test before they become pregnant to determine if they are immune to the disease.

Syphilis has more damaging effects later in prenatal development—four months or later after conception—than rubella. Thus, rather than affecting organogenesis like rubella does, syphilis damages organs after they already have been formed. Such damage occurs in the form of lesions in the eye, which can produce blindness, and lesions on the skin. When syphilis is present at birth, other problems involving the central nervous system and gastrointestinal tract may develop. Most states require a pregnant woman to be given a blood test to detect the presence of syphilis.

As we see next, in recent years, another infection has received widespread attention because of its possible transmission to the offspring.

Herpes Simplex Virus

Two infections that are members of the herpes simplex virus family—CMV and HVH—can be transmitted from the mother to the infant at birth. **CMV** (which stands for cytomegalovirus) infects the genitalia, urinary tract, and breasts, and usually does not produce overt symptoms. The disease is latent and can become reactivated during pregnancy. It is active or reactivated in approximately 12 percent of pregnant women near the point of the infant's birth. The virus is most likely to infect the cervix, which is the opening from the uterus to the vagina. The infant becomes infected when he or she passes through the cervix during the birth process. The infant does not always become infected, however, with about 1 percent of newborns in the United States contracting the disease. CMV is estimated to be the major cause of damage to the sensory parts of the nervous system in children in the United States (Stagno, 1980).

HVH (which stands for herpes virus hominis) is mainly transmitted venereally and infects the vagina or cervix. If the virus is active in the mother when the child is born, it can be transmitted to the offspring as the infant passes through the cervix and vagina during the birth process. Approximately half of neonates who are exposed to the HVH virus during the birth process contract the disease. In such instances, death of the infant is very possible. If the exposed infant does not die, a number of very serious problems may result, ranging from brain damage to blindness.

Clearly, transmission of the herpes simplex viruses to offspring must be prevented. This often is not as easy as it might seem because, in a majority of cases, there are no active lesions to indicate the presence of the herpes virus. Medications are available to reduce the chance of an active outbreak of HVH, but no cure for the virus has been discovered. If a pregnant woman is detected as having an active case of HVH close to her delivery date, a cesarean section birth (in which the infant is delivered through the mother's abdomen) can often be performed to keep the virus from infecting the newborn.

Now that we have seen how maternal diseases and infections can be transmitted during prenatal development and the birth process, we turn our attention to another aspect of the mother-to-be that has generated considerable interest—her age.

The Mother's Age

When the age of the mother is considered in terms of possible harmful effects on the fetus and infant, two time periods are of particular interest: adolescence and the 30s and beyond.

Adolescence

In recent years, approximately one of every five births has been to an adolescent, and in some urban areas, the figure reaches as high as one in every two births. Infants born to adolescents are often premature, with the mortality rate of infants born to adolescent mothers double that of infants born to mothers over the age of 20 (Graham, 1981). While such figures may reflect the mother's immature reproductive system, they also may involve such factors as poor nutrition, lack of prenatal care, and low socioeconomic status. Prenatal care decreases the likelihood that a child born to an adolescent girl will have physical problems, but adolescents are the least likely of all age groups to obtain prenatal assistance from clinics, pediatricians, and health services (Blum & Goldhagen, 1981).

The 30s and Beyond   Increasingly, women seek to establish a career before beginning a family, and thus delay childbearing until their 30s. Down's syndrome, a congenital deficiency, is related to the mother's age. A baby with Down's syndrome rarely is born to a mother under the age of 30, but the risk increases after the mother reaches 30. By age 40, the probability is slightly over 1 in 100, and by the age of 50, it is almost 1 in 10.

There also is evidence that women may have more difficulty becoming pregnant after the age of 30. In one investigation (Schwartz & Mayaux, 1982), the clients of a French fertility clinic all had husbands who were sterile. To increase their chances of having a child, they were artificially inseminated once a month for one year. Each woman had 12 chances to become pregnant. The results indicated that 75 percent of the women in their 20s became pregnant, while only 62 percent of the women in the 31 to 35-year-old group were successful, and only 54 percent in the over-35 group.

Nonetheless, we still have much to learn about the role of the mother's age in pregnancy and childbirth. As women become more active, exercise regularly, and are careful about their nutrition, their reproductive systems may remain healthier at older ages than was thought possible some years ago. Indeed, as we see next, the mother's nutrition may have a significant impact on prenatal development.

Nutrition

The developing fetus is completely dependent on the mother for its nutrition, which comes from the mother's blood. While nutritional state is not determined by any specific aspect of diet, among the important factors are believed to be the total number of calories and appropriate levels of protein, vitamins, and minerals. The mother's nutrition even has a significant impact on her ability to reproduce. For example, in extreme instances of malnutrition, women stop menstruating, thus precluding conception. And children born to malnourished mothers are more likely to have malformations (Hurley, 1980).

One investigation of mothers in Iowa provided further evidence of the role nutrition plays in prenatal development and birth (Jeans, Smith, & Stearns, 1955). The diets of 400 pregnant women were studied, and the status of the newborns was assessed. The mothers with the poorest diets were more likely to have offspring who weighed the least, had the least vitality, and were most likely to die. Also, a greater percentage of the infants born to the poor-diet mothers were premature.

Malnutrition is characteristic of many countries in our world. Many women are not adequately nourished before, during, and after pregnancy, and their offspring are not well fed after they are born. Some research efforts have revealed that diet supplements given to malnourished mothers during pregnancy are associated with their infants' improved performance on psychological tests during the first three years of life (Klein, Forbes, & Nadar, 1976; Werner, 1979).

Nutrition is an important aspect of both the mother and offspring's life. As we see next, the mother's emotional state and stress also are linked to prenatal development.

Emotional State and Stress

Tales abound about the way the mother's emotional makeup or experiences can affect the fetus. For example, for many centuries, it was thought that frightening experiences, such as a severe thunderstorm or the death of a family member, would leave birthmarks on the child or affect the child in more serious ways.

Today, we believe that the mother's stressful experiences can be transmitted to the fetus, although we have gone beyond thinking that these happenings are magically produced. We now know that, when a pregnant woman experiences intense fears, anxieties, and other emotions, a number of physiological changes occur. These physiological changes involve heart rate, respiration, and glandular secretions. For example, the production of adrenaline in response to fear may restrict blood flow to the uterine area and thus deprive the fetus of optimal levels of oxygen.

The mother's emotional state during pregnancy can influence the birth process as well. An emotionally distraught mother may have irregular contractions and a more difficult labor. This may produce irregularities in the baby's oxygen supply, or it may lead to irregularities after birth. Babies born after extended labor may adjust more slowly to their world and show more irritability. One investigation revealed a clear connection between the mother's anxiety during pregnancy and the condition of her newborn (Ottinger & Simmons, 1964). In this study, mothers answered a questionnaire about their anxiety every three months during their pregnancy. When their babies were born, the babies' weights, activity levels, and crying were assessed. The babies of the more anxious mothers cried more before feedings and were more active than the babies born to the less anxious mothers.

While the maternal diseases and conditions already described can have a negative effect on the developing fetus, perhaps scientists' greatest current interest is in the drugs that can affect the fetus.

Drugs

To learn about the effects of drugs on prenatal development, we examine the thalidomide tragedy and the use of alcohol and cigarettes.

The Thalidomide Tragedy

In the early 1960s, it was discovered that the mothers of a number of children who were born with malformations (many of which involved arm and/or leg deformities) had taken a mild tranquilizer prescribed by their doctor to reduce their anxiety or morning sickness. The drug was **thalidomide.** Most of the cases of malformation were in Europe since thalidomide had not yet been approved for use in the United States.

Alcohol

Alcohol intake by pregnant mothers involves a wide range of drinking behavior. Some pregnant mothers may be alcoholics, while others may drink only moderately. The amount that the pregnant woman drinks appears to be related to how extensively the developing fetus may be affected.

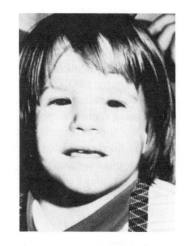

FIGURE 3.14 This child has fetal alcohol syndrome. What are the characteristics of fetal alcohol syndrome?

Fetal Alcohol Syndrome   A cluster of characteristics known as **fetal alcohol syndrome (FAS)** has been identified in the children born to mothers who are heavy drinkers (Jones, Smith, Ulleland, & Streissguth, 1973). FAS is characterized by microencephaly (small head) and defective limbs, joints, face, and heart (see Figure 3.14). Children with FAS may show abnormal behavior, such as hyperactivity or seizures. Also, the majority of FAS children score below average on intelligence, with a number of them in the mentally retarded range (Abel, 1981).

Moderate Versus Heavy Drinking Patterns   How much alcohol is too much for a pregnant woman? Does she have to drink three or four mixed drinks a day during her pregnancy for the fetus to be adversely affected? Can she get by with one or two glasses of wine a day? Or should she abstain altogether?

Even moderate drinking has been linked to changes in the neonate and infant. For example, moderate drinking is related to lower birth weight of infants (Streissguth, Martin, Martin, & Barr, 1981). However, no serious malformations, like those of FAS, have been found in infants born to mothers who are moderate or light drinkers (e.g., Harlap & Shiono, 1980). Nonetheless, some behavioral effects of moderate alcohol intake by pregnant women on infants even as far along in development as four years of age have been found. To learn more about this interesting research, read Focus on Child Development 3.1.

FOCUS ON CHILD DEVELOPMENT 3.1

AA SCORES AT MID-PREGNANCY, NEONATAL AROUSAL, AND PRESCHOOL VIGILANCE

It is one month before she is to become pregnant. The future mother has a difficult job, and she has become accustomed to having several mixed drinks every evening when she comes home from work. Five months into her pregnancy, she is interviewed about her drinking patterns. The interviewer asks how much she drank in the month or so before she became pregnant and how much she drinks now, midway through the pregnancy. She reports that she still has one to two drinks a day about four to five times a week. An AA (absolute alcohol consumed per day) score based on this information is computed by the researcher. For the AA score, 1 ounce of alcohol is defined as two drinks of wine or beer or liquor per day on the average. The figure could be derived from drinking two glasses of wine every day or from drinking 14 cans of beer on Saturday night.

Such was the procedure in a **prospective study** of the effects of alcohol intake by pregnant women on the behavior of their infants and children. The study is called "prospective" because the data about the mother's alcohol intake were collected before the infants' development was assessed some months and years later. This contrasts with a retrospective study, which would have assessed the infants' development and then possibly interviewed the mothers about their drinking patterns a number of months or years earlier. In reality, though, one portion of the maternal interview was retrospective, since the interviewer asked the pregnant women to recall the nature of their alcohol intake a month or so before pregnancy.

This investigation, conducted by Ann Streissguth and her colleagues (Streissguth, Barr, & Martin, 1983), focused on 417 mothers and their offspring. The AA score was computed at midpregnancy. Then, the infants of these mothers were individually administered the Brazelton Neonatal Behavioral Assessment Scale 9 to 35 hours after birth. On the basis of this assessment, the mother's use of alcohol during the fifth month of pregnancy was negatively correlated with the infant's state of arousal—that is, the more alcohol the mother drank, the less alert and attentive the infant was (see the figure).

Further data from Ann Streissguth's laboratory (Streissguth et al., 1984) have assessed children at four years of age in terms of their behavior and its possible link to their mothers' drinking patterns during pregnancy. In this study, the mothers' drinking patterns during pregnancy were related to less efficient reaction time and poorer attention in the offspring at four years of age.

Thus, research indicates that even moderate alcohol intake during pregnancy is related to behavioral changes in the infant shortly after birth and for as long as four years after birth. At this time, there is no clear consensus on how much alcohol intake is necessary to damage the fetus and infant, but findings such as these suggest that pregnant women should at least consider reducing their alcohol use.

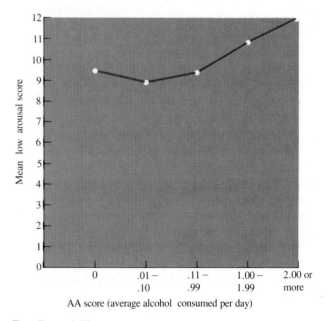

The effects of different levels of alcohol intake during pregnancy on the infant's level of arousal. A higher score indicates lower arousal. When high scores were obtained, the infant tended to fluctuate between being awake and being drowsy. When low scores were obtained, the infant more often seemed to swing back and forth between being awake and crying.

Now we turn our attention to another common concern in prenatal development—cigarette smoking by the pregnant woman.

Cigarette Smoking

Cigarette smoking by the pregnant woman also can have an adverse effect on prenatal development, birth, and infant development. Fetal and neonatal death rates are higher among smoking mothers. Also prevalent are higher preterm rates and lower birth weights. How extensively cigarette smoking affects surviving infants is not entirely clear, with the long-term effects on such important variables as intelligence being somewhat mixed (e.g., Broman & Nichols, 1981; Naeye, 1979). Sleeping and wakefulness patterns in infancy have been found to be related to the mother's smoking habits during her pregnancy, however. For example, in one investigation (Landesman-Dwyer & Sackett, 1983), 271 infant-mother pairs were studied during the infant's 8th, 12th, and 16th weeks of life by having each mother keep a diary of her infant's activity patterns. Mothers who smoked during pregnancy had infants who were awake on a more consistent basis, a finding one might suspect since the active chemical ingredient in cigarettes—nicotine—is a stimulant. Respiratory problems and even **sudden infant death syndrome** (**SIDS**) (also known as crib death) also are more common in the offspring of mothers who smoke.

Precisely how cigarette smoking affects prenatal and infant development is not entirely known. Is it the nicotine? Are the tars in cigarettes involved? Are the poorer nutritional habits associated with cigarette smoking implicated? And is the inadequate oxygen supply sometimes linked with cigarette smoking possibly a factor? All of these may be contributing factors.

Child Development Concept Table 3.3 summarizes our discussion of the field of teratology and hazards to prenatal development. Now we examine the birth process itself.

THE BIRTH PROCESS

In this section, we study a number of childbirth strategies, the stages of birth and delivery complications, the use of drugs during childbirth, preterm infants and age-weight considerations, and the fascinating topic of bonding.

Childbirth Strategies

A controversy currently exists over how the childbirth process should proceed. Some critics argue that the standard delivery practices of most hospitals and physicians need to be overhauled; others suggest that the entire family—especially the father—should be more involved in childbirth; and others argue that procedures that ensure mother-infant bonding should be followed. Here, we examine standard childbirth, the Leboyer method, and the Lamaze method.

Standard Childbirth

In the standard childbirth procedure that was practiced for many years, the expectant mother was taken to a hospital, where a doctor was responsible for the delivery of the baby. The pregnant woman was prepared for labor by having her pubic hair shaved and by having an enema. She then was placed in a labor room often filled with other pregnant women, some of whom were screaming. When she was ready to deliver, she was taken to a delivery room, which looked very much like an operating room. She was laid on a table with her legs in the air, and the physician, along with an anesthetist and a nurse, delivered the baby.

Judy Rosenblith and Judith Sims-Knight (1985) described three major criticisms of this standard procedure. First, important persons related to the mother are excluded from the birth process. Second, the mother is separated from her infant in the first minutes and hours after birth. And, third, giving birth is treated like a disease, and a woman in labor is considered a sick patient. As we see next, two procedures differ radically from this standard procedure.

Child Development Concept Table 3.3   Teratology and Hazards to Prenatal Development

Concept	Processes/Related Ideas	Characteristics/Description
Teratology	Overview	Teratology is the field that investigates the causes of congenital (birth) defects. Any agent that causes birth defects is called a teratogen. The greatest damage to embryonic structures is likely to occur during organogenesis. Exposure during the later fetal period is likely to stunt growth or to create problems in how organs function. Environmental agents may cause problems at the genetic level, at the level of organogenesis, or after organogenesis is complete.
Maternal diseases and conditions	Diseases and infections	Maternal diseases and infections can cause damage by crossing the placental barrier, or they can be destructive during the birth process itself.
	Rubella and syphilis	Rubella (German measles) has its most negative impact in the third and fourth weeks of pregnancy. Elaborate efforts have been made to ensure its control. Syphilis is more damaging later in prenatal development, usually four months or later after conception. Most states require pregnant women to have a syphilis blood test.
	Herpes simplex virus	Two members of the herpes simplex virus family—CMV and HVH—can be transmitted from the mother to the infant at birth. CMV is the major cause of damage to the sensory parts of the nervous system among children in the United States. Approximately half of newborns who are exposed to the HVH virus during the birth process contract the disease, which often results in the death of the infant. A cesarean section may help to prevent problems when the herpes virus is active.
	The mother's age	More premature infants are born to adolescent mothers than other age groups, and the infant mortality rate is much higher in this age group as well. More women now are having babies after the age of 30 than in the past. This increases the risk of Down's syndrome, although most women over 30 give birth to healthy infants. The current increase in exercise and nutritional awareness may have a beneficial effect on the health of a female's reproductive system after the age of 30.
	Nutrition	The developing fetus is completely dependent on its mother for nutrition, so the mother's diet is of obvious importance in prenatal development. In extreme cases of malnutrition, women cannot even have babies. Serious malnutrition has very dire consequences for prenatal development, increasing the likelihood of malformations and death.
	Emotional state and stress	Today it is believed that stressful experiences of the mother can be transmitted to the fetus.
Drugs	The thalidomide tragedy	Thalidomide was a tranquilizer given to pregnant mothers to reduce their anxiety or morning sickness. In the early 1960s, thousands of babies turned up malformed as a consequence of their mothers taking this drug.
	Alcohol	Offspring born to alcoholic mothers or to mothers with heavy drinking patterns may have a cluster of characteristics known as fetal alcohol syndrome (FAS). FAS is characterized by microencephaly and defective limbs, joints, face, and heart. Even moderate drinking patterns have been linked to changes in the neonate and infant—these changes often involve alertness and attention and usually do not involve structural damage. At this time, no firm conclusion has been reached about how much a pregnant mother can safely drink.
	Cigarette smoking	Fetal and neonatal death rates are higher among smoking mothers. Also prevalent are higher preterm rates and lower birth weights. Respiratory problems and sudden infant death syndrome also are more common in the offspring of mothers who smoke.

The Leboyer Method

The **Leboyer method,** developed by French obstetrician Frederick Leboyer, is intended to make the birth experience less stressful for infants. Leboyer's procedure often is referred to as "birth without violence." He describes standard delivery procedures as tortuous for the infant (Leboyer, 1975). He vehemently objects to such practices as holding newborns upside down and slapping or spanking them, putting silver nitrite into their eyes, separating them immediately from their mothers, and scaring them with bright lights and harsh noises in the traditional delivery room. Leboyer also criticizes the traditional habit of cutting the umbilical cord as soon as the infant is born, a situation that forces the infant to immediately take in oxygen from the air to breathe. Leboyer believes that the umbilical cord should be left intact for several minutes to allow the newborn a chance to adjust to his or her new world of air and breathing. With the Leboyer method, the baby often is placed on the mother's stomach immediately after birth so that the mother can caress the infant. Then the infant is placed in a bath of warm water to relax.

While most hospitals do not use the soft lights and warm baths for the newborn that Leboyer suggests, they frequently do allow the newborn to be placed on the mother's stomach immediately after birth in the belief that it will stimulate mother-infant bonding.

The Lamaze Method

Another well-known birth procedure that deviates markedly from the standard practice is the **Lamaze method.** The Lamaze method is a form of prepared or natural childbirth developed by Fernand Lamaze, a pioneering French obstetrician. It has become widely accepted by the medical profession and involves helping the pregnant mother to cope with the pain of childbirth in an active way to avoid or reduce medication. Lamaze classes are widely dispersed across the United States, often consisting of six weekly classes. In these classes, the pregnant woman learns about the birth process and is trained in breathing and relaxation exercises.

As the Lamaze method grew in popularity in the United States, it became more common for the father to participate in the exercises and to assist in the birth process. To learn more about the father's role in the Lamaze method and his participation in the birth process in general, read Focus on Child Development 3.2.

Stages of Birth and Delivery Complications

The birth process has been divided into three stages. The first birth stage lasts an average of 12 to 24 hours for a woman having her first child—it is the longest of the three stages. In this first stage, uterine contractions are from 15 to 20 minutes apart at the beginning and last up to a minute. These contractions cause the woman's cervix to stretch and open. As the first stage progresses, the contractions come closer together, often appearing every 2 to 5 minutes. Their intensity increases as well. By the end of the first birth stage, contractions have dilated the cervix to an opening of about 4 inches so that the baby can move from the uterus to the birth canal.

The second birth stage begins when the baby's head starts to move through the cervix and the birth canal. It terminates when the baby completely emerges from the mother's body. This stage lasts for approximately 1½ hours. With each contraction, the mother bears down very hard to help push the baby out of her body. By the time the baby's head is out of the mother's body, the contractions are coming almost every minute and last for about one minute as well. Figure 3.15 vividly portrays the first stage and the early part of the second stage of the birth process.

The third birth stage, known as **afterbirth,** involves the detachment and expelling of the placenta, umbilical cord, and other membranes. This final stage is the shortest of the three birth stages, lasting only several minutes.

A number of complications can accompany the baby's delivery. When the baby moves through the birth canal too rapidly, the delivery is called **precipitate.** Usually, a precipitate delivery is defined as one that takes the baby less than 10 minutes to be squeezed through the birth canal. This deviation in delivery may disturb the normal flow of blood in the infant, and the pressure on the head may lead to hemorrhaging. If the delivery takes very long, brain damage also may occur, in this case because of **anoxia,** meaning insufficient oxygen was available to the infant.

FOCUS ON CHILD DEVELOPMENT 3.2

A FATHER IN THE DELIVERY ROOM: "IT WAS OUT OF THIS WORLD!"

An interesting historical accident led to a major part of Lamaze training as it now is practiced in the United States (Rosenblith & Sims-Knight, 1985). In France, trained women assist the woman in labor. Since in the United States such assistants are not available, fathers have assumed the function of the assistant. Fathers attend childbirth classes with their wives, learn the strategies required, and assist in such important matters as timing contractions, massaging the mother, and giving psychological support.

The father's participation in the birth process through such procedures as the Lamaze method may help to strengthen his relationship with his wife and also to increase the likelihood that he will develop a strong attachment bond with the infant. Data supporting the belief that participation of the father in Lamaze classes and in the birth process will benefit the infant's long-term development have not been generated. However, there seems to be something intuitively positive about the father's involvement in the birth process, if he is motivated to participate. Such participation by motivated fathers is unlikely to have any adverse effects, and it may increase the sense of the family as a cohesive, interdependent unit that does things together. A survey by Pawson and Morris (1972) indicated that the father's presence in the delivery room is a positive experience. Only one of the 544 fathers sampled said that he regretted participating in the birth process.

What are some reactions of fathers who have participated in the Lamaze-type natural childbirth classes and in the birth process in the delivery room? Some years ago, I was allowed in the delivery room by a progressive physician at a hospital that did not permit such practices. I still have a very vivid image of those moments. It truly inspires a sense of awe and excitement in a father when he sees his child being born.

One father who participated in natural childbirth classes proudly described how he felt at his accomplishments and his sense of involvement in helping his wife with the birth of the baby:

It made me feel good to be able to help out. I know it is a painful experience, and I wanted to make it as easy for her as possible. She was willing to have the baby and go through the nine months of carrying it around. The least I could do was go to the childbirth classes once a week with her and give her my support. There were times during her pregnancy when she did not feel very good physically, and I know she really appreciated my willingness to assist her in the birth of the baby. Then, in the hospital room itself—what a great, uplifting experience. It was out of this world! I would not have missed it for the world.

What might be some of the effects of a husband's participation in a natural childbirth class with his wife?

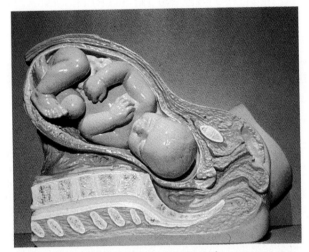

a. The uterus at term; cervix not dilated.

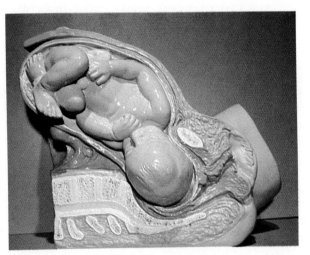

b. Cervix dilates as the uterus contracts.

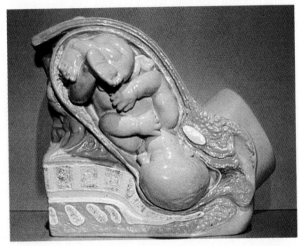

c. Progress of the head to pelvic floor.

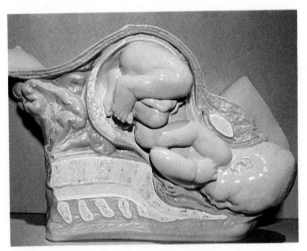

d. Emergence of the head as it rotates.

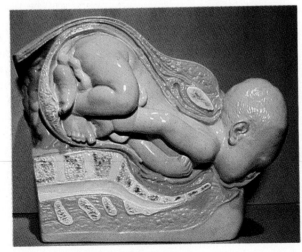

e. Further extension of the head.

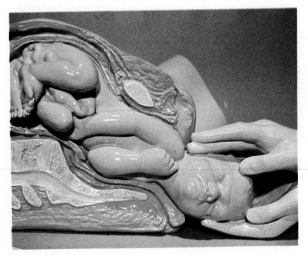

f. The shoulder begins to emerge.

FIGURE 3.15   Stages of the birth process.

Another delivery complication involves the position of the baby in the uterus. In normal circumstances, the crown of the baby's head comes through the vagina first. However, about 1 in every 25 babies is not in the head-first position. Some come with their buttocks first, which is referred to as the **breech position.** A breech baby is likely to have difficulties if delivered in this position because his or her head will still be in the uterus when the rest of the body is not, which may produce respiratory difficulties. Some breech babies cannot be passed through the cervix and must be delivered by cesarean section.

The Use of Drugs During Childbirth

Drugs may be used to relieve pain and anxiety as well as to speed up delivery during the birth process. The widest use of drugs during delivery is to relieve the expectant mother's pain or anxiety. A wide variety of tranquilizers, sedatives, and analgesics are used for this purpose. Researchers are interested in the effects of such drugs because the drugs can cross the placental barrier and because of the drugs' prevalent use during the delivery process. One survey of hospitals found that only 5 percent of deliveries were carried out without anesthesia (Brackbill, 1979).

Drugs also are used to speed up delivery. One drug that has been widely used for this purpose is called **oxytocin.** Oxytocin is a hormone that stimulates uterine contractions. Controversy surrounds the use of this drug. Some physicians argue that it may help to save the mother's life or to keep the infant from being damaged. They also point out that using such a drug allows the mother to be well rested and prepared for the birth process. Critics argue that babies born to mothers who have taken oxytocin are more likely to have jaundice, that induced labor requires more pain-killing drugs, and that greater medical care is required after the birth, resulting in separation of the infant and mother. A research study involving the use of oxytocin as well as other drugs is described in Focus on Child Development 3.3.

Among the conclusions about the influence of drugs during delivery are (Rosenblith & Sims-Knight, 1985):

1. It is difficult to arrive at specific conclusions about the use of drugs during delivery because there have not been a large number of research studies

and those that have been completed often have methodological problems. However, it can be said that all drugs do not have similar effects. Some drugs, such as tranquilizers, sedatives, and analgesics, do not seem to have long-term effects. Other drugs are suspected of having long-term effects (oxytocin is in this category).
2. The degree to which a drug influences the infant is usually very small. Birth weight and social class, for example, are more powerful predictors of infant difficulties than drugs.
3. A specific drug may have an effect on some infants but not on others. And in some cases, the drug may have a beneficial effect, while in others it may produce disadvantages.
4. The overall amount of the medication may be an important factor in understanding drug effects during delivery.

Child Development Concept Table 3.4 summarizes our discussion of childbirth strategies, stages of birth, delivery complications, and the use of drugs during childbirth. Now we examine two other aspects of the birth process: preterm infants and bonding.

Preterm Infants and Age-Weight Considerations

What are preterm infants like? How should they be handled by caregivers? Do parents and hospital personnel interact with preterm infants differently than with their full-term counterparts? These are some of the questions we now explore.

Birth Date and Weight

A full-term infant is one who has grown in the womb for the full 37 to 40 weeks between conception and delivery. Not all babies are born on schedule, however. In the past, babies born before 37 weeks in the womb were considered premature. More recently, the term **premature birth** has lost favor with scientists because it does not sufficiently distinguish early birth from retarded prenatal growth (Kopp & Parmalee, 1979). The trend now is to refer to babies born after a briefer than regular time period in the womb as **short-gestation babies.** (The term **gestation** refers to the length of time between conception

FOCUS ON CHILD DEVELOPMENT 3.3

ANESTHESIA, OXYTOCIN, AND INFANT STATES

Ann Murray and her colleagues (Murray, Dolby, Nation, & Thomas, 1981) investigated the effects of epidural anesthesia on newborns. Epidural anesthesia is a pain-relief technique used during childbirth that involves a local anesthetic blocking transmission of nerve impulses to and from the pelvic region. Compared with other more centrally acting drugs, such as sedatives, tranquilizers, or general anesthetics, local anesthetics usually have been found to have fewer depressant effects on the baby (Brackbill, 1979).

In Murray's research, three samples of babies were studied: Group 1 consisted of 15 infants whose mothers received little or no medication during childbirth; Group 2 consisted of 20 infants whose mothers were given an epidural anesthetic involving the drug bupivacaine; and Group 3 consisted of 20 infants whose mothers were given both an epidural anesthetic and oxytocin (to speed up the delivery process). The outcome measures included assessments of newborn behavior using the Brazelton Neonatal Behavioral Assessment Scale (NBAS) (Brazelton, 1973), mother-infant interaction during feeding, and the mother's perception of her infant's behavior during the first month after delivery.

Results showed that the effects of the drugs were strongest on the first day of the infant's life and were considerably reduced by the fifth day, although the babies of medicated mothers continued to show poor state organization at this time. The table reveals these changes from Day 1 to Day 5 as measured by four scales on the NBAS. At one month, observers detected few differences between the groups, although unmedicated mothers did report that their infants were more sociable, rewarding, and easy to take care of, and these mothers were more responsive to their infant's cries.

Effects of Anesthesia and Oxytocin on Neonatal Development One and Five Days After Birth

Measures	Group		
	Unmedicated	Epidural Anesthetic Only	Epidural Anesthetic Plus Oxytocin
Day 1 NBAS			
Interactive	1.9	2.0	2.8
Motoric	2.3	2.6	3.2
State control	2.5	3.7	3.6
Physiological	1.0	1.5	1.8
Total	7.7	9.8	11.4
Day 5 NBAS			
Interactive	2.6	3.1	2.9
Motoric	2.3	2.4	2.8
State control	3.1	4.0	3.8
Physiological	.3	.6	.8
Total	8.3	10.1	10.3

From Murray, A. D., et al., "Effects of epidural anesthesia on newborns and their mothers" in *Child Development, 52,* 71–82, 1981. © 1981 by The Society for Research in Child Development, Inc. Reprinted by permission.

Child Development Concept Table 3.4   Childbirth Strategies, Stages of Birth and Delivery Complications, and the Use of Drugs

Concept	Processes/Related Ideas	Characteristics/Description
Childbirth strategies	Overview	A controversy currently exists over how the childbirth process should proceed.
	Standard childbirth	The standard childbirth procedure has been criticized because significant people are excluded from participation, mother-infant separation occurs, and giving birth is treated like a disease.
	The Leboyer method	Developed by the French physician Frederick Leboyer, this procedure is designed to make the birth process less stressful for the infant. It often is referred to as "birth without violence."
	The Lamaze method	This form of natural childbirth, developed by the French physician Fernand Lamaze, has become widely accepted. In Lamaze classes, pregnant women are trained in breathing and relaxation techniques and often are helped by their husbands, who participate in the birth process.
Stages of birth and delivery complications	Three stages of birth have been defined.	The first birth stage lasts about 12 to 24 hours for a woman having her first child. It is the longest of the three stages. During this stage, uterine contractions cause the cervix to dilate to about 4 inches. The second stage begins when the baby's head starts to move through the cervix and ends with the complete emergence of the baby from the mother's body. The third and final stage, called afterbirth, is brief and consists of the detachment and expelling of the placenta, umbilical cord, and other membranes.
	Delivery complications include speed of delivery and baby positioning.	A baby can move through the birth canal too rapidly or too slowly. A delivery that is too rapid is called precipitate—blood flow and head pressure may be problems. When delivery is too slow, anoxia may occur. About 1 in 25 babies is not positioned to come out headfirst. When buttocks are positioned first, it is called the breech position. Respiratory difficulties may develop if the baby is delivered in this position.
Use of drugs during childbirth	Drugs are used to relieve pain and anxiety as well as to speed up delivery during the birth process.	A wide variety of tranquilizers, sedatives, and analgesics are used to relieve the expectant mother's pain or anxiety, while oxytocin is the drug most widely used to speed up delivery. Some general conclusions about the effects of drugs during delivery suggest that it is difficult to come up with overall effect statements because of methodological problems in the research. It can be said, however, that some drugs have short-term effects, while others have long-term effects. Overall, though, the degree to which a drug influences the infant is less than for such factors as birth weight and social class. A specific drug may have mixed effects, and the overall amount of medication needs to be considered.

and birth.) By contrast, infants born after a regular gestation period of 37 to 40 weeks, but who weigh less than 5½ pounds, are called **low-birth-weight** or **high-risk infants.** In one investigation (Milham, Widmayer, Bauer, & Peterson, 1983), children were assessed at least once per year through the first four years of life. The most severe cognitive deficits appeared among those who had been short-gestation or low-birth-weight babies and who came from an impoverished rather than a middle-class family.

A short gestation period does not necessarily harm the infant and is distinguished from retarded prenatal growth, in which the fetus has been damaged in some way (Kopp, 1983). The neurological development of the short-gestation infant continues after birth on approximately the same timetable as if the infant still were in the womb. For example, consider an infant born after a gestation period of 30 weeks. At 38 weeks, approximately two months after birth, this infant shows the same level of brain development as a 38-week-old fetus who is yet to be born.

TABLE 3.1   The Apgar Scale

	Score		
	0	1	2
Heart rate	Absent	Slow—less than 100 beats per minute	Fast—100–140 beats per minute
Respiratory effort	No breathing for more than one minute	Irregular and slow	Good breathing with normal crying
Muscle tone	Limp and flaccid	Weak, inactive, but some flexion of extremities	Strong, active motion
Body color	Blue and pale	Body pink, but extremities blue	Entire body pink
Reflex irritability	No response	Grimace	Coughing, sneezing, and crying

From Apgar, Virginia, ''A proposal for a new method of evaluation of a newborn infant'' in *Anesthesia and Analgesia, 32,* 260–267, 1975. © 1975 International Anesthesia Research Society. Reprinted by permission.

As scientists have explored the world of the neonate, they have recognized the need for better measures of the newborn's condition. It is to these measures that we now turn.

Measures of Neonatal Health and Responsiveness

For many years, the **Apgar Scale** shown in Table 3.1 has been used to assess the health of the newborn. One minute and five minutes after birth, the obstetrician or nurse gives the newborn a reading of 0, 1, or 2 on each of five signs: heart rate, respiratory effort, muscle tone, body color, and reflex irritability. A high total score of 7 to 10 suggests that the newborn's condition is good, a score of 5 indicates that there may be developmental difficulties, and a score of 3 or below signals an emergency and indicates that survival may be in doubt.

A test that is more subtle than the Apgar Scale in detecting an infant's neurological integrity is the **Brazelton Neonatal Behavioral Assessment Scale.** This scale includes an evaluation of the infant's reaction to people. The Brazelton scale usually is given on the third day of life and then repeated two to three days later. Twenty reflexes are assessed along with reactions to circumstances, such as the neonate's reaction to a rattle. A very low Brazelton score can indicate brain damage. But if the infant merely seems sluggish in responding to social circumstances, the parents often are encouraged to make a special effort to observe and provide attention to the infant (Brazelton, 1979). For sluggish infants, **Brazelton training** frequently is suggested. This involves using the Brazelton scale to show parents how their newborn responds to people. As part of the training, parents are shown how the neonate can respond positively to people and how such responses can be stimulated. The Brazelton training has been shown to improve the social interaction of high-risk infants as well as the social skills of healthy, responsive infants (Brazelton, 1979; Myers, 1982; Widmayer & Field, 1980; Worobey & Belsky, 1982).

Measures of neonatal health are of particular interest in the case of preterm infants. Let's now try to draw some conclusions about what preterm infants are like.

Conclusions About Preterm Infants

Claire Kopp (1983) reviewed the converging results of several longitudinal studies on preterm infants. Four important conclusions about preterm infants grew out of these studies:

1. As intensive care technology has improved, there have been fewer serious consequences of preterm births. For instance, from 1961 to 1965, the manner of feeding preterm infants changed and intravenous fluid therapy came into use. From 1966 to 1968, better control of hypoxemia (oxygen deficiency) resulted. In 1971, artificial ventilation was introduced. And in the mid-1970s, neonatal support systems became less intrusive and damaging to the infant.

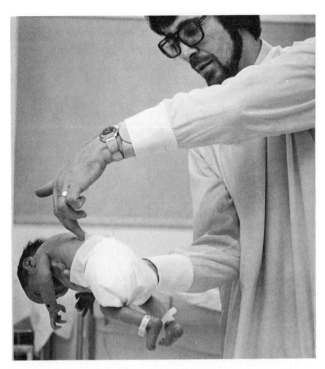

As intensive care technology has improved, fewer serious consequences of preterm births have occurred.

2. Infants born with an identifiable problem are likely to have a poorer developmental future than infants born without a recognizable problem. For instance, extremely sick or very tiny babies are less likely to survive than healthy or normal-weight babies.
3. Social class differences are linked with the preterm infant's development. Put simply, the higher the socioeconomic status, the more favorable is the developmental outcome for a newborn. Social class differences are tied to a number of other differences likely to affect the newborn. For instance, quality of environment, cigarette and alcohol consumption, IQ, and knowledge of competent parenting strategies are linked with social class; less positive characteristics are associated with lower-class families.

4. We do not have solid evidence that preterm infants, as a rule, have difficulty later in school. Nor is there good evidence that these preterm children perform poorly on IQ and information-processing tests. Such claims to the contrary were made just one or two decades ago.

Helping preterm infants to adjust to their world involves more than improved medical care. As suggested in Focus on Child Development 3.4, parent-child relationships make important contributions to the development of the preterm infant.

As we see next, another aspect of social interaction—bonding—also has generated a considerable amount of interest.

Bonding

Perhaps the most controversial strategy focusing on the role of the mother in the neonate's life involves what has been referred to as **bonding.** It has been argued that long-term consequences for the infant's development are set in motion during the first minutes, hours, or days of the neonate's interaction with his or her social world. Situations surrounding the delivery may prevent or make difficult the occurrence of an emotional bond between the infant and the mother. For example, preterm infants are often isolated from their mothers to an even greater degree than full-term infants. In many hospitals, it also has been common to give the mother sufficient drugs to make the delivery of the baby less painful. Such drugs often make the mother drowsy and may interfere with her ability to respond to and stimulate the neonate.

Pediatricians have been the most adamant about the importance of bonding during the initial hours and days of the neonate's life. In particular, Marshall Klaus and John Kennell (1976) have been influential in introducing bonding to many hospital settings. They argue that the first few days of life represent a critical period in development. During this period, close contact, particularly physical contact, between the neonate and the mother is believed to create an important emotional attachment that provides a foundation for optimal development for years to come.

FOCUS ON CHILD DEVELOPMENT 3.4

PREEMIES ARE DIFFERENT

Without a doubt, preterm infants are perceived differently by the adults in their world. Consider the medical community—they know a great deal about the problems confronting preterm infants. The staff-patient ratio for preterm infants is often one of the most favorable in the entire hospital. And the preterm infant often is immersed in an exotic environment of high-technology life-support equipment. Parents undoubtedly also perceive their preterm infant differently than the parents of full-term infants. Parents know that their preterm infant is different and have reasonable fears about the infant's health and future. Preterm infants frequently remain in the hospital for a long time, making the role of the parent as a competent caregiver difficult. Parents must cope with a great deal of uncertainty for a lengthy time period.

How do parents actually deal with their preterm infants? A recent review by Joe Campos and his colleagues (Campos, Barrett, Lamb, Goldsmith, & Stenberg, 1983) summarized the research on this question. Some studies suggest that, even before the newborn goes home from the hospital, mothers show less confidence as a parent in dealing with their preterm infant than the mothers of full-term infants. Even though they have less confidence, do these mothers actually behave differently toward their preterm infant? Research studies indicate that the mothers of preterm infants are less likely to hold the baby close, cuddle, and smile at the infant than the mothers of full-term infants. Possibly such mothers feel awkward or perceive the preterm baby as more fragile than a full-term baby.

Susan Goldberg (1977, 1980) has studied preterm babies and their mothers on several occasions. She speculates that these mothers may harbor a sense of inadequacy because the anticipated interaction with their infant has been frustrated and the close attachment bond has been shut off. As infants go home from the hospital, differences in handling preterm and full-term infants continue. In early infancy, mothers of preterm infants are more intrusive. For example, mothers actively intervened and tried almost desperately to make things happen with their preterm babies more so than the mothers of full-term babies.

While it is appealing to discover differences in the interaction of mothers and their preterm infants compared with mothers and their full-term infants, it is just as likely that preterm infant behavior and responsiveness may be the reason their mothers treat them differently. In some of the longitudinal studies described by Claire Kopp (1983), evidence suggests that preterm infants have a different profile than full-term infants. For instance, Tiffany Field (1979) discovered that four-month-old preterm infants had lower scores on the Denver Developmental Screening Test, a widely used infant development measure. The preterm infants vocalized less, fussed more, and tended to avoid eye contact with their mother more than their full-term infant counterparts. Thus, because they have to deal with infants who are physically and behaviorally different from full-term infants, possibly the differences in the way mothers handle preterm babies are based on their sincere motivation to negotiate this infant difference.

In what ways are the interactions between mothers and premature infants different than those between mothers and full-term infants?

Is there evidence that such close contact between the mother and the neonate is absolutely critical for optimal development later in life? While some research has been offered in support of the bonding hypothesis (e.g., Klaus et al., 1972; Klaus & Kennell, 1976; Carlson et al., 1979; Leifer, Leiderman, Barnett, & Williams, 1972), a growing body of research challenges the significance of the first few days of life as a critical period (e.g., Bakeman & Brown, 1980; Brown & Bakeman, 1980; Campbell, 1977; Crawford, 1982; Field, 1977; Rode, Chang, Fisch, & Sroufe, 1981; Zeskind, 1980). Clearly, strong conclusions about the positive effects of bonding are not possible at this time. Indeed, the extreme form of the bonding hypothesis—namely, that the neonate must have close contact with the mother in the first few days of life to develop—simply is not true.

Some expectant parents fear that, if bonding does not occur, their neonate will later develop problems adjusting to the world and likely will never form a close attachment to the mother. And parents with infants and older children may look back to when their child was born and worry that bonding was not practiced. Such parents should not worry. Most mother-infant pairs seem to compensate for any negative effects that might have occurred during their separation in the postpartum period (Grossman, Thane, & Grossman, 1981).

Nevertheless, the weakness of the maternal-infant bonding research should not be used as an excuse to keep motivated mothers from interacting with their infants in the postpartum period because such contact brings pleasure to many mothers (McCall, 1982; Rosenblith & Sims-Knight, 1985). In the case of some mother-infant pairs (such as preterm infants, adolescent mothers, or mothers from disadvantaged circumstances), the practice of bonding may set in motion a climate for improved mother-infant interaction after the mother and infant leave the hospital (Maccoby & Martin, 1983).

THINKING BACK, LOOKING AHEAD

We always will be, and always have been, biological beings, as well as social beings, with a genetic and evolutionary history. In this chapter, you learned that, in terms of the calendar year, humans arrived late in December, that porcupines and human

infants are biologically adapted, that both genes and environment are necessary for a child even to exist, and that there are a number of intriguing ways to assess genetic-environmental influences. The chapter discussion of prenatal development took us from when the organism is a single cell (not a brain cell) to birth (when the infant has some 10 to 100 billion brain cells). It has been found that, during this masterful development, brain cells are produced at rates of up to 25,000 a minute! From zygote to neonate, conception to bonding, preemies to full-terms, organogenesis to Leboyer and Lamaze, the world of prenatal development is eventful and awe-inspiring.

You also learned in this chapter that information being collected as part of the scientific process is finding its way into the lives of families who want to increase their chances of having a healthy offspring. Genetic counseling has become far more frequent, and expectant mothers are far more likely to question whether they should smoke or drink during their pregnancy. Technological advances are expanding the survival chances of preterm infants, and increased knowledge of drugs is allowing more intelligent choices to be made regarding their use during prenatal development or the delivery process. Amniocentesis and, more recently, the chorionic villus test are providing a "window" into the makeup of the organism earlier in prenatal development. Much yet is to be learned about prenatal development and the birth process, but the gains made in the last several decades are impressive.

In the next chapter, you will read much more about the infant's states soon after birth. Chapter 4 also portrays many of the other fascinating aspects of physical and perceptual/motor development during the first two years of life. And in other chapters in Section 2, you will learn about cognitive and social/personality development during infancy. But before we leave our discussion of prenatal development and the birth process, reflect for a moment on the fact that, of the more than 300 million sperm that are released in a single ejaculation, only one sperm penetrates the ovum. Aldous Huxley spoke eloquently about this in the "Fifth Philosopher's Song":

A million, million spermatozoa,
    All of them alive
Out of their cataclysm but one poor Noah
    Dare hope to survive
And among the billion minus one
    might have chanced to be
Shakespeare, another Newton, one Donne
    But the one was me.

SUMMARY

I. Charles Darwin proposed his theory of evolution after traveling around the world and observing the adaptation of a variety of species to their natural habitats. The principle of natural selection emphasizes the existence of genetic diversity in a species. Because of this diversity, some organisms have beneficial characteristics that help them to adapt to their environment. These beneficial characteristics are likely to be perpetuated. Most scientists today believe that natural selection provides the best explanation of evolution and that evolution occurs at a slow pace.

II. To understand the role of genetics in the child's development, we need to know what genes are, some important genetic principles, methods of behavior geneticists, and the nature of genetic-environmental interaction.

   A. Each human cell contains 46 chromosomes and 50,000 or more genes. Chromosomes come in pairs (23 pairs in humans) and are made up of DNA, which has a double helix shape. A gene is a short segment of the DNA ladder and is distinguished by its unique sequences of "rungs," called bases. Genes are transmitted from parents to offspring by gametes, or sex cells. Gametes are formed by the splitting of cells, a process called meiosis. Reproduction takes place when a female gamete (ovum) is fertilized by a male gamete (sperm) to create a single-celled zygote. The actual combination of genes is called a genotype, while the behavioral manifestations of the genes are called phenotypes.

   B. Some important genetic principles are dominant-recessive genes, sex-linked genes, polygenic inheritance, reaction range, and canalization.

      1. A dominant gene exerts its full effect, regardless of its genetic partner. A recessive gene's code is masked by a dominant gene and is only expressed when the recessive gene is paired with another recessive gene.

      2. Some characteristics are determined by genes located on the 23rd chromosome pair, the one determining the sex of the offspring. The result is that these characteristics are more or less likely to appear in members of one sex.

      3. Few psychological characteristics are the result of the actions of single gene pairs. Traits produced by the mixing of genes are said to be polygenically determined.

      4. Given any individual genotype, there is a range of phenotypes that can be expressed—this is called reaction range.

      5. Canalization refers to the narrow path or developmental course that certain characteristics take.

   C. Among the methods used by behavior geneticists are the twin study, the family-of-twins design, the kinship study, and the adoption study. Heritability refers to a mathematical estimate of the degree to which a characteristic is inherited. It is by no means flawless, and unfortunately, the nature of genetic-environmental interaction gets lost in heritability computation.

   D. A general conclusion about genetic-environmental interaction is: No genes, no organism; no environment, no organism. Both genes and environment are necessary even for a child to exist.

III. The course of prenatal development includes conception and the zygote, the germinal period, the embryonic period, and the fetal period.

   A. Standard conception occurs when a single sperm cell unites with the ovum in the female's fallopian tube, a process called fertilization. The single-celled zygote created by this process has 50 percent of its chromosomes from the mother and 50 percent from the father. Early cell divisions are called cleavage divisions. The first three to four days after conception is called the zygote period. Since the first in-vitro fertilization in the 1970s, a variety of procedures have been developed to allow otherwise infertile couples to have a child.

   B. The germinal period is defined as the period from conception until about 10 to 14 days later. Cell division continues, and a cell mass of about 100 to 150 cells is formed at about one week after conception. This cell mass is called the blastula. The blastula differentiates into inner (blastocyst) and outer (trophoblast) layers. At about 10 to 14 days after conception, the zygote attaches to the uterine wall.

   C. The embryonic period is defined as the period that lasts from approximately two weeks to eight weeks after conception. During the embryonic period, the embryo differentiates into three layers, life support systems develop, and organ systems form (organogenesis). At two to three weeks after conception, the outer layer of the embryo differentiates into the ectoderm and mesoderm, and the inner layer of the embryo differentiates into the endoderm. The placenta matures, and the umbilical cord is forming. At three to four weeks after conception, the neural tube is forming, eyes are appearing, the heart is being differentiated, arm and leg buds emerge, and heart chambers take shape. At five to eight weeks after conception, the arms and legs are more differentiated, the face starts to form, the intestinal tract develops, and the facial structures fuse. At eight weeks, the organism weighs about 1/30 of an ounce and is slightly more than 1 inch long.

D. The fetal period lasts from about two months after conception until nine months or when the infant is born. Organ systems mature to the point where life can be sustained outside the womb. The fetus grows from 3 inches in length and 1 ounce in weight at three months after conception to 12 inches and 1 pound at five months and then 16 inches and 2 pounds at seven months. By four months after conception, prenatal reflexes are becoming apparent, and the mother likely feels movement for the first time. By seven months after conception, the fetus's chances for survival are excellent. In the last two months, the fetus grows longer and gains considerable weight. Fatty tissues develop, and the functioning of various organ systems is stepped up. The average American baby weighs 7 pounds and is 20 inches long at birth.

IV. An understanding of teratology and hazards to prenatal development requires information about what teratology is, maternal diseases and conditions, and drugs.

A. Teratology is the field that investigates the causes of congenital (birth) defects. The greatest damage to embryonic structures is likely to occur during organogenesis. Exposure during the later fetal period is likely to stunt growth or to create problems in how organs function. Environmental agents may cause problems at the genetic level, at the level of organogenesis, or after organogenesis is complete.

B. Maternal diseases and conditions that can influence prenatal development include diseases and infections, rubella and syphilis, herpes simplex virus, the mother's age, nutrition, and emotional state and stress.

1. Maternal diseases and infections can cause damage by crossing the placental barrier, or they can be destructive during the birth process itself.

2. Rubella (German measles) is most destructive during the third to fourth week of pregnancy. Syphilis is more damaging four months or later after conception.

3. Two members of the herpes simplex virus family—CMV and HVH—can be transmitted from the mother to the infant at birth.

4. More premature infants are born to adolescent mothers than other age groups. Women over 30 have an increased risk of giving birth to a baby with Down's syndrome.

5. The developing fetus is completely dependent on the mother for nutrition. Serious malnutrition can produce death or malformations of the fetus.

6. Today it is believed that stressful experiences of the mother can be transmitted to the fetus.

C. Drugs that affect prenatal development include thalidomide, alcohol, and cigarettes.

1. Thalidomide is a tranquilizer that was given to pregnant women to reduce their anxiety or morning sickness. In the early 1960s, it was responsible for thousands of deformed babies.

2. Fetal alcohol syndrome refers to a cluster of characteristics, such as microencephaly and deformed limbs, that often appear in the offspring of alcoholic or heavy-drinking mothers. Even moderate drinking patterns of pregnant women have been associated with behavioral deficiencies in children as old as four years of age, but moderate drinking does not seem to cause structural damage.

3. Fetal and neonatal death rates are higher among smoking mothers. Also prevalent are higher preterm rates and lower birth weights. Respiratory problems and sudden infant death syndrome also are more common in the offspring of mothers who smoke.

V. To learn about the birth process, it is important to consider childbirth strategies, the stages of birth and delivery complications, the use of drugs during childbirth, preterm infants and age-weight considerations, and bonding.

A. A controversy currently exists over how the childbirth process should proceed. The standard childbirth procedure has been criticized, and the Leboyer and Lamaze methods are two alternatives. The Lamaze method has gained popularity in the United States, and many fathers have become involved in the birth process through this technique.

B. Three stages of birth have been defined. The first birth stage lasts about 12 to 24 hours in the first pregnancy. During this stage, uterine contractions cause the cervix to dilate. The second stage begins when the baby's head starts to move through the cervix and ends with the complete emergence of the baby from the mother's body. The third stage, called afterbirth, is brief and consists of the detachment and expelling of the placenta, umbilical cord, and other membranes.

C. A baby can move through the birth canal too rapidly or too slowly. A delivery that is too rapid is called precipitate—blood flow and head pressure may be problems. When delivery is too slow, anoxia may occur. About 1 in 25 babies is not positioned headfirst. When buttocks are positioned first, it is called the breech position. Respiratory difficulties may develop if the baby is delivered in this position.

D. Drugs are used to relieve pain and anxiety as well as to speed up delivery during the birth process. A wide variety of tranquilizers, sedatives, and analgesics are used to relieve the expectant mother's pain or anxiety, while oxytocin is the drug most widely used to speed up delivery. Some general conclusions about the effects of drugs during delivery suggest that it often is difficult to come up with overall statements about drug effects because of methodological problems in the research. It can be said, however, that some drugs have short-term effects, while others have long-term effects. In general, though, the degree to which a drug influences the infant usually is less than for such variables as birth weight and social class. A specific drug may have mixed effects, and the overall amount of medication needs to be considered.

E. Short-gestation babies are those born after a briefer than regular time period in the womb. Infants who are born after a regular gestation period of 37 to 40 weeks but who weigh less than 5½ pounds are called low-birth-weight or high-risk infants. As intensive care technology has improved, preterm babies have benefited considerably. Infants born with an identifiable problem are likely to have a poorer developmental future than infants born without a recognizable problem. Social class differences are associated with the preterm infant's development. There is no solid evidence that preterm infants perform more poorly than full-term infants when they are assessed years later in school.

F. There is evidence that bonding, defined as the establishment of a close mother-infant bond in the first hours or days after birth, is not critical for optimal development, although for some mother-infant pairs, it may stimulate interaction after they leave the hospital. Thus, while bonding certainly does no harm, it does not seem to possess the magical characteristics that some pediatricians ascribe to it.

KEY TERMS

adoption studies 90
afterbirth 108
amniocentesis 84
amnion 96
anoxia 108
Apgar Scale 114
behavior genetics 89
blastocyst 95
blastula 95
bonding 115
Brazelton Neonatal Behavioral Assessment Scale 114
Brazelton training 114
breech position 111
canalization 89
chorionic villus test 84
chromosomes 86
cleavage divisions 94
CMV 102
conception 92
dizygotic 90
DNA 86
dominant-recessive genes 87
ectoderm 96
embryonic period 96
endoderm 96
family-of-twins design 90
fetal alcohol syndrome (FAS) 104
fetal period 97
gametes 86
gene 86
genotype 87
germinal period 95
gestation 111

heritability 90
HVH 102
implantation 95
in-vitro fertilization 94
kinship studies 90
Lamaze method 108
Leboyer method 108
low-birth-weight (high-risk) infants 113
meiosis 86
mesoderm 96
monozygotic 90
natural selection 85
organogenesis 97
oxytocin 111
phenotypes 87
placenta 96
polygenic inheritance 88
precipitate 108
premature birth 111
prospective study 105
reaction range 89
reproduction 86
sex-linked genes 88
short-gestation babies 111
sudden infant death syndrome (SIDS) 106
teratogen 100
teratology 100
thalidomide 104
trophoblast 95
twin study 90
umbilical cord 96
zygote 87
zygote period 94

SUGGESTED READINGS

Brazelton, T. B., & Lester, B. M. (1982). *New approaches to developmental screenings of infants*. New York: Elsevier.
A group of experts on infant development relate new developments in the assessment of newborns.

Child Development, April 1983, Vol. 54.
A major portion of this issue of *Child Development* is devoted to research on behavior genetics from a developmental perspective. Here you can read about current twin studies and longitudinal studies of adoption.

Falkner, F., & Macy, C. (1980). *Pregnancy and birth*. New York: Harper & Row.
An easy-to-read description of experiences during pregnancy and the nature of childbearing.

Goldberg, S., & Divitto, B. A. (1983). *Born too soon: Preterm birth and early development*. San Francisco: W. H. Freeman.
Gives recent information about the nature of preterm infants and ways to socially interact with them.

Gould, S. (1983). *Hen's teeth and horse's toes: Reflections on natural history*. New York: Norton.
A collection of fascinating articles by a biologist interested in evolution. The essays originally were published in the magazine *Natural History*.

Leboyer, F. (1975). *Birth without violence*. New York: Alfred A. Knopf.
The French physician describes his highly influential practice of delivery and his opinions about its value. Written in easy-to-read language and accompanied by illustrative photographs.

Nilsson, L. (1966). *A child is born*. New York: Delacourt.
Contains an abundance of breathtaking photographs that take you inside the mother's womb to see the developmental unfolding of the zygote, embryo, and fetus.

Walters, W., & Singer, P. (Eds.). (1982). *Test-tube babies*. New York: Oxford University Press.
Focuses on the ethics of in-vitro fertilization with varying perspectives being expressed.

PHYSICAL AND PERCEPTUAL MOTOR DEVELOPMENT OF INFANTS

IMAGINE . . . YOU ARE FROM OUTER SPACE AND HAVE COME UPON A CREATURE THAT SEEMS HELPLESS

PREVIEW

PHYSICAL DEVELOPMENT

Reflexes, States, and Activities
Reflexes
States

FOCUS ON CHILD DEVELOPMENT 4.1: RATTLES, BELLS, PINPRICKS, AND CUDDLES

Eating Behavior

CHILD DEVELOPMENT CONCEPT TABLE 4.1: REFLEXES, STATES, AND ACTIVITIES

Physical Growth and Motor Development
The First Year
The Second Year
Rhythmic Motor Behavior
The Brain

CHILD DEVELOPMENT CONCEPT TABLE 4.2: PHYSICAL GROWTH AND MOTOR DEVELOPMENT

SENSORY AND PERCEPTUAL DEVELOPMENT

What Are Sensation and Perception?

FOCUS ON CHILD DEVELOPMENT 4.2: "SLICES" OF SPACE AND "EYES" IN THE BACK OF YOUR HEAD

Visual Perception
Visual Preferences
Visual Acuity and Accommodation
Perception of Color
Perception of Objects and Faces
Perception of Depth
Perception of Spatial Relations

Other Senses
Hearing

FOCUS ON CHILD DEVELOPMENT 4.3: YELLOW KANGAROOS, GRAY DONKEYS, THUMPS, GONGS, AND FOUR-MONTH-OLD INFANTS

CHILD DEVELOPMENT CONCEPT TABLE 4.3: THE NATURE OF SENSATION AND PERCEPTION, THEORIES OF PERCEPTUAL DEVELOPMENT, VISUAL PERCEPTION, AND AUDITORY PERCEPTION

Smell
Taste
Touch
Pain

FOCUS ON CHILD DEVELOPMENT 4.4: THE THREE-DAY-OLD MALE INFANT AND THE CIRCUMSTRAINT BOARD

The Relatedness of Different Sensory Dimensions

THINKING BACK, LOOKING AHEAD

SUMMARY

KEY TERMS

SUGGESTED READINGS

CHAPTER 4

IMAGINE . . . YOU ARE FROM OUTER SPACE AND HAVE COME UPON A CREATURE THAT SEEMS HELPLESS

The creature has very poor motor coordination and can move itself only with great difficulty. Its general behavior appears to be unorganized, and though it cries when uncomfortable, it has few other vocalizations. In fact, it sleeps most of the time, about 16 to 17 hours a day. You are curious about this creature and want to know more about what it can do. You think to yourself, "I wonder if it can see? How could I find out?"

You obviously have a communication problem with the creature. You must devise a way that will allow the creature to "tell" you that it can see. While examining the creature one day, you make an interesting discovery: When you move a large object toward it, it moves its head backward, as if to avoid a collision with the object. The head movement of the creature suggests that it has at least some vision, so you begin to evaluate the visual information that induces a natural reaction on a regular basis. Does the creature actually perceive an approaching object? Or does it simply respond to changes in the height and width of an object? You launch a series of inquiries to find out.

You soon discover another way to study the creature's visual perception. You notice that it looks at some objects for rather extensive periods and at others hardly at all. There is little apparent rhyme or reason to these preferences, but this gives you a powerful tool: you can present the creature with pairs of objects, carefully controlling the differences between them. By studying the minimum differences necessary for the creature to show a preference, you can make an estimate of its visual acuity.

This preference method you have discovered is helpful, but limited to cases in which one object is preferred over another. How can you test discrimination between two objects that are preferred equally by the creature? This has you stumped for awhile, but then you think that you might be able to determine how bored the creature gets with an object. You put an object in front of the creature, and it looks at it for awhile. But then it seems to get bored, and the looking time drops off. Now you present a subtly different object, one that is just slightly different in color. Will the creature look at it longer? Will its interest increase? If it does, the creature has communicated to you that it sees the two objects differently. You then decide to use this strategy with chips of different colors, and you discover that the creature has color vision. Using the same technique with faces, you learn that it can tell faces apart. Apparently, you conclude, the creature can recognize people. This creature is beginning to appear much more complex than you originally thought. While its motor abilities seem very limited, it can see a great deal!

In case you haven't already guessed, the creature you have been reading about is the human infant and the role you played from outer space is that of a scientist interested in devising techniques to learn about the infant's visual perception. The strategies described (in order) were **natural reaction, preference,** and **habituation.** Later in the chapter, as we discuss perceptual development in infancy, you will see that techniques such as these have led to some very clever studies that allow child developmentalists to communicate with the very young infant.

PREVIEW

Have you seen a baby in the last several years? What did the baby look like? How big was the baby? What could it do? Could the infant walk, talk, frown, think? If you have not observed infants for some time, do so as soon as possible. The time you spend with a baby will help you a great deal in understanding our description of infant development.

In this chapter, we discuss many interesting aspects of the infant's physical development and then turn to the fascinating world of sensory/perceptual development. You will discover that developmental psychologists have varying views of how information gets inside the infant's head, and they also have varying beliefs about how important cognitive processes are in knowing the sensory world. The following words of Aldous Huxley stimulate consideration of such issues:

Systematic reasoning is something we could not, as a species of individuals, do without. But neither, if we are to remain sane, can we do without direct perception . . . of the inner and outer world into which we have been born.

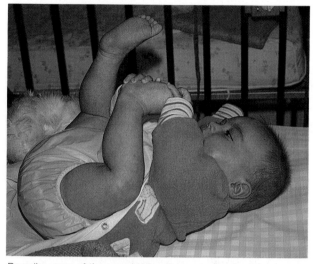

Describe some of the remarkable reflexes young infants possess.

PHYSICAL DEVELOPMENT

How do infants respond to their world? What kind of states do they experience? What are the different kind of activities they engage in?

Reflexes, States, and Activities

The newborn is not an empty-headed organism. Among other things, it has some basic reflexes that are genetically carried survival mechanisms. For example, the newborn has no fear of water. It will naturally hold its breath and contract its throat to keep water from coming in. Let's look at more of the remarkable reflexes that the young infant possesses.

Reflexes

Reflexes govern the infant's movements, which are automatic and beyond the infant's control. For example, if you stroke the newborn's hand or foot on the back or top, the whole arm or leg withdraws slightly and the hand or foot flexes and then returns so that fingers or toes may grasp your finger. This withdrawal reflex only exists until

the baby begins to use his or her limbs in a different way—legs for standing and stepping, arms for reaching.

The newborn also has many other reflexes. If you hold the infant in a standing position and gently press the sole of one foot and then the other to the bed, the infant will draw up each leg successively as if walking. The newborn can actually "walk" across a bed. Almost a year after the newborn's walk reflex vanishes, it reappears as the voluntary, complex art of walking.

One of the most frequent and dramatic reflexes of the newborn is the **Moro reflex,** a vestige from our primate ancestry. If infants are handled roughly, hear a very loud noise, see a bright light, or feel a sudden change in position, they startle, arch their back, and throw their head back. At the same time, they fling out their arms and legs, then rapidly close them to the center of their body, and then flex as if they were falling. As they cry, they startle, then cry because of the startle. This reflex, normal in all newborns, tends to disappear at three to four months of age. Steady pressure on any part of the infant's body will calm the infant. If you hold the infant's arm firmly flexed at his or her shoulder, the infant will quiet even though undressed and free of restraints. Table 4.1 presents additional information about the neonate's repertoire of reflexes.

Table 4.1 The Neonate's Reflex Repertoire

If You	Then the Baby's
Tap the bridge of the nose, shine a bright light suddenly into the eyes, clap hands about 18 inches from the infant's head, or touch the white of the eye with cotton	Eyes close tightly.
Make sudden contact or noise	Head drops backward, neck extends, arms and legs fling outward and back sharply (Moro reflex).
Extend forearms at elbow	Arms flex briskly.
Lightly prick soles of feet	Knee and foot flex.
Stand infant; press foot to bed	Feet step.
Pull baby to sit	Eyes snap open, shoulders tense. Baby tries unsuccessfully to right head (China doll reflex).
Pull baby on tummy on flat surface	Head turns to side and lifts. Baby crawls, lifts self with arms.
Support chest on water surface	Arms and legs "swim."
Place baby on back and turn head to side	Body arches away from face side; arm on face side extends, leg draws up; other arm flexes (tonic neck reflex).
Stroke foot or hand on top	Limb withdraws, arches, returns to grasp.
Stroke palm or sole at base of digits	Limb grasps.
Stroke outside of sole	Toes spread, large toe sticks up.
Tap upper lips sharply	Lips protrude.
Stroke cheek or mouth	Mouth roots; head turns, and tongue moves toward stroking object; mouth sucks.
Stroke cheek or palm	Mouth roots; arm flexes: hand goes to open mouth.
Place object over nose and mouth	Mouth works vigorously; head twists, arms fling across face.
Stroke leg, upper part of body	Opposite leg or hand crosses to push your hand away; withdraws.
Rotate baby to side	Head turns, eyes precede direction of rotation.
Suspend by legs	Body curls to upside-down ball, legs extend, arms drop into straight line; neck arches backward.

From Caplan, F., *The First Twelve Months of Life*. Copyright © 1981 Bantam Books, Inc.

Some reflexes are important in the baby's life—crying in response to pain, and sucking, for instance. Although the usefulness of many neonatal reflexes is not completely clear, if some reflexes, such as the Moro reflex, are very weak, it may indicate brain damage. Reflexes often are tested in the neonate as a means of discovering whether the neonate's nervous system is working properly.

A number of reflexes that are present in the newborn, such as coughing, blinking, and yawning, persist throughout our lives. They are important for the adult's life just as they are for the infant's. Other reflexes, however, often disappear in the several months following birth as the infant's higher brain functions mature and voluntary control over many behaviors develops. Let's look at three reflexes in greater detail—sucking, crying, and smiling.

Sucking   Sucking is an important means of obtaining nutrition, as well as an enjoyable, soothing activity, for infants. One early study by T. Berry Brazelton (1956) involved observations of infants for over one year to determine their incidence of sucking when they were not nursing and how their sucking behavior changed as they grew older. More than 85 percent of the infants engaged in considerable sucking behavior unrelated to feeding. They sucked on their fingers, their fists, and pacifiers. By the time the infants were one year old, most of them had stopped the sucking behavior.

Thus, parents clearly should not become worried when infants suck their thumbs, fist, or even a pacifier. Many parents begin to worry more, of course, when thumb sucking persists through the early childhood years and even into the elementary school setting. As many as 40 percent of children continue to suck their thumbs after they have started school (Kessen, Haith, & Salapatek, 1970). Most developmental psychologists do not attach a great deal of significance to this behavior and are not aware of any parenting strategies that might have contributed to it. There are considerable individual differences in the biological makeup of children, and these differences may be to some degree involved in this late continuation of sucking behavior.

Infant researchers are interested in nonnutritive sucking for another reason. **Nonnutritive sucking** shows up in a surprisingly large number of research studies with young infants because it has been found that young infants quit sucking when they attend to something in their environment, such as a picture or a vocalization. Thus, infant researchers may include nonnutritive sucking as a dependent variable in studies of the infant's attention.

In contrast to nonnutritive sucking, nutritive sucking is the infant's route to nourishment. Neonates' sucking capabilities vary considerably—some newborns are quite efficient at forceful sucking and getting milk while others are not as adept and also get tired before they are full. It takes most newborns several weeks to establish a sucking style that is coordinated with such matters as the way the mother is holding the infant, the way milk is coming out of the bottle or breast, and the infant's speed and temperament.

Crying and Smiling   Crying and smiling are emotional behaviors that are very important in the infant's communication with the world. Crying is the infant's first affective behavior. Newborns spend 6 to 7 percent of their day crying, although there is considerable individual variation (Korner, Hutchinson, Koperski, Kraemer, & Schneider, 1981). Infants' earliest cries are reflexive reactions to discomfort. Thus, cries are one of the most important ways in which the infant is biologically equipped to communicate with adults. The cries may signify information about the infant's biological state and possibly indicate distress. They also are highly differentiated and involve different patterns of frequency, intensity, and pause.

Recent research has demonstrated that most adults can determine whether the infant's cries signify anger or pain. In one study, even for brief segments of infant crying, adults were able to distinguish between aversive and arousing cries (more distressful) and those indicating hunger (less distressful) (Zeskind, Sale, Maio, Huntington, & Weiseman, 1984). Thus, the infant's cries even shortly after birth communicate information to the world.

Should a crying infant be given attention and be soothed, or does such parental behavior spoil the infant? Many years ago, behaviorist John Watson (1928) argued that parents spend too much time responding to the crying of the infant and as a consequence reward the crying and increase its incidence. By contrast, recent arguments by ethologists such as Mary Ainsworth (e.g., Ainsworth, 1979) stress that it is difficult to respond too much to the infant's crying. Ainsworth views caregivers' responsiveness to infant crying as contributing to the formation of a secure attachment between the infant and the caregiver. One research project found that mothers who responded quickly to their infant's crying at three months of age had infants who cried less when assessed at a later point in the first year of life (Bell & Ainsworth, 1972). Other research by those from the behavioral viewpoint (e.g., Gewirtz, 1977) suggests that quick, soothing responses by caregivers to crying increases the infant's subsequent crying. In sum, controversy still surrounds the issue of when and how caregivers should respond to infant crying.

Smiling is another important communication behavior of infants. Researchers distinguish between two kinds of smiling in infants—one reflexive, the other social. At some time in the first month after birth, an expression appears on the infant's face that adults refer to as a smile. This smile is a **reflexive smile** because it does not occur in response to external stimuli. The reflexive smile occurs most often during irregular patterns of sleep and does not appear when the infant is in an alert state. **Social smiling,** which usually occurs in response to a face, usually does not occur until two to three months of age (e.g., Emde, Gaensbauer, & Harmon, 1976). Others, however, feel that the social aspects of smiling appear earlier than two months of age, as when an infant grins in response to voices as early as three weeks of age (Sroufe & Waters, 1976).

Now that we have investigated a number of different reflexes in early infancy and seen the beginning of social responsiveness, we turn our attention to the nature of the infant's states.

When does social smiling first occur during infancy?

States

Researchers who study infant states are concerned with just how such states can be classified and the nature of the sleeping-waking cycle.

The Classification of Infant States In an effort to chart and understand the nature of the infant's development, researchers have put together different classification schemes of the infant's states (e.g., Brown, 1964; Prechtl, 1965; Wolff, 1966). One classification scheme (Brown, 1964) describes the following seven infant states:

1. *Deep sleep.* The infant lies motionless with eyes closed, has regular breathing, shows no vocalization, and does not respond to outside stimulation.

2. *Regular sleep.* The infant moves very little, breathing might be raspy or involve wheezing, and respirations may be normal or move from normal to irregular.

3. *Disturbed sleep.* There is a variable amount of movement, the infant's eyelids are closed but might flutter, breathing is regular or irregular, and there may be some squawks, sobs, and sighs.

4. *Drowsy.* The infant's eyes are open or partly open and appear glassy, there is little movement (although startles and free movement may occur), vocalizations are more regular than in disturbed sleep, and some transitional sounds may be heard.

5. *Alert activity.* This is the state most often viewed by parents as being awake. The infant's eyes are open and bright, he or she shows a variety of free movements, fretting may occur, skin may redden, and there may be irregular breathing when the infant feels tension.

6. *Alert and focused.* This kind of attention is often seen in older children but is unusual in the neonate. The child's eyes are open and bright. Some motor activity may occur, but it is integrated around a specific activity. This state may occur when focusing on some sound or some visual stimulus.

7. *Inflexibly focused.* In this state, the infant is awake but does not react to external stimuli—two examples are sucking and wild crying. During wild crying, for instance, the infant may thrash about, but the eyes usually are closed as he or she screams.

Using classification schemes such as the one just described, researchers have investigated many different aspects of the baby's life. As we see next, one such aspect has been the infant's sleeping-waking cycle.

The Sleeping-Waking Cycle Each night, something lures us from our work, our play, our loved ones, into a solitary state called sleep—the sandman's spell claims more of our time than any other pursuit. As a baby, sleep consumed even more of our time than it does now. Newborns sleep for 16 to 17 hours a day, although there is considerable individual variation, ranging from a low of about 10 hours to a high of approximately 21 hours

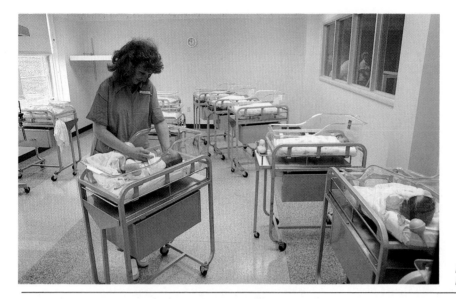

How much do newborns sleep? What is their REM sleep like?

(Parmelee, Schulz, & Disbrow, 1961; Parmelee, Wenne, & Schulz, 1964). Research data also indicate that when newborns and young infants sleep is not always when their parents like to sleep. In one of the studies by Arthur Parmelee and his colleagues (Parmelee, Schulz, & Disbrow, 1961), slightly fewer than half of the young infants did not have their longest period of sleep between 11 P.M. and 7 A.M. And while total sleep remains somewhat consistent for young infants, the patterns of sleep during the day do not always follow a rhythmic pattern—an infant might change from sleeping several long bouts of seven or eight hours to three or four shorter sessions only several hours in duration. By approximately one month of age, most infants have begun to sleep longer at night, and by about four months of age, they usually have moved even closer to adultlike sleep patterns, spending their longest span of sleeping time at night and their longest bouts of waking time during the day (e.g., Parmelee & Stern, 1972).

Infant researchers also have been fascinated by the kind of sleep young infants engage in. This fascination has focused on how much of the infant's sleep involves **REM sleep,** which refers to rapid eye movement sleep. Children and adults who have been awakened in sleep laboratories after being in a state of REM sleep report that they have been dreaming (Foulkes, 1972; Webb, 1975). Most adults spend about one-fifth of their night in REM sleep, and REM sleep usually appears about an hour after non-REM sleep has occurred. It has been found, however, that about half of an infant's sleep involves REM sleep and that infants often begin their sleep cycle with REM rather than non-REM sleep (Roffwarg, Muzio, & Dement, 1966). By the time infants have reached three months of age, the percentage of time spent in REM sleep has fallen to about 40 percent, and they no longer begin their sleep cycle with REM sleep (Minard, Coleman, Williams, & Ingledyne, 1968). Some sleep researchers believe that the large amount of time spent in REM sleep by young infants provides them with added self-stimulation since they spend less time awake than older infants. Others suggest that REM sleep promotes the development of the brain.

Chapter 3 indicated that the Brazelton Neonatal Behavioral Assessment Scale provides a more sensitive index of the newborn's neurological integrity than the traditionally used Apgar Scale. We also saw in Chapter 3 that the Brazelton scale can be used as a basis for training the responsiveness of young infants and that the scale is used in a number of research studies. One of the major indices on the Brazelton scale involves the assessment of infant states. The Brazelton Neonatal Behavioral Assessment Scale is described in more detail in Focus on Child Development 4.1.

FOCUS ON CHILD DEVELOPMENT 4.1

RATTLES, BELLS, PINPRICKS, AND CUDDLES

The **Brazelton Neonatal- Behavioral Assessment Scale** (named after well-known pediatrician T. Berry Brazelton) is being used as a more sensitive index of the neurological integrity of newborns for clinical purposes. But it also is receiving widespread recognition as an important assessment device in research studies on neonatal development. For example, Chapter 3 reported that the Brazelton Neonatal Behavioral Assessment Scale (known as the NBAS) was used to assess newborns' level of development after their mothers had received anesthesia during the birth process (Murray et al., 1981).

The NBAS has a category to assess infant reflexes, but it is mainly concerned with infant states. In particular, it is valuable in pinpointing behaviors that interfere with competent mother-infant interaction (Lester & Brazelton, 1982). The examiner rates the infant on each of 26 different categories (see the first table). As an indication of the detailed nature of how one of these characteristics is assessed, consider item 14 in the table—"cuddliness." As shown in the second table, nine steps are involved in assessing this item, with infant behavior scored on a continuum that ranges from the infant being very resistant to being held to the infant being extremely cuddly and clinging.

In recent versions of scoring the Brazelton scale, Brazelton and his colleagues have been categorizing the 26 items into four different scales—physiological, motoric, state, or interaction. They also have been categorizing the baby in global terms, such as "worrisome," "normal," or "superior," based on these four scales.

The 26 Categories on the Brazelton Neonatal Behavioral Assessment Scale (NBAS)

1. Response decrement to repeated visual stimuli
2. Response decrement to rattle
3. Response decrement to bell
4. Response decrement to pinprick
5. Orienting response to inanimate visual stimuli
6. Orienting response to inanimate auditory stimuli
7. Orienting response to animate visual stimuli—examiner's face
8. Orienting response to animate auditory stimuli—examiner's voice
9. Orienting responses to animate visual and auditory stimuli
10. Quality and duration of alert periods
11. General muscle tone—in resting and in response to being handled, passive and active
12. Motor activity
13. Traction responses as he or she is pulled to sit
14. Cuddliness—responses to being cuddled by examiner
15. Defensive movements—reactions to a cloth over his or her face
16. Consolability with intervention by examiner
17. Peak of excitement and capacity to control self
18. Rapidity of buildup to crying state
19. Irritability during the examination
20. General assessment of kind and degree of activity
21. Tremulousness
22. Amount of startling
23. Lability of skin color—measuring autonomic lability
24. Lability of states during entire examination
25. Self-quieting activity—attempts to console self and control state
26. Hand-to-mouth activity

From Lester, B. M. and T. B. Brazelton, "Cross-cultural assessment of neonatal behavior" in D. A. Wagner and H. W. Stevenson, (Eds.), *Cultural Perspective on Child Development.* © 1982 W. H. Freeman and Company, New York. Reprinted by permission.

So far, we have discussed a number of different reflexes of the newborn and also outlined several important infant states. Next, we discuss an important activity of infants—eating—focusing on the pros and cons of breast feeding and the scheduled feeding versus demand feeding controversy.

Eating Behavior

Because young infants are growing so rapidly, they must consume approximately 50 calories per day for each pound they weigh—more than twice an adult's requirement per pound. Most experts agree that young infants should be fed several times a day, but there is controversy as to just how this should be accomplished.

For years, psychologists have debated whether breast feeding of an infant has substantial benefits over bottle feeding. The growing consensus is that breast feeding is superior for the infant's health (e.g., Nutrition Committee, 1978). It is believed that breast feeding allows the neonate to obtain milk that is clean and digestible and that helps to immunize the newborn from diseases. Breast-fed babies also gain weight more rapidly than bottle-fed babies. Nonetheless, even with such strong recommendations for breast feeding, it has been estimated that only about half of mothers nurse their newborns, and even fewer do so several months into infancy. The dramatic increase in working mothers undoubtedly has contributed to the failure of many women to breast-feed their young infant. Convenience is the reason most often cited by mothers as to why they do not breast-feed their offspring.

Some years ago, a great deal of controversy surrounded the issue of whether a baby should be fed on demand or on a regular schedule. For example, John Watson (1928) argued that **scheduled feeding** was superior because he believed that it would increase the likelihood that the child would become orderly and controlled. An example of a recommended schedule for newborns was four ounces of formula every six hours. In recent years, **demand feeding,** in which the timing of the feeding as well as the amount are determined by the infant, has become more popular.

Child Development Concept Table 4.1 summarizes our discussion of the infant's reflexes, states, and activities. Now, we discuss the course of physical growth and motor development during the infant years.

The Assessment of Cuddliness on the Brazelton Neonatal Behavioral Assessment Scale

Score	Infant Behavior
1	The infant resists being held and continually pushes away, thrashes, and stiffens.
2	The infant resists being held most of the time.
3	The infant does not resist but does not participate either, acting like a rag doll.
4	The infant eventually molds into the examiner's arms after considerable nestling and cuddling efforts by the examiner.
5	The infant usually molds and relaxes when initially held, nestling into the examiner's neck or crook of the elbow. The infant leans forward when held on the examiner's shoulder.
6	The infant always molds at the beginning, as described above.
7	The infant always molds initially with nestling and turns toward body and leans forward.
8	The infant molds and relaxes, nestles and turns head, leans forward on the shoulder, fits feet into cavity of other arm, and all of the body participates.
9	All of the above take place, and in addition, the infant grasps the examiner and clings.

From *In the Beginning: Development in the First Two Years,* by J. F. Rosenblith and J. E. Sim-Knight. Copyright © 1985 by Wadsworth, Inc. Reprinted by permission of Brooks/Cole Publishing Company, Monterey, California.

Child Development Concept Table 4.1   Reflexes, States, and Activities

Concept	Processes/Related Ideas	Characteristics/Description
Reflexes	Their nature	The newborn no longer is viewed as a passive, empty-headed organism. The activities to sustain life are present at birth. Physically, newborns are limited, and reflexes govern the neonate's movements. The Moro reflex is a vestige of our primate ancestry. Some reflexes are important in the baby's life, such as crying in response to pain, and sucking. Others are less useful. A number of reflexes present at birth, such as blinking and coughing, persist through life, while others disappear in several months.
	Sucking	Sucking is an important means of obtaining nutrition, as well as a pleasurable, soothing activity, for infants. Nonnutritive sucking is of interest to some infant researchers because infants stop sucking when they attend to something. There is considerable individual variation in the infant's nutritive sucking, and it often takes an infant several weeks to develop a coordinated sucking style.
	Crying and smiling	Crying and smiling are affective behaviors that are important in the infant's communication with the world. Infants' earliest cries are reactions to discomfort. The sounds of infant crying are highly differentiated. Considerable debate has been generated—especially by behaviorists and ethologists—regarding how much parents should soothe and attend to infant crying. A reflexive smile appears early in the life of the infant, while social smiling occurs later, usually by two to three months of age.
States	Classification	Researchers have put together different classifications of infant states. One such classification that is widely used involves seven categories of infant states, including deep sleep, drowsy, alert and focused, and inflexibly focused.
	The sleeping-waking cycle	Newborns usually sleep for 16 to 17 hours a day. This sleep does not always follow a rhythmic pattern. By one month, most infants are sleeping longer at night, and by four months, they usually have moved even closer to adultlike sleeping patterns. Researchers have been interested in the REM sleep of infants. This rapid eye movement sleep, during which children and adults are most likely to dream, occurs much more in early infancy than in adulthood, accounting for about half of neonatal sleep. The high percentage of REM sleep may function as a self-stimulatory device, or it may promote brain development.
	The Brazelton Neonatal Behavioral Assessment Scale	This measure, named after well-known pediatrician T. Berry Brazelton, not only is being widely used as a clinical device to assess the neurological integrity of the newborn but also is used as a measure of infant development in many research studies. The NBAS consists of 26 categories and involves extensive assessment of infant states.
Eating behavior	Breast versus bottle feeding	There are many health advantages to breast feeding, but a large portion of American mothers choose to bottle-feed their infants, mainly for reasons of convenience.
	Scheduled versus demand feeding	Some years ago, scheduled feeding was thought to increase the likelihood that a child would become controlled. In recent years, however, demand feeding, in which the timing of the feeding as well as the amount are determined by the infant, has become more popular.

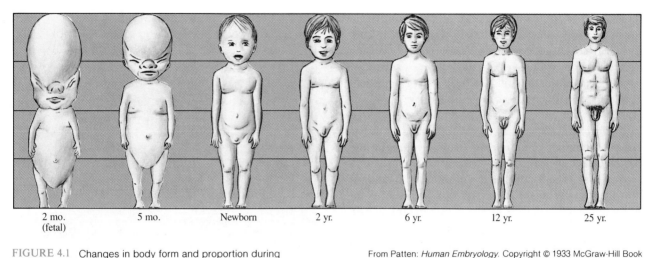

| 2 mo. (fetal) | 5 mo. | Newborn | 2 yr. | 6 yr. | 12 yr. | 25 yr. |

FIGURE 4.1 Changes in body form and proportion during prenatal and postnatal growth.

From Patten: *Human Embryology.* Copyright © 1933 McGraw-Hill Book Company. Reprinted by permission.

Physical Growth and Motor Development

Physically, newborns are admittedly limited. Newborns are tiny. From head to heels, they may be about 20 inches long and weigh seven pounds. They are bound by where you put them, and they are at the mercy of their bodily needs. Their heart beats twice as fast as a grownup's—120 beats a minute—and they breathe twice as fast as an adult does—about 33 times a minute. They may urinate as many as 18 times and move their bowels from 4 to 7 times in 24 hours. They sleep 14 to 18 hours of their 24-hour day. On the average, they are alert and comfortable for only 30 minutes in a 4-hour period.

The infant's pattern of physical development during the first two years of life is exciting. At birth, the neonate has a gigantic head (relative to the rest of its body) that flops around in an uncontrollable fashion; he or she also possesses reflexes that are dominated by evolutionary movements. In the span of twelve months, the infant becomes capable of sitting anywhere, standing, stooping, climbing, and probably walking. During the second year, growth decelerates, but rapid increases in such activities as running and climbing occur.

In this section, we examine how the infant's physical growth and motor development increases rapidly over the first two years of life.

The First Year

Among the important growth patterns that characterize life in the first year are those pertaining to cephalocaudal and proximodistal sequences, gross motor skills, and fine motor skills.

Cephalocaudal and Proximodistal Patterns   The **cephalocaudal pattern** suggests that the greatest growth always occurs at the top of the person—the head—with physical growth in size, weight, and feature differentiation gradually working its way down from top to bottom (e.g., neck, shoulders, middle trunk, and so on). This same pattern is manifested within the head area because the top parts of the head—the eyes and brain, for example—grow faster than the lower portions—such as the jaw. An illustration of this type of growth pattern is shown in Figure 4.1. As shown in the figure, an extraordinary proportion of the total body is occupied by the head at birth, but by the time the individual reaches maturity, this proportion is almost cut in half.

A second pattern of development—called the **proximodistal pattern**—suggests that the pattern of growth starts at the center of the body and moves toward the extremities. An example of this is the early maturation of muscular control of the trunk and arms as compared with that of the hands and fingers.

In addition to cephalocaudal and proximodistal growth patterns in infancy, it also is important to consider what are called **gross motor skills** (those involving large muscle activities, like moving one's arms or walking) and **fine motor skills** (those involving more fine-grained movements, such as finger dexterity).

Gross Motor Skills   At birth, the infant has no appreciable coordination of the chest or arms. By three or four months of age, however, two striking accomplishments occur in turn. The first is the infant's ability to hold the chest up while in a facedown position. The other is the ability to reach for objects placed within the infant's direct line of vision, without, of course, making any consistent contact with the objects (because the two hands don't work together and the coordination of vision and grasping is not yet possible). A little later, there is further progress in motor control: By five months, the infant can sit up with some support and grasp objects, and by six months, the child can roll over when lying in a prone position.

At birth, the newborn is capable of supporting some weight with the legs. This is proven by formal tests of muscular strength. These tests use a specially constructed apparatus to measure the infant's leg resistance as the foot is pulled with a calibrated spring device. This ability is also evidenced by the infant's partial support of its own weight when held upright by an adult. If the child is given enough support by the adult, some forward movement can actually be seen in a built-in stepping reflex, which disappears in a few months. Each leg is lifted, moved forward, and placed down, as if the infant were taking a series of steps. However, the sequence lasts only two or three steps, and, of course, the infant does not have sufficient balance or strength to execute the movement independently.

It is not until 8 or 9 months of age that the infant can walk with limited help from an adult. Sometime later (perhaps 10 or 11 months), the infant can support himself or herself standing alone, pull up into a standing position, and finally (perhaps by 13 or 14 months) walk.

At what age can infants hold up their chests?

The actual month at which some milestone occurs may vary by as much as 2 to 4 months, particularly among older infants. What remains fairly uniform, however, is the sequence of accomplishments.

A summary of important gross motor skills that reflect a cephalocaudal sequence is shown in Table 4.2.

Fine Motor Skills   The motor pathways to the brain mature sooner for areas in the center of the body than for areas at the extremities. However, coordination also progresses on the basis of sensorimotor linkages in the central nervous system. The sensory and motor control centers in the brain develop faster than the brain's ability to coordinate them. Environmental information picked up through the five senses (and registered in the **sensory cortex**) must be coordinated with an action stimulated by the **motor cortex.** When the infant reaches for an object, for example, the brain center that directs the movement must be in touch with the center that detects where the object is (perhaps the visual cortex). But that communication is governed by the **association areas of the cortex,** which develop later than the sensory and motor areas.

Some specific landmarks in the development of motor control and sensorimotor coordination follow. The focus on "eye and hand" is dictated by the importance placed

Table 4.2 Milestones of Gross Motor Development in the First Year of Life Reflecting a Cephalocaudal Sequence

Age in Months	Control of		
	Head	Trunk and Arms	Legs
Birth			
1	Side to side movement		Limited support stepping reflex
2	Hold head and chin up		
3		Hold chest up in facedown position	
4		Reach for objects in sight (without success)	
5	Head erect in sitting position		
6		Sit up with some support	
7		Roll over in prone position	
8			Walk with assistance
9			
10			Support self alone
11			Pull self up in standing position
12			
13			Walk alone
14			

on this system in many theories of development (e.g., Piaget, 1954; Bruner, 1973) and by our greater knowledge of this as opposed to other sensorimotor systems. Sensorimotor coordination is considered again in the next chapter, where we explore Piaget's theory of cognitive development in greater detail.

From birth to one month, the infant shows little coordination of any sort but will briefly follow a slowly moving object, such as a hand or a light, until the object is out of the immediate perceptual field. In the next two or three months, visual pursuit becomes more intricate; the infant may follow the object in different directions and planes and will persist in viewing it for longer periods of time.

Manipulation of objects lags somewhat behind visual pursuit and exploration of objects. For example, the infant does not systematically grasp and hold onto objects until four or five months. Prior to this, the infant might make brief contact with objects, reach for them, or hold them briefly if they are placed in the hands by someone. Toward the end of the first year (9 to 12 months), the infant becomes able to grasp, finger, and manipulate objects with more subtle use of the thumb, palm, and forefinger. The child may also hold an object in each hand, alternately inspect each, and bang the objects together.

An overview of some of the important developments in fine motor skills during the first year is presented in Table 4.3.

The Second Year

There is a deceleration in growth during the second year of the infant's life. The average infant gains approximately 5 inches in height and 5 to 6 pounds in weight. Somewhere around the last few months of the first year of life, and extending well into the second year, the infant begins to eat less. The plump infant gradually changes into a leaner, more muscular child during the second year. The brain also grows more slowly now. Head circumference, which increased by approximately 4 inches during the first year, increases only by about 2 inches this year. By the end of the first year, the brain has attained approximately two-thirds of its adult size, and by the end of the second year, about four-fifths of its adult size. During the second year, eight more teeth erupt to go along with the six to eight that appeared during the first year. By their first birthday, many infants have moved from an awkward, upright standing position to walking without support. Gross motor skills, such as walking, are considerably refined in the second year.

Table 4.3	Important Developments in the First Year of Life in Fine Motor Skills	

Age in Months	Coordinations	
	Visual Pursuit	Use of Hands
1	Follow slowly moving object	
2		
3	Sustain viewing of objects	
4	Follow object in different	Systematically grasp and hold
5	directions and planes	objects
6		
7		
8		
9		Finger objects
10		
11		Hold objects in each hand and
12		inspect them

Gross Motor Skills   Several months into the second year, the infant may be able to run and can sit down on a chair unassisted if the chair is short (when the seat is about 10 inches off the floor). At about 18 months, the infant can climb stairs, by 20 months walk downstairs with one hand held, and by 24 months run efficiently without falling very often. Between 18 and 24 months, the toddler (the name often given to the infant who is in the second year of life) enters the "runabout age"—scurrying from place to place, throwing caution to the wind, and evidencing no concern for the danger of his or her ventures.

The development of walking and running skills is important for the infant's emotional as well as physical development. They provide infants with a sense of mastery of their world. Initially, the infant performs very poorly at walking and running, but during the course of the second year will pick himself or herself up time and time again to face the world and test reality.

Fine Motor Skills   What is the development of fine motor skills during the second year of life like? Frank and Teresa Caplan (1981) describe it this way:

The way she handles objects that go together is a good illustration of the halfway state the baby has reached.

She puts her doll's sock next to its foot, for example, but cannot carry the operation further. She does the same thing with her own shoe, indicating that she knows where it belongs by holding it against her foot. She recognizes that her action is incomplete, gestures to any nearby adult for help, and gives a grunt of satisfaction when the task is performed for her. Her intentions clearly outrace her abilities at this point, a most frustrating state of affairs. From the baby's point of view, unfamiliar objects are expressly made to be investigated, usually by being pulled apart. Doors that open and shut and drawers that pull out are much more interesting than his own small toys. If he can reach nothing else, his clothing will do. A period of silence in the playpen can often mean that he is busily pulling his garments off. Mothers who do not look on this particular activity with favor may come to tolerate it more easily if they regard it as an important prelude to their child's learning to dress himself. (p. 7)

An overview of both second-year gross and fine motor skills is shown in Table 4.4. We have described how gross and fine motor skills unfold during the first and second years of life. Next, we look at another important consideration about the development of motor skills—their rhythmic nature.

Table 4.4 Gross and Fine Motor Development During the Second Year	
Gross Motor	**Fine Motor**
Visually monitors walking, watching placement of feet in order to be able to deal with obstacles in path by avoiding them	Turns pages of a book, one at a time
Runs, but generally lacks ability to start efficiently or stop quickly	Manipulates more freely with one hand; alternates from one hand to the other
Jumps crudely with two-foot takeoff	Has fully developed right- or left-handedness
Walking rhythm stabilizes and becomes even	Increased smoothness of coordination in fine motor movements
Goes up and down stairs alone without alternating feet	
Can walk approximately on line	
Likes to walk on low walls with one hand held	
Can walk a few steps on tiptoe	
Can be trusted alone on stairs	
Can walk backward 10 feet	
Can quickly alternate between sitting and standing	
Tries to balance self on either foot, not yet successfully	
Is sturdy on feet; less likely to fall	
Still geared to gross motor activity	

Reprinted by permission of Grosset & Dunlop from *The Second Twelve Months of Life* by Frank and Theresa Caplan. Copyright © 1977 by Frank and Theresa Caplan.

Rhythmic Motor Behavior

During the first year of life, rapid, repetitive movement of the limbs, torso, and head is common. Such **rhythmic motor behavior**—kicking, rocking, waving, bouncing, banging, rubbing, scratching, swaying—has intrigued scientists for many years. These infant motor behaviors stand out not only because they occur frequently, but also because of the pleasure infants seem to derive from performing the acts.

Explanations of rhythmic motor behavior have been numerous. Arnold Gesell (1954) saw rocking as a specific stage in development, but warned (Gesell & Amatruda, 1941) that persistent rhythmic motor behavior was a sign of developmental delay or an impoverished environment. Jean Piaget (1952) referred to kicking and waving as "secondary circular reactions," a stage of sensorimotor development when infants attempt to repeat a behavior that has an interesting effect on their environment. Psychoanalysts have interpreted rocking as the infant's attempt to establish relations with an "aloof" mother (Brody & Axelrad, 1970). And pediatricians have suggested that head banging is due to a bad temper (Levy & Patrick, 1928). In one investigation, mothers

of 200 infants were questioned about their infants' rhythmic behavior (Kravitz & Boehm, 1971). It was concluded that rhythmic behavior has no neurological explanation, a conclusion similar to that reached in a review of the functions of rhythmic behavior (Mitchell & Etches, 1977).

Esther Thelen (1981), however, believes that rhythmic behavior in infancy serves a more important developmental function than it has been ascribed in the past. She believes that rhythmic motor cycles serve an important adaptive function for infants in their first year of life; namely, they represent an important transition between uncoordinated activity and complex, coordinated motor behavior. She conducted extraordinarily detailed observations of 20 normal infants from the time they were four weeks old until they were one year old. More than 16,000 bouts of rhythmic behavior were observed. Infants generally spent about 5 percent of their time performing this type of behavior, but some infants at some ages performed rhythmic movements as much as 40 percent of the time they were being observed. The 47 distinct movements observed included variations of kicking, waving, bouncing, scratching, banging, rubbing, thrusting, swaying, and twisting. When stereotyped movements were grouped by body part and posture, their frequencies showed characteristic developmental profiles over the first year, as shown in Figure 4.2. Rhythmic leg behavior, for example, gradually increased at about one month, peaked at five to six months, and then declined. Rhythmic arm movements also gradually increased, but their first occurrence and peak frequency were later than for rhythmic leg movements. If all rhythmic cycles are summed, the age of peak frequency is six to seven months, with a small but real decline in the last few months of the year (Thelen, 1979).

Rhythmic stereotypies do seem to represent an important transition between uncoordinated activity and complex, coordinated, voluntary motor control. For example, kicking movements peaked just before the onset of locomotion and declined dramatically in the last third of the year. Rocking on hands and knees appeared just before crawling, and rhythmic hand and arm movements appeared before complex manual skills.

If rhythmic stereotypies indeed span the stages between immature motor coordination and full voluntary behavior, infants with developmental delays should show not only retarded onset ages but also comparatively slower onsets of integrated behavior. Thus, once acquired, rhythmic stereotypies should tend to persist longer in these infants. Although systematic observations of the full developmental course, both onset and decline, of stereotypies in retarded infants have not been reported, stereotypies in general are common in retarded children, especially those in institutions. Stereotypies were observed to be the primary mode of expression of affect, social encounter, and object exploration in Down's syndrome infants (Wolff, 1968).

A dramatic confirmation of the developmental prediction of persistent stereotypy comes from Selma Fraiberg's (1977) studies of infants blind from birth. Motor development in blind infants was characteristically uneven. Blind infants attained postural milestones such as sitting alone, "bridging" on hands and knees, and standing at ages comparable to sighted infants. Their locomotor development was severely delayed, however,

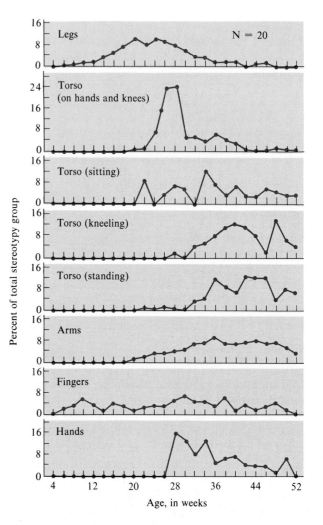

FIGURE 4.2 Frequency of rhythmic motor behavior in the first year of life. Frequencies are expressed as a percentage of the total bouts of rhythmical behavior observed in the sterotypy group at each age. The bouts are grouped by body parts. Data have been pooled for the sample.

probably due to a lack of visual motivation to move forward. In normal infants, for example, crawling follows very soon after the infant assumes the hands and knees posture. In blind infants, there may be four or more months delay between these events. Nonetheless, all the infants rocked vigorously in sitting, hands and knees, and

standing postures, and unlike in normal infants, this rocking did not disappear. In Selma Fraiberg's words,

> In the blind infant, it (rhythmic activity) may be more prolonged because, at each point along the gross motor sequence, the self-initiated mobility that should follow upon the new posture is delayed. (p. 217)
>
> Thus, a child with good control of his trunk in a bridging posture, with "readiness" we would say for creeping, might be observed on all fours, rocking steadily, "ready to go" with "no place to go." The motor impetus, which normally leads to mobility was exercised in a vacuum. Again, typically, when mobility was achieved, the stereotyped rocking was extinguished. (p. 278)

As we have seen thus far, infancy is a period of considerable physical growth and development. Next, we look at some important changes in the brain and nervous system during this time frame.

The Brain

As the infant walks, talks, runs, shakes a rattle, smiles, and frowns, changes in the brain are occurring. Consider that the infant began life as a single cell and that in nine months was born with a brain and nervous system that contained some 10 to 100 billion neurons. Indeed, at birth, the infant likely had all of the neurons it was going to have in its entire life. But at birth and in early infancy,

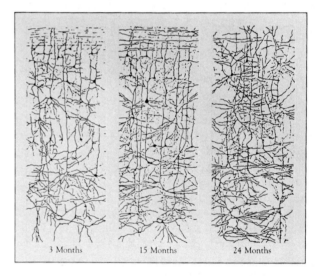

FIGURE 4.3 Notice the dramatic spreading of dendrites during the first two years of life. Dendrites are the receiving part of the neuron, the basic cellular unit of the brain. The dendrites make up about 95 percent of the surface area of neurons.

the connectedness of all of these neurons was impoverished. As shown in Figure 4.3, as the infant moves from birth to two years of age, the interconnections of neurons increase dramatically as the dendrites of neurons branch out.

Child Development Concept Table 4.2   Physical Growth and Motor Development

Concept	Processes/Related Ideas	Characteristics/Description
First year	Its nature	Growth during the first year is very rapid.
	Principles of growth	The cephalocaudal pattern refers to growth from the top down, and the proximodistal pattern indexes growth from the center out. These two growth patterns are apparent in the infant's development.
	Development of motor skills	Both gross (large muscle) and fine (more delicate, fine-grained) motor skills undergo considerable change in the first year. By the eighth to ninth month, the infant can walk with assistance. At 4 months of age, the infant can hold objects, and by 11 to 12 months of age, the infant can hold objects in each hand and inspect them.
Second year	Its nature	Growth decelerates during the second year. The average infant gains 5 inches in height and 5 to 6 pounds in weight. The brain grows more slowly. Gross motor skills, such as walking, are considerably refined in the second year.
	Gross and fine motor skills	The infant becomes much more proficient at walking and running by the second birthday. There also is increased refinement of fine motor skills, as evidenced by the infant turning the pages of a book one page at a time and developing right- or left-handedness.
Rhythmic motor behavior	Its nature	During the first year of life, rapid, repetitive movement of the limbs, torso, and head is common. There have been many explanations of its purpose.
	The role of rhythmic stereotypies in development	Thelen believes that rhythmic stereotypies represent an important link between reflexive, uncoordinated motor behavior in early infancy and later, more coordinated, more mature voluntary motor actions. Such stereotypies are much more frequent in the second half of the first year than in the first half. Rhythmic stereotypies may persist longer in abnormal infants.
The brain	Nature of change	There is a great deal of brain development in the first two years of life. Dendritic spreading is dramatic in these first two years. Some important changes in neurotransmitters likely are occurring as well, but their precise determination has yet to be accurately charted.

Undoubtedly, neurotransmitters are changing during prenatal and the infant years as well, but very little is known about such changes at this time (Parmelee & Sigman, 1983). However, with regard to one area of the brain (prefrontal region) and one neurotransmitter (dopamine), researchers have found some interesting changes in developing monkeys (Goldman-Rakic, Isseroff, Schartz, & Bugbee, 1983). The concentration of dopamine in the prefrontal region, generally viewed as the area where higher cognitive functions such as problem solving occur, peaks at 5 months of age, declines until 18 to 24 months, and then increases again at two to three years of age. These changes in concentrations of dopamine may reflect a switching from growth and nutritional functions to neurotransmitter function for this substance. Such speculation only begins to scratch the surface of the important role that neurotransmitters might play in the early development of the brain.

Child Development Concept Table 4.2 summarizes our discussion of the many different aspects of physical growth and motor development during the infant years. Next, we explore the infant's fascinating sensory and perceptual development.

SENSORY AND PERCEPTUAL DEVELOPMENT

Because the newborn is capable of very few responses, for a long time it was difficult to assess what the infant sensed, perceived, or learned. In the past two decades, scientists have developed sophisticated techniques to make inferences about these matters. The prevailing view used to be that the newborn was a passive, empty-headed organism that perceived nothing, did nothing, and learned nothing. New evidence, however, has reversed this notion. The neonate is now regarded as an active individual exploring the environment and picking up information through primitive but nonetheless effective perceptual apparatus—that is, the eyes, ears, nose, mouth, and skin.

In the "Imagine" section that opened this chapter, you read about how the newborn comes into the world equipped with some very important sensory capabilities that serve him or her in dealing with the world. But what are sensation and perception anyway? Can a newborn see, and if so, what can it perceive? And what about the other senses—hearing, smell, taste, touch, and pain— what are they like in the newborn, and what is the nature of their development? These are among the intriguing questions we now explore.

What Are Sensation and Perception?

How does a newborn know that his mother's skin is soft, rather than rough? How does a 5-year-old know what color her hair is? How does an 8-year-old know that summer is warmer than winter? How does a 10-year-old know that a firecracker is louder than a cat's meow? These infants and children "know" these things because of their senses. All information comes to the infant through the senses. Without vision, hearing, touch, taste, smell, and other senses, the infant's brain would be isolated from the world, and he or she would live in dark silence—a tasteless, colorless, feelingless void. Quite clearly, understanding the nature of these senses and how infants perceive their world is an important aspect of understanding their development.

Sensation occurs when information contacts sensory receptors—for example, the eyes, ears, tongue, nostrils, and skin. The sensation of hearing occurs when waves of pulsating air are collected by the outer ear and transmitted through the bones of the middle ear to the cochlear nerve. The visual sensation occurs as rays of light contact the two eyes and become focused on the retina. **Perception** is the interpretation of what is sensed. For example, the information about physical events that contacts the ears may be interpreted as musical sounds, a human voice, or noise. The physical energy transmitted to the retina may be interpreted as a particular color, pattern, or shape.

As with most aspects of development, child developmentalists have different theories about the nature of perceptual development. The two most often discussed theories of perceptual development are examined in Focus on Child Development 4.2, which presents an overview of the constructivist approach of Jean Piaget and the ecological view of James and Eleanor Gibson. Next, we study the aspect of infant perception that has been given the most attention—visual perception.

Visual Perception

How do we see? Anyone who has ever taken photographs while on vacation can appreciate the miracle of vision. The camera is no match for it. Consider a favorite scenic spot that you visited and photographed some time in the past. Compare your memory of this spot to your snapshot. Although your memory may be faulty, there is little doubt that the richness of your perceptual experience is not captured in the picture. The sense of depth that you felt at this spot probably is not conveyed by the snapshot. Nor is the subtlety of the colors you perceived or the intricacies of textures and shapes. Human vision is highly complex, and its development is complex as well.

Psychologist William James called the perceptual world of the newborn "a great blooming, buzzing confusion" (James, 1890, p. 488). Is visual perception by newborn infants actually consistent with this quote? Almost 100 years later, we have learned that the answer is no. There recently has been a burst of research on visual perception by infants, including newborn infants only minutes or hours old. To sum up this research with one simple statement: Infants' perception of visual information is *much* more advanced than previously thought.

FOCUS ON CHILD DEVELOPMENT 4.2

"SLICES" OF SPACE AND "EYES" IN THE BACK OF YOUR HEAD

Sit up and look around the room that surrounds you. Although you may not realize it, as you take in the room, your eyes are almost constantly moving. They move two or three times a second, and they provide visual data only when they pause between movements. The angle of highest acuity is extremely small—only about 2 degrees. So, each fixation is giving you high-resolution information about only a very limited "slice" of space. It is as if you were trying to examine a totally dark room armed only with a narrow-beam flashlight that you could move around. But think for a moment. Rapid fixations are not what you experience—what you experience is a stable room extended in space around you (Hochberg, 1978). You even experience the room behind your head where you cannot visually sense it (Attneave & Farrar, 1977). What is the basis for such experience?

The **constructivist approach** has a provocative answer—what you experience is a construction based on the sensory input from your eyes plus information retrieved from your memory. It is a kind of **representation** of the world you build up in your mind, as shown in the bottom left figure.

The constructivist view has important implications for the study of perceptual development. It suggests that many changes in perception reflect changes in how the infant or child constructs a representation of his or her world. The constructivist approach argues that, as the infant and child's memory develops, changes in long-term memory knowledge play an important role in how the infant or child perceives the world.

In the next chapter, we explore the exciting question of whether young infants have memory, and if so, when it emerges. While developmental psychologist Jean Piaget is

Jean Piaget, the famous Swiss psychologist. What was Piaget's view of children's perception?

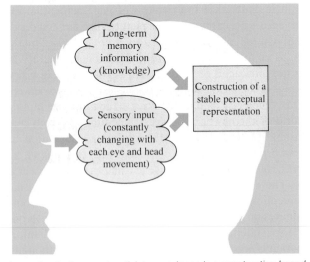

According to the constructivist, experience is a construction based on visual sensory input plus information retrieved from memory.

best known for his constructivist view of intelligence in children (which we also discuss in the next chapter), he also viewed perceptual development in constructivist terms (Bornstein, 1984).

Another group of perception theorists, however, believes that the constructivist approach does not accurately portray the development of perception. The **direct perception** or **ecological view** of James J. and Eleanor Gibson has stimulated a great deal of interest among child developmentalists and also has spawned a number of intriguing research inquiries. To understand the ecological approach, look at the figure below and ask yourself this question: Are the telephone poles of equal height? If you answered, "Yes," you are correct (assuming that the ground is flat). But how did you know? Gibson (1979) points out that there is an invariant in the visual information in the environment and that this invariant specifies the constancy in height—indeed, it specifies your own height in relation to the telephone poles. Note the point in the figure where the horizon line intersects each of the poles—there is a constant ratio between the length of a pole above this point and the length of a pole below it (the ratio is about 2:1 in this drawing). This ratio is a **perceptual invariant,** and, according to Gibson, is what tells you that the height of the poles is constant. Further, the point where the horizon intersects each pole shows the height of your eyes above the ground (the point would be even with your eyes if you were standing right next to the pole). If you do not believe this, find some level ground with telephone poles and look at the point where the horizon intersects each pole. Then stand on something (maybe your car) and look at the poles again— the point of intersection will be noticeably higher.

Eleanor Gibson (1969), James J. Gibson (1979), and other ecological theorists argue that the invariants in stimulation to the infant's sensory receptors provide rich information about the world in which the infant lives. These aspects of the environment involve places (a room), objects (a face), and pictures (a picture of a face). Since these things are actually in the world, and since perceptual invariants specify their properties, the ecological theorists do not believe that the infant or child has to build up internal representations to perceive them. The infant or child needs only to attend to the appropriate information.

An important feature of the direct perception or ecological approach is its assumption that even complex things (such as the spatial layout of a room) can be perceived "directly" by picking up the invariants rather than engaging in any complex constructive activity (Michaels & Carello, 1981). If complex things can be perceived directly, perhaps they can be perceived at young ages, maybe even by very young infants. Thus, the direct perception or ecological approach has inspired investigators to search for the competencies of very young infants (Bower, 1982). These theorists and researchers do not deny that perception develops as infants and children grow. In fact, it is assumed that, as perceptual processes mature, a child becomes more efficient at discovering invariant properties in the environment that are available to his or her senses (Bornstein, 1984).

An example of invariants in a direct perception, ecological framework. The telephone poles in this display are all cut by the horizon in the same ratio. The proportion differs for objects of different heights. The line where the horizon cuts the tree is just as high above the ground as the point of observation, that is, the height of the observer's eye. Hence everyone can see his own eye-height on the standing objects of the terrain.

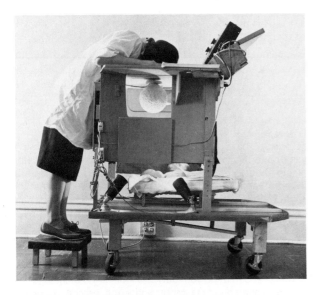

FIGURE 4.4 The "looking chamber" has been used to study visual preference in infants.

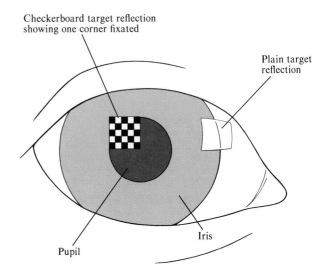

FIGURE 4.5 Schematic drawing of an infant's eye as seen by the experimenter in the test chamber when the infant has been visually exposed to checked and plain squares. The more the target reflection overlays the pupil, the greater the degree of fixation.

In the pages that follow, we first examine visual preferences in infancy, describing an important line of research that was pioneered by Robert Fantz. Then we turn to studies of a similar nature on perceiving simple, "lower-order" types of visual information, such as detail (visual acuity) and color. We will see that perception of these lower-order variables develops rather rapidly in some infants, sometimes by two months of age. The section continues with research on perception of "higher-order" information—information such as perceiving faces, objects, and aspects of objects, such as their "depth" or distance from the viewer, and their spatial relations to other objects in the environment. Much of this work on perceiving higher-order information was influenced by the direct perception or ecological approach to visual perception, pioneered by James J. and Eleanor Gibson, who you read about in Focus on Child Development 4.2.

Visual Preferences

Our tour of infant visual perception begins with the work of Robert Fantz (1958, 1961). In his research, Fantz placed infants in a "looking chamber," which had two visual displays on the ceiling of the chamber above the infant's head (see Figure 4.4). An experimenter viewed the infant's eyes by looking through a peephole. If the infant was fixating on one of the displays, the experimenter could see the display's reflection in the infant's eyes (as shown in Figure 4.5). In this manner, the experimenter could determine how long the infant looked at each display. The basic findings were simple: When presented with a pair of visual displays, an infant looks at one longer than the other. For instance, infants look longer at a display of stripes than at a display of a solid gray patch. This demonstrates that newborns can *see* and also that they can discriminate (tell the difference) between two dissimilar stimuli. Thus, the newborn's visual world is not completely a blooming confusion as James had thought.

Visual Acuity and Accommodation

Just how well can infants see? How good is a neonate's **visual acuity,** and how does it change through infancy? How effective is **visual accommodation** in newborns and very young infants? That is, how well can infants see patterns and objects at different distances?

"What you're looking at could make you a very rich man."

Extensions of Fantz's preference method have been used to measure the visual acuity of newborns. This technique takes advantage of the fact that infants prefer patterned to unpatterned displays. The adult observer monitors the infant's looking behavior—preferential looking at the patterned display is carefully evaluated and believed to indicate the visual acuity of the infant. In a review of the many studies evaluating the infant's visual acuity, it was concluded that the visual acuity of the newborn is about 20/600 in Snellen notation (the kind of notation used by optometrists) (Banks & Salapatek, 1983). This is about 30 times lower than adult visual acuity (20/20). But by six months of age, acuity appears to be 20/100 or higher (Banks & Salapatek, 1983).

A question related to visual acuity regards the effectiveness of visual accommodation, that is, maintenance of maximal visual acuity over a range of viewing distances. It was once believed that infant acuity was best for objects about 8 inches away and became much worse for objects nearer or further away. You may have read in books or magazines that a newborn baby might not see your face clearly unless you positioned your face about 8 inches away. Indeed, focusing errors by the eye of a newborn are much greater than those of a three-month-old. Surprisingly, however, this has little direct impact on infants' perception of near and far objects.

Perception of Color

Do one-month-old infants see colors? If so, do they see colors as well as normal adults? Or do they resemble adults who are partially color-blind in that only two out of three color receptors in the eye are functioning?

Normal adults with full color vision are referred to as "trichromats," in that three types of cones in the eye are functioning (cones are the receptors in the retina that underlie color vision). Many color-blind adults are "dichromats" in that only two of the three types of cones are functioning. There are three types of dichromats: (1) "protanopes," who lack cones most sensitive to red; (2) "deuteranopes," who lack cones most sensitive to green; and (3) "tritanopes," who lack cones most sensitive to blue. Thus, if infants are partially color-blind, do they resemble most closely protanopes, deuteranopes, or tritanopes?

Although a number of studies have addressed early development of color vision, most of the data have been ambiguous. Many earlier studies assessed infants' abilities to distinguish different colors but failed to control for the brightness of stimuli. The more recent investigations have suggested that (1) infants are not entirely color-blind, but (2) they might be partially color-blind, in the fashion of tritanopes (Bornstein, 1976; Pulos, Teller, & Buck, 1980).

Perception of Objects and Faces

The visual world of an adult human being contains much more than abstract patterns and colors. It is populated with objects in spatial arrangements. We perceive these objects as separate from the background as well as from other objects in our field of vision. Objects in our visual world maintain a kind of unity even when partially hidden from view. For example, if a chair in your living room is partly occluded by the coffee table in front of it, you still see the chair as complete. It does not look like *part* of a chair, but like a *whole* chair that is only partly visible from where you stand (Gibson, 1979).

How do infants perceive objects and faces?

Does the infant's visual world also consist of objects, or is the integrity of objects something that infants must learn? Some classic work on this fascinating problem was initiated by T. G. R. Bower in the 1960s. More recently, Bower's work has been extended and clarified by several investigators, including Elizabeth Spelke and her colleagues (Kellman & Spelke, 1979, 1981; Spelke & Born, 1982). In one condition of the Kellman and Spelke experiment, a habituation method was used. An infant viewed a rod with a block placed in front of it. The rod moved slightly to the left and to the right during viewing. After this first viewing episode, two test stimuli were shown to the infant. These were: (1) a complete rod with nothing in front of it, and (2) a rod with a gap and nothing in front of it. The result was that the infants looked longer at the rod with a gap than the complete rod. This suggests that the first phase of the experiment produced habituation. More importantly, habituation apparently was to the complete rod, even though only part of the rod was seen. Thus, the Kellman and Spelke experiment provides impressive evidence that partly occluded objects are perceived as units, even at only four months of age.

An important type of visual object is the face of another person. In an early study of perception of faces, Fantz (1966) found that two-month-old infants showed a preference for viewing a normal versus a rearranged

drawing of a face (see Figure 4.6). Furthermore, even newborns show differences in visual tracking when a moving face is shown as opposed to when a moving rearranged face is shown (Goren, Sarty, & Wu, 1975). So there is evidence suggesting that even newborns are sensitive to properties of faces.

Perception of Depth

The classic study of depth perception in infants was conducted by Eleanor Gibson and Richard Walk (1960) using the "visual cliff." A photograph of the visual cliff is shown in Figure 4.7. There is a central board above two checkerboard floors, forming a high "cliff" on one side and a shallow "cliff" on the other. But a sheet of glass is above both checkerboard floors, at roughly the same level as the central board. Thus, an infant can crawl all over the apparatus and never suffer a fall; yet, crawling on the deep side *appears* to be dangerous. An infant between 6 and 14 months of age is less likely to crawl on this deep side of the cliff than on the shallow side of the cliff. Apparently, then, 6- to 14-month-old infants have some ability to see depth.

Exactly how early in life does depth perception develop? Since younger infants do not crawl, this question has proven difficult to answer. Research with two- to four-month-olds has shown differences in heart rate when the

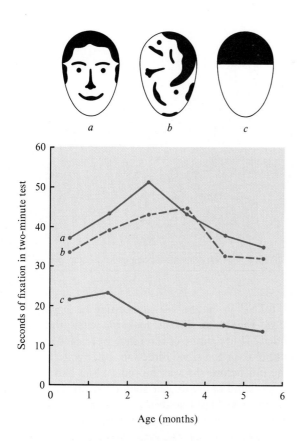

FIGURE 4.6   Adaptive significance of form perception was indicated by the preference that infants showed for a "real" face (a) over a scrambled face (b), and for both over a control (c). These results show the average time scores for infants of various ages when presented with the three face-shaped objects paired in all the possible combinations.

FIGURE 4.7   A child's depth perception is tested on the visual cliff. The apparatus consists of a board laid across a sheet of heavy glass, with a patterned material directly beneath the glass on one side and several feet below it on the other. Placed on the center board the child crawls to his mother across the "shallow" side. Called from the "deep" side, he pats the glass but despite this tactual evidence that the "cliff" is in fact a solid surface, he refuses to cross over to the mother.

infants are placed directly on the deep side of the visual cliff versus the shallow side of the cliff (Campos, Langer, & Krowitz, 1970). These heart-rate differences might imply depth perception at two to four months. However, an alternative interpretation is that young infants are responding to differences in some visual characteristic of the deep and shallow cliffs, with no actual knowledge of depth.

Fortunately, alternative techniques may reveal the depth-perception abilities of very young infants. For example, some recent studies by Albert Yonas, Carl Granrud, and their colleagues have taken advantage of the fact that infants tend to reach toward the *nearer* of two objects that they see. In one of their studies, the researchers found that five-and-a-half- and seven-month-olds also reach toward the *larger* of two objects, *if* these objects are viewed through one eye (Yonas, Granrud, & Pettersen, 1985). This finding suggests that, in the absence of binocular (two-eye) information, infants as young as five-and-a-half months (1) perceive depth and (2) use size as a cue for depth. Although infants under five-and-a-half months do not use size as a depth cue, they apparently can use other types of cues for depth (Granrud, Yonas, Smith, Arterberry, Glicksman, & Snorknes, 1984). Moreover, research using the habituation technique suggests that even twelve-week-old infants can perceive size independent of distance when viewing moving objects (Granrud, Arterberry, & Yonas, 1985).

Perception of Spatial Relations

As we move around through a new environment, we develop a sense of where things are located. But when we have learned where something is located, just what exactly have we learned? The question is: What frame of reference has been used in our learning the locations of objects? We might learn the location of an object relative to ourselves ("the box is directly to my right"). This is an example of using an "egocentric" frame of reference. Or we might learn the location of this same object relative to other objects either near or far away. This is an example of using a nonegocentric or "objective" frame of reference. Jean Mandler (1983) argues that adults use both egocentric and objective frames of reference, depending on the situation. For example, many of us learn the routes to new places in an egocentric way ("Go to Main Street, turn right, and then go straight ahead until you get to the shopping mall. Then turn right at the first light, and left at the light after that, and you will see my house on the corner on your right"). Yet, in other situations, an objective framework dominates (we realize that there must be a more direct route to a place we have visited before and then discover this route using "sense of direction").

If adults can use both egocentric and objective frames of reference, what about young infants? Jean Piaget (1971) argued that, in the first year of life, infants are restricted to egocentric orientation. Indeed, a number of recent empirical studies lend some support to this claim. For example, in a study conducted by Linda Acredolo (1978), infants 6, 11, and 16 months old were placed at one end of a room, from which position they could view two windows. The setup is shown in Figure 4.8.

A trial proceeded as follows: Three seconds after the sound of a buzzer, an experimenter appeared in one of the two windows, calling the infant's name and entertaining her with toys. The window at which the experimenter appeared was always the same (for a given infant). Thus, the infant learned to look toward that window when the buzzer was sounded. After an infant had learned which window to look toward, she was moved (by her mother) to the opposite side of the room (from

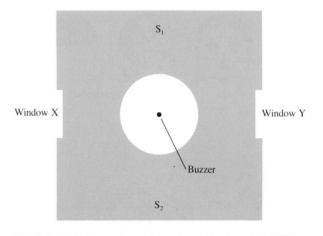

FIGURE 4.8   The experimental space used by Acredolo (1978).

"S_1" to "S_2" in Figure 4.8), and testing resumed. Which window should an infant look at when the buzzer sounded? If her frame of reference were egocentric, she should look in the same direction, relative to her body, as she did before she was moved (if she looked at the left-most window before, she should look at the left-most window now). This would be an incorrect response. If, however, the infant used an objective frame of reference, she should look in the opposite direction, relative to her body. This would be a correct response. The authors discovered egocentric responses were dominant for the 6- and 11-month-old infants. Only the 16-month-old infants consistently looked toward the correct window, indicating an objective frame of reference.

Acredolo's research supports Piaget's idea of egocentric reference in the first year of life. However, it should not be concluded that objective frames of reference are impossible for one-year-old infants. We must consider some additional factors, one of which is landmarks. As adults learning our way around a city, we are aware that landmarks help us to maintain our orientation. A similar principle holds true for young infants who are learning where in a room some event might occur. Acredolo (1978, Acredolo & Evans, 1980) has found a reduction in egocentric responding when landmarks are provided (one of the landmarks was a star around one of the windows).

Another important factor was discovered as well (Acredolo, 1979): Reduced levels of egocentric responding were found in infants tested in their own homes, as opposed to those tested in an unfamiliar environment. (Acredolo's original studies were conducted in laboratory environments.) Thus, the presence of landmarks and a familiar environment might help young infants to use objective frames of reference. Despite this qualification, infants' use of an objective frame of reference appears to show substantial development between 6 and 18 months of age.

The early emergence of objective frames of reference may derive from infants' body movements. As an infant starts to crawl around, the changing (egocentric) directions of stationary objects may become quite noticeable (what was on the right is now on the left after turning around). This may lead the infant to start attending to landmarks, and this puts him or her on the road to establishing true objective reference frames (Bremnar, 1985; Bryant, 1985). In any event, objective frames of reference are clearly in evidence by the end of the infancy period (two years). Indeed, there appear to be cases in which preschoolers find it difficult to use an egocentric frame of reference (Allen, Kirasic, & King, 1985).

We have covered a good deal of research on visual perception in infancy. Many fundamental aspects of vision are in working order by birth, and others are present by two months of age. Yet, perception is not complete by one or even two years of age. Many aspects of perception continue to grow more efficient and accurate during the childhood years.

Now that we have studied visual perception in some detail, let's focus on the development of other senses in infancy.

Other Senses

Humans have a number of senses other than vision that help to get information from "out there" to inside their heads. How powerful are these other senses in infancy? To find out, let's investigate the senses of hearing, smell, taste, touch, and pain.

Hearing

Scientists have been fascinated with the possibility that a fetus in the mother's womb can hear auditory stimuli. Pregnant mothers have reported movements by their babies in response to loud noises, and several weeks before birth, investigators have found that an auditory stimulus produces changes in the auditory system of the fetus (Sakabe, Arayama, & Suzuki, 1969).

It has been documented that, immediately after birth, infants can hear, although their sensory thresholds are somewhat higher than those of adults. That is, a stimulus must be louder to be heard by newborns than by adults. Given that hearing is less sensitive in newborns than adults, when and at what rate does it improve? We still do not have good information about this question in infants below the age of 6 months, but it appears that by the age of 24 months, infants are capable of hearing very high frequency sounds (19,000 Hz) just as effectively as adults (Aslin, Pisoni, & Jusczyk, 1983).

It may be somewhat misleading to discuss auditory perception as if it were completely separate from visual perception or from perception in any other modality. As Elizabeth Spelke (1979) points out, humans live in a world of objects and events that are heard, seen, and felt. When individuals look at and listen to an event simultaneously, they experience a unitary episode, not one that is visually and auditorily separated. Spelke (1979) has conducted research demonstrating that infants only four months old have **intermodal perception**—the ability to perceive auditory and visual events in a related, unified manner. We do not know if the human newborn has intermodal perception, but the finding that newborns make eye movements toward sounds (Wertheimer, 1961) suggests this possibility. Focus on Child Development 4.3 reveals some fascinating ideas about the intermodal world of the young infant.

Child Development Concept Table 4.3 summarizes our discussion of the infant's perception, including what sensation and perception are, theories of perceptual development, visual perception, and auditory perception. Now we look further at other senses, first studying the sense of smell.

FOCUS ON CHILD DEVELOPMENT 4.3

YELLOW KANGAROOS, GRAY DONKEYS, THUMPS, GONGS, AND FOUR-MONTH-OLD INFANTS

Imagine yourself playing basketball or tennis. There are obviously many visual inputs: the ball coming and going, other players moving around, etc. But there also are many auditory inputs: the sound of the ball bouncing or being hit and the grunts, groans, and curses emitted by yourself and others. There is also good correspondence between much of the visual and auditory information: When you see the ball bounce, you also hear a bouncing sound; when a player leaps, you hear his or her groan.

As Elizabeth Spelke (1979) has pointed out:

Humans live in a world of objects and events that can be seen, heard, and felt. When mature perceivers look and listen to an event simultaneously, they experience a unitary episode. (p. 626)

All of this is so commonplace that it scarcely seems worth mentioning. But consider the task of a very young infant with little practice at perceiving. Can he or she put vision and sound together as precisely as adults? Jean Piaget (1952), along with earlier thinkers (Berkeley, 1709; Mill, 1869), believed that the answer is no. Piaget claimed that intermodal perception is achieved only after a considerable period of learning to piece together visual and auditory information. However, the direct perception or ecological approach of James J. Gibson (1979) and Eleanor J. Gibson (1969; Gibson & Spelke, 1983) suggests an alternative view: Perhaps there is higher-order information that is *invariant* over the auditory or visual modalities. If so, it is possible that even young infants can perceive such information. Intermodal information might simply be another type of higher-order information that is readily perceived in infancy.

To test intermodal perception, Spelke (1979) performed three experiments with the following structure: Two simple films were shown side-by-side in front of a four-month-old infant. One film showed a yellow kangaroo bouncing up and down, and the other showed a gray donkey bouncing up and down (see the photo). There also was an auditory sound track—a repeating thump or gong sound. A variety of measures assessed the tendency of the infant to look at one film versus the other.

In Experiment 1, the animal in one of the films bounced at a slower rate than the animal in the other. And the sound track was in synchrony either with the film of the slow-bouncing animal or with the film of the fast-bouncing animal. Infants' first looks were more frequently toward the film that was "specified" by the sound track.

Experiments 2 and 3 explored two components of the relationship between the sound track and the matching film: common tempo and simultaneity of sounds and bounces. The findings showed that infants are sensitive to both of these components.

Spelke's clever demonstration suggests that infants only four months old "do not appear to experience a world of unrelated visual and auditory sensations. They can perceive unitary audible and visible events" (p. 636). However, a cautionary note comes from David Lewkowicz (1985), who failed to find evidence that four-month-old infants have bisensory perception of frequency of events. As Lewkowicz points out, the problem may have been that his procedure, which involved flashing checks and simple tones, was less naturalistic than Spelke's. On the positive side, Arlene Walker-Andrews and Elizabeth Lennon (1985) have reported evidence that five-month-olds have bisensory perception of information concerning changing distance of objects. Faced with a film of an approaching car and another film of a car driving away, a five-month-old will tend to look at the film that corresponds to a sound track (if the sound track is of a car sound getting louder, the infant tends to look more at the film of an approaching car).

Child Development Concept Table 4.3   The Nature of Sensation and Perception, Theories of Perceptual Development, Visual Perception, and Auditory Perception

Concept	Processes/Related Ideas	Characteristics/Description
What are sensation and perception?	Sensation	Sensation occurs when information contacts sensory receptors—for example, the eyes, ears, tongue, nostrils, and skin.
	Perception	Perception is the interpretation of what is sensed.
Theories of perception	Constructivist approach	The constructivist approach, advocated by Piaget, argues that what the child experiences is a construction based on a combination of sensory input and information retrieved from memory. Representation in the mind is important.
	Direct perception or ecological view	The Gibsons argue that such representation is not the way perception works. They believe that the infant picks up perceptual invariants in the environment. This view has generated considerable research on infant perception, particularly in terms of the infant's ability to perceive complex things. This view stresses that perceptual development occurs because the infant and child become more efficient at discovering invariant properties in the environment.
Visual perception	William James's perception	James believed that the world of the newborn was "a great blooming, buzzing confusion." Now we believe that the infant's visual perception is more advanced than previously thought. This view has been pioneered by the Gibsons' work.
	Visual preferences	Robert Fantz's research—by showing how infants prefer striped to solid patches—demonstrated that newborns can see.
	Visual acuity and accommodation	Acuity refers to how well an organism can see. Visual acuity is about 20/600 in the newborn, and by six months of age has improved to 20/100. Accommodation refers to acuity over a range of viewing distances. Focusing errors in this regard decrease with age.
	Color	Newborns likely are not entirely color-blind, but they might be partially color-blind.
	Perception of objects and faces	Infants as young as four months of age perceive partly masked objects as wholes. Infants as young as two months of age prefer to look at a normal rather than a rearranged face.
	Perception of depth	A classic study by Gibson and Walk demonstrated through the use of a visual cliff apparatus that infants as young as six months have depth perception.
	Spatial relations	An egocentric frame of reference characterizes the first year of life, with landmarks and familiarity being important variables in understanding spatial relations. The early emergence of objective frames of reference may derive from infants' body movements. Spatial perception develops throughout childhood.
Auditory perception	The fetus and newborn	Some research suggests that the fetus can hear several weeks before birth. It has been documented that, immediately following birth, newborns can hear, although their sensory thresholds are higher than those of adults.
	Intermodal perception	Much of our information comes through more than one sensory channel. Spelke's research suggests that infants as young as four months of age have intermodal perception because they perceive auditory and visual events in related, unitary episodes rather than in unrelated ways.

Smell

Asafetida is a substance obtained from the roots of plants from the *Ferula* genus. Once used in medicine, asafetida is bitter and extremely offensive to the adult nose. If you were forced to smell this substance, you would be likely to grimace and move away. Apparently, one-day-old infants have a similar reaction. An important study by Trygg Engen and his colleagues showed that infants less than 24 hours old make body and leg movements and show changes in respiration (breathing) when exposed to asafetida (Lipsitt, Engen, & Kaye, 1963). Further, the concentration of asafetida needed to produce these responses drops markedly over the first four days of life. Thus, the sense of smell is present at birth, and it appears to develop in the days immediately afterward. Other research by the same group of scientists showed that very young infants (32 to 68 hours of age) are not only sensitive to unpleasant odors, they can discriminate between two different unpleasant odors (Engen & Lipsitt, 1965).

Infants' sense of smell is fortunately not only for unpleasant odors. They apparently can recognize the smell of their mother's breasts (presumably pleasant). One study used the following procedure (MacFarlane, 1975): Two- to seven-day-old infants were exposed to two breast pads, one to their right and one to their left. One of these breast pads had been used by the infant's mother, while the other was clean. The finding was that infants spent more time turned toward their mother's pad than toward the clean pad, clearly demonstrating some sense of smell. However, it has not been shown that infants this young can actually recognize the smell of their own mother as opposed to that of other mothers. To test for such refined discrimination, MacFarlane (1975) conducted a study in which the clean breast pad was replaced by another mother's breast pad. Two-day-old infants showed no difference in turning to the breast pad of their own mother versus pads of other infants' mothers. It may not be until two weeks of age that infants can recognize their own mother's smell.

Taste

Anatomical studies of the taste buds in fetuses (Bradley & Stern, 1977) suggest that there might be taste sensitivity prior to birth (Acredolo & Hake, 1982). Indeed, one investigator found that, when saccharin was added to the amniotic fluid of a near-term fetus, increased swallowing was observed (Windle, 1940). In any event, sensitivity to sweetness is very well demonstrated in the sucking behavior of newborn infants (Lipsitt, Reilly, Butcher, & Greenwood, 1976; Crook & Lipsitt, 1976). When sucks on a nipple are rewarded with a water and sweetener (sucrose) solution, the amount of sucking increases. Yet, within a "burst" of sucking, the rate of sucking is slower for more-sweetened solutions than for less-sweetened solutions. This pattern suggests a form of "savoring" of sweet tastes by young infants (note that when you savor a taste, you swallow slowly, not quickly). Thus, it appears not only that newborns can taste sweet substances—they appear to enjoy such substances. Our "sweet tooth" comes early.

Taste in newborns also can be demonstrated by movements of face muscles. One researcher found that sweet stimulation was followed by movements that resulted in a smilelike expression, while sour stimulation caused a pursing of the lips (Steiner, 1979). And this was with infants only a few hours old! Indeed, similar facial responses to tastes were observed in premature infants, as well as in developmentally malformed neonates who lacked an intact cortex. Thus, distinguishing some tastes may not require much in the way of "higher mental processes." (Tell this to one of your gourmet friends.)

Touch

Just as newborns make reflexive movements in response to taste, they also perform such movements in response to touch. A touch to the cheek can produce a head-turning response, while a touch to the lips can produce sucking movements (Acredolo & Hake, 1982). An important use of touch is to perceive the physical features of objects, establishing connections with visual information. It is widely documented that one-year-old infants are able to use touch in this manner, and it appears that even six-month-old infants can use touch in this way (Acredolo & Hake, 1982). For example, in one study, six-month-old infants either looked at an object or explored it haptically (by touch) for 30 seconds. The object was either a cube or a ball. After the 30 seconds, the infants saw the object that they had played with beside another object, during which time their looking behavior was monitored. The infants preferred to look at the familiar object, even those who had only touched the object previously. Thus, it was concluded that six-month-old infants can perceive objects haptically and can relate haptic and visual information (Ruff & Kohler, 1978). Whether still younger infants can accomplish this feat has not yet been documented.

Pain

If and when you have a son and need to consider whether he should be circumcised, the issue of infants' pain perception will probably be important to you. Circumcision is usually performed on young boys about the third day of life. Will your young son experience pain if he is circumcised when he is three days old? Two investigations directed at this question indicated an increase in crying and fussing during the circumcision procedure (Anders & Chalemian, 1974; Emde, Harmon, Metcalf, Koenig, & Wagonfield, 1971). Another recent investigation also revealed that, when the male infant is circumcised, he experiences a considerable amount of stress (Gunnar, Malone, & Fisch, in press). Focus on Child Development 4.4 examines how this investigation was conducted as well as how the circumcision procedure provides information about the neonate's ways of coping with stress.

In our tour of the perceptual world of the infant, we have discussed a number of senses—vision, hearing, smell, taste, touch, and pain. For the most part, we have discussed these senses in isolation from each other. Next, we explore the fascinating idea that even very young infants can relate information about different sensory modalities.

The Relatedness of Different Sensory Dimensions

Is the young infant so competent that he or she can relate and integrate information from several different sensory dimensions? A growing group of developmental psychologists in the perception area (e.g., Gibson &

Spelke, 1983; Kagan, 1986) believe that the young infant possesses more sophisticated methods for processing information about the sensory world than was previously thought possible. One such area of sophisticated information processing for the young infant is the ability to relate information from different sensory domains. Spelke's (1979) finding (discussed in Focus on Child Development 4.3) that four-month-old infants experience a related auditory and visual world is consistent with a growing body of research that indicates that young infants can integrate information about different sensory modalities (Bahrick, 1983; Meltzoff & Borton, 1979; Rose, Gottfried, & Bridger, 1981; Starkey, Spelke, & Gelman, 1983; Wagner, Winner, Cicchetti, & Gardner, 1981).

The claim that a young infant can relate information from one sensory dimension to another has important theoretical ties. For example, let's see how the two main theoretical views described in Focus on Child Development 4.2 handle the idea of intermodal perception among young infants: The constructivist view of perception, reflected in Piaget's theory, argues that the main perceptual abilities, such as visual, auditory, and tactile, are completely uncoordinated at birth, and further, that young infants do not have intermodal perceptual abilities. According to Piaget, it only is through many months of sensorimotor interactions with the world that such intermodal perception is possible. By contrast, the direct perception or ecological perspective on perception offered by the Gibsons stresses that infants are born with some intermodal perceptual abilities or predispositions that enhance the early development of such abilities through experience.

The recent research pushing back the age barriers of when an infant can coordinate information from different senses is beginning to provide support for the direct perception or ecological view of the Gibsons. Still, there are enough inconsistencies and sufficient methodological difficulties in this research to keep alive a debate on the degree to which such complex perceptual capabilities are inborn or are constructed over a longer period of time through interaction with the world. Nonetheless, if research on intermodal perception continues to be verified with very young infants, the ecological interpretation will be difficult to refute.

FOCUS ON CHILD DEVELOPMENT 4.4

THE THREE-DAY-OLD MALE INFANT AND THE CIRCUMSTRAINT BOARD

The infant is one of 80 newborn males participating in a study of circumcision and his perception of pain. It is the third day of his life. One-half hour before blood is to be sampled from capillary veins in his heel, his behavioral state is observed. Using Brazelton's (1973) scale, the researchers rate the infant on a six-point scale ranging from deep sleep to crying every 30 seconds for 30 minutes. Then after the baseline blood sample is obtained, the infant is strapped to a circumstraint board so that the circumcision can be performed. A Gomco clamp procedure is used, and the boy is given a pacifier and the researchers attempt to soothe him during the surgery. During circumcision, the newborn's behavioral state continues to be rated along with other behaviors, such as straining against the circumstraint straps. Then 10 or more minutes after the circumcision, blood sampling is again performed. The researchers' primary interest is in the cortisol levels in the blood (Gunnar, Malone, & Fisch, in press). Prior research (e.g., Talbert, Kraybill, & Potter, 1976) has shown that it takes 10 or more minutes for blood cortisol levels to reach peak values after a stressful encounter. The infant's behavioral state also continues to be observed for up to four hours after the circumcision.

The researchers believe that routine circumcision provides an opportunity to evaluate the coping process of healthy neonates when faced with an apparently intense stressor in the absence of drugs or illness. The results indicated that the surgical procedure was clearly stressful. The infants cried intensely during the procedure, and adrenocortical steroids (measured by the cortisol level) were massively produced. The researchers indicated that it is rather remarkable that the newborn infant does not suffer serious consequences from the surgery. Rather, the circumcised infant displays remarkable resiliency and ability to cope. Even during the aversive surgery, soothing by caregivers seems to help calm the infant. Within several minutes after the surgery, the infant can nurse and interact in a normal manner with his mother (Marshall et al., 1982). And, if allowed, the newly circumcised neonate drifts into a deep state of sleep that seems to serve as a coping mechanism. As shown in the figure below, the percentage of time spent in deep sleep was greater in the 60 to 240 minutes after the circumcision than prior to the circumcision (when the baseline was assessed). The increase in deep sleep was occurring at the same time that blood cortisol levels were falling. Thus, deep sleep seems to function as an exquisite coping mechanism that allows the neonate to clear the high levels of cortisol that were produced during the stressful circumcision.

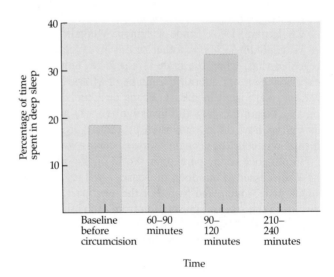

Percentage of time spent in deep sleep by male newborns before and after circumcision.

THINKING BACK, LOOKING AHEAD

Charting the course of growth processes and trying to determine how knowledge "out there" gets inside of the infant's head have fascinated developmental psychologists for many years. The infant's world is one of sensing and perceiving, of watching and listening, of touching and sensing warmth and coldness and pain, of tasting and smelling, of negotiating movement and space in this world. Among the intriguing themes of these aspects of the infant's world are those pertaining to the creature from outer space who seemed helpless, the Moro reflex (a vestige from the newborn's primate ancestry), sucking, crying, smiling, the rhythmic patterns of the sandman's spell, rattles, bells, pinpricks, cuddles, bottle feeding, breast feeding, cephalocaudal and proximodistal patterns, gross and fine motor skills, rhythmic stereotypies, "a great blooming, buzzing confusion," "slices" of space and "eyes" in the back of your head, the Gibsons and Piaget, directly perceiving and constructing the world, the looking chamber, 20/600 vision, distorted faces, visual cliffs, hearing fetuses, yellow kangaroos, gray donkeys, thumps, gongs, asafetida, taste buds, haptic exploration, the three-day-old male and the circumstraint board, and the relatedness of different sensory dimensions.

In the next chapter, we continue our study of the infant's world, turning to information about how infants learn, the nature of their cognition, and the manner in which they acquire language. Before we leave this chapter, though, consider the words of W. H. Auden in *Mundus et Infans:*

> . . . he cooperates
> With a universe of large and noisy feeling states
>   Without troubling to place
> Them anywhere special, for, to his eyes, Funnyface
>   Or Elephant as yet
> Mean nothing. His distinction between Me and Us
> Is a matter of taste; his seasons are Dry and Wet;
>   He thinks as his mouth does.

SUMMARY

I. Reflexes, states, and activities are important aspects of the newborn's development.
   A. The newborn no longer is viewed as a passive empty-headed organism. The activities to sustain life are present at birth. Physically, however, newborns are limited, and reflexes govern the neonate's movements. The Moro reflex is a vestige of our primate ancestry. Some reflexes are important in the baby's life, such as crying in response to pain, and sucking. Others are less useful. A number of reflexes present at birth, such as blinking and coughing, persist through life, while others disappear in several months.
      1. Sucking is an important means of obtaining nutrition, as well as a pleasurable, soothing activity, for infants. Nonnutritive sucking is of interest to some infant researchers because infants stop sucking when they attend to something. There is considerable individual variation in the infant's nutritive sucking, and it often takes an infant several weeks to develop a coordinated sucking style.
      2. Crying and smiling are affective behaviors that are important in the infant's communication with the world. Infants' earliest cries are reactions to discomfort. The sounds of infant crying are highly differentiated. Considerable debate has been generated—especially by behaviorists and ethologists—regarding how much parents should soothe and attend to infant crying. A reflexive smile appears early in the life of the infant, while social smiling occurs later, usually by two to three months of age.
   B. Information about states and activities emphasizes their classification, the sleeping-waking cycle, the Brazelton Neonatal Behavioral Assessment Scale, and eating behavior.
      1. Researchers have put together different classifications of infant states. One such classification that is widely used involves seven categories of infant states, including deep sleep, drowsy, alert and focused, and inflexibly focused.
      2. Newborns usually sleep for 16 to 17 hours a day. This sleep does not always follow a rhythmic pattern. By one month, most infants are sleeping longer at night, and by four months, they usually have moved even closer to adultlike sleeping patterns. Researchers have been interested in the REM sleep of infants. This rapid eye movement sleep, during which children and adults are most likely to dream, occurs much more in early infancy than in adulthood, accounting for about half of neonatal sleep. The high percentage of REM sleep may function as a self-stimulatory device, or it may promote brain development.

3. The Brazelton Neonatal Behavioral Assessment Scale not only is being widely used as a clinical measure to assess the neurological integrity of the newborn but also is used as a measure of infant development in many research studies. The NBAS consists of 26 categories and involves extensive assessment of infant states.

4. Interest in neonatal eating behavior has focused on breast versus bottle feeding as well as scheduled versus demand feeding. There are many health advantages to breast feeding, but most American mothers choose to bottle-feed their infants, mainly for reasons of convenience. Some years ago, scheduled feeding was thought to increase the likelihood that a child would become controlled. In recent years, however, demand feeding, in which the timing of the feeding as well as the amount are determined by the infant, has become more popular.

II. The infant's physical and motor development increases rapidly over the first two years of life.

A. Growth during the first year is very rapid. The cephalocaudal pattern of growth refers to growth from the top down, and the proximodistal pattern indexes growth from the center out. These two growth patterns are apparent in the infant's development. Both gross and fine motor skills undergo considerable change in the first year. By the eighth to ninth month, most infants can walk with assistance, and by 11 to 12 months of age, the infant can hold objects in each hand and inspect them.

B. During the second year, growth decelerates, and gross and fine motor skills are considerably refined. The infant becomes much more proficient at walking and running and develops such fine motor skills as being able to turn the pages of a book one page at a time.

C. During the first year, rhythmic motor behavior, involving rapid, repetitive movement of the limbs, torso, and head, is common, and there have been many explanations of its purpose. Thelen believes that these rhythmic stereotypies represent an important link between reflexive, uncoordinated motor behavior in early infancy and later, more mature, voluntary motor actions. Such stereotypies are much more frequent in the second half of the first year than in the first half. Rhythmic stereotypies may persist longer in abnormal infants.

D. There is a great deal of brain development in the first two years of life. Dendritic spreading is dramatic in these first two years. Some important changes in neurotransmitters likely are occurring as well, but their precise determination has yet to be accurately charted.

III. An understanding of the infant's sensory and perceptual development requires an examination of sensation and perception, the theories of perceptual development, visual perception, and the other senses.

A. Sensation occurs when information contacts sensory receptors (for example, the eyes, ears, tongue, nostrils, and skin), while perception is the interpretation of what is sensed.

B. Two important theories of perception are the constructivist approach and the direct perception or ecological view.

1. The constructivist approach, advocated by Piaget, argues that what the child experiences is a construction based on a combination of sensory input and information retrieved from memory. Representation in the mind is important.

2. The direct perception or ecological view, promoted by the Gibsons, argues that representation is not the way perception works. The Gibsons believe that there are perceptual invariants in the environment that the infant picks up. This view stresses that perceptual development occurs because the infant and child become more efficient at discovering invariant properties in the environment. This view has generated considerable research on infant perception, particularly in terms of the infant's ability to perceive complex things.

C. Information about visual perception focuses on William James's view, visual preferences, visual acuity and accommodation, color, perception of objects and faces, perception of depth, and spatial relations.

1. James believed that the world of the newborn was "a great blooming, buzzing confusion." Now we believe that the infant's visual perception is more advanced than previously thought. This view has been pioneered by the Gibsons' work.

2. With regard to visual preferences, Fantz's research—by showing how infants prefer striped to solid patches—demonstrated that newborns can see.

3. Visual acuity refers to how well an organism can see. Visual acuity is about 20/600 in the newborn, and by six months of age has improved to 20/100. Accommodation refers to acuity over a range of viewing distances. Focusing errors in this regard decrease with age.

4. Newborns likely are not entirely color-blind, but they might be partially color-blind.

5. Infants as young as four months of age perceive partly masked objects as whole. Infants as young as two months of age prefer to look at a normal rather than a rearranged face.

6. A classic study by Gibson and Walk demonstrated through the use of a visual cliff apparatus that infants as young as six months have depth perception.

7. An egocentric frame of reference characterizes the first year of life, with landmarks and familiarity being important variables in understanding spatial relations. The early emergence of objective frames of reference may derive from infants' body movements. Spatial perception develops throughout childhood.

D. Information about the other senses focuses on auditory perception (hearing), smell, taste, touch, and pain.

1. Some research suggests that the fetus can hear several weeks before birth. It has been documented that, immediately following birth, newborns can hear, although their sensory thresholds are higher than those of adults. Intermodal perception refers to information that comes through more than one sensory channel. Spelke's research suggests that infants as young as four months old have intermodal perception because they perceive auditory and visual events in related, unitary episodes rather than in unrelated ways.

2. The development of the other senses—smell, taste, touch, and pain—in the infant have not been thoroughly investigated. However, we do know that these four senses are present in newborns. Research investigations regarding circumcision have shown that newborns experience the sense of pain, yet can adapt to cope with the stress.

E. Considerable research interest focuses on the infant's ability to relate information across perceptual modalities. Research documenting the very young infant's ability to engage in intermodal perception supports the direct perception or ecological view of the Gibsons, although there still is lively debate on the role of innate and experiential factors in early perceptual development.

KEY TERMS

association areas of the cortex 134	perception 141
Brazelton Neonatal Behavioral Assessment Scale 130	perceptual invariant 143
	preference 124
cephalocaudal pattern 133	proximodistal pattern 133
constructivist approach 142	reflexive smile 127
demand feeding 131	REM sleep 129
direct perception or ecological view 135	representation 142
fine motor skills 134	rhythmic motor behavior 137
gross motor skills 134	rhythmic stereotypies 138
habituation 124	scheduled feeding 131
intermodal perception 149	sensation 141
Moro reflex 125	sensory cortex 134
motor cortex 134	social smiling 127
natural reaction 124	visual accommodation 144
nonnutritive sucking 127	visual acuity 144

SUGGESTED READINGS

Banks, M. S., & Salapatek, P. (1983). Infant visual perception. In P. E. Mussen (Ed.), *Handbook of child psychology* (4th ed.), Vol. 2. New York: Wiley. This authoritative version of research on infant perception covers in great detail the topics discussed in this chapter.

Bower, T. G. R. (1977). *The perceptual world of the child.* Cambridge, MA: Harvard University Press. A scholarly introduction to the study of infant perception, including the topics of space perception, distance perception, and size constancy.

Caplan, F. (1981). *The first twelve months of life.* New York: Bantam. An easy-to-read, well-written account of each of the first twelve months of life.

Lamb, M. E., & Bornstein, M. C. (1987). *Development in infancy.* New York: Random House. This portrayal of the infant by two leading researchers includes individual chapters on perceptual development as well as the ecology of the infant's development.

LEARNING, COGNITION, AND LANGUAGE IN INFANCY

IMAGINE . . . YOUR SON IS ONE
YEAR OLD AND IS LEARNING
MATH AND A FOREIGN
LANGUAGE

PREVIEW

LEARNING

What Is Learning?
Classical Conditioning
*The Basic Classical Conditioning
Experiment and Its Elements
Why Does Classical Conditioning Work?
Classical Conditioning in Infancy
Evaluation of Classical Conditioning*
Operant Conditioning
Imitation

FOCUS ON CHILD DEVELOPMENT
5.1: SMILES, FROWNS, AND
SURPRISES

Evaluation of the Learning Approaches

CHILD DEVELOPMENT CONCEPT
TABLE 5.1: LEARNING

PIAGET'S THEORY OF INFANT
DEVELOPMENT

An Overview of Piaget's View of
Development
The Stage of Sensorimotor Development
*Simple Reflexes (Birth to One Month of
Age)
First Habits and Primary Circular Reactions
(One to Four Months of Age)
Secondary Circular Reactions (Four to Eight
Months of Age)
Coordination of Secondary Circular
Reactions (8 to 12 Months of Age)
Tertiary Circular Reactions, Novelty, and
Curiosity (12 to 18 Months of Age)
Internalization of Schemes (18 Months to
Two Years of Age)*
Object Permanence

FOCUS ON CHILD DEVELOPMENT
5.2: FATHOMING THE
PERMANENCE OF THINGS IN THE
WORLD

ATTENTION AND MEMORY

Attention
*The Orienting Response
Scanning Visual Patterns*
Memory
*Conjugate Reinforcement
Conscious Memory*

FOCUS ON CHILD DEVELOPMENT
5.3: INFANTILE AMNESIA, A
SIBLING'S BIRTH, AND RATS

INDIVIDUAL DIFFERENCES,
DEVELOPMENTAL SCALES, AND
THE MEASUREMENT OF INFANT
INTELLIGENCE

History of Interest in Infant Testing
The Bayley Scales of Infant
Development
Other Developmental Scales
Conclusions About Infant Testing of
Intelligence and Continuity in Mental
Development

CHILD DEVELOPMENT CONCEPT
TABLE 5.2: PIAGET'S THEORY,
ATTENTION AND MEMORY, AND
INFANT INTELLIGENCE TESTS

LANGUAGE DEVELOPMENT

The Nature of Language
The Rule Systems of Language
*Phonology
Morphology
Syntax
Semantics
Pragmatics*
Theoretical Views of Language
Acquisition
*The Behavioral View
Nativist Theory*

FOCUS ON CHILD DEVELOPMENT
5.4: THE CURIOUS CASE OF GENIE

*Cognitive Theory
Conclusions About Theories of Language*
Environmental Influences on Language

FOCUS ON CHILD DEVELOPMENT
5.5: BABY TALK

CHILD DEVELOPMENT CONCEPT
TABLE 5.3: THE NATURE OF
LANGUAGE, RULE SYSTEMS OF
LANGUAGE, THEORETICAL VIEWS
OF LANGUAGE ACQUISITION, AND
ENVIRONMENTAL INFLUENCES
ON LANGUAGE

Milestones in Language Development
During Infancy
*Preverbal Developments
One-Word Utterances
Two-Word Utterances*

THINKING BACK, LOOKING
AHEAD

SUMMARY

KEY TERMS

SUGGESTED READINGS

CHAPTER 5

IMAGINE . . . YOUR SON IS ONE YEAR OLD AND IS LEARNING MATH AND A FOREIGN LANGUAGE

Matthew is one year old. He already has seen over 1,000 flash cards with pictures of shells, flowers, insects, flags, countries, words—you name it—on them. His mother, Billie, has made close to 10,000 such 11-inch square cards for Matthew and his four-year-old brother Mark. Billie has religiously followed the regimen recommended by Glenn Doman, the director of the Philadelphia Institute for the Achievement of Human Potential and the author of *How to Teach Your Baby to Read.* Using his methods, learned in a $400 week-long course called "How to Multiply Your Baby's Intelligence," Billie is teaching Matthew Japanese and even a little math. Mark is learning geography, natural science, engineering, and fine arts as well.

Parents using the card approach print one word on each card using a bright red felt-tipped pen. The parent repeatedly shows the card to the infant while saying the word. The first word usually is *mommy,* then comes *daddy,* the baby's name, parts of the body, and all things the infant can touch. The infant is lavishly praised when he or she can recognize the word. The idea is to imprint the large red words in the infant's memory, so that in time, he or she accumulates an impressive vocabulary and begins to read. Subsequently, the parent continues to feed the infant and young child with all manner of data in small, assimilable bits, just as Billie Rash has done with her two boys.

With this method, the child should be reading by two years of age, and by four or five, should have begun mastering some math and be able to play the violin, not to mention the vast knowledge of the world he or she should be able to display because of a monumental vocabulary. Maybe the SAT test you labored through on your way to college might have been taken easily at the age of six if your parents had only been enrolled in the "How to Multiply Your Baby's Intelligence" course and had made 10,000 flash cards for you.

It is too soon to tell whether programs like the Doman method will be successful or have a substantial impact on children's later development. Some developmental psychologists believe that Doman's so-called "better baby" institute is a money-making scheme and is not based on sound scientific information. Before we invest extensive effort in trying to teach such skills to infants, we must first determine what their basic capacities are.

What evidence do we have, for example, that infants can work with numerical concepts? Mark Strauss and Lynn Curtis (1982) demonstrated that infants as young as 10 to 12 months of age are able to discriminate between a complex stimulus containing three items and one containing either two or four items. One possible conclusion from this rather startling discovery is that one-year-old infants can count up to three or four items but no higher. Such a conclusion, however, is probably false. More likely, infants are able to notice in a single perceptual act up to five variations in the number of objects.

While it seems important to evaluate whether numerical concepts can be taught to infants and also whether maternal communication patterns are related to the infant and child's development, considerable debate exists about whether we should be trying to accelerate the infant's development along the lines of the 10,000 flash cards used to teach language. Jean Piaget called "What should we do to foster cognitive development?" the American question because it was asked of him so often when he lectured to American audiences. Piaget, as well as many other cognitive developmentalists, believe that there is something fundamentally wrong with the intense tutorial practicing that characterizes methods such as Doman's. As you read this chapter, you will see that Piaget stresses the importance of letting infants actively organize their experiences themselves and spontaneously explore their environment.

PREVIEW

The excitement and enthusiasm surrounding research on infant learning and cognition has been fueled by interests in such matters as what an infant knows at birth and soon after, by continued fascination about innate and learned factors in the infant's cognitive development, and by controversies over whether infants construct their knowledge, as Piaget believed, or whether they know their world more directly, as the Gibsons argue. Primary topics of interest include what and how infants learn, the nature of their attention and memory, measurement of their intelligence, and where their language comes from and how it develops. The capacities for learning and cognition were recognized by Rousseau, who said:

We are born capable of learning. . . .

and by Walt Whitman, when he wrote:

There was a child who went forth every day
And the first object he looked upon,
    that object he became.
And that object became part of him for
    the day, or a certain
part of the day, or for many years,
    or stretching cycles of years. . . .

LEARNING

Learning builds on an evolutionary base and permits infants to face the challenge of survival and adaptation with the information they acquire. Infants learn to ignore stimuli that are unimportant, to anticipate changes in their world, to modify their environment, and to benefit from the experience.

What Is Learning?

First, learning anything new involves a *change*. For instance, a child learning to use a computer likely will make some mistakes along the way, but at some point, the child's mind and behavior are likely to change enough so that an understanding of how to use the computer is attained. In other words, the child changes from someone who could not operate a computer to someone who can.

Second, learning has a *relatively permanent* influence on the child's mind and behavior. Thus, once the child learns how to use the computer, the skill does not usually go away. Once the child has learned how to add and subtract, this ability becomes a relatively permanent part of the mind and behavior.

Third, learning involves *experience*. Through experiences with other people, children learn how to behave in a mannerly or not-so-mannerly way. Through experiences, children learn positive or negative attitudes. Behavior and thought due to maturation, reflexes, and instincts or to the influence of fatigue, injury, disease, or drugs do not involve learning.

Thus, **learning** can be defined as a relatively permanent change in the mind or behavior that occurs through experience and cannot be accounted for by reflexes, instincts, and maturation, or the influence of fatigue, injury, disease, or drugs. Now that we have defined learning, let's look at three different kinds of learning: classical conditioning, operant conditioning, and imitation.

Classical Conditioning

In this section, we examine the basic classical conditioning experiment and its elements, explore why classical conditioning works, investigate classical conditioning in infancy, and evaluate the contributions and limitations of classical conditioning.

The Basic Classical Conditioning Experiment and Its Elements

Ivan Pavlov's (1927) experiments with salivating dogs are among the best-known studies in psychology. In his original experiment, Pavlov discovered that he could change behavior by presenting stimuli to an organism. Before an experimental session began, Pavlov had a dog's cheek surgically treated so that its saliva could be measured (see Figure 5.1). During the experiment, the dog

FIGURE 5.1 Surgical preparation for studying the salivary reflex. When the dog salivated, the saliva collected in a glass funnel attached to the dog's cheek. In this way the strength of the salivary response was precisely measured.

was restrained in a harness (see Figure 5.2). Next, Pavlov sounded a tuning fork. (At this point in the experiment, the dog did not salivate.) Soon after, while the tuning fork was still being sounded, Pavlov gave the dog some meat powder. As the dog ate the meat powder, it salivated. By repeatedly pairing the sound of the tuning fork with the meat powder, Pavlov soon discovered that the dog began to salivate at the appearance of the sound alone. Prior to this, the dog had only salivated when the food was presented. Through the association of the meat powder and the sound, the dog learned to salivate to the sound of the tuning fork alone. This process of association is called **classical conditioning.**

There are four important elements in the classical conditioning experiment: (1) the unconditioned stimulus, (2) the unconditioned response, (3) the conditioned stimulus, and (4) the conditioned response. An **unconditioned stimulus (UCS)** can elicit a response before learning occurs, usually through a reflex. In Pavlov's experiment, the meat powder was the unconditioned

stimulus. Because the tuning fork was not able to produce salivation before it was paired with the food, the tuning fork was the **conditioned stimulus (CS),** which acquires the ability to elicit a response by being associated with an unconditioned stimulus. In Pavlov's experiment, the dog's salivating was the **unconditioned response (UCR)**—behavior that is unlearned and occurs in response to an unconditioned stimulus. When the dog began salivating to the tuning fork, the salivating became a **conditioned response (CR)** rather than an unconditioned response. Thus, the conditioned response was learned through a pairing of the tuning fork and the food.

To keep these terms straight, it is a good idea to go over them several times. Also, the diagram in Figure 5.3 should provide further help in your understanding of the terms and procedures of classical conditioning. The key aspect of classical conditioning focuses on the UCS-CS association. Because this pairing is so important in classical conditioning, the process often is referred to as **S-S learning** to emphasize the significance of the association between stimuli.

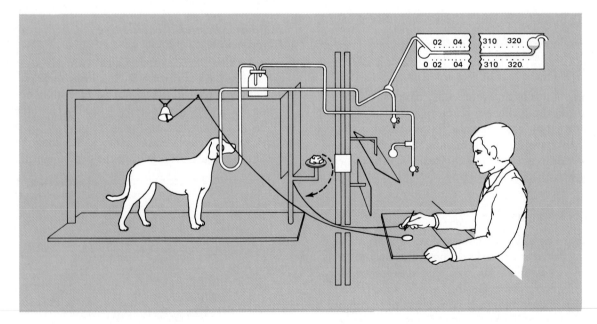

FIGURE 5.2   A modern apparatus for Pavlov's experiment in classical conditioning.

Pavlov demonstrated that behavior can not only be acquired but can be extinguished as well. He showed that a conditioned response will gradually disappear if the conditioned stimulus is presented repeatedly without reinforcement. This process is called **extinction.** In Pavlov's experiment, when the sound of the tuning fork and the food were no longer paired, the dogs eventually stopped salivating.

However, a conditioned response that has been extinguished can recur with no further conditioning. This process is referred to as **spontaneous recovery.** In a classical conditioning experiment, spontaneous recovery occurs when a rest period is allowed to follow the extinction of the response. The processes of extinction and spontaneous recovery are shown in Figure 5.4. This figure reveals how spontaneous recovery may occur several times during extinction. However, if the CS continues to be unreinforced, the recovered conditioned response will be extinguished gradually until it ceases to occur.

Now that we have seen *how* classical conditioning works, let's study *why* it works.

Why Does Classical Conditioning Work?

The two reasons given to explain why classical conditioning works involve stimulus substitution and information theory (Tarpy & Mayer, 1978). The traditional explanation of classical conditioning is based on the **stimulus substitution theory.** Pavlov himself subscribed to this theory, arguing that the nervous system is structured in such a manner that the contiguity between the CS and the UCS creates a bond between them and eventually the CS substitutes for the UCS. If indeed the CS can substitute for the UCS, then the two stimuli should evoke very similar responses. However, researchers have found that the CS and UCS are not as similar as Pavlov believed. For example, a shock UCS produces flinching and jumping in rats (that is, highly activated behavior), whereas a CS paired with shock invariably elicits freezing and immobility (Bindra & Palfai, 1967; Blanchard & Blanchard, 1969).

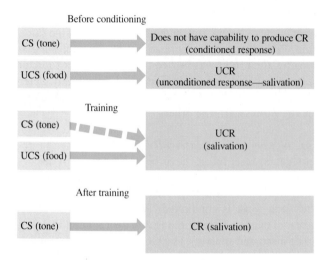

FIGURE 5.3 Diagram of the classical conditioning procedure. At the start of training, the UCS will evoke the UCR, but the CS does not have the capacity to evoke the appropriate response. During training the CS and the UCS are presented such that the CS comes to evoke the response. Remember, the key to classical conditioning, or S-S learning, is the strength of the association between the unconditioned stimulus and the conditioned stimulus.

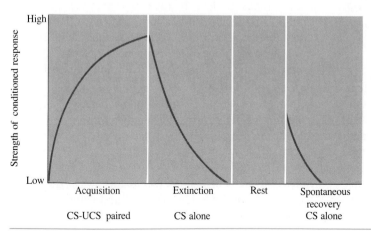

FIGURE 5.4 The strength of a conditioned response during acquisition, extinction, and spontaneous recovery. During acquisition the conditioned stimulus and unconditioned stimulus are paired, thus increasing the strength of the conditioned response. During extinction the conditioned stimulus is presented alone and, as can be seen, the strength of the conditioned response decreases. After a rest period, spontaneous recovery often takes place, although the conditioned response is not nearly as strong as it is after a number of UCS-CS pairings. When the CS is presented alone again, after spontaneous recovery, the response is extinguished rapidly.

A second explanation of why classical conditioning works is based on **information theory** (Rescorla, 1967). This view stresses that the CS acquires information value, meaning that the child learns information about whatever event follows it in time. Put another way, the child uses the CS as a sign or expectancy that a UCS will follow (Tolman, 1932). The view of the CS having informational value goes beyond the original meaning of Pavlov's classical conditioning.

Emphasis on the information the child processes in a classically conditioned context is reflected in many contemporary learning studies (Dickinson, 1980; Mackintosh, 1983). Rather than viewing a classical conditioning context in the manner of Pavlov, such studies have taken on a cognitive flavor, as classical conditioning researchers describe the child's memory or image of past events and how the child has processed these events.

Now we examine some specific research studies of classical conditioning with infants.

Classical Conditioning in Infancy

Early research in classical conditioning with human infants and children focused on the role classical conditioning might play in phobias and counterconditioning. More recent research has studied whether newborns can be classically conditioned.

Phobias and Counterconditioning   Phobias are irrational fears, which many psychologists believe are generated by classical conditioning. Behaviorists John Watson and Rosalie Rayner (1920) conducted an experiment to demonstrate this. A little boy named Albert was shown a white laboratory rat to see if he was afraid of it. He was not. Subsequently, as Albert played with the rat, a loud noise was sounded behind Albert's head. As you might imagine, the loud noise caused little Albert to cry loud and long. After only seven pairings of the loud noise with the white rat, Albert began to fear the rat even when the noise was not sounded. Through stimulus generalization, Albert's fear was also produced by objects similar to the white rat—a rabbit, a dog, and a sealskin coat. Today an experiment conducted in this manner would be unethical, especially since Watson and Rayner did not remove Albert's fear of rats, so presumably this phobia remained with him after the experiment. If we can produce fears by means of classical conditioning, we should also be able to eliminate them.

Counterconditioning is a procedure for weakening a classically conditioned CR by associating the stimuli that currently elicit it to a new response incompatible with the CR. Watson (with Mary Cover Jones, 1924) used a counterconditioning procedure to eliminate fear in a three-year-old boy named Peter. Peter had many of the same fears Albert had, but they were not produced by Watson. Peter was afraid of such things as white rats, fur coats, frogs, fish, and mechanical toys. To get rid of these fears, a rabbit was brought into Peter's view, but far enough away that it would not upset him. At the same time, Peter was fed crackers and milk. On each successive day, the rabbit was moved closer and closer to Peter as Peter was simultaneously given food. Eventually, Peter reached the point where he would eat with one hand and pet the rabbit with the other.

Can Newborns Be Classically Conditioned?   In recent years, researchers have been interested in discovering whether newborns can be classically conditioned. The research of Hans Papoušek (1961, 1976) illustrates how such work is conducted. Papoušek used a combination of classical conditioning and operant conditioning (to be discussed shortly). His UCS was a tactile stimulus that touched the side of the newborn's mouth—this elicited the UCR of head turning about one-fourth of the time. A sound was used as the CS and was paired with the touch of the mouth. Then the experimenter introduced the operant conditioning component of the study—the newborn was rewarded for the head turning with milk. Papoušek was successful with this procedure, but it took something on the order of 150 to 200 trials over a three-week period. It appears that classical conditioning is possible with newborns but that it is very difficult to demonstrate, that it often takes considerable time to occur, and that it often is open to alternative interpretations, such as the operant conditioning possibilities in Papoušek's research.

Now that we have studied many facets of classical conditioning, let's evaluate where it stands in the scheme of children's learning.

Evaluation of Classical Conditioning

Since Pavlov's original experiments with dogs, researchers have made rabbits blink and children jerk to the sound of a buzzer, a glimpse of light, or the touch of a hand. The adaptability that classical conditioning brings has a great deal of survival value for the child.

Through the process of classical conditioning, children jerk their hands away before they are burned by fire and get off the street when a truck rapidly approaches. As children acquire language, the words that stand for objects also serve as important signals for classical conditioning. A peer yells, "Snake," and a little girl runs crying to her mother, for example.

Although Pavlov described all learning in terms of classical conditioning, it has become apparent that classical conditioning is a simple type of learning and that we learn in a number of other ways. Nonetheless, classical conditioning does help a child to learn about his or her environment, and as we have just seen, it has been used successfully in the elimination of fears. However, a view of learning that only describes the child as responding to its environment fails to capture the active nature of the child in influencing the environment. It is to such an active form of learning that we turn next.

Operant Conditioning

Operant conditioning, first described in Chapter 2 with regard to the behavioral perspective of B. F. Skinner, involves the organism acting or operating on the environment. In contrast, classical conditioning is a process in which the organism responds to the environment. While classical conditioning and operant conditioning are similar in the sense that they both involve experience and a stimulus that is important in determining behavior, there are some distinct differences in the two forms of learning as well. First, with operant conditioning, the reinforcement depends on the appropriate response of the organism. If the infant does not kick its foot, it does not get smiled at, for example. Second, classical conditioning involves reflexive involuntary behavior controlled by the spinal column or the autonomic nervous system. Such behavior includes eye blinks, salivation, and heart rate. Operant conditioning, on the other hand, focuses less on reflexive behavior and more on spontaneous behavior related to the voluntary nervous system.

Much research indicates that operant conditioning can alter a variety of behaviors during childhood (Bijou, 1976). There are also many demonstrations that show how infant behavior changes as a result of operant processes (Papoušek, 1976; Rheingold, Gewirtz, & Ross, 1959; Lipsitt, 1979). A classic study by Harriet Rheingold and associates (1959) demonstrated that vocalization in infants may be increased through simple

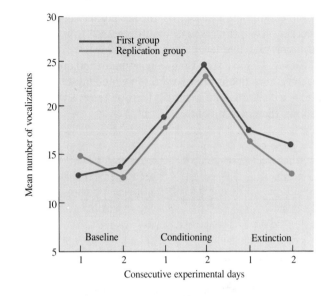

FIGURE 5.5 Changes in the level of infant vocalization through the phases of operant conditioning.

contingencies of reinforcement. In the study, three-month-old infants were tested with a now familiar operant-conditioning procedure. In a **baseline** period, the investigators charted the frequency of vocalizations in children before reinforcement was introduced. In the **conditioning trials** that followed, all vocalizations were rewarded. Following the conditioning procedure, an extinction phase occurred. (Extinction is similar to baseline. The investigators simply observed the amount of vocalization without reinforcing it.) Each of the three phases of the experiment—baseline, conditioning, and extinction—was conducted over a period of two days. On each day, a woman visited the infant nine times, each time for about three minutes. During the sessions in the baseline and extinction phases, the woman remained neutral. Standing passively in front of the child, she showed no expression and did nothing when the child vocalized. During the conditioning phase, the woman stood passively only until the infant vocalized. She followed the vocalizations with a series of socially pleasant events—smiles, soothing sounds, and gentle caresses.

The results of this study are shown in Figure 5.5. Notice that, during the baseline period, the infants produced about 13 vocalizations on each day. The number of vocalizations increased to almost 25 by the second day of the conditioning phase. By the second day of the extinction phase, the response had decreased to its previously low baseline level.

So far, we have seen that responding to and operating on the environment are two ways in which infants learn. Next, we see that infants also learn extensively by observing the environment.

Imitation

In the discussion of social learning theory in Chapter 2, information about the importance of imitation was presented. Albert Bandura (1977) believes that **imitation** (sometimes also called **modeling** or **observational learning**) requires the coordination of motor activity with a mental picture of the act being imitated. It sometimes

---

FOCUS ON CHILD DEVELOPMENT 5.1

SMILES, FROWNS, AND SURPRISES

The adult smiles. Then the newborn smiles. The adult protrudes her lower lip, wrinkles her forehead, and frowns. The baby does something very similar. Next, the adult opens her mouth and eyes widely and raises her eyebrows. The baby then displays an expression very much like the one shown by the adult. Is it possible that these observations could be made with babies as young as one or two weeks old? Could a baby as young as 36 hours old perform these behaviors that reflect the emotional expressions of happiness, sadness, and surprise?

Tiffany Field and her colleagues conducted a research investigation with newborns averaging 36 hours old (Field, Woodson, Greenberg, & Cohen, 1982). The model held the newborn's head upright, with the model and the newborn's faces separated by about 10 inches. The newborn's facial movement patterns were recorded by an observer who stood behind the model to see the newborn's face but who was unaware of which facial expression the model was showing. The model expressed one of three emotions: happiness, sadness, or surprise. The figure at the bottom right of the following page shows the proportion of trials on which different mouth movements occurred when the neonate was exposed to a happy, sad, or surprised model. As indicated, the most

noticeable difference occurred in the surprise condition, with the newborns frequently following the surprised model's facial expression with a wide opening of their own mouths. Also notice that widened lips were most likely to be observed on the part of the neonate after he or she had observed a happy model. And the neonate was more likely to show pouting lips after a sad model had been seen.

The results of this investigation coincide with data from other studies (e.g., Meltzoff & Moore, 1977), suggesting that young infants and even newborns are capable of discriminating different facial expressions. Field and her colleagues believe that their research supports the argument that newborns have an innate ability to compare the sensory information of a visually perceived expression.

There has been considerable interest in studying the nature of imitation in young infants (e.g., Martin & Clark, 1982; Meltzoff & Moore, 1977). Researchers believe that to show that true imitation, rather than pseudo-imitation, has occurred, it is necessary to demonstrate that infants can imitate behaviors they cannot see themselves perform (that is, hand movements would not qualify), as well as behaviors that are not just spontaneous or coincidental. Further, there is the question of whether the infant has learned to acquire new information through imitation or whether an innate ability is simply being released, as ethologists might argue. And, if we rely on the definition of imitation given by Bandura and Piaget, there clearly is no evidence that the young infant or newborn is imaging the model's behaviors.

has been argued that very young infants cannot engage in imitation because they either cannot form a mental picture of another individual or cannot coordinate their motor actions with that picture.

Piaget also was interested in the role of imitation in infant cognition. In his view, infants cannot imagine objects until approximately nine months of age. Before then, said Piaget, it is possible to get a baby to imitate such responses as opening and closing the hands, which babies can master early in life and can see themselves doing. Piaget called this type of behavior pseudo-imitation. Much research has tried to demonstrate the existence of imitation, rather than pseudo-imitation, in young infants. Focus on Child Development 5.1 examines how researchers inquire about the existence of imitation in early infancy.

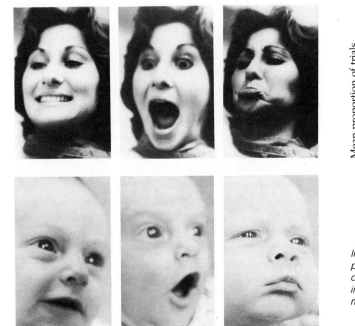

Can newborns imitate an adult's emotional facial expressions?

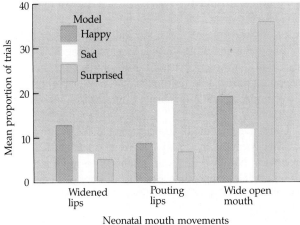

Imitation of facial expressions by neonates. Shown above is the proportion of time during which neonates moved their mouths after different facial expressions had been modeled. Mouth movements included widened lips (happy), pouting lips (sad), and widened mouth (surprise).

Now that we have considered how infants respond, operate, and observe in their environment, let's draw some overall conclusions about the different learning approaches.

Evaluation of the Learning Approaches

Classical conditioning does represent how a limited set of infant behaviors are learned, but it provides a view that is too reflexive and mechanical to provide an overall perspective of the major way infants learn. The operant conditioning perspective accurately describes the organism as active in its world, moving away from the more reflexive view of Pavlov. Skinner's perspective greatly broadened the scope of learning by revealing how many spontaneous voluntary behaviors can be learned through reinforcement. Reinforcement is an important process in the infant's life and provides an explanation of many behaviors. However, the fact that the operant approach rules out the role of the mind and cognition in determining behavior limits its use in explaining how much of infant learning occurs. Imitation is an important learning process, taking into account how the infant cognitively processes information in learning about the world.

Child Development Concept Table 5.1 summarizes our discussion of the many different aspects of learning processes. Now we turn our attention to some views of infant development that provide a stronger cognitive interpretation than do operant or classical conditioning approaches.

PIAGET'S THEORY OF INFANT DEVELOPMENT

Piaget had a very different view of infants than either Watson or Skinner. Before we tackle Piaget's more precise insights about infant development, let's review some of the main ideas in his theory of cognitive development.

An Overview of Piaget's View of Development

Piaget believed that the child passed through a series of stages of thought from infancy to adolescence. Passage through the stages is the result of biological pressures to *adapt* to the environment (assimilation and accommodation) and to organize structures of thinking. These stages of thought are described as *qualitatively* different from one another, which means that the way a child reasons at one stage is very different from the way a child reasons at another. This contrasts with the *quantitative* assessments of intellect made in standardized intelligence tests, where the focus is on how much the child knows, or how many questions the child answers correctly. Recall from Chapter 2 that, according to Piaget, the development of thought is divided into the following major stages: sensorimotor, preoperational, concrete operational, and formal operational. We now explore the infant stage of sensorimotor development in detail.

The Stage of Sensorimotor Development

Piaget's sensorimotor stage lasts from birth to about two years of age, corresponding to the period of infancy. During this time, mental development is characterized by considerable progression in the infant's ability to organize and coordinate sensations and perceptions with his or her physical movements and actions—hence, the term *sensorimotor* (Piaget, 1952).

At the beginning of the sensorimotor stage, the newborn has little more than reflexive patterns with which to work. At the end of the stage, the two-year-old has complex sensoriaction patterns and is beginning to operate with a primitive symbol system. Unlike other stages, the sensorimotor stage is subdivided into six substages, which delineate qualitative changes in the nature of sensorimotor organization. The term **scheme,** or **schema,** is used to refer to the basic unit for an organized pattern of sensorimotor functioning. Within a given substage, there may be many different schemes—for example, sucking, rooting, and blinking in Substage 1—but all have the same organization. In Substage 1, they are basically reflexive in nature. From substage to substage, the schemes change in organization. This change is at the heart of Piaget's descriptions of the substages.

The six substages of sensorimotor development are: (1) simple reflexes; (2) first habits and primary circular reactions; (3) secondary circular reactions; (4) coordination of secondary, circular reactions; (5) tertiary circular reactions, novelty, and curiosity; and (6) internalization of schemes.

Child Development Concept Table 5.1   Learning

Concept	Processes/Related Ideas	Characteristics/Description
What is learning?	Change, permanence, experience	Learning can be defined as a relatively permanent change in the mind or behavior that occurs through experience and cannot be accounted for by reflexes, instincts, and maturation, or the influence of fatigue, injury, disease, or drugs.
Classical conditioning	The basic classical conditioning experiment and its elements	Classical conditioning is a procedure by which a neutral stimulus comes to elicit a response by being paired with a stimulus that regularly evokes the response. The basic classical conditioning experiment was conducted by Pavlov and involved an unconditional stimulus (UCS), an unconditioned response (UCR), a conditioned stimulus (CS), and a conditioned response (CR). Responses can be acquired or eliminated through classical conditioning. Extinction refers to the presentation of the CS alone and results in a decrease of the CR. After a rest period, spontaneous recovery occurs.
	Why does classical conditioning work?	Two possible explanations for classical conditioning are stimulus substitution (the traditional explanation) and information theory (a more modern interpretation).
	Classical conditioning in infancy	Early research focused on phobias and counterconditioning, as emphasized in the work of John Watson. More recent research has examined whether newborns can be classically conditioned. It appears that classical conditioning of infants is possible, but not without great difficulty.
	Evaluation of classical conditioning	The adaptability that classical conditioning brings has survival value for the young child. However, classical conditioning is a rather simple form of learning and fails to capture the active nature of the child in the learning process.
Operant conditioning	Its nature	Operant conditioning emphasizes the infant's operating or acting on the environment, with behavior being controlled by external consequences. Operant conditioning has been demonstrated with young infants.
Imitation	Its nature	Imitation sometimes is called modeling or observational learning. Some experts, such as Bandura, believe that imitation requires the coordination of motor activity with a mental picture of the act being imitated.
	Imitation in infancy	Considerable interest has been generated in whether newborns and young infants can engage in imitation. Debate focuses on what is pseudo-imitation and what is imitation. Researchers believe that it is important to show that infants can imitate behaviors they cannot see themselves perform, as well as behaviors that are not just spontaneous or coincidental. Some researchers believe that true imitation has been demonstrated in very young infants; others disagree.
Evaluation of the learning approaches	Positive and negative features	Classical conditioning, operant conditioning, and imitation are three ways infants learn. As grand theories of the developing infant and child, however, classical conditioning and operant conditioning miss the importance of cognitive factors in either mediating environmental-behavior relations or in causing behavior.

Simple Reflexes (Birth to One Month of Age)

The basic means of coordinating sensation and action is through reflexive behaviors, such as sucking and rooting, that the newborn has at birth. During Substage 1, the infant exercises these reflexes. More importantly, he or she develops an ability to produce behaviors that resemble reflexes in the absence of obvious reflex stimuli. For example, the newborn may suck when a bottle or nipple is only nearby. The bottle or nipple would have produced the sucking pattern only when placed directly in the newborn's mouth or touched to the newborn's lips when the baby was just born. Therefore, reflexlike action in the absence of a triggering stimulus is evidence that the infant is initiating action and actively structuring experiences in the first month of life.

First Habits and Primary Circular Reactions (One to Four Months of Age)

The infant learns to coordinate sensation and types of schemes or structures, that is, habits and primary circular reactions, during Substage 2. A *habit* is a scheme based upon a simple reflex, such as sucking, that has become completely divorced from its eliciting stimulus. For example, an infant in Substage 1 might suck when orally stimulated by a bottle or when visually shown the bottle, but an infant in Substage 2 may exercise the sucking scheme even when no bottle is present.

A **primary circular reaction** is a scheme based upon the infant's attempt to reproduce an interesting or pleasurable event that initially occurred by chance. In a popular Piagetian example, a child accidentally sucks his fingers when they are placed near his mouth; later, he searches for the fingers to suck them again, but the fingers do not cooperate in the search because the child cannot coordinate visual and manual actions.

Habits and circular reactions are stereotyped in that the infant repeats them the same way each time. The infant's own body remains the center of attention; there is no outward pull by environmental events.

This infant is engaging in a secondary circular reaction. What did Piaget mean by secondary circular reactions?

Secondary Circular Reactions (Four to Eight Months of Age)

In Substage 3—**secondary circular reactions**—the infant becomes more object oriented or focused on the world, and moves beyond preoccupation with the self in sense-action interactions. The chance shaking of a rattle, for example, may fascinate the child, and the child repeats this action for the sake of again experiencing fascination. The infant imitates some simple actions of others, such as the baby talk or burbling of adults, and some physical gestures. However, these imitations are limited to actions the infant is already able to produce. Although directed toward objects in the world, the infant's schemes lack an intentional, goal-directed quality.

Coordination of Secondary Circular Reactions (8 to 12 Months of Age)

Several significant changes take place in Substage 4, the **coordination of secondary circular reactions.** The infant readily combines and recombines previously learned schemes in a *coordinated* fashion. He or she may look at an object and grasp it simultaneously, or visually inspect a toy, such as a rattle, and finger it simultaneously in obvious tactile exploration. Actions are even more outward directed than before.

This child is engaging in a tertiary circular reaction. What are tertiary circular reactions?

A block can be made to fall, spin, hit another object, slide across the ground, and so on. **Tertiary circular reactions** are schemes in which the infant purposefully explores new possibilities with objects, continuously changing what is done to them and exploring the results. Piaget speaks of this period as marking the developmental starting point for human curiosity and interest in novelty. Previous circular reactions have been devoted exclusively to reproducing former events, with the exception of imitation of novel acts, which occurs as early as Substage 4. The tertiary circular reaction is the first to be concerned with novelty. As such, it is the mechanism par excellence for trial-and-error learning.

Internalization of Schemes (18 Months to Two Years of Age)

The infant's mental functioning shifts from a purely sensorimotor plane to a symbolic plane in Substage 6 (the **internalization of schemes**), and the infant develops the ability to use primitive symbols. For Piaget, a **symbol** is an internalized sensory image or word that represents an event. Primitive symbols permit the child to think about concrete events without directly acting them out or perceiving them. Moreover, symbols allow the child to manipulate and transform the represented events in simple ways. In a favorite Piagetian example, Piaget's young daughter saw a matchbox being opened and closed and sometime later mimicked the event by opening and closing her mouth. This was an obvious expression of her image of the event. In another example, a child opened a door slowly to avoid disturbing a piece of paper lying on the floor on the other side. Clearly, the child had an image of the unseen paper and what would happen to it if the door were opened quickly. Recently, however, scholars have debated whether two-year-olds really have such representations of action sequences at their command (Corrigan, 1981; Fischer & Jennings, 1981).

We have seen that Piaget divided the infant years into six substages. Next, we examine what Piaget saw as one of the hallmarks of infant development—object permanence—which Piaget believed also unfolded in six substages.

Related to this coordination is the second achievement—the presence of **intentionality,** the separation of means and goals in accomplishing simple feats. For example, the infant may manipulate a stick (the means) to bring a desired toy within reach (the goal). He or she may knock over one block to reach and play with another one.

As will be seen later, this substage has generated a great deal of interest on the part of investigators who wish to examine the logic and validity of the infant stages (e.g., Gratch, 1977; Fischer, 1980).

Tertiary Circular Reactions, Novelty, and Curiosity (12 to 18 Months of Age)

In Substage 5, the infant becomes intrigued by the variety of properties that objects possess and by the multiplicity of things he or she can make happen to objects.

Object Permanence

One of the infant's most significant accomplishments is the development of object concept, which generally has been studied through research on object permanence (Flavell, 1985). **Object permanence** focuses on the development of the ability to understand that objects and events continue to exist even though the child is not in direct contact with them. Imagine what thought would be like if you could not distinguish between yourself and your world. Your thought would be highly chaotic, disorderly, and unpredictable. This is what the mental life of the newborn is like; there is no self-world differentiation and no sense of object permanence (Piaget, 1952). By the end of the sensorimotor period, however, both are clearly present. The transition between these states is not abrupt; rather, it is marked by qualitative changes that reflect movement through each of the substages of sensorimotor thought.

The principal way in which object permanence is studied is by watching the infant's reaction when an attractive object or event disappears. If the infant shows no reaction, it is assumed that he or she has no belief in its continued existence. On the other hand, if the infant is surprised at the disappearance and searches for the object, it is assumed that he or she has a belief in its continued existence.

According to Piaget, six distinct stages characterize the development of object permanence. Table 5.1 shows how Piaget's sensorimotor substages of infant development are applied to object permanence.

Focus on Child Development 5.2 presents other views of object permanence, in particular, how some scholars do not agree with many of Piaget's conclusions about the timing of different aspects of object permanence.

While Piaget's theory has been an important force in generating research on infant cognitive development, we have seen that Piaget has a number of detractors. Some of the detractors believe that more time should be spent investigating such processes as attention and memory and that less time should be given to a search for cognitive structures and stages. Let's now look at the nature of attention and memory in infancy.

Table 5.1   The Six Substages of Object Permanence

Stage	Behavior
Sensorimotor Substage 1	There is no apparent object permanence. When a spot of light moves across the visual field, the infant follows it but quickly ignores its disappearance.
Sensorimotor Substage 2	A primitive form of object permanence develops. Given the same experience, the infant looks briefly at the spot where the light disappeared, with an expression of passive expectancy.
Sensorimotor Substage 3	The infant's sense of object permanence undergoes further development. With the newfound ability to coordinate simple schemes, the infant shows clear patterns of searching for a missing object, with sustained visual and manual examination of the spot where the object apparently disappeared.
Sensorimotor Substage 4	The infant actively searches for a missing object in the spot where it disappeared, with new actions to achieve the goal of searching effectively. For example, if an attractive toy has been hidden behind a screen, the child may look at the screen and try to push it away with a hand. If the screen is too heavy to move or is permanently fixed, the child readily substitutes a secondary scheme—for example, crawling around it or kicking it. These new actions signal that the infant's belief in the continued existence of the missing object is strengthening.
Sensorimotor Substage 5	The infant now is able to track an object that disappears and reappears in several locations in rapid succession. For example, a toy may be hidden under different boxes in succession in front of the infant, who succeeds in finding it. The infant is apparently able to hold an image of the missing object in mind longer than before.
Sensorimotor Substage 6	The infant can search for a missing object that disappeared and reappeared in several locations in succession, as before. In addition, the infant searches in the appropriate place even when the object has been hidden from view as it is being moved. This activity indicates that the infant is able to "imagine" the missing object and to follow the image from one location to the next.

FOCUS ON CHILD DEVELOPMENT 5.2

FATHOMING THE PERMANENCE OF THINGS IN THE WORLD

Although Piaget's stage sequence is the best summary of what might happen as the infant comes to fathom the permanence of things in the world, it cannot adequately handle the weight of many contradictory findings that have surfaced over a number of years (Yussen & Santrock, 1982). Piaget's stages broadly describe the interesting changes reasonably well, but the infant's life is not so neatly packaged into six distinct organizations as Piaget believed. And some of Piaget's explanations for the causes of change simply are not very accurate. In the spirit of constructive criticism, let's now look at four different areas that reflect shortcomings in Piaget's view of object permanence.

First, Ina Uzgiris and J. McVicker Hunt (1972, 1975; Hunt, 1976) offered convincing evidence that there are more than six landmarks in the general course of sensorimotor growth and in the development of object permanence in particular. These researchers detected more than a dozen behavioral accomplishments of the infant in a developmental sequence. In their view, infant change is more gradual and continuous than Piaget thought.

Second, Piaget's account ignores many psychological ''performance variables'' that influence what the infant might do. The manner in which an object is hidden, the amount of time it is hidden, and the way the adult alternates hiding places are among the factors that influence how the infant performs in an object permanence experiment (Bower, 1974; Corrigan, 1981; Harris, 1975).

Third, Piaget argued that certain processes are crucial in stage transitions. The data do not always support his explanations, however. For instance, according to Piaget, the critical requirement for the infant to progress into Substage 4 is the coordination of vision and the sense of touch, or hand-eye coordination. Another important feature of Substage 4 transition for Piaget is the infant's inclination to search for an object hidden in a familiar location, rather than looking for the object in a new location. If new locations serve as hiding places, the infant progressing into Substage 4 should make frequent mistakes, selecting the familiar hiding place (A) instead of the new location (B). This phenomenon is often referred to as the **A-B error** in object permanence, and it involves perseveration. Unfortunately, perseveration does not occur consistently in an infant's behavior (Corrigan, 1981; Harris, 1975; Sophian, 1985). Sometimes it occurs; some-

How does object permanence develop in infancy?

times it does not. Further, there is accumulating evidence that A-B errors are sensitive to the delay between the hiding of an object at B and the infant's attempt to find it (Diamond, 1985). Thus, the A-B error might be due partly to memory failure.

Finally, infant competencies may sometimes be described incorrectly by Piaget. According to Piaget, the infant in Substage 6 is able to mentally conceive of a series of actions and operate with this mental scheme over time. For example, suppose an object is made invisible by placing it inside a covered container. Then the object is removed from one hiding place to another so that the infant cannot see it directly. According to Piaget, the infant should be able to follow the unseen object's movement, since he or she supposedly has the object in mind. A close look at such tasks, however, reveals that in Substage 6 the infant may succeed at finding objects without using a specific image or memory of the object (Corrigan, 1981). Instead, he or she may rely on understanding what the person hiding the objects is doing and simply look in those locations where the adult has been. Such performances, then, depend on learning how to search, not on where the invisible object is. Some critics go so far as to argue that two-year-olds probably do not readily call on mental images of absent events at all (Fischer & Jennings, 1981).

ATTENTION AND MEMORY

Two of the most prominent processes used by the infant to deal with information in the world are attention and memory.

Attention

Attention involves focusing perception to produce increased awareness of a stimulus. Among the interests of scientists who study infant attention are the nature of the orienting response and the infant's ability to scan patterns.

The Orienting Response

Besides the rather obvious signs of attention, such as turning the head, a number of physiological responses accompany increased attention to a stimulus. Collectively, these physiological changes are referred to as the **orienting response (OR)** (Sokolov, 1976). Among these physiological changes are dilation of pupils in the eyes, an increase in muscle tone, changes in the electrical activity of the brain, perspiration, constriction of blood vessels in the limbs and dilation of blood vessels in the head (which produces increased blood flow in the brain), and a change in heart rate. Such physiological changes seem to increase the organism's ability to perceive and respond to a stimulus. For instance, dilated pupils allow more light to come into the eyes, thus enhancing visual sensitivity.

Researchers have used the orienting response in many research attempts to communicate with very young infants. This strategy focuses on the process called **habituation** (first encountered in our discussion of perceptual development in Chapter 4). Habituation of the OR goes like this: Whenever an infant experiences a change in stimulation, he or she looks and listens, and his or her heart rate becomes slower. If the stimulation remains unchanged for some period of time, then the infant stops orienting toward it. This decrease in attention (which is something like getting bored) is called habituation of the orienting response. When a new stimulus is presented after habituation has occurred, the process of reorienting is called **dishabituation.** Among the many responses infant researchers have studied in evaluating the orienting response are heart and respiration rates (measured by instruments) and observable behaviors, such as sucking behavior (sucking stops when the very young infant attends to an object) and the length of time the infant will look at a stimulus.

Newborns do show an orienting response and the orienting response does show habituation, but only in very limited situations. For example, using heart rate deceleration in response to novel stimulation has not been very productive in eliciting an OR in newborns (e.g., Berg & Berg, 1979). Recently, habituation of eye movements has been shown in newborns (e.g., Kisilevsky & Muir, 1984).

A knowledge of habituation and dishabituation can be beneficial in parent-infant interaction (Rosenblith & Sims-Knight, 1985). Infants do respond to changes in stimulation. If stimulation is repeated often, the infant's response often will decrease to the point that the infant no longer responds to the parent. In parent-infant interactions, it is important for parents to do novel things and to repeat them often until the infant quits responding. The wise parent senses that the infant's orienting response shows an interest and that many repetitions of the stimulus may be necessary for the infant to process the information. The parent stops or changes behaviors when the infant redirects his or her attention.

In addition to studying the OR, habituation, and dishabituation, researchers investigate attention by examining how infants scan visual patterns.

Scanning Visual Patterns

When we look at a complex pattern, our eyes do not stay still. Rather, they make what are called **saccadic movements,** fixating first on one part of the pattern, then on another, then another, and so on. The location of these eye fixations provides clues as to how a pattern is processed.

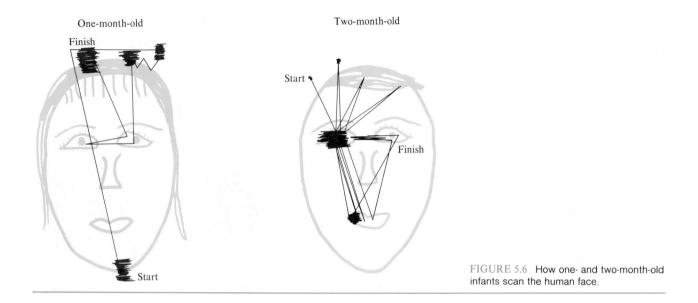

FIGURE 5.6 How one- and two-month-old infants scan the human face.

How do infants scan patterns? Three conclusions stand out (Banks & Salapatek, 1983): First, even newborns can detect a contour and fixate on it. Second, both the orientation and size of the stimulus affect fixation. Third, as infants get older, they scan a pattern more thoroughly, fixating on internal parts as well as on external parts. Up to one month, infants tend to fixate on the external parts of a pattern and exclude the internal parts. This has been called the **externality effect.** This effect has been demonstrated with stimuli as meaningful as the mother's face. For example, in one investigation, one- and two-month-old infants were exposed to the faces of their mothers while the mothers maintained a stationary and expressionless pose (Mauer & Salapatek, 1976). With both the faces of the mother as well as a stranger, the one-month-olds concentrated on the external details, such as the hairline and chin. By contrast, the two-month-olds looked more at the internal features, such as the eyes (see Figure 5.6).

By studying the orienting response and examining how infants scan visual patterns, researchers have learned that attention is a powerful way in which the infant learns about the world. But what would the infant's world be like if the infant had no memory of what had gone on before? Next, we examine memory processes in the infant.

Memory

Memory is a central feature of cognitive development, pertaining to all situations in which we retain information over time. Sometimes, information is retained for only a few seconds or less, whereas at other times it is retained for a lifetime. Memory is involved when we look up a telephone number and dial it. Memory also is involved when we remember the name of our best friend from elementary school. Considerable information about memory is provided throughout this book as we discuss cognitive development through childhood and adolescence. Here, we focus on whether infants have memory, and if so, how long it lasts.

Since memory abilities are usually assessed by examining some type of verbal response, it is not an easy task to study infant memory. First, we discuss a procedure called conjugate reinforcement that has been used to investigate infant memory, and second, we study the extent to which infants have conscious memory.

Conjugate Reinforcement

In the **conjugate reinforcement technique,** which is illustrated in Figure 5.7, one end of a ribbon is tied to an infant's ankle and the other end to a mobile (Rovee-Collier, 1984). When the infant kicks, the mobile moves. This is rewarding for the infant, who soon doubles his or her kicking rate. After the infant's kicking behavior has increased, the mobile is removed from the crib for some period of time. Later, the mobile is reattached to the crib, the infant's ankle and mobile are ribboned once again, and the infant's kicking behavior is again observed. If the infant "remembers" that his or her kicks in this situation were enjoyable, the infant should immediately increase his or her rate of kicking. This is what three-month-olds do even up to an interval of one week of remembering.

Use of the conjugate reinforcement technique to investigate memory has indicated that infants as young as two months of age can remember for as long as three days (Earley, Griesler, & Rovee-Collier, 1985). And the duration of remembering can be extended through the use of a reactivation technique. If the mobile is reexposed to the infant 24 hours before the test (it is reattached to the crib but not tied to the infant's ankle), retention over four or five weeks can be demonstrated (Earley, Griesler, & Rovee-Collier, 1985; Fagan, Ohr, & Fleckenstein, 1985; Hayne & Rovee-Collier, 1985). Apparently, if a 12-week-old views a mobile that he or she played with four weeks earlier, the infant can be "reminded" of the kicking responses he or she learned through such playing.

Now that we have studied how the conjugate reinforcement technique can be used to study infant memory, let's turn our attention to the infant's conscious memory.

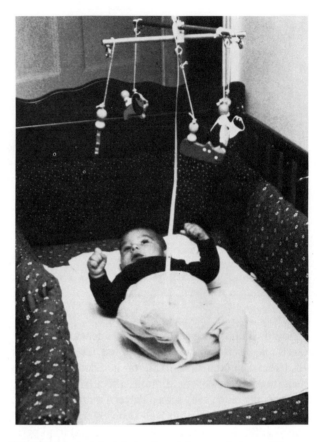

FIGURE 5.7   An infant during the reinforcement phase of the conjugate reinforcement paradigm. The mobile is connected to the infant's ankle by the ribbon and moves in direct proportion to the frequency and vigor of the infant's kicks.

Conscious Memory

Although it is interesting to show that infants "remember" in the conjugate reinforcement setting, certain key aspects of adult memory are not really demonstrated by this technique. John Flavell (1985) and others (Lockhart, 1984) argue that memory in children and adults involves conscious feelings of "I have seen that before," as well as additional retrieval abilities (such as, "Where have I seen that before—was it at the zoo?") that are not present in young infants. And while recall in children may entail a conscious representation or image of something not present ("I recall our first meeting as if it were yesterday"), recall in young infants might not. Flavell argues—as did Jean Piaget—that young infants do not have this ability to "consciously recall" or "reflect on" objects when they are not perceptually available.

Just when do infants acquire the ability to consciously remember the past? In one investigation, parents kept diaries of memory behavior in their 7- to 11-month-old infants (Ashmead & Perlmutter, 1979). An entry in one of the diaries describes the behavior of a 9-month-old girl who was looking for ribbons that had been moved from the drawer where they had been kept. She first looked in the "old" drawer. Failing to find the ribbons, she searched other drawers until she found them. The next day, the young girl went directly to the "new" drawer to find the ribbons. More formal experiments support the existence of such memory in infants over six months of age (Fox, Kagan, & Weiskopf, 1979). For example, when an object is shown to an infant and then subsequently removed, the infant of seven months of age or older will search for the object, but younger infants will not (Kail, 1984). Thus, the data suggest that the memory of infants in the first six months of life is not what adults usually mean by memory—that is, a conscious recollection of prior events. The type of memory evidenced in the conjugate reinforcement technique with two-month-olds is referred to as the learning of adaptive responses or skills, rather than the conscious recollection of specific past episodes.

Some psychologists—Piaget, for instance—refer to the learning of adaptive responses or skills as *memory in the wide sense*, while reserving the label *memory in the strict sense* to the conscious recollection of past episodes. Piaget believed that memory in the wide sense might be present quite early but that memory in the strict sense does not occur until 18 months to two years of age. As we have seen, though, memory in the strict sense is likely to occur earlier than Piaget believed.

It is interesting to speculate about why memory in the strict sense, or conscious memory, develops later than other learning and memory skills. One possibility is that conscious memory must await the maturation of certain brain structures, such as the hippocampus (Schacter & Moscovitch, 1984). Another possibility is that conscious memory may depend on the development of structures of knowledge called schemata (Mandler, 1983; Olson & Strauss, 1984), a view in agreement with Piaget's theory of cognitive structure.

Despite evidence of conscious memory within the first year of life, there is a sense that such recall remains minimal until the child is about three years old. Think about your own infancy. Try to recall a specific episode, like the birth of a sibling. Can you remember anything about such events in your first two years of life? Probably, you can't. Focus on Child Development 5.3 examines this fascinating issue of infantile amnesia.

So far in this chapter, our study of infants has taken us through how they respond to, operate on, observe, attend to, and retain information about their environment. But, as we see next, it is also important to evaluate how infants differ from each other and how we can measure those differences.

INDIVIDUAL DIFFERENCES, DEVELOPMENTAL SCALES, AND THE MEASUREMENT OF INFANT INTELLIGENCE

We have studied different learning approaches, the cognitive developmental perspective, and the information processing approach (attention and memory) to understanding infant development. None of these approaches emphasizes individual differences and the assessment of infant intelligence. Rather, they stress general statements about behavior and thought, summarizing what is typical of the largest number of subjects or for the average members of the species. However, the results obtained for most infants do not apply to all infants— the concept of individual differences. Let's now look at how individual differences in infant development have been studied through the use of developmental scales or infant intelligence tests.

FOCUS ON CHILD DEVELOPMENT 5.3

INFANTILE AMNESIA, A SIBLING'S BIRTH, AND RATS

As children and adults, we have little or no memory of events we experienced before three years of age. This is the phenomenon of **infantile amnesia.** It is not a simple matter to examine how well a child or an adult remembers events from infancy—some events may be reported, but these may or may not be remembered accurately. The clever technique used in one investigation involved asking children and adults if they remembered specific information about the birth of a younger sibling (Sheingold & Tenney, 1982). Each of the subjects had at least one younger sibling. Examples of the questions asked were: "Who told you your mother was leaving to go to the hospital?" "What time of day was it when she left to go to the hospital?" "Did you visit your mother while she was in the hospital?"

Both children and adults were tested, and the reports of the children were checked against their mothers' recall. Fortunately, there was good agreement between children and their mothers, supporting true memory for the type of information tested. The information from the adults involved siblings one year and three months to seventeen years and five months younger than they were. Recall by these subjects is shown in the top right figure. It was virtually zero unless their siblings were three years younger or more. This finding suggests that, if a child is less than three when a certain event occurs, the child will be unlikely to remember it when he or she is an adult.

Infantile amnesia might not be restricted to humans. For example, in one investigation, young and old rats were trained to jump across a barrier to avoid an electric shock (Feigley & Spear, 1970). Twenty-eight days later, the older rats demonstrated memory of the training, but the younger rats did not. This and other studies using nonhuman subjects might help us to determine the mechanisms responsible for infantile amnesia, but the phenomenon at present remains unexplained (Kail, 1984). Although Sigmund Freud (1905/1953) thought that infantile amnesia is the result of repressing memories of sexual feelings experienced early in life, it is unlikely that this explanation could be applied to rats.

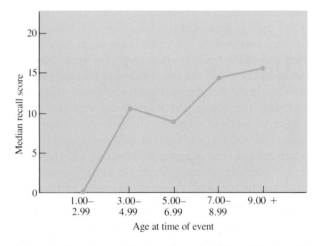

Median recall scores as a function of age for sibling births reported by college students.

What is meant by infantile amnesia?

History of Interest in Infant Testing

It is advantageous to know whether an infant is advancing at a slow, normal, or fast rate of development. In Chapter 4, we discussed the Brazelton Neonatal Behavioral Assessment Scale, which now is being widely used to evaluate neonates. However, developmental psychologists also want to know how development is proceeding during the course of the infant years as well. If the infant is advancing at a particularly slow rate of development, then some form of cognitive enrichment may be necessary. And if an infant is progressing at an advanced rate of development, parents may be advised to provide toys that are designed to stimulate cognitive growth in slightly older infants. To assess development in infancy, measures called **developmental scales** have been devised.

The infant testing movement grew out of the tradition of IQ testing with older children. However, the measures used to assess infants are necessarily less verbal than IQ tests used to assess intelligence in older children. Instead, the infant developmental scales contain far more items pertaining to sensory/perceptual and motor development. And they include measures of social interaction as well.

The most important early contributor to the developmental testing of infants was Arnold Gesell (1934). Gesell developed a measure that was used as a clinical tool to help sort out potentially normal babies from abnormal ones. This was especially useful to adoption agencies who had large numbers of babies awaiting placement. Gesell's examination was widely used for many years and still is called on frequently by pediatricians in their assessment of normal and abnormal infant development.

The version of the Gesell test now used involves four categories of behavior: motor, language, adaptive, and personal-social. If the examiner wishes, the scores in these four domains can be combined into one overall developmental score for the infant, called the **developmental quotient** (or **DQ**). Gesell's intention was to provide a means of giving the infant an overall score, much like the IQ score given older children. However, it has been found that scores on tests like the Gesell that arrive at an overall DQ for the infant do not correlate very highly with IQ scores obtained later in childhood. This is not surprising since the nature of items on the developmental scales, as indicated earlier, are much less verbal than those on intelligence tests used with older children.

As we see next, however, it is not the Gesell test, but rather the **Bayley Scales of Infant Development,** that have been given the most attention by child developmentalists.

The Bayley Scales of Infant Development

The developmental scales most widely used today were developed by Nancy Bayley (1969). Unlike Gesell, whose scales were clinically motivated, Bayley wanted to develop scales that could document infant behavior and predict later development. The early version of the Bayley Scales of Infant Development only covered the first 12 months. It was not until the 1950s that the scales were extended.

The version of the scales used today has three components—a Mental scale, a Motor scale, and an Infant Behavior Profile (which is based on the examiner's observations of the infant during testing). Our major interest here is in the **Mental scale.** This scale focuses on the following aspects of the infant's mental development:

1. Auditory and visual attention to stimuli
2. Manipulation, such as combining objects or shaking a rattle
3. Examiner interaction, such as babbling and imitation
4. Relation with toys, such as banging spoons together
5. Memory/awareness of object permanence, such as when the infant finds a hidden toy
6. Goal-directed tasks that involve persistence, such as putting pegs in a board
7. Ability to follow directions and knowledge of the names of objects, such as whether the infant knows the concept of "one"

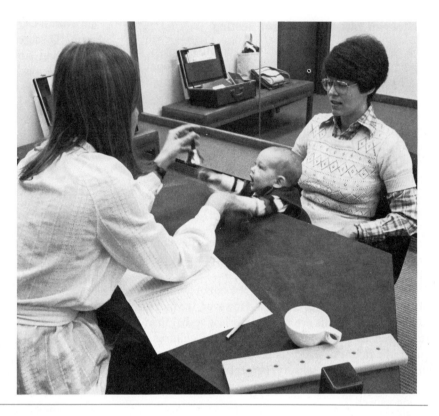

FIGURE 5.8 Administering the Bayley Mental scale.

As an example of the developmental nature of such components of Bayley's Mental scale, consider that the average six-month-old infant should be able to vocalize pleasure and displeasure, persistently reach for objects that are just out of immediate reach, and approach a mirror when the examiner places it in front of the infant. By 12 months of age, the infant who is progressing at an average rate should be able to inhibit behavior when commanded to do so, imitate words the examiner says (such as "Mama"), and respond to simple requests, such as "Take a drink." Figure 5.8 shows the Bayley Mental scale being administered to an infant.

While the Bayley Scales of Infant Development have been the most widely used developmental scales, other scales have also surfaced. In particular, one interesting

scale attempts to precisely measure many of the components of intelligence that Piaget believed were important.

Other Developmental Scales

There have been a number of other attempts to measure the development of infants (Rosenblith & Sims-Knight, 1985). One test—called the Measurement of Intelligence in Infants and Young Children—by Cattell (1940) models the format of the Stanford-Binet Intelligence Test that is used with older children. The Cattell test never has been standardized, but it is a reasonably short test and can be used with infants from 2 to 30 months of age.

An interesting test that some child developmentalists believe possibly captures the flavor of the infant's intellectual development better than most other developmental scales was developed by Ina Uzgiris and J.

McVicker Hunt (1975). Piaget himself was not interested in studying individual differences in intelligence but rather the general manner in which all infants progress through a cognitive developmental sequence. Nonetheless, Piaget's theory and observations stimulated Uzgiris and Hunt to develop a standardized Piagetian infant test. This measure assesses such aspects of the infant's cognitive development as sensorimotor schemes, imitation, and object permanence and classifies the child according to substages of sensorimotor intelligence.

Now that we have considered many different measures of infants, let's draw some conclusions about such tests.

Conclusions About Infant Testing of Intelligence and Continuity in Mental Development

Infant tests of intelligence have been more valuable in assessing the effects of malnutrition, drugs, maternal deprivation, and environmental stimulation than they have been in predicting later intelligence. While they often seem to predict reasonably well the intelligence of older children who have been badly damaged as infants, in the normal range of intelligence, the infant tests have not been very accurate in long-range forecasts of intelligence later in childhood and adolescence. As researchers become more precise in their investigation of what constitutes intellectual development in infancy, it may be that future infant intelligence tests may become better predictors of later intelligence.

The explosion of research interest in infant development has led to many new measures, especially tasks that evaluate the manner in which the infant processes information. In particular, evidence is beginning to accumulate showing a relation between the young infant's attention and intelligence later in the childhood years. In a recent review, Marc Bornstein and Marian Sigman (1986) provided evidence that, when more precise measures of information processing are used to assess intelligence in early infancy, there is greater continuity with measures of intelligence in the childhood years than when the more global Bayley Scales of Infant Development

are used. In reviewing a large number of studies, Bornstein and Sigman concluded that infants who more efficiently encode visual stimuli or who more effectively recollect visual or auditory stimuli are more likely to perform more competently on traditional psychometric measures of intelligence and language during childhood (e.g., Bornstein, 1984, 1985a, 1985b; Sigman, 1983). In particular, they believe that two aspects of information processing—decrement of attention and recovery of attention—are better at predicting intelligence later in childhood than the Bayley Scales of Infant Development. **Decrement of attention** is what we have been calling habituation—that is, the amount or rate of decay in looking at a repeated or constant stimulus. **Recovery of attention** is frequently referred to as novelty preference or response to novelty and is indexed by the relative amount of looking infants give to novel, rather than familiar, stimuli. Quicker decays or less cumulative looking in the habituation situation and greater amounts of looking in the novelty situation are generally thought to reflect more efficient information processing. Both types of attention—decrement and recovery—when measured in the first six months of infancy, are moderately linked with more efficient performance on standard intelligence tests assessed at various times between the ages of two and eight (Bornstein & Sigman, 1986). Thus, more precise assessments of the infant's cognitive functioning through the use of information processing tasks involving attention have led to the conclusion that there is greater continuity between infant and childhood intelligence than previously was believed.

Child Development Concept Table 5.2 summarizes our discussion of the Piagetian perspective on infant development, aspects of the information processing approach (such as attention and memory), and infant developmental scales, intelligence tests, and continuity in mental development. Next, we turn our attention to the infant's fascinating development of language.

Child Development Concept Table 5.2   Piaget's Theory, Attention and Memory, and Infant Intelligence Tests

Concept	Processes/Related Ideas	Characteristics/Description
Piaget's theory of infant development	Overview of theory	Piaget believed that the child passes through four stages of cognitive development from infancy through adolescence due to biological pressures to adapt to the environment and to organize structures of thinking. Piaget's four stages—sensorimotor, preoperational, concrete operational, and formal operational—are qualitatively different.
	Sensorimotor stage	The sensorimotor stage lasts from birth to about two years of age and involves progression in the infant's ability to organize and coordinate sensations and perceptions with physical movements and actions. The six substages of the sensorimotor stage are: simple reflexes; first habits and primary circular reactions; secondary circular reactions; coordination of secondary circular reactions; tertiary circular reactions, novelty, and curiosity; and internalization of schemes.
	Object permanence	Object permanence refers to the development of the ability to understand that objects and events continue to exist even though a child is not in direct contact with them. Piaget developed this perspective and described the development of object permanence over the course of the first two years of life. In recent years, some researchers have disagreed with Piaget about the timing of different aspects of object permanence.
Attention and memory	Attention	Attention plays an important role in information processing—it involves focusing perception to produce increased awareness of a stimulus. In studying attention in infants, researchers have been interested in the orienting response and the infant's ability to scan visual patterns. The orienting response (OR) involves a number of physiological changes, and it accompanies attention to a stimulus. Habituation and dishabituation of the OR have been widely used in infant research to index attention. Habituation of the OR in newborns has been shown with some responses but not others. When we look at patterns, our eyes make saccadic movements. Infants' pattern scanning involves an externality effect up to one month of age, but by two months, infants are focusing on internal features.
	Memory	Memory is a central process in cognitive development, involving the retention of information over time. Conjugate reinforcement is a procedure used to investigate memory in infants. With conjugate reinforcement, infants as young as two months of age remember for as long as three days. This procedure seems to produce adaptive responses or skills that sometimes are called "memory in the wide sense." It does not seem to produce conscious memory. Piaget called conscious memory "memory in the strict sense," that is, a type of memory that involves conscious feelings. Conscious memory is present as early as seven months of age, which is earlier than Piaget believed it to develop. Children and adults have little or no memory for events experienced before the age of three, a phenomenon known as infantile amnesia.
Individual differences, developmental scales, and the measurement of infant intelligence	Historical background	Developmental scales for infants grew out of the tradition of IQ testing with older children. These scales are less verbal than the IQ tests and involve more sensory/perceptual and motor items. The most important early contributor in this area was Gesell, whose scale still is widely used by pediatricians today. He developed the idea of a developmental quotient (DQ).
	Bayley Scales of Infant Development	The developmental scales most widely used today were devised by Nancy Bayley. Her scales consist of a Motor scale, a Mental scale, and an Infant Behavior Profile.

Child Development Concept Table 5.2 Continued		
Concept	**Processes/Related Ideas**	**Characteristics/Description**
Individual differences, developmental scales, and the measurement of infant intelligence (cont.)	Other scales	A number of other developmental scales also have been created, such as those by Cattell and Uzgiris-Hunt. The Uzgiris-Hunt scale assesses the infant's cognitive development according to Piaget's six substages of sensorimotor thought.
	Conclusions about infant tests and continuity in mental development	Infant intelligence tests have been better at assessing the effects of such matters as malnutrition, drugs, and maternal deprivation than at predicting intelligence later in childhood. However, recent research on two aspects of attention in infancy—decrement of attention and recovery of attention—suggests more continuity with intelligence in childhood.

LANGUAGE DEVELOPMENT

As mentioned in an earlier chapter, newborn birds come into the world prepared to sing the song of their species. They only have to listen to it several times early in their life and to practice it for awhile before they can sing it as well as their parents. They are predisposed to learn some song in some way at a certain time. And so it is also with humans, regardless of the native language they are to learn, according to many contemporary researchers who study language development. But as we will see, there is more to language development than this analogy with newborn birds suggests. Let's begin by studying the nature of language, its rule systems, some theories of language development, environmental influences on language, and milestones in language development during the infant years.

The Nature of Language

According to one definition, language is a complex set of rules used in speaking, listening, and writing. Although you may not really know the rules in the sense that you could recite them to someone, as a speaker, listener, and writer, you nonetheless "know" the rules necessary to speak, listen, and write.

Using language is a highly creative process. For example, you can understand this sentence even though you have never seen or heard it before. You can create a unique sentence you have never written or heard before. You can use words to symbolize many different things. And you can use language to communicate ideas. This

What is the nature of children's language development?

creative quality of language is called **infinite generativity,** referring to a finite set of rules used by the speaker, listener, and writer to generate an infinite number of meaningful sentences.

Although we often talk to other people about what is going on in our immediate environment, language also allows us to communicate information about another time and place. This characteristic of language is called **displacement.**

Already, then, we can expand our original brief definition of language. We can say that language is a complex set of rules used in speaking, listening, and writing and that is characterized by infinite generativity and displacement. Let's look at this complex set of rules in more detail.

The Rule Systems of Language

The five most prominent rule systems that characterize language are: phonology, morphology, syntax, semantics, and pragmatics.

Phonology

Language is comprised of basic, elementary sounds, or **phonemes.** In the English language, there are approximately 36 phonemes (other languages have more or fewer). The study of the sound system of a language is called **phonology,** and for every language, there are phonological rules that make some sound sequences (e.g., *sp, ar,* and *ba* in the English language) permissible and others (e.g., *zx* and *qp* in the English language) not permissible.

Morphology

Language is also characterized by a string of sounds that provide meaning for what we say and hear. The string of sounds is a **morpheme,** and **morphology** refers to rules involved in combining morphemes. Every word in a language is made up of one or more morphemes pieced together. Not all morphemes are words, however (e.g., *pre-, -tion,* and *-ing*). Some words consist of a single morpheme (e.g., *help*), whereas other words are made up of more than one morpheme (e.g., *helper,* which has two morphemes—*help + er*—with the morpheme *er* meaning "one who"—in this case, "one who helps"). Just as phonemes are restricted in specific ways, so are morphemes.

Syntax

Another set of language rules involves the combining of words into acceptable phrases and sentences. Because you and I share the same rules of **syntax,** if I say to you,

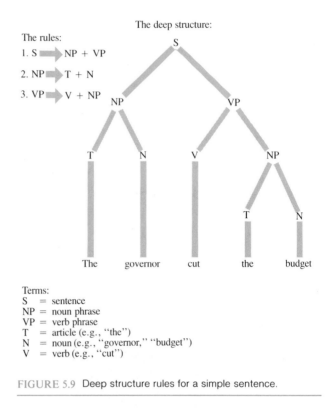

FIGURE 5.9   Deep structure rules for a simple sentence.

"Bob slugged Tom," and "Bob was slugged by Tom," you know who did the slugging in each case. You also understand that the sentence "You didn't say that, did you?" is syntactically correct, but that "You didn't say that, didn't you?" is unacceptable English.

A concept closely related to syntax is **grammar,** which refers to the formal description of syntactic rules. In school, most of us learned rules of grammar about how sentences are structured. Linguists devise grammatical rules that are similar in some ways to those you learned in school, but that are much more complex and powerful.

Many contemporary linguistic grammars (e.g., Chomsky, 1965) distinguish between the deep structure and the surface structure of sentences. **Surface structure** is the actual order of words in a spoken sentence. **Deep structure** concerns the syntactic relationships between the words in a sentence. Deep structure employs syntactic categories, such as noun phrase, verb phrase, noun, verb, and article (see Figure 5.9).

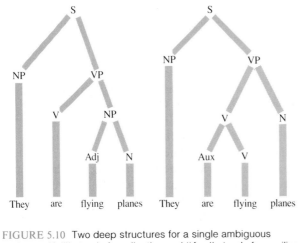

FIGURE 5.10 Two deep structures for a single ambiguous sentence. ("Adj" stands for adjective and "Aux" stands for auxiliary verb.)

Applying syntactic rules in different ways, one can give one and the same sentence (or surface structure) two different deep structures, and this is one reason why sentences can be ambiguous. Consider the following fictional headline (it was the winner in a contest for ambiguous headlines): "Mrs. Nixon Found Drunk on White House Lawn." Was Mrs. Nixon intoxicated, or did she spot a drunk on the lawn? Either interpretation can fit the sentence, depending upon the deep structure applied. Other examples of deep-structure ambiguity can be found in the sentences, "Visiting relatives can be boring," and "They are flying planes." The two deep structures for the "flying planes" sentence are shown in Figure 5.10.

Semantics

Another set of language rules is **semantics,** which refers to the study of the meaning of words and sentences. Every word has a set of semantic features. The words *girl* and *woman,* for example, share the same semantic features of female and human but differ with regard to age. There are semantic restrictions on how words can be used to form meaningful sentences as well. The sentence, "The bicycle talked the boy into buying it a candy bar" is syntactically correct but semantically incorrect. The sentence violates our semantic knowledge—bicycles do not talk.

Pragmatics

Rules of **pragmatics** pertain to the social context of language and to how people use language in conversation. Such rules allow us both to convey intended meanings and to "get along" with those with whom we are talking. The domain of pragmatics is broad indeed. It covers such things as (1) taking turns in discussions (instead of everyone talking at once), (2) using questions to convey commands ("Why is it so noisy in here?" "What is this, Grand Central Station?"), (3) using words like *the* and *a* in a way that enhances understanding ("I read *a* book last night. *The* plot was boring."), (4) using polite language in appropriate situations (e.g., when talking to one's boss), and even (5) telling stories that are interesting, jokes that are funny, and lies that convince.

Now that you have some idea of the rules that govern the language children learn, let's consider some different theories of language acquisition—some environmental, some biological, and some cognitive.

Theoretical Views of Language Acquisition

No mystery is deeper than how a child manages to learn the infinite number of things there are to learn about language. The language characteristic of infinite generativity has an important implication in the complexity of what the child must do—simple memorization of utterances will not work. Since the number of meaningful utterances is infinite, no child could possibly memorize them all. Instead, children must do something much more amazing—they must build in their head a kind of "language engine" (Miller, 1981) that can generate the infinity of admissible sound sequences of language. How a child manages to construct this engine is a question researchers are trying to answer.

Historically, there have been three major theories of how a child learns language: the behavioral view, the nativist view, and the cognitive view.

The Behavioral View

Imagine that you are a pigeon (or some other simple creature) and that you have been placed in a small wooden box. At one end of the box is a small circular disc. You do not know why you have been placed there, but you do know that you are hungry. Simply by chance, you turn your head toward the disc—and some food pellets fall out of a hole below the disc. You eat the pellets.

This event repeats itself again and again. However, at a certain point in the process, turning toward the disc no longer suffices for food to appear—a step or two toward the disc is required. Obligingly, you begin to produce this behavior to obtain the food pellets. At a still later point in time, it becomes necessary to come right up to the disc to obtain the food pellets. Still later, it is necessary to actually peck at the disc to get some food. So you learn these behaviors, too.

What has happened? According to the behavioral view of B. F. Skinner, your behavior has been "shaped." That is, you have been trained to respond so that you can obtain a reward. Would it be possible for human infants to learn language in this way? Could an infant be shaped to produce the words of a language, and then later shaped to produce appropriate sequences of words, and in this way learn to speak and understand? According to behavioral theory, the answer might be yes (Skinner, 1953). But many scientific findings, as well as what we know about the structure of language, suggest strongly that the answer is no.

Let's now look at three aspects of language development that provide information about the viability of the behavioral view—shaping and reinforcement, imitation, and the creative generalization of rules.

Shaping and Reinforcement   In a landmark experiment by Roger Brown, the interchanges between mothers and their children in the early stages of learning to speak were tape-recorded (Brown & Hanlon, 1970). Although the speech of the children included many ungrammatical sequences, the mothers appeared to understand them quite well. Not only that, the mothers responded to most of these ill-formed utterances in a positive (reinforcing) manner. In short, there was no evidence for "shaping" in the direction of good grammar.

It also is important to point out that there is no a priori way for the child to know what he or she is being reinforced for—Correct grammar? Correct pronounciation? For speaking at all? And the same holds true if the child is punished for a response. Thus, reinforcement only allows the child to know that he or she is globally correct or incorrect. And once the child produces an error, reinforcement does not inform the child as to how the error should be corrected.

Imitation   Other relevant research has focused on imitation, another important process in learning theory (Bandura, 1971, 1986). On the surface, it is plausible that young children learn language by imitating the speech of their parents. Indeed, there is no question that young children sometimes imitate. We even have evidence that if children practice imitating certain sentence structures—that of the passive voice, for example—they increase their spontaneous use of such structures and grow more proficient at comprehending such structures when spoken by others (Whitehurst & Vasta, 1975).

More recent evidence suggests that there are different forms of imitation, ranging from rote repetition of a parent's speech production to more creative forms of modeling and rehearsal (Moerk, 1985). Further, whereas some instances of imitation may have a "consolidation" function—facilitating the storage of particular words or expressions in memory—others may have a "looped replay" function, providing more time for the child to analyze and understand an utterance (Snow, 1985). Some promising findings indicate that children's tendencies to imitate language can be exploited to facilitate the process of learning a language. Specifically, a child who is delayed in his or her expressive language ability can be helped if the parents start using carefully selected lists of words and grammatical constructions in their speech to the child (Whitehurst, 1985).

Although imitation may contribute to the acquisition of language, there are individual differences in its nature and extent (Bloom, Hood, & Lightbown, 1974). In fact, Eric Lenneberg (1962) described a case of a child who was physically unable to speak, and therefore unable to engage in imitation, but who nonetheless learned language. Catherine Snow's (1985) observations show that imitation of language occurs infrequently in the home and that it is highly variable from one individual to the next. Children also have great difficulty in (or in some cases, simply cannot engage in) direct imitation of grammatical structures they have not mastered on their own. In sum, while imitation helps in the language learning process, its role is facilitative, rather than necessary (de Villiers & de Villiers, 1978).

Creative Generalization of Rules   Other problems with the behavioral learning theory of language acquisition pertain to the infinite generativity of language. This generativity is difficult to handle with concepts like shaping and reinforcement. What happens in language acquisition is more than just repetition of responses—it involves the generalization of complex rules to produce novel utterances. For example, a child might hear the sentence, "The plate fell on the floor," and later might spontaneously remark, "My mirror fell on the blanket." The learning-theory mechanisms of shaping and reinforcement are poorly suited to explain such creative generalization of rules.

Since the environmental explanation does not seem to explain the nature of language completely and accurately, let's look at the biological explanation.

Nativist Theory

If language is impossible to acquire through learning-theory mechanisms such as shaping and reinforcement, perhaps it simply is innate, that is, inherited as part of our genetic makeup. Of course, no specific language such as English is innate. Still, human infants might come equipped with a prewired "language acquisition device" (McNeill, 1970) that helps them to learn the language around them. Linguist Noam Chomsky (1957) has been a foremost advocate of this nativist idea. He claims that young children acquire language very quickly and that they do this under learning conditions that are much less than ideal (there is no effective shaping, for example). How could this occur unless children are born with a good deal of language-related machinery already in place in their brains? Aside from the rapidity with which children learn language, four compelling arguments favor Chomsky's nativist view: (1) language universals, (2) lateralization of language function in the brain, (3) critical or sensitive periods, and (4) communication in nonhuman species.

Language Universals   One type of argument for the nativist position is that there are "universals" of languages around the world. These **language universals** include certain phonological categories (consonants, vowels, syllables), syntactic categories (sentences, noun phrases, verb phrases, and so on), and even semantic categories (number). Since all human languages appear to

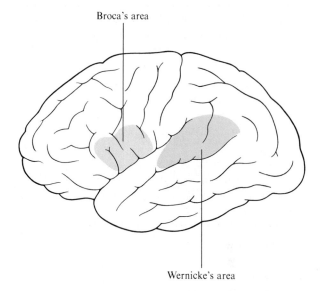

FIGURE 5.11   Speech and language functions are localized in Broca's and Wernicke's areas in the left hemisphere of the human brain. Broca's area plays a role in the production of speech, translating information from other speech areas of the brain into actual speech. Wernicke's area is involved in the comprehension of auditory input and the monitoring of speech output. Damage to these regions can seriously interfere with the ability either to produce or to understand speech.

have such categories (Maratsos, 1983), these language universals may be what comprise the young child's "language acquisition device."

Lateralization of Language Function in the Brain   A second argument for the nativist position concerns **lateralization of language** in the human brain. Current evidence suggests that language processing in the vast majority of people is controlled by the left hemisphere of the brain. Indeed, studies of language in brain-damaged individuals have pinpointed two areas of the left hemisphere of the brain that are especially critical. One of these areas—called **Broca's area**—is important for speech production, whereas the other area—called **Wernicke's area**—is more heavily involved in speech comprehension (Figure 5.11). Thus, damage to these areas in the brain (as a result of stroke, for example) can seriously interfere with a person's ability either to produce or to understand speech.

FOCUS ON CHILD DEVELOPMENT 5.4

THE CURIOUS CASE OF GENIE

Until she was 13½ years old, Genie was raised with virtually no linguistic (or any other) input. Her prior life has been vividly described by Jill and Peter de Villiers (1978):

Genie's first months seemed to have been medically unremarkable, at least as revealed by scanty pediatric records. However, from the age of about 20 months until she was discovered, Genie was kept in a small, closed and curtained room, either tied to a potty-chair or laid in a covered infant crib, confined from the waist down. Her mother, who was almost blind, visited her for only a few minutes each day to feed her with soft infant food. There was no opportunity for Genie to hear television or radio, for there was neither in the house. If she made noises, she was liable to be beaten by her father, who could not tolerate noise. The father and elder brother of

Genie did not speak to her but were wont to bark at her like dogs. It was the father's belief that Genie was hopelessly retarded, based on the fact that she was delayed in starting to walk because of a congenital hip dislocation that was treated during her first year.

It is unnecessary to explain that such circumstances did not leave Genie intact in body and mind. However, although she was malnourished, there was no evidence of physical abnormalities sufficient to account for her behavior, for she had adequate hearing, vision, and eye-hand coordination. She was severely disturbed emotionally, having frequent but silent tantrums, yet there were no other symptoms of childhood autism. The most likely explanation of her behavior was the chronic social deprivation she had suffered for those twelve years (Fromkin, Krashen, Curtiss, Rigler, & Rigler, 1974).

Shortly after her rescue, Genie was tested on a series of language comprehension tests. Although

---

Lateralization of language in the human brain is detectable at several months after birth, perhaps even earlier (Entus, 1975). These developmental findings, together with the discoveries of Broca and Wernicke's areas, suggest some inborn capacity to construct linguistic mechanisms in certain distinct parts of the brain (Miller, 1981).

Critical or Sensitive Periods   A third type of evidence for the nativist position concerns the concept of critical or sensitive periods for acquiring language (Lenneberg, 1967). If you have heard Henry Kissinger speak, you have some evidence for critical or sensitive periods. If an immigrant over 12 years old arrives in a new country and starts to learn its language, it is likely that, for the rest of his or her life, the immigrant will speak the language

with a foreign "accent." But this is not true for those who immigrate as young children (Asher & Garcia, 1969). Similarly, speaking like a native New Yorker is less related to how long you have lived in the city than to the age at which you moved there. Speaking with a New York "dialect" is more likely if you moved there at an age of less than 12 (Labov, 1970). Apparently, puberty marks the close of a critical or sensitive period for fully acquiring the phonological rules of different languages and dialects.

Eric Lenneberg (1967) has speculated that lateralization of language in the brain is subject to a similar critical or sensitive period. Up until the age of 12 years or so, a child who has suffered left-hemisphere brain damage might be able to shift language to the right side of the brain. But after this point, such a shift becomes within a very short time she began imitating words and learning names, her comprehension of grammar was completely absent. So Genie qualifies as the most satisfactory case to date to test Lenneberg's critical age hypothesis for first-language acquisition.

After her emergence into the world, Genie was placed in a foster home, where she began to acquire a first language primarily by exposure rather than by training, like a normal child. (pp. 215–216)

Genie's linguistic progress over a five-year period occurred at phonological, morphological, syntactic, and semantic levels (Fromkin, Krashen, Curtiss, Rigler, & Rigler, 1974). Her progress at the phonological level was similar to that of young normal children, and eventually she was able to produce all of the phonemes of English. However, her speech remained difficult for others to understand, apparently due to articulatory difficulties—she perceived phonemes better than she produced them.

With respect to the morphological level, Genie learned to use word endings to put words in the plural (*s*) or progressive (*ing*) forms, and she also mastered articles such as *a* and *the*. However, she had trouble with word endings for the past tense (*ed*). Genie's knowledge of syntax advanced her as far as the production of three-word utterances. However, it is unclear whether her knowledge of syntactic rules surpassed that of Sarah, the chimpanzee trained to talk with colored plastic shapes (Premack & Premack, 1972).

Genie's achievements at the semantic level were by far her most impressive. She showed good knowledge of how to classify words (e.g., she needed no training to know that words like *shirt* and *pants* meant types of clothes) and was advanced compared to young normal children in her knowledge of color and number concepts. Apparently, she was more advanced conceptually than linguistically (de Villiers & de Villiers, 1978).

---

impossible. Unfortunately, a critical or sensitive period for shifting lateralization of language is quite controversial and is not as well supported as a critical or sensitive period for phonological rules (de Villiers & de Villiers, 1978).

The experiences of a girl named Genie add further support to the belief that a reasonably long critical or sensitive period for language development exists (see Focus on Child Development 5.4).

Communication in Nonhuman Species   A fourth sort of nativist argument is that communication systems found in other species of animals do not approach the languages of humans in richness and complexity. Nonhuman primates gesture at each other, cats meow and purr, birds have songs and various calls, and bees perform elaborate ritualistic dances (see Figure 5.12). While

some of these systems might be called languages—this has been debated—not one of them has all five of the characteristics of human language that we described at the start of this section.

But what about animals higher on the evolutionary scale, such as chimpanzees? Do chimpanzees have languages that are more humanoid? Apparently, they do not, at least when one focuses on their natural way of life. Certainly, chimpanzees in the wild have identifiable calls—various hoots, howls, grunts, and so on. However, there are not very many of these—only about two dozen, in fact—and they are unlike human words in that they simply express emotions and are probably instinctive responses, not learned utterances with conventional relationships to their referents. Infinite generativity is apparently lacking in chimpanzee communication.

(a) Round dance

(b) Tail-wagging dance

FIGURE 5.12   The language dances of honey bees. The round dance indicates that nectar is within 100 meters of the hive. The tail-wagging dance points in the direction of the nectar when it's more than 200 meters away. Distances between 100 and 200 meters are signalled by a third dance.

The absence of language in chimpanzees is striking, especially in view of their high level of intelligence (Miller, 1981). But their intelligence raises an interesting question: Although chimpanzees in the wild do not have advanced language, could chimpanzees be taught an advanced form of language?

A number of psychologists have spent years trying to teach language to apes. For example, the Kelloggs adopted a 7-month-old chimpanzee and named her Gua (Kellogg & Kellogg, 1933). They tried to rear her alongside their 10-month-old son Donald. Gua was treated in very much the same way we rear infants and young children—she was dressed, talked with, and played with. Nine months after she was adopted, Gua knew 95 words and Donald only a few more. The Kelloggs discontinued the project because they were afraid that Gua's talents were slowing down Donald's progress!

The Hayeses adopted a chimpanzee named Viki when she was only a few days old (Hayes & Hayes, 1951). Their goal was to teach Viki to speak. They eventually taught her to say "Mama," but it was a painstaking effort. The Hayeses would sit day after day holding and shaping Viki's mouth to make the desired sounds. She eventually learned three other words—Papa, cup, and up—but she never learned the meanings of these words, and her speech was not very clear.

The chimpanzee's articulatory structures are not capable of producing all of the phonemes of the English language. Thus, efforts to teach nonhuman primates spoken language were abandoned. This led others to the idea of teaching chimpanzees language in a different form.

FIGURE 5.13 Washow is learning to ask for objects by means of sign language.

Another famous chimpanzee named Washoe was adopted by the Gardners when she was 10 months old (Gardner & Gardner, 1971). Having recognized that the Kelloggs and the Hayeses had not really been able to demonstrate that chimpanzees have language with human qualities, they tried to teach Washoe the American Sign Language, which is the sign language of the deaf. People conversed with Washoe only with the manual gestures of American Sign Language. The events of the daily routine, such as meals and washups, household chores, play with toys, and car rides to interesting places provided many opportunities for the use of sign language. (See Figure 5.13.)

There is yet another way to teach "language" to chimpanzees. The Premacks constructed a set of plastic shapes that symbolized different objects and were able to teach the meanings of the shapes to Sarah, a six-year-old chimpanzee (Premack & Premack, 1972). Sarah was able to respond correctly, using such abstract symbols as "same as" or "different from." For example, she could tell you that "banana is yellow" is the same as "yellow color of banana." Sarah eventually was able to "name" objects, respond "yes," "no," "same as," and "different from" and to tell you about certain events by using symbols (such as putting a banana on a tray). Did Sarah learn a generative language capable of productivity? Did the signs Washoe learned have an underlying system of language rules?

Herbert Terrace (1979) doubts that these apes have been taught language. Terrace was part of a research project focused on teaching language to an ape by the name of Nim Chimpsky (named for Noam Chomsky). Initially, Terrace was optimistic about Nim's ability to use language as humans use it, but after further evaluation, he concluded that Nim really did not have language in the sense that humans do. Terrace argues that apes do not spontaneously expand on a trainer's statements like humans do; rather, the apes essentially *imitate* their trainer. Terrace also believes that apes do not understand what they are saying when they speak; instead, they are responding to cues from the trainer of which the trainer is unaware. The apes also do not seem to have an appreciation of syntax.

In sum, it seems that chimpanzees can learn to use signs to communicate meanings. This used to be the old boundary for language. However, the question of whether chimpanzees can use ordered grammars that have significant characteristics of human grammar is more difficult to answer. Thus, the capacity for infinite generativity of language has not yet been demonstrated in chimpanzees. See VanCantfort & Rimpau, 1982 for a counter argument.

Now that we have seen the importance of the biological basis of language acquisition, let's consider the role that cognition plays.

Cognitive Theory

Noam Chomsky's idea of the young language learner as richly endowed with prewired equipment is today quite widely accepted. However, there is question about the type of equipment that the young learner possesses. Is such equipment specifically linguistic—a specialized "language acquisition device" (McNeill, 1970)—or is it more generally cognitive—deriving from the generally high level of intelligence of human beings (Maratsos, 1983)? A growing contingent of language researchers are beginning to argue that language derives less from specifically linguistic abilities than from more general cognitive abilities (e.g., Anderson, 1976, 1980; Bates & MacWhinney, 1982; Maratsos & Chalkey, 1980; Slobin, 1973). The basic claim is that a child's growing intelligence and his or her desire to express meanings—together with language input provided by parents—are what "drives" the acquisition of language. Thus, the

Table 5.2	Fourteen Meanings of Children's Two-Word Utterances
Meaning	**Example of Utterance**
Identification	"See doggie"
Location	"Book there"
Repetition	"More milk"
Nonexistence	"Allgone thing"
Negation	"Not wolf"
Possession	"My candy"
Attribution	"Big car"
Agent-action	"Mama walk"
Agent-object	"Mama book" (meaning, "Mama read book")
Action-location	"Sit chair"
Action-direct object	"Hit you"
Action-indirect object	"Give papa"
Action-instrument	"Cut knife"
Question	"Where ball?"

From Slobin, D., "Children and language: They learn the same around the world" in *Psychology Today.* Reprinted with permission from *Psychology Today Magazine.* © 1972 American Psychological Association.

focus is on the semantic and pragmatic levels of language, as opposed to the syntactic, morphological, or phonological levels.

One type of evidence for the cognitive view is that a child's early utterances seem to indicate knowledge of semantic categories—such as "agent" and "action"—rather than linguistic categories—such as "noun" and "verb" (Maratsos, 1983). For example, Daniel Slobin (1972) analyzed the early speech productions of children learning 18 different languages in countries all over the world. He found that all of these children started with one-word utterances and then advanced to two-word utterances. Further, the two-word utterances consistently fell into categories of meaning listed in Table 5.2.

Slobin concluded from his research that "A child easily figures out that the speech he hears around him contains discrete, meaningful elements and that these elements can be combined." According to Slobin, the child is concerned with how combining known words can convey certain meanings—syntactic rules and categories are not yet important to him or her. Indeed, rules that are purely syntactic in nature—such as rules for noun gender that exist in some languages—are mastered by children relatively late in their development (Slobin, 1973).

In support of Slobin's semantics-before-syntax view, there is evidence that children can tell that semantically deviant sentences are wrong before they can tell that syntactically deviant sentences are wrong (Washburn & Hakes, 1985). This evidence implies that a 5½-year-old might detect the unacceptability of "The bicycle talked to the boy" (semantically deviant) and yet fail to reject such sentences as, "The boy ride the bicycle" and "What you are doing today?" (syntactically deviant).

Another sort of argument for cognitive theory (and against nativist theory) concerns what we have learned about how language has evolved. Since a spoken language leaves no physical trace, the age of human language is difficult to determine. However, according to some estimates, language evolved as recently as 10,000 to 100,000 years ago (Swadesh, 1971). This is indeed quite recent in evolutionary time—perhaps too recent for a large amount of purely linguistic machinery to have evolved in the brain. From an evolutionary perspective, cognition is much older than human language. For example, tool-making activity—clearly a sign of high intellectual functioning—is at least 2 million years old (Miller, 1981). Considerations like these tend to favor the view that language is at least partly a product of rather general cognitive abilities, not just specific linguistic abilities.

We have studied at length the behavioral, nativist, and cognitive views of language. It is time to draw some conclusions about the viability of these views.

Conclusions About Theories of Language

To conclude our discussion of theories of language learning, we should note that all of the theories probably carry some truth. Imitation and reinforcement occur to an extent and probably have important functions (e.g., learning of words and expressions). Further, the evidence on lateralization and critical and sensitive periods supports some prewired linguistic machinery, especially for the phonological, morphological, and syntactic levels of language. Finally, cognitive learning strategies are also quite likely to facilitate language learning, especially learning of semantic and pragmatic rules. Moreover, since none of these theories is by itself adequate to handle all aspects of language acquisition, we might do well to keep all three.

Environmental Influences on Language

Environmental factors also play a role in a child's acquisition of language. Perhaps the most fascinating of these environmental factors is known as **motherese,** a characteristic way in which mothers, fathers, and people in general talk to young language learners. (Read Focus on Child Development 5.5.) If you pay attention to your behavior when talking to a two-year-old, you will notice some interesting things. Your sentences will be simple and short, you will use exaggerated intonation contours (speaking with great ups and downs in pitch), you will pause for long periods between sentences, and you will place great stress on the more important words. You also will probably repeat yourself frequently and engage in the behaviors of **prompting** (rephrasing a sentence you have spoken if it appears that the child has not understood), **echoing** (repeating what the child says to you, especially if it is an incomplete phrase or sentence), and **expanding** (restating what the child has said in a more linguistically sophisticated form). The term *motherese* is a misnomer in that you need not be a mother to speak in this way. Fathers' and mothers' speech to their three- to nine-month-old children has been found to be quite similar (Kruper, 1985). Even four-year-olds will speak

differently to two-year-olds than to children their own age (Shatz & Gelman, 1973).

Two prosodic characteristics of motherese—exaggerated intonation contours and the occurrence of whispering—have been extensively examined by Anne Fernald (Fernald, 1983; Fernald & Simon, 1984). She has performed highly sophisticated acoustic analyses of mothers' speech to their three- to five-day-old babies versus other adults. According to these analyses, mothers' speech to infants has higher pitch, wider pitch excursions, longer pauses, shorter utterance lengths, and more repetitions of pitch contours and whispering than does their speech to other adults. Most remarkably, 77 percent of mothers' utterances to their babies involved expanded pitch contours and/or whispering, while almost none of their utterances to other adults contained these features. When mothers simply imagine that they are talking to their babies, their speech resembles that of true motherese, but only to an extent. Thus, the reactions of a physically present baby apparently contribute to motherese-type speech.

What might be the functions of the exaggerated contour and other features of motherese to infants? In general, there can be no question that these aspects of motherese help to get messages across. For example, Fernald (1985) has documented that the intonation contours in motherese provide clues concerning the emotional content of what a mother is saying. Further, James Morgan (1985) has found that exaggerated contours tend to occur at syntactic phrase boundaries. Thus, pitch contours offer clues about the syntax as well as the meaning of the message.

The functions of prompting, echoing, and expanding have also been examined. Expansion in particular has been extensively discussed. When a young child utters a short, primitive sentence, such as "Brush teeth," or "Dog bark," an adult is quite likely to expand it syntactically. The adult might say: "Oh, you want to brush your teeth," or "Yes, the dog is barking." It would seem on the surface that this technique of expansion could not help but improve the child's knowledge of syntax. However, research on this question has not been encouraging (de Villiers & de Villiers, 1978), and some researchers wonder if expansion helps at all (Flavell, 1985).

FOCUS ON CHILD DEVELOPMENT 5.5

BABY TALK

Roger Brown has been one of the pioneers in our understanding of language development in infancy. He recently described an experience in William James Hall at Harvard University:

> My office . . . is next door to the Child Development Research Laboratory. We are pretty well insulated against sound transmission, so the voices in the laboratory are content-filtered for me, but I can nevertheless always tell when someone is talking to a baby. That is because everyone, all adults and even children as young as three to four years . . . speak to babies in a special "register" (the baby talk register or BT).   (Brown, 1986, p. 518)

Brown (1986) goes on to discuss the nature of the baby talk register and research documenting its existence. A **register** is a way of speaking to address a particular category, such as babies, pets, or foreigners. The **baby talk register** has six distinguishing features (Garnica, 1977):

1. A higher than normal frequency (about 267 Hz)
2. Greater than normal range of pitch
3. Rising final intonation on imperatives ("push in?")
4. Occasional whispering
5. Longer than normal duration in speaking separable verbs (such as "puuuush—in")
6. Two main syllabic stresses on words calling for one (such as "pú-úsh-ín")

It is hard to talk baby talk when not in the presence of a baby. But as soon as you start talking with a baby, you immediately shift into the BT register. Much of this register is automatic and something that parents are not aware of. The BT register seems to serve an important function in capturing the infant's attention and maintaining communication as well.

The BT register appears to be universal (Ferguson, 1977). It was documented as early as the first century B.C. and has been described as present in highly diverse languages. Some characteristics of the BT register, such as high pitch, exaggerated intonation, and simple sentences, are virtually the same in different languages.

When parents are asked why they use baby talk, they usually point out that it is designed to teach their child to talk. Brown (1977) believes that there are two basic features of BT—(1) simplification features, such as short sentences and references to what is here and now and (2) affectional features, such as diminutives, pet names, and nursery tone.

While older peers often talk BT with infants, observations of siblings indicate that certain features of BT are not always used. The extensive sibling observations of Judy Dunn and Carol Kendrick (1982) revealed that the older sibling often drops the affectional features when rivalry is sensed.

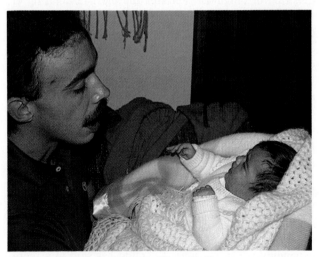

What are some examples of the BT register?

Babies make a great captive audience with whom to share those brilliant ideas no one else appreciates.

A positive role for a type of echoing was suggested by a study of communicative competence of adopted and nonadopted one-year-olds (Hardy-Brown & Plomin, 1985). Communicative competence of one-year-olds was assessed by (1) analyzing video recordings of the infants interacting with their mothers, (2) examining productive vocabulary of the infants as reported by their mothers, and (3) evaluating infants' performance on eight language-relevant items from the Bayley Scale of Infant Development. It was found that mothers' tendency to imitate (echo) the vocalizations of their babies was positively correlated with the communicative competence of these babies. That is, mothers who tended to imitate more were likely to have babies who were advanced in their language. Of course, future research must address the issue of whether mothers' echoing actually causes improvements in language acquisition or whether mothers of more linguistically competent infants tend to imitate more.

Recasting appears to be a promising technique for speeding language learning (Nelson, 1975; Nelson, Carskaddon, & Bonvillian, 1973). In response to a sentence uttered by a young child, an adult can recast the sentence, phrasing the same or a similar meaning in a different way, perhaps turning it into a question. For example, if a child says, "The dog was barking," the adult can respond by asking, "When was the dog barking?" Recasting has had some positive effects on children's use of linguistic structures, and—interestingly—parents do not use it as spontaneously as they use expansion (Flavell,

1985). Perhaps recasting might be used in programs for improving "motherese" of parents of slow language learners.

The effects of recasting fit with suggestions that "following in order to lead" a child helps the child to learn language (Schaffer, 1977). That is, letting a child initially indicate an interest and then proceeding to elaborate that interest—commenting, demonstrating, and explaining—may enhance communication and help language acquisition. In contrast, an overly active, directive approach to communicating with the child may be harmful (Schaffer, 1977).

To conclude our discussion of the many aspects of the environment that can influence language learning, we consider the process of **labeling.** Young children are forever being asked to identify the names of objects. Roger Brown once called this the great word game and claimed that much of the early vocabulary acquired by children is motivated by this adult pressure to identify the words associated with objects.

Child Development Concept Table 5.3 summarizes our discussion of the nature of language, rule systems of language, theoretical views of language, and environmental influences on language acquisition. Now we turn our attention to the developmental unfolding of language during the infant years.

Milestones in Language Development During Infancy

Milestones in language development during infancy include some preverbal accomplishments that are precursors to language, one-word utterances, and two-word utterances.

Preverbal Developments

It is a happy event for a young child's parents when he or she utters a first word. (It might be a happy event for the child as well, but this is hard to tell.) The event usually occurs when the child is 10 to 13 months old (de Villiers & de Villiers, 1978), although some children take longer. Some parents view the onset of language as coincident with this first word. But a number of highly significant accomplishments precede this dramatic event.

Child Development Concept Table 5.3   The Nature of Language, Rule Systems of Language, Theoretical Views of Language Acquisition, and Environmental Influences on Language

Concept	Processes/Related Ideas	Description/Characteristics
Nature of language	Infinite generativity	Infinite generativity involves using a finite set of rules to generate an infinite number of meaningful sentences.
	Displacement	Displacement allows us to communicate information about a different time and context.
Language rules	Phonology	Phonology is the study of the sound system of a language.
	Morphology	Morphology refers to rules involved in combining morphemes—strings of sounds that provide meaning to what we say and hear.
	Syntax	Syntax is a complex aspect of language referring to the manner in which words are combined to form acceptable phrases and sentences. It involves grammar and deep and surface structures.
	Semantics	Semantics is the study of the meaning of words and sentences.
	Pragmatics	Pragmatics refers to the social context of language and to how people use language in conversations.
Theoretical views of language acquisition	Behavioral	The behavioral view argues that children learn language through imitation, shaping, and reinforcement. Some learning through imitation occurs, but the evidence is stacked against the behavioral view, particularly information about the infinite generativity of language.
	Nativist	The nativist theory is supported by evidence about language universals, the lateralization of language function in the brain, critical or sensitive periods in phonological development, and the absence of humanlike language in other species.
	Cognitive	The cognitive theory argues that young children's speech shows more evidence of semantic than syntactic categories. Further, language may be recent in evolutionary time. Thus, cognitive machinery seems to be used for language.
	Conclusions	None of these theories is by itself adequate to handle all aspects of language acquisition, but all of the theories probably carry some truth.
Environmental influences on language	Their nature	Aspects of the environment that are important in language learning are "motherese," prompting, echoing, expanding, recasting, following in order to lead, and labeling. Research studies on imitation and shaping also have a strong environmental flavor.

These preverbal accomplishments fall into three main areas: vocalization, communication, and cognition (Flavell, 1985).

Vocalization, Babbling   Vocalization begins with the infant's **babbling,** somewhere between three and six months of age. The onset of babbling is controlled by biological maturation, not reinforcement or even the ability to hear. Even deaf babies will babble for a time (Lenneberg, Rebelsky, & Nichols, 1965).

It once was assumed that all possible phonemes in all the world's languages were produced by babies in the

babbling stage. Now we know that this is not true (Flavell, 1985). Perhaps the best guess about the function of babbling is that it exercises the child's vocal apparatus and helps him or her to develop articulatory skills that later will be useful in producing words and sentences (Clark & Clark, 1977).

Pragmatic Communication Skills   A baby's earliest communication skills have little to do with his or her babbling; instead, they consist of a number of interesting pragmatic skills that support communication (Flavell, 1985). Some of these skills pertain to attracting attention from parents and other people in the environment.

Infants can engage the attention of others through (1) their looking behavior, specifically their ability to make and break eye contact with others, and also through (2) vocalizing sounds and making manual actions, such as pointing.

One 14-month-old displayed—even flaunted—his knowledge of using eye contact for attention. At a family gathering of several adult relatives, he picked out one adult, established eye contact with her, and then ran over for a hug. Then he picked another adult and repeated the procedure. This went on for several minutes, and he eventually engaged every adult in the room, *except* for Grandpa. This avoidance of Grandpa was apparently on purpose, as despite repeated entreaties from Grandpa, little David avoided making eye contact with him. And he never ran over to his grandpa for a hug (this apparently was a kind of game on David's part, as he was very fond of his grandpa). David's skill at avoiding eye contact with Grandpa was very impressive—it reminded David's father of an overworked waiter who skillfully avoids eye contact with customers who are waiting for their checks. Both overworked waiters and 14-month-old babies appear to have knowledge of how eye contact establishes reciprocal attention between two people.

Another type of pragmatic knowledge is revealed by the ability to *request* and *assert*. Before the age of about nine months, a child who wants a toy might look toward it while reaching and fussing. An older child, however, is likely to establish eye contact with a nearby adult and begin alternating eye contact between the adult and the toy while fussing (Bates, 1979). Such behavior is easily understood as a request to bring the object. Assertions are a bit harder to identify (Flavell, 1985). But, frequently, babies will point toward an object while showing no particular interest in picking it up or playing with it. This sort of behavior might be an invitation for another simply to look at the thing pointed to. It appears to be an early form of asserting—communicating about things in the world.

Cognitive Development   For a child to master language, some achievements in the cognitive area probably are required. A necessary skill for such a required achievement is the ability to use and comprehend symbols—that is, to have knowledge that one thing can stand for another. Words are symbols that relate arbitrarily to their referents. Unless a child can think symbolically, he or she would be unlikely to learn how words and symbols relate and would find it difficult to advance far in his or her language. As Jean Piaget has theorized, the capacity for symbolic thought is not present at birth but must develop over the first two years of life. Thus, it may be no coincidence that a child's language competence begins to develop quite rapidly around the end of the second year.

Now that we have studied preverbal accomplishments in infant language, let's move on to the infant's first words.

One-Word Utterances

A child's first words include those naming important people (*Dada* and *Mama*), familiar animals (e.g., *dog, kittie*), vehicles (e.g., *car, boat*), toys (e.g., *ball, doll*), foods (e.g., *milk, cookie*), body parts (e.g., *eye, nose*), clothes (e.g., *hat*), household items (e.g., *clock*), greeting terms (e.g., *bye*), and others. And the first words of babies born 50 years ago were similar to those of babies born recently (Clark, 1979; 1983). Babies seem to differ in that some use more "referential terms" (i.e., object names), while others use more "expressive terms" (e.g., "bye bye, naughty") (Nelson, 1978). Although "referential babies" appear initially to learn new words faster, they are no more advanced than "expressive babies" in their knowledge of linguistic rules (de Villiers & de Villiers, 1978).

Next we consider what these one-word utterances might mean.

The Holophrase Hypothesis

One hypothesis for the meaning of the child's one-word utterances is that the single word stands for a complete sentence in the young child's mind: He or she thinks a complete sentence but—because of limited cognitive or linguistic skills—can only produce one word at a time. According to this view, the one-word utterance is a **holophrase**—a single word that implies a whole sentence (de Villiers & de Villiers, 1978; Dale, 1976).

MARVIN by Tom Armstrong. © by and permission of News America Syndicate, 1985.

An alternative hypothesis is that a one-word utterance really is what it appears to be—a thought corresponding to just one word. Consider a case in which a young child hears a footstep in the hall and utters "Mama." According to the holophrase hypothesis, the child might actually mean "Here comes Mama," or "That's the sound of Mama coming," or even "I'm glad Mama is coming because I'm starting to get hungry." But an alternative interpretation is that the sound of the footstep makes the child think of his or her mother, which evoked the corresponding word (Flavell, 1985).

Eve Clark's Theory of Meaning   It seems likely that the truth about one-word utterances does not fit either the holophrase hypothesis or the one-word/one-idea hypothesis. Consider a child who shoves a glass in your face and cries, "Milk" (Flavell, 1985). The child clearly means more than the simple word *milk*—but has he or she actually formulated a sentence in his or her mind? Eve Clark's (1983) theory offers some insight into the meaning of one-word utterances.

According to Clark, it is important to distinguish between *words* on the one hand and *concepts* on the other. Beginning around nine months of age or even earlier,

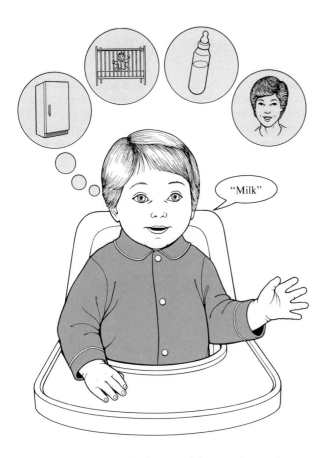

"Milk"

FIGURE 5.14 A child's mind may contain several concepts expressed by a single word.

So what happens when a child wants to say something? The child has some concepts in mind—perhaps quite a few—and tries to choose some word to express them. He does the best that he can in choosing a word, but probably the word does not capture all of his concepts. Although he is thinking about more than just one word, he may not have a full sentence in mind. What he has in mind are concepts, some of them concepts that he has not verbalized to himself. Figure 5.14 illustrates this idea.

Over- and Underextensions of Words   Clark's interesting theory is also useful for explaining how children can "know" a word and yet use it incorrectly. One way that children can misuse words is by **overextending** the word's meaning. For example, the word *ball* might be used not only for balls, but also for (1) other toys, (2) radishes, and (3) stone spheres on park gates; and the word *watch* might be used for (1) a clock, (2) a gas meter, (3) a fire hose wound on a spool, and (4) a bathroom scale with a round dial (Clark, 1983). In both of these cases, a word's meaning has been overextended to include a set of objects that (according to adults) does not fit within it. Another way of misusing a word is by **underextending** its meaning. For example, a child might use the word *car* when she is looking out the window and a car goes by, but not when she is on the street and a car goes by (Bloom, 1973). Apparently, the child's use of "car" has been underextended to cases in which cars are seen from windows.

Overextensions and underextensions are more prevalent in children's *production* of words than in their *comprehension* of words. For example, a child might call many round objects "ball." Yet, if you put her in front of several round objects, including a ball, a clock and a Frisbee, she might be able to tell you which one is the "ball" (Clark, 1983). This finding seems puzzling at first—does the child know the extension of "ball" or not? However, if we remember the distinction between concepts and words, the finding can be understood. The child probably has the concept of ball, as well as the concept of clock and Frisbee. However, she may have learned the word *ball* much better than *clock* or *Frisbee*. Hence, when she wants to name a clock or Frisbee, she might

children begin acquiring concepts. They learn that sets of physically different stimuli (e.g., different views of their mother's face) can be the same person or thing (mother). Children acquire more and more new concepts in succeeding months, while they are learning words. When they are learning words, children are learning how different sequences of phonemes map onto their store of concepts. Of course, learning words may help children to add to their store of concepts. The processes of learning words and learning concepts are highly intertwined (Kuczaj, 1985). Nonetheless, there are many concepts—perhaps especially when the language learning process has only just begun—that a child has not yet associated with words.

not recall their proper (adult) names and so she settles for *ball,* a term she knows well that maps onto similar concepts. Although the child may know that clocks and Frisbees are not "balls," she also wants to communicate—hence, she overextends a little. From this analysis, we see how the child's "misuses" of words arise from her active attempts to communicate.

Two-Word Utterances

By the time children are 18 to 24 months old, they usually begin uttering two-word statements. During this two-word stage, they quickly grasp the importance of expressing concepts and the role language plays in communicating with others. It is not unusual for as many as a thousand two-word utterances to appear on a monthly basis at this point in development (Braine, 1976). These two-word utterances can convey a wealth of meaning, as we discussed earlier (Table 5.2). However, they differ substantially from adult word combinations. Language usage at this time has been referred to as **telegraphic speech**—articles, auxiliary verbs, and other connectives are usually omitted. When we send telegrams to people, we try to be short and precise, excluding any unnecessary words. Children in the two-word stage are doing something quite similar. Of course, telegraphic speech is not limited to two-word utterances; three- and four-word utterances can also be telegraphic (e.g., "Mommy give ice cream," "Mommy give Tommy ice cream").

A question that has not yet been answered is whether children at the two-word-utterance stage have a grasp of syntactic rules. On the positive side, some children appear to use word order to help them communicate and interpret different meanings. For example, a child might say "Daddy pat" when her father is patting her, and "pat Daddy" when she is patting her father (de Villiers & de Villiers, 1978; Flavell, 1985). However, not all children appear to use word order in this way. Thus, we simply do not know how much syntactic knowledge we can attribute to children in the two-word stage.

We have taken some time to chart the foundations of language and its development during infancy. Keep in mind as you read about children's development that language is an important domain of study. We discuss language again in Chapters 7, 10, and 12.

THINKING BACK, LOOKING AHEAD

The world of learning, cognition, and language in infancy is an intriguing one—for the infants who are acquiring skills, learning about the world, saying words, attending to events, and remembering what had happened to them in the past and also for the scientists who have devised ingenious ways to investigate this fascinating world. It is a world of interest in moving, colored patterns; fears of furry objects; frowns at a frowning model; patterns of sucking; knowledge that a rabbit is out of sight but not out of mind; kicks to make a mobile whirl; memories of a sibling's birth; response to a request to take a drink; the curious cases of Genie, Gua, Viki, Washoe, Sarah, and Nim Chimpsky; as well as progress from babbling to the one-word utterance "knife" to the two-word utterance "cut knife."

In the last two chapters, you have learned about the infant's physical and perceptual motor development as well as about his or her learning, cognition, and language development. In Chapter 6, we tackle the infant's social and personality development. But before we leave the world of infant learning, cognition, and language, reflect for a moment on some words by Longfellow that capture the beauty of the infant's development:

Ye are better than all the ballads
    That ever were sung or said;
For ye are living poems,
    And all the rest are dead.

SUMMARY

I. Information about learning focuses on what learning is, classical conditioning, operant conditioning, imitation, and conclusions about the learning approaches.
  A. Learning can be defined as a relatively permanent change in the mind or behavior that occurs through experience and cannot be accounted for by reflexes, instincts, and maturation, or the influence of drugs, fatigue, injury, or disease.
  B. Classical conditioning is a procedure by which a neutral stimulus comes to elicit a response by being paired with a stimulus that regularly evokes the response.
    1. The basic classical conditioning experiment was conducted by Pavlov and involved an unconditioned stimulus (UCS), an unconditioned response (UCR), a conditioned

stimulus (CS), and a conditioned response (CR). Responses can be acquired or eliminated through classical conditioning. Extinction refers to the presentation of the CS alone and results in a decrease of the CR. After a rest period, spontaneous recovery occurs.

2. Two possible explanations for classical conditioning are stimulus substitution (the traditional view) and information theory (a more modern interpretation).

3. Early research on classical conditioning in infancy by John Watson focused on phobias and how they could be reduced or eliminated through counterconditioning. More recent research has examined whether newborns can be classically conditioned. It appears that classical conditioning of infants is possible, but not without great difficulty.

4. The adaptability that classical conditioning brings has survival value for the young child. However, classical conditioning is a rather simple form of learning and fails to capture the child's active nature in the learning process.

C. Operant conditioning emphasizes the infant's operating or acting on the environment, with behavior being controlled by external consequences. Operant conditioning has been demonstrated with young infants.

D. Imitation is sometimes called modeling or observational learning. Some experts, such as Bandura, believe that imitation requires the coordination of motor activity with a mental picture of the act being imitated. Considerable interest has been generated in whether newborns and young infants can engage in imitation. Debate focuses on what is pseudo-imitation and what is imitation. Researchers believe that it is important to show that infants can imitate behaviors they cannot see themselves perform, as well as behaviors that are not spontaneous or coincidental. Some researchers believe that true imitation has been demonstrated in very young infants; others disagree.

E. Classical conditioning, operant conditioning, and imitation are three ways infants learn. As grand theories of the developing infant and child, however, classical and operant conditioning miss the importance of cognitive factors in either mediating environmental-behavior relations or in causing behavior.

II. Information about infant cognition focuses on Piaget's theory of infant development, attention and memory, and infant intelligence tests.

A. An understanding of Piaget's theory requires information about the theory's basic features, what the sensorimotor stage is like, and the nature of object permanence.

1. According to Piaget, the child passes through four stages of cognitive development from infancy through adolescence due to biological pressures to adapt to the environment and to organize structures of thinking. Piaget's four stages—sensorimotor, preoperational, concrete operational, and formal operational—are qualitatively different.

2. The sensorimotor stage lasts from birth to about two years of age and involves progression in the infant's ability to organize and coordinate sensations and perceptions with physical movements and actions. The six substages of the sensorimotor stage are: simple reflexes; first habits and primary circular reactions; secondary circular reactions; coordination of secondary circular reactions; tertiary circular reactions, novelty, and curiosity; and internalization of schemes.

3. Object permanence refers to the development of the ability to understand that objects and events continue to exist even though a child is not in direct contact with them. Piaget developed this perspective and described the development of object permanence over the course of the first two years of life. In recent years, some researchers have disagreed with Piaget about the timing of different aspects of object permanence.

B. Two of the most prominent processes used by the infant to deal with information in the world are attention and memory.

1. Attention plays an important role in information processing—it involves focusing perception to produce increased awareness of a stimulus. In studying attention in infants, researchers have been interested in the orienting response and the infant's ability to scan visual patterns. The orienting response (OR) involves a number of physiological changes, and it accompanies attention to a stimulus. Habituation and dishabituation of the

OR have been widely used in infant research to index attention. Habituation of the OR in newborns has been shown with some responses but not others. When we look at patterns, our eyes make saccadic movements. Infants' pattern scanning involves an externality effect up to one month of age, but by two months of age, infants are focusing on internal features.

2. Memory is a central process in cognitive development, involving the retention of information over time. Conjugate reinforcement is a procedure used to investigate memory in infants. With conjugate reinforcement, infants as young as two months of age remember for as long as three days. This procedure seems to produce adaptive responses or skills that sometimes are called "memory in the wide sense." It does not seem to produce conscious memory. Piaget called conscious memory "memory in the strict sense," that is, a type of memory that involves conscious feelings. Conscious memory is present as early as seven months of age, which is earlier than Piaget believed it to develop. Children and adults have little or no memory for events experienced before the age of three, a phenomenon known as infantile amnesia.

C. Individual differences in infant development have been studied through the use of developmental scales or infant intelligence tests.
1. Developmental scales for infants grew out of the tradition of IQ testing with older children. These scales are less verbal than the IQ tests and involve more sensory/perceptual and motor items. The most important early contributor in this area was Gesell, whose scale still is widely used by pediatricians today. He developed the idea of a developmental quotient (DQ).
2. The developmental scales most widely used today were devised by Nancy Bayley. Her scales consist of a Motor scale, a Mental scale, and an Infant Behavior Profile.
3. A number of other developmental scales also have been devised, such as those by Cattell and Uzgiris-Hunt. The Uzgiris-Hunt scale assesses the infant's cognitive development according to Piaget's six substages of sensorimotor thought.
4. Infant intelligence tests have been better at assessing the effects of such matters as malnutrition, drugs, and maternal deprivation than at predicting intelligence later in childhood. However, recent research on two aspects of attention in infancy—decrement of attention and recovery of attention—suggests more continuity with intelligence in childhood.

III. An understanding of language development requires information about its basic nature, language rules, theories of language development, environmental influences on language, and milestones in language development during the infant years.
A. Two characteristics of language are infinite generativity and displacement.
B. Language rules include phonology (study of the sound system), morphology (rules involved in combining morphemes—strings of sounds providing meaning to what we say and hear), syntax (a complex aspect referring to how words are combined to form acceptable phrases and sentences; involves grammar and deep and surface structures), semantics (study of the meaning of words and sentences), and pragmatics (which refers to the social context of language and to how people use language in conversation).
C. Theoretical views of language acquisition include the behavioral, nativist, and cognitive perspectives.
1. The behavioral view argues that children learn language through imitation, shaping, and reinforcement. Some learning through imitation occurs, but the evidence is stacked against the behavioral view, particularly information about the infinite generativity of language.
2. The nativist theory is supported by evidence about language universals, the lateralization of language function in the brain, critical or sensitive periods in phonological development, and the absence of humanlike language in other species.
3. The cognitive theory argues that young children's speech shows more evidence of semantic than syntactic categories. Further, language may be recent in evolutionary time. Thus, cognitive machinery seems to be used for language.
4. None of these theories is by itself adequate to handle all aspects of language acquisition, but all of the theories probably carry some truth.
D. Aspects of the environment that are important in language learning are "motherese," prompting, echoing, expanding, recasting, following in order to lead, and labeling. Research studies on imitation and shaping also have a strong environmental flavor.

E. Milestones in language development during infancy include preverbal accomplishments, one-word utterances, and two-word utterances.
  1. Vocalization begins with babbling, somewhere between three and six months of age. A baby's earliest communication skills consist of a number of interesting pragmatic skills. Some cognitive development is likely to be necessary for a child to master language.
  2. The holophrase hypothesis, the one-word/one-idea hypothesis, and Eve Clark's theory of meaning are all possible explanations for the meaning of one-word utterances.
  3. By 18 to 24 months of age, infants usually begin uttering two-word statements. Language at this point is often referred to as telegraphic.

phonemes (phonology) 184
pragmatics 185
primary circular reaction 170
prompting 193
recasting 195
recovery of attention 181
saccadic movements 174
scheme (schema) 168
secondary circular reaction 170
semantics 185
spontaneous recovery 163

S-S learning 162
stimulus substitution theory 163
surface structure 184
symbol 171
syntax 184
telegraphic speech 200
tertiary circular reactions 171
unconditioned response (UCR) 162
unconditioned stimulus (UCS) 162
underextending 199
Wernicke's area 187

KEY TERMS

A-B error 173
babbling 196
baby talk register 194
baseline 165
Bayley Scales of Infant Development 179
Broca's area 187
classical conditioning 162
conditioned response (CR) 162
conditioned stimulus (CS) 162
conditioning trials 165
conjugate reinforcement technique 176
coordination of secondary circular reactions 170
counterconditioning 164
decrement of attention 181
deep structure 184
developmental quotient (DQ) 179
developmental scales 179
dishabituation 174
displacement 183
echoing 193
expanding 193

externality effect 175
extinction 163
grammar 184
habituation 174
holophrase 197
imitation (modeling, observational learning) 166
infantile amnesia 178
infinite generativity 183
information theory 164
intentionality 171
internalization of schemes 171
labeling 195
language universals 187
lateralization of language 187
learning 161
memory 175
Mental scale 179
morphemes (morphology) 184
"motherese" 193
object permanence 172
orienting response (OR) 174
overextending 199
phobias 164

SUGGESTED READINGS

Brown, A. L., Bransford, J. D., Ferrara, R. A., & Campione, J. C. (1983). Learning, remembering, and understanding. In P. H. Mussen (Ed.), *Handbook of child psychology* (4th ed.), Vol. 3. New York: Wiley. These leaders in the field of learning and cognition describe trends and theory in research, the nature of learning activities, as well as intervention research.
Bruner, J. (1983). *Child talk*. New York: Norton. A fascinating view of the child's language development by one of the leading cognitive theorists.
Flavell, J. H. (1985). *Cognitive development* (2nd ed.). Englewood Cliffs, NJ: Prentice-Hall. An outstanding statement of the major contemporary ideas about cognitive development by one of the leading scholars. Although inspired by Piaget's work, the author goes beyond it, offering new insights, critical evaluation, and reflections about his own research.
Ginsburg, H., & Opper, S. (1979). *Piaget's theory of intellectual development* (2nd ed.). Englewood Cliffs, NJ: Prentice-Hall. One of the best explanations and descriptions of Piaget's theory of infant development.
Maratsos, M. (1983). Some current issues in the study of the acquisition of grammar. In P. H. Mussen (Ed.), *Handbook of child psychology* (4th ed.), Vol. 3. New York: Wiley. A very thorough, informative, up-to-date review of what is known about language development.

SOCIAL AND PERSONALITY FOUNDATIONS AND DEVELOPMENT IN INFANCY

IMAGINE. . .YOU ARE FACED WITH CHOOSING A DAY-CARE CENTER FOR YOUR ONE-YEAR-OLD CHILD

PREVIEW

THE ROLE OF BIOLOGY AND CULTURE IN UNDERSTANDING SOCIAL AND PERSONALITY DEVELOPMENT IN INFANCY

Biological Influences
Sociocultural Influences

FAMILY PROCESSES

The Beginnings of Parenthood
Reciprocal Socialization and Mutual Regulation
The Family as a System
The Construction of Relationships

CHILD DEVELOPMENT CONCEPT TABLE 6.1: BIOLOGY, CULTURE, AND FAMILY PROCESSES

ATTACHMENT

What Is Attachment?
Theories of Attachment
Ethological Theory
Psychoanalytic Theory
Social Learning Theory
Cognitive Developmental Theory
Evaluation of Attachment Theories
The Developmental Course of Attachment, Individual Differences, and Situational Influences
The Developmental Course of Attachment
Individual Differences and Situational Influences
Attachment and the Construction of Relationships

FOCUS ON CHILD DEVELOPMENT 6.1: ATTACHMENT BONDS, PEER RELATIONS, DEPRESSION, AND SCHIZOID BEHAVIOR
Attachment and Temperament

FOCUS ON CHILD·DEVELOPMENT 6.2: INTENSE MOTHERS AND AVOIDANT BABIES—THE IMPORTANCE OF TEMPERAMENT
Infant-Father Attachment and Involvement
The Father's Role and Involvement With the Child
Father Attachment
Attachment and Other Social Influences on Development

CHILD DEVELOPMENT CONCEPT TABLE 6.2: ATTACHMENT

SIBLING AND PEER INFLUENCES DURING INFANCY
Sibling Influences
Peer Influences

DAY CARE DURING INFANCY
The Scope and Nature of Day Care
The Effects of Day Care on the Infant's Development
Some Conclusions About Day Care

EMOTIONAL AND PERSONALITY DEVELOPMENT DURING INFANCY
The Functions of Emotions in Infancy
Communication of Emotions in Preverbal Infants
Display of Emotions
Recognition of Emotions
Further Developments in Emotions During Infancy
Personality Development in Infancy
Trust
The Developing Sense of Self and Independence
Self-Control

CHILD DEVELOPMENT CONCEPT TABLE 6.3: SIBLINGS AND PEERS, DAY CARE, EMOTIONAL DEVELOPMENT, AND PERSONALITY DEVELOPMENT

PROBLEMS AND DISTURBANCES IN INFANCY
Genetics and Early Experience Revisited
Early Experience
Child Abuse
Autism

FOCUS ON CHILD DEVELOPMENT 6.3: A CHILD CALLED NOAH

THINKING BACK, LOOKING AHEAD

SUMMARY

KEY TERMS

SUGGESTED READINGS

CHAPTER 6

205

IMAGINE . . . YOU ARE FACED WITH CHOOSING A DAY-CARE CENTER FOR YOUR ONE-YEAR-OLD CHILD

Each weekday at 8:00 A.M., Ellen Smith takes her one-year-old daughter, Tanya, to the day-care center at Brookhaven College in Dallas. Then Mrs. Smith goes off to work and returns in the afternoon to take Tanya home. Tanya has excelled in day care, according to Mrs. Smith. Now, after three years at the center, Mrs. Smith reports that her daughter is very adventuresome and interacts confidently with peers and adults. Mrs. Smith believes that day care has been a wonderful way to raise Tanya.

In Los Angeles, however, day care has been a series of "horror stories" for Barbara Jones. After two years of unpleasant experiences with sitters, day-care centers, and day-care homes, Mrs. Jones has quit her job as a successful real estate agent to stay home and take care of her two-and-a-half-year-old daughter, Gretchen. "I didn't want to sacrifice my baby for my job," says Mrs. Jones, who was unable to find good substitute care in day-care homes. And, when she put Gretchen in a day-care center, she said that she felt like her daughter was being treated like a piece of merchandise—dropped off and picked up.

Many mothers worry whether day care will adversely affect their children. They fear that day-care centers may lessen the emotional attachment of the infant to the mother, retard the infant's cognitive development, fail to teach the child how to control his or her anger, and allow the child to be unduly influenced by other children.

Traditionally, it has been argued that effective socialization of the child into a mature individual depends on the development of a strong attachment bond between the infant and his or her mother or primary caretaker. If this relationship is severed for a lengthy period of time on a daily basis, the child's attachment to the caretaker may be weakened. Selma Fraiberg (1977), in her book *Every Child's Birthright: In Defense of Mothering,* supports this traditional belief. Fraiberg says that she worries about babies and small children who are delivered like packages to neighbors, strangers, and storage houses. Fraiberg is not against all day care, though. She says that children between the ages of three and six can benefit from half-day nursery school programs that entail small groups and qualified teachers. The problem, according to Fraiberg, is that children in most day-care centers are there 9 to 11 hours a day and are being cared for by poorly educated, unqualified personnel.

Many more day-care centers that are run by professionally trained, committed staff are needed. Opinions differ, however, on who should be responsible for developing the competent baby centers. Many individuals oppose public support for the care of the babies because they feel that it would lead to too much government control over families. Many middle-class families would prefer privately developed, self-supporting day-care centers that would incorporate the features of the superior university-based centers, but poorer working-class families would not be able to afford to place their infants in such centers. This dilemma remains unsolved, and for the most part, a high quality of day care is not available in most communities.

More about day care appears later in the chapter as we explore the impact of day care on such important matters as the infant's attachment to the mother, peer relationships, and socially competent behavior.

PREVIEW

The newborns of varying species vary in their ability to function independently in the world. The newborn opossum is still fetal, capable of finding its way around only in the pouch of its mother, where it attaches itself to her nipple and continues to develop in this soft, warm protective environment that is similar to still being in the uterus. By contrast, the wildebeest, moments after birth, must be able to run with the herd. The neonatal wildebeest's behavior is much more adultlike than the opossum's, but the wildebeest still has to get its food through suckling. The maturation of the human infant is at some point between these two extremes—the infant must develop and learn a great deal before it can sustain itself without adult help (Maccoby, 1980).

Because it cannot sustain its own life, the human infant requires a considerable amount of caregiving. This chapter discusses that caregiving and also the infant's development of the foundations of social maturity.

We begin by examining the important roles of both biological and sociocultural factors in infants' social and personality development. Then aspects of family processes and attachment, as well as sibling, peer, and daycare influences are considered. Emotional and personality development are discussed, and some important problems and disturbances of infancy also are highlighted. Before we begin, though, consider the following Chinese proverb that portrays the adaptability of the human infant: "A young branch takes all the bends that one gives it."

THE ROLE OF BIOLOGY AND CULTURE IN UNDERSTANDING SOCIAL AND PERSONALITY DEVELOPMENT IN INFANCY

In the early part of this century, developmental psychologists were interested in the role of biology in social and personality development. However, as John Watson's behaviorism rose to prominence in the 1920s and 1930s, the importance of biological factors in social and personality development took a backseat to environment. Even through the 1960s, the primary, often sole, purpose of inquiries about the socialization of the infant and child involved the role of the environment. Since the 1970s, however, the concept that social and personality development are influenced by an interplay of biological and environmental inputs has been "rediscovered." The "rediscovery" is not that biological factors are more important than environmental influences; rather, it involves the renewed understanding that social and personality development can be predicted more accurately by studying the interaction of biological and environmental influences instead of either alone.

Biological Influences

The discussion of genetic influences in Chapter 3 is relevant to our understanding of social and personality development here. For example, Jerome Kagan (1986) believes that inhibition and the lack of inhibition have a genetic basis. The inhibited infant or child is shy and introverted, while the disinhibited child seeks social stimulation, feels much more at ease during social interaction, and is extraverted.

Kagan believes that we are born with a predisposition to behave in a socially inhibited or socially facilitative way. According to Kagan, environmental experiences, such as sensitivity of parents to the shyness of the infant and child, modify the developmental path of the infant and child's inhibition, but not as extensively and completely as behaviorists such as Watson and Skinner believed. Kagan argues that the extremely introverted young child is not likely to turn into an extraverted older child and that, similarly, an extremely extraverted young child is not likely to become an introvert as he or she grows older.

It should be pointed out that Kagan's research involved only the extremes of children—the 10 percent who were the most extraverted and the 10 percent who were the most introverted. Further, the children were not studied until they were three years of age. Thus, environmental contributions before the age of three, rather than genetic factors only, could be involved, and the 80 percent of the children who were not extremely introverted or extraverted may have been more susceptible to environmental changes than the extreme 20 percent studied.

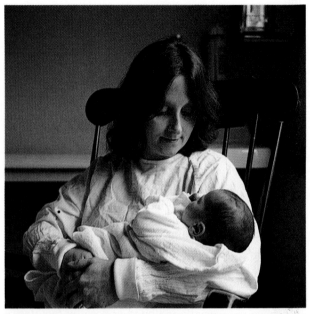

Is there a sensitive period for the development of attachment?

The views of ethologists also are important in our consideration of social and personality development in infancy. As discussed in Chapter 2 in the overview of ethological theory, Robert Hinde (1983) believes that biological factors play an important role in understanding social and personality development. For example, the concept of a sensitive period offers a useful label for suggesting that early infant-mother interaction is important in the development of attachment, a topic we discuss in considerable detail later in the chapter. But as we see next, these biological factors need to be considered in the context of sociocultural influences.

Sociocultural Influences

Sociocultural influences on social and personality development are numerous and complex. They range from the broad-based, global inputs of culture to a mother or father's affectionate touch. Cultural influences can have direct or indirect effects; comparisons across cultures can help us to decide whether information we have discovered about development in one culture generalizes to other cultures; and within a culture, it is important to consider the socioeconomic circumstances that might influence development.

A view that captures the complexity of this sociocultural world has been presented by Urie Bronfenbrenner (1979, 1983). His ecological perspective on children stresses the importance of understanding the child's relationship with many different aspects of the sociocultural world. A portrayal of Bronfenbrenner's model is presented in Figure 6.1. Notice that the child is placed in the center of the model and that the most direct interactions are with the **microsystem,** defined as the actual social setting in which the child lives. Such contexts as the child's family, school, peers, and neighborhood are important in this respect. The child is not viewed as a passive recipient of such experiences, but as one who helps to construct the environment. Most research on sociocultural influences has focused on the microsystem, emphasizing such matters as the attachment of the infant to parents, parenting strategies, sibling relationships, peer relations and friendships, and the nature of schooling experiences.

According to Bronfenbrenner, the **mesosystem** refers to relations between microsystems or connections between contexts. Examples include the relation of family experiences to school experiences, school experiences to church experiences, or family experiences to peer experiences. Bronfenbrenner accurately points out that, too often, our observations are focused on only one setting, such as the family, rather than on multiple settings, such as family, school, and peer contexts.

Children also experience culture in a more indirect way. Bronfenbrenner refers to the **exosystem** as the contexts that influence the child's development even though the child does not have an active role in those contexts. Such indirect effects of culture occur when experiences in another social setting influence what the child is experiencing in an immediate context. For example, experiences at work may influence a woman's relationship with her husband and children. She may receive a promotion that requires her to travel more. This circumstance might increase marital conflict and lead to a change in the child's caregiving (e.g., increased father

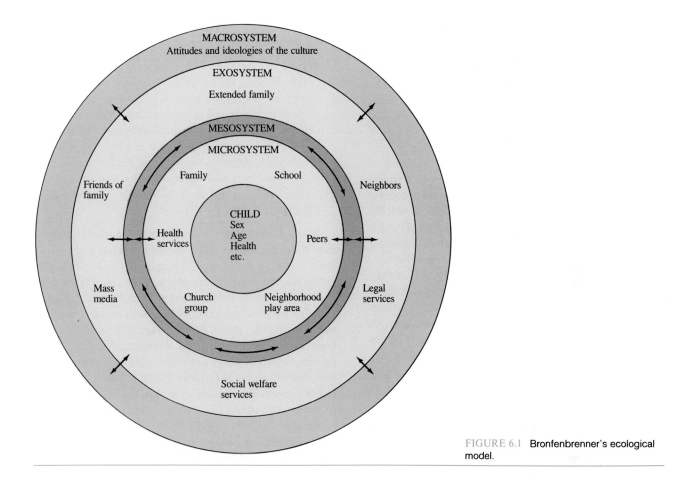

FIGURE 6.1 Bronfenbrenner's ecological model.

care, increased day care, and so on). Another example of an exosystem is the city government, which is responsible for such matters as the quality of parks and recreation facilities available to children and adolescents.

The most abstract level in Bronfenbrenner's portrayal of culture is the **macrosystem,** which refers to the attitudes and ideologies of the culture. People in a particular culture or subculture often share some broad-based beliefs. For example, there are certain beliefs and attitudes that people in Russia, China, or a South Sea island culture have that differ from those we have in the United States. And within countries, there are shared beliefs within subcultures. The values and attitudes of children growing up in an urban ghetto may differ considerably from those of children growing up in a wealthy suburb.

For example, in Brazil, almost every middle-class family can afford a nanny, and there is no such thing as a baby-sitting problem. However, because many of the nannies believe in black magic, it is not beyond the realm of possibility for Brazilian parents to return home from a movie and find their infant screaming, presumably, according to the nanny, from a voodoo curse. Contrast the world of the middle-class Brazilian family with the world of the child in Thailand, where farm families are large and can only afford to educate their most promising child (determined by which child is most capable of learning English). Let's now explore the nature of these family processes in much greater detail.

FAMILY PROCESSES

Among the important ideas about family processes in infancy are those pertaining to the beginnings of parenthood, reciprocal socialization and mutual regulation, the family as a system, and the construction of relationships.

The Beginnings of Parenthood

When individuals become parents through pregnancy or adoption, or by becoming a stepparent, they find themselves facing a disequilibrium in their lives that requires a great deal of adaptation. While the parents (or parent) want to develop a strong bond with their infant, they still want to maintain a healthy, intimate adult relationship and adult friendships and, possibly, to continue their careers. Prospective parents often ask themselves what they will be like as parents and examine their experiences as children to see if they want to adopt a different strategy in child rearing than their parents had. Parents also ask how this new being will change their life. A baby places new restrictions on partners—no longer will they be able to rush off to a movie on a moment's notice, and money is not likely to be as readily available for trips, nights on the town, and so forth. If the mother has a career, she wonders how her infant will change her vocational life. She may ask, "Will it be harmful to put the baby in a day-care center during the first year of life? Will I be able to find responsible baby-sitters?"

More fathers have become sensitive to the important role they play during pregnancy as well as in child rearing. An increasing number of fathers have completed Lamaze training, in which the father assists the mother in the delivery of the baby. When the events surrounding the birth of the baby unfold in a smooth manner, with both man and woman feeling a strong sense of involvement, the parenting process is off to a positive start.

The excitement and joy that accompany the birth of a healthy baby are often followed by what are called "postpartum blues" in mothers, a depressed state that sometimes lasts as long as nine months into the infant's life. The early months of the baby's physical demands may bring not only rewarding intimacy but also exhaustion for the mother. Pregnancy and childbirth are demanding physical events that require recovery time for the mother. As one mother tells it:

> When I was pregnant, I felt more tired that ever before in my life. Since my baby was born, I am 100 percent more tired. It's not just physical exhaustion from the stress of childbirth and subsequent days of interrupted sleep, but I'm slowed down emotionally and intellectually as well. I'm too tired to make calls to find a baby-sitter. I see a scrap of paper on the floor, and I'm too tired to pick it up. I want to be taken care of and have no demands made of me other than the baby's. (*Ourselves and our Children,* 1978, pp. 42–43)

Many fathers are not aware of or sensitive to these extreme demands placed on the mother's body and mind. Busy trying to make enough money to pay the bills, the father may not be at home much of the time. His ability to sense and adapt to the stress placed on his wife during this first year of the child's life has important implications for the success of the marriage and family. In several research studies, it was demonstrated that, when fathers helped mothers more and gave them strong support, the mothers were more likely to show competent mother-infant interaction in which they were sensitive to the infant's needs (Feiring & Lewis, 1978; Pedersen, Anderson, & Cain, 1980).

Once children are two to three years of age, they no longer are the sleeping bundles that people stop to admire in the supermarket. Active, curious, mobile young children require parents to be more than holders, feeders, and comforters. Toddlers and preschoolers won't sit in carts, want to choose food for themselves, and ask difficult questions—behaviors that require adaptation on the part of the parents, who find themselves thrown into new child-rearing roles as limit-setters, authority figures, teachers, and guides.

At some point during the early years of the child's life, parents need to recognize that they must learn how to successfully juggle their roles as parents and self-actualizing adults. Until recent years in our American culture, nurturing our children and having a career were seen as incompatible. Fortunately, we have come to recognize that the balance between caring and achieving, nurturing and working—although difficult to manage—can be successfully accomplished and often results in competent and well-adjusted children and parents.

Now that we have considered the beginnings of parenthood, we study some ideas that are important in how we conceptualize parent influences on children.

Reciprocal Socialization and Mutual Regulation

For many years, the socialization process between parents and children was viewed as a one-way affair. Children were considered to be products of their parents' socialization techniques. Willard Hartup (1979) refers to such perspectives as **social mold theories** because they describe the way the child is molded by his or her environment, particularly within the family. In such theories (the behavioral view of Skinner being the most prominent example), maturation processes have been given little attention. Instead, the child is looked upon as infinitely malleable—parents, as well as other adults, can supposedly shape children by effectively managing and manipulating their environments.

By contrast, the socialization process between parents and their children is now viewed as reciprocal—children socialize parents just as parents socialize children. This process is called **reciprocal socialization.** For instance, the interaction of mothers and their infants has been symbolized as a dance or dialogue in which successive actions of the partners are closely coordinated.

This coordinated dance or dialogue can assume the form of mutual contingency or synchrony (each person's behavior depends on the partner's previous behavior), or it can be reciprocal in a more precise sense—the actions of the partners can be matched, as when one partner imitates the other or there is mutual smiling. The exchange between a parent and infant has been investigated in terms of specific behaviors as well as clusters of social behavior (at a more molar level).

One of the most frequently investigated aspects of reciprocal socialization in infancy is mutual gazing or eye contact. Microanalytic studies suggest that mutual visual regard is an important part of early social interaction. For example, in one investigation, the mother and infant engaged in a variety of behavioral actions while they looked at each other. By contrast, when they looked away from each other, the rate of such behaviors was reduced considerably (Stern, Beebe, Jaffe, & Bennett, 1977). These episodes of mutual gazing were referred to as "episodes of maintained engagement," a term reflecting how mutual gazing increases the variety of behaviors engaged in.

Recently, researchers have focused on global clusters of responses, or **molar exchanges,** rather than specific behaviors in reciprocal interchanges between parents and infants. For example, rather than observing only smiles, an investigator may observe positive affective behavior of which a smile is only one component. In one investigation, mothers and infants matched each other's affective tone (Lewis, 1972). For example, the amount of positive affective behavior on the part of the mother was correlated with the amount of such positive behavior on the part of the three-month-old infant. The same pattern of findings occurred for negative affective behavior (frowns and the like) as well.

We have seen that the behaviors of mothers and infants are interconnected. Behaviors such as gazing are synchronized, and affective states are reciprocal. The question arises as to which partner is driving the relationship—is the mother doing most of the work in the partnership, being sensitive to the infant's states and changing her behavior according to her perception of the infant's needs?

Eleanor Maccoby and John Martin (1983), after reviewing a number of mother-infant studies, concluded that, when the infant is very young, the mother is performing more work in facilitating interaction than the infant. Through all of the first year and into the second, the mother is more likely to join the infant's nonsocial behavior than vice versa (Bronson, 1974; Thomas & Martin, 1976). Over time, as the child becomes more capable of regulating his or her behavior, the mother and the child interact with each other on more equal terms; that is, both "drive" or initiate the relationship.

In this section, we have seen that socialization is a two-way process. However, so far we only have been considering socialization as a dyadic process, between two people. Next, we see that it is important to consider the entire family system in our study of social processes.

The Family as a System

As we have seen, the nature of parent-child relationships is very complex. Not only should the reciprocal nature of parent-child relationships be considered when explaining the child's social behavior, but we should also look at the entire system of interacting individuals in the family. As a social system, the family can be thought of as a constellation of subsystems defined in terms of generation, gender, and role (Feiring & Lewis, 1978). Divisions of labor among family members define particular subunits, and attachments define others. Each family member is a participant in several subsystems—some dyadic, some polyadic.

As fathers have become recognized as important socialization agents, it has become obvious that we should be studying more than two-party social interactions (Lamb, 1976). Children interact with more than one

Describe some units of the family system that are important in the child's development.

parent or adult most days of their lives, yet we know very little about how parents serve each other as sources of support or dissatisfaction. One attempt to understand the link between spouse relationships and parent-infant relationships was conducted by Frank Pedersen and his colleagues (Pedersen, Anderson, & Cain, 1977). They believe that the three dyadic units of interaction—mother-father, mother-child, and father-child—are interrelated. Using the husband-wife relationship as a point of reference, they set out to investigate the connections among family members. Forty-one families were observed on three separate occasions at home, with separate observations of husband-wife and parent-infant dyads. The infants were firstborn, five-month-old middle-class boys and girls.

The first hypothesis investigated was that positive interaction between the husband and wife, such as smiling and affection, would be positively linked with the expression of positive affect toward the infant by each parent. The results: There was little relationship between measures of positive husband-wife interaction and their positive interaction with the infant. However, when negative social interaction between the husband and wife was observed (e.g., verbal criticism, blame), it was strongly linked to the negative affect shown by the father toward the infant. These findings suggest that the family is a network of interacting individuals functioning as a system.

One subsystem of the family system that merits additional comment is the husband-wife support system. Since many mothers now work outside the home, the extent to which husbands share in what once were traditional female duties may go a long way toward developing a healthy family system. Husbands who adapt to such changes in the female role in our society reduce marital and family conflict and increase the likelihood that children will experience competent child rearing.

Jay Belsky (1981) developed an organizational scheme of the family system that highlights the possible reciprocal influences that marital relations, parenting, and infant behavior/development may have on each other. As can be seen by following the arrows in Figure 6.2, these three aspects of the family system may have both direct and indirect effects on each other. An example of a direct effect is the influence of the parent's behavior on the child, while an example of an indirect effect is how the relationship between spouses mediates the way a parent acts toward the child. Sometimes, such indirect effects are labeled **second-order effects** by child development researchers.

Note in Figure 6.2 that the infant's behavior can influence the parenting he or she experiences. And the infant also can have a strong effect on the nature of the marital relationship. For example, the actual birth of the infant, particularly the first child in the family, has a major effect on the family, as was indicated in our earlier discussion of the beginnings of parenthood. Researchers have found that pregnancy and the birth of a first child promote a shift toward a more traditional division of roles in the family (Cowan & Cowan, 1983). This shift occurs regardless of whether the initial husband and wife roles were traditional or not. Thus, even in families where the mother has assumed a strong career role, the pregnancy and birth of the child often produces an orientation in which the mother assumes a more traditional female caregiving role and the husband becomes more responsible for providing the family's income.

In an attempt to understand the contemporary flavor of scientific inquiry about families, we have discussed the beginnings of parenthood, reciprocal socialization and mutual regulation, and the family as a system. Recently, a great deal of interest has been generated in understanding how family relationships are constructed and carried forward in time.

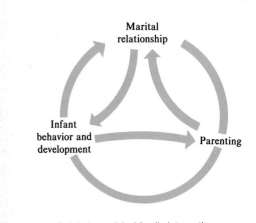

FIGURE 6.2 Belsky's model of family interaction.

The Construction of Relationships

We no longer see socialization as a process through which parents simply mold children into mature beings. At the same time, we do not believe that the child constructs a vision of reality and social maturity apart from interactions with parents and other socializing agents. Rather, the contemporary view of socialization adopts a view of the child that emphasizes the transactions between a changing child and a changing social environment (Hartup, 1983).

One proposal describing how we construct relationships and carry them forward in time was made by Alan Sroufe and June Fleeson (1986). They believe that the following propositions describe relationships:

1. A continuity and coherence characterize close relationships over time.
2. Previous relationship patterns are carried forward to influence later relationships.

Changes in the child's behaviors are very extensive in the infant and early childhood years. Sroufe and Fleeson believe, however, that, through all of this change, there is a remarkable coherence and system. Over time, there is a continuity in such close relationships as the mother-child relationship. Some infants come to learn that their caregiver will be emotionally available; others expect their caregiver not to be available. What goes on in the relationship between caregivers and a child leads the child to construct a picture of relationships in social situations.

According to Sroufe and Fleeson, relationships also are carried forward to influence new relationships. For example, children who have a history of secure attachment have been observed to be more socially competent in preschool settings (Waters, Wippman, & Sroufe, 1979). It is not known exactly how relationship histories are carried forward. It may be that an important part of this process is the motivation to maintain a consistency or coherence of self. An important part of this coherence and consistency may be continuing or re-establishing relationships that are similar to past relationship experiences.

For example, Sroufe and Fleeson (1986) point to observations of when preschool teachers became so angry that they were ready to shove a child across the hall. Invariably, such a child was one who had experienced chronic maternal rejection. When a teacher was observed to be strongly drawn to cuddle or caress a child, invariably, this child came from a family with a history of seductive maternal behavior. Thus, the rejected child misbehaves until he or she is punished, a situation that reproduces a familiar family relationship. By contrast, the seductive child has been treated as cute and charming—he or she knows how to elicit seductiveness from adults. When teachers were informed about their relationships with these children, they were able to modify their behavior toward them.

Child Development Concept Table 6.1 summarizes our discussion of biological and cultural influences on infants' social and personality development as well as several important issues regarding family processes. Our discussion so far has made several references to the attachment process between an infant and a caregiver, particularly the infant and the mother. Next, we look in greater detail at the important process of attachment in infancy and learn more precisely what is meant by such terms as insecure and secure attachment.

ATTACHMENT

During the 1970s and 1980s, a great deal of research attention has been devoted to the study of infant attachment. The interest has included pinning down what attachment really is, developing theoretical ideas about attachment, charting the developmental course of attachment, and describing individual differences as well as situational influences. In this section, we also discuss attachment and the construction of relationships, the role of temperament in attachment, and the debate on the degree to which secure attachment, particularly to the mother, is responsible for psychologically healthy development later in childhood. The father's role in the infant's development also is examined.

What Is Attachment?

In everyday language, an attachment refers to a relationship between two individuals in which each person feels strongly about the other and does a number of things to ensure the continuation of the relationship. Many pairs of people are attached: relatives, lovers, a teacher and

Child Development Concept Table 6.1	Biology, Culture, and Family Processes	
Concept	**Processes/Related Ideas**	**Characteristics/Description**
Biological and sociocultural influences on social and personality development	Biological influences	The "rediscovery" in the 1970s and 1980s of biological factors in social and personality development has led to the belief that both biological and sociocultural factors are important in the infant's socialization. Genetic influences, temperament, and ethological ideas are currently viewed as important contributions to the study of childhood socialization.
	Sociocultural influences	Bronfenbrenner's model has been helpful in describing the complexity of the child's sociocultural world. He describes the microsystem, mesosystem, exosystem, and macrosystem. This perspective provides insights into the direct and indirect ways in which sociocultural experiences influence children's development.
Family processes	The beginnings of parenthood	Becoming a parent produces a disequilibrium in the family that requires a great deal of adaptation.
	Reciprocal socialization and mutual regulation	Infants socialize parents just as parents socialize infants. Parent-child relationships are mutually regulated by the parent and the child. It is important to study parent-child relationships at both micro and molar levels. In infancy, much of the relationship is driven by the parent, but as the child gains self-control and self-regulation, the relationship is initiated by both on a more equal basis.
	The family as a system	The family is made up of interactions and relationships—some of which are dyadic, others polyadic—between individuals. Belsky has described a model of development that shows the importance of both direct and indirect effects involving family interaction. The husband-wife support system seems to be important in the family system, and the contribution of the infant should not be forgotten either.
	The construction of relationships	Relationships are constructed through the child's interactions with parents. Such relationships reflect continuity and coherence, and are carried forward to influence new relationships. The mother-child relationship seems to be particularly salient in this regard.

student. In the language of developmental psychology, however, **attachment** is often restricted to a relationship between particular social figures, and to a particular phenomenon thought to reflect unique characteristics of the relationship. The developmental period is infancy (roughly birth to two years), the social figures are the infant and one or more adult caregivers, and the phenomenon in question involves a bonding.

As we see next, as with most phenomena that generate considerable interest, a number of theories of attachment have been proposed.

Theories of Attachment

While the most prominent theory of attachment in recent years has been John Bowlby's ethological view, psychoanalytic, social learning, and cognitive theories also have stimulated research and understanding of infant attachment.

Ethological Theory

The most comprehensive account of attachment is that of John Bowlby (1958, 1969, 1973). Bowlby has set forth a theoretically elegant and eclectic account of attachment, based upon a synthesis of ethology and several other traditions in psychology. In his view, the infant and mother instinctively trigger each other's behavior to form an attachment bond. The neonate is biologically equipped with signals to elicit responses from the mother; he or she cries, clings, smiles, and coos, and later crawls, walks, and follows the mother. Such behavior is often elicited by the mother's specific action, such as leaving the room or putting the infant down. The infant's behavior is directed by the primary goal of maintaining the mother's proximity. The baby *processes information* about the mother's location, and his or her behavior changes on the basis of this feedback. Thus, as with other ethological explanations of behavior, *instinct* (or a fixed action pattern) is the primary force for developmental change, but it is transformed through social experience.

Bowlby has classified attachment into two main classes of action: executor and signalling responses. **Executor responses** include clinging, following, sucking, and physical approach; they bring the infant and mother in close contact and, functionally speaking, the infant is the main actor. **Signalling responses** refer to the infant's smiling, crying, and calling; they also bring the infant and mother together, but in this case, the infant attempts to elicit (reciprocal) behaviors from the mother.

According to Bowlby, the development of attachment as an integrated system of behaviors occurs in four phases during the first year of life. During the first phase, extending from birth to two or three months of age, the infant directs his or her attachment to human figures on the basis of an instinctual bias; strangers, siblings, mothers, and fathers are equally likely to elicit smiling or crying since the infant is not yet discriminating. In phase two, from three to six months, attachment focuses on one figure, typically the primary caregiver (e.g., mother). In phase three, extending from six to nine months, the intensity of attachment to the mother increases; because of increased locomotor skills, the infant now more readily seeks proximity to the mother. Finally, in the fourth phase, which extends from nine months to a year, the elements of attachment discussed previously—such as executor responses and signalling responses—become integrated into a mutual system of attachment to which the infant and mother both contribute.

Psychoanalytic Theory

According to Freud, the infant becomes attached to a person or object that provides oral satisfaction. Recall that Freud labeled the first stage of development the oral stage because he believed that infants obtain considerable pleasure from sucking and biting objects. Freud argued that infants are likely to become attached to their mothers because it is mothers who are most likely to feed them.

Erikson also believed that the feeding situation was an important contributor to attachment, but he also emphasized the infant's development of trust. Erikson

(1968) stressed that mothers who are warmly involved in caregiving activities with their infants are likely to have infants who show trust rather than mistrust. Difficulties during these early infant years are believed by psychoanalytic theorists to often have lifelong influences on relationships. Thus, psychoanalytic theorists predict that infants who have problems with the feeding situation and who have not developed a sense of trust may have difficulty establishing close relationships with others later in life.

Social Learning Theory

Social learning theorists often explain attachment with the processes of primary and secondary reinforcement. Primary reinforcement is unlearned, and secondary reinforcement is learned. The feeding situation involves primary reinforcement, since food is innately satisfying. By becoming associated with the feeding process, the mother (or caregiver) becomes a secondary reinforcer for the infant. The mother's smiles, pats on the head, and mere presence become associated with the positive effect of food and the satisfaction of the infant's hunger drive. Now the infant will do what he or she can to maintain the mother's presence because she has become a rewarding individual. In the past, many social learning theorists, like psychoanalytic theorists, have believed that the feeding situation plays a central role in attachment.

Is feeding really such a critical factor in the development of attachment? A classic study by Harry Harlow and Robert Zimmerman (1959) tested the importance of feeding and **contact comfort** in the development of attachment. Infant monkeys were taken away from their mothers at birth and brought up during the next six months with surrogate (substitute) mothers. As shown in Figure 6.3, one of the substitute mothers was wire while the other was covered with a soft cloth. Half of the infant monkeys were fed by the wire mother, half by the cloth mother. Periodically during the study, the amount of time the infant monkeys spent with either the wire or cloth mother was assessed. Also, the researchers created an experimental situation in which they introduced a stressful circumstance by placing a strange-looking creature in with the monkeys. This situation was designed to see which mother the infant would prefer in a stressful encounter. As shown in Figure 6.4, regardless of whether they were fed by the wire or the cloth mother,

FIGURE 6.3 The classic Harlow infant monkey study revealed the importance of contact in attachment. Here, the infant monkey clings to the cloth ''mother,'' but feeds from the wire ''mother.''

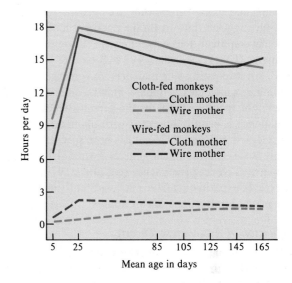

FIGURE 6.4 Harlow and Zimmerman's wire and cloth monkey study. The average amount of time infant monkeys spent in contact with their cloth and wire mothers is shown. The infant monkeys spent most of their time with the cloth monkey regardless of which mother fed them (Harlow and Zimmerman, 1959).

the infant monkeys spent considerably more time with the cloth mother. Further, when they were frightened by the strange creature, the infant monkeys invariably ran to the cloth mother and clung to her. Then, after seeming to gain confidence, they would approach the strange creature and explore it.

In sum, the Harlow monkey study provides strong evidence that feeding is not the crucial factor in the attachment process but that contact comfort, as Harlow referred to it, is. Most contemporary learning theorists now agree that feeding is not the key variable in attachment. Rather, they argue that there are many rewarding aspects to the infant-caregiver interaction—satisfying the infant's hunger is but one of a number of behaviors

that the caregiver performs. Others include the contact comfort, or tactile stimulation, described by Harlow, as well as visual and vocal stimulation. Taken together, all of these behaviors make the caregiver a rewarding object to become attached to (Gewirtz, 1969).

Cognitive Developmental Theory

Some cognitive psychologists (e.g., Kohlberg, 1969) have interpreted attachment as a motivational system based on the need to express competence (as opposed to achieving biological pleasure) in interpersonal exchanges. Attachment from this perspective reflects the infant's intellectual development. So, for example, the infant must first acquire the ability to appreciate objects as existing beyond momentary reach (object permanence) before particular objects (e.g., a caregiver) can become part of a stable motivational system.

To achieve a strong emotional bond with significant caregivers, goes the argument, the infant must at least first perceive object permanence with respect to those people. That is, the infant must first perceive that people are permanent fixtures in the world, existing beyond the moments and places where they are encountered. Some research suggests that an infant's general level of cognitive development does correlate with the degree of attachment (Clarke-Stewart, 1973; Stone & Chesney, 1978). An interesting side issue has also emerged. Since the time at which clear attachments first emerge (about six to eight months) predates the time at which object permanence is usually observed with inanimate objects (e.g., Uzgiris & Hunt, 1975), it has been speculated that the presence of attachment reflects a special, uniquely early case of object permanence (e.g., Bell, 1970). However, clever experiments have not consistently confirmed some of the implications of this notion.

Evaluation of Attachment Theories

Each attachment theory has provided a useful addition to the notion of attachment as a whole. From psychoanalysis has come the idea that the infant is born with a number of needs and that the individuals who help satisfy these needs exert a powerful emotional pull on the child. From ethology, we have learned that these needs are instincts obeying laws and principles, much like the instincts in the nonhuman animal kingdom. Ethology has also taught us to examine instinctual response systems carefully and to observe their naturalistic patterning over time. Social learning theory has been useful in demonstrating that specific response categories (e.g., smiling, vocalizing) can be shaped between the caregiver and the infant, but its focus on specific classes of behavior has also been its theoretical undoing because attachment is a more global phenomenon, cutting across many behavioral categories. Finally, from cognitive psychology has come the notion that the emotional bond of attachment presupposes certain cognitive prerequisites in the infant (e.g., identification and discrimination of different people). However, this latter theory has not been particularly illuminating about how the specific course of cognitive growth is linked with the specific growth of attachment, and it also fails to account for the vast individual differences in attachment. In the final analysis, the approach taken by Bowlby seems to hold the most promise since it offers the most general and subtle account of the development of attachment.

The Developmental Course of Attachment, Individual Differences, and Situational Influences

What is the developmental course of attachment in infancy—that is, when do infants become attached to a parent or primary caregiver? Are there individual differences in attachment? And are there situational variations in attachment as well?

The Developmental Course of Attachment

Perhaps the most widely cited longitudinal study of attachment is the one reported by Schaffer and Emerson (1964). The investigators followed 60 Scottish infants from the ages of 5 to 23 weeks at the outset of the study until the infants were 18 months old. The researchers periodically interviewed the mothers about the infants' responses to separation episodes and observed the infants' responses to several standardized situations in which the interviewer (a stranger) slowly approached the infant. Figure 6.5 depicts the course of infant attachment behavior over time. It indicates that the infants protested separation from anyone (indiscriminate attachment) during the first months of life. Beginning at about 6 months (25 to 28 weeks), attachment to the mother became more focused and remained strong from 10 months through the remainder of the 18-month period. Importantly, attachments to other specific caregivers were about as intense as attachment to the mother. Among the additional findings not shown in the figure, from 7 months until almost the end of the first year, the specific attachment to the mother became more intense, and fear of strangers generally occurred at about 8 months, approximately one to two months after the onset of attachment to the mother.

In another well-known study of infant attachment, Mary Ainsworth (1967) observed 29 infant-mother pairs in Uganda, Africa, for a period of nine months. The children ranged in age from 2 to 14 months during the investigation. Her observations included as indicators of attachment, smiling, crying, vocalization, separation protest, following, touching, greeting gestures, and using the mother as a base of exploration. As with infants in the Schaffer and Emerson study, the Ugandan infants

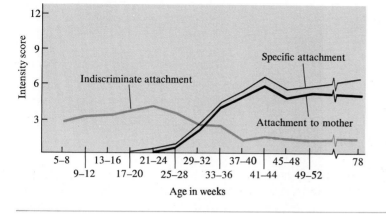

FIGURE 6.5   Developmental course of attachment.

began to show the most intense signs of attachment to their mothers around 7 months of age. But as we see next, there is some variation in the developmental course of attachment.

Individual Differences and Situational Influences

To speak of attachment as being experienced in the same way or to the same degree by all infant-caregiver pairs is, of course, a convenient fiction. There are striking individual differences among infants.

To return to the Schaffer and Emerson (1964) investigation, for example, one-fourth of the infants showed fear of strangers before specific attachment to the mother. This is quite a striking and significant variation in the normal pattern of development. And in Mary Ainsworth's (1967) research, 5 of the 29 infants never did display positive affiliation with their mothers (e.g., clinging, proximity seeking, visual contact). Other investigators have found similar patterns of individual variation (e.g., Waters, 1978; Main, 1973).

Mary Ainsworth (1973, 1979) has offered a number of ideas about attachment. First, she believes that there are vast individual differences in the patterning of caregiver-infant interactions that have profound consequences for the nature of the attachment that develops. Second, the resulting attachment seems to fall into distinct categories that are relatively enduring for the child. The two most important categories, according to Ainsworth, are **secure attachment** and **insecure attachment.**

What does Ainsworth mean by *secure?* An infant who is securely attached uses the caregiver, or mother, as a secure base from which to explore the environment. The infant may move away from the mother freely, but generally processes her location by occasionally glancing in her direction. The infant responds positively to being picked up; when put back down, he or she moves away freely to play. An insecurely attached infant, by contrast, shows ambivalent attachment behavior, particularly with regard to physical contact. He or she shows heightened separation anxiety in strange situations or in response to minor, everyday separations. The infant also tends to avoid proximity with the caregiver, a behavior that sometimes results in premature and inappropriate independence.

Among those infants Ainsworth designated as insecurely attached, a further distinction is made: One subgroup exhibits insecurity by avoiding the mother, that is, for example, by ignoring her, averting her gaze, and failing to seek proximity; the other subgroup exhibits insecurity by resisting the mother, that is, clinging to her but at the same time fighting against the closeness by, for example, kicking and pushing away. Finer subdivisions of these categories are possible, as shown in Table 6.1. However, most investigators find the major subdivisions easier to work with and to score reliably. In most groups of infants, it is assumed that the majority will be securely attached (two-thirds of Ainsworth's babies were). It is the minority of infants who evidence some maladaptive attachment.

Table 6.1 Ainsworth's Classification of Attachment: Individual Differences	
	Characteristics
Securely Attached	
Group 1	Seeks interaction on reunion but not proximity. Does not resist when held. Little or no distress during separation episodes.
Group 2	Seeks interaction and more proximity on reunion. Does not resist when held. Little or no distress during separation episodes.
Group 3	Approaches mother on reunion. May also cry. Clutches when held, resists release. May or may not be distressed. Very active in seeking contact and resisting release.
Group 4	Greatest desire for proximity, interaction, and being held throughout. Distress evident in separation episodes.
Insecurely Attached—Avoidant	
Group 1	Infant fails to greet mother upon return. Fails to approach mother, or attempt is abortive. If picked up, likely to squirm to get down and does not cling.
Group 2	Infant greets mother with mixed response, both approaching and turning and looking away. If picked up, always shows mixed response, momentarily clinging but also slipping away.
Insecurely Attached— Resistant	
Group 1	May reach or approach mother on reunion and seek contact. But great ambivalence shown, with hitting, kicking, and pushing.
Group 2	Fails even to contact mother. If approached or held, ambivalence shown.

How would you classify the attachment of this infant-mother pair?

Research by Jay Belsky and his colleagues provides further clarification of the nature of secure and insecure attachment (Belsky, Rovine, & Taylor, 1984). Infant-mother attachment was observed during naturalistic home situations when the infant was one, three, and nine months of age. Securely attached infants had experienced an intermediate amount of reciprocal interaction and maternal stimulation, believed to reflect sensitive care. Resistant babies experienced less responsive care than securely attached babies. No support was found for the idea that avoidant babies experienced less physical contact with their mothers than the securely attached babies. Belsky believes that the mother plays an important role in individual differences in attachment, with overstimulation leading to avoidance, understimulation producing resistance, and intermediate levels generating security.

While Ainsworth and many other researchers have pursued the importance of individual differences in attachment, it also is necessary to investigate whether there are situational influences on attachment. Alison Clarke-Stewart (1978) offered a penetrating analysis of the importance of situational variability when studying infant behavior. She focused on "fear of the stranger" and analyzed the factors that determine how much fear or wariness will surface in the stranger's presence. The one-year-old infant does not show as much distress toward a stranger when sitting on his or her mother's lap as he or she does when sitting on a table (Morgan & Ricciuti, 1969). Infants fuss less and explore their environment more when a novel toy is present (Rheingold & Samuels, 1969). The readiness of infants to explore an unfamiliar object depends in part on how closely the mother is positioned to the baby (Schwartz, 1978). Eye contact may also be important. Adults who maintain visual attention to the infant may give him or her a sense of security. For example, five-month-old infants smile and vocalize more

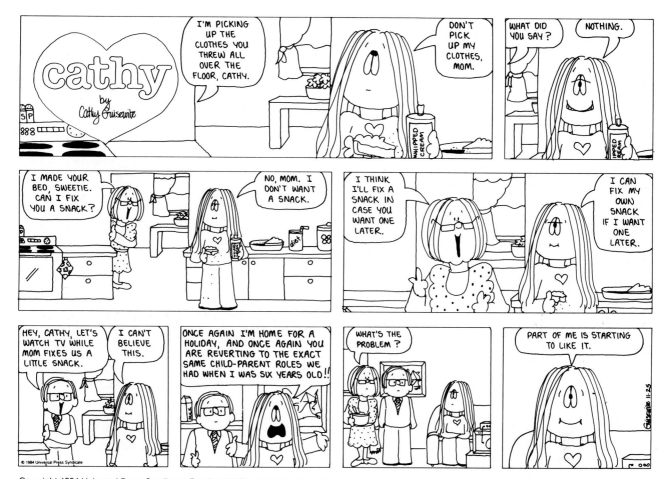

and cry less when their mothers or a female stranger maintain direct eye contact with them (Lasky & Klein, 1979). Also, infants respond more positively (approaching, smiling, and touching) to *nice* strangers and more negatively (avoiding, crying, aggressing) to *nasty* ones (Clarke-Stewart, 1978).

Now that we have seen what attachment is, discussed theories of attachment, described its developmental course, looked at the importance of individual differences and the role of situational variation, we turn our attention once again to the construction of relationships and how this process is a key ingredient in the formation of attachments.

Attachment and the Construction of Relationships

In discussing the construction of relationships earlier in the chapter, it was pointed out that relationships are carried forward to influence the development of new relationships. Work by Alan Sroufe and his colleagues supports this argument (Waters, Wippman, & Sroufe, 1979). More about their research is presented in Focus on Child Development 6.1.

FOCUS ON CHILD DEVELOPMENT 6.1

ATTACHMENT BONDS, PEER RELATIONS, DEPRESSION, AND SCHIZOID BEHAVIOR

If, as the major theories claim, the first social bond(s) of attachment is critical for later development, it should be possible to determine a link between the degree or quality of attachment achieved in infancy and later social development. Such evidence is available from research conducted by Alan Sroufe.

In one investigation, two such important links were established (Waters, Wippman, & Sroufe, 1979). First, 18-month-old infants who were or were not securely attached (see Table 6.1 for what is meant by secure and insecure attachment) displayed different types of free play six months later. During a 10-minute free play period in which infants were placed in a room with their mothers and a number of toys, it was found that the secure infants showed and gave toys to their mothers—affectively shared—much more than either avoidant or resistant children did. Second, an independent group of 15-month-olds who were distinguished as securely or insecurely attached showed different levels of personal and interpersonal competence when they were three-and-one-half years old. Competence was assessed by means of a Q-sort technique in which a series of "descriptors" were evaluated by judges who observed children in preschool. Secure children received higher scores for "other children seek his or her company," "suggests activities," "peer leader," and "sympathetic to peer distress"; insecure children received higher scores for "basically withdrawn," "hesitates to engage," and "spectator (versus participant) in social activities." This link between attachment and later social competence has been verified by other investigators as well (e.g., Main & Louderville, 1977; Lieberman, 1977).

Other research from Alan Sroufe's laboratory supports the link between attachment and later behaviors. For example, in one investigation, a relationship was shown wherein more securely attached infants at 18 months of age were more capable of using specially designed tools and in solving simple problems six months later (Matas, Arend, & Sroufe, 1978). Infants who had displayed a secure attachment at 18 months of age showed less frustration and were rated as happier at two years of age than their avoidant and ambivalent counterparts (see the figure at the right).

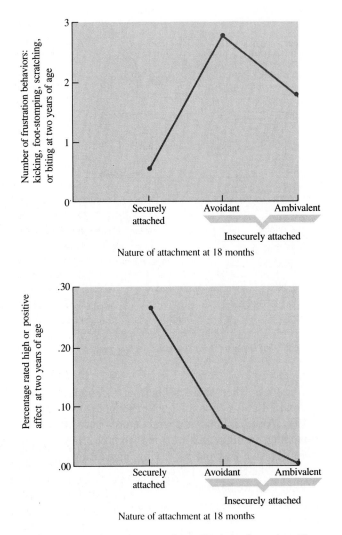

Relation of type of attachment to frustration behavior and positive affect.

How could this boy's attachment history with his parents affect his happiness?

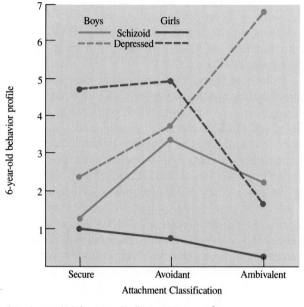

Attachment in infancy and adjustment at age 6.

Van Pancake (1985) recently has provided further evidence of the importance of secure attachment in infancy for the emergence of competent peer relations in early childhood. Twenty-four children (mean age four years, six months), for whom information about secure and insecure attachment had been obtained between 12 and 18 months of age, were videotaped in a number of dyadic play sessions. Raters observed the videotape and coded the quality of the peer relationships. Children with a history of anxious-avoidant attachment were observed to have a less positive relationship with peers than their securely attached counterparts.

However, other research conducted by Michael Lewis and his colleagues suggests that secure and insecure attachment sometimes is related to adjustment later in development and sometimes is not (Lewis, Feiring, McGuffog, & Jaskir, 1984). These researchers studied 100 children at one and six years of age and investigated the link between attachment in infancy and adjustment at six years of age. Boys who were insecurely attached in infancy were more poorly adjusted,

showing more symptoms of psychopathology, at age six. However, no relation between attachment classification in infancy and adjustment in the elementary school years was found for girls. The boys who were classified in the avoidant category in infancy had more schizoid tendencies (bizarre affective behavior often involving withdrawal and variability) at age six, while the boys who were rated as ambivalent in infancy were more likely to be depressive and withdrawn at age six (see the figure above for the schizoid and depressive data). But even among the boys, attachment was not the only factor that was related to later adjustment. Stressful life events and environmental changes also influenced the nature of adjustment in the elementary school years. Thus, secure attachment is an important factor in development, but as Lewis and his colleagues note, it is not the *only* predictor of later adjustment, and insecure attachment does not always lead to maladjustment.

To fully understand the construction of relationships, it also is helpful to consider the role intergenerational relationships might play in attachment. Researchers are beginning to accumulate evidence about the transmission of relationships across generations from middle-aged grandparents through their young adult children and then to the offspring of the young adult parents (Hartup, 1986; Sroufe & Fleeson, 1986). For example, in one investigation, mothers who indicated that they had poor relationships with their own parents more often reported problems with their one-year-old infants than mothers who reported no such problems with their parents (Frommer & O'Shea, 1973).

In another study, 95 mothers were interviewed four months after their babies were born and when the offspring reached four-and-one-half years of age (Uddenberg, 1974). The maternal grandmothers also were interviewed with regard to parent-child relationships 20 years earlier. The nature of the mother's relationship with her own mother was linked with psychiatric difficulties in the postpartum period, feelings of inadequacy as a parent, and ambivalent or negative feelings toward the infant. And such problems in relationships with the mother and grandmother were associated with the child's perception of the mother four years after delivery.

In another investigation, the mothers and fathers of infants whose attachments had been classified according to Ainsworth's categories were interviewed (Main, Kaplan, & Cassidy, 1985). The child's avoidance of the parent following separation was related to parental reports of rejection in their own childhoods. Resistance of the infant toward the mother was associated with continuing anger and conflict with regard to the mother's own parents. And infants showing secure attachment had parents whose own relationships with their parents were described as secure. These results provide increasing evidence of the importance of studying relationships in an intergenerational manner.

So far, we have spent considerable time outlining the main ideas of the concept of attachment and emphasizing research revealing the importance of attachment in influencing later development. In particular, there is an emphasis in attachment theory on the biological orientation of the child to the caregiver (mother) and the sensitivity of the mother to the infant's signals. As we see next, some theorists and researchers believe that this conception of attachment gives too little attention to temperament characteristics of the infant and the mother.

Attachment and Temperament

There has been a flourish of interest in the 1980s regarding whether attachment might possibly be related to temperamental characteristics of the infant (e.g., Campos, Barrett, Lamb, Goldsmith, & Sternberg, 1983; Chess & Thomas, 1982; Kagan, 1982, 1984; Weber & Levitt, 1986). The attachment theorists and researchers who follow the scheme of Bowlby and Ainsworth argue that infant temperament is not related in any causal manner to attachment classifications, such as insecure and secure attachment (e.g., Sroufe, 1985; Sroufe & Waters, 1982). By contrast, other theorists and researchers argue that the classifications suggested by Ainsworth reflect the infant's temperamental responses to stressful situations, rather than attachment quality (e.g., Kagan, 1984; Weber, Levitt, & Clark, 1986).

Alan Sroufe (1985) argues that the temperament approach is unfortunate because it emphasizes a stable trait approach to development—that is, it suggests that the infant is born with a genetic predisposition to behave in a particular temperamental style and that this behavior is modified within some limited way by environmental interactions. Sroufe stresses that the Ainsworth approach is superior because Ainsworth's system captures the nature of the relationship between the caregiver and the infant, as derived from the history of their interaction.

Those who argue for the temperament side of this disagreement, such as Jerome Kagan (1984), believe that it is not that environmental interchanges are unimportant. Rather, they stress that theorists such as Ainsworth and Bowlby have underplayed the role that genetic, temperament characteristics of the infant have in the development of parent-infant relationships. And, as we see in Focus on Child Development 6.2, recent research has revealed not only a relation between infant temperament and the Ainsworth attachment classifications, but also a suggestion that the temperament of the mother may be a factor in the development of close relationships, such as attachment, as well.

FOCUS ON CHILD DEVELOPMENT 6.2

INTENSE MOTHERS AND AVOIDANT BABIES—THE IMPORTANCE OF TEMPERAMENT

If the temperament theorists are correct, then we would expect that both the infant and the mother's temperaments would influence the infant's mode of interacting not only with the mother but also with unfamiliar adults. These possibilities were studied by Ruth Weber, Mary Levitt, and Cherie Clark (1986), who videotaped 36 mother-infant dyads when the infants were 13 months old. The videotapes were scored for crying intensity and duration, interactive behavior, and attachment classifications. Richard Lerner's Dimensions of Temperament Survey was used to evaluate the temperament of both the mothers and their infants. The dimensions on the temperament scale are closely related to those suggested by Thomas and Chess (1977) in their well-known longitudinal study of temperament. The dimensions include activity level, attention span, adaptability, rhythmicity, and reactivity. Attention span includes both attention span/persistence and distractibility; adaptability includes both adaptability and approach/withdrawal; and reactivity includes intensity of reaction, threshold of responsiveness, and some aspects of activity.

The results of this investigation suggested that the mothers of the avoidant babies were more likely to have a temperament involving intensity of reaction than the mothers of the secure and ambivalent babies (see the bottom left figure). Maternal adaptability also was a significant predictor of infant crying, indicating that the mother's own hesitancy in new situations may be transmitted to the infant. Further, infant temperament, particularly adaptability, was related to the infant's behavior toward the stranger. And an overall summary rating of the infant's temperament of difficulty was linked to resistance to the mother and the stranger. These results suggest that infant and maternal temperament are factors that need to be considered when classification of attachment patterns is at issue.

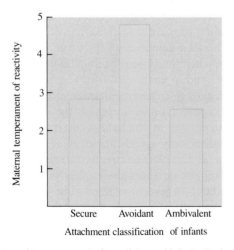

The maternal temperament of reactivity and infant attachment classification.

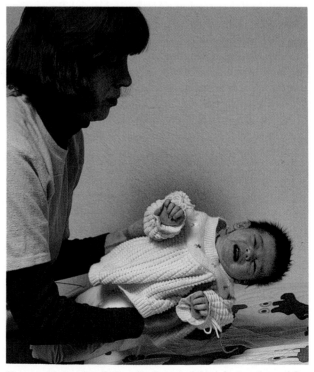

How would you classify the attachment of this infant-mother pair?

So far in our discussion of attachment, we have talked primarily about mothers and infants. As we see next, researchers have become intrigued by the nature of father-infant attachment and the importance of the father's involvement in the child's development.

Infant-Father Attachment and Involvement

What is the father's role in the infant and child's development? Are the attachment patterns of infants to their fathers different than those to their mothers?

The Father's Role and Involvement With the Child

Historically, the role of the father in the child's development has gone through four different changes (Lamb, 1986; Pleck, 1984). The earliest phase extended from the time of the Puritans through the Colonial period, a lengthy era in which the father's role was primarily one of responsibility for moral teaching. Fathers were viewed as providing moral guidance and values, particularly through religious means. As the Industrial Revolution progressed, the father's role changed—he now had the responsibility as the breadwinner, a role that continued through the Great Depression. During the emergence of the breadwinning role, the father continued to serve an important role in moral training. By the end of World War II, a third role of fathers became important, that of a sex-role model. While being a breadwinner and moral guardian continued to be important father roles, attention shifted to his role as a male, particularly for sons. Then, in the 1970s, the current interest in the role of the father as an active, nurturant, caregiving parent emerged. Rather than only being concerned with the discipline and control of older children and with providing the economic basis of the family, the father now is being evaluated in terms of his active, nurturant involvement with his children, even infants.

Are fathers more actively involved with their children today than they were 10 to 20 years ago? To provide a more detailed analysis of this question, Michael

How has the father's role in child rearing changed?

Lamb (1986) described involvement in terms of (1) engagement/interaction, (2) accessibility, and (3) responsibility. Engagement/interaction involves actual one-to-one interaction with the child (feeding, doing homework, or passing a ball back and forth). Accessibility refers to a less intense degree of interaction, such as cooking in the kitchen while the child plays in the living room, or watching television while the child does his or her homework close by. Responsibility is the most difficult to define but may be the most important categorization—it refers to the extent that the parent takes ultimate responsibility for the child's welfare and care. Responsibility consists of such matters as knowing when the child needs a dental checkup, when the child needs new shoes, when the child is having difficulty in peer relationships, and so forth.

With regard to engagement/interaction, it is important to compare families in which the mother is employed with families in which she is not. It has been found that the father only spends about 20 to 25 percent as much time as the mother directly interacting with the child in families in which the mother is a homemaker and only about 33 percent as much time being as accessible as the mother. By far the biggest discrepancy is in

"Are you going to believe me, your own flesh and blood, or some stranger you married?"

Reprinted by permission of Jerry Marcus.

the area of responsibility—a number of studies suggest that fathers assume little or no responsibility for the child's care or rearing. For two-parent families in which the mother works, levels of paternal interaction and accessibility increase, with figures improving to about one-third and two-thirds of the mother's involvement, respectively. There seems to be little or no increase in the father's responsibility role, however.

Very few data document changes in the father's involvement from one point in history to another. One recent study, however, compared the father's involvement in 1975 and 1981 (Juster, in press). In 1981, fathers spent about one-fourth more time in direct interaction with the child than in 1975. Mothers increased their direct interaction about 7 percent over this time frame, so fathers, while increasing their direct interaction, still were far below mothers in this regard. In this study, the father's involvement was about one-third of the mother's in both 1975 and 1981.

In sum, there does seem to be some increase in the father's active involvement in the child's development. However, this active involvement does not approach the mother's involvement, even when she is employed. And in the area of responsibility, fathers do not seem to be more involved. Next, we consider the extent to which infants are attached to fathers, seeing that fathers may play a different role in the attachment process than mothers.

Father Attachment

We may gain a better understanding of the father's function in the human family by considering the behavior of the father in nonhuman species where, after procreation, his function primarily involves protection of the mother and offspring. Except for isolated instances in the animal kingdom, such as that of the mountain gorilla (Schaller, 1963), the father does not engage in the daily responsibilities of child rearing. However, the male wolf has occasionally been known to baby-sit and feed the young while the mother is away from the den (Morris, 1967; Mowat, 1963). In most nonmammalian species, the father rarely assumes any important functions related to the offspring after fertilization.

Studies of human fathers and their infants confirm that many fathers can and do act sensitively and responsively with their infants (Parke & Sawin, 1980) and that infants form attachments to both their mothers and fathers at roughly the same age (Lamb, 1976). In both humans and primates, adult male behavior toward infants appears to be highly flexible and adaptive. Probably the strongest evidence of the plasticity of male caretaking abilities is derived from studies in which the males from primate species that are notoriously low in male interest in offspring are forced to live with infants whose female caretakers are absent; under these circumstances, the adult males show considerable competence in rearing the infants (Parke & Suomi, 1983).

Mothers and fathers seem to play different roles in the infant's life. Mothers are more likely to be the primary caregivers. Babies who are wet, hungry, tired, or sick are more likely to seek out their mothers than their fathers for this reason. By contrast, fathers are more likely to be sought out by infants for play. Thus, both the mother and the father are important attachment figures for the infant, but the circumstances that lead an infant to show a preference for one or the other seem to differ.

Another important question is whether infants prefer their mother or father under stressful circumstances. This question has been the focus of a research investigation by Michael Lamb (1977). Twenty 12-month-olds were observed interacting with their parents in a laboratory playroom equipped with one-way mirrors behind which observers stood. Initially, with both parents present, infants showed no preference for either the mother or father. The same was true when the baby was alone with the mother or father. However, the entrance of a stranger, combined with fatigue and boredom, produced a shift in the infant's social behavior toward the mother. Thus, under stressful circumstances, infants show a stronger attachment to their mother.

In their naturalistic observations of attachment in the home, Belsky and his colleagues made additional comparisons of the infant's attachment to the father (Belsky, Gilstrap & Rovine, 1984). When observed under naturalistic circumstances in the home, fathers were strikingly less involved with their infants than mothers were. Thus, while there is clear evidence that fathers can and sometimes do become highly active participants in their infants' lives, a number of experts believe that, when the large population of fathers in the United States are considered, there are clear differences in the degree of involvement fathers and mothers have with their infants, with mothers being far more participant.

Further evidence of the different kind of socialization infants experience with mothers and fathers is offered by Michael Lamb and his associates (Lamb, Frodi, Hwayng, Frodi, & Steinberg, 1982). They were intrigued by whether mothers and fathers with nontraditional gender roles would act differently with their infants than their counterparts with traditional gender roles. They studied Swedish families in which the fathers were the primary caretakers of their firstborn, eight-month-old infants. The mothers were working full-time. In all of the researchers' naturalistic observations of the parents at home with their infants, the mothers were more likely to discipline, vocalize to, hold, soothe, and kiss the infants than fathers (see Figure 6.6 for data on discipline and soothing). Thus, mothers and fathers dealt with their infants differently, along the lines that often are found with traditional gender role American fathers and mothers. Having fathers assume the primary caretaking role did not seem to lead to great changes in the way the fathers interacted with the infant. Such findings may be due to biological reasons or to deeply ingrained socialization patterns in cultures.

In sum, while fathers have seemed to increase their active interaction with their infants and young children,

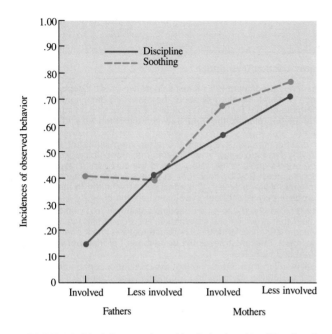

FIGURE 6.6 Disciplinary and soothing behavior of traditional and nontraditional parents in Sweden.

they are more identified with a play role than a caregiving role. Next, we look at how the degree of attachment to the primary caregiver, as well as other aspects of the complex sociocultural world the child experiences, may predict later development.

Attachment and Other Social Influences on Development

We have spent considerable time exploring the nature of the attachment process. On the one hand, we have seen that theorists and researchers such as Bowlby, Ainsworth, and Sroufe have argued that attachment plays a key, if not almost exclusive role, in promoting optimal, psychologically healthy development both in infancy and later in development. A large number of research projects have been directed at determining how the attachment process works and the degree that attachment in infancy, particularly with the mother, predicts development later in childhood.

In contrast to the ideas of the secure attachment theorists and researchers, other experts, such as Jerome Kagan, argue that genetic influences, such as those represented in temperament characteristics of the infant and mother, have been left out of the attachment description too often. Further, a number of social development theorists and researchers believe that too much weight has been placed on the infant's attachment to the mother as the key socializing experience in the child's development (e.g., Lamb, Thompson, Gardner, Charnov, & Estes, 1984). The argument is that the infant and child grow up in a complex social world with many different social agents and in many different social settings. The infant is viewed as a malleable being, one capable of adapting to many different social circumstances. According to these theorists and researchers, experiences with fathers, siblings, and peers, the quality of day care and schooling, and socioeconomic and cultural factors also affect the infant's development. Quite clearly, this alternative perspective does not deny the important role that caregivers play in the early years of the child's development. However, it does stress that secure attachment to the mother does not have exclusive rights on determining the child's healthy course of development. This view is very compatible with the ecological perspective provided by Urie Bronfenbrenner earlier in the chapter, in which a wide variety of direct and indirect sociocultural influences on the child were discussed. Keep in mind, then, that there currently is a great deal of controversy surrounding the attachment process—some experts arguing for its primacy in influencing other aspects of the child's development, other experts emphasizing that it has been given too much weight in determining the course of the child's social development.

Child Development Concept Table 6.2 summarizes our discussion of attachment. Let's now turn our attention to some of the other influences on the infant's development, first studying sibling and peer influences.

Child Development Concept Table 6.2   Attachment

Concept	Processes/Related Ideas	Characteristics/Description
The nature of attachment	What is attachment?	In general, attachment is a relationship between two people in which each person feels strongly about the other and does a number of things to ensure the continuation of the relationship. In infancy, attachment refers to the bond between the caregiver and the infant.
Theories of attachment	Ethological theory	The most comprehensive account of attachment is that of John Bowlby. His ethological view stresses the infant's biologically equipped signals to the caregiver and the caregiver's responses to those signals. Bowlby describes the course of attachment over the first year of life, believing that a focused attachment to the caregiver begins at about three to six months of age.
	Psychoanalytic theory	According to Freud, the infant becomes attached to a person or object that provides oral satisfaction. He argued that infants become attached to mothers because mothers most often feed the infant. Erikson stresses the development of trust between the infant and caregiver.
	Social learning theory	Social learning theorists argue that attachment occurs because of the link between primary and secondary reinforcement. They believe that, by becoming associated with the feeding process, the caregiver becomes a secondary reinforcer. Harlow demonstrated the importance of contact comfort in attachment.
	Cognitive developmental theory	Kohlberg argues that attachment is a motivational system based on the need to express competence in interpersonal exchanges. Cognitive theorists often point to the development of object and person permanence in the first year of life as important precursors of attachment.
	Evaluation of the attachment theories	While ethological theory has become the most widely debated and provocative attachment view, each of the theories has provided useful additions to the notion of attachment as a whole.
The developmental course of attachment, individual differences, situational influences, and the construction of relationships	Developmental course of attachment	Several investigations suggest that between the ages of six to nine months, infant attachment becomes focused on the primary caregiver.
	Individual differences	Mary Ainsworth's classification of attachment into secure, avoidant, and resistant categories has generated considerable research inquiry. Ainsworth argues that securely attached infants use the caregiver as a base for exploring the wider social world. Sroufe's research has found that secure attachment in infancy is linked to social competence in the preschool years. Lewis's research suggests that insecurely attached infants do not always become maladjusted in the elementary school years. Belsky argues that intermediate levels of stimulation produce secure attachment.
	Situational influences	Situational influences refer to the extent that environmental settings are capable of modifying attachment. For example, by modifying the behavior of a stranger, the infant's attachment behavior may be changed.
	The construction of relationships	The attachment relationship is carried forward over time to influence the development of new relationships, such as those with peers. The infant's attachment pattern also is sometimes linked to intergenerational relationships.

Child Development Concept Table Continued		
Concept	**Processes/Related Ideas**	**Characteristics/Description**
Attachment and temperament, infant-father attachment and involvement, and the wider social world	Attachment and temperament	Attachment theorists and researchers who follow the scheme of Bowlby and Ainsworth believe that infant temperament is not involved in a causal way to attachment classifications. By contrast, other theorists and researchers, such as Kagan, emphasize that the infant's inherited temperament plays an important role in how the infant's attachment is classified. Research reveals that infant and maternal temperaments are factors that need to be taken into account when attachment is at issue.
	Infant-father attachment and involvement	Over time, the father's role in the child's development has evolved from moral teacher to breadwinner to sex-role model to active, nurturant caregiver. Involvement can be analyzed in terms of engagement/interaction, accessibility, and responsibility. While fathers have increased their active interaction with their children, there seems to be little or no increase in the father's responsibility role. Infants seem to develop attachments to mothers and fathers at about the same time, but fathers seem to be more identified with a play role with infants, while mothers are identified as having a caretaking role.
	Attachment and the wider social world	A current controversy about attachment focuses on how critical attachment is for optimal development later in childhood. While the ethological view of attachment stresses that attachment to the caregiver, particularly the mother, is the key factor in healthy psychological development, others believe that this view ignores the complexity of the child's sociocultural world. This latter view, which has much in common with Bronfenbrenner's ecological perspective, sees early social interactions with the mother as important in development, but stresses that other social agents and social contexts need to be considered over the long course of development.

SIBLING AND PEER INFLUENCES DURING INFANCY

The socialization of infants is often attributed to parents. But in many instances, siblings and peers also are involved.

Sibling Influences

Studies of sibling interaction indicate that the behavior of both members of the sibling dyad and their development must be considered. Judith Dunn and Carol Kendrick (1982, in preparation) have conducted highly focused assessments of both siblings as they interacted in naturalistic settings, such as at home and at play. In particular, their research has revealed how the developmental status of the sibling is related to how siblings interact. Observations of young pairs of siblings over time have suggested that, at some point between the ages of

one and two years, younger siblings begin to initiate more sibling conflict than in their first year. During the second year of life, they are physically more aggressive toward their older sibling and show anger in different ways, such as biting themselves and throwing things, actions that are not observed in the first year. The behavior of the older siblings also changes as they develop. As they move through the preschool years (being about two years older than their younger siblings), the older siblings tend to express more concern about social rules and rationales, increase the number of their prohibitions and moral references toward the younger sibling, and voice more interest in their own needs and feelings. The Dunn and Kendrick research is particularly important in signalling the manner in which focused assessments of both members in close relationships over time provide insight into individual sources of change in the relationship.

What is the nature of social interaction in young siblings?

Peer Influences

While in the past, peer relations were not a major consideration in infant development, they are today since, now more than ever before, infants are being placed together in day-care centers as more mothers work outside the home. Infants as young as six months of age do interact with each other when placed together (Vandell, Wilson, & Buchanan, 1980). Six-month-old babies primarily interact by smiling, touching, and vocalizing. In the second year of life, toys become a focus of peer interaction. In one investigation, observations of 8- to 10-month-old infants in a day-care center suggested that one infant seemed to be liked by her peers more than any others and that one boy was more likely to be avoided than the others (Lee, 1973). On close inspection, some reasons for these individual differences appeared: The boy often initiated encounters with other infants by grabbing their toys, while the girl approached her peers in a positive way, by smiling, for example.

Toys seem to be very important in peer interaction during the second year of life (Mueller, 1979). Infants less than one year old seem not to use toys in peer interaction; at approximately 12 to 14 months of age, the presence of toys actually seems to decrease peer interaction; and at about 14 months of age, toddlers begin to use toys as a medium for play and peer involvement (Jacobson, 1981). It apparently takes time for the toddler to coordinate play that involves both an object (toy) and a person (peer).

When positive peer interaction begins to occur in the second year, it is likely to be accompanied by a display of affect, which is usually absent from peer exchanges in the first year (Mueller & Brenner, 1977). For example, when an 18-month-old touches another age-mate, he or she may smile. However, although positive interactions and affective displays are more common in the second year, so are negative interchanges; that is, more fights over toys, hitting, biting, and hair pulling occur in the second year (Eckerman, Whatley, & Kutz, 1975).

Recent research on early peer relationships has provided further support for the belief that, rather than being merely a curious new phenomenon in human relationships, early peer relationships can be of enduring significance in the child's social and cognitive growth (Mueller, 1985; Hay, 1985; Vandell, 1985; Brownell & Brown, 1985). For example, in one investigation, early peer skills were related to sociometric status in the preschool years (Howes, 1985). Two three-year longitudinal studies were conducted. In both studies, positive affect during peer interaction in the toddler period predicted easy access to peer play groups and popularity with peers in the preschool period.

DAY CARE DURING INFANCY

An understanding of day care requires information about its scope and nature as well as its effects on the infant's development.

The Scope and Nature of Day Care

The number of women in the labor force with children under six (with spouse present in home) has increased from 2.5 million in 1960 to 4.4 million in 1975 to 6.2 million in 1984. And the number of women in the labor force with children under six (with no spouse present in

How strongly do you think the quality of day care influences children's development?

the home) has increased from .42 million in 1960 to .96 million in 1975 to 1.8 million in 1984. In the 1980s, far more young children are being placed in day care than at any time in history—about 2 million children currently receive formal, licensed day care, and more than 5 million children attend nursery schools or kindergartens. Furthermore, uncounted millions of children are taken care of by unlicensed baby-sitters. Day care clearly is becoming a basic need of the American family.

Much of day care is informal and unregulated, consisting of whatever day-care arrangements the hurried parent can muster up. For example, a mother may get a neighbor to baby-sit three afternoons a week and may take the child to her mother's house two days a week. Formal day care is usually of two types—a center or home care. Centers invariably monitor large groups of young children and often have elaborate facilities. Some are commercial operations, others nonprofit centers run by churches, civic groups, and employers. Home care frequently is provided in private homes, at times by child-care professionals, at others by mothers who want to earn extra money. Let's now study what the effects of these varying day-care arrangements have on the infant's development.

The Effects of Day Care on the Infant's Development

United States government figures indicate that approximately 1.3 million babies are cared for by relatives in relatives' homes, 938,000 by relatives in the child's home, 1.2 million by nonrelatives in "family" day-care homes, and 620,000 by unrelated baby-sitters in the child's own home. Certainly, not all such day care is of poor quality, but there is some indication that these types of day care require careful attention by parents. In one investigation, the effects of routine daily separations involved in day care on the attachment of infants to mothers in economically disadvantaged families were evaluated (Vaughn, Gove, & Egeland, 1980). Many of the infants were cared for by an adult female in a nonrelative's home. Significant disruption in the infant-mother attachment relationship was found in the day-care group. Many such day-care arrangements clearly fail to meet the psychological needs of infants.

In many of the day-care/home-rearing comparisons, the day-care centers are university based or staffed. Such centers serve many different types of families, and while the programs differ, they do have some features in common. Babies are taken care of in small groups, and a caretaker is assigned to each infant who is younger than two years of age. The caretaker changes the baby's diapers and feeds the infant and is trained to enrich such routines by communicating with the infant. Periodically during the day, the caretaker seeks out the infant and engages him or her in some form of lively social interaction. The general conclusion from the comparisons of the high-quality university-staffed day care and home-reared children is that there are few if any differences in the attachment behavior of the children growing up under these two different circumstances (Belsky & Steinberg, 1978).

Demonstration programs, such as Jerome Kagan's (Kagan, Kearsley, & Zelazo, 1978), show that it is possible to provide group care for infants that will not harm them, and in some cases, will actually aid their social development. Kagan's day-care center included a pediatrician, a nonteaching director, and an infant-teacher ratio of three to one. And teachers' aides assisted at the center. The teachers and aides were trained to smile frequently, to talk with the infants, and to provide them with a safe environment that included many stimulating toys.

Kagan and his colleagues assessed many variables, including the results for peer play. To assess peer play, an unfamiliar peer of the same age, sex, and ethnicity of the child entered the room with the peer's mother. A new set of toys was then brought in. The child's behavior was observed for 21 minutes to assess such matters as the time spent in peer play and the duration of time spent looking at the peer. Particularly at 20 months of age, the home-reared children spent less time in play and more time looking at the peer (a likely indicator of wariness about the peer) than their day-care counterparts. At 13 and 29 months, these differences did not appear. However, in looking at the overall indicators of social competence in children, Kagan and his colleagues concluded that there were few differences in the global measures

of cognitive or social development. Good quality day care had neither positive nor negative effects. The day care that most babies receive, however, does not approach the quality of Kagan's program or other university-based day-care programs.

Some Conclusions About Day Care

The area of social development that has been studied most extensively in relation to day care is attachment. Sometimes, the quality of attachment to the mother is influenced by day care (Clarke-Stewart & Fein, 1983). In many instances, these differences involve greater distance, avoidance, or independence from the mother, and they appear in mildly stressful circumstances with unfamiliar people in uncertain places. They appear to be more extreme when day care is begun in the infant's first year of life, probably before a secure and stable attachment to the mother has developed. These differences are likely to appear not just because of time spent away from the mother but also because of the amount of time spent with other caregivers and the differences in maternal attitudes and emotional accessibility that are involved in combining a job and family. For many children, this pattern of increased distance from the mother is more likely to represent an adaptive pattern to the circumstances of being away from the mother a large part of the day rather than a pathological disturbance.

At this time, it is virtually impossible to answer the question of whether day care has a positive or negative effect on young children's development. Some investigations show positive effects, others negative effects, and others no effects. Trying to combine these results into an overall conclusion about day-care effects is a problem because of the different types of day care children experience and the different measures used to assess the outcome in different day-care studies (Clarke-Stewart & Fein, 1983).

We have discussed many different aspects of the social world of infants—from the broader culture into which they are born to their everyday interactions within the family to the role of day care in the infant's development. Two other important aspects of the infant's development still need to be considered—their emotional and personality development.

EMOTIONAL AND PERSONALITY DEVELOPMENT DURING INFANCY

Emotions are an important part of infant development—infants laugh and cry, smile and frown, and sometimes act surprised. In this section, we explore the functions of such emotions in the infant's development, describe the communication of emotions in preverbal infants, and outline the onset of verbal communication about emotions in later infancy. An understanding of emotions requires consideration of the infant's physical, cognitive, and social development, and there is interest in integrating these different aspects of development in studying emotional development.

Discussion of infancy also would not be complete without a discussion of the infant's personality development. In this regard, we discuss the infant's development of trust, a sense of self, independence, and self-control.

There often are close connections between emotional and personality development, as well as between these two domains and ideas we already have discussed pertaining to social development. For example, attachment sometimes is discussed as emotional, rather than social, development. Also, the emotion of crying is an important part of the attachment system, and the emotion of smiling is viewed as an important aspect of the infant's social world. Chapter 4 examined the development of crying and smiling in early infancy as part of an overview of the reflexes, states, and activities of the young infant. Thus, the emotions of the infant are involved in many aspects of his or her development, having important ties with biological, cognitive, social, and personality development. Let's now explore some of these important connections as we investigate the functions of emotions in infancy.

The Functions of Emotions in Infancy

While there is still some disagreement about the exact functions of emotions in the infant's development, most views claim that emotions have adaptive and survival-promoting functions, serve as a form of communication, and provide important regulative functions (Bretherton, Fritz, Zahn-Waxler, & Ridgeway, 1986).

Concerning the function of emotions as adaptive and survival-promoting, various fears, such as fear of the dark, fear of being alone, and fear of sudden changes in the environment are adaptive because there are clear linkages between such events and possible danger (Bowlby, 1973).

Emotions also serve a communication function: Infants use emotions to inform others about their feelings and needs. The infant who smiles likely is telling others that he or she is feeling pleasant, while the infant who cries may be communicating that something is unpleasant.

With regard to the regulative function of emotions, infants may call on emotions to increase or decrease the distance between themselves and others. The infant who smiles may be encouraging someone to come closer, while one who displays anger may be suggesting that an intruder should go away. As part of the regulative function of emotions, infants appraise and categorize the meaning of events, such as whether the events are dangerous or beneficial (Izard, 1978; Lazarus, 1974; Stein & Levine, in press). Also, emotions may regulate internal psychological processes by influencing the information the infant selects from the perceptual world, the flow and processing of the information once it has been detected, and the selection of behaviors the infant displays. In this way, emotions both energize and guide the infant's behavior (Campos, Barrett, Lamb, Goldsmith, & Stenberg, 1983).

In sum, emotions serve important adaptive/survival, communicative, and regulative functions in the infant's development. Let's now look at the developmental unfolding of emotions in infancy, first outlining the communication of emotions in preverbal infants.

Communication of Emotions in Preverbal Infants

In studying the communication of emotions in young infants, it is helpful to distinguish between the display of emotions and the recognition of emotions.

Display of Emotions

Researchers have demonstrated that young infants display a rather wide range of emotional expressions. In one investigation, mothers were interviewed about the expression of various emotions by their one-month-old infants (Johnson, Emde, Pannabecker, Stenberg, & Davis, 1982). Virtually all of the mothers said that their offspring showed joy and interest; more than 80 percent said that anger was present; almost three out of four mothers reported that the infants displayed surprise; more than half said that fear was shown; and slightly more than one-third indicated that the one-month-olds showed sadness.

Other research by Carol Malatesta and Jeannette Haviland (1982, 1985) provides even more direct evidence of young infants' wide expression of emotions. They videotaped the playful interactions of infants at three and six months of age with their mothers. Judges were able to reliably code the expression of joy, interest, sadness, anger, and pain in three-month-old infants. In another research study, judges could recognize the emotions of interest, joy, surprise, sadness, anger, disgust, contempt, and fear in infants one to nine months of age (Izard, Huebner, Risser, McGinnes, & Dougherty, 1980). Thus, even by one month of age, infants seem capable of displaying a wide range of emotional expressions. The researchers point out that such displays cannot be used to infer the presence of internal emotional states but that the muscle configurations shown by the infants are those commonly associated with emotional states.

Researchers also have been interested in determining the order in which emotions emerge. A prominent theorist and researcher in the study of emotional development, Carroll Izard (1982), described the developmental appearance of a number of emotions. Some displays, such as a startle, distress, disgust, and a reflexive smile, seem to be present even at birth. Social smiling (smiling in response to a face) does not seem to appear until several months of age. At approximately three to four months of age, such emotional expressions as surprise, anger, and sadness emerge. The infant does not seem to show fear until approximately halfway through the first year.

Recognition of Emotions

Researchers not only are interested in charting when infants can display emotions—they also are fascinated by the appearance of the ability to recognize emotions in others. It appears that infants as young as four months of age can distinguish between different emotions. In one investigation, four- to six-month-old infants were shown sides of a face displaying joy, anger, or a neutral emotion. The infants spent more time looking at the facial expression of joy than at the other two expressions (La Barbera, Izard, Vietze, & Parisi, 1976). Apparently, infants can detect positive emotions, such as smiling, earlier than they can negative emotions, such as anger. And it appears that they are able to display emotions earlier in development than they are capable of recognizing them in others.

Further Developments in Emotions During Infancy

In the latter half of the first year and continuing through the second year of life, infants gradually develop an understanding of themselves and others as experiencers and communicators of emotions (Bretherton, Fritz, Zahn-Waxler, & Ridgeway, 1986). Also, toward the end of the first year and into the second year, infants make considerable progress in producing and comprehending intentional communicative gestures and affective signals (Bretherton, 1984; Stern, 1985). And as we see next, during the toddler years, emotional development progresses through advances in verbal communication.

The onset of emotion language appears to emerge at about 18 to 20 months of age (Bretherton, Fritz, Zahn-Waxler, & Ridgeway, 1986). During the third year, the use of such words rapidly increases. At some point between 18 and 36 months of age, infants and toddlers become capable of labeling the emotions of others as well as their own, discussing past and future emotions, and talking appropriately about the antecedents and consequences of emotional states.

Our developmental tour of emotions during infancy reveals that the infant's world is filled with a great deal of emotion. While some rudimentary emotions, such as the startle response and reflexive smiling, appear to be present at birth, there is considerable growth and development in emotions over the course of the infant years. These emotions seem to serve important adaptive/survival, communicative, and regulative functions in the infant's development. Such functions reveal the connectedness of emotional development to other important aspects of development, such as biological, cognitive, and social development. As we discuss the development of personality in infancy, you will be able to detect how emotional development also has important ties with personality. For example, in the discussion of trust, you will discover how Erik Erikson argues that the infant who develops a sense of trust has a minimum of fear. In the description of the development of a sense of self, you will learn about corresponding changes in the infant's emotional development. In the discussion of the development of self-control, you will find references to the regulation of emotions.

Personality Development in Infancy

The individual characteristics of the infant that often are thought of as central to personality development are trust, the self, independence, and self-control.

Trust

According to Erik Erikson (1968), infancy is characterized by the stage of development called trust versus mistrust. Following a life of regularity, warmth, and protection in the mother's womb, the infant faces a world that is less secure. From Erikson's perspective, infants learn trust when they are cared for in a consistent, warm manner. If the infant is not well fed and kept warm on a consistent basis, a sense of mistrust is likely to develop. What is developed is an expectancy—if the infant experiences a feeling of physical comfort and a minimum of fear or uncertainty, a sense of trust will emerge, trust that can be extended to new experiences. By contrast, a sense of mistrust develops from unsatisfactory physical and psychological experiences, producing fearful apprehension of new experiences.

Erikson's ideas about trust are very compatible with the view of attachment developed by Mary Ainsworth (1979), who described the importance of the infant's

sense of secure attachment and how it can be formed through considerable involvement, warmth, and care on the part of the caregiver. The infant who has a sense of trust is likely to be securely attached and have confidence to explore new circumstances, whereas the infant who has a sense of mistrust is more likely to be insecurely attached and to not have such confidence and positive expectations.

Erikson believes that trust is an important aspect of a developing sense of self in infancy. As we see next, there also have been a number of other ideas about the infant's developing sense of self.

The Developing Sense of Self and Independence

When do infants develop a sense of self, and how can this be studied? What are some major theories of the development of self and independence in infancy? What does research on infants and young children tell us about the nature of their independence?

Sense of Self   Individuals carry within them a sense of who they are and what makes them different from everyone else. They cling to this identity and begin to feel secure in the knowledge that this identity is becoming more stable. Real or imagined, the individual's developing sense of identity and uniqueness is a strong motivating force in life. But when exactly does the individual begin to sense a separate existence from others?

Children begin the process of developing a sense of self by learning to distinguish themselves from others. To determine whether, in fact, infants are able to recognize themselves, psychologists have traditionally relied on mirrors. In the animal kingdom, only the great apes can learn to recognize their reflection in a mirror, but human infants can accomplish this feat by approximately 18 months of age.

The mirror technique, initially used with animals, has been modified for use with human infants. The mother puts a dot of rouge on her infant's nose. During a pretest, an observer watches to see how frequently the infant touches his or her nose. Next, the infant is placed in front of a mirror, and observers detect whether nose touching increases. Figure 6.7 presents the results of two separate investigations of self-recognition using the rouge-and-mirror technique. Thus, in the second half of the second year of life, there is good evidence that infants recognize their own image and coordinate the image they see with the actions of touching their own body (Amsterdam, 1968; Lewis & Brooks-Gunn, 1979).

The toddler's ability to recognize a mirrored reflection seems to be linked to the ability to form a mental image of his or her own face. This development of a sense of self does not occur in a single step but is rather the product of a complex understanding that develops very gradually.

Two Theories of Self-Development and Independence

The theories of Margaret Mahler and Erik Erikson have important implications for our understanding and study of self-development and independence in infancy. Margaret Mahler (1979) is a well-known psychoanalyst who has conducted very detailed clinical observations of infants and their mothers with the goal of finding out how infants and toddlers develop independence. Mahler believes that the child acquires a sense of separateness along with a sense of relatedness to the world through the process of **separation-individuation.** The process is characterized by the child's emergence from the symbiotic relationship with the mother (separation) and the child's acquisition of individual characteristics in the first three years of life. At the end of three years, the child has an independent, autonomous self.

Mahler (1979) described how mother-child interaction can interfere with the development of individuation with the example of Anna. Anna's mother's marked emotional unavailability made Anna's practicing and exploratory period brief and subdued. Never certain of her mother's availability, and therefore always preoccupied with it, Anna found it difficult to explore her surroundings. After a brief spurt of practicing, she would

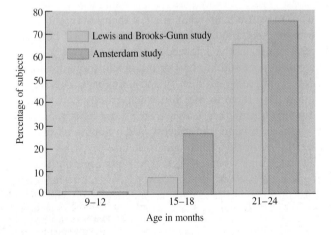

FIGURE 6.7 The development of self-recognition in infancy. The graph gives the findings of two studies in which infants of different ages showed recognition of rouge by touching, wiping, or verbally referring to it.

return to her mother and try to interact with her in an intense manner. From such relatively direct expressions of need for her mother as bringing a book to read to her or hitting the mother's ever-present book in which she was engrossed, Anna turned to more desperate measures, such as spilling cookies on the floor and stomping on them, always with an eye to gaining her mother's attention, if not involvement. Anna's mother was absorbed in her own interests, which were anything but child-centered. In addition to her inability to let her mother out of her sight, Anna's activities were very low-keyed: They lacked the vivacity and luster that characterized other children her age.

Anna was observed during the preschool years at the nursery school she attended. When her mother would leave after dropping her off at school, Anna often threw a temper tantrum and would cling to her teacher. But the clinging frequently turned to hitting and yelling. In Mahler's view, Anna wanted only one thing to happen— her mother to return through the door. But when her mother did return, Anna did not show even a flicker of radiance or happiness. Her first words were, "What did you bring me?" and the whining and discontent started all over again. As can be seen in Anna's case, a very unsatisfactory mother-infant relationship led to problems in her development of independence.

While Mahler's account of the separation-individuation process has stimulated thought about the development of independence in infancy and early childhood and given us a vivid picture of mother-infant interaction, it is not without problems. Susan Harter (1983) summarized some of the problems that surface in Mahler's perspective. Mahler's goal, at first glance, appears to be similar to that of cognitive-structural theorists, who are interested in how the infant develops a sense of self as an active, independent individual. According to the cognitive-structural perspective, the infant is an inquisitive young scientist who is preoccupied with the serious business of locating objects and people in space and coordinating sensorimotor schemes. Susan Harter (1983), however, believes that this conflicts with Mahler's perspective:

The budding terrible two as described by Mahler is faced with different developmental hurdles and tends to evoke more sympathy. The infant is wrenched from the blissful stage of need gratification, must endure separation distress, struggle to create a soothing image of mother, tolerate the fickleness of an environment which initially seemed to yield to the infant's every whim only to frustrate the infant in a subsequent developmental hour of need; and finally, to make matters worse, the toddler is greeted with social approbation for throwing him/herself, red-faced and screaming on the supermarket floor. (p. 23)

Harter feels that Mahler puts too much singular emphasis on the mother. Harter also believes that many of Mahler's observations of mother-infant relationships have not been systematically documented.

Erik Erikson (1968), like Mahler, argues that the relationship between the mother and the infant is important in determining the extent to which the toddler develops a sense of autonomy. Autonomy versus shame and doubt represents the second stage in Erikson's theory of development. The major significance of this stage in the life cycle lies in rapid gains in muscular maturation, verbalization, and the coordination of a number of conflicting action patterns characterized by tendencies to hold on and let go. Through such changes, the highly dependent child begins to experience autonomous will. Mutual regulation between adult and child faces a severe test. This stage becomes decisive in whether the child will feel comfortable in self-expression or feel anxious and show extensive self-restraint. Erikson believes that, if the child does not develop a sense of self-control and free will at this point in development, he or she may become saddled with a lasting propensity for doubt and shame.

According to Erikson, for the toddler to develop independence, a firmly developed early trust is necessary. The sense of autonomy parents are able to grant their small children depends on the dignity and sense of personal independence they derive from their own lives. In other words, the toddler's sense of autonomy is a reflection of the parents' dignity as autonomous beings. Erikson believes that much of the lasting sense of doubt developed in the toddler is a consequence of the parents' frustrations in marriage, work, and citizenship.

BLOOM COUNTY   by Berke Breathed

© 1986 Washington Post Writers Group. Reprinted with permission.

Erikson also describes how the struggles and triumphs of this stage of development contribute to the identity crisis all adolescents undergo, either by supporting the formation of a healthy identity or by contributing to estrangement and confusion. According to Erikson, the development of a sense of autonomy during the toddler years helps to give the adolescent the courage to be an independent individual who can choose and guide his or her own future.

Research on Independence   Research on independence in infancy and childhood has received far less attention than attachment. Harriet Rheingold (1973) describes how, in reflecting on her earliest work on infants, it was only after a number of years that she began to recognize how independent many of the youngsters' behaviors were:

> Some eight years ago, I began a series of studies designed to measure the effect of a strange environment on the behavior of infants at 10 months of age. Only after the last sentence of the discussion of the study was written did I realize that it was not so much the strange environment that caused the distress of the children placed in it without their mothers, nor even the absence of their mothers, as it was being *placed* and *left alone* (Rheingold, 1969). That this was so was demonstrated in a later study in which infants the same age were given the opportunity to leave their mothers and enter that same strange environment by themselves. All the children did enter on their own initiative, even when the environment contained no toy. Not only did they enter, but they crept to places in the room from which they could not see the mother. They returned to the mother's room, left again, and returned again—some infants many times—but on a third of the returns, they did not contact the mother. (pp. 182–83)

Rheingold (1973) indicated that, in the process of investigating the influence of different environments, it was becoming clear that she was seeing infants move away from their mothers. A review of the nonhuman primate research on independence provided support for the belief that the infant detaches himself or herself from the mother (Rheingold & Eckerman, 1970). As the nonhuman primate grows older, it leaves the mother more frequently, goes farther, and stays away longer. To find out how far from the mother a human child would stray, Rheingold and Eckerman (1970) placed a mother and her child in a backyard—the mother was seated and the child was left free. They found a positive relationship between the age of the children (from one to five years) and the distance they traveled from their mothers. However, the continuing relationship to the mother was evidenced in the observations that older children brought small items to their mothers—pebbles and leaves, for example.

Table 6.2 Kopp's Four Phases in the Development of Self-Control During Infancy

Phases	Approximate Ages	Features	Cognitive Requisites
Neurophysiological modulation	Birth to 2–3 mo.	Modulation of arousal, activation of organized patterns of behavior	
Sensorimotor modulation	3–9 + mo.	Change ongoing behavior in response to events and stimuli in environment	
Control	12–18 + mo.	Awareness of social demands of a situation and initiate, maintain, cease physical acts, communication, etc. accordingly; compliance, self-initiated monitoring	Intentionality, goal-directed behavior, conscious awareness of action, memory of existential self
Self-control	24 + mo.	As above; delay upon request; behave according to social expectations in the absence of external monitors	Representational thinking and recall memory, symbolic thinking, continuing sense of identity

From Kopp, Claire B., "Antecedents of self-regulation: A developmental perspective in *Developmental Psychology, 18*, 199–215, 1982. Copyright © 1982 American Psychological Association. Reprinted by permission of the author.

We have seen that, during the second year of life, infants show increasing signs of self and independence. As we discuss next, during this time, infants also begin to sense the requirements of social situations and to monitor their behavior accordingly.

Self-Control

Self-control seems to emerge during late infancy. There seem to be some important developmental milestones in the development of self-control, and parent-infant relationships might influence this development.

Claire Kopp (1982) described four phases in the development of self-control during infancy: neurophysiological modulation, sensorimotor modulation, control, and self-control. The approximate ages, features, and possible cognitive requisites for these milestones are presented in Table 6.2.

Long before the child is capable of self-control, there is a form of control in which arousal states are modulated and reflex patterns become more organized in terms of functional behavior—Kopp calls this phase, occurring roughly from birth through 2 to 3 months of age, **neurophysiological modulation.**

From 3 months to approximately 9–12 months of age, the infant develops the ability to engage in a voluntary act (such as reach and grasp) and to change the act in response to events that might arise. By the midpoint of the first year, infants actively use their sensorimotor abilities to modulate such important matters as attention and social exchanges (Salapatek, 1975; Stern, 1974). This phase is called **sensorimotor modulation.**

Kopp believes that **control** occurs from approximately 12 months to about 18+ months—this phase characterizes the emerging ability of infants to show awareness of social or task demands that have been defined by caregivers, and to initiate, maintain, modulate, or cease physical acts, communication, and emotional signals accordingly. Thus, control represents an important transition period in the infant's journey toward self-regulation.

Kopp believes that these behaviors do not represent true self-control in the sense that the infant does not yet have awareness of a continuing identity. **Self-control** differs from control, according to Kopp, by virtue of the appearance of representational thinking and recall memory. With representational thinking, the older infant uses a symbol to stand for an object; with recall memory, the older infant evokes and sustains the image of the absent object. Kopp argues that representational thinking and recall memory are the necessary cognitive mechanisms that permit the older infant to form an integrated sense of his or her continuing independent identity and therefore to link his or her acts with caregivers' demands for acceptable behavior. Thus, the older infant's pattern of behavior begins to reflect knowledge of social rules as well as the demand characteristics of situations, even when caregivers are not present. Self-control also represents something beyond awareness—the term indicates self-initiated modifications of remembered information. And, self-control indexes an important shift to an internally generated monitoring system.

Child Development Concept Table 6.3	Siblings and Peers, Day Care, Emotional Development, and Personality Development	

Concept	Processes/Related Ideas	Characteristics/Description
Siblings and peers, day care	Sibling influences	When a sibling is present, the nature of family interaction changes. Dunn and Kendrick have conducted highly focused assessments of infant/sibling pairs in the naturalistic setting of siblings' homes. Their research stresses how the developmental status of each sibling is related to how siblings interact. At some point between one and two years of age, the younger sibling initiates more sibling conflict.
	Peer influences	Infants as young as six months of age interact with each other—primarily through smiling, touching, and vocalizing. In the second year of life, toys become a stronger focus of peer interaction. Recent research has shown that early peer skills are linked to popularity and social competence in the peer group during the preschool period.
	Day care	About 2 million children currently receive formal day care, more than 5 million attend nursery schools or kindergartens, and uncounted millions are cared for by unlicensed baby-sitters. There is some indication that day care may disrupt mother-infant attachment, but this often varies with the quality of the day care. At this time, no conclusions can be drawn about overall positive or negative effects of day care, although many more high-quality day-care centers are badly needed.
Emotional development	Functions of emotions in infancy	Emotions serve important adaptive/survival, communicative, and regulative functions in the infant's development.
	Communication of emotions in preverbal infants	Very young infants display a variety of emotions. As early as one to three months of age, researchers can reliably code such expressions as joy and interest. Rudimentary emotions, such as the startle response and reflexive smiling, seem to be present at birth. Surprise, anger, and sadness are likely to emerge at three to four months of age. Fear may not be present until midway through the first year. Researchers also are interested in the ability of infants to recognize emotions in others. By four to six months of age, infants seem capable of recognizing such emotions as joy in others. Infants are able to display emotions earlier than they can recognize them in others, and they tend to recognize positive emotions (such as smiling) earlier than negative emotions (such as anger).
	Further developments in emotions during infancy	During the last half of the first year and into the second year, infants make considerable progress in understanding that they and others in their world are experiencers and communicators of emotions. At about 18 to 20 months of age, the onset of emotion language appears, and between 18 and 36 months of age, infants and toddlers become capable of labeling the emotions of others as well as their own, discussing past and future emotions, and talking appropriately about the antecedents and consequences of emotions.
Personality development	Trust	Erikson stresses that the first stage of personality development, roughly corresponding to the first year of life, is trust versus mistrust.
	The developing sense of self and independence	At some point between 18 and 24 months of age, the infant develops a sense of self. The development of the self likely is a gradually unfolding process. Two theories of independence have been offered by Mahler and Erikson. Mahler emphasizes the process of separation-individuation in the first three years of life, while Erikson stresses the stage of autonomy versus shame and doubt in the second year. Some critics believe that Mahler places too much emphasis on the mother.

Child Development Concept Table 6.3 Continued		
Concept	Processes/Related Ideas	Characteristics/Description
Personality development (cont.)	Research on independence	Research on independence has lagged behind research on attachment. As infants age from one to five years, they show more independence from their parents.
	Self-control	Self-control seems to emerge during late infancy. Claire Kopp believes that there are four phases in the development of self-control: neurophysiological modulation, sensorimotor modulation, control, and self-control. Self-control involves the appearance of representational thinking and recall memory, and is characterized by awareness, self-initiated modifications of remembered information, and an internally generated monitoring system. Parent-child relationships likely are involved in the child's development of self-control, but clearly there are some important biogenetic and cognitive milestones as well.

Can caregivers' interactions with the infant influence the development of the infant's self-control? In one study parents' use of language and their general positive involvement with the infant was linked with compliance skills in two-year-olds (Lytton, 1976). However, much yet is to be learned about the role of family processes in the infant's development of self-control. More about self-control appears later in the book when we discuss the early childhood years.

Child Development Concept Table 6.3 summarizes our discussions of sibling and peer relations, day care, and emotional and personality development in infancy. We now focus on problems and disturbances in infancy.

PROBLEMS AND DISTURBANCES IN INFANCY

An understanding of problems and disturbances in infancy requires revisiting the areas of genetic influences and early experience. Other aspects of problems and disturbances in infancy include the nature of child abuse and autism.

Genetics and Early Experience Revisited

All development—abnormal as well as normal—is influenced by an interaction of heredity and environment. As discussed in Chapter 3, genetic influences have been determined for many disorders, including some forms of

mental retardation. The role that genes play in temperament may be an important factor in the development of some problems and disturbances. For example, a shy, introverted individual is likely to produce very different reactions from his or her environment than the socially at ease infant who is extraverted. The nature of such temperamental contributions to problems in infancy, however, has not yet been accurately pinpointed by research.

In addition to genetic influences, prenatal development may also contribute to problems and disturbances in infancy. In one of the most comprehensive studies of children at risk, a variety of biological, social, and developmental characteristics were identified as predictors of incompetent behavior at the age of 18. Among the factors were moderate to severe perinatal (at or near birth) stress and congenital defects. Also among the predictors were low socioeconomic status at 2 and 10 years of age, level of maternal education below 8 years, low family stability between 2 and 8 years of age, very low or very high infant responsiveness at age 1 year, a Cattell score below 80 at age 2 years (the Cattell is one of the early measures of infant intelligence), and the need for long-term mental health services or placement in a learning disability class at age 10. When four or more of these variables were present, the stage was set for serious coping problems in the second decade of life (Kopp, 1983; Werner & Smith, 1982).

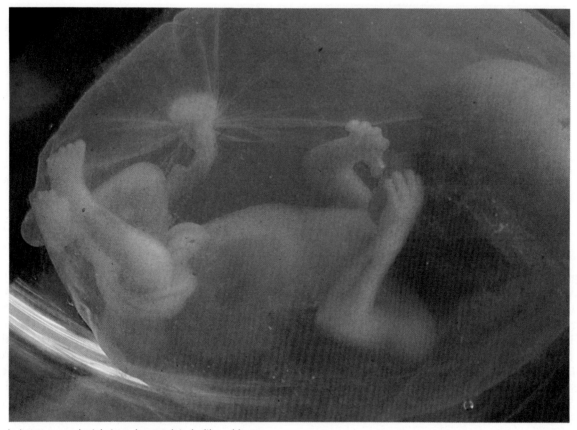

Moderate to severe perinatal stress is associated with problems and disturbances during later development.

In summarizing what we know about children at risk, Claire Kopp (1983) pointed out that a variety of biological risk conditions can impinge on the organism at the time of conception or during prenatal, perinatal, and postnatal life. The outcome of this assault varies and depends on the particular type and timing of the influence, but in general, the earlier the insult, the greater the effects. The range of outcome for all perinatal and postnatal insults is from severe impairment to normal development, although the processes accounting for variability are not fully documented. Factors in the environment act upon biological risk by heightening or attenuating its effects. In some instances, such as in perinatal stress, environmental influences may outweigh biological risk. Biological risk and adverse rearing conditions combine to have more negative impact than either factor would alone.

Early Experience

Michael Rutter (1981) has listed a number of ways that earlier experience might be connected to later disorders: (1) experience produces the disorder at the time, and the disorder persists; (2) experience creates bodily changes that affect later functioning; (3) experience alters patterns of behavior at the time, which later take the form

TABLE 6.3 Salient Developmental Issues	
Age (Years)	Issues
0–1	Biological regulation; harmonious dyadic interaction; formation of an effective attachment relationship
1–2½	Exploration, experimentation, and mastery of the object world (caregiver as secure base); individuation and autonomy; responding to external control of impulses
3–5	Flexible self-control; self-reliance; initiative; identification and gender concept; establishing effective peer contacts (empathy)
6–12	Social understanding (equity, fairness); gender constancy; same-sex chumships; sense of "industry" (competence); school adjustment
13 +	"Formal operations" (flexible perspective taking; "as if" thinking); loyal friendships (same sex); beginning heterosexual relationships; emancipation; identity

From Sroufe, L. A. and M. Rutter, "The domain of developmental psychology" in *Child Development, 56,* 17–29, 1984. © 1984 by The Society for Research in Child Development. Reprinted by permission.

of a disorder; (4) early experiences can change family relationships and circumstances, which over time lead to a disorder; (5) sensitivities to stress or coping strategies are changes, which then later predispose the person to disorder, or buffer the person from stress; (6) experiences change the child's self-concept or attitudes, which in turn influence behavior in later circumstances; and (7) experience influences behavior by affecting the selection of environments or the opening up or closing of opportunities.

Alan Sroufe (1979) has listed a number of salient developmental issues that need to be considered in the study of developmental psychopathology. As can be seen in Table 6.3, during the first year of life, biological regulation, harmonious dyadic relationships, and the formation of an attachment relationship are central developmental tasks. As the infant progresses through the second year of life, exploration, experimentation, and mastery of the object world, as well as individuation and autonomy become prominent developmental tasks. Sroufe and Rutter (1984) believe that issues at one developmental period lay the groundwork for subsequent issues, just as they do in the life-cycle framework proposed by Erik Erikson (1968).

Thus, we can see that genetics, biological conditions, attachment, and early experiences are important contributors to problems and disturbances in infancy. Let's now study several specific problems—first, child abuse, and second, the autistic child.

Child Abuse

Unfortunately, parental hostility toward children in some families reaches the point where one or both parents abuse the child. Child abuse is an increasing problem in the United States (Parke & Lewis, 1980). Estimates of its incidence vary according to different sources, but some authorities say that as many as 500,000 children are physically abused in the United States each year. Laws in many states now require doctors and teachers to report suspected cases of child abuse. Yet, many cases go unreported, particularly those of "battered" infants.

For several years, it was believed that parents who committed child abuse were severely disturbed, "sick" individuals. Recent research, however, reveals that parents who abuse their children are rarely psychotic (Blumberg, 1974). Ross Parke (Parke, 1976; Parke & Lewis, 1980) has developed a model for understanding child abuse that shifts the focus from the personality traits of the parents to an analysis of three aspects of the social environment—cultural, familial, and community influences.

The extensive violence in the American culture is reflected in the occurrence of violence in the family. Violence occurs regularly on television, and parents frequently resort to power assertion as a disciplinary technique. Cross-cultural studies indicate that American television contains more violence than British television (Geis & Monahan, 1976) and that in China, where physical punishment is rarely used to discipline children, the incidence of child abuse is very low (Stevenson, 1974).

To understand child abuse in the family, the interaction of all family members should be considered, regardless of who actually performs the violent acts against the child. Even though the father, for example, may be the person who has physically abused the child, contributions of the mother, the father, and the child should be evaluated.

Many parents who abuse their children come from families in which physical punishment was used. They may view physical punishment as a legitimate way of controlling the children's behavior, and physical abuse may be a part of this sanctioning. Thus, the parents' experiences as children in their own families may contribute to their child-abuse punishment techniques.

Many aspects of the ongoing interaction among immediate family members also affect the incidence of child abuse. The child himself or herself may have some effect—for example, an unattractive child experiences more physical punishment than an attractive child does (Dion, 1974), and a child from an unwanted pregnancy may be especially vulnerable to abuse (Birrell & Birrell, 1968).

The interaction of the parents with each other may lead to child abuse as well. Dominant-submissive husband-wife pairs have been linked with child abuse (Terr, 1970). Husband-wife violence or such stressful family situations as those caused by financial problems, for example, may erupt in the form of aggression directed against the defenseless child. Such displaced aggression, whereby a person shifts an aggressive reaction from the original target person or situation to some other person or situation, is a common cause of child abuse.

Community-based support systems are extremely important in alleviating stressful family situations and thereby preventing child abuse. A study of the support systems in 58 counties in New York State revealed a relationship between the incidence of child abuse and the presence of support systems available to the family. Both family resources—relatives and friends, for example—and such formal community support systems as crisis centers and child-abuse counseling were associated with a reduction in child abuse (Garbarino, 1976). Parke (1976) commented that "the family should not be treated as an independent social unit, but as embedded in a broader social network of informal and formal community-based support systems" (p. 14).

Now that we have some sense of what contributes to child abuse, let's study another perplexing disturbance that shows up in infancy.

Autism

Infantile **autism,** often diagnosed during infancy, may persist well into childhood. Probably the most distinguishing characteristic of autistic children is their inability to relate to other people (Wing, 1977). As babies, they require very little from their parents: They do not demand much attention, and they do not reach out (literally or figuratively) for their parents. They rarely smile. When someone attempts to hold them, they often try to withdraw by arching their backs and pushing away from the person. In their cribs or playpens, they appear oblivious to what is going on around them, often sitting and staring into space for long periods of time.

In addition to deficits in attachment to others, autistic children often have speech problems. As many as one out of every two autistic children never learns to speak. Those who do learn to speak may engage in a type of speech called **echolalia**—the child echoes rather than responds to what he or she hears. Thus, if you ask, "How are you, Chuck?" Chuck will respond with, "How are you, Chuck?" Autistic children also tend to confuse pronouns, inappropriately substituting *you* for *I,* for example.

A third major characteristic of autistic children is the degree to which they become upset over a change in their daily routine or their physical environment. Rearrangement of a sequence of events or even furniture in the course of their "normal" day often causes them to become extremely upset. Thus, autistic children are not flexible in adapting to new routines and changes in their daily life.

Autism is a severe disorder. Michael Rutter and Norman Garmezy (1983) recently summarized some of the most important research on causes of autism. Autism seems to involve some form of organic brain dysfunction and may have genetic ties as well. There has been no satisfactory evidence developed to suggest that family processes are linked to autism. To learn more about the everyday lives of autistic children and their parents, read Focus on Child Development 6.3.

FOCUS ON CHILD DEVELOPMENT 6.3

A CHILD CALLED NOAH

The impact an autistic child can have on parents is described in the following excerpts from the popular book *A Child Called Noah,* written in 1972 by Josh Greenfield about his autistic son Noah.

4–16–67: We've decided to stop worrying about Noah. He isn't retarded, he's just pushing the clock hands about at his own slow speed. Yet . . .

8–16–67: We took Noah to a pediatrician in the next town, who specializes in neurology. He said that, since Noah is talking now, there was little cause to worry; that Noah seemed "hypertonic," a floppy baby, a slow developer, but that time would be the maturing agent. We came away relieved. But I also have to admit that lately I haven't worried that much.

6–6–69: Noah is two. He still doesn't walk, but I do think he's trying to teach himself how to stand up. We're still concerned. And I guess we'll remain concerned until he stands up and walks like a boy.

7–14–69: Our fears about Noah continue to undergo dramatic ups and downs. Because of his increased opacity, the fact that he doesn't respond when we call his name and fails to relate completely to his immediate environment—pattern of retardation or autism—we took him to a nearby hospital. . . . I guess we both fear that what we dread is so, that Noah is not a normal child, that he is a freak, and his condition is getting worse.

2–19–70: I'm a lousy father. I anger too easily. I get hot with Karl and take on a four-year-old kid. I shout at Noah and further upset an already disturbed one. Perhaps I am responsible for Noah's problems.

8–70: I also must note how very few people can actually understand our situation as a family, how they assume we are aloof when we tend not to accept or extend the usual social invitations. Nor have I mentioned the extra expenses a child like Noah entails—those expenses I keep in another book.

8–71: Even more heartbreaking has been the three-year period it has taken us to pierce the organized-medicine, institutionalized-mental-health gauze curtain. Most doctors, if they were unable to prescribe any form of curative aid, did their best to deter us from seeking it. Freudian-oriented psychiatrists and psychologists, if ill-equipped to deal with the problems of those not verbal, tried to inflict great feelings of guilt upon us as all-too-vulnerable parents. Neurologists and pediatricians, if not having the foggiest notions about the effects of diet and nutrition, vitamins and enzymes, and their biochemical workings, would always suggest such forms of therapy as practiced only by quacks. And county mental-health boards, we discovered, who have charge of the moneys that might be spent helping children like Noah, usually tossed their skimpy fundings away through existing channels that do not offer proper treatment for children like Noah. (pp. 91–92)

The specific cause of autistic behavior still is the focus of extensive speculation. Some experts stress the importance of underlying hereditary and biological mechanisms, while other experts believe that social experiences are at fault.

THINKING BACK, LOOKING AHEAD

Our tour of the social world of the infant has taken us through genetic and biological contributions, microsystems, mesosystems, exosystems, macrosystems, reciprocal socialization and mutual regulation, the construction of relationships, the contact comfort of monkeys, secure and insecure attachment, intense mothers and avoidant babies, the father's interaction, accessibility and responsibility, siblings, peers, warehouses for infants, smiles and cries, joy and interest, anger and disgust, trust, mistrust, self-recognition, separation-individuation, independence, and self-control. This is the infant's social world—fascinating and multifaceted.

In Section 3, we move on to the early childhood years, describing the remarkable physical, cognitive, and social changes that occur from the ages of approximately three to five. But before you move on, reflect for a moment on Erik Erikson's belief that experiences in the first and second year of life are carried forward to influence a person's identity later in development:

> (Trust versus mistrust) leaves a residue in the growing being which will echo something of the conviction "I am what hope I have and give." The analogous residue of the stage of autonomy appears to be "I am what I can will freely."

SUMMARY

I. To understand the infant's social and personality development, it is important to consider both biological and sociocultural influences.
   A. The "rediscovery" in the 1970s and 1980s of biological factors in social and personality development has led to the belief that both biological and sociocultural factors are important in the infant's socialization. Genetic influences, temperament, and ethological ideas are among the important contributors to the study of childhood socialization.
   B. Bronfenbrenner's model has been helpful in describing the complexity of the child's sociocultural world. He describes the microsystem, mesosystem, exosystem, and macrosystem. This perspective provides insight into the direct and indirect ways in which sociocultural experiences influence children's development.

II. Family processes that are important in understanding infancy include the beginnings of parenthood, reciprocal socialization and mutual regulation, the family as a system, and the construction of relationships.
   A. Becoming a parent produces a disequilibrium in the family that requires a great deal of adaptation.
   B. Infants socialize parents just as parents socialize infants. Parent-infant relationships are mutually regulated by the parent and the infant. It is important to study parent-child relationships at both micro and molar levels. In infancy, much of the relationship is driven by the parent, but as the child gains self-control and self-regulation, the relationship is initiated on a more equal basis.
   C. The family is made up of interactions and relationships—some of which are dyadic, others polyadic—between individuals. Belsky has described a model of development that shows the importance of both direct and indirect effects involving family interaction. The husband-wife support system seems to be important in the family system, and the contributon of the infant should not be forgotten either.
   D. Relationships are constructed through the child's interactions with parents. Such relationships reflect continuity and coherence, and are carried forward to influence new relationships. The mother-child relationship seems to be particularly salient in this regard.

III. In general, attachment is a relationship between two people in which each person feels strongly about the other and does a number of things to ensure the continuation of the relationship. In infancy, attachment refers to the bond between the caregiver and the infant.
   A. Theories of attachment include ethological, psychoanalytic, social learning, and cognitive developmental perspectives.
      1. The most comprehensive account of attachment is that of John Bowlby. His ethological view stresses the infant's biologically equipped signals to the caregiver and the caregiver's responses to those signals. Bowlby describes the course of attachment over the first year of life, believing a focused attachment to the caregiver begins at about three to six months of age.
      2. According to Freud, the infant becomes attached to a person or object that provides oral satisfaction. He argued that infants become attached to mothers because mothers most often feed the infant. Erikson stresses the development of trust between the infant and caregiver.

3. Social learning theorists argue that attachment occurs because of the link between primary and secondary reinforcement. They believe that, by becoming associated with the feeding process, the caregiver becomes a secondary reinforcer. Harlow demonstrated the importance of contact comfort in attachment.

4. Kohlberg argues that attachment is a motivational system based on the need to express competence in interpersonal exchanges. Cognitive theorists often point to the development of object and person permanence in the first year of life as important precursors of attachment.

5. While ethological theory has become the most widely debated and provocative attachment view, each of the theories has provided a useful addition to the notion of attachment as a whole.

B. Researchers have been interested in charting the developmental course of attachment, discovering individual differences in attachment, and noting situational influences on attachment.

1. Several investigations suggest that between the ages of six to nine months, infant attachment becomes focused on the primary caregiver.

2. Mary Ainsworth's classification of attachment into secure, avoidant, and resistant categories has generated considerable research inquiry. Ainsworth argues that securely attached infants use the caregiver as a base for exploring the wider social world. Sroufe's research has found that secure attachment in infancy is linked to social competence in the preschool years. Lewis's research suggests that insecurely attached infants do not always become maladjusted in the elementary school years. And Belsky argues that intermediate levels of stimulation produce secure attachment.

3. Situational influences refer to the extent that environmental settings are capable of modifying attachment. For example, by modifying the behavior of a stranger, the infant's attachment behavior may be changed.

C. The attachment relationship is carried forward over time to influence the development of new relationships, such as those with peers. The infant's attachment pattern also is sometimes linked to intergenerational relationships.

D. Temperament, the father's role, and the importance of attachment in relation to other aspects of the child's complex sociocultural world raise questions about the role of attachment—particularly secure attachment to the mother—in the child's development.

1. Attachment theorists and researchers who follow the scheme of Bowlby and Ainsworth believe that infant temperament is not involved in a causal way to attachment classifications. By contrast, other theorists and researchers, such as Kagan, emphasize that the infant's inherited temperament plays an important role in how the infant's attachment is classified. Research reveals that infant and maternal temperaments are factors that need to be taken into account when attachment is at issue.

2. Over time, the father's role in the child's development has evolved from moral teacher to breadwinner to sex-role model to active, nurturant caregiver. Involvement can be analyzed in terms of engagement/interaction, accessibility, and responsibility. While fathers have increased their active interaction with their children, there seems to be little or no increase in the father's responsibility role. Infants seem to develop attachments to fathers and mothers at about the same time, but fathers seem to be more identified with a play role with infants, while mothers are identified as having a caretaking role.

3. A current controversy about attachment focuses on how critical attachment is for optimal development later in childhood. While the ethological view of attachment stresses that attachment to the caregiver, especially the mother, is the key factor in healthy psychological development, others believe that this view ignores the complexity of the child's sociocultural world. This latter view, which has much in common with Bronfenbrenner's ecological perspective, sees early social interactions with the mother as important in development, but stresses that other social agents and social contexts need to be considered over the long course of development.

IV. Sibling influences, peer influences, and day care are other important aspects of the infant's social world.

A. When a sibling is present, the nature of family interaction changes. Dunn and Kendrick have conducted highly focused assessments of infant/sibling pairs in the naturalistic setting of siblings' homes. Their research stresses how the developmental status of each sibling is related to how siblings interact. At some point between one and two years of age, the younger sibling initiates more sibling conflict.

B. Infants as young as six months of age interact with each other—primarily through smiling, touching, and vocalizing. In the second year of life, toys become a stronger focus of peer interaction. Recent research has shown that early peer skills are linked to popularity and social competence in the peer group during the preschool period.

C. About 2 million children currently receive formal day care, more than 5 million attend nursery schools or kindergartens, and uncounted millions are cared for by unlicensed baby-sitters. There is some indication that day care may disrupt mother-infant attachment, but this often varies with the quality of the day care. At this time, no conclusions can be drawn about overall positive or negative effects of day care, although many more high-quality day-care centers are badly needed.

V. Emotional and personality development are other important aspects of the infant's development.

A. Among the important aspects of emotional development are its functions, communication of emotions in preverbal infants, and further developments in emotions later in infancy.

1. Emotions serve important adaptive/survival, communicative, and regulative functions in the infant's development.

2. Very young infants display a variety of emotions. As early as one to three months of age, researchers can reliably code such expressions as joy and interest. Rudimentary emotions, such as the startle response and reflexive smiling, seem to be present at birth. Surprise, anger, and sadness are likely to emerge at three to four months of age. Fear may not be present until midway through the first year. Researchers also are interested in the ability of infants to recognize emotions in others. By four to six months of age, infants seem capable of recognizing such emotions as joy in others. Infants are able to display emotions earlier than they can recognize them in others, and they tend to recognize positive emotions (such as smiling) earlier than negative emotions (such as anger).

3. During the last half of the first year and into the second year, infants make considerable progress in understanding that they and others in their world are experiencers and communicators of emotions. At about 18 to 20 months of age, the onset of emotion language appears, and between 18 and 36 months of age, infants and toddlers become capable of labeling the emotions of others as well as their own, discussing past and future emotions, and talking appropriately about the antecedents and consequences of emotions.

B. Among the important aspects of personality development in infancy are trust, a sense of self, independence, and self-control.

1. Erikson stresses that the first stage of personality development, roughly corresponding to the first year of life, is trust versus mistrust.

2. At some point between 18 and 24 months of age, the infant develops a sense of self. The development of the self likely is a gradually unfolding process. Two theories of independence have been offered by Mahler and Erikson. Mahler emphasizes the process of separation-individuation in the first three years of life, while Erikson stresses the stage of autonomy versus shame and doubt in the second year. Some critics believe that Mahler places too much emphasis on the mother.

3. Research on independence has lagged behind research on attachment. As infants age from one to five years, they show more independence from their parents.

4. Self-control seems to emerge during late infancy. Claire Kopp believes that there are four phases in the development of self-control: neurophysiological modulation, sensorimotor modulation, control, and self-control. Self-control involves the appearance of representational thinking and recall memory, and is characterized by awareness, self-initiated modifications of remembered information, and an internally generated monitoring system. Parent-child relationships likely are involved in the child's development of self-control, but clearly there are important biogenetic and cognitive milestones as well.

VI. An understanding of problems and disturbances in infancy requires revisiting the areas of genetic influences and early experience. Other aspects of problems and disturbances in infancy include the nature of child abuse and autism.

A. All development—abnormal as well as normal—is influenced by an interaction of heredity and environment. Prenatal and perinatal influences have been documented as significant factors in adjustment later in development. Socioeconomic factors are involved in whether such prenatal and perinatal factors will produce maladjustment. Rutter has described a number of reasons why early experience might be important to understanding the development of problems and disturbances. And Sroufe has outlined salient developmental issues for infants and children of different ages.

B. An understanding of child abuse requires an analysis of cultural, familial, and community influences.

C. Autism is a severe disorder involving an inability to relate to people, speech problems, and upset over change in daily routine or physical environment. Autism seems to involve some form of organic brain dysfunction and genetic disorder.

KEY TERMS

attachment 215
autism 246
contact comfort 216
control 241
echolalia 246
executor responses 216
exosystem 208
insecure attachment 219
macrosystem 209
mesosystem 208
microsystem 208

molar exchanges 211
neurophysiological modulation 241
reciprocal socialization 211
second-order effects 213
secure attachment 219
self-control 241
sensorimotor modulation 241
separation-individuation 238
signalling responses 216
social mold theories 211

SUGGESTED READINGS

Bronfenbrenner, U., & Crouter, A. C. (1983). The evolution of environmental models in developmental research. In P. H. Mussen (Ed.), *Handbook of child psychology* (4th ed.), Vol. I. New York: Wiley.
Bronfenbrenner, a leading figure in the ecological approach, presents his views on how developmental psychology has been too constrained in its thinking and assessment regarding the contexts of development.

Hartup, W. W., & Rubin, Z. (Eds.). (1986). *Relationships and development*. Hillsdale, NJ: Erlbaum.
This compendium of articles provides considerable insight into the study of children's relationships. Includes articles by Hartup, Hinde, Sroufe, Pattern, and Weiss. Pays particular attention to the role of development in understanding relationships.

Izard, C. E. (1982). *Measuring emotions in infants and children*. New York: Cambridge University Press.
Izard, one of the leading figures in the study of infant emotions, describes in fascinating detail how to assess the emotions of infants and young children.

Lamb, M. E. (Ed.). (1986). *The father's role: Applied perspectives*. New York: Wiley.
A very up-to-date, broad-based overview of what is known about the father's role in the child's development. Includes many applications to the real world of families.

Maccoby, E. E., & Martin, J. A. (1983). Socialization in the context of the family: Parent-child interaction. In P. Mussen (Ed.), *Handbook of child psychology* (4th ed.), Vol. 4. New York: Wiley.
An extensive, competent overview of what we know about children's socialization in families. Provides many new ideas about research on children and their families.

Plomin, R., & Dunn, J. (1986). *The study of temperament*. Hillsdale, NJ: Erlbaum.
A number of leading experts detail the importance of biogenetic factors in the study of infant and children's socialization. Includes articles by Kagan, Hinde, and Dunn.

Sroufe, L. A., & Fleeson, J. (1986). Attachment and the construction of relationships. In W. Hartup and Z. Rubin (Eds.), *Relationships and development*. Hillsdale, NJ: Erlbaum.
In this article, the very important idea that in order to understand family development we need to study how people construct relationships is presented. Details from research on child development as well as clinical studies across generations are provided.

SECTION 3
EARLY CHILDHOOD

The childhood shows the man, as morning shows the day.
Milton

PHYSICAL AND COGNITIVE DEVELOPMENT IN EARLY CHILDHOOD

CHAPTER 7

IMAGINE . . . YOU ARE FOUR YEARS OLD AND ATTENDING A MONTESSORI PRESCHOOL

PREVIEW

PHYSICAL DEVELOPMENT IN EARLY CHILDHOOD

Height, Weight, Fat, Muscle, and Other Bodily Parts
Individual Variation in Physical Development
Motor and Perceptual Development
Nutrition, Health, and Exercise
Nutrition
Health and Illness

FOCUS ON CHILD DEVELOPMENT 7.1: "FEET NOT COLD NOW"

Exercise

CHILD DEVELOPMENT CONCEPT TABLE 7.1: PHYSICAL DEVELOPMENT IN EARLY CHILDHOOD

COGNITIVE DEVELOPMENT IN EARLY CHILDHOOD

Preoperational Thought
The General Nature of Preoperational Thought
The Symbolic Function Substage

FOCUS ON CHILD DEVELOPMENT 7.2: WHERE PELICANS KISS SEALS, CARS FLOAT ON CLOUDS, AND HUMANS ARE TADPOLES

The Substage of Intuitive Thought
Some Criticisms of Piaget's Ideas on Preschool Thought
Information Processing
Attention
Memory
Task Dimensions and Analyses

FOCUS ON CHILD DEVELOPMENT 7.3: MERDS THAT LAUGH DON'T LIKE MUSHROOMS

LANGUAGE DEVELOPMENT IN EARLY CHILDHOOD

The Mean Length of Utterance
Further Development in the Basic Properties of Language
Phonology
Morphology

FOCUS ON CHILD DEVELOPMENT 7.4: FOOTS, FEETS, AND WUGS

Syntax
Semantics
Pragmatics

CHILD DEVELOPMENT CONCEPT TABLE 7.2: COGNITIVE DEVELOPMENT IN EARLY CHILDHOOD

EARLY CHILDHOOD EDUCATION

The Nature and Effects of Early Childhood Education
Compensatory Education
Project Follow Through

FOCUS ON CHILD DEVELOPMENT 7.5: VARIATIONS IN EARLY EDUCATION WITH IMPOVERISHED CHILDREN

The Long-Term Effects of Project Head Start and Preschool Education With Low-Income Children

THINKING BACK, LOOKING AHEAD

SUMMARY

KEY TERMS

SUGGESTED READINGS

IMAGINE . . . YOU ARE FOUR YEARS OLD AND ATTENDING A MONTESSORI PRESCHOOL

Amy began attending a Montessori school when she was three years old and has been attending the school for more than a year now. Her mother was interested in a preschool program for Amy that involved academic instruction rather than a program focused on play. Amy's mother talked to a number of mothers in her neighborhood, read extensively about different approaches to early childhood education, and visited eight different preschool programs to observe a typical school day and talk with teachers before making her decision about which school would be best for Amy.

Montessori schools are patterned after the educational philosophy of Maria Montessori, an Italian physician-turned-educator, who crafted a revolutionary approach to the education of young children at the beginning of the 20th century. Her work began with a group of mentally retarded children in Rome. She was very successful in teaching them to read, write, and pass examinations designed for normal children. Some time later, she turned her attention to poor children from the slums of Rome and had similar success in teaching them. Her approach has since been adopted extensively in private nursery schools in the United States.

The **Montessori approach** is at once a philosophy of education, a psychology of the child, and a group of practical educational exercises that can be used to teach children. Children are permitted considerable freedom and spontaneity in choosing intellectual activities, and they can move from one activity to another when they desire. Each child is encouraged to work independently, to complete tasks in a prescribed manner once they have been undertaken, and to put materials away in assigned places. The teacher serves as a facilitator, rather than a director or controller of learning. He or she shows the child how to perform intellectual activities, demonstrates interesting ways to explore curriculum materials, and offers help when the child requests.

During her morning activities at Montessori, Amy works at a task designed to promote sensory and perceptual development. The materials Amy is working with facilitate the discrimination of different textures through the sense of touch. The materials include:

1. A long rectangular board divided into two rectangles—one with smooth paper, the other with rough paper
2. A second board of the same shape as the first but covered with alternating strips of smooth and rough paper
3. A third board with strips of emery paper and sandpaper in decreasing grades of coarseness
4. A fourth board with pieces of paper of varying grades of smoothness, ranging from parchment to the very smooth paper of the first board.

Amy also is working with materials that facilitate the perception of sound. Cardboard boxes are constructed in a series so that they will produce graduated noises. The boxes are jumbled together. By judging the different sounds the boxes make when she hits them with her hand, Amy is able to place the boxes in a graduated order.

These children are attending a Montessori school. What experiences are they likely to have there?

Amy subsequently goes over to a table where a series of bells are located. She carefully and quietly takes the bells to her workstation. Amy shakes each of the bells to determine the individual notes. Then, just as with the cardboard boxes, she places them in an order designed to show a gradation of sounds. When she is finished with this task, she places the bells back in their location on the table where she obtained them originally.

These are just a few of the many exercises used in the Montessori curriculum to teach children about the senses of touch, hearing, smell, and taste. They constitute a unique approach to the education of young children's senses and perception. Many of these techniques are used in contemporary preschool education.

While the Montessori approach to preschool education is favored by some psychologists and educators, others believe that the social development of children is neglected. For example, while Montessori attempts to foster independence and the development of cognitive skills, verbal interaction between the teacher and child and extensive peer interaction are deemphasized. The critics of Montessori also argue that imaginative play is restricted. Later in this chapter, various types of preschool programs other than Montessori's are described. Keep the Montessori approach in mind so that you can compare its focus with that of these other programs.

PREVIEW

The physical and cognitive world of the preschool child is creative, free, and fanciful. Striking, catching, throwing, kicking, balancing, rolling objects, rolling oneself, zipping, lacing, buttoning, cutting, locking, latching, snapping, buckling, stacking, fitting, pushing, pulling, dancing, and swimming—preschool children do all of these things and much more. A fascinating part of the ''much more'' is their drawing and symbolic thought. Suns sometime show up as green, skies yellow. Cars float in the sky, pelicans kiss seals, and people are represented by tadpoles (Winner, 1986). As Picasso once said, ''I used to draw like Raphael, but it has taken me a whole lifetime to learn to draw like children.''

PHYSICAL DEVELOPMENT IN EARLY CHILDHOOD

Remember from Chapter 4 that the infant's growth in the first year is extremely rapid and follows cephalocaudal and proximodistal patterns. By 13 to 14 months of age, most infants have begun to walk. During the infant's second year, the growth rate begins to slow down, but both gross and fine motor skills progress rapidly. The infant develops a sense of mastery through increased proficiency in walking and running. Increased fine motor skills, such as being able to turn the pages of a book one at a time, also contribute to the infant's sense of mastery during the second year.

While the growth rate continues to slow down during early childhood, there is growth in height, weight, fat, muscle, and other bodily parts. There are some general growth trends among most children, but considerable individual variation is apparent. Changes in motor and perceptual development also characterize the preschool years, although changes in perceptual development in this age span do not seem nearly as dramatic as those documented in the first year of life. Other issues of interest regarding physical development in early childhood are nutrition, health, and exercise.

Table 7.1   Physical Growth, Ages Three to Six (50th Percentile)

Age	Height (Inches)		Weight (Pounds)	
	Boys	Girls	Boys	Girls
3	38	37¾	32¼	31¾
3½	39¼	39¼	34¼	34
4	40¼	40½	36½	36¼
4½	42	42	38½	38½
5	43¼	43	41½	41
5½	45	44½	45½	44
6	46	46	48	47

From *Growth and Development of Children*, 8th edition, by George H. Lowrey. Copyright © 1986 by Year Book Medical Publishers, Inc., Chicago. Used with permission of Year Book Medical Publishers, Inc.

Height, Weight, Fat, Muscle, and Other Bodily Parts

The average child grows 2½ inches in height and gains between five and seven pounds a year during early childhood. As the preschool child grows older, the percentage of increase in height and weight decreases with each additional year of age. Table 7.1 shows the average height and weight of children as they age from three to six years. Girls are only slightly smaller and lighter than boys during this age frame, a difference that continues until puberty. During the preschool years, both boys and girls slim down as the trunk of their bodies becomes longer. Although their heads are still somewhat large for their bodies, by the end of the preschool years, most children have lost their top-heavy look. Body fat also shows a slow, steady decline during the preschool years, so that the chubby baby often looks much leaner by the end of early childhood. Girls have more fatty tissue than do boys, and boys have more muscle tissue.

During early childhood, some body systems show signs of maturing—for instance, the child's heart rate slows down and becomes more stable (Eichorn, 1970). Nonetheless, there still are signs of immaturity in many body systems, including bones, joints, and muscles, which are much more susceptible to injury than those of children in middle and late childhood (Lundsteen & Bernstein-Tarrow, 1981).

Individual Variation in Physical Development

Clearly, growth patterns vary individually. Think back to your preschool years. You may recall that this was the first time you noticed that some other children were taller than you, some shorter; that some were fatter, some thinner; that some were stronger, some weaker.

Much of the variation in height is due to genetic factors, but there is evidence that environmental experiences contribute as well. In reviewing more than 200 studies of the heights of preschool children around the world, researchers concluded that two very important contributors to height differences are ethnic origin and nutrition (Meredith, 1978). Urban, middle-class, and firstborn children were taller than rural, lower-class, and later-born children, possibly because the former experience better health care and nutrition. The researchers also noted that children at the age of five were approximately ½ inch shorter if their mother smoked during pregnancy. In the United States, height differences among preschool children are mainly due to genetic inheritance because most children receive enough food for their bodies to grow appropriately. On the average, black children are taller than white children in the United States (Krogman, 1970).

Children who experience growth problems, being unusually short or unusually tall (which is less frequent), usually do so for one of three reasons: (1) a congenital reason, (2) a physical problem that develops during childhood, or (3) an emotional difficulty. In many instances, individuals with congenital growth problems (those due to genetic conditions or prenatal difficulties) can be treated with hormones. Usually, such treatment is directed at a master gland, the pituitary, located at the base of the brain. This gland secretes hormones that control growth. With regard to physical problems that develop during childhood, malnutrition and chronic infections can stunt growth, although if they are properly treated, normal growth usually is achieved (Lowrey, 1978). Finally, some psychologists believe that emotional problems can produce growth abnormalities. For instance, Lita Gardner (1972) argues that children who are deprived of affection may experience alterations in the release of hormones by the pituitary gland. This type of growth retardation is called **deprivation dwarfism.** Some children who are small and weak but who are not dwarfs also may show the effects of an impoverished emotional environment—although most parents of such children generally say that they are small and weak because they have a poor body structure or constitution.

Now that we have examined some common patterns, as well as some individual variations, in physical growth, let's discuss the nature of motor and perceptual development in early childhood.

Motor and Perceptual Development

Building towers with blocks . . . running as fast as you could, falling down, getting right back up, and running just as fast again . . . scribbling, scribbling, and then scribbling some more on lots of pieces of paper . . . cutting paper with scissors—during your preschool years, you probably developed all of these motor activities. A summary of the manner in which a number of gross and fine motor skills change during the course of early childhood is presented in Table 7.2.

Three- to five-year-olds often experience considerable large-muscle development, particularly in the arms and legs, and thus, daily exercise is recommended to increase gross motor skills. Sedentary periods should be brief and few. Although fine motor skills also are increasing during this period, they seem to show more growth during the beginning of middle childhood than during early childhood (Robinson, 1977).

How is motor development assessed? The Bayley Motor Scale can be used for children through the age of 2½; the Gesell Developmental Schedules and the Denver Developmental Screening Test can be used for children through the age of six. The Bayley test was designed primarily for very young children, mainly infants, so it is not surprising that postural control, locomotion, and prehensile activity are emphasized and that there is an absence of attention to such important aspects of movement as striking, catching, throwing, jumping, running, and kicking behaviors, which are included on the Gesell and Denver tests.

Table 7.2   Motor and Perceptual Development in Early Childhood

The following tasks are reasonable to expect in 75 to 80 percent of the children of the indicated ages. Children should be tested individually. The data upon which this is based have been collected from children in white middle-class neighborhoods.
A child failing to master four to six of the tasks for his or her age probably needs (a) a more thorough evaluation and (b) some kind of remedial help. Various sex differences are indicated.

Two to Three Years	Yes	No
1. Displays a variety of scribbling behavior	___	___
2. Can walk rhythmically at an even pace	___	___
3. Can step off low object, one foot ahead of the other	___	___
4. Can name hands, feet, head, and some face parts	___	___
5. Opposes thumb to fingers when grasping objects and releases objects smoothly from finger-thumb grasp	___	___
6. Can walk a 2-inch wide line placed on ground, for 10 feet	___	___

Four to Four-and-a-Half	Yes	No
1. Forward broad jump, both feet together and clear of ground at the same time	___	___
2. Can hop two or three times on one foot without precision or rhythm	___	___
3. Walks and runs with arm action coordinated with leg action	___	___
4. Can walk a circular line a short distance	___	___
5. Can draw a crude circle	___	___
6. Can imitate a simple line cross using a vertical and horizontal line	___	___

Five to Five-and-a-Half	Yes	No
1. Runs 30 yards in just over 8 seconds	___	___
2. Balances on one foot (girls 6 to 8 seconds) (boys 4 to 6 seconds)	___	___
3. Child catches large playground ball bounced to him or her chest-high from 15 feet away, four to five times out of five	___	___
4. Rectangle and square drawn differently (one side at a time)	___	___
5. Can high-jump 8 inches or higher over bar with simultaneous two-foot takeoff	___	___
6. Bounces playground ball, using one or two hands, a distance of 3 to 4 feet	___	___

Six to Six-and-a-Half	Yes	No
1. Can block-print first name in letters 1½ to 2 inches high	___	___
2. Can gallop, if it is demonstrated	___	___
3. Can exert 6 pounds or more of pressure in grip strength measure	___	___
4. Can walk balance beam 2 inches wide, 6 inches high, and 10 to 12 inches long	___	___
5. Can run 60 feet in about 5 seconds	___	___
6. Can arise from ground from back lying position, when asked to do so as fast as he or she can, in 2 seconds or under	___	___

From Cratty, B., *Psychomotor Behavior in Education and Sport.* © 1974 Charles C. Thomas, Publisher, Springfield, Illinois. Reprinted by permission.

The Denver Developmental Screening Test deserves further mention because it was created as a simple, inexpensive, and fast way to diagnose delayed development in children from birth through six years of age. The test is individually administered and includes an evaluation of language and personal-social ability in addition to separate assessments of gross and fine motor skills. Gross motor skills that are evaluated include the child's ability to sit, walk, broad-jump, pedal a tricycle, throw a ball overhand, catch a bounced ball, hop on one foot, and balance on one foot. Fine motor-adaptive skills that are evaluated include the child's ability to stack cubes, reach for objects, and draw a person.

One promising test that provides a more detailed assessment of gross motor skills is the DeOreo Fundamental Motor Skills Inventory (DeOreo, 1976). Performance is evaluated in 11 categories: striking, balancing, skipping, jumping, galloping, hopping, catching, running, climbing, throwing, and kicking. Items are divided into product components, such as, "Can the child run 35 yards in less than 10 seconds?" and process components, such as, "While running, does the child keep his or her body erect or inclined backward?"

Another important development in early childhood is how children perceive the space they live in. If you are sitting in your bedroom and the door is shut, can you identify what lies beyond each wall? Can you point toward the TV in the living area or the stove in the kitchen?

What kinds of motor skills would you want to assess if you were developing a motor skills test for preschool children?

And what about the spatial locations of your house, your school, and the downtown area of the city where you live? Can you sketch a map showing all of these locations? Chances are you can perform all of these tasks with some degree of accuracy. But some of us—those with a "good sense of direction"—are much better at such tasks than others (Kozlowski & Bryant, 1977). The rest of us—those with a mediocre or poor sense of direction—generally regard this as a significant failing. The study of the development of "mapping" in young children may help us to discover why individual differences in sense of direction occur. Further, mapping in children is important in its own right. How many cases of children getting lost are due to their difficulties in mapping large-scale spaces (those too large to be seen all at once)?

In an experiment on the development of mapping ability, three- to five-year-old children were led on a route through four rooms, each containing a toy. After training in identifying which doors to use and which toys would be encountered in successive rooms, the children were given a reversed-route test. All of the children showed some ability to choose which doors to go through and to identify toys that would be encountered when they took the reverse route. However, younger children made more errors. Furthermore, all of the children were relatively

poor at making inference judgments—that is, judgments of the toy behind a door that they had not traveled through during training (Hazen, Lockman, & Pick, 1978). Thus, there are deficiencies in young children's learning of large-scale layouts, though what perhaps is more surprising is that children as young as three years old learn such layouts as well as they do.

So far, we have charted some basic changes in young children's physical growth patterns and also looked at several intriguing ideas about their motor and perceptual development. As we see next, however, other important aspects of the preschool child's physical development include nutrition, health, and exercise.

Nutrition, Health, and Exercise

We have become a very health-conscious nation. In the last decade, we have become much more aware of what we eat and what effect it might have on our bodies. Considerable interest also has been generated in the role that exercise may play in the development of a healthy body. What is the nature of such concerns with regard to young children?

Table 7.3   Fat and Calorie Intake of Selected Fast-Food Meals

Selected Meal	Calories	Percent of Calories from Fat
Burger King Whopper, fries, vanilla shake	1,250	43
Big Mac, fries, chocolate shake	1,100	41
McDonald's Quarter-Pounder with cheese	418	52
Pizza Hut 10-inch pizza with sausage, mushrooms, pepperoni, and green pepper	1,035	35
Arby's roast beef plate (roast beef sandwich, two potato patties, and coleslaw), chocolate shake	1,200	30
Kentucky Fried Chicken dinner (three pieces chicken, mashed potatoes and gravy, coleslaw, roll)	830	50
Arthur Treacher's fish and chips (two pieces breaded, fried fish, french fries, cola drink)	900	42
Typical restaurant "diet plate" (hamburger patty, cottage cheese, etc.)	638	63

From Virginia Demoss, "Good, the Bad and the Edible" in *Runner's World,* June 1980. Copyright Virginia Demoss. Reprinted with permission.

Nutrition

Feeding and eating habits are important aspects of development during early childhood. It is widely recognized that what we eat affects our skeletal growth, body shape, and susceptibility to disease. Recognizing that nutrition is important for the child's growth and development, the federal government provides money for school lunch programs. On the average, the preschool child requires approximately 1,400 to 1,800 calories a day. Children with unbalanced or malnourished diets show below-average physical development by the third year of life. Some evidence suggests that, when the appropriate nutrients are introduced into the diet of the malnourished child, physical development improves. For instance, when provided milk supplements over a 20-month period, deprived children between the ages of 4 and 15 showed gains of 3.6 percent in height and 29 percent in weight.

A particular concern in our culture is the amount of fat in our diet. Table 7.3 lists the number of calories and the percentage of fat in the offerings of a number of fast-food restaurants. Most fast-food meals are high in protein, especially meat and dairy products. But the average American does not need to be concerned about obtaining protein. What must be of concern is the vast number of young children who are being weaned on fast foods that are not only high in protein but also high in

How might early nutritional patterns influence later development?

fat. (It is during the preschool years that many individuals get their first taste of fast foods, and, unfortunately, eating habits become ingrained very early in life.) The American Heart Association recommends that the daily limit for calories from fat should be approximately 35 percent. Compare this figure with the figures in Table 7.3. Clearly, many fast-food meals contribute to excessive fat intake by young children.

Perhaps the most direct evidence of the effects of nutrition on development is provided by animal studies, which, for example, have shown that the development of the brain is related to protein intake. In one study, one month before impregnation, one group of female rats was placed on a high-protein diet, and a similar group was placed on a low-protein diet. When the brain and body weights of the offspring were measured, the weights of the offspring of mothers on the high-protein diet were greater than those of the offspring of mothers on the low-protein diet. The brains of the mothers themselves were subsequently analyzed: The brains of the mothers on the high-protein diet had more cells than did those of the mothers on the low-protein diet (Zamenhof, van Marthens, & Margolis, 1968). Thus, we may conclude that the nutrition of the mother may affect not only the development of her own brain but the development of her offspring's brain as well.

In another study, two groups of black South African infants, all one year old, were extremely malnourished. The children in one group were given adequate nourishment during the next six years; there was no intervention in the poor nutrition of the other group. After the seventh year, the poorly nourished group of children had significantly lower IQs than the adequately nourished group did (Bayley, 1970).

What is an appropriate diet for a preschool child? Clearly, there is individual variation, and experts may disagree on detail, but in general, the diet should include fats, carbohydrates, protein, vitamins, and minerals.

Health and Illness

While there has been great national interest in and considerable attention given during the last decade to psychological aspects of health among adults (e.g., Stone, 1983), only very recently has a developmental perspective on psychological aspects of health among children been set forth. James Maddux and his colleagues believe that a developmental approach to children's health care consists of two main elements: First, a future orientation focuses on early intervention as optimal for preventing health problems later in childhood, adolescence, and adulthood. This viewpoint seems to be well represented in health psychology. However, the second aspect of the developmental viewpoint has been chronically ignored. That is, each period of development needs to be given attention for the particular problems evident in that period. The uniqueness of health care needs of young children can be further understood by considering issues of health in relation to motor, cognitive, and social development (Maddux, Roberts, Sledden, & Wright, 1986).

Health and Motor Development

As the preschool child's motor development increases, the child has greater risk of accidents and exposure to sources of disease. Since accidents are the leading cause of death and disability among children (Califano, 1979), information about children's motor development may shed light on the points at which certain problems occur and which ages of children are more at risk.

Since the infant and young preschool child do not have adequate motor control to ensure his or her personal safety while riding in an automobile, adults must take preventive measures to restrain infants and young children in car seats. The importance of this preventive measure becomes even clearer when we consider that the infant is more susceptible to brain injury because of a softer skull and a greater proportion of body weight centered in the head (which pulls the head forward in collisions).

Pediatric medicine has argued that anticipatory guidance can be helpful in preventing accidents. Anticipatory guidance involves discussions with parents about behavioral characteristics of children at different ages and precautions that can be taken (Brazelton, 1975; Roberts & Wright, 1982).

Morbidity and mortality rates can provide clues about prevention as well. For instance, children one to four years of age have higher rates of accident poisoning (Nelson, Vaughn, & McKay, 1975), those five to nine years of age have higher rates of pedestrian accidents (Yeaton & Bailey, 1978), and older children and adolescents have higher rates of accidents on recreational equipment (Werner, 1982).

More than an understanding of motor development is involved in preventing accidents in young children, however. Young children may lack the intellectual skills, including reading ability, to discriminate between safe and unsafe household substances. And they may lack the impulse control to keep them from running out into a busy street while going after a ball or a toy.

Health and Cognitive Development   There has been considerable interest in linkages between the child's cognitive development and his or her understanding of the relation between behavior and health/illness (Bibace & Walsh, 1979; Potter & Roberts, 1984; Willis, Elliott, & Jay, 1982). Increased cognitive sophistication should improve the child's self-protective behavior and encourage him or her to take responsibility for preventing problems and promoting health and safety. Cognitive development also likely influences the child's psychological and behavioral responses to injury and illness and their treatment.

One model of the link between health and cognition focuses on Piaget's stages of development (Bibace & Walsh, 1979). In the **phenomenistic stage,** preoperational thought dominates. The child often explains the relation between sources of illness and the body in magiclike terms or believes that the relation is due to mere association. In the **contagion stage,** concrete operational thought is dominant. The child believes that there is at least temporal or spatial proximity between illness and its source. The concrete nature of the stage is particularly seen in the child's views of illness being transmitted through physical contact with the source, such as dirt. At this point, the child begins to assume some self-responsibility for his or her health by simply avoiding such agents as dirt and germs. It is believed that, as children and adolescents move beyond the contagion stage, they increasingly internalize the belief of being responsible for their health behavior and develop more sophisticated understanding of the role of avoidance behaviors and proper care in the maintenance of health. The development of formal operational thinking during the adolescent years allows the individual to perceive that there are multiple causes of health and multiple cures for illness. Hypothetical thinking begins, in which the adolescent entertains which course among many to take in pursuing a healthy existence. Further, the adolescent is likely to begin sensing that cognitions and feelings may influence the nature of health behavior.

Health education programs for preschool children need to be cognitively simple. For example, Parcel, Tiernan, Nadar, & Gottlob (1979) stress three simple but important goals in a health education program for nursery school children: (1) identifying feelings of wellness and illness and being able to express them to adults, (2) identifying appropriate sources of assistance for health programs, and (3) independently initiating the use of sources of assistance for health-related problems. The first recommendation deserves further consideration. As seen in Focus on Child Development 7.1, a sense of self, language development, and the use of internal-state words (words that describe inner states, like *feeling*) are important in the young child's ability to communicate information about health and illness.

Further evidence of the importance of cognitive development in health, illness, and injury involves the child's reactions to severe burns. Children under the age of four are most vulnerable to burns, and children in this age group have the most difficulty understanding the condition and its treatment (Feck, Baptiste, & Tate, 1978; Wisely, Masur, & Morgan, 1983). Other research reveals that children's reactions to painful medical procedures likely are related to the children's cognitive development (Jay & Elliott, 1984). A dramatic decrease around the ages of six to seven occurs in the level of distress displayed by children during bone marrow aspirations—children under age five showed distress levels five times that of the older children. The older children likely have a more logical and realistic understanding of medical procedures and are better able to control their impulses.

Health and Social Development   In terms of the social development of the preschool child, caregivers play an important health role. For example, by controlling the speed of the vehicles they drive, by decreasing their drinking—particularly before driving—and by not smoking around children, caregivers can enhance the children's health. Caregivers also can actively affect the child's health and safety more directly by training the child in appropriate dental hygiene, proper nutrition, recreational safety, and self-protection skills.

FOCUS ON CHILD DEVELOPMENT 7.1

"FEET NOT COLD NOW"

At some time between 18 and 24 months of age, infants develop a sense of self. During their third year of life, they also seem to develop the ability to use internal-state words to refer to themselves and others. Inge Bretherton and Marjorie Beeghly (1982) studied the development of the spontaneous use of internal-state words with 28-month-old children. While the researchers studied a wide variety of cognitions, such as those pertaining to moral matters, ability, and perception, our concern here is with their research on young children's communication about internal bodily states/sensations that are most closely related to illness and health.

The data reported in the table are based on both direct observations of the child's use of internal-state words and an interview with the mother about her child's use of such words. The table includes information about specific words, verbatim examples heard, the percentage of children who had acquired the word, and the percentage of children who used a specific word for both self and others. As can be seen in the table, the children's abilities to identify internal states that might be related to health and illness varied, but nonetheless it does appear that they understood the existence of such internal states and could communicate about them at least in a rudimentary way.

Arthur Parmelee (1986), however, worries about how such young children may confuse such terms as "feel bad" with bad behavior and "feel good" with good behavior. For example, he took the statements from the Bretherton and Beeghly (1982) study that might be related to feelings due to physical illness or injury and juxtaposed them with statements involving similar words but that are related to emotional feelings. Some examples follow:

"I feel bad. I want aspirin."
"I feel bad. My tummy hurts."
"Bobby hurt me."
"I bad girl. I wet my pants."
"Me can do it, me good girl."
"I'm hurting your feeling, cause I was mean to you."
"Stop, it doesn't feel good."

In fact, young children often attribute their illness to what they view as a transgression, such as having eaten the wrong food

At what age can young children report the inner states of their illnesses?

or played outdoors in the cold when told not to (Blos, 1978; Brewster, 1982; Kister & Patterson, 1980).

Parmelee (1986) goes on to show the potential in illness and wellness situations for adults to help children sort out distress feelings and state changes due to emotional upsets and those due to physical illness. For instance, a mother might say to her young child, "I know you feel bad because you are sick like your sister was last week, but you will be well soon just like she is now." Or a mother might comment, "I know you feel bad because I am going on a trip and can't take you with me, but I will be back in a few days."

(continued on following page)

FOCUS ON CHILD DEVELOPMENT 7.1

Words About Internal States That Might Be Related to Health and Illness by 28-Month-Old Children

Words	Verbatim Example	Children Who Acquired the Word (%)	Children Who Used a Specific Word for Self and Others (%)
Perceptual Words			
Cold (feeling cold, having cold feet—not about objects being cold)	"Feet not cold now." (past)	83	67
Hot (same as for cold)	"I'm too hot. I'm sweating."	67	27
Hurt	"Does it hurt, Billy?"	90	80
Physiological Words			
Hungry	"I not hungry now." (past)	77	70
Thirsty	"I'm not thirsty anymore." (past)	80	70
Tired	"I'm not tired anymore." (past)	83	70
Sick	"If I eat poison, it will make me sick."	73	63
Emotional, Affective Words			
Feel (good, bad, all right)	"Don't feel bad, Bob."	60	47
Good (feel good)	"Feel good now." (about self)	47	27
Dirty	"My hands dirty?"	87	63

From Bretherton, Inge and M. Beeghly, "Talking about internal states: The acquisition of an explicit theory of mind" in *Developmental Psychology, 18,* 906–921, 1982. Copyright © 1982 American Psychological Association. Reprinted by permission of the author.

Caretakers' monitoring of the child's health behavior is an important long-term project. Thus, while the child's internalization and self-responsibility for his or her health-related behavior should be the goal of every parent, such self-control only comes through thousands of hours of interaction and relationships with parents who are competent models of health behavior themselves, who are knowledgeable about health-related matters, who can communicate this knowledge in effective ways to their children, and who carefully monitor their children's lives to prevent injury and illness. In one area of illness—diabetes—it has been found that diabetic children must be 12 years old for self-management of both insulin injection and urine testing (Johnson, 1984).

It also is important to consider how illness and hospitalization may influence the attachment process. Extensive separation of the infant from the parents may disrupt the attachment process and produce insecure attachment. Further, hospitalization and extensive illness during the toddler and early childhood years may restrict the child's development of independence and exploration (Willis, Elliott, & Jay, 1982).

As mentioned in Focus on Child Development 7.1, Parmelee (1986) believes that illnesses, particularly minor illnesses that are not life threatening, provide an excellent opportunity for the young child to expand his or her development. Parmelee points out that the preschool period is a time when such illnesses as respiratory infections (colds, flu) and gastrointestinal upsets (nausea, diarrhea) are at their peak. The illnesses usually are of short duration and are handled for the most part outside of the medical community through the family, day care, or school. Parmelee believes that such minor illnesses can stimulate an increase in the young child's self-knowledge, sense of empathy, and realistic understanding of the sick role. This knowledge is gained not only by children encountering such illnesses themselves but also by children observing parents, siblings, and peers as they become ill and recover, often in quick succession, after the child's own experience.

So far, we have discussed how the child's nutrition and health are important aspects of the preschool child's physical development. As we see next, exercise is another component that deserves attention.

What is the physical fitness level of our nation's children?

Exercise

By the time they reach elementary school, many children already are out of shape. While we currently are in the midst of a trend toward greater exercise by adults, the exercise revolution apparently is not filtering down to children. The 1985 School Fitness Survey tested 18,857 children, ages 6 to 17, on nine fitness tasks. The 1985 results, when compared with a similar survey in 1975, showed virtually no improvement. For example, 40 percent of boys ages 6 to 12 could not do more than one pull-up, and 25 percent couldn't do any! Fifty percent of the girls ages 6 to 17 and 30 percent of the boys ages 6 to 12 could not run a mile in less than 10 minutes. One difference in the 1985 and 1975 comparisons suggested that, by adolescence, girls were in better shape 10 years ago. In a 50-yard dash, the adolescent girls of 1985 were significantly slower than their 1975 counterparts. Such information suggests that there likely is a long history of exercise neglect and that the preschool years may be a good time to have children begin a regular exercise program.

Child Development Concept Table 7.1 summarizes our discussion of the many different dimensions of physical development in early childhood. Now we focus on cognitive changes during the preschool years.

Child Development Concept Table 7.1   Physical Development in Early Childhood

Concept	Processes/Related Ideas	Characteristics/Description
Height, weight, fat, muscle, and other bodily parts	Developmental changes	Growth is slower in early childhood than in infancy. The average child grows 2½ inches in height and gains between five and seven pounds a year during early childhood. Bones, muscles, and joints are more susceptible to injury than in middle and late childhood.
	Individual variation	Both genetic and environmental factors contribute to considerable variation in physical development during early childhood. Ethnic origin and nutrition are very important influences on height. Urban, middle-class, and firstborn children are taller than rural, lower-class, and later-born children. Children who experience growth problems usually do so because of a congenital reason, a physical problem that develops in childhood, or an emotional difficulty.
Motor and perceptual development	Motor skills	Considerable progress is made in gross motor skills during early childhood. This progress is particularly noticeable in arms and legs. The DeOreo Fundamental Motor Skills Inventory is a comprehensive assessment measure that evaluates 11 gross motor skills. Fine motor skills also are increasing during the preschool years.
	Perceptual mapping of large-scale spaces	Children's ability to develop a map of large-scale spaces (those too large to be seen all at once) improves markedly in the preschool years. But even children as young as three years of age have a rudimentary ability to map such large-scale spaces.
Nutrition, health, and exercise	Nutrition	Feeding and eating habits are important aspects of development during early childhood. The average preschool child requires 1,400 to 1,800 calories per day. Poor nutrition and malnutrition can influence not only physical development but cognitive development as well.
	Health and illness	Only recently has a developmental perspective on psychological aspects of health among children appeared. Interest in young children's health involves consideration of its role in later development—a future orientation—as well as a focus on health problems in a particular developmental period, such as early childhood—a current orientation. The effects of health and illness can be studied in terms of their relation to motor development, cognitive development, and social development. Increased motor activity in the preschool child exposes him or her to greater risk of accident and more sources of disease. Increased cognitive sophistication should improve the child's self-protective behavior and encourage him or her to take responsibility for preventing problems and promoting health and safety. Cognitive development also likely influences the child's psychological and behavioral responses to injury and illness and their treatment. In terms of social development, caregivers play an important health role. Indirectly, they serve as important role models for health, and more directly, they can train the child in appropriate health habits.
	Exercise	By the age of six, many children already are not in very good physical shape. Comparisons with 1975 data suggest that, in the mid-1980s, schoolchildren were still in poor physical condition—for example, 25 percent of all elementary school boys could not even do one pull-up! Such information suggests that the preschool years are an important time for beginning physical fitness programs.

These children are in the stage of preoperational thought.

COGNITIVE DEVELOPMENT IN EARLY CHILDHOOD

Dramatic cognitive progress is made during the pre-school years. Among the cognitive feats of the preschool child is that a four-year-old has a vocabulary that has grown to approximately 1,500 words. By age five, the child's vocabulary has expanded to 2,200 words. Five-year-olds can remember a long sentence and repeat the plot to a story. The three- to five-year-old child engages in symbolic thinking on a regular basis, evidenced in such highly enjoyable activities as pretend play. Our study of the preschool child's cognitive development begins with a discussion of Piaget's stages of development. Subsequently, important information processing changes during the preschool years are outlined.

Preoperational Thought

Remember from Chapter 5 that, during Piaget's sen-sorimotor stage of development, the infant progresses in the ability to organize and coordinate sensations and perceptions with physical movements and actions. Ac-cording to Piaget, by the end of this stage, at about 18 to 24 months of age, the infant becomes capable of prim-itive symbolic thinking. The child's use of symbolism in

thought greatly advances during the preschool years. In-deed, as we soon will see, this stage of preoperational thought has sometimes been divided into two sub-periods—symbolic function (approximately two to four years of age) and intuitive thought (approximately four to seven years of age). But first let's consider in more detail just what preoperational thought really is.

The General Nature of Preoperational Thought

Since this stage of thought is called preoperational, it would seem that not much of importance is occurring until full-fledged operational thought appears. The pre-operational stage spans the time frame of approximately two to seven years of age and is a time when stable con-cepts are formed, mental reasoning emerges, egocen-trism (stronger in the beginning) eventually decreases, and magical belief systems are constructed. Thus, pre-operational thought is anything but a convenient waiting period for concrete operational thought, although the label "preoperational" does suggest that, from two to seven years of age, the child does not yet think in an op-erational manner. **Operations** are internalized sets of ac-tions that allow the child to do mentally what before was done physically. They are highly organized and conform to certain rules and principles of logic. The operations appear in one form in the concrete operational period and in another form in the formal operational period. In sum, while stable concepts are formed, mental reasoning emerges, egocentrism decreases, and magical belief systems are constructed during the preoperational stage, these thoughts are still flawed and not well organized. Thus, the preoperational stage should be viewed as the beginning of the ability to reconstruct at the level of thought what has been established in behavior and as a transition from a primitive to a more sophisticated use of symbols.

The Symbolic Function Substage

The **symbolic function substage** of preoperational thought exists roughly between the ages of two to four years. By two years of age, the child has the ability to develop a mental representation of an object in his or her head. The child at this point has begun to use symbols to represent objects that are not present. The ability to engage in such symbolic thought is sometimes referred to as symbolic function, and it greatly broadens the child's mental world during the two-to-four-year age period. Young children use shapes and scribbles to represent people, houses, and so forth. Such scribbling and drawing is an example of how symbolic function develops during the preschool years. More on young children's scribbles and art is presented in Focus on Child Development 7.2.

Other examples of the use of symbolism in the early childhood years are the prevalence of pretend play, which is discussed in Chapter 8, and language, more about which appears later in this chapter. Thus, during this early substage of preoperational thought, the ability to think in symbolic ways and represent the world mentally predominates.

However, while the child makes distinct progress during the symbolic function substage, there also are several important limitations to this point in development. Two such limitations are egocentrism and animism.

Egocentrism   One of the most salient features of preoperational thought is **egocentrism,** the inability to distinguish between one's own perspective and the perspective of someone else. The following telephone conversation between four-year-old Mary, who is at

"Look what I can do, Grandma!"

home, and her father, who is at work, typifies Mary's egocentric thought:

Father: Mary, is Mommy there?
Mary: (Silently nods)
Father: Mary, may I speak to Mommy?
Mary: (Nods again silently)

Mary's response is egocentric in the sense that she fails to consider her father's perspective before replying. A nonegocentric thinker would have responded verbally.

Piaget and Barbara Inhelder (1969) initially studied young children's egocentrism by devising the **three mountains task** (see Figure 7.1). The child walks around the mountains and becomes familiar with what mountains look like from different perspectives. The child can see that there are different objects on the mountains as well. The child then is seated on one side of the table on which the mountains are placed. The experimenter takes a doll and moves it to different locations around the table, at each location asking the child to pick one photo from a series of photos that most accurately reflects the view the doll is seeing. Children in the preoperational stage often pick the view they have from where they are sitting rather than the view that the doll has.

FOCUS ON CHILD DEVELOPMENT 7.2

WHERE PELICANS KISS SEALS, CARS FLOAT ON CLOUDS, AND HUMANS ARE TADPOLES

Usually at about the age of three but sometimes even at two, children's spontaneous scribbles begin to resemble pictures. One 3½-year-old looked at the scribble he had just drawn and said that it was a pelican kissing a seal. Then he added eyes and freckles, and the drawing began to take on more of the characteristics of a pelican and a seal. (See figure below.)

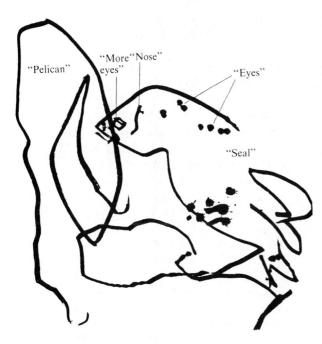

Halfway into this drawing, the 3½-year-old artist said it was "a pelican kissing a seal."

D. Wolf/J. Nove

At about three to four years of age, children begin to create their first symbolism of human beings in their drawings. Invariably, the drawings look like tadpoles, being comprised of a circle that probably stands for a head and trunk and two lines for legs. (See figure below.) These observations of young children's drawings were made by Denise Wolf, Carol Fucigna, and Howard Gardner of Project Zero at Harvard University. Many people think young children draw a human in

The 3-year-old's first drawing of a person: a "tadpole" consisting of a circle with two lines for legs.

(continued on following page)

FOCUS ON CHILD DEVELOPMENT 7.2

A young child, asked to draw people playing ball, includes only a single arm on the figures playing ball; the fourth figure, an observer, is armless.

this rather odd way because it is the best that children can do—the tadpole is just a failed attempt to capture a real human. Piaget said that children's drawings are intended to be realistic but that children draw what they know rather than what they see. So, the tadpole, with its strange exemptions of trunk and arms, might indicate children's lack of knowledge of the parts of the human body and how they go together.

However, Claire Golomb believes that children know more about the human body than they know how to draw. One three-year-old drew a tadpole but described it in complete detail, including the parts she had not drawn, such as feet, cheeks, and chin. Her simple figure symbolized a complex human being. And when children were asked to draw

someone playing ball, the three- and four-year-olds' symbols of humans included arms, possibly because the task implicitly requires arms. (See figure above.)

Conceivably because preschool children are not very concerned with realism, their drawings may become fanciful and inventive. Suns may be blue, skies may be yellow, and cars may float on clouds. The children produce simple but very strong symbolisms of the world that are not too unlike abstractions found in some contemporary art. (See top figure on next page.) By the time the child has moved on to the later elementary school years, the symbols that stand for the child's world are now more realistic, neat, and precise. (See bottom figure on next page.) Suns are yellow, skies are blue, and cars move on roads. Children's drawings and their ability to represent their world symbolically on paper are related to their development of perceptual motor skills.

This 6-year-old's drawing (top) *is free, fanciful and inventive. An 11-year-old's drawing* (bottom) *is neater and more realistic but also less inventive.*

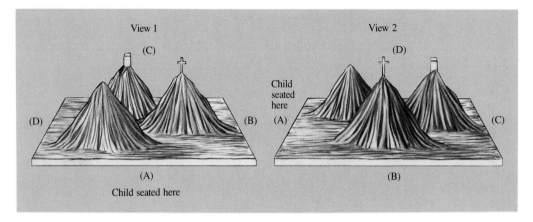

FIGURE 7.1   The three mountains problem

Note: The Three Mountains Task devised by Piaget and Inhelder (1967). In view 1 the child's perspective from where he or she is sitting is shown. View 2 is an example of the photograph the child would be shown mixed in with others from different perspectives. For the child to correctly identify this view, he or she has to take the perspective of a person sitting at spot (B). Invariably the preschool child, who thinks in a preoperational way, cannot perform this task. When asked what the perspective or view of the mountains will look like from position (B), the child selects a photograph taken from location (A), the view he or she has at that time.

One research question focuses on whether egocentrism actually decreases as the child becomes older or whether this simply reflects general intelligence. According to Rubin (1978), perspective-taking ability does increase with age and does not seem to be influenced strongly by general intelligence, since scores on perspective-taking tasks are only weakly related to scores on general intelligence tests.

Researchers also ask the extent to which children who show perspective-taking skills in one dimension also reveal them in other dimensions. For example, does the preschool child who reveals a lack of perspective-taking skill on Piaget's three mountain problem also show an inability to take another child's perspective in a peer discussion? Researchers have found only moderate to weak relations between children's responses on different kinds of perspective-taking tasks, suggesting that different types of cognitive skills or levels may be needed for performing these tasks (Shantz, 1983).

An interesting additional question involves whether there might be a cognitive primacy operating among different dimensions of perspective taking. Just as some cognitive developmentalists have argued that the development of object concept in infancy might be an important precursor of person permanence and attachment in infancy, so too has it been speculated that spatial perspective taking might be an antecedent of social perspective taking (Shantz, 1983). While this is an intriguing possibility and merits further research attention, no evidence for the cognitive primacy of spatial perspective taking has been generated as yet.

Animism   Another facet of preoperational thought is **animism,** the belief that inanimate objects have "life-like" qualities and are capable of action. Remarks like, "That tree pushed the leaf off, and it fell down," or "The sidewalk was angry with me. It made me fall down," reveal this notion. Animism is a failure to distinguish the appropriate occasions for employing the human and the nonhuman perspectives.

Several recent investigations, however, have questioned the pervasiveness of the animism phenomenon. In many cases, animistic statements may reflect children's incomplete knowledge of the objects referred to (Dolgin & Behrend, 1984), their incomplete knowledge of how animate and inanimate things differ (Bullock, 1985), or their assumption that they are playing a game when an adult questioner wants them to be serious (Gelman & Spelke, 1981). Perhaps animism should be viewed as incomplete knowledge and understanding, not as a child's general conception of the world in which he or she lives.

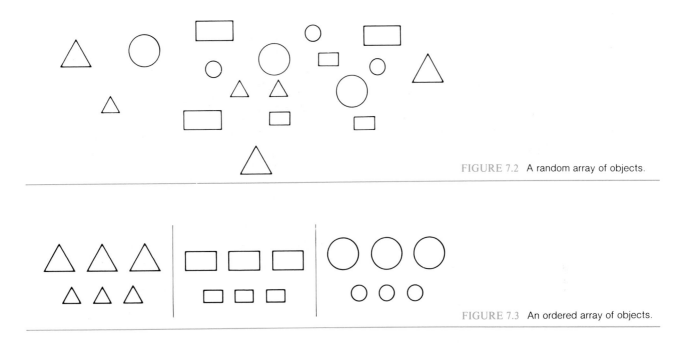

FIGURE 7.2 A random array of objects.

FIGURE 7.3 An ordered array of objects.

As the preschool child becomes older, he or she is likely to move from the substage of symbolic thought to an inner world of thinking that is more intuitive in nature.

The Substage of Intuitive Thought

The preoperational stage of thought continues from four to seven years of age for most children, but a new substage, called **intuitive thought,** emerges. During this time frame, the child begins to reason about various matters and wants to know the answers to all sorts of questions. Children's thinking in this substage is viewed as prelogical. While reasoning and a search for answers to many questions are prevalent, such reasoning is very imperfect compared to adult standards. Piaget referred to this time period as intuitive because, on the one hand, young children seem so sure about their knowledge and understanding, yet on the other hand, they are so unaware of how they know what they know.

An important limitation of the young child's reasoning ability is the difficulties he or she has putting things into their correct classes. Faced with a random collection of objects that can be grouped together on the basis of two or more properties, the preoperational child is seldom capable of using these properties consistently to sort the objects into what could be referred to as a competent classification.

For example, look at the collection of objects shown in Figure 7.2. You would respond to the direction, "Put the things together that you believe belong together" by sorting the characteristics of size and shape together. Your sorting might look something like that shown in Figure 7.3. In the social realm, a five-year-old girl might be given the task of dividing her peers into groups according to whether they are friends and whether they are boys or girls. She would be unlikely to arrive at the following classification: friendly boys, friendly girls, unfriendly boys, and unfriendly girls. Another such example, one developed by David Elkind (1976), illustrates the preoperational child's shortcomings in reasoning in terms of understanding religious concepts. When asked the question, "Can you be a Protestant and an American at the same time?" six- and seven-year-olds usually say no, while nine-year-olds are much more likely to say yes, understanding that objects can be cross-classified simultaneously.

The child's earliest questions begin to occur around the age of three, and by the age of five or six, he or she has just about exhausted the adults around with persistent inquiries, particularly with questions involving "why?" The child's questions provide clues to mental development and reflect his or her intellectual curiosity. Such questions indicate an emergence of the child's interest in reasoning and figuring out why things are the way they are. A sample of the kinds of questions children ask during this question-asking period of four to six years of age are (Elkind, 1976):

"What makes you grow up?"
"What makes you stop growing up?"
"Why does a lady have to be married to have a baby?"
"Who was the mother when everybody was a baby?"
"Why do leaves fall?"
"Why does the sun shine?"

We have discussed how Piaget envisioned all young children to think about the world. However, research during the 1970s and 1980s produced many challenges to some of Piaget's basic ideas about cognitive development. In Chapter 9, where we discuss Piaget's view of concrete operational thought, a number of contemporary criticisms of his work are provided. Here, we focus more precisely on some of the problems that child developmentalists believe relate to Piaget's ideas on preschool thought.

Some Criticisms of Piaget's Ideas on Preschool Thought

Some developmental psychologists believe that characteristics of concrete operational thought occur earlier than Piaget predicted and that some dimensions of concrete operational thought can be accelerated through changes in environmental experiences. In Chapter 9, we consider in some detail Piaget's ideas on conservation because they form such an important part of concrete operational thought, which Piaget argued occurs approximately between the ages of 7 and 11. However, as we see next, the Piagetian revisionists believe that, when preschool children do not show concrete operational thought, it may be due to characteristics of the tasks and inadequate learning opportunities rather than the absence of concrete operational thought.

At what age does a child begin to ask questions?

Briefly, conservation refers to the child's ability to understand that quantities remain the same even if changes are made in their appearance. For example, in Chapter 9, we describe a number of domains in which conservation can occur, such as number, liquid, and matter. The research strategy involves the experimenter making superficial changes in an object or situation. The child at the preoperational stage of thought is unable to understand that certain characteristics of the object or situation remain the same, or in the language of Piaget, have been conserved. For example, a child may be shown two equal lines of six checkers each. The experimenter then may lengthen the spaces between one line and ask the child which line has more checkers. The preoperational child typically responds incorrectly that the longer line has more checkers.

Rochel Gelman's research and analysis (e.g., Gelman, 1969, 1972, 1979; Gelman & Baillargeon, 1983; Gelman & Gallistel, 1978) has led to a more refined understanding of preschool thought, in particular revealing that, when the circumstances surrounding the evaluation of the child's conservation are carefully scrutinized and modified, changes in the child's ability to conserve may be observed. For instance, Gelman (1969) has shown that, by improving the child's attention to relevant aspects of the conservation task, the child is more likely to conserve than when such attentional training is not present. And she has demonstrated that attentional training on one type of task, such as number, is likely to improve the preschool child's performance on another type of task, such as mass.

In another investigation, Gelman provided further evidence that preschool children likely know more about the concept of number than Piaget believed (Gelman, 1972). The children were three to six years of age, and each saw two plates with a row of mice on each plate. There were three mice in one row and two in the other. For some children, the lengths of the rows were identical—the two-mouse rows were less dense than the three-mouse rows. For other children, the spaces between the mice were identical; that is, the three-mouse row was longer than the two-mouse row. Gelman made the task into a game by asking the children which of the mouse-plates was the "winner" and which was the "loser." In this way, the child could determine which plate was the winner without paying any attention to number or number differences. In the first situation, the winner was both denser and more numerous, while in the second situation, the winner was both longer and more numerous. The children were reinforced for correct responses but never told why their choice was correct. Subsequently, after a number of trials, the experimenter, out of view of the child, altered the winning row. In some situations, one mouse was removed from the end or center, making the two rows numerically the same. The children's surprise reactions were observed, and they were asked a number of questions about what had occurred. Gelman's (1972) results indicated that even the three- and four-year-olds perceived the winner in terms of number rather than density or length.

Thus, Gelman's research has demonstrated that children may fail Piagetian tasks because of their failure to attend to relevant dimensions of the task, such as length, shape, density, and so forth, and because the tasks and procedures may not be sensitive to the child's cognitive abilities. Thus, rather than limitations on cognitive ability, the limitations may be related to the tasks and procedures themselves. Gelman's research reflects the thinking of information processing psychologists, who place considerable importance on the tasks and procedures involved in assessing the child's cognition.

Next, we study further the interest of information processing psychologists in task analysis as well as other important aspects of how the child processes information about his or her world.

Information Processing

Two possible limitations on the preschool child's thought are attention and memory. Nonetheless, considerable advances are made with regard to these two very important cognitive processes during the preschool years.

Attention

Remember from Chapter 5 that attention plays an important role in information processing. Attention was defined as focusing perception to produce increased awareness of a stimulus. Habituation and dishabituation were discussed as having been widely used in studying attention in infants. Habituation involves something almost like being bored in the sense that the infant becomes disinterested in a stimulus, while dishabituation involves reorienting to a new stimulus. Some researchers refer to habituation as a decrement in attention while calling dishabituation recovery of attention or novelty preference. The importance of these aspects of attention in infancy for our discussion of cognitive development in the preschool years was underscored by research revealing that both types of attention, decrement and recovery, when measured in the first six months of infancy, are linked with more efficient performance on standardized tests of intelligence in the preschool and elementary school years.

But while these aspects of the infant's attention clearly are important for later development, there also seem to be great changes in the child's ability to pay attention during the early childhood years. The toddler, for example, wanders around a good deal, shifts attention from one activity to another, and generally seems to spend very little time focused on any one object or event. The preschooler, by comparison, is often seen playing a game or watching a television program for a half hour. A number of people researching the impact of educational television on young children have combined an interest in measuring the child's television viewing behavior with an interest in measuring the child's learning of television material.

In one study, the attention of children from two to four years of age to an episode of "Sesame Street" was examined (Anderson & Levin, 1976). The children watched the program with their mothers in a setting resembling a living room. The youngest children often got up to play with toys or turned and talked to other people in the room. These patterns of distraction declined among the older children.

The young preschool child who spends long periods of time at play or watching television does not have the same extended attention span for learning problems presented by psychologists, however. Researchers feel fortunate when they can sustain a three-year-old's attention for 10 minutes and a two-year-old's for even 2 minutes (Perlmutter, 1980; Wellman, Ritter, & Flavell, 1975).

The changes in ability to pay attention continue beyond the preschool years into the first or second year of school. In the classroom, children are able to observe the teacher for extended periods of time, and they can pore over their books in long periods of independent study. These demands on attention exceed what was required of the preschooler, who is generally free to move about in various play activities. These apparent changes in attention have a dramatic influence on the child's learning (Stevenson, 1972).

The development of strategic use of attention is aptly shown in a study of visual scanning (Vurpillot, 1968). Children were shown two similar pictures and were asked to judge if the two were identical (see Figure 7.4). To perform well on this task, the child has to systematically

FIGURE 7.4 Sample of the stimuli: a pair of identical houses and a pair of different houses.

scan the pictures, comparing them feature by feature. Observation of the eye-movement patterns of the six- and nine-year-old children suggested that they were engaging in systematic scanning of the pictures, but the four-year-old children were not.

It appears that, after the age of six or seven, there is a shift to cognitive control of attention so that children act less precipitously and reflect more (Paris & Lindauer, 1982). In other words, older children attend to stimulus features that are relevant to a particular task and scan information in a more systematic and organized manner than preschool children. Preschool children, by contrast, are more influenced by features that stand out or are *salient* than those that are relevant to solving a problem or performing well at a task. The development of attentional strategies is important for practical reasons—low-achieving students often are deficient in attentional skills (Piontkowski & Calfee, 1979; Zelnicker & Jeffrey, 1979).

Memory

Recall from our discussion in Chapter 5 that memory is a central process in cognitive development and involves the retention of information over time. Conscious memory may come into play as early as seven months of age, although as children and adults, we have little or no memory of events experienced before the age of three. Among the interesting questions about memory in the preschool years are those involving the distinction between short-term and long-term memory and the degree to which short-term memory improves.

Short-Term and Long-Term Memory Short-term memory appears to retain information for up to 20 to 30 seconds, assuming that there is no rehearsal. With rehearsal, **short-term memory** can retain information for considerably longer periods. As an example of short-term memory, what happens when you try to remember a telephone number you just heard? If you attempt to remember the number five seconds after hearing it, you probably will be successful. But what occurs if you try to do the same thing four to five minutes later? Unless you have been rehearsing the phone number, your memory is likely to fail. This is because short-term memory for unrehearsed information does not exceed 20 to 30 seconds, and the processes needed for long-term retention, what psychologists refer to as encoding information into long-term memory, are difficult and often error prone.

Although we are capable of memorizing a number in a more-or-less permanent way (many people claim that they can recall their own telephone numbers from three or more previous residences), this generally is not accomplished easily or quickly. Thus, while short-term retention of information seems to be somewhat effortless, encoding information for long-term retention is much

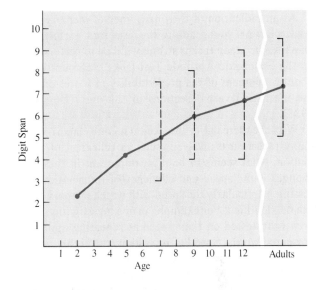

FIGURE 7.5 Memory span and age.

more difficult. Long-term memory involves more effortful use of retrieval as well. We often struggle to recall information that (we think) is in long-term memory but that for some reason cannot be "found." In sum, there seem to be adequate reasons for making a distinction between short-term and long-term memory. Now let's see how short-term memory improves in preschoolers.

The Increase in Short-Term Memory One method of assessing short-term memory involves the **memory span task.** If you have ever taken an IQ test, you have likely been exposed to a memory span task. You simply hear a short list of stimuli, usually digits, presented at a rapid pace (typically one per second). Then you are asked to repeat the digits back. Research with the memory span task indicates that short-term memory increases during early childhood. For example, as shown in Figure 7.5, memory span increases from about two digits in two- to three-year-old children to about five digits in seven-year-old children. Yet, between 7 and 13 years of age, memory span only increases by 1½ digits (Dempster, 1981). Keep in mind, though, that there are individual differences in memory span, which is why IQ tests and various aptitude tests are used.

As an indication of the importance of memory span, research with young adults suggests that performance on a memory span task is strongly linked to performance on the Scholastic Aptitude Test (SAT), accounting for about 50 percent of the predictability of scores on both the math and verbal sections of this test (Dempster, 1985).

Why are there age differences in memory span? While many factors are involved, such as rehearsal of information, what seems to be most important in these age changes is the speed and efficiency of information processing, particularly the speed with which memory items can be identified. For example, in one investigation, children were tested on their speed at repeating auditorily presented words. Speed of repetition was highly predictive of memory span using these same words. Indeed, when speed of repetition was controlled, the memory spans of the six-year-old children were equal to those of young adults (the adults were tested with nonsense words so that their repetition times equaled those of children) (Case, Kurland, & Goldberg, 1982).

The speed-of-processing explanation for the increase in memory span highlights an important point in the information processing perspective. That is, the speed with which a child processes information is an important aspect of his or her cognitive abilities. However, speed of processing is only one of a number of components of cognitive tasks. As we see next, another of the major emphases in the information processing perspective is to identify the components of the task the child is performing.

Task Dimensions and Analyses

Let's see how identifying task dimensions might work with a typical Piagetian problem involving what is known as class inclusion reasoning. **Class inclusion reasoning** calls for the child to compare the relative number of objects in a subset with the number of objects in the larger set. If, as in Figure 7.6, there is a set of rectangular bars—some colored, some black—can the child compare the number of colored bars with the total number

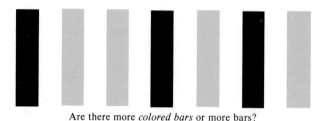

Are there more *colored bars* or more bars?

FIGURE 7.6   Class inclusion figure and question.

of bars present in the total set? The question posed to the child in this classic experiment by Piaget is, "Are there more colored bars or more bars?" According to Piaget, concrete operational thinkers answer the question correctly, while preoperational thinkers do not. He suggests that the underlying problem involves some form of ability to deal with whole-part comparisons.

The information processing psychologist takes a different view. The information processing psychologist suggests that we need to understand the component steps required to solve the task. For example, first the child must encode the key elements in the question. Roughly speaking, this means that the child must attend to and store some key pieces of information. There are at least three concepts in the question about the bars: (1) which of the two sets has *more,* (2) the *colored* bars, or (3) all the *bars.*

Next, according to the information processing psychologist, the child must formulate a *plan* to answer the question. One good plan is to take the first concept as a goal (that is, find the set with *more* items) and proceed with two *counting* steps: (1) count the colored bars and (2) count all the bars. Finally, a *comparison* must be made between the outcome of counting step (1) (i.e., How many colored ones were there?) and counting step (2) (i.e., How many bars were there altogether?).

Notice, then, that in the information processing analysis, the child must do a number of things to solve the problem—he or she must encode the problem correctly, formulate a goal, engage in at least two counting steps, and compare the results of counting. There are a host of reasons, then, for the young child to fail to solve the problem. Tom Trabasso (1977) has shown that young children often encode the problem incorrectly, perhaps because they find the form of the question unusual or unexpected. For example, usually when we are asked to compare sets of objects in the world, the sets do not overlap. If one set is described by reference to its color, perhaps the child assumes that the other set also was meant to have a color in its description, even if the adult asking the question forgot to mention it.

Young children may have difficulty *counting* because, once they have counted an object, they have trouble counting it a second time to represent a place in its alternate set (Wilkinson, 1976). Many young children have just mastered a one-to-one correspondence rule in counting—that is, each counting number goes with one and only one object. To ask the child to disregard this rule and engage in double counting is to tamper with a fragile skill the child has just mastered.

Finally, we note that the information processing steps outlined in the model require the child to hold the problem in his or her mind while it is being solved. Suppose the steps of planning, counting, and comparing, for example, require 5 to 10 seconds to complete. Remembering the different parts of the problem may interfere with the counting operations, confuse the child about which step to take next, or make the child lose track of the overall goal of the task.

Information processing psychologists have subjected a number of other important cognitive problems to task analysis, including conservation (Brainerd, 1978), arithmetic problems (Resnick, 1980), and reading and ordering stories (Yussen, 1982). They have come up with a number of suggestions for teaching young children important skills and have shown that young children are capable of surprising competence in these tasks.

Piagetian theory will often explain a young child's inability to offer a "grownup" response to some task by citing the child's early stage of development. The child does not yet have the cognitive skills and understanding

to respond otherwise, in this view. In contrast, the information processing view focuses on the task requirements and considers the complexity of what the child is being asked to do. By understanding the components of the task, one may eventually discover how to simplify them so that even young children can respond to a problem intelligently. Focus on Child Development 7.3 explains how researchers ingeniously followed this strategy with the high-level cognitive ability of deductive reasoning.

So far, we have discussed important ideas about pre-operational thought and information processing. Yet, the story of cognitive development in early childhood would not be complete without consideration of the next topic—language development.

LANGUAGE DEVELOPMENT IN EARLY CHILDHOOD

In Chapter 5, we discussed the biological, cognitive, and social foundations of language development and described the course of language development in the first two years of life. Here we outline the nature of language development during early childhood, focusing on Roger Brown's concept of the mean length of utterance and continuing our overview from Chapter 5 of how the basic properties of language develop.

The Mean Length of Utterance

Psychologist Roger Brown (1973) has developed a way to chart a child's language progress using the **mean length of utterance (MLU)** in the everyday speech of a child. To compute MLU, you simply tape-record a sample of speech (say, 50 to 100 utterances), count the number of morphemes in each utterance, and then calculate the average. MLU has turned out to be useful in measuring the progress of language development—it is a much better criterion than chronological age, for example.

FOCUS ON CHILD DEVELOPMENT 7.3

MERDS THAT LAUGH DON'T LIKE MUSHROOMS

Developmental psychologists are interested in analyzing the nature of tasks and how tasks might be involved in making children look more advanced or less advanced in their development. In particular, they have been fascinated by the possibility that, if the task requirements are made appropriate and simple, the child may show more cognitive maturity than previously thought.

One investigation used this strategy to determine if preschool children could engage in deductive reasoning (Hawkins, Pea, Glick, & Scribner, 1984). In particular, the task content, complexity, and organization were manipulated in ways that might enhance a preschool child's ability to handle the complex problem of solving a syllogism. A **syllogism** is a type of reasoning problem, consisting of two premises, or statements, that are assumed to be true, plus a conclusion. The problem usually involves quantities and often includes the words *all, some, none,* and so forth. As shown in the table,

three different forms of syllogisms were presented to children. And three different types of problems were constructed: (1) fantasy problems, in which premises described mythical creatures alien from practical knowledge; (2) congruent problems, in which premises were compatible with practical knowledge; and (3) incongruent problems, in which premises contradicted practical knowledge. To simplify the problems, quantifiers such as "some" and "all" were made implicit rather than explicit. The form of the problems was consistently controlled.

A total of 24 syllogisms were presented to 40 preschool children four to five years of age in four different sequences—fantasy first, congruent first, incongruent first, or mixed. The instructions were:

"I am going to read you some little stories. Some of them are about make-believe animals and things, and some of them are about real animals and things. Some of the stories are going to sound sort of funny. I want you to pretend that everything the stories say is true. . . ." (p. 587)

Examples of Syllogisms Given to Preschool Children

Form	Model	Affirmative Example	Negative Example
A. Universal	A is B	Every banga is purple.	Bears have big teeth.
	B is C	Purple animals always sneeze at people.	Animals with big teeth can't read books.
	A is C	Do bangas sneeze at people?	Can bears read books?
B. Particular	A has B	Pogs wear blue boots.	Rabbits never bite.
	C is an A	Tom is a pog.	Cuddly is a rabbit.
	C has B	Does Tom wear blue boots?	Does Cuddly bite?
C. Action-functional	A does B when . . .	Glasses bounce when they fall.	Merds laugh when they're happy.
	B is C	Everything that bounces is made of rubber.	Animals that laugh don't like mushrooms.
	A has C	Are glasses made of rubber?	Do merds like mushrooms?

From Hawkins, J., et al., "Merds that laugh don't like mushrooms: Evidence for deductive reasoning by preschoolers" in *Developmental Psychology, 20,* 584–594, 1984. Copyright © American Psychological Association. Reprinted by permission of the author.

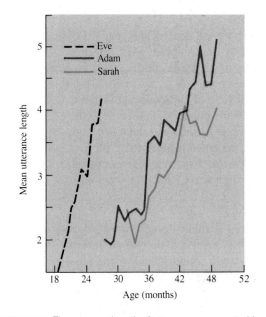

As shown in the figure below, the results suggested that, when the fantasy problems were encountered first, the preschool children gave more correct responses. The researchers believed that having the children experience the fantasy condition first effectively eliminated the intrusion of real-world knowledge. They argued that, in prior research, young children may have been too concerned about the empirical truth value of the premises and that this likely interfered with their ability to demonstrate syllogistic reasoning. Thus, by simplifying the tasks, investigating appropriate dimensions of the problem, and varying the sequence of material presentation, the researchers were able to demonstrate the existence of a higher form of cognition in preschool children—syllogistic reasoning.

FIGURE 7.7 The average length of utterances generated by three children who ranged in age from one-and-one-half to four years.

Figure 7.7 shows MLU as a function of age for three different children studied by Roger Brown and his colleagues (Brown, Cazden, & Bellugi-Klima, 1969). Note that Eve attained an MLU of 3 when she was only two years old. In contrast, Adam and Sarah attained this same MLU when they were around three years old. There are large individual differences in attaining later stages of language development.

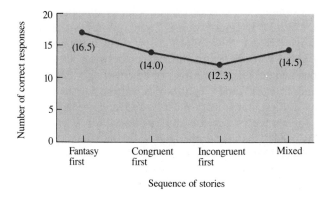

Syllogistic reasoning in preschool children.

Further Development in the Basic Properties of Language

Language development in the preschool child involves specific accomplishments in phonology, morphology, syntax, semantics and pragmatics. Recall from Chapter 5 that phonology involves the sound system of language, morphology focuses on rules for combining morphemes (strings of sounds that provide meaning for what we say and hear), syntax consists of the manner in which words are combined to form acceptable phrases and sentences, semantics deals with the meaning of words and sentences, and pragmatics indexes the ability to engage in appropriate conversation.

Phonology

Although a good deal of phonological development has occurred by the time that MLU reaches 3, there is still some way to go. Some children have problems speaking consonant clusters (e.g., *str* as in *string*) throughout the preschool years. Furthermore, pronouncing some of the more difficult phonemes—such as *r*, for example—can cause problems even into the school-age years. Finally, some of the phonological rules for pronouncing word endings (in the past tense, for example) are not mastered until children are six to eight years old.

Morphology

As children advance beyond two-word utterances, there is clear evidence that they know morphological rules. Children begin using the plural and possessive forms of nouns (e.g., *dogs* and *dog's*), putting appropriate endings on verbs (e.g., *s* when the subject is third-person singular, *ed* for the past tense, and *ing* for the present progressive tense), and using prepositions (e.g., *in* and *on*), articles (e.g., *a* and *the*), and various forms of the verb *to be* (e.g., "I was going to the store"). In a classic study of these and other "grammatical morphemes," Roger Brown (1973) found evidence of a consistent pattern of development. One of his findings was that children learn to make nouns plural (e.g., *dogs*) before they learn to make nouns possessive (e.g., *dog's*). And only after this do children learn to put verbs in the third-person singular form (e.g., *runs* in the sentence, "He runs fast"). What makes this pattern intriguing is that the same basic word ending (*s*) is involved in all three cases. We can see, therefore, that it is not the ending that is learned, but rather the rules for applying this ending.

Some of the most important evidence for morphological rules comes from overgeneralizations of these rules. A preschool child will often say "foots" instead of "feet," or "goed" instead of "went." These errors frequently follow from rules. More information about such errors and the rules that they follow is presented in Focus on Child Development 7.4.

Syntax

Similar evidence that children learn and actively apply rules can be found at the level of syntax. After advancing beyond two-word utterances, the child utters

Smithereens

"If you don't mind my asking, about how much does a sentence diagrammer pull down a year?"

word sequences that display a growing mastery of complex rules for how words should be ordered. Consider, for example, the case of *wh-* questions—questions such as, "Where is Daddy going?" and "What is that boy doing?" To ask these questions properly, it is necessary to know two important differences between *wh-* questions and simple affirmative statements (e.g., "Daddy is going to work" and "That boy is waiting for the school bus"). First, a *wh-* word must be added at the beginning of the sentence. Second, the auxiliary verb *is* must be "inverted," that is, exchanged with the subject of the sentence. Young children appear to learn quite early where to put the *wh-* word, but they take much longer to learn the auxiliary-inversion rule. Hence, it is common to hear preschool children asking such questions as, "Where Daddy is going?" and "What that boy is doing?"

Interestingly, once children have mastered the auxiliary-inversion rule, they sometimes overgeneralize it to "how come" questions (Kuczaj & Brannick, 1979). Although it is correct to ask, "How come that boy is running?" children will sometimes ask, "How come is that boy running?" The sequence of words, "is that boy running," would be correct if it came after "why." But coming after "how come," it is a highly intelligent, rule-governed error.

FOOTS, FEETS, AND WUGS

In considering the type of "error" made by a child who uses *foots*, note that the *s* ending is appropriate for pluralizing many English words. When a child says "foots," the child is demonstrating knowledge of a rule; the "error" lies in failing to honor one of this rule's exceptions.

Interestingly, overgeneralization often follows a three-stage sequence: First, the child correctly produces an irregular form (says "feet"). Then, after learning a general rule, the child overgeneralizes this rule (e.g., says "foots" or "feets"). Finally, the child produces the appropriate forms, having learned the rule as well as its exceptions (e.g., says "feet" but also "fingers" and "toes") (Flavell, 1985).

In a classic experiment, Jean Berko (1958) presented preschool and first grade children with cards such as the one shown in the figure. A child was asked to look at the card while the experimenter read the words on the card aloud. Then the child was asked to supply the missing word. This might sound easy, but Berko was interested not just in the child's ability to recall the right word but also in his or her ability to say it "correctly" (with the ending that was dictated by morphological rules). "Wugs" would be the correct response for the card in the figure. Although the children were not perfectly accurate, they were certainly much better than chance. Moreover, they showed their knowledge of morphological rules not only with plural forms of nouns ("There are two wugs") but also with the possessive forms of nouns and with the third-person singular and past-tense forms of verbs.

This is a wug.

Now there is another one.
There are two of them.
There are two _____.

The plural allomorph of / -z /.

What makes this study by Berko impressive is that most of the "words" were fictional. They were created especially for the experiment. Thus, the children could not base their responses on remembering past instances of hearing the words. It seems that they were forced to rely upon *rules*. Their performance suggests that they did so successfully.

Some interesting cross-cultural findings suggest that how children learn syntactical rules depends upon their language. For example, Michael Akiyami (1984) showed that English-speaking preschoolers find it more difficult to understand true-negative statements ("You are not a baby") than false-negative statements ("You are not a child"). The differing results suggest different strategies for processing the sentences, which in turn reflect subtle differences in syntactic rules for negation in English versus Japanese. Akiyami concluded:

> It seems that children are so sensitive to fine differences in languages that they do develop strategies best suited for their language. The belief that children all over the world learn their language the same way needs to be corrected. (p. 227)

Semantics

As children advance beyond the two-word stage, it is not just phonology, morphology, and syntax that improve—knowledge of meanings is rapidly advancing as well. In the first place, the sheer number of word meanings that children know is increasing. The speaking vocabulary of a six-year-old has been estimated as ranging from 8,000 to 14,000 words (Carey, 1977). Assuming that the learning of words starts when a child is 12 months old, this translates into a learning rate for new word meanings of five to eight words a day between the ages of one and six. After five years of word learning, the six-year-old child is not slowing down. According to some estimates, the average child of this age is moving along at the awe-inspiring rate of 22 words per day (Miller, 1981)! It truly is miraculous how quickly children learn language.

One way that children achieve such rapid new-word learning is through a "fast mapping" process (Carey, 1977). Hearing a new word being used in a sentence can provide many clues as to what the word means, and young children apparently make use of these cues effectively. For example, consider a child who is entirely unfamiliar with the color term *chartreuse*. Suppose you say to this child, in the course of some activity, "Bring me the chartreuse one, not the red one." The child might figure out which one you mean, particularly if there are only two objects present and only one of them is red. At the same time, the child might start to learn the meaning of *chartreuse* (Heibeck & Markman, 1985).

Despite the rapid course of new-word learning, some classes of words are not fully understood until well into the childhood years. One such class is relational words. **Relational words** are words that specify relationships. The relationships can be among objects (e.g., *more* as in, "The piano weighs more than the table"), events (e.g., *longer* as in, "Today's game went longer than the one last week"), or people (e.g., *borrowed* as in, "The lady borrowed her friend's new Porsche").

One important subset of relational words is that of *spatial adjectives,* including *big* and *small,* and *thick* and *thin.* Studies have shown that, while some of these adjectives are well understood by preschool children, others are not. For example, Eve Clark (1972) examined how well four-year-old children could supply opposites for words like *big* (*small*) and *deep* (*shallow*). Her results showed an excellent understanding of the *big–small* pair (all of her subjects could supply *small* as the opposite of *big* and vice versa). Furthermore, there was weaker but still good understanding of the pairs *long–short* and *tall–short.* However, there was only moderate understanding of *high–low,* poorer understanding of *thick–thin* and *wide–narrow,* and almost no understanding of *deep–shallow.*

Why are spatial adjectives such as *thick, wide,* and *deep* so difficult for preschoolers to understand? One popular view is that such terms are semantically complex in their internal representations. An alternative view is that they simply are used less frequently than other spatial adjectives, so children have less experience with them. In any case, some spatial adjectives take a long time to master (Clark, 1983).

The same conclusion holds for *possessive verbs,* another subset of relational words. Possessive verbs offer or imply transfer of possession (e.g., *trade, spend, buy,* and *sell*) (Gentner, 1975). A preschooler may talk of buying something when he or she really is thinking of getting something for free.

Pragmatics

Although there are many great differences between a two-year-old's language and a six-year-old's language, none are more important than those pertaining to pragmatics—that is, rules of conversation. There is no question that, apart from many differences at phonological, morphological, syntactical, and semantic levels of language, a six-year-old is simply a much better conversationalist than a two-year-old. The development of this conversational skill occurs in several areas (de Villiers & de Villiers, 1978): At around three years of age, children show an improved ability to talk about things not physically present. Thus, they improve their command of the characteristic of language referred to as displacement. One way in which such displacement is revealed is in games of pretend. Although two-year-olds may know the word *table,* they are unlikely to use this word to refer to an imaginary table that they pretend is standing in front of them. However, most children over three have this ability, even if they do not always use it. (There are large individual differences in preschoolers' talk of imaginary people and things.)

At what age do children begin to show sensitivity to the needs of others in conversation?

Somewhat later in the preschool years, at around age four, children begin to show remarkable sensitivity to the needs of others in conversation. One way in which they show such sensitivity is in their use of the articles *the* and *an* (or *a*). When adults are telling a story or describing an event, they generally use *an* (or *a*) when they first refer to an object or animal and then use *the* when referring to it later (e.g., "Two boys were walking through the jungle when *a* fierce lion appeared. *The* lion lunged at one boy while the other ran for cover"). Even three-year-olds follow part of this rule (they consistently use *the* when referring to previously mentioned things). However, using the word *a* when something is initially mentioned develops much more slowly. Although five-year-olds follow this rule on some occasions, they fail to follow it on others (Warden, 1976).

Another important pragmatic ability that emerges around four or five years of age has to do with speech style. As adults, we have an excellent ability to change our speech style in accordance with the social situation and the person with whom we are speaking. An obvious example is that adults speak in a simpler way to a two-year-old than to an older child or an adult. Interestingly, even four-year-olds speak differently to a two-year-old than to a same-aged peer. They "talk down" to the two-year-old, using shorter utterance lengths (Shatz & Gelman, 1973). However, children in this age range do show some deficiencies in communicating with one- and two-year-olds (Tomasello & Mannle, 1985). For example, they appear less adept than adults at providing an infant with nonverbal cues (gestures) to the meaning of what they are saying. They also use fewer conversational devices to keep a dialogue with an infant running smoothly. For example, children will frequently ignore an infant's most recent utterance or at least fail to continue conversing about the topic of this utterance.

Although pragmatic abilities develop quite rapidly during the preschool years, they continue developing in later years as well. One interesting set of late-developing abilities are those pertaining to making requests. Although five-year-olds can comprehend requests, they are unlikely themselves to generate requests, particularly politely worded requests for someone to help them with some difficulty they face. However, older children show developing knowledge of the pragmatics of making requests. By the time children are nine years old, they show an impressive ability to take into account both the difficulty of satisfying the request and the status of the person of whom they are making the request (Axia & Baroni, 1985; Wilkinson, Wilkinson, Spinelli, & Chiang, 1984).

Our journey through cognitive development in early childhood has been a rather long one. Child Development Concept Table 7.2 summarizes our discussion of preoperational thought, information processing, and language development in the preschool years. Next, we consider one final aspect of the preschool child's development—early childhood education.

Child Development Concept Table 7.2   Cognitive Development in Early Childhood

Concept	Processes/Related Ideas	Characteristics/Description
Preoperational thought	General nature	Preoperational thought is the second major stage of Piaget's theory of cognitive development and roughly spans the ages of two to seven. This period is a time when stable concepts are formed, mental reasoning emerges, egocentrism is prominent, and magical belief systems are constructed. The child does not yet think in an operational manner. Thought is still flawed and not well organized. This period also is characterized by a shift from a primitive to a more sophisticated use of symbols.
	The symbolic function substage	The symbolic function substage occurs between two and four years of age. During this time, symbolic thought occurs on a regular basis in the form of language, pretend play, and scribbling and drawing. Symbols are frequently used to represent objects that are not present. Egocentrism is highly prominent in this substage. Children at this point have considerable difficulty in spatial and social perspective taking. Piaget and Inhelder investigated spatial perspective taking with the three mountains task. Researchers have shown that perspective taking is only weakly related to general intelligence and that different dimensions of perspective taking appear to be only moderately to weakly related. They are intrigued by the possibility that spatial perspective taking might be an antecedent of social perspective taking, although no research data have documented this latter point. Animism is another prominent characteristic of the symbolic function substage—it refers to the belief that inanimate objects have lifelike qualities and are capable of action.
	Intuitive thought substage	The intuitive thought substage lasts from approximately four to seven years of age. Reasoning is present but in a prelogical form. Question asking is prevalent. Children seem sure of their knowledge and understanding but are unaware of how they know what they know. Children in this substage have difficulty sorting objects into what could be referred to as a competent classification.
	Some criticisms of Piaget's ideas on preschool thought	Cognitive psychologists such as Gelman have revealed that the preschool child may have a more developed concept of conservation than Piaget envisioned. Gelman's research has called attention to the importance of task analysis and other dimensions of the situation, such as the child's attention, in evaluating preoperational and concrete operational thought.
Information processing	Attention	The child's attention span increases substantially during early childhood, and distraction decreases. After age six, there appears to be a shift to cognitive control of attention. While preschool children focus more on the salient features of a task, elementary school children are more likely to attend to task-relevant features.
	Memory	Short-term memory involves retention up to 20 to 30 seconds and is more effortless than long-term memory. Encoding information for long-term retention is much more difficult, and long-term memory involves more effortful use of retrieval as well. Memory span tasks have been used to assess short-term memory. Memory span increases substantially in early childhood and is related to speed of information processing.
	Task dimensions and analyses	The information processing perspective emphasizes the importance of analyzing task requirements, such as the encoding of key pieces of information, the storing of information, the formulation of plans for analyses, and the size of working memory required. Emphasis on task dimensions and analyses has led researchers to simplify tasks and to make them more appropriate for very young children. This has helped researchers to determine if younger children are more cognitively mature than previously was thought. For example, this strategy has revealed that even four-year-old children can reason syllogistically.

Child Development Concept Table 7.2   Continued

Concept	Processes/Related Ideas	Characteristics/Description
Language development	Mean length of utterance	The mean length of utterance (MLU) concept was developed by Roger Brown and is useful in measuring the progress of language development.
	Phonology	The ability to pronounce consonant clusters as well as difficult phonemes and word endings improves during the preschool years.
	Morphology	During the preschool years, children begin to apply rules for combining morphemes (e.g., correct word endings for plural, possessive, and third-person singular forms of words). Overgeneralizations of these rules also appear and are later corrected.
	Syntax	Mastery of *wh-* questions and other complex syntactic forms is attained during the preschool years.
	Semantics	Children between the ages of one and six have a learning rate for new word meanings of five to eight words a day. Six-year-olds may acquire as many as 22 new words per day. The understanding of complex meanings of relational terms, such as spatial adjectives (e.g., thick–thin), improves during the preschool years.
	Pragmatics	Improvements in displacement (talking about things not physically present, as in games of pretend) are evident during the preschool years. Also, knowledge of using articles (*the, a*) to enhance communication increases, as do modifications of speech style depending on the age and status of the listener.

EARLY CHILDHOOD EDUCATION

Early childhood education has become a pervasive experience for children in our society—even children from lower socioeconomic backgrounds have been widely exposed to education at the preschool level.

The Nature and Effects of Early Childhood Education

The term **child-centered** has been used to describe the most popular form of education before the first grade. Child-centered means an emphasis on the individual child that provides each child with a number of experiences to make education a fun-filled adventure in exploration. But the term includes a diversity of goals and curricula in thousands of so-classified nursery schools. While some nursery schools emphasize social development, others emphasize cognitive development. While some stress daily structured activities, others stress much more flexible activities. Nonetheless, some attempts have been made to come up with an answer to the question of whether attending nursery school has a positive effect on young children's development.

The general conclusions about the effects of preschool education on children's development are these (Clarke-Stewart & Fein, 1983): (1) Children attending preschools interact more with peers—both positively and, often, negatively; (2) They are less cooperative with and responsive to adults than home-reared children; (3) They are more socially competent and mature in that they are more confident and extraverted (Ramey, MacPhee, & Yeates, 1982), more assertive (Rubenstein, Howes, & Boyle, 1981), more self-sufficient and independent (Fowler, 1978), more verbally expressive and more knowledgeable about their social world (Clarke-Stewart & Fein, 1983), more comfortable in stressful circumstances (Kagan, Kearsley, & Zelazo, 1978), and better adjusted when they go to school—for example, exhibiting more task persistence, leadership, and goal direction (Fowler & Kahn, 1974; Ramey, MacPhee, & Yeates, 1982).

But while children attending early childhood education programs show greater social competence, they also exhibit some negative behaviors. While they are more independent, they also tend to be less polite and less compliant with teacher demands. They not only have been found to be more assertive, but also louder, more aggressive, and bossy, particularly if the school or family standards support such behavior (Lally & Honig, 1977; Ramey, MacPhee, & Yeates, 1982). While such behaviors are not positive, they seem to be in a direction that shows greater developmental maturity since these behaviors increase as the child ages through the preschool years (Clarke-Stewart & Fein, 1983).

In sum, early childhood education generally has a positive effect on children's development. Now we turn our attention to the nature of compensatory education and several more specific types of early childhood programs.

Compensatory Education

For many years, children from low-income families did not receive any education before they entered the first grade. In the 1960s, an effort was made to try to break the poverty/poor education cycle for young children in the United States through **compensatory education.** As part of this effort, **Project Head Start** began in the summer of 1965, funded by the Economic Opportunity Act. The program was designed to provide children from low-income families with an opportunity to experience an enriched early environment. It was hoped that the early intervention might counteract the disadvantages these children had experienced and place them on an equal level with other children when they entered the first grade.

Project Follow Through

Project Head Start consisted of many different types of preschool programs in different parts of the country. Initially, little effort was made to find out whether some types of programs worked better than others. However, it soon became apparent that this was the case. Consequently, **Project Follow Through** was established in 1967. A significant aspect of this program was planned variation, in which different kinds of educational programs

This child is on his way to a Project Head Start program. What are his experiences there likely to be?

were devised to see whether specific programs were effective. In the Follow Through programs, the enriched planned variation was carried through the first few years of elementary school as well. Information about Project Follow Through is presented in Focus on Child Development 7.5, including a description of five Follow Through models and research evaluation of Project Follow Through.

FOCUS ON CHILD DEVELOPMENT 7.5

VARIATIONS IN EARLY EDUCATION WITH IMPOVERISHED CHILDREN

The table describes five Follow Through models. National research assessment of the effects of planned variation, such as that exhibited by the five models in the table, supported the belief that such programs can enhance the child's social and cognitive development. Jane Stallings (1975) commented on how many of the different variations were able to obtain the desired effects on children. For example, children in the academically oriented, direct instruction approaches, such as the University of Oregon model, seemed to do better on achievement tests and were more persistent on tasks than children in other approaches that placed more emphasis on affective development. However, children in the affective education approaches, such as the Far West Laboratory model, were absent from school less and showed more independence than children in other approaches, such as those that were highly structured.

As shown in the figures below, children experiencing the highly structured academic orientation of the University of Kansas model (much like the University of Oregon model) persisted on tasks but were less independent than children involved in the Far West affective education program. *Task persistence* was defined as the child engaging in self-instruction over a specified period of time. *Independence* was defined as a child or a group of children engaging in any task without an adult.

Thus, Project Follow Through was important in demonstrating that variation in early education does have important effects on a wide range of social and cognitive behaviors.

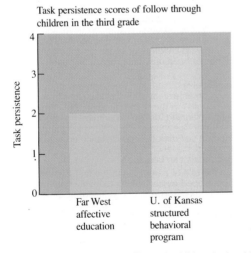

Task persistence scores of follow through children in the third grade

Task persistence scores of Follow Through children in the third grade.

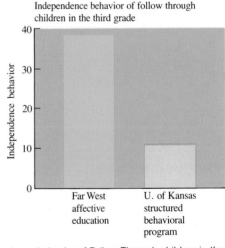

Independence behavior of follow through children in the third grade

Independence behavior of Follow Through children in the third grade.

(continued on following page)

FOCUS ON CHILD DEVELOPMENT 7.5

These children are in a Follow Through classroom. What effects has Project Follow Through shown on children's development?

Five Follow Through Models

Model	Description
University of Oregon Engelmann/Becker Model for Direct Instruction	Emphasizes that children fail in school because they have not been instructed properly. Disadvantaged children lag behind other children in developing appropriate skills. It is a highly structured program, with sequentially programmed lessons. Teachers systematically reward children for success and monitor them closely so that learning failures do not build up. This program is based on learning theory and behavior modification.
High/Scope: Cognitively Oriented Curriculum Model	Developed by Dave Weikart, this model is based on Piaget's theory of cognitive development. The child is seen as an active learner who discovers things about the world. He or she should not be "taught" in the sense of being told information; rather, he or she should "learn" by planning, doing, experimenting, exploring, and talking about what he or she is doing. Communication and thinking skills are nurtured, and emphasis is placed on self-direction, not reliance on external reinforcement from others. Each child's level of development is continuously monitored so that appropriate materials can be used.
Florida Parent-Education Program	Places more direct importance on the role of parents than the first two models mentioned. This program was developed by Ira Gordon to involve parents in the emotional and intellectual growth of their children. It assumes that the child's learning habits and personality are formed primarily through experiences in the early home environment; thus, parents are trained to supervise the child's learning at home. Parent educators work in the classroom and visit parents on a weekly basis.
Far West Laboratory Responsive Educational Program	Emphasizes the development of a healthy self-concept in the child and the freedom to decide his or her own course of learning. Teachers try to build up the child's confidence in his or her ability to succeed and provide many different alternatives in the classroom so that the child can choose and direct activities. This program has much in common with a humanistic view of child development.
Bank Street College of Education Approach	An eclectic approach in which academic skills are seen as acquired within a broader context of planned activities. The program focuses on the child's interests at school, at home, and in the community, and views the child as an active learner seeking to become independent and to understand the world. The child is encouraged to select from different alternatives, to make decisions, and to cope with the world. The individual nature of the child also is taken into account; learning experiences are constantly restructured to meet the needs of each child.

So far, we have looked primarily at the short-term effects of these important educational programs. But what about their long-term effects?

The Long-Term Effects of Project Head Start and Preschool Education With Low-Income Children

The effects of compensatory education in early childhood continue to be studied. Of particular interest is the long-term effect such early intervention might have on children. Sex differences have appeared on these long-term assessments. While differences favor children who attended Head Start compared with those who did not, by the time early adulthood is reached, the advantages favor males more than females. This is one of the findings of an ongoing large study of poor, black children who participated in Head Start in Harlem during the early 1960s (Deutsch, Deutsch, Jordan, & Grallo, 1981). More than 150 adults currently are involved in this study, half of whom entered Head Start when they were four years old. The others did not get this training and serve as a comparison group. All have been interviewed by psychologists every two to three years since the Head Start experience.

For the most part, the Head Start males have been successful in school and the job market: 32 percent are attending college, while only 20 percent of the non-Head Start group are; 57 percent are employed full- or part-time, compared with only 44 percent of the comparison group. These positive benefits did not emerge for the females, who seem to be no better off than those who started school at the usual age. The researchers are not sure why the young adult females are not doing as well as their male counterparts. The school system, however, may have to absorb some of the blame. The preschool program stressed verbal skills, inquisitiveness, and self-confidence. In elementary school, boys were rewarded for showing these characteristics, but in many instances, girls were punished for showing similar behaviors. Some teachers, for instance, even complained that the girls were too assertive and asked too many questions. But there are some indications that Head Start may indeed have left a positive impression on the females as well. Many females had to leave school because they became pregnant, but preliminary indications suggest that those who were in the preschool program are more likely to return to school and continue their education (Trotter, 1981).

In addition to the long-term effects in the study just discussed, another set of analyses also reveals that competent programs with low-income preschool children can have lasting effects many years later. Irving Lazar, Richard Darlington, and their collaborators (1982) established a number of different model programs for educating preschool low-income children in the 1960s and 1970s. They pooled their resources into what they called a consortium for longitudinal studies, developed to share information about the long-term effects of preschool programs so that better designs and methods could be created. At the time the data from the 11 different early education studies were analyzed together, the children ranged in age from 9 to 19 years. The early education models varied substantially, but all were carefully planned and carried out by experts in the field of early childhood education. Outcome measures included: (1) indicators of school competence, such as special education and grade retention; (2) abilities, as measured by standardized intelligence and achievement tests; (3) children's attitudes and values; and (4) impact on the family. The results indicated substantial effects of competent preschool education with low-income children on all four dimensions investigated.

In sum, there is substantial evidence that well-designed and implemented preschool education programs with low-income children are successful.

THINKING BACK, LOOKING AHEAD

Our journey through the physical and cognitive world of early childhood has taken us through green suns and yellow skies; pelicans that kiss seals; cars that float in the sky; throwing, kicking, balancing, building towers with blocks; a Big Mac, fries, and a chocolate shake; "Feet not cold now"; "I feel bad. My tummy hurts"; the three mountains task; "That tree pushed the leaf off"; "Why does the sun shine?"; watching "Sesame Street"; developing a better short-term memory; "Merds that laugh don't like mushrooms"; foots, feets, and wugs; Head Start and Follow Through. The free, fanciful, and creative world of young children comes through clearly as they become more adept at using their physical skills of movement and coordination and their cognitive skills of symbolic thought and language.

While we have covered a great deal about early childhood in this chapter, there is much more to be told. It is to the social aspects of development in the preschool years that we turn next. Before going on to the next chapter, though, think for a moment about the beauty of early childhood that is conveyed in these words:

The greatest poem ever known
Is one all poets have outgrown:
The poetry, innate, untold,
Of being only four years old.

Christopher Morley

SUMMARY

I. Physical development in early childhood encompasses increases in height, weight, fat, muscle, and other bodily parts; motor and perceptual development; and nutrition, health, and exercise.
   A. While virtually all children go through a number of developmental changes in early childhood, there are individual variations as well.
      1. Growth is slower in early childhood than in infancy. The average child grows 2½ inches in height and gains between five and seven pounds a year during early childhood. Bones, muscles, and joints are more susceptible to injury than in middle and late childhood.
      2. Both genetic and environmental factors contribute to considerable individual variation in physical development during early childhood. Ethnic origin and nutrition are very important influences on height. Urban, middle-class, and firstborn children are taller than rural, lower-class, and later-born children. Children who experience growth problems usually do so because of a congenital reason, a physical problem that develops in childhood, or an emotional difficulty.
   B. Changes in motor and perceptual development during early childhood involve gross motor skills, fine motor skills, and perceptual mapping of large-scale places.
      1. Considerable progress is made in gross motor skills during early childhood. This progress is particularly noticeable in arms and legs. The DeOreo Fundamental Motor Skills Inventory is a comprehensive assessment measure that evaluates 11 gross motor skills. Fine motor skills also are increasing during the preschool years.
      2. Children's ability to develop a map of large-scale spaces (those too large to be seen all at once) improves markedly in the preschool years. But even children as young as three years of age have a rudimentary ability to map such large-scale spaces.
   C. Nutrition, health, and exercise are important concerns of development during early childhood.
      1. Feeding and eating habits are important aspects of development during early childhood. The average preschool child requires 1,400 to 1,800 calories per day. Poor nutrition and malnutrition can influence not only physical development but cognitive development as well.
      2. Only recently has a developmental perspective on psychological aspects of health among children appeared. Interest in young children's health involves consideration of its role in later development—a future orientation—as well as a focus on health problems in a particular developmental period, such as early childhood—a current orientation. The effects of health and illness can be studied in terms of their relation to motor, cognitive, and social development. Increased motor activity by the preschool child exposes him or her to greater risk of accident and more sources of disease. Increased cognitive sophistication should improve the child's self-protective behavior and encourage him or her to take responsibility for preventing problems and promoting health and safety. Cognitive development also likely influences the child's psychological and behavioral responses to injury and illness and their treatment. In terms of social development, caregivers play an important health role. Indirectly, they serve as important role models for health, and more directly, they can train the child in appropriate health habits.

3. By the age of six, many children already are not in very good physical shape. Comparisons with 1975 data suggest that, in the mid-1980s, schoolchildren were still in poor physical condition—for example, 25 percent of all elementary school boys could not even do one pull-up! Such information suggests that the preschool years are an important time for beginning physical fitness programs.

II. Ideas about cognitive development in early childhood include Piaget's stage of preoperational thought, information processing, and language development.

  A. Preoperational thought encompasses a number of characteristics and includes two substages.

    1. Preoperational thought is the second major stage of Piaget's theory of cognitive development and roughly spans the ages of two to seven. This period is a time when stable concepts are formed, mental reasoning emerges, egocentrism is prominent, and magical belief systems are constructed. The child does not yet think in an operational manner. Thought is still flawed and not well organized. This stage also is characterized by a shift from a primitive to a more sophisticated use of symbols.

    2. The symbolic function substage occurs between two and four years of age. During this time, symbolic thought occurs on a regular basis in the form of language, pretend play, and scribbling and drawing. Symbols are frequently used to represent objects that are not present. Egocentrism is highly prominent in this substage. Children at this point have considerable difficulty in spatial and social perspective taking. Piaget and Inhelder investigated spatial perspective taking with the three mountains task. Researchers have shown that perspective taking is only weakly related to general intelligence and that different dimensions of perspective taking appear to be only moderately to weakly related. They are intrigued by the possibility that spatial perspective taking might be an antecedent of social perspective taking, although no research data have documented this latter point. Animism is another prominent characteristic of the symbolic function substage—it refers to the belief that inanimate objects have lifelike qualities and are capable of action.

3. The intuitive thought substage lasts from approximately four to seven years of age. Reasoning is present but in a prelogical form. Question asking is prevalent. Children seem sure of their knowledge and understanding but are unaware of how they know what they know. Children in this substage have difficulty sorting objects into what could be referred to as a competent classification.

4. Cognitive psychologists such as Gelman have revealed that the preschool child may have a more developed concept of conservation than Piaget envisioned. Gelman's research has called attention to the importance of task analysis and other dimensions of the situation, such as the child's attention, in evaluating preoperational and concrete operational thought.

  B. Changes in children's information processing during the preschool years focus on attention, memory, and the role of task dimensions and analyses.

    1. The child's attention span increases substantially during early childhood, and distraction decreases. After age six, there appears to be a shift to cognitive control of attention. While preschool children focus more on the salient features of a task, elementary school children are more likely to attend to task-relevant features.

    2. Short-term memory involves retention up to 20 to 30 seconds and is more effortless than long-term memory. Encoding information for long-term retention is much more difficult, and long-term memory involves more effortful use of retrieval as well. Memory span tasks have been used to assess short-term memory. Memory span increases considerably during early childhood and is related to speed of information processing.

    3. The information processing perspective emphasizes the importance of analyzing task requirements, such as the encoding of key pieces of information, the storing of information, the formulation of plans for analyses, and the size of working memory required. Emphasis on task dimensions and analyses has led researchers to simplify tasks and to make them more appropriate for very young children. This has helped researchers to determine if younger children are more cognitively mature than previously was thought.

For example, this strategy has revealed that even four-year-old children can reason syllogistically.

C. Changes in language development during the preschool years focus on the mean length of utterance, phonology, morphology, syntax, semantics, and pragmatics.

1. The mean length of utterance concept was developed by Roger Brown and is useful in measuring the progress of language development.

2. With regard to phonology, the ability to pronounce consonant clusters as well as difficult phonemes and word endings improves during the preschool years.

3. With regard to morphology, during the preschool years, children begin to apply rules for combining morphemes (e.g., correct word endings for plural, possessive, and third-person singular forms of words). Overgeneralizations of these rules also appear and are later corrected.

4. With regard to syntax, wh- questions and other complex syntactic forms are mastered during the preschool years.

5. With regard to semantics, children between the ages of one and six have a learning rate for new word meanings of five to eight words a day. Six-year-olds may acquire as many as 22 new words per day. The understanding of complex meanings of relational terms, such as spatial adjectives (e.g., thin–thick), improves during the preschool years.

6. Changes in pragmatics include improvements in displacement (talking about things not physically present, as in games of pretend). Knowledge of using articles (*the, a*) to enhance communication increases, as do modifications of speech style depending on the age and status of the listener.

III. The child-centered approach to early childhood education can result in the highest quality of education when all developmental levels are considered. Children who attend preschool are more competent than those who do not attend, although they show more negative behaviors as well. Compensatory education has tried to break through the poverty cycle in the form of such programs as Head Start and Follow Through. The Montessori approach to early childhood education has been very popular.

KEY TERMS

animism 274
child-centered education 289
class inclusion reasoning 280
compensatory education 290
contagion stage 264
deprivation dwarfism 259
egocentrism 270
intuitive thought 275
mean length of utterance (MLU) 281
memory span task 279

Montessori approach 256
operations 269
phenomenistic stage 264
Project Follow Through 290
Project Head Start 290
relational words 286
short-term memory 279
syllogism 282
symbolic function substage 270
three mountains task 270

SUGGESTED READINGS

Clarke-Stewart, K. A., & Fein, G. G. (1983). Early childhood programs. In P. H. Mussen (Ed.), *Handbook of Child Psychology,* 4th ed., Vol. 2. New York: Wiley.
A comprehensive review of what is known about early childhood education programs is presented.

Daehler, M. W., & Bukatko, D. (1985). *Cognitive development.* New York: Random House.
A thorough overview of children's cognitive development is provided. Topics include the development of attention, basic memory processes, and reasoning.

Piaget, J. (1987) (Translated from the French by Helga Feider). *Possibility and necessity.* Minneapolis, MN: U. of Minnesota Press.
Children's understanding of possibility and how they learn to choose among alternatives was a major interest of Piaget's late in his life. This book includes a description of a number of problems Piaget devised to assess these possibilities and choices.

Stevenson, H. W., & Siegel, A. E. (eds.), (1987). *Child development research and social policy.* Chicago: U. of Chicago Press.
This book offers a number of important ideas about social policies pertaining to children. Included are chapters focused on nutrition and public policy and child health policy.

SOCIAL AND PERSONALITY DEVELOPMENT IN EARLY CHILDHOOD

IMAGINE . . . TWO FOUR-YEAR-
OLDS ARE PLAYING AND ONE
SAYS TO THE OTHER: "YOU STAY
HERE WITH THE BABY WHILE I
GO FISHING."

PREVIEW

FAMILIES

Parenting Styles
Sibling Relationships
Sibling and Parent–Child Relationships
Birth Order
Siblings as Models and Teachers
The Changing Family in a Changing
Society
Working Mothers
Effects of Divorce on Children

**CHILD DEVELOPMENT CONCEPT
TABLE 8.1: PARENTING STYLES,
SIBLING RELATIONSHIPS, AND
THE CHANGING FAMILY**

PEER RELATIONS AND PLAY IN
EARLY CHILDHOOD

The Nature of Peer Relations
The Meaning of the Term Peers
Peers and Competent Social Development
*Cross-Cultural Comparisons of Peer
Relations*
Peer Relations and Perspective Taking
The Development of Peer Relations

**FOCUS ON CHILD
DEVELOPMENT 8.1: NOSE
PUNCHERS, PINCHERS, AND
ISOLATES**

The Distinct but Coordinated Worlds of
Parents and Peers
Play
Functions of Play
Types of Play
Pretend Play

**FOCUS ON CHILD
DEVELOPMENT 8.2: THE
SYMBOLIC WORLD OF
CHILDREN'S PLAY**

*New Directions in Research on Children's
Play*

TELEVISION

Functions of Television
Children's Exposure to Television
The Role of Television as a Social Agent
Aggression
Prosocial Behavior
The Social Context of Viewing Television
Commercials
Formal Features of Television

**CHILD DEVELOPMENT CONCEPT
TABLE 8.2: PEERS, PLAY, AND
TELEVISION**

THE SELF, SEX ROLES, AND
MORAL DEVELOPMENT IN
EARLY CHILDHOOD

The Self
"I" and "Me"
Sex Roles
Biological Influences
Cognitive Factors

**FOCUS ON CHILD
DEVELOPMENT 8.3: HOW GOOD
ARE GIRLS AT WUDGEMAKING IF
THE WUDGEMAKER IS A "HE"?**
Environmental Influences
The Development of Sex Roles

**CHILD DEVELOPMENT CONCEPT
TABLE 8.3: THE SELF AND SEX-
ROLE DEVELOPMENT**

Moral Development
Piaget's View of Moral Reasoning
Moral Behavior
Moral Feelings and Guilt
Altruism

THINKING BACK, LOOKING
AHEAD

SUMMARY

KEY TERMS

SUGGESTED READINGS

CHAPTER 8

IMAGINE . . . TWO FOUR-YEAR-OLDS ARE PLAYING AND ONE SAYS TO THE OTHER: "YOU STAY HERE WITH THE BABY WHILE I GO FISHING."

Don't you immediately assume that one of the preschool children is a boy and the other is a girl? And don't you also infer that the sex of the child speaking is male? If you made these inferences, you are correct. These two preschool children—Shane and Barbara—were playing at their nursery school. As Shane walked away, Barbara called to him: "I want to go fishing, too." Shane replied, "No. Girls don't go fishing. But I will take you out to a French restaurant when I get back."

Barbara returned to playing with her dolls as Shane left. The director of the nursery school talked with Shane's mother about his behavior. She wanted to know whether Shane was merely mimicking his father's behavior. Shane's mother said that he was not, because the entire family went fishing together. The sex roles children display, then, are not merely a replication of parental actions.

Another play scene observed by the nursery school director focused on three boys sitting around a play table in a play kitchen. The boys began issuing orders like, "I want a cup of coffee," or "Some more jelly for the toast over here." Girls were running back and forth between the stove and table as they cooked and served breakfast. In one scenario, the boys got out of hand, demanding cups of coffee one after another as the four-year-old girl, Ann, raced around in a dizzy state. Finally, she gained some control of the situation by announcing that the coffee was all gone. It didn't seem to occur to Ann to sit down at the table and demand coffee from the boys.

Sexist behavior from young children is nothing new, but viewing it as a problem is something that only has occurred in recent years. Such behavior has become somewhat of an obsession with preschool teachers and directors, and it bothers many parents who are trying to rear their offspring free of sexual bias. The parents may carefully screen out books in which mothers primarily tie shoelaces and bake cookies, and buy sports equipment for their daughters as well as (or in place of) dolls.

One of the main tasks facing the young child is the development of a sense of self, and attaining a sexual identity is an important part of such development. As children move from the toddler years into early childhood, they begin making generalizations about sex-related matters that may not be accurate. William, for instance, went with his mother to a doctor's office when he was 2½ years old. As they sat in the waiting room, a man in a white coat walked by, and William said, "Hi, Doc." Then a woman in a white coat walked by, and William said, "Hi, Nurse." His mother asked how he knew which person was a doctor and which was a nurse. William replied, "Doctors are daddies and nurses are mommies." However, William's own pediatrician was a female who had cared for him since birth. Many preschool children show some confusion about sex roles, just as they reveal fuzzy, often inaccurate perceptions of their entire social world (Carper, 1978).

One of the focuses in this chapter is the role of children's development in obtaining a sexual identity. We will see that such identity is determined by an interaction of biological heritage and culture. Nowhere in the study of child development has there been greater cultural change in recent years than in the area of sex roles. Whereas, at one time in history, it was accepted that boys should grow up to be masculine and girls to be feminine and that the many pieces of information they encountered from parents, teachers, siblings, and the media were consistent in portraying this course of development, today many boys and girls are likely to be getting more conflicting information about sex roles. A preschool girl may have a mother who is promoting her femininity, yet become friends with a "tomboy" at her nursery school and have a teacher who is promoting assertiveness in young girls. The chapter discussion of the development of sex roles provides much more information about the aspects of sex roles detailed so far.

PREVIEW

There is a vigorous nature to the preschool child's social ventures—Erikson (1968) calls it "initiative." The preschool child has a surplus of energy that allows failures to be forgotten quickly and desirable things to be approached with enthusiasm. Interactions and relationships with parents, siblings, and peers are prominent in the preschool child's day. Time also often is spent watching television. Such interactions and relationships with people and the time spent watching television are important in determining the nature of the preschool child's self, sex-role orientation, and moral development. This chapter continues to stress that parents have a very important investment in the future—their child. Carl Jung once captured the importance of parenting by suggesting that we reach backward to our parents and forward to our children, and through their children to a future we never will see, but about which we need to care.

FAMILIES

In Chapter 6, we learned that attachment is an important aspect of family relationships during infancy. We discovered that some experts believe that attachment, particularly to the mother, during the first several years of life is the key ingredient in the child's social development and increases the likelihood that the child will be socially competent and well adjusted in the preschool years and beyond. We also learned that other experts believe that infant attachment to the mother has been overemphasized and that the child's temperament, other social agents and contexts, and the complexity of the child's social world are also important in the assessment of what contributes to the child's social competence and well-being. Some child developmentalists, however, believe that the infancy years have been overemphasized as determinants of later social development, arguing that social experiences in the early childhood years and later have sometimes not been given the attention they deserve.

In this chapter, we move beyond the attachment process as we explore the different types of parenting styles to which children are exposed, additional information about sibling relationships, and how, as we are moving through the latter part of the 20th century, more children are experiencing socialization in a greater variety of family structures than at any point in history. Keep in mind as we discuss these aspects of families the importance of the family as a system of interacting individuals who reciprocally socialize and mutually regulate each other.

Parenting Styles

Parents want their children to grow into socially mature individuals, and they often feel a great deal of frustration in knowing the best way to accomplish this. Child psychologists have long searched for ingredients of parenting that will promote competent social development in children. For example, in the 1930s, the behaviorist John Watson argued that parents were too affectionate with their children. Early research in child development focused on a distinction between physical and psychological discipline or between controlling and permissive parenting. More recently, the dimensions of competent parenting have become more precise.

Diana Baumrind's (1971) research has revealed that parents should be neither punitive toward their children nor aloof from them but rather should develop and enforce rules and regulations for their children. She emphasizes three types of parenting that are associated with different aspects of the child's social behavior: authoritarian, authoritative, and laissez-faire (permissive). More recently, developmental psychologists have argued that permissive parenting comes in two different forms. Thus, the overview of parenting styles that follows focuses on authoritarian, authoritative, and two forms of permissive parenting.

Authoritarian parents are restrictive, have a punitive orientation, exhort the child to follow their directions, respect work and effort, place limits and controls on the child, and offer little verbal give-and-take between the child and the parent. **Authoritarian parenting** is linked with the following social behaviors of the child: an anxiety about social comparison, failure to initiate activity, and ineffective social interaction.

Authoritative parenting encourages the child to be independent but still places limits, demands, and controls on his or her actions. There is extensive verbal give-and-take, and parents demonstrate a high degree of warmth and nurturance toward the child. Authoritative parenting is associated with social competency of the child, particularly self-reliance and social responsibility.

Eleanor Maccoby and John Martin (1983) proposed a scheme for categorizing parenting styles that involves various combinations of a demanding–undemanding dimension and an accepting–rejecting dimension. As shown in Figure 8.1, an authoritarian parent (also called power assertive in the sense that the parent exercises considerable power over the child and/or the child's resources) is demanding and controlling as well as rejecting, unresponsive, and parent-centered. An authoritative parent is also demanding and controlling but is accepting, responsive, and child-centered. This parenting style is called authoritative-reciprocal by Maccoby and Martin.

Notice in the fourfold scheme of parenting described by Maccoby and Martin in Figure 8.1 that indulgent parents are undemanding but accepting and responsive, while neglecting parents are also undemanding but rejecting as well. The **permissive-indulgent pattern,** on the whole, seems to have more negative than positive effects on children. Consider the parents who are highly involved in their children's lives but who allow them a great deal of freedom and do not control their negative behaviors. These children often grow up learning that they can get by with just about anything and often show a disregard for rules and regulations. Consider also the **permissive-indifferent** parent, who is very uninvolved in his or her children's lives. This type of parenting has consistently been linked to a lack of self-control on the part of the children. In sum, a lack of self-control seems to be one of the prominent results of children who experience permissive-indulgent or permissive-indifferent parenting.

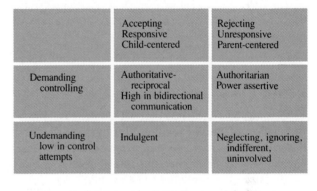

	Accepting Responsive Child-centered	Rejecting Unresponsive Parent-centered
Demanding controlling	Authoritative-reciprocal High in bidirectional communication	Authoritarian Power assertive
Undemanding low in control attempts	Indulgent	Neglecting, ignoring, indifferent, uninvolved

FIGURE 8.1   A two-dimensional classification of parenting patterns.

One factor that should not be overlooked in considering the parent's behavior toward the child is the child's maturation. Mothers obviously do not treat a five-year-old in the same way as a two-year-old. The two-year-old and the five-year-old have different needs and abilities, and the mother has different expectancies for the two children. According to Eleanor Maccoby (1980):

During the first year of a child's life, the parent–child interaction moves from a heavy focus on routine caretaking—feeding, changing, bathing, and soothing—and comes to include more noncaretaking activities like play and visual-vocal exchanges. During children's second and third years, parents often handle disciplinary issues by physical manipulation: They carry the child away from a mischievous activity to the place they want the child to go; they put fragile and dangerous objects out of reach; they sometimes spank. But as the child grows older, parents turn increasingly to reasoning, moral exhortation, and giving or withholding special privileges. As children move from infancy to middle childhood, parents show them less physical affection, become less protective, and spend less time with them (Baldwin, 1946; Lasko, 1954).

Eleanor Maccoby (1980) believes that these changes in parental behavior are clearly linked to the child's physical and mental growth—to changes in the child's motor skill, language, judgment, and perspective-taking ability. As the child grows larger and heavier, parents seem less likely to resort to physical manipulation. Parents seem unlikely to reason with a child who doesn't yet talk and who seems to have a limited understanding of other people's speech.

As we discussed in Chapter 6, children are socialized by their parents, but the socialization is reciprocal: Children also socialize their parents. As we see next, in most families, there also are siblings to be socialized and to be socialized by.

Sibling Relationships

Sandra describes to her mother what happened in a conflict with her sister:

> We had just come home from the ball game. I sat down on the sofa next to the light so I could read. Sally (the sister) said, "Get up. I was sitting there first. I just got up for a second to get a drink." I told her I was not going to get up and that I didn't see her name on the chair. I got mad at her and started pushing her—her drink spilled all over her. Then she got really mad and started shoving me up against the wall and hitting me. I managed to grab her hair.

At this point, Sally comes into the room and begins to tell her side of the story. Sandra interrupts, "Mother, you always take her side."

Competition among **siblings**—that is, brothers and/or sisters—along with concern about being treated fairly and equally by parents are among the most pervasive characteristics of sibling relationships (Santrock, Smith, & Bourbeau, 1976).

More than 80 percent of American children have one or more siblings. Because there are so many possible sibling combinations in a family, it is difficult to generalize about sibling influence and conflict. Among a variety of important factors to be considered in studying sibling relationships are number of siblings, age of siblings, birth order, age spacing, sex of siblings, and whether sibling relationships are different than parent–child relationships.

Sibling and Parent–Child Relationships

Is sibling interaction more influential than parent–child interaction? There is some evidence that it is. Linda Baskett (1974; Baskett & Johnson, 1982) observed the members of 47 families, each of which had two or three children. The siblings ranged from 5 to 10 years of age. Observations were made for 45 minutes on five different occasions. The children's observed behaviors included teasing, whining, yelling, commanding, talking, touching, nonverbal interacting, laughing, and complying. The interaction of the children with their parents was far more positive than their interaction with each other. Children and their parents had more varied and positive interchanges—they talked, laughed, and comforted one another more than siblings did. Children also tended to follow the dictates of their parents more than those of their siblings, and they behaved more negatively and punitively during interaction with their siblings than with their parents.

In some instances, siblings are a stronger socializing influence on the child than parents are. Victor Cicirelli (1977) believes, in particular, that older siblings teach their younger siblings. Someone close in age to the child may understand his or her problems more readily and be able to communicate more effectively with him or her than parents can. In such areas as dealing with peers, coping with difficult teachers, and discussing taboo subjects, siblings are often more influential than parents in the socialization process. Older siblings also may serve effectively in teaching younger siblings about identity problems, sexual behavior, and physical appearance—areas in which the parents may be unwilling or incapable of helping an adolescent.

The potential benefits of using siblings as therapists have been demonstrated by Miller and Cantwell (1976). They found that, in families where siblings are involved, therapy is more effective than in families where only the parents and the disturbed child are included. When siblings are not included, they may unknowingly encourage and perpetuate unwanted behaviors in the disturbed child. Instructing siblings in ways that they and their parents can more effectively manage their disturbed brother or sister produces more positive outcomes in family therapy.

An area of research attention in recent years involves the interaction of mothers with young siblings. Carol Kendrick and Judith Dunn (1980; Dunn & Kendrick, 1982) observed that older toddlers and preschool children were given less attention by their mothers after a younger sibling was born. They believe that the older sibling responds to such decreased attention by placing increased demands on the mother or by engaging in behavior that will attract the mother's attention. Toward the end of the first year of the younger sibling's life, the older sibling may sometimes begin to act aggressively toward the younger sibling, even hitting him or her on occasion. Arguments typically are triggered by the older sibling and are likely to increase as the younger sibling ages and is more likely to fend for himself or herself (Pepler, Ambramovitch, & Corter, 1981).

In infancy and the toddler years, there is evidence that more sibling rivalry appears between opposite-sex siblings than same-sex siblings (Dunn & Kendrick, 1981). It is argued that such differences are a consequence of the mother's behavior. Mothers were observed to spend considerably more time playing with the younger child when his or her sex was opposite that of the older sibling. However, one research investigation with siblings in the elementary school years revealed greater sibling rivalry between same-sex than opposite-sex siblings (Minnett, Vandell, & Santrock, 1983). In this study, more coercive interaction also appeared between 8- and 12-year-old female siblings than between 4- and 8-year-old female siblings, suggesting the possibility that same-sex sibling rivalry increases during the elementary school years.

How does sibling rivalry develop?

Many parents of siblings who took part in the Minnett, Vandell, and Santrock (1983) study expressed concern about their children's constant bickering and fighting, hoping that participation in the study would shed some light on sibling rivalry. Indeed, the process of social comparison is intensified in any sibling relationship. The child has a built-in need to know where he or she stands vis-à-vis a brother or sister: Is he as strong, is he as smart, is he as worthwhile a person? All children are concerned about where they stand in these matters, but a sibling provides a more concrete reminder to the child to question his or her status in the family. Competitive sibling interaction, then, is a fact of sibling life, but so, too, are positive and neutral interactions. However, parents may overlook many of the positive and neutral sibling exchanges, responding instead to negative behaviors that require parental intervention.

So far, we have focused heavily on the nature of social interaction in sibling interaction, but what about birth order? How is it related to the child's development?

Birth Order

Think about your birth order. Are you the eldest? the youngest? the middle child? Do you think being born in a particular sibling order has influenced your development? Birth order has been studied extensively over many years. To summarize some of the main conclusions of this large body of literature, it seems that firstborn children are more achievement oriented (Glass, Neulinger, & Brim, 1974; Schachter, 1963) and more socially responsible than children born later (Sutton-Smith & Rosenberg, 1970). It also seems that firstborns are more affiliative and sociable than children born later (Schachter, 1963). Nevertheless, there are some mixed findings in the sociability–affiliation domain since later-born children often have better peer relationships, and in the case of boys, may have fewer behavior problems (Lahey, Hammer, Crumrine, & Forehand, 1980; Miller & Maruyama, 1976). It is important to point out that birth order findings often account for a small percentage of variance when trying to predict the social competence of the child. Birth order, then, is best viewed as one of many variables that influence the child's development. It clearly is erroneous to conclude that, because you are a firstborn, you will be more achievement oriented than your friend who is a later-born child. Also remember that when differences between firstborn and later-born children are reported, they represent average differences. There clearly are many later-born children who are highly achievement oriented because their birth order did not produce a rigid social script that their parents followed.

Nevertheless, many mothers do seem to give different amounts of attention to firstborn siblings compared to later-born siblings, a finding that is often called on to explain firstborn findings. For example, in observations of mother–sibling interaction, mothers consistently gave more attention to their firstborn children than to children born later (Cushna, 1966; Gewirtz & Gewirtz, 1965; Rothbart, 1967). This is perhaps explained by the fact that many mothers anxiously await the birth of their first child and that both parents often have high expec-tations for the child. By the time the second child is born, much of the novelty and intrigue of rearing a child probably has worn off.

As we see next, siblings also can be studied in terms of their roles as models and teachers.

Siblings as Models and Teachers

Older siblings are often effective models and teachers for their younger siblings. Helen Samuels (1977) observed siblings' social interaction in a 20-minute play situation of infants (mean age, 19 months) with their older pre-school siblings (mean age, 4½ years). She predicted that the infants would find the older siblings attractive and treat them as models. A comparison of the siblings' behavior supported her prediction. The infant tended to look at, imitate, and follow the older sibling about, whereas the older sibling tended to show comparatively little interest of this sort in the infant. More recent research confirms the observation that younger siblings imitate older siblings more than vice versa (Abramovitch, Corter, Pepler, & Stanhope, 1986).

In one investigation of siblings as teachers, researchers found that older siblings were much more likely to assume a teaching role than were younger siblings. However, when these older siblings were studied in terms of their relationships with equal-status peers, the older siblings were much less likely to assume a stance of dominance toward the peers as they engaged in less teaching behavior (Brody, Stoneman, & MacKinnon, 1982). Other research on siblings as teachers has found that some siblings are better teachers than others (Cicirelli, 1972). In particular, older sisters seem to be more competent than older brothers at teaching younger siblings. In the Cicirelli study, the older sisters were more likely to demonstrate, explain, give feedback, and provide clues and hints when teaching a younger sibling how to solve a problem.

So far, we have been discussing parenting styles and sibling relations, but as we see next, one of the most important considerations in family processes focuses on the hodgepodge of family structures in which children now are growing up.

The Changing Family in a Changing Society

Children are growing up in a greater variety of family structures than ever before in history. Many mothers spend the greatest part of their day away from their children, even their infants. More than one out of every three mothers with a child under the age of three is employed, and almost 42 percent of the mothers of preschoolers work outside the home (U.S. Department of Commerce, 1979). The increasing number of children growing up in single-parent families is staggering. One estimate indicates that about 25 percent of the children born between 1910 and 1960 lived in a single-parent family sometime during their development. However, 40 to 50 percent of the individuals born during the 1970s will spend some part of their childhood in a single-parent family (Bane, 1978). Furthermore, about 11 percent of all American households now are made up of so-called blended families; that is, families with stepparents or those consisting of cohabitating adults. Also, while there has been a slight trend for fathers to engage in more child-rearing duties in recent years, when we look back at earlier times, we see that most American fathers spend far less time with their families than at any other time in history. Consider the frontier father, who was the sole provider of the family's welfare—he performed virtually all of the decision making and probably demanded a high degree of respect from his children. Today's father often operates in the background, supporting the mother's handling of daily family problems. In this section, we look more closely at some of the family changes that are occurring, first describing the impact of working mothers on children, and second, outlining the expanding interest in the effects of divorce on children.

Working Mothers

Because household operations have become more efficient and family size has decreased in America, it is not certain that children with mothers who work outside the home actually receive less attention than children in the past whose mothers were not employed. Outside employment, at least for mothers with school-age children and adolescents, may simply be filling time previously taken up by added household burdens and more children. Also, it cannot be assumed that, if the mother did not go to work, the child or adolescent would benefit from the time freed by streamlined household operations and smaller families. Mothering does not always have a positive effect on the child. In one longitudinal study, it was found that boys who experienced full-time mothering during the preschool years were more competent intellectually but were also more ready to conform, more fearful, and more inhibited as adolescents (Moore, 1975). The educated, nonworking mother may overinvest her energies in her children, fostering an excess of worry and discouraging the children's independence. In such situations, the mother may inject more mothering into parent–child relationships than the child can profitably handle (Hoffman, 1974).

Recent research efforts have begun to chart the effects that the mother's employment patterns may have on the father's interaction and relationship with the child (e.g., Cowan & Cowan, 1985; Crouter & Huston, 1985; Piotrkowski & Stark, 1985). The complexity of the mother's work patterns and the father's role in the child's development is evident when we consider that it is important to take into account such matters as (Berman, 1985): (1) both the qualitative and quantitative aspects of the father and mother's work circumstances, (2) the number of hours worked and the overlap of parent work schedules, (3) the age and sex of the child, (4) the values and attitudes of each parent, (5) the stage of career and family development that each parent is in, (6) changing values in the culture, and (7) changing employment patterns.

Lois Hoffman (1979), who has been charting the effects of working mothers on children's development for a number of years, concluded that:

Maternal employment is a part of modern life. It is not an aberrant aspect of it, but a response to other social changes and, as such, meets the needs that the previous family ideal of a full-time mother and homemaker cannot. Not only does it meet the parent's needs, but in many ways, it is a pattern better suited to socializing the child for the adult roles he or she will occupy. This is particularly true for the daughter, but for the son, too, the broader range of emotions and skills that each parent presents are more consistent with this adult role. Just as his father shares the breadwinning role and the child-rearing role with his mother, so the son, too, will be likely to share these roles. The rigid sex-role stereotyping perpetuated by the divisions of labor in the traditional family is not appropriate for the demands children of either sex will have made on them as adults. Furthermore, the needs of the growing child require the mother to loosen her hold on the child, and this task may be easier for the working woman whose job is an additional source of identity and self-esteem.

Effects of Divorce on Children

The effects of divorce on the child are mediated by a host of factors, including the relationship of the child to the custodial parent; the availability of and reliance on family support systems, such as friends, relatives, and other adults; peer support; and whether there is an ongoing, positive relationship with the noncustodial parent. Many generalizations about the effects that divorced parents have on children are stereotypical and do not take into account the uniqueness of many single-parent family structures. One study vividly demonstrated that boys from divorced homes are often treated differently than boys in two-parent homes (Santrock & Tracy, 1978). Thirty teachers were shown a videotape that focused on the social interaction of a boy. Half of the teachers were informed that the boy was from an "intact" home, and the other half were told that the boy's parents were divorced. The teachers were asked to rate the boy on 11 personality traits (e.g., anxiety, social deviance, and happiness) and to predict what his behavior would be like in five different school situations (e.g., ability to cope with stress, popularity). The teachers rated the "divorced" boy more negatively on three counts: happiness, emotional adjustment, and ability to cope with stress (see Figure 8.2).

Many separations and divorces are highly emotional affairs that immerse the child in conflict. Conflict is a critical aspect of family functioning that appears to even outweigh the influence of family structure on the child's development. Children in single-parent families function better than those in conflict-ridden nuclear families (Hetherington, Cox, & Cox, 1978; Rutter, 1983). Although escape from conflict may be a positive benefit of divorce for children, unfortunately, in the year immediately following the divorce, conflict does not decline but rather increases (Hetherington, Cox, & Cox, 1978). At this time, children—particularly boys—in divorced families show more adjustment problems than children in homes in which both parents are present.

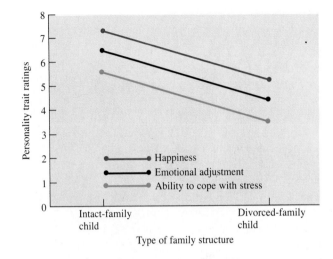

FIGURE 8.2 How teachers stereotype boys from mother-custody divorced homes.

The child's relationship with both parents after the divorce influences the ability to cope with stress (Hetherington, Cox, & Cox, 1978). During the first year after the divorce, the quality of parenting that the child experiences is often very poor; parents seem to be preoccupied with their own needs and adjustment, experiencing anger, depression, confusion, and emotional instability, which inhibits their ability to respond sensitively to the child's needs. During this period, parents tend to discipline the child inconsistently, to be less affectionate, and to be ineffective in controlling the child. But during the second year after the divorce, parents are more effective in the important child-rearing duties, and the degree to which there is a continuous harmonious relationship between the custodial parent and the ex-spouse is an important predictor of the child's adjustment (Hetherington, Cox, & Cox, 1978).

The majority of information we have about divorced families emphasizes the absent father or the relationship between the custodial parent and the child, but child psychologists have become increasingly interested in the role of support systems available to the child and the family. Support systems for divorced families seem more important for low-income than for middle-income families (Colletta, 1978). The extended family and community services may play a critical role in the functioning

How might the sex of the custodial parent be related to the child's adjustment?

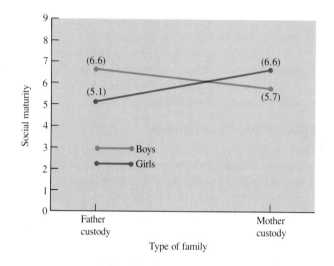

FIGURE 8.3   Ratings of social maturity in children based on observations of behavior during social interaction with the custodial parent in father- and mother-custody families.

of low-income families. Competent support systems may be particularly important for divorced parents with infant and preschool children because the majority of these parents must work full-time to make ends meet.

The age of the child at the time of the divorce is also a factor in what effects the divorce will have on the child. Little is known about the effects of divorce on infants. The early onset of divorce, however, does seem to have a more negative effect on development than later onset. During infancy, divorce may disrupt the attachment bond because many mothers have to go to work to provide support for the family. Strapped financially, many divorced mothers may not be able to afford quality day care. Therefore, many infants of divorced mothers are not only not being cared for by their mothers during most

of the day, but are likely to be in day-care centers of questionable quality.

Preschool children are not as accurate as elementary school children and adolescents in evaluating the cause of divorce, their own role in the divorce, and possible outcomes. Consequently, young children may blame themselves more for the divorce and distort the feelings and behavior of their parents, including having hopes for their parents' reconciliation (Wallerstein & Kelly, 1980).

In addition to conflict, relationships with parents, and the age of the child as factors affecting the effects of divorce on children, it also is important to consider the sex of the child and the sex of the custodial parent. One research study has directly compared children living in father-custody and mother-custody families (Santrock & Warshak, 1979, 1986). Children were videotaped during social interaction with their same-sex parent as the parent and child discussed a weekend plan and problems surfaced. The videotapes were rated by two people to ensure a high degree of reliability. On a number of ratings of observed behavior, children living with a same-sex parent were characterized as having greater social competence than those living with an opposite-sex parent. For example, as shown in Figure 8.3, father-custody boys

Child Development Concept Table 8.1 Parenting Styles, Sibling Relationships, and the Changing Family		

Concept	Processes/Related Ideas	Characteristics/Description
Parenting styles	Authoritarian	Authoritarian parenting is linked with parents who are restrictive, have a punitive orientation, exhort the child to follow their directions, respect work and effort, place limits and controls on the child, and offer little verbal give-and-take with the child. This parenting style is associated with the child's anxiety about social comparison, failure to initiate activity, and ineffective social interaction.
	Authoritative	Authoritative parents encourage the child to be independent but still place limits. Extensive verbal give-and-take is present, as is a high degree of warmth. Authoritative parenting is linked with the child's social competence, particularly self-reliance and social responsibility.
	Permissive-indulgent	Permissive-indulgent parents are undemanding but accepting and responsive. On the whole, this type of parenting seems to have more negative than positive effects, being linked to impulsivity, aggressiveness, lack of independence, and lack of responsibility.
	Permissive-indifferent	Permissive-indifferent parents are undemanding and rejecting as well. This style of parenting has negative effects on children, including disruption of the attachment bond and lack of self-control.
	Maturation of child	Parents need to adapt their interaction strategies as the child grows older, using less physical manipulation and more reasoning in the process.
Sibling relationships	Their nature	More than 80 percent of American children have one or more siblings. Sibling relationships are an important part of children's socialization.
	Sibling and parent–child interaction	In some instances, siblings are stronger socializing influences than parents—older siblings may be particularly influential in teaching younger siblings about identity problems and physical appearance, for example. Mothers give more attention to firstborn children than to later-borns.
The changing family	Working mothers	A mother's working full-time outside the home can have both positive and negative effects on the child. There is no indication of long-term negative effects overall.
	Divorce	Family conflict seems to outweigh the family structure in its impact on the child; conflict is greatest in the first year after the divorce. A continuing ongoing positive relationship with the ex-spouse is important for the child's adjustment. Support systems are significant in the child's adaptation to divorce. Divorce is a highly stressful experience for a child of any age. Boys fare better in father-custody families, while girls are more socially competent in mother-custody families.

and mother-custody girls were rated the highest in social maturity, and father-custody girls were rated the lowest. Possible explanations for this are the importance of the child's identification with the same-sex parent, the coercive interaction that may characterize mother–son relations because boys are more aggressive than girls,

and the possibility that the child in an opposite-sex custodial situation may be pushed into adult roles too soon by substituting for the absent spouse.

Child Development Concept Table 8.1 summarizes our discussion of the role the family plays in the preschool child's development. Next, we study the nature of peer relations and play in early childhood.

PEER RELATIONS AND PLAY IN EARLY CHILDHOOD

In Chapter 6, we discussed how child psychologists now are studying peer relations in infancy more than in the past. We learned that six-month-old infants interact with each other primarily through touching, smiling, and vocalizing. In the second year of life, toys become a focus of peer interaction. Peer relations during early childhood take up an increasing amount of time. In particular, play becomes a central aspect of the child's life, and cognitive processes influence how the preschool child plays and interacts with peers.

The Nature of Peer Relations

To learn more about the nature of peer relations, we define the term *peers,* study the necessity of peers for competent social development, make cross-cultural comparisons of peers, and discuss the importance of peer relations in children's perspective taking.

The Meaning of the Term Peers

Children spend a great deal of time with their peers; many of their greatest frustrations and happiest moments come when they are with peers. The term **peers** usually refers to children who are about the same age, but children often interact with other children who are three or four years older or younger. Peers have also been described as children who interact at about the same behavioral level (Lewis & Rosenblum, 1975). Defining peers in terms of behavioral level places more emphasis on the maturity of the children than on their age. For example, consider the precociously developed 13-year-old female adolescent who feels very uncomfortable around underdeveloped girls her own age. She may well find more satisfaction in spending time with 17- or 18-year-olds than with people her own age.

The influence of children who are the same age may be quite different from that of younger or older peers. For example, mixed-age groups often produce more dominant and altruistic behavior than do groups of children of the same age. Social contacts and aggression, however, are more characteristic of same-age peers.

Willard Hartup (1976) has emphasized that same-age peer interaction serves a unique role in our culture:

> I am convinced that age grading would occur even if our schools were not age graded and children were left alone to determine the composition of their own societies. After all, one can only learn to be a good fighter among age-mates: The bigger guys will kill you, and the little ones are no challenge. Perhaps one of the most important functions of the peer group is to provide a source of information and comparison about the world outside the family. From the peer group, the child receives feedback about his or her abilities. The child evaluates what he or she does in terms of whether it is better than, as good as, or worse than what other children do. It is hard to do this at home because siblings are usually older or younger. (p. 10)

Peers and Competent Social Development

Studies about the necessity of peers for competent social development have been limited primarily to animals. For example, when peer monkeys who have been reared together are separated from one another, indications of depression and less advanced social development are observed (Suomi, Harlow, & Domek, 1970). Attempts to use peer monkeys to counteract the effects of social isolation prove more beneficial when the deprived monkeys are placed with younger peers (Suomi & Harlow, 1972). Willard Hartup (Furman, Rahe, & Hartup, 1979) is trying out the younger-peer therapeutic technique with human peer isolates in a nursery school. Initial reports indicate that the technique is as effective with humans as it has been with monkeys.

The human development literature contains a classic example of the importance of peers in social development. Anna Freud (Freud & Dann, 1951) studied six children from different families who banded together after their parents were killed in World War II. Intensive peer attachment was observed; the children were a tightly knit group, dependent on one another and aloof with outsiders. Even though deprived of parental care, they became neither delinquent nor psychotic.

Now that we have seen how peers contribute to the child's social competence, let's explore the nature of peer relations in different cultures.

Cross-Cultural Comparisons of Peer Relations

Probably no other cross-cultural work with children is more widely cited than the work of Beatrice and John Whiting. In 1954, the Whitings and their colleagues began reporting their observations of children in six different cultures. Their most recent publication is *Children of Six Cultures: A Psychocultural Analysis* (1975). For these observations, the Whitings placed six teams of anthropologists in six different cultures, five of which were primarily farming communities: northern India; the Philippines; Okinawa, Japan; Oaxaca, Mexico; and western Kenya. The sixth setting was a small, non-farming town in New England. The teams interviewed the mothers and conducted standardized observations of the children in the six cultures.

Among the most intriguing findings of the project were the consistent differences in adult–child and peer interactions across the cultures. Dependency, nurturance, and intimacy were rarely observed in peer relations but were frequently observed in adult–child interaction. By contrast, aggressiveness, prosocial activity, and sociable behavior were the most frequently occurring behaviors in peer relations across the six cultures. Such findings support the belief that there may be universal differences between adult–child and peer interactions.

Next, we study another cross-cultural investigation of peers, in this instance involving perspective taking.

Peer Relations and Perspective Taking

A research investigation that took place in Norway and Hungary provides further support for the belief that peer relations serve important developmental functions (Hollis, 1975). In this study, the main interest focused on **perspective taking,** which can be defined as the ability to take someone else's point of view (perspective). The Norwegian and Hungarian children were seven to nine years old and lived in one of three settings in each country—an isolated, dispersed farm community, a village, or a town—which varied in terms of the relative physical isolation of the children from one another.

The children were assessed on three measures of perspective taking: visual perspective taking, communication accuracy, and role taking. In the visual (spatial)

perspective-taking task, the children observed a three-dimensional display of buildings and were asked to tell what the view of the buildings would look like if the children were seated at different locations around the table on which the buildings were placed. This is the widely used Piagetian task discussed in Chapter 7 and provides an index of how egocentric a child is. The child who has advanced beyond the egocentrism of preoperational thought is able to provide a perspective of how the buildings look from other locations than where he or she is seated. Communication accuracy was assessed by telling each child a story and then having the child repeat the story to another person. Role taking was investigated by showing the child a seven-picture cartoon sequence that told an obvious story. Three pictures were then removed from the sequence and the child was told to tell the story to another person who had not seen all seven pictures.

To analyze the results, the researchers combined the scores on these measures to obtain a total perspective-taking score. As shown in Figure 8.4, in both Norway and Hungary, children from the isolated farm regions were much poorer at perspective taking than the children from the villages and towns. This suggests that children with few peers with whom to interact are poorer at perspective taking.

Now let's investigate how peer relations change over the preschool years.

The Development of Peer Relations

The frequency of peer interaction, both positive and negative, continues to increase throughout early childhood (Hartup, 1983). Although aggressive interaction and rough-and-tumble play increase, the *proportion* of aggressive exchanges to friendly interactions decreases, especially among middle-class boys. With age, children tend to abandon this immature and inefficient social interaction and acquire more mature methods of relating to peers.

Nonetheless, some children show high rates of aggressive behavior with their peers. At times, such behavior can be very disruptive in a preschool classroom.

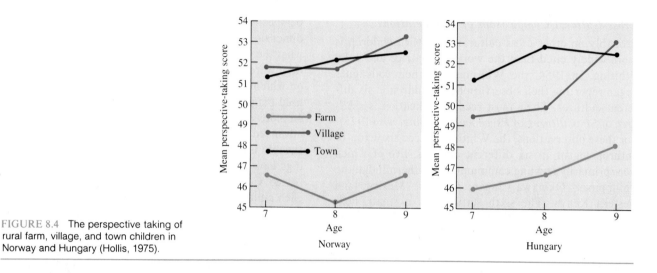

FIGURE 8.4   The perspective taking of rural farm, village, and town children in Norway and Hungary (Hollis, 1975).

If you were a teacher and a boy in your preschool classroom was engaging in extensive bouts of aggressive conduct, what would you do? And what if a girl rarely interacted with any other children during the course of virtually every day at the school? What kind of procedures might you use to change her behavior? Focus on Child Development 8.1 presents some possible solutions to improving such preschool children's behavior.

Socialization cannot be described solely in terms of the quality of social activity, however. Evidence suggests that social differentiation is also a major achievement of the maturing child. Children become more adept at using social skills, so that by the end of the preschool years, a rudimentary peer system has emerged.

As we see next, however, it is always important to keep in mind the roles that parents have in peer relations.

The Distinct but Coordinated Worlds of Parents and Peers

Peer relations are both similar to and different from parent–child relations. For example, infants touch, smile, and vocalize when they interact with both parents and other children (Eckerman, Whatley, & Kutz, 1975). However, rough-and-tumble play occurs mainly with other children and not with adults. Another difference

in children's orientation toward peers and parents is that, in times of stress, children usually move toward their parents rather than their peers (Maccoby & Masters, 1970). Willard Hartup (1979) described some of the most important ideas about the interrelation of the worlds of child–child and parent–child relations:

As children grow older, their interactions with adult associates and with child associates become more extensively differentiated: (a) Different actions are used to express affection to child associates and to adults, and (b) dominance and nurturance are directed from adults to children, but appeals and submissions are directed more frequently by children to adults than vice versa.

The evidence, then, suggests that children live in distinctive, albeit coordinate, social worlds. Family relations and peer relations constitute similar sociobehavioral contexts in some ways and different ones in others. Children may not conceive of separate normative worlds until early adolescence, because child associates are not used extensively as normative models before that time (Emmerich, Goldman, & Shore, 1971). But the family system and the peer system elicit distinctive socioemotional activity many years before these normative distinctions are made. The complex interrelations between the family and peer systems thus work themselves out over long periods of time (Hill, 1980). (pp. 947–48)

FOCUS ON CHILD DEVELOPMENT 8.1

NOSE PUNCHERS, PINCHERS, AND ISOLATES

Put yourself in this situation. You are a preschool teacher, and a boy in your classroom is showing high rates of aggressive behavior. Yesterday, he punched a classmate in the nose, and today he beat up a younger boy on the playground. What can you do?

A lot depends on the situation. What is your relationship with the boy? What are the other children like—are many of them aggressive, or is he the only major aggression problem? Would it help to work with his parents, or has his home situation deteriorated to the point where the parents are out of touch with the boy or are uncooperative? How old is he? What is his history of aggressive behavior? Are there any clues to what might have helped reduce or eliminate his aggressive actions in similar situations? Is he getting reinforcement through an increase in status or through attention from peers and from you for his hostile actions? How much and in what ways does he reinforce himself for the aggressive actions? Could he get more attention from peers and from you by performing prosocial (socially desirable) acts that may include assertive but nonhostile behavior?

To what extent are painful and aversive frustrative stimuli precipitating his aggression? Can you identify these? Can some of them be removed? If there are sudden outbursts of extreme aggression and violence with no apparent cause, a medical checkup or perhaps even a neurological examination might be considered (in unusual cases). What kinds of aggressive cues are present in the child's environment? Can some or most of them be removed or reduced? What is the subculture like in which he lives? What are his peers like?

We could ask many other questions and speculate further about sources and controls for the child's aggression. It is important, however, to recognize that the control of aggression is no easy task, that there are probably multiple causes and controls for the child's aggressions, and that, as a teacher or a parent, you alone will probably not be able to gain complete control over his aggressive actions. But you can help, and you are one of the significant social agents in the child's life; you may be able to make a difference in the child's social development by some combination of the answers to the questions asked here. The aggression should not be allowed to continue if it begins to disrupt the class.

How might a preschool teacher control this aggression?

As just mentioned, a possible contributor to the preschool child's aggression in the classroom may be that attention is given to the aggressive behavior. In one of the earliest behavior modification studies with children, a group of behaviorists looked at the possibility that the teacher's attention might be contributing to a number of children's problems in the preschool classroom (Harris, Wolf, & Baer, 1964). One boy repeatedly threw his glasses on the floor and broke them a number of times; another loved to pinch adults, including the teacher; one girl spent over 80 percent of her time on the floor; and another girl isolated herself from other children at least 85 percent of her school day. The teacher's reinforcement of desirable behaviors and the removal of her attention from undesirable ones had a powerful effect on increasing "isolate" children's interactions with peers. Researchers, however, have found that behavior modification often is more successful with withdrawn, isolated children than with children who are engaging in acting out, aggressive behaviors. While the teacher's attention may be removed from the aggressive behaviors, those behaviors may still be rewarded through peer attention.

More specifically, it has been argued by ethologists that the role of the mother is to provide a "secure" base for the child's early attachment, which in turn reduces the child's fears and promotes exploration of the environment. The reduction in fear and increase in exploratory behavior could be expected to increase the likelihood that the child would seek out age-mates with whom to play. And, while parents are not usually as good at playing with their children as children are among themselves, parents, and particularly mothers, often take an active role in monitoring their children's choice of playmates and the form of their play.

We saw in Chapter 6 that recent research supports the contention that a secure early attachment to the mother promotes positive peer relations (Matas, Arend, & Sroufe, 1978). However, Hartup (1983) cautions that it is risky to conclude that healthy parent–child relations are a prerequisite for healthy peer relations. Nonetheless, the data are consistent with the theory that the child's relationships with his or her parents serve as emotional bases for exploring and enjoying peer relations.

Peer relations provide an important context for early childhood development. As we see next, so does play.

Play

An extensive amount of time spent with peers during the preschool years involves play. Play can serve many functions for the child, and there are many different types of play. While play is a very important part of the child's social world, cognition and language serve important roles in understanding the nature of play.

Functions of Play

The functions of play include affiliation with peers, tension release, advances in cognitive development, and exploration. Play increases the likelihood that children will affiliate with one another. During this interaction, children practice the roles they will assume later in life.

Like Sigmund Freud, Erik Erikson (1950) believes that play permits the child to work off past emotions and to find imaginary relief for past frustrations. Because these tensions are relieved in play, the child (or adult) is better able to cope with problems in life and to work efficiently. Thus, psychoanalytic theorists believe that play

permits an individual to let off excess physical energy and to release pent-up tensions that he or she has repressed. On the basis of this view of play, many psychologists and psychiatrists have children engage in **play therapy.** In their opinion, play therapy not only allows the child to work off his or her frustrations but also serves as a medium through which the therapist can analyze many of the child's conflicts and methods of coping with them. It is believed that the child feels less threatened and is more likely to display his or her true feelings in the context of play.

Jean Piaget (1962) saw play as a medium that helps to advance the child's cognitive development. At the same time, he stressed that the level of cognitive development the child has attained may constrain the way in which he or she plays. Play allows children to practice their competencies and acquired skills in a relaxed, pleasurable way. According to Piaget, cognitive structures need to be used and exercised, and play provides a perfect medium for such use. For example, a young child who has just learned how to add or multiply numbers begins to play with the numbers in different ways as she perfects these operations, laughing as she does so.

Daniel Berlyne (1960) sees play as exciting and pleasurable in itself because it satisfies the exploratory drive that each person has. This drive involves curiosity and a desire for information about something new or unusual. Play serves as a means whereby children can safely explore and seek out new information—something they might not otherwise do. Play promotes this exploratory behavior by offering children the possibilities of novelty, complexity, uncertainty, surprise, and incongruity. When these elements are components of play, children can be expected to engage in more exploratory behavior. Whether the objects or situations involved in play have these properties depends on the child's age and his or her prior experience with those objects. Play with a squeaking ball, for example, may hold the element of novelty for a 4-month-old but not for a 10-month-old, who has played with such toys often.

Play is an elusive concept. It can range from an infant's simple exercise of a newfound sensorimotor talent to a preschool child's riding a tricycle to an older child's participation in organized games. One expert on play and games has observed that there is no universally accepted definition of play, probably because it can encompass so many different kinds of activities (Sutton-Smith, 1973).

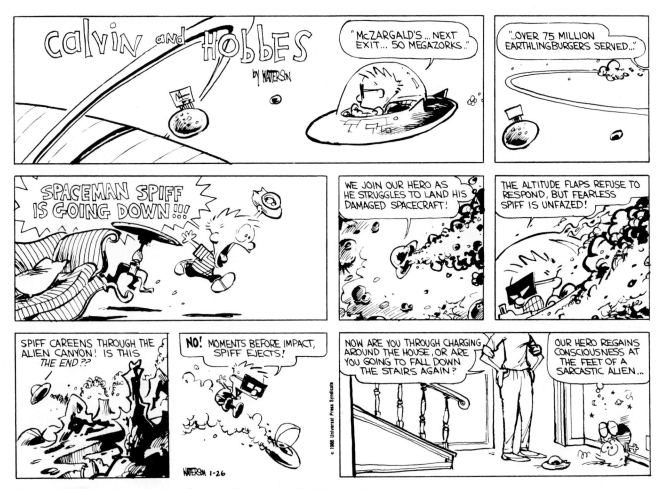

Types of Play

One of the most elaborate attempts to examine developmental changes in children's social play was conducted many years ago by Mildred Parten (1932). She developed the following categories of play, based on observations of children in free play at nursery school:

Unoccupied The child is not engaging in play as it is commonly understood. He or she may stand in one spot, look around the room, or perform random movements that seem to have no goal. In most nursery schools, **unoccupied play** is less frequent than other types of play.

Solitary The child plays alone and independently of those around him or her. The child seems engrossed in what he or she is doing and does not care much about anything else that is going on. Parten found that two- and three-year-olds engage more frequently in **solitary play** than older preschoolers do.

Onlooker The child watches other children playing. He or she may talk with them or ask them questions but does not enter into their play behavior. The child's active interest in other children's play distinguishes this **onlooker play** from unoccupied play.

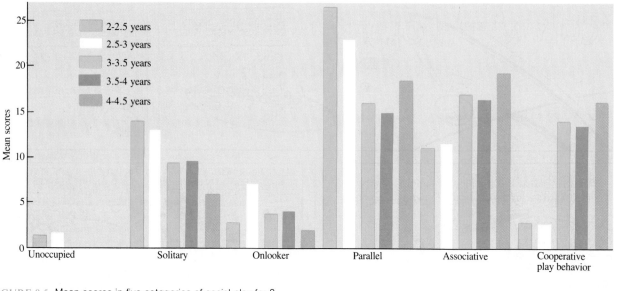

FIGURE 8.5 Mean scores in five categories of social play for 2-, 3-, and 4-year-olds.

Parallel The child plays alone, but with toys like those that other children are using or in a manner that mimics the behavior of other playing children. The older the child, the less frequently he or she engages in this type of play; even older preschool children, however, engage in **parallel play** relatively often.

Associative Social interaction with little or no organization is involved in **associative play.** Children engage in play activities similar to those of other children; however, they appear to be more interested in being associated with one another than in the tasks they are involved with. Borrowing or lending toys and materials and following or leading one another in a line are examples of associative play. Each child plays as he or she wishes; there is no effort to place the group first and himself or herself last.

Cooperative Social interaction in a group with a sense of group identity and organized activity characterizes **cooperative play.** Children's formal games, competition aimed at winning something, and groups formed by the teacher for doing things together usually are examples of this type of play. Cooperative play is the prototype for the games of middle childhood; little of it is seen in the preschool years.

Parten's research on developmental changes in play was conducted more than 50 years ago. To determine whether her findings are now out-of-date, Keith Barnes (1971) observed a group of preschoolers, using Parten's categories of play. He watched the children's activities during an hour-long free-play period each school day for 12 weeks. He found that children in the 1970s did not engage in as much associative or cooperative play as they did in the 1930s. Barnes advanced several reasons to explain this difference: (1) children have become more passive because of television viewing; (2) toys today are more abundant and attractive than they were 40 years ago, so solitary play may be more natural; and (3) parents today may encourage children to play by themselves more than parents did years ago.

The developmental changes in social play that were observed by Parten were also observed by Barnes (Hartup, 1976). That is, three-year-old children engaged in solitary and parallel play more than five-year-old children did, and five-year-old children engaged more frequently in cooperative and associative play than in other kinds of play (see Figure 8.5).

During the preschool years, peer interaction may involve highly ritualized social interchanges. **A ritual** is a form of spontaneous play that involves controlled repetition. These interchanges have been referred to as *turns* and *rounds* by Catherine Garvey (1977). The contribution of each child is called a turn, while the total sequence of alternating turns constitutes a round. The following is an example of a round between two five-year-olds (Garvey, 1977):

Boy: Can you carry this?
Girl: Yeah, if I weighed 50 pounds.
Boy: You can't even carry it.
Ritual
Boy: Can you carry it by the string?
Girl: Yeah. Yes, I can. (lifts toy fish overhead by string)
Boy: Can you carry it by the eye?
Girl: (carries it by eye)
Boy: Can you carry it by the nose?
Girl: Where's the nose?
Boy: That yellow one.
Girl: This? (carries it by nose)
Ritual
Boy: Can you carry it by its tail?
Girl: Yeah. (carries it by tail)
Boy: Can you carry it by its fur?
Girl: (carries it by fur)
Boy: Can you carry it by its body?
Girl: (carries it by body)
Boy: Can you carry it like this? (shows how to carry it by fin)
Girl: (carries it by fin)
Boy: Right.
Girl: I weigh 50 pounds almost, right?
(pp. 118–19)

In this ritual between a boy and girl, both language and motion were involved. The boy's turns were verbal; the girl's were mainly variations of picking up and carrying the object. In Garvey's (1977) work, there was a tendency for the five-year-old children to engage in more complex rituals than younger children, but three-year-old children were more likely to participate in longer rituals than their older counterparts. For example, a ritual between three-year-olds might involve the sequence "You're a girl."—"No, I'm not." repeated for as long as several minutes. As children become older and enter the elementary school years, rituals may become more formal and be found in games like Red Rover and London Bridge.

Now that we have studied the functions of play and different forms of play, we focus on the type of play that is symbolic in nature—pretend play.

Pretend Play

When children engage in **pretend play,** they have transformed the physical environment into a symbol (Fein, 1975). Make-believe play appears rather abruptly in the toddler's development, at about 18 months of age, continues to develop between ages three and four, peaks between ages five and six, and then declines. In the early elementary school years, children's interests begin to shift to games.

In pretend play, children try out many different roles—they may be the mother, the father, the teacher, the next-door neighbor, and so forth. Sometimes, their pretend play reflects an adult role; at other times, it may make fun of it. Here is one example of pretend play:

Harvey was playing with Karen, his twin sister. Karen began to push the carriage. Harvey said, "Let me be the baby, Karen," and started to talk like a baby. He got into the carriage. Karen pushed him around the room as he squinted his eyes and cried. She stopped the carriage, patted his shoulder, saying, "Don't cry, baby." He squirmed around, put his thumb in his mouth, and swayed his body.

Josie came to the carriage and wanted to push Harvey. He jumped out and hit her in the face. She walked away almost crying. He went to her, put his arm around her, and said, in a sympathetic manner, "Come, you be the baby. I'll push you in the carriage." She climbed in. He ran and got the dog and gave it to her saying, "Here, baby." She smiled and began to play with the dog. He went to the housekeeping corner, got a cup, and held it to her mouth. He smacked his lips, looking at her, smiling. He pushed her around in the carriage. Karen ran to him and said, "Harvey, let me push the carriage. I'll be the mamma, you be the daddy." Harvey said, "O.K.," and reached his hand in his pocket and gave her money. He said, "Bye, baby," waving his hand. (Hartley, Frank, & Goldenson, 1952, pp. 70–72)

You probably can remember many episodes of pretend play from your own childhood—playing doctor, teacher, and so on. As you think about your early childhood years, play is probably one of the predominant things you remember. Further information about pretend play and the role of cognitive development in such play appears in Focus on Child Development 8.2.

FOCUS ON CHILD DEVELOPMENT 8.2

THE SYMBOLIC WORLD OF CHILDREN'S PLAY

Piaget believed that play is an important aspect of sensori-motor development in infancy. For example, Piaget argued that play is evident when infants repeat acts that are satisfying. Acts such as banging, mouthing, and waving are examples of such play behaviors in infancy. During the second year of life, infants are more likely to play with objects in the manner in which the objects are used in daily life. Accompanying this play is an increase in the amount of pretense involved. For example, between 14 and 19 months of age, there is an increase in the use of realistic objects in pretend play (Fein & Apfel, 1979); between 19 and 24 months, there is an increase in the use of a substitute object, such as a block for a doll (Ungerer, Zelazo, Kearsley, & O'Leary, 1981). By 24 months, 75 percent of the infants in one investigation showed substitution behavior (Watson & Fischer, 1977).

During the preschool years, most children become pre-operational thinkers, according to Piaget's framework. It has been suggested that pretend play becomes more and more social with age, at least up to the elementary school years. For example, Piaget (1962) saw symbolic play as solitary through the first two years of life. He also indicated that, by the concrete operational period, at about seven years of age, pretend play declines and is replaced by games with rules.

Research designed to evaluate such claims as those made by Piaget has often involved the observation of children during free play in familiar surroundings. A typical strategy was followed by Kenneth Rubin (1977, 1982), who coded play behavior in terms of the following categories: (1) functional or sensorimotor play (which includes simple, repetitive muscular activities with or without objects); (2) constructive play (the manipulation of objects to construct something); (3) dramatic or pretense play; and (4) games-with-rules (in which the child accepts prearranged rules and adjusts his or

What are some of the characteristics of the symbolic world of children's play?

her behavior to the rules). When these four categories were recorded, each was further subdivided in terms of social context. Did the play occur when the child was alone (solitary—functional play), when the child was in close proximity but not interacting with others (parallel—functional play), or when playing with others in joint activity (group—games-with-rules)?

For the most part, research following this strategy does document the belief that the portion of pretend play to other play types increases with age from three years up to approximately six to seven years of age (Rubin, Fein, & Vandenberg, 1983). More precisely, interactive pretend play increases with age during the preschool years, then decreases somewhat at the beginning of the elementary school years. However, the frequency of solitary pretend play actually decreases during the preschool years, but then increases in the late preschool or early elementary school years. This increase in solitary pretend play may come about as a result of the practice of social games-with-rules, which often emerges at about six years of age. For example, when away from the group, the child may practice and consolidate the skills required to participate effectively in group game circumstances.

Several other comments about the increase in pretend play that characterizes the preschool years provide further illumination of the importance of cognitive development in play. The language development of preschool children undoubtedly is involved in their increase in pretend play. As they become more proficient at using language, preschool children use words in creative ways as they generate a world of fantasy. It is also at this time, the preschool period, that children often develop imaginary companions or playmates. As preschool children construct a play world that is highly symbolic in nature, from Piaget's perspective, they are practicing their cognitive skills in a relaxed, nonthreatening atmosphere. From the cognitive developmental perspective, then, play is an important context for the growth of cognitive skills.

The increased research interest in cognitive changes involved in symbolic play is part of the new look in research on play. Let's now explore this new look in more detail.

New Directions in Research on Children's Play

In recent years, play has been given considerable research attention in an effort to understand the nature of children's development. In particular, there has been a keen interest in how play is assessed, as well as in the interface of cognition and play and the interface of language and play.

Play and Its Assessment   If norms for the development of play could be worked out and appropriate measures developed to assess those norms, an important addition to diagnosing normal and abnormal development could be achieved. If Piaget and Freud were correct, then play represents a window to the child's mind. Play may be an important index of the child's socioemotional and intellectual status. Thus, play can be an important addition or alternative to formal testing procedures administered to children, particularly those who are very young or severely impaired. Until recently, play assessment has been somewhat informal, lacking the rigor necessary for such evaluation. However, some signs of measures with psychometric respectability are emerging (e.g., Enslein & Fein, 1981; Roper & Hinde, 1978).

If valid assessment measures of play are to be developed, three problems must be solved. First, the elusive definition of play must be pinned down more precisely. Second, children's play is sensitive to ecological or contextual variation; thus, standardized settings need to be formulated to allow replication of assessment to be high. Third, interpretation of children's play content must be agreed upon by observers. For instance, when a child is aggressive while being observed during the assessment, does the aggression involve imitation, does it consist of a characteristic response style, or is it a cathartic release of inhibited impulses? Interpretation could be facilitated by supplementing standardized setting information with data from observations in natural settings, parental reports of play at home, and child interviews that probe for the child's motivation.

Not only are researchers who study play intrigued by how play can be measured more precisely, but they also are fascinated by the inner cognitive world of play.

Play and Cognition   There are two main directions of contemporary research on play and cognition. The first concerns the extent to which play can be used as an index of the child's cognitive or intellectual status. The second concerns the nature of children's cognitions about play.

Several standardized procedures have been developed to measure the cognitive complexity of the child's play (Belsky & Most, 1981; Fein, 1975; Nicolich, 1977; Rosenblatt, 1977; Watson & Fischer, 1980). Such procedures permit the investigator to infer cognitive competencies from observations of play. These procedures have also precipitated the reformulation of age norms for the onset of cognitive competencies associated with play (Rubin & Pepler, 1980). In particular, the assessment of cognitive competencies through play has underscored the importance of not overloading the child with complicated instructions and not relying too heavily on verbal reports. For example, it has been found that children's conception of roles is more complex and is reasoned about at a higher level when assessed through formal, but simple, nonverbal play measures than when assessed via observations of spontaneous play (Watson & Fischer, 1980).

Researchers in child development have also become increasingly intrigued by children's thoughts about play. For example, in one investigation, children from 5 to 11 years of age were asked whether they could pretend to be a doctor, mother/father, teacher, friend, or the interviewer. At five years of age, virtually all of the children said that they could enact the roles of doctor, parent, and teacher but could not be the friend or interviewer. Also, young children were found to comment about props (e.g., costumes) when enacting roles, while older children were more likely to refer to actions carried out by the pretense target. In addition, younger children were more likely to use toys as part of their description of pretend play than were older children (Chaillé, 1978). These findings suggest a move from material to nonmaterial or ideational conceptions of pretend play as children develop (see Figure 8.6).

Play and Language   There has also been increased research interest in the interface of symbolic play and language. While theorists have stressed for some time that early pretend play and early language development have some common dimensions or have some influence on each other (Piaget, 1962; Vygotsky, 1978; Werner & Kaplan, 1963), only recently has this intersection been the focus of actual research. In particular, the research has been dominated by Piaget's belief that pretend play signals the beginning of representational thinking and the appearance of a special function (called the **semiotic function**) that overlays meaning on sound patterns, gestures, or images. For both Piaget and Vygotsky, the main issue focuses on the child's awareness that one thing can signify something else, even when the something else is not present.

So far, researchers have not been able to provide convincing data that pretend play is either a prerequisite for language development or cognitive abilities, a concurrent achievement, or a consequence of having developed such abilities. It may be, as Kurt Fischer (1980) has noted, that precise correspondence between play and language and play and cognition is unlikely since development usually does not unfold evenly across different task domains. Future research in this area, however, should illuminate more precisely the line between play and language and play and cognition.

Our discussion of the preschool child's world has focused heavily on families, peers, and play. And in Chapter 7, we found that preschool education is an important part of this world as well. Now, however, we turn our attention to an influence on the young child that has come about only in the last half of the 20th century. In a very short time span, however, it has assumed a prominent place in our effort to understand children's socialization.

TELEVISION

Few developments in society over the last 25 years have had greater impact on children than television has. Many children spend more time in front of the television set than they do with their parents. Although only one of the vehicles of the mass media that affect children's behavior—books, comic books, movies, and newspapers also have some impact—television is the most influential.

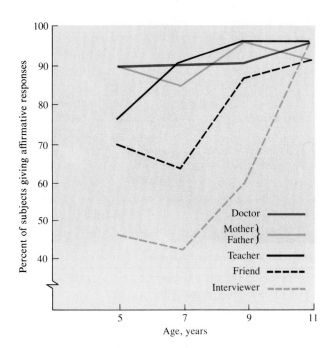
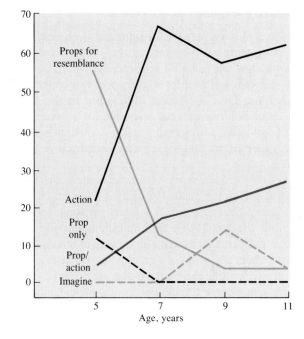

FIGURE 8.6 Affirmative responses to the question 'Can you pretend to be *someone else?*' by age and item, in percentages. Responses by category to the question 'Can you pretend to be a *mother/father?*' by age, in percentages.

Functions of Television

Television has been called a lot of things, not all of them good. Depending on one's point of view, it may be a "window on the world," "the one-eyed monster," or "the boob tube." Television has been attacked as one of the reasons that scores on national achievement tests in reading and mathematics are lower now than they have been in the past. Television, it is claimed, attracts children away from books and schoolwork. Furthermore, it is argued that television trains the child to become a passive learner; rarely, if ever, does television call for active responses from the observer.

Television also is said to deceive; that is, it teaches children that problems are easily resolved and that everything always comes out right in the end. For example, it usually takes only from 30 to 90 minutes for detectives to sort through a complex array of clues and discover the killer—and they always find the killer. Violence is pictured as a way of life in many shows. It is

all right for police to use violence and to break moral codes in their fight against evildoers. And the lasting results of violence are rarely brought home to the viewer. A person who is injured appears to suffer for only a few seconds, even though in real life a person with such an injury may not recover for several weeks or months or perhaps not at all. Yet, one out of every two first-grade children says that the adults on television are like adults in real life (Lyle & Hoffman, 1972).

However, there are some possible positive aspects to television's influence on children as well. For one, television presents the child with a world that is often different than the one in which he or she lives. This means that, through television, the child is exposed to a wider variety of views and knowledge than may be the case when the child is informed only by his or her parents, teachers, and peers.

Children's Exposure to Television

Children watch a lot of television, and they seem to be watching more all the time. In the 1950s, three-year-olds watched television for less than one hour a day, and five-year-olds watched for slightly over two hours a day (Schramm, Lyle, & Parker, 1961). But in the 1970s, preschool children watched television for an average of four hours a day, and elementary school children watched for as long as six hours each day (Friedrich & Stein, 1973).

According to one major commercial television ratings service, during the 1980–1981 viewing season, children ages 2 to 5 years viewed 27.8 hours per week (Nielson Television Index, 1981). Both questionnaire and diary studies indicate that systematic viewing of television begins at about 2½ years of age, rapidly increases during the preschool and early school-age years, and declines during adolescence (Anderson, Lorch, Field, Collins, & Nathan, 1985). A number of investigations have directly observed television viewing behavior in the laboratory (e.g., Anderson, Lorch, Smith, Bradford, & Levin, 1981; Field & Anderson, in press; Sporull, 1973; Huston & Wright, 1983). The evidence suggests that visual attention to television dramatically rises over the preschool years.

Researchers have begun to observe the television viewing behavior of children in the naturalistic context of their home (Allen, 1965; Anderson, Lorch, Field, Collins, & Nathan, 1985; Bechtel, Achelpohl, & Akers, 1972). In the Anderson, Lorch, Field, Collins, & Nathan (1985) study, an elaborate assessment involved the use of several video cameras and a time-lapse video recorder. A full-screen image of the viewing room was recorded in every frame. Diaries were filled out in conjunction with the videotaping of television viewing behavior. Ninety-nine families with a total of 460 persons were observed, and time sample analyses of 4,672 hours of recordings were analyzed. The most important finding in this elaborate evaluation of children's television viewing behavior was verification of the dramatic increase in visual attention to the television during the preschool years (see Figure 8.7).

How much television do children watch?

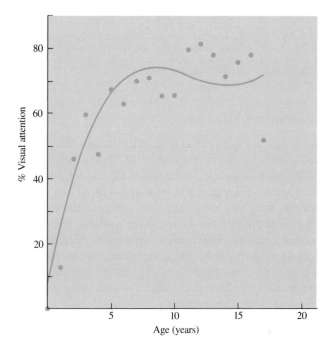

FIGURE 8.7 Increase in visual attention to TV during the preschool years.

"Mrs. Horton, could you stop by school today?"

© 1981 Martha F. Campbell.

An additional important point is made by Daniel Anderson and his colleagues—children spent about a third of their time with television not looking at the television. Children not only left the viewing room and returned in the middle of programs, but they also played with toys, other children, read, and interacted with their parents. Thus, surveys and diaries filled out about number of hours spent watching television may substantially overestimate the amount of time actually spent looking at the television set.

It also is instructive to investigate children's exposure to media other than television. According to Aletha Stein (1972), other than television, the only medium reaching large portions of children in the United States is books. Children also read comic books, magazines, and some newspaper comic strips; they go to movies; and they listen to the radio and to their records and tapes. Television, comic books, movies, and comic strips can be thought of as pictorial media; the children who use one of these pictorial media regularly tend to use the others also. But children who frequently use pictorial media are not nec-

essarily frequent consumers of the printed media, such as books and the written, nonpictorial parts of newspapers and magazines (Greenberg & Domonick, 1969). Their use of the pictorial media increases until they are about 12, after which time it declines. Children from low-income backgrounds use pictorial media more than children from middle-income homes do, and black children are exposed to pictorial media more than white children are (Schramm, Lyle, & Parker, 1961).

Of particular concern has been the extent to which children are exposed to violence and aggression on television. Up to 80 percent of the prime-time shows include such violent acts as beatings, shootings, or stabbings. And there are usually about five of these violent acts per hour on prime-time shows. The frequency of violence is even greater on the Saturday morning cartoon shows, where there is an average of more than 25 violent episodes per hour.

Children, then, watch large doses of television. Can such large doses make television function like a social agent for children?

The Role of Television as a Social Agent

Television can influence a wide variety of children's social behaviors. To what extent does television violence contribute to children's aggression? Can positive, prosocial behaviors be increased by watching television shows emphasizing altruism, caring, and consideration for others? And what is the nature of the social context in which young children view television?

Aggression

Television violence contributes to antisocial behavior in children, particularly aggression toward other children. Let's look at one example that demonstrates this fact clearly. One group of children was exposed to cartoons of the violent Saturday morning type; another group was shown the same cartoons with the violence removed. Children who saw the violent cartoons later kicked, choked, and pushed their friends more than children did who saw the same cartoons without the violent acts (Steuer, Applefield, & Smith, 1971).

Prosocial Behavior

Television can also teach children that it is better to behave in prosocial rather than antisocial ways. Aimee Leifer (1973) has demonstrated how television can instill prosocial behaviors in young children. From the television show "Sesame Street," she selected a number of episodes that reflected positive social interchanges. She was particularly interested in situations that taught the child how to use his or her social skills. For example, in one exchange, two men were fighting over the amount of space available to them; they gradually began to cooperate and to share the space. Children who watched these episodes copied these behaviors and in later social situations applied the lessons they had learned.

Now that we have seen how much television is watched and how television influences social behavior, let's examine the context in which children watch television.

The Social Context of Viewing Television

It is important to evaluate television-viewing patterns in the context of parental and peer influences. For example, one survey indicated that parents rarely discuss the content of television shows with their children (Leifer, Gordon, & Graves, 1974). In studying the home environment of children's television viewing, the age period of 2½ to 6 seems to be an important formative period for television viewing habits. In one investigation, families kept a one-week diary of television viewing for each family member (Huston, Seigle, & Bremer, 1983). A home interview was conducted prior to the diary week to obtain information about various child and family characteristics. Although parents with higher occupational status and more education had children who watched less television than their lower socioeconomic status counterparts, maternal employment was not linked with young children's television viewing. Low viewing time was characteristic of children who attended preschool and day care. Furthermore, children with younger siblings watched television more than those with older siblings, possibly because they were at home more. Mothers of those with high viewing time reported more arguments about television rules and discussions about television content than did mothers of those with low

viewing time. Maternal regulation of television watching was only related to low viewing for the five-year-olds. At age five, boys watched more television than girls, and children who used books and the printed media watched less than those who did not. Such looks into the social contexts of children's behavior provide a clearer picture of how social processes influence children's development.

Earlier, we saw that television influences aggressive and prosocial behavior. Let's now evaluate whether it can influence children's eating behavior.

Commercials

When we watch television, we are exposed to commercials as well as regular programming. For example, the average television-viewing child sees more than 20,000 commercials per year! A significant portion of the commercials shown during children's television shows involve food products that are high in sugar (Barcus, 1978). To investigate the effects of television food commercials and pronutritional public service announcements on children's snack choices, Joann Galst (1980) exposed three- to six-year-old children to television cartoons over a four-week period. The advertising content of the shows consisted of either commercials for food products with added sugar, food products with no added sugar, or pronutritional public service announcements, with or without adult comments about the portrayed product. As shown in Table 8.1, the most effective treatment in reducing the child's selection of snacks with added sugar was exposure to commercials for food products without added sugar and pronutritional public service announcements with accompanying positive comments by an adult.

We have studied a number of features of television and their influence on many aspects of children's lives, but we need to consider one final set of features—those that are formal.

Formal Features of Television

There is increasing interest in studying how the formal features of television affect children's understanding of the content of television shows (Calvert, Huston, Watkins, & Wright, 1982; Wright & Huston, 1985). Such

Table 8.1   Average Proportion of Snacks With Added Sugar Selected During Four Weeks of Experimental Intervention

Intervention Week	Condition				
	S-NC	NS-NC	S-C	NS-C	CT
3	.86	.88	.80	.71	.90
4	.74	.80	.73	.58	.84
5	.77	.86	.76	.68	.87
6	.83	.81	.83	.71	.88

Note: S-NC   Commercials for food products with added sugar viewed without adult commentary
NS-NC   No sugar added and public service announcement without adult commentary
S-C   Sugar added and adult commentary
NS-C   No sugar added and pronutritional public service announcement with adult commentary
CT   The control condition, in which children had no television exposure
From Galst, J. P., "Television food commercials and pro-nutritional public service announcements as determinants of young children's snack choices" in *Child Development*, 51, 935–938, 1980. © 1980 by The Society for Research in Child Development. Reprinted by permission.

formal features include animation, movement, pace, visual techniques (like fades and special effects), and auditory features (such as music and sound effects). In particular, this research has been tied closely to the information processing model of cognition. For example, initial research focused on the relation of form to children's attention but more recently has emphasized the informational functions of formal features. John Wright and Aletha Huston (1985) stress that form can affect what aspects of a content message are processed and can influence how actively the child engages in such processing.

Children learn rather early in their development that certain formal features of television programs index certain kinds of content. Animation, unusual voices, and sound effects often are associated with child-oriented content. Such features attempt to make the message funny and comprehensible. By contrast, adult male voices, low action, and talking heads are associated with adult-oriented content, which is uninteresting and incomprehensible. Dan Anderson (e.g., Anderson & Lorch, 1983) has argued that the association of specific formal features with comprehensible or incomprehensible content is one reason children attend differently to these features. The research of John Wright, Aletha Huston, and their colleagues has expanded Anderson's work to reveal how formal features index entertainment value, humor, and interest level, as well as comprehensibility.

Formal features of television programming that signal child-oriented content not only enhance children's attention, but they increase the likelihood that children will process the content more actively and, it is hoped, learn the content more thoroughly. One investigation clearly revealed this process (Campbell, Wright, & Huston, 1983). Two parallel sets of public service announcements containing nutritional information were developed. The content of the two announcements was virtually identical, but the forms were different. One set was produced with child-oriented forms—animation, character voices, and lively music. The second set was made with adult-oriented forms—live photography, adult male narration, and soft music. Five- and six-year-old children attended more to the child-oriented than the adult-oriented version. And children recalled more of the content of the child-oriented version, regardless of how difficult the message was. The implication is that the form of television shows can lure children into doing some cognitive work when the forms signal that the content is age-appropriate, interesting, comprehensible, or in some other ways worth some mental effort (Wright & Huston, 1985).

Child Development Concept Table 8.2 summarizes our discussion of the child's peer world, play, and television. Next, we continue our study of young children's social and personality development as we explore various dimensions of personality.

Child Development Concept Table 8.2   Peers, Play, and Television

Concept	Processes/Related Ideas	Characteristics/Description
Peers	The nature of peer relations	Peers are very powerful social agents. The term *peers* refers to children who are about the same age or who act at about the same behavioral level. Peers provide a source of information and social comparison about the world outside the family. Peers have been shown to have an important influence on the child's development of socially competent behavior. Cross-cultural comparisons of peer relations suggest that aggressiveness, prosocial activity, and sociable behavior are more likely in peer than in parent–child relations. Peer relations also play an important role in perspective taking.
	The development of peer relations	The frequency of peer interaction, both positive and negative, increases during the preschool years. By the end of the preschool years, a rudimentary peer system has emerged.
	The distinct but coordinated worlds of parents and peers	Peer relations are both similar to and different from family relations. Children touch, smile, and vocalize while they interact with parents and peers. However, rough-and-tumble play occurs mainly with peers. In times of stress, children generally seek out their parents rather than their peers. Peers and parents live in distinct but coordinated worlds. Healthy family relations often promote healthy peer relations.
Play	Functions of play	The functions of play include affiliation with peers, tension release, advances in cognitive development, and exploration.
	Types of play	Unoccupied, solitary, onlooker, parallel, associative, and cooperative play are among the most characteristic play styles. A ritual is a form of play that involves controlled repetition. One of the most enjoyable forms of play in early childhood is pretend play, in which the child transforms the physical environment into a symbol.
	New directions in play research	Three new directions in play research involve: (1) better ways to assess play, (2) the interface of cognition and play, and (3) the role of language in play.
Television	Functions of television	The basic functions of television are to provide information and entertainment. Television provides a portrayal of the world beyond the family, teachers, and peers. However, television may train children to become passive learners, may be deceiving, and often takes children away from reading or studying.
	Children's exposure to television	Children watch huge amounts of television, with preschool children watching about four hours a day. Up to 80 percent of prime-time shows have violent episodes. Visual attention to television dramatically increases during the preschool years. Videotaped naturalistic observations of children's television viewing, however, suggest that time spent actually looking at the television is far less than surveys might suggest.
	Television as a social agent	Television influences children's aggression and prosocial behaviors. Parents rarely monitor or discuss the content of children's television viewing. Children who read books watch less television than those who don't.
	Commercials	The average television-viewing child sees more than 20,000 commercials per year! Commercials seem to influence children's food preferences.
	Formal features of television	Children's attention and memory are influenced by the formal features of television programming, such as animation, movement, pace, visual techniques, and auditory features.

THE SELF, SEX ROLES, AND MORAL DEVELOPMENT IN EARLY CHILDHOOD

In this section, we examine the continuing development of the self, the development of sex roles, and the emergence of moral development during the early childhood years.

The Self

We saw in Chapter 6 that, toward the end of the second year of life, the child develops a sense of self. Here, we make a distinction between the self as knower and as the object of what is known and chart the development of self during the early childhood years.

"I" and "Me"

Most scholars who have devoted thoughtful attention to understanding the self have concluded that two distinct but closely intertwined aspects of self exist (Harter, 1983). Such a distinction was made very early in psychology by William James (1890/1963), who described the "I" as knower in contrast to the "me" as aggregate of things objectively known. More recently, Ruth Wylie (1979) has continued the distinction between "I" and "me" in understanding the self. She contrasts the self as active agent or process with the self as the object of one's knowledge and evaluation. The "I," then, is the active observer, while the "me" is the observed (that is, the product of the observing process when attention to the self occurs). However, most research attention has been given to the self as an object of one's knowledge and evaluation, as indicated by the many studies of children's self-concept and self-esteem (Wylie, 1979). As we see next, self-concept and self-esteem are viewed as objects of one's knowledge in this categorization of the self.

Self-Concept and Self-Esteem   While early in the history of psychology, William James showed a strong interest in the self, during the 20th century, the psychologists most interested in the self have followed the tradition of **humanism,** which places a strong emphasis on the role of the self and self-concept as central to understanding the child's development (Maslow, 1970; Rogers, 1951). The humanistic approaches have little scientific credibility. Indeed, the humanists believe that

How do we differentiate "I" and "me" in self-development?

scientific approaches keep the investigator from learning the most important facts about the child's existence—his or her uniqueness as a person and creative potential, for instance. In this regard, the humanists believe that science is too concerned with general principles that are common to all children, rather than the unique nature of each child. Humanists also believe that, to understand the child, it is necessary to grasp the essence of the child's global self. In particular, they believe that the child's **global self-concept,** how he or she generally perceives himself or herself, is a key organizing principle of personality.

Theorists such as the humanists, who advocate the importance of perceptions such as self-concept, are taking a **phenomenological approach** to the study of children's development. That is, the child's perception of the world is more important in understanding his or her development than is his or her actual behavior. From this view, reality exists as the perceptions of the child, not in the child's actual behavior. This approach to the child directly conflicts with the behavioral approach, which advocates that the key ingredients of the child's development are his or her behaviors, not perceptions of behavior.

One recent study of parenting practices and the self-esteem of preschool children revealed the importance of the consistency of parenting and the sensitivity of the parents to the young child's signals (Burkett, 1985). In particular, the parents' respect for their children as individuals separate from them and as having their own needs were the best predictors of the preschool child's self-esteem.

Now that we have studied the self as the object of what is known, let's evaluate the self as knower.

The Self as Knower   A number of contemporary researchers are beginning to develop insight into the **self as knower** (Broughton, 1981; Dickstein, 1977; Gergen, in press; Greenwald & Pratkanis, in press; Harter, 1983; Lapsley & Quintana, 1985; Lewis & Brooks-Gunn, 1979). The interest is in crafting an account of the self that not only encompasses the self as object of knowledge, attention, and evaluation, but one that also includes the self as an active observing process. Thus, there is interest in combining "I" and "me" into a common theoretical account of the self. One of the first steps is to establish the domain of the self as knower. The approach in contemporary psychology that offers the most help in such a project is information processing (Lapsley & Quintana, 1985).

One area of interest that is emerging in the investigation of the self as knower is memory development. Two aspects of memory thought to reflect the self as knower are self-generation and self-reference. Self-generation describes instances when information that is self-generated is more easily retrieved and recalled than information that is passively encountered (Bobrow & Bower, 1969; Jacoby, 1978). For instance, individuals are more likely to recall their own contributions to a discussion of a controversial topic than the inputs of others (Greenwald & Albert, 1968).

Self-reference refers to the efficient retrieval of information encoded in terms of the self as opposed to information not self-encoded. There is a clear indication in a number of memory studies that individuals are more likely to remember information that is encoded about the self than information that is not self-referenced (Markus, 1977; Rogers, 1981). For example, in one

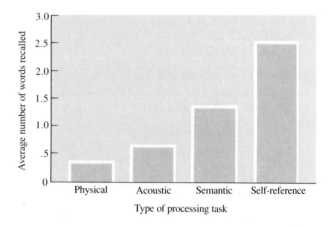

FIGURE 8.8   Number of words recalled as a function of type of processing.

investigation, individuals were given either physical, acoustic, or semantic-meaning kinds of tasks. Another group of people were asked whether a particular word could be related to themselves. As suggested by Figure 8.8, self-reference was the most effective strategy. For example, if the word *win* were on the list, they might think of the time they won a bicycle race, and if the word *cook* appeared, they might image the last time they cooked dinner (Rogers, Kuiper, & Kirker, 1977).

An important developmental implication from research on memory for understanding the self as knower is the rather consistent finding that young children do not spontaneously use encoding and retrieval strategies (e.g., Flavell, Beach, & Chinsky, 1966; Siegler, 1983). The weak performance of young children on memory tasks may be due to a production deficiency; that is, they may not know how or when to use appropriate memory strategies, although they often can be taught such strategies. Thus, we would not anticipate that young children would encode to-be-remembered information with reference to the self (self-reference) or to construct information in a way that would help retrieval (self-generation). For instance, young children do not always produce their own elaborations of to-be-remembered information (Pressley, 1982). However, when the children are provided elaboration by the experimenter, or are given an encoding or retrieval strategy, their memory improves (Levin, 1976). Older children, however, are much better when they generate their own strategies than when they use strategies provided by the experimenter (Pressley, 1982; Siegler, 1983). One possibility is that developmental differences in strategy use by children reflect the differential availability of a self schema for organizing memory input (Lapsley & Quintana, 1985).

As we see next, two important developmental changes in the self during the early childhood years are an emerging sense of a private, inner self and a description of the self in terms of external characteristics.

The Emerging Sense of a Private, Inner Self   Investigators such as John Flavell (Flavell, Shipstead, & Croft, 1978) have found that children as young as three years of age have a basic idea that they have a private self to which others do not have access. Flavell reports the following exchange between an experimenter and a three-year-old:

> (Can I see you thinking?) "No." (Even if I look in your eyes, do I see you thinking?) "No." (Why not?) "Cause I don't have any big holes." (You mean there would have to be a hole there for me to see you thinking?) Child nods. (p. 16)

Another child said that the experimenter could not see his thinking processes because he had skin over his head.

Young children also distinguish this inner self from their bodily self or outer self, a distinction that seems to emerge sometime between three and four years of age. After they have developed an understanding that they have a private self, children then set about the task of defining the characteristics of their private self.

Describing the Self's External Characteristics   Even though preschool children begin to detect that they have a private inner self, they nonetheless, when asked to describe themselves, present a self-portrait focused on external characteristics. During early childhood, children describe themselves in terms of how they look, where they live, and what activities they are involved in. It is not until about six to seven years of age that children begin to describe themselves more in terms of psychological traits, such as how they feel, their personality characteristics, and their relationships with others.

An important part of the self in childhood is that aspect of development called sex roles. Whether children are boys or girls, and how they view their roles as male and female are key ingredients of personality.

Sex Roles

Each of us is curious about his or her sex. Even during the preschool years, children are curious about how girls are different than boys. In this section, we consider the biological and cognitive underpinnings of sex-role development, discuss a number of environmental contributions to sex roles, and conclude with a portrayal of the developmental unfolding of sex roles in the early years of childhood.

Biological Influences

One of Freud's basic assumptions is that human behavior and history are directly related to reproductive processes. From this assumption arises the belief that sexuality is essentially unlearned and *instinctual*. Erik Erikson (1950) has extended this argument, claiming that psychological differences in males and females stem from anatomical differences between the two groups. Erikson argues that, because of genital structure, males are more intrusive and aggressive, while females are more inclusive and passive. Erikson's belief is sometimes referred to as the "anatomy is destiny" doctrine.

One period during which sex hormones are produced extensively is before birth. Anna Ehrhardt has extensively studied the influence of prenatal hormonal changes on sex-role development (Ehrhardt & Baker, 1973). In the 1950s, a number of expectant mothers were given doses of androgen (a male sex hormone); these women had a history of miscarriage, and the hormone is believed to ameliorate conditions that cause this problem. Six offspring, ranging from 4 to 26 years of age, of these mothers were studied. They were compared with siblings of the same sex whose mothers had not been treated with androgen during the prenatal period.

Results indicated that hormones are an important factor in sex-role development. The girls whose mothers received androgen expended comparatively more energy in their play and seemed to prefer boys over girls as playmates. Instead of dolls, they chose male sex-typed toys for play. They displayed little interest in future marriage and did not enjoy taking care of babies. They also preferred functional over attractive clothes and were generally unconcerned with their appearance. The boys whose mothers received androgen engaged in rough-and-tumble play and outdoor sports to a greater extent than their unaffected brothers did.

Ehrhardt's work has been criticized for a number of reasons. First, the inflated androgen levels require that these individuals be treated with cortisone for the remainder of their lives. One of the side effects of cortisone is a high activity level. The high energy and activity levels of the girls and boys, then, may have been due to the cortisone treatment rather than to high levels of androgen (Quadagno, Briscoe, & Quadagno, 1977). Second, "masculinized" girls may be perceived as deviant by their parents, siblings, and peers. Those around them may have thought of them as "boys" and treated them accordingly.

No one argues the existence of genetic, biochemical, and anatomical differences between the sexes. Even environmentally oriented psychologists acknowledge that boys and girls are treated differently because of their physical differences and their different roles in reproduction. Consequently, the importance of biological factors is not at issue; what is at issue is the directness or indirectness of the effect of biological factors on social behavior.

According to Aletha Huston (1983), if a high androgen level directly influences the central nervous system, which in turn produces a higher activity level, then the effect is reasonably direct. By contrast, if a high level of androgen produces strong muscle development, which in turn causes others to expect the child to be a good athlete and in turn leads him or her to participate in sports, then the biological effect is more indirect.

Next, we see that, in addition to biological factors, cognitive factors also are important in understanding sex roles.

Cognitive Factors

The role of cognition in sex roles involves the importance of self-categorization and language. The ideas of Lawrence Kohlberg and others suggest that children must establish a stable gender identity before they can achieve a sense of masculinity or femininity.

Self-Categorization and Stable Gender Identity

Lawrence Kohlberg (1966) argued that, to have an idea of what is masculine or feminine, a child must be able to categorize objects into these two groups—masculine or feminine. According to Kohlberg, the categories become relatively stable for a child by the age of six. That

What is the cognitive view of children's sex-role development?

is, by the age of six, children have a fairly definite idea of which category they belong to. Further, they understand what is entailed by belonging to one category or the other and seldom fluctuate in their category judgments. According to Kohlberg, this self-categorization is the impetus for the unfolding of sex-role development.

Kohlberg reasons that sex-role development proceeds in the following sequence: "I am a boy, I want to do boy things; therefore, the opportunity to do boy things is rewarding" (1966, p. 89). According to Kohlberg, the child, having acquired the ability to categorize, strives toward consistency between use of the categories and actual behavior. This striving for consistency forms the basis for the development of sex typing.

Others have expanded on Kohlberg's cognitive developmental theme (e.g., Block, 1973; Pleck, 1975; Rebecca, Hefner, & Oleshansky, 1976). For example, one proposal suggests that there initially is a stage of undifferentiated sex-role concepts among very young children and that in the next stage (about the time of the preschool years) children adopt very rigid, conventional sex roles (Pleck, 1975). This rigidity is believed to peak during the early adolescent years. Then, at some point later in development, often not until the adult years, a more flexible orientation emerges, one that has both masculine and feminine characteristics (e.g., Block, 1973; Pleck, 1975).

Language, Cognition, and Sex Roles   What is the nature of sexism in language? That is, does the English language contain sex bias, particularly in terms of such usages as "he" and "man" referring to everyone? Focus on Child Development 8.3 examines intriguing research on children's interpretation of various sex-related aspects of language, along with a discussion of whether sexist language produces sexist thought or vice versa.

Cognitive capacities are extremely important in the development of sex roles, but as we see next, they do not explain entirely the wide variation in behavior observed in members of the same sex. Such individual variation undoubtedly is strongly influenced by environmental experiences, which we consider next.

Environmental Influences

In our culture, adults begin to discriminate between sexes shortly after the infant's birth. The "pink and blue treatment" is often applied to girls and boys even before they leave the hospital. Soon afterward, the differences in hairstyles, clothes, and toys become obvious. Adults and other children reinforce these differences throughout childhood, but boys and girls also learn appropriate role behavior by watching what other people say and do. For example, a seven-year-old boy who knows he is a boy readily labels appropriate objects as male or female, but he has parents who support the feminist movement and stress equality between the sexes. His behavior will be less stereotyped along masculine lines than that of boys reared in more traditional homes.

In recent years, the idea that parents are the critical socialization agents with regard to sex-role development has been de-emphasized. Parents clearly are only one of many sources, such as schools, peers, the media, and other family members, through which children learn about sex-role development. Yet, it is important to guard against swinging too far in this direction, because particularly in the early years of life, parents do play a very important role in the sex-role development of their child.

Parent–Child Relationships   Fathers and mothers both are psychologically important for children even during infancy. Fathers seem to play a particularly important role in the sex typing of both boys and girls. Reviews of sex-typing research indicate that fathers are more likely to act differently toward sons and daughters than mothers are (Huston, 1983). And most reviews of the father-absence literature conclude that boys show a more feminine patterning of behavior in father-absent than in father-present homes (Lamb, 1981); however, close inspection of those studies suggests that this conclusion is more appropriate for young children, while the findings for elementary and secondary school children are mixed. For example, Hetherington, Cox, and Cox (1978) found that children's sex-typed behavior reflected more than the unavailability of a consistent adult male model. While many single-parent mothers were overprotective and apprehensive about their son's independence, when single parents encouraged masculine and exploratory behavior and did not have a negative attitude toward the absent father, the son's sex-typed behavior was not disrupted.

Many parents encourage boys and girls to engage in different types of play activities, even during infancy. In particular, many parents emphasize that doll play is for girls only, while boys are more likely to be rewarded for engaging in gross motor activities. Parents often play more actively with male babies and respond more positively to physical activity by boys. There also is some evidence that parents encourage girls to be more dependent, show more affection, and express more tender emotions than boys; but there is no indication that parents show different reactions to aggression according to their child's sex. Also, with increasing age, boys are permitted more freedom by parents (Huston, 1983).

Thus, we can see that parents, by action and example, influence their child's sex-role development. In the psychoanalytic view, this influence stems principally from the child's identification with the parent of the same sex. The child develops a sense of likeness to the parent of the same sex and strives to emulate that parent.

Parents provide the earliest discrimination of sex-typed behavior in the child's development, but before long, peers and teachers join the societal process of providing substantial feedback about masculine and feminine roles.

FOCUS ON CHILD DEVELOPMENT 8.3

HOW GOOD ARE GIRLS AT WUDGEMAKING IF THE WUDGEMAKER IS A "HE"?

One manner in which the role of language in sex-role development can be investigated is by studying children's interpretation of the "gender neutral" use of *he* and *his*. Janet Hyde (1984) investigated this issue by presenting cue sentences to first, third, and fifth graders, as well as college students. The individuals then told stories in response to a cue sentence containing *he, he or she,* or *they*. The individuals also supplied pronouns in a fill-in task and were questioned about their knowledge of the gender-neutral use of *he*. It was found that 12, 18, and 42 percent of the stories were about females when *he, she,* and *he or she* were used, respectively. Even first graders supplied *he* in gender-neutral fill-in sentences. Only 28 percent of the first graders, but 84 percent of the college students, seemed to understand the grammatical rule for the gender use of *he*.

In a second experiment, Hyde (1984) replicated some aspects of the first experiment and expanded the design to include third and fifth graders. *She* was included as a fourth pronoun condition in the storytelling and produced 77 percent female stories. The experiment also involved the following description of a fictitious, gender-neutral occupation,

wudgemaker, which was read to the children, with repeated references either to *he, they, he or she,* or *she:*

> Few people have heard of a job in factories, being a wudgemaker. Wudges are made of plastic, oddly shaped, and are an important part of video games. The wudgemaker works from a plan or pattern posted at eye level as *he or she* puts together the pieces at a table while *he or she* is sitting down. Eleven plastic pieces must be snapped together. Some of the pieces are tiny, so the *he or she* must have good coordination in *his or her* fingers. Once all eleven pieces are put together, *he or she* must test out the wudge to make sure that all of the moving pieces move properly. The wudgemaker is well paid and must be a high school graduate, but *he or she* does not have to have gone to college to get the job. (Hyde, 1984, p. 702)

One-fourth of the children were given *he* as the pronoun, one-fourth *they*, one-fourth *he or she* (as shown in the previous "wudgemaker" description), and one-fourth *she*. They were asked to rate on a three-point scale how well women could do the job and how well men could do the job. As shown in the figure on the next page, subject ratings of how well women could make wudges were influenced by pronoun, with

---

Peers   Most children have already acquired a preference for sex-typed toys and activities before they are exposed to school. During the preschool and elementary school years, teachers and peers usually maintain these preferences through feedback to the boy or girl.

Children who play in sex-appropriate activities tend to be rewarded for doing so by their peers, while those

who play in cross-sex activities tend to be criticized by their peers or left to play alone. Indeed, children seem to differentiate their peers very early on the basis of sex, with such patterns reflecting the preschool child's increasing awareness of culturally prescribed expectancies for males and females.

One of the most frequent observations of elementary school children's play groups is their gender segregation. Boys tend to play with boys, and girls are much more ratings being lowest for *he,* intermediate for *they* and *he or she.* These data indicate that the use of gender-neutral *he,* compared to other pronouns, influences the formation of gender schema in children.

The research conducted by Janet Hyde (1984) touches on an important classic issue in developmental psychology. That is, to what extent does language influence thought or vice versa? In Hyde's research, the issue is whether sexist language is primary and influences thought, or whether sexist thought is primary and produces sexist language. Stated in the language of schema theory, does sexist language produce the schema, or does the schema produce the sexist language? Hyde presented further data that address this issue. When the cue pronoun was *he,* the percentage of female stories was very low (12 percent in one experiment and 17 percent in another). However, when the truly neutral pronoun *they* was used, the percentage of female stories still was significantly below 50 percent (18 percent and 31 percent in the two experiments). Such results led Hyde to the conclusion that sexism in thought might be primary since an overwhelming majority of people think of males even when presented with the neutral pronoun *they.* However, it is important to note that even the youngest subjects had been exposed to sexist language for most of their lives, including hearing *he* and *they* used interchangeably in sentences. Thus, sexist thought may be the product of years of exposure to sexist language or other factors.

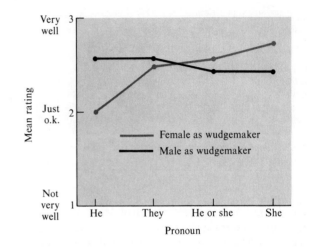

Mean ratings of how well women and men would do as wudgemakers, according to pronoun used in the description.

likely to play with girls. In one recent investigation, children's free play was observed in several contexts—during lunch, on a museum trip, and at public and private schools, for example—and with different ages of children—three- and four-year-olds and fourth, fifth, and sixth graders (Luria & Herzog, 1985). All-female, all-male, and cross-sexed groups of children were observed in all settings and at all ages. Interestingly, public school fourth through sixth graders showed much less cross-sex

peer grouping than their private school counterparts. And it was only in the public school groupings that an overt ideology of cross-sex exclusion was ever heard. Overall, however, there appears to be an acceptance of cross-sex play in most children's peer groups, even though the majority of elementary school children express a same-sex play group preference.

How extensive is gender segregation in peer groups during middle and late childhood?

Teachers   Actual observations of teacher behavior in both preschool and elementary school classes suggest that boys are given more disapproval, scolding, and other forms of negative attention than girls (e.g., Cherry, 1975; Serbin, O'Leary, Kent, & Tonick, 1973). However, the findings for positive teacher behavior are mixed: Some investigators find that teachers give more attention to girls (Fagot, 1973), while others find that boys get more positive attention (e.g., Serbin, O'Leary, Kent, & Tonick, 1973). Similarly, there is no consistent evidence that teachers reward sex-typed social behaviors differently for boys and girls (Huston, 1983). Sometimes, however, the fact that boys do not do as well as girls in school early in their development is attributed to the possibilities that either female teachers treat boys differently from girls or that boys have few male models as teachers.

Female teachers are more likely to reward "feminine" behavior than "masculine" behavior. Beverly Fagot (1975) reasoned that teachers would most probably support student behaviors that were a part of the teacher's own behavioral system. Since most preschool and elementary school teachers are female, they would be expected to reward behaviors consistent with the feminine, or "good girl," stereotype. As expected, Fagot found that teachers reinforced both boys' and girls' feminine behaviors 83 percent of the time. In a similar study, Boyd

McCandless (1973) found that female teachers rewarded feminine behaviors 51 percent of the time and masculine behaviors 49 percent of the time. Perhaps if more male adults were involved in early education, there would be more support of masculine behavior and activity.

So far, we have studied the roles of parents, peers, and teachers as environmental influences on sex roles. But it also is intriguing to ask the general question of just how easily sex-typed behavior can be changed.

Changing Sex-Typed Behavior   Efforts to change children's sex-typed behavior have taken two directions (Huston, 1983): "Gender-deviant" children are trained to show more appropriate sex-typed behavior, and attempts are made to free normal children from rigidly sex-typed patterns. Both types of intervention create ethical concerns; yet, both produce valuable information about sex typing, that is, about psychological aspects of being male or female.

Most studies of gender deviance have included only boys, who are diagnosed as gender deviant when they play mostly with feminine sex-typed toys, dress up in female clothes, choose girls rather than boys as playmates, engage in female role playing, fantasize about being a girl, and express themselves with feminine gestures (Green, 1974; Rekers, 1979). One investigation based on detailed observations showed that girls use very different gestural patterns than boys, such as hanging their wrists, limply holding books with their arms folded toward their body, and so forth (Rekers, 1979). Gender-deviant boys not only prefer feminine activities but also purposely avoid masculine activities. In particular, they indicate that the rough-and-tumble play of other boys either disinterests or frightens them (Green, 1974).

Both behavioral and psychoanalytic treatment procedures have been used in attempts to alter the sex-typed behavior of gender-deviant children. These treatment procedures have led to changes in children's play patterns but usually only in the situation where the treatment occurred. Consequently, clinical treatment has been augmented by direct interventions at home and at school. Parents and teachers have been taught behavior modification techniques, and young male adults have visited the children at home or at school, attempting to teach the gender-deviant boys athletic skills, an area in which feminine boys tend to perform very poorly. Indications are that such programs have led to more normal sex-typed behavior in boys, lasting for as long as one to three years after the intervention (Rekers, 1979).

While gender deviance has been diagnosed and treated, there is little knowledge of the origins of such patterns. One possibility is that many parents are indifferent to the occurrence of gender-deviant patterns of behavior in young children. Some parents think that it is cute when little boys continue to dress up as females and play with dolls. Such children are often referred for treatment only after someone outside the family points out the child's effeminate characteristics. Other factors that show up in the case histories of some gender-deviant boys are maternal overprotection of boys and restrictions on rough-and-tumble play, absence of an adult male, weak father–son relationship, physical beauty of the small boy that leads to his being treated as a girl, absence of male playmates, and maternal dominance.

In addition to attempts to change the sex-typed behavior of gender-deviant children, another effort has focused on teaching children about androgyny. Believing that rigid sex roles may be detrimental to both males and females, a number of educators and social scientists have developed materials and created courses involving the teaching of androgyny to students. Among the curricula developed have been resource guides and examples of materials that can be used to study sex roles (Biemer, 1975; Hahn, 1975; Holman, 1975; Nickerson, 1975), as well as courses with outlines and lesson plans (Emma Willard Task Force on Education, 1971; Gaskell & Knapp, 1976; National Education Association, 1974; Stein, 1972).

The results of these intervention efforts are mixed. Generally, they meet with more success when girls, rather than boys, are involved. Ethical concerns, however, are aroused when the issue is one of teaching children to depart from socially approved behavior patterns, particularly when there is no evidence of extreme sex typing in the groups of children to whom the interventions are applied. The advocates of androgyny programs believe that traditional sex typing is psychologically harmful for all children and that it has prevented many girls and women from experiencing equal opportunity. Huston (1983) concluded that, while some people believe that androgyny is more adaptive than either a traditional masculine or feminine pattern, it is not possible to ignore the imbalance within our culture that values masculinity more than femininity.

Now that we have considered many different aspects of sex roles, we chart the unfolding of different dimensions of sex roles in the early years of children's lives.

The Development of Sex Roles

The majority of research studies that have focused on sex-role development have been conducted with children ages two to nine years. While some sex typing likely occurs during the first several years of life, it is difficult to assess. However, during the 18-month to three-year-old age period, children begin to show a great deal of interest in sex-typed play and activities. In home observations of toddlers, girls were more likely to play with soft toys, dolls, and dress-up clothes and to dance more, whereas boys were more likely to play with blocks and transportation toys and to manipulate the objects (Fagot, 1974). During the 18-month to three-year-old age period, children also begin to classify themselves and others according to gender (Marcus & Corsini, 1978; McConaghy, 1979). At this same time, young children interpret many of the activities and objects around them in culturally defined sex-appropriate ways. By the time children are three years of age, they know the sex stereotypes for toys, games, household objects, clothing, and work (Ruble & Ruble, 1980). Of all of these content areas of sex typing, sex-typed interests and activities appear earliest in the child's development (Huston, 1983).

During the three- to seven-year-old age period, children begin to acquire an understanding of gender constancy and increasingly enjoy being with same-sex peers (Hartup, 1983). At this time, they gain knowledge about stereotypes of sex-typed personal and social attributes. Masculine stereotypes include such traits as strength, robustness, aggression, adventurousness, and dominance; female stereotypes include such characteristics as the ability to express emotions, gentleness, submission, fretfulness, and coquetry (Best et al., 1977). Sex differences in response to these stereotyped attributes begin to appear in this age range, and boys consistently hold more stereotyped views than girls (Emmerich, 1979; Gold, Andres, & Glorieux, 1979). During the three- to seven-year-old period, there is also evidence that children increasingly prefer same-sex models and attachment figures (Slaby & Frey, 1975).

Child Development Concept Table 8.3 summarizes our overview of the self and the development of sex roles. Now we consider one final dimension of personality in early childhood—moral development.

Moral Development

In one sense, moral development has a longer history than virtually any aspect of development discussed in this text. In prescientific periods, philosophers and theologians heatedly debated the child's moral status at birth, which they felt had important implications for how the child was to be reared. Today, people are hardly neutral about moral development. Most have very strong opinions about acceptable and unacceptable behavior, ethical and unethical conduct, and the ways that acceptable and ethical behaviors are to be fostered in children.

Moral development concerns rules and conventions about what people should do in their interactions with other people. In studying these rules, psychologists examine three different domains of moral development. First, how do children reason or think about rules for ethical conduct? For example, cheating is generally considered unacceptable. The child can be presented with a story in which someone has a conflict about whether or not to cheat in a specific situation. The child is asked to decide what is appropriate for the character to do, and why. The focus is thereby placed on the rationale, the type of reasoning the child uses to justify his or her moral decision.

A second domain concerns how children actually behave in the face of rules for ethical conduct. Here, for example, the concern is whether the child actually cheats in different situations and what factors influence this behavior.

A third domain concerns how the child feels after making a moral decision. There has been more interest in a child's feelings after doing something wrong than after doing something right. For example, does the child feel guilty as the result of having cheated?

In the remainder of this section, we focus on these three facets of moral development—thought, action, and feeling. Then to conclude the discussion of moral development, we consider the positive side of moral development—altruism. First, we discuss Piaget's view of moral thought, or reasoning.

Piaget's View of Moral Reasoning

Interest in how the child thinks about ethical issues has been stimulated by the work of Piaget (1932), who conducted extensive observations and interviews with children from 4 to 12 years of age. He watched them in natural play with marbles, trying to understand the manner in which they used and thought about the rules of the game. Later, he asked them several questions about ethical concepts (e.g., theft, lies, punishment, justice) to arrive at a similar understanding of how they thought about ethical rules. He concluded that there are two different modes (or stages) of moral thought. The more primitive one, **moral realism,** is associated with younger children (from 4 to 7 years old); the more advanced one, **moral autonomy,** is associated with older children (10 years old and older). Children from 7 to 10 years of age are in a transition period between the two stages, evidencing some features of each stage.

What are some of the characteristics of these two stages? The moral realist judges the rightness or goodness of behavior by considering the consequences of the behavior, not the intentions of the actor. For example, a realist would say that breaking twelve cups accidentally is worse than breaking one cup intentionally while trying to steal a cookie. For the moral autonomist, the reverse is true; the intention of the actor becomes more important.

The moral realist believes that all rules are unchangeable and are handed down by all-powerful authorities. When Piaget suggested that new rules be introduced into the game of marbles, the young children became troubled; they insisted that the rules had always existed as they were and could not be changed. The moral autonomist, by contrast, accepts change and recognizes that rules are merely convenient, socially agreed upon conventions, subject to change by consensus.

A third characteristic is the moral realist's belief in **immanent justice**—if a rule is broken, punishment will be meted out immediately. The realist believes that the violation is connected in some mechanical or reflexlike way to the punishment. Thus, young children often look around worriedly after committing a transgression, expecting inevitable punishment. Recent research (e.g., Jose, 1985) verifies that immanent justice responses decline during the latter part of the elementary school years. The moral autonomist recognizes that punishment is a socially mediated event that occurs only if a relevant

Child Development Concept Table 8.3 The Self and Sex-Role Development		
Concept	**Processes/Related Ideas**	**Characteristics/Description**
The self	The self as knower and the object of what is known	There are two basic ways of describing the self—in terms of the self as knower ("I") and as the object of what is known ("me"). Historically, most research has focused on the object of what is known and involved the assessment of self-concept or self-esteem. In particular, this phenomenological approach has been advocated by the humanists. Only recently has research on the self as knower been emphasized. This research has been conducted by information processing psychologists and, in particular, has emphasized the development of memory.
	Development of the self in early childhood	During early childhood, the child develops a sense of a private, inner self, yet basically describes himself or herself in terms of external characteristics.
Sex roles	Biological influences	Freud and Erikson argued that sex-role development is tied to anatomy and reproductive forces. No one argues the existence of genetic, biochemical, and anatomical differences between the sexes. What is at issue is the directness or indirectness of the effect of biological factors on social behavior.
	Cognitive influences	Kohlberg argued that, by age six, the child's cognitive ability leads to categorization in sex-role terms. The cognitive developmental theory of Kohlberg has suggested that self-categorization and the development of a stable gender identity are precursors for sex-typed behavior. Others have expanded on this view and believe that a rigidity of sex roles often occurs during early adolescence. Hyde's research reveals links between language and thought in sex roles.
	Environmental influences	Historically, parents have been thought to be the most important influences on the child's sex-role development, but more recently, there has been a trend toward evaluating a wide spectrum of environmental influences, such as peers, school, the media, and other family members. Nonetheless, parents by action and example influence children's sex-role development. Children tend to differentiate their peers very early on the basis of sex and continue to prefer same-sex peer groups throughout childhood. Nonetheless, cross-sex peer play often is acceptable. Teachers react more negatively to boys than to girls in early schooling and are more likely to reward "feminine" behaviors in boys and girls. Gender-deviant behavior, particularly among boys, has been studied. Changing such behavior through treatment involves ethical issues. School interventions focus on training children to become androgynous. The results of this research are mixed, although the programs usually are more successful with girls than boys.
	Sex-role development	During the 18-month to three-year-old age period, children start expressing considerable interest in sex-typed activities and classify themselves according to gender. From three to seven years of age, children begin to acquire an understanding of gender constancy and increasingly enjoy being with same-sex peers.

person witnesses the wrongdoing and that, even then, punishment is not inevitable.

Piaget's theory of moral judgment was crafted as a counterargument to sociologist Emile Durkheim's view that the socialization process should instill respect in each individual for the social group. In Durkheim's view, each member of the group should accept the group's constraints and rules. Piaget's main thrust was to reveal the limitations of Durkheim's view (which was basically heteronomous in nature) by arguing that, as the child develops, she or he becomes more sophisticated in thinking about social matters, particularly about the possibilities and conditions of cooperation. Piaget believed that this social understanding comes about through the mutual give-and-take of peer relations. In the peer group, where others have similar status and power as the individual, plans are negotiated and coordinated, and disagreements are reasoned about and eventually settled. It is in the peer group that the child learns of the possibilities for cooperation not based on unilateral respect (as is typically the case in parent–child relationships, relationships in which the child simply acquiesces to the demands of more powerful social agents). In peer relationships, the child learns about cooperation through collaboration and commerce with others. Through such relationships, the fundamental nature of the child's moral nature changes.

Moral Behavior

The study of moral behavior has been influenced primarily by social learning theory. The familiar processes of reinforcement, punishment, and imitation have been invoked to explain how and why children learn certain responses and why their responses differ from one another; the general conclusions to be drawn are the same as elsewhere. When children are reinforced for behavior that is consistent with laws and social conventions, they are likely to repeat that behavior. When models who behave "morally" are provided, children are likely to adopt their actions. Finally, when children are punished for "immoral" or unacceptable behaviors, those behaviors can be eliminated, but at the expense of sanctioning punishment, which by its very use can cause emotional side effects for the child.

To these general conclusions, we add the usual qualifiers. The effectiveness of reward and punishment depends on the consistency with which they are administered and the schedule (e.g., continuous, partial) that is adopted. The effectiveness of modeling depends on the characteristics of the model (e.g., esteem, power) and the presence of symbolic codes to enhance retention of the modeled behavior.

A key ingredient of moral development from the social learning perspective is the child's ability to resist temptation and to develop self-control. When pressures mount for the child to cheat, to lie, or to steal, has he or she developed the ability to control himself or herself and resist such temptations?

What influences moral behavior?

Child developmentalists have invented a number of ways to investigate such temptations. In one procedure frequently employed, a child is shown an attractive set of toys and told that the toys belong to someone else, who has requested that they not be touched. The child then experiences some social influence, perhaps in the form of a discussion of the virtues of respecting other people's property or a model shown resisting or giving in to the temptation to play with prohibited objects. The child is left alone in the room to amuse himself or herself when the experimenter departs (under some pretext), announcing that he or she will return in 10 or 15 minutes. The experimenter then watches through a one-way mirror to see whether the child resists or gives in to the temptation to play with the toys.

In particular, there has been considerable interest in examining the effects of punishment on children's ability to resist temptation (Parke, 1972, 1977). For the most part, it has been found that a cognitive rationale enhances almost any form of punishment. Such rationales provide reasons as to why, for example, the child should not touch a forbidden toy. In particular, such cognitive rationales have been more effective in getting children to resist temptation over a period of time than strategies that do not use such reasoning, such as when the parent puts the child in his or her room without explaining the consequences of the deviant behavior for others.

The ability to resist temptation is closely tied to delay of gratification. Self-control is involved in both the ability to resist temptation and the ability to delay gratification. The child must overcome his or her impulses to get something that is desired but is known to be prohibitive in the case of resistance to temptation. Similarly, the child must exhibit a sense of patience and self-control in delaying gratification for something more desirable in the future rather than succumbing to the immediate pressures of pursuing a smaller reward now.

Considerable research has been conducted on children's self-control. Walter Mischel (1974) believes that self-control is strongly influenced by cognitive factors. Children's cognitive transformations of desired objects have a strong impact on how patient children are. Research has shown that children can instruct themselves to be more patient and in the process exhibit more self-control. In one investigation, preschool children were asked to engage in a very dull task. Close by was a very enticing mechanical clown who tried to persuade the children to come play with him. The children who had been trained to say to themselves, "I'm not going to look at Mr. Clown when Mr. Clown says to look at him," were much more likely to control their behavior and continue working on the dull task than children who were not given the self-instructional strategy (Mischel & Patterson, 1976).

Social learning theorists are increasingly interested in the manner in which such cognitive factors as resistance to temptation, delay of gratification, and self-control mediate the relation between environmental experiences and moral behavior.

Moral Feelings and Guilt

Moral feelings have traditionally been thought of in terms of guilt, but recently there has been a great deal of interest in the role of empathy. **Empathy** is the ability to understand the feelings or ideas of another person. Emphasizing empathic response stresses the positive side of moral development more than its negative side.

In psychoanalytic accounts, the development of **guilt** occurs in the following way: Through identification with parents and the parents' use of love-withdrawal for disciplinary purposes, the child turns his or her hostility inward and experiences guilt. This guilt is primarily unconscious and reflects the structure of the personality known as the *superego*.

It is assumed that guilt-prone individuals avoid transgressing in order to avoid *anxiety;* on the other hand, the person with little guilt has little reason to resist temptation. Thus, in this view, guilt is responsible for harnessing the evil drives of the *id* and for maintaining the world as a safe place in which to live. In the psychoanalytic perspective, early childhood is a particularly important period for the child's moral development. Recall that Erik Erikson even refers to early childhood as the initiative versus guilt stage.

In studying guilt, as well as such matters as cheating, lying, and stealing, we are investigating the antisocial, inhibitive aspects of morality. As we see next, however, it also is important to consider the prosocial aspects.

Altruism

In general, altruism increases as children develop (Underwood & Moore, 1980): Older children usually are more likely to be helpful or to share than are younger children, and older children show a greater variety of prosocial behaviors. However, as the following vivid episode suggests, very young children—even as young as the second year of life—may display altruistic behavior (Zahn-Waxler, Radke-Yarrow, & King, 1979):

> Today, Jerry was kind of cranky; he just started completely bawling and he wouldn't stop. John kept coming over and handing Jerry toys, trying to cheer him up, so to speak. He'd say things like, "Here, Jerry," and I said to John: "Jerry's sad; he doesn't feel good; he had a shot today." John would look at me with his eyebrows kind of wrinkled together like he really understood that Jerry was crying because he was unhappy, not that he was just being a crybaby. He went over and rubbed Jerry's arm and said, "Nice Jerry" and continued to give him toys. (pp. 321–22)

Clearly, John was touched by his friend Jerry's disturbed state and acted in an altruistic manner toward him. Rather amazingly, John was not quite two years old when this incident occurred.

Empathic responding is viewed as a critical building block in forming a basic motive to help others, hence its important role in moral development. For example, very young children, approximately two to four years old, typically show empathy toward a hurt child, even though they sometimes do nothing or act inappropriately (e.g., Zahn-Waxler, Radke-Yarrow, & King, 1979). In addition to empathy, another factor important in promoting altruistic tendencies in children is role taking or perspective taking.

Role-taking or **perspective-taking skills** refer to the understanding that other people have feelings and perceptions different from one's own. By seven or eight years of age, the child has mastered complex role-taking skills (Flavell, Botkin, Fry, Wright, & Jarvis, 1968; Selman, 1971), but others are mastered as early as the age of two or three (Flavell, 1985). Elementary school children's empathy is directed toward helping the other person, but they seek to find the true source of the other person's distress. And they are likely to discover the tentative and hypothetical nature of their inferences. Thus, their motivation to relieve the other's distress is less egocentric and based to a greater degree on the accurate assessment of the other's needs, trial and error, and response to corrective feedback (Hoffman, 1975).

Research on the link between role taking and altruism suggests that children who have well-developed role-taking skills show more kindness and helping behaviors toward other children (e.g., Rubin & Schneider, 1973). One investigator has successfully trained six-year-old children in role-taking skills and found that they subsequently have more altruistic tendencies than a nontrained group (Ianotti, 1978).

THINKING BACK, LOOKING AHEAD

We touched many bases in our portrayal of the preschool child's social worlds—"You stay here with the baby while I go fishing"; Erikson's "initiative"; Jung's description of the importance of parental investment; parenting styles; the sibling who said, "Mother, you always take her side"; working mothers; the effects of divorce on children; nose punchers, pinchers, and isolates; "You're a girl—No I'm not!" repeated for several minutes; playing doctor and teacher; "the one-eyed monster" of television that also is a "window on the world"; the "I" and "me" of the self; the emerging sense of a private inner self ("I can't see you thinking because you don't have any holes in your head"); wudgemaking done by a he, she, or they; and moral realists and autonomists.

In Section 4, we move on to the middle and late childhood years, which range from approximately 6 to 11 years of age and are sometimes called the elementary school years. But before you turn to Section 4, think for several moments about the 18th-century words of Jean-Jacques Rousseau that capture some of the marvels of childhood years:

> You are troubled at seeing him spend his early years in doing nothing. What! Is it nothing to be happy? Is it nothing to skip, to play, to run about all day long? Never in his life will he be so busy as now.

SUMMARY

I. Our study of families emphasized parenting styles, sibling relationships, and the changing family.
  A. Four parenting styles are authoritarian, authoritative, permissive-indulgent, and permissive-indifferent.
    1. Authoritarian and permissive styles generally have negative effects on children, while authoritative parenting is associated with social competence in children. Authoritative parents encourage the child to be independent but still place limits on the child. Extensive verbal give-and-take is present, as is a high degree of warmth. The parenting styles involve different combinations of acceptance-rejection and demanding-undemanding behavior.
    2. Parents need to adapt their interaction strategies as the child grows older, using less physical manipulation and more reasoning.
  B. Information about sibling relationships focuses on such matters as their nature and sibling and parent-child interaction.
    1. More than 80 percent of American children have one or more siblings. Sibling relationships are an important part of children's socialization.
    2. In some instances, siblings are stronger socializing agents than parents—older siblings may be particularly influential in teaching younger siblings about identity problems and physical appearance, for example. Mothers give more attention to firstborn children than to later-born children.
  C. Family changes include the increase in working mothers and the effects of divorce.

1. A mother's working full-time outside the home can have positive or negative effects on children. Overall, however, there do not seem to be long-term negative effects associated with working mothers.

2. Understanding the effects of divorce on children requires attention to family conflict, the role of support systems, how much time has passed since the divorce, the stress of divorce, the child's age, and the sex of the child and the sex of the custodial parent. Clearly, divorce is a complex process and its effects on the child are mediated by many factors.

II. Peers, play, and television occupy a considerable amount of the preschool child's time.

   A. Ideas about peers focus on the nature of peer relations, the development of peer relations, and the distinct but coordinated worlds of parents and peers.

      1. Peers are very powerful social agents. The term *peers* refers to children who are about the same age or who act at about the same behavioral level. Peers provide a source of information and social comparison about the world outside the family. Peers have been shown to have an important influence on the child's development of socially competent behavior. Cross-cultural comparisons of peer relations suggest that aggressiveness, prosocial activity, and sociable behavior are more likely in peer than in parent–child relations. Peer relations also play an important role in perspective taking.

      2. The frequency of peer interaction, both positive and negative, increases during the preschool years. By the end of the preschool years, a rudimentary peer system has emerged.

      3. Peer relations are both similar to and different from family relations. Children touch, smile, and vocalize while they interact with parents and peers: However, rough-and-tumble play occurs mainly with peers. In times of stress, children generally seek out their parents rather than their peers. Peers and parents live in distinct but coordinated worlds. Healthy family relations often promote healthy peer relations.

   B. Information about play involves the functions of play, types of play, and new directions in play research.

      1. The functions of play include affiliation with peers, tension release, advances in cognitive development, and exploration.

      2. The types of play include unoccupied, solitary, onlooker, parallel, associative, and cooperative. A ritual is a form of play that involves controlled repetition. One of the most enjoyable forms of play in early childhood is pretend play, in which the child transforms the physical environment into a symbol.

      3. Three new directions in play research involve: (1) better ways to assess play, (2) the interface of cognition and play, and (3) the role of language in play.

   C. Ideas about television include its functions, children's exposure to television, television's role as a social agent, commercials, and television's formal features.

      1. The basic functions of television are to provide information and entertainment. Television provides a portrayal of the world beyond the family, teachers, and peers. However, television may train children to become passive learners, may be deceiving, and frequently takes children away from reading or studying.

      2. Children watch huge amounts of television, with preschool children watching about four hours a day. Up to 80 percent of prime-time television shows have violent episodes. Visual attention to television dramatically increases during the preschool years. Videotaped naturalistic observations of children's television viewing, however, suggest that time spent actually looking at the television set is far less than surveys might suggest.

      3. Television influences children's aggression and prosocial behaviors. Parents rarely monitor or discuss the content of children's television viewing. Children who read books watch less television than those who don't.

      4. The average television-viewing child sees more than 20,000 commercials per year! Commercials seem to influence children's food preferences.

      5. Children's attention and memory are influenced by the formal features of television programming, such as animation, movement, pace, visual techniques, and auditory features.

III. Changes in the self, sex roles, and moral development occur during the preschool years.

A. Ideas about the self involve the self as knower and as the object of what is known, as well as the development of the self in early childhood.

1. There are two basic ways of describing the self—in terms of the self as knower ("I") and as the object of what is known ("me"). Historically, most research has focused on the object of what is known and involved the assessment of self-concept or self-esteem. In particular, this phenomenological approach has been advocated by the humanists. Only recently has research on the self as knower been emphasized. This research has been conducted by information processing psychologists and, in particular, has emphasized the development of memory.

2. During early childhood, the child develops a sense of a private, inner self, yet basically describes himself or herself in terms of external characteristics.

B. Information about sex roles focuses on biological, cognitive, and environmental influences, as well as sex-role developmental sequences in early childhood.

1. Freud and Erikson argued that sex-role development is tied to anatomy and reproductive forces. No one argues the existence of genetic, biochemical, and anatomical differences between the sexes. What is at issue is the directness or indirectness of the effect of biological factors on social behavior.

2. Kohlberg argued that, by age six, the child's cognitive ability leads to categorization in sex-role terms. The cognitive developmental theory of Kohlberg has suggested that self-categorization and the development of a stable gender identity are precursors for sex-typed behavior. Others have expanded on this view and believe that a rigidity of sex roles often occurs during early adolescence. Hyde's research reveals links between language and thought in sex roles.

3. Historically, parents have been thought to be the most important influences on the child's sex-role development, but more recently, there has been a trend toward evaluating a wide spectrum of environmental influences, such as peers, school, the media, and other family members. Nonetheless, parents by action and example influence children's sex-role development. Children tend to differentiate their peers very early on the basis of sex and continue to prefer same-sex peer groups throughout childhood. Nonetheless, cross-sex peer play often is acceptable. Teachers react more negatively to boys than to girls in early schooling and are more likely to reward "feminine" behaviors in boys and girls. Gender-deviant behavior, particularly among boys—has been studied. Changing such behavior through treatment involves ethical issues. School interventions focus on training children to become more androgynous. The results of this research are mixed, although the programs usually are more successful with girls than boys.

4. During the 18-month to three-year-old age period, children start expressing considerable interest in sex-typed activities and classify themselves according to gender. From three to seven years of age, children begin to acquire an understanding of gender constancy and increasingly enjoy being with same-sex peers.

C. Moral development concerns rules and regulations about what people should do in their interactions with other people. Developmental psychologists study how people think, behave, and feel about such rules and regulations. In recent years, considerable attention has been given to the study of altruism.

1. Piaget distinguished between the moral realism of younger children and the moral autonomy of older children.

2. The study of moral behavior focuses on what children do, rather than what they think. Social learning theory has influenced the study of moral behavior.

3. Psychoanalytic theorists emphasize the role of guilt in moral development. More recently, the study of moral feelings has focused on empathy.

4. The discussion of altruism focuses on the development of altruism and on role-taking or perspective-taking skills.

KEY TERMS

associative play 316
authoritarian parenting 301
authoritative parenting 301
cooperative play 316
empathy 339
global self-concept 327
guilt 339
humanism 327
immanent justice 336
moral autonomy 336
moral development 336
moral realism 336
onlooker play 315
parallel play 316
peers 310
permissive-indifferent pattern 302

permissive-indulgent pattern 302
perspective taking 311
phenomenological approach 327
play therapy 314
pretend play 317
ritual 316
role-taking and perspective-taking skills 340
self as knower 328
semiotic function 320
siblings 303
solitary play 315
unoccupied play 315

SUGGESTED READINGS

Becker, W. (1971). *Parents are teachers.* Champaign, IL: Research Press.
Wesley Becker has studied parental influences on children for many years. In his book, he outlines some principles of behavior modification that can be taught to parents and includes a number of exercises for observing family interaction.

Children of divorce. (1979). *Journal of Social Issues 35* (4).
The entire issue is devoted to information about children from divorced families. Included is an excellent introduction that summarizes some of the most important issues involved in the study of the effects of divorce on children.

Hartup, W. W. (1983). The peer system. In P. H. Mussen (Ed.), *Handbook of child psychology* (4th ed.), Vol. 4. New York: Wiley.
A detailed look at the development of peer relations from infancy through adolescence by one of the leading researchers on peer relations.

Liebert, R. M., Neale, J. M., & Davidson, E. S. (1973). *The early window: Effects of television on children and youth.* Elmsford, NY: Pergamon.
Excellent overview of the effects of television on youth. Provides ideas about the psychological processes underlying the influence of television as well as critical analysis of whether television has a positive or negative influence on children.

Rubin, K. H., Gein, G. G., & Vandenberg, B. (1983). Play. In P. H. Mussen (Ed.), *Handbook of child psychology* (4th ed.), Vol. 4. New York: Wiley.
A very thorough, detailed analysis of what is known about children's play, provided by leading researchers in child development. Includes numerous insights into conducting research on children's play and the directions in which research on play is moving.

Childhood is the sleep of reason
Jean-Jacques Rousseau

PHYSICAL AND COGNITIVE DEVELOPMENT IN MIDDLE AND LATE CHILDHOOD

IMAGINE . . . YOU ARE NINE YEARS OLD AND ARE HAVING A "CONVERSATION" WITH YOUR COMPUTER

PREVIEW

PHYSICAL DEVELOPMENT IN MIDDLE AND LATE CHILDHOOD

Basic Physical Attributes
Health and Fitness

FOCUS ON CHILD DEVELOPMENT 9.1: TYPE A CHILDREN, ILLNESS, STRESS, AND ACHIEVEMENT

Handicapped Children

The Prevalence of Handicapped Children
Issues in the Special Education of the Handicapped
Learning Disabilities
Hyperactive Children

CHILD DEVELOPMENT CONCEPT TABLE 9.1: PHYSICAL DEVELOPMENT IN MIDDLE AND LATE CHILDHOOD

PIAGET'S THEORY AND COGNITIVE DEVELOPMENTAL CHANGE IN MIDDLE AND LATE CHILDHOOD

Concrete Operational Thought

The Beaker Task—Studying the Conservation of Liquid
Reversibility and the Nature of a Concrete Operation
Classification
Constraints on Concrete Operational Thought

Piaget and Education
Piaget's Contributions and the Neo-Piagetian Critiques

FOCUS ON CHILD DEVELOPMENT 9.2: 10 + 12 = __?__ : THE IMPORTANCE OF SHORT-TERM MEMORY AND AUTOMATIZATION

CHILD DEVELOPMENT CONCEPT TABLE 9.2: PIAGET'S THEORY AND COGNITIVE DEVELOPMENTAL CHANGE IN MIDDLE AND LATE CHILDHOOD

INFORMATION PROCESSING

Memory

Control Processes
Characteristics of the Learner

FOCUS ON CHILD DEVELOPMENT 9.3: METAMEMORY—PREDICTING MEMORY SPAN AND KNOWING HOW MUCH TO STUDY

Drawing Inferences

Schemata and Scripts
The Development of Scripts in Children

FOCUS ON CHILD DEVELOPMENT 9.4: SCRIPTS FOR SANDBOXES, SNACKS, AND SPELLING

An Information Processing Conception of Intelligence
Knowledge Versus Process Views of Intelligence

CHILD DEVELOPMENT CONCEPT TABLE 9.3: INFORMATION PROCESSING

Information Processing and Education

FOCUS ON CHILD DEVELOPMENT 9.5: INFORMATION PROCESSING, EDUCATION, AND THE INFORMATION AGE

THINKING BACK, LOOKING AHEAD

SUMMARY

KEY TERMS

SUGGESTED READINGS

CHAPTER 9

IMAGINE . . . YOU ARE NINE YEARS OLD AND ARE HAVING A "CONVERSATION" WITH YOUR COMPUTER

Bobby: "Hi, how are you?"
Robert: "I'm fine, thank you. What can I do for you today?"
Bobby: "I'm in a big hurry. My math answers are due tomorrow, and I don't have time to finish them. Do you think you can help me with them?"
Robert: "Yes. Math is no problem for me."
Bobby: "O.K. I'll give you the problems and come back for them later."

This conversation was between nine-year-old Bobby and his computer, which he named Robert. Unlikely? Well, human beings have been enthralled by the idea that they might in some way construct lifelike mechanisms in their own image—robots, androids, thinking machines. The plots of various movies often go something like this: The machine at first obeys its human creator, then becomes sophisticated and outgrows its maker, becoming more impudent and dangerous, but in the end is defeated by the wisdom of the human being.

Until recently, this scenario was science fiction, but today an electronic network can come precariously close to having power over us. Computer scientists have created programs that mimic human intelligence in a number of ways and even outdo human intellect in certain areas. We know that computers can calculate numbers much faster and more accurately than we could ever hope to do. Some computers can summarize news stories, comprehend spoken sentences, follow orders, and play games.

Artificial intelligence (AI) refers to the field of inquiry involved with developing computers and robots that perform intellectual tasks that we commonly think of as characterizing human thought. Are child and adult minds likely to be taken over by the superminds of computers and robots? Edward Fredkin, Professor of Electrical Engineering and Computer Science at MIT, comments:

Eventually, no matter what we do, there will be artificial intelligences with independent goals. It's very hard to imagine a machine that's a million times smarter than

you as your slave. Once artificial intelligences start getting smart, their smartness will grow with explosive speed. If that happens at Stanford, say, the Stanford AI lab may have immense power all of a sudden. It's not that the United States might take over the world, it's that the Stanford AI lab might. (Hunt, 1982, p. 318)

The computer should, in theory, be able to translate verbal and other symbols into its own kind of symbols, rework them according to its own programmed instructions, and thus process information in ways that are said to be intelligent and to be called thinking. However, there are some things that children's minds can do that computers cannot. First, it is important to recognize that all artificial intelligence works toward known end states, goals defined by their creators. A machine can learn and improve its own program, but it does not have any means of developing a new goal for itself. Second, computers seem to be better at simulating the logical processes of our mind than the nonlogical, intuitive, and possibly unconscious aspects of our mind. Many of our most creative efforts seem to be based on such nonlogical, intuitive mental processes. Third, the extraordinary multiple pathways in the brain probably produce thinking that cannot be mimicked by a computer. A computer can be made to look like it is performing **parallel processing,** the simultaneous consideration of a number of lines of thought, as it pursues one line of thought for a millisecond and then switches to another point and considers it for another several milliseconds. But the computer really is not engaging in parallel processing. We do much of this processing at a nonconscious level, and multiple simultaneous considerations seem to be responsible for many of the new ideas that children and adults develop.

Donald Norman (1982), cognitive psychologist at the University of California at San Diego, also points out that we do not have any programs that are self-aware or that begin to approach the consciousness that even children have. The child's mind can examine its own ideas and react to them—not just with thoughts about the ideas but with emotions as well. We are not even close to simulating consciousness on a computer and possibly never will.

PREVIEW

We now live in an information society, which is reflected in the conversation between Bobby and his computer. Children's ability to process information efficiently is important if they are to do well in this society.

In the middle of the 18th century, philosopher David Hume anticipated that philosophical discovery would soon provide an understanding of the operations of the mind. But yet, even today, our knowledge about how children's minds work is far from complete. However, we know much more than we did a century ago or even a decade ago, which makes it an exciting time to investigate the manner in which children process information about their world.

In this chapter, we discuss not only the cognitive changes that characterize children during the elementary school years, but also their physical changes, including information about the many children who have physical handicaps. At 18 months of age, Helen Keller was afflicted with a near-fatal disease that resulted in her total loss of sight and hearing. But through the dedication of her teacher and friend, Anne Sullivan, Helen learned to speak, later becoming an honors graduate of Radcliffe College. Her words create powerful images of changes in thought as we develop:

But whatever the process, the result is wonderful. Gradually from naming an object we advance step by step until we have traversed the vast distance between our first stammered syllable and the sweep of thought in a line of Shakespeare.

What is the nature of physical development in middle and late childhood?

PHYSICAL DEVELOPMENT IN MIDDLE AND LATE CHILDHOOD

The period of middle and late childhood involves slow, consistent growth—the calm before the rapid growth spurt that appears in adolescence. Among the important topics related to physical development during this age period are basic physical attributes, health and fitness, and handicapped children.

Basic Physical Attributes

During the elementary school years, children grow an average of 2 to 3 inches per year until, at the age of 11, the average girl is 4 feet, 10 inches tall and the average boy is 4 feet, 9½ inches tall. Weight increases range from 3 to 5 pounds per year until, at the age of 11, the average girl weighs 88½ pounds and the average boy weighs 85½ pounds (Krogman, 1970).

During middle and late childhood, children's legs become longer and their trunks slimmer, and they are steadier on their feet. Fat tissue tends to develop more rapidly than muscle tissue (which increases substantially in adolescence). Children who had a rounded, somewhat "chubby" body build (sometimes referred to as **endomorphic**) have noticeably more fat tissue than muscle tissue, while the reverse is true of children with **mesomorphic** body builds (athletic, muscular). **Ectomorphs** (skinny, thin body build) do not have a predominance of fat or muscle, which accounts for their tendency to appear somewhat scrawny.

During middle and late childhood, the motor development of children becomes much smoother and more coordinated than was the case in early childhood. For example, only one child in a thousand can hit a tennis ball over the net at the age of 4, yet by the age of 11, most children can learn to play this sport. In the early elementary school years, children can become competent at running, climbing, throwing and catching a ball, skipping rope, swimming, bicycle riding, and skating, to name just some of the many physical skills that, when mastered, are sources of pleasure and accomplishment. Developing competence in these physical skills indicates increases in children's strength, speed, flexibility, and precision, including steadiness, balance, and aiming (Lundsteen & Bernstein-Tarrow, 1981). There usually are marked sex differences in these gross motor skills, with boys outperforming girls rather handily. However, in fine motor skills, girls generally outperform boys.

During middle and late childhood, sensory mechanisms continue to mature. Early farsightedness is overcome, binocular vision becomes well-developed, and hearing acuity increases. Children of this age have fewer illnesses than younger children, particularly fewer respiratory and gastrointestinal problems. Widespread immunization has considerably reduced the incidence of disease, and many illnesses can be prevented by practicing good health, safety, and nutrition habits.

Now that we know something about some general physical attributes of elementary school children, let's evaluate the nature of their health and fitness.

Health and Fitness

When elementary school children are asked about their health, they seem to understand that it is not just something that will stay positive but rather that good health is something they have to work at almost continually. Children recognize that nutrition and physical fitness are important in maintaining their health. Interestingly, most children do not define health in terms of illness. And as they grow through the middle and late childhood years, boys and girls are likely to define health in more abstract and global terms (O'Connor-Francoeur, 1983).

However, while elementary school children may recognize the contributions of nutrition and exercise to their health, the national survey on physical fitness described in Chapter 7 suggests a gap between this awareness and behavior. The survey indicated that our nation's children

are in rather poor physical shape by the time they enter the first grade and that such poor physical fitness seems to continue through the remainder of their childhood and adolescence.

One way a number of elementary school children do get a considerable amount of exercise is through competitive sports. Competitive sports programs for boys and girls have increased in recent years, and parents often place their children in such programs at very young ages. Anywhere in the United States, you are likely to find preschool and elementary school children engaged in competitive sports—in Minnesota, it might be hockey, in Texas football, in Florida soccer. While there is surprisingly little empirical information about the effects that such competitive activities have on physical and emotional development, some researchers have investigated possible links between physical skills competition and the child's maturing bone structure, as well as the possible stress of early physical overload on the young child.

Bryant Cratty (1978) concluded that, of all competitive sports, there is no team sport anywhere in the world in which the occurrence of injury is greater than in football. Soccer, baseball, and basketball, for example, appear to be far less damaging to the child's body. However, bone breaks, if properly set, are likely to heal and not cause growth retardation or malformation.

In addition to information about the effects of competitive sports on bone development, scientists have been interested in the exposure of young children's cardiovascular systems to moderate or severe stress. It appears that vigorous exercise in young children whose cardiovascular systems are sound (tested under exercise stress), if not carried to extremes (exercise that gives the child's system time to recover between "bouts" or sessions not so severe as to produce chronic fatigue), is likely to be beneficial exercise and will probably provide a sound base for later superior endurance performance.

Probably the greatest interest in cardiovascular disease in recent years has focused on the contribution that life-style might make to the disease. Research with adults has demonstrated rather convincingly that the adult with a **Type A behavioral pattern** is more likely to develop cardiovascular disease. The Type A individual is excessively

Table 9.1   Estimates of the Percent and Number of Handicapped Children in the United States

Handicap	Percent of Population	Number of Children Ages 5 to 18*
Visually impaired (includes blind)	0.1	55,000
Hearing impaired (includes deaf)	0.5 to 0.7	275,000 to 385,000
Speech handicapped	3.0 to 4.0	1,650,000 to 2,200,000
Orthopedic and health impairments	0.5	275,000
Emotionally disturbed	2.0 to 3.0	1,100,000 to 1,650,000
Mentally retarded (both educable and trainable)	2.0 to 3.0	1,100,000 to 1,650,000
Learning disabilities	2.0 to 3.0	1,100,000 to 1,650,000
Multi-handicapped	0.5 to 0.7	275,000 to 385,000
Total	10.6 to 15.0	5,830,000 to 8,250,000

*Number of children based on 1985 population estimates
Data from *The Exceptional Student in the Regular Classroom*, Third Edition, by Bill R. Gearhart and Mel W. Weishahn. Copyright © 1984 C. V. Mosby Co. Copyright © 1986 Merrill Publishing Co., Columbus, Ohio. Reprinted by permission.

competitive, has an accelerated pace of ordinary activities, is impatient with the rate at which most events occur, often thinks about doing several things at the same time, shows hostility, and cannot hide the fact that time is a struggle in his or her life. By contrast, the Type B person is typified by the absence of these behavioral tendencies. In adult studies, about 10 percent are clearly Type A or Type B (Rosenman et al., 1970; Matthews, 1982). Can we identify such behavioral patterns in childhood? And if so, are they related to cardiovascular problems in childhood as well? What factors contribute to Type A behavior in children? Focus on Child Development 9.1 examines these questions.

So far, our study of physical development in middle and late childhood has focused on some general physical changes and the roles that health and fitness play. But there are many individual variations in physical development, some of which involve severe physical handicaps, which we study next.

Handicapped Children

A number of children have serious physical handicaps— such as blindness, deafness, speech impairments, learning disabilities, and hyperactivity.

The Prevalence of Handicapped Children

Approximately 10 to 15 percent of the U.S. population of children ages 5 to 18 are estimated to be handicapped in some way (see Table 9.1). The estimates range from the 0.1 percent who are visually impaired to the 3 to 4 percent who have speech handicaps. Estimates vary because of problems in classification and testing. Experts differ in how they define the various categories of handicapped children. And different tests may be used by different school systems or psychologists to assess whether a child is handicapped.

FOCUS ON CHILD DEVELOPMENT 9.1

TYPE A CHILDREN, ILLNESS, STRESS, AND ACHIEVEMENT

A recent research investigation by Carl Thoresen and his colleagues studied children and young adolescents in grades 5, 7, and 9 (Thoresen, Eagleston, Kirmil-Gray, & Bracke, 1985; Eagleston et al., in press). The students were screened for placement in high or low Type A categories based on a Type A behavior scale adapted for students, structured interviews evaluating verbal and behavioral responses, and a test of health.

As shown in the top left figure on the next page, children who rated high in Type A behavior reported higher levels of overall physical symptoms of stress, specifically cardiovascular symptoms, muscle tension, and sleep disturbance. High Type A children also reported more symptoms of illness, particularly headaches and sore throats. The high and low Type A children, however, did not differ on number of visits to physicians or school absences due to illness. They also did not differ in terms of either acute or chronic conditions.

Interviews with the high and low Type A children indicated that the high Type A children overwhelmingly reported having much more stress and tension in their lives. And in most instances, just as in studies of adults, the high Type A children were rated as higher in anger and hostility than the low Type A children. Further, the high Type A children were more likely to be characterized by lower self-esteem and less secure feelings. High Type A adults are not more likely to have lower self-esteem than their low Type A counterparts. One reason for this difference between high Type A children and adults involves the importance of peer acceptance to children. The high Type A children may also be more prone to arousal and to reacting emotionally, since they were more likely to show both hostility and anxiety.

Ties of the Type A children to their parents also were investigated. Of boys in the high Type A group, 80 percent had fathers who scored high in Type A behavior. Only 30 percent of the fathers of the boys in the low Type A group scored high in Type A behavior. Both the mothers and fathers of the high Type A girls showed more Type A behavior than did the parents of low Type A girls. When the parents were observed interacting with their children on laboratory tasks involving block stacking and ring tossing, the parents of the high Type A boys criticized their sons' early failures more than the parents of the other children. The parents of both high and low

All states have now been ordered by the federal government to make every effort to educate handicapped and nonhandicapped children in the same setting (that is, in the public school classroom). If the child's handicap is too severe, then the state must educate the child in special education classes at no cost to the parents or provide funds for the education of the child at home. Each handicapped child must have an individually prescribed educational program. This program must meet with the acceptance of the child's parents, counselors, a local education agency representative, and (when feasible) the child himself or herself. The program must include short- and long-term objectives, and it must be evaluated periodically. Within the last several years, universities and colleges have added to their special education staffs to handle the large numbers of students who are seeking special training in teaching handicapped children.

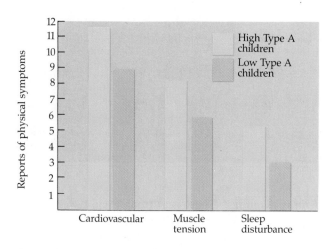

Reported presence of selected physical symptoms in high and low Type A children.

What kind of experiences might determine whether this boy exhibits Type A behavior?

Type A children gave equal amounts of praise to their children. However, the parents of the high Type A children were more likely to compare their children to others in evaluating the children's performance. The authors concluded that the parents of high Type A children, particularly boys, may be promoting a high need for achievement, a fear of failure, and a tendency to overreact to competitive situations.

Issues in the Special Education of the Handicapped

Of the many controversial issues in special education, two that have had overriding importance in recent years are labeling and mainstreaming. **Labeling** refers to the assignment of a label, or category, to a child and the effects that label or category may then have. (If, for example, a child is labeled "learning-disabled" rather than "mentally retarded," will it lead people to treat the child differently?) **Mainstreaming** refers to the process in which children in need of special education are placed in regular classrooms rather than special classrooms.

Labeling   Thomas Szasz (1970) believes that labeling should be abandoned. He argues that labeling a person as having a mental problem (such as a behavioral disorder or learning disability) produces a public stigma.

What are some of the most important issues in the special education of the handicapped?

Everybody then expects the child with the label to be slow, crazy, strange, or even violent, regardless of whether the child actually behaves this way. The expectations others have for the child's behavior may make the behavior worse than it was before.

Labeling may cause children with problems real harm, but some experts believe that abandoning all attempts at classification would be an overreaction (e.g., Martin, 1977). They argue that the public use of labels should definitely be minimized, but that "judicious and sensitive use of classification categories by researchers and clinicians who are aware of these pitfalls still seems desirable—for the long-term benefit of the [child] as well as for general scientific goals" (Martin, 1977, p. 111).

There is a trend in educational circles to no longer categorize children with special problems as "learning-disabled," "behaviorally disordered," and "mentally retarded." Instead, diagnosticians refer to the skills and functioning level of the special education child without attaching a label. Hence, instead of labeling the child who has a learning problem as "LD" or "learning-disabled," the child in question might be said to have attentional difficulties and problems in auditorially decoding words.

Mainstreaming   There is a strong trend toward mainstreaming children who need special education. As mentioned earlier, most school systems have no choice because federal legislation now requires all states to provide for the education of handicapped children in the regular classroom if at all possible.

Some people believe that mainstreaming means that there will be a number of profoundly retarded, drugged children and adolescents sitting in classrooms in dazed, unresponsive states. Others are concerned that special education students will be given so much attention by the teacher that too much class time will be taken away from "normal" children. Some even believe that special education children will have negative effects on the social interactions of the normal children in the class.

The actual picture is not as bleak as many of these critics suggest. Virtually all profoundly retarded children are institutionalized and will never appear in public school classrooms; those who are being mainstreamed are only mildly retarded. Interestingly, not too long ago, there were no elementary and high school special education classes for mildly retarded, learning disabled, and behaviorally disordered children and adolescents. They were mainstreamed, although the label and process of mainstreaming was not an issue then. It only has been in recent years that self-contained classrooms for special education children have been created (Turnbull & Schulz, 1979).

In the 1970s, there was a trend toward placing learning disabled, mentally retarded, and behaviorally disordered children into separate special education classes. Now there is a trend toward using one or more special education resource teachers to work with children with any of these problems. The amount of time children with problems spend outside of their regular classroom varies with the severity of their problems and the particular school system.

But should special education children spend most or all of their time in the regular classroom? Some people believe that placing such children in a special class singles them out as "different" and prevents them from having the opportunity to learn from children who are brighter and more competent than they are. Furthermore, the majority of their social interactions will be with other special education children rather than with normal children. Others argue that retarded children who are placed in a classroom with normal children will experience many failures and will constantly engage in negative social comparisons with the other children. In one review of segregated versus integrated classrooms for special education students, it was concluded that segregated classrooms demonstrated no benefits, either academically or socially (Bartel & Guskin, 1971).

The stigma attached to being a member of a special education class is illustrated by the following incident: A seventh grader had been in self-contained special education classes part of each school day for about one year. One of his special education teachers spoke to him in the hall during lunch hour. Later in the day, he called her aside in the special education class and said: "If you ever speak to me again in the hall, I'll kill you! Act like you don't know who I am!" When she asked why, he responded that none of his friends knew he was in the "tard" class, and he wanted to keep it that way. Later in the year, this seventh grader broke his leg, and a friend pushed him around in a wheelchair to his various classes. He reported to the special education teacher that "the kids will probably call me a crippled tard now." This case illustrates that children and adolescents do feel defensive and sensitive about being in special education classes—special education carries a label that may embarrass them.

Next, we look at two of the most prevalent types of learning handicaps that elementary school children experience—learning disabilities and hyperactivity.

Learning Disabilities

Pediatricians, school psychologists, psychiatrists, and clinical psychologists are being called on more frequently to determine whether a child has a learning disability. While there seems to be no universal agreement on just what a learning disability is, a child diagnosed as learning-disabled generally has: (1) significant deficits in some area of educational achievement, (2) a normal overall score on a standardized intelligence test, (3) no primary emotional-behavioral disturbances, (4) no uncorrected sensory deficits, and (5) no history of severe emotional deprivation (Gearheart, 1973).

This global definition of **learning disabilities** would probably include children diagnosed as dyslexic, children with minimal brain dysfunction, and children who are hyperactive. The following statement by the National Advisory Committee on Handicapped Children (1968) refines the definition further:

> Children with special learning disabilities exhibit a disorder in one or more of the basic psychological processes involved in understanding or in using spoken or written languages. These may be manifested in disorders of listening, thinking, talking, reading, writing, spelling, or arithmetic. They include conditions which have been referred to as perceptual handicaps, brain injury, minimal brain dysfunction, dyslexia, developmental aphasia, etc. They do not include learning problems which are due primarily to visual, hearing, or motor handicaps, to mental retardation, to emotional disturbance, or to environmental disadvantage.

Behavioral Characteristics of Learning-Disabled Children

Although the definition of learning disability is fairly broad, it does allow for reasonably consistent agreement on which children should be diagnosed as learning-disabled. As a result of this broadness of the defining criteria, however, the children so classified are a heterogeneous group. For example, a checklist completed by the teachers of 284 learning-disabled children reveals an extremely wide range of behavioral characteristics for these children (Meier, 1971). Table 9.2 includes the characteristics that were checked for at least one third of the children.

Table 9.2   Descriptions of Behavior Most Frequently Checked by Teachers for Second-Grade Children Meeting Diagnostic Guidelines for Learning Disabilities

Description of Behavior	Percentage of Children for Whom Description Was Checked	Description of Behavior	Percentage of Children for Whom Description Was Checked
1. Substitutes words which distort meaning (''when'' for ''where'')	70%	19. Reverses and/or rotates letters and numbers (reads b for d, u for n, and 6 for 9) far more than most peers	47%
2. Reads silently or aloud far more slowly than peers (word by word while reading aloud)	68%	20. Difficulty with arithmetic (e.g., can't determine what number follows 8 or 16, may begin to add in the middle of a subtraction problem)	46%
3. Unusually short attention span for daily work	67%	21. Poor drawing of crossing, wavy lines compared with peers' drawing	46%
4. Easily distracted from schoolwork (can't concentrate with even the slightest disturbances from other students' moving around or talking quietly)	66%	22. Omits words while reading grade-level material aloud (omits more than one of every 10)	44%
5. Can't follow written directions, which most peers can follow, when read orally or silently	65%	23. Poor drawing of a person compared with peers' drawings	43%
6. Does very poorly in written spelling tests compared with peers	64%	24. Can read orally but does not comprehend the meaning of written grade-level words (word-caller)	43%
7. Can't sound out or ''unlock'' words	64%	25. Excessive inconsistency in quality of performance from day to day and even hour to hour	43%
8. Reading ability at least ¾ of a year below most peers	63%	26. Seems quite immature (doesn't act his or her age)	43%
9. Has trouble telling time	62%	27. Unable to learn the sounds of letters (can't associate appropriate phoneme with its grapheme)	41%
10. Doesn't seem to listen to daily classroom instructions or directions (often asks to have them repeated whereas rest of class goes ahead)	61%	28. Avoids work calling for concentrated visual attention	39%
11. Is slow to finish work (doesn't apply self, daydreams a lot, falls asleep in school)	56%	29. Mistakes own left from right (confuses left-hand side of paper)	39%
12. Repeats the same behavior over and over again	56%	30. Demands unusual amount of attention during regular classroom activities	39%
13. Has trouble organizing written work (seems scatterbrained, confused)	56%	31. Loses place more than once while reading aloud for more than one minute	38%
14. Can't correctly recall oral directions (e.g., item 10 above) when asked to repeat them	54%	32. Cannot apply the classroom or school regulations to own behavior whereas peers can	37%
15. Poor handwriting compared with peers' writing	52%	33. Tense or disturbed (bites lip, needs to go to the bathroom often, twists hair, high-strung)	36%
16. Reverses and/or rotates letters, numbers, or words (writes p for q, saw for was, 2 for 7) far more frequently than peers	52%	34. Poor drawing of diamond compared with peers' drawings	36%
17. Seems very bright in many ways but does poorly in school	50%	35. Overactive (can't sit still in class—shakes or swings legs, fidgety)	34%
18. Points at words while reading silently or aloud	49%		

From Meier, J. H., ''Prevalence and characteristics of learning disabilities found in second-grade children'' in *Journal of Learning Disabilities, 4,* 1–16, 1971. Copyright © 1971 PRO ED, Inc., Austin, Texas. Reprinted by permission.

As we see next, some young children with learning disabilities may be experiencing a developmental lag.

Developmental Lag   Many young children in learning disabilities programs experience a **developmental lag;** in other words, they are slow in developing. Lerner (1971) has even gone so far as to say that most children who are labeled learning-disabled early (e.g., in kindergarten) are not very different from normal children. He believes that these children do not have a dysfunction of the central nervous system but are experiencing a developmental, or maturational, lag involving important brain functions. They do not have less ability than others have; their ability is simply developing more slowly.

Lauretta Bender (1968) argues that children with reading disabilities usually show immaturity in other areas of development as well. For example, their motor development is usually immature; they appear to be very clumsy, even though they are diagnosed as free of neurological problems. These children more often than not are left-handed, which is one indication of a maturational lag in the development of cortical dominance in the brain. Furthermore, they are often described as having a "less mature" personality than that of their peers, which contributes to their learning difficulties.

It is not hard to imagine how damaging it would be for the teacher to think that these children are "dumb," "not trying," "permanently brain-damaged," and the like. Experts suggest that patience and reassuring words from both teachers and parents greatly benefit children with a developmental lag.

Hyperactive Children

Hyperactive children are often viewed as children with learning disabilities (Havighurst, 1976). It has been estimated that as many as 5 percent of American children (about four times as many boys as girls) are diagnosed as hyperactive. In 1971, the Office of Child Development defined the symptoms of **hyperactivity** as "an increase of purposeless physical activity and a significant impaired span of focused attention which may generate other conditions, such as disturbed mood and behavior, within the home, at play with peers, and in the schoolroom." Frequently, excessive physical activity and distractibility are believed to interfere with the child's ability to read and do well in academic settings.

Drugs are increasingly used to control the behavior of hyperactive children. Best guesses by experts on the number of hyperactive children being treated by drugs is about 2 percent of the children in kindergarten and in first through eighth grades (Sprague & Gadow, 1976)—about 500,000 children. The drugs most widely prescribed for hyperactive children are **amphetamines,** particularly the amphetamine Ritalin. For most people, amphetamines act as a stimulant, but for the hyperactive child, they have a calming effect. Over a period of time, their effectiveness is reduced, so the dosage must be increased gradually to continue control of the child's behavior.

What are the results of this use of drugs? Do the amphetamines improve school performance? Ritalin does have a calming effect on the hyperactive child; however, sometimes the dosage given is too great, and teachers report that the child goes about as if in a daze. Some studies indicate that Ritalin has a positive effect on classroom performance, while others indicate no positive effect. One study demonstrated that Ritalin had positive effects on hyperactive children's school performance (Sprague & Sleator, 1975), but these effects varied according to the size of the dose administered. A low dose had a more positive effect than a high dose in an assessment of learning performance. However, when social behavior was evaluated, a high dose had a more positive effect. These researchers have found similar results in other investigations. As many as 20 percent of the hyperactive children treated with Ritalin do not respond to it.

Child Development Concept Table 9.1 summarizes our discussion of physical development in middle and late childhood. Next, we study cognitive developmental changes during this age period.

Child Development Concept Table 9.1 Physical Development in Middle and Late Childhood		
Concept	**Processes/Related Ideas**	**Characteristics/Description**
Basic physical attributes and health and fitness	Changes in physical development	The period of middle and late childhood involves slow, consistent growth—the calm before the rapid growth spurt that appears in adolescence. With regard to body build, children can be characterized as endomorphs, ectomorphs, and mesomorphs. During middle and late childhood, motor development becomes much smoother, and sensory mechanisms continue to mature.
	Health and fitness	Our nation's elementary school children are, for the most part, in poor physical shape. While they cognitively recognize the importance of nutrition and exercise in health, their behavior does not reflect this recognition. Competitive sports programs for elementary school children have increased in recent years and represent one way in which children get consistent exercise. Recent interest has focused on the identification of Type A children. These children experience more stress, in some instances have more illnesses, exhibit more anger, and have parents who often show similar behavior patterns, but a specific link to cardiovascular disease, which has been established with adults, has not yet been discovered with children.
Handicapped children	Their prevalence	Estimates suggest that somewhere between 10 to 15 percent of children between the ages of 5 and 18 are handicapped in some way, ranging from the 0.1 percent who are visually impaired to the 3 to 4 percent with speech handicaps.
	Issues in special education	Two important issues in special education are labeling and mainstreaming. Labeling refers to the assignment of a label, or category, to a child and the effects that label or category may then have. Extreme caution needs to be exercised in the labels given to handicapped children. Mainstreaming refers to the process in which children in need of special education are placed in regular rather than special classrooms. There has been a strong trend toward mainstreaming in recent years.
	Learning disabilities	Between 2 and 3 percent of children are estimated to have a learning disability—this often includes children who are dyslexic, have minimal brain dysfunction, and who are hyperactive. Such children are often a heterogeneous group, showing a wide variety of characteristics. It has been speculated that some children have a learning disability because of developmental lag; that is, they are slow in developing.
	Hyperactive children	Hyperactive children show an increase in purposeless physical activity and an impaired span of attention. Such behavior may interfere with the child's ability to do well in school. Drugs, particularly amphetamines, have been used to treat many hyperactive children. Evidence is mixed on the effectiveness of such drugs, and careful monitoring of dosages is necessary.

PIAGET'S THEORY AND COGNITIVE DEVELOPMENTAL CHANGE IN MIDDLE AND LATE CHILDHOOD

As discussed in Chapter 7, according to Piaget (1967), the preschool child is primarily characterized by preoperational thought. Preoperational thought is a time when stable concepts are formed, mental reasoning emerges, egocentrism is often prominent, and magical belief systems are constructed. Thought during the preschool years is still flawed and not well organized. Piaget believed that concrete operational thought does not appear until about the age of seven, although as we saw in Chapter 7, Piaget may have underestimated some of the cognitive skills of preschool children. For example, by carefully and cleverly designing experiments on understanding the concept of number, Rochel Gelman (1972) demonstrated that some preschool children are able to demonstrate conservation, a concrete operational skill.

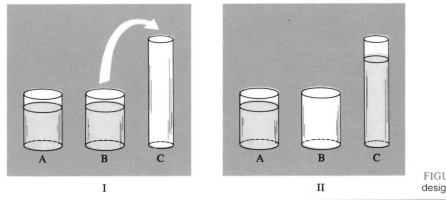

FIGURE 9.1 Piaget's beaker test, designed to assess conservation of liquid.

In this chapter, we explore in greater detail the third major stage of Piaget's view of cognitive development—concrete operational thought. We study the basic aspects of this stage, focus on the application of Piaget's ideas to education, and then provide an overall evaluation of Piaget's contributions to our understanding of cognitive development.

Concrete Operational Thought

According to Piaget (1967), as the child enters the concrete operational stage of thought, he or she is not as egocentric as earlier, does not show animistic thought, reveals conservation skills, and is characterized by decentered and reversible thought.

The Beaker Task—Studying the Conservation of Liquid

Perhaps the most famous of all of Piaget's tasks are those of conservation, the hallmark of concrete operations. Liquids, number, matter, length, volume, and area are among the different conservation dimensions that children can be tested on. Of these conservation tasks, conservation of liquid amount is perhaps the most researched. In this task, which is illustrated in Figure 9.1, the child is presented with two identical beakers, each filled to the same level with liquid (often, milk). The child is asked if these beakers have the same amount of liquid, and he or she usually says yes. Then, the liquid from one beaker is poured into a third beaker, which is taller and thinner than the first two (see Figure 9.1). The child is then asked if the amount of liquid in the tall, thin beaker

is equal to that which remains in one of the original beakers. If the child is less than seven or eight years old, he or she is likely to say no and to justify his or her answer in terms of the differing height or width of the beakers. Older children usually answer yes and can justify their answers appropriately (e.g., "If you poured the milk back, it would show that the amount is the same").

In Piaget's theory, failing the conservation of liquid quantity task is a sign that a child is at the preoperational stage of development, while passing this test is a sign that the child has reached the concrete operational stage. However, this interpretation has been subject to dispute and has been compromised by a number of findings. The ability of the child to conserve, for example, does not happen in a single moment. For instance, the child's ability to conserve area and volume generally develops only a number of years after conservation of matter and length has appeared. Despite problems of interpretation, Piaget's conservation tasks have had a dramatic impact on the field of cognitive development.

Reversibility and the Nature of a Concrete Operation

According to Piaget, concrete operational thought is made up of **operations**—that is, mental actions or representations that are reversible (Piaget, 1967). For example, a well-known test of reversibility of thought involving the conservation of matter involves two identical balls of clay. The experimenter rolls one ball into a long, thin shape, and the other remains in its original ball shape. The child is then asked if there is more clay in the ball or the long, thin piece of clay. By the time children reach the age of seven or eight, most answer that the amount of clay is the same. To answer this problem correctly, children have to be able to imagine that the clay ball is rolled out into a long, thin strip and then returned to its original round shape. Such imagination involves a reversible mental action. Thus, a **concrete operation** is a reversible mental action on real, concrete objects. Such concrete operations allow the child to coordinate several characteristics rather than focusing on a single property of an object. In the clay example, the preoperational child is likely to focus on height *or* width, while the concrete operational child coordinates information about both dimensions.

As we see next, classification is an important aspect of concrete operations as well.

Classification

Many of the concrete operations identified by Piaget focus on the way children reason about the properties of objects. One important skill that characterizes the concrete operational thinker is the ability to classify or divide things into different sets and subsets and to consider their interrelationships. An example of the concrete operational child's classification skills involves a family tree of four generations (see Figure 9.2) (Furth & Wachs, 1975). This family tree suggests that the grandfather (A) has three children (B, C, and D), each of whom has two children (E through J), and that one of these children (J) has three children (K, L, and M). A child who comprehends the classification system can move up or down a level (vertically), across a given level (horizontally), and up and down and across (obliquely) within the system. He or she understands that person J can at the same time be father, brother, son, and grandson, for example.

While we have seen that concrete operational thought is much more advanced than preoperational thought, as discussed next, it has limitations, too.

Constraints on Concrete Operational Thought

Concrete operational thought is limited in that the child needs to have clearly available perceptual physical supports. That is, the child needs to have objects and events present in order to think about them. The concrete operational thinker is not capable of imagining the necessary steps to complete an algebraic equation, for

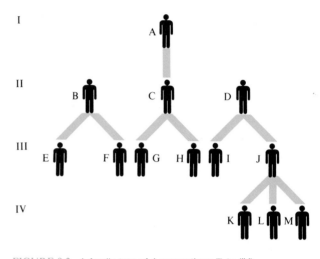

FIGURE 9.2   A family tree of 4 generations (I) to (IV).

example. More information about thought beyond concrete operations appears in Chapter 12, where we discuss formal operational thought.

Piaget and Education

Hardly a day passes without the appearance of a new article applying the principles of Piaget's theory of cognitive development to the education of American children. Frank Murray (1978) describes why Americans have moved so swiftly to embrace Piaget. Two social crises, the proliferation of behaviorism and the dominance of the psychometric approach to intelligence (IQ testing), have made the adoption of Piagetian theory inevitable, he says. The first social crisis was the post-Sputnik concern of a country preoccupied with its deteriorating position as the engineering and scientific leader in the world, and the second was the need for compensatory education for minority groups and the poor. Curriculum projects that soon came into being after these social crises included the "new math," Science Curriculum Improvement Study, Project Physics, "discovery learning," and Man: A Course of Study. All of these projects were based upon Piaget's notion of cognitive developmental changes in thought structure. Piaget's theory contains a great deal of information about the young person's reasoning in the areas of math, science, and logic—material not found anywhere else in the literature of developmental psychology.

How have Piaget's ideas been applied to education?

Piaget was not an educator, and he was not principally concerned with problems of education. However, he provided a scientifically sound conceptual framework from which to view educational problems. In summarizing the general principles of education implicit in Piaget's image of the child, David Elkind (1976) concluded:

> First of all . . . the foremost problem of education is *communication*. According to the Piaget image, the child's mind is not an empty slate. Quite the contrary, the child has a host of ideas about the physical and natural world, but these ideas differ from those of adults and are expressed in a different linguistic mode. . . . We must learn to comprehend what children are saying and to respond in the same mode of discourse.
>
> A second implication is that the child is always unlearning and relearning as well as acquiring entirely new knowledge. The child comes to school with his own ideas about space, time, causality, quantity, and number. . . .
>
> Still a third implication for educational philosophy . . . is that the child is by nature a knowing creature. If the child has ideas about the world which he has not been taught (because they are foreign to adults) and which he has not inherited (because they change with age) then he must have acquired these notions through his spontaneous interactions with the environment . . . education needs to insure that it does not dull this eagerness to know by overly rigid curricula that disrupt the child's own rhythm and pace of learning. (pp. 108–9)

Now that we have seen how provocative and influential Piaget's ideas have been in the study of children's cognition, it is time to take stock of just what Piaget's major contributions have been, as well as where his theory may have fallen short.

Piaget's Contributions and the Neo-Piagetian Critiques

Piaget was a genius when it came to observing children, and his insights are often surprisingly easy to verify. Piaget showed us some important things to look for in development, including the shift to object permanence in infancy and the change from thinking in a concrete manner during the elementary school years to thinking in a more abstract way during adolescence. He also showed us how we must make experiences fit our cognitive framework, yet simultaneously adapt our cognitive orientation to experience. Piaget also revealed how cognitive change is likely to occur if the situation is structured to allow gradual movement to the next higher level.

Four sorts of research findings cause questioning of the Piagetian perspective (Gelman & Baillargeon, 1983; Mandler, 1983; Kuhn, 1984). First, Piaget conceived of stages as unitary structures of thought, so his theory assumes that there is a type of "synchrony" in development. That is, various aspects of a stage should emerge at about the same time. However, researchers have found that several concrete operational concepts do not appear in such synchrony—for example, children do not learn to conserve at the same time they learn to cross-classify (Fischer, 1980).

Second, very small changes in the procedures involving a Piagetian problem have significant effects on a child's cognition. To some degree, this is due to the fact that such matters as remembering the various parts of a task can determine the likelihood that it will be completed correctly (Trabasso, 1977). Thus, a child's stage is at best characterized by one of several factors involved in the solving of Piagetian tasks.

Third, it has been possible to take a child who seems to be at one Piagetian stage, such as preoperational thought, and train the child to pass tasks at the concrete operational level (Gelman, 1969). Such findings pose

$10 + 12 = \underline{\quad?\quad}$: THE IMPORTANCE OF SHORT-TERM MEMORY AND AUTOMATIZATION

Robbie Case (1984) describes himself as a neo-Piagetian, supporting his claim as follows:

Like Piaget, I believe that children's intellectual functioning at different stages of development is most usefully depicted as a sequence of increasingly sophisticated mental structures. Also like Piaget, I believe that the underlying form and complexity of these structures is constant across a wide variety of content domains (provided that children are exposed to the appropriate opportunities for learning). (p. 20)

But Case departs from Piaget's theory in holding the view that:

Stage transition takes place by a set of processes that are oriented toward achieving particular results [e.g., solving problems], in particular physical and social environments. (p. 41)

Case reapproaches Piagetian theory by assuming an age-related constraint that restricts the complexity of mental structures. This age-related constraint is the "space" for storage in short-term memory. Case assumes that structures of knowledge must be assembled in short-term memory. Thus, the storage space available in short-term memory limits the complexity that these structures can attain. He further assumes (as does Pascual-Leone, 1970, another neo-Piagetian) that short-term memory storage space increases as children get older. It follows that the complexity of internal structures of knowledge increases as children get older.

It is worthwhile to consider in more detail the role of information processing concepts in Case's neo-Piagetian theory. In Case's theory, there is a type of limit on information processing capacity; it results from the fact that both forming mental structures and performing mental operations require space in short-term memory. The former takes "storage space," while the latter takes "operating space." The total space in short-term memory does not change with age. However, storage space increases because, as children get older, they become more efficient in their information processing. In other words, many types of mental operation become more automatic as children grow up. As performing operations become more automatic, less of the total short-term memory space is devoted to such operations, and hence more space is left over for forming mental structures that add to the child's

problems for Piaget, who has argued that such training only works on a superficial level and is ineffective unless the child is at a transitional point from one stage to the next.

Fourth, recent studies of infants and young children have shown how certain cognitive abilities emerge earlier than Piaget believed, and their subsequent development may be more prolonged than he thought as well (Gelman & Baillargeon, 1983; Mandler, 1983). One example is symbolic thought, as indicated by the ability to think about objects in their absence. Thinking about objects in their absence seems to appear prior to 12 months of age, not by 18 to 24 months as Piaget believed. For example, infants under one year of age can recall the locations of previously viewed objects (Ashmead & Perlmutter, 1980). Another example is conservation of number (Gelman, 1979). Piaget claimed that conservation of number (like conservation of liquid) does not appear until about seven or eight years of age. Yet we have evidence of number conservation by children three knowledge. In other words, as a result of automatization, there is a developmental decrease in operational space and a corresponding increase in storage space, making more complex knowledge structures possible.

Let's consider the short-term memory and automatization ideas further (Yussen & Santrock, 1982). Suppose a problem required an elementary school child to first add two numbers together (Step 1: 10 + 12) and to next divide the sum by 2 (Step 2: Divide sum by 2). If the elementary school child could do this problem in his or her head, he or she would need to preserve the result of Step 1 (22) momentarily while applying the next step (divide by 2). Some space in the child's short-term memory is necessary to preserve the results of Step 1. A second grader might have to work at the addition problem for several seconds before solving it. By contrast, a sixth grader might quickly solve the problem in one rapid step. In other words, the sixth grader performs the task more automatically with less time and effort. As children become more automatic in performing particular strategies or steps in a task, "free-up" space is created to handle other strategies or steps.

In sum, in Case's model, short-term memory and automatization account for a great deal of the cognitive change going on during the elementary school years—cognitive change that allows students to be much more efficient in solving school-related tasks as they age.

What would Case's neo-Piagetian approach say about the way these children solve math problems?

years of age. Not only do such cognitive skills appear earlier than Piaget believed, but several cognitive developmental experts (Gelman & Baillargeon, 1983; Mandler, 1983) argue that their development is spread out over a longer period of time than Piaget believed. That is, the younger child can do more and the older child less than should be possible according to the Piagetian stages.

Focus on Child Development 9.2 examines Robbie Case's neo-Piagetian theory, a view that places a pre-

mium on short-term memory in understanding children's cognitive development.

Child Development Concept Table 9.2 summarizes our discussion of Piaget's view of cognitive change in middle and late childhood as well as the neo-Piagetian critiques of his view. Now we turn our attention to the information processing perspective and development during middle and late childhood.

Child Development Concept Table 9.2	Piaget's Theory and Cognitive Developmental Change in Middle and Late Childhood	
Concept	**Processes/Related Ideas**	**Characteristics/Description**
Concrete operational thought	The beaker task	The beaker task likely is the most famous of the Piagetian tasks. It assesses conservation of liquid. Failing this task is a sign that the child is still a preoperational, rather than a concrete operational, thinker, although this interpretation has been disputed.
	Reversibility and the nature of a concrete operation	Concrete operational thought is made up of operations, which are mental actions or representations that are reversible. The concrete operational child can coordinate several characteristics, rather than focusing on a single property of an object.
	Classification	One important skill that characterizes the concrete operational thinker is the ability to classify or divide things into different sets or subsets and to consider their interrelationships.
	Constraints on concrete operational thought	The child in the concrete operational stage needs clearly available perceptual supports to reason. Later in development, thought becomes more abstract.
Piaget and education	Its nature	There have been widespread applications of Piaget's ideas to the education of children. These applications emphasize that the child has many ideas about the world, that the child is always unlearning and relearning, and that the child is by nature a knowing creature.
Piaget's contributions and the neo-Piagetian critiques	Piaget's contributions	Piaget was a genius when it came to observing children and developing new insights about their thoughts. He showed us important things to look for in development and mapped out some general cognitive changes in development.
	Neo-Piagetian critiques	The neo-Piagetian critiques focus on the beliefs that the stages of thought are not as unitary as Piaget believed, that small changes in procedures affect the child's cognition, that children sometimes can be trained to reason at higher stages, and that some cognitive skills appear much earlier than Piaget thought while others seem to be more prolonged than Piaget believed. Case, a neo-Piagetian, argues that short-term memory and automatization may explain age-related cognitive changes rather than the cognitive structures advocated by Piaget.

INFORMATION PROCESSING

Among the highlights of the information processing view that provide us with greater insights into cognitive changes during middle and late childhood are those involving memory and drawing inferences, how the information processing perspective views intelligence, the distinction between process and knowledge in development, and the interface of information processing and the education of children. Remember that, without question, the attention of most children improves considerably during middle and late childhood. Also, as mentioned in Chapter 7, elementary school children are more likely to focus on the task-relevant dimensions of a problem rather than its most salient features and are able to maintain their attention for much longer periods of time than preschool children.

Memory

In Chapter 7, we concluded that tests involving short-term memory—for instance, the memory span task—reveal a considerable increase in short-term memory during early childhood but after the age of seven do not show much increase. However, tests of long-term memory frequently show age-related changes during middle and late childhood. We now look more closely at two aspects of memory that seem to be linked to age-related changes in long-term memory during middle and late childhood—control processes in learning and learner characteristics.

Control Processes

If we know anything at all about long-term memory, it is that such memory depends on the learning activities that people engage in when learning and remembering information. Most learning activities fit under the category of effortful **control processes.** Such activities are under the learner's conscious control—they are appropriately referred to as strategies. Five such control processes involved in memory are: (1) rehearsal, (2) organization, (3) semantic elaboration, (4) imagery, and (5) retrieval or search processes.

What all **rehearsal** has in common is extended processing of to-be-remembered material after it has been presented. If someone tells you their phone number and you run through it in your mind while frantically searching for a pencil, you are using rehearsal. If after hearing the number you notice that it includes the year that Columbus discovered America ("1492" as in "690–1492"), you also are rehearsing. In the first instance—with no association involving "1492" and Columbus—you are engaging in what is called **maintenance rehearsal,** while in the second instance—in which you do make the association with Columbus—you are performing **elaborative rehearsal** (Craik & Lockhart, 1972). Maintenance rehearsal simply involves a rote restatement, as in repeating items, while elaborative rehearsal can include organizational, elaborative, and imaginative activities.

In Chapter 8, we referred to a classic memory study by John Flavell and his colleagues to provide support for the belief that cognitive developmental changes possibly underlie changes in the self as knower of the world (Flavell, Beach, & Chinsky, 1966). The basic results of the investigation are reported again here because they have important implications for our understanding of memory development in childhood. In the research, children from five to ten years old were given the task of remembering a set of from two to five pictures of nameable objects for a short (15-second) retention interval. The novel feature of the experiment was that the experimenter was a trained lip-reader. The critical result was that some of the children made lip movements that evidenced rehearsal of the names of the pictures. Furthermore, the percentage of children making such movements increased with age—10 percent of the five-year-olds, 60 percent of the seven-year-olds, and 85 percent of the ten-year-olds made lip movements suggesting rehearsal. A subsequent study of six-year-old children found that those children who engaged in rehearsal showed better recall than those who did not. If nonrehearsers were taught to rehearse, their performance rose to that of the spontaneous rehearsers (Keeney, Cannizzo, & Flavell, 1967).

Although the Flavell, Beach, and Chinsky (1966) study showed an increase with age in the extent of rehearsal, it was uninformative regarding the nature of rehearsal. However, more recent experiments have shown that rehearsal not only increases as children get older—it changes qualitatively. That is, rehearsal changes from simple maintenance or rote rehearsal to more advanced forms of elaborative rehearsal.

The use of organization improves long-term memory. Do children show increased **organizational processing** in middle and late childhood? In one investigation, children were presented with a circular array of pictures from four different categories: clothing, furniture, animals, and vehicles. The children were told to study the pictures so that later they could tell the experimenter the names of the objects in the picture. They also were told that they could move the pictures around in order to remember them better. The results showed that while 10- and 11-year-old children performed such grouping, younger children did not. Importantly, when younger children were put through a brief training procedure that encouraged semantic grouping, they were also able to follow this strategy, and their memory for the pictures improved (Moely, Olson, Halwes, & Flavell, 1969).

Semantic elaboration refers to a process in which information is encoded in a form that preserves the meaning of words and sounds. Semantic elaboration increases during middle and late childhood and is an important factor in long-term memory. Research on memory for meaningful sentences is instructive. In experiments by Scott Paris and his colleagues, children heard sentences that implied the use of but did not actually mention certain tools or instruments (Paris & Lindauer, 1976; Paris, Lindauer, & Cox, 1977). One of the sentences was, "Her friend swept the floor." It clearly implies but does not actually mention the instrument "broom." The critical question asked by Paris and his colleagues was this: If a child hears a sentence such as "Her friend swept the floor," will the child spontaneously infer that a broom was used? If so, we can make a prediction about recall performance in a subsequent test. Specifically, we can make the prediction that a word like *broom* should be a good cue for reminding the child of the sentence. In fact, the results obtained by Paris and his colleagues supported the prediction for 11-year-old children but not for 7-year-old children. This suggested that the use of spontaneous inferential processing increases from 7 to 11 years of age.

Another control process that develops as children move through the middle and late childhood years is **mental imagery.** However, imagery is a process that even adults sometimes fail to use spontaneously (Paivio, 1971). A typical experiment that examined this process used the paired-associates recall procedure (Pressley & Levin, 1977). A list of 18 pairs of words was presented to second-grade and sixth-grade children. Half of the children were told to construct mental images for each of the pairs to help their learning (they were given practice at image construction and were shown drawings of the types of images most helpful to paired-associates recall—these are images in which the two objects interact in some way, e.g., an image of a dog with a kite in its mouth). The older children benefited from the imagery instructions. So also did the younger children in most of the experimental conditions. However, when the pairs were difficult to image and the presentation rate was fast (six seconds per pair), the younger children showed little or no benefit from imagery. Apparently, seven- and eight-year-old children can sometimes use imagery strategies, but not with difficult pairs and fast presentation. Children four or five years old appear to have still greater difficulties in using an imagery strategy (Pressley & Levin, 1977).

Not all learning activities occur at the time of presentation of to-be-remembered material—some occur at the time of testing. There are developmental differences in such **retrieval** activities, as evidenced by another investigation of imagery and memory (Pressley & Levin, 1980). Younger (first grade) and older (sixth grade) children were tested on paired-associates recall. However, there actually were two different imagery groups.

In one imagery group, the children were instructed to use imagery not only when they were learning the pairs but also when they were recalling the pairs. In the other imagery group, the children were instructed to use imagery when learning but were not instructed to use imagery when recalling. Older children performed identically in the two imagery groups. But younger children in the first imagery group showed better recall than those in the second imagery group. Apparently, the younger children engaged in imagery-based learning and yet failed to capitalize on such learning unless instructed to use imagery in recall. They suffered a deficit in spontaneous use of an effective retrieval strategy.

Retrieval strategies are not limited to situations involving mental imagery. For example, Kobasigawa (1974) has shown that, as children get older, they make more and better use of category information in the process of remembering. Children from 6 to 11 years old were shown three different pictures from each of eight different categories (e.g., three zoo animals, three fruits, etc.). A test followed in which children attempted to recall the pictures. In one condition, they were given a deck containing category cues (e.g., a picture of a zoo was the cue for the animals—these category cues had also been shown during learning). These category cues were used by only 33 percent of the 6-year-old subjects. But they were used by 75 percent of the 8-year-old subjects, and by over 90 percent of the 11-year-old subjects.

So far, we have seen that long-term memory shows considerable improvement during middle and late childhood. Control processes, such as rehearsal, organization, semantic elaboration, imagery, and retrieval or search processes, are among the most important influences on the increase in long-term memory. Now we turn our attention to another important influence on memory—characteristics of the learner.

Characteristics of the Learner

Apart from the obvious variable of age, many characteristics of a learner can determine the level of his or her memory performance. These characteristics include attitudes, motivations, and health-related factors. However, the characteristic that has been examined most thoroughly is the previously acquired knowledge of the learner.

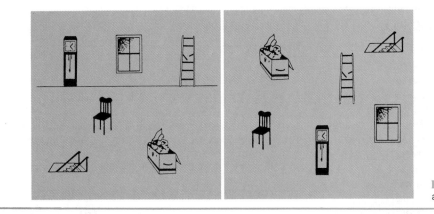

FIGURE 9.3   An example of an organized and unorganized version of a picture.

The knowledge that a learner possesses probably contributes to most memory tasks. And since knowledge is something that increases with age, it clearly should contribute to development of memory. In support of this reasoning, Mandler and Robinson (1977) compared memory for meaningful scenes and disorganized arrays of objects in first, third, and fifth graders (see Figure 9.3). One interesting finding was that the meaningful scenes were recognized better than the disorganized arrays and that this difference grew larger with age. That is, the benefit of viewing organized scenes was less for the first graders than for the older children. This suggests that a child's growing knowledge of scenes can be beneficial to his or her memory for scenes.

The effects that knowledge can have upon memory are impressively strong. In one study, a group of children and a group of adults were tested on memory for chessboard displays (Chi, 1978). After viewing a chessboard, all subjects attempted to recall the locations of pieces. The results should strike you as quite unusual, given the research we have covered thus far in the chapter: The children were better, and by a substantial margin. How could this be so? The answer is simple: The children were all skilled chess players, whereas the adults were novices. What this study shows is that, when children's knowledge of stimuli to be remembered exceeds that of adults, children's memory for the stimuli can be superior. Such is the power of the effects of knowledge on memory.

What are the effects of knowledge on memory?

Given the strength of knowledge effects, one might ask whether the learner's knowledge is a more important determinant of memory than the control processes (e.g., organization, imagery) that he or she employs. Although this question sounds reasonable, it probably is unanswerable. The reason is that the subject's knowledge and his or her control processes do not function independently. They interact with each other and together

FOCUS ON CHILD DEVELOPMENT 9.3

METAMEMORY: PREDICTING MEMORY SPAN AND KNOWING HOW MUCH TO STUDY

The two factors of knowledge and control processes are tightly intertwined. Indeed, one important type of memory knowledge actually concerns control processes. Such knowledge is that of **metamemory,** which can be loosely defined as knowledge about one's own memory (Brown, Bransford, Ferrara, & Campione, 1983; Flavell, 1985; Flavell & Wellman, 1977). More specifically, metamemory comprises (1) knowledge that learning information is different from simply perceiving information, in that specific memory strategies are sometimes necessary for the former; (2) diagnostic knowledge of the various factors (e.g., rehearsal, recall versus recognition testing) contributing to performance of different memory tasks; and (3) knowledge of how to monitor memory during the course of learning (e.g., the ability to tell when one has studied sufficiently to pass an exam).

The sophistication of children's metamemory—as assessed through their answers on verbal test batteries—improves from the preschool years through adolescence and beyond (Brown, Bransford, Ferrara, & Campione, 1983; Flavell, 1985). However, a basic question has been raised: Does children's metamemorial knowledge of memory strategies actually predict their use of such strategies and their level of performance in learning and remembering tasks? The answer appears to be yes. Although the relationship of metamemory to memory performance is often weak or absent in younger children (e.g., second graders), it appears to grow stronger in older children (sixth graders) (Ledger & Graff, 1985;

Short, 1985). Moreover, the weak associations that are found with younger children may reflect difficulties of measuring metamemory rather than a true absence of metamemory—memory connections. If metamemory questions are carefully worded and given after children have had some exposure to a task, the answers to these questions may be more valid. For example, in one study of first and second graders, it was shown that children's causal attributions regarding organizational processing—that is, their ideas about whether organizing information improves its memorability—were related to organizational processing in a subsequent memory task (Fabricius & Hagen, 1984). An important feature of this experiment was that children were asked about the effects of organization on memory only after some experience in tasks requiring both organization and memory.

Of the three different types of metamemorial functioning, perhaps the most crucial from a practical standpoint is that of memory monitoring. Whether or not children know the most efficient memory strategies, it is crucial for them to know when they have finally mastered a body of information so that they can safely stop studying. Yet, memory monitoring appears to be deficient in young children. In an investigation of memory monitoring, Flavell, Friedrichs, and Hoyt (1970) studied the memory spans of children in nursery school through the fourth grade. Initially, children were presented with strips of paper with different-length series of pictures of familiar objects (such as toys, blocks, scissors, and houses). The children were then asked how many of the objects they could remember if the objects were covered up (a strip with one picture, two pictures, and so on). Next, each child's actual memory span was evaluated by reading aloud to the child a series of object names of pictures and determining how many he or she could

determine efficiency of learning and memory. Some support for interactions between knowledge and control processes comes from a study by Mary Zembar and Mary Naus (1985). They tested recall memory in third and sixth graders, using three different types of materials: "kiddie" materials, consisting of very common words;

"typical experimental" materials, consisting of nouns of intermediate difficulty; and "advanced adult" materials, consisting of very difficult words. Their results showed that children in both age groups showed good recall and used efficient memory strategies when given materials that were easy for them but not when given materials

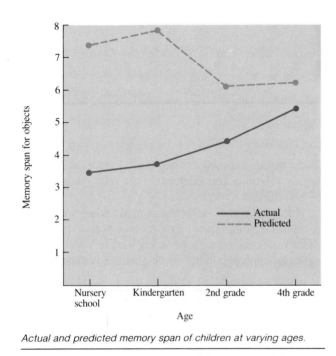

Actual and predicted memory span of children at varying ages.

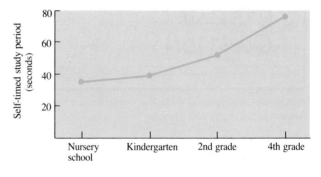

Self-timed study for memory span task by children of different ages.

recall. In addition to assessing the children's memory spans, the experimenter also asked the children to predict how long their memory span would be. As shown in the figure above, the older children's memory span, not surprisingly, was superior, but these children were also better able than the younger children to accurately predict their memory span, an aspect of metamemory or knowledge about one's memory.

Then, in a second phase, each child was given a new set of pictures equal in length to his or her predetermined memory span. The children were told to study the objects on the strip of paper as long as was necessary to recall them perfectly. The results suggested that the younger children often stopped studying before they were ready to recall. As shown in the figure above, the younger children were much less likely to study as long as the older children.

Thus, the research of Flavell and his colleagues showed that younger children are much less efficient than older children at monitoring their memory, both in terms of memory span predictability and in the degree of study time required for recall readiness.

that were difficult for them. That is, subjects' knowledge of the materials affected their use of efficient memory strategies.

Focus on Child Development 9.3 examines a very widely researched aspect of children's knowledge of efficient memory strategies—metamemory. Now that we have seen how important memory is in children's processing of information, we consider another aspect of cognition that involves children's ability to draw inferences.

MISS PEACH   By Mell Lazarus

MISS PEACH by Mell Lazarus. Courtesy of Mell Lazarus and News America Syndicate.

Drawing Inferences

An **inference** is a relationship noted between one event and another that is not directly stated. Thus far, we have considered the importance of attending to something, perceiving it, and remembering it. Our world would be a rather simple place if our mental activity stopped there. It would consist of unconnected and unrelated events. So what does it mean that the sun rises and then people wake up and get on with the day's business? What is the connection between a child's falling off a bicycle one moment and an adult's holding the child the next moment while the youngster cries? Throughout our lives, we experience events that are logically or matter-of-factly related to one another. The study of inferencing helps us to understand how people construct these relationships.

Sometimes, the connection between events is logical. We need not even experience the events directly to understand how they are related to one another. Thus, suppose we hear someone describe a situation as follows:

There was an older man, a man, and a boy.
The older man said to the man, "I'm glad you're my son."
The man said to the boy, "And I'm glad you're my son."
What is the relationship between the older man and the boy?

The answer is based on our logical understanding of family relations and inference—the relationship is one of grandfather and grandson.

Another type of inference is made when we rely on substantial prior knowledge to interpret experiences. Substantial reliance on prior knowledge is required to make an appropriate inference about the following:

Albert spotted a worm in the water. He swam over to the worm and bit into him. Albert was caught and pulled through the water. Who is Albert? Why did he bite the worm? Who caught him and how?

The paragraph provides no clues to answer these questions, but our own experiences and prior knowledge offer some help. Albert is probably a fish who was hungry and was caught on the hook of a fisherman.

Children improve dramatically in their abilities to draw certain types of inferences as they mature. For example, their understanding of relationships in narrative folktales improves across the elementary school years. Children also improve in making a variety of linguistic inferences and analogical inferences (that is, drawing analogies) throughout the elementary school years. They improve in making inferences on a host of traditional reading comprehension and cognitive assessment measures as well (Wechsler, 1974; Yussen, 1982).

No topic, perhaps, has received greater attention in contemporary circles of information processing than the importance of what the individual already knows as an influence on what he or she will get out of some cognitive encounter (Schank & Abelson, 1977; Chi, 1978; Kintsch, 1982). As we see next, some of the most fascinating inquiries about how children organize such knowledge involves schemata and scripts.

Schemata and Scripts

Many psychologists believe that it is necessary to call on a concept called **schemata** as well as **scripts** when we try to explain children's activation of long-term memory knowledge (Bartlett, 1932; Mandler, 1983). Schemata (*schema* is the singular) are active organizations of past experiences that provide a structure from which new information can be judged.

There are schemata for scenes or spatial layouts (you may have a schema for a typical kitchen), as well as schemata for common events (you may have schemata for going to a restaurant, playing baseball, and writing a term paper). Schemata for events are often called *scripts* (Schank & Abelson, 1977), and these have been the focus of some interesting research. A typical script includes information about physical features, people, and typical happenings. This type of generalized knowledge is useful to people when they are trying to interpret what is going on around them.

A standard example of a script is our generalized understanding of what takes place when we visit a restaurant. The major events that occur include entering the restaurant, being seated, ordering, eating, paying the bill, and leaving. An event that touches on a restaurant episode, then, would be expected to evoke the person's highly ritualized understanding of the activities mentioned. Consider this paragraph, for example:

> The hungry man saw the sign for the steak house. An hour later, he had wolfed down a delicious tenderloin and was on his way.

Since we all have common knowledge about restaurants, we can draw several inferences, such as that the man ordered a meal from a waiter or waitress and later paid for it. Now that we have some idea of what scripts are like in our lives, let's see how they develop in children's lives.

The Development of Scripts in Children

Current evidence suggests that scripts emerge quite early in life, perhaps by one year of age if not sooner (Nelson, 1977; Schank & Abelson, 1977). Scripts may explain why young infants grow distressed when there is a change in their daily routine (Mandler, 1983). And certainly there is very clear evidence that children have scripts and other types of schemata by the time they start school. In one study, four- and five-year-old children were asked to describe what happens when eating in different locations (at home, in a day-care center, and at McDonald's) (Nelson, 1978). The descriptions they gave were impressively detailed and in good correspondence with those given by adults in other studies (Bower, Black, & Turner, 1979). The children showed knowledge of the beginnings and endings of the various types of eating episodes and of events that were central versus optional in an episode.

Not only can children describe their scripts, they spontaneously make inferences based on those scripts. For example, if children hear a story that conforms to a script and later are given a recognition test, they will falsely recognize objects and actions that are typical of the script, even though these items were not actually presented in the story (Brown, 1976; Rabinowitz, Valentine, & Mandler, 1981). Apparently, children infer from their scripts that the typical actions occurred, and this leads them to judge that the actions were actually part of the story. For example, after hearing a story about lunch time at school, children may think that they heard something about opening a lunch box, even though they did not. Adults show this same sort of error, and so it appears that scripts govern inferencing at all phases of development. Of course, scripts and other types of schemata can grow more complex and differentiated as children learn more about their world (Gruendel, 1980). As adults, we may have separate scripts for Chinese and French restaurants and for fancy restaurants versus diners. A young child who has not experienced many restaurants obviously would lack such detailed scripts.

We mentioned earlier that the knowledge of the world that children carry in their minds increases dramatically throughout the preschool and elementary school years. Recent research suggests that schemata and scripts are intimately involved in this development of knowledge.

Specifically, some provocative new findings support the conclusion that a child's world knowledge initially is organized in terms of schemata and scripts for familiar events and activities. Only later do taxonomic categories emerge (Lucariello & Nelson, 1985; Mandler, 1980; Nelson, 1981).

An example helps to clarify the distinction between schematic/scriptal categories and taxonomic categories. As adults, we realize that elephant, dog, and cow all fit within the taxonomic category of animals. However, they do not fit naturally within the same script—whereas elephant fits within a visiting-the-zoo script, dog fits more naturally within a playing-with-pets script, and cow within an on-the-farm script. In contrast, elephant, tiger and camel all fit within a visiting-the-zoo script. Now, if preschool children rely primarily on schematic and scriptal categories, as opposed to taxonomic categories, they might fail to recognize that elephant, dog, and cow all are examples of a single category (animals). Yet, they should have no difficulty in recognizing that elephant, tiger, and camel all fit together (zoo animals). In fact, Joan Lucariello and Katherine Nelson (1985) have provided evidence for this line of reasoning. They presented three- and four-year-olds with a nine-word list containing three members of each of three taxonomic categories (animals, clothes, and foods) or a list containing three members of each of three scriptal categories (zoo animals, clothes to put on in the morning, and lunch foods). Recall was higher in the scriptal condition than in the taxonomic condition. Further, children in the scriptal condition showed more "clustering"—a stronger tendency to recall the three words of a category together. Research conducted with older children shows that script-based categorization continues into the childhood years (Mistry & Lange, 1985). Focus on Child Development 9.4 presents more about the nature of scripts in children.

So far, we have learned a great deal about how children process information about their world. Through a number of chapters, we have studied how they attend to information, perceive it, retain it over time, and draw inferences about it. As we see next, information processing psychologists believe that many of these things also are likely to be important in understanding children's intelligence.

R. J. Sternberg, whose information processing view of intelligence has gained considerable recognition in recent years.

An Information Processing Conception of Intelligence

In Chapter 10, we explore a number of ideas about the nature of intelligence and how it is measured. However, some of the most recent and provocative ideas about intelligence have come from information processing psychologists.

Robert Sternberg (1982, 1984) has described how the psychometric, measurement-based approach—the use of tests to uncover the structure of abilities—focuses on the products of intellectual performance. In the information processing revolution, the emphasis shifted to the study of processes of intellectual behavior and away from products. Psychometricians were criticized for their lack of attention to the cognitive processes that produce the products measured by the tests.

FOCUS ON CHILD DEVELOPMENT 9.4

SCRIPTS FOR SANDBOXES, SNACKS, AND SPELLING

Changes in children's everyday routines are common. Some activities are added, some are deleted, and the order of occurrence of ongoing activities may be modified. Children's memory for such preschool routines was the focus of an investigation by Marina Myles-Worsley, Cindy Cromer, and David Dodd (1986). Both preschool and nonpreschool activities were studied according to script modification possibilities. The modifications were labeled as early deletions (deleted from the school-day script after preschool), later deletions (deleted from the school-day script after kindergarten), or nondeletions (continuing to occur in the school-day script but with temporal order changed). Nonpreschool activities were categorized as early additions (added to the school-day script after preschool), later additions (added to the school-day

script after kindergarten), or nonadditions (not occurring in the school-day script for preschool through the third grade). Teachers were asked to identify the preschool activities that occurred on a routine basis two or more times per week during the five-year period of the study. Based on these data, four activities in each of the three preschool and nonpreschool script modification categories were chosen to indicate routine school activities as shown in the table.

Visual memory cues consisting of 24 line drawings showing routine school activities were given to 50 children, 10 in each of five grade levels (preschool, kindergarten, and first, second, and third grades). Each of these children had attended the same structured preschool for one year. Examples of the stimulus cues are shown in the figure below. A control group of nonattendees also were shown the same stimulus cards. As shown in the first graph, the most frequent sources of errors were early deletions and additions, activities that either are deleted or added to the school-day script at the early script

Routine School Activities

Script Modification Category	Activities Depicted
Preschool activities	
Early deletions	Health check, putting on name tags, playing in the sandbox, using carpentry tools
Later deletions	Having a snack, playing house, building with blocks, playing cars and trucks
Nondeletions	Playground/recess, cleaning up, painting, rugtime/circle
Nonpreschool activities	
Early additions	Doing workbooks, saying the Pledge of Allegiance, spelling, math
Later additions	Having lunch, cursive writing, tests, tidying own desk
Nonadditions	Naptime, sitting in the corner, chemistry lessons, computer lessons

From Myles-Worsley, Marina, et al., "Children's preschool script reconstruction: Reliance on general knowledge as memory fades" in *Developmental Psychology, 22,* 22–30, 1986. Copyright © 1986 American Psychological Association. Reprinted by permission of the author.

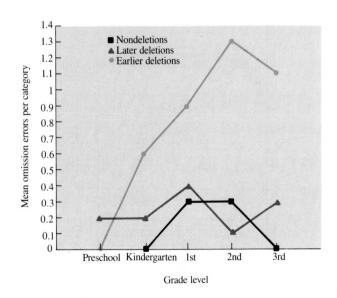

Errors in preschool script made by children of different ages.

(continued on following page)

FOCUS ON CHILD DEVELOPMENT 9.4

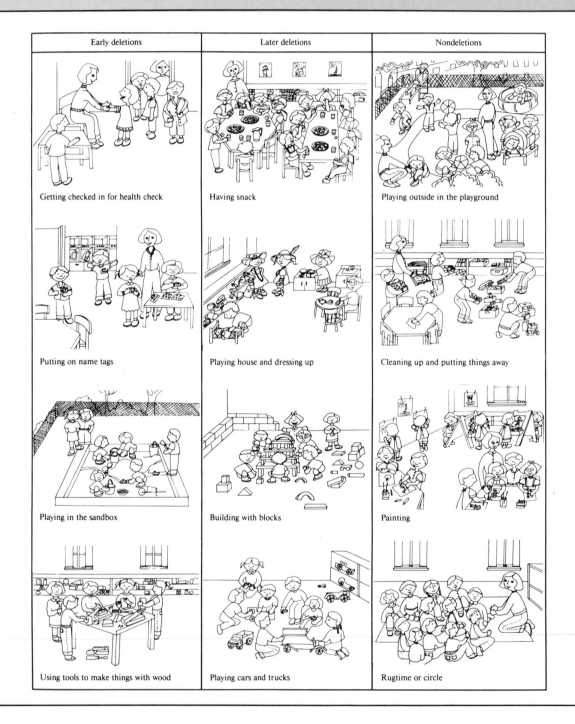

Early deletions	Later deletions	Nondeletions
Getting checked in for health check	Having snack	Playing outside in the playground
Putting on name tags	Playing house and dressing up	Cleaning up and putting things away
Playing in the sandbox	Building with blocks	Painting
Using tools to make things with wood	Playing cars and trucks	Rugtime or circle

modification stage immediately after preschool. For example, an early error would be the failure to recognize preschool activities from script modification categories. Thus, a child might fail to remember that "playing in the sandbox," an early deletion, was a regular preschool activity. A possible explanation is that, as children progress through school, a general school-day script evolves that biases memory away from activities that distinguish one grade level from another and toward activities common to most grades.

The comparison of the children who attended preschool with those who did not suggested that, over time, children's reconstructions are based more on growing general knowledge than specific, event-based memories. As shown in the second graph, the younger, direct-experience children had a significant advantage over the no-experience children. However, by the third grade, recognition errors for the two groups were very close. Recognition errors for the direct experience faded as the children became older, while the general knowledge of school-related matters decreased the number of errors of the no-experience children.

In sum, a process of generalization in memory for the preschool script evolves over many years. As memory for preschool experiences fades, information about such experiences is reconstructed from an evolving, general school-day script that becomes part of the child's general knowledge. Because of their growing general knowledge, even children who did not attend preschool are able to develop inferences that virtually match the accuracy of their counterparts who attended preschool when they are queried about the nature of preschool scripts.

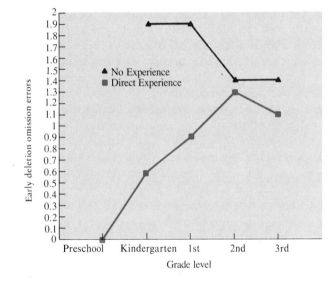

The effects of preschool experience on memory for scripts.

Sternberg has proposed that we might better understand intelligence if it is viewed in terms of information processing components. Thus, his **componential analysis** attempts to understand the availability, accessibility, and ease of execution of a number of different information processing components. The basic concept in this approach is the **component,** an elementary information process that operates on internal representations of objects (Newell & Simon, 1972; Sternberg, 1982). A component may translate sensory input into conceptual representation, transform one conceptual representation into another, or translate conceptual representation into some form of motor output. In Sternberg's perspective, we see the familiar model of receiving, processing, and reacting that neuroscientists use to describe the transmission of information within the brain and nervous system. According to Sternberg, a component can be classified according to function (what it does) and level (whether it has a higher-level function in terms of planning and decision making or a lower-level, more precise function).

Sternberg has identified the following five information processing components, each performing a different function:

1. **Metacomponents** are higher-order control processes used for executive planning and decision making when problem solving is called for. The decisions of which problem to solve and how to solve it are metacomponential decisions.
2. **Performance components** are processes used to carry out a problem-solving strategy. A set of performance components involves the actual working through of a problem.
3. **Acquisition (or storage) components** are processes used in learning new information. For example, this might involve rehearsing new information to transfer a trace of it into long-term memory.
4. **Retention (or retrieval) components** index processes involved in accessing previously stored information. For example, you might search through your long-term memory store in an organized manner to find a fact you need at a particular moment.
5. **Transfer components** are processes used in generalization, such as using information learned on one task to help solve another task. For example, having learned how to use a typewriter should expedite your ability to use a computer.

The shift in interest to information processing and away from products as measured by intelligence tests does not mean that information processing theorists are uninterested in products (Sternberg, 1982). Rather, these theorists are suggesting that attention should be given to the knowledge base generated by the processes.

Knowledge Versus Process Views of Intelligence

The information processing approach raises two very important questions about intelligence: (1) What are the information processing abilities that occur in development? and (2) What are the changes in world knowledge or "expertise" that occur in development?

Few would deny that both changes in processing and changes in knowledge occur in development. However, there is disagreement about which is more fundamental. For example, though there is accumulation of knowledge in childhood, this accumulation may simply be the consequence of a growing reserve of "processing capacity." That is, the older child's greater capacity may be what allows him or her to learn more sophisticated knowledge. Alternatively, though processing efficiency clearly increases as children get older, perhaps this reflects older children's greater knowledge and the fact that greater knowledge allows more efficient information processing activities. It has been difficult to decide between these two possibilities, creating what Frank Keil (1984) calls the structure/process dilemma of cognitive development. The dilemma concerns the basic issue of what the "mechanisms" of intellectual development are (Sternberg, 1984). Are they those of changing information processing abilities? Are they those of changing knowledge and expertise? Or are they both?

To make the structure/process dilemma somewhat more concrete, consider a simple computer metaphor. Suppose that we have two computers and that each is capable of solving multiplication problems (e.g., 13 × 24, 45 × 21). However, one computer works much faster than the other. What could be the explanation? One possibility is that the "faster" computer truly is faster—it has faster subroutines for performing arithmetic computations, or more core (that is, short-term memory), allowing two or more computations to proceed at once. Alternatively, the "faster" computer might have a greater store of relevant knowledge—perhaps it has in

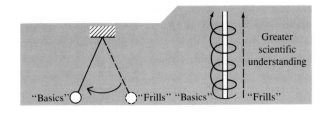

FIGURE 9.4   There may always be tension between two functions of schooling—cognitive development versus the more social enterprises such as athletics, band, and drivers' education. Undoubtedly this tension will produce shifts of emphasis, as with a swinging pendulum. But if we are successful in developing an instructional psychology, we might achieve something similar to a spiral staircase, as opposed to a pendulum that just swings back and forth. That is, we might continually develop more sophisticated ways of fulfilling the varied and changing functions of schooling.

its data bank (long-term memory) a complete multiplication table going up to 99 × 99. The "slower" computer might be forced to get by (as do most humans) with a smaller table going up to only 12 × 12. In this case, the "faster" computer need not be fundamentally faster—its subroutines may be relatively slow—but it is able to perform the multiplication task relying on knowledge instead of computation. The issue we face in the development of intelligence is similar to that of explaining the difference between the "fast" and "slow" computers. Is it processing or knowledge that is responsible for how intelligence changes with age? Recent research on memory indicates that the answer may be both (Zembar & Naus, 1985). If so, the essential task for researchers is to determine how processing and knowledge interact in the course of intellectual development.

Child Development Concept Table 9.3 summarizes our discussion of children's information processing during the elementary school years. Next, we consider one final intriguing question about information processing—its importance in the education of children.

Information Processing and Education

Elementary and secondary schools in the United States are in serious need of reform. This point has been recognized by a number of states in which educational reform movements are already underway or at least in the planning stages. But just what sort of reform is needed? The main thrust of many current proposals is that there is a great deal of wasted time and fluff in our school curricula; children need to work more on the "basics," such as English and math, instead of the "frills," such as athletics and band. Many such proposals call for extensions in the school day and school year, as well as more homework. Many also argue that teachers should be given more power and prestige to enforce a rigorous regimen of study (though these teachers also should be tested to

ensure that they are competent and worthy of the prestige they are given). The essential notion seems to be that more time and work—enforced by tough and competent teachers—is a large part of the answer to our problems in educating children.

But these proposals are not novel. As Patricia Cross (1984) points out:

. . . similar recommendations in the recent wave of reports on school reform foster a sense of deja vu. Our collective memories are short. Yet we have only to look back one decade to find a school reform movement of today; more than a dozen books and reports calling for the reform of education were published between 1970 and 1976. Why can't we find excellence in education and then hang onto it? The pattern of educational reform has been to generate a lot of enthusiasm, reform the curriculum, raise the standards, restore prestige to teaching—and then somehow have improvements swept away again by the rising tide of mediocrity. (p. 168)

Later in her provocative article, Cross calls this the "swinging pendulum solution": We "get tough" in education, then grow lax in our enforcement of standards, then grow alarmed and "get tough" again ad infinitum. Clearly, this is not satisfactory, so what *really* is the problem? Why can't we aim for a "spiral staircase solution" (Figure 9.4)? If we must discard and then return to old issues and approaches—and probably we must in a democratic society in which fads come and go—can't we at least have a more advanced perspective on each "return trip"? With all of the advances in science and technology in other areas of our life, why have we failed to find lasting improvements in how we educate our children?

An answer to this rather depressing question was suggested by Robert Glaser (1982). Glaser pointed out that, since the early part of this century, the fields of education and psychology have not interacted as much as they

Child Development Concept Table 9.3 Information Processing		
Concepts	**Processes/Related Ideas**	**Characteristics/Description**
Memory	Long-term memory and control processes	Long-term memory shows considerable improvement during middle and late childhood. Control processes, such as rehearsal, organization, semantic elaboration, imagery, and retrieval or search processes, are among the most important influences on the increase in long-term memory.
	Characteristics of the learner	Apart from the obvious characteristic of age, many individual characteristics determine the level of the child's memory performance. These characteristics include attitudes, motivations, and health-related factors. However, the characteristic that has been most widely examined is the previously acquired knowledge of the learner. In particular, developmental psychologists have been interested in children's ability to monitor their memory activities. Metamemory (children's knowledge of memory processes) seems to increase during the middle and late childhood years.
Drawing inferences	The nature of inferences, schemata, and scripts	An inference is a relationship noted between one event and another that is not directly stated. Children improve dramatically in their ability to draw inferences during the elementary school years. Schemata are active organizations of past experiences that provide a structure from which new information can be judged. Scripts are schemata for events. While scripts emerge quite early in life, perhaps by one year of age, and are prominent in preschool as well, the increased knowledge base of elementary school children likely contributes strongly to the prevalence and complexity of scripts. Older children rely on such general knowledge to develop inferences about scripts for experiences they never encountered themselves.
An information processing conception of intelligence	Sternberg's componential analysis	Robert Sternberg has demonstrated the importance of studying the processes of intellectual behavior rather than relying only on the products of intelligence (which psychometricians do). Sternberg has developed the strategy of componential analysis to evaluate how we receive, process, and react to information. A component is an elementary information process that operates on internal representations of objects. According to Sternberg, five such components in intelligence are: metacomponents, performance components, acquisition (or storage) components, retention (or retrieval) components, and transfer components.
Knowledge versus process views of intelligence	What are the information processing abilities that occur in development, and what are the changes in world knowledge or "expertise" that occur in development?	A critical issue raised by information processing psychologists is whether intelligence and development occur primarily through a growth in knowledge or through changes in processing. Some recent research suggests that both knowledge and processing are involved.

might. The consequence has been that educational policy, unlike policy in many other areas of life, has been affected only slightly by scientific and technological advances. Without the influence of such advances, the swinging pendulum solution is about all that is possible in changing educational curricula. On the bright side, however, there have been many recent advances in our understanding of human cognition and information processing, and the time seems ripe to exploit these advances by applying them to education. Some further ideas about the interface of information processing and the education of children are presented in Focus on Child Development 9.5.

FOCUS ON CHILD DEVELOPMENT 9.5

INFORMATION PROCESSING, EDUCATION, AND THE INFORMATION AGE

When you were in elementary school, did any teacher at any time work with you on improving your memory strategies? Did any of your teachers work with you on your reading skills after the first few grades of elementary school? Did any of your teachers work with you on trying to improve your speed of information processing? Did any of your teachers discuss with you ways in which imagery could be used to enhance your processing of information? Did any of your teachers work with you on developing your ability to make inferences about information you encountered in the classroom and outside of school? If you are like most people, you spent little or no time during elementary school on improving these important processes involved in our everyday encounters with our world.

Why is it important to have an educational goal of improving the information processing skills of children? Think for a moment about yourself and the skills that likely are necessary for you to be successful in adapting to your environment and in improving your chances for getting a good job and having a successful career. To some extent, knowledge itself is important; more precisely, content knowledge in particular areas is important. Our schools have done a much better job of imparting knowledge to students, particularly content knowledge about a particular subject (basically, schools have been in the business of pouring knowledge into children's heads), than in instructing them in how to process information about their world.

Another important situation in your life where instruction in information processing skills would have helped you tremendously was when you took the SAT or ACT test. SAT cram courses are popping up everywhere in the United States because our schools, for the most part, have not done a good job of developing information processing skills. Is speed of processing important on the SAT? Most of you likely felt that you did not have as much time as you would have liked to handle difficult questions. Are memory strategies important on the SAT? You had to read paragraphs and hold a considerable amount of information in your mind to answer some of

the questions. And you certainly had to remember how to solve a variety of math problems. Also, didn't you have to remember the definitions of a tremendous number of vocabulary words? And what about problem solving, inferencing, and understanding? Remember the difficult verbal problems you had to answer and the inferences you had to make when reasoning was called for? Also, remember how it was necessary for you to read several paragraphs and process the selection's key points?

The story of information processing is one of attention, perception, memory (particularly the control processes involved in memory), thinking, and the like. Such information processing skills become even more important in education when we consider that we are now in the midst of a transition from an industrial society to a post-industrial, information processing society, with approximately 65 to 70 percent of all workers involved in services. The information revolution in our society has placed stressful demands on workers who are called on daily to process huge amounts of information in a rapid fashion, to have efficient memories, to attend to relevant details, to reason logically about difficult issues, and to make inferences about information that may be fuzzy and unclear. Students graduate from high school, college, or postgraduate education and move into such jobs calling for efficient skills in information processing and often have had little or no instruction in improving such skills.

At this time, we do not have a specified curriculum of information processing that can be taught in a stepwise, developmental fashion to children and adolescents. We also do not have the trained personnel for this instruction. Further, some information processing experts believe that such processes as attention and memory cannot be trained in a general way. Rather, these experts argue that information processing often is domain- or content-specific. They do believe, however, that an infusion of the information processing orientation into all parts of the curriculum in secondary schools would greatly benefit adolescent cognition.

Research in educational psychology is beginning to look seriously at the importance of information processing in school learning. A recent book by Ellen Gagne (1985), in particular,

(continued on following page)

FOCUS ON CHILD DEVELOPMENT 9.5

How might information processing skills be taught in schools?

provides a menu of information processing strategies that need to be given attention when instructing children in specific content areas, such as reading, writing, math, and science. She concludes that research has shown that successful students (e.g., those who make better grades, get higher achievement test scores) are better than their unsuccessful counterparts at such information processing components as focusing their attention, elaborating and organizing information, and monitoring their study strategies. As yet, however, the extent to which these important information processing abilities can be taught is unknown. Nonetheless, Gagne recently demonstrated how seventh-grade students can be taught effective ways to elaborate on information so that it can be remembered more efficiently (Gagne, Weidemann, Bell, & Ander, in press).

Patricia Cross (1984) has also addressed how information processing instruction might benefit individuals. According to Cross, the goal of schools should be to develop a lifetime learner who has the information processing skills to acquire new information efficiently throughout life. Schooling has been shown to improve the information processing skills of children when children who attend schools in rural and isolated communities are compared with children in the same communities who do not attend schools. For example, Harold Stevenson (1982) found that Peruvian children who attended school were better than their nonschool counterparts at many different memory and conceptualization tasks. However, while significant, the effects were small. Perhaps if a concentrated effort was made to begin instructing individuals from kindergarten through the college years in ways to improve their information processing skills, the effects of schooling would be much more pronounced. Several prominent universities, such as Carnegie-Mellon and UCLA, encourage students to take courses in information processing and try to teach such

Copyright © 1981 United Feature Syndicate, Inc.

higher-level information processing skills as problem solving. And, Robert Sternberg, whose ideas about intelligence were discussed earlier in this chapter, is working on a book to be published soon (*Intelligence Applied*) that describes how to teach intelligence. Frank Barron (1985) also believes that critical thinking skills can be taught. He is especially interested in how individuals can be taught to think in less irrational ways. For example, Barron argues that adolescents should be more critical of the first ideas that pop into their heads—they should be instructed to think longer about important things and to search in more organized ways for evidence to support their views.

The possibilities that the information processing perspective offers for the education of children are exciting. In the next several decades, there likely will be increased commerce between the fields of information processing and education, although there may be limits to how extensively information processing skills can be taught.

THINKING BACK, LOOKING AHEAD

The physical and cognitive world of middle and late childhood is an exciting one, capturing such imaginative themes as a nine-year-old boy having a conversation with his computer, Helen Keller's awe at being able to traverse the great distance between a first syllable and "the sweep of thought in a line of Shakespeare," hockey in Minnesota, football in Texas, soccer in Florida, Type A behavioral patterns, labeling, mainstreaming, learning disabilities, hyperactivity, reasoning about water in beakers and a family tree of four generations, salutes to and disenchantments with Piaget, short-term memory and automatization, imagery, expert child chess players, predicting memory span and knowing how much to study, drawing inferences about Albert and the worm, scripts for restaurants, sandboxes, snacks, and spelling, Sternberg's information processing conception of intelligence, the distinction between knowledge and process, the swinging pendulum of educational reform, and the importance of improving the information processing skills of children as a predominant aspect of education.

In Chapter 10, we continue our inquiry about the child's cognitive world as we explore further ideas about intelligence and spend considerable time describing achievement. But before we leave this chapter, think for a moment about how important memory, one of the central features of information processing, is in our lives and the lives of children. This importance was imaginatively captured by Dylan Thomas, who reconstructed some of the highlights of his childhood:

And that park grew up with me; that small world widened as I learned its secret boundaries, as I discovered new refuges in its woods and jungles; hidden homes and lairs for the multitudes of imagination, for cowboys and Indians, and the tall-terrible half-people who rode on nightmares through my bedroom. But it was not the only world—that world of rockery, gravel path, playbank, bowling green, bandstands, reservoir, dahlia garden, where an ancient keeper named Smoky, was the whiskered snake in the grass one must keep off. There was another world where with my friends I used to dawdle on half holidays along the bent and Devon-facing seashore, hoping for gold watches or the skull of a sheep or a message in a bottle to be washed up with the tide.

SUMMARY

I. Topics related to physical development during middle and late childhood include basic physical attributes, health and fitness, and handicapped children.
  A. The period of middle and late childhood involves slow, consistent growth—the calm before the rapid growth spurt that appears in adolescence. With regard to body build, children can be characterized as endomorphs, ectomorphs, and mesomorphs. During middle and late childhood, motor development becomes much smoother, and sensory mechanisms continue to mature.
  B. Our nation's elementary school children are, for the most part, in poor physical shape. While they cognitively recognize the importance of nutrition and exercise in health, their behavior does not reflect this recognition. Competitive sports programs for elementary school children have increased in recent years and represent one way in which children get consistent exercise. Recent interest has focused on the identification of Type A children. These children experience more stress, in some instances have more illnesses, exhibit more anger, and have parents who often show similar behavior patterns, but a specific link to cardiovascular disease, which has been established with adults, has not yet been discovered with children.
  C. Information about handicapped children focuses on the prevalence of these children, issues in special education, learning disabilities, and hyperactive children.
    1. Estimates suggest that somewhere between 10 to 15 percent of children between the ages of 5 and 18 are handicapped in some way, ranging from the 0.1 percent who are visually impaired to the 3 to 4 percent with speech handicaps.
    2. Two important issues in special education are labeling and mainstreaming. Labeling refers to the assignment of a label, or category, to a child and the effects that label or category may then have. Extreme caution needs to be exercised in the labels given to handicapped children. Mainstreaming refers to the process in which children in need of special education are placed in regular rather than special classrooms. There has been a strong trend toward mainstreaming in recent years.

3. Between 2 and 3 percent of children are estimated to have a learning disability—this often includes children who are dyslexic, have minimal brain dysfunction, and who are hyperactive. Such children are often a heterogeneous group, showing a wide variety of characteristics. It has been speculated that some children have a learning disability because of a developmental lag; that is, they are slow in developing.

4. Hyperactive children show an increase in purposeless physical activity and an impaired span of attention. Such behavior may interfere with the child's ability to do well in school. Drugs, particularly amphetamines, have been used to treat many hyperactive children. Evidence is mixed on the effectiveness of such drugs, and careful monitoring of dosages is necessary.

II. Information about Piaget's theory and cognitive developmental change focus on concrete operational thought, the application of Piaget's ideas to education, and Piaget's contributions and the neo-Piagetian critiques.

A. Topics related to concrete operational thought include the beaker task, reversibility and the nature of a concrete operation, classification, and constraints on concrete operational thought.

1. The beaker task likely is the most famous of the Piagetian tasks. It assesses conservation of liquid. Failing this task is a sign that the child is still a preoperational, rather than a concrete operational, thinker, although this interpretation has been disputed.

2. Concrete operational thought is made up of operations, which are mental actions or representations that are reversible. The concrete operational child can coordinate several characteristics, rather than focusing on a single property of an object.

3. One important skill that characterizes concrete operational thought is the ability to classify or divide things into different sets or subsets and to consider their interrelationships.

4. The child in the concrete operational stage needs clearly available perceptual supports to reason. Later in development, thought becomes more abstract.

B. There have been widespread applications of Piaget's ideas to the education of children. These applications emphasize that the child has many ideas about the world, that the child is always unlearning and relearning, and that the child is by nature a knowing creature.

C. Piaget was a genius at observing children and developed fascinating new insights about children's thoughts. He showed us some important things to look for in development and mapped out some general cognitive changes in development. The neo-Piagetian critiques focus on the beliefs that the stages of thought are not as unitary as Piaget believed, that small changes in procedures affect the child's cognition, that children can sometimes be trained to reason at higher stages, and that some cognitive skills appear much earlier than Piaget thought while others seem to be more prolonged than Piaget believed. Case, a neo-Piagetian, argues that short-term memory and automatization may explain age-related cognitive changes rather than the cognitive structures advocated by Piaget.

III. Ideas about information processing in the elementary school years involve memory, drawing inferences, an information processing conception of intelligence, knowledge versus process views of intelligence, and the interface of information processing and the education of children.

A. An understanding of changes in memory development requires knowledge about long-term memory and control processes as well as characteristics of the learner.

1. Long-term memory shows considerable improvement during middle and late childhood. Control processes, such as rehearsal, organization, semantic elaboration, imagery, and retrieval or search processes, are among the most important influences on the increase in long-term memory.

2. Apart from the obvious characteristic of age, many individual characteristics determine the level of the child's memory performance. These characteristics include attitudes, motivations, and health-related factors. However, the characteristic that has been most widely examined is the previously acquired knowledge of the learner. In particular, developmental psychologists have been interested in children's ability to monitor their memory activities.

Metamemory (children's knowledge of memory processes) seems to increase during the middle and late childhood years.

B. An inference is a relationship noted between one event and another that is not directly stated. Children improve dramatically in their ability to draw inferences during the elementary school years. Schemata are active organizations of past experiences that provide a structure from which new information can be judged. Scripts are schemata for events. While scripts emerge quite early in life, perhaps by one year of age, and are prominent in preschool as well, the increased knowledge base of elementary school children likely contributes to the prevalence and complexity of scripts. Older children rely on such general knowledge to develop inferences about scripts for experiences they never encountered themselves.

C. Robert Sternberg has demonstrated the importance of studying the processes of intellectual behavior rather than relying only on the products of intelligence (which psychometricians do). Sternberg has developed the strategy of componential analysis to evaluate how we receive, process, and react to information. A component is an elementary information process that operates on internal representations of objects. Five such components in intelligence are: metacomponents, performance components, acquisition (or storage) components, retention (or retrieval) components, and transfer components.

D. A critical issue raised by information processing psychologists is whether intelligence and development occur primarily through a growth in knowledge or through changes in processing. Some recent research suggests that both knowledge and processing are involved.

E. An important issue pertains to the interface of information processing, the education of children, and the information age in which we now live. Some experts believe that information processing skills in general are very difficult, if not impossible, to train, although such experts as Sternberg argue that we can teach intelligence at least to some degree. Information processing psychologists believe that children's cognition would be improved by an infusion of the information processing perspective into all areas of the elementary school curricula.

KEY TERMS

acquisition (or storage) components 376
amphetamines 357
artificial intelligence (AI) 348
component 376
componential analysis 376
concrete operation 360
control processes 365
developmental lag 357
ectomorphs 349
elaborative rehearsal 365
endomorphic 349
hyperactivity 357
inferences 370
labeling 353
learning disabilities 355
mainstreaming 353
maintenance rehearsal 365
mental imagery 366
mesomorphic 349
metacomponents 376
metamemory 368
operations 359
organizational processing 365
parallel processing 348
performance components 376
rehearsal 365
retention (or retrieval) components 376
retrieval 366
schemata 371
scripts 371
semantic elaboration 365
transfer components 376
Type A behavioral pattern 350

SUGGESTED READINGS

Cratty, B. (1979). *Perceptual and motor development in infants and children* (2nd ed.). Englewood Cliffs, NJ: Prentice-Hall.
This book provides a detailed description of many different aspects of physical development in middle and late childhood. Extensive information is given about the awkward child and the child in competitive sports.

Davis, G. A., and Scott, J. A. (Eds.). (1981). *Training creative thinking.* New York: Holt, Rinehart & Winston.
A collection of articles by several psychologists who study creativity, with practical suggestions on how to stimulate creativity in the classroom.

Furth, H. G., & Wachs, H. (1975). *Thinking goes to school.* New York: Oxford.
An easy-to-read application of Piaget's view to education in the middle and late childhood years. Includes 179 thinking games that can be incorporated in the day-to-day teaching of children.

Gearheart, B. R., & Weishahan, M. W. (1984). *The exceptional student in the regular classroom* (3rd ed.). St. Louis, MO: Times Mirror/Mosby.
This book provides a broad overview of ideas pertaining to mainstreaming and other important issues involved in the education of handicapped students.

Hunt, M. (1982). *The universe within.* New York: Simon & Schuster.
Hunt traveled to many universities and talked to top scholars in the cognitive area; this book represents his distillation of their ideas. The outcome is an extraordinarily insightful and well-written overview of the current state of knowledge on cognition. Includes many intriguing comments about the relation of the mind to a computer.

Kail, R. (1984). *The development of memory in children.* San Francisco: W. H. Freeman.
A readable overview of developmental changes in children's memory. Includes information about many aspects of memory, such as metamemory, control processes, and short-term, long-term memory distinctions.

Sternberg, R. J. (1984). Mechanisms of cognitive development: A componential approach. In R. S. Sternberg (Ed.), *Mechanisms of cognitive development.* San Francisco: W. H. Freeman.
Sternberg, one of the leading figures in the modern information processing view of intelligence, describes in considerable detail the information processing perspective on intelligence.

INTELLIGENCE
AND
ACHIEVEMENT

CHAPTER 10

IMAGINE . . . YOU MUST DETERMINE WHETHER OR NOT A CHILD IS MENTALLY RETARDED

PREVIEW

INTELLIGENCE

Theories, Definition, and Measurement

Binet and the Concept of Intelligence
The Wechsler Scales
The Many Faces of Intelligence

FOCUS ON CHILD DEVELOPMENT 10.1: BIRD TO BEETHOVEN— SEVEN FRAMES OF MIND

Alternatives and Supplements to Standardized Intelligence Tests

Culture-Fair Tests
Social Intelligence
Stability and Change in Intelligence
Genetic-Environmental Influences on Intelligence

Genetic Influences on Intelligence

FOCUS ON CHILD DEVELOPMENT 10.2: DORAN, DR. GRAHAM, AND THE REPOSITORY FOR GERMINAL CHOICE

Environmental Influences on Intelligence
The Complex Interaction of Genetic-Environmental Influences on Intelligence
Mental Retardation, Giftedness, and Creativity

Mental Retardation
Gifted Children

FOCUS ON CHILD DEVELOPMENT 10.3: NOVEL THINKING, INSIGHT, AND AUTOMATIZATION IN THE GIFTED AND THE RETARDED

Creativity

CHILD DEVELOPMENT CONCEPT TABLE 10.1: THE PSYCHOMETRIC APPROACH TO INTELLIGENCE

THE 3 Rs AND BILINGUALISM

Writing and Reading

Writing Systems
Techniques for Teaching Reading
Bilingualism
Simultaneous Acquisition of Two Languages
Successive Acquisition of Two Languages

Mathematics

Educational Goals for Children's Mathematics
Cross-Cultural Comparisons of Achievement in Mathematics

FOCUS ON CHILD DEVELOPMENT 10.4: ACHIEVEMENT IN MATH REQUIRES TIME AND PRACTICE— COMPARISONS OF CHILDREN IN THE UNITED STATES AND JAPAN

CHILD DEVELOPMENT CONCEPT TABLE 10.2: THE 3 Rs AND BILINGUALISM

MOTIVATION AND ACHIEVEMENT

Motivation and Its Importance in Children's Development
Theories of Achievement Motivation and Achievement-Related Factors

The Achievement Motivation Views of McClelland and Atkinson
Attribution Theory
Delay of Gratification

FOCUS ON CHILD DEVELOPMENT 10.5: PRETZELS AND MARSHMALLOWS—DELAY OF GRATIFICATION IN CHILDHOOD AND ADJUSTMENT IN ADOLESCENCE

CHILD DEVELOPMENT CONCEPT TABLE 10.3: MOTIVATION, ACHIEVEMENT MOTIVATION, AND ACHIEVEMENT-RELATED FACTORS

Sociocultural Influences

Cultural Standards of Achievement
Parental and Peer Influences
School/Teacher Influences

FOCUS ON CHILD DEVELOPMENT 10.6: REVISITING THE INTERNAL-EXTERNAL DIMENSION OF ACHIEVEMENT

THINKING BACK, LOOKING AHEAD

SUMMARY

KEY TERMS

SUGGESTED READINGS

387

IMAGINE . . . YOU MUST DETERMINE WHETHER OR NOT A CHILD IS MENTALLY RETARDED

The place is a new institution for the mentally retarded, and it is in an uproar. Sam, a student at the institution, had evaded supervision long enough to sneak into the woods and take off for home. Sam is not the first to make such an escape; other mentally retarded individuals at the institution have been similarly successful at these escape acts. A psychologist at the mental retardation center is curious about Sam and the other escape artists, particularly as he reflects on the results of the Porteus Maze Test that he has been giving to the students. This test is used as a measure of intelligence and often is given to mentally retarded people because it requires no language—you only have to find your way out of printed mazes. Somewhat to the psychologist's amazement, when given the test, many of the escape artists had not been able to work even the simplest of the mazes. They had not been able to get from point A to point B on the paper in front of them. The psychologist is forced to conclude that the intelligence that Sam and the other escape artists displayed in planning and executing an escape from the institution must not have been adequately captured by the test they had been given (McKean, 1985).

Larry P. is black and comes from a low-income background. When he was six years old, he was placed in a class for the educable mentally retarded (EMR). The primary reason Larry was placed in the EMR class was his very low score of 64 on an intelligence test.

Is there a possibility that the intelligence test Larry was given is culturally biased? Psychologists still debate this issue. The controversy has been the target of a major class action challenging the use of standardized IQ tests to place black elementary school students in classes for the educable mentally retarded. The initial lawsuit, filed on behalf of Larry P., claimed that the IQ test he took underestimated his learning ability. The lawyers for Larry P. argued that IQ tests place too much emphasis on verbal skills and fail to account for the background of black children. Therefore, it was argued, Larry was incorrectly labeled mentally retarded and may forever be saddled with the stigma of being called retarded.

As part of the lengthy court battle involving Larry P., six black EMR students were independently retested by members of the Bay Area Association of Black Psychologists in California. The psychologists made sure that they estab-

lished good rapport with the students and made special efforts to overcome defeatism and distraction on the part of the students. Certain items were rewarded in terms more consistent with the children's social background, and recognition was given to nonstandard answers that showed a logical, intelligent approach to problems. The retesting produced scores of 79 to 104—17 to 38 points higher than the scores the students received when initially tested by school psychologists. The retest scores were above the ceiling for placement in an EMR class.

In Larry's case, it was ruled that IQ tests are biased and their use discriminates against blacks and other ethnic minorities. The ruling continued the moratorium on the use of IQ tests in decisions about placement of a child in an EMR class. During the Larry P. trial, it was revealed that 66 percent of elementary school students in EMR classes in San Francisco were black, whereas blacks only make up 28.5 percent of the San Francisco school population.

What was the state's argument for using intelligence tests as part of the criteria for placing children in EMR classes? At one point, the state suggested that, because blacks tend to be poor and poor pregnant women tend to suffer from inadequate nutrition, it is possible that the brain development of many black children has been retarded by their mothers' poor diets during pregnancy. However, from the beginning of the trial, a basic point made by the state was that blacks are genetically inferior to whites intellectually.

The decision in favor of Larry P. was upheld by a three-judge appeals panel in 1984, but in another court case, *Pase v. Hannon* in Illinois, it was ruled that IQ tests are not culturally biased. Many psychologists continue to take exception to the ruling in the *Larry P.* case, arguing that the required method for determining overrepresentation of minority children in special classes is not flawed, that the evidence does not suggest the tests are biased, and that informed consent procedures and regular review of children's progress in special education would protect rights to equal protection under the law, as well as rights to special education services when needed.

It should be pointed out that before intelligence tests were available, teachers relied on their own biases in assigning students. Thus intelligence tests, by themselves, are not to blame. Rather, such tests can be misused by people who lack competent psychological training.

Both the cases of Sam and Larry P. raise the issue of how accurate intelligence tests are at determining a child's true intellectual abilities. The use and misuse of intelligence tests is a prominent issue in studying the intelligence of children, and one we address further in this chapter.

PREVIEW

Robert Sternberg recalls being terrified of taking IQ tests as a child. He says he literally froze when the time came to take such tests. When he was in the sixth grade, he was sent to take an IQ test with the fifth graders and still talks about how embarrassing and humiliating the experience was. Sternberg recalls that maybe he was dumb, but he knows he wasn't *that* dumb. He finally overcame his anxieties about IQ tests and performed much better on them. Sternberg became so fascinated with IQ tests that he devised his own at the age of 13 and began assessing the intellectual abilities of his classmates until the school psychologist found out and scolded him.

Intellectual performance and achievement are highly prized by our society and are heavily promoted by parents who enthusiastically encourage their charges to become brighter and strongly motivated to gain success. During the elementary school years, the push for intellectual performance and achievement becomes more apparent to children than earlier in their development. Now, they usually are spending far more of their time in the achievement setting of school and are placed in circumstances that call on them to exhibit their intellectual skills in more pressurized ways than when they were in early childhood. Intelligence is often equated more with ability, and achievement usually is equated more with motivation.

Striking images of children's intelligence are apparent in the words of Aldous Huxley:

Children are remarkable for their intelligence and ardor, for their curiosity, their intolerance of shams, the clarity . . . of their vision.

INTELLIGENCE

In everyday conversation, we often equate intelligence with IQ. When asked what IQ and intelligence are, many of us respond, "That's how smart you are." But intelligence must be more than IQ (an abbreviation for the intelligence quotient derived from performance on intelligence tests). Although most of us have some idea of what intelligence is, not everybody defines it in the same way. For many years, psychologists have been trying to pin down a definition of intelligence and also to find better ways to measure it.

Theories, Definition, and Measurement

Extensive effort has been expended to develop a comprehensive theory of intelligence and to create the ultimate test of intelligence. The effort has been highlighted by the early work of Alfred Binet, the creation of the Wechsler scales, and the factor analytic approach.

Binet and the Concept of Intelligence

Alfred Binet was a true pioneer in the development of intelligence testing, the hallmark of the psychometric approach to psychology. By **psychometric** is meant the use of measurement to assess a concept of psychology. People who give tests or measures of tests are called **psychometricians.**

Alfred Binet and Theodore Simon devised the first intelligence test in 1905 to determine which students in the schools of Paris would not benefit from regular classes and consequently should be placed in special classes. Binet and Simon did not work from a basic definition of intelligence but proceeded in a trial-and-error fashion, simply relying on the test's ability to discriminate between children who were successful in school and those who were not. On this basis, they found that "higher" mental abilities (memory, attention, and comprehension) were better means for making this distinction than "lower" mental abilities (reaction time, speed of hand movement in a specified amount of space, and the like). The latter measures had been used by the American psychologist James McKeen Cattell as indicators of intelligence, but Binet found that they were not very good at predicting which children would succeed in French schools.

Although the Binet test was made up of items that tested several different mental capacities (including memory comprehension, attention, moral judgment, and aesthetic appreciation), Binet was primarily concerned with the child's general intelligence, which he noted simply as the letter *g,* rather than the child's specific mental abilities.

Binet developed the concept of **mental age (MA)** to describe the general level of the child's intellectual functioning. This term was devised to refer to the number of items a child of a given age answered correctly. It was believed that an **IQ,** or intelligence quotient, could be calculated by using the concept of mental age and comparing it with the child's chronological age. The formula for calculating IQ became:

$$IQ = \frac{\text{Mental age}}{\text{Chronological age}} \times 100$$

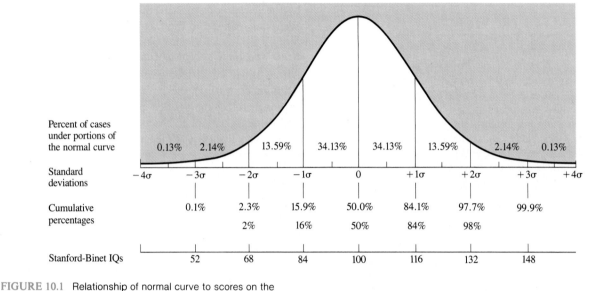

Percent of cases under portions of the normal curve	0.13%	2.14%	13.59%	34.13%	34.13%	13.59%	2.14%	0.13%
Standard deviations	−4σ −3σ		−2σ	−1σ	0	+1σ	+2σ	+3σ +4σ

Cumulative percentages 0.1% 2.3% 15.9% 50.0% 84.1% 97.7% 99.9%

2% 16% 50% 84% 98%

Stanford-Binet IQs 52 68 84 100 116 132 148

FIGURE 10.1   Relationship of normal curve to scores on the Stanford-Binet Intelligence Test.

Standardization of the Binet   Over the years, there has been an effort to standardize the Binet test, which has been given to thousands of children and adults of different ages, selected at random from different parts of the United States. Through administration of the test to large numbers of people and recording of the results, it has been found that intelligence as measured by the Binet has an almost **normal distribution** (see Figure 10.1). A normal distribution is reflected in a frequency distribution that is very symmetrical, with a majority of the cases falling in the middle of the possible range of scores and fewer scores appearing toward the ends of the range.

Revisions of the Binet test have resulted in what are now called the Stanford-Binet tests (Stanford for Stanford University, where the revisions were done). The Stanford-Binet has a mean of 100 and a standard deviation of 16. The **mean** is the average score, and the **standard deviation** is how much the scores vary. As you can see by looking at Figure 10.1, about 68 percent of the scores fall within what is called the average range: 84–116.

In the 1972 revision of the Stanford-Binet, preschool children scored an average of about 110 on the test, compared with a mean of 100. The 1972 sampling included more children from minority groups than did earlier

samplings. Possible explanations for the 1972 increase may be that preschool children today are experiencing more visual and verbal stimulation from books, television, toys, and other educational materials, and their parents average two to three more years of education than was true of earlier generations.

Historically, labels have been used to reflect how far away from the mean a person scored on an IQ test. Someone who scored 102 was labeled "average"; someone who scored 60 was labeled "mentally retarded"; and someone who scored 156 was labeled "genius." The evaluation of intelligence is rapidly moving away from such categorization. Many experts believe that an intelligence quotient based on the results of a single intelligence test should not be the basis for so classifying a child. Such labels have often remained with the child for many years, even though circumstances of the testing may have led to inappropriate measurement.

The Binet Today   The current Stanford-Binet test can be given to individuals from the age of two years through adulthood. It includes many different types of items, some requiring verbal responses and some calling for nonverbal performance. For example, items that characterize the six-year-old's performance on the test include

Alfred Binet (1857–1911), who constructed the first intelligence test.

Table 10.1   Examples of Subtests of the Wechsler Intelligence Scale for Children

Verbal	Performance
Similarities: The child must think abstractly and logically to answer 16 questions. Example: ''How are a skunk and a rabbit the same?''	*Picture arrangement:* With each of 11 items, the child is to rearrange parts of a figure or picture to make it complete or to tell a meaningful story. This test of nonverbal reasoning requires that the child understand how parts of a picture or a story go together. The pictures are shown to the child, who manually arranges the pieces in the right order.
Vocabulary: Forty words are used to test word knowledge. This subtest is thought to be an excellent indicator of general intelligence, measuring a variety of cognitive functions, including concept formation, memory, and language development. Example: ''Tell me what the word *cabinet* means.''	*Block design:* The child must put together a set of different-colored blocks 10 times to match each of 10 designs the examiner shows. Visual-motor coordination, perceptual organization, and an ability to visualize spatially are among the cognitive functions measured. This subtest is one of the best for measuring general intelligence.

the verbal ability to define at least six words, such as *orange* and *envelope,* and the nonverbal ability to trace a path through a maze. Items that reflect an average adult's intelligence include defining such words as *regard* and *disproportionate,* explaining a proverb, and comparing idleness and laziness.

The fourth edition of the Stanford-Binet was published in 1985 (Thorndike, Hagan, & Sattler). One important addition to the latest edition is the analysis of the individual's responses into four separate area scores: verbal reasoning, quantitative reasoning, abstract/visual reasoning, and short-term memory. In addition, a composite score is also computed.

Now that we have some feel for the Stanford-Binet test, let's examine the other major test of intelligence given to children—the Wechsler scales.

The Wechsler Scales

Like Binet, David Wechsler subscribed to a view of intelligence that emphasized its general nature. Wechsler defined intelligence as "the global capacity of the individual to act purposefully, to think rationally, and to deal effectively with the environment" (1958, p. 7). In using the term *global capacity,* Wechsler was referring to the general structure of intelligence. Like the Binet, the Wechsler scales provide a score that reflects general intelligence. However, Wechsler was more systematic than Binet in organizing the component parts of intelligence. Unlike the Binet, which is organized by age levels, the Wechsler scales are divided into verbal and nonverbal

categories, which in turn are further subdivided to reflect specific aspects of intelligence. Table 10.1 presents examples of the various subtests of the Wechsler Intelligence Scale for Children. Remember that, even though the Wechsler provides an evaluation of specific mental abilities, it also provides a general score for overall intelligence. Currently, three main versions of the Wechsler tests are being used: the Wechsler Adult Intelligence Scale (WAIS), used for adults; the Wechsler Intelligence Scale for Children (WISC-R), used for those ages 5 to 18; and the Wechsler Preschool and Primary Intelligence Scale (WPPIS), devised for children ages 4 to 6½.

The Stanford-Binet test and the Wechsler scales are the most widely used tests of intelligence with children. But as we see next, other ideas about what intelligence is and how it should be measured have been proposed.

VERBAL REASONING

Choose the correct pair of words to fill the blanks. The first word of the pair goes in the blank space at the beginning of the sentence; the second word of the pair goes in the blank at the end of the sentence.

. . . . . . is to night as breakfast is to . . . . . .

A. supper — corner
B. gentle — morning
C. door — corner
D. flow — enjoy
E. supper — morning

The correct answer is E.

NUMERICAL ABILITY

Choose the correct answer for each problem.

Add 13	A 14	Subtract 30	A 15
12	B 25	20	B 26
	C 16		C 16
	D 59		D 8
	E none of these		E none of these

The correct answer for the first problem is B; for the second, E.

ABSTRACT REASONING

The four "problem figures" in each row make a series. Find the one among the "answer figures" that would be next in the series.

Problem figures   Answer figures

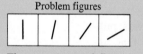   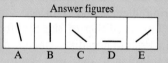

The correct answer is D.   A   B   C   D   E

CLERICAL SPEED AND ACCURACY

In each test item, one of the five combinations is underlined. Find the same combination on the answer sheet and mark it.

V. AB AC AD AE AF		AC AE AF AB AD
W. aA aB BA Ba Bb	V.	▮
X. A7 7A B7 7B AB	W. BA Ba Bb aA aB	▮
Y. Aa Ba bA BA bB	X. 7B B7 AB 7A A7	▮
Z. 3A 3B 33 B3 BB	Y. Aa bA bB Ba BA	▮
	Z. BB 3B B3 3A 33	▮

FIGURE 10.2 Sample items from the Differential Aptitude Tests, which seek to measure intelligence through analysis of specific intelligence factors.

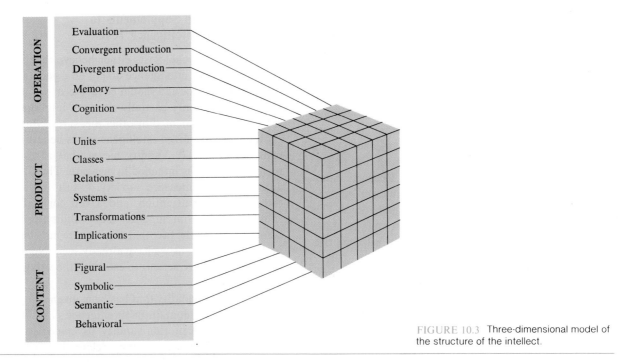

FIGURE 10.3 Three-dimensional model of the structure of the intellect.

From Guilford, J. P., The Nature of Human Intelligence. Copyright © 1967 McGraw-Hill Book Company. Reprinted by permission.

The Many Faces of Intelligence

Many years before Wechsler began analyzing intelligence in terms of its general and specific nature, C. E. Spearman (1927) proposed that intelligence has two factors. His was called a **two-factor theory** and suggested that intelligence consists of *g,* standing for general intelligence, and *s,* standing for specific factor. Spearman believed that these two factors could explain an individual's performance on an intelligence test. However, some factor approaches abandoned the idea of a general structure for intelligence and instead searched for specific factors only.

L. L. Thurstone (1938) developed an elaborate framework for understanding the idea that there are many specific types of intelligence. This view that a number of specific factors, rather than one general and one specific factor, make up intelligence is called **multiple-factor theory.** Thurstone consistently discovered 6 to 12 abilities; the seven that appeared most consistently when Thurstone analyzed people's test responses were: (1) verbal comprehension, (2) number ability, (3) word fluency, (4) spatial visualization, (5) associative memory, (6) reasoning, and (7) perceptual speed. Figure 10.2

provides examples of the types of items that are included on tests designed to assess specific factors.

Yet another entrant in the search for the structure of intelligence is the theory of fluid and crystallized intelligence proposed by Raymond Cattell. Cattell (1963) proposed that two forms of intelligence act to influence the primary mental abilities described by Thurstone. Cattell labeled the two forms fluid and crystallized. **Fluid intelligence** focuses on the individual's adaptability and capacity to perceive things and integrate them mentally. It appears to be independent of education and experience. For example, some individuals seem to intuitively think through problems with strategies they have never been taught. In comparison, schooling and environment are said to determine **crystallized intelligence,** which involves skills, abilities, and understanding. Instruction and observation are thought to enhance such skills. For example, an individual may learn how to play a particular game only after he or she has seen someone else do it or has been given instructions on how to proceed.

J. P. Guilford (1967) proposed 120 mental abilities, calling his perspective the **structure of intellect.** As shown in Figure 10.3, the 120 mental abilities are made up of all the possible combinations of five operations, four contents, and six products ($5 \times 4 \times 6 = 120$). **Operations** are intellectual activities or processes, that is, what one does with information. Guilford's five cognitive operations focus on cognition (such as discovery, recognition, and awareness), memory, divergent production (generation of many different ideas), convergent production (finding a single best answer), and evaluation. **Contents** can be figural (such as visual or spatial), symbolic (e.g., letters, numbers, or words), semantic (word meanings), or behavioral (nonverbal performance). **Products** index the form in which information occurs—units, classes, relations, systems, transformations, or implications. The products dimension is hierarchical in that units combine into classes, classes form relations, relations comprise systems, and so on.

Today, most psychologists still believe that it is important to look at the different aspects of intelligence rather than general intelligence alone. From time to time, psychologists have attempted to distinguish academic from nonacademic intelligence, social from nonsocial (abstract) intelligence, and so on. (Many people who do very well when it comes to verbal reasoning may not be able to replace a fuse. Others can take one look at an automobile engine and tell what is wrong with it but are not able to make verbal analogies.) The factor analytic approach to intelligence has fostered the belief that we should be searching for different kinds of intelligence rather than one general intelligence.

Two contemporary psychologists who believe that there are a number of processes involved in intelligence are Robert J. Sternberg (1977, 1984, in press) and Howard Gardner (1983). You read about Sternberg's ideas in our discussion of the information processing approach to intelligence in Chapter 9. Focus on Child Development 10.1, relates Gardner's beliefs about how many intelligences we possess.

So far, we have seen that a diverse set of ideas has developed regarding what intelligence is and how it should be measured. Next, we add to that diversity by discussing alternatives and supplements to standardized intelligence tests.

Alternatives and Supplements to Standardized Intelligence Tests

A number of psychologists either believe that the standardized tests of intelligence do not do a good job of assessing intelligence and should be replaced, or they argue that such tests only partially evaluate intelligence and should be supplemented by other measures. Many of the critics of standardized intelligence tests believe that the tests are not valid. **Validity** means that a test should measure what it is intended to measure. Thus, a test for anxiety should measure anxiety, a test for attention should measure attention, and a test for intelligence should measure intelligence. The validity problem is compounded by the fact that intelligence may be defined in different ways, as we have already seen. Nonetheless, psychologists have set out to establish the validity of intelligence tests.

One form of validity that has been given considerable attention in the domain of intelligence is **criterion validity.** To assess criterion validity, psychologists have to measure intelligence and then relate that measure to some other measure. The second measure, or criterion, varies in how closely it is related to the first measure. It is not unusual for validity studies to include other tests of intelligence as the second or third measures to relate the first measure to. For example, a study might try to show how people's scores on the Stanford-Binet are positively related to the same people's scores on the Wechsler tests. In most instances, these measures are positively correlated to each other to a high degree. (This is not surprising because many of the items are similar from test to test.)

However, many psychologists have shown an interest in whether intelligence tests can accurately predict a criterion that is very different from the intelligence measure itself, such as grades in school, occupational success, ability to get along with people, creativity, and so forth. To make a long story short, intelligence tests are reasonably good at predicting grades in school (Stevenson, Hale, Klein, & Miller, 1968) and not bad at predicting occupational success (Cronbach, 1970). There is much less evidence that they can predict the ability to get along with people or predict creativity, although intelligence and creativity are positively related (Richards, 1976).

Next, we see that the validity of traditional intelligence tests has been questioned in terms of how culturally fair these tests are.

FOCUS ON CHILD DEVELOPMENT 10.1

BIRD TO BEETHOVEN—SEVEN FRAMES OF MIND

Larry Bird, the 6-foot, 9-inch superstar of the Boston Celtics, springs into motion. Grabbing a rebound off the defensive board, he quickly traverses two thirds of the 94-foot basketball court, all the while processing the whereabouts of his five opponents as well as his four teammates. The crowd is screaming as Bird calmly looks one way, finesses his way past a defender, and whirls a behind-the-back pass to a fast-breaking teammate who dunks the ball for two points. Is there an intelligence to Bird's movement and perception of the spatial layout of the basketball court?

Now we turn back the clock some 200 years. A tiny, four-year-old boy is standing on a footstool in front of a piano keyboard and diligently practicing. At the age of six, the young boy has the honor of playing concertos and trios at a concert. The young boy is Ludwig von Beethoven, whose musical genius was evident from a very early age. Does he have a special type of intelligence?

Bird and Beethoven, two very different types of people with different sets of abilities . . . Howard Gardner (1983), writing in his book *Frames of Mind,* believes that Bird and Beethoven's talents represent two of seven intelligences we possess. Beyond the verbal and mathematical intelligences tapped by such tests as the SAT and most traditional intelligence tests, Gardner thinks we also need to include in our conception of intelligence the ability to spatially analyze the visual world, movement skills, insightful skills for analyzing ourselves, skills for understanding others, and musical skills.

Gardner believes that each of the seven intelligences can be destroyed by particular brain damage, that each involves unique cognitive skills (he believes, for example, that there is reasoning present in Bird's great passing ability since Bird has to know where his teammates and opponents are, anticipate where they are going to move to, and use analysis, inference, and planning to decide what he will do next), and that each shows up in highlighted ways in both the gifted and *idiots savants,* the latter being people who are mentally retarded but who have unbelievable skills in a particular domain, such as drawing, music, or computing. (I remember vividly one such person from my childhood who could respond simultaneously with the correct day of the week—say Tuesday or Saturday—when given any date in history, such as June 4, 1926 or December 15, 1746. Astonishing!)

Gardner, in particular, has been fascinated by musical intelligence, especially the very early age at which some children show this ability. He points out that musically inclined preschool children not only have a remarkable ability to learn musical patterns easily, but they also rarely forget them. He points to a story about Stravinsky, who as an adult could still remember the musical patterns of the tuba, drums, and piccolos of the fife-and-drum band that marched outside of his window when he was in early childhood.

To measure such musical talent in young children, Gardner may ask a child to listen to a melody and then to re-create the tune on some bells that Gardner provides. He believes that such evaluations can be used to develop a profile of children's intelligences and that it is during this early time in the life cycle that feedback to parents can make important differences in whether we develop our intelligences (McKean, 1985).

Culture-Fair Tests

In our discussion of Larry P. in the "Imagine" section at the beginning of this chapter, it was argued that traditional standardized intelligence tests, such as the Stanford-Binet and the Wechsler scales, favor children from white, middle-class backgrounds over children from lower-class, minority backgrounds. The argument is that the standardized tests are not culturally fair to the latter individuals because these people have not had the same experience and exposure to the information that the tests measure as middle-class whites have. For example, individuals with greater exposure to verbal knowledge and verbal reasoning are likely to perform better on such tests.

Two types of **culture-fair tests** have been developed to eliminate or reduce cultural bias. In the first, verbal items are removed (Raven, 1960). Figure 10.4 shows a sample item from this type of test (the Raven Progressive Matrices Test). However, while tests such as the Raven Progressive Matrices Test are designed to be culture-fair, there is evidence that individuals with more education do better on them than individuals with less education (Anastasi, 1976). A second type of culture-fair test focuses on the development of items that are familiar to people from all socioeconomic and ethnic backgrounds, or items that are at least familiar to the people who are taking the test. For example, a child might be asked how a bird and a dog are different—on the assumption that virtually all children have had exposure to birds and dogs.

In the United States, particular concern has been voiced about the lack of intelligence tests that are culturally fair to blacks. The Dove Counterbalance General Intelligence Test (see Table 10.2), sometimes referred to as the Chitling Test, was developed by a black sociologist, Adrian Dove, as a sarcastic rejoinder to the middle-class bias of most intelligence tests. Dove's test was not presented as a serious effort to develop a culture-free test for blacks; it was designed to illustrate how the language used by many blacks differs from that of middle-class whites.

A recently developed intelligence test, the Kaufman Assessment Battery for Children (K-ABC), has been promoted as an improvement over past culture-fair tests (Kaufman & Kaufman, 1983). It can be administered to children from 2½ to 12½ years of age. This test has been standardized on a more representative sample than most tests, including more minority and handicapped children. The intelligence portion of this test focuses less on language than the Stanford-Binet does, and this test includes an achievement section involving such subtests as arithmetic and reading. Nonetheless, like other culture-fair intelligence tests, the K-ABC test already has found some detractors (Bracken, 1985; Keith, 1985).

Although cultural bias exists in intelligence testing, the available culture-fair tests have not provided a satisfactory alternative. Creating a truly culture-fair test, one that rules out the role of experiences due to socioeconomic and ethnic background, not only has been difficult but it may be impossible.

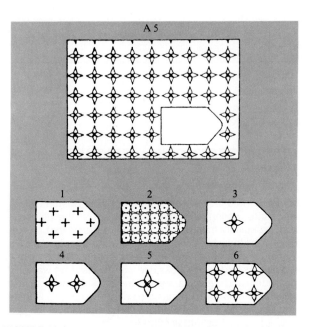

FIGURE 10.4   Sample item from the Raven Progressive Matrices Test. The individual is presented with a matrix arrangement of symbols, such as the one at the top of this figure, and must then complete the matrix by selecting the appropriate missing symbol from a group of symbols.

Social Intelligence

Children's lives are more than solving verbal and numerical problems. They also need to get along with others and to be able to adapt to the social world in which they live. An increasing number of psychologists argue that the construct of intelligence should be construed to include social variables, such as interpersonal skills (e.g., Ford, 1986; Gardner, 1983; Mercer & Lewis, 1978; Sternberg, 1984).

Jane Mercer (e.g., Mercer & Lewis, 1978) has put together a battery of measures that she believes provides a more complete assessment of intelligence than a single traditional intelligence test. Her battery of tests is called **SOMPA**, which stands for System of Multicultural Pluralistic Assessment. It can be given to children from 5 to 11 years of age. SOMPA was particularly designed for use with children from an impoverished background. Instead of relying on a single test, SOMPA includes information about the child's intellectual functioning in four main areas: (1) verbal and nonverbal intelligence in the traditional intelligence test vein, assessed by the WISC-R; (2) social and economic background of the

Table 10.2   The Chitling Intelligence Test

1. A "gas head" is a person who has a:
   (a) fast-moving car
   (b) stable of "lace"
   (c) "process"
   (d) habit of stealing cars
   (e) long jail record for arson
2. "Bo Diddley" is a:
   (a) game for children
   (b) down-home cheap wine
   (c) down-home singer
   (d) new dance
   (e) Moejoe call
3. If a pimp is uptight with a woman who gets state aid, what does he mean when he talks about "Mother's day"?
   (a) second Sunday in May
   (b) third Sunday in June
   (c) first of every month
   (d) none of these
   (e) first and fifteenth of every month

4. A "handkerchief head" is:
   (a) a cool cat
   (b) a porter
   (c) an Uncle Tom
   (d) a hoddi
   (e) a preacher
5. If a man is called a "blood," then he is a:
   (a) fighter
   (b) Mexican-American
   (c) Negro
   (d) hungry hemophile
   (e) red man, or Indian
6. Cheap chitlings (not the kind you purchase at a frozen-food counter) will taste rubbery unless they are cooked long enough. How soon can you quit cooking them to eat and enjoy them?
   (a) 45 minutes
   (b) 2 hours
   (c) 24 hours
   (d) 1 week (on a low flame)
   (e) 1 hour

Answers: 1. c   2. c   3. e   4. c   5. c   6. c

family, obtained via a one-hour parental interview; (3) social adjustment to school, evaluated by an adaptive behavior inventory filled out by parents; and (4) physical health, ascertained by a medical examination. Thus, Mercer hopes to obtain a more complete picture of the experiences and environmental background of the child than would be possible from giving the WISC-R alone. She also shows a concern for assessing the child's health, which might interfere with intellectual performance.

At this point, we have covered many facets of intelligence, including its theories, definition, and measurement, as well as alternatives and supplements to standardized intelligence tests. Next, we consider another important facet of children's intelligence—its stability and change.

Stability and Change in Intelligence

Can psychologists predict what a child's IQ will be when the child is 10 or 18 years old from the child's scores on an IQ test administered when he or she is 2, 3, and 4 years old? IQ tests still do not provide very reliable predictions of this sort. IQ scores obtained at 2 and 3 years of age are statistically related to the IQ scores of the same individuals even at 10 and 18 years of age, but they are not very strongly related. IQ scores obtained at the

age of 4 are much better at predicting IQ at the age of 10 than at the age of 18 (Honzik, MacFarlane, & Allen, 1948).

There is a strong relation between IQ scores obtained at the ages of 6, 8, and 9 and IQ scores obtained at the age of 10. For example, in one study, the correlation between IQ at the age of 8 and IQ at the age of 10 was .88. The correlation between IQ at the age of 9 and IQ at the age of 10 was .90. These figures show a very high relation between IQ scores obtained in these years. The correlation of IQ in the preadolescent years and IQ at the age of 18 is slightly less, but still statistically significant. For example, the correlation between IQ at the age of 10 and IQ at the age of 18 was .70 in one study (Honzik, MacFarlane, & Allen, 1948).

The figures on the stability of intelligence have been based on measures of groups of individuals. The stability of intelligence also can be evaluated through studies of individual persons. There can be considerable variability in an individual's scores on IQ tests. Robert McCall and his associates studied 140 individuals and found that, between 2½ and 17 years of age, the average range of IQ scores was more than 28 points (McCall, Applebaum, & Hogarty, 1973). The scores of one out of three children changed by as much as 30 points, and one out of seven by as much as 40 points.

According to researchers, what aspects of infant intelligence predict intelligence later in childhood?

How should intelligence be assessed in infancy and in middle and late childhood?

When individuals are assessed over long periods of time, their scores on intelligence tests often fluctuate considerably. Some experts also point out that, while intelligence tests (and virtually all psychological tests) were designed to measure stable attributes of the individual, data like those collected by McCall indicate that intelligence is not as stable as the original theories of intelligence predicted.

Nonetheless, in contrast to the poor predictive power of early indices of IQ with regard to later IQ, other aspects of the infant's behavior seem to be linked to intelligence at a later point in development. Specifically, a number of recent studies have suggested that an infant's response to novel stimulation—what we have referred to as dishabituation (Chapter 4)—is significantly correlated with later IQ. One impressive study by Susan Rose and Ina Wallace (1985) assessed the amount of time that six-month-old infants spent looking at novel versus previously viewed visual stimuli. "Novelty scores," which

measured the preference for viewing novel stimuli, predicted WISC-R IQ scores at six years of age ($r = .56$). Infant preferences for novel auditory stimuli are similarly predictive of later IQ. Mary O'Connor, Sarale Cohen, and Arthur Parmelee (1984) found that four-month-old infants' cardiac (heart rate) responses to repetitive versus novel sounds predicted Stanford-Binet IQ at five years ($r = .60$). These findings are provocative in supporting the claim that the nature of intelligence—measured appropriately—is fundamentally continuous from infancy through childhood (Fagan, 1985). They also suggest that intelligence may be conceptualized as including the component of responsiveness to novelty (Berg & Sternberg, 1985), not only in infancy but in childhood as well (Marr & Sternberg, 1985). Although some loose ends remain in the data on novelty-intelligence associations (McCall, 1985), the emerging findings promise some important new insights on the emergence and development of intelligence.

Next, we evaluate the extent to which the intelligence of children is genetically and environmentally determined.

Genetic-Environmental Influences on Intelligence

As we saw in Chapter 3 in our discussion of genetic influences on children's development, both genes and environment are necessary just for the child to survive. But psychologists have been trying to nail down more precise

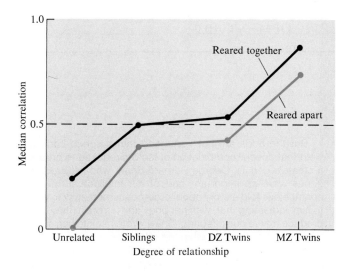

FIGURE 10.5   Influence of environmental similarity and biological relatedness on the similarity of IQ.

estimates of the contribution of heredity and environment to intelligence. Let's look at some of the investigations that have addressed this issue and then describe the complex interaction of genetic-environmental influences on intelligence.

Genetic Influences on Intelligence

What is the influence of heredity in the broad range of normal and superior intelligence? Arthur Jensen (1969) examined the research literature that addresses this question. The most compelling information concerns the similiarity of IQ for individuals who vary on a dimension of genetic similarity. If hereditary variation among people contributes to differences in IQ, then individuals who have very similar genetic endowments should have very similar IQs, whereas individuals with very different endowments should have very different IQs. Identical twins have identical genetic endowments, so their IQs should be very similar. Nonidentical (fraternal) twins and ordinary siblings are less similar genetically and so should have less similar IQs. Children from different parents are the least similar genetically and should have the least similar IQs. If relevant groups existed in each of these categories, the correlation based on pairs of children should be high for identical twins, lower for fraternal twins and ordinary siblings, and lowest for unrelated children. The graph in Figure 10.5 illustrates these correlations.

On the basis of this kind of thinking and some complex calculations, Jensen places the heritability quotient at about .80 for intelligence. However, many scholars criticize Jensen's work, and few accept his estimate without qualification.

What is perhaps the most important criticism involves the very definition of intelligence. Standard IQ tests tap a very narrow range of intellectual functioning, most of it based on specific things learned at school and at home. There are many facets of mental life related to everyday problem solving, work performance, and social adaptability that are not covered in IQ tests. At best, then, the genetic arguments apply only to a limited part of mental life (Kamin, 1974).

Second, there are substantive disagreements on just how much variation can be fairly attributed to the environment. Some critics claim that most heritability studies have not included environments that differ from one another in radical ways, so it is not surprising that results support the interpretation that environment contributes little to variation. If studies were to include environments that differ significantly from one another, then greater variation would be attributable to the environment (Bronfenbrenner, 1972; Scarr & Weinberg, 1976).

Although there is strong evidence for the heritability of IQ, there are also strong doubts that the actual figure is as high as Jensen claims. In a review of the heritability of intelligence, behavior-genetics expert Norman Henderson (1982) argued that a figure of about .50 seems more reasonable. And in keeping with a recent trend of providing a range rather than a point estimate of heritability for intelligence, .30 to .60 is given. Nonetheless, as described in Focus on Child Development 10.2, belief in the importance of genetics in intelligence has led to the creation of a sperm bank for Nobel Prize winners.

Because heritability is an incomplete explanation of IQ, we can now explore in detail some of the most important environmental influences that interact with heredity to affect the child's intelligence.

Environmental Influences on Intelligence

Important environmental influences on intelligence include experiences at home, the effects of being institutionalized, education, and social class.

FOCUS ON CHILD DEVELOPMENT 10.2

DORAN, DR. GRAHAM, AND THE REPOSITORY FOR GERMINAL CHOICE

Doran (from the Greek, meaning *gift*) learned to use all the appropriate parts of speech by the time he was two years of age, and on a traditional intelligence test, he tested as a four-year-old at the age of one. Doran was the second child born through the Nobel Prize sperm bank, which began in 1980. The sperm bank was founded by Robert Graham in Escondido, California, for the primary intent of producing geniuses. Graham has collected the sperm of Nobel prize winning scientists and offered it free of charge to intelligent women who seem to come from good stock themselves and whose husbands are infertile.

One of the Nobel contributors to the sperm bank is physicist William Shockley, who shared the Nobel Prize in 1956 for inventing the transistor. During the 1960s and 1970s, Shockley was criticized for preaching the genetic basis of intelligence on a widespread basis. There actually have been only two other Nobel Prize winners who have donated sperm to the bank. Shockley is the only one who has been identified.

So far, more than 20 children have been sired through the sperm bank. Are the progeny prodigies? It may be too early to tell. Except for the child named Doran, little has been revealed about the children.

Doran's genetic father is designated as 28 Red in the sperm bank (the color apparently has no meaning) and is listed in the sperm bank's catalog as handsome, blond, athletic, with a math SAT score of 800, who also has won prizes for classical music performances. One of his few drawbacks is that there is almost a one in three chance that he has passed along a tendency for hemorrhoids to Doran. Doran's mother says that her genetic contribution goes back to the royal court of Norway and to the poet William Blake. The mother believes that Doran's genetic heritage already is obvious. At the age of two, he was on the cover of *Newsweek*, shown playing the piano!

But the odds are not very good that a sperm bank will yield that special combination of factors required to produce a creative genius. George Bernard Shaw, who believed that genes were an important part of our intellectual makeup, nonetheless told a story about a gorgeous woman who wrote to him, indicating that, with her body and his brain, they could produce marvelous offspring. Shaw wrote back to her, saying that, unfortunately, the offspring might get his body and her brains!

Not surprisingly, the Nobel Prize sperm bank has been criticized. Some say that brighter does not mean better and that IQ is not a good index of social competence or of human contribution to the world. Other critics say that intelligence is an elusive concept to measure and that it can't be reliably reproduced like the sperm bank is trying to do. Visions of the German gene program of the 1930s and 1940s have surfaced. The Nazi Germans thought certain traits were superior, tried to breed children with such traits, and at times killed people who did not have the traits.

While Graham's Repository of Germinal Choice (as the sperm bank is formally known) has been heavily criticized, we should consider its possible contributions as well. The repository provides a social service for parents who cannot have children by themselves, and people who go to the sperm bank may be those who are likely to provide a very enriched environment for their offspring. To once childless parents, the offspring possible through the sperm bank, or through any other of the new methods of conception available, are invariably viewed as a miracle (Garelik, 1985).

Home   Families influence their children's intellectual development both genetically and environmentally; untangling these two sources of influence is a formidable task. While psychologists do not know how much of the variance in intellectual development is due to enriched surroundings provided by parents, family structure, and other environmental factors, they do know that these factors are significant. Recent efforts have focused on intervention with parents of children with low IQs to see whether working with the parents as well as the child can advance the child's intelligence. Other work has evaluated the influence of the size of the family and sibling order on the child's intelligence.

Investigations have shown that, in low-income families, the intelligence of children can be raised by intervening with the mother early in the child's development (e.g., Andrews, Blumenthal, Bache, & Weiner, 1975; Lasater, Briggs, Malone, Gilliom, & Weisburg, 1975; Leler, Johnson, Kahn, Hines, & Tones, 1975). And children from smaller families, those who are firstborn, and those who come from intact families tend to perform better on intelligence tests than their counterparts from larger families, of younger sibling status, who live in single-parent families (e.g., Santrock, 1972; Zajonc & Markus, 1975). Nonetheless, a number of developmental psychologists believe that the nature of interaction going on in families, such as how parents socialize their children, how involved they are, how much verbal give-and-take is happening, is a better predictor of intelligence than family structure characteristics like family size, birth order, and intact versus divorce status.

Institutionalization   In one widely quoted study, Harold Skeels (1966) removed children from an unstimulating orphanage and placed them in an institution where they received individual attention. The change in institutions significantly raised their level of intellectual functioning. In the Skeels study, children were assigned an "adoptive mother"—an older, mentally retarded girl—who was given the responsibility of caring for them. At the end of 2½ years, the children with the mentally retarded "mother" showed an average gain of 32 points in IQ; the children who remained in the inferior institution dropped an average of 21 points in IQ.

Many studies of **institutionalization** have been criticized heavily on methodological grounds. For example, some of the early studies (e.g., Spitz, 1945) interpreted the negative effects of institutionalization in terms of the lack of mother love. Studies of institutionalization, however, do not provide accurate tests of the intrinsic importance of the mother or the family in the child's development. Multiple mothering in the institution, separation from the mother, and such distortions in mothering as rejection and overprotection are possible explanations for the observed effects of institutionalization (Yarrow, 1964).

Descriptions of several institutions in the Soviet Union by Yvonne Brackbill (1962) and Urie Bronfenbrenner (1970) further support the belief that qualitative aspects of institutional care are important in determining whether the child will show intellectual deficits. Where nurses give considerable individual attention to the infants and provide them with many visual-motor opportunities, where toddlers are trained to become self-reliant and to engage in appropriate peer interaction, institutionalized children show normal intellectual and personality patterns.

Education and Social Class   Education and social class are other important environmental factors that influence intelligence. In one recent investigation, 63 disadvantaged black children were followed for 6½ years after birth (Breitmayer & Ramey, 1983). They were selected for study on the basis of low maternal IQ and family income. Half of them were assigned to an educational day-care program designed to prevent socially induced mental retardation, and the other half were assigned to a control group that received day care only. It was found that poor Apgar scores at birth as well as relatively low birth weight had a negative influence on intelligence at both 5 and 6½ years only in the group of children who received day care only. The children with low Apgar scores who received enriched educational day care did not show depressed intelligence. Further assessment revealed that IQ deficits were influenced by the impoverished conditions in which the children were growing up but that enriched educational day-care experiences often were successful in remediating the effects of poverty on intelligence.

The Complex Interaction of Genetic-Environmental Influences on Intelligence

In our discussion of environmental influences on intelligence, we have been concerned primarily with the role of the family, institutionalization, and sociocultural factors. It is becoming clearer that there are many psychological and biological factors that influence children's intelligence. Intelligence, like all other aspects of the child's life, is multiply determined. For example, maternal deprivation alone does not cause a child to have a low IQ. Nor does father absence. Nor does attending a poor-quality school. Children's intelligence is influenced by a complex interaction of genetic, biological, psychological, and social factors. We have seen that the child's experiences at home influence his or her intelligence. So, too, do school experiences, nutrition, a healthy birth process, a childhood free of traumatic head injury, and the inheritance of "bright" genes.

So far in our discussion of intelligence, we have talked primarily about normal intelligence. As we see next, there also has been considerable interest in the exceptional aspects of intelligence.

Mental Retardation, Giftedness, and Creativity

In this section, we explore extremes in intelligence by evaluating the concepts of mental retardation and giftedness, examine R. J. Sternberg's conception of intelligence and what he has to say about mental retardation and giftedness, and discuss what we mean by creativity and the distinction between intelligence and creativity.

Mental Retardation

What is mental retardation? How is it determined that one child is mentally retarded and another is not? Not everyone agrees on this important matter. In 1977, the American Association on Mental Deficiency defined **mental retardation** as "significantly subaverage general intellectual functioning existing concurrently with deficits in adaptive behavior and manifested during the developmental period" (Grossman, 1977, p. 11). Traditionally, IQ has been the primary criterion for identifying a child as mentally retarded.

However, cultural and socioeconomic differences can influence performance on IQ tests. Such differences may result in the categorization of blacks, Mexican Americans, and children from non-English-speaking backgrounds, for example, as mentally retarded even though they actually are not. Therefore, assessment for retardation should go beyond standardized IQ tests to include observations of children in everyday circumstances and environments—at home, in the community, in the classroom with an understanding teacher—to reveal whether or not they can follow instructions and handle problems successfully. Aspects of social competence should be considered in addition to intellectual competence.

Further consideration of mental retardation emphasizes the process of labeling and the causes of retardation.

Labeling Mental retardation is not some kind of disease; it is a label that describes the child's position in relation to other children on the basis of some standard (or standards) of performance. Thus, if a child scores below 70 on the WISC-R, he or she is demonstrating less efficient performance than that of a large majority of same-age children who have taken the test. The child is likely to be labeled "mentally retarded," generating a number of inferences (Ross, 1974).

For example, the term *trainable* has been applied to children whose scores are between 25 and 45, and the term *educable* to those whose scores are between 55 and 69. An educable mentally retarded child is supposed to be able to successfully perform academic work at the third- to sixth-grade level by the time he or she is 16 years old. A trainable mentally retarded child is supposed to be unable to perform academic work at all; he or she is generally taught personal care and how to cope with some basic, simple routines in life. These children are not taught to read and write. Thus, a child's score on an IQ test has important implications for the type of treatment program to which he or she is assigned.

It is important to remember that an IQ score reflects a child's *current* performance; it does not always indicate academic *potential*. Therefore, the use of diagnostic labels that suggest assumptions about a child's potential can be dangerous. Remarkable strides are sometimes made in teaching retarded children to perform academic tasks that were thought to be impossible.

Many experts believe that the terms *trainable* and *educable,* as well as *mental retardation,* should always be thought of as labels that index only current performance. Because a child's level of performance may well change later, it may be wise to discard the label.

A score in the mentally retarded range on an IQ test reveals nothing about why the child is retarded. Next, we find that the most widely used classification of the causes of mental retardation distinguishes between organic and cultural-familial causes.

Causes of Retardation   Damage to the central nervous system, particularly the brain, can produce mental retardation. Damage to the brain may occur during prenatal or postnatal development or as a result of an abnormal chromosome configuration. Down's syndrome is a well-known example of mental retardation that has an organic cause—the presence of an extra chromosome. Another type of organic disturbance that results in severe mental retardation is inadequate production of hormones, as in **cretinism.** Cretinism is caused by a hormone deficiency in the thyroid gland. When this deficiency is untreated, physical and mental development is stunted.

Many *organic* causes of mental retardation are linked to pregnancy and birth. For example, overdoses of radiation or the contraction of syphilis during pregnancy can cause retardation. Accidental injury to the brain of the fetus, as through a bad fall by the mother or the birth process itself, can cause mental retardation. Furthermore, although no clear link to mental retardation itself has been uncovered, inadequate protein intake on the part of the mother may be a contributing factor.

Most instances of mental retardation do not have a known organic cause. Such retardation is termed **cultural-familial.** For retardation to be considered cultural-familial, there can be no detectable brain abnormality, the retardation must be mild, and at least one of the parents or one of the siblings must also be mentally retarded (Davison & Neale, 1975). It has been estimated that the mental retardation of about 75 percent of the retarded population is cultural-familial. Their intelligence test scores generally fall between 50 and 70, whereas the scores of those with organic retardation are likely to be much lower.

Both genetic and environmental factors contribute to the occurrence of cultural-familial retardation. For instance, parents who have low IQs not only are more likely to transmit genes for a lower intelligence to their offspring but also tend to provide them with a less enriched environment (Ross, 1974).

Some experts believe that replacing the impoverished environment of the cultural-familial retarded child with a more enriched one may stimulate normal or even superior intellectual growth. Even though such children may make intellectual gains, however, the gains are usually limited. Of course, intensive effort at teaching mentally retarded children should not be abandoned. To the contrary, every effort should be made to encourage retarded children to learn and to achieve to the best of their abilities. However, the process of change is usually an arduous one that requires great teacher patience and commitment.

At the other end of the intelligence spectrum are those children with well-above-average intelligence, often referred to as gifted children. In the next section, we look at what it means for a child to be gifted.

Gifted Children
Many years ago, the label "gifted" had a single meaning, namely, high intelligence (White House Conference on Children, 1931). The **gifted child** still is described as an individual with well-above-average intellectual capacity (an IQ of 120 or more, for example), but he or she may also be a child with a superior talent for something (Owen, Froman, & Moscow, 1981). In their selection of children for gifted programs, most school systems still place the heaviest weight on intellectual superiority and academic aptitude and do not look as carefully at such areas of competence as the visual and performing arts, psychomotor abilities, and other specific aptitudes.

One classic study dominates our knowledge about gifted children, that of Lewis Terman (1925). In the 1920s, Terman began to study approximately 1,500 children whose Stanford-Binet IQ scores averaged 150. Terman's research was designed to follow these children through their adulthood—it will not be complete until the year 2010.

The accomplishments of the 1,500 children in Terman's study are remarkable. Of the 800 males, 78 have obtained Ph.D.s, 48 have earned M.D.s, and 85 have been granted law degrees. Nearly all of these figures are 10 to 30 times greater than would have been found among 800 men of the same age chosen randomly (Getzels & Dillon, 1973).

Scrutiny of the gifted 1,500 continues. The most recent investigation focused on whether the gifted individuals were satisfied with their lives (Sears, 1977). When the average age of the Terman gifted population was 62, four target factors were assessed: (1) life-cycle satisfaction with occupation, (2) satisfaction with family life, (3) degree of work persistence into their sixties, and (4) unbroken marriage versus a history of divorce. The recorded events and expressions of feelings have been obtained at decade intervals since 1922. One of the most interesting findings of the study is that, in spite of their autonomy and extensive success in their occupations, these people placed more importance on achieving satisfaction in their family life than in their work. Furthermore, the gifted individuals felt that they had found such satisfaction. As Terman suggested, they are not only superior intellectually, but are physically, emotionally, morally, and socially more able as well.

Individuals who turn out to have exceptional talents as adults suggest that there is more to becoming a "star" in their respective fields than gifted programs. In one inquiry, 120 individuals who had achieved stardom in six different areas—concert pianists and sculptors (arts), Olympic swimmers and tennis champions (psychomotor), and research mathematicians and research neurologists (cognitive)—were interviewed to learn what they felt was responsible for their lofty accomplishments (Bloom, 1983). It seems that exceptional accomplishments require particular kinds of environmental support, special experiences, excellent teaching, and motivational encouragement throughout development. Regardless of the quality of their gifts, each of the individuals experienced many years of special attention under the tutelage and supervision of a remarkable series of teachers and coaches. They also were given considerable support and attention by their parents. All of the "stars" devoted great amounts of time to practice and training, easily outrivaling the amount of time spent in other activities.

R. J. Sternberg has made some important contributions to our understanding of intelligence in recent years. Focus on Child Development 10.3 outlines some of his ideas involving giftedness and mental retardation.

Closely related to the study of gifted children is creativity, an important aspect of mental functioning that is not measured by traditional IQ tests, a fact that has triggered considerable criticism of intelligence tests. As we see in the next section, children not only think, they think creatively.

Creativity

Most of us would like to be creative, and parents and teachers would like to be able to develop situations that promote creative thinking in children. Why was Thomas Edison able to invent so many things? Was he simply more intelligent than most people? Did he spend long hours toiling away in private? Somewhat surprisingly, when Edison was a young boy, his teacher told him that he was too dumb to learn anything! There are other examples of famous individuals whose creative genius went unnoticed when they were younger (Larson, 1973): Walt Disney was fired from a newspaper because he did not have any good ideas; Enrico Caruso's music teacher informed him that he could not sing and that he didn't have any voice at all; Albert Einstein was four years old before he could speak and seven before he could read; and Winston Churchill failed one year of secondary school. Among the reasons such individuals are overlooked as youngsters is the difficulty psychologists have in defining and measuring **creativity**.

Definition and Measurement　The prevailing belief of experts who study creativity is that intelligence and creativity are not the same (Wallach, 1973). For example, scores on widely used tests of creativity developed by J. P. Guilford are only weakly related to intelligence scores (Richards, 1976). Yet it is as difficult to define creativity as it is to define intelligence. Just as intelligence consists of many disparate elements, so also is creativity a many-faceted phenomenon. An important question is whether measuring general creative functioning is appropriate or even possible.

David Ausubel (1968) emphasized that *creativity* is one of the most ambiguous and confusing terms in psychology and education. He believes that the term *creative* should not be applied to as many people as it is but

FOCUS ON CHILD DEVELOPMENT 10.3

NOVEL THINKING, INSIGHT, AND AUTOMATIZATION IN THE GIFTED AND THE RETARDED

In addition to describing a number of components of intelligence, R. J. Sternberg (1984) has proposed a dual-facet conception of intelligence: skill at coping with novel tasks and situations and skill at "automatizing" information processing.

The ability to cope with novelty can be tapped in tests of "insight problems" such as the following:

> Water lilies double in area every 24 hours. At the beginning of the summer, there is one water lily on the lake. It takes 60 days for the lake to become covered with water lilies. On what day is the lake half covered? (Sternberg, 1984, p. 177)

Although this problem is difficult, a single insight provides you with the answer. You need only realize that 24 hours before the lake becomes fully covered, it must be only half covered (since water lilies double in area every 24 hours). Thus, the answer must be the 59th day. Presumably, intelligent behavior in everyday life sometimes involves the formulation of insights into novel situations or tasks. Certainly, all of us have some intuition of how good we are—compared to others— at dealing with the unexpected. Sternberg is suggesting that this is one basic type of intelligence.

Automatization can be measured in such tasks as the "synonyms task." The subject takes a multiple-choice test in which each item consists of a word alongside some alternative words, one of which is its synonym. Some people can perform such tasks more quickly and accurately than others, presumably because they can automatize the processes of retrieving and comparing the meanings of the words. There may be different types of automatization, tapped by different types of tasks. In any event, Sternberg argues that automatization skills are an important facet of intelligence, not just in the laboratory but in real life. Presumably, individuals who quickly master complex tasks and learn information easily are good automatizers.

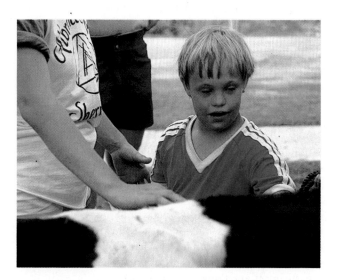

How might the information processing of mentally retarded children differ from children of normal intellect?

Sternberg's dual-facet view of intelligence has some important implications for thinking about giftedness and mental retardation. Sternberg and Davidson (1983) have argued that giftedness involves the ability of gifted children to think in novel ways and to do so in an insightful manner. Exceptional intellectual accomplishments—for example, major scientific discoveries, important inventions, and special literary and philosophical works—invariably involve major intellectual insights.

If gifted people are high in insightfulness, are the mentally retarded unusually low in this attribute? Sternberg argues that the answer is no. While the mentally retarded may not have many insights, neither do people of average intelligence. Thus, Sternberg (1984) argues that retardation is not a failure to be insightful, but that it is better understood in terms of (1) inadequate automatization of processes (that is, the second facet of intelligence) or (2) other deficits in the efficiency of information processing.

should be reserved for describing people who make unique and original contributions to society.

The term *creativity* has been used in many ways. Next, we look at how one well-known figure—J.P. Guilford—defined creativity and attempted to measure it in individuals.

Guilford's Concept of Divergent Thinking Creative thinking is part of J. P. Guilford's model of intelligence (Guilford, 1967). The aspect of his theory of intelligence that is most closely related to creativity is what he called **divergent thinking,** a type of thinking that produces many different answers to a single question. Divergent thinking is distinguished from **convergent thinking,** a type of thinking that goes toward one correct answer. For example, there is one correct answer to this intellectual problem-solving task: "How many quarters can you get from 60 dimes?" It calls for convergent thinking. But there are many possible answers to this question: "What are some unique things a coat hanger can be used for?" This question requires divergent thinking. Going off in different directions may sometimes lead to more productive answers. Examples of what Guilford means by divergent thinking (his term for creativity) and ways of measuring it are shown in Figure 10.6.

Encouraging Creativity If you were an elementary school teacher, how might you go about fostering creativity on the part of your students? **Brainstorming** is one technique that has been effective in several programs developed to stimulate creativity in children. In brainstorming sessions, a topic is presented for consideration and participants are encouraged to suggest ideas related to it. Criticism of ideas contributed must be withheld initially to prevent stopping the flow of ideas. The more freewheeling the ideas, the better. Participants are also encouraged to combine ideas that have already been suggested. Studies with children in regular classrooms (e.g., Torrance & Torrance, 1972) and in classrooms with educationally handicapped children (e.g., Sharpe, 1976) indicate that brainstorming can be an effective strategy for increasing creative thinking.

Another useful technique for encouraging creativity is called **playing with improbabilities.** This method forces children to think about the events that might follow an

1. *Sketches:* Add just enough detail to the circle below to make a recognizable object (two examples of acceptable responses are shown).

2. *Word fluency:* Write as many words as you can think of with the first and last letters R_____M ("rim" would be one).

3. *Name grouping:* Classify the following six names in as many different ways as you can (a person might group 1, 3 and 4 together because each has two syllables).
   1. GERTRUDE   2. BILL
   3. ALEX   4. CARRIE
   5. BELLE   6. DON

4. *Making objects:* Using two or more of the forms shown below, make a face. Now make a lamp (examples of good responses are shown).

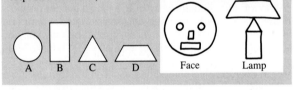

FIGURE 10.6 Sample items from Guilford's (1967) Divergent Productions Tests.

unlikely occurrence. The following are examples of questions that can be used to foster classroom discussion:

> What could happen if it always rained on Saturday?
> What could happen if it were against the law to sing?
> . . . Just suppose you could visit the prehistoric section of the museum and the animals could come alive? Just suppose you could enter into the life of a pond and become whatever you wanted to become? (Davis, 1981, pp. 436–437)

To answer these questions, the child must break out of conventional modes of thought and wander through fantasyland.

More important, perhaps, than any specific technique, however, is the need to foster a *creative atmosphere* in the classroom. Children need to feel that they can try out ideas, even if the ideas seem crazy or far-fetched, without being criticized by the teacher. The only way to produce a creative environment on a sustained basis is to *do* things creatively on a regular basis.

Creative thinking can be encouraged in any type of curriculum and in any kind of classroom situation; neither an open classroom nor progressive education is required. A word of caution, however: Although experts believe that creative thinking exercises should be practiced in every classroom, they caution against spending too much time on creative activities at the expense of other equally important learning activities. Michael Wallach (1973), for one, has commented that many children do not need to read more creatively, they just need to learn how to read.

Child Development Concept Table 10.1 summarizes our discussion of the psychometric approach to intelligence. Next, we focus on several other important dimensions of the child's intellectual and achievement world.

THE 3 Rs AND BILINGUALISM

The 3 Rs—they have been around for a long time in the education of children. Let's look more closely at the nature of their development in children and some recent information about how they might be taught effectively.

Writing and Reading

A very important language-related task that the child must tackle in the preschool or elementary school years is learning to read. First, however, we consider writing systems, which differ in how visual symbols map on to different levels of language. Subsequently, we describe the major ways children are taught to read.

Writing Systems

Robert Crowder (1982) has summarized a good deal of what is known about the variety and evolution of writing systems. According to the best archeological evidence, making visual marks to represent experiences has been occurring for some 50,000 years. However, the appearance of writing, as opposed to art, probably is much more

How did writing systems evolve?

recent. At least five major writing systems have been invented, but the current systems of the world have evolved from just two sources: the Egyptian system, which originated around 3500 B.C., and the Chinese system, which originated around 2000 B.C. Our own **alphabetic system** evolved from the Egyptian.

Our alphabetic system is one of three basic types of systems that are used in the world today. It is a system in which the visual symbols (letters) correspond—but only roughly—to the phonemes of our speech. That is, letters refer to phonemes, but with compromises and exceptions that we call spelling irregularities.

Two alternatives to our alphabetic system are the **syllabic** and **logographic** writing systems. In a syllabic system, such as that of the Japanese Katakana, each written symbol corresponds to a spoken syllable. If we used such a system in English, we might have a letter for "bas" and another for "ket," and might spell "basket" by writing these two letters side by side. In a logographic system, which is found in Chinese, each visual symbol corresponds to a word—so in such a system, we might have a single visual symbol for "basket."

Child Development Concept Table 10.1   The Psychometric Approach to Intelligence

Concept	Processes/Related Ideas	Characteristics/Description
Theories, definition, and measurement	Binet and the concept of general intelligence	Alfred Binet (with Theodore Simon) developed the first intelligence test in 1905 to determine which students in Paris would not benefit from regular classes. Binet also developed the concept of mental age to describe the general level of the child's intellectual functioning. The Binet has gone through a lengthy standardization process (which has resulted in its now being called the Stanford-Binet) and today can be given to individuals from the age of two years through adulthood. The Stanford-Binet measures overall or general level of intellectual functioning, which is then indicated by a certain IQ score. The 1985 version of the Stanford-Binet also provides for an analysis of several intellectual processes.
	The Wechsler scales	Wechsler also emphasizes the general nature of intelligence, but his WAIS, WISC-R, and WPPIS tests provide not only an overall IQ score, but also are divided into verbal and nonverbal categories, which are further subdivided to reflect specific aspects of intelligence.
	The many faces of intelligence	Spearman's two-factor theory stressed the existence of g (for general intelligence) and s (for specific factor); Thurstone developed a multiple-factor theory; Cattell described intelligence in terms of two factors—fluid intelligence and crystallized intelligence; and Guilford's structure of intellect model lists 120 factors involved in intelligence. Both Sternberg and Gardner, while not placing a premium on the factor analytic statistical technique, like many of these theorists argue that there are a number of intelligences and intellectual processes rather than a single unitary intelligence.
Alternatives and supplements to standardized intelligence tests	Validity	Critics have argued that intelligence tests are not valid in the sense that IQ tests may not be accurately measuring what they purport to measure—intelligence. Criterion validity is particularly important in this respect. IQ tests are reasonably good at predicting grades in school.
	Culture-fair tests	Culture-fair tests have been developed in an attempt to reduce or eliminate cultural bias in tests. In particular, it has been argued that traditional IQ tests favor children from white, middle-class backgrounds. Creating a truly culture-fair test has so far proven to be beyond the ability of test makers.
	Social intelligence	Children's lives involve more than solving verbal and numerical problems. Recently, efforts have been made to assess social intelligence as well as the more traditional cognitive and academic forms of intelligence. SOMPA has been a widely used test in this regard.
Stability and change in intelligence	Stability	IQ scores at 2 and 3 years of age do not reliably predict IQ at 10 or 18 years of age. However, recent research has shown that novelty scores based on dishabituation in infancy are reasonably good predictors of IQ in early childhood. Also, IQ scores obtained at 6, 8, and 9 years of age are somewhat accurate predictors of IQ at 10 and 18 years of age.
	Individual change	Between the ages of 2½ and 17, the IQ scores of one out of every three individuals change by as much as 30 points.
Genetic-environmental influences on intelligence	Genetic influences	Heredity is a strong influence on intelligence, although not as strong as Jensen believed.
	Environmental influences	Among the most important environmental influences on intelligence are those involving home, institutionalization, education, and social class.
	Conclusions about genetic-environmental interaction and intelligence	As with all other aspects of the child's development, genes and environment interact to produce intelligence.

Child Development Concept Table 10.1   Continued

Concept	Processes/Related Ideas	Characteristics/Description
Mental retardation, giftedness, and creativity	Mental retardation	Mental retardation is defined as significantly subaverage general intellectual functioning existing concurrently with deficits in adaptive behavior and manifested during the developmental period. Such labels as "mentally retarded," "trainable," and "educable" have often been applied to individuals who score significantly below average on IQ tests. Such labels need to be used cautiously. The causes of retardation often are categorized as organic or cultural-familial.
	Gifted children	The gifted child still is described as a child with well-above-average intelligence (IQ of 120 or more), but he or she may also be a child with a superior talent in the arts, psychomotor abilities, or other specific aptitudes. Research suggests that the gifted often are superior to others in nonacademic areas as well. Sternberg believes that giftedness involves insight and the ability to think in novel ways.
	Creativity	Creativity is very difficult to define and measure. Guilford defines it in terms of divergent thinking, a type of thinking that produces many different answers to the same question. Brainstorming and playing with improbabilities are two examples of ways creativity can be encouraged in the classroom. A creative atmosphere needs to be fostered in the classroom, keeping in mind the caution that some children do not need to read creatively, they simply need to learn how to read.

It is interesting to note that, in the evolution of writing, there has been a trend to move downward from meaning to sound, and from longer segments of sound (words) to shorter segments of sound (syllables, phonemes), in linking the language to visual symbols. In the earliest logographic systems, the visual symbols looked like (were drawings of) what they represented. But these symbols often became streamlined and highly abstract, sometimes to the extent that they no longer resembled their referents at all. Figure 10.7 shows the evolution of some written symbols in Sumerian cuneiform writing.

The evolution from a logographic to a syllabic writing system often involves a recognition of homophones (words that sound alike but have different meanings). As a hypothetical example, a symbol for a word like *sun* might begin to be used for "son." Another important evolutionary step is the taking of two word-symbols and combining them to form a longer word (symbols for the words *sun* and *day* might be combined to make *Sunday*). At this point, we have begun to form a syllabary. It apparently happened only once in ancient history—around 1000 B.C. in the Near East—that the transition was made from a syllabic to an alphabetic system.

Now that we have seen how writing systems evolved, let's study how this might help us instruct children in learning to read more effectively.

Techniques for Teaching Reading

The evolution of writing is historically interesting, but it also is important for practical reasons—it may provide a clue as to how best to teach reading to young children. This is the argument of Paul Rozin and Lila Gleitman (1977), two experts in the field of reading research. Rozin and Gleitman have developed a method for the teaching of reading in which children begin with pictographic representations, which they then learn to relate to sounds and, subsequently, to syllables. After this, the children move to using the alphabetic system of spelling out words. There are five separate stages in all:

In the first, "semasiographic" stage of the Rozin and Gleitman method, children are taught that meaning can be represented visually. They send and try to understand messages using only a pencil and paper or a chalkboard. Speaking in these "communication games" is strictly against the rules. Hence, children are trained to code and decode meaning using only visual markings. An example

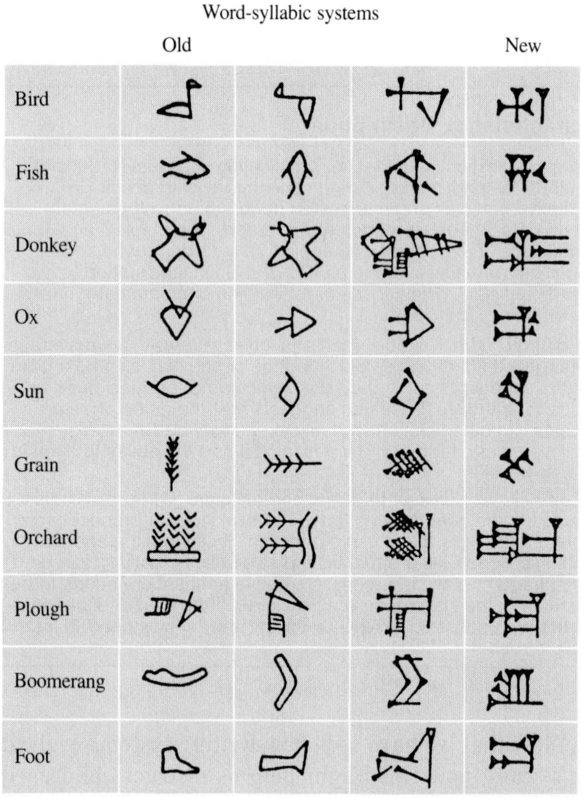

Word-syllabic systems

FIGURE 10.7 Pictorial origins of ten cuneiform signs.

of a communication game is to "say" where an object is hidden in a room simply by drawing some sort of picture (e.g., a map). Such games are fun for five- and six-year-old children (and even for much older people).

In the second, "logographic" stage, children learn that certain pictures stand for certain words. Furthermore, they practice reading and writing simple sentences made up of these pictures. Some examples of picture-sentences are shown in Figure 10.8. Note that each picture is printed on a card. Note also that the word is spelled out below each picture—this is to get the children familiar with the look of English orthography and perhaps to get them started in learning this orthography.

In the third, "phoneticization" stage, children are taught that written symbols can correspond to sounds, not just meanings. Specifically, they learn that, if two different words sound the same, they also may be written

the same (e.g., a picture of a can is used to stand for *can*, even when *can* is used as a verb, as in "The man can saw the can," see Figure 10.8).

In the fourth, "syllabary" stage, children learn symbols that correspond to spoken syllables. In the course of such learning, children come to realize that two one-syllable words can be "put together" to form a completely new two-syllable word (e.g., *sand* and *witch* can combine to form *sandwich*, see Figure 10.8). The children also learn to read and write some syllables that have no meaning by themselves, such as *y* and *er*. Pictures are not much use for representing such syllables. Hence, the children are taught adult-type spellings for them (Figure 10.8).

In the fifth, "alphabet" stage, the children are taught that syllables can be broken down into phonemes and that alphabetic characters roughly correspond (with compromises and exceptions) to these phonemes. This is done through various "blending" exercises, in which a given alphabetic symbol (e.g., *s*) is combined with different combinations of letters (*ing, and*) to produce different words (see Figure 10.8).

An important aspect of this approach pertains to problems with linguistic awareness of phonemes. Awareness of the phonemes contained within syllables is difficult for children to attain and can be a serious stumbling block in reading. In the method proposed by Rozin and Gleitman, care is taken to instill in children four other aspects of reading before this final task is faced.

But does the method actually work? Some preliminary data are quite encouraging. Specifically, stages 1 through 4 appear to be learnable by first-grade students, even those who have a poor prognosis for reading. Stage 5, however, causes more problems. Thus, it is not yet clear that the five-stage program actually facilitates the linguistic awareness that children need to learn our alphabetic system of reading.

There is good reason for optimism, however. In the first place, the five-stage method has not yet been refined—improvements in the materials and procedures might increase its effectiveness enormously. Second, a side benefit of the method is that it is fun for children and motivates them to read. Since motivation is doubtlessly important in overcoming reading difficulties, the motivational aspect of the five-stage method might be its strongest feature.

Logographic-stage
sentence:

Phoneticization-
stage sentence:

Syllabary-stage
words:

Alphabet-stage
words:

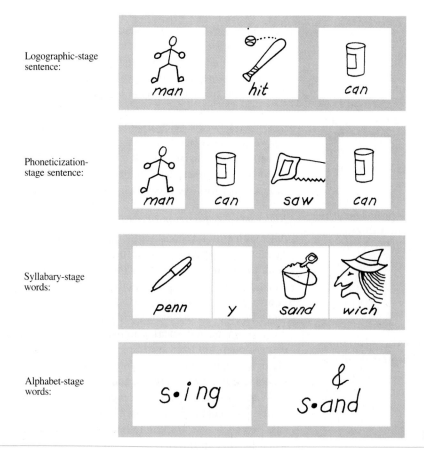

FIGURE 10.8 Examples of materials used
by Rozin and Gleitman.

Rozin and Gleitman (1977) were hardly the first to devise a technique for the teaching of reading. In the history of learning-to-read techniques, three approaches have been dominant: (1) the **ABC method,** which emphasizes memorization of the names of the letters of the alphabet; (2) the **whole-word method,** which focuses on learning direct associations between whole words and their meanings; and (3) the **phonics method,** which stresses the sounds that letters make when in words— such sounds can differ from the names of these letters (e.g., the sound of the name of the letter *C* is not to be found in *cat*). The ABC method is today in ill repute. Because of the imperfect relationship between the names of letters and their sounds in words, the technique is viewed as ineffective in teaching if not actually harmful to children. Despite its poor reputation, the ABC method was that by which many children in past generations successfully learned to read.

Most disputes in recent times have centered on the merits of the whole-word and phonics methods. Although there has been some research comparing these two techniques, the findings have not been conclusive (Crowder, 1982). However, there is evidence suggesting that drilling the sounds made by letters in words (part of some phonics methods) can be helpful to an extent in some aspects of reading (e.g., spelling and reading aloud) (Chall, 1967; Williams, 1979). In any case, many current techniques of reading instruction incorporate both whole-word and phonics components. The Rozin and Gleitman technique also has both sorts of components— children initially learn single symbols for words (clearly a whole-word approach) but later attend to the phonemes that make up words and learn to associate visual symbols with these phonemes (clearly a phonics approach).

Bilingualism

For many children, in addition to reading and writing, an additional concern that involves language development and schooling is bilingualism. Learning a first language is, for the vast majority of humanity, an affair of infancy and childhood. However, learning a second language is a very different matter. This can occur at any time of life, from young childhood through old age. Though learning a new language is difficult for most of us, it is hardly impossible. We may never shake our first-language accents, but we can grow fluent in the second language nonetheless.

Just how is it possible to attain great proficiency in more than one language? We now turn to a discussion of two different types of bilingual individuals: (1) those who learn two languages simultaneously in young childhood and (2) those who learn two languages successively in time.

Simultaneous Acquisition of Two Languages

An excellent analysis of the simultaneous acquisition of two languages has been provided by Virginia Volterra and Traute Taeschner (1978). They considered the language development of three children, each of whom acquired mastery of two languages, from one to four years of age. The goal was to identify "stages" in the children's early usage and mastery. One child grew up in an English-speaking environment where her mother spoke to her mostly in English and her father spoke to her only in German. The other children were two sisters, living in Rome, who had been immersed in two languages since birth. Their father spoke German to them. The data used in the study consisted of extensive tape recordings of the two sisters and a detailed diary of the first girl made by her father. Volterra and Taeschner (1978) believe that there are three distinct stages in learning two languages:

> In the first stage, the child seems to have one mixed vocabulary, or lexicon. Words from the two languages are often used together in short phrases, and for any single word in one language, there is not always a corresponding word in the other. The child seems to move freely among the two languages without clearly discriminating between them.

> In the second stage, the child has separate vocabularies for the two languages and does not mix them. Phrases contain words from only one language, and for any single word in one language, there is a corresponding one in the other language. Generally, one child uses the same syntactic rules for both languages.

> In the third stage, the child advances significantly in syntax. Different rules for producing utterances in the two languages emerge and there is a differentiation between the languages in all other ways. To help keep the languages distinct, the child only speaks the language associated with the person being addressed.

Successive Acquisition of Two Languages

Although simultaneous acquisition of two different languages is undeniably fascinating, successive acquisition is at the heart of some pressing educational problems. Consider the case of a hypothetical but quite typical young boy named Octavio. Octavio's Mexican parents moved to the United States one year before Octavio was born. They do not speak English fluently and have always spoken to Octavio in Spanish. At six years of age, Octavio has just entered the first grade at an elementary school in San Antonio, Texas, and does not speak English.

What is the best way to reach Octavio? How much easier would elementary school be for Octavio if his parents had been able to speak to him in Spanish and English when he was an infant?

According to the 1980 census, well over six million children in the United States come from homes where the primary language is not English. Often, like Octavio, they live in a community where this same non-English language is the major means of communication. These children face a more difficult task than most of us—they must master the native tongue of their family to be effective at home and in their own community, and they must also master English to make their way in and contribute to the larger society. The number of bilingual children is expanding at such a rapid rate in our country (some experts, for example, predict a tripling in their numbers by early in the 21st century) that they constitute an important subgroup of language learners to be dealt with by society. Although the education of such children in the public schools has a long history, only recently has a national policy evolved to guarantee a quality language experience for them.

How do children acquire languages successively?

Widespread efforts in the early 1960s to incorporate bilingual education components into the American school curricula resulted in the enactment by Congress in 1967 of the Bilingual Education Act (as title VII of the Elementary and Secondary Education Act). The Educational Amendments Act of 1974 revised and strengthened the 1967 statute: In federal fiscal year 1975, congressional appropriations for bilingual education were $85 million. This figure nearly doubled within three to four years.

Great debates have raged concerning how best to conduct this bilingual education. Does one teach English as a foreign language, adopting the child's native tongue as the language of the classroom, or does one treat English as a second, equal language and strive for balance in usage of English and the native tongue? The answer to this has important consequences for the way in which school curricula and texts are written in cities with large concentrations of Spanish-speaking children (e.g., New York, Miami, San Antonio, and Los Angeles).

Practical educational decisions about bilingual education ideally should rest on a sound understanding of how second-language learning comes about. Research in this area is only beginning, but already we have learned enough to question many previously held beliefs. Barry McLaughlin (1978) considers several popular notions about second-language learning, including the three following:

1. The young child acquires a language more quickly and easily than an adult because the child is biologically programmed to acquire languages, whereas the adult is not.
2. The younger the child, the more skilled in acquiring a second language.
3. Second-language acquisition is a qualitatively different process than first-language acquisition. (pp. 197–200)

Although these ideas sound plausible, it may surprise you to learn that the bulk of research evidence weighs against all three! It certainly is true that young children are impressive at the task of language learning. But so are adults who are highly motivated and are also extensively exposed to a new language. Although a college student might feel quite the moron when trying to learn French, consider the number of hours per day (or week) he or she actually spends with this language. In contrast, a young child learning his or her first language is almost literally immersed in it, hearing it and trying to use it to communicate every day. Motivation is probably also involved. Although a college student might have difficulty actually opening up that French book, there can be no doubt that a young child is simply driven to learn his or her first language. When studies have controlled these critical variables of exposure time and motivation and have measured language competence by objective criteria, the evidence does not favor superiority of younger children over older children and adults, but rather the reverse. Furthermore, there has been no strong evidence that the basic mechanisms of language learning are different in young children than in older children and adults.

Of course, the foregoing is not meant to deny that there are benefits to beginning second-language learning early. As McLaughlin (1978) remarks:

The success of young children in acquiring two languages under such conditions need not be attributed to superior language learning skills. Given the same amount and quality of exposure, an older child (or an adult) would presumably do just as well, most likely better. This, of course, is not to denigrate the young child's achievement or to downgrade the advantages of early introduction to a second language. Older children and adults do not have the amount of time at their disposal for learning a second language that the young child does. There is no reason not to utilize this advantage and to begin language instruction early. The practice of total immersion programs of introducing children to a second language in kindergarten through games, songs, rhymes, and so forth has produced extremely favorable results and is in all likelihood a more pleasant way to acquire a second language for the child than the repetitious drills that often characterize later classroom instruction. (p. 200)

A qualification on McLaughlin's conclusions concerns the phonological level of language. As mentioned in an earlier chapter, it appears to be difficult to acquire new accents after the time of puberty. Thus, the learning of phonemes may indeed be better in young children than in the rest of us, perhaps because of a critical period tied to biological maturation.

Reading and writing are important developments in middle and late childhood. But so also is the development of mathematical abilities, as we see next.

Mathematics

What kind of educational goals should we have for children's mathematical skills? How do American children stack up against children from other cultures when achievement in math is at issue? Let's explore some possible answers to these questions.

Educational Goals for Children's Mathematics

The National Assessment of Educational Progress suggests that the following mathematical objectives should be strived for: mathematical knowledge, mathematical skills (such as how well students can perform computations, make measurements, read graphs and tables), mathematical understanding, and mathematical application. Applying these objectives to a third grader, we would expect him or her to be able to (Biehler & Snowman, 1986):

Identify plus and minus signs in problems

Describe how to add and subtract numbers

Show the actual ability to add and subtract numbers

Demonstrate the ability to take sets of numbers supplied and arrange them to be added or subtracted by self or others

Explain how to use knowledge of addition and subtraction to handle situations outside of school (for instance, deciding how much money it takes to buy three different objects at a store)

Cross-Cultural Comparisons of Achievement in Mathematics

Quite clearly, American schoolchildren are more achievement oriented than children in many cultures. However, there has been recent concern about the achievement of American children in comparison to children in other countries that have developed very strong educational orientations, such as Russia and Japan. In particular, recent data suggest that, in comparison to Japanese children, American children are not faring well in math achievement. Focus on Child Development 10. 4 examines this issue.

FOCUS ON CHILD DEVELOPMENT 10.4

ACHIEVEMENT IN MATH REQUIRES TIME AND PRACTICE—COMPARISONS OF CHILDREN IN THE UNITED STATES AND JAPAN

Children in Japan frequently are superior to children from other countries in math achievement (Comber & Keeves, 1973; Glaser, 1976; Walberg, Harnisch, & Tsai, 1984). Recently, Harold Stevenson and his colleagues conducted a very detailed research investigation focused on math achievement in first- and fifth-grade children from Japan and the United States (Stevenson, Stigler, & Lee, 1986). Representative samples of children were evaluated in two economically successful cities in the two countries, both of which have little heavy industry and are more culturally traditional than many cities in their respective countries. The final sample included 240 first graders and 240 fifth graders from each country. Ten elementary schools were sampled in each city, and two first- and two fifth-grade classrooms were studied at each school. From each of these classrooms, six boys and six girls were randomly selected. Extensive time was spent in developing a mathematics test that was given to the children, the children were observed in their classrooms, and additional information was obtained from mothers, teachers, and the children themselves.

As shown in the following table, the results clearly indicated that the Japanese children scored higher than American children on the mathematics test in both the first and fifth grades. And interestingly, by the fifth grade, the highest average score of any of the American classrooms sampled fell *below* the worst performing score of the Japanese classrooms sampled!

What are some of the reasons for these dramatic differences between American and Japanese children with regard to mathematics achievement?

Average Mathematics Achievement by Japanese and American Children

Country	Boys	Girls
Grade 1		
Japan	20.7	19.5
United States	16.6	17.6
Grade 5		
Japan	53.0	53.5
United States	45.0	43.8

From Stevenson, H. W., et al., "Achievement in Mathematics" in H. W. Stevenson, et al., (Eds.), *Child Development and Education in Japan.* © 1986 W. H. Freeman and Company, New York. Reprinted by permission.

Stevenson and his associates considered a number of possible factors. First, according to the researchers, the curriculum did not seem to be a factor. For example, in the first grade, 15 of the early items in the math test appeared in the curricula in both countries. And similar situations occurred in the fifth grade. For example, items 35 through 38 were identical for children from both nations. The average grade placement of these items was 2.6 and 3.2 for American and Japanese children, far below fifth grade. Just as with the similar first-grade math items, the American children did more poorly than the Japanese children on the items even though both sets of children had been taught the math concepts.

(continued on following page)

FOCUS ON CHILD DEVELOPMENT 10.4

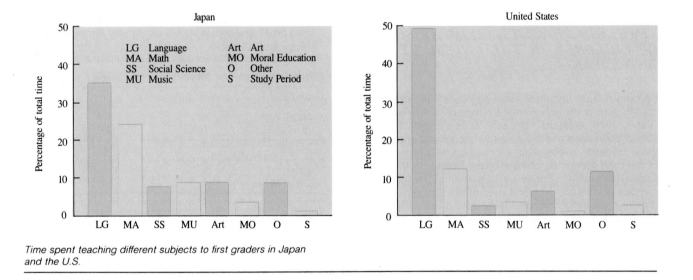

Time spent teaching different subjects to first graders in Japan and the U.S.

Parental educational status typically is related to children's level of achievement. However, when the researchers compared the educational status of the Japanese and American parents, they found that this could not be used to explain the discrepancy in the children's math achievement. For example, more than half of the American mothers had attended college or graduate school, but only 22 percent of the Japanese mothers had. About two thirds of the American fathers were college graduates, but only slightly more than one third of the Japanese fathers had completed college.

A positive relation between children's intellectual level and their academic achievement usually is found. Possibly, the researchers thought, the Japanese children were merely brighter than their American counterparts. A battery of 10 cognitive tasks constructed for this project focused on such categories as vocabulary, general information, verbal memory (which are tests of verbal ability), and categories of coding, spatial, and perceptual speed (which are tests of nonverbal intelligence). There were some differences on these cognitive tasks when they were given to the children, but they tended to be opposite the results on the mathematics test, with the American sample being more intelligent on the cognitive measures reflecting intelligence.

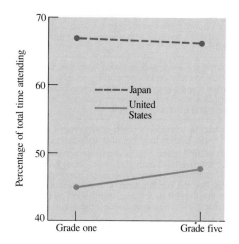

Proportion of time spent attending to teacher in teacher-led activities by Japanese and American children.

Possibly the teachers of the Japanese children had more experience than the teachers of the American children? The results indicated that this was not the case, both in terms of the educational degrees of the teachers and the number of years teaching experience.

The Japanese school year consists of 240 days of instruction, and there are 5½ days in each school week. By contrast, the American school year is made up of 178 days of instruction, and students attend school only 5 days a week. In the first grade, teachers reported no differences in the number of hours spent each week in school, but the fifth-grade teachers said that the Japanese children were in school an average of 37.3 hours per week, compared to only 30.4 hours for their American counterparts.

Observations of the children's behavior in their classrooms also were revealing. These observations provided information about the amount of time spent on mathematics compared to other subjects. As shown in the bar graph on p. 416, the Japanese teachers spent far more time teaching math to their first graders than did American teachers. (The difference decreased by the fifth grade but was still significant.)

Also, it is important to point out that instruction does not always ensure that children will learn. Attention is an important aspect of learning. Were there differences in the Japanese and American children's attention to their teachers? As shown in the line graph at the left, in both the first and fifth grades, Japanese children were far more likely to attend to the teacher in teacher-led activities than American children were. American children also were observed to be more likely to be engaging in inappropriate activities than the Japanese children. An activity was coded as inappropriate when the child was not doing what he or she was expected or supposed to be doing but was instead talking to peers, wandering about the classroom, or staring into space.

A final factor studied by Stevenson and his colleagues focused on homework. Learning happens at home as well as at school, and homework is part of this learning. From interview responses, the researchers concluded that neither American teachers nor parents viewed homework as very important. In marked contrast, both the Japanese teachers and parents remarked how they believed that homework was a very important part of learning. As expected, then, the researchers found that the Japanese children spent far more time doing homework than the American children. On weekends, for example, American children studied an average of 18 minutes, while the Japanese children did homework for an average of 66 minutes.

The conclusion of the researchers: Learning requires time and practice. When either is reduced, learning is impaired. Such seems to be the case in American children's poor mathematics achievement in comparison to Japanese children.

Child Development Concept Table 10.2 The 3 Rs and Bilingualism		
Concept	**Processes/Related Ideas**	**Characteristics/Description**
Writing and reading	Writing systems	Our alphabetic writing system is one of three basic kinds in the world today. The other two are syllabic and logographic. The evolution of writing has followed a trend to move downward from meaning to sound, and from longer to shorter segments of sound.
	Techniques for teaching reading	The Rozin-Gleitman technique for teaching reading follows a progression of from meaning to sound, and from longer to shorter segments of sound. Other strategies for teaching reading are the now ill-favored ABC method, the whole-word method, and the phonics method.
Bilingualism	Its nature	Bilinguals include those individuals who learn two languages simultaneously in early childhood and those who learn a second language after having learned the first. There is no evidence that second language learning is better in younger children than in older children and adults.
Mathematics	Educational goals	Educational goals for children's math achievement include knowledge, skills, understanding, and application.
	Cross-cultural comparisons	While children in the United States are more achievement oriented than their counterparts in many cultures, Japanese children considerably outdistance their American counterparts in mathematics. Recent research has shown that time spent in math classes and time spent practicing math (such as in homework) are possible explanations for these cultural differences in math achievement.

Child Development Concept Table 10.2 summarizes our discussion of reading, writing, bilingualism, and mathematics. Next, we focus on a number of concepts pertaining to achievement and motivation.

MOTIVATION AND ACHIEVEMENT

Even though Japanese children show higher achievement in mathematics than American children, the cultural standard in the United States suggests that success is important in life and that such success involves a competitive spirit, a desire to win, a motivation to do well what one attempts, and the wherewithal to cope with adversity and persist with effort until obstacles are overcome. Quite clearly, some children develop these talents while others do not. Indeed, some psychologists believe that our culture places too high a premium on achieving and succeeding, to the point where we have reared a nation of "wired" children with a strong fear of failure and an uptightness about comparisons with others. In this section, we study the concept of motivation itself, and then investigate different theoretical views of achievement motivation and achievement-related factors. Sociocultural influences on achievement also are explored.

Motivation and Its Importance in Children's Development

Some children are bored, others highly enthusiastic. And some children seem to work relentlessly, struggling through incredibly difficult matters, while others may take one look at a difficult or time-consuming problem and not lift a finger to solve it. What accounts for these wide individual differences?

Motivation involves the question of *why* people behave, think, and feel the way they do. When a child is motivated, his or her behavior is energized and directed. For example, if an adolescent is sexually motivated, he or she may want to stay at a dance long after it is over so that someone whose affection is desired can be pursued. Similarly, if a child is hungry, the book being studied likely will be put down and a trip to the refrigerator will transpire. And, likewise, if a person is motivated to achieve, long hours may be spent studying for an exam. The child's motivation pushes him or her into action.

It is important to make a distinction between motivation and learning. Psychologists often say that learning focuses on the issue of how behavior occurs, while motivation focuses on why it happens. In our discussions of

What question does motivation ask?

Piaget's cognitive developmental theory and the information processing perspective in earlier chapters, the *why* question was touched on. Both of these cognitive perspectives believe that motivation rests with the individual's desire for information and knowledge and that this desire is wired into the nature of the child's mind. From the cognitive developmental perspective, the child's mind is viewed as motivated to function at a higher, more efficient level. Therefore, it is argued that providing the child with information that is slightly above where the child is mentally should stimulate the child to think at a higher level and thus motivate the child. The information processing perspective implies that an analysis of the cognitive processes that make up the child's cognitive system should help. Then, by providing environmental stimulation aimed at improving such processes as attention, memory, and problem solving, the child's motivation should improve as his or her information processing abilities work more efficiently. Our discussion of information processing and education in Chapter 9 emphasized that schools need to concentrate on ways to improve children's information processing skills. However,

there seems to be much more to motivation than these basic points about cognition and its inherent motivating capacity made by the major cognitive theorists.

According to the perspective of such behaviorists as Skinner, the issue of motivation is one of arranging the child's environment so that it is rewarding. Cognitive processes are unimportant in this view of motivation—rather, motivation is seen as external to the child. According to the traditional psychoanalytic view of Freud, motivation is primarily unconscious, with such important matters as achievement motivation being wedded to biological processes housed in the id, particularly sexual motivation. Freud, for example, saw even great works as those crafted by Michelangelo as basically a sublimation, or repressing, of sexual, instinctual forces in order to engage in socially accepted and desirable conduct.

Thus, according to some of the major theoretical perspectives in psychology, motivation is seen primarily as a biological, internal force that is either cognitive (cognitive developmental, information processing), instinctual and unconscious (psychoanalytic theory), or behavioral/environmental (behaviorism) in nature. The view taken in this text is that biological and environmental factors contribute to the child's motivation, that both internal and external factors need to be examined, and that there are cognitive, affective, and behavioral aspects to the child's motivation. Next, we focus in greater detail on a very important aspect of the child's motivation—his or her achievement motivation.

Theories of Achievement Motivation and Achievement-Related Factors

Theories that specifically focus on achievement motivation include the achievement motivation views of McClelland and Atkinson, attribution theory, and the delay of gratification.

The Achievement Motivation Views of McClelland and Atkinson

David McClelland argued that achievement motivation is a property of the individual's psychological makeup and need system. Borrowing from the personality theory of Henry Murray (1938), McClelland stressed that individuals vary in how much achievement motivation they have and further that such motivation can be measured. He referred to achievement motivation as **_n_ achievement**

(standing for need for achievement), which meant the individual's internal striving for success. McClelland viewed this need for achievement as a general property of the individual, one that should be reasonably consistent across a number of different domains and across time. It was believed to develop primarily through the child and adolescent's interactions with parents and from the cultural standards in which the child lives. McClelland frequently mentioned two factors that he believed to be influential in promoting achievement motivation: independence training by parents and living in a democratic culture that emphasizes achievement orientation and individuality (McClelland, Atkinson, Clark, & Lowell, 1953; Winterbottem, 1958).

The concept of need for achievement has been criticized because research suggests that it is not as stable as McClelland predicted (e.g., Mischel, 1976). For example, children identified as high in need for achievement do not always behave in accordance with this trait in all situations. The same can be said about students low in need for achievement. Children usually do show consistent achievement behavior in different school subjects, but grades and standardized achievement test scores in those subjects are not always linked with behavior outside the classroom (e.g., Holland & Richards, 1965). Such criticisms use the behaviorist argument that concepts such as achievement motivation are too global and do not adequately pay attention to situational variation in behavior and, further, may ignore important environmental determinants of behavior. Therefore, in analyzing the child's achievement orientation, it is important to conduct a thorough observation of different achievement domains, both those related to academic and nonacademic functioning.

John Atkinson believes that the extent to which children believe that they will succeed and the degree to which they feel they are likely to fail are important components of achievement motivation (Atkinson & Feather, 1966; Atkinson & Raynor, 1974). According to Atkinson, **hope for success** is the equivalent of achievement motivation—the child's underlying drive for success. **Fear of failure** refers to the child's anxiety about not doing well. Motivation is believed to be a function of expectancy for success and the incentive value of success or failure. Thus, if children think that they will do well on a math test, and if this outcome is very rewarding, then their achievement motivation for the math test is likely to be high. On the other hand, if their anxiety about the test is also high, it can counteract their motivation to do well.

How do hope for success and fear of failure combine to produce or inhibit the desire to achieve? Atkinson believes that motivation should be behaviorally measured by assessing children's aspiration levels and/or their persistence at a task. A child's aspiration level is how well the child expects or hopes to perform. (In the case of a math test, the girl who throws away her paper in disgust may have hoped to get an A on the test; the girl who is pleased with her test score may have hoped or expected to get a C.) Persistence is measured by how long children maintain effort. For instance, students may be given a difficult science project and be evaluated on how long they work at solving it.

Researchers generally believe that moderate levels of aspiration and persistence are signs of healthy achievement orientation. It has been found that children whose hope for success is greater than their fear of failure develop moderate levels of aspiration and show lengthy persistence on problem-solving tasks (Atkinson and Feather, 1966). Thus, the achievement motivation can be increased if the child's hopes for success are encouraged.

In Atkinson's conceptualization of achievement, high levels of anxiety can have a debilitating effect on achievement behavior. Even though anxiety is a difficult concept to pin down, it is one of the most widely used terms in psychology. Most psychologists agree that anxiety is an unpleasant state, that it is linked to the physiological arousal of the child, and that it involves anticipation of something uncomfortable or painful (Sarason and Spielberger, 1975).

Anxiety can have an adaptive, or positive, influence as well as a maladaptive, or negative, influence; therefore, the removal of all achievement anxiety from the child's experiences is not a desirable goal. A moderate level of anxiety can motivate the child to do better on an examination, for example. The act of overcoming anxiety can also enhance development; mastery and competence in dealing with the world may be positive outcomes of such anxiety. You yourself have probably experienced the exhilaration that follows the completion of a task that made you extremely nervous. Some philosophers have even argued that anxiety is one of the necessary engines for social progress.

Anxiety can impede or enhance learning and school achievement. An extensive amount of work has been conducted to determine the relation between anxiety and school performance. Charles Spielberger and his colleagues (e.g., Spielberger, Gorsuch, & Lushene, 1970) have developed an anxiety measure that distinguishes between trait anxiety and state anxiety. **Trait anxiety** is the more or less stable and permanent tendency to experience a certain level of anxiety across time and circumstances; by contrast, **state anxiety** comes and goes depending upon particular experiences. Spielberger and his fellow researchers developed the State-Trait Anxiety Inventory to measure these two different types of anxiety. Trait anxiety is measured by asking individuals how they generally feel about specific situations. State anxiety is evaluated by asking, "How do you feel right now?" about specific situations. Examples of answers on the state-trait anxiety scale are "I feel pleasant," "I feel regretful," "I find myself worrying," and "I am calm."

It is possible for a child to have a high state anxiety but a low trait anxiety. Such children are generally calm and easygoing, but once in a while they become intensely upset for some reason that may be difficult for other people to understand.

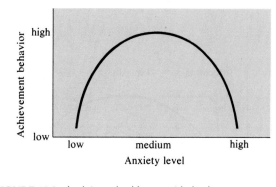

FIGURE 10.9   Anxiety and achievement behavior.

Trait anxiety is not consistently linked to the student's learning or school performance, but state anxiety is (e.g., Spielberger, 1966). The relation between state anxiety and performance is a curvilinear one for most tasks—that is, achievement behavior is maximized by moderate levels of anxiety (see Figure 10.9). Either high or low levels of anxiety result in less-than-maximum efficiency. At the low end of the anxiety continuum, the child may be too lethargic to attend to the cues necessary to efficiently perform the task. At extremely high levels of anxiety, irrelevant responses often appear to compete with task-oriented behavior. At high levels of anxiety, discrimination between appropriate and inappropriate cues also breaks down, resulting in behavioral inefficiency.

While the curvilinear relation between anxiety and achievement behavior is presumed to hold for most tasks, the exact nature of the relation may depend on the difficulty of the task for the child. For well-learned or simple tasks (signing one's name, pushing a button on request), the optimal level of anxiety is quite high, as shown in Figure 10.10. On the other hand, when the child is just learning a task (learning to ride a bicycle) or when the task is extremely complex (solving a math problem), the optimal level of anxiety is much lower. For these tasks, achievement is enhanced by the ability to relax, yet be alert and attentive.

Atkinson's work helped to pave the way for a more detailed look at the components that comprise achievement motivation. However, as we see next, it has been attribution theory that has provided the impetus for increased research on achievement.

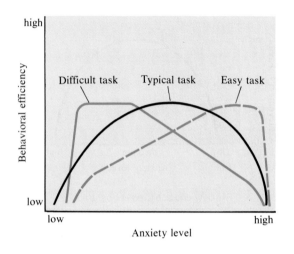

FIGURE 10.10 Achievement, anxiety, and task difficulty.

Attribution Theory

Attribution theory argues that we are cognitive beings who want to know why we behave the way we do because it will help us to cope more effectively with situations that confront us. Further, when we do not know the causes of our own or others' behavior, such behavior may not make sense to us. Thus, attribution theorists interested in achievement motivation want to know how children infer causes that underlie achievement behavior and their attempts to make sense out of that behavior.

The Internal-External Factor

We can classify the reasons why we and others behave in a number of ways, but we make one basic distinction more than any other—between internal causes (such as personality traits or motives) and external causes (environmental, situational factors, such as rewards or how difficult a task is). If a child does not do well on a test, does he or she attribute it to the fact that the teacher plotted against him or her and made the test too difficult (external cause) or to the fact that he or she didn't study hard enough (internal cause)? The answer to such a question influences how the child feels about himself or herself—if the child believes that his or her performance was the teacher's fault, then the child probably does not feel as bad as when he or she doesn't spend enough time studying.

Now that we have some general ideas about what attribution theory is and the importance of the internal-external factor in achievement, we examine a specific attributional theory of achievement.

Weiner's View: Attribution and Emotion

Bernard Weiner (Weiner, 1984; Weiner, Kun, & Benesh-Weiner, 1980) believes that we tend to attribute the causes of success and failure to four elements described by Fritz Heider (1958): ability, effort, task difficulty, and luck. Weiner's work focuses on the relation of these causal attributions to our feelings. For example, we tend to feel pleased, happy, satisfied, good, and so on after success, and unpleasant, sad, dissatisfied, and bad after failure. The following examples represent the reasoning you might go through if you were asked to interpret the causes and feelings experienced in an achievement circumstance:

"I just received an A on this exam. That's a very high grade" (generating happiness). "I received this grade because I worked hard during the entire school year" (producing contentment and relaxation). "I really do have some positive qualities that will persist in the future" (followed by high self-esteem, feelings of self-worth, and optimism).

"I just received a D on the exam. That's a very low grade" (generating feelings of unhappiness, frustration, and upset). "I received this grade because I just am not smart enough" (followed by feelings of incompetence). "There is really something lacking in me, and it is likely to remain that way" (leading to feelings of low self-esteem and hopelessness). (Weiner, Kun, & Benesh-Weiner, 1980, p. 112) These comments suggest that emotional reactions differ considerably, depending on the cognitive interpretations people make about attributes in themselves and others in the situation.

As we saw earlier, attribution theorists believe that it is important to distinguish between external and internal causes of behavior. Next, we explore the concept of internal locus of control, a closely related idea.

Locus of Control

Attribution theory stresses that the causes that children ascribe success and failure to are important determinants of achievement behavior. Closely linked to the way a child views achievement is the child's sense of personal responsibility. Children who believe that they are in control of their world, that they can cause

How is social class related to locus of control?

things to happen if they choose, and that they command their own rewards have an **internal locus of control.** Children who perceive that others have more control over them than they do over themselves have an **external locus of control.** The perceived locus of control, internal or external, has important implications for how the child can be expected to behave in a variety of situations. The child who is more internally than externally controlled is generally considered more socially competent.

The type of subculture in which boys and girls live is a significant determinant of their locus of control. Children who grow up in lower-class environments demonstrate a less internal locus of control than those from middle-class backgrounds do (Stephens & Delys, 1973). Important to the development of an internal locus of control is the quality of a child's social interactions with important people in his or her life. Brenda Bryant (1974) discovered that boys and girls with an external locus of control ascribe more negative attributes to themselves and to their teachers than those with an internal locus of control do.

Children with an internal locus of control seem to process information about themselves and their environments differently. Jerry Phares (1976) has conducted a number of research projects with individuals, focusing on the relation between their locus-of-control orientations and their use of psychological defenses. In one investigation, externally oriented individuals actually preferred a task with a built-in reason for failure, while those internally oriented did not (Phares & Lamiell, 1975). In general, externally oriented individuals tend to be threatened by possible failure but still believe that failure is not their fault.

At the same time that Bernard Weiner and others have argued for the importance of understanding the attributions that children make about achievement-related matters, an equally important aspect of achievement has been emphasized by another leading psychologist. As we see next, Walter Mischel believes that the ability to delay gratification is a key ingredient in evaluating the child's achievement orientation.

Delay of Gratification

Walter Mischel has intensively studied delay of gratification, a process he believes is a fundamental aspect of the child's personality, including his or her achievement orientation. **Delay of gratification** refers to purposefully deferring immediate gratification for delayed but more desired future gratification. For instance, delay of gratification is at work when you turn off your stereo each evening to study for two hours so that the likelihood that you will get better grades at the end of the semester will be enhanced. The entire educational enterprise is built around the belief that the child who puts considerable effort and work into study and school while denying some alluring, immediate pleasures increases the likelihood that, years into the future, he or she will graduate from college and obtain a better job than children who give in to immediate pleasures and do not delay gratification.

Mischel's research has focused on the mechanisms that are involved in self-control, both in terms of the person and the situational influences on the person (Mischel, 1974, 1984). An enduring concern of the research is how children and adolescents can overcome stimulus control—the power of situations—and attain an ever-increasing volitional control over their own behavior when faced with tempting situations.

Mischel's investigations have helped to specify how mental representations influence delay of gratification regardless of the power of the situation facing the person at the moment. In a typical experiment, children are given the opportunity to have a desired goal object now or to wait until a later time to get an even more preferred object. For example, children may be told that they can have one marshmallow now or two marshmallows if they wait a specified amount of time (such as until the experimenter returns). The results of one experiment involving such delay of gratification are shown in Figure 10.11. The data reported in this figure reflect how long the child was willing to wait by himself or herself for a preferred but delayed gratification (e.g., two marshmallows rather than one). When the rewards were unavailable for attention (obscured from view during the delay period), children waited more than 10 times longer than when the rewards were exposed and could be observed. This suggests that individuals can gain control over their ability to delay gratification by keeping desired objects out of sight.

Further exploration of how individuals can control the situation involves their use of cognitive strategies to represent the environment. For example, Mischel's research has revealed that, if individuals represent rewards mentally in consummatory or "hot" ways (such as focusing on their taste, as thinking about how yummy, crunchy, and tasty pretzels are), they cannot delay gratification very long (Mischel & Baker, 1975). However, if they focus on the nonconsummatory or "cool" features (such as thinking of pretzels as if they were sticks or tiny

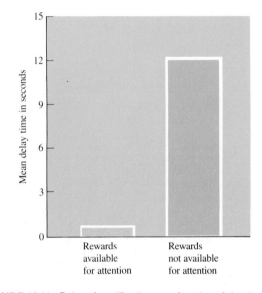

FIGURE 10.11   Delay of gratification as a function of the desired goal object being available for attention.

logs), they can wait for them easily. How people mentally represent the outcomes of a situation is very important in determining their ability to delay gratification.

Focus on Child Development 10.5 examines Mischel's recent study of the extent to which the ability to delay gratification in childhood is a good predictor of adjustment during the adolescent years.

Child Development Concept Table 10.3 summarizes our discussion of motivation, achievement motivation, attribution theory, and delay of gratification. Remember from our discussion of locus of control that lower-class children seem to have a stronger external locus than internal locus. As we see next, social class is one of a number of important sociocultural factors to consider in evaluating the achievement of children.

Sociocultural Influences

Among the most important aspects of the environment that influence the child's achievement are cultural standards of achievement, parental and peer influences, and school/teacher influences.

FOCUS ON CHILD DEVELOPMENT 10.5

PRETZELS AND MARSHMALLOWS— DELAY OF GRATIFICATION IN CHILDHOOD AND ADJUSTMENT IN ADOLESCENCE

Walter Mischel's research concerning how attention and cognitive strategies can modify delay of gratification is process-oriented research. It focuses on how personality or some aspect of personality—in this case, delay of gratification—can be changed. An equally important aspect of research on personality and achievement is the study of the individual, including differences between one child and another. Recently, Mischel has turned his attention to the stability of individual differences in delay of gratification from childhood through the adolescent years.

Mischel's research on the stability of individual differences (e.g., Mischel, 1983; Mischel, Peake, & Zeiss, 1984) reveals impressive contiguity between a preschool child's delay of gratification for pretzels or marshmallows and independent ratings of the adolescent's perceived cognitive and social competence by his or her parents some 12 years later. Mischel (1984) points out that, while his research has shown that the preschool child who delays behavior in one situation may not do so in even slightly different contexts, he is now finding significant links between the preschool child's delay of gratification and cognitive and social competence in adolescence. As shown in the table, the correlations between delay of gratification in early childhood and cognitive and social competence in adolescence suggest a general picture of a child who delayed gratification in the preschool years as developing into an adolescent who is seen as attentive and able

The Relation Between Delay of Gratification in Early Childhood and Rated Cognitive and Social Competence During Adolescence

Items	Correlation	Items	Correlation
Positive		Negative	
Is attentive and able to concentrate	.49	Tends to go to pieces under stress, becomes rattled	−.49
Is verbally fluent, can express ideas well	.40	Reverts to more immature behavior under stress	−.39
Uses and responds to reason	.38	Appears to feel unworthy, thinks of himself or herself as bad	−.33
Is competent, skillful	.38	Is restless and fidgety	−.32
Is planful, thinks ahead	.35	Is shy and reserved, makes social contacts slowly	−.31
Is self-reliant, confident, trusts own judgment	.33	Tends to withdraw and disengage himself or herself under stress	−.30
Is curious and exploring, eager to learn, open	.32	Shows specific mannerisms or behavioral rituals	−.27
Is resourceful in initiating activities	.29	Is stubborn	−.25
Is self-assertive	.29	Turns anxious when his or her environment is unpredictable	−.25
Appears to have high intellectual capacity	.28	Is unable to delay gratification	−.25
Has high standards of performance for self	.27	Attempts to transfer blame to others	−.24
Can be trusted, is dependable	.25	Teases other children	−.22
Becomes strongly involved in what he or she does	.25	Tends to be indecisive and vacillating	−.22
Is creative in perception, thought, work, or play	.24		
Is persistent in his or her activities	.23		

From Mischel, Walter, "Convergences and challenges in the search for consistency" in *American Psychologist, 39,* 355, 1984. Copyright © 1984 American Psychological Association. Reprinted by permission of the author.

(continued on following page)

FOCUS ON CHILD DEVELOPMENT 10.5

What is the nature of delay of gratification?

to concentrate, able to express ideas well, responsive to reason, competent, skillful, able to plan ahead and think ahead, and able to cope with stress in a mature way.

Mischel (1984) argues that, taken together, the results of the process-oriented experimental laboratory studies in conjunction with the investigations of individual differences across the childhood and adolescent years portray personality as both adaptive to situations and consistent over time. They also suggest that the development of delay of gratification skills during the childhood years is linked with achievement-related matters in adolescence, such as the ability to plan ahead, to be persistent in work efforts, to have high achievement standards, and to be competent and skillful.

Child Development Concept Table 10.3   Motivation, Achievement Motivation, and Achievement-Related Factors

Concept	Processes/Related Ideas	Characteristics/Description
Motivation	Its nature	Motivation involves the question of *why* people behave, think, and feel the way they do. Motivated behavior is energized and directed.
	The grand theories	Both the cognitive developmental and information processing perspectives do not deal heavily with motivation. In their views, it is evident that motivation rests within the child's desire for knowledge and information. For behaviorists, motivation rests in making the environment of the individual more rewarding. For psychoanalytic theorists like Freud, motivation is biologically based, with instincts like sex dominating achievement-related matters.
Theories of achievement and achievement-related factors	The achievement motivation views of McClelland and Atkinson	McClelland argued that achievement motivation is a property of the individual's psychological makeup and need system. He described *n* achievement as the individual's internal striving for success. Atkinson elaborated on McClelland's ideas, specifying more clearly the importance of such processes as hope for success and fear of failure. In this regard, he believes that children's expectations for success should outweigh their anxiety about failing if they are to show a strong achievement orientation. In many instances, it has been found that moderate anxiety is optimal for achievement, although there are exceptions.
	Attribution theory	There has been considerable interest in attribution theory in recent years. Attribution theory argues that we are cognitive beings who want to know why we behave in a particular way. In particular, attribution theorists have analyzed achievement circumstances in terms of the individual's perception of internal-external factors involved in achievement. In general, they argue that achievement is enhanced when the child is internally rather than externally oriented, particularly when such achievement is effort based. Weiner believes that it is important to understand emotional reactions to attributions. Locus of control is a concept linked to internal-external aspects of achievement.
	Delay of gratification	Delay of gratification is another important process in understanding achievement. Mischel argues that delay of gratification can be influenced by situational factors but also often can be predicted in adolescence from information about delay of gratification behavior in childhood. Such a view suggests that personality is both adaptive to situations and consistent over time.

Cultural Standards of Achievement

We commented earlier that, compared to most other cultures, the United States is a very achievement-oriented culture. Within our culture, though, achievement standards often vary, depending on the social class background the child comes from.

Middle-class and lower-class parents differ in the way that they socialize their children in achievement situations. Middle-class parents tend to emphasize the future more than lower-class parents do (Strodtbeck, 1958). An important part of this orientation toward the future is the ability to delay gratification until a later time when rewards will be greater than they are at present—middle-class children are more likely to delay gratification than lower-class children are (Mischel, 1976). Lower-class children are motivated more by rewards external to a learning task than to the intrinsic rewards built into the task. Further, they show less achievement motivation when they are asked to tell stories about achievement-related situations (Rosen, 1959). And lower-class children support values that promote family loyalty more than independent striving for achievement (e.g., Rosen, 1959; Strodtbeck, 1958).

Parental and Peer Influences

As we just saw, middle-class and lower-class parents have different achievement expectations for their children and often socialize them differently in terms of achievement orientation. While early studies of achievement motivation suggested that independence training was an important factor, subsequent research seemed to indicate that parental standards for achievement are even more important than independence training (e.g., Crandall & Battle, 1970).

Indeed, the standards against which children judge their performance are key ingredients of achievement. Some children have very low standards of success and are exposed to models, including parents, who have low standards of success. Other children have high standards of success and are exposed to models who have high standards of success. Albert Bandura (1977) has demonstrated that boys and girls who are exposed to models who adopt lenient standards (for example, parents who reward themselves for mediocre work) also tend to adopt lenient standards of achievement. By contrast, children who are around models who adopt stringent standards (e.g., parents who reward themselves only for a high level of performance) are likely to adopt high standards themselves. Children, of course, also are exposed to the achievement standards that peers bring to the peer group and that teachers and school administrators bring to schools.

However, it is important to consider just how high the standards are that parents set in relation to such matters as the child's abilities, the amount of involvement and support parents are willing to give the child, and so forth. David Elkind (1979), for example, believes that many children are being hurried to achieve too much too soon in their development.

With regard to peers' influence on achievement, two processes that should be considered are social comparison and competitiveness. While it has been commonly believed that social comparison, and particularly competitiveness, enhance achievement motivation, a spate of recent studies suggest that this may not be the case (e.g., Ames, 1984; Cooper & Tom, 1984; Covington, 1984; Maeher, 1984; Nichols, 1984). The argument of these researchers is that competition may be debilitating because it puts the child in an ego-involved, threatening,

self-focused state rather than a task-involved, effort- or strategy-focused state. These debilitating effects are most clearly seen as negative self-esteem and corresponding low effort behavior that produce ineffective performance (Ames & Ames, 1984).

Quite clearly, whether children performing alongside each other hold similar or dissimilar interpersonal perceptions of ability and worthiness is likely to influence achievement behavior (Ames, 1984). Such social comparison may produce avoidance of achievement or reduced achievement behavior if one perceives that one's abilities are less than a peer's, or may generate self-aggrandizement if one perceives that one's abilities are superior to those of peer competitors. John Nichols (1979), for example, stresses that such inequalities are a part of academic settings and invariably evolve in competitive circumstances probably because of perceived differences in abilities.

Thus, while cooperative classroom settings are important considerations, particularly in the case of low-ability students, and seem intuitively right—in reality, they do not always work. The parents of high-ability students may undermine the efforts of teachers to develop cooperative achievement settings. In such circumstances, the achievement standards of a culture, transmitted through family relationships, are brought to the classroom setting and influence the nature of students' achievement orientation.

School/Teacher Influences

With regard to school/teacher influences on achievement motivation, Joan Lipsitz (1983) commented that, while the nature of effective schools varies, those schools where students are highly motivated to achieve have similar themes. She concluded that schools likely to be successful at motivating students take seriously individual differences in physical, cognitive, and social development and reveal a deep concern for what is known about children's development. Also, in effective schools that are able to motivate students, there often is a strong sense of caring and commitment on the part of the administrators and teachers—principals and teachers willing to spend long hours beyond the beginning and end of class hours to come up with ingenious ways to make school both an enjoyable and challenging learning experience. For example, Author's Week was created at

How can schools successfully motivate students?

one school, Black History Week was established at another, and a simulated rock music station was put together at yet another school. These were contexts that required considerable effort on the part of their architects but that were highly effective in influencing student motivation.

Attribution in the School Setting   Can students learn to attribute failure to lack of effort and success to appropriate effort? If they can, then it would be predicted from attribution theory that these students would persist longer at difficult tasks.

Several investigations have shown that students can learn to modify their achievement attributions and that there are corresponding changes in persistence (e.g., Andrews & Debus, 1978; Chapin & Dyck, 1976; Dweck, 1975). One investigation involved 42 sixth-grade boys who were below average in attributing their failure to lack of effort. A training program was developed for two thirds of these students. In this program, they were allowed to experience success half of the time. When the students experienced success and attributed it to effort or when they experienced failure and attributed it to a lack of effort, they were rewarded by being told such things as, "That's good!" or "Very good!" If the student

attributed success or failure to something besides effort, then no reinforcement was given and the instructor simply went on to the next task. The students were trained until they made effort evaluations 80 percent of the time or for 60 trials, whichever came first. After this attribution training, they were given block design and anagram tasks, as well as a third unsolvable task. The students who received attribution training were much more likely than the control group (the one third who did not get attribution training) to attribute both success and failure to effort and to persist at the unsolvable task. Another testing one week later produced similar results (Andrews & Debus, 1978).

Ellen Gagne (1985), however, warns that teachers who try to change students' attributions need to be careful and patient. Such attributions, which sometimes are tied to self-conceptions of low ability (Ames, Ames, & Garrison, 1977; Ames & Ames, 1984), usually have been built up over a long number of years through many experiences. Thus, a quick fix that will be maintained over many years without careful monitoring is not likely. Care needs to be given to the selection of tasks at which the student can succeed with effort. Given the behavioral principle of shaping, it may be best to start with tasks that require only a small amount of effort and then, as the student shows a greater willingness to work, increase the amount required for success. It also seems likely that students showing low amounts of effort should be encouraged to be more ability-focused and to set individualistic goals rather than to be competitively oriented and interested in social comparison (Ames & Ames, 1984). Such teacher strategies require a great deal of planning, organization, and classroom management abilities.

Observational Learning A tremendous amount of achievement-related learning goes on during the course of a school year simply by being in proximity to other people. Children watch and listen to what teachers and peers are like and may be motivated to model their behavior after these individuals (Bandura, 1977).

For students to be motivated by a teacher, it generally is very important that the students like the teacher. Students form teacher impressions very early in the school year. Some research has shown that the first two weeks of the semester are very important in setting the achievement tone for the entire semester and are critical in the development of a student's achievement orientation (e.g., Emmer, Evertson, & Anderson, 1980). Effective teachers who know how to motivate students seem to know how to get things off to a good start. As shown in Table 10.3, observations of teacher behavior during the first three weeks of the school year revealed that effective teachers were more likely to use a variety of rewards, to signal appropriate behavior, to maintain eye contact, and to state desired attitudes. The effectiveness was measured by more on-task behavior throughout the semester and by improvements on achievement tests at the end of the semester. These effective teachers also were more organized on the first day of school than their ineffective counterparts. Competent teachers provide an important achievement-related model for their students to imitate: as someone who is organized; who values achievement, work, and effort; and who is self-disciplined. Students pick up on such characteristics of models very quickly and see the expectations of these important people in their lives. It also is important while setting an achievement-oriented tone early in the semester for the teacher to establish a classroom climate of warmth and mutual respect.

Table 10.3 Differences Between Effective and Ineffective Teachers During the First Three Weeks of the Semester

Variable	More Effective Teachers	Less Effective Teachers
Provides variety of rewards	4.3	3.1
Signals appropriate behavior	5.4	3.8
Maintains eye contact	6.1	4.9
States desired attitudes	5.5	3.9
Stops if disruptive behavior occurs	4.9	3.5
Ignores disruptive behavior	2.9	3.6

From Emmer, E. T., C. M. Everston, and L. M. Anderson, "Effective classroom management at the beginning of the school year" in *Elementary School Journal, 80,* 219–231, 1980. Copyright © 1980 University of Chicago Press, Reprinted by permission.

The most imitated person in many classrooms is not the teacher but the most popular student(s). If the most popular students are not very achievement oriented, this likely will influence some other students in the class to follow suit. In such circumstances, teachers should determine early in the school year which students are the most popular and seek to get them academically oriented.

In sum, both teachers and peers serve as achievement-oriented or nonachievement-oriented models for students. When a student sits down to solve a difficult problem and considers possibly giving up, these models likely will influence the student's decision to persist or quit. Through memories and continued observation of such models (including parents), the child's achievement orientation is strongly influenced.

Reinforcement In our discussion of observational learning, it was pointed out that effective teachers seem to provide a variety of rewards. One dilemma faced by many teachers is whether to emphasize the intrinsic motivation of the child and not give external rewards for work and effort or whether to emphasize the extrinsic motivation of the child and be sure to give external rewards. Psychologists define **intrinsic motivation** as behavior that is motivated by an underlying need for competence and self-determination (mastery and competence motivation are two other terms commonly used in this regard). By contrast, **extrinsic motivation** refers

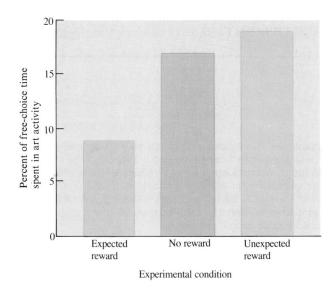

FIGURE 10.12 Amount of time spent in art activity following expected reward, no reward, and unexpected reward for engaging in same activity.

to behavior that is influenced by external rewards. If a child works hard at school to get a monetary reward from parents, then extrinsic motivation is at work. If a child works hard at school because of a personal standard of excellence, then intrinsic motivation is involved.

Incentives are external cues that stimulate motivation. They can be positive in the sense of a teacher telling the class that students who do a specified level of work will get certain privileges or they can be negative in the sense of a teacher taking away privileges if certain levels of work are not reached. Though it often is difficult to decide whether to introduce incentives to motivate a child, several guidelines are available. If the child is not doing competent work, seems bored with what he or she is doing, and has a negative attitude, then it may be an appropriate time for introducing incentives to improve performance. However, sometimes, extrinsic rewards can get in the way of intrinsic rewards, particularly if the child already is showing competent achievement motivation. In one investigation, baseline observations of initial intrinsic interest in artistic activity were conducted. Students with a high interest in the artistic work were exposed to one of three conditions. In the expected-reward condition, students agreed to engage in the art

activity to obtain a reward. In the unexpected-reward condition, they had no knowledge of the reward until they had finished the art work. And in the no-reward condition, the students neither expected nor received a reward. As shown in Figure 10.12, the students in the expected-reward condition showed less subsequent intrinsic interest in the art activity than students in either of the other two conditions, presumably because their intrinsic motivation was detracted by the extrinsic motives. (Lepper, Greene, & Nisbett, 1973).

A key point to be made about when extrinsic rewards will likely enhance or diminish motivation involves a distinction between the information and controlling functions of the rewards (Deci, 1975). It may be that, when a child receives extrinsic rewards for engaging in intrinsically interesting activities, the child's beliefs about why he or she is performing the activity may change. If the controlling aspect of external rewards is made salient, then the child may think that external factors are causing his or her behavior. But if informational aspects of external rewards are prominent, then the child may develop feelings of competence and self-determination. Thus, external rewards that indicate to the child that he or she is performing competently would be expected to enhance, rather than diminish, intrinsic motivation. Thus, a trophy for the best performance as an indication of superiority should not undermine motivation. In general, when external rewards are not related to good performance, but rather are linked to simply performing a task, they tend to decrease motivation. In such circumstances, the child may just whiz through the task as fast as possible to obtain the external reward.

In our discussion of achievement motivation, the issue of external and internal factors has appeared in the theoretical views of motivation in general, in the more specific theories related to achievement motivation, and in research on children's achievement in classroom settings. In Focus on Child Development 10.6, we revisit the internal-external controversy in achievement and provide further research data suggesting that external and internal factors may have a synergistic effect on achievement when they occur in certain ways in achievement situations.

FOCUS ON CHILD DEVELOPMENT 10.6

REVISITING THE INTERNAL-EXTERNAL DIMENSION OF ACHIEVEMENT

While attribution theorists emphasize the importance of studying both external and internal causes of achievement, they tend to favor internal factors. Recall the recent work by attribution theorists documenting that an emphasis on social comparison and competition seems to be detrimental to achievement. However, we pointed out that this finding likely holds for comparison and competitiveness with peers having more ability and being more successful than the student in question, rather than with peers with less ability and less success. We also have seen that external rewards sometimes get in the way of intrinsic motivation and that this may be particularly true for a student who already is highly motivated. We concluded that incentives may be more helpful to students with low achievement motivation who are showing little effort. And we also indicated that the most effective

teachers—those whose students show the most achievement gains—are those who give out a variety of rewards early in the semester. Continuing on through other aspects of external reasons for achievement behavior, we found that cultural standards, parent and peer influences, and the school context were important environmental contributors to the child's achievement orientation.

Let's look at an example of research on children's achievement revealing how both external and internal factors may work together to produce the highest achievement behavior in some situations. Dale Schunk (1983) has investigated the roles of both social comparison and individual goal setting in children's achievement. Low-achieving boys and girls in math classes were given instruction in math skills. One group was given social comparative information indicating the number of problems solved by their classmates (external factor). A second group worked under conditions involving a goal of completing a given number of problems (self-determination, internal factor). A third group received both treatments. A fourth group, the control group, was given no treatment.

The Effects of a Combined Treatment of Social Comparison and Individual Goal Setting on Achievement-Related Performance

Measure	Phase	Experimental Condition			
		Information Only	Goals Only	Information and Goals	Training Control
Skill[a]	Pretest	3.4	3.4	4.4	4.0
	Posttest	5.2	4.0	9.5	6.2
Persistence[b]	Pretest	43.1	40.8	64.8	58.0
	Posttest	65.5	81.2	68.3	94.1
Self-efficacy[c]	Pretest	45.6	54.1	54.5	53.6
	Posttest	59.0	74.2	79.4	65.5
Training progress[d]	Total	37.4	36.2	44.0	33.9

[a]Number of correct solutions on 14 problems
[b]Average number of seconds per problem
[c]Average judgment per problem; range of scale, 10 (low)–100
[d]Number of problems worked
From Schunk, D. H., "Developing children's self-efficacy and skills: The roles of social comparative information and goal setting" in *Contemporary Educational Psychology, 8*, 76–86, 1983. Copyright © 1983 Academic Press, Inc., Orlando, Florida. Reprinted by permission.

The boys and girls' self-efficacy judgments were assessed before and after the conditions, as were their math skills on a test, and how long they persisted at working math problems. (**Self-efficacy** is a term generated by Bandura (1981) to index judgments of how well one can execute courses of actions required in situations.) In addition, their training progress was assessed in terms of how many math problems they worked. As shown in the table, in most instances, those children who experienced *both* the social comparison and self-determined goal conditions combined showed superior performance compared to their internal-, external-, or no-treatment-condition counterparts.

It seems likely, then, that there are a variety of external and internal factors related to achievement behavior. It is instructive to point out that the issue of external and internal causes of behavior is one of the oldest dilemmas faced by psychologists. This issue is so prevalent that it will come up again later in the text. For example, in the next chapter

when we discuss moral development, you will find that Lawrence Kohlberg argues moral development becomes more internalized as development progresses. However, you also will see that Carol Gilligan disagrees with Kohlberg, believing that the highest form of moral development consists of a connectedness with others and emphasizes relationships.

It seems that, too often, internal and external factors are pitted against each other as opposites in studies of achievement attribution and achievement orientation. In reality, the child's achievement orientation likely is influenced by a composite of internal and external factors, and even when internal factors are strong, they are not entirely divorced from the sociocultural context. It is important to recognize that some very competent children who show a strong internal motivation for success with very lofty personal standards may be highly competitive persons who also are very motivated to outperform their peers.

How might competitiveness and social comparison be involved in achievement?

THINKING BACK, LOOKING AHEAD

Intelligence and achievement are important aspects of the cognitive worlds children experience in the middle and late childhood years. Among the intriguing themes we have encountered are those involving the lawsuit of Larry P.; intelligence being how smart you are; the intelligence constructionists and measurers; the intelligence of Larry Bird's spatial and bodily skills; Bo Diddley, a hungry hemophile, and cheap chitlings; mental retardation; children who are "stars" in their fields; novel thinking, insight, and automatization in the gifted and the retarded; the 3 Rs; Octavio's bilingualism; time and practice in the math skills of Japanese and American children; attributions of ability and effort; delay of gratification for pretzels and marshmallows; times when external rewards may get in the way; and the importance of internal-external dimensions in understanding achievement.

In Chapter 11, we focus on social and personality development in middle and late childhood. Before you turn to these thoughts about the child's social worlds, however, consider for several moments the stimulating words of Erik Erikson (1968), as he spoke about the middle and late childhood years:

> Such is the wisdom of the ground plan that at no time is the child more ready to learn quickly and avidly . . . than at the end of the period of expansive imagination . . . sooner or later (children) become dissatisfied and disgruntled without a sense of being able to make things and make them well and even perfectly: it is this that I have called the "sense of industry." (pp. 122–123)

SUMMARY

I. Information about the psychometric approach to intelligence focuses on theories, definition, and measurement; alternatives and supplements to standardized intelligence tests; stability and change in intelligence; genetic-environmental influences on intelligence; and mental retardation, giftedness, and creativity.
   A. Ideas about theories, definition, and measurement involve Binet and the concept of general intelligence, the Wechsler scales, and the factor analytic approach.
      1. Alfred Binet (with Theodore Simon) devised the first intelligence test in 1905 to determine which students in Paris would not benefit from regular classes. Binet also developed the concept of mental age to describe the general level of the child's intellectual functioning. The Binet has gone through a lengthy standardization process (which has resulted in its now being called the Stanford-Binet) and today can be given to individuals from the age of two years through adulthood. The Stanford-Binet measures overall or general level of intellectual functioning, which is then indicated by a certain IQ score. The 1985 version of the Stanford-Binet also provides for an analysis of several intellectual processes.
      2. Wechsler also emphasizes the general nature of intelligence, but his WAIS, WISC-R, and WPPIS tests provide not only an overall IQ score, but also are divided into verbal and nonverbal categories, which are further subdivided to reflect specific aspects of intelligence.
      3. Psychologists have searched for how many factors make up intelligence. Spearman's two-factor theory stressed the existence of g (for general intelligence) and s (for specific factor); Thurstone developed a multiple-factor theory; Cattell described intelligence in terms of two factors—fluid intelligence and crystallized intelligence; and Guilford's structure of intellect model lists 120 factors involved in intelligence. Both Sternberg and Gardner, while not placing a premium on the factor analytic statistical technique, argue that there are a number of intelligences and intellectual processes rather than a single unitary intelligence.
   B. Ideas about alternatives and supplements to standardized intelligence tests stress validity, culture-fair tests, and social intelligence.
      1. Critics have argued that intelligence tests are not valid in the sense that IQ tests may not be accurately measuring what they purport to measure—intelligence. Criterion validity is particularly important in this respect. IQ tests are reasonably good at predicting grades in school.
      2. Culture-fair tests have been developed in an attempt to reduce or eliminate cultural bias in tests. In particular, it has been argued that traditional IQ tests favor children from white, middle-class backgrounds. Creating a truly culture-fair test has so far proven to be beyond the ability of test makers.

3. Assessing social intelligence is compatible with the belief that children's lives and competence involve more than solving verbal and numerical problems. Recently, efforts have been made to assess social intelligence as well as the more traditional cognitive and academic forms of intelligence. The SOMPA has been a widely used test in this regard.

C. IQ scores at 2 and 3 years of age do not reliably predict IQ at 10 or 18 years of age. However, recent research has shown that novelty scores based on dishabituation in infancy are reasonably good predictors of IQ in early childhood. Also, IQ scores obtained at 6, 8, and 9 years of age are somewhat accurate predictors of IQ at 10 and 18 years of age. Between the ages of 2½ and 17, the IQ scores of one out of every three individuals change by as much as 30 points.

D. Genetics have a powerful impact on intelligence, although not as strong as Jensen believed. Among the important environmental influences on intelligence are those involving home, institutionalization, education, and social class. As with all other aspects of the child's development, genes and environment interact to produce intelligence.

E. Mental retardation, giftedness, and creativity represent variations in intellectual abilities.

1. Mental retardation is defined as significantly subaverage general intellectual functioning existing concurrently with deficits in adaptive behavior and manifested during the developmental period. Such labels as "mentally retarded," "trainable," and "educable" have often been applied to individuals who score significantly below average on IQ tests. Such labels need to be used cautiously. The causes of retardation often are categorized as organic or cultural-familial.

2. The gifted child still is described as a child with well-above-average intelligence (IQ of 120 or more), but he or she may also be a child with a superior talent in the arts, psychomotor abilities, or other specific aptitudes. Research suggests that the gifted often are superior to others in nonacademic matters as well. Sternberg believes that giftedness involves insight and the ability to think in novel ways.

3. Creativity is very difficult to define and measure. Guilford defines it in terms of divergent thinking, a type of thinking that produces many different answers to the same question. Brainstorming and playing with improbabilities are two examples of ways creativity can be encouraged in the classroom. A creative atmosphere needs to be fostered in schools, keeping in mind the caution that some children do not need to read creatively, they simply need to learn to read.

II. Ideas about the 3 Rs and bilingualism focus on the nature of writing and reading, the simultaneous and successive acquisition of a second language, and math achievement.

A. Our alphabetic writing system is one of three basic kinds in the world today. The other two are syllabic and logographic. The evolution of writing has followed a trend to move downward from meaning to sound, and from longer to shorter segments of sound. The Rozin-Gleitman technique for teaching reading follows a progression of from meaning to sound, and from longer to shorter segments of sound. Other strategies for teaching reading are the now ill-favored ABC method, the whole-word method, and the phonics method.

B. Bilinguals include those individuals who learn two languages simultaneously in early childhood and those who learn a second language after having learned the first. There is no evidence that second language learning is better in younger children than in older children and adults.

C. Educational goals for children's math achievement include knowledge, skills, understanding, and application. Cross-cultural data suggest that, while children in the United States are more achievement oriented than their counterparts in many cultures, Japanese children considerably outdistance their American counterparts in mathematics. Recent research has shown that time spent in math classes and time spent practicing math (such as in homework) are possible explanations for these cultural differences in math achievement.

III. Ideas about motivation and achievement involve the concept of motivation, theories of achievement motivation and achievement-related factors, and sociocultural factors.

A. Motivation involves the question of *why* people behave, think, and feel the way they do. Motivated behavior is energized and directed. Both the cognitive developmental and information processing perspectives do not deal heavily with motivation. In their views, it is evident that motivation rests within the child's desire for knowledge and information.

For behaviorists, motivation rests in making the environment of the individual more rewarding. For psychoanalytic theorists like Freud, motivation is biologically based, with instincts like sex dominating achievement-related matters.

B. Information about theories of achievement motivation and achievement-related matters includes the views of McClelland and Atkinson, attribution theory, and delay of gratification.

1. McClelland argued that achievement motivation is a property of the individual's psychological makeup and need system. He described *n* achievement as the individual's internal striving for success. Atkinson elaborated on McClelland's ideas, specifying more clearly the importance of such processes as hope for success and fear of failure. In this regard, he believes that children's expectations for success should outweigh their anxiety about failure if they are to show a strong achievement orientation. In many instances, it has been found that moderate anxiety is optimal for achievement, although there are exceptions.

2. There has been considerable interest in attribution theory in recent years. Attribution theory argues that we are cognitive beings who want to know why we behave in a particular way. In particular, attribution theorists have analyzed achievement circumstances in terms of the individual's perception of internal-external factors involved in achievement. In general, they argue that achievement is enhanced when the child is internally rather than externally oriented, particularly when such achievement is effort based. Weiner believes that it is important to understand emotional reactions to attributions. Locus of control is a concept linked to internal-external aspects of achievement.

3. Delay of gratification has been promoted as an important variable in achievement research. Mischel argues that delay of gratification can be influenced by situational factors but also often can be predicted in adolescence from information about delay of gratification behavior in childhood. Such a view suggests that personality is both adaptive to situations and consistent over time.

C. Ideas about sociocultural factors in children's achievement include cultural standards of achievement, parental and peer influences, schools and teachers, and revisiting internal/external factors in achievement.

1. Adolescents in the United States are characteristically more achievement oriented than their counterparts in other cultures. The ingredients for achievement often are much stronger for children from middle- rather than lower-class backgrounds.

2. The models of achievement that parents present for children are important contributors to children's achievement orientation. Parents who model stringent standards for achievement are more likely to have achievement-oriented children than those who model lax standards. Some parents, however, push too hard and too early for achievement. This circumstance, according to Elkind, is particularly hazardous when parents do not provide adequate support for their lofty expectations. Social comparison and competitiveness often are in operation between children and their peers. Children who compare themselves favorably with their peers are likely to feel better about their own achievement behavior than those who compare themselves less favorably. Some educational strategists argue that competitiveness and social comparison should be discouraged and cooperativeness and internal striving emphasized. Trying to implement this strategy, however, is not easy.

3. Lipsitz has described some effective schools likely to promote achievement—these schools often reveal a strong sense of involvement and commitment on the part of teachers and school personnel as well an appreciation of individual variation and knowledge of children's development. Getting students to attribute their successes and failures to effort rather than to external factors has improved the achievement orientation of students, although this process is often difficult and lengthy. Observational learning is very important in the school setting as well as at home. Children often are motivated to behave like a teacher or the most popular peer in the class. With regard to reinforcement, it seems that intrinsic motivation is best when students already show a strong achievement orientation but that some form of extrinsic motivation, or use of external rewards, may benefit students showing low motivation.

4. The implication from attribution theory is that internal factors should be promoted when getting the child to understand the causes of his or her achievement behavior. However, it is important to recognize that achievement behavior is motivated by both internal and external factors and the child is never truly divorced from commerce with the social world. Thus, it is somewhat of an artificial distinction when internal and external factors are pitted against each other in the battle for determining the cause of achievement behavior. The internal-external motivation argument is a very old one in psychology and cuts across many different domains of psychology. It does seem wise to emphasize that the child learn to attribute the causes of his or her success or failure to effort, but also it seems intelligent to argue that achievement is determined by multiple internal and external factors. Further, some of the most achievement-oriented and competent children are those who have *both* a high personal standard of achievement (internal) and who are very competitive (external) as well.

KEY TERMS

ABC method 411
alphabetic system 407
attribution theory 422
brainstorming 406
contents 394
convergent thinking 406
creativity 404
cretinism 403
criterion validity 394
crystallized intelligence 393
cultural-familial 403
culture-fair tests 396
delay of gratification 423
divergent thinking 406
external locus of control 423
extrinsic motivation 430
fear of failure 420
fluid intelligence 393
gifted child 403
hope for success 420

incentives 431
institutionalization 401
internal locus of control 423
intrinsic motivation 430
IQ 389
logographic writing system 407
mean 390
mental age (MA) 389
mental retardation 402
motivation 418
multiple-factor theory 393
n achievement 419
normal distribution 390
operations 394
phonics method 411
playing with improbabilities 406
products 394
psychometric 389

psychometricians 389
self-efficacy 433
SOMPA 396
standard deviation 390
state anxiety 421
structure of intellect 393

syllabic writing system 407
trait anxiety 421
two-factor theory 393
validity 394
whole-word method 411

SUGGESTED READINGS

Ames, R. E., & Ames, C. (Eds.). (1984). *Motivation in education.* New York: Academic Press.
Includes many ideas by leading scholars on the topic of achievement orientation. A number of chapters are devoted to ideas on attributions.

Dweck, C., & Eliot, E. S. (1983). Achievement motivation. In P. H. Mussen (Ed.), *Handbook of child psychology* (4th ed.), Vol. 4, New York: Wiley.
This detailed chapter provides a contemporary overview of attribution theory and achievement.

Gowan, J. C., Khatena, J., and Torrance, E. P. (Eds.). (1979). *Educating the ablest* (2d ed.). Itasca, IL: F. E. Peacock.
A selected book of readings on a variety of topics that relate to gifted children and the process of creativity. Includes sections on programs and curricula for gifted and creative children, the role of imagery, and developmental characteristics. Easy to read.

Sattler, J. (1980). *Assessment of children's intelligence* (2nd ed.). Philadelphia: Saunders.
Provides extensive information about the history of intelligence testing, with emphasis on the Binet and WISC-R tests, and also about a variety of intelligence tests currently used with children.

Special issue testing: concepts, policy, practice, and research. (1981, October). *American Psychologist, 36.*
American Psychologist is the journal of the American Psychological Association. This entire issue is devoted to psychological testing and includes articles written by a number of experts.

SOCIAL AND PERSONALITY DEVELOPMENT IN MIDDLE AND LATE CHILDHOOD

IMAGINE . . . YOU ARE
TEACHING A FOURTH-GRADE
CLASS AND A BOY YELLS, "YOU
JERK!"

PREVIEW

FAMILY PROCESSES AND
RELATIONSHIPS IN MIDDLE AND
LATE CHILDHOOD

Amount of Parent-Child Interaction
Parent-Child Issues
Discipline Techniques
Changes in Control Processes
Mutual Cognitions
Changes in Parental Maturation
Societal Changes in the Types of
Families
Stepfamilies
Latchkey Children

PEER RELATIONS IN MIDDLE
AND LATE CHILDHOOD

Amount and Form of Peer Interaction
Popular, Rejected, and Neglected
Children
Social Cognition
Social Information Processing

FOCUS ON CHILD DEVELOPMENT
11.1: DESTROYING A BLOCK
TOWER WHILE CLEANING UP A
ROOM—INTENTION-CUE
DETECTION SKILLS IN CHILDREN

Social Knowledge
Friendships
*The Incidence of Friendship and Cognitive
Factors*
Intimacy and Similarity in Friendships
Shared Support and Knowledge
Conversational Skills
Children's Groups

SCHOOLS

The Impact of Schooling and the
Elementary School Setting
Open Versus Traditional Classrooms and
Schools
Teachers
Teaching Styles and Traits
Erikson's Criteria for a Good Teacher

Aptitude-Treatment Interaction
Social Class and Ethnicity
Social Class
Ethnicity

CHILD DEVELOPMENT CONCEPT
TABLE 11.1: FAMILIES, PEERS,
AND SCHOOLS IN MIDDLE AND
LATE CHILDHOOD

THE SELF, SEX ROLES, AND
MORAL DEVELOPMENT IN
MIDDLE AND LATE CHILDHOOD

The Self
*Selman's Ideas on the Self and Perspective
Taking*
Self-Esteem
Measuring Self-Concept
Social Competence
Sex Roles
Masculinity, Femininity, and Androgyny
Sex-Role Stereotypes and Sex Differences

FOCUS ON CHILD DEVELOPMENT
11.2: BRIGHT GIRLS, LEARNED
HELPLESSNESS, AND
EXPECTATIONS

Moral Development
Kohlberg's Stages of Moral Development
*Research on Kohlberg's Stages and
Influences on the Stages*

FOCUS ON CHILD DEVELOPMENT
11.3: NOT JUST ANY PEER
COMMUNICATION WILL DO—THE
ROLE OF TRANSACTIVE
DISCUSSION

Critics of Kohlberg

FOCUS ON CHILD DEVELOPMENT
11.4: AMY SAYS THEY SHOULD
JUST TALK IT OUT AND FIND
SOME OTHER WAY TO MAKE
MONEY

Social Conventional Reasoning
Moral Education

CHILD DEVELOPMENT CONCEPT
TABLE 11.2: THE SELF, SEX ROLES,
AND MORAL DEVELOPMENT

IMAGINE . . . YOU ARE TEACHING A FOURTH-GRADE CLASS AND A BOY YELLS, "YOU JERK!"

"You Jerk, what are you trying to do to me," Jess yelled at his teacher. "I got no use for this school and people like you. Leave me alone and quit hassling me."

Jess was ten years old and had already gotten into lots of trouble. He had been arrested three times for stealing, been suspended from school twice, and had a great deal of difficulty getting along with people in social circumstances. He had particular difficulty with authority figures. No longer able to cope with his outbursts in class, his teacher recommended that he be suspended from school once again. The principal was aware of a different kind of school that she thought might help Jess.

Jess began attending the Manville School, a clinic in the Judge Baker Guidance Center in Boston for learning-disabled and emotionally disturbed 7- to 15-year-old children. Jess, like many other students at the Manville School, had shown considerable difficulty in interpersonal relationships. Since peer relationships become a crucial aspect of development during the elementary school years, Robert Selman designed a peer therapy program at the Manville School to help students like Jess to improve their peer relations in classroom settings, group activities, and sports (Selman, Newberger, & Jacquette, 1977). The staff at the Manville School has been trained to help peers to provide support and encouragement to each other in such group settings, a process referred to as **peer sociotherapy.**

Structured programs at the Manville School are designed to help the children to assist each other in such areas as cooperation, trust, leadership, and conformity. Four school activities have been developed to improve students' social reasoning skills in these areas:

First, there is a weekly peer problem-solving session in the classroom in which the peers work cooperatively to plan activities and relate problems. At the end of each week, the peers evaluate their improvements in areas like cooperation, conflict resolution, and so forth.

Second, the members of a class, numbering from six to eight students, plan a series of weekly field trips—for example, going to the movies or visiting historical sites. While the counselor provides some assistance, peer decision making dominates. When each activity is completed, the students discuss how things went and what might have been done to improve social relations with each other on the outings.

Third, when a student finds himself or herself in a highly frustrating situation (e.g., angry enough to strike out at a classmate), he or she is allowed to go to a private "time-out" area of the school to regain composure. In time-out, the student also is given the opportunity to discuss the problems with a counselor who has been trained to help the child or adolescent to improve social reasoning skills.

Fourth, during social studies and current events discussion sessions, the students evaluate a number of moral and societal issues that incorporate the thinking of such theorists as Lawrence Kohlberg.

PREVIEW

Plato, in approximately 350 B.C., expressed strong views on discipline and sex roles:

> Of all the animals, the boy is the most unmanageable, inasmuch as he has the fountain of reason in him not yet regulated; he is the most insidious, sharp-witted, and insubordinate of animals. Wherefore he must be bound with many bridles.

In this chapter, we study parenting and family processes of the middle and late childhood years, and considerable time is spent discussing sex-role development as well. The social worlds of schools and peers also are examined, as are further aspects of self and moral development. The chapter concludes with problems and disturbances that sometimes emerge during the elementary school years.

How does parent-child interaction change in middle and late childhood?

FAMILY PROCESSES AND RELATIONSHIPS IN MIDDLE AND LATE CHILDHOOD

Among the important aspects of family processes and relationships in middle and late childhood are the amount of parent-child interaction, a number of parent-child issues, discipline techniques, changes in control processes, mutual cognitions, changes in parental maturation, and societal changes in the types of families children are growing up in.

Amount of Parent-Child Interaction

As children move into the elementary school years, parents spend considerably less time with them. For example, in one investigation, parents spent less than half as much time with their children ages 5 to 12 years in caregiving, instruction, reading, talking, and playing than when the children were younger (Hill & Stafford, 1980). It appears that this drop in parent-child interaction time is even more extensive in families with little parental education.

Parent-Child Issues

There also are important changes in the type of issues parents deal with on a daily basis with their children during the elementary school years (Maccoby, 1984).

The focus of parent-child interaction during early childhood is on such matters as modesty, bedtime regularities, control of temper, fighting with siblings and peers, eating behavior and manners, autonomy in dressing, and attention seeking (Newson & Newson, 1968; Sears, Maccoby, & Levin, 1957). While some of these issues, such as fighting and children's reactions to discipline, are carried forward to the elementary school years, many new issues appear by the age of seven. These include such issues as whether children should be made to perform chores and, if so, whether they should be paid for them; how to help children to learn to entertain themselves rather than relying on parents for everything; and how to monitor children's lives outside the family in school and peer settings.

School-related matters are important in families during middle and late childhood. Later in this chapter, we see that school-related difficulties are the major reason children in this period are referred for clinical help. Children must learn to relate to adults outside the family on a regular basis—adults who interact with the child in a much different manner than parents. While increasing numbers of children encounter other adults on a regular basis in day care and preschool, these interactions are often not in a setting that is as achievement oriented as elementary school and do not involve as much formal control.

Now let's return to the theme of Plato's comments and discuss the discipline techniques prominent during middle and late childhood.

Discipline Techniques

Discipline during the elementary school years is often easier for parents than was the case during the preschool years and also may be easier than during the adolescent years. The elementary school child's cognitive development often has matured to the point where it is possible for parents to reason with the child about disciplinary matters. By adolescence, the child's reasoning has become more sophisticated, and he or she is more likely not to accept parental reasons regarding disciplinary issues. The adolescent also pushes much more strongly for independence than the elementary school child, which contributes to parents' disciplinary problems.

Parents of elementary school children use less physical punishment than the parents of preschool children (Newson & Newson, 1976). By contrast, parents are more likely to use deprivation of privileges, appeals directed at the child's esteem, comments designed to increase the child's sense of guilt, and statements indicating to the child that he or she is responsible for his or her actions (Clifford, 1959; Roberts, Block, & Block, 1981).

Changes in Control Processes

During the elementary school years, there appears to be some transfer of control from parent to child, although the process is more gradual than often is thought and should be viewed as a **coregulation process** rather than control by the child or by the parent alone (Maccoby, 1984). It appears that the major shift to autonomy for the child does not occur until the age of 12 or later. During the elementary school years, parents continue to exert general supervision and control, while children are allowed to engage in moment-to-moment self-regulation. This coregulation process seems to be a transition period between the strong parental control of the preschool years and the increased relinquishment of general supervision that occurs during adolescence.

During this coregulation process, parents should (Maccoby, 1984):

1. Monitor, guide, and support elementary school children at a distance
2. Effectively use the times when they have direct contact with the child
3. Strengthen in their children the ability to monitor their own behavior, to adopt appropriate standards of conduct, to avoid hazardous risks, and to sense when parental support and contact is appropriate

As we see next, parent-child relationships during middle and late childhood also are influenced by the cognitions of both children and their parents.

Mutual Cognitions

There is an increasing interest in the way parents and children label each other, as well as in the attributions they make about each other regarding motives (Hess, 1981; Maccoby, 1984; Maccoby & Martin, 1983). Such cognitions seem to play a more important role in parent-child relationships during the elementary school years than the preschool years. Parents and children do not react to each other only on the basis of each others' past behavior. Rather, their reactions to each other are based on how they interpret such behavior and their expectations of behavior.

By the middle childhood years, parents have developed expectations of how they think their children will behave, and children have developed similar expectations for parents. Parents and children are likely to broadly label each other—for example, a parent is likely to label his or her child as "smart" or "dumb," "introverted" or "extraverted," "mannerly" or "unruly," and "lazy" or "hard worker." The child is likely to label his or her parent as "cold" or "warm," "understanding and easy to talk to" or "not understanding and difficult to talk to," "strict" or "permissive," and so forth. Even though there may be specific circumstances when the child or parent does not conform to these labels, such labels seem to represent many hours, days, months, and years of learning about what each other is like as a person. While to some extent these labels may represent stereotypes, in the sense that some behaviors do not conform to the labels, the labels are likely to provide a global sense of the parent's/child's behavior.

Parents with more than one child are likely to label the children differently as part of a social comparison process. Ask any parent about their two children and you will get responses like, "Tommy listens well, but Terry doesn't listen to a thing I say" or "Bobby follows through with everything, but Barbara quits almost the moment she starts something" and "Tammy never gives me any trouble, but Jerry keeps the family in constant turmoil." Given such expectations and sibling comparison, parents may interact in very different ways with one child compared to another. The mother may be willing to take more time to explain something to Tommy but be less likely to take the time with Terry, for example.

A final consideration about parent-child relationships during middle and late childhood focuses on maturational changes in parents.

Changes in Parental Maturation

In Chapter 8, we saw how the family has changed in recent years as we explored such matters as the role of the working mother and the effects of divorce on children. Such life changes in parents influence the development of the elementary school child as well. Parents undergo life-span developmental changes that sometimes are carried out in concert with the maturation of their children. For instance, the parents of elementary school children are more experienced in child rearing than they were when their children were infants or preschoolers. As child-rearing demands become more reduced in middle and late childhood, the mother is more likely to consider returning to a career or beginning a career. Marital relationships often change as less time is spent in child rearing and more time is spent on achieving occupational success, particularly for women. Also, as children age through the elementary and secondary school years, many parents are faced with the care of their own parents.

Societal Changes in the Types of Families

As we discussed in Chapter 8, an increased number of children today grow up in divorced and working-mother families. But there are several other major shifts in the composition of family life that especially affect elementary school children. For example, parents are getting divorced in greater numbers than ever before, but many of them remarry. It takes time for parents to marry, have children, get divorced, and then get remarried. Consequently, there are far more elementary and secondary school children living in stepfamilies than infants or preschool children. In addition, an increasing number of elementary and secondary school children have become what are known as latchkey children.

Stepfamilies

The number of remarriages in which children are involved has been steadily growing. Projections into the 1990s estimate that approximately 25 to 30 percent of all children will be part of a stepfamily before their 18th birthday (Glick, 1977). Remarried families are usually referred to as stepfamilies, blended families, or reconstituted families.

When a remarriage occurs, adjustment to the new family may be overwhelming. The mother who remarries not only has to adjust to having another father for her children but also to being a wife again. There may not be much time for the husband–wife relationship to develop in stepfamilies. The children are a part of this new family from the beginning, a situation that leaves little time for the couple to be alone and to grow with each other (Visher & Visher, 1978).

There is not nearly as much research information about stepparent families as divorced families, but recently, attention has been given to the increasing number of children growing up in stepparent families. Researchers have found that children show more adjustment problems when they are in a complex, rather than a simple, stepfamily (Hetherington, Cox, & Cox, 1982). A **complex stepfamily** is one in which both the stepparent and the biological parent have brought children to the newly formed stepfamily; a **simple stepfamily** is one in which the stepparent has not brought children from a previous marriage to live in the newly formed stepfamily.

In another investigation, children in stepfather, stepmother, and intact families were observed interacting with their parents, and both the parents and the children were interviewed about family relationships (Santrock, Warshak, Sitterle, Dozier, & Stephens, 1985). When differences appeared, they invariably suggested that the intact family atmosphere was more positive than in a stepparent family. Within the stepparent families, relationships between the child and the stepfather or stepmother were more strained than between the child and his or her biological parent. The relationship between the child and the stepfather was a very distant, somewhat unpleasant one, while the relationship between the child and the stepmother appeared to involve an extensive but sometimes abrasive set of interactions. In stepfather families, the remarried mother was performing the bulk of the child-rearing duties, while in stepmother families, the stepmother was receiving much more parenting support from the biological father, who undoubtedly gained considerable parenting experience as a single father. The continuity of attachment to a biological, remarried parent was clearly evident in the child's life, as was the difficulty in establishing an attachment to the stepparent.

Latchkey Children

While Lois Hoffman (1979) and others have concluded that the mother's working is not associated with negative child outcomes, a certain set of children from working-mother families bear further scrutiny; these are the so-called "latchkey" children. A very important point to consider when we study the effects of working mothers on children is what is happening to the children when they are away from their parents. During the course of the day, children of elementary school age and adolescents are at school. Infants are placed in some form of day care, and preschool-aged children usually attend nursery school or are in some form of day care. As we saw in Chapter 6, the quality of day care many young children receive is far from optimal. Thus, negative effects on young children may not be due to the fact that their mothers are working per se but rather to the inferior quality of care the children are receiving when they are not with their parents.

Still, there is more to be said about latchkey children. These children typically do not see their parents from the time the children leave for school in the morning until about 6:00 or 7:00 P.M. They are called latchkey children because they are given the key to their home, take the key with them to school, and use it after school to let themselves into the home while their parents are still at work. Latchkey children are largely unsupervised for two to four hours a day during the school week. In addition, during the summer months, many children who only spent two to four hours each day unsupervised now spend whole days, five days a week, unsupervised. Very little is known about the possible adverse effects of being a latchkey child, although interviews with latchkey children suggest some of the negative influences.

Thomas and Lynette Long (1983) conducted interviews with more than 1,500 latchkey children. They concluded that "a slight majority of these children have negative latchkey experiences." For example, some latchkey children may grow up too fast, hurried by the responsibility placed on them. David Elkind (1981) points out that latchkey children are stressed by taking on the psychological trappings of adulthood before they are prepared to deal with them. Still, some latchkey children may thrive on such responsibility, developing a mature sense of independence and accountability. One of the major problems for latchkey children is the lack of limits and structure in their lives during their latchkey hours. Without such limits and parental involvement, it becomes easier for latchkey children to find their way into trouble—possibly abusing a sibling, stealing, or vandalizing. The Longs point out that 90 percent of the adjudicated juvenile delinquents in Montgomery County, Maryland, were latchkey children.

All too often, self-care is forced on children because of a divorce or death of a spouse. The custodial parent, now the main breadwinner, must work. The child, already having to deal with the stress of divorce or death, must also cope with further loss of time spent with the custodial parent.

It is very difficult to predict how a particular child will respond to the stress of divorce and simultaneously being pushed into self-care. The stress that promotes psychological disturbance in one child may strengthen the sense of competency in another child. Nevertheless, the huge number of latchkey children now present in the United States warrants further research attention.

Family relationships continue to exert powerful influences on development in middle and late childhood. But as we see next, the world of peers is very prominent as well.

PEER RELATIONS IN MIDDLE AND LATE CHILDHOOD

Our discussion of peer relations during the elementary school years focuses on the amount and form of peer interaction; popular, rejected, and neglected children; social cognition; friendships; and children's groups.

Amount and Form of Peer Interaction

It appears that a considerable portion of a child's day during middle and late childhood is spent in peer interaction. The naturalistic observations of eight children indicated that, at age two, only 10 percent of all interaction involved peers. However, the amount of peer interaction rose to 20 percent at age 4 and increased to more than 40 percent between the ages of 7 and 11 (Barker & Wright, 1955). In a typical school day, the school-aged children engaged in approximately 299 behavioral episodes. Many of these episodes involved playing and "fooling around." Many of the interchanges involved play and dominance-focused issues.

In a recent investigation of 764 sixth-graders, the children were asked what they liked to do when they were with their friends (Medrich, Rosen, Ruben, & Buckley, 1982). Team sports accounted for 45 percent of the nominations of boys but for only 26 percent of those activities listed by girls. General play, going places, and socializing were common listings for both boys and girls. Most such interactions occurred outside the home (although close to home), occurred more often in private than public places (such as parks), and were more likely to be same-sex interactions.

Another investigation documented the prominent amount of time spent with peers by 766 sixth-graders (Condry, Simon, & Bronfenbrenner, 1968). It was found that, over the course of a weekend, children spent more than twice as much time with peers as with parents.

Now that we have seen that elementary school children spend an extensive amount of time with peers and that much of this time involves play and socializing, we turn our attention to the status of children with their peers—whether they are popular, rejected, or neglected.

Popular, Rejected, and Neglected Children

Elementary and secondary school children often think, "What can I do to have all of the kids at school like me?" "How can I be popular with both girls and guys?" "What's wrong with me? There must be something wrong, or I would be more popular." Sometimes, children go to great lengths to be popular; and in some cases, parents go to even greater lengths to try to insulate their offspring from rejection and to increase the likelihood that they will be popular.

What makes a child popular with peers? In one study, children who gave the most reinforcements were found to gain popularity among their peers (e.g., Hartup, 1970). In coaching sessions designed to help children become better integrated in the peer group, students are encouraged to overcome their difficulty in interacting with their peers by listening carefully to their peers' conversation and by maintaining open lines of communication with their peers (Oden & Asher, 1975). Being yourself, being happy, showing enthusiasm and concern for others, and showing self-confidence but not conceit are among the characteristics that lead to popularity (Hartup, 1983). In many instances, the opposites of these behaviors invite rejection from peers (Hollingshead, 1975).

Certain physical and cultural factors also can affect a child's popularity. Some research has shown that children who are physically attractive are more popular than those who are not; and contrary to what some believe, brighter children are more popular than less intelligent ones. Children growing up in middle-class surroundings tend to be more popular than those growing up in lower-class surroundings, presumably in part because they are more in control of establishing standards for popularity (e.g., Hollingshead, 1975). But findings such as these reflect group averages; there are many physically attractive children who are unpopular and physically unattractive children who are very well liked. Also, with the increased concern for equal treatment of minority groups, lower-class and ethnic group children can be expected to gain more influence in establishing the standards of popularity. Finally, popularity may fluctuate, and children sense its tenuous nature; even the child who is very popular with peers may have doubts about his or her ability to maintain that popularity.

In recent years, researchers have tried to distinguish between two sets of children who are not popular with their peers—those who are neglected or rejected (Asher & Dodge, 1986). **Neglected children,** while they may not have friends, are not particularly disliked by their peers. However, **rejected children** are overtly disliked by their peers. Rejected children are much more likely to demonstrate disruptive and aggressive behavior than neglected children. And rejected children are much more likely to continue to be unaccepted by their peers as they move into a new setting, while neglected children seem to get a new social life in new groups (Coie & Dodge,

1983; Coie & Kupersmidt, 1983; Newcomb & Bukowski, 1984). Also, neglected and rejected children differ in the amount of loneliness and social unhappiness they experience, with rejected children reporting more problems in this area (Asher & Wheeler, 1985). Further, rejected children seem to have more serious adjustment problems later in life (Cowen, Pederson, Babigian, Izzo, & Trost, 1973; Kupersmidt, 1983; Roff, Sells, & Golden, 1972). In sum, it appears that rejected children are more at risk for adjustment problems, while the risk status of neglected children is less clear.

Social Cognition

In our earlier discussion of family relationships, we found that mutual cognitions of parents and children become increasingly important during middle and late childhood. The social cognitions of children with regard to peer relationships also have received considerable attention in recent years. As part of this trend, developmental psychologists are interested in discovering how children cognitively construct information about peers. We look at two important aspects of social cognition in peer relations—social information processing and social knowledge.

Social Information Processing

As children process information about the social world of peers, a number of steps are likely to be involved. One intriguing application of the information processing approach to social matters is the relation of processing style to aggressive behavior. For example, Kenneth Dodge (1983) argues that children go through five steps in processing social information: decoding of social cues, interpretation, response search, selecting an optimal response, and enactment. Dodge has found that aggressive boys are more likely than nonaggressive boys to perceive another child's actions as hostile when there is considerable ambiguity in the peer's intention. Also, when aggressive boys are allowed to search for cues to determine a peer's intention, they respond more rapidly and engage in a less efficient, less reflective search than nonaggressive children. Focus on Child Development 11.1

presents more information about the importance of the child's information processing skills in peer interaction.

Social Knowledge

The cognitive influence in research on social processes also involves information about social knowledge. As children become more cognitively advanced, they acquire more social knowledge. One of the most interesting aspects of social knowledge research involves the concept of scripts (Nelson, 1981), described in Chapter 9. Children's scripts involve plans for particular goals. An important part of children's social life involves an assessment of what goals to pursue in poorly defined or ambiguous social situations. Also, social relationship goals are important, such as initiating or maintaining a social bond. For example, does the child have the social knowledge to put together a script that will get a particular child to become his or her friend? As part of this script, does the child know that saying nice things to the peer will make the peer like him or her more?

From a social cognitive perspective, children who are maladjusted likely do not have adequate social cognitive skills necessary for skillful social interaction (Asarnow & Asarnow, 1982; Asher & Renshaw, 1981; Butler & Meichenbaum, 1981; Spivack, Platt, & Shure, 1976). One recent investigation explored the possibility that social cognitive skill deficits characterize maladjusted children (Asarnow & Callan, 1985). Boys with and without peer adjustment difficulties were identified and then a number of social cognitive processes or skills were assessed. These included the boy's ability to generate alternative solutions to hypothetical problems, to evaluate these solutions in terms of their effectiveness, to describe self-statements, and to rate the likelihood of self-statements. It was found that boys without peer adjustment problems generated more alternative solutions, proposed more assertive and mature solutions, gave less intense aggressive solutions, showed more adaptive planning, and evaluated physically aggressive responses less positively than the boys with peer adjustment problems. For example, as shown in Figure 11.1, negative peer status sixth-grade boys were not as likely to generate alternative solutions and much less likely to adaptively plan ahead than their positive peer status counterparts.

FOCUS ON CHILD DEVELOPMENT 11.1

DESTROYING A BLOCK TOWER WHILE CLEANING UP A ROOM—INTENTION-CUE DETECTION SKILLS IN CHILDREN

A peer accidentally trips and knocks the boy's soft drink out of his hand. The boy misinterprets the encounter as hostile, which leads him to retaliate aggressively against the peer. His aggression is viewed as inappropriate by peers who observed the encounter. Through repeated encounters of this nature, peers come to perceive the boy as having a habit of acting inappropriately. In a recent investigation, Kenneth Dodge and his colleagues studied boys like the one just mentioned who misinterpreted social cues on a consistent basis (Dodge, Murphy, & Buchsbaum, 1984). They developed a measure to assess **intention-cue detection,** investigated whether this skill develops throughout the elementary school years, examined the relation between intention-cue detection and deviant behavior on the part of children, and described the role of intention-cue detection in developing a model of developmental psychopathology.

The measure of intention-cue detection skill was a discrimination task in which a child was presented with 14 sets of three short videotaped vignettes, each showing social interaction between two children in which one child provokes the other. In two of the three vignettes, the actor shows the same intention, but in the third, he shows a different intention. The subject's task is to identify the different vignette. Intentions included those that were hostile, prosocial, accidental, and others.

This measure was given to 176 children in kindergarten, second, and fourth grades who were identified as having a peer status of popular, average, socially rejected, or socially neglected. Scores on the intention-cue measure increased with age, and normal children (popular and average) had higher scores than deviant children (neglected and rejected). The mistakes made by the deviant children consistently involved erroneously labeling prosocial intentions as hostile (see the figure on the following page). A hostile intention was represented by a display of obviously purposeful destructive be-

How might social information processing be involved in children's aggression?

havior accompanied by corresponding verbalizations and facial expressions. A prosocial intention was reflected in a purposeful destruction of a peer's play object, but in an effort to help someone else (such as destroying a block tower while cleaning up the room).

Thus, children who are deficient (relative to their age-mates) in intention-cue detection are likely to show behavior viewed as inappropriate by their peers. Since children are capable of identifying hostile intentions at an earlier age than they can prosocial intentions, children deficient in intention-cue detection are likely to make errors in judging nonhostile actions as hostile. This error is likely to lead some children to act aggressively. Other children who make this attributional error may respond by withdrawing. Either response is likely to be judged by peers as inappropriate to the situation. Those who respond aggressively have a high probability of being rejected by peers, while those who withdraw have a high probability of being neglected by peers (Dodge, 1983).

(continued on following page)

FOCUS ON CHILD DEVELOPMENT 11.1

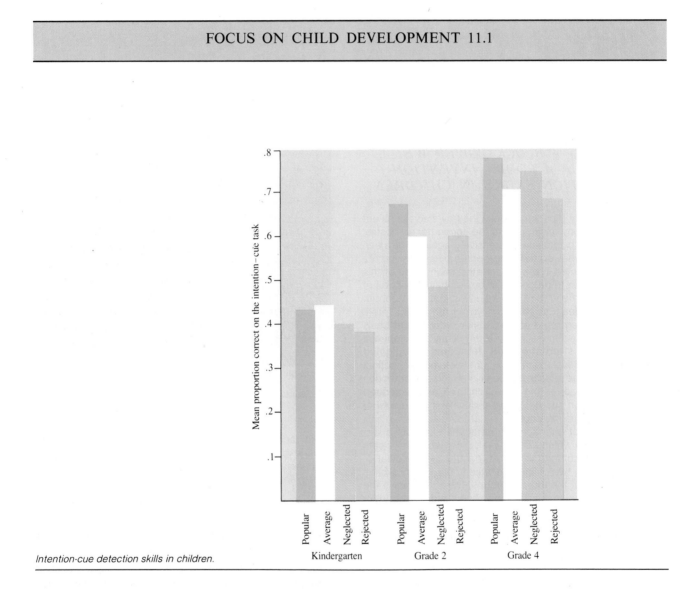

Intention-cue detection skills in children.

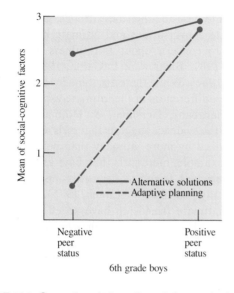

FIGURE 11.1 Generation of alternative solutions and adaptive planning by negative and positive peer status boys.

While it is becoming clear that social cognitive knowledge is a very important ingredient of peer relations, psychologists have not yet developed a precise body of social cognitive knowledge believed to be beneficial to children at different developmental levels. However, it seems clear that children who get along better with others, both peers and adults, likely have significantly greater knowledge about social skills than those who are not popular and not well-liked.

The world of peers is one of varying acquaintances—children interact with some children they barely know and with others for hours every day. It is to the latter type—friends—that we turn now.

Friendships

"My best friend is nice. She's honest, and I can trust her. I can tell her my innermost secrets and know that nobody else will find out about them. I have other friends, too, but she is my best friend. We consider each other's feelings and don't want to hurt each other. We help each other out when we have problems. We make up funny names for people and laugh ourselves silly. We make lists of which boys we think are the ugliest, which are the biggest jerks, and so on. Some of these things we share with other friends, some we don't." This description of

the nature of friendship by a 10-year-old girl suggests the importance of intimacy in friendship—telling a friend your innermost secrets. We will see that intimacy is one of the most important characteristics of friendships.

The Incidence of Friendship and Cognitive Factors

For many children, their most important encounters are with a friend or friends. While there may be warm and trusting relationships that develop in large groups, friendships involve specific attachments that have several characteristics not unlike those found in parent-infant attachment (Hartup, 1983). For example, friends are a source of security in strange, upsetting circumstances, and separation from them arouses anxiety. Children enjoy being with their friends, develop a sense of trust in them, and derive a great deal of pleasure from being with them. Of course, unlike the parent-infant attachment system, friendship attachments are often not permanent. Despite their fragile nature, however, friendships can be as intense as attachments with parents and siblings.

While friendships exist in early childhood, they become much more predominant in the elementary school years and adolescence. Particularly around the ages of 8 to 10, children begin developing a real sensitivity to the feelings of another child (Sullivan, 1953). Unfortunately, however, many children do not have a best friend, or even a circle of friends, in whom they can confide. One school psychologist always made a practice of asking children and adolescents about their friends. One 11-year-old boy, when asked who his best friend was, replied, "My kite." Further discussion revealed that his parents had rejected him and insulated him from the world of his peers as well. This circumstance suggests how attachment histories and relationships are carried forward to influence friendship attachments. In one investigation of college-aged youths, as many as one of every three students surveyed said that they had not found or were not sure they had found a close, meaningful relationship with a same-sex peer (Katz, 1968).

The cognitive orientation in social processes also has begun to characterize the study of friendships. During middle and late childhood and adolescence, when children are asked about their friends, they use more interpersonal constructs; as they get older, they are more flexible and precise in the use of these constructs, provide more complex and organized information about their friends, and understand that particular attributes characterize their friends as compared to acquaintances. These changes undoubtedly are tied to general changes in cognitive and language development (Hartup, 1983; Shantz, 1983).

Intimacy and Similarity in Friendships

Intimacy in friendships has been defined in different ways; for example, it has been broadly defined to include everything in a relationship that makes it seem close or intense (Huston & Burgess, 1980). But in most research studies, **intimacy in friendship** has been defined more narrowly in terms of intimate self-disclosure and the sharing of private thoughts. Another factor in intimacy is private and personal knowledge about a friend (Selman, 1980; Sullivan, 1953).

Most efforts to obtain information about friendships simply involve asking children such questions as, "What is a friend?" or "How can you tell that someone is your best friend?" (Berndt, 1982). Researchers find that intimate friendships rarely appear during childhood but are most likely to first arise during early adolescence. For example, in one investigation, fourth- and eighth-graders were asked about external or observable characteristics of their best friends, such as their friends' birthdates, and about more intimate information, such as their friends' preferences and personality characteristics (for example, what the friend worried about the most). To determine the accuracy of the reports, they were compared with their best friends' self-reports. Fourth- and eighth-graders did not differ in their knowledge of external or observable characteristics of their friends, but the eighth-graders knew more intimate things about their best friends than the fourth-graders did (Diaz & Berndt, 1982).

It has been said that girls have more intimate friendships than boys do (Douvan & Adelson, 1966). The assumption behind this suggested sex-role difference is that girls are more oriented toward interpersonal relationships, while boys are more interested in assertiveness and achievement than in warmth and empathy. Also, intimacy between boys may be discouraged because of the fear that it may lead to homosexuality. When children are asked to describe their best friends, girls refer more to intimate conversations and intimate knowledge and show more concern about faithfulness and rejection (Berndt, 1981; Bieglow & LaGaipa, 1980; Douvan & Adelson, 1966). While there are some investigations that find no sex differences in the intimate aspects of friendships (Sharabany, Gershoni, & Hofman, 1981), the weight of the evidence suggests that girls' friendships are characterized by more intimacy than boys' friendships are. For example, more girls than boys are likely to describe their best friend as "sensitive just like me" or "trustworthy just like me" (Duck, 1975).

Does intimate friendship have an effect on personality? There is some evidence that having a close and stable best friend is positively associated with self-esteem (Mannarino, 1978, 1979), but psychologists do not know whether the differences between youths are caused by self-esteem or intimacy in friendship. In other words, children with high self-esteem may be more likely to be able to develop a close, intimate friendship, just as easily as having a close friend could promote self-esteem.

The extent to which there is similarity between friends in a variety of characteristics has been of interest to psychologists for many years. Throughout the childhood and adolescent years, friends are generally similar in terms of age, sex, and race (Hallinan, 1979). Usually, friends also have similar attitudes toward school, similar educational aspirations, and closely aligned achievement orientations (Ball, 1981). Such findings reveal the importance of schooling in children's lives and the tendency toward agreement between friends on its importance. As Thomas Berndt (1982) suggests, if friends have different attitudes about school, one of them may want to play basketball or go shopping while the other does homework. If one friend insists on completing his or her homework while the other persists at playing basketball, conflicts are likely to weaken the friendship.

Friends also tend to be similar in their orientations toward teenage or youth culture. Friends generally like the same kinds of music, the same kinds of clothes, and the same kinds of leisure activities (Ball, 1981). However, some friendships are based on specific interests, such as horseback riding or playing golf. These types of friends often do not share as many similar ideas and attitudes.

Shared Support and Knowledge

Friendships involve a great deal of sharing. This shared support often appears very early in development. Friendships are also characterized by shared knowledge.

John Gottman and Jennifer Parkhurst (1978) maintain that young children's abilities to provide mutual support and to resolve conflict in imaginative fantasies are critical in establishing and maintaining intimacy among young friends. In coping with conflict, young friends express considerable emotion, sympathy and support, and anguish. One excerpt from the fantasy play of two four-year-old best friends, Eric and Naomi, reveals extensive emotional support from Naomi:

Naomi: No, it's time for our birthday. We better clean up quickly.

Eric: Well, I'd rather play with my skeleton. Hold on there everyone. Snappers. I am the skeleton. I'm the skeleton. Ooh, hee. Hugh, ha, ha. You're hiding.

Naomi: Hey, in the top drawer, there's the . . .

Eric: I am, the skeleton, whoa.

Naomi: There's the feet. (clattering)

Eric: (screams) A skeleton. Everyone a skeleton.

Naomi: I'm your friend. The dinosaur.

Eric: Oh, hi, dinosaur. You know, no one likes me.

Naomi: But I like you. I'm your friend.

Eric: But none of my other friends like me. They don't like my new suit. They don't like my skeleton suit. It's really just me. They think I'm a dumb-dumb.

Naomi: I know what. He's a good skeleton.

Eric: I am not a dumb-dumb.

Naomi: I'm not calling you a dumb-dumb. I'm calling you a friendly skeleton.

By the middle of the elementary school years, friendships involve a considerable amount of reciprocal information about each other's personal and social characteristics. One investigation by Gary Ladd and Elizabeth Emerson (1984) found that the friendships of first-grade children were less likely to include a reciprocal awareness of their friend's differences from the self, but that by the fourth grade, such awareness had developed. This suggests that the friendships of older children broaden to include characteristics that do not overlap with self-interests and coincide with the decrease in egocentrism that characterizes development during the elementary school years.

So far, we have described the incidence of friendships and the cognitive factors involved, seen that friendships involve similarity and intimacy, and observed the role of shared support and knowledge in friendships. As we see next, though, communication skills are especially important in constructing friendships.

Conversational Skills

Yet another important factor in friendship is conversational skills. In one recent investigation, the researchers devised a clever strategy for evaluating the role of conversational skills in friendship formation (Parker & Gottman, 1985). Four- and five-year-old children were brought individually to a playroom where they played for 30 minutes with a talking doll that resembled a green human wearing silver clothes. The doll housed a wireless, hidden receiver/speaker that allowed a concealed assistant to act as its voice and converse with the subject. The assistant was trained to talk in age-appropriate ways while systematically varying the competence/incompetence of her speech with regard to a number of friendship skills. This strategy produced two experimental conditions—skilled and unskilled. Following the exposure of the children to the skilled and unskilled conversationalist from outer space (that is, "the green extraterrestrial"), the experimenters evaluated the path of friendship formation. They found that children who met the skilled doll were more likely to "hit it off" and progress toward friendship, while those who met the unskilled doll tended not to hit it off. These findings provide evidence for the importance of conversational skills in friendship formation. Other research on communication skills and children's social relationships suggests that comforting and listening skills are key factors in peer popularity (Burleson, 1985).

We have been describing the nature of children's peer relationships as well as their more intimate interactions with friends. Children also spend time in larger assemblages as part of groups.

Children's Groups

What is the nature of children's groups? How have they been studied naturalistically? An assemblage of children is not necessarily a group or clique. A group exists when several children interact with one another on an ongoing basis, sharing values and goals. In addition to shared values and goals, norms and status positions are also important to the functioning of the group. Norms are the standards, rules, and guidelines by which the group abides; and status positions are positions of greater or lesser power and control within the group. Stable groups have values or norms that become established and maintained over time. And when leaders and followers become differentiated, an aggregation takes on the distinctive flavor of a group (Hartup, 1970).

The most extensive work conducted on the formation of children and adolescent groups is that of Muzafer Sherif and his colleagues (Sherif, Harvey, White, Hood, & Sherif, 1961). The Sherif naturalistic experiments often proceeded according to a particular format. Middle-class, white, Protestant boys were recruited and removed to a campsite during the summer. There they were exposed to an experiment in the natural setting of the camp. The observers were members of the camp staff.

In the first phase of the experiment, in-group formation was established by placing two groups of boys who did not know one another together for a few days. In the second phase, the two groups were brought together for the intergroup conflict phase. This conflict included win-lose competition and planned frustration that was expected to increase the tension between the groups. In the third phase, ways to reduce intergroup conflict were explored. The observers used such strategies as experiencing a common enemy or constructing superordinate goals that the two groups could only achieve together to reduce conflict.

Some of the important findings to come out of Sherif's naturalistic experiments are: (1) Hierarchical structures invariably emerged within the groups. The top and bottom status positions were filled first, then the middle positions. (2) Norms developed in all groups. "We-they" talk was a frequent part of the groups' conversations. The groups often adopted nicknames, like the Bulldogs or the Sorcerers. (3) Frustration and competition contributed to hostility between the groups. (4) Intergroup hostility often was reduced by setting up a superordinate goal that

What is the nature of children's groups?

required the mutual efforts of both groups. For example, Sherif's camp directors deliberately broke a waterline so that both groups of boys would have to pitch in together to help. Another time, the camp truck taking the boys to a movie in town was driven into a muddy ditch, requiring considerable team effort to get it out.

We have discussed a number of important ideas about family and peer relationships in middle and late childhood. Now we turn our attention to another important aspect of middle and late childhood—schools.

SCHOOLS

Our study of schools in middle and late childhood focuses on the nature of the child's schooling, open versus traditional classrooms, teachers, aptitude-treatment interaction, and social class and ethnicity.

The Impact of Schooling and the Elementary School Setting

It is justifiable to be concerned about the impact of schools on children because of the degree of influence schools have on their lives. By the time an individual has graduated from high school, he or she will have spent 10,000 hours in the classroom.

Children spend many years in schools as members of a small society in which there are tasks to be accomplished, people to be socialized with and to be socialized by, and rules that define and limit behavior, feelings, and attitudes. The experiences children have in this society are likely to have a strong influence in such areas as identity development, belief in one's competence, images of life and career possibilities, social relationships, standards of right and wrong, and conceptions of how a social system beyond the family functions.

The classroom is still the major context for the elementary school child, although it is more likely to be experienced as a social unit than in the preschool. Furthermore, the network of social expression is more complex now. Teachers and peers have a prominent influence on the child during the middle childhood years, with teachers symbolizing authority and establishing the climate of the classroom, conditions of interaction with students, and the nature of group functioning. The peer group takes on a very prominent status in the lives of elementary school children. Not only is there interest in friendship, belonging, and status in peer groups at school, but the peer group is also a learning community in which social roles and standards related to work and achievement are formed.

Open Versus Traditional Classrooms and Schools

There has been a great deal of debate in educational circles on how classroom structure and climate influence development. Perhaps the most widely discussed aspect of this debate focuses on open versus traditional classrooms. **Open classroom** (or open education) programs have been characterized by a number of features (Giaconia & Hedges, 1982; Marshall, 1981):

Free choice by students of activities they will participate in

Space flexibility

Varied, enriched learning materials

Emphasis on individual and small-group instruction

The teacher as more of a facilitator than a director of learning

Students learning to assume responsibility for their learning

Multi-age grouping of children

Team teaching

Classrooms without walls, in which the physical nature of the school is more open

Some open classroom programs have more of these features than others. Thus, research that compares open with traditional classrooms is difficult to interpret because there are so many variations of open classrooms. Part of the problem with studies of open and traditional classrooms also is that these terms are not always reflected directly in the classroom. As a result, in some classrooms defined as open, the teachers may be using a teaching style more characteristic of traditional classrooms. One inadequate strategy that has been used too often is simply to ask teachers or school officials (who may have varying definitions of what constitutes open and traditional classrooms) to rate classroom climate.

In many instances, the measures that have been used to assess the effects of classroom climate have been standardized tests of intelligence and achievement. However, Rudolf Moos (Moos & Moos, 1978; Tricket & Moos, 1974) believes that it may be wise to assess educational effects other than those evaluated by standardized tests. Cognitive preferences, school satisfaction, and persistent motivation to learn are several other factors that adolescents should be measured on as well.

Furthermore, experts believe that, not only should different measures be used to assess the effects of classroom climate, but that better instruments to evaluate classroom climate are needed. One such measure is the **Classroom Environment Scale (CES)** developed by Trickett and Moos (1974). The CES assesses teacher-student and peer relationships, as well as the organization of the classroom. Students are asked to respond to a number of questions concerning nine different categories: teacher support, affiliation, task orientation, competition, order and organization, rule clarity, involvement, teacher control, and innovation.

Because open classrooms have been defined in so many different ways, some researchers have recommended that the concept of the open classroom be evaluated in terms of its components, or some combination of the components, rather than as a whole. In one evaluation of the components of open classrooms, the researchers performed a meta-analysis of approximately 150 studies

(Giaconia & Hedges, 1982). A **meta-analysis** involves the application of statistical techniques to already existing research studies. The investigator sorts through the research literature looking for common results of many different studies to discover some consistent themes. The results indicated that the open classroom concept seems to have the following characteristics:

Lowered language achievement but by a very small amount

Little effect on math, reading, and other types of academic achievement

Moderately enhanced achievement motivation, cooperativeness, creativity, and independence

No effect on adjustment, anxiety, locus of control, or self-concept

Slightly improved student attitudes toward school, the teacher, curiosity, and general mental ability

However, the results tell us nothing about the particular dimensions of the open classroom concept. To identify these more precise effects, the following characteristics were investigated:

Role of the child (the degree of activity in learning)

Diagnostic evaluation (use of work samples and observations but rare use of tests to guide instruction)

Materials to manipulate

Individualized instruction (adjusting rate, methods, materials; calling on small-group methods)

Multi-age groupings of students (two or more grades in the same area)

Open space (flexible use of areas, activity centers; no interior walls; flexible seating)

Team teaching (two or more teachers combining to plan and instruct the same students; use of parents as teaching aids)

Among the most important results of this meta-analysis was the finding that, when open classrooms had a strong effect on the child's self-concept, the role of the child was a criterion in all investigations. Other aspects of open classrooms linked to positive effects on the child's self-concept were: diagnostic evaluation, materials to manipulate, and individualized instruction. With regard to nonachievement outcomes, all features except team teaching and open space were present in the open classrooms. For achievement outcomes, materials to manipulate and team teaching were the key ingredients of open classsrooms.

Our discussion of elementary schools so far has focused on the impact of schooling, the nature of the school setting, and open versus traditional classrooms and schools. But, of course, a key ingredient of understanding schools is the teacher.

Teachers

Virtually everyone's life is affected in one way or another by teachers: You were probably influenced by teachers as you grew up; you may become a teacher yourself or work with teachers through counseling or psychological services; and you may one day have children whose education will be guided by many different teachers through the years. How much influence do teachers really have on children? What were some characteristics of the teachers you have liked or disliked, particularly their communication and social interaction styles? You can probably remember several of your teachers vividly: Perhaps one never smiled, another required you to memorize everything in sight, and yet another always appeared happy and vibrant and encouraged verbal interaction. Our further discussion of teachers focuses on teaching styles and traits as well as Erik Erikson's criteria for a good teacher.

Teaching Styles and Traits

For many years, psychologists and educators have been trying to create a profile of the personality traits of a good teacher. Because of the complexity of the task, a definitive profile may never be produced; yet, several studies suggest that some traits are better for teachers than others. Teacher traits that relate positively to the student's intellectual development are enthusiasm, the ability to plan, poise, adaptability, and awareness of individual differences (Gage, 1965). Teachers who are impulsive tend to produce more impulsive students who are less reflective in solving school tasks (Yando & Kagan, 1968). Teachers who are warm and flexible and who encourage responsibility tend to produce students who respond constructively to failure and who usually engage willingly in class activities (Thompson, 1944).

© 1976 United Feature Syndicate, Inc.

Erikson's Criteria for a Good Teacher

Erik Erikson (1968) believes that good teachers are able to produce a sense of industry, rather than inferiority, in their students. Good teachers are trusted and respected by the community and know how to alternate play and work, games and study. They know how to recognize special efforts and to encourage special abilities. They also know how to give a child time and how to handle those children to whom school is not important.

Good teachers, in Erikson's view, allow a student to engage in peer interaction when academic work is getting to the student and his or her interaction with the teacher seems to be deteriorating. At stake is the child's development of identification with those who know things and know how to do things. Time after time in interviews with talented and creative people, spontaneous comments reveal that one teacher helped to spark hidden talent. Without such teachers, many children never develop their abilities.

Erikson believes that many teachers emphasize self-restraint and a strict allegiance to duty, as opposed to encouraging children to make discoveries on their own. Erikson remarks that either method may work well with some children but not with others. He also stresses that, if the first method is carried to the extreme, children may develop too much self-restraint and sense of duty in conforming to what others do. If the opposite method is used, Erikson believes that children should be "mildly but firmly coerced into the adventure of finding out that one can learn to accomplish things which one would never have thought of by oneself" (1968, p.127).

There is another possible hazard in the child's development that Erikson feels teachers need to watch for. When the child conforms too much, he or she may view work as the only worthwhile activity in life. This type of child probably will not engage in imaginative activities and games to the extent that an individual with better identity development would. There are times when the grind of hard work should be left behind, and teachers can encourage students to do so.

Teacher characteristics and styles are important aspects of understanding the influence of schools on children. However, such characteristics need to be considered in concert with what the child brings to the school situation.

Aptitude-Treatment Interaction

Some children may benefit more from structure than others, and some teachers may be able to handle a flexible curriculum better than others. As a result, a whole field of educational research has sprung up, referred to as **Aptitude-Treatment Interaction (ATI)**. The term **aptitude** refers to academic potential and personality dimensions in which students differ; **treatment** refers to the educational technique (e.g., structured class or flexible class) adopted in the classroom. Lee Cronbach and Richard Snow (1977), as well as other education experts, believe that ATI is the best way to study teaching effectiveness.

Research has shown that a child's achievement level (aptitude) may interact directly with classroom structure (treatment) to produce the best learning and the most enjoyable learning environment (Peterson, 1977; Porteus, 1976). That is, students with high-achievement orientation often do well in a flexible classroom and enjoy it; students with low-achievement orientation do not usually do as well and dislike the flexibility. The reverse

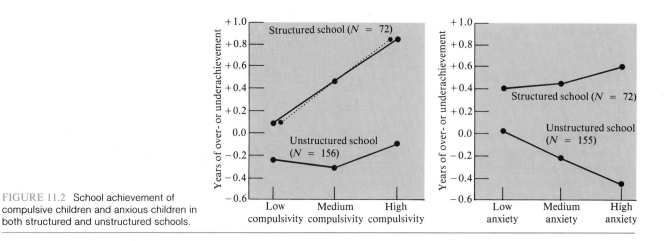

FIGURE 11.2 School achievement of compulsive children and anxious children in both structured and unstructured schools.

is true in a structured classroom. There are many other ATI factors operating in the classroom. Education experts are just beginning to pin some of these down; further clarification of aptitude-treatment interaction should lead to useful information about how children can be taught more effectively.

In one study, the academic performance of two types of children learning to read was assessed in two different settings (Grimes & Allinsmith, 1961). One group of children was labeled "anxious," the other "compulsive" on the basis of assessments of individual differences among the children. One classroom was highly structured, the other relatively unstructured. Children who were neither very compulsive (e.g., upset by disorder) nor anxious (e.g., restless) were not influenced by the type of classroom organization. But the high-anxiety group of children did very poorly in the unstructured classroom and somewhat better than the low-anxiety group in the highly structured classroom. The highly compulsive group performed best in a highly structured classroom, while relatively uncompulsive children were not influenced by classroom organization. These results, shown in Figure 11.2, clearly suggest the importance of considering aptitude-treatment interaction in the design of classroom environments and teaching strategies. Richard Snow (1977) points out that individual differences (aptitudes) were ignored for many years in the design of instruction and curriculum. Now, individual differences

in student aptitudes, learning styles, cultural backgrounds, and so forth are forcing curriculum teams to consider more specific instructional situations and more specific groups of children.

Two ways the teacher's orientation can be classified are as challenging and demanding, or as encouraging good performance. Jere Brophy (1979) reviewed several studies focused on these types of teacher orientations. Teachers who work with higher-socioeconomic-status/high-ability students usually are more successful if they move at a quick pace, frequently communicating high expectations and enforcing high standards. These teachers try to keep students challenged, will not accept inferior work, and occasionally criticize the students' work when it does not meet their standards. Teachers who generally are successful with lower-socioeconomic-status/low-ability students also are interested in getting the most out of their students, but they usually do so by being warm and encouraging rather than demanding. They are friendly with their students, take more time out from academic subject matter to motivate the youth, praise and encourage more often, rarely criticize poor work, and move the curriculum along at a slower pace. When they call on individual students, they allow more time for the student to respond; they may provide hints to help the student get the correct answer (Brophy & Evertson, 1974). As can be readily seen by this example, successful teaching varies according to the type of student being taught—one teaching strategy is superior with lower-class students, another with higher-socioeconomic-status students.

Social Class and Ethnicity

Consideration of social class as well as ethnicity provides further insight into the nature of the child's schooling.

Social Class

It often seems as though one of the major functions of schools in this country is to train children to function in and contribute to middle-class society. This happens because politicians who vote on school funding are usually middle class, school-board members are predominantly middle class, and principals and teachers are often middle class. In fact, it has been stated many times that schools function in a middle-class society, and critics believe that schools have not done a good job of educating lower-class children to overcome the cultural barriers that make it difficult to enhance their social position. This theme characterized the educational protest literature in the 1960s and early 1970s.

In *Dark Ghetto,* Kenneth Clark (1965) described some of the ways lower- and middle-class children are treated differently in school. Teachers in the middle-class school spent more time teaching their students and evaluated students' work more than twice as often as teachers did in the low-income school. Teachers in the low-income school made three times as many negative comments to students as teachers did in the middle-class school; the latter made more positive than negative comments to their students.

Teachers have lower expectations for children from low-income families than for children from middle-income families. A teacher who knows that a child comes from a lower-class background may spend less time trying to help the child solve a problem and may anticipate that the child will frequently get into trouble. The teacher may also perceive a gap between his or her own middle-class position and the lower-class status of the child's parents; as a result, the teacher may believe that the parents are not interested in helping the child and may make fewer efforts to communicate with them.

The maturational experiences of teachers with a middle-class background are quite different from those of children or teachers with a lower-class background. A teacher from the middle class has probably not gone hungry for weeks at a time or experienced the conditions of an overcrowded apartment, perhaps without electricity or plumbing, where several children may sleep with one or two adults in one small room.

There is evidence from at least one study that teachers with lower-class origins may have different attitudes toward lower-class students than middle-class teachers have (Gottlieb, 1966). Perhaps because they have experienced many inequities themselves, teachers with lower-class origins tend to be empathetic to problems that lower-class children encounter. In Gottlieb's study, for example, the teachers were asked to indicate the most outstanding characteristics of their lower-class students. The middle-class teachers checked adjectives like *lazy, rebellious,* and *fun-loving;* the lower-class teachers, however, checked such adjectives as *happy, cooperative, energetic,* and *ambitious.* The teachers with lower-class backgrounds perceived the behaviors of the lower-class children as adaptive, whereas the middle-class teachers viewed the same behaviors as falling short of middle-class standards.

Ethnicity

Not only do students from lower-class backgrounds often experience discrimination in our schools; children from many different ethnic backgrounds do as well. In most American schools, blacks, Mexican Americans, Puerto Ricans, Native Americans, Japanese, and Asian Indians are minorities. Teachers have often been ignorant of different cultural meanings that non-Anglo children have learned in their communities. The problems that boys and girls from non-Anglo backgrounds have had in conventional schools are well-documented (Casteñada, Ramirez, Cortes, & Barrera, 1971; Minuchin & Shapiro, 1983).

The social and academic development of children from minority groups depends on such factors as teacher expectations; the teacher's preparation for working with children from different backgrounds; the nature of the curriculum; the presence of role models in the school for minority students; the quality of relations between school personnel and parents from different ethnic, economic, and educational backgrounds; and the relations between the school and the community (Minuchin & Shapiro, 1983).

How can the social and academic development of children from minority groups be improved?

By far the largest effort to study the role of ethnicity in schools has dealt with desegregation (Bell, 1980). The focus of desegregation has been on improving the proportions of black and white student populations in schools. Efforts to improve this ratio have typically involved busing students, usually the minority-group members, from their home neighborhoods to more distant schools. The underlying belief in such efforts is that bringing different groups together reduces stereotyped attitudes and improves intergroup relationships. But busing tells us nothing about what is going on inside the school. Black adolescents bused to a predominantly white school are usually resegregated in the classroom by seating patterns, ability grouping, and tracking systems (Epstein, 1980).

In one comprehensive national study focused on factors that contribute to positive interracial relations, over 5,000 fifth-grade students in more than 90 elementary schools and over 400 tenth-graders in 72 high schools were evaluated (Forehand, Ragosta, & Rock, 1976). It was concluded that multi-ethnic curricula, projects focused on racial issues, and mixed work groups lead to positive changes, and that improved relationships are enhanced by the presence of supportive principals and teachers.

Overall, however, the findings pertaining to desegregation have not been encouraging (Minuchin & Shapiro, 1983). Desegregation in itself does not necessarily improve race relations—positive consequences depend on what goes on in the classroom once children get there. School personnel who support the advancement of minority student curricula acknowledge that ethnic pluralism, and the participation of students in cooperative activities and learning situations, are likely to improve the minority student's development.

Our discussion of social development in middle and late childhood has covered many aspects of families, peers, and schools and is summarized in Child Development Concept Table 11.1. Now we turn our attention to information about personality development in middle and late childhood.

Child Development Concept Table 11.1   Families, Peers, and Schools in Middle and Late Childhood

Concept	Processes/Related Ideas	Characteristics/Description
Family	Amount of parent-child interaction	Parents spend less time with children during middle and late childhood than during early childhood, including less time in caregiving, instruction, reading, talking, and playing.
	Parent-child issues	New parent-child issues during middle and late childhood include chores, material reinforcement, children's self-entertainment, and monitoring outside the family. School-related matters are particularly salient.
	Discipline techniques	Discipline during middle and late childhood involves more reasoning than in early childhood, as well as more deprivation of privileges, appeals to the child's self-esteem, comments directed at the child's guilt, and information about the child's responsibility.
	Control processes	During the elementary school years, there is a gradual transfer of control from parent to child, but this process should be viewed as coregulatory in the sense that parental control of moment-to-moment activities may be relinquished but general supervisory control is still prevalent.
	Mutual cognitions	During middle and late childhood, children increasingly categorize their parents in terms of labels. They often react to their parents according to these categorizations, and parents likewise react to their children based on labels they have developed for them.
	Parental maturation	Not only are children maturing but so are parents. The parents of elementary school children are more experienced at parenting than the parents of preschool children. The fact that child-rearing demands become somewhat lessened in the elementary school years may produce changes in parents.
	Societal changes in the types of families	During the elementary and secondary school years, two major changes in children's lives are the increasing number of children growing up in stepparent families as well as the increase in latchkey children.
Peer relations	Amount and form of peer interaction	A considerable portion of a child's day during middle and late childhood is spent in the company of peers. Play and socialization are frequent components of peer interaction.
	Popular, rejected, and neglected children	Listening skills and effective communication, being yourself, being happy, showing enthusiasm and concern for others, and indicating self-confidence but not conceit are predictors of peer popularity. Rejected children are at risk for adjustment problems, while the risk status of neglected children is less clear.
	Social cognition	There has been increased interest in social cognition in peer relations. Social information processing and social knowledge are two important aspects of social cognition in peer relations.
	Friendships	Friendships become a more salient feature of peer relationships in the elementary school years. Among the most important features of friendships are intimacy and similarity, shared support and knowledge, an increased cognitive orientation, and conversational skills.
	Children's groups	An understanding of children's groups requires focusing on their nature and the naturalistic study of group formation.

(continued on following page)

Child Development Concept Table 11.1 Continued		
Concept	**Processes/Related Ideas**	**Characteristics/Description**
Schools	Nature of schooling	Children spend more than 10,000 hours in the classroom as members of a small society in which there are tasks to be accomplished, people to be socialized with and socialized by, and rules that define and limit behavior, feelings, and attitudes.
	Open versus traditional classrooms and schools	The open classroom concept is multi-dimensional, and the criteria for evaluation often have varied from one study to the next. The Classroom Environment Scale has improved assessment. Through meta-analysis, investigators have found that open classrooms are associated with lower language achievement but improved attitudes toward school. What seems most important here is linking specific dimensions of open classrooms with specific dimensions of the child. In this regard, individualized instruction and emphasis on the role of the child are associated with positive effects on the child's self-concept.
	Teachers	A definitive profile of a competent teacher is difficult to create, although positive teacher traits include enthusiasm, planning, poise, adaptability, and awareness of individual differences. Erikson believes that good teachers are capable of producing a sense of industry, rather than inferiority, in children.
	Aptitude-treatment interaction	Aptitude-treatment interaction (ATI) refers to the importance of looking at the interaction of aptitude and treatment factors rather than focusing on each factor in isolation when evaluating educational outcomes.
	Social class and ethnicity	Schools have a stronger middle-class than lower-class orientation. Teachers from a lower-class socioeconomic background seem to have different orientations toward students than those from middle-class backgrounds. And many teachers seem to have different expectations for children from lower- and middle-class backgrounds. The major investigation of ethnicity and schooling has focused on desegregation through busing, a procedure that has not produced any consistent benefits for minority group children.

THE SELF, SEX ROLES, AND MORAL DEVELOPMENT IN MIDDLE AND LATE CHILDHOOD

Our exploration of personality development in middle and late childhood focuses on changes in the self, sex roles, and moral development. The child's expanding social world and increased cognitive sophistication contribute to how the child sees himself or herself in the social world, the sex-role stereotypes and sex differences that develop, and the nature of the child's behavior, thoughts, and feelings about standards of right and wrong.

The Self

Among the most important changes in self-conception during middle and late childhood are: the child's in-creasing ability to understand how he or she is viewed by others, differentiation, individuation, and stability.

A very important part of the development of self-concept is the child's increasing ability to understand how he or she is viewed by others (Maccoby, 1980). Very young children have difficulty in understanding others' perspective of them, and they often are not aware of the impressions their behavior makes on others. But gradually, children begin to understand that their behavior triggers reactions from others, and they begin to monitor their actions, acting differently depending on whom they are with and which aspect of their social-self they want to be seen. This represents a time at which children are more cautious about revealing themselves to others.

Children also develop a more differentiated view of themselves as they grow older (McCandless & Evans,

1973). As young children, they may simply have perceived themselves as "good" or "bad." By late childhood and adolescence, they are likely to perceive themselves in more detailed ways, such as "I am a good person most of the time, except when my older sister bugs me, or when my father won't let me have the car, or when I have to study for an exam."

Older children also develop a more individuated view of themselves than they had as young children. This indicates that older children have a more distinct view of themselves as unique persons and more readily differentiate themselves from others than young children. As young children, they may have labeled themselves in terms of how they were similar to their peers, but as they approach adolescence, they tend to describe themselves more in terms of how they are different from their peers.

Also, the older child's self-concept is likely to be more stable than the young child's. But in an extreme form, stability can lead to rigidity and unrealistic self-appraisals. Even though we say that the self-concept of the child becomes more stable, this does not imply that self-concept does not change. It clearly does change, but as children and adolescents mature cognitively, they become more capable of integrating incoming information into a stable sense of who they are.

So far, our discussion of the self in middle and late childhood has focused on changes in self-conception. But, as we observe next, during middle and late childhood, changes in self-other perspectives are prominent as well.

Selman's Ideas on the Self and Perspective Taking

Robert Selman has considerably expanded our knowledge of the child's perception of self-other relationships. This expansion focuses on a developmental sequence of perspective taking. Selman (1976, 1980) believes that perspective taking moves through a series of five stages, ranging from three years of age through the adolescent years. As shown in Table 11.1, these stages span the egocentric viewpoint of the preschool child to the in-depth societal perspective-taking view of the adolescent. Selman (1980) has shown how these stages of perspective taking can be applied to four dimensions of individual and social development: concepts of individuals, concepts of friendships, concepts of peers, and concepts of parent-child relationships. These concepts have often

Table 11.1 Selman's Stages of Perspective Taking	
Social Role-Taking Stage	**Description**
Stage 0— Egocentric viewpoint (age range 3 to 6)	Child has a sense of differentiation of self and other but fails to distinguish between the social perspective (thoughts, feelings) of other and self. Child can label other's overt feelings but does not see the cause-and-effect relation of reasons to social actions.
Stage 1—Social-informational role taking (age range 6 to 8)	Child is aware that other has a social perspective based on other's own reasoning, which may or may not be similar to child's. However, child tends to focus on one perspective rather than coordinating viewpoints.
Stage 2—Self-reflective role taking (age range 8 to 10)	Child is conscious that each individual is aware of the other's perspective and that this awareness influences self and other's view of each other. Putting self in other's place is a way of judging other's intentions, purposes, and actions. Child can form a coordinated chain of perspectives, but cannot yet abstract from this process to the level of simultaneous mutuality.
Stage 3—Mutual role taking (age range 10 to 12)	Child realizes that both self and other can view each other mutually and simultaneously as subjects. Child can step outside the two-person dyad and view the interaction from a third-person perspective.
Stage 4—Social and conventional system role taking (age range 12 to 15)	Person realizes mutual perspective taking does not always lead to complete understanding. Social conventions are seen as necessary because they are understood by all members of the group (the generalized other), regardless of their position, role, or experience.

From Selman, R. L., "The development of social-cognitive understanding: A guide to educational and clinical practice" in T. Lickona, (Ed.), *Moral Development and Behavior: Theory, Research and Social Issues.* Copyright © 1976 Holt, Rinehart & Winston, Inc., New York. Reprinted by permission of Dr. Thomas Lickona.

been assessed by Selman through individual interviews with the child focusing on the following dilemma:

Eight-year-old Tom is trying to decide what to buy his best friend, Mike, for his birthday party. By chance, he meets Mike on the street and learns that Mike is extremely upset because his dog, Pepper, has been lost for two weeks. In fact, Mike is so upset he tells Tom, "I miss Pepper so much I never want to look at another dog again." Tom goes off, only to pass a store with a sale on puppies; only two are left and these soon will be gone. (Selman, 1980, p. 94)

The dilemma is whether to buy the puppy and how this will influence Mike psychologically.

To explore the issue of self-awareness, the interviewer now begins with a general question, such as, "Mike said he never wants to see another puppy again. Why did he say that?" Depending in part on the child's response, the interviewer subsequently chooses from a range of questions related to stages.

In addition to changing views of self and others in middle and late childhood, psychologists also have shown an interest in the elementary school child's self-esteem.

Self-Esteem

Many theorists and researchers use the labels self-concept and self-esteem interchangeably. For example, one definition explains self-esteem as the value children place on themselves and their behavior, which would be evaluated by finding out whether the children feel good or bad about themselves (McCandless & Evans, 1973). Other definitions of self-esteem embrace only the positive parts of self-concept, such as feeling proud of oneself or evaluating one's attributes highly (Wylie, 1974).

Stanley Coopersmith (1967) has developed a personality scale that attempts to measure boys' and girls' self-esteem. Like other measures of self-concept, Coopersmith's inventory (called the Self-Esteem Inventory, or SEI) asks the child to read a number of statements and to check whether each of these is "like me" or "unlike me." The statements include the extent to which the children worry about themselves, the degree to which they are proud of their school performances, how popular they are with peers, how happy they are, and so on.

In one investigation, the Self-Esteem Inventory was administered to a large group of elementary school boys (Coopersmith, 1967). In addition, the boys, their mothers, and the boys' teachers at school were interviewed about various matters relating to the social experiences and self-perceptions of the boys. The following parental attributes were linked with the development of high self-esteem in the boys:

1. Expression of affection
2. Concern about the youth's problems
3. Harmony in the home
4. Participation in friendly joint activities
5. Availability to give competent, organized help to the boys when they need it

6. Setting clear and fair rules
7. Abiding by these rules
8. Allowing the youth freedom within well-prescribed limits

Efforts to measure self-esteem and self-concept have been numerous, and a number of paper-and-pencil scales have been developed. However, as we see next, accurate assessment of self-concept is a very difficult task.

Measuring Self-Concept

While it is recognized that every child has a self-concept and that self-evaluation is an important part of personality, psychologists have had a difficult time trying to measure self-concept. One method that frequently has been used is the Piers-Harris Scale (Piers & Harris, 1964), which consists of 80 items designed to measure the child's overall self-concept. School psychologists often use the scale with boys and girls who have been referred to them for evaluation. By responding yes or no to such items as "I have good ideas," children reveal how they view themselves. The Piers-Harris Scale requires 15 to 20 minutes for completion and can be administered to groups as well as to individuals.

Children's self-perception often changes according to the situation, although self-concept measures like the Piers-Harris Scale are designed to measure a stable, consistent aspect of personality. Also, with self-reporting, it is difficult to determine whether children are telling about the way they really are or the way they want someone else to think they are. Even though the instructions on the Piers-Harris Scale and other measures of self-concept direct children to respond as they really are, there is no assurance that they will do so (Wylie, 1974).

A promising measure of self-concept has been developed by Susan Harter (1982). Her scale is called the **Perceived Competence Scale for Children.** Emphasis is placed on assessing the child's sense of competence across different domains rather than viewing perceived competence as a unitary concept. Three types of skills are assessed on separate subscales: cognitive (good at schoolwork; remember things easily); social (have a lot of friends; most kids like me); and physical (do well at sports; first chosen for games). A fourth subscale measures general self-worth (sure of myself; happy the way I am) independent of any particular skill domain. The importance of Harter's measure is that prior measures

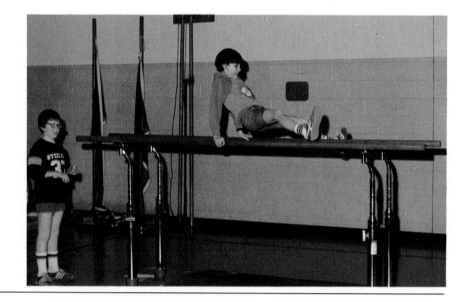

What categories does Harter's Perceived Competence Scale for Children assess?

of self-concept, such as the Piers-Harris, lump together the child's perceptions of his or her competencies in a variety of domains in an effort to come up with an overall measure of the child's self-concept. Harter's scale does an excellent job of separating the child's self-perceptions of his or her abilities in different skill areas; and when general self-worth is assessed, questions that focus on overall perceptions of the self are used rather than questions that are directed at specific skill domains.

Recently, Susan Harter and Robin Pike (1984) developed the Pictorial Scale of Perceived Competence and Social Acceptance for Young Children, a downward extension of the Perceived Competence Scale for Children. There are two versions of the measure, one for preschool children and the other for first- and second-grade children. Each version taps four domains: cognitive competence, physical competence, peer acceptance, and maternal acceptance (see Table 11.2). Analysis of preschool and early elementary school children's responses suggest that two factors are present: first, a general competence factor (physical and cognitive), and second, a general social acceptance factor (peer and maternal). The measure should not be viewed as a general self-concept scale but rather as a measure that evaluates perceived competence and social acceptance.

Some assessment experts believe that a combination of several methods should be used in measuring self-concept and other personality traits. In addition to self-

reporting, rating of a child's self-concept by others and careful observation of behavior in various settings could give a more complete, and hence, more accurate, picture of self-concept. Peers, teachers, parents, and even others who do not know the child well should be asked for their perceptions. Peers are particularly good at rating each other, so it may be helpful to listen carefully to what children have to say about each other.

When we discuss the self, we are talking about the child's personality in a very broad way. As seen in our discussion of Selman's view, there currently is a great deal of interest in understanding developmental sequences involved in the child's perception of self-other relationships. Another global aspect of the child's development and an area that also focuses on the child's personality as reflected in his or her ability to engage in the social world effectively is the domain of social competence.

Notice that rather than calling her scale a measure of self-concept or merely the self, Harter refers to her scale as an assessment of "perceived competence." Also note that one important domain of perceived competence is social competence. Indeed, in recent years, there has been an increased amount of interest in mapping out what social competence is.

Table 11.2   Pictorial Scale of Perceived Competence and Social Acceptance for Young Children—Items Grouped According to Subscale for Each Form

Subscale and Item No.	Preschool–Kindergarten	First–Second Grades
Cognitive competence		
1	Good at puzzles	Good at numbers
5	Gets stars on paper	Knows a lot in school
9	Knows names of colors	Can read alone
13	Good at counting	Can write words
17	Knows alphabet	Good at spelling
21	Knows first letter of name	Good at adding
Physical competence		
3	Good at swinging	Good at swinging
7*	Good at climbing	Good at climbing
11	Can tie shoes	Good at bouncing ball
15*	Good at skipping	Good at skipping
19*	Good at running	Good at running
23	Good at hopping	Good at jump-roping
Peer acceptance		
2*	Has lots of friends	Has lots of friends
6	Stays overnight at friends'	Others share their toys
10*	Has friends to play with	Has friends to play with
14*	Has friends on playground	Has friends on playground
18*	Gets asked to play with others	Gets asked to play with others
22	Eats dinner at friends' house	Others sit next to you
Maternal acceptance		
4	Mom smiles	Mom lets you eat at friends'
8*	Mom takes you places you like	Mom takes you places you like
12*	Mom cooks favorite foods	Mom cooks favorite foods
16*	Mom reads to you	Mom reads to you
20	Mom plays with you	Mom plays with you
24*	Mom talks to you	Mom talks to you

Note: Item number refers to position of the item in the order administered to the child. Asterisk designates items common to both forms.

From Harter, R. and S. Pike, "The pictorial scale of perceived competence and social acceptance for young children" in *Child Development*, pp. 1969, 1982, 1984. © by The Society for Research in Child Development. Reprinted by permission.

Social Competence

It is the goal of most parents to rear a child who becomes socially competent. The concept of social competence has presented problems for conceptualization and assessment, however. In this section, we follow the thinking of Everett Waters and Alan Sroufe (1983), first defining the socially competent child and then providing a portrayal of how social competence might be assessed more effectively.

What Is Social Competence? Waters and Sroufe (1983) define the socially competent child as "one who is able to make use of environmental resources to achieve a good developmental outcome" (p. 81). Resources in the environment are those things that can support or develop the ability to coordinate affect, cognition, and behavior in the service of short-term adaptation and long-term developmental progress. In infancy, adult social agents clearly are salient. In early childhood and beyond, play and peer relations may be very important. From early childhood on, the range of potential resources expands.

Resources within the individual are an important part of social competence as well. The possibilities range from specific skills and abilities to general constructs, such as self-esteem. Delay of gratification, ego resiliency (adaptability, flexibility), and ego control (self-control) are important strengths of the socially competent child. Need for achievement, or the motivation to do something well, is also an important dimension of the socially competent child, particularly in an achievement-oriented society such as the United States (McClelland, 1961). In addition, the entire class of constructs labeled self, self-esteem, self-concept, and so on denote resources within the child, not in terms of stable traits but more in terms of theories the child has about his or her actions and abilities. It is important to remember that, as with resources in the environment, resources within the child usually have to be referenced to a particular point in development (for example, dependency is probably a positive characteristic in infancy but is more closely tied to a lack of social competence by adolescence).

Assessment of Social Competence   In describing the important features of assessing social competence, Waters and Sroufe (1983) point out four considerations: (1) broadband versus narrow assessments; (2) real behavior versus laboratory tasks; (3) assessments emphasizing the coordination of affect, cognition, and behavior; and (4) taxing behavioral and integrative/adaptive capacity.

It is important to assess both the global and more fine-grained aspects of the child's social behavior. Waters and Sroufe (1983) argue that, at least initially, it would be wise to understand broadly what the child's social competence is like. For example, in studying toddler problem solving, the focus might be on enthusiasm, persistence, flexibility, and enjoyment in dealing with the problem rather than the part of the problem first addressed, the tool used first, or even the time required to solve the problem. In the attachment literature, researchers have often assessed the infant's tendency to stay close to its mother in terms of specific discrete behaviors. Often, counts of touching the mother, looking at her, and the like are selected for measurement. However, such measures tend to be more situation-specific than broad-based measures. An alternative approach is to select more broadly defined measures of proximity-seeking or contact-maintaining behaviors. Assessments of this nature usually do not involve frequency counts of behaviors but rather rating scales. Thus, in assessing attachment, Ainsworth, Sroufe, Waters, Main, and others have begun to use ratings of secure and insecure attachment rather than frequency counts of proximity seeking in their attempt to accurately capture the nature of social competence in infants. Keep in mind, however, that in our assessment of the child's development it is wise to consider both fine-grained, behavioral measures of the child and the more broadly based measures Waters and Sroufe recommend (e.g., Maccoby & Martin, 1983).

A second issue in assessment focuses on whether we should be assessing social competence through specific tasks in controlled laboratory contexts or designing more naturalistic and ecologically valid measures. As discussed in Chapter 1 in the description of methods, advantages and costs are associated with either choice. Developmental psychologists interested in assessing social competence are likely to find themselves going into and out of laboratory situations. However, Waters and Sroufe (1983) argue that, early in the development of assessment devices for measuring social competence, it is particularly important to conduct ecologically valid assessment in real-life circumstances. They reason that laboratory measures often evaluate a narrow dimension of social competence, whereas real-life, naturalistic assessments typically are more broadly based, which fits with their first assessment recommendation.

A third assessment issue in social competence focuses on the evaluation of how the child coordinates affect, cognition, and behavior. Waters and Sroufe believe that information about early social behavior (social attachment, problem solving, peer interaction, and self/behavior relationships) suggests that psychologists should be studying how affect, cognition, and behavior are coordinated. Assessing the coordination of these three dimensions rather than each dimension alone fits nicely with the belief that broad-based measures of social competence are needed. This also meshes with the belief that the affective world of the child is important, just as his or her cognitive and behavioral worlds are. Cognition and behavior are obviously important dimensions of the child's development, but in isolation, they may not effectively reflect social competence. Social competence clearly is linked to motivation and control, and in circumstances where these are relevant, affect often is involved and frequently arises from either success or failure. As we see next, inclusion of affect in the assessment of social competence is important when critical events or transactions occur in the child's world.

Waters and Sroufe (1983) also believe that assessment of social competence needs to include measures that plug into the child's integrative/adaptive capacity in dealing with critical events or transactions in his or her world. Even within the range of typical behaviors, there are circumstances that challenge or tax the child's integrative capacity: for example, temperature change, sustained face-to-face interaction, response to separation and union, exploration of new environments, responses to success and failure, and sustained social play.

In sum, while the construct of social competence presents problems in conceptualization and assessment, the work of Waters and Sroufe (1983) is an important step toward defining the concept, describing its development, and providing ideas about how it should be assessed.

Next we explore changes in the child's sex roles during the elementary school years.

Sex Roles

In the middle childhood years, two divergent trends in sex typing occur. Children increase their understanding of culturally defined expectations for males and females, and simultaneously, the behavior and attitude of boys increasingly reflect masculine sex typing. However, during the middle years of childhood, girls do not show an increased interest in feminine activities. Actually, many girls begin to show a stronger preference for masculine interests and activities, a finding that has appeared in research studies conducted from the 1920s to the present.

In one research study, the toy preferences of 750 children five to nine years old were assessed by evaluating their letters to Santa Claus (Richardson & Simpson, 1982). As shown in Table 11.3, while such requests for toys were sex typed, more girls than boys asked for cross-sex items. Boys and girls, though, do begin to show more flexibility in their understanding of sex-role stereotypes in the elementary school years, seeing that stereotypes are not absolute and that alternatives are feasible.

Huston (1983) calls attention to an additional developmental trend in sex typing. Interests, play activities, and social and occupational roles are sex typed earlier and in a more clearly defined way than are personality characteristics and social behaviors. Parents and other socialization agents also place more emphasis on sex-typed interests and activities than on personal-social sex differences.

So far in our discussion of sex roles, we have charted a number of developmental characteristics. As we see next, there is a great deal of interest in conceptualizing the nature of sex roles.

Table 11.3 Proportions of Males and Females Requesting Items in Each Category

	Male (%)	Female (%)
Classes of items requested by significantly more males:		
Vehicles	43.5	8.2
Sport	25.1	15.1
Spatial-temporal	24.5	15.6
Military toys	23.4	.8
Race cars	23.4	5.1
Doll (humanoid)	22.8	6.6
Real vehicles	15.3	9.7
Doll (male)	10.0	2.8
Outer space toys	7.5	.3
Depots	6.4	.5
Machines	4.5	.8
Classes of items requested by significantly more females:		
Doll (female)	.6	27.4
Doll (baby)	.6	23.0
Domestic	1.7	21.7
Educational-art	11.4	21.4
Clothes	1.9	18.9
Dollhouses	2.2	16.1
Clothing accessories	1.1	15.3
Doll accessories	5.0	12.5
Stuffed animals	1.9	9.7
Furnishings		5.4

From Richardson, J. G. and C. H. Simpson, "Children, Gender, and Social Structure: An Analysis of the Contents of Letters to Santa Claus" in *Child Development*, 53, 429–436, 1982. © 1982 by The Society for Research in Child Development. Reprinted by permission.

Masculinity, Femininity, and Androgyny

In the past, research on sex roles involved classifying children as being either masculine or feminine. In recent years, though, there has been a tremendous amount of interest in looking at children in terms of combinations of masculine and feminine characteristics. We look first at the masculinity-femininity tradition and subsequently at the more recently developed idea of androgyny.

Masculinity and Femininity For many years, it was believed that the well-adjusted child behaved in a sex-appropriate way; that is, a male child was supposed to be masculine and a female child was supposed to be feminine. A wide variety of characteristics have been classified as "masculine," and many others have been referred to as "feminine." Basically, these characteristics are those that are stereotypically masculine or feminine in a particular culture. Thus, in the United States, it has been masculine to be independent and aggressive, and it has been feminine to be dependent and unaggressive. It has been masculine to be oriented toward math and feminine to be interested in verbal skills. And it also has been masculine to become power-oriented and feminine to not be power-oriented.

Androgyny   By the mid-1970s, the landscape of sex roles had changed considerably. It had become obvious that increased numbers of females in our culture were unhappy with being labeled "feminine" and stigmatized with such adjectives as passive, dependent, and unassertive. And there were a number of males who likewise were unhappy with being labeled with such "masculine" characteristics as rugged, aggressive, and power-oriented. It seemed apparent to a number of laypeople and scientists that traditional concepts of "masculinity" and "femininity" no longer were as useful as they once were because the sex roles of society were changing so rapidly. The byword in sex/gender roles in the 1970s became **androgyny,** which refers to a combination of both masculine and feminine characteristics in the same individual. The androgynous child is referred to as an individual who has both positive features of masculinity and femininity, rather than only having strong masculine or strong feminine characteristics.

Among the measures that are used to assess androgyny are the Bem Sex-Role Inventory (called the BSRI) (Bem, 1974), the Personal Attributes Questionnaire (called the PAQ) (Spence, Helmreich, & Stapp, 1974), the masculinity and femininity scales of the Adjective Check List (called the ACL) (Heilbrun, 1976), the masculinity and femininity scales of the California Psychological Inventory (called the CPI) (Baucom, 1976), and the Personality Research Form ANDRO scale (called the PRF ANDRO) (Berzins, Wellings, & Wetter, 1978), as well as children's versions of the PAQ (called the CPAQ) (Hall & Halberstadt, 1980) and the BSRI (called the CSRI) (Trupin, 1979).

The core dimensions of these measures appear to be related to self-assertion and integration (Ford, 1986). For example, the masculinity items on the BSRI and the PRF ANDRO tend to be similar and reflect self-assertion. They include: acts as leader, has leadership qualities, dominant, willing to take a stand, willing to take risks, independent, forceful, competitive, strong personality,

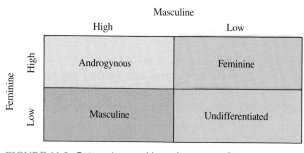

FIGURE 11.3   Categories used in androgyny scales.

and individualistic. The items for femininity on the BSRI and the PRF ANDRO also are similar and reflect integration: sympathetic, eager to soothe hurt feelings, sensitive to the needs of others, tender, compassionate, affectionate, gentle, warm, and understanding.

Thus, it is important to recognize that new items and new characteristics have not been developed to characterize the individual with an androgynous orientation. Rather, the androgynous child is simply either a male or a female who has a high degree of both masculine and feminine characteristics. That is, there is no third set of items on the sex-role measures that tap androgyny—categorizing the child as androgynous comes from his or her responses that are masculine as well as feminine. On most androgyny scales, a fourth category also is possible. The child who says that neither the masculine nor the feminine characteristics portray him or her is often referred to as **undifferentiated.** Figure 11.3 shows the four categories used on most androgyny scales—masculine, feminine, androgynous, and undifferentiated, as well as the kind of responses to the items required to be placed in one of the categories.

Do androgynous children just have a different sex-role classification and orientation, or are they also more competent than other children?

Masculinity, Femininity, Androgyny, and Competence
Which children are the most competent—those who are masculine, feminine, or androgynous? The answer to this question is difficult for several reasons. There has been a failure to untangle the multiple meanings of sex/gender roles and masculinity/femininity and androgyny. Second, there has not been a clear specification of why and when masculinity, femininity, and androgyny should be linked

with greater personal and social competence. Far too many research studies on androgyny have lacked any theoretical foundation (Worrell, 1978). What has happened in the androgyny area is that researchers have developed a rash of new scales and related androgyny to anything and everything! The anything and everything includes variables as diverse as self-esteem, achievement, health, sexual maturity, hypnotic suggestibility, fantasy content, personal space, menstrual distress, appreciation of sexual humor, arousal, and the list goes on.

An important task for masculinity/femininity and androgyny research is the specification of dimensions involved. Some researchers (e.g., Block, 1973; Ford, 1986) argue that, when we limit our discussion of androgyny to the dimensions of self-assertion and integration, we have gone further in specifying the nature of the androgyny concept than frequently has been the case in research on the topic. As Jeanne Block (1973) has argued, the competent male should temper his self-assertion with mutuality in social encounters, and the competent female should modify her integrative tendencies with a stronger sense of self-assertion.

However, it is important to recognize that competence criteria are often governed by more than just self-assertion and integration. The idea that androgynous individuals should be better at everything is very simplistic. For example, androgyny likely is not closely linked with factors that are heavily cognitive or biological in nature, such as intelligence, physical health, and creativity. These factors are likely dependent on other powerful forces, such as genetic potential, quality of schooling, nutrition, life stress, and many other variables. Even outcomes focusing on social and personality development are likely to be related to many factors unrelated to self-assertive and integrative qualities of the individual. In particular, this seems to occur under two types of conditions: First, when distinct gender-related criteria (such as attitudes toward women, sexual orientation, vocational choice) are used as outcome variables (Helmreich, Spence, & Holahan, 1979; Storms, 1980; Wolfe & Betz, 1981; Zeldow, 1976), and second, when the outcome variables involve attitudes, perceptions, or beliefs (such as expectancies or attributions) rather than

performance, adjustment, or development (Baucom & Danker-Brown, 1979; Bem, 1977; Crimmings, 1978; Cummings, 1979; Pritscher, 1980).

Further refinement of when androgyny may or may not be an advantageous sex-role makeup involves consideration of the relevant contexts in a culture that promote and value self-assertive and integrative behaviors. Some behaviors that are adaptive in one setting may not be adaptive in another setting. For example, in achievement-oriented settings, self-assertion usually is promoted and valued. And for that matter, in our entire American culture, self-assertion tends to be valued more than integration. Thus, along this line of thinking, such self-assertive qualities as initiative and competitiveness are adaptive, but in other contexts, they may not be as adaptive. For example, most religious contexts emphasize fellowship and interdependence rather than self-reliance or self-interest. In such contexts, androgynous individuals may not be judged as competent as feminine or integratively oriented individuals.

The implications of our discussion on androgyny suggest that androgynous children will not be more competent than other children in all circumstances. If the criteria for competence primarily involve self-assertion *and* integration, then we would expect the androgynous child to fare better than children of other sex-role makeups. For criteria that primarily involve self-assertion, we would anticipate both masculine and androgynous children to perform effectively. For criteria focusing on integration, we would expect feminine and androgynous children to do well. And for criteria unrelated to self-assertion and integration, we would anticipate that androgynous children would not perform more competently than nonandrogynous children.

Yet another important point to be made about the androgyny research literature is that the self-assertive dimension has been valued as more important than the integrative dimension. Thus, just as our culture has been biased toward the masculine, self-assertive dimension, so have the criteria used to assess competence been oriented in this direction as well. For example, an analysis of the criteria used to assess social competence when it is linked to androgyny suggests that self-assertive dimensions outnumber integrative dimensions by about a two-to-one margin (Ford, 1986). A disturbing outcome

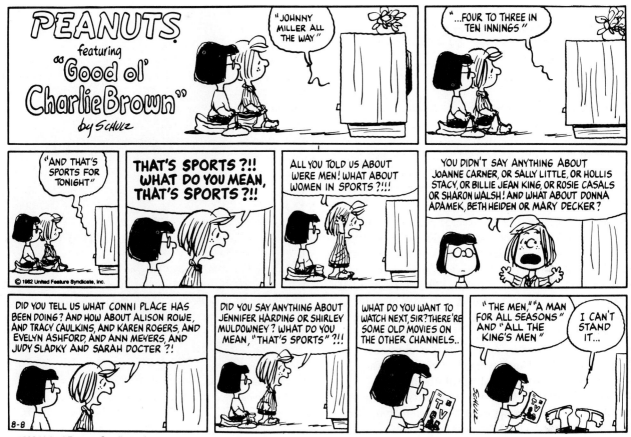

© 1982 United Feature Syndicate, Inc.

of this tendency is that overgeneralizations about the desirability of masculine, self-assertive characteristics are sometimes made, along with comments about the undesirability of feminine or integrative characteristics when social competence is at issue (e.g., Antill & Cunningham, 1979; Deutsch & Gilbert, 1976; Hansson, O'Conner, Jones, & Mihelich, 1980; Jones, Chernovetz, & Hansson, 1978; Kelly & Worrell, 1977; Kenworthy, 1979; Olds & Shaver, 1980; Silvern & Ryan, 1979; Williams, 1979).

Sex-Role Stereotypes and Sex Differences

How do sex-role stereotypes work? And what are some actual sex differences in children? In particular, the latter question has been the focus of considerable research among child developmentalists.

Sex-Role Stereotypes

Sex-role stereotypes are broad categories that reflect our impressions about people, events, and ourselves. The world is extremely complex; every day, we are confronted with thousands of different stimuli. The use of stereotypes is one way we simplify this complexity. If we simply assign a label (e.g., the quality of "softness" in women) to someone, we then have much less to consider when we think about the person. However, once these labels have been assigned, we find it remarkably difficult to abandon them, even in the face of contradictory evidence. Do you have a repertory of sex-role stereotypes? Table 11.4 provides a brief exercise in understanding sex-role behavior. Record your answers on a separate sheet of paper so that you can check them later when they are discussed.

Table 11.4   Knowing the Sexes

How well do you know the sexes? For each of the adjectives listed below, indicate whether you think it best describes women or men—or neither—in our society. Be honest with yourself, and follow your first impulse in responding.

a. Verbal	g. Mathematical
b. Sensitive	h. Suggestible
c. Active	i. Analytic
d. Competitive	j. Social
e. Compliant	k. Aggressive
f. Dominant	

After recording your answers, continue reading this chapter for an interpretation of your responses.

Many stereotypes are so general that they are extremely ambiguous. Take, for example, the stereotypes "masculine" and "feminine." Very diverse behaviors may be called up to support the stereotype, such as scoring a touchdown or growing facial hair. The stereotype, of course, may also be modified in the face of cultural change; whereas at one time muscular development might be thought masculine, at another time masculinity may be typified by a lithe, slender physique. The behaviors popularly agreed upon as reflecting the stereotype may fluctuate according to subculture.

Walter Mischel (1970) comments that, even though the behaviors that are supposed to fit the stereotype often do not, the label itself may have significant consequences for the individual. Labeling a person "homosexual," "queer," or "sissy" can produce dire social consequences in terms of status and acceptance in groups, even when the person so labeled is not a homosexual, queer, or sissy. Regardless of their accuracy, stereotypes can cause tremendous emotional upheaval in an individual and undermine the individual's opinions about himself or herself and his or her status.

So far, we've been talking about stereotypes—but what about the real sex differences?

Sex Differences   How well did you do with the adjectives in Table 11.4? According to Eleanor Maccoby and Carol Jacklin (1974), here are the facts: females are more verbal (a); males are more mathematical (g) and aggressive (k); all the others are really characteristic of neither.

What is the nature of boys' superiority in math skills?

With regard to verbal ability, girls tend to understand and produce language more competently than boys do. Girls are superior to boys in higher-order verbal tasks, such as making analogies, understanding difficult written material, and writing creatively, as well as on lower-order verbal tasks, such as spelling. Maccoby and Jacklin speculated that girls probably get an early start on boys in the use of language, but studies indicate that differences in the verbal abilities of boys and girls are not consistent until about the age of 11. A similar developmental trend can be seen for mathematical skills, but this time in favor of boys. Boys' superiority in math skills does not usually appear until the age of 12 or 13 and does not seem to be entirely influenced by the fact that boys take more math courses. Likewise, male superiority on visual-spatial tasks does not consistently appear until adolescence. However, sex differences in aggression appear early, by the age of two or three, and continue through

**"Don't be too rough with Dolly! Remember——
she's just a little GIRL!"**

Reprinted with special permission of King Features Syndicate, Inc.

adolescence. The differences are not confined to physical aggression—boys also show more verbal aggression as well as more fantasy aggression (imagining harm to someone or to some object rather than actually performing an aggressive act).

Two of the myths about the sexes merit further examination: that girls are more social than boys and that girls are more suggestible than boys. The measure of sociability was based upon diverse aspects of social interaction, which included interest in social events (e.g., faces and voices), responsiveness to social reward, dependence on caregivers, time spent with playmates, and understanding of the emotional needs of others. There simply was no evidence to suggest that girls engaged in these practices more than boys did. In some cases, the reverse was observed; for example, boys spent more time with playmates than girls did. Suggestibility was indexed by children's spontaneous imitation of models, susceptibility to persuasive communication, and social conformity to group norms. There were no consistent sex differences in a large number of studies measuring these characteristics.

Even though research tells us that girls are not more social and not more suggestible than boys, do you believe it? If you do not, you have a firsthand example of how difficult it is to discard stereotypes.

Not everyone agrees with all of the conclusions of Maccoby and Jacklin's widely quoted work on sex differences. Jeanne Block (1976) acknowledges that Maccoby and Jacklin have made an important contribution to information about sex roles, but she also believes that some of their conclusions, and some of the data on which the conclusions are based, are shakier than Maccoby and Jacklin lead readers to believe. She argues that Maccoby and Jacklin did not differentiate between those studies that were methodologically sound and those that were not. She further criticizes the decisions they made about what kinds of studies should go into a particular category. For example, Maccoby and Jacklin lumped together many measures in their assessment of parental pressure on achievement motivation, including the following: amount of praise or criticism for intellectual performance, parental standards for intellectual performance as expressed on a questionnaire item, expectations of household help from youth, the ages at which parents feel it is appropriate to teach a boy or girl more mature behaviors, number of anxious intrusions in the youth's task performance, and pressure for success on memory tasks. While many of the measures are clearly linked with the achievement dimension, others may be more peripheral.

Although Block does commend Maccoby and Jacklin for their completion of the long, difficult task of organizing a sprawling, unruly body of information, she also suggests that such data are open to error and reasonable argument at virtually every step of the analysis. In other words, anyone attempting to impose structure and meaning on some 1,600 disparate studies of sex roles is bound to make a few questionable decisions. For those of you interested in reading more about sex differences in adolescence, both Maccoby and Jacklin's book and Block's critique are highly recommended.

Another critic of Maccoby and Jacklin (Tieger, 1980) argues that sex differences in aggression are not biologically based but are instead learned. Tieger argues that consistent sex differences do not emerge until about the age of six and that there are ample conditions in the first six years of the child's life for aggression to be learned.

In a rejoinder to Tieger, Maccoby and Jacklin (1980) reviewed their data and conducted some further analyses. The reassessment supported their earlier claim that greater aggression in boys occurs well before the age of six, is present in studies of nonhuman male primates, and appears in cross-cultural studies of children.

Now that we have studied some general ideas about sex-role stereotypes and sex differences, let's focus on one characteristic more intensely, one that has been given considerable attention recently—achievement.

Achievement   Achievement was one area where Block (1976) questioned the conclusions of the Maccoby and Jacklin report. And achievement also is an area of children's development that has generated considerable controversy in our society as well as among researchers. Let's explore further the issue of whether boys are more achievement oriented than girls.

Diana Baumrind (1972) has distinguished between instrumental competence and incompetence. Boys, she says, are trained to become instrumentally competent, while girls learn how to become instrumentally incompetent. By instrumental competence, Baumrind means behavior that is socially responsible and purposive. Instrumental incompetence is more aimless behavior.

The following evidence is offered by Baumrind (1972) in support of her argument: (1) few women obtain jobs in science, and of those who do, few achieve high positions; (2) being a female is devalued by society; (3) being independent and achieving intellectual status causes the female to lose her "femininity" in society's eyes—both men and women devalue such behaviors in women; (4) parents usually have lower achievement aspirations for girls than boys (for example, parents expect their boys to become doctors and their girls to become nurses); and (5) girls and women are more oriented toward expressive behavior than boys and men are.

There is reason to believe that differences in the achievement orientations of adolescent boys and girls are learned—not innately determined by sex. Aletha Stein and Margaret Bailey (1973) have listed several parental characteristics or attributes that are associated with the development of achievement orientation in girls. For example, achievement orientation can be encouraged

through the modeling of a mother who has a career. In some instances, particularly when the mother assumes a traditional female role, the social interaction of the father takes on greater importance. Stein and Bailey also point out that socialization practices fostering so-called femininity in girls are often counter to those practices producing achievement orientation. Moderate parental permissiveness, coupled with attempts to accelerate achievement, is related to achievement orientation in girls. This kind of parenting is not compatible with what is usually prescribed for rearing a young woman.

In their review of the achievement orientation of females, Stein and Bailey (1973) concluded that females have lower expectancies for success across many different tasks than males do, lower levels of aspiration, more anxiety about failure, less willingness to risk failure, and more feelings of personal responsibility when failure occurs. It is important that these differences are more pronounced during the adolescent years than during the middle or early childhood years. In one set of investigations, late-adolescent females and males attributed male success to ability and female success to effort and luck (Feldman-Summers & Kiesler, 1974; Frieze, 1975).

Aletha Huston-Stein and Ann Higgens-Trenk (1978) have discussed the developmental precursors of sex differences in achievement orientation. Women who as adults are career and achievement oriented usually showed the signs of this orientation early in their childhood years. Adult women who are attracted to traditionally feminine activities were likely attracted to such activities during middle childhood and adolescence (Crandall & Battle, 1970; Kagan & Moss, 1962). Achievement behavior was more consistent over the childhood, adolescent, and young adult years than any other personality attribute studied in these longitudinal investigations. Interest in "masculine" play activities in childhood (Crandall & Battle, 1970) and in "masculine" subject matter (Sears & Barbee, 1975) is linked with achievement orientation in females during adolescence and young adulthood. In sum, childhood socialization experiences seem to be critical in influencing the achievement orientation of females during adolescence and even into young adulthood. Focus on Child Development 11.2 examines an additional reason why girls might be less achievement oriented than boys.

FOCUS ON CHILD DEVELOPMENT 11.2

BRIGHT GIRLS, LEARNED HELPLESSNESS, AND EXPECTATIONS

A state of **learned helplessness** develops when a child believes that the rewards she or he receives are beyond personal control (Seligman, 1975). Two major systems of learned helplessness are a lack of motivation and negative affect. For example, if the child in a failure situation sees his or her behavior as irrelevant to the outcome, the child is displaying learned helplessness. Such perceptions lead to attributions that are seen as incontrollable or unchangeable, such as lack of ability, difficulty of the task, or presumably fixed attitudes of other people. In addition, attributions of failure to these factors are often linked with deterioration of performance in the face of failure. Individuals who attribute their failure to controllable or changeable factors, such as effort or luck, are more likely to show improvement in their performance (Dweck, 1975; Dweck & Reppucci, 1973; Weiner, 1974).

A number of investigations of achievement behavior suggest that girls are more likely to attribute failure to uncontrollable factors, like lack of ability, than boys (Dweck & Reppucci, 1973); to display disrupted performance or decreased effort under the pressure of impending failure or evaluation (Dweck & Gilliard, 1975); and to avoid situations in which failure is likely (Crandall & Rabson, 1960).

These sex differences in the effects of failure feedback on achievement behavior generally are attributed to girls' greater dependency on external social evaluation. However, some investigators believe that different evaluations of boys and girls by adults and peers may influence such sex differences. For example, Dweck and Bush (1976) found that, when failure feedback for girls came from adults, little change in the girls' achievement behavior resulted; but when the feedback came from peers, the girls' achievement behavior increased substantially.

There does seem to be evidence that girls form lower expectancies for success than their past performance warrants (Dweck & Eliot, 1983). Girls, even when they outperform boys on a task, report that they do not feel they did as well when queried later. And it is often the *brightest* girls who underestimate their skills the most. For example, in one investigation, the highest-achieving girls actually had lower

Expectations of High-, Average-, and Low-Achieving Boys and Girls

Group	Initial Expectation		
	Grade 1	Grade 3	Total
Girls			
High achievers	6.2	2.6	4.4
Average achievers	6.6	7.8	7.2
Low achievers	6.6	8.2	7.4
Boys			
High achievers	7.6	6.6	7.1
Average achievers	8.8	6.4	7.6
Low achievers	4.6	4.8	4.7

From Stipek, J. D. and J. M. Hoffman, "Children's achievement-related expectancies as a function of academic performance histories and sex" in *Journal of Educational Psychology, 72,* 861–865, 1980. Copyright © 1980 by American Psychological Association. Reprinted by permission of the author.

expectancies for success than the average- or low-achieving girls (Stipek & Hoffman, 1980). For boys, the expected results were obtained; that is, higher-achieving boys generated higher expectancies of success (see the table above).

In research on the gifted at Johns Hopkins University (Fox, Brody, & Tobin, 1979), while many female junior high school students identified through a talent search for mathematically precocious youth did aspire to scientific and medical careers, only 46 percent of these girls aspired to having a full-time career (compared to 98 percent of the boys in the study). Gifted girls, perceiving a conflict between family and career, may decide against an occupation that requires an extensive personal commitment, precisely those careers that offer the highest status and salary. This decision to drop out of education or a career to marry and raise a family has been found to be detrimental to career advancement and income, with such females rarely ever catching up with their male counterparts (Card, Steele, & Abeles, 1980).

(continued on following page)

FOCUS ON CHILD DEVELOPMENT 11.2

To counter such developmental sequences in females, several career education programs have been drafted and, in some instances, their effectiveness evaluated. An intervention program with gifted females was developed by Barbara Kerr (1983). The participants were 23 gifted girls and 25 gifted boys, all in the 11th grade, who voluntarily attended the Guidance Laboratory at the University of Nebraska. They initially were given career interest tests and then were allowed to select any part of the university to visit, such as the library or computer center, and were accompanied there by a university student host. Next, they were asked to select and attend a university class related to their career interest area, and arrangements were made for them to sit in on the class. After class visitation, the students lunched with the guidance center staff and university faculty members, discussing such matters as the morning's activities, school activities, and future career plans.

In the afternoon, the students participated in individual and group counseling sessions. In the individual sessions, the counselors interpreted test results and discussed career interests. Counselors then helped the talented students set tentative career goals. The counselor attempted to raise the student's career aspirations if such aspirations (1) were clearly below the student's abilities as evidenced by grade point average and achievement test scores; (2) were a sex-role stereotyped response by a female that was based on a lack of awareness; and (3) were related to a low-paying, low-status occupation. The counseling session ended with the discussion and completion of three forms: (1) "Personal Map of the Future," a goal-setting exercise; (2) "Suggestions for Parents," in which participants listed three ways in which parents could help them to achieve their career goals; and (3) "Suggestions to a Significant Teacher or Counselor," an exercise similar to the "Suggestions for Parents."

After individual counseling, all students participated in a life-planning group. In this exercise, the talented students were led on a guided fantasy into a "Perfect Future Day." The students shared fantasies with each other and then were moved toward a discussion of possible barriers that might impede their fantasies. The counselors focused on both internal and

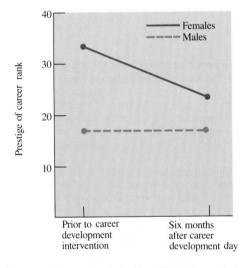

Prestigiousness of careers selected by gifted 11th grade boys and girls before and six months after an intensive, day-long career orientation at a university. (The higher the number, the lower the prestige of the occupation. For example, physician ranks 2, lawyer ranks 11, teacher ranks 27.5, store clerk ranks 70, and nightclub singer ranks 74.)

external constraints to career success. Sex-role stereotypes were discussed, and high aspirations were encouraged. Counselors then distributed a "Fact Sheet for Gifted Women and Men" that briefly described the importance of high aspirations and the possibilities of combining both a family and a career. The afternoon ended with an evaluation of the workshop and an invitation to come to the guidance facility in the future and to continue to use its resources.

Approximately six months after the one-day career development orientation, the gifted students responded to the question, "What occupation have you most recently considered?" The response to this question was compared to the gifted student's earlier response to his or her main career interest, assessed prior to the daylong career orientation. As shown in the figure above, the results suggested that the girls

What can we do to encourage career development in gifted girls?

increased their choices of prestigious careers over the six-month period, while the boys did not. It is not surprising that the prestige of the boys' aspirations did not change because their aspirations initially were very high. While other experiences in the six months besides the intensive career guidance seminar may account for the increase in choices of prestigious careers among the girls, it seems likely that the daylong program is at least to some degree responsible. Still, it is important to be cautious about the long-term benefits of such programs, because as has been shown in some studies (e.g., Fox, 1976), there is a tendency for such effects to fade when intervention is discontinued.

It would seem from the discussion so far that it might be possible to conclude that females are less achievement oriented and less competent than males in our society. Yet, this conclusion is not justified. In our earlier discussion of androgyny and sex roles, social competence was described in terms of many different dimensions. In particular, two dimensions believed to be particularly important in interpreting competence are self-assertion and integration (Ford, 1986). In our culture, self-assertion has been emphasized to a greater degree than integration. And measures of social competence have included far more self-assertive than integrative items. The conclusions about lower achievement and social competence too often are made in terms of self-assertive dimensions. In particular, achievement and competence have been described frequently in terms of occupational success. It may be more instructive to think of achievement and competence in terms of success in many different roles, not just the occupational role. Females and males quite clearly have been socialized into different roles—males often showing a stronger motivation for self-assertive roles, while females reveal a stronger motivation for integrative roles. Females also seem to show a stronger interest in balancing multiple roles than males do (e.g., Fassinger, 1985). Thus, it is inaccurate to conclude that females are less achievement and competence oriented than males are—it depends on the domain of achievement and competence being evaluated and the cultural proscriptions for success.

Now that we have studied a number of ideas about children's sex roles, we focus on children's moral development. In our discussion, we will see that, just as self-other orientations are important in understanding the self, social competence, and sex roles, so do they also represent key aspects of children's moral development.

Moral Development

Remember from Chapter 8 our description of Piaget's stage view of moral development. He believes that younger children are characterized by moral realism but that by 10 years of age have moved into a higher stage called moral autonomy. According to Piaget, older elementary school children consider the intentions of a person, believe that rules are subject to change, and are aware that punishment does not always follow a deviation. As we see next, a second major cognitive perspective on moral development has been developed by Lawrence Kohlberg.

Kohlberg's Stages of Moral Development

The most provocative view of moral development to come along in recent years was crafted by Lawrence Kohlberg (1958, 1976). Kohlberg believes that moral development is primarily based on moral reasoning and unfolds in a stagelike manner. Kohlberg arrived at this view after some 20 years of using a unique procedure in interviewing children, adolescents, and adults: In an interview, the individual is presented with a series of stories in which characters face moral dilemmas. The following is one of the more popular Kohlberg dilemmas (Kohlberg, 1969):

> In Europe, a woman was near death from a special kind of cancer. There was one drug that the doctors thought might save her. It was a form of radium that a druggist in the same town had recently discovered. The drug was expensive to make, but the druggist was charging 10 times what the drug cost him to make. He paid $200 for the radium and charged $2,000 for a small dose of the drug. The sick woman's husband, Heinz, went to everyone he knew to borrow the money, but he could only get together $1,000, which is half of what it cost. He told the druggist that his wife was dying and asked him to sell it cheaper or let him pay later. But the druggist said, "No, I discovered the drug, and I am going to make money from it." So Heinz got desperate and broke into the man's store to steal the drug for his wife. (p. 379)

The interviewee is then asked a series of questions about each dilemma. For the Heinz dilemma, Kohlberg asks such questions as: Should Heinz have done that? Was it actually wrong or right? Why? Is it a husband's duty to steal the drug for his wife if he can get it no other way? Would a good husband do it? Did the druggist have the right to charge that much when there was no law actually setting a limit on the price? Why?

Based on the types of reasons individuals have given to this and other moral dilemmas, Kohlberg arrived at

Lawrence Kohlberg, shown above, has advanced our knowledge of the role cognition plays in social development.

three levels of moral development, each of which is characterized by two stages:

1. **Preconventional level** At this low level, the child shows no internalization of moral values—his or her moral thinking is based on the punishments (stage 1) and rewards (stage 2) he or she experiences in the environment.
2. **Conventional level** At this level of morality, the child's internalization of moral values is intermediate. He or she abides by certain standards of other people, such as parents (stage 3) or the rules of society (stage 4).
3. **Postconventional level** At the highest level, morality is completely internalized and not based on the standards of others. The individual recognizes alternative moral courses, explores the options, and then develops a moral code that is his or hers. The code may be among the principles generally accepted by the community (stage 5) or it may be more individualized (stage 6).

Table 11.5	Examples of Kohlberg's Six Stages of Moral Development	
Stage	**Pro**	**Con**
1	He should steal the drug. It is not really bad to take it. It is not like he did not ask to pay for it first. The drug he would take is only worth $200; he is not really taking a $2,000 drug.	He should not steal the drug; it is a big crime. He did not get permission; he used force and broke in and entered. He did a lot of damage, stealing a very expensive drug and breaking up the store, too.
2	It is all right to steal the drug because she needs it and he wants her to live. It is not that he wants to steal, but it is the way he has to use to get the drug to save her.	He should not steal it. The druggist is not wrong or bad, he just wants to make a profit. That is what you are in business for, to make money.
3	He should steal the drug. He was only doing something that was natural for a good husband to do. You cannot blame him for doing something out of love for his wife; you would blame him if he did not love his wife enough to save her.	He should not steal. If his wife dies, he cannot be blamed. It is not because he is heartless or that he does not love her enough to do everything that he legally can. The druggist is the selfish or heartless one.
4	You should steal it. If you did nothing, you would be letting your wife die; it is your responsibility if she dies. You have to take it with the idea of paying the druggist.	It is a natural thing for Heinz to want to save his wife, but it is still always wrong to steal. He still knows he is stealing and taking a valuable drug from the man who made it.
5	The law was not set up for these circumstances. Taking the drug in this situation is not really right, but it is justified to do it.	You cannot completely blame someone for stealing, but extreme circumstances do not really justify taking the law in your own hands. You cannot have everyone stealing whenever they get desperate. The end may be good, but the ends do not justify the means.
6	This is a situation which forces him to choose between stealing and letting his wife die. In a situation where the choice must be made, it is morally right to steal. He has to act in terms of the principle of preserving and respecting life.	Heinz is faced with the decision of whether to consider the other people who need the drug just as badly as his wife. Heinz ought to act not according to his particular feelings toward his wife, but considering the value of all the lives involved.

From Kohlberg, Lawrence, "Stage and Sequences: The Cognitive Developmental Approach to Socialization" in *Handbook of Socialization Theory and Research*, David A. Goslin, (Ed.). © 1969 Houghton Mifflin Company, Boston. Reprinted by permission of the editor.

For an individual at the postconventional level, the rules of the society have to mesh with underlying moral principles. In cases where the rules of the society come into conflict with the individual's principles, the individual will follow his or her own principles rather than the conventions of the society. Some specific responses to the Heinz and the druggist dilemma are presented in Table 11.5, which should provide you with a better sense of moral reasoning at the six stages in Kohlberg's theory.

Now that we have briefly reviewed Kohlberg's theory, let's turn to research on the topic of moral stages.

Research on Kohlberg's Stages and Influences on the Stages

What has Kohlberg's research revealed about his theoretical account of moral development? What are the main influences that move children through the stages of moral development? Let's explore these questions now.

The Kohlberg Research In his original work, Kohlberg (1958) found that, as the age of the child increased, his or her moral judgments become more advanced. Kohlberg (1969) also reported that age changes in children's responses to moral judgment items have been found in most industrialized Western countries, such as the United States, France, and Great Britain. And these changes occur regardless of the child's sex or social class. The stages are also significantly related to intelligence (Kohlberg, 1969). Kohlberg (1958) also found support for his belief that social participation in groups is one way to advance the moral judgment of children.

While Kohlberg's original research was conducted in 1958, he subsequently charted moral development in a longitudinal manner (Colby, Kohlberg, Gibbs, & Lieberman, 1980). This 20-year longitudinal study charted moral development from late childhood through the early

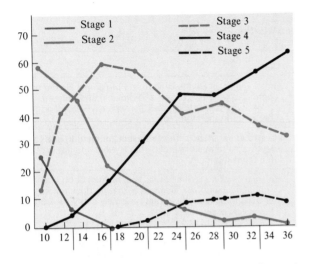

FIGURE 11.4   Mean percentage of each type (stage) of reasoning for each age group.

adulthood years. The mean percentage of individuals reasoning at each of Kohlberg's stages at a given age is shown in Figure 11.4.

The data show a clear relation between age and moral judgment. Over the 20-year period, the use of stages 1 and 2 decreased. Stage 4, which did not appear at all in the moral reasoning of the 10-year-olds, was reflected in 62 percent of the moral thinking of the 36-year-olds. Stage 5 did not appear until the age of 20 or 22 and never characterized more than about 10 percent of the individuals interviewed. Thus, just as formal operational thought does not always emerge in adolescence, neither do the higher stages of Kohlberg's theory of moral development. Reasoning about moral dilemmas does seem to change in adulthood—adults in their 30s reason at more advanced levels than adolescents or children.

Cognitive Development   Kohlberg believes that the child's moral orientation unfolds as a consequence of cognitive development. As you will recall, cognitive development is dependent upon the interaction of genetic endowment and social experiences. The child passes through the six stages in an invariant sequence, from less to more advanced. The child acts constructively on the world as he or she proceeds from one stage to the next, rather than passively accepting a cultural norm of morality.

Modeling and Cognitive Conflict   Several investigators have attempted to advance an individual's level of moral development by providing arguments that reflect moral thinking one stage above the individual's established level. These studies are based on the cognitive developmental concepts of equilibrium and conflict. By finding the correct environmental match slightly beyond the child's cognitive level, a disequilibrium is created that motivates the child to restructure his or her moral thought. The resolution of the disequilibrium and conflict should be toward increased competence, but the data are mixed on this question. In one of the pioneer studies on this topic, Eliot Turiel (1966) discovered that children preferred a response one stage above their current level over a response two stages above it. However, they actually chose a response one stage below their level more often than a response one stage above it. Apparently, the children were motivated more by security needs than by the need to reorganize thought to a higher level. Other studies indicate that children do prefer a more advanced stage over a less advanced stage (e.g., Rest, Turiel, & Kohlberg, 1969).

Since the early studies of stage modeling, a number of investigations have attempted to more precisely determine the effectiveness of various forms of stage modeling (Lapsley & Quintana, in press). The upshot of these studies is that virtually any plus-stage discussion format, for any length of time, seems to promote more advanced moral reasoning. For example, in one investigation, exposure to plus-two stage reasoning (arguments two stages above the child's current stage of moral thought) was just as effective in advancing moral thought as plus-one stage reasoning (Walker, 1982). Exposure to plus-two stage reasoning did not produce more plus-two stage reasoning but rather, like exposure to plus-one stage reasoning, increased the likelihood that the child would reason one stage above his or her current stage. Other research has found that exposure to reasoning only one third of a stage higher than the individual's current level of moral thought will advance moral thought (Berkowitz & Gibbs, 1983). In sum, current research on modeling and cognitive conflict reveals that moral thought can be advanced to a higher level through exposure to models or discussion that is more advanced than the child's.

As we see next, there also is considerable interest in the role of peers in advancing moral judgments.

Peer Relations and Role/Perspective-Taking Opportunities   Kohlberg believes that peer interaction is a critical part of the social stimulation that challenges children to change their moral orientations. Whereas adults characteristically impose rules and regulations on children, the mutual give-and-take in peer interaction provides the child with an opportunity to take the role of another person and to generate rules democratically. Kohlberg stresses that role-taking opportunities can, in principle, be engendered by any peer group encounter. While Kohlberg believes that such role-taking opportunities are ideal for moral development, he also believes that certain types of parent-child experiences can induce children to think at more advanced levels of moral thinking. In particular, parents who allow or encourage conversation about value-laden issues promote more advanced moral thought in their children. Unfortunately, many parents do not systematically provide their children or adolescents with such role-taking opportunities.

More information about the importance of peer relations, particularly the nature of peer discussion, is presented in Focus on Child Development 11.3.

So far we have covered a number of ideas about Kohlberg's theory and research. But as we see next, Kohlberg's provocative theory has its share of critics.

Critics of Kohlberg

Kohlberg's theory has not gone unchallenged. Among the criticisms are those involving the link between moral thought, moral behavior, and moral feeling; the quality of the research; sex differences and the care perspective; and societal contributions. We consider each of these criticisms in turn.

Kohlberg and Cognitive Primacy   Moral reasons can always be a shelter for immoral behavior. That is, some critics believe that Kohlberg has placed too much emphasis on moral thought and not paid enough attention to what children morally do or morally feel (Gibbs & Schnell, 1985). No one wants a nation of individuals who can reason at stages 5 and 6 of Kohlberg's model but who are liars, cheaters, and stealers lacking empathy.

Thus, the critics stress that Kohlberg's view is too cognitive and too cold. Elizabeth Simpson (1976) captured this point nicely:

> Reasons can be a shelter, as we all know, especially when they are developed after the fact and are applied to our own behavior or to that of someone in whom we have an ego investment. In any case, reasons are inseparable from the personality of the reasoner, whether they apply to his own behavior or that of others. They are grounded not in the situation in which decisions are made, but in the reasoner's psychic definition of past experience, and that psychic definition frequently crosses all boundaries of rationality. Passionate irrationality in the name of impassioned reason occurs in the market, the classroom, and in science, as well as elsewhere, and often unconsciously. (pp. 162–163)

Quality of the Research   James Rest (1976, 1977, 1983) believes that more attention should be paid to the way in which moral judgment is assessed. Rest (1976) points out that alternative methods should be used to collect information about moral thinking rather than relying on a single method that requires individuals to reason about hypothetical moral dilemmas. Rest further points out that the Kohlberg stories are exceedingly difficult to score. To help remedy this problem, Rest (1976, 1977, 1983) has devised his own measure of moral development, called the Defining Issue Test, or the DIT.

In the DIT, an attempt is made to determine which moral issues individuals feel are most crucial in a given situation by presenting them with a series of dilemmas and a list of definitions of the major issues involved (Kohlberg's procedure does not make use of such a list). In the dilemma of Heinz and the druggist, for example, individuals might be asked whether a community's laws should be upheld or whether Heinz should be willing to risk being injured or caught as a burglar; they might also be asked to list the most important values that govern human interaction. They are given six stories and asked to rate the importance of each issue involved in deciding what ought to be done. Then the subjects are asked to list what they believe are the four most important issues. Rest believes that this method provides a more consistent and accurate measurement of moral thinking than Kohlberg's system.

FOCUS ON CHILD DEVELOPMENT 11.3

NOT JUST ANY PEER COMMUNICATION WILL DO—THE ROLE OF TRANSACTIVE DISCUSSION

Recall how researchers have found that modeling and discussion of moral matters above the child's moral stage often advance the child's moral reasoning. Research also suggests that an important factor in whether discussion of moral matters will advance children's moral reasoning is the quality of peer interaction and discussion involved (Berkowitz, 1981; Berkowitz & Gibbs, 1983; Berkowitz, Gibbs, & Broughton, 1980). For example, in one investigation, 30 dyads were observed and the nature of their discussion about moral issues assessed. The nature of the discourse focused on solutions to moral dilemmas in Kohlberg's moral judgment interview. Of the 30 dyads, 16 showed stage change in moral development while 14 of the dyads did not change (Berkowitz &

Gibbs, 1983). The researchers concluded that moral advances were made by certain dyads and not others because of the style of reasoning of both members of the dyad. Such reasoning was termed **transactive discussion,** meaning reasoning that operates on the reasoning of another individual.

In the investigation of transactive discussion, it was found that such discussion can follow one of two forms: representation of another's reasoning (such as feedback request, paraphrase, justification request, dyad paraphrase, and the like) or operation upon another's reasoning (such as clarification, contradiction, competitive extension, common ground/integration, comparative critique, and so on). Operational transactions are presumed to reflect more sophisticated discussion patterns than representation transactions. In this research effort, operational transaction was observed to advance moral reasoning more than representation transaction (Berkowitz & Gibbs, 1983) (see the table on the following page).

Another research investigation provides further criticism of the nature of the Kohlberg stories (Yussen, 1977). Most of the Kohlberg stories focus on the family and authority. However, when adolescents were invited to write stories about their own moral dilemmas, adolescents generated dilemmas that were broader in scope, focusing on such matters as friends, acquaintances, and other issues, as well as family and authority. The moral dilemmas were also analyzed in terms of the issues that concerned adolescents the most. As shown in Table 11.6, the moral issue that concerned adolescents more than any other was interpersonal relationships. As can be seen, there is reason to be concerned about the manner in which Kohlberg's data on moral development were collected.

Next, we find that, in recent years, one of the hottest controversies pertaining to Kohlberg's work involves the area of sex roles.

Table 11.6   Actual Moral Dilemmas Generated by Adolescents

Story Subject	Grade		
	7	9	12
	Percentage		
Alcohol	2	0	5
Civil rights	0	6	7
Drugs	7	10	5
Interpersonal relations	38	24	35
Physical safety	22	8	3
Sexual relations	2	20	10
Smoking	7	2	0
Stealing	9	2	0
Working	2	2	15
Other	11	26	20

From Yussen, Steven R., "Characteristics of moral dilemmas written by adolescents" in *Developmental Psychology, 13,* 162–163, 1977. Copyright © 1977 American Psychological Association. Reprinted by permission of the author.

This investigation of transactive discussion was conducted with college students, but it is probable that such a strategy would be beneficial for children as well. The lesson to be learned here is the importance of communication in peer discussion. In particular, it appears that the language and listening skills of the peer discussants are important factors in whether the peer discussion promotes advances in moral judgment. Many children have substandard vocabularies, a fact that undoubtedly contributes to their lack of ability to engage in transactive discussion. Indeed, children and adolescents have been found to have difficulty conducting competent discussion in general (Danner, 1986). In sum, it appears that an important new avenue of inquiry in moral development has been unveiled, one that emphasizes the importance of children's communication skills in peer discussion aimed at advancing moral development (Lapsley, Enright, & Serlin, 1986).

Percentages of Total Statements in Each Transact Category for Pre- to Posttest Moral Stage Changers and Nonchangers

Group	Transact Type		
	All Transacts	**Representational Transacts**	**Operational Transacts**
Nonchangers	19.9	7.2	12.9
Changers	26.6	8.8	17.8

From Berkowitz, M. and J. Gibbs, "Measuring the developmental features of moral discussion" in *Merrill-Palmer Quarterly, 29,* 399–410, 1983. Copyright © 1983 The Wayne State University Press, Detroit, Michigan. Reprinted by permission.

Sex Differences and the Care Perspective   No other aspect of Kohlberg's theory has generated as much recent controversy as the extent to which Kohlberg's stages are more characteristic of the moral development of males than of females. Carol Gilligan (1982), writing in her book *In a Different Voice,* argues that Kohlberg's theory and research are heavily sex-biased. She argues that females, because of their unique perspectives and concerns, should be included in the study of moral development. She reasons that their inclusion might produce a different perspective on moral development for both females and males. Gilligan thinks that individuals move from a level of selfishness focused on personal survival and practical needs to a level involving sacrificing one's own wishes for what other people want and then finally to the third and highest level, in which moral equality is sought between oneself and others. (See Table

11.7 for a comparison of Gilligan's and Kohlberg's levels.) Woven through Gilligan's concerns is her belief that Kohlberg has grossly underestimated the importance of interpersonal relationships and caring in moral development, regardless of whether males or females are under consideration. More details about Gilligan's views on the construction of moral thought are presented in Focus on Child Development 11.4.

Are there sex differences in moral development? A recent review of a large number of studies of sex differences in moral development by Lawrence Walker (1984) concluded that the overall pattern is one of nonsignificance. Of the 108 studies reviewed, only 8 revealed sex differences favoring males. Walker argues that, rather than debating whether sex bias is inherent in Kohlberg's theory, it might be more fruitful to ask why the myth that males are more advanced in moral development than

Table 11.7   Kohlberg's Versus Gilligan's Understanding of Moral Development

Kohlberg's Levels and Stages	Kohlberg's Definition	Gilligan's Levels
Level I. Preconventional morality		*Level I. Preconventional morality*
Stage 1. Punishment orientation	Obey rules to avoid punishment	Concern for the self and survival
Stage 2. Naive reward orientation	Obey rules to get rewards, share in order to get returns	
Level II. Conventional morality		*Level II. Conventional morality*
Stage 3. Good-boy/good-girl orientation	Conform to rules that are defined by others' approval/disapproval	Concern for being responsible, caring for others
Stage 4. Authority orientation	Rigid conformity to society's rules, law-and-order mentality, avoid censure for rule-breaking	
Level III. Postconventional morality		*Level III. Postconventional morality*
Stage 5. Social-contract orientation	More flexible understanding that we obey rules because they are necessary for social order, but the rules could be changed if there were better alternatives	Concern for self and others as interdependent
Stage 6. Morality of individual principles and conscience	Behavior conforms to internal principles (justice, equality) to avoid self-condemnation, and sometimes may violate society's rules	

From *Half the Human Experience: The Psychology of Women* by Janet Shibley Hyde. Copyright © 1985 by D. C. Heath and Company. Reprinted by permission of the publisher.

females persists in light of so little evidence. Gilligan (1985a, 1985b) believes that Walker has missed her main point. She states that her orientation focuses on the differences between two moral perspectives, one a justice perspective, the other a care perspective. She is quick to argue that her orientation does not stress whether males and females will differ on Kohlberg's stages of justice reasoning; that is, a feminine "voice" is not necessarily spoken more often by girls than boys (in a statistical sense). Rather, the feminine "voice" is associated with a feminine stereotype of caring and relationships. Gilligan fears that because so much empirical attention has been focused on sex differences in the expression of the feminine "voice," her view that a concern for caring and relationships is a key ingredient of the moral development of both females and males will be lost (Gilligan, 1985b).

Thus, we see that Gilligan senses that Kohlberg's theory does not adequately encompass relationships among people. Next we see that a related criticism of Kohlberg's theory—namely, that it is based too much on the individual—can be found in research and thinking about the role of culture and society in generating moral development.

Culture and Society   Many critics argue that moral development is more culture-specific than Kohlberg believes. As Urie Bronfenbrenner and James Garbarino (1976) have observed, moral standards in other cultures are not always consistent with the standards that children abide by in the United States. Bronfenbrenner and Garbarino believe that one of the key ingredients of moral development is the developmental unfolding of social relationships and cultural experiences. Bronfenbrenner and Garbarino (1976) created a model for understanding the link between developmental period, socialization experiences, and the extent to which individuals are exposed to different social agents and different sociopolitical views. The main theme of Bronfenbrenner and Garbarino's model is that, the greater the exposure to multiple social agents and multiple sociopolitical views, the more advanced is the child and adolescent's moral development. Their research suggests that individuals who grow up in a culture that is more sociopolitically plural (United States, West Germany) are less likely to be authority oriented and to have more plural ideas about moral dilemmas than their counterparts who grow up in less sociopolitically plural cultures (Poland, Hungary).

FOCUS ON CHILD DEVELOPMENT 11.4

AMY SAYS THEY SHOULD JUST TALK IT OUT AND FIND SOME OTHER WAY TO MAKE MONEY

Carol Gilligan (1982) notes that the main character in Kohlberg's dilemma is Heinz, a male. Possibly, females have a difficult time identifying with him. While some of the other Kohlberg dilemmas are gender neutral, one is about the captain of a company of marines. Gilligan also points out that subjects in Kohlberg's original research, those he has followed for 20 years, were all males. Gilligan also believes that Kohlberg's interpretations are flawed: The finding that females often only reach stage 3 is described as a deficiency by Kohlberg, yet it easily could be analyzed as a deficiency in Kohlberg's theory.

Going beyond her critique of Kohlberg's failure to consider females, Gilligan has provided a reformulation of Kohlberg's theory based on the premise that an important voice is not present in his view. Following are two excerpts from her book, one from 11-year-old Jake and one from 11-year-old Amy, which reflect the importance of this voice. First, Jake's comments:

> For one thing, human life is worth more than money, and if the druggist only makes $1,000, he is still going to live, but if Heinz doesn't steal the drug, his wife is going to die. *(Why is life worth more than money?)* Because the druggist can get $1,000 later from rich people with cancer, but Heinz can't get his wife again. (Gilligan, 1982, p. 26)

Now Amy's comments:

> Well, I don't think so. I think there might be other ways besides stealing it, like if he could borrow the money or make a loan or something, but he really shouldn't steal the drug—but his wife shouldn't die either. *(Why shouldn't he steal the drug?)* If he stole the drug, he might save his wife then, but if he did, he might have to go to jail, and then his wife might get sicker again, and he couldn't get more of the drug, and it might not be good. So, they should really just talk it out and find some other way to make the money. (Gilligan, 1982, p. 28)

How does Carol Gilligan believe moral development should be conceptualized?

Jake's comments would likely be scored as a mixture of Kohlberg's stages 3 and 4, but also include some of the components of a mature level III moral thinker. Amy, by contrast, does not fit into Kohlberg's scoring system as well. Jake sees the problems as one of rules and balancing the rights of people. However, Amy views the problem as one involving relationships—the druggist fails to live up to his relationship to the needy woman, the need to maintain the relationship between Heinz and his wife, and the hope that a bad relationship between Heinz and the druggist can be avoided. Amy concludes that the characters should talk it out and try to repair their relationships.

Gilligan (1982, 1985a, 1985b) concludes that there are two basic approaches to moral reasoning. In the **justice perspective,** people are differentiated and seen as standing alone—the focus is on the rights of the individual (that is, on justice). In the **care perspective,** people are viewed in terms of their connectedness with other people, and the focus is on their communication with others. From Gilligan's view, Kohlberg has greatly underplayed the importance of the care perspective in the moral development of both females and males.

Bronfenbrenner and Garbarino have also commented on the kinds of families children are likely to be exposed to in eastern European countries, which are less sociopolitically plural, and western European countries and the United States, which are more sociopolitically plural. In the former, the family is expected to support the governmental regime, and family styles are likely to be more monolithic. In the latter countries, where more individual freedom is allowed, more diverse family styles are common, and thus children are exposed to more varied cultural experiences.

As part of the belief that culture contributes to moral development more than Kohlberg allows, some social scientists stress that Kohlberg's view is too individualistic. The social theorists argue that, from Kohlberg's perspective, morality is basically a property of the individual, when in reality, moral development more appropriately should be construed as a matter of the individual's accommodation to the values and requirements of society. This assumption basically argues that society is the source of all values, not the individual. This view of morality has been referred to as **societalism.** However, while Kohlberg's cognitive developmental view is more individualistic than traditional socialization views of morality that place a primary emphasis on social relationships and conventions, it is inappropriate to describe Kohlberg's theory as completely individualistic (Gibbs & Schnell, 1985). As we have seen, Kohlberg, while arguing about the importance of moral reasoning in understanding morality, nonetheless does not argue that social matters are unimportant in generating moral thought. As we will see later in the chapter, for example, in the section on moral education, Kohlberg has recently placed added emphasis on the social climate in which moral thought is produced.

In this section, we have seen that one issue surrounding Kohlberg's theory of moral development is the extent to which moral reasoning is a property of the individual versus the degree to which it is generated by societal considerations. In the next section, we find that such considerations have led to attempts to distinguish moral reasoning and social conventional reasoning.

Social Conventional Reasoning

In recent years, considerable interest has been generated in whether reasoning about social matters is distinct from reasoning about moral matters (Nucci, 1982; Smetana, 1983, 1985; Turiel, 1977, 1978). Adherents of the belief that social reasoning is distinct from moral reasoning cast their thoughts within a cognitive developmental framework (Enright, Lapsley, & Olson, 1984).

The architects of the social reasoning approach argue that conventional rules are created to control behavioral irregularities. In this manner, the actions of individuals can be controlled and the existing social system maintained. Such conventional rules are thought to be arbitrary, with no prescription necessary. For example, not eating food with our fingers is a social conventional rule, as is not talking before raising one's hand in class.

By contrast, it is argued that moral rules are not arbitrary and certainly do involve prescription. Furthermore, moral rules are not created through any social consensus but rather are obligatory, virtually universally applicable, and somewhat impersonal (Turiel, 1978). Thus, rules pertaining to lying, stealing, cheating, and physically harming another person are moral rules because violation of these rules confronts ethical standards that exist apart from social consensus and convention. In sum, moral judgments are constructed as concepts of justice, whereas social conventional judgments are structured as concepts of social organization (Lapsley, Enright, & Serlin, 1986).

Moral Education

Some years ago, John Dewey (1933) argued that the most important values taught in school focus on how the school is organized and governed. Educational experts sometimes refer to this as the "hidden curriculum." In the hidden curriculum, students learn about obedience and defiance of authority rather than about democratic principles. As Dewey suggested, schools were in the business of moral education long before the current "new morality" programs came on the scene. In the 1800s, youth who were exposed to McGuffey's Readers were taught how to behave as well as how to read.

Dewey was correct in arguing that the school is a moral system. Schools, like families, are settings for moral development. Teachers serve as models of ethical behavior. Classroom rules and peer relations transmit attitudes about cheating, lying, stealing, and consideration of others. And the school administration, through its rules and regulations, represents a specific value system to children.

Some educational theorists believe that, while it is difficult to specify the appropriate moral virtues to instill in children, it is possible to identify generally accepted moral virtues and to didactically inform students about them (e.g., Hamm, 1977). But other theorists believe that there are no universally agreed upon moral virtues and that "subjective" virtues should not be taught to children. Led by Lawrence Kohlberg, this group stresses that the moral-reasoning skills of children—rather than adherence to any value system—should be developed. While moral education programs embodying Kohlberg's beliefs vary from school to school, most have emphasized the role of the teacher as a facilitator rather than a lecturer, the importance of discussing moral dilemmas, and the importance of give-and-take peer-group discussion.

In 1974, Kohlberg established the "Just Community," a small school for black and white students from different socioeconomic backgrounds. In the Just Community, consideration of realistic issues that arise in school, the nature of moral behavior as well as moral thought, and an active role for teachers as moral advocates were emphasized.

The Just Community shared with other alternative schools a belief in self-governance, mutual caring, and group solidarity. The goal for moral development was geared toward increasing students' responsibility to the community (stage 4 in Kohlberg's theory) rather than self-principled reasoning. In a recent investigation of the effectiveness of the Just Community—actually named the Cluster School—(Power, 1984), it was found that a more positive orientation toward the community did develop and that students were likely to adhere to the rules they had established. However, although the moral reasoning of the students at the Cluster School did advance, students who simply participated in moral discussion programs advanced their moral reasoning just as much as the students at the Cluster School.

With the development of the Cluster School in the mid-1970s, Kohlberg himself seemed to change his ideas about moral education. Kohlberg (1981) reported that he was not satisfied with the discussion approach to moral education. He realized that attempts to instill principled reasoning about morality in adolescents might be unrealistic because most people do not reach this level of cognitive maturity even in adulthood. And he began to believe that the moral climate of the country was shifting to an emphasis on the self and away from a concern for

others in the 1970s. As a consequence, Kohlberg began to show a stronger interest in the school as a social system and in creating moral school communities (Minuchin & Shapiro, 1983).

As a further indication of Kohlberg's belief in the importance of the moral atmosphere of the school, he has developed the Moral Atmosphere Interview. This interview poses dilemmas that deal with typically occurring problems in high schools, problems that are likely to involve social responsibility. In a recent investigation, the Moral Atmosphere Interview was administered to samples of approximately 20 students from three democratic alternative high schools and three more traditional, authoritarian high schools (Higgins, Power, & Kohlberg, 1983). Students in the democratic schools perceived the rules of their schools to be more collective and described themselves and their peers as more willing to act responsibly than did students from the traditional schools.

Child Development Concept Table 11.2 summarizes our discussion of the self, sex roles, and moral development in middle and late childhood. Now we turn to one final topic in this chapter—the nature of problems and disturbances during the elementary school years.

PROBLEMS AND DISTURBANCES IN MIDDLE AND LATE CHILDHOOD

In this section, we focus on the wide spectrum of problems and disturbances that characterize not only the elementary school years but other points in child development as well, childhood depression, school-related problems, and resilient children.

The Wide Spectrum of Problems and Disturbances

Thomas Achenbach and Craig Edelbrock (1981) investigated the prevalence of specific behavioral problems and competencies in children. Parents of 1,300 children being evaluated in 29 outpatient mental health settings and parents of 1,300 nonreferred children filled out the Child Behavior Checklist, which assesses behavioral problems and competencies. Problems and disturbances were evaluated in terms of the following ages: 4 to 5, 6 to 7, 8 to 9, 10 to 11, 12 to 13, 14 to 15, and 16.

Child Development Concept Table 11.2   The Self, Sex Roles, and Moral Development

Concept	Processes/Related Ideas	Characteristics/Description
The self	Differentiation, individuation, and stability	As the child develops through the elementary school years, his or her self-concept becomes more differentiated, individuated, and stable, and the child has an increasing ability to understand how he or she is viewed by others.
	Conceptions of self-other relations	As the child's social world expands and his or her cognitive development becomes more sophisticated, the child's conception of self-other relations advances. Selman has proposed a view of developing self-other relations that focuses on perspective taking.
	Self-esteem	Many researchers and the measures they have devised study self-concept and self-esteem in closely related ways. The child's self-esteem is linked to positive family experiences.
	Measuring self-concept	Measuring self-concept is a very difficult task. One promising measure is Harter's Perceived Competence Scale for Children.
	Social competence	Social competence is one of the four domains assessed by Harter's scale and has become recognized as an important aspect of the child to evaluate. Its conception and measurement, as in the case of self-concept, are difficult tasks. Waters and Sroufe recommend that social competence be defined in terms of effective uses of resources in the environment and resources in the individual. They believe that four important issues in the assessment of social competence involve: (1) broadband versus narrow assessments; (2) real behavior versus laboratory tasks; (3) assessments emphasizing the coordination of affect, cognition, and behavior; and (4) taxing behavioral and integrative/adaptive capacity.
Sex roles	Development in middle and late childhood	Two major changes in sex typing occur during middle and late childhood. Children increase their understanding of culturally defined expectations for males and females, and simultaneously, the behavior and attitudes of boys increasingly reflect masculine sex typing. However, girls do not show an increased interest in feminine activities during this developmental period.
	Masculinity, femininity, and androgyny	For many years, the male- and female-related aspects of sex/gender roles were categorized either as feminine or masculine. The competent male child was described as "masculine" (for example, being independent and aggressive), while the competent female child was characterized as "feminine" (for example, being dependent and unaggressive). Androgyny became an important part of sex-role research during the 1970s. Androgyny refers to a combination of both masculine and feminine characteristics in the same child. Most androgyny scales allow the child to be categorized as masculine, feminine, androgynous, or undifferentiated. Considerable interest has been generated in whether children of a particular sex-role makeup are more competent than others. In instances where the criteria for competence involve both self-assertion and integration, androgynous children often are more competent. However, it is very important to specify the contexts in which androgyny is being evaluated. In contexts where feminine characteristics are valued, for example, we would expect "feminine" children to perform more competently than others. It is important to specify the criteria for social competence as well as the criteria for the makeup of sex/gender roles. There has been a tendency to value the masculine and self-assertive role as more competent in our culture, and the criteria for competence have been tilted in this direction as well.

Child Development Concept Table 11.2   Continued

Concept	Processes/Related Ideas	Characteristics/Description
Sex roles (cont.)	Sex-role stereotypes	Sex-role stereotypes are broad categories that reflect our impressions about people, events, and ourselves. Regardless of their accuracy, stereotypes can cause tremendous emotional upheaval in an individual and undermine the individual's opinions about himself or herself and his or her status.
	Sex differences	Maccoby and Jacklin concluded that there are four main sex differences: Boys are better at math and at visual-spatial reasoning and are more aggressive, while girls are better at verbal activities. Some critics have faulted their conclusions.
	Achievement	Information about sex differences in achievement focuses on cultural standards, ideas about instrumental competence/incompetence, parenting orientation, developmental precursors, learned helplessness, and conclusions about whether there actually are sex differences in achievement and competence. Such conclusions must be described in terms of specific domains of achievement and competence and take into account sociohistorical proscriptions for success.
Moral development	Piaget's view	Piaget argued that children from 4 to 7 years of age are in the stage of moral realism and that from about the age of 10 years move into the stage of moral autonomy.
	Kohlberg's theory	Kohlberg proposed a provocative theory of moral development with three levels and six stages. According to Kohlberg, as the individual moves through the levels, he or she shows increased internalization.
	Kohlberg's research and influences on the stages	Kohlberg's original research documented age changes in moral thought. His more recent longitudinal data continue to show a relation to age and the fact that the higher stages often do not emerge in adolescence or even adulthood in many cases. Among the most important influences on the stages are cognitive development, modeling and cognitive conflict, and peer relations, and opportunities for role/perspective taking.
	Criticism of Kohlberg's theory	Kohlberg's views have been criticized on a number of grounds, including an overemphasis on cognition and a lack of emphasis on behavior and feeling, the quality of the research, failure to consider females and an underevaluation of a care perspective and relationships, and too much individualistic emphasis with too little attention given to cultural and societal contributions.
	Distinction between moral and social conventional reasoning	Moral reasoning pertains to ethical matters, while social conventional reasoning focuses on social consensus and convention. Moral reasoning is prescriptive, while social conventional reasoning is more arbitrary. Moral reasoning emphasizes justice, while social conventional reasoning focuses more on social regulation and the control of behavioral irregularities so that the social system can be maintained.
	Moral education	Moral education has a long history. Some years ago, John Dewey described the moral atmosphere that exists in every school. During the 1970s, Kohlberg proposed that children should be morally educated. Kohlberg has revised his views in the last decade and now is more in agreement with Dewey that the entire school has a moral atmosphere that must be considered.

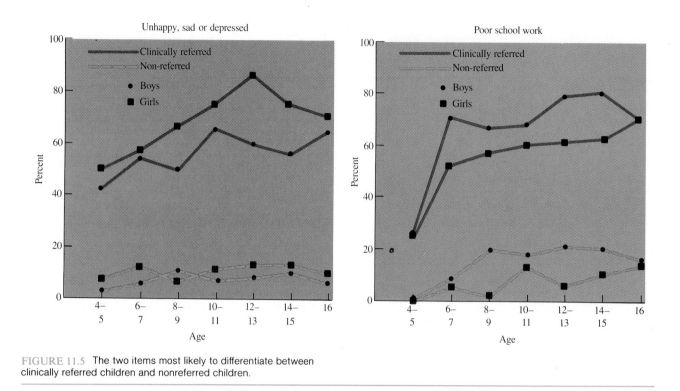

FIGURE 11.5   The two items most likely to differentiate between clinically referred children and nonreferred children.

There was a general tendency for behavioral problems to decline somewhat with age and for parents of lower-socioeconomic-status children to report more problems and fewer competencies than parents of middle-socioeconomic-status children, although there was no overall tendency for more problems to be reported for one gender than the other. Most of the problems reported for lower-socioeconomic-status children and for boys were undercontrolled, externalizing behaviors (e.g., destroys others' things, fighting), while the problems reported for girls tended to be either overcontrolled, internalizing behaviors (e.g., unhappy, sad, or depressed) or not clearly classifiable as undercontrolled. Racial differences were few and small.

The behavioral problems revealing the largest effects of clinical status across age and gender groups were unhappy, sad, or depressed, and poor schoolwork (see Figure 11.5). Both were reported by large proportions of the parents of referred children and very small proportions of the parents of nonreferred children. Certain problems that have been the subject of considerable interest by

clinical psychologists, such as fears of certain animals, situations, or places, and bed-wetting, showed very small differences between referred and nonreferred children (see Figure 11.6).

Let's now take a closer look at two of the problems that surface the most in clinical referrals of elementary school children—depression and school-related problems.

Childhood Depression

Alan Sroufe and Michael Rutter (1984) point to a number of reasons why depressive disorders reflect the importance of taking a developmental perspective in understanding psychopathology: (1) there are clear age-related changes in depression; (2) depression seems to have both biological and environmental determinants, calling for a developmental perspective possibly to integrate findings; and (3) while depressive disorders exist in childhood, they occur much more frequently in adulthood, suggesting that there is no simple link between

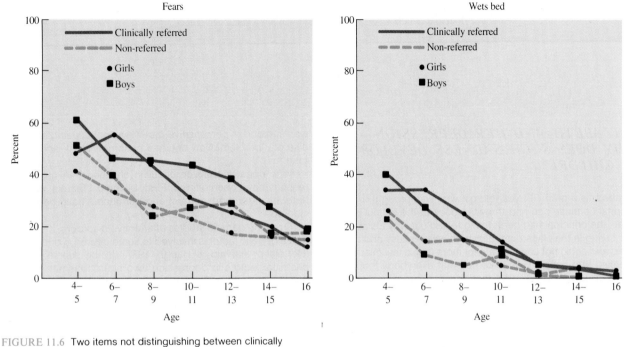

FIGURE 11.6 Two items not distinguishing between clinically referred children and nonreferred children.

childhood and adult conditions. Among the age-related aspects of depression are the facts that: (1) before the second half of the first year, infants show no grief reaction to loss; (2) infantile sequences of protest, despair, and detachment in the face of loss continue until about four or five years of age; (3) disorders with both cognitive and affective components of depression probably emerge after infancy; (4) the frequency of depression increases sharply during puberty, being more characteristic of girls than boys; and (5) depression becomes even more frequent during adulthood.

In childhood, the features of depression are mixed with a broader array of behaviors than in adulthood. For example, during childhood, aggression, school failure, anxiety, antisocial behavior, and poor peer relations are often related to depression, which makes its diagnosis more difficult (Weiner, 1980). Focus on Child Development 11.5 presents more information about the nature of children's depression.

School-Related Problems

Difficulties in school achievement, whether secondary to other kinds of disturbances or primary problems in themselves, seem to account for more referrals to clinical treatment than any other child problem (Weiner, 1980). This fact alone demonstrates the importance our society places on achievement. Because underachievement is so frequently associated with problems and disturbances, we will discuss it further.

Underachievement in school refers to the child's failure to receive grades commensurate with his or her intellectual abilities. Unexpected poor school performance has been estimated to occur in 25 percent of schoolchildren. It also appears that approximately one third of children and adolescents seen in psychiatric clinics are referred because of learning problems. Further, more than 50 percent of college students who request counseling and psychotherapy do so because of worries about studying and grades (Blaine & McArthur, 1971).

FOCUS ON CHILD DEVELOPMENT 11.5

ELIZABETH AND HER DEPRESSION—
WHY DOES SUCH SADNESS DEVELOP
IN CHILDREN?

Elizabeth is a pretty 11-year-old girl who was brought to the hospital because she had thrown a book at the school principal. The principal had been trying to find out why Elizabeth was crying in the classroom. Elizabeth was restless and confused and could not concentrate for more than a few minutes. She said that people didn't like her, that everybody thought she was ugly. She believed that she had been justified in throwing the book at the principal: "He was bugging me; I was nervous." While Elizabeth's mother was interviewed in another room at the hospital, Elizabeth began to pace up and down, saying that she was feeling hot. She showed someone her clammy, perspiring hands and began to cry, saying, "I'm dying. Something in my throat doesn't let me breathe. My stomach isn't pumping. People are trying to kill me. I'll die if I stay here. I was normal before I came. Now I am dying. . . ." During the next three days, Elizabeth had one or two severe anxiety attacks a day. Between the attacks, she was anxious, restless, and depressed. She did not show any signs of psychosis in clinical or psychological testings.

The background history obtained on Elizabeth revealed that she had been an insecure, timid, and friendless child since entering school. When Elizabeth was 7 years old, her father had been charged with attempting to seduce a 13-year-old female neighbor; and though the charges had been dismissed, the family was alienated and ostracized from the neighborhood. Elizabeth's father had then deserted the family, leaving Elizabeth, her 13-year-old brother, and her mother with no source of income. Elizabeth's mother was a tense, depressed woman, who felt harassed by the responsibilities of finding a job and caring for her children. Six months before Elizabeth's admission to the hospital, her mother had found a job that kept her away from home from 8:00 A.M. to 6:00 P.M. She had not had time to go over to school when Elizabeth brought a letter from her teacher reporting that Elizabeth seemed very unhappy, that her schoolwork had deteriorated, and that she was frequently absent. Elizabeth's mother was now extremely angry at Elizabeth. She explained, "I knew she

was sad and hypersensitive, but it was not causing anybody else any problem. Now she has become violent, and I can't take that."

Why does depression occur in childhood? A number of reasons have been offered. First, biological factors, such as heredity, neurotransmitters, and hormones, have been considered.

From the genetic studies of affective disorders, it appears that a genetic factor is involved to some degree in depression (Bertelsen, Harvald, & Hauge, 1977). In the search for biochemical factors in depression, two neurotransmitters have been proposed as culprits: norepinephrine (Goodwin & Athanascious, 1979) and serotonin (Asberg, Thoren, Traskman, Bertilsson, & Ringberger, 1976).

As researchers explore the nature of depression in the childhood and adolescent years, they have also discovered that the greatest changes in depression seem to emerge during adolescence (Kendell, Rennie, Clarke, & Dean, 1981). Because depression is more common in girls than boys, the question is raised as to whether depression is related to hormonal changes that accompany puberty. So far, the findings on hormonal changes have not led to any clear conclusions about their role in depression during adolescence.

Psychoanalytic theories generally attribute the development of depression to early mother-child relationships, particularly oral difficulties or loss of a love object (Bowlby, 1980; Isenberg & Schatzberg, 1978). While positive evidence for the role of maternal loss or difficulties in oral matters during infancy is not available, the psychoanalytic emphasis on the importance of loss in the development of depression, regardless of the developmental time period, is an important contribution.

In recent years, cognitive theories have been crafted to provide a further understanding of depression. For example, Aaron Beck (1967, 1973) argues that people become depressed because early in their development they acquired cognitive schemata that are characterized by self-devaluation and lack of confidence about the future. Another view of depression suggests that it develops because the individual perceives that she or he cannot control undesirable events and attributes the causes of her or his depression to internal rather than external causes (Seligman & Peterson, in press).

John Bowlby (1980) argues that insecure mother-infant attachment, a lack of love and affection in child rearing, or the actual loss of a parent during childhood leads to a negative

Why do some children develop depression?

cognitive set. This schema that is built up during the infant and/or childhood years causes the child to interpret later losses as yet other failures to create an enduring and close positive relationship. From Bowlby's perspective, then, early childhood experiences, particularly those involving loss, produce cognitive schemata that are carried forward to influence the way in which the child or adolescent interprets new experiences. When these new experiences involve further loss, the loss serves as the immediate precipitant of depression.

The theories suggest that vulnerabilities (genetic, biochemical, and earlier experiences), cognitive sets, and precipitating stress events, particularly those involving loss, are involved in understanding depression. Psychologists still know little about how cognitive changes in childhood might influence the onset and development of depression. Nevertheless, the fact that depression in infancy is rare and increases considerably during adolescence indicates that cognitive developmental changes are likely candidates for further understanding of the developmental nature of depression (Rutter & Garmezy, 1983).

According to Irving Weiner (1980), school underachievement may occur because of sociocultural factors, such as family and neighborhood value systems that minimize the importance of education and peer group attitudes that stamp academic success as unmanly for boys and unfeminine for girls. From Weiner's perspective, this type of underachievement does not constitute a psychological disturbance. Rather, school problems that involve psychological disturbances can be traced to two circumstances: First, attention, concentration, and specific learning handicaps, often associated with neurological problems, usually are detected in the elementary school years. Second, neurotic patterns of family interaction may produce a pattern of what is referred to as passive-aggressive underachievement. A child who is passive-aggressive is purposely inactive, working hard at making sure nothing happens that will raise his or her grades too far. It is the second pattern of underachievement that is more characteristic of children with achievement problems; this is the pattern we will focus on.

From Weiner's perspective, three factors usually contribute to the development of passive-aggressive underachievement:

1. Extensive hostility, usually toward parents, that cannot be expressed directly
2. Worry about rivalry with parents and siblings that produces fear of failure or fear of success
3. Adoption of a passive-aggressive pattern of behavior in coping with difficult, stressful situations

Investigations of underachieving children frequently reveal that they are more likely than their achieving counterparts to feel hostility that they cannot express directly (Davids & Hainsworth, 1967). Parental demands for extraordinarily high standards for academic achievement are likely to trigger poor school performance (which may be an indirect retaliation toward the achievement-oriented parents).

Passive-aggressive underachieving children often either fear failure or fear success, which restricts their achievement. Children who fear failure usually have negative perceptions of their abilities and feel that they will never be able to equal the achievements of their parents or siblings. Such children usually have a very low tolerance for criticism; the more that parents or teachers tell them that they should be earning better grades, the more they withdraw from trying to compete in school. Children who fear failure often set unrealistically high goals but rarely work hard in trying to achieve them. They are usually unwilling to risk making a mistake, and they often pride themselves on being able to accomplish something with a minimum of effort.

We have seen that depression and school-related problems stand out as the most frequent reason children are referred for clinical help. But as we see next, some children who would be expected to have serious problems are highly resilient.

Resilient Children

The 10-year-old child had everything against him: extreme poverty, an ex-convict father who was dying of chronic disease, an illiterate mother who sometimes abused him, two mentally retarded siblings. Yet his teachers described him as a charming boy, loved by everyone at school, a good student, and a natural leader. How can we explain such outstanding resilience?

Norman Garmezy (1981; Garmezy, Masten, & Tellegen, 1984) has been studying the competence and incompetence of children at risk for psychopathology for more than a decade. Approximately 200 children and their families have participated in the full project. Measures include six hours of parent interviews, two hours of interviews with the child, a variety of laboratory assessments of the child, and indices of stress and competence. The measures of stress include the Life Events Questionnaire, a parent interview about stress-related circumstances, and socioeconomic status. Measures of school-based competence include two indices of academic achievement (e.g., grades and the Peabody Individual Achievement Test), classroom competence (teacher ratings), interpersonal competence (peer assessments), and a measure of general intellectual ability (the WISC-R). Further, both the parent and the child interviews contain extensive information about the child's competence.

Garmezy is now studying these "invulnerable" children in some depth, both in the classroom and through family interviews, in the hope of identifying the core variables that produce resilience. Among his early findings is that much depends upon the quality of the child's attention. "Attentional dysfunction is the basic substitute out of which incompetence arises," Garmezy believes. The next question is: How modifiable is this defect? at what age? and in what way?

THINKING BACK, LOOKING AHEAD

Our coverage of social and personality development in middle and late childhood has included a number of interesting circumstances—A boy who called his teacher a jerk, a child who destroyed a block tower while cleaning up a room, a child whose best friend was his kite, a talking doll that resembled a green human wearing silver clothes, children spending many years in schools as members of a small society, social reasoning about a lost dog named Pepper, social competence and the Perceived Competence Scale for Children, sex roles from androgynous to undifferentiated, bright girls, learned helplessness and achievement expectations, Heinz the druggist, transactive discussion, Amy's comment that they should just talk it out and find some other way to make money, good manners as well as good morals, the hidden curriculum, internalized problems, externalized problems, and the invulnerables.

In Section 5, we discuss adolescence. About the people we will be studying next, Aristotle once said, "They think they know everything, and are quite sure about it." But before we go on to Section 5 and determine whether Aristotle's perception of adolescents was accurate, reflect on the following words of Alistair Reed as we exit childhood:

> Children know nothing about childhood and have little to say about it. They are too busy becoming something they have not quite grasped yet, something which keeps changing . . . Nor will they realize what is happening to them until they are too far beyond it to remember how it felt.

SUMMARY

I. Ideas about family processes in middle and late childhood focus on amount of parent-child interaction, parent-child issues, discipline techniques, control processes, mutual cognitions, parental maturation, and societal changes in families.

A. Parents spend less time with children during middle and late childhood than during early childhood, including less time in caregiving, instruction, reading, talking, and playing.

B. New parent-child issues during middle and late childhood include chores, material reinforcement, children's self-entertainment, and monitoring outside the family. School-related matters are particularly salient.

C. Discipline during middle and late childhood involves more reasoning than in early childhood, as well as more deprivation of privileges, appeals to the child's self-esteem, comments directed at the child's guilt, and information about the child's responsibility.

D. During the elementary school years, there is a gradual transfer of control from parent to child, but this process should be viewed as coregulatory in the sense that parental control of moment-to-moment activities may be relinquished but general supervisory control is still prevalent.

E. During middle and late childhood, children increasingly categorize their parents in terms of labels. They often react to their parents according to these categorizations, and parents likewise react to their children based on labels they have developed for them.

F. Not only are children maturing but so are parents. The parents of elementary school children are more experienced at parenting than the parents of preschool children. The fact that child-rearing demands become somewhat lessened in the elementary school years may produce changes in parents.

G. During the elementary and secondary school years, two major changes in children's lives are the increasing number of children growing up in stepparent families as well as the increase in latchkey children.

II. Information about peer relations in middle and late childhood involves the amount and form of peer interaction; popular, rejected, and neglected children; social cognition; friendships; and children's groups.

A. A considerable portion of a child's day during middle and late childhood is spent in the company of peers. Play and socialization are frequent components of peer interaction.

B. Listening skills and effective communication, being yourself, being happy, showing enthusiasm and concern for others, and indicating self-confidence but not conceit are predictors of peer popularity. Rejected children are at risk for adjustment problems, while the risk status of neglected children is less clear.

C. There has been increased interest in social cognition in peer relations. Social information processing and social knowledge are two important aspects of social cognition in peer relations.

D. Friendships become a more salient feature of peer relationships in the elementary school years. Among the most important features of friendships are intimacy and similarity, shared support and knowledge, an increased cognitive orientation, and conversational skills.

E. An understanding of children's groups requires focusing on their nature and the naturalistic study of group formation.

III. Schooling becomes a very important aspect of the child's life during middle and late childhood. Discussion focuses on the nature of schooling, open versus traditional classrooms and schools, teachers, aptitude-treatment interaction, and social class and ethnicity.

A. Children spend more than 10,000 hours in the classroom as members of a small society in which there are tasks to be accomplished, people to be socialized with and socialized by, and rules that define and limit behavior, feelings, and attitudes.

B. The open classroom concept is multi-dimensional, and the criteria for evaluation often have varied from one study to the next. The Classroom Environment Scale has improved assessment. Through meta-analysis, investigators have found that open classrooms are associated with lower language achievement but improved attitudes toward school. What seems most important here is linking specific dimensions of open classrooms with specific dimensions of the child. In this regard, individualized instruction and emphasis on the role of the child are associated with positive effects on the child's self-concept.

C. A definitive profile of a competent teacher is difficult to create, although positive teacher traits include enthusiasm, planning, poise, adaptability, and awareness of individual differences. Erikson believes that good teachers are capable of producing a sense of industry, rather than inferiority, in children.

D. Aptitude-treatment interaction (ATI) refers to the importance of looking at the interaction of aptitude and treatment factors rather than focusing on each factor in isolation when evaluating educational outcomes.

E. Schools have a stronger middle-class than lower-class orientation. Teachers from a lower-class socioeconomic background seem to have different orientations toward students than those from middle-class backgrounds. And many teachers seem to have different expectations for children from lower- and middle-class backgrounds. The major investigation of ethnicity and schooling has focused on desegregation through busing, a procedure that has not produced any consistent benefits for minority group children.

IV. Ideas about the self involve differentiation, individuation, and stability; concept of self-other relations; self-esteem; measuring self-concept; and social competence.

A. As the child develops through the elementary school years, his or her self-concept becomes more differentiated, individuated, and stable, and the child has an increasing ability to understand how he or she is viewed by others.

B. As the child's social world expands and his or her cognitive development becomes more sophisticated, the child's conception of self-other relations advances. Selman has proposed a view of developing self-other relations that emphasizes perspective taking.

C. Many researchers and the measures they have devised study self-concept and self-esteem in closely related ways. The child's self-esteem is linked to positive family experiences.

D. Measuring self-concept is a very difficult task. One promising measure is Harter's Perceived Competence Scale for Children.

E. Social competence is one of the four domains assessed by Harter's scale and has become recognized as an important aspect of the child to evaluate. Its conception and measurement, as in the case of self-concept, are difficult tasks. Waters and Sroufe recommend that social competence be defined in terms of effective uses of resources in the environment and resources in the individual. They believe that four important issues in the assessment of social competence involve: (1) broadband versus narrow assessments; (2) real behavior versus laboratory tasks; (3) assessments emphasizing the coordination of affect, cognition, and behavior; and (4) taxing behavioral and integrative/adaptive capacity.

V. Aspects of sex roles involve developmental concerns, the nature of sex roles, sex-role stereotypes, sex differences, and achievement.

A. Two major changes in sex typing occur during middle and late childhood. Children increase their understanding of culturally defined expectations for males and females, and simultaneously, the behavior and attitudes of boys increasingly reflect masculine sex typing. However, girls do not show an increased interest in feminine activities during this developmental period.

B. For many years, the male- and female-related aspects of sex/gender roles were categorized either as feminine or masculine. The competent male child was described as "masculine" (for example, being independent and aggressive), while the competent female child was characterized as "feminine" (for example, being dependent and unaggressive). Androgyny became an important part of sex-role research during the 1970s. Androgyny refers to a combination of both masculine and feminine characteristics in the same child. Most androgyny scales allow the child to be classified as masculine, feminine, androgynous, or undifferentiated. Considerable interest has been generated in whether children of a particular sex-role makeup are more competent than others. In instances where the criteria for competence involve both self-assertion and integration, androgynous children often are more competent. However, it is very important to specify the contexts in which androgyny is being evaluated. In contexts where feminine characteristics are valued, for example, we would expect "feminine" children to perform more competently than others. It is important to specify the criteria for social competence as well as the criteria for the makeup of gender/sex roles. There has been a tendency to value the masculine and self-assertive role as more competent in our culture, and the criteria for competence often have been tilted in this direction as well.

C. Sex-role stereotypes are broad categories that reflect our impressions about people, events, and ourselves. Regardless of their accuracy, stereotypes can cause tremendous emotional upheaval in an individual and undermine the individual's opinions about himself or herself and his or her status.

D. Maccoby and Jacklin concluded that there are four main sex differences: Boys are better at math and at visual-spatial reasoning and are more aggressive, while girls are better at verbal abilities. Some critics have faulted their conclusions.

E. Information about sex differences in achievement focuses on cultural standards, ideas about instrumental competence/incompetence, parenting orientation, developmental precursors, learned helplessness, and conclusions about whether there actually are sex differences in achievement and competence. Such conclusions must be described in terms of specific domains of achievement and competence and take into account sociohistorical proscriptions for success.

VI. Ideas about moral development involve Piaget's view, Kohlberg's theory, Kohlberg's research and influences on the stages, Kohlberg's critics, the distinction between moral and social conventional reasoning, and moral education.

A. Piaget argued that children from 4 to 7 years of age are in the stage of moral realism and that from about the age of 10 years move into the stage of moral autonomy.

B. Kohlberg proposed a provocative theory of moral development with three levels and six stages. According to Kohlberg as the individual moves through the levels, he or she shows increased internalization.

C. Kohlberg's original research documented age changes in moral thought. His more recent longitudinal data continue to show a relation to age and the fact that the higher stages often do not emerge in adolescence or even adulthood in many cases. Among the most important influences on the stages are cognitive development, modeling and cognitive conflict, and peer relations and opportunities for role/perspective taking.

D. Kohlberg's ideas have been attacked on a number of grounds, including an overemphasis on cognition and a lack of emphasis on behavior and feeling, the quality of the research, failure to consider females and an underevaluation of a care perspective and relationships, and too much individualistic emphasis with insufficient attention given to societal and cultural contributions.

E. Moral reasoning pertains to ethical matters, while social conventional reasoning focuses on social consensus and convention.

F. Moral education has a long history. Some years ago, John Dewey described the moral atmosphere that exists in every school. During the 1970s, Kohlberg proposed that children should be morally educated. Kohlberg has revised his views in the last decade and now is more in agreement with Dewey that the entire school is an arena for moral development.

VII. A wide spectrum of problems and disturbances are possible in middle and late childhood.

A. Lower-socioeconomic-status parents report their children as having more disturbances than middle-socioeconomic-status parents. Most problems for lower-socioeconomic-status children and boys are undercontrolled, externalizing problems, while those for girls involve either overcontrolled, internalizing problems or those that cannot be clearly classified in one of these domains.

B. Children likely are referred for psychological help for two reasons: being unhappy and depressed, or poor schoolwork. Diagnosing childhood depression often is difficult, and a number of causes have been offered to explain its occurrence. School-related problems include underachievement, which can involve passive-aggressive behavior.

C. Some psychologists, such as Garmezy, are interested in studying resilient children—those who should develop problems, but do not. The quality of the child's attention seems to be one important factor that helps such resilient children.

KEY TERMS

androgyny 467
aptitude 455
Aptitude-Treatment
Interaction 455
care perspective 483
Classroom Environment
Scale 453
complex stepfamily 443
conventional level 476
coregulation process 442
intention-cue detection 447
intimacy in friendship 450
justice perspective 483
learned helplessness 473
meta-analysis 454
neglected children 445

open classroom 453
peer sociotherapy 440
Perceived Competence Scale
for Children 462
postconventional level 476
preconventional level 476
rejected children 445
sex-role stereotypes 469
simple stepfamily 443
societalism 484
transactive discussion 480
treatment 455
undifferentiated 467

SUGGESTED READINGS

Development during middle childhood. (1984). Washington, DC: National Academy Press.
An excellent collection of essays about what currently is known about the development of children in the elementary school years. Includes chapters by Maccoby on families and Hartup on peers, as well as other chapters on schools, the self, and psychopathology.

Gilligan, C. (1982). *In a different voice.* Cambridge, MA: Harvard University Press.
Advances Gilligan's provocative view that a care perspective is underrepresented in Kohlberg's theory and research.

Hyde, J. S. (1985). *Half the human experience* (3rd ed.). Lexington, MA: D. C. Heath.
An excellent overview of sex roles related to the development of females.

Minuchin, P. P., & Shapiro, E. K. (1983). The school as a context for social development. In P. H. Mussen (Ed.), *Handbook of child psychology* (4th ed.), Vol. 4. New York: Wiley.
An authoritative, up-to-date review of the role of the school in the child's development.

Rest, J. R. (1983). Morality. In P. H. Mussen (Ed.), *Handbook of child psychology* (4th ed.), Vol. 3. New York: Wiley.
Recent information about moral reasoning is evaluated, with considerable attention devoted to methodological issues in assessment. Valuable ideas about the importance of information processing in understanding moral reasoning are also offered.

Rutter, M., and Garmezy, N. (1983). Developmental psychopathology. In P. H. Mussen (Ed.), *Handbook of child psychology* (4th ed.), Vol. 4. New York: Wiley.
This lengthy, highly detailed chapter spells out many important dimensions of the field of developmental psychopathology. Includes considerable discussion of Rutter's and Garmezy's important research.

Sex Roles. This journal is likely to be in your library.
Look at the issues during the 1980s to see the kind of research being conducted on the development of children's sex roles.

SECTION 5
ADOLESCENCE

In no order of things is adolescence the time of simple life.

Jean Erskine Stewart

PHYSICAL AND COGNITIVE DEVELOPMENT IN ADOLESCENCE

IMAGINE . . . A 14-YEAR-OLD GIRL THINKING, "GET PREGNANT? IT WON'T HAPPEN TO ME!"

PREVIEW

HISTORICAL BACKGROUND, BIOLOGY/CULTURE, AND CONTINUITY/DISCONTINUITY

Historical Background

G. Stanley Hall—The Storm and Stress View
The Inventionist View of Adolescence
Stereotyping Adolescents

Biology/Culture and Continuity/Discontinuity

Biology/Culture
Continuity/Discontinuity in Development

CHILD DEVELOPMENT CONCEPT TABLE 12.1: HISTORICAL BACKGROUND, BIOLOGY/CULTURE, AND CONTINUITY/DISCONTINUITY

PHYSICAL DEVELOPMENT IN ADOLESCENCE

The Nature of the Pubertal Process
The Endocrine System

FOCUS ON CHILD DEVELOPMENT 12.1: GONADOTROPINS, SEX STEROIDS, ADRENAL ANDROGENS, AND THE ADOLESCENT

Physical Changes

Height and Weight
Sexual Maturation and Behavior

Psychological Accompaniments of Physical Changes

Body Image
Early and Late Maturation

FOCUS ON CHILD DEVELOPMENT 12.2: PHYSICAL ATTRACTIVENESS, PUBERTAL CHANGE, AND SELF-ESTEEM IN ADOLESCENT GIRLS

On-Time/Off-Time in Pubertal Development

CHILD DEVELOPMENT CONCEPT TABLE 12.2: PHYSICAL DEVELOPMENT IN ADOLESCENCE

COGNITIVE DEVELOPMENT IN ADOLESCENCE

Formal Operational Thought

The Characteristics of Formal Operational Thought

FOCUS ON CHILD DEVELOPMENT 12.3: JAY AND HIS HAIRCUT—THE DEVELOPMENT OF SARCASM

Early and Late Formal Operational Thought
Individual Variation in Formal Operational Thought

Social Cognition

Egocentrism

FOCUS ON CHILD DEVELOPMENT 12.4: IMAGINARY AUDIENCES

Implicit Personality Theory
Social Monitoring

CHILD DEVELOPMENT CONCEPT TABLE 12.3: COGNITIVE DEVELOPMENT IN ADOLESCENCE

Career Orientation and Work

Exploration and Cognitive Factors in Career Development
Work

THINKING BACK, LOOKING AHEAD

SUMMARY

KEY TERMS

SUGGESTED READINGS

CHAPTER 12

IMAGINE . . . A 14-YEAR-OLD GIRL THINKING, "GET PREGNANT? IT WON'T HAPPEN TO ME!"

Fourteen-year-old Jennifer is talking to her best friend, Anne, about something she just heard. "Anne, did you hear about Barbara? You know she fools around a lot. Well, the word is that she's pregnant. Can you believe it? That would never happen to me." The conversation between Jennifer and Anne then turns to Anne's relationship with her boyfriend, Bob. Anne says, "I really like Bob, but sometimes he is a jerk. I don't think he understands what I am all about. He just doesn't know my true feelings."

The conversation between Jennifer and Anne has the ingredients of the "personal fable" that characterizes development in early adolescence. A personal fable refers to an adolescent's sense of uniqueness and indestructibility. To retain their sense of uniqueness and to preserve their feeling that they are seen in a positive and powerful way by others, adolescents often construct a personal fable about themselves that is not true. With their developing idealism and ability to think in more abstract and hypothetical ways, young adolescents often get caught up in a mental world far removed from reality, one that may involve a belief that things just can't or won't happen to them and that they are omnipotent and indestructible.

These cognitive changes, as well as others, have interesting implications for the sex education of adolescents. With regard to the importance of cognitive development in sex education, Joan Lipsitz (1980) points out that having information about contraceptives is not enough—what seems to predict whether adolescents will use contraceptives or not depends on their acceptance of themselves and their sexuality. Such acceptance likely requires cognitive as well as emotional maturity.

Most discussions of adolescent pregnancy and its prevention assume that adolescents have the ability to anticipate consequences, to weigh the probable outcome of behavior, and to project into the future what will happen if they engage in certain acts, such as sexual intercourse. That is, prevention is based on the belief that adolescents have the cognitive ability to approach problem solving in a planned, organized, and analytical manner. However, many adolescents are just beginning to develop such capacities, and others have not developed them at all.

Lipsitz (1980), in addressing the American Association of Sex Educators, Counselors, and Therapists, described the personal fable and how it may be linked to adolescent pregnancy. The young adolescent often says, "Hey, it won't happen to me." If the adolescent is locked into this personal fable, he or she may not respond well to a course on sex education that preaches prevention. Lipsitz points out that the best of what we know about prevention is not appropriate for early adolescents. A developmental perspective on cognition may provide some insight into what can be taught in sex education courses for early adolescents.

Late adolescents (those 18 to 19 years of age) are at least to some degree realistic and future-oriented about sexual experiences, just as they are about careers and marriage. Middle adolescents (those 15 to 17 years of age) often romanticize sexuality. However, young adolescents (those 10 to 15 years of age) appear to experience sex in a depersonalized way that is filled with anxiety and denial. At the same time, even college students who are anxious and guilty about sex have been shown to be more likely to risk pregnancy than their less uptight counterparts. Thus, it seems that the somewhat depersonalized way in which young adolescents experience sexuality is not very likely to lead to preventive behavior.

Consider the outcome if the following are combined: the nature of early adolescent cognition, the personal fable, anxiety about sex, sex-role definitions about what is masculine and feminine, the sexual themes of music in the adolescent culture, the sexual overtones that are rampant on television and in magazines, and a societal standard that says sex is appropriate for adults but promiscuous for adolescents. That is, as Lipsitz (1980) says:

> Sex is fun, harmless, adult—and forbidden . . . the combination of early physical maturation, risk-taking behavior, egocentrism, the inability to think futuristically, and this ambivalent contradictory culture is more than most of us want to face up to. Add to that the growing need young adolescents have, as they mature, for meaningful social commitment in a society which puts its young people on "hold" in order to reduce the strain on the glutted job market. To be a young adolescent with a newly forming sense of destiny facing a 35 percent youth unemployment rate is to be turned away from the future, intensively toward the present. . . . Put together early adolescent development, America's sexual ambivalence, and adolescents' vulnerability to economic forces, and I think you have social dynamite. (p. 31)

PREVIEW

Throughout history, adolescence has been the focus of many interesting thoughts. At the end of the last chapter, we read about Aristotle's perception that adolescents are megalomanical. Late in the 19th century, Joseph Conrad's words conveyed the image of indestructibility that is part of the adolescent's personal fable: "I remember my youth and the feeling that never came back anymore—the feeling that I could last forever, outlast the sea, the earth, and all men." And, more recently, the *Wall Street Journal* portrayed the material orientation of today's adolescents: "The key to success, according to today's youth, is the one that fits in the ignition."

In this chapter, we study the historical interest in adolescents, revisit two important issues—those of biology/culture and continuity/discontinuity, and then turn to the dramatic physical and cognitive changes that characterize adolescence.

HISTORICAL BACKGROUND, BIOLOGY/CULTURE, AND CONTINUITY/DISCONTINUITY

In Chapter 1, we portrayed the historical background of interest in the child's development. Here, we describe the intriguing history of interest in the adolescent's development. We also discuss how adolescent development, like child development, is always influenced by an interaction of biology and culture, rather than being determined by either factor alone. The important issue of continuity/discontinuity in development is revisited in this section as well.

Historical Background

It was not until the turn of the 20th century that the period we now call adolescence was extensively studied and scientifically investigated. Our exploration of the interest in adolescence from a historical perspective will include the important contributions of G. Stanley Hall, the inventionist view of adolescence, and the issue of stereotyping adolescents.

G. Stanley Hall—The Storm and Stress View

Most historians label G. Stanley Hall (1844–1924) the father of the scientific study of adolescence. Hall's ideas were published in the two-volume set *Adolescence* in 1904.

Charles Darwin, the famous evolutionary theorist, had a tremendous impact on Hall's thinking. Hall applied the scientific, biological aspects of Darwin's views to the study of adolescent development. He believed that all development is controlled by genetically determined physiological factors. Environmental influences on development were minimized in his view, particularly in infancy and childhood. Hall did acknowledge that the environment accounts for more change in development during adolescence than in earlier age periods. Thus, Hall believed—as we do today—that at least during adolescence, heredity interacts with environmental influences to determine the individual's development.

Hall subscribed to a four-stage approach to development: infancy, childhood, youth, and adolescence. Adolescence is the period of time from about 12 to 23 years of age, or when adulthood is achieved. Hall saw adolescence as a period of *Sturm und Drang,* which means storm and stress. This label was borrowed from the German writings of Goethe and Schiller, who wrote novels full of idealism, commitment to goals, revolution, passion, and feeling. Hall sensed that there was a parallel between the themes of the German authors and the psychological development of adolescents.

According to Hall, the adolescent period of storm and stress is full of contradictions and wide swings in mood and emotion. Thoughts, feelings, and actions oscillate between conceit and humility, goodness and temptation, and happiness and sadness. One moment, the adolescent may be nasty to a peer, yet in the next moment be extremely nice to him or her. At one time, the adolescent may want to be left alone, but shortly thereafter desire to cling to somebody. In sum, G. Stanley Hall viewed adolescence as a turbulent time charged with conflict (Ross, 1972), a perspective labeled the **storm and stress view** of adolescence.

Hall's view also had implications for social development and education (White, 1985). Hall conceived of development as a biological process directed toward a series of possibilities of social organization. As children moved into adolescence, they were thought to be capable of entering progressively more complicated and powerful social arrangements. In the terminology of today, we might call Hall a "sociobiological developmentalist." Hall's analysis of the adolescent years also led him to believe that the time to begin strenuously educating such faculties as civility, scientific thinking, and morality is after the age of 15. However, Hall's developmental vision of education rested mainly on highly speculative theory rather than empirical data. While Hall believed that systematic methods should be developed to study adolescents, his research efforts usually resorted to the creation of rather weak and unconvincing questionnaires. But while the quality of his research was suspect, Hall was a giant in the history of understanding adolescent development. It was he who began the theorizing, the systematizing, the inquiry that went beyond mere speculation and philosophy. To Hall we owe the scientific beginnings of the study of adolescent development.

But while Hall was arguing strongly for a biological interpretation of adolescence, others emphasized that the period of development we now call adolescence actually was invented through a combination of social and historical conditions, as we see next.

The Inventionist View of Adolescence

A. K. Cohen suggests that teenagers may have sneaked up on us in our own lifetime:

> . . . not quite children and certainly not adults, in many ways privileged, wielding unprecedented economic power as consumers of clothing, entertainment, and other amenities, the object of a peculiar blend of tenderness, indulgence, distrust, hostility, moving through a seemingly endless course of "preparation for life" . . ., playing furiously at "adult" games but resolutely confined to a society of their own peers and excluded from serious and responsible participation in the world of their elders. . . . a few years ago, it occurred to me that, when I was a teenager, in the early Depression years, there were no teenagers! The teenager has sneaked up on us in our own lifetime, and yet it seems to us that he always has been with us. . . . The teenager had not yet been invented [though, and] there did not yet exist a special class of beings, bounded in a certain way . . . not quite children and certainly not adults. (Cohen, 1964, p. ix)

Thus, in Cohen's perspective, at a point not too long ago in history—the Depression years—the teenager had not yet been invented.

Social and historical conditions have led a number of writers and experts on adolescence to agree that adolescence indeed has been "invented" (Elder, 1975; Field, 1981; Finley, 1985; Hill, 1980; Lapsley, Enright, &

Serlin, 1985). Thus, while adolescence clearly has biological foundations, there nonetheless are many social and historical occurrences that have contributed to the acceptance of adolescence as the transitional time between childhood and adulthood. These social and historical occurrences include the decline in apprenticeship, increased mechanization during the Industrial Revolution (including upgraded skill requirements of labor and specialized divisions of labor), separation of work from the home, the writings of G. Stanley Hall and the increased interest in child guidance, changes in fertility patterns and family structure, urbanization, the appearance of such youth groups as the YMCA and Boy Scouts, and age-segregated schools.

The roles of schools, work, and economics have figured prominently in the current flourish of interest that has developed in the historical invention of adolescence. Some contributors argue that the institutionalization of adolescence was a by-product of the cultural motivation to create a system of compulsory public education. From this view, secondary schools are seen mainly as vehicles for transmitting intellectual skills to youth (e.g., Callahan, 1962; Cremin, 1961; Stedman & Smith, 1983). However, others argue that the primary purpose of secondary schools has been to deploy youth within the economic sphere and to serve as an important cog in the authority structure of the culture. Daniel Lapsley, Robert Enright, and Ronald Serlin (1985) adopt the latter stance. They believe that American society "inflicted" the status of adolescence on its youth and argue that the history of child-saving legislation is actually the history of the origins of adolescence. According to Lapsley, Enright, and Serlin, by developing laws for youth, the adult power structure placed young people in a submissive position on the authority hierarchy of the culture, a location restricting their options, encouraging dependency, and making their move into the world of work more manageable.

The period of 1890–1920 is now viewed as the age of adolescence—the time when adolescence was invented. It was during this time period that a great deal of compulsory legislation was enacted (Tyack, 1976). In virtually every state, laws requiring that secondary school be attended excluded youth from most employment. Extensive enforcement provisions characterized most of this legislation.

Two clear changes resulted from such legislation—decreased employment and increased school attendance by youth. From 1910 to 1930, there was a dramatic decrease in the number of 10- to 15-year-olds who were gainfully employed, dropping about 75 percent in this time frame. And between 1900 and 1930, there also was a tremendous increase in the number of high school graduates. Approximately 600 percent more individuals graduated from high school, and there was approximately a 450 percent increase in enrollment in high schools during this historical period.

As this historical look at adolescence indicates, school and work figured prominently in the invention of adolescence. In considering the historical interest in adolescence, it also is important to focus on another issue—the stereotyping of adolescents.

Stereotyping Adolescents

A study by Daniel Yankelovich (1974) indicates that many stereotypes about youth are false. Yankelovich compared the attitudes of adolescents with those of their parents about different values, life-styles, and codes of personal conduct. There was little or no difference in the attitudes of the adolescents and their parents toward self-control, hard work, saving money, competition, compromise, legal authority, and private property. There was a substantial difference between the adolescents and their parents with regard to religion (89 percent of the parents said that religion was important to them, compared to only 66 percent of the adolescents). But a majority of the adolescents still subscribed to the belief that religion is important.

John Hill (1983) also believes that many of the ideas the layperson has about adolescents are based on stereotypes that develop in a particular culture. For example, he points out that independence from and conflict with parents is likely overestimated in most views of the adolescent's development. In reality, many individuals move through the adolescent period in a reasonably smooth fashion. Similarly, we have gone through an era when adolescents as a group were branded as rebellious and deviant, while in reality, many of them were plugging along efficiently and competently toward mature adulthood. Hill thinks that adolescents would benefit if there was less dramatization of the adolescent period. Then, the majority of adolescents—who do not follow the pattern of the deviant minority—would not be penalized as heavily.

Joseph Adelson (1979) also stresses that far too many stereotypes about adolescents exist—many of which, he says, are based on the visible, rebellious adolescents of the 1960s. Adelson points out that there is an **adolescent "generalization gap"** rather than a "generation gap," meaning that widespread generalizations have developed that are based on information about a limited set of adolescents.

There has been a tendency to study the abnormalities and deviancies of adolescence more than the normalities. Consider the images and descriptions of adolescents that come to mind when you think about this group—rebellious, in conflict, impulsive, faddish, and so forth. Adelson (1979) argues, just as Yankelovich (1974) and Hill (1980) do, that the majority of adolescents are not experiencing a generation gap any more than the adolescents of any other era. Most adolescents do not experience intense turmoil or deep emotional disturbances. Neither are they completely controlled by their immediate impulses; nor do they totally reject parental values.

Before we examine the major physical changes that characterize adolescent development, there are two important issues to revisit.

Biology/Culture and Continuity/Discontinuity

As we consider development during the adolescent years, it is important to keep in mind two important issues that first were described in Chapter 1—the implications of biology/culture and continuity/discontinuity for understanding adolescent development.

Biology/Culture

On the one hand, G. Stanley Hall argued for a very strong biological explanation of adolescence, but the inventionist view stresses the importance of sociohistorical conditions. Which view is correct?

Development throughout the human life cycle is determined by an interaction of biological and cultural factors—for example, puberty is not an environmentally produced accident of development, yet its onset and continuation can be influenced by such factors as nutrition, health, cultural experiences, and the like. Thus, while the basic evolutionary and genetic program for puberty is wired into the species biologically, there is considerable room for environmental modification of the nature of the pubertal process. More about the nature of puberty and factors that influence its onset appears shortly in our discussion of physical development in adolescence.

As we discuss the nature of biological and cultural influences on adolescent development, it also is helpful to think once again about Urie Bronfenbrenner's ecological model of how sociocultural experiences influence development (Bronfenbrenner, 1979; Bronfenbrenner & Crouter, 1983). Recall from Chapter 6 that Bronfenbrenner believes that many experiences occur through direct interactions in a social setting, such as with family members, with peers, and with teachers. He also argues that there are important connections between contexts, such as the relation of family and peer experiences, that influence development. Bronfenbrenner also stresses that individuals can experience culture indirectly—for example, marital conflict or divorce might produce changes in the degree to which the adolescent's life is monitored effectively. And he also emphasizes that, to understand the impact of social experiences, we have to consider the attitudes and ideologies present in a culture, such as those present in lower- and middle-class situations and those that exist in countries such as Russia and the United States.

As we explore the nature of adolescent development, remember that, just like the child's development, the adolescent's development is influenced by an interaction of biology and culture, rather than solely by either factor alone.

Continuity/Discontinuity in Development

A second important issue for us to consider as we begin our study of adolescence is continuity/discontinuity in development. It is very easy to think that only the biological and social experiences occurring during adolescence determine the course of adolescent development. However, by the time the child enters adolescence, he or she has spent some 10 to 13 years in many different social settings with many different social agents and also carries with him or her the genetic code that was transmitted from parents. The thousands and thousands of hours of interaction with parents, peers, and at school that have occurred before adolescence do not just go away as the child enters and moves through adolescence. And the genetic inheritance of the individual still contributes in significant ways to the nature of adolescent development.

Still, the child experiences many new facets of the world during adolescence. Continued experiences with family members, peers, and at school, and new experiences in dating and sexual relationships in many other social settings and with many other people contribute to the makeup of the adolescent's development. The stance on continuity/discontinuity taken in Chapter 1 remains intact as we explore adolescent development—that is, there is continuity between childhood experiences and development in adolescence, but new experiences may influence development in adolescence as well.

Thus, as we begin our discussion of the adolescent's physical development, keep in mind that much development and many experiences are carried forward to influence the nature of adolescent development and also that adolescent development is best viewed as a product of an interaction of biological and cultural experiences. A summary of these ideas as well as the historical background of interest in adolescence is presented in Child Development Concept Table 12.1.

Now that we have some sense of the historical interest in adolescents and discussed two important issues related to development during adolescence, we turn our attention to more specific aspects of development, beginning with physical changes.

PHYSICAL DEVELOPMENT IN ADOLESCENCE

Immense physical changes characterize adolescent development, particularly early adolescence. To understand these physical changes, we examine the nature of the pubertal process, the endocrine system that is such an important part of pubertal change, physical changes, and psychological accompaniments of these physical changes.

The Nature of the Pubertal Process

Imagine a toddler displaying all the features of puberty. Think about a three-year-old girl with fully developed breasts or a boy just slightly older with a deep male voice. That is what we would see by the year 2250 if the age at which puberty arrives kept getting younger at its present pace.

In Norway, **menarche** (the first menstruation) occurs at just over 13 years of age, as opposed to 17 years of

Child Development Concept Table 12.1   Historical Background, Biology/Culture, and Continuity/Discontinuity

Concept	Processes/Related Ideas	Characteristics/Description
Historical background	G. Stanley Hall	G. Stanley Hall is viewed as the father of the scientific study of adolescence. His view is a storm and stress perspective, suggesting that adolescence is a turbulent time for all of us. His biological deterministic view of adolescence is now perceived as too strong a statement.
	The inventionist view	Between 1890 and 1920, a cadre of urban reformers, youth workers, and counselors began to mold the concept of adolescence. A number of scholars argue for an inventionist view of adolescence—one emphasizing that adolescence was constructed out of sociohistorical conditions. They believe that legislation ensured the dependency of youth and made their move into the economic sphere more manageable.
	Stereotyping adolescents	Widespread generalizations that are based on information about a limited set of highly visible adolescents have resulted in a number of inaccurate stereotypes about adolescents.
Biology/culture and continuity/ discontinuity	Biology/culture	Adolescence, just like childhood, is influenced by an interaction of biological and cultural factors, rather than either factor alone.
	Continuity/discontinuity	There is continuity between childhood experiences and development in adolescence, but new experiences may influence development in adolescence as well.

age in the 1840s. In the United States—where children mature up to a year earlier than children in European countries—the average age of menarche has declined from 14.2 in 1900 to about 12.45 today. The age of menarche has been declining at an average of about four months per decade for the past century (see Figure 12.1).

Fortunately, however, we are unlikely to see pubescent toddlers, since what has happened in the past century is special. The best guess is that the something special is a higher level of nutrition and health. The available information suggests that menarche began to occur earlier at about the time of the Industrial Revolution, a period linked with increased standards of living and advances in medical science.

Menarche also is associated with weight. For example, Rose Frisch and Roger Revelle (1970) have documented that menarche occurs at a relatively constant weight. (They also found that the adolescent growth spurt begins at relatively constant weights for boys and girls.) They suggest that, for menarche to occur and continue, fat must make up about 17 percent of the body weight. Thus, both teenage anorexics (who starve themselves) and female athletes in certain sports, such as track and gymnastics, may experience **amenorrhea,** that is, they have an abnormal absence or suppression of menstrual discharge.

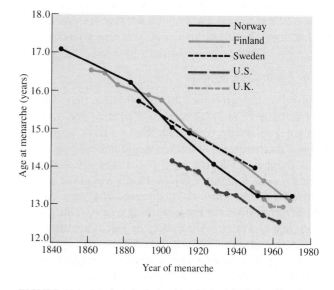

FIGURE 12.1   Age (median) at menarche in selected northern European countries and the United States from 1845 to 1969.

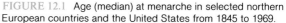

Defining puberty has complicated the search for its trigger. While **puberty** can be defined as a rapid change to maturation, it is not a single, sudden event, but part of a slow, gradually unfolding process that begins at conception (about 10 to 15 percent of the variation in age

at menarche is believed to be genetic in nature). We know when a young person is going through puberty, but pinpointing its onset and end is difficult. Except for menarche, which occurs rather late in the pubertal process, there is no single marker heralding puberty. For boys, the first wet dream and the first whisker are events that could mark its appearance, but both may go unnoticed.

The Endocrine System

Before we describe the physical changes that characterize puberty, such as sexual maturation and gains in height and weight, it is important to know something about the hormonal system that stimulates these physical changes. Endocrinology, or the study of the endocrine system, is highly complex. Here we examine several basic ideas about how the endocrine system works.

The endocrine system is made up of endocrine glands and their secretions. The endocrine glands are often less noticeable than other glands because their secretions are carried in the bloodstream instead of through ducts. Glands with ducts are called exocrine glands and secrete such substances as saliva, sweat, and breast milk. The secretions of endocrine glands are **hormones,** which are powerful chemical substances that regulate organs that are often far from the endocrine glands where the secretions are first emitted.

The aspects of the endocrine system that are most important in puberty involve the **hypothalamic-pituitary-gonadal axis** (Nottelmann et al., 1985; Nottelmann et al., in press). The **hypothalamus** is a structure in the higher portion of the brain. The **pituitary gland** is often referred to as a master gland and is located at the base of the brain. Its reference as a master gland comes from its regulation of a number of other glands. The term **gonadal** refers to the sex glands—the testes in males and the ovaries in females. The hormonal system involving the hypothalamus, pituitary gland, and gonads works like this: While the pituitary monitors endocrine levels, it is regulated by the hypothalamus. The pituitary sends a signal via a **gonadotropin** (a hormone that stimulates the testes or ovaries) to the appropriate gland to manufacture the hormone. Then, the pituitary, through interaction with the hypothalamus, detects when the optimal level is reached and responds by maintaining gonadotropin and sex-hormone secretion (Petersen & Taylor, 1980).

There are two general classes of sex hormones that are important in understanding pubertal development—androgens and estrogens. **Androgens** mature primarily in males, and **estrogens** mature mainly in females. Current research has been able to pinpoint more precisely which androgens and estrogens seem to play the most important roles in pubertal development. For example, **testosterone** appears to assume an important role in the pubertal development of males. Throughout puberty, increasing testosterone levels are clearly linked with a number of physical changes in boys: development of external genitals, increase in height, and voice changes (Fregly & Luttge, 1982). In females, **estradiol** is likely the most important hormone responsible for pubertal development. The level of estradiol increases throughout

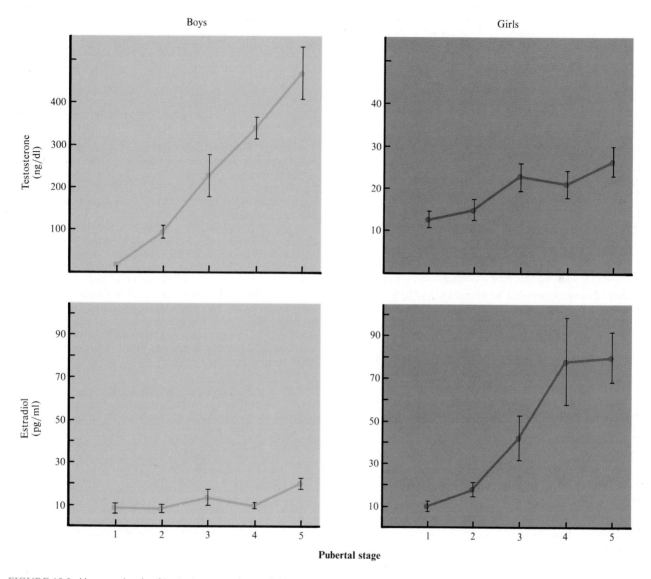

FIGURE 12.2   Hormone levels of testosterone and estradiol by sex and pubertal stage.

puberty and then varies in women across their menstrual cycle. As the estradiol level rises, breast and uterine development occur and skeletal changes also appear (Dillon, 1980; Fregly & Luttge, 1982).

As shown in Figure 12.2, in one study, testosterone levels were found to increase 18-fold in boys but only 2-fold in girls across the pubertal period (Nottelmann et al., 1985). For girls in the same study, there was an 8-fold increase in estradiol, but the increase for this hormone in boys was only 2-fold. Note that both testos-

terone and estradiol are present in the hormonal makeup of both boys and girls but that testosterone is dominant for boys, while estradiol is stronger in girls. It should be mentioned that testosterone and estradiol are part of a complex hormonal system and that, alone, each hormone is not solely responsible for pubertal change. Nonetheless, their strong association with the physical changes of puberty suggests that they clearly play a very important role in the pubertal process.

FOCUS ON CHILD DEVELOPMENT 12.1

GONADOTROPINS, SEX STEROIDS, ADRENAL ANDROGENS, AND THE ADOLESCENT

The same influx of hormones that put hair on a male's chest and impart curvature to a female's breasts also may be linked to psychological adjustment during adolescence. As we have seen, it is during puberty that hormone levels increase dramatically, setting in motion physical changes that transform a child's body into an adult's body. In an effort to determine the role of hormones in the adolescent's adjustment, Edith Nottelmann, Elizabeth Susman, and their colleagues (1985, in press) have studied the hormone levels, physical development, and behavioral characteristics of 108 normal adolescent boys and girls, ages 9 to 14. They focused on three types of hormones—**gonadotropins, sex steroids** (testosterone and estradiol), and **adrenal androgens** (secreted by the adrenal gland). The researchers created a hormone "profile" for each adolescent, and, in addition, the adolescents and their parents filled out a variety of questionnaires related to the adolescent's personality traits, moods, self-image, behavior problems, and competence in physical, social, and cognitive activities.

Nottelmann and her colleagues have concluded from their research that, first, hormone levels are associated with adolescent adjustment. The most consistent finding is that higher sex steroid and lower adrenal androgen levels are associated with competent adjustment. For example, a higher sex steroid level in boys was associated with whether boys rated themselves as competent in social matters, while a higher adrenal androgen level was linked with adolescent boys' negative perception of their competence in social affairs (see the figure in the next column). Further, the mothers of adolescent boys with higher adrenal androgen and lower sex steroid levels rated the boys as showing more delinquent behavior than their lower adrenal androgen/higher sex steroid counterparts (see the figure on the following page).

Second, the links between hormone levels and adjustment were stronger for boys than girls. This could be due either to biological or environmental factors. It also could be due to the fact that hormonal levels are more difficult to measure accurately in girls, probably because female hormone levels are cyclical (move up and down).

Third, in a number of instances, the timing of changes in hormone levels was more likely to be associated with the adjustment of adolescents than the actual pubertal stage in which the adolescents were classified due to their external physical characteristics. The onset of hormonal changes often precedes changes in external physical characteristics that usually are called on as an index of pubertal maturity (such as breast development in girls and testicular volume in boys). Thus, only using external physical characteristics as pubertal markers may obscure important relations between pubertal change and adjustment.

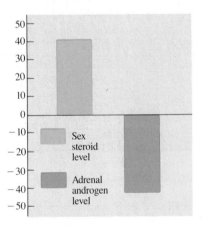

Relations of adolescent boys' perceived social competence to sex steroid and adrenal androgen levels.

Fourth, the researchers determined that the adrenal androgens were associated in important ways with the adjustment of adolescent boys. Previously, the adrenal androgens had been thought to play only a minor role in pubertal development, but the Nottelmann research suggests that perhaps they should be studied more closely in future inquiries about the nature of relations between hormones, puberty, and adolescent adjustment.

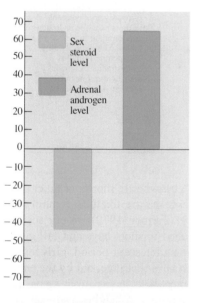

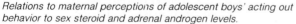

Relations to maternal perceptions of adolescent boys' acting out behavior to sex steroid and adrenal androgen levels.

While it has been known for some time that hormones play a very powerful role in the development of puberty, only recently has research demonstrated the manner in which hormones might not only be associated with pubertal changes but also with the behavior of adolescents. As described in Focus on Child Development 12.1, hormonal level may turn out to be an important predictor of adolescent behavior and adjustment.

Before we leave the discussion of hormones and puberty, one additional aspect of the pituitary gland's master role in development needs to be portrayed. Not only does the pituitary gland release gonadotropins that stimulate the testes and ovaries, but through its interaction with the hypothalamus, it also secretes hormones that either directly lead to growth and skeletal maturation or that produce such growth effects through interaction with the **thyroid gland,** located in the neck region.

Figure 12.3 shows the location and functions of the major endocrine glands. Now that we have studied the important role of the endocrine system in pubertal development, we turn our attention to the external physical changes that characterize puberty.

Physical Changes

Among the important ideas about physical changes are those pertaining to height and weight, sexual maturation, individual variation, and sexual attitudes and behavior.

Height and Weight

As individuals undergo the adolescent growth spurt, they make rapid gains in height and weight. But as indicated in Figure 12.4, the growth spurt for girls occurs approximately two years earlier than for boys. The growth spurt in girls begins at approximately age 10½ and lasts for about two years. During this time period, girls increase in height by about 3½ inches per year. The growth spurt for boys usually begins at about age 12½ and also lasts for approximately two years. Boys usually grow about 4 inches per year in height during this growth spurt (Tanner, 1970). These averages do not reflect the fairly wide range of time within which the adolescent growth spurt begins. Girls may start the growth spurt as early as age 7½ or as late as age 11½, while boys may begin as early as age 10½ or as late as age 16 (Faust, 1977).

Pituitary gland: The master gland, producing hormones that stimulate other glands. Also more directly influences growth by producing growth hormones. Sends gonadotropins to testes and ovaries, and a thyroid stimulating hormone to thyroid gland. And sends hormone to adrenal gland as well.

Hypothalamus: Structure in brain that interacts with pituitary gland in monitoring bodily regulation of hormones.

Thyroid gland: Interacts with pituitary gland to influence growth.

Adrenal gland: Interacts with pituitary, likely plays some role in pubertal development but less is known about its function than sex glands. Recent research, however, suggests it may be involved in adolescent behavior, particularly for boys.

The sex glands: Testes in males, ovaries in females. Heavily involved in the appearance of secondary sex characteristics, such as facial hair in males, and breast development in females. The general class of hormones called estrogens are dominant in females while androgens are dominant in males. More specifically, testosterone in males and estradiol in females are key hormones in pubertal development.

FIGURE 12.3   The major endocrine glands involved in pubertal development.

What is the nature of height and weight changes in puberty?

Boys and girls who are shorter or taller than their peers before adolescence are likely to remain so during adolescence (e.g., Tanner, 1970). In our society, there is a stigma attached to short boys and tall girls. At the beginning of the adolescent period, girls tend to be as tall or taller than boys their age, but by the end of the junior high years, most boys have caught up or, in many cases, even surpassed girls in height. And even though height in the elementary school years is a good predictor of height later in adolescence, there is still room for the individual's height to change in relation to the height of his or her peers.

The rate at which adolescents gain weight follows approximately the same developmental timetable as the rate at which they gain height. Marked weight gains coincide with the onset of puberty. During early adolescence, girls tend to outweigh boys, but by about age 14, just as with height, boys tend to surpass girls (Faust, 1977; Tanner, 1970).

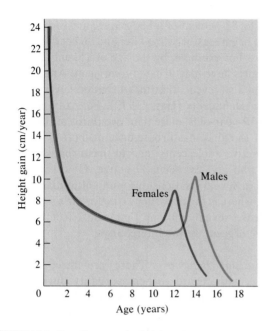

FIGURE 12.4 Growth curves for height in boys and girls. These curves represent the rate of growth of typical boy and girl at a given age.

Sexual Maturation and Behavior

Think back to your last few years of childhood and then to your first few years of adolescence. Probably nothing comes to mind more strikingly than the sexual maturation that began to occur during the first two years of adolescence. You are also likely to recall that, during the last several years of childhood, your interest in sexual activity and sexual relationships was nowhere near the level it reached during the first few years of adolescence. Few aspects of development throughout the life cycle attract more curiosity and are as mysterious as the onset of sexual maturation during early adolescence.

Three of the most noticeable aspects of sexual maturation in boys are penis elongation, testes development, and the growth of pubic hair. The normal range and average age of development for these sexual characteristics is shown in Figure 12.5. Two of the most marked aspects of the female's sexual maturation are the growth of pubic hair and breast development. Figure 12.6 illustrates the normal range and average age of development for these female characteristics, as well as information about menarche and height gain, two other prominent features of female pubertal change.

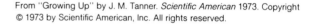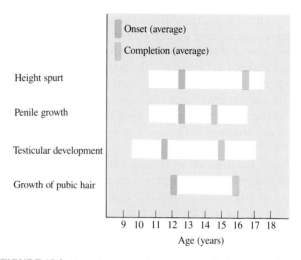

FIGURE 12.5 Normal range and average age of development of sexual characteristics in males.

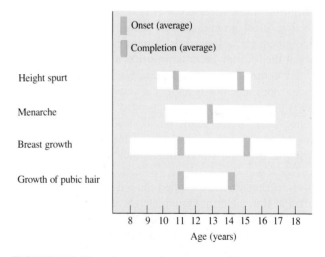

FIGURE 12.6 Normal range and average age of development of sexual characteristics in females.

For most boys, the pubertal sequence may begin as early as age 10 and as late as age 13½, at which time there is an acceleration in the growth of the testes. If this sequence ends at the time of the first ejaculation, the average age at termination is 13½ to 14 (although ejaculation could happen much earlier or later, depending upon when the process started). Among the most remarkable normal variations is the fact that two boys may be the same chronological age, and yet one may complete the pubertal sequence before the other has begun it. For most girls, the first menstrual period may occur at the age of 10 or as late as the age of 15½ (Hill, 1980).

During the time of rapid maturation of sexual characteristics, most adolescents, as we see next, engage in sexual fantasies.

Sexual Fantasies   Are the sexual fantasies of adolescent males and females different? As a rule, adolescent females are more sexually inhibited than adolescent males are. Most adolescent girls are not encouraged to acknowledge their sexual needs. Although they are taught to make themselves attractive, their own sexual feelings often go undiscussed. Thus, the sexual drive of adolescent girls often tends to manifest itself in fantasies about the future—becoming a bride, a lover, and so forth.

By contrast, the sexual fantasies of adolescent boys focus more specifically on sexual activity itself. Some experts suggest that it is only toward the end of adolescence that males begin to see sex as an important component of human communication and that females discover the robust potential of their bodies (Haeberle, 1978).

Now that we have studied the nature of the pubertal process, the endocrine system, height and weight changes, sexual maturation, and sexual fantasies, let's investigate the nature of actual sexual behavior among adolescents, looking at self-stimulation, homosexual behavior, and heterosexual behavior.

Self-Stimulation   The most extensive data collected about adolescent sexual behavior are those reported by Alfred Kinsey, (Kinsey, Pomeroy, & Martin, 1948). A rapid increase in the incidence of masturbation occurs for boys between the ages of 13 and 15. By age 15, for

example, 82 percent of all boys have masturbated. Girls tend to begin masturbating later and do not do so as often as boys. For example, by the age of 15, only 25 percent of all girls have masturbated to orgasm. Another investigation also reveals that masturbation is very common among adolescents (Hass, 1979). For example, among 16- to 19-year-olds, more than two thirds of the boys and half of the girls masturbate once or more a week. Sexually active adolescents tend to masturbate more than those who are less sexually active. However, boys involved in sexual relationships tend not to masturbate as much, whereas the opposite is true for girls—apparently to release sexual tensions that result from failure to achieve orgasm during intercourse.

Homosexual Behavior   There are three consistent findings with regard to homosexuality during adolescence (Dreyer, 1982). First, homosexual contacts occur more frequently before the age of 15 and involve boys more than girls (Hass, 1979).

Second, acceptance of homosexuality is widespread. Nearly 70 percent of 16- to 19-year-olds accept sexual relationships between two girls and only slightly fewer adolescents accept such contacts between boys. As a rule, boys accept female homosexuality more than male homosexuality, whereas girls accept both about equally (Hass, 1979).

Third, in spite of liberal attitudes about homosexuality, less than 15 percent of boys and 10 percent of girls report that they have ever had even one homosexual contact during adolescence. Only 3 percent of the boys and 2 percent of the girls report participating in an ongoing homosexual relationship (Chilman, 1979; Hass, 1979). Although many other types of sexual behavior in adolescence seem to have increased during recent years, participation in homosexual relationships appears to have remained the same or possibly even declined (Chilman, 1979).

One point needs to be made about the acceptance and incidence of homosexual behavior. The data on the increase in acceptance of homosexual behavior were collected prior to the recent fear created by AIDS. It is likely that, when surveys of homosexual acceptance are conducted in the future, acceptance may be reduced.

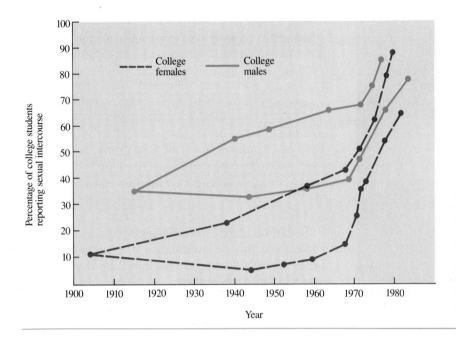

FIGURE 12.7   Percentage of twentieth-century college youth reporting having sexual intercourse.

(Note: This graph is based on a large number of studies of the sexual intercourse of college students at different points in the twentieth century, beginning in 1903 and continuing through 1980. Based on data presented by Darling, Kallen, & VanDusen, 1984, p. 388.)

Heterosexual Behavior and Attitudes   In a review of sexual practices and attitudes involving college females and males from 1900 to 1980 (Darling, Kallen, & VanDusen, 1984), two major trends were apparent. First, there has been a major increase in the proportion of young people reporting intercourse, and second, the proportion of females reporting coital involvement has increased more rapidly than the proportion of males, although the initial basis for males is greater (see Figure 12.7). Previous to 1970, about twice as many college males as females reported coital involvement, but since 1970, the proportions of males and females are almost equal.

Such changes are viewed as supporting major shifts in the standards governing sexual behavior. That is, there has been a move away from a double standard in which it was more appropriate for males to have intercourse than females. This seemed to characterize sexual standards through the late 1940s and early 1950s. There followed an era of permissiveness with affection (Reiss, 1967). This standard allowed sexual intercourse as long as a love relationship was present and the relationship was expected to lead to marriage. This standard lasted until approximately 1970, at which time the present era

appeared. This new standard has focused on the belief that sexual intercourse is a natural and expected part of a love relationship, a relationship that does not necessarily lead to marriage. Under this current standard, while intercourse also is acceptable for both males and females in a nonlove relationship, physical or emotional exploitation of the partner is not.

The majority of inquiries about heterosexual relationships have focused on college students and adults. Recently, however, some investigators have queried adolescents about their sexual behavior as well (Chilman, 1979; Cvetkovich & Grote, 1975; Hass, 1979; Kantner & Zelnick, 1973; Sorenson, 1973; Vener & Stewart, 1974; Zelnick & Kantner, 1978a, 1978b). Philip Dreyer (1982) points out that, while the new norm suggests to adolescents that sex is acceptable, it is acceptable mainly within the boundary of a loving and affectionate relationship. By contrast, promiscuity, exploitation, and unprotected sexual intercourse are often perceived as unacceptable by adolescents. However, there still seems to be a tendency for society to accept and promote sexual activity for male adolescents and not female adolescents. The double standard seems to persist. Thus, there still may be considerable pressure on adolescent males to have

How have the standards of heterosexual relationships changed?

Table 12.1	Age at First Intercourse by Age Group			
	Females (Percent)		Males (Percent)	
Present Age	15–16	17–18	15–16	17–18
Age of first intercourse				
13	7	3	18	7
16	31	41	43	42

Reprinted with permission of Macmillan Publishing Company from *Teenage Sexuality: A Survey of Teenage Sex* by Aaron Hass. Copyright © 1979 by Aaron Hass, Ph.D.

So far, we mainly have discussed physical changes in adolescence. But the investigation of sexual attitudes and behaviors calls attention to the important psychological aspects of physical changes.

Psychological Accompaniments of Physical Changes

A host of psychological characteristics and social consequences accompany changes in the adolescent's physical development. Think about your own changing body as you began puberty. Not only did you probably begin to think in different ways about yourself, but important individuals in your life, such as peers and parents, probably began acting differently toward you as well. Maybe you were proud of your changing body, even though you may have been perplexed about what was going on. Or maybe you felt embarrassed about the changes that were taking place and experienced a lot of anxiety. Perhaps you looked in the mirror on a daily or sometimes even on an hourly basis to see if you were maturing physically and to see if you could detect anything different about your changing body.

Body Image

One thing is certain about the psychological aspects of physical development—adolescents show a great deal of preoccupation with their bodies and develop individual images of what their bodies are like. Surveys of adolescents reveal that young adolescents are more preoccupied and dissatisfied with their bodies than late adolescents (Hamburg, 1974). And in another investigation, girls who were judged as being attractive, and who generally had positive attitudes about their bodies,

sexual intercourse. As one adolescent male recently remarked, "Look, I feel a lot of pressure from my buddies to go for the score." One stereotype among contemporary male adolescents is that they will be perceived as homosexual if they have not had sexual intercourse—a fear that is referred to as **homophobia.**

At the behavioral level, there seems to be an increase in sexual behavior among adolescents and at an earlier age than in the past. Many adolescents believe that mid- to late adolescence is the best time to first have sexual intercourse. In one investigation, at age 16, slightly over 40 percent of the males had engaged in sexual intercourse, while approximately 30 to 40 percent of the females had (see Table 12.1) (Hass, 1979). Also note in Table 12.1 that, at age 13, more than twice as many males as females had engaged in sexual intercourse. This finding that male adolescents engage in sexual intercourse at an earlier age than females has been discovered by other researchers as well. Such results are curious in light of the fact that females reach puberty, on the average, two years earlier than males. The curious findings undoubtedly are related to the different standards we have in our culture for males and females and the distinctive way we socialize children and adolescents because of their sex.

Table 12.2 The Average Importance of Selected Body Characteristics for Personal Physical Attractiveness for Males and Females (Lower Numbers Indicate *Greatest* Importance)		
	Males' Own Importance	Females' Own Importance
Body Characteristics	*Mean*	*Mean*
Facial complexion	1.8	1.6
Ears	3.5	3.9
Chest	2.6	2.4
Profile	2.3	2.5
Distribution of weight	2.0	1.7
Eyes	2.4	1.9
Height	2.7	2.9
Ankles	4.2	4.1
Waist	2.4	2.3
Arms	3.0	3.1
Shape of legs	2.8	2.2
General appearance	1.5	1.3
Hips	2.8	2.2
Width of shoulders	2.9	3.4
Mouth	2.4	2.4
Neck	2.8	3.2
Teeth	2.0	1.9
Nose	2.4	2.4
Chin	2.8	3.1
Hair texture	2.3	2.3
Body build	1.9	1.7
Hair color	3.2	3.2
Thighs	2.9	2.5
Face	1.5	1.4

From Lerner, R. M. and S. A. Karabenick, "Physical attractiveness, body attitudes and self-concept in late adolescence" in *Journal of Youth and Adolescence, 3*, 307–316, 1974. Copyright © 1974 Plenum Publishing Corporation, New York. Reprinted by permission.

How acutely concerned are young adolescents about their body images?

were found to have higher opinions of themselves in general (Lerner & Karabenick, 1974). Boys with athletic physiques also had more positive self-concepts, and those who were overweight had more negative self-images. Table 12.2 provides an overview of some of the bodily characteristics adolescents rate as important. Note that boys and girls do not differ much in their ratings of which parts of their bodies are important to them.

Early and Late Maturation

The majority of research that has addressed the issue of early and late maturation in adolescence has been collected as part of a longitudinal growth study at the University of California. The upshot of the California investigations concerning early and late maturation is that boys who mature early in adolescence (as measured by their skeletal growth) perceive themselves more positively and are more successful in peer relations than their late-maturing counterparts. The findings for early-maturing girls are also positive but not as strong as for boys (Mussen & Jones, 1958).

However, while early maturation seems to favor boys when they are studied in adolescence, this advantage may wane in later years. Indeed, when the early and late maturers were followed into their 30s and their identity formation evaluated, it was the late maturers who seemed to have an advantage (Jones, 1965; Peskin, 1967). It is argued that early maturers may be pushed into decisions about their identity too soon. By contrast, those adolescents who mature later may have more time to handle the physical changes and therefore may be more flexible in their identity development.

Another longitudinal investigation of early and late maturation was conducted by Dale Blyth and his colleagues (Blyth, Bulcroft, & Simmons, 1981). In this study, the presence or absence of menstruation and the relative onset of menses were used to classify girls as early, middle, and late maturers. For boys, the classification was made on the basis of peak rate of height growth. More than 450 individuals were followed for five years, beginning in the 6th grade and continuing through the 10th grade in Milwaukee, Wisconsin, from 1974 through 1979. Students were individually interviewed, and achievement-test scores and grade point averages were obtained.

LUANN   BY GREG EVANS

LUANN by Greg Evans. © by and permission of News America Syndicate, Inc.

The findings for early-maturing boys confirmed the California results, whereas the data for early-maturing girls were mixed. Early maturation in girls seemed to be disadvantageous for grades and achievement-test performance at school. Early-maturing girls also were more likely to show problem behavior at school, such as skipping classes. However, early maturation was advantageous for girls in terms of independence and opposite-sex relationships. Some of the most intriguing findings, though, pertained to the girl's body image.

One of the most important tasks of adolescence is to incorporate dramatic physical changes into a positive body image. With regard to satisfaction with one's figure, a complex pattern developed for adolescent girls (see Figure 12.8). More developed, menstruating girls showed greater satisfaction with their figures in the 6th grade than did late-maturing girls. But by the 9th and 10th grade, the pattern was reversed. When all girls were developed, it was the late maturers who were more satisfied with their figures. One reason for this pattern of findings is that, by the 9th and 10th grade, early maturers are usually shorter and stockier and late maturers are often taller and thinner. Possibly, the late-maturing female in the 9th and 10th grades more closely approximates the American ideal of feminine beauty—tall and slim.

Thus, early and late maturation during the adolescent years is a complex topic. And it is important to consider the point in development when the effects are being assessed and the specific outcomes or dimensions that are being evaluated before arriving at any conclusions.

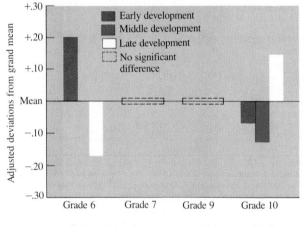

FIGURE 12.8   Pubertal development and satisfaction with figure.

Recently, another aspect of the adolescent's development was investigated in relation to early and late maturation. As seen in Focus on Child Development 12.2, the physical attractiveness of girls is a factor that likely mediates the effects of early and late maturation on self-esteem.

On-Time/Off-Time in Pubertal Development

We have seen that not all boys and girls move through the pubertal sequence at the same time and that they often are acutely aware of their pubertal status vis-à-vis their age-mates. Jeanne Brooks-Gunn, Anne Peterson, and Dorothy Eichorn (1985) recently evaluated the

FOCUS ON CHILD DEVELOPMENT 12.2

PHYSICAL ATTRACTIVENESS, PUBERTAL CHANGE, AND SELF-ESTEEM IN ADOLESCENT GIRLS

The body as a social stimulus has been given increased research attention in recent years (e.g., Berscheid & Walster, 1974; Dion, Berscheid, & Walster, 1972). Individual differences in physical attractiveness may mediate the effects of early and late maturation on adolescent development. As part of the Milwaukee Longitudinal Study focused on early and late maturation, David Zakin, Dale Blyth, and Roberta Simmons (1984) examined the effects of early pubertal development and physical attractiveness on the popularity, body image, and self-esteem of more than 200 sixth-grade girls. Attractiveness was rated by an adult nurse using two five-point scales, one ranging from fat to skinny, the other from ugly to very good-looking. Attractive girls were defined as those observers rated as both above average in looks and average to thin in body build. Unattractive girls were defined as those observers rated as both chubby in body build and below average in looks. Girls who fell between these categories were labeled as average in attractiveness. With regard to the assessment of self-esteem, girls were asked to answer six questions from the Rosenberg Self-Esteem Scale specifically designed for children and young adolescents. High scores on this scale suggest that the girl considers herself to be a person of worth, while low scores indicate that she experiences some degree of self-rejection or dissatisfaction.

The results of this inquiry indicated that, regardless of puberty status, unattractive girls perceived themselves as less popular and had a less satisfactory body image than attractive girls. However, when the unattractive girls were in the midst of pubertal change, (that is, developing), they exhibited higher self-esteem than their attractive counterparts (see the figure). This finding may be explained by considering the degree of risk or uncertainty involved in making the transition through early adolescence. The attractive girl, prior to experiencing pubertal change, is accustomed to preferential treatment because of her looks. Presumably, her self-esteem is to some extent tied to her physical appearance. Thus, when the attractive girl begins to experience the pubertal transition, the physical changes may be more threatening to her

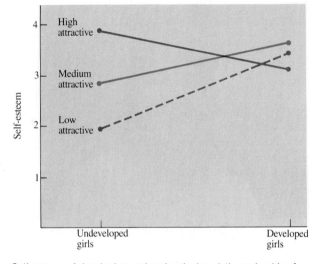

Self-esteem of developing and undeveloping sixth grade girls of varying degrees of attractiveness.

because of the possible risk of losing her attractiveness. She does not know at this point in development what the final outcome will be. By contrast, the unattractive girl may welcome the onset of puberty. From her view, she has nothing to lose. The popular myth of the ugly duckling who turns into a beautiful swan may offer her some hope. Because she believes that puberty may result in a more beautiful body, she may cope relatively better during the pubertal change process than the girl who initially was more attractive.

An alternative explanation also is possible. Developing, attractive girls face a different arena of social circumstances than developing, unattractive girls. The developing girl's bodily changes, including breast development, alter the nature of her interactions with the opposite sex, imbuing them with sexual overtones. Young, physically maturing girls may not yet be emotionally mature enough to handle the adultlike pressures of dating and opposite-sex relationships. Physically attractive girls, due to their greater appeal, are especially likely to receive more attention from boys. Because of

(continued on following page)

During puberty, how might attractiveness be related to self-esteem?

these reactions, they may become more acutely aware that they face the transition to new roles in life. This realization, combined with an increase in emotional demands, may lead to a change in self-image, which is reflected in lower self-esteem. For example, in the Milwaukee study, early involvement with boys was linked with lower self-esteem and poor school performance. However, this alternative interpretation does not account for the unattractive developing girl's higher self-esteem.

In sum, this investigation reveals that puberty may have different meanings for girls differing in physical attractiveness. It is particularly interesting that, at least during the peak of physical change in puberty, the attractive girl has more difficulty adjusting than the unattractive girl.

timing of maturational events and its implications for pubertal development. They found that being on-time or off-time in terms of pubertal events is a complex affair. In terms of such timing, it is important to consider not just biological status or pubertal age, but also chronological age, grade in school, cognitive functioning, and social maturity. Such complexity in the development of the adolescent suggests that it may be inappropriate to categorize the individual on only one dimension of development, such as pubertal age. A seventh-grade girl may be on-time for pubertal age (i.e., biological growth) but off-time socially or cognitively in terms of comparison with her age-mates. Or, the girl may be on-time socially but off-time cognitively and biologically.

And variability may occur within a particular domain—such as biological changes. For example, when investigators use different measures to index pubertal events, variability among various characteristics often is considerable. A girl may be on-time with regard to breast development but not pubic hair development. In too many investigations, only one measure is used to index puberty—thus, in such studies, asynchrony in pubertal development may be hidden. One investigation found that the onset of breast development, but not pubic hair, was linked with the social development of fifth- and sixth-grade girls (Brooks-Gunn & Warren, 1985).

Bernice Neugarten and Nancy Datan (1973) argue that social time is just as important as chronological time in understanding adolescence. They believe that off-time and on-time events can be thought of both in terms of biological and social markers. Historical time also is stressed in their view. The findings by Dale Blyth and his colleagues (Blyth, Bulcroft, & Simmons, 1981) described earlier in the chapter call attention to the importance of historical time, as do the data on the earlier occurrence of puberty in recent years. Blyth's interpretation of the body image differences of early- and late-maturing girls pertained to the fact that the current model of the ideal female body image involves a tall, slender figure.

Given that a number of different domains must be considered when evaluating the nature of pubertal timing, the **goodness-of-fit model** proposed by Richard Lerner (1985) takes on added meaning. Lerner believes that adolescents may be at risk when the demands of a particular social context and the adolescents' physical and behavioral characteristics are mismatched. On-time dancers are one such example (Brooks-Gunn & Warren, 1985). With regard to general peer comparisons, on-time dancers should not show adjustment problems. However, they do not have the ideal characteristics thought to be important in the world of dancers. That is, the ideal characteristics of dancers are those generally associated with late maturity—a thin, lithe body build. The dancers, then, are on-time in terms of their peer group in general, but there is an asynchrony to their development in terms of their more focused peer group—dancers. Clearly, as we have seen throughout this chapter, understanding pubertal timing is a complex affair with many different domains and no simple conclusions.

Child Development Concept Table 12.2 summarizes our discussion of physical development in adolescence. Next, we consider the cognitive gains made during the adolescent years.

Child Development Concept Table 12.2   Physical Development in Adolescence

Concept	Processes/Related Ideas	Characteristics/Description
Puberty	Its nature	Puberty is a rapid change to maturation that does not involve a single event but rather is part of a long developmental process. Menarche is the girl's first menstruation and has been occurring earlier in recent decades probably because of improved nutrition and health.
The endocrine system	The hypothalamic-pituitary-gonadal axis	The endocrine glands secrete hormones. Hormones are powerful chemical substances that regulate organs. The aspects of the endocrine system that are primarily involved in puberty make up what is called the hypothalamic-pituitary-gonadal axis.
	Sex hormones	There are two general classes of sex hormones—androgens, which mature primarily in males, and estrogens, which mature mainly in females. More precisely, testosterone appears to be the sex hormone that increases the most during male pubertal development, while estradiol assumes this role in female pubertal development. Research by Nottelmann and her colleagues focused on three types of hormones—gonadotropins, sex steroids, and adrenal androgens. Their research revealed that the secretion of sex hormones is related to adolescent psychological characteristics and behavior, although more so for boys than for girls. The thyroid gland, another important part of the endocrine system, communicates with the pituitary gland and influences growth and skeletal maturation.
Physical changes	Height and weight	As adolescents undergo a growth spurt, they make rapid gains in height and weight. The spurt occurs approximately two years earlier in girls (at age 10½) than in boys (at age 12½).
	Sexual maturation and behavior	Sexual maturation is one of the hallmarks of pubertal development. Three of the most noticeable changes in boys are penis elongation, testes growth, and pubic hair. Three of the most obvious changes in girls are menarche and the menstrual cycle, breast development, and pubic hair. Adolescent males' sexual fantasies are more explicit than those of females. The frequency of masturbation increases between the ages of 13 and 15, but much more so for boys than girls. Homosexual contacts occur more in boys than girls, and acceptance of homosexuality is greater than the incidence of the behavior, although the AIDS epidemic may decrease acceptance. There has been a rapid increase in sexual intercourse reported by young people during the 20th century, with the increase more pronounced for females than males. The current sexual standard stresses that physical and emotional exploitation of the partner is unacceptable.

(continued on following page)

Child Development Concept Table 12.2   Continued

Concept	Processes/Related Ideas	Characteristics/Description
Psychological accompaniments of physical changes	Body image	Adolescents show a considerable increase in interest in their body image. Young adolescents are more preoccupied and dissatisfied with their bodies than late adolescents.
	Early and late maturation	While early maturation has seemed to favor boys when they are studied during adolescence, when they are studied as adults, early maturers are less likely to have achieved a successful identity. Research on girls suggests that, with regard to body image, early maturers show greater satisfaction with their figures in early adolescence, but by late adolescence, the pattern is reversed. Recent research has revealed that, when attractive girls are in the midst of pubertal change, they have lower self-esteem than their unattractive counterparts. It clearly is important to specify a number of dimensions that early and late maturation might influence—results often are not consistent across different dimensions and age spans.
	On-time/off-time in pubertal development	Being on-time or off-time in terms of pubertal events is a complex affair. For example, the dimensions may involve not just biological status and pubertal age, but also chronological age, grade in school, cognitive functioning, and social maturity. Variability in such dimensions may be obscured when limited indices of puberty and psychological functioning are assessed. Lerner has argued that adolescents may be at risk when the demands of a particular social context and the adolescents' physical and behavioral characteristics are mismatched—his model is called the goodness-of-fit model.

COGNITIVE DEVELOPMENT IN ADOLESCENCE

In addition to the dramatic physical changes that characterize adolescent development, there are equally impressive cognitive changes. Our consideration of adolescent cognition focuses on formal operational thought and social cognition, as well as careers and work.

Formal Operational Thought

It seems that more research papers have been published on adolescent thought in the past decade than in the six previous decades all together. This impressive growth in interest is due almost entirely to Piaget's theory about formal operational thought (Hill, 1985).

The Characteristics of Formal Operational Thought

According to Piaget, the formal operational stage comes into play between the ages of 11 and 14. The characteristics of formal operational thought that make it qualitatively different than concrete operational thought include abstractness, idealism and extended possibilities, problem solving governed by hypothetical deductive reasoning and logical thought, advanced understanding of language, and perspective taking.

Abstractness   Most significantly, adolescent thought is more abstract than child thought. The adolescent no longer is limited to actual, concrete experience as the anchor of thought. Instead, she or he may conjure up make-believe situations, strictly hypothetical possibilities, or purely abstract propositions and proceed to reason logically about them.

The abstract quality of the adolescent's thought at the formal operational level is evident in the adolescent's verbal problem-solving ability. While the concrete operational thinker would need to see the concrete elements A, B, and C to make the logical inference that if $A > B$ and $B > C$, then $A > C$, the formal operational thinker can solve this problem merely through verbal presentation.

Another indication of the abstract quality of the adolescent's thought is his or her increased tendency to think about thought itself. One adolescent commented,

What is the nature of adolescent cognitive development?

"I began thinking about why I was thinking what I was. Then I began thinking about why I was thinking about why I was thinking about what I was." If this sounds abstract, it is, and it characterizes the adolescent's enhanced focus on thought and its abstract qualities.

Idealism and What Is Possible Accompanying the abstract nature of formal operational thought in adolescence is thought full of idealism and possibilities. Adolescents often think in idealistic ways and about what is possible; in contrast, children frequently think in concrete ways, or in terms of what is real and limited. Adolescents begin to engage in extended speculation about ideal characteristics—qualities they desire in themselves and also in others. During adolescence, such thoughts often lead adolescents to compare themselves and others to such ideal standards. The thought of adolescents also often takes wings as fantasy flights into the future of possibilities. It is not unusual for the adolescent to become impatient with these newfound ideal standards and to be perplexed over which of many ideal standards to adopt.

Hypothetical-Deductive and Logical Reasoning Adolescents are more likely than children to think in hypothetical-deductive ways and to reason in more logical

ways about problems than children. It sometimes is said that the adolescent's thought is more like a scientist's than a child's, meaning that the adolescent often entertains many possibilities and tests many solutions in a planful way when faced with solving a problem. This kind of problem solving has been called **hypothetical-deductive reasoning.** Basically, this means that, in solving a problem, an individual develops hypotheses or hunches about what will be a correct solution to the problem and then in a planned manner tests one or more of the hypotheses, discarding the ones that do not work. (See Table 12.3 for one example of hypothetical-deductive reasoning.)

Consider also a modification of the familiar game "Twenty Questions" that Jerome Bruner and his associates have used in extensive work on cognitive skills (Bruner, 1966). The adolescent is given a set of 42 colorful pictures displayed in a rectangular array (six rows of seven pictures each) and is asked to determine which picture the experimenter has in mind (that is, which is "correct"). The person is allowed to ask only questions to which the experimenter can reply yes or no. The object of the game is to select the correct picture by asking as few questions as possible. The person who is a deductive hypothesis tester formulates a plan to propose and test a series of hypotheses, each of which narrows the field of choices considerably. The most effective plan consists in a "halving" strategy (*Q:* Is it in the right half of the array? *A:* No. *Q:* Okay; is it in the top half? And so on.). Used correctly, the halving strategy guarantees the questioner the correct solution in seven questions or less, no matter where the correct picture is located in the array. Even if he or she is using a less elegant strategy than the optimal "halving" one, the deductive hypothesis tester understands that, when the experimenter answers no to one of his or her guesses, several possibilities are immediately eliminated.

By contrast, the concrete operational thinker may persist with questions that continue to test some of the same possibilities that previous questions should have eliminated. For example, the child may have asked whether the correct picture was in row 1 and received the answer no, but later asks whether the correct picture is *x,* which is in row 1.

Thus, the formal operational thinker tests his or her hypotheses with judiciously chosen questions and tests.

Table 12.3   An Exemplary Task of Hypothetical-Deductive Reasoning

---

A common task for all of us is to determine what can logically be inferred from a statement made by someone else. Young children are often told by teachers that, if they work hard, they will receive good grades. Regardless of the empirical truth of the claim, the children may believe that good grades are the result of hard work, and that if they do not get good grades, they did not work hard enough. (Establishing the direction of the relationship between variables is an important issue.)

Children in the late concrete operational stage, too, are concerned with understanding the relations between their behavior and their teachers' grading practices. However, they are beginning to question the "truths" of their childhood. First, they now know that there are four possible combinations if two variables are dichotomized (work hard—not work hard; good grades—not good grades):

Behavior	Consequences
1. Work hard	Good grades
2. Work hard	Not good grades
3. Not work hard	Good grades
4. Not work hard	Not good grades

Two combinations are consistent with the hypothesis that a student's hard work is necessarily related to good grades: (1) they work hard and get good grades, and (4) they do not work hard and do not get good grades. When the presumed "cause" is present, the effect is present; when the cause is absent, the effect is absent. There are also two combinations that do not fit the hypothesis of a direct relation between hard work and good grades: (2) they work hard and do not get good grades, and (3) they get good grades without working hard.

The adolescent's notion of possibility allows him or her to take this analysis of combinations one important step further. Each of the four basic combinations of binary variables may be true or it may not. If 1, 2, 3, or 4 are true alone or in combination, there are 16 possible patterns of truth values:

1 or 2 or 3 or 4 is true	4 patterns
1–2 or 1–3 or 1–4 or 2–3 or 2–4 or 3–4 are true	6 patterns
1–2–3 or 1–2–4 or 1–3–4 or 2–3–4 are true	4 patterns
All (1–2–3–4) are true	1 pattern
All are false	1 pattern
Total	16 patterns

The list is critically important because each pattern leads to a different conclusion about the possible relation between two variables.

From *Piaget with Feeling: Cognitive, Social and Emotional Dimensions* by Philip A. Cowan. Copyright © 1978 by Holt, Rinehart & Winston. Reprinted by permission of Holt, Rinehart & Winston, Inc.

Often, a single question or test will help to eliminate an untenable hypothesis. By contrast, the concrete operational thinker often fails to understand the relation between a hypothesis and a well-chosen test of it— stubbornly clinging to the idea despite clear, logical disconfirmation of it.

As we see next, other changes in adolescence involve language.

Advanced Understanding of Language   Piaget himself did not write extensively about adolescent changes in language development. For example, Piaget (1952) believed that cognition always directed language and that what was most important about understanding changes in development were primary changes in cognition, not secondary changes in language. However, debate still exists over whether cognition directs language, language directs cognition, or both possibilities exist (e.g., Jenkins, 1969). Nonetheless, it appears that there are more significant changes in language development during adolescence than Piaget believed. Many scholars believe that these changes occur within the context of the stage of formal operational thought and its abstract qualities (Bereiter & Scardamalia, 1982; Fischer & Lazerson, 1984; Gardner, 1983; Labov, 1972; Brown & Smiley, 1977; Werner & Kaplan, 1952). Among the significant language changes during adolescence are those pertaining to words and concepts, prose and writing, and pragmatics.

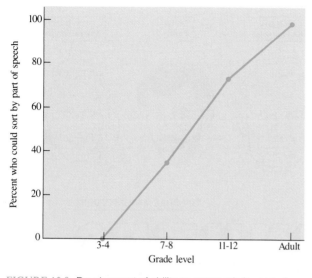

FIGURE 12.9   Development of ability to sort words by part of speech.

Adolescents are more sophisticated in their ability to understand words and related abstract concepts (Fischer & Lazerson, 1984). The understanding of grammar is a case in point. While children can learn the definition of a part of speech, such as what a noun is, and can become fairly adept at imitating model sentences in English workbooks, it appears that it is not until adolescence that a true understanding of grammar appears. With the increase in abstract thinking, adolescents seem to be far superior to children in analyzing a word's function in a sentence.

For instance, in one research study, elementary school children, adolescents, and adults were asked whether they knew what nouns, verbs, adjectives, and prepositions were (Anglin, 1970). Since parts of speech are taught in most schools by the third grade, it was not surprising that most of the subjects, including the third- and fourth-graders, for the most part gave correct definitions. However, when the subjects were required to sort 20 words (such as *during, flower, dead, poor, cry, listen,* and *white*) according to parts of speech, none of the elementary school children could do this task. As shown in Figure 12.9, many of the adolescents and adults were successful at this task.

Another aspect of language that increases during adolescence and that is related to words and concepts is **metaphor.** A metaphor is an implied comparison between two ideas that is conveyed by the abstract meaning contained in the words used to make the comparison. A person's faith and a piece of glass may be alike in that both can be shattered easily. A runner's performance and a politician's speech may be alike in that both are predictable. Concrete operational thinkers have a difficult time understanding such metaphorical relations. Consequently, many elementary school children are puzzled by the meanings of parables and fables (Elkind, 1976).

Adolescents also have an increased understanding of another aspect of language called **satire,** which refers to a literary work in which irony, derision, or wit in any form is used to expose folly or wickedness. Caricatures are an example of such satire. During adolescence, satire often takes on rhythmical qualities. Junior high school students may sit in school and make up satirical labels for teachers, such as "the walking wilt Wilkie and his wilking machine" and "the magnificent Manifred and his manifest morbidity." They also substantially increase their use of satirical and derisive nicknames—"stilt," "the refrigerator," and "spaz" are three examples. The satire of *Mad Magazine* also is more likely to be understood by adolescents than children (see Figure 12.10). This magazine relies on double meaning, exaggerations, and parody to highlight absurd circumstances and contradictory happenings. Such complexities in the use of language and caricature are lost on children but begin to find an audience in adolescents.

The written language of adolescents is often very different from their spoken language (Bereiter & Scardamalia, 1982; Fischer & Lazerson, 1984; Olson, 1977). When adolescents talk with each other, they typically are face-to-face so that they can monitor each other's interest and understanding. When an adolescent writes, however, no other person is present. Therefore, the writer must create an abstract idea of what his or her audience is like. Further, spoken communication is broken up by the replies of the person with whom we are communicating, while in written communication, it may be necessary to write a number of paragraphs without interruption or a response.

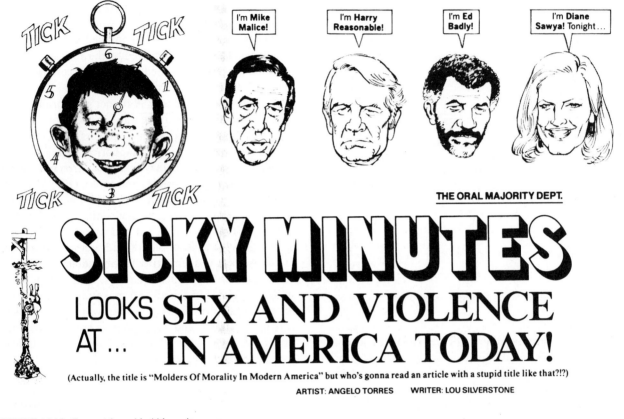

FIGURE 12.10 Excerpt from *Mad Magazine*.

As can be seen, writing is a complex aspect of language and communication, and it is not surprising that children are very poor at writing (Hunt, 1970; Scardamalia, Bereiter, & Goelman, 1982). An organization of ideas is very important in writing—logical thought processes help the writer to provide a hierarchical organization for the reader, letting him or her know which ideas are more general, which are more specific, and which are more important than others. Children are very poor at organizing their ideas before they write, and they also have considerable difficulty detecting the most salient points in a prose passage (Brown & Smiley, 1977).

While many adolescents are not yet Pulitzer Prize winning novelists, they do seem to be more capable than children of distinguishing more general from more specific points and of highlighting important points as they write. The increased logical thought of adolescents allows them to string sentences together in a way that makes more sense than the sentences children often put

one after the other. Further, adolescents' essays are more likely to include an introduction, several paragraphs that represent a body of the paper, and concluding remarks (Fischer & Lazerson, 1984).

Most adolescents are much better conversationalists than children. **Pragmatics** refers to the rules of conversation. Such rules allow adolescents to convey intended meanings and to "get along" with those they are talking to. The domain of pragmatics is broad and includes (1) taking turns in discussions instead of everyone talking at once, (2) using questions to convey commands ("Why is it so noisy in here?"), (3) using words like *the* and *a* in ways that enhance understanding ("He is *the* living end! He is not just *a* person."), (4) using polite language in appropriate situations (e.g., when a guest comes to the house), and even (5) telling stories that are interesting, jokes that are funny, and lies that convince. Focus on Child Development 12.3 discusses the ability of children and adolescents to detect when someone is lying or being sarcastic.

FOCUS ON CHILD DEVELOPMENT 12.3

JAY AND HIS HAIRCUT—THE DEVELOPMENT OF SARCASM

To comprehend the full meaning of a speaker's message, an adolescent needs to be sensitive to the speaker's belief and purpose. In most instances, people say what they believe. However, sometimes they don't. Consider the swimmer, who after diving into a pool, comes to the surface and says, "Come on in. The water is warm." The statement may be sincere or deliberately false. To distinguish between these possibilities, the listener must determine the facts and the speaker's belief about the facts. In addition, the speaker also may try to signal to the listener that the statement is false by using sarcasm.

To test the possibility that understanding the sincerity, deception, and sarcasm in a speaker's message follows a developmental sequence, Amy Demorest and her colleagues studied 6-, 9-, and 13-year-olds, and adults (Demorest, Meyer, Phelps, Gardner, & Winner, 1984). The subjects were given stories about a conversation between two people containing sincere, deceptive, or sarcastic statements. (The table shows what the conversations between the story characters were like.) The subjects' ability to identify speaker belief and communicative purpose in sincere, deceptive, and sarcastic remarks was assessed. As shown in the figure below, all of the six-year-old children took remarks as sincere by assuming that a speaker's belief and purpose were consistent with his or her statement. By nine years of age, though, children were able to appreciate the deliberate deception of the speaker.

Three Versions of Character Conversations Designed to Be Sincere, Deceptive, or Sarcastic

	Versions
Sincere	Jay needed to get his hair cut. A new barbershop had just opened in town. Jay went to the new barbershop for a haircut. *Jay got the best haircut he had ever had. It was just the right length.* Jay walked home from the barbershop. He saw Mike walking down the street. Mike noticed Jay's new haircut. He crossed the street to speak to Jay. Mike said to Jay, "That new haircut you got looks terrific."
Deceptive	*Jay got the worst haircut he had ever had. It was so short that his ears seemed to stick out.* He [Mike] put his arm around Jay's shoulder and smiled at Jay.
Sarcastic	*Jay got the worst haircut he had ever had. It was so short that his ears seemed to stick out.* He [Mike] laughed and pointed to Jay's head.

From Demorest, A., et al., "Words speak louder than actions: Understanding deliberately false remarks" in *Child Development, 55,* 152–154, 1984. © 1984 by The Society for Research in Child Development. Reprinted by permission.

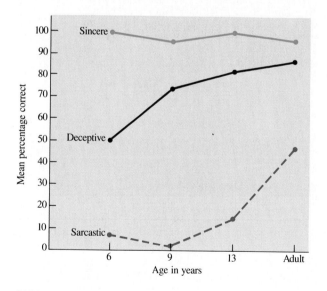

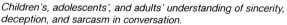

Children's, adolescents', and adults' understanding of sincerity, deception, and sarcasm in conversation.

(continued on following page)

However, at this age, deception and sarcasm were both seen as deceptive. The researchers concluded that, at some point between 13 years of age and adulthood, adolescents become capable of better appreciating that a speaker's purpose may not be consistent with his or her statement. That is, it is during adolescence that sarcasm and deception are distinguished. When sarcasm is detected, the listener gives more weight to the speaker's behavior than to his or her statement.

When developmentally is sarcasm understood?

Perspective Taking   Adolescents not only think about thought—they also develop an awareness that others often are thinking in different ways than they are. Piaget has shown that young children are basically egocentric in that they often perceive that others have the same view of the world they do. That is, young children have considerable difficulty taking the perspective of another individual. The ability to take the perspective of another person and to recognize that others have different viewpoints than our own improves during the adolescent years. There has been a considerable amount of research interest in the topics of egocentrism and perspective taking during the adolescent years, and we describe this interest in greater detail later in the chapter when we discuss social cognition.

Early and Late Formal Operational Thought

Early formal operational thought typically comes into play between the ages of 12 and 14, and late formal operational thought appears from about 15 to 18 years of age. Recall that Piaget's ideas about formal operational thought focus on the development of the adolescent's ability to consider all possible combinations of events and situations when given a problem to solve. In the early formal operational stage, adolescents begin to see many of the possible combinations necessary to solve a problem, but they are not as likely as the late formal operational thinker to start with a plan and to organize their search for a solution. In other words, early formal operational thinkers experiment with many different strategies, but they don't seem to have a systematic strategy from the start, as late formal operational thinkers do.

The changing relation between observations and hypotheses also reveals differences in the way early formal operational thinkers pursue a solution to a problem when compared with late formal operational thinkers. Piaget describes significant changes in the way adolescents deal with the relation between observations and hypotheses when tested with a pendulum problem. A weight is placed at the bottom of a string, which is fastened to the top of a rod. Boys and girls are asked to discover what causes the pendulum to move faster or slower. The subjects may change the length of the string, the weight of the object, the height from which they drop it, or the force with which they push it. Only the length of the string, however, influences the speed of oscillation.

Early formal operational thinkers go beyond providing a summary statement about their observations; they look for a general hypothesis that will explain what happened. For example, early formal operational thinkers might mention their idea that the length of the string may influence the speed of the pendulum after experimenting with it. But early formal operational thinkers are hardly ever concerned with trying out ideas that do not influence the pendulum. Consequently, the length of the string usually is not separated from the other variables when the causes of velocity are investigated, and early formal operational thinkers are left with uncertainty about the validity of their hypothesis. They are unable to systematically test their ideas against their observations.

By the late formal operational stage, adolescents think differently about such matters. Their hypotheses are not always derived from the data but are sometimes created at the beginning of the experiment to guide their investigation. Also, late formal operational thinkers are not satisfied with just a general statement about cause and effect—they search for something that tells them what is *necessary* and what is *sufficient* to account for what has happened. In the pendulum problem, this leads them to further separate the weight and length variables to ascertain what the necessary and sufficient causes of velocity are. Is the length of the string acting alone, or is it interacting to produce the effect? Formal operational thinkers might design an experiment to test these speculations (Cowan, 1978).

Individual Variation in Formal Operational Thought

For the most part, Piaget emphasized universal and consistent patterns of formal operational thought. Piaget's theory does not adequately account for the unique, individual differences that characterize the cognitive development of adolescents. These differences have been documented in a far-ranging set of research studies, meaning that certain modifications in Piaget's theory of formal operational thought need to be pursued (e.g., Bart, 1971; Berzonsky, Weiner, & Raphael, 1975; Higgens-Trenk & Gaite, 1971; Neimark, 1982; Overton & Meehan, 1982; Stone & Day, 1980).

The studies suggest that formal operational thought does develop during early adolescence for many boys and girls, but that this stage of thinking is far from pervasive.

Instead, early adolescence is more likely to be characterized by a consolidation of concrete operational thought (Hill, 1983). One limitation of formal reasoning may involve the content of the reasoning; while 14-year-olds may reason at the formal operational level when it comes to analyzing algebraic equations, they may not be able to do so with verbal problem-solving tasks or when reasoning about interpersonal relations.

Now that we have some idea of some basic cognitive changes in adolescence, let's turn our attention to the fascinating world of adolescents' social cognitions—their thoughts about social matters.

Social Cognition

Impressive changes in social cognition characterize adolescent development, including ideas about egocentrism, implicit personality theory, and social monitoring.

Egocentrism

David Elkind (1967, 1976, 1978) believes that two types of thinking—the imaginary audience and the personal fable—represent the emergence of a unique kind of **egocentrism in adolescence** and that underlying this egocentric thought is the emergence of formal operational thought.

The **imaginary audience** is the belief that others are as preoccupied with the adolescent's behavior as he or she is. Attention-getting behavior, so common in early adolescence, may reflect this interest in an imaginary audience, that is, the desire to be noticed, visible, and "on stage." An adolescent boy may think that others are as aware of a small spot on his trousers as he is and that they may possibly know or think that he has masturbated. The adolescent girl, walking into her eighth-grade classroom, thinks that all eyes are riveted on her complexion. Thus, particularly during early adolescence, individuals see themselves as constantly on stage. They believe that they are the main actors and that all others are the audience. More about the nature of the imaginary audience in adolescence appears in Focus on Child Development 12.4.

Recall from the "Imagine" section at the beginning of this chapter that the **personal fable** refers to the adolescent's sense of personal uniqueness and indestructibility. Their sense of personal uniqueness suggests that

FOCUS ON CHILD DEVELOPMENT 12.4

IMAGINARY AUDIENCES

Presumably, younger adolescents are more prone to play to an imaginary audience—that is, to be more self-conscious—than older ones, because they are less experienced at using formal operational thinking. This egocentric self-consciousness should diminish during the adolescent years.

Roberta Simmons and her colleagues (Simmons, Rosenberg, & Rosenberg, 1973) developed a clever device to measure this possibility. They created a self-inventory questionnaire called the Imaginary Audience Scale (IAS). The items pose situations about hypothetical teenagers who must perform in the presence of an audience and ask actual teenagers how willing they might be to do these things. Several items similar to those in the following table were used in the study.

Working with children and adolescents ranging from 8 to 18 years of age, the researchers found that the 12-year-olds were the most likely to choose the more self-conscious alternatives.

More recently, David Elkind (Elkind & Bowen, 1979) distinguished between two facets of the imaginary audience. One centers on a subject's willingness to reveal characteristics of the self that are believed to be permanent or stable over time. For example, most people view their levels of intelligence or features of personality as relatively constant over time. The other facet centers on the person's willingness to reveal characteristics of the self that are believed to vary considerably over time. For example, showing up dressed inappropriately, saying something inappropriate, or getting a bad haircut are all occasional occurrences, not permanent fixtures of the self. Elkind labeled the first phenomenon the **abiding self** and the latter one the **transient self.** He predicted that adolescent

---

The Imaginary Audience Scale (IAS)

Instructions: Please read the following stories carefully and assume that the events actually happened to you. Place a check next to the answer that best describes what you would do or feel in the real situation.

AS scale
1. Let's say some adult visitors came to your school and you were asked to tell them a little bit about yourself.
   _____ I would like that.
   _____ I would not like that.
   _____ I wouldn't care.

AS scale
2. If you went to a party where you did not know most of the kids, would you wonder what they were thinking about you?
   _____ I wouldn't think about it.
   _____ I would wonder about that a lot.
   _____ I would wonder about that a little.

TS scale
3. You are sitting in class and have discovered that your jeans have a small but noticeable split along the side seam. Your teacher has offered extra credit toward his or her course grade to anyone who can write the correct answer to a question on the blackboard. Would you get up in front of the class and go to the blackboard, or would you remain seated?
   _____ Go to the blackboard as though nothing had happened.
   _____ Go to the blackboard and try to hide the split.
   _____ Remain seated.

TS scale
4. Your class is supposed to have their picture taken, but you fell the day before and scraped your face. You would like to be in the picture, but your cheek is red and swollen. Would you have your picture taken anyway or stay out of the picture?
   _____ Get my picture taken even though I'd be embarrassed.
   _____ Stay out of the picture.
   _____ Get my picture taken and not worry about it.

From Elkind, David and R. Bowen, ''Imaginary audience behavior in children and adolescents'' in *Developmental Psychology, 15,* 38–44, 1979. Copyright © 1979 American Psychological Association. Reprinted by permission of the author.

What are some traits of adolescent egocentrism?

self-consciousness would be more pronounced with regard to the abiding self than for the transient self. Correspondingly, he predicted that only the abiding self is related to the individual's self-esteem.

Elkind and Bowen constructed two scales. Items 1 and 2 in the previous table both represent the abiding self (AS), while items 3 and 4 represent the transient self (TS). In all, there were six items on each scale. Following pilot work, the authors tested 697 boys and girls in the 4th, 6th, 8th, and 12th grades in a large, middle-class, suburban school district. Each child was asked to complete the two scales of imaginary audience along with other scales, including a measure of self-esteem and self-concept.

The major finding was that young adolescents were significantly less willing than children or older adolescents to reveal either the transient or the abiding self to an audience (see the figure below). This finding provides additional support for the hypothesis of heightened self-consciousness in early adolescence and for the construct of an imaginary audience during this age period. To the extent that the two subscales are comparable, the data also suggest that young adolescents are a little more self-conscious about their abiding than about their transient selves.

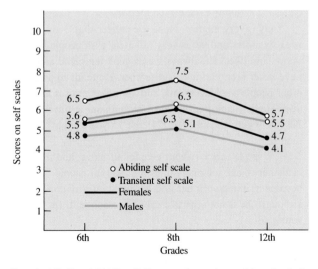

Transient Self and Abiding Self scores for males and females in the sixth, eighth, and twelfth grades.

no one can understand how they really feel. For example, an adolescent girl thinks that her mother can in no way sense the hurt she feels because her boyfriend broke up with her. Another aspect of the personal fable involves the adolescents' belief that they are indestructible. As part of their effort to retain this sense of personal uniqueness and indestructibility, adolescents often craft a story about the self that is not true.

There has been a flourish of research interest in the phenomenon of adolescent egocentrism in recent years (e.g., Adams & Jones, 1981; Damon & Hart, 1982; Elkind, in press; Elkind & Bowen, 1979; Enright, Shukla, & Lapsley, 1980; Gray & Hudson, 1984; Lapsley, 1985; Lapsley & Murphy, in press; Selman, 1980; Stephenson & Wicklund, 1983; Walker, 1980; Wicklund, 1979). Much of the thrust of this research interest has focused on such matters as determining the components of egocentrism, the nature of self-other relationships in adolescence, and why egocentric thought emerges in adolescence.

While Elkind (in press) continues to argue that egocentrism and the adolescent's construction of an imaginary audience come about because of the emergence of formal operational thought, others believe that the nature of interpersonal understanding is involved as well.

Lapsley (1985; Lapsley & Murphy, in press) argues that the imaginary audience is due both to the ability to think hypothetically (formal operations) and the ability to mentally step outside of one's self and anticipate what the reactions of others will be in imaginative circumstances (perspective taking). Lapsley, for example, argues that Robert Selman's view of the development of perspective taking and interpersonal understanding (see Chapter 11) provides a context for analyzing egocentrism.

Implicit Personality Theory

In addition to egocentrism, developmental psychologists also are interested in the emergence of implicit personality theory in adolescence. **Implicit personality theory** refers to individuals' ideas about what their own and other people's personalities are like. Carl Barenboim (1977, 1981, 1985) has investigated the developmental unfolding of implicit personality theory in children and adolescents.

It appears that, between the ages of 6 and 9, children increasingly are able to infer personality characteristics in others and to treat them as stable and causative factors that help to account for people's behavior (Livesley & Bromley, 1973; Rholes & Ruble, 1984; Rotenberg, 1980). Barenboim (1985) argues that the creation of personality constructs are something like a social-cognitive version of concrete operational thought. That is, the concrete attributes of people, including their behaviors, are classified. The resulting personality constructs are much like the beginning of a concrete classification of objects.

What kinds of changes during adolescence index the individual's development of an implicit personality theory? The development of an implicit personality theory during adolescence seems to consist of several elements that appear to be absent during the elementary school years. First, when adolescents are given information about another person, they consider previously acquired information as well, not relying solely on the concrete information at hand. Second, adolescents have more of a tendency than elementary school children to detect the contextual or situational variability in their and others' behavior, rather than thinking that they and others always behave consistently. Third, rather than merely accepting surface traits as a valid description of another person or themselves, adolescents begin to look

for deeper, more complex—even hidden—causes of personality. These factors are not merely considered in isolation, but as interacting forces that determine personality. This complex way of thinking about themselves and others does not appear until adolescence in most individuals. As is the case with formal operational thought, though, these implicit personality theories are not always employed—whether adolescents use such a strategy to understand themselves and others may depend upon a number of specific factors. It is important to note here, though, that the individual does not appear to be capable of such thought until the beginning of the adolescent age period (e.g., Barenboim, 1977; Livesley & Bromley, 1973).

In the following comments obtained in one developmental investigation of how individuals perceive others (Livesley & Bromley, 1973), we can see how the development of an implicit personality theory proceeds:

Max sits next to me, his eyes are hazel and he is tall. He hasn't got a very big head, he's got a big pointed nose. (p. 213; age seven years, six months)

He smells very much and is very nasty. He has no sense of humor and is very dull. He is always fighting and he is cruel. He does silly things and is very stupid. He has brown hair and cruel eyes. He is sulky and 11 years old and has lots of sisters. I think he is the most horrible boy in the class. He has a croaky voice and always chews his pencil and picks his teeth and I think he is disgusting. (p. 217; age nine years, eleven months)

Andy is very modest. He is even shyer than I am when near strangers and yet is very talkative with people he knows and likes. He always seems good tempered and I have never seen him in a bad temper. He tends to degrade other people's achievements, and yet never praises his own. He does not seem to voice his opinions to anyone. He easily gets nervous. (p. 221; age 15 years, eight months)

. . . she is curious about people but naive, and this leads her to ask too many questions so that people become irritated with her and withhold information, although she is not sensitive enough to notice it. (p. 225; young adult)

As part of their increased awareness of others—including what others are doing and what they are thinking—adolescents engage in a great deal of social monitoring.

What is the nature of social monitoring in adolescence?

Social Monitoring

Bob, a 16-year-old, feels that he does not know as much as he wants or needs to know about Sally, another 16-year-old. He also wants and needs to know more about Sally's relationship with Brian, a 17-year-old. In his effort to learn about Sally, Bob decides that he wants to know more about the groups that Sally belongs to—her student council friends, the clique she belongs to, and so forth. Bob thinks about what he already knows about all these people and groups and decides he needs to find out how close he is to his goal of understanding them by taking some appropriate, feedback-producing action. What he discovers by taking that action will determine his social-cognitive progress and how difficult his social-cognitive task is. Notice that the immediate aim of this feedback-producing action is not to make progress toward the main goal but to monitor that progress.

There are a number of cognitive monitoring methods that adolescents engage in on virtually a daily basis. A student may meet someone new and quickly think, "It's going to be hard to really get to know this guy." Another adolescent may check incoming information about an organization (school, club, group of friends) to determine if it is consistent with the adolescent's impressions of the club or the group. Still another adolescent may question someone or paraphrase what that person has just said about her feelings to ensure that he has understood them correctly.

An important aspect of social cognition is the individual's development of conscious self-awareness. John Flavell (1979) believes that developing differentiated thoughts about oneself is a gradual process. Statements such as, "I think I am not easily fooled by others" or "I tend to give people the benefit of the doubt" evidence the development of such self- and social awareness. And although children may distinguish only between succeeding or failing to learn something they want to know about someone else, adolescents may understand the more complex notion that what they have learned may be either accurate or inaccurate. Acquiring this latter distinction can serve as the basis for still further development in monitoring social thought. For example, later in development, the individual may recognize that the accuracy of social thought is difficult to assess and that knowledge of certain aspects of the self or of others may actually decrease accuracy. For instance, prejudice, intense emotions, or mental or physical illness might produce inaccurate perceptions of oneself and others. While some forms of social-cognitive knowledge do not develop until later, other aspects of this awareness may emerge quite early in development, according to Flavell. Thus, a young child may be entirely able to recognize that his or her friend is not thinking clearly about people because the friend is upset or in a bad mood.

Individuals also learn to evaluate the social behavior of others and to recognize when this behavior is not accompanied by social thought. Flavell argues that, in the early years of development, the child attributes no social cognitions to others. Later on, the child may automatically assume that others' social thoughts always coincide with their social behavior. For example, the child may assume that helpful actions reflect an intent to help and harmful actions the intent to harm. Still later, the child may think that both types of actions portray either no intent at all or an incongruent one, such as a helpful action performed unintentionally for purely selfish reasons, or even with an intent to achieve ultimate harm.

Flavell goes on to talk about the implications of children's and adolescents' ability to monitor their social cognitions as an indicator of their social maturity and competence:

> In many real-life situations, the monitoring problem is not to determine how well you understand what a message means but rather to determine how much you ought to believe it or do what it says to do. I am thinking of the persuasive appeals the young receive from all quarters to smoke, drink, commit aggressive or criminal acts, have casual sex without contraceptives, have or not have the casual babies that often result, quit school, and become unthinking followers of this year's flaky cults, sects, and movements. (Feel free to revise this list in accordance with *your* values and prejudices.) Perhaps it is stretching the meanings of . . . cognitive monitoring too far to include the critical appraisal of message source, quality of appeal, and probable consequences needed to cope with these inputs sensibly, but I do not think so. It is at least conceivable that the ideas currently brewing in this area could some day be parlayed into a method of teaching children (and adults) to make wise and thoughtful life decisions as well as to comprehend and learn better in formal educational settings. (Flavell, 1979, p. 910)

Child Development Concept Table 12.3 summarizes our discussion of the nature of formal operational thought and social cognition during adolescence. Now we turn to several final ideas about the development of adolescents—career orientation and work.

Career Orientation and Work

During adolescence, young people begin thinking much more about careers than they did as children. And an increasing number of adolescents decide to work on a part-time basis and still go to school.

Exploration and Cognitive Factors in Career Development

Donald Super and Douglas Hall (1978) believe that in countries where equal employment opportunities have developed—such as the United States, Great Britain, and France—exploration of various career paths is critical for the adolescent's career development. The role of the school is especially important in career exploration, since families and friends tend to be from the same social class and are more knowledgeable about career opportunities within their own social class (Reynolds & Shister, 1949).

Students often approach career exploration and decision making with a great deal of ambiguity, uncertainty, and stress (e.g., Jordaan, 1963; Jordaan & Heyde, 1978). In one investigation, Donald Super and his colleagues studied late adolescents and young adults after they left high school (Super, Kowalski, & Gotkin, 1967). In their career pattern study, they found that over half the position changes (such as student to student, student to job, job to job) made between leaving school and the age of 25 involved floundering and unplanned changes. In other words, the young adults were neither systematic nor intentional in their exploration and decision making about careers.

Most high school students have not explored the world of work adequately on their own, and receive very little direction from high school guidance counselors about how to do this. According to the National Assessment of Educational Progress report (1976), high school students not only do not know what information to seek about careers, they do not know how to seek it. Just as discouraging is the fact that, on the average, high school students spend less than three hours per year with the guidance counselors at their schools (Super & Hall, 1978).

While adolescents have not been adequately exposed to future career worlds, they do frequently participate in the world of work, as we see next.

Work

In 1974, the government Panel on Youth, headed by James Coleman, concluded that work has a positive influence on adolescents. According to Coleman and his colleagues, a job during adolescence creates a positive attitude toward work, allows students to learn from adults other than teachers or parents, and may help keep them out of trouble. The Panel on Youth recommended that more youth should be included in the work force of our country. To accomplish this goal, the panel suggested that more work/study programs be developed, that the minimum wage be lowered, and that more flexible school/work schedules be allowed.

Over the past hundred years, the percentage of youth who work full-time as opposed to those who are in school has decreased dramatically. During the last half of the

Child Development Concept Table 12.3   Cognitive Development in Adolescence

Concept	Processes/Related Ideas	Characteristics/Description
Formal operational thought	Abstractness	Most significantly, formal operational thought is more abstract than concrete operational thought. Adolescents may conjure up make-believe situations, strictly hypothetical possibilities, and purely abstract propositions. Verbal problem-solving ability improves dramatically.
	Idealism and what is possible	Formal operational thought is full of idealism and possibilities, rather than always focusing on what is real and limited, as is the case with concrete operational thought. Adolescents often compare themselves and others to ideal standards. Thoughts often take wings as fantasy flights into the future.
	Hypothetical-deductive and logical reasoning	Formal operational thought involves hypothetical-deductive reasoning, reasoning that is more logical than that of concrete operational thought. Such logical thought is more often planful than that of concrete operational thought.
	Advanced understanding of language	Formal operational thought includes more advanced understanding of language. Adolescents are better than children at understanding the abstract meanings of words, including the parts of speech, metaphors, and satire. Formal operational thinkers, with their more logical reasoning, are much better at writing than concrete operational thinkers, and they also are much better at understanding the key points when reading prose. Adolescent thinkers understand pragmatics—the rules of conversation—more easily than children.
	Perspective taking	Formal operational thinkers are better than concrete operational thinkers at perspective taking, such as considering and understanding another person's point of view.
Early and late formal operational thought and individual variation	Early and late formal operational thought	Early formal operational thought often comes into play between the ages of 12 and 14, and late formal operational thought appears from about 15 to 18 years of age. Planful and organized thought prior to solution of problems is more characteristic of late formal operational thought.
	Individual variation	There is a great deal of individual variation in adolescent thought— Piaget inadequately recognized such variation. Many adolescents still primarily are concrete operational thinkers.
Social cognition	Egocentrism	Elkind proposed that adolescents, particularly those in early adolescence, develop a curious sort of egocentrism that includes the construction of an imaginary audience and a personal fable. While Elkind believes that egocentrism emerges because of formal operational thought, others argue that perspective taking and interpersonal understanding, as described by Selman, are involved.
	Implicit personality theory	It is during adolescence that, for the first time, individuals construct an implicit personality theory, one that becomes more contextual, more interested in piecing the past and present together, and more focused on uncovering hidden, complex causes of personality.
	Social monitoring	Adolescents are superior to children in their ability to monitor their social world, including "detectivelike" strategy in getting desired information.

1800s, fewer than 1 out of every 20 high school–aged adolescents were in school, whereas more than 9 out of every 10 adolescents receive high school diplomas today. In the 19th century, many adolescents learned a trade from their father or some other adult member of the community. Now a much more prolonged period of educational training keeps most adolescents out of the full-time work force. The part-time work force, however, is another story. Huge numbers of adolescents combine part-time work with school.

What is the relationship between part-time work and school achievement?

Part-Time Work and Its Relation to School Most high school seniors already have had some experience in the world of work. In a national survey of 17,000 high school seniors, three out of four reported that they had some job income during the average school week (Bachman, 1982). For 41 percent of the males and 30 percent of the females, this income exceeded $50 a week. The typical part-time job for high school seniors involves 16 to 20 hours a week, although 10 percent work 30 or more hours a week.

Clearly, more adolescent students are working today than in past years. For example, in 1940, only 1 out of 25 tenth-grade males attended school and simultaneously worked part-time, whereas in 1970, the number had increased to more than 1 out of 4. More recent estimates suggest that 1 out of 3 ninth- and tenth-graders are combining school and work (Cole, 1981).

Adolescents also are working longer hours now than in the past. For instance, the number of 14- and 15-year-olds who work more than 14 hours per week has increased substantially in the last 20 years. A similar picture emerges for 16-year-olds. In 1960, 44 percent of the 16-year-old males who attended school worked more than 14 hours a week, but by 1970, the figure had increased to 56 percent.

Does this increase in work have a positive influence on adolescents? In some cases yes, in others no. Ellen Greenberger and Laurence Steinberg (1981) gave a questionnaire focusing on work experiences to students in four California high schools. Their findings disproved some common myths. For example, it generally is assumed that adolescents get extensive on-the-job training when they are hired for work—the reality is that they get little training at all, according to the researchers. Also, it is assumed that youths, through work experiences, learn to get along better with adults. However, adolescents reported that they rarely feel close to the adults they work with. The work experiences of the adolescents did help them to understand how the business world works, how to get and keep a job, and how to manage money. Working also helped the youths to learn to budget their time, to take pride in their accomplishments, and to evaluate their goals. Working adolescents often have to give up sports, social affairs with peers, and sometimes sleep. And they have to balance the demands of work, school, and family.

In their investigation, Greenberger and Steinberg asked adolescents about their grade point averages, school attendance, satisfaction from school, and the number of hours spent studying and in extracurricular activities since they began working. They found that working adolescents had lower grade point averages than nonworkers. More than one out of four students reported that their grades dropped when they began working; whereas only one out of nine said that their grades improved. But it wasn't just working that affected the adolescent's grades—more importantly, it was the number of hours worked. Tenth-graders who worked more than 14 hours a week suffered a drop in grades; whereas 11th-graders worked up to 20 hours a week before their grades began to drop. When adolescents spend more than 20 hours a week working, there is little time to study for tests and to do homework assignments.

In addition to the effect of work on grades, working adolescents also feel less involved in school, are absent more, and say they don't enjoy school as much (compared to their nonworking peers). Adolescents who work also spend less time with their families—but just as much time with their peers—as their nonworking counterparts.

Adolescent Unemployment   A considerable amount of media attention has focused on unemployment among teenagers in recent years. Overall, however, it appears that such unemployment is not as widespread as the media suggest. For example, based on data collected by the U.S. Department of Labor, one study revealed that more than 9 out of 10 adolescent boys either were in school, working at a job, or both, with only 5 percent out of school, without a job, and looking for full-time employment (Feldstein & Ellwood, 1982). And most of the adolescents who did not have a job were not unemployed for prolonged periods of time. For instance, almost half of the unemployed adolescents had been out of work for one month or less, and only 10 percent had been without a job for six months or more. It is important to note that the major portion of adolescents who are unemployed are individuals who have dropped out of school.

However, while it appears that the media have over-exaggerated the extent of unemployment among adolescents, a disproportionate number of unemployed adolescents are black. As indicated in Table 12.4, the unemployment situation is particularly acute for blacks and other minorities between the ages of 16 and 19. One survey revealed that, in 1979, only 50 percent of Hispanic adolescents held jobs (Rosenbaum, 1983). Since 1960, though, the job situation has improved for black adolescents, particularly black males. For example, in 1960, 44 percent of black male adolescents were unemployed, but by 1979, the figure had been reduced to 30 percent (Rosenbaum, 1983).

Thus, while the world of adolescent unemployment is not as bleak as the media suggest, there is reason to be concerned about the disproportionate number of blacks and other minority adolescents, particularly those from low socioeconomic backgrounds, in the unemployed adolescent pool.

Table 12.4	Percentages of Unemployed Youths and Adults	
	Whites	**Blacks and Other Minorities**
Men 20 years and older	5.1	8.3
Women 20 years and older	3.5	10.2
Men 16 to 19 years old	14.1	34.8
Women 16 to 19 years old	13.9	35.9

Source: U.S. Department of Labor, *Special Labor Force Report No. 218* (Washington D.C.: U.S. Government Printing Office, 1979), p. 9.

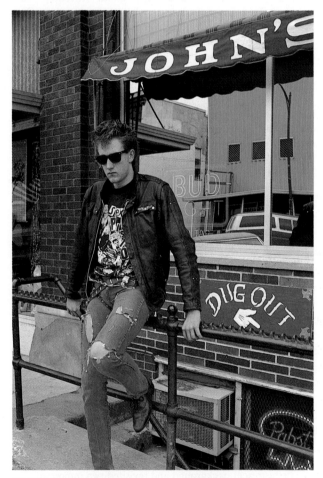

What is the nature of unemployment in adolescence?

THINKING BACK, LOOKING AHEAD

As the words that opened Section 5 suggested, adolescence is not a time of simple life . . . in no order of things. Our exploration of historical ideas and issues in adolescence included G. Stanley Hall and his storm and stress view, the teenager who has sneaked up on us in our lifetime, the adolescent "generalization gap," and considerations of biology/culture and continuity/discontinuity. Our interest in the physical changes of adolescence encompassed menarche and pubescent toddlers, the hypothalamic-pituitary-gonadal axis, first pubic hairs and enlargement of breasts, sexual fantasies, masturbation, homosexual behavior, changing heterosexual attitudes, body image, and on-time/off-time in pubertal development. Our overview of cognitive changes in adolescence focused on such matters as abstractness, idealism and what is possible, the game of "Twenty Questions," the satire and caricatures of *Mad Magazine,* Jay and his "great" haircut, the girl who thinks that all eyes are riveted on her complexion and also the girl who thinks that her mother can't possibly sense the hurt she is feeling, becoming a personality theorist, and monitoring a world of social behaviors and thoughts. Our coverage of the world of careers and work in adolescence took us through such intriguing themes as the failure of adolescents to adequately explore future career options, the history of work experiences, 11th-graders who worked more than 20 hours per week and saw their grades drop, and the exaggeration of overall unemployment in adolescents but the alarmingly high rate of unemployment among certain subcultures.

In Chapter 13, we turn our attention to the social contexts of adolescent development. But first, reflect for a moment on the words of Anne Frank, as she pondered the physical changes of her puberty:

> I think what is happening to me is so wonderful, and not only what can be seen on my body, but all that is taking place inside. I never discuss myself with anybody; that is why I have to talk to myself about them.

SUMMARY

I. Our introduction to adolescent development focused on its historical background and revisited two important issues—the implications of biology/culture and continuity/discontinuity for understanding adolescent development.

A. G. Stanley Hall is viewed as the father of the scientific study of adolescent development. His storm and stress view suggests that adolescence is a turbulent time for all of us. His biological deterministic view is now perceived as too strong a statement.

B. Between 1890 and 1920, a cadre of urban reformers, youth workers, and counselors began to mold the concept of adolescence. A number of scholars argue for an inventionist view of adolescence, one emphasizing that adolescence was constructed out of sociohistorical conditions. They believe that legislation ensured the dependency of youth and made their move into the economic sphere more manageable.

C. Widespread generalizations based on information about a limited set of highly visible adolescents have resulted in a number of inaccurate stereotypes about adolescents.

D. Adolescence, just like childhood, is influenced by an interaction of biological and cultural factors, rather than either factor alone.

E. There is continuity between childhood experiences and development in adolescence, but new experiences may influence development in adolescence as well.

II. Ideas about physical development in adolescence focus on puberty, the endocrine system, physical changes, and the psychological accompaniments of puberty.

A. Puberty is a rapid change to maturation that does not involve a single event but rather is part of a long developmental process. Menarche is the girl's first menstruation and has been occurring earlier in recent decades probably because of improved nutrition and health.

B. The endocrine glands secrete hormones. Hormones are powerful chemical substances that regulate organs. The aspects of the endocrine system that are primarily involved in puberty make up what is called the hypothalamic-pituitary-gonadal axis. There are two general classes of sex hormones—androgens, which mature primarily in males, and estrogens, which mature mainly in females. More precisely, testosterone appears to be the sex hormone that increases the most during male pubertal development, while estradiol assumes this role in female pubertal change. Research by Nottelmann and her colleagues focused on three types of hormones—gonadotropins, sex steroids, and adrenal androgens. Their research revealed that the secretion of sex hormones is related to adolescent psychological and behavioral characteristics, although more so for boys than for girls. The thyroid gland, another important part of the endocrine system, communicates with the pituitary gland and influences growth and skeletal maturation.

C. Physical changes involve those pertaining to height and weight as well as sexual maturation.

   1. As adolescents undergo a growth spurt, they make rapid gains in height and weight. The spurt occurs approximately two years earlier in girls (at age 10½) than boys (at age 12½).

   2. Sexual maturation is one of the hallmarks of pubertal development. Three of the most noticeable changes in boys are penis elongation, testes growth, and pubic hair. Three of the most obvious changes in girls are menarche and the menstrual cycle, breast development, and pubic hair. Adolescent males' sexual fantasies are more explicit than those of females. The frequency of masturbation increases between the ages of 13 and 15, but much more so for boys than girls. Homosexual contacts occur more in boys than girls, and acceptance of homosexuality is greater than the incidence of its behavior, although the AIDS epidemic may decrease acceptance. There has been a rapid increase in sexual intercourse reported by young people during the 20th century, with the increase more pronounced for females than males. The current sexual standard stresses that physical and emotional exploitation of the partner is unacceptable.

D. Ideas about psychological accompaniments of physical changes involve body image, early and late maturation, and on-time/off-time in pubertal development.

   1. Adolescents show a considerable increase in interest in their body image. Young adolescents are more preoccupied and dissatisfied with their bodies than late adolescents.

   2. While early maturation has seemed to favor boys when they are studied during adolescence, when they are assessed in adulthood, early maturers are less likely to have achieved a successful identity. Research on girls suggests that, with regard to body image, early maturers show greater satisfaction with their figures in early adolescence, but by late adolescence, the pattern is reversed. Recent research has

revealed that, when attractive girls are in the midst of pubertal change, their self-esteem is lower than their unattractive counterparts. It clearly is important to specify a number of dimensions that early and late maturation might influence—results often are not consistent across different dimensions and age spans.

   3. Being on-time or off-time in terms of pubertal events is a complex affair. For example, the dimensions may involve not just biological status and pubertal age, but also chronological age, grade in school, cognitive functioning, and social maturity. Variability in such dimensions may be obscured when limited indices of puberty and psychological functioning are assessed. Lerner has argued that adolescents may be at risk when the demands of a particular social context and the adolescents' physical and behavioral characteristics are mismatched—his model is called the goodness-of-fit model.

III. Ideas about cognitive development in adolescence involve the nature of formal operational thought, variations in such thought, social cognition, and careers and work.

A. Formal operational thought is related to abstractness, idealism and what is possible, hypothetical-deductive and logical reasoning, advanced understanding of language, and perspective taking.

   1. Most significantly, formal operational thought is more abstract than concrete operational thought. Adolescents may conjure up make-believe situations, strictly hypothetical possibilities, and purely abstract propositions. Verbal problem-solving ability improves dramatically.

   2. Formal operational thought is full of idealism and possibilities, rather than always focusing on what is real and limited, as is the case with concrete operational thought. Adolescents often compare themselves and others to ideal standards. Thoughts often take wings as fantasy flights into the future.

   3. Formal operational thought involves hypothetical-deductive reasoning, reasoning that is more logical than that of concrete operational thought. Such logical thought is more often planful than that of concrete operational thought.

4. Formal operational thought includes more advanced understanding of language. Adolescents are better than children at understanding the abstract meanings of words, including the parts of speech, metaphors, and satire. Formal operational thinkers, with their more logical reasoning, are much better at writing than concrete operational thinkers, and they also are much better at understanding the key points when reading prose. Adolescent thinkers also understand pragmatics—the rules of conversation—more easily than children.

5. Formal operational thinkers are better than concrete operational thinkers at perspective taking, such as considering and understanding another person's point of view.

B. Early formal operational thought often comes into play between the ages of 12 and 14, and late formal operational thought appears from about 15 to 18 years of age. Planful and organized thought prior to solution of problems is more characteristic of late formal operational thought. There is a great deal of individual variation in adolescent thought—Piaget inadequately recognized such individual variation. Many adolescents still primarily are concrete operational thinkers.

C. Ideas about social cognition in adolescence include egocentrism, implicit personality theory, and social monitoring.

1. Elkind proposed that adolescents, particularly young adolescents, develop a curious sort of egocentrism that includes the construction of an imaginary audience and a personal fable. While Elkind argues that such egocentrism emerges because of formal operational thought, others argue that perspective taking and interpersonal understanding, as described by Selman, are involved.

2. It is during adolescence that, for the first time, individuals construct an implicit personality theory, one that becomes more contextual, more interested in piecing together the past and the present, and more focused on covert, complex causes of personality.

3. Adolescents are superior to children in their ability to monitor their social world, including "detectivelike" strategy in getting desired information.

D. Two other important changes in adolescence involve career orientation and work.

1. Many adolescents do not have adequate career information. Wide exploration of a variety of career paths is one of the most consistently emphasized aspects of career development in adolescence.

2. There has been a tremendous increase in the number of adolescents who have part-time jobs and continue to go to school. The jobs adolescents have are both advantageous and disadvantageous to their development. With regard to school, working more than 14 hours a week seems to lower the grades of 10th-graders, while the figure is 20 hours a week for 11th-graders. While there has been widespread media attention on youth unemployment, the fact is that such unemployment in general is not that pervasive. The major portion of unemployed youth are high school dropouts. The most acute unemployment problem resides with black and other minority group adolescents, as well as youth from the lower socioeconomic class.

KEY TERMS

abiding self 530
adolescent generalization gap 505
adrenal androgens 510
amenorrhea 507
androgens 508
egocentrism in adolescence 529
estradiol 508
estrogens 508
gonadal 508
gonadotropin 508, 510
goodness-of-fit model 520
homophobia 516
hormones 508
hypothalamic-pituitary-gonadal axis 508
hypothalamus 508
hypothetical-deductive reasoning 523
imaginary audience 529
implicit personality theory 532
menarche 506
metaphor 525
personal fable 529
pituitary gland 508
pragmatics 526
puberty 507
satire 525
sex steroids 510
storm and stress view 503
testosterone 508
thyroid gland 511
transient self 530

SUGGESTED READINGS

Brooks-Gunn, J., & Petersen, A. (Eds.). (1983). *Girls at puberty*. New York: Plenum.

This book of readings written by experts in different areas of adolescent development provides considerable insight into current thinking about the role of puberty in the psychological life of girls.

Early adolescent sexuality: Resources for parents, professionals, and young people. (1983). Chapel Hill, NC: Center for Early Adolescence, University of North Carolina.

This compendium of resources provides an excellent annotated bibliography of a wide variety of topics related to sexuality in early adolescence.

Journal of Early Adolescence.

This journal focuses primarily on the 10- to 15-year age range and includes research articles on a wide variety of issues pertaining to physical, cognitive, social, and personality development in early adolescence. Leaf through the issues of the last several years to see the kinds of research being conducted with young adolescents.

Journal of Occupational Behavior.

This research journal has many articles that pertain to career development in adolescence. Look at the issues of the last several years to get a feel for the topics that are interesting to researchers who study the nature of career development.

Journal of Youth and Adolescence (1985) *14*, (3,4).

Two issues of this excellent research journal have been devoted to the study of maturational timing in adolescence. Includes many insights into how puberty is experienced and the complexity of studying early and late maturation.

Selman, R. L. (1981). What children understand of intrapsychic processes: The child as a budding personality theorist. In E. K. Shapiro & E. Weber (Eds.), *Cognitive and affective growth*. Hillsdale, NJ: Erlbaum.

This article contains Selman's account of how he thinks the adolescent forms a theory of personality. Includes an overview of his ideas about role taking.

SOCIAL
DEVELOPMENT
IN
ADOLESCENCE

IMAGINE . . . YOU ARE
OBSERVING AN EIGHTH-GRADE
CLASS AND THE TEACHER SAYS,
"I DON'T WANT ANY MORE
'WHAT IF' QUESTIONS."

PREVIEW

FAMILIES AND ADOLESCENT
DEVELOPMENT

Autonomy and Attachment-
Connectedness

The Multidimensionality of Autonomy
*Parenting Strategies for Promoting Healthy
Autonomy*
*Attachment, the Coordinated Worlds of
Parents and Peers, and Connectedness*

FOCUS ON CHILD DEVELOPMENT
13.1: MOTHERS, DAUGHTERS, AND
GIRLFRIENDS

Parenting Strategies and Parent-
Adolescent Conflict

Parenting Strategies with Adolescents

FOCUS ON CHILD DEVELOPMENT
13.2: MONITORING THE LIVES OF
ADOLESCENTS AFTER SCHOOL

Parent-Adolescent Conflict

The Maturation of the Adolescent and
the Maturation of Parents

The Maturation of the Adolescent
The Maturation of Parents

The Effects of Divorce on Adolescents

*Wallerstein and Kelly: Carrying Forward the
Divorce Experience*
*Hetherington: Effects of Divorce on the
Heterosexual Behavior of Adolescent Girls*

CHILD DEVELOPMENT CONCEPT
TABLE 13.1: FAMILIES AND
ADOLESCENT DEVELOPMENT

PEERS AND ADOLESCENT
DEVELOPMENT

Peer Pressure and Conformity
Peer Modeling and Social Comparison
Cliques and Crowds

Distinguishing Cliques and Crowds
*Coleman's Study of Leading Adolescent
Groups*
Cliques, Crowds, and Self-Esteem

FOCUS ON CHILD DEVELOPMENT
13.3: JOCKS, POPULARS,
NORMALS, DRUGGIES/TOUGHS,
INDEPENDENTS, AND NOBODIES

Children and Adolescent Groups

Dating

The Functions of Dating
Incidence of Dating and Age Trends
Sex Differences and Similarities in Dating
*The Construction of Dating Relationships:
Family and Peer Factors*

CHILD DEVELOPMENT CONCEPT
TABLE 13.2: PEERS AND
ADOLESCENT DEVELOPMENT

SCHOOLS

The Controversy Surrounding the
Function of Secondary Schools
Effective Schools

FOCUS ON CHILD DEVELOPMENT
13.4: BEYOND THE ZOO

School Organization

The Organization of Secondary Schools
*The Transition to Middle or Junior High
School*

FOCUS ON CHILD DEVELOPMENT
13.5: FACILITATING THE
TRANSITION TO JUNIOR HIGH
SCHOOL

After-School Needs of Adolescents

THINKING BACK, LOOKING
AHEAD

SUMMARY

KEY TERMS

SUGGESTED READINGS

CHAPTER **13**

IMAGINE . . . YOU ARE OBSERVING AN EIGHTH-GRADE CLASS AND THE TEACHER SAYS, "I DON'T WANT ANY MORE 'WHAT IF' QUESTIONS."

—A teacher sits in the back of the room, her legs up on her desk, asking students questions from a textbook. The students, bored and listless, sit in straight rows facing no one in the front of the room, answering laconically to a blank blackboard. When the principal enters the room, the teacher lowers her legs to the floor. Nothing else changes.

—A teacher drills students for a seemingly endless amount of time on prime numbers. After the lesson, not one of them can say why it is important to learn prime numbers.

—A visitor asks a teacher if hers is an eighth-grade class. "It's called eighth grade," she answers archly, "but we know it's really kindergarten—right, class?"

—In a predominantly Hispanic school, only the one adult hired as a bilingual teacher speaks Spanish.

—In a biracial school, the principal and the guidance counselor cite test scores with pride. They are asked if the difference between the test scores of black and white students is narrowing. "Oh, that's an interesting question!" the guidance counselor says in surprise. The principal agrees. It has never been asked by or of them before.

—A teacher in a social studies class squelches several imaginative questions, exclaiming, "You're always asking 'what if' questions. Stop asking 'what if'!" When a visitor asks who will become president if the president-elect dies before the electoral college meets, the teacher explodes: "You're as bad as they are! That's another 'what if' question!"   (Lipsitz, 1984, pp. 169–170)

The foregoing vignettes are from middle schools where life seems to be difficult and unhappy for students. By contrast, consider the following circumstances in effective middle schools:

—Everything is peaceful. There are open cubbies instead of locked lockers. There is no theft. Students walk quietly in the corridors. "Why?" they are asked. "So as not to disturb the media center," they answer, which is self-evident to them but not the visitor who is left wondering. . . . When asked, "Do you like this school?" (They) answer: "No, we don't like it. We love it!"   (Lipsitz, 1984, p. 27)

—When asked how the school feels, one student answered, "It feels smart. We're smart. Look at our test scores." Comments from one of the parents of a student at the school are revealing: "My child would have been a dropout. In elementary school, his teacher said to me: 'That child isn't going to give you anything but heartaches.' He had perfect attendance here. He didn't want to miss a day. Summer vacation was too long and boring. Now he's majoring in communications at the University of Texas. He got here and all of a sudden someone cared for him. I had been getting notes about Roger every other day, with threats about expulsion. Here, the first note said: 'It's just a joy to have him in the classroom.' " (Lipsitz, 1984, p. 84)

—The humane environment that encourages teachers' growth . . . is translated by the teachers . . . into a humane environment that encourages students' growth. The school feels cold when one first enters. It has the institutional feeling of any large school building with metal lockers and impersonal halls. Then one opens the door to a team area, and it is filled with energy, movement, productivity, doing. There is a lot of informal relating among students and between students and teachers. Visible from one vantage point are students working on written projects, putting the last touches on posters, watching a film, and working independently from reading kits. . . . Most know what they are doing, can say why it is important, and go back to work immediately after being interrupted. (Lipsitz, 1984, p. 109)

—Authors' Week is yet another special activity built into the school's curriculum that entices students to consider themselves in relation to the rich variety of making and doing in people's lives. Based on student interest, availability, and diversity, authors are invited . . . to discuss their craft. Students sign up to meet with individual authors. They must have read one individual book by the author. . . . Students prepare questions for their sessions with the authors. . . . Sometimes, an author stays several days to work with a group of students on his or her manuscript. (Lipsitz, 1984, p. 141)

These excerpts about a variety of middle schools in different areas of the United States reveal the great diversity among schools for adolescents. They also tell us that, despite the inefficiency of many schools for adolescents, others are very effective. One of the themes of this chapter is that schools can be breeding grounds for competent academic and social development. Our discussion of schools later in the chapter includes a more detailed look at the qualities that make middle schools effective.

PREVIEW

The social worlds of adolescence are many and fascinating—through experiences with parents, siblings, peers, friends, clique members, teachers, and other adults, adolescents make the transition from being a child to being an adult. There are many hills and valleys in this transition, and there are times when parent-adolescent relationships become exacerbated, as reflected in the comments of Mark Twain:

> When I was a boy of 14, my father was so ignorant I could hardly stand to have the man around. But when I got to be 21, I was astonished at how much he had learnt in 7 years.

FAMILIES AND ADOLESCENT DEVELOPMENT

In Chapter 11, we discussed how, during middle and late childhood, parents spend less time with their children than in the preschool years, discipline involves an increased use of reasoning and deprivation of privileges, there is a gradual transfer of control from parents to children but a coregulatory environment is prevalent, and parents and children increasingly respond to each other on the basis of categorizations of each other. Our discussion of family relationships in the adolescent years focuses on the adolescent's push for autonomy and how it affects family processes, parenting strategies and parent-adolescent conflict, maturational changes in adolescents as well as parents, and the effects of divorce on adolescents.

Autonomy and Attachment-Connectedness

The adolescent's quest for autonomy and a sense of responsibility creates puzzlement and conflict for many parents. Parents begin to see their teenager slipping away from their grasp. Often, the urge is to take stronger control as the adolescent seeks autonomy and responsibility for himself or herself. Heated emotional exchanges may ensue, with either side calling names, making threats, and doing whatever seems necessary to gain control. Often, parents are frustrated because they expected their teenager to heed their advice, to want to spend time with his or her family, and to grow up to do what is right. To be sure, they anticipated that their teenager would have some difficulty adjusting to the changes that adolescence brings, but few parents are able to accurately imagine and predict just how strong the adolescent's desire will be to spend time with peers and how much the adolescent will want to show that it is he or she, not they, who is responsible for his or her success or failure.

At the same time that adolescents are beginning to show signs of independence from parental influence, they rapidly come under more intense peer influence. But it is incorrect to think that adolescent autonomy from parents is synonymous with the adolescent's total conformity to his or her peer culture. Instead, the adolescent's autonomy is influenced by a variety of social agents, the two most important being parents and peers.

Let's now see how autonomy is made up of various dimensions.

The Multidimensionality of Autonomy

Trying to define adolescent autonomy is more complex and elusive than it might seem at first. For most people, the term *autonomy* connotes self-direction and independence. But what does it really mean? Is it an internal personality trait that consistently characterizes the adolescent's immunity from parental influence? Is it the ability to make responsible personal decisions? Does autonomy imply consistent behavior in all areas of adolescent life, including school, finances, dating, and peer relations? What are the relative contributions of peers and other adults to the development of the adolescent's autonomy?

It is clear that adolescent autonomy is *not* a unitary personality dimension that consistently comes out in all behaviors (Hill & Holmbeck, in press). For example, in one investigation, high school students were asked 25 questions about their independence from their families (Psathas, 1957). Four distinct patterns of adolescent autonomy emerged from analyses of the high school students' responses. One dimension was labeled "permissiveness in outside activities" and was represented by such questions as, "Do you have to account to parents for the way you spend your money?" A second dimension was called "permissiveness in age-related activities" and was reflected in such questions as, "Do your

LUANN   BY GREG EVANS

LUANN by Greg Evans. © by and permission of News America Syndicate, 1986.

parents help you buy your clothes?" A third independent aspect of adolescent autonomy was referred to as "parental regard for judgment," indicted by responses to items like, "In family discussions, do your parents encourage you to give your opinion?" And a fourth dimension was characterized as "activities with status implications" and was indexed by parental influence on choice of occupation.

Further support for the multidimensionality of adolescent autonomy came from an investigation of college freshmen and sophomores between the ages of 18 and 21 (Moore, 1985). At issue was the nature of parent-adolescent separation when adolescents leave home. Eight factors reflected the diversity of how late adolescents viewed leaving home: (1) autonomy (movement toward adult status, making independent decisions), (2) emotional detachment (feelings of not belonging or not close), (3) financial independence, (4) separate residence (moving to an apartment and not living with parents in the summer), (5) disengagement (parents no longer telling individual what to do, being physically away), (6) school affiliation, (7) starting a family, and (8) graduation. Adolescent autonomy, then, is not a unitary phenomenon but a summary label for a variety of adolescent interests, behaviors, thoughts, and feelings.

Now that we have some idea of the multidimensionality of autonomy, we next discuss how autonomy is related to the way in which parents interact with their adolescents.

Parenting Strategies for Promoting Healthy Autonomy

There is consistent evidence that authoritarian parenting restricts the adolescent's development of independence. In a cross-cultural study of adolescents and their families in the United States and Denmark, authoritarian parenting was related to a lack of autonomy in adolescents (Kandel & Lesser, 1969). The structure of the average American family is much more authoritarian than the structure of a typical family in Denmark. This difference in family structure generally indicates that Danish adolescents are more autonomous than their American counterparts.

While there is agreement that an authoritarian family structure restricts the adolescent's development of autonomy, there is not as much consistency in pinpointing the parenting practices that increase autonomy. Some investigations have found that a permissive parenting strategy allows the adolescent to become more independent (Elder, 1968). Others suggest that a democratic parenting strategy is best (Kandel & Lesser, 1969). While investigators vary in how they define permissive and democratic parenting techniques, in most instances, a permissive strategy generally entails little parental involvement and few parental standards. By contrast, a democratic strategy usually consists of equal involvement on the part of parents and adolescents, with the parents having the final authority to set limits on their teenagers. When the overall competence and adjustment of the adolescent is evaluated (rather than just autonomy), an even more clear-cut advantage can be attributed to democratic over permissive strategies of parenting.

In summary, adolescence is a period of development when the individual pushes for autonomy (or the perception that he or she has control over his or her behavior) and gradually develops the ability to take that control. This ability may be acquired through appropriate adult reactions to the adolescent's desire for control. At the onset of adolescence, the average person does not have the knowledge to make appropriate or mature decisions in all areas of his or her life. As the adolescent pushes for autonomy, the wise adult will relinquish control in areas where the adolescent can make mature decisions and help the adolescent to make reasonable decisions in areas where his or her knowledge is more limited. Gradually, the adolescent will acquire the ability to make mature decisions on his or her own.

So far, we have seen that autonomy is multidimensional and that some parenting strategies are better than others in promoting healthy autonomy. As we observe next, it also is important to consider the coordination of autonomy with connectedness and attachment with parents.

Attachment, the Coordinated Worlds of Parents and Peers, and Connectedness

Adolescents do not simply move away from parental influence into a decision-making process all their own. There is continued connectedness to parents as adolescents move toward autonomy.

Attachment in Adolescence Attachment theorists (e.g., Ainsworth, 1979; Bowlby, 1969; Sroufe & Fleeson, 1985) have argued that secure attachment is central to the infant's relationship with his or her caregiver, as we saw in Chapter 6. The attachment bond is believed to promote the healthy exploration of the world because the caregiver provides a secure base to which the infant can return if stressors are encountered. By contrast, insecure attachment to the caregiver is believed to be associated with an incompetent exploration of the world.

It may well be that secure attachment also is important in understanding the nature of the adolescent's development. A secure attachment in infancy and childhood

likely is carried forward to influence the adolescent's continuing relationships with parents. And a continuing secure attachment in adolescence likely promotes the healthy exploration of the environment, including relationships with peers, friends, and the opposite sex, as well as identity development. Adolescents who do not sense that there is a predictable home base to return to in times of considerable stress are more likely to pursue autonomy in an unhealthy manner and to possibly develop a negative rather than a positive identity.

Very few investigations have studied the nature of secure attachment in adolescence and its link to adolescent adjustment. One study, however, investigated the possibility that secure attachment to parents might be associated with healthy adjustment in late adolescence (Armsden & Greenberg, 1982). In this study, 179 individuals ages 16 to 20 years were asked to describe the nature of their relationships with their parents by indicating the extent to which a number of statements characterized such relationships. For example, they were asked the extent to which their parents respected their feelings, the degree to which parents respected their judgment, how much they could talk to their parents about problems, and the likelihood that parents would question them if the parents knew that something was bothering them. In particular, the element of trust in relationships between adolescents and parents was weighted heavily in assessing secure attachment. In addition to assessing secure and insecure attachment, the researchers also evaluated the self-esteem and life satisfaction of the adolescents. As predicted, adolescents who were securely attached to their parents had higher self-esteem and life satisfaction than their insecurely attached counterparts.

The Coordinated Worlds of Parents and Peers The worlds of parent-adolescent relationships and peer relationships are distinct, but coordinated. In the Armsden & Greenberg (1982) investigation described previously, attachment to peers was assessed, in addition to attachment to parents. It was found that adolescents who were securely attached to parents also were more likely to show a secure pattern of attachment to peers. For example, 45 percent of the adolescents who were securely attached to parents were also securely attached to peers, while only 16 percent of the securely attached parent group of adolescents showed insecure attachment with peers (not all adolescents could be clearly categorized as either securely or insecurely attached to parents or peers).

Another investigation also revealed the continuing importance of both parents and peers in the adolescent's development (Brittain, 1963). Adolescents were queried about whether they were influenced more by their peers or their parents in a variety of contexts, such as taking different classes at school, selecting different styles of clothing, or choosing to decline or accept a part-time job offer. In some situations, the adolescents chose to adhere to the wishes of their friends, while in other contexts, they chose to rely on their parents' advice. For example, when decisions involved basic values and vocation orientations, adolescents were more likely to listen to their parents, but when peer activities were involved, they were more likely to accede to the influence of their friends.

Focus on Child Development 13.1 provides information about yet another study of the coordinated worlds of parents and peers. Now let's look further at the connectedness of adolescents and their parents.

Connectedness of Adolescents and Parents   A review of parent-adolescent and peer relationships by Catherine Cooper and Susan Ayers-Lopez (1985) stresses that early models of adolescents and their relationships emphasized the differences and distinctiveness of parent and peer worlds. Traditionally, adolescents have been described as attempting to separate themselves from their parents while at the same time trying to engage themselves with peers. The process of separation characteristically has been studied in relation to parents, and engagement and connectedness have been evaluated almost exclusively in relation to peers. Cooper and Ayers-Lopez argue that this is an artificial distinction and an oversimplification of the complex, coordinated relationships of adolescents with parents and peers. They go on to describe the ideas of ethologist Robert Hinde (1983), who emphasizes a distinction between interactions, relationships, and groups.

Hinde believes that **interactions** involve patterns of communications that occur between persons who may or may not be intimates. **Relationships,** by contrast, occur between people with enduring bonds to each other and are often marked by histories of past interactions as well

as commitments to the future. **Groups** carry with them normative expectations about acceptable and unacceptable aspects of behavior and influence both the interactions and relationships of group members (Hartup, 1985).

For example, one key aspect of adolescent peer relations can be traced to basic decisions by parents at the group level. Parents' choices of neighborhoods, churches, schools, and their own friends influence the pool from which their adolescents might select possible friends. For instance, choice of schools can lead to differences in grouping policies, academic and extracurricular activities, and classroom organization (e.g., open, teacher-centered, and so forth). In turn, such factors affect which students the adolescent is likely to meet, their purpose in interacting, and eventually who become friends. For instance, classrooms in which teachers encourage more cooperative peer interchanges have fewer isolates (Epstein, in press).

At the interaction level, parents may model or coach their adolescents in ways of relating to peers. For instance, in one investigation, parents revealed that they recommended specific strategies to their children with regard to their children's relationships with peers (Rubin & Sloman, 1984). For example, parents told their children how to mediate disputes or how to become less shy with others. They also encouraged them to be tolerant and to resist peer pressure. However, while such strategies may be beneficial with children, there may be times, particularly in early adolescence, when adolescents resist such coaching strategies by parents.

Nonetheless, it is quite clear that a *connectedness,* rather than a separateness, exists between the world of parent-adolescent relationships and peer relationships. For example, when positive relationships exist between parents and adolescents, parents may coach their offspring, particularly same-sex offspring, in dating relationships. During late adolescence, it is not unusual for mothers and daughters and fathers and sons to converse about the nature of relationships with the opposite sex. Such conversations may be cross-sexed as well, with fathers coaching their daughters about the type of guys to watch out for, what to look for in a relationship, and so forth.

FOCUS ON CHILD DEVELOPMENT 13.1

MOTHERS, DAUGHTERS, AND GIRLFRIENDS

Martin Gold and Denise Yanof (1985) investigated the relation between adolescent girls' relationships with their mothers and their relationships with their closest girlfriends. They gave questionnaires to 134 high school girls, asking them about mother-daughter affection, democratic treatment by their mothers, and appropriateness of their mothers as models. In addition, they asked the high school girls about the intimacy of their relationships with their closest girlfriends, the mutual influence in these peer relationships, and their identification with their girlfriends.

The results of the study clearly revealed that consideration of their mothers as appropriate models was positively related to not only the girls' identification with their closest girlfriends but also to the intimacy of those friendships. This intimacy involved high levels of affection. The general extent to which the girl identified with her mother was significantly related to her identification with her girlfriend(s). Identification with mothers was assessed by such items as the extent to which the girl said that she "would like to become like" her mother with regard to such characteristics as career attainment, appearance, relationships with people, and the like. Identification with a girlfriend(s) was evaluated by asking the girl to rate the general extent to which she wanted to be like her girlfriend. Also, the more that the girls perceived that their mothers treated them in a democratic way, the more the girls reported mutual influence in relationships with their girlfriends.

Gold and Yanof concluded that these data support a developmental, rather than a compensatory, model of adolescent relationships. A developmental model suggests that parents, through close, positive relationships with adolescents, influence adolescents' construction of positive relationships with others. A compensatory model indicates that adolescents immerse themselves in relationships with peers

How might adolescent girls' friendship patterns be associated with parent-adolescent relationships?

when they lack close, positive relationships with parents. Quite clearly, such data support the argument that connectedness and attachment to parents continue as adolescents form relationships outside of their family and that the positive nature of parent-adolescent relationships contributes to healthy peer relationships.

Now that we have some sense of what autonomy is, its multidimensional nature, parenting strategies for promoting healthy autonomy, and the coordinated, connected worlds of parents and peers, let's turn our attention to some more general ideas about parenting in adolescence and also explore the nature of parent-adolescent conflict.

Parenting Strategies and Parent-Adolescent Conflict

We saw in Chapter 8 that authoritative parenting often seems to be a wise strategy for rearing children. Let's explore whether this parenting strategy remains the best choice with adolescents and also look at the degree to which conflict with parents increases during adolescence.

Parenting Strategies with Adolescents

The expectations of adolescents and their parents often seem to conflict as adolescents change dramatically during the course of puberty. Many parents see their child changing from being a compliant being to being someone who is noncompliant, oppositional, and resistant to parental standards. Parents often tend to clamp down tighter and to put more pressure on the adolescent to conform to parental standards. They tend to deal with the young adolescent as if they expect the adolescent to become a mature being within the next 10 to 15 minutes. Of course, the transition from childhood to adulthood is a long one. Adolescents are not going to conform to adult standards immediately.

Parents who recognize that adolescents take a long time "to get it right" may be able to more competently and calmly deal with adolescent transgressions than parents who demand immediate conformity to parental standards. Yet, other parents, rather than placing heavy demands on their adolescents for compliance, do virtually the opposite, letting the adolescent do as he or she pleases. Just as with children, neither high-intensity demands for compliance nor an unwillingness to monitor and be involved in the adolescent's development are likely to be wise parenting strategies. Focus on Child Development 13.2 describes recent research on the latchkey experiences of adolescents and the importance of parenting strategy and adolescent monitoring in these circumstances.

How extensive is parent-adolescent conflict?

Parent-Adolescent Conflict

Conflict between parents and adolescents often seems to increase during early adolescence, although the degree of the conflict often is not as intense and pervasive as the media generally portray it.

Why Is There an Increase in Parent-Adolescent Conflict? Possible explanations for increased parent-adolescent conflict during early adolescence focus on changes in the adolescent and include biological changes in levels of aggression, the appearance of sexuality, the push for independence, and the quest for identity. Other explanations emphasize parental characteristics. For example, the parents of many adolescents are entering middle age and may encounter more difficult life circumstances themselves, which may contribute to parent-adolescent conflict. And parents, particularly the mother, may be unwilling to let go and allow the adolescent to autonomously develop an identity. Still other explanations focus on the disequilibrium that occurs in the family social system with the onset of adolescence, an upheaval that replaces the relatively smoothly functioning family system that existed during childhood.

FOCUS ON CHILD DEVELOPMENT 13.2

MONITORING THE LIVES OF ADOLESCENTS AFTER SCHOOL

Sandra is a 14-year-old adolescent. Both her parents work and do not get home until after 6:00 P.M. each weekday evening. Sandra is involved in a club on Tuesdays after school, but she does not participate in any organized activities on the other four days of the week. On this particular Wednesday, she is at her home around 4:00 P.M., and two girlfriends and three boys have been invited over to watch MTV. One of the boys is 17 years of age and has brought some beer for an after-school party at Sandra's home.

Barbara also is a 14-year-old adolescent whose parents work and get home on weekdays at about the same time as Sandra's parents. Barbara is a member of the tennis team at her school, and the team practices until 5:00 P.M. five days a week. She usually remains at school until her mother or father picks her up between 6:00 and 6:30 P.M. Barbara's mother has organized a study group of students in Barbara's school whose parents work and cannot get home until late in the evening. The parents have gone together to pay one of the coaches to monitor the study hall after practice until the adolescents are picked up and taken home.

Both Barbara and Sandra have working parents who cannot themselves directly monitor the adolescents' lives after school, but the after-school lives of the two girls are very different. To investigate variations in the after-school experiences of latchkey adolescents, Laurence Steinberg (1986) recently studied 865 adolescents in the fifth through ninth grades. Consistent with the findings of other research (e.g., Rodman, Pratto, & Nelson, 1985), the latchkey adolescents as a group were not significantly different from a control group of adolescents whose parents supervised them at home in the after-school hours. However, when the research was expanded to include greater variation in after-school experiences, latchkey adolescents who were more removed from adult supervision were more susceptible to peer pressure than those who were at a friend's house after school. Further, latchkey adolescents who were at a friend's house were also

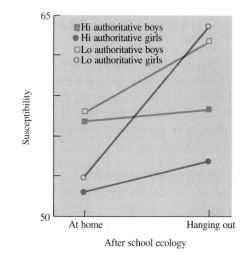

Susceptibility to peer pressure of latchkey boys and girls who are at home or "hanging out" after school as a function of parental authoritativeness.

less susceptible to peer influence than latchkey adolescents who simply described themselves as just "hanging out." And latchkey adolescents whose parents knew their whereabouts and those who had been reared in an authoritative manner were less susceptible to peer pressure than their counterparts whose parents did not know where they were and what they were doing and who used other parenting strategies, such as authoritarian and permissive. Even when the latchkey adolescents whose parents knew their whereabouts and had reared them in an authoritative way were in situations in which adult supervision was lax and susceptibility to peer pressure was high, these adolescents showed an ability to resist peer influence. The figure above shows the results pertaining to authoritative parenting and susceptibility to peer pressure for latchkey adolescents who were either at home or just "hanging out."

Research on Parent-Adolescent Conflict   Research on parent-adolescent conflict has suggested a developmental patterning for such conflict, has provided information about the kinds of conflicts parents and adolescents have, and has indicated how such conflict can serve a positive developmental function.

It is not unusual to talk to the parents of early adolescents and hear them say, "Is it ever going to get better?" A review of research on the developmental patterning of parent-adolescent conflict suggests that things generally do get better as individuals move from the early part of adolescence toward the end (Montemayor, 1982). Conflict between parents and adolescents seems to escalate during early adolescence, remain somewhat stable during the high school years, and then lessen as the adolescent reaches 17 to 20 years of age. Parent-adolescent relationships become more positive if adolescents go away to college than if they stay at home while they go to college (Sullivan & Sullivan, 1980).

Most arguments between parents and their adolescents focus on normal, everyday goings-on, such as schoolwork, social life, peers, home chores, disobedience, sibling fights, and personal hygiene (Montemayor, 1982). Although many of these conflicts are a result of the adolescent's push for independence, they often are a product of parents' continuing efforts to teach their adolescent offspring to delay gratification and to conform to a set of societal and family rules and regulations.

When you talk to the parents of young adolescents, it is difficult to convince them that the parent-adolescent conflict they are experiencing serves a positive developmental function. However, in one recent investigation parent-adolescent conflict did just that (Cooper, Grotevant, Moore, & Condon, 1982). Adolescent identity exploration was positively related to the frequency of expression of disagreement with parents during a family discussion task. Within some normal range, then, conflict with parents may be psychologically healthy for the adolescent's development. A virtually conflict-free relationship may indicate that an adolescent has a fear of separation, exploration, and independence.

As suggested earlier, one way for parents to cope with the adolescent's push for independence and identity is to recognize that adolescence is a 10- to 15-year transition period rather than an overnight accomplishment. Realizing that conflict can serve a positive developmental function can tone down parental hostility as well. Understanding parent-adolescent conflict, though, is not simple. As we observe next, both the maturation of the adolescent and the maturation of the parents likely are wrapped up in such conflict.

The Maturation of the Adolescent and the Maturation of Parents

The overview of biological and cognitive changes during adolescence presented in Chapter 12 suggested that the adolescent is a changing being, particularly in the early adolescent years. Successful parenting requires at least some adaptation to these changes. And it also is important to consider that the parent, as well as the adolescent, is changing.

The Maturation of the Adolescent

Let's look at some of the physical, cognitive, and social changes during adolescence that might call for changes in the way parents relate to the adolescent.

Physical Changes   There are universal physical changes in individuals as they move from childhood into the early adolescent years. Pubertal change brings with it dramatic increases in height and weight as well as sexual maturation. By the age of 14 or 15, many adolescents are as large as or larger than their parents, while some three to five years earlier they were much shorter and smaller. Thus, parents must now look at eye level or upward as they communicate with the adolescent. They are no longer able to look downward and feel a sense of physical power over their offspring. Given their sheer physical size and power, adolescents, much more so than children, are physical equals of their parents.

The sexual maturation of the adolescent also calls for parental adaptation. No longer can the son or daughter crawl into bed with an opposite-sex parent and be cuddled. And parents must now deal with questions of sexuality—how much freedom should the adolescent be allowed in dating curfews? If and what kind of sexual information should be given to the adolescent? How much and how should sexual activity be monitored?

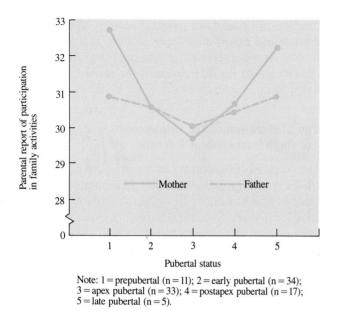

Note: 1 = prepubertal (n = 11); 2 = early pubertal (n = 34); 3 = apex pubertal (n = 33); 4 = postapex pubertal (n = 17); 5 = late pubertal (n = 5).

FIGURE 13.1   Pubertal development and parents' perception of sons' participation in family activity.

Several recent investigations have revealed that relationships between mothers and sons are most stressful during the apex of pubertal growth, while father-son relationships seem to be less influenced by the son's transition through puberty (Hill, Holmbeck, Marlow, Green, & Lynch, 1985; Steinberg, 1981; Steinberg & Hill, 1978). For example, as shown in Figure 13.1, mothers were less satisfied with their sons' participation in family activities during the apex of pubertal change (Hill, Holmbeck, Marlow, Green, & Lynch, 1985). And actual observations of parent-adolescent relationships reveal that the father retains his influence over family decision making throughout the pubertal transition and asserts his dominance by requiring increasing deference from the son. However, mothers and sons interrupted each other more, explained themselves less, and deferred less to each other. Ultimately, though, toward the end of the pubertal change process, as sons grew much larger and became more powerful, mothers were more likely to defer to their sons and were engaged in less conflict with them than during the apex of pubertal change. Less is known about the pubertal change of girls and the nature of

parent-adolescent relationships. Clearly, though, it appears that where the adolescent is in the pubertal cycle is to some degree linked with the nature of parent-adolescent relationships.

Cognitive Changes   The adolescent, compared to when he or she was a child, can reason in more logical ways with parents. During childhood, a parent may be able to get by with saying, "O.K. That's it. We do it my way or else," and the child conforms. But with increased cognitive skills, the adolescent no longer is likely to accept such a statement as a reason for conforming to parental dictates. The adolescent wants to know, often in fine detail, why he or she is being disciplined. And even when the parent gives what, to the parent, seems to be a logical reason, the adolescent's cognitive sophistication may call attention to a deficiency in the parent's reasoning. Such prolonged bouts of discourse with parents usually do not characterize parent-child relationships but are a frequent occurrence in parent-adolescent relationships.

In addition to increased logical reasoning skills, the idealistic nature of the adolescent's thought, compared to when he or she was a child, also affects the nature of parent-adolescent relationships. Parents often are now evaluated vis-à-vis what an ideal parent would be like. The very real interactions with parents, any of which inevitably contain negative interchanges and flaws, are placed next to the adolescent's schema of the characteristics of an ideal parent. Also, as part of his or her egocentrism, the adolescent's concern with how others view him or her is likely to lead to an overreaction to parental comments. A mother may suggest that her adolescent daughter buy a new blouse. The daughter may respond, "What's the matter? You don't think I have good taste? You think I look gross, don't you?" The same comment made to the daughter during the late childhood years likely would not have evoked such a response.

Yet another aspect of the changing cognitive world of the adolescent and his or her parents is the expectations they have for each other. Andrew Collins (1985) has described how expectations may be violated because the adolescent is changing so rapidly that the adolescent's past behavior may be an unreliable predictor of future behavior. For instance, consider the common situation of the preadolescent child who has been compliant and easy to manage. As he or she enters puberty, the child begins

"*I want to talk to you about the way you're frittering away your life.*"

"*Oh, I know what you're going to say: 'You just don't understand.' Well, I understand this, my friend. You're headed down a dead-end street!*"

"*I'm talking about a sense of purpose. You've got to look for direction to find direction.*"

"*I suppose it's my fault. What kind of example have I been, right? Well, I'm not ashamed of the modest success I've had with my materialistic orientation.*"

"*O.K., so I suppose I'm wrong. Put down that paper and tell me how I've failed.*"

Drawing by Saxon; © 1970 The New Yorker Magazine, Inc.

to question or seek rationales for parental demands (Maccoby, 1984). Parents often perceive such behavior to be resistant and oppositional because it departs from the child's usual compliant behavior, and they may respond with increased pressure for compliance. In this situation, expectations that were prematurely stabilized in a period of relatively slow developmental change are now lagging behind as the adolescent's behavior is changing more rapidly. Collins (1985) also gives another example of how violation of expectations can influence parent-adolescent relationships. The adolescent may interpret the parent's behavior as unfair or repressive because of the adolescent's experiences in other social settings, such as the peer group or school, where questioning and challenging are more typical forms of communication. Or the adolescent may have partial, but not fully recognized, ideas about reciprocity and mutuality in parent-adolescent relationships (e.g., Selman, 1980). Thus, Collins suggests that parents and adolescents are frequently violating and modifying each other's expectations as they move from childhood to adulthood.

We have discussed several important changes in the adolescent's cognition that may contribute to changes in parent-adolescent relationships—among them, the expanded logical reasoning of the adolescent, the increased idealistic and egocentric thought of the adolescent, and violated expectations (on the part of both the adolescent and parents). Next, we look at social changes in the adolescent that may contribute to parent-adolescent relationships.

Social Changes   John Hill (1980) has pointed to a number of social changes in the adolescent's world that might contribute to understanding the nature of parent-adolescent relationships. Adolescence usually brings with it new definitions of socially appropriate behavior. In our society, such definitions often are linked with changes in schooling arrangements—transitions to middle or junior high school. The adolescent is required to function in a more anonymous, larger environment with multiple and varying teachers. More work is required, as is more initiative and responsibility to be successful.

The social world of adolescents at school is not the only arena likely to influence parent-adolescent relationships. Adolescents, compared to children, spend more time with peers and develop more sophisticated friendships. Further, in the social realm, adolescents begin to push for more autonomy. Parents, then, must adapt to changing worlds of adolescent schooling and peer relations, as well as movements toward independence in this expanding environment.

The Maturation of Parents

There are some interesting complementarities in the developmental issues confronting both adolescents and their parents (Hill, 1980; Steinberg, 1980). The intriguing issues focus on the beliefs that:

1. Marital dissatisfaction is greater when the offspring is an adolescent (as opposed to when the offspring is a child or an adult).
2. A greater economic burden is placed on parents during their rearing of adolescents.
3. Parents often re-evaluate occupational achievement when the offspring is an adolescent. The parents of adolescents often evaluate whether they have met their youthful aspirations for success. Further, the parents often look to the future in terms of how much time they have left to accomplish what they want. With regard to career orientation and time perspective, adolescents, however, often look mainly to the future, and do so with unbounded optimism. Adolescents sense that they have an unlimited amount of time to accomplish what they desire.
4. Health concerns, as well as interest in body integrity and sexual attractiveness, become prominent themes of the parents of adolescents. Even when their body and sexual attractiveness are not deteriorating, many parents of adolescents perceive that they are. By contrast, adolescents are at or are beginning to reach the peak of their physical attractiveness, strength, and health. Thus, while both the adolescent and his or her parents often show a heightened preoccupation with their bodies, the adolescent's view likely is a more positive one.

It is important to note that the parents of adolescents either are in mid-life or are rapidly approaching the middle adulthood years. And, if current trends continue, the parents of adolescents will be even older in the future. As shown in Table 13.1, adults are waiting longer to get married, with the median age of marriage changing from 20.8 to 23.0 years for females just in the 1970 to 1984 time frame. Also, there currently is a trend for married couples to delay having children so that they can stabilize and advance their careers. The upshot of these trends is that the parents of adolescents in the future are likely to be further into the middle adulthood years than parents of adolescents today. What do we know about how the age of parents influences parent-adolescent relationships? Very little research has been conducted, but several studies reveal some insights. In one set of studies, younger and older fathers were compared (Nydegger, 1975, 1981; Mitteness & Nydegger, 1982). The older fathers seemed to fare better than the younger fathers in some ways, being warmer, communicating better, encouraging more achievement, and showing less rejection. However, the older fathers were less likely to place demands on their children and were less likely to enforce rules.

Table 13.1   Median Age at First Marriage

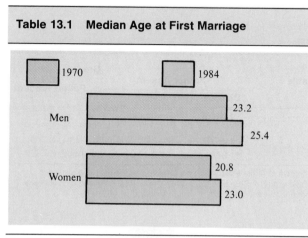

Source: U.S. Bureau of the Census.

While we have described a number of aspects of family processes and adolescent development, it is important to consider one final set of changes that an increasing number of adolescents are experiencing—life in a divorced family.

The Effects of Divorce on Adolescents

In Chapter 8, we saw that divorce is a highly stressful matter for children. Here we will discover that divorce is a stressful circumstance for adolescents as well. First, we study the intriguing work of Judith Wallerstein and Joan Kelly and then that of E. Mavis Hetherington.

Wallerstein and Kelly: Carrying Forward the Divorce Experience

The Wallerstein and Kelly research reveals the stress of divorce for adolescents as well as how the divorce experience in adolescence continues to influence individuals as they move into their adult years. In the Wallerstein and Kelly (1980) investigation, 21 of the individuals were 13 years old or older at the time of the divorce decision. Almost without exception, these adolescents perceived the divorce as painful. The adolescents who distanced themselves from parental conflict seemed to be coping more effectively than others. In many instances, the parents of these adolescents kept them as uninvolved as possible in the divorce proceedings. The parents of these adolescents also allowed them to maintain strong ties with their peers. At first, these adolescents seemed insensitive in their counselors' eyes, but over

time, they were better able than other adolescents to realistically assess their family situation.

In a 10-year follow-up of these adolescents as they moved into their early adulthood years (Wallerstein, 1982), they continued to report that the divorce of their parents a decade or more earlier had been carried forward and had a lasting impact on their lives. Many of the young adults sensed that the divorce of their parents during the adolescent years had burdened their efforts at growing up and becoming mature adults. As adults, they looked backward with emotions filled with sadness and with wishes that they had grown up in an intact family. They also showed considerable concern about repeating the divorce in their own marriages and were anxious to avoid having their own children grow up in divorced circumstances.

Hetherington: Effects of Divorce on the Heterosexual Behavior of Adolescent Girls

Mavis Hetherington (1972) has shown that the heterosexual behavior of adolescent girls from father-absent and father-present homes is different. In her study, the adolescent girls with absent fathers acted in one of two extreme ways: They were either very withdrawn, passive, and subdued around boys or were overly active, aggressive, and flirtatious. The girls who were inhibited, rigid, and restrained around males were more likely to have come from widowed homes. Those who sought the attention of males, who showed early heterosexual behavior, and who seemed more open and uninhibited were more likely to have come from homes in which the parents were divorced. In addition, early separation from fathers usually was associated with more profound effects, and the mothers' attitudes toward themselves and marriage differed from that of widows. Divorced women were more anxious, unhappy, hostile toward males, and more negative about marriage than were the widows. And perhaps not surprisingly, daughters of divorcees had more negative attitudes about men than did the daughters of widows.

Several examples of the actual behavior of the girls should provide a clearer picture of the study. One technique used to investigate the girls' behavior was to interview them sometimes with a male interviewer and sometimes with a female interviewer. Four chairs were

Table 13.2   Group Means for Observational Variables in the Recreational Center

Observational Variable	Group Father Absent		Group Father Present
	Divorce	Death	
Subject-initiated physical contact and nearness with male peers	3.08	1.71	1.79
Male areas	7.75	2.25	4.71
Female areas	11.67	17.42	14.42

From Hetherington, E. Mavis, "Effects of father-absence on personality development in adolescent daughters" in *Developmental Psychology, 7,* 313–326, 1972. Copyright © 1972 American Psychological Association. Reprinted by permission of the author.

placed in the room, including one for the interviewer. Daughters of widows most frequently chose the chair farthest from the male interviewer, while daughters of divorcees generally selected the chair closest to him. There were no differences when the interviewer was a female. The interviewer also observed the girls at a dance and during activities at the recreational center. At the dance, the daughters of widows often refused to dance when asked. One widow's daughter even spent the entire evening in the restroom. The daughters of the divorcees were more likely to accept the boys' invitations to dance. At the recreation center, the daughters of divorcees were more frequently observed outside the gym where boys were playing, while the daughters of widows more often engaged in traditional "female" activities, like sewing and cooking (see Table 13.2).

Hetherington (1977) continued to study these girls, following them into young adulthood to determine their sexual behavior, marital choices, and marital behavior. The daughters of divorcees tended to marry younger (eight of the daughters of widowed mothers still were not married at the time of the report) and to select marital partners who more frequently had drug problems and inconsistent work histories. In contrast, daughters of widows tended to marry men with a more puritanical makeup. In addition, both the daughters of widows and divorcees reported more sexual adjustment problems than the daughters from intact homes; for example, the daughters from homes where the father was absent generally experienced fewer orgasms than daughters from intact homes. The daughters from intact homes also showed more variation in their sex-role behavior and

How might family experiences influence heterosexual behavior in adolescence?

marital adjustment. They seemed to be more relaxed and dealt more competently with their roles as wives, suggesting that they had worked through their relationships with their fathers and were more psychologically free to deal successfully in their relationships with other males. On the other hand, the daughters of the divorcees and widows appeared to be marrying images of their fathers.

It should be recognized that findings such as Hetherington's (1972) may not hold as the woman's role in society continues to change. Also, the findings are from a restricted sample of middle-class families living in one

Child Development Concept Table 13.1 Families and Adolescent Development		
Concept	**Processes/Related Ideas**	**Characteristics/Description**
Autonomy and attachment-connectedness	The multidimensionality of autonomy	Many parents have a difficult time handling the adolescent's strong push for autonomy, even though this push is one of the hallmarks of adolescent development. Trying to define autonomy is difficult; conceptualizing autonomy as multidimensional is important.
	Parenting strategies for promoting healthy autonomy	Democratic parenting is associated with enhanced autonomy of adolescents, while authoritarian parenting is related to a lack of autonomy. The wise parent relinquishes control in areas where the adolescent shows maturity but monitors the adolescent's life more closely in those domains where immature behavior is shown.
	Attachment, the coordinated worlds of parents and peers, and connectedness	There is an increased interest in the connectedness of adolescents and their parents. Historically, connectedness has been reserved for peer relations, while separation has been used to describe parent-adolescent relationships. Now, there is considerable enthusiasm in looking at parent-adolescent relationships in terms of attachment and connectedness, as well as at the coordinated worlds of parents and peers. It is likely that secure attachment to parents through the childhood and adolescent years promotes a healthy exploration of independence and identity. Hinde's view that interactions, relationships, and groups can be distinguished has led to further emphasis on the connectedness of family relationships to the wider social world of the adolescent.
Parenting strategies and parent-adolescent conflict	Parenting strategies with adolescents	Too often, parents do not stop to think about how much time it takes to make the long transition from child to adult. As the individual moves into the later years of adolescence, the parent may be wise to relinquish more control and to monitor the adolescent's life more indirectly while still maintaining a strong connectedness with the adolescent.
	Parent-adolescent conflict	Interest in parent-adolescent conflict has a long history, and many explanations have been offered for the belief that conflict increases between parents and their offspring as the children become adolescents. Conflict with parents does seem to increase in the early adolescent years. Such conflict usually is of the moderate variety, rather than the prolonged, intense type. The moderate increase in conflict likely serves the positive developmental function of promoting independence and identity.
The maturation of the adolescent and the maturation of parents	The maturation of the adolescent	Physical, cognitive, and social changes in the adolescent's development influence parent-adolescent relationships. Among these are the nature of pubertal change; the adolescent's expanded logical reasoning and increased idealistic and egocentric thought; violated expectations; changes in schooling, peers, friendships, and dating; and movement toward independence.
	The maturation of parents	Parental changes include those involving marital dissatisfaction, economic burdens, career reevaluation and time perspective, as well as health and bodily concerns.
The effects of divorce on adolescents	Its nature	Divorce is a stressful experience for adolescents, just as it is for children. Adolescents carry forward the experience of their parents' divorce into their adult years. Divorce influences the heterosexual behavior of girls.

city—hence, the results may not be as clear when adolescents from other subcultures are studied. Nonetheless, Hetherington's results do point to some likely vulnerabilities of adolescent girls growing up in divorced and widowed families.

Child Development Concept Table 13.1 summarizes our discussion of family processes and adolescent development. Next, we look at the pervasive influence of peers in adolescent development.

PEERS AND ADOLESCENT DEVELOPMENT

In Chapter 11, we discussed how, in middle and late childhood, children spend more time with their peers than in the preschool years. We also found that friendships become more important in the elementary school years and that popularity with peers is a strong motivation for most children. Advances in cognitive development during the middle and late childhood years also allow children to take the perspective of peers and friends more easily, and their social knowledge of how to make and maintain friends increases.

Think about when you were in junior and senior high school—especially your good times. Chances are that what comes to mind are your relationships with friends and age-mates. Adolescents spend huge chunks of time with peers. We now look at peer pressure and conformity, peer modeling and social comparison, cliques and crowds, and dating during the adolescent years.

Peer Pressure and Conformity

Consider the following statement made by an adolescent girl:

> Peer pressure is extremely influential in my life. I have never had very many friends, and I spend quite a bit of time alone. The friends I have are older. . . . The closest friend I have had is a lot like me in that we are both sad and depressed a lot. I began to act even more depressed than before when I was with her. I would call her up and try to act even more depressed than I was because that is what I thought she liked. In that relationship, I felt pressure to be like her. . . .

Because adolescents spend more time with peers, do they conform more to the ideas and behaviors of their peers than to those advocated by parents? There are several ways to look at peer conformity. First, the influences that are exerted by parents and peers may be contradictory, and adolescents may choose to conform to the perspectives of those they are with the most; or they may simply choose to rebel against parental authority. Second, adolescents may become more responsible for themselves, seeing themselves as more independent of their

What is the nature of conformity to peers in adolescence?

parents and capable of making their own decisions. A third possibility is that a combination of both of these perspectives may come into play.

In an effort to explore the developmental patterns of parental and peer conformity, Thomas Berndt (1979) studied 273 3rd- through 12th-grade students. Hypothetical dilemmas were presented to the students, requiring them to make choices about conformity with friends on prosocial and antisocial behaviors and conformity with parents on neutral and prosocial behaviors. For example, one prosocial item questioned whether students relied on their parents' advice in such situations as deciding about helping at the library or instructing another child to swim. An antisocial question asked a boy what he would do if one of his peers wanted him to help steal some candy. A neutral question asked a girl if she would follow peer suggestions to engage in an activity she wasn't interested in—for example, going to a movie she didn't want to see.

Some interesting developmental patterns were found in this investigation. In the 3rd grade, parent and peer influences often directly contradicted each other. Since parent conformity is much greater for 3rd-grade children, children of this age are probably still closely tied

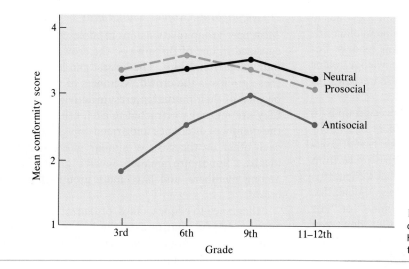

FIGURE 13.2 Mean scores of peer conformity for different types of behavior. Higher scores indicate greater conformity; the neutral point is 3.5.

to and dependent on their parents. However, by the 6th grade, parent and peer influences were found to be no longer in direct opposition. Peer conformity had increased, but parent and peer influences were operating in different situations—parents had more impact in some situations, while peers had more clout in others. For example, parents are more influential in a discussion of political parties, but peers seem to have more say when sexual behavior and attitudes are at issue (Hyman, 1959; Vandiver, 1972).

By the 9th grade, parent and peer influences were once again in strong opposition to one another, probably because the increased conformity of adolescents to the social behavior of peers is stronger at this grade level than at any other. Figure 13.2 displays the increased conformity to antisocial peer standards in the 9th grade. At this time, adolescent adoption of antisocial standards endorsed by the peer group inevitably leads to conflict between adolescents and parents. Researchers have also found that the adolescent's attempt to gain independence meets with more parental opposition around the 9th grade than at any other time (Douvan & Adelson, 1966; Kandel & Lesser, 1969).

Other recent research also has focused on a distinction between different kinds of conformity. For instance, Bradford Brown and his colleagues have studied peer involvement (the degree of socializing with friends) and misconduct (drug/alcohol use, sexual intercourse, and minor delinquent behavior) (Brown, Clasen, & Eicher, in press). Adolescents perceived less peer pressure toward misconduct than they did regarding peer involvement and also were less willing to follow peers in misconduct. Males were more likely to accede to antisocial peer pressures than females.

So far, we have looked only at how adolescents conform to peer pressure and societal standards. While the majority of adolescents are conformity oriented, some could best be described as independent or rebellious. The truly *independent* or **nonconformist** adolescents know what the people around them expect, but they don't use these expectations to guide their behavior. However, *rebellious* or **anticonformist** teenagers react counter to the group's expectations and deliberately move away from the actions or beliefs the group advocates.

Peer Modeling and Social Comparison

Adolescents also are influenced by the models that peers provide. Positive relationships between models and observers tend to enhance models' effectiveness (Hartup, 1970), as does the extent to which individuals perceive models as similar to themselves (Rosenkrans, 1967). Models who are more powerful are often more likely to be followed than those who are less powerful (Bandura, 1977). Thus, school leaders—captains of the football and drill teams, the president of the student council, and so forth—are more likely to be imitated than those not in school leadership positions. In some instances, older adolescents are more likely to be adopted as models. Because of their age, experience, and knowledge, older adolescents are likely to come across as more powerful than younger adolescents.

One of the primary functions of the peer group is to provide a means of **social comparison** about one's abilities, talents, characteristics, and the like. Social comparison seems to heighten as boys and girls move from the elementary school years into early adolescence. It is not unusual to daily hear such comments as, "I don't like her hair. It's not as natural as yours and mine." or "His car is a piece of junk. Mine is much better, don't you think?" or "I got an A on the biology test. What did you get?" Consider also the following comments of a person describing her girlfriend as a social comparison source:

> Girlfriends were as essential as mothers . . . girlfriends provided a sense of security, as belonging to any group does . . .·(but) a best friend was more complicated: using a friend as a mirror or as a model, expanding your own knowledge through someone else's, painfully acquiring social skills. What little we learned about living with another person in an equal relationship, outside our own families, we learned from our girlfriends. (Toth, 1981, p. 60)

Social comparison, of course, can have either negative or positive effects. As adolescents look around their peer world and compare themselves with others, they likely find some things about themselves that they like and some that they don't like. Adolescents who see themselves more positively than most others likely have higher self-esteem than those who compare themselves more negatively to others. Quite clearly, though, social comparison is a highly motivating aspect of adolescent life, as adolescents strive to find out where they stand vis-à-vis their peers on many different abilities and characteristics.

Cliques and Crowds

What are adolescent cliques and crowds like? Does clique membership affect the adolescent's self-esteem? How do children's groups differ from adolescents' groups? Let's explore these and other questions.

Distinguishing Cliques and Crowds

Most peer group relationships in adolescence can be categorized in one of three ways: the **crowd,** the **clique,** or individual friendships. The largest and least personal of these groups is the crowd. Members of the crowd meet because of their mutual interest in activities, not because they are mutually attracted to each other. By contrast, the members of cliques and friendships are attracted to each other on the basis of similar interests and social ideals. Cliques are smaller, involve greater intimacy among members, and have more group cohesion than crowds.

Allegiance to cliques, clubs, organizations, and teams exerts powerful control over the lives of many adolescents. Group identity often overrides personal identity. The leader of a group may place a member in a position of considerable moral conflict by asking, in effect, "What's more important, our code or your parents'?" or "Are you looking out for yourself, or for the members of the group?" Labels like "brother" and "sister" sometimes are adopted and used in group members' conversations with one another. These labels symbolize the intensity of the bond between the members and suggest the high status of group membership.

Now let's examine some research on cliques and crowds, first studying a well-known early investigation of leading groups and then a very recent inquiry about how clique membership may be related to self-esteem.

Coleman's Study of Leading Adolescent Groups

One of the most widely quoted studies of adolescent cliques and crowds is that of James Coleman (1961). Students in 10 different high schools were asked to identify the leading crowds in their schools. They also were asked to name the students who were the most outstanding in athletics, popularity, and different school activities. Regardless of the school sampled, the leading crowds were likely to be composed of athletes and popular girls. Much less power in the leading crowd was attributed to the bright student. Coleman's finding that being an athlete contributes to popularity for boys was reconfirmed in a more recent investigation by Eitzen (1975).

Cliques, Crowds, and Self-Esteem

Crowds and cliques have been portrayed as playing a pivotal role in the adolescent's maintenance of self-esteem and development of a sense of identity (e.g., Coleman, 1961; Erikson, 1968). Several theoretical perspectives suggest how crowd and clique membership might be linked with the adolescent's self-esteem (Brown & Lohr, in press). In an extension of Erikson's identity development theory, it is argued that virtually all 13- to 17-year-olds regard clique and crowd membership as highly salient and that self-esteem is higher among clique and crowd members (at least those satisfied with the crowd) than nonmembers. The peer group is viewed as a "way station" between relinquishing childhood dependence on parents and adult self-definition, achievement, and autonomy. Group affiliation and acceptance by the crowd is seen as important in keeping the adolescent's self-concept positive during this long transition period. Social comparison theory also has implications for understanding crowd attachment and self-esteem. It implies that, while group members as a whole might have higher self-esteem than nonmembers, there are differences among group members according to the position of their crowd in the peer group status hierarchy. This argument is based on the belief that individuals often evaluate the adequacy of their ideas or characteristics with those of significant others (Festinger, 1954). Focus on Child Development 13.3 describes a recent investigation that evaluated the importance of crowd identification in the adolescent's self-esteem.

FOCUS ON CHILD DEVELOPMENT 13.3

JOCKS, POPULARS, NORMALS, DRUGGIES/TOUGHS, INDEPENDENTS, AND NOBODIES

Bradford Brown and Mary Jane Lohr (in press) examined the self-esteem of 221 7th- through 12th-graders. These adolescents were either associated with one of five major school crowds or were relatively unknown by classmates and not associated with any school crowd. Adolescents were asked to identify in their own words the major crowds that they perceived as existing in their school. They then described the stereotypic traits of each group, rank-ordered the crowds in terms of status, and listed five classmates they considered to be members of each crowd. Listed from highest to lowest in peer status, the crowds were: "jocks" (athletically oriented), "populars" (well-known students who lead social activities), "normals" (middle-of-the-road students who make up the "masses"), "druggies/toughs" (known for illicit drug use and/or delinquent activities), and "nobodies" (low in social skills and/or intellectual abilities). Self-esteem was measured by a 10-item scale developed by Rosenberg (1965).

The results confirmed the belief that the self-esteem of crowd members is higher than nonmembers and also that the higher-rated a crowd is the more likely that the adolescent's

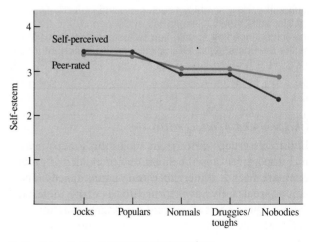

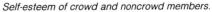

Self-esteem of crowd and noncrowd members.

self-esteem also will be higher (see the figure above). Adolescents who were members of crowds had higher self-esteem than nonmembers, and the members of the crowds rated the most prestigious by peers (such as "jocks") had the highest self-esteem among the various crowds.

(continued on following page)

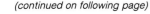

FOCUS ON CHILD DEVELOPMENT 13.3

Other information collected by Brown and Lohr further elaborated on the link between crowd affiliation and self-esteem. For example, a group of adolescents who were labeled outsiders also were studied. Those who realized that they were outsiders but who placed little importance on crowd membership (that is, the "independents") had higher self-esteem than those who perceived themselves as crowd members but whose peers did not (called the "distorters") or those who recognized that they were not part of a crowd but who rated crowd affiliation as important (called the "envious"). The self-esteem of "independents" was not significantly lower than any of the crowds, while the self-esteem of the "distorters" and the "envious" was lower than the two leading crowds.

In considering the linkages between crowd affiliation and self-esteem, it is important to keep several things in mind. First, it is not possible to conclude that crowd affiliation causes enhanced self-esteem. These data are correlational in nature. Indeed, self-esteem probably improves the likelihood that an adolescent will be included in a leading crowd, while at the same time, membership in such a crowd also is likely to engender self-esteem. Second, as evidenced by the fact that the "independents" actually had self-esteem that was as high as the members of the leading crowds, it is important to rec-

How is clique membership or being independent related to the adolescent's self-esteem?

ognize that while crowd affiliation often is a viable path to increased self-esteem in adolescence, there are other avenues as well.

Children and Adolescent Groups

Children's groups differ from adolescent groups in several important ways. The members of children's groups often are friends or neighborhood acquaintances. Their groups are usually not as formalized as many adolescent groups. During the adolescent years, groups tend to include a broader array of members—in other words, adolescents other than friends or neighborhood acquaintances often are members of the adolescent groups. Try to recall the student council, honor society, or football team at your junior high school. If you were a member of any of these junior high organizations, you are likely to recall that they were comprised of a number of individuals you had not met before and that they were

a·more heterogeneous group than your childhood peer groups. Rules and regulations were likely to be well defined, and captains or leaders were formally elected or appointed. Formalized structure and definition of status positions probably did not characterize many of your childhood peer groups.

A well-known observational study by Dexter Dunphy (1963) in Australia provides support for the development of opposite-sex group participation during adolescence. In late childhood, boys and girls participate in small, same-sex cliques. As they move into the early adolescent years, the same-sex cliques begin to interact with each other. Gradually, the leaders and high-status members form further cliques based on heterosexual relationships. Eventually, the newly created heterosexual

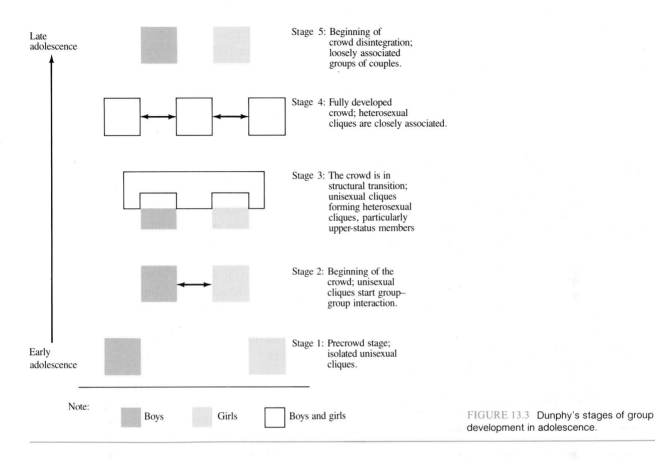

FIGURE 13.3 Dunphy's stages of group development in adolescence.

cliques replace the same-sex cliques. The heterosexual cliques interact with each other in larger crowd activities as well, such as during dances and at athletic events. Dunphy believes that, in late adolescence, the crowd begins to dissolve as couples begin to develop more serious relationships and make long-range plans that often include engagement and marriage. A summary of Dunphy's ideas is presented in Figure 13.3.

Dunphy's research also appears in our discussion of adolescent dating, which follows.

Dating

While many adolescent boys and girls have social interchanges through formal and informal peer groups, it is through dating that more serious contacts between the sexes occur. Many agonizing moments are spent by young male adolescents worrying about whether they should call a certain girl and ask her out—"Will she turn me down?" "What if she says yes, what do I say next?" "How am I going to get her to the dance? I don't want my mother to take us!" "I want to kiss her, but what if she pushes me away?" "How can I get to be alone with her?" And, on the other side of the coin: "What if no one asks me to the dance?" "What do I do if he tries to kiss me?" "I really don't want to go with him. Maybe I should wait two more days and see if Bill will call me." Think about your junior high, high school, and early college years. You probably spent a lot of time thinking about how you were going to get a particular girl or boy to go out with you. And many of your weekend evenings were probably spent on dates, or envying others who had dates. Some of you went steady, perhaps even during junior high school—others of you may have been engaged to be married by the end of high school. Certainly, dating is an important aspect of adolescent development, but what functions does it serve?

The Functions of Dating

Dating is a relatively recent phenomenon. It wasn't until the 1920s that dating as we know it became a reality, and even then, its primary role was for the purpose of selecting and winning a mate. Prior to this period, mate selection was the sole purpose of dating, and "dates" were carefully monitored by parents, who completely controlled the nature of any heterosexual companionship. Often, parents bargained with each other about the merits of their adolescents as potential marriage partners and even chose mates for their children. In recent times, of course, adolescents themselves have gained much more control over the dating process; today's adolescents are not as much at the mercy of their parents with regard to whom they go out with. Furthermore, dating has evolved into something more than just courtship for marriage. Dating today serves four main functions for adolescents (Skipper & Nass, 1966):

1. Dating can be a form of recreation. Adolescents who date seem to have fun and see dating as a source of enjoyment and recreation.
2. Dating is a source of status and achievement. Part of the social comparison process in adolescence involves evaluating the status of the people one dates—are they the best looking, the most popular, and so forth.
3. Dating is part of the socialization process in adolescence—it helps the adolescent to learn how to get along with others and assists in learning manners and sociable behavior.
4. Dating can be a means of mate sorting and selection—it retains its original courtship function.

Dating, then, can be an important part of the adolescent's social development. Just when and how much do adolescents date?

Incidence of Dating and Age Trends

Most girls in the United States begin dating at the age of 14, while most boys begin sometime between the ages of 14 and 15 (Douvan & Adelson, 1966; Sorenson, 1973). Most adolescents have their first date sometime between the ages of 12 and 16. Fewer than 10 percent have a first date before the age of 10, and by the age of 16, more than 90 percent have had at least one date. More than 50 percent of the 10th-, 11th-, and 12th-graders in one study averaged one or more dates per week (Dickinson, 1975). About 15 percent of these high school students dated less than once per month, and about three out of every four students had gone steady at least once.

Dating and going steady, then, are standard fare on the menu of most teenagers' social relationships. Adolescents who do not date very much may feel left out of the mainstream in their high school and community. Just as social skills training programs have been developed for adolescents who have difficulty in peer relations, so have programs been created to improve the ability of the adolescent to obtain a date and to interact more effectively during social relationships with the opposite sex (e.g., Curran, 1975; Rehm & Marston, 1968).

So far, we have seen that dating serves some important functions and that it either is pursued or is in the back of most adolescents' minds. As we see next, males and females may bring different interests to the dating relationship.

Sex Differences and Similarities in Dating

It generally has been believed that females are more strongly oriented toward affection in opposite-sex relationships, while males are more interested in sexual matters. With regard to sexual interest, it does appear that, during adolescence, males show a stronger sexual motivation than females do, although both males and females show a heightened desire for sexual involvement as the relationship deepens. For example, both male and female adolescents who go steady show a stronger desire for sexual involvement than their counterparts who have only had several dates with the same person (McCabe & Collins, 1979).

With regard to affectional and personality aspects of dating, there does seem to be a tendency for females to show more interest in personality exploration and self-disclosure than males (e.g., Douvan & Adelson, 1966; Simon & Gagnon, 1969). However, in one investigation, both males and females said that they begin a dating relationship with an affectional orientation (McCabe & Collins, 1979). Further, as with sexual interest, the deeper the relationship becomes (as when adolescents go steady), the more this affectional orientation increases.

The Construction of Dating Relationships: Family and Peer Factors

Close relationships influence the nature of other relationships. It is likely, for example, that the commerce of adolescents with family members and peers contributes in meaningful ways to how adolescents construct their dating relationships.

Peter Blos (1962) sees adolescent dating as tied to parental relationships. At the beginning of adolescence, Blos says, adolescents attempt to separate themselves from the opposite-sex parent as a love object. As the adolescent separates himself or herself, the adolescent is seen as very narcissistic. Blos believes that this narcissism helps to give the adolescent a sense of personal strength as separation from parents develops. Particularly in early adolescence, this narcissistic, self-orientation likely produces self-serving, highly idealized, tenuous, and superficial heterosexual relationships.

Psychoanalytic theorists, such as Blos, also believe that relationships with parents are carried forward to influence the construction of dating relationships. Thus, the adolescent's relationships with his or her opposite-sex parent, as well as the relationships with parents of the person the adolescent dates, likely contribute to the nature of dating relationships. For example, an adolescent male whose mother has been very nurturant, warm, and involved with him, yet not smothering, likely feels that dating relationships with females will be rewarding. By contrast, the adolescent male whose mother has been somewhat unloving and aloof may not trust females and may perceive that relationships with females will be unrewarding.

In addition to the adolescent's relationship with his or her parents, the adolescent's observation of his or her parents' marital relationship also likely contributes to the adolescent's dating relationships. Consider an adolescent girl who has come from a divorced family and grew up seeing her parents fight on many occasions. She may immerse herself in dating relationships to insulate herself from the stress she has experienced, or she may become aloof and untrusting with males and not wish to become involved heavily in dating relationships. Even when she does date, it may be difficult for her to develop a trusting relationship with males because she has seen promises broken by her parents.

Unfortunately, there has been little empirical investigation of the influence of parents on the manner in which adolescents construct dating relationships. As mentioned earlier in the chapter, Hetherington (1972, 1977) found that divorce was associated with a stronger heterosexual orientation of adolescent daughters than was the death of a parent or coming from an intact family. Hetherington also suggested that the daughters of divorcees had a more negative opinion of males than did the girls from other family structures. Girls from divorced and widowed families also were more likely to marry images of their fathers than girls from intact families. The argument was made that females from intact families likely have had a greater opportunity to work through relationships with their father and therefore are more psychologically free to date and marry someone different than their father.

It also appears that girls are more likely to have their parents involved or interested in their dating patterns and relationships than males. For example, in one investigation, college females were much more likely than their male counterparts to say that their parents tried to influence who they dated during adolescence (Knox & Wilson, 1981). They also indicated that it was not unusual for their parents to try to interfere with their dating choices and relationships.

Birth order and sibling relationships also could be expected to be linked with dating relationships. While a number of studies of birth order and attraction in dating have been conducted (e.g., Altus, 1970; Critelli & Baldwin, 1979; Toman, 1971), the results have been somewhat inconclusive. Sometimes, older siblings are attracted to opposite-sex persons who are younger siblings, while sometimes they like opposite-sex persons who are also older siblings themselves. Thus, the actual nature of sibling relationships, rather than birth order alone, may need to be studied to determine how sibling relationships influence dating relationships. Nonetheless, it is likely that younger siblings learn a great deal from the triumphs and failings of their older siblings' dating practices. Younger siblings may date earlier than older siblings, being influenced by the model of their older siblings. And younger siblings with opposite-sex older siblings may find the transition to dating easier because they have already learned much about the opposite sex from their older siblings. One investigation revealed that girls often used sibling relationships to their advantage when dealing with parents. Younger siblings pointed to how older siblings were given dating privileges that they had been denied. And an adolescent would sometimes side with a sibling when the sibling was having an argument with parents in the hope that the sibling would do likewise when the adolescent was seeking dating privileges (Place, 1975).

Peer relationships also are involved in the adolescent's dating relationships. Dunphy (1963) found that all large adolescent crowds were heterosexual and that males in these crowds consistently were older than females. Dunphy also noted the dominant role of the group leader in dating relationships. Both the leaders of large crowds and smaller cliques had a high degree of involvement with the opposite sex. Leaders dated more frequently, were more likely to go steady, and achieved these characteristics earlier than other members of the cliques. Also, leaders were ascribed the task of maintaining a certain level of heterosexual involvement in the peer group. They functioned as confidants and advisors with regard to dating and even put partners together for the "slow learners."

Child Development Concept Table 13.2 summarizes our discussion of peers, friendships, cliques, crowds, groups, and dating in adolescence. Next, we examine a context in which adolescents spend much of their time—school.

SCHOOLS

In Chapter 11, we described many different ideas about the effects of schools on children's development. Here we focus more precisely on the nature of secondary schools, as we investigate the continuing controversy that surrounds the function of secondary schools for adolescents, study effective schools for young adolescents, examine the nature of school organization (particularly being interested in the transition from elementary to middle or junior high school), and conclude with some comments about the after-school needs of adolescents.

How might sibling relationships influence dating relationships during adolescence?

The Controversy Surrounding the Function of Secondary Schools

Secondary schools seem to have always been wrapped in controversy. One of the controversies has revolved around whether adolescents should be treated more like children or more like adults (Stipek, 1981). For the most part, in the United States, adolescents have been kept in school for as long as possible. This policy has had practical applications because it has delayed the entry of youth into the labor force. Further, high schools have been perceived as the most competent environment for adolescents to gain the maturity and skills they need to function in the adult world. For more than 150 years, there has been a consistent trend toward compulsory school attendance.

However, in the 1960s, the distress over alienated and rebellious youth brought up the issue of whether secondary schools were actually beneficial to adolescents. During the early 1970s, three independent panels agreed that high school contributed to adolescent alienation and actually restricted the transition to adulthood (Brown, 1973; Coleman et al., 1974; Martin, 1976). These prestigious panels argued that adolescents should be given educational alternatives to the comprehensive high

Child Development Concept Table 13.2   Peers and Adolescent Development

Concept	Processes/Related Ideas	Characteristics/Description
Peer pressure and conformity	Its nature	The pressure to conform to peers becomes very strong during the adolescent years. It seems to be stronger in early adolescence than late adolescence. By about the ninth grade, conformity to antisocial peer norms seems to peak. Boys show more conformity to antisocial peer standards than girls. Most conformity focuses on peer involvement, such as socializing with friends, rather than antisocial standards.
Peer modeling and social comparison	Their importance	Peers serve as important models during adolescence. In particular, popular adolescents are likely to be imitated. Social comparison seems to increase in early adolescence, as individuals seek information about where they stand vis-à-vis other adolescents.
Cliques and crowds	Distinguishing cliques and crowds	Crowds are less personal than cliques. Members of cliques are attracted to each other on the basis of similar interests and social ideals. Allegiance to cliques exerts powerful control over the adolescent's life.
	Coleman's study of leading adolescent groups	In the Coleman study, the leading crowds were likely to be composed of athletes and popular girls.
	Cliques, crowds, and self-esteem	There usually are three to six well-defined crowds in most high schools. Membership in crowds is generally associated with higher self-esteem. However, independents (those who place little importance on crowd membership) show self-esteem as high as the members of the leading crowds.
	Children and adolescent groups	Children's groups are not as formal, are less heterogeneous, and are less heterosexual than adolescent groups. Dunphy found that the development of adolescent groups moves through five stages, during which heterosexual groups replace same-sex cliques. By late adolescence, the crowds begin to dissipate.
Dating	Functions of dating	Dating can be a form of recreation, is a source of status and achievement, is part of the socialization process, and can be a means of mate sorting and selection.
	Incidence of dating and age trends	Most adolescents are involved in dating. Most girls begin dating around the age of 14, while most boys begin at about 14 to 15 years of age. Going steady is an important aspect of adolescent dating.
	Sex differences and similarities in dating	It appears that adolescent females are more interested in the affectional aspects of dating, while their male counterparts show more sexual motivation.
	Construction of dating relationships: Family and peer factors	Relationships with parents, siblings, and peers influence the manner in which adolescents construct dating relationships. Dunphy's study revealed that group leaders serve an important role in dating.

school, such as on-the-job community work, to increase their exposure to adult roles and to decrease their sense of isolation from the adult world. To some degree in response to these reports, a number of states lowered the age at which adolescents could leave school from 16 to 14.

Now in the 1980s, the back-to-basics movement has gained momentum, arguing that the main function of schools should be a rigorous training of intellectual skills through subjects like English, math, and science. Proponents of the back-to-basics movement emphasize that there is too much fluff in the secondary school curricula, with students being allowed to select from many alternatives that will not give them a basic education in intellectual subjects. Critics of the fluff in secondary schools also often argue that the school day should be longer and that the school year should be extended into the summer months. Some critics of schools believe that too much

What changes in the philosophy of educating adolescents have taken place?

emphasis is placed on extracurricular activities. Such arguments suggest that schools should be in the business of imparting knowledge to adolescents and should evidence little or no concern for their social and emotional development. Related to the issue of the function of schools is the proverbial dilemma of whether schools should include a vocational curriculum in addition to training in such basic subjects as English, math, science, and history.

Should the main and perhaps only major goal of schooling for adolescents be the development of an intellectually mature person? Or should schools also show a strong concern for the development of a maturity in social and emotional matters as well? And should schools be very comprehensive and provide a multifaceted curriculum that includes many elective and alternative subjects in addition to a basic set of core subjects? These provocative questions continue to be heatedly debated in educational and community circles (Cross, 1984; Goodlad, 1983; Sizer, 1984).

There may always be tension between the various functions of schooling thought to be important by educators, psychologists, and parents. Is true cognitive development the main function? Should cognitive

development be only one of the functions, with preparation for work, social and emotional development, and the development of a lifelong learner assuming importance as well?

Now that we have considered the functions of secondary schools, let's see what makes schools effective.

Effective Schools

Joan Lipsitz (1984), director of the Center for Early Adolescence at the University of North Carolina, in a book called *Successful Schools for Young Adolescents,* has tried to answer the question of what an effective school for adolescents is and to provide examples of such effective schools. Letters were sent to leading researchers and practitioners in diverse fields related to early adolescence and education. Each respondent was asked to recommend schools for visitation and to answer the question, "What are five characteristics of effective schools for young adolescents?" Respondents, interestingly, focused primarily on the developmental appropriateness of the schools with only one or two of the five answers being devoted to academic matters. The respondents emphasized such characteristics as the development of self-discipline, industriousness, respect for authority, persistence, patience, honesty, ability to work toward goals, a sense of respect for self and others, assertiveness, enthusiasm and interest in learning, confidence, ability to function in the peer group, individuality, communication skills, knowledge, and the like. From the respondents' recommendations of effective schools that were able to engender such characteristics in young adolescents, one dozen schools were selected for two-day visits. After these initial two-day visits, four schools were selected for more detailed, seven-day observation. Lipsitz focused on nine categories of observation and discussion:

1. **Purposes, goals, definitions**—The underlying rationale or purpose of the school
2. **School climate**—The school's norms, beliefs, responsiveness to developmental needs, academic purpose, learning, socialization for discipline, working conditions, and physical setting
3. **Organization**—Staff organization, graded or multi-aged organization, scheduling, grouping, open or contained classroom structure, and responsiveness to the school's clientele

4. **Curriculum**—Issues of balance in the curriculum, interface with elementary and senior high schools, and consideration of adaptation to the nature of the school population

5. **Instructional practices**—The work process, how objectives were identified and accepted, student participation in decisions, allocation of time, rewards, and the assessment process

6. **Leadership**—The principal's leadership, how authority was created and norms were established, as well as the principal's role as interpreter of the school for the community

7. **The community context**—The external pressures that impinged on the school, its history, the role of parents in the school, and the school's response to the community, as perceived by the principal, superintendent, school board members, community leaders, and parents

8. **Public policy questions**—The school's response to desegregation, the education of handicapped students, and the equal treatment of boys and girls

9. **Self-evaluation**—The school's motivation to scrutinize its own practices and to hold itself accountable for the effectiveness of the school

Lipsitz and her observational team found that the most striking feature of the four best middle schools was their willingness and ability to adapt all school practices to the individual differences in intellectual, biological, and social development of their students. The schools took information about early adolescent development seriously. This seriousness was reflected in decisions about many different aspects of school life. For example, one middle school fought to keep its schedule of mini-courses on Friday so that every student could be with friends and pursue personal interests. Two other middle schools expended considerable energy on a complex school organization so that small groups of students worked with small groups of teachers who could vary the tone and pace of the school day, depending on the students' needs. Another middle school developed an advisory scheme so that each student had daily contact with an adult who was willing to listen, explain, comfort, and prod the adolescent. Such school policies reflect thoughtfulness and personal concern about individuals whose developmental needs are compelling.

Another aspect of the effective middle schools observed was that, very early in their existence (the first year in three of the schools and the second year in the fourth school), they emphasized the importance of creating an environment that was positive for the adolescent's social and personality development. This goal was established not only because such environments contribute to academic excellence but also because social and personality development are intrinsically valued as important in themselves in the schooling of adolescents. Focus on Child Development 13.4 presents more information about the nature of the four effective middle schools.

School Organization

Let's now look at how schools are organized and see if this organization is linked with the adolescent's development. In particular, we highlight the importance of the transition from the elementary school to the middle or junior high school.

The Organization of Secondary Schools

The organization of junior high schools, and more recently, middle schools, has been justified on the basis of the physical, cognitive, and social changes that characterize early adolescence. As John Hill (1980) points out, the growth spurt and the onset of puberty were the basis for removing seventh- and eighth-grade students from elementary schools. And because puberty has been occurring earlier in recent decades, the same kind of thinking has lead to the creation of middle schools that house sixth- and sometimes fifth-graders in separate buildings along with seventh- and eighth-graders.

Many educators and psychologists believe that junior high schools have merely become watered-down versions of high schools, simply mimicking their curricular and extracurricular schedules. These critics argue that unique curricular and extracurricular activities reflecting the wide range of individual differences in biological and psychological development in early adolescence should be incorporated into junior high schools. It also has been argued that most secondary schools foster passivity rather than autonomy and that schools should develop a variety of pathways for junior high and high school students to achieve an identity. But there is little evidence that schools have made much headway in accomplishing these difficult tasks (Hill, 1980).

FOCUS ON CHILD DEVELOPMENT 13.4

BEYOND THE ZOO

Joan Lipsitz (1984) evaluated the nature of leadership, school climate, curriculum, school organization, and the school in the community for effective schools for young adolescents.

Leadership The principal served as an important leader in each of the effective middle schools. She or he often was an independent and resourceful person. From motley sources often came dinners, trips, extra supplies, and other perks for outstanding teachers. Students, teachers, and parents were made to feel that their school was a very special place. These principals recognized the important principle that, when people are made to feel special and they are in a special situation, they usually respond and perform competently.

School climate Many young adolescents are impulsive, self-absorbed, antagonistic toward adult authority, alternately energetic and enervated, and so on. When teachers complain about young adolescents, animal imagery is extensive: "That school is a zoo," "Those students are like animals," and "It's a jungle in that classroom." How did the successful schools get their young adolescents to behave in more humane ways? They insisted on the common humanity of their inhabitants. They emphasized the school context as a community in which there is a great deal of caring. Hours upon hours of time were spent in and outside of school on the students' personal welfare—on canoeing expeditions, at baseball games, and in promoting rock concerts. This level of caring is important at any age group, but it is particularly valuable for an age where individuals feel so fragile about their development of independence and identity. These schools recognized that young adolescents are not ready for the strong independence foisted on them by secondary school organization. The schools granted more independence than elementary schools do, but established strong support groups (houses, teams, wings, advisory groups) to help adolescents in their transition from childhood to more mature status.

What are the characteristics of successful middle schools?

Curriculum The curriculum at each of the four effective middle schools was diverse and exciting. The schools emphasized creating numerous opportunities for competence and achievement, self-exploration and definition, social interaction, and effective school participation. There were spectacular instances of curricular success, such as a camping trip, a Fifties Week, Authors' Week, and the like. These schools recognized the importance of flamboyance in educating young adolescents. An awards ceremony for campers, Black History Week, and WNOE (a simulated rock music station) all represent the school as theater. Such brilliant moments in these schools gave variety to what otherwise would be regarded as a rather dull, uninspired curriculum.

School organization None of the four effective middle schools used the same method of grouping students. A particular practice distinguishes each school, such as a full period for advisory at one school, multi-aging in core subjects as in another school, and a variety of teaming options in yet another school. Each principal was creative in fashioning the school organization and school day to enhance communication, personalization, and continuity in relationships. Each school's organization evolved over a number of years. Each school has had at least one major overhaul in organization and many minor tune-ups. Each of the schools adopted a house and team structure so that groups of students live together for several hours each school day, sometimes for two to three years.

The school in the community Schools often thrive or fail depending on their particular community context. The public makes tremendous demands on schools. While each of the four effective middle schools functioned in different contexts, all four schools were responsive to the particular social and political milieu in those communities. One school survives because of its strict discipline and substantial curricular predictability; another because it has turned inward, away from a contentious district; another school has developed strong math and science programs and prepares students for success on the SAT. The distinctiveness of each effective school is the result of an interplay between a coherent concept of schooling for the age group, particular personalities, and the constraints and demands of the community context.

The secondary school years can be packaged in many ways. For example, as we entered the 1980s, there were at least 34 different grade combinations that encompassed the middle grades (Lipsitz, 1984). Several examples include: grades 7 through 9, 7 through 12, 6 through 8, 5 through 8, and kindergarten through grade 8.

The Transition to Middle or Junior High School

A number of research inquiries are beginning to chart children's development as they move from an elementary school into a middle or junior high school (e.g., Blyth, Simmons, & Bush, 1978; Douvan & Adelson, 1966; Simmons, Rosenberg, & Rosenberg, 1973; Goodlad, 1983; Gump, 1983; Hawkins & Berndt, 1985). The transition to middle school or junior high school from an elementary school is of interest to developmental psychologists because, even though it is a normative experience for virtually all children in our society, this transition can be stressful due to the point in development at which the transition takes place (Hawkins & Berndt, 1985; Nottelmann, 1982). Transition to middle or junior high school occurs at a time in the development of children when a number of simultaneous changes are occurring, including (1) the occurrence of puberty and related concerns about body image; (2) the emergence of at least some aspects of formal operational thought, including accompanying changes in social cognition; (3) increased responsibility and independence in association with decreased dependency on parents; (4) change from a small, contained classroom structure to a larger, more impersonal school structure; (5) change from one teacher to many teachers and from a small, homogeneous set of peers to a larger, more heterogeneous group of peers; (6) and increased focus on achievement and performance (and assessment of such achievement and performance). Another reason cited for the difficulty that new middle or junior high school students encounter is what is referred to as the **"top-dog" phenomenon** (Blyth, Simmons, & Carleton-Ford, 1983).

FACILITATING THE TRANSITION TO JUNIOR HIGH SCHOOL

Jacquelyn Hawkins and Thomas Berndt (1985) were interested in the transition from elementary to junior high school, in particular how the nature of the school environment and friendship formations influence this transition. They studied 101 students at three points in time: the spring of the sixth grade (pretransition), and twice in the seventh grade (early and late posttransition). The sample consisted of students in two different kinds of schools, one being a traditional junior high school, the other a school in which the students were grouped into small teams (100 students, 4 teachers). A number of different measures were used to assess the students' adjustment, including self-reports, peer ratings, and teacher ratings. The results indicated that adjustment dropped during posttransition, that is, during the seventh grade. For example, the self-esteem of students in both schools dropped in the seventh grade. However, the nature of the school environment influenced the results. For instance, in the traditional junior high school, students reported that they received less teacher support than in the sixth grade,

How important are friendships in the transition to middle or junior high school?

but in the junior high with smaller student classes, more teacher support was reported during early posttransition (see the table on the following page). Also, friendships (as mea-

Moving from the top position (in elementary school, as the oldest, biggest, and most powerful students in the school) to the bottom or lowest position (in middle or junior high school, as the youngest, smallest, and least powerful group of students) may create a number of difficulties for students.

There also are positive aspects of the transition to middle or junior high school. Students are more likely to feel grown up, to have more subjects to select from, to have more opportunities to spend time with peers and more chances to locate compatible friends, to enjoy increased independence from direct parental and teacher monitoring, and to be more challenged intellectually by academic work (Hawkins & Berndt, 1985).

Fortunately, there is increased interest in the nature of schooling experiences that might produce better adjustment for children as they move from elementary school to middle or junior high schools. Schools providing more supportiveness, less anonymity, more stability, and less complexity have been found to have a salutary effect on student adjustment in middle and junior high school transition.

Adjustment to the transition to middle or junior high school may be somewhat different for boys than girls in that boys may be at a disadvantage with regard to social matters. Since girls enter puberty, on the average, about two years earlier than boys, a much larger percentage of girls in the first year of middle or junior high school have entered puberty than boys. The girls' sexual maturation and growth spurt may put them more on par with

Classroom Environment in the Transition From Elementary School to Junior High School

		Pretransition	Early Posttransition	Late Posttransition
Total Sample	Involvement	.57	.55	.51
	Affiliation	.71	.66	.67
	Support	.48	.44	.41
Traditional Junior High School	Involvement	.50	.47	.45
	Affiliation	.71	.68	.68
	Support	.47	.38	.35
Team-Organized Junior High School	Involvement	.66	.65	.57
	Affiliation	.75	.71	.70
	Support	.49	.53	.49

From Hawkins, J. A. and T. J. Berndt, "Adjustment following the transition to junior high school", paper presented to SRCD biennial meeting, Toronto, April 1985. Reprinted by permission of the author.

sured by the quality of relationship and contact with friends) improved by late posttransition and influenced adjustment to junior high school. Students with higher scores on friendship measures had a more positive perception of themselves and more positive attitudes toward school in general. These data show how a supportive, more intimate school environment and friendship formation and maintenance can ease the transition for students as they move from the elementary to middle or junior high school years.

the older girls and boys in middle and junior high schools. And since it is in middle and junior high school that dating pressures begin to emerge, girls, many of whom already are moving well along the path to physical maturity, are likely to fare better.

It also is helpful to consider whether students making the transition to middle or junior high school are maturing early, on time, or late. Recall from our discussion of early and late maturation in Chapter 12 that early-maturing girls, while they seemed to get along better with male adolescents, nonetheless seemed to have more difficulty in achievement- and academic-related matters.

Focus on Child Develoment 13.5 examines a recent research study that highlights the importance of friendships and the nature of the school in the transition to middle or junior high school.

While we don't often think of schools as a support system for families, they are. While parents work, schools monitor the adolescent's life during school hours. But what about the after-school needs of adolescents?

After-School Needs of Adolescents

Joan Lipsitz (1983) spent one year trying to identify the after-school needs of adolescents. She found that no network of professionals or volunteers to help youth in the after-school hours exists. Adolescents who are not part of a specific national organization, like Boy Scouts or Girl Scouts, have no one to turn to for new ideas, mutual support, and information about what works and why. Parents of these adolescents seem even more isolated, not having printed materials that tell them what exists in their community and what criteria they should be using to guide them in selecting after-school programs. Lipsitz did find that adolescents often spend after-school hours in places like community centers, libraries, schools, churches and synagogues, Boys Clubs, Girls Clubs, 4-H, and such. They go to these places mainly because there is an adult present who knows and understands them. While a particular activity may be the "hook" that gets the adolescent into the community setting, their loyalty to the program seems to be linked to the sensitivity and caring of an adult who has the time to listen and provide advice.

Lipsitz found that such community settings have been and could continue to serve as providers of safe, supervised recreation, academic and cultural enrichment, and counseling. However, inflation, cutbacks in funding, and taxpayer revolts are not encouraging. For example, given cutbacks in Title XX funds, day-care programs have been forced to institute increased fee schedules. Parents have been forced to decide which of their children they will send to after-school programs. Understandably, they usually choose to pay for younger children and withdraw older siblings, who typically become latchkey children. Libraries are finding that more and more young adolescents are dropping in during the after-school hours. Parents approve of their adolescents going to libraries because a library is perceived as a warm, safe, supervised environment where nothing disastrous will happen to the adolescent. Ideally, libraries would increase the number of adults who specialize in understanding young adolescents. However, with budget cuts, libraries often have had to cut back in hours and acquisitions. At the same time, municipal recreation departments have had to cut back the number of their youth worker positions at exactly the time when more such positions are needed. Quite clearly, the after-school needs of adolescents represent an important agenda for communities in the remainder of the 20th century.

THINKING BACK, LOOKING AHEAD

When adults look backward to their adolescence, they often can vividly recall important adolescent events. Recent research on autobiographical memory suggests that the night of your high school graduation, the night of your senior prom (whether you went or not), your first date (the moment you met him or her), and an early romantic memory are likely to be of a flash-bulb variety—that is, even after many years, these events will still be represented by vivid and emotional images (Rubin & Kozin, 1984).

Schools and dating are important contexts of adolescence, and our coverage of social development in adolescence examined many such themes, including: no more "what if" questions; Mark Twain's perceptive comments about his father; the push for independence and connectedness with parents; the coordinated worlds of adolescent peer-parent relationships; mothers, daughters, and girlfriends; parent-adolescent conflict; the maturation of adolescents and their parents; violated expectations of adolescents and their parents; carrying forward the divorce experience; a widow's daughter who spent the entire evening in the restroom; peer pressure and conformity; the captains of the football and drill teams; "His car is a piece of junk. Mine is much better, don't you think?"; jocks, populars, normals, druggies/toughs, independents, and nobodies; the construction of dating relationships; why there are secondary schools; why there are middle schools; beyond the zoo; the top-dog phenomenon; and the importance of developing support systems for families, particularly in the after-school hours.

In Chapter 14, we conclude our study of the adolescent years as we explore the personality development of adolescents as well as the problems and disturbances they may encounter. But before we turn to those ideas, consider for several moments the insightful words of Erma Bombeck:

This half-child, half-adult groping . . . to weigh life's inconsistencies, hypocrisy, . . . independence, advice, rules, and responsibilities. . . . The blind date that never showed. The captaincy that went to the best friend. The college reject, the drill team have-nots, the class office also-rans, the honors that went to someone else. And they turned to me for an answer. . . . And there were joys. Moments of closeness . . . an awkward hug; a look in the semidarkness as you turned off the test pattern as they slept. . . . The strange, warm feeling of seeing them pick up a baby and seeing a wistfulness in their faces I have never seen before. . . . Did they ever know I smiled? Did they ever understand my tears? Did I talk too much? Did I say too little? Did I ever look at them and really see them? Do I know them at all? Or was it all a lifetime of "Why don't you grow up?"

SUMMARY

I. Information about families and adolescent development focuses on autonomy and attachment-connectedness, parenting strategies and parent-adolescent conflict, the maturation of the adolescent and the maturation of parents, and the effects of divorce on adolescents.
   A. Ideas about autonomy and attachment-connectedness involve the multidimensionality of autonomy, parenting strategies for promoting healthy autonomy, and attachment, the coordinated worlds of parents and peers, and connectedness.
      1. Many parents have a difficult time handling the adolescent's strong push for autonomy, even though this push is one of the hallmarks of adolescent development. Trying to define autonomy is difficult; conceptualizing autonomy as multidimensional is important.
      2. Democratic parenting is associated with enhanced autonomy of adolescents, while authoritarian parenting is related to a lack of autonomy. The wise parent relinquishes control in areas where the adolescent shows maturity but monitors the adolescent's life more closely in those domains where immature behavior is shown.
      3. There is an increased interest in the connectedness of adolescents and their parents. Historically, connectedness has been reserved for peer relations, while separation has been used to describe parent-adolescent relationships. Now, there is considerable enthusiasm in looking at parent-adolescent relationships in terms of attachment and connectedness, as well as at the coordination of parent and peer worlds. It is likely that secure attachment to parents through the childhood and adolescent years promotes a healthy exploration of independence and identity. Hinde's view that interactions, relationships, and groups can be distinguished has led to further emphasis on the connectedness of family relationships to the wider social world of the adolescent.
   B. Parenting strategies and parent-adolescent conflict are other important aspects of parent-adolescent relationships.
      1. Too often, parents do not stop to think about how much time it takes to make the long transition from child to adult. As the individual

moves into the later years of adolescence, the parent may be wise to relinquish more control and to monitor the adolescent's life more indirectly while still maintaining a strong connectedness with the adolescent.
      2. Interest in parent-adolescent conflict has a long history, and many explanations have been offered for the belief that conflict increases between parents and their offspring as the children become adolescents. Conflict with parents does seem to increase during the early adolescent years. Such conflict usually is of the moderate variety, rather than the prolonged, intense type. The moderate increase in conflict likely serves the positive developmental function of promoting independence and identity.
   C. Parent-adolescent relationships are influenced by the maturation of the adolescent and the maturation of the parents.
      1. Physical, cognitive, and social changes in the adolescent's development influence parent-adolescent relationships. Among these are the nature of pubertal change; the adolescent's expanded logical reasoning and increased idealistic and egocentric thought; violated expectations; changes in schooling, peers, friendships, and dating; and movement toward independence.
      2. Parental changes include those involving marital dissatisfaction, economic burdens, career reevaluation and time perspective, as well as health and bodily concerns.
   D. Divorce is a stressful experience for adolescents, just as it is for children. Adolescents carry forward the experience of their parents' divorce into their adult years. Divorce influences the heterosexual behavior of girls.
II. Ideas about peers and adolescent development involve peer pressure and conformity, peer modeling and social comparison, cliques and crowds, group behavior, and dating.
   A. The pressure to conform to peers becomes very strong during the adolescent years. It seems to be stronger in early adolescence than late adolescence. By about the ninth grade, conformity to antisocial peer standards seems to peak. Boys show more conformity to antisocial peer standards than girls. Most conformity focuses on peer involvement, such as socializing with friends, rather than antisocial standards.

B. Peers serve as important models during adolescence. In particular, popular adolescents are likely to be imitated. Social comparison seems to increase in early adolescence, as individuals seek information about where they stand vis-à-vis other adolescents.

C. Crowds are less personal than cliques. Members of cliques are attracted to each other on the basis of similar interests and social ideals. Allegiance to cliques exerts powerful control over the adolescent's life. In the Coleman study, the leading crowds were likely to be composed of athletes and popular girls. There usually are three to six well-defined crowds in most high schools. Membership in crowds is generally associated with higher self-esteem. However, independents (those who place little importance on crowd membership) show self-esteem as high as the members of the leading crowds.

D. Children's groups are not as formal, are less heterogeneous, and are less heterosexual than adolescent groups. Dunphy found that the development of adolescent groups moves through five stages, during which heterosexual groups replace same-sex cliques. By late adolescence, the crowds begin to dissipate.

E. Ideas about dating focus on the functions of dating, the incidence of dating and age trends, sex differences and similarities in dating, and the construction of dating relationships.
1. Dating can be a form of recreation, is a source of status and achievement, is part of the socialization process, and can be a means of mate sorting and selection.
2. Most adolescents are involved in dating. Most girls begin dating around the age of 14, while boys begin at about age 14 or 15. Going steady is an important aspect of adolescent dating.
3. It appears that adolescent females are more interested in the affectional aspects of dating, while their male counterparts show more sexual motivation.
4. Relationships with parents, siblings, and peers influence the manner in which adolescents construct dating relationships. Dunphy's study revealed that group leaders serve an important role in dating.

III. Information about adolescents and schools focuses on the controversy surrounding the function of secondary schools, effective schools, the nature of school organization, and after-school needs of adolescents.
A. The function of secondary schools is wrapped in controversy. Some maintain that the function of secondary schools should be the intellectual development of the adolescent. Others suggest that secondary schools should have more comprehensive functions—that is, in addition to intellectual development, secondary schools should be promoting social and emotional development, as well as preparing the adolescent for adult work and existence as a lifelong learner.
B. Effective schools for young adolescents take individual differences in development seriously and show a deep concern for what is known about early adolescence. These successful schools emphasize social development as much as intellectual development.
C. The organization of junior high schools and, more recently, middle schools has been justified on the basis of physical, cognitive, and social changes in the adolescent. The earlier onset of puberty has had a strong impact on the increased appearance of middle schools. There are many different ways to organize secondary schools, such as grades 7 through 9, 7 through 12, 6 through 8, and kindergarten through grade 8. The transition from elementary to middle or junior high school coincides with a number of individual, familial, and societal changes. The transition is associated with adjustment difficulties for many children, although intimate, supportive school environments, as well as friendships, seem to make such adjustment less taxing. Sex differences and the timing of puberty likely are other factors that mediate this transition.
D. The after-school needs of adolescents have not been given adequate attention and represent an important community concern.

KEY TERMS

anticonformist 561
clique 562
crowd 562
groups 549
interactions 549

nonconformist 561
relationships 549
social comparison 562
top-dog phenomenon 573

SUGGESTED READINGS

Goldstein, A. P., Sprafkin, R. P., Gershaw, N. J., & Klein, P. (1981). *Skillstreaming the adolescent*. Champaign, IL: Research Press.
    Provides an excellent set of exercises that can be used to improve the social skills of adolescents.
Journal of Early Adolescence (Spring 1985), *5,* (1).
    The entire issue is devoted to contemporary approaches to the study of families with adolescents. Includes articles by Catherine Cooper and Susan Ayers-Lopez on the connectedness of adolescents and their families, by Raymond Montemayor on parent-adolescent conflict, by John Hill and his colleagues on pubertal status and parent-adolescent relationships, and many others.
Lipsitz, J. (1984). *Successful schools for young adolescents*. New Brunswick, NJ: Transaction Books.
    Must reading for anyone interested in better schools for young adolescents. Filled with rich examples of successful schools and the many factors that contribute to success in the education of young adolescents.
Review of Educational Research.
    This journal publishes reviews of educational research. By leafing through the issues of the last several years in your library, you will come across research summaries with references to many of the topics in this chapter.
Steinberg, L. D. (1980). *Understanding families with young adolescents*. Carrboro, NC: Center for Early Adolescence.
    An easy-to-read overview of the maturation of adolescents and the simultaneous maturation of parents. Offers ideas for coping with adolescent change in families.

PERSONALITY DEVELOPMENT IN ADOLESCENCE

IMAGINE . . . YOU ARE
GROUCHO MARX DEVELOPING
AN IDENTITY

PREVIEW

IDENTITY
Erikson's Ideas on Identity

**FOCUS ON CHILD DEVELOPMENT
14.1: SAWYER, HITLER, LUTHER,
AND GANDHI**
Personality and Role Experimentation
The Complexity of Erikson's Theory
A Contemporary View of Identity
Development
The Four Statuses of Identity
Developmental Changes in Identity
Sex Differences and Similarities in
Identity
Family Influences on the Adolescent's
Identity

**FOCUS ON CHILD DEVELOPMENT
14.2: INDIVIDUATION AND
CONNECTEDNESS IN FAMILIES**
The Measurement of Identity
Identity and Intimacy
Erikson's Views of Identity and Intimacy
The Five Statuses of Intimacy
Research on Intimacy
Complexity of Identity-Intimacy Pathways

**CHILD DEVELOPMENT CONCEPT
TABLE 14.1: IDENTITY**

PROBLEMS AND DISTURBANCES
Drugs
Actual Drug Use by Adolescents
Alcohol
Marijuana
Preventive Health Efforts

**FOCUS ON CHILD DEVELOPMENT
14.3: AGENT, ENVIRONMENT, AND
HOST**
Delinquency
What Is Juvenile Delinquency?
What Causes Delinquency?
Sociocultural Influences on Delinquency

**FOCUS ON CHILD DEVELOPMENT
14.4: DELINQUENCY AND FAMILY
PROCESSES—CAUSE, CORRELATE,
OR CONSEQUENCE?**

**CHILD DEVELOPMENT CONCEPT
TABLE 14.2: DRUGS AND
DELINQUENCY**
Suicide
Incidence of Suicide
Causes of Suicide
Prevention of Suicide
Eating Disorders
Incidence of Eating Disorders
Anorexia Nervosa

**FOCUS ON CHILD DEVELOPMENT
14.5: JANE, A 16-YEAR-OLD
ANOREXIC**
Bulimia
Obesity
Adolescent Problems Versus Childhood
Problems

THE TRANSITION FROM
ADOLESCENCE TO ADULTHOOD

THINKING BACK, LOOKING
AHEAD

SUMMARY

KEY TERMS

SUGGESTED READINGS

CHAPTER **14**

IMAGINE . . . YOU ARE GROUCHO MARX DEVELOPING AN IDENTITY

". . . they left school to help support the family . . . Minnie's Boys. In the beginning, they were five brothers, . . . the sons of a lovable, forceful, well-upholstered German lady and her handsome, diffident, French-born husband. She looked after her boys and their careers with the ferocity of a mother lion.

". . . (But) it was a topsy-turvy family. Minnie traveled with the boys while Frenchy stayed home banking the fires, if not any great amount of money. You could say she wore the pants, though Minnie was too much a product of her time and her femininity to do so literally.

"Groucho, the serious one, with his head always buried in a book, took up the leadership by default. . . . Chico, the eldest, . . . was the biggest headache, . . . as irresponsible as he was naturally charming (Chico played truant, as well as the piano). It wasn't Harpo's peaceful nature to take up the cudgels, so he passed. It was (Groucho) who led the brothers into show business, influenced and impressed by the success in vaudeville of their uncle, Al Shean, Minnie's brother. Only after Groucho had achieved a modicum of success on his own did Minnie decide that the act should be expanded to include one, then two, then three other brothers." (Marx, 1977, pp. xiii, xiv)

"I was Sam and Minnie's fourth son. The oldest, Manfred, died of old age. He was three at the time. Leonard and Adolph were the second and third sons. You know them as Chico and Harpo respectively. . . . Milton (Gummo) and Herbert (Zeppo) would come later. . . .

"Uncle Al was a dandy and a bon vivant. He would visit us, reeking of bay rum and good cheer. Soon, he'd also be reeking of Limburger cheese he'd send us out to buy for him. He may have been the first person I ever saw wearing spats. At the end of the visit, each nephew would get a quarter. The kids in the neighborhood would be waiting outside, for Uncle Al made a ritual of taking 100 pennies out of a bag and throwing them in the air. The boys would scramble for them. I longed to be like Uncle Al. He made $200 a week. He had style. And a pretty wife, Aunt Joanna. . . . Through (Minnie) and Uncle Al, I develop(ed) a love for the stage. . . .

"The first real job I ever got was on Coney Island. I sang a song on a beer keg and made a dollar. Later, I sang in a Protestant church choir—until they found out what was wrong with it. For that I got a dollar every Sunday. Before long, I had to get a full-time job and leave school. There wasn't enough money to feed five brothers, parents, grandparents, Cousin Polly, Aunt Hannah, and Uncle Julius. That's when I got into the big money, making $3.50 a week at the Hepner Wig Company. I lugged the big cans in which the wigs were washed. I'd been promised that someday, after I had worked my way up, I'd be able to comb the wigs and put them on some famous actress's head. . . .

"I was a little nervous as to how the announcement of my departure would be received at home. I had visualized a family group, bent with sorrow, or if not quite bent, at least saddened by the thought of my leaving them. . . . When I said goodbye, my mother cried a little, but the rest of the family seemed able to contain themselves without too much effort. As a parting gesture, just as I was leaving, the dog bit me.

"My luggage consisted of a paper suitcase and a shoe box filled with pumpernickel, bananas, and hard-boiled eggs. Eggs must have been cheap that year, for I never saw so many in one box. Though I was only going as far as Grand Rapids, I had enough eggs to carry me all the way to Frisco.

"Later, after the Grand Rapids tour failed, Minnie decided we brothers should stage our own act. Chico was successfully employed as a piano salesman at Shapiro and Berstein. Harpo was working at a nickelodeon, a job he'd inherited from Chico. . . . Consequently, Gummo and I formed the basis of the act, with Lou Levy and Mabel O'Donnell being hired to fill out the complement of four. When Mabel left the act, Harpo stepped in. The Four Nightingales toured the country from 1907 to 1910. Because we were a kid act, we traveled at half-fare, despite the fact that we were all around 20. Minnie insisted that we were 13. 'That kid of yours in the dining car is smoking a cigar,' the conductor told her. 'And another one is in the washroom shaving.' Minnie shook her head sadly, 'They grow so fast.'

"It was around this time that Minnie decided we should move to Chicago, which was more central to the small-time vaudeville circuits we were working. . . . Each of us had a motor scooter. . . . We would travel from town to town, usually with a girl straddling the back. Harpo had a Harley-Davidson, and one day we had a race. We hit a mule. It didn't help the mule any. It was while we were touring that our singing act became intentionally funny. Harpo said in his autobiography that this happened in Ada, Oklahoma. I insist it was Nacogdoches, Texas. Who's right? I am; I'm still living. Another mule disrupted the show, which was being held in an outdoor theatre. We lost most of the audience, and when some of them straggled back, they heard some smart remarks that they took to be funny. We thought we were talking over their heads, but the audience laughed, and a new era began for the Marx brothers plus Lou." (Marx, 1977, pp. 7, 11, 15, 18)

In these excerpts from Groucho Marx's autobiography, we can see some of the important ingredients of identity—family relationships, the importance of vocational orientation, and the complexity of the development of identity over many years.

PREVIEW

In this chapter, we explore some of the themes captured in Groucho Marx's pursuit of identity in greater detail. We will discover that, more than any other perspective, Erik Erikson's ideas provide the richest portrayal of adolescents' search for who they are and what they are all about. Like the other periods of development that we have studied, adolescence is also a time when problems and disturbances can surface, and we examine a number of these. What is considered a disturbance of adolescence at one point in history may not be conceived that way at another point. Consider G. Stanley Hall's deep concern about the evils of masturbation at the beginning of this century:

> One of the very saddest of all the aspects of human weakness and sin is (masturbation). . . . Tissot, in 1759, found every pupil guilty. . . . Dr. G. Bachin (1895) argued that growth, especially in the moral and intellectual regions, is dwarfed and stunted (by masturbation). Bachin also felt that masturbation caused gray hairs, and especially baldness, a stooping and enfeebled gait. . . .
>
> Prominent among predisposing causes are often placed erotic reading, pictures, and theatrical presentations. . . . Schiller protests against trouser pockets for boys, as do others against feather beds, while even horseback riding and the bicycle have been placed under the ban by a few extremist writers. . . .
>
> The medical cures of masturbation that have been prescribed are almost without number: bromide, ergot, lupin, blistering, clitoridectomy, sections of certain nerves, small mechanical appliances, which the Patent Office at Washington has quite a collection. Regimen rather than special treatment, must, however, be chiefly relied on. Work reduces temptation, and so does early rising. . . . Good music is a moral tonic. . . . (Hall, 1904, Vol. I, pp. 411–471)

IDENTITY

By far the most comprehensive and provocative story of identity development has been told by Erik Erikson. We study his view of identity in some detail, consider four statuses of identity and developmental changes in identity, evaluate sex differences and similarities in identity, focus on family influences on the adolescent's identity, describe the measurement of identity, and conclude with a discussion of the intriguing link between identity and intimacy.

Erikson's Ideas on Identity

The description of identity development can be traced directly to the thinking and writing of the famous psychoanalyst Erik Erikson (1963, 1968). As you may recall from Chapter 2, identity versus identity confusion (diffusion) represents the fifth stage in Erikson's eight stages of the life cycle, occurring at about the same time as adolescence. (A review of Chapter 2's discussion of Erikson's eight stages of development would provide you with a developmental setting for understanding identity development.) The following passage from *Identity: Youth and Crisis,* Erikson's most detailed work on identity, should give you some sense of Erikson's ideas on adolescent development:

> The youth of today is not the youth of 20 years ago. This much an elderly person would say, at any point in history, and think it was both new and true. But here we mean something very specifically related to our theories. For whereas 20 years ago, we gingerly suggested that some young people might be suffering from a more or less unconscious identity conflict, a certain type today tells us in no uncertain terms, and with the dramatic outer display of what we once considered to be inner secrets, that yes, indeed, they have an identity conflict—and they wear it on their sleeves, Edwardian or leather. Sexual identity confusion? Yes, indeed; sometimes when we see them walking down the street, it is impossible for us to tell without indelicate scrutiny who is a boy and who is a girl. Negative identity? Oh, yes; they want to be everything which "society" tells them not to be: in this, at least, they "conform." And for such fancy terms as psychosocial moratorium, they will certainly take their time, and take it with vengeance, until they are sure whether or not they want any of the identity offered in a conformist world. (1968, p. 26)

Also from *Identity: Youth and Crisis* is this commentary about the adolescent's search for truth, virtue, and fidelity:

> The evidence in young lives of the search for something and somebody to be true to can be seen in a variety of pursuits more or less sanctioned by society. It is often hidden in a bewildering combination of shifting devotion and sudden perversity, sometimes more devotedly perverse, sometimes more perversely devoted. Yet in all youth's seeming shiftiness, a seeking after some durability in change can be detected, whether in the accuracy of scientific and technical method or in the sincerity of obedience; in the veracity of historical and fictional accounts or in the fairness of the rules of the game; in the authenticity of artistic production, and the high fidelity of reproduction, or in the genuineness of convictions and the reliability of commitments. This search is easily misunderstood, and often it is only dimly perceived by the individual himself, because youth, always set to grasp both diversity in principle and principle in diversity, must often test extremes before setting on a considered course. These extremes, particularly in times of ideological confusion and widespread marginality of identity, may include not only rebellious but also deviant, delinquent, and self-destructive tendencies. However, all of this can be in the nature of a moratorium, a period of delay in which to test the rock bottom of some truth before committing the powers of the mind and body to a segment of the existing (or a coming) order. (1968, pp. 235–236)

During adolescence, world views become important to an individual, who enters what Erikson terms a "psychological moratorium"—a gap between the security of childhood and the new autonomy of approaching adulthood. Numerous identities can be drawn from the surrounding culture. Adolescents can experiment with different roles, trying them out and seeing which ones they like. The youth who successfully copes with these conflicting identities during adolescence emerges with a new sense of self that is both refreshing and acceptable. The adolescent who is not successful in resolving this identity crisis becomes confused, suffering what Erikson refers to as identity confusion. This confusion may take one of two courses: individuals may withdraw, isolating themselves from peers and family, or they may lose their own identity in that of the crowd.

Adolescents want to be able to decide freely for themselves such matters as what careers they will pursue, whether they will go to college or into military service, and whether or not they will marry. In other words, they want to free themselves from the shackles of their parents and other adults and make their own choices. At the same time, however, many adolescents have a deep fear of making the wrong decisions and of failing.

The choice of an occupation is particularly important in identity development. Erikson (1968) remarks that, in a highly technological society like that of the United States, students who have been well trained to enter a work force that offers the potential of reasonably high self-esteem will experience the least stress during the development of identity. Some students have rejected jobs offering good pay and traditionally high social status, choosing instead to work in situations that allow them to be more genuinely helpful to their fellow humans, such as in the Peace Corps, in mental health clinics, or in schools for children from low-income backgrounds. Some adolescents prefer unemployment to the prospect of working at a job they would be unable to perform well or at which they would feel useless. To Erikson, this attitude reflects the desire to achieve a meaningful identity through being true to oneself (rather than burying one's identity in that of society at large).

Identity confusion may account for the large number of adolescents who run away from home, drop out of school, quit their jobs, stay out all night, or assume bizarre moods. Before Erikson's ideas became popular, these adolescents were often labeled delinquents and looked at with a disapproving eye. As a result of Erikson's writings and analyses, the problems these youth encounter are now viewed in a more positive light. Not only do runaways, school dropouts, and job quitters struggle with identity—virtually all adolescents go through an identity crisis, and some are simply able to resolve the crisis more easily than others.

Certainly, the idea of the **identity crisis** has permeated our society. The term is applied to practically anyone of any age who feels a loss of identification or self-image—teenagers who cannot "find" themselves; teachers who have lost their jobs; the newly divorced;

Reprinted with special permission of King Features Syndicate, Inc.

business executives who are questioning their values. The term has even been applied to companies and institutions. For example, the federal government might be undergoing an "identity crisis" when it has been rocked by scandal, or a school system may be having an identity crisis when it must choose between a traditional and an innovative curriculum. In fact, the use of the term *identity crisis* has become so pervasive that defining it is difficult.

These general applications have gone far beyond Erikson's original use of the term; for Erikson (1968), identity is primarily the property of an individual person, not a group or an institution. According to Erikson, although identity is important throughout a person's life, it is only in adolescence that identity development reaches crisis proportions. A positive or negative identity is being developed throughout childhood as a result of the way various crises have been handled. The positive resolution of earlier crises, such as trust versus mistrust and industry versus inferiority, helps the individual to cope positively with the identity crisis that, Erikson believes, occurs in adolescence.

Because Erikson's ideas about identity are so prevalent in today's social and educational systems, and because they reveal such rich insight into the thoughts and feelings of adolescents, you are strongly advised to read one or more of his original writings. A good starting point is *Childhood and Society* (1963) or *Identity: Youth and Crisis* (1968). Other works that portray identity crises successfully resolved include *Young Man Luther* (1962) and *Gandhi's Truth* (1969)—the latter won a Pulitzer

Prize. A sampling of Erikson's writings from these books is presented in Focus on Child Development 14.1.

Now that we have some feel for the nature of Erikson's ideas on identity, let's focus on more specific aspects of his claims.

Personality and Role Experimentation

Two ingredients at the core of the adolescent's developing identity are personality and role experimentation. As was previously stated, Erikson believes that adolescents are faced by an overwhelming number of choices and at some point during their youth enter a period of "psychological moratorium." During this moratorium, they try out different roles and personalities before they reach a stable sense of self. They may be argumentive one moment and pleasant the next; they may dress neatly one day and look sloppy the next; they may like a friend or acquaintance one week and hate the person the next. Such personality experimentation is a deliberate effort on the part of adolescents to find out where they fit in the world.

As they begin to realize that they will be responsible for themselves and their own lives, adolescents search for what those lives are going to be. Many parents and other adults, accustomed to having their children go along with what they say, fail to change their methods of interaction as the children become adolescents. Adults are often bewildered or incensed by the wisecracks, the rebelliousness, and the rapid mood changes that accompany adolescence. They must learn to give young adolescents the time and opportunity to explore different roles and personalities. In turn, adolescents will often eventually discard undesirable roles.

FOCUS ON CHILD DEVELOPMENT 14.1

SAWYER, HITLER, LUTHER, AND GANDHI

Erik Erikson is a master at using the psychoanalytic method to uncover historical clues about identity formation. Erikson has used the psychoanalytic method both with the youths he treats in psychotherapy sessions and in the analysis of the lives of famous individuals. Erikson (1963) believes that the psychoanalytic technique sheds light on human psychological evolution. He also believes that the history of the world is a composite of individual life cycles.

In the excerpts that follow from Erikson's writings, the psychoanalytic method is used to analyze the youths of Tom Sawyer, Adolf Hitler, Martin Luther, and Mahatma Gandhi.

The occasion, while not pathological, is nevertheless a tragic one: a boy named Tom Sawyer, by verdict of his aunt, must whitewash a fence on an otherwise faultless spring morning. His predicament is intensified by the appearance of an age-mate named Ben Rogers, who indulges in a game. It is Ben, the man of leisure, whom we want to observe with the eyes of Tom, the working man.

"He took up his brush and went tranquilly to work. Ben Rogers hove in sight presently—the very boy, of all boys, whose ridicule he had been dreading. Ben was impersonating the *Big Missouri,* and considered himself to be drawing nine feet of water. He was boat and captain and engine-bells combined. Tom went on whitewashing—paid no attention to the steamboat. Ben stared a moment, and then said: 'Hiyi! You're a stump, ain't you! You got to work, hey?' " (Erikson, quoting Twain, 1963, pp. 209–210)

Erikson presented this conversation between Tom and Ben to a class of psychiatric social work students and asked them to interpret Ben's behavior. They indicated that Ben must have been a frustrated boy to take so much trouble to play so strenuously. They went on to say that the frustrations likely emerged as a consequence of having a tyrannical father. But Erikson provided them with a more positive analysis—namely,

Hitler in elementary schools. He is in the center of the top row.

that Ben was a growing boy, and growing means that he has to gradually master his gangling body and divided mind. Flexible and happy might be better labels to place on Tom's friend Ben.

In other passages, Erikson (1962) describes the youth of Adolf Hitler:

I will not go into the symbolism of Hitler's urge to build except to say that his shiftless and brutal father had consistently denied the mother a steady residence; one must read how Adolf took care of his mother when she wasted away from breast cancer to get an inkling of this young man's desperate urge to cure. But it would take a very extensive analysis, indeed, to indicate in what way a single boy can daydream his way into history and emerge a sinister genius, and how a whole nation

(continued on following page)

FOCUS ON CHILD DEVELOPMENT 14.1

becomes ready to accept the emotive power of that genius as a hope of fulfillment for its national aspirations and as a warrant for national criminality. . . .

The memoirs of young Hitler's friend indicate an almost pitiful fear on the part of the future dictator that he might be nothing. He had to challenge this possibility by being deliberately and totally anonymous; and only out of this self-chosen nothingness could he become everything. (Erikson, 1962, pp. 108–109)

But while the identity crisis of Adolf Hitler led him to turn toward politics in a pathological effort to create a world order, the identity crisis of Martin Luther in a different era led him to turn toward theology in an attempt to deal systematically with human nothingness or lack of identity:

In confession, for example, he was so meticulous in the attempt to be truthful that he spelled out every intention as well as every deed; he splintered relatively acceptable purities into smaller and smaller impurities; he reported temptations in historical sequence, starting back in childhood; and after having confessed for hours, would ask for special appointments in order to correct previous statements. In doing this, he was obviously both exceedingly compulsive and, at least unconsciously, rebellious. . . .

At this point, we must note a characteristic of great young rebels: their inner split between the temptation to surrender and the need to dominate. A great young rebel is torn between, on the other hand, tendencies to give in and fantasies of defeat (Luther used to resign himself to an early death at times of impending success), and the absolute need, on the other hand, to take the lead, not only over himself but over all the forces and people who impinge on him. (Erikson, 1968, pp. 155–157)

And in his Pulitzer Prize winning novel on Mahatma Gandhi's life, Erikson (1969) describes the personality formation of Gandhi during his youth:

Straight and yet not stiff; shy and yet not withdrawn; intelligent and yet not bookish; willful and yet not stubborn; sensual and yet not soft. . . . We must try to

What did Erikson believe were some of the key ingredients in Mahatma Gandhi's development of identity?

reflect on the relation of such a youth to his father, because the Mahatma places service to the father and the crushing guilt of failing in such service in the center of his adolescent turbulence. Some historians and political scientists seem to find it easy to interpret this account in psychoanalytic terms; I do not. For the question is not how a particular version of the Oedipal complex "causes" a man to be both great and neurotic in a particular way, but rather how such a young person . . . manages the complexes which constrict other men. (Erikson, 1969, p. 113)

In these passages, the workings of an insightful, sensitive mind is shown looking for a historical perspective on personality development. Through analysis of the lives of such famous individuals as Hitler, Luther, and Gandhi, and through the thousands of youth he has talked with in person, Erikson has pieced together a descriptive picture of identity development.

There are literally hundreds of roles for the adolescent to try out, and probably as many ways to pursue each role. Erikson believes that, by late adolescence, occupational choices are central to the development of identity. Other important role choices involve sexuality (including decisions on dating, marriage, and sexual behavior), politics, religion, and moral values. For example, many adolescents have been indoctrinated in the religious beliefs of their parents. By late adolescence, youth come to understand that they can make their own decisions about religion. The same can be said of political identity—most children report that they adopt their parents' political choices. But by late adolescence, youth make their own decisions. Unfortunately, some adolescents consistently and deliberately adopt choices that are opposite those of their parents as a means of attaining "independence." Such behavior does not meet the criteria for successful development of autonomy or identity, but represents a negative identity.

At the same time adolescents are struggling to come to grips with occupational, political, and religious identities, they also are trying to achieve a stable sexual identity. One means of exploring sex roles is cohabitation, or living with a member of the opposite sex outside of marriage. Other issues involve the adoption of "masculine" and "feminine" roles.

Thus, the development of an integrated sense of identity is a complex and difficult task. Adolescents are expected to master many different roles in our culture. It is the rare, perhaps even nonexistent, adolescent who doesn't experience serious doubts about his or her capabilities in handling at least some of these roles competently.

The Complexity of Erikson's Theory

Edmund Bourne (1978) analyzed the complexity of Erikson's developmental view of identity and proposed seven components to Erikson's definition of identity: genetic, adaptive, structural, dynamic, subjective or experiential, psychosocial reciprocity, and existential status.

With regard to what Bourne refers to as a genetic component, identity is often described as a developmental product or outcome incorporating the individual's experiences over the first five years of Erikson's life-cycle stages. Also, Erikson refers to the **epigenetic principle,** which states that anything that grows has a ground

plan, and out of this ground plan the parts arise, each one having its special time of ascendancy. Identity development reflects the way the adolescent has resolved prior stages, such as trust versus mistrust, and industry versus inferiority.

Concerning the adaptive dimension of identity, the adolescent's identity development can be viewed as an adaptive accomplishment or achievement. It is the adaptation of the adolescent's special skills, capacities, and strengths to the society in which he or she lives.

Erikson also described identity in structural ways. The possibility of identity confusion or diffusion suggests a breakdown in the adolescent's time perspective, initiative, and ability to coordinate present behavior toward future goals. This kind of breakdown implies a structural deficit.

The dynamic aspects of identity development are reflected in Erikson's view that

> Identity formation begins where the usefulness of identification ends. It arises from the selective repudiation and mutual assimilation of childhood identifications, and their absorption in a new configuration . . . which in turn, is dependent upon the process by which a society . . . identifies the young individual. (Erikson, 1968)

The subjective or experiential aspects of identity involve the individual sensing an inner feeling of cohesiveness or lack of cohesiveness. This subjective feeling may produce a great deal of confidence or a lack of assuredness.

Concerning psychosocial reciprocity, identity development implies a mutual relationship of the adolescent with his or her social world and community. Thus, identity development is not just an intrapsychic self-representation but rather also involves a particular relationship with people, community, and society.

Finally, the existential aspect of identity development is seen in Erikson's belief that identity is a way of "being in the world." In the existentialist mold, the adolescent seeks the meaning to his or her life as well as the meaning of life in general, much like an existential philosopher. As we have seen, the concept of identity as developed by Erikson includes many complex components.

A Contemporary View of Identity Development

James Marcia (1980), an expert on identity development, has described some ideas that provide insight into the role of identity in contemporary life:

> The identity process neither begins nor ends with adolescence. It begins with the self-object differentiation at infancy and reaches its final phase with the self-humankind integration at old age. What is important about identity in adolescence, particularly late adolescence, is that this is the first time that physical development, cognitive skills, and social expectations coincide to enable young persons to sort through and synthesize their childhood identifications in order to construct a viable pathway toward their adulthood. Resolution of the identity issue at adolescence guarantees only that one will be faced with subsequent identity "crises." A well-developed identity structure, like a well-developed superego, is flexible. It is open to changes in society and to changes in relationships. This openness assures numerous reorganizations of identity *contents* throughout the "identity-achieved" person's life, although the essential identity *process* remains the same, growing stronger through each crisis.
>
> Identity formation does not happen neatly. At the bare minimum, it involves commitment to a sexual orientation, an ideological stance, and a vocational direction. Synthesizing the identity components is as much a process of negation as affirmation. One must relinquish one's parents as psychosexual objects, relinquish childhood ideology based on one's position as a "taker," and relinquish the fantasized possibilities of multiple, glamorous life-styles. In the ongoing construction of an identity, that which one negates is known; what one affirms and chooses contains an element of the unknown. That is one of the reasons why some young people either do not form an identity or form only a partial one. They cannot risk saying "no" to elements of their past of which they are certain and make the affirmative leap into an uncertain future.
>
> Although some identity crises are cataclysmic and totally preoccupying, identity formation usually proceeds in a much more gradual and nonconscious way. It gets done by bits and pieces. Decisions are not made once and for all, but have to be made again and again. And the decisions may seem trivial at the time: whom to date, whether or not to break up, having intercourse, taking drugs, going to college or working, which college, what major, studying or playing, being politically active, and so on. Each of these decisions has identity-forming implications. The decisions and the bases on which one decides begin to form themselves into a more or less consistent core or structure. Of course, there are ways in which one can circumvent the decison-making process: one can let previously incorporated, parentally based values determine one's actions; one can permit oneself to be pushed one way or the other by external pressures; or one can become mired in indecision. (pp. 60–61)

Marcia's comments emphasize his view that considering identity a crisis in adolescence may be too strong a label. His belief that identity proceeds in a more gradual fashion and is a lifelong process seems intuitively correct. Nonetheless, remember that it is during adolescence that physical, cognitive, and social skills are sufficiently advanced to allow a questioning and a synthesis of who one is and what one is all about as a person.

Next, we see that Marcia also believes that adolescents can wear four different faces in their effort to achieve identity.

The Four Statuses of Identity

James Marcia (1966, 1980) also analyzed Erikson's identity theory of adolescence and concluded that four identity statuses, or *modes of resolution,* appear in the theory—identity diffusion, foreclosure, moratorium, and identity achievement. The extent of an adolescent's commitment and crisis is used to classify him or her as having one of the four identity statuses. Marcia (1966) defines crisis as a period during which the adolescent is choosing among meaningful alternatives. (Most researchers now use the term *exploration* rather than *crisis,* although in the spirit of Marcia's original formulation, we will refer to crisis.) He defines commitment as the extent to which an adolescent shows a personal investment in what he or she is doing or is going to do.

Adolescents classified as **identity diffused** (or **confused**) have not experienced any crisis (that is, they haven't explored meaningful alternatives) or made any commitments. Not only are they undecided upon occupational or ideological choices, they also are likely to show little or no interest in such matters.

Table 14.1   The Four Statuses of Identity

	Identity Status			
Position on Occupation and Ideology	Identity Moratorium	Identity Foreclosure	Identity Diffusion	Identity Achievement
Crisis	Present	Absent	Absent	Present
Commitment	Absent	Present	Absent	Present

The adolescent experiencing **identity foreclosure** has made a commitment but has not experienced a crisis. This occurs most often when parents simply hand down commitments to their adolescents, more often than not in an authoritarian manner. In such circumstances, adolescents may not have had enough opportunities to explore different approaches, ideologies, and vocations on their own. Some experts on adolescence, such as Kenneth Kenniston (1971), believe that experiencing a crisis is necessary for the development of a mature and self-integrated identity.

Marcia (1966) states that adolescents in the **identity moratorium** status are in the midst of a crisis but that their commitments are either absent or only vaguely defined. Such adolescents are searching for commitments by actively questioning alternatives.

Adolescents who have undergone a crisis and made a commitment are referred to as **identity achieved.** In other words, to reach the identity achievement status, it is necessary to first experience a psychological moratorium—exploring different roles and experimenting with different personalities—and then make an enduring commitment. An overview of Marcia's four identity statuses is provided in Table 14.1.

Now we turn our attention to research on identity development, studying developmental changes in identity, sex differences and similarities in identity, and sociocultural influences, particularly the family. We will see that Marcia's four statuses of identity have figured prominently in research on identity development.

Developmental Changes in Identity

Research on identity development has focused primarily on college students and to some extent high school students, with little attention given to early adolescence (Adams & Montemayor, 1983). Several investigations do reveal that early adolescents primarily are in the identity diffusion and identity foreclosure states.

In one recent investigation of the lower age boundaries of identity development, Sally Archer (1982) interviewed early and midadolescent males and females in the 6th, 8th, 10th, and 12th grades with regard to such aspects of identity development as vocational choice, religious beliefs, political philosophies, and sex-role preferences. She found that the frequency of identity achievement went up with an increase in grade level. The diffusion and foreclosure statuses were most apparent at all grade levels. Similar patterns were found for both girls and boys.

Another investigation of Marcia's four identity statuses focused on five age-groups of males: 12, 15, 18, 21, and 24 years of age (Meilman, 1979). Most of the subjects studied were found to be in identity diffusion or foreclosure. The most significant changes in identity status occurred between the ages of 18 and 21. The most prominent shifts at this time were from identity diffusion and foreclosure to identity achievement.

James Marcia (1983) believes that three aspects of the adolescent's life are important in the development of identity during early adolescence. He argues that young adolescents must establish confidence in parental support, develop a sense of industry, and gain a self-reflective perspective into their future. These are viewed by Marcia as early-adolescent precursors to the achievement of an identity in late adolescence.

Note that in Meilman's (1979) study, the most significant changes in identity status occurred between the ages of 18 and 21. The upshot of most studies focused on age changes in identity find that it is in the post-high-school years that the main changes in identity status take place. Over time during the college years, individuals are

When do the most significant changes in identity status take place?

likely to move in the direction of identity achievement (Marcia, 1976; Waterman, Geary, & Waterman, 1974). One investigation studied 148 freshmen, sophomore, and junior college students (Adams & Fitch, 1982). While half of the students remained stable in their identity status from 1976 to 1977, the other half either regressed or advanced. Few who were judged as having an identity diffusion status in 1976 remained at the same point in 1977. Moratorium-status students also advanced toward identity achievement. Identity-achieved students either remained that way, or in some cases, regressed to a moratorium status. In view of the research discussed here, then, identity achievement is more common in post-high-school youth, whereas early adolescents are more likely to be identity diffused and foreclosed.

Some experts on adolescence argue that college experiences increase the likelihood that adolescents will enter a status of identity moratorium. The theory is that professors and peers stimulate older adolescents to rethink their vocational and ideological orientations (e.g., Waterman & Waterman, 1971). In one investigation, as many as four out of every five adolescents in a moratorium status switched their occupational orientation during their college years (Waterman & Waterman, 1972). As a rule, the incidence of successful resolution

to the identity crisis and successful development of an identity commitment increases from the first year to the final year of college (Constantinople, 1969).

As Erikson's provocative view of identity development has been evaluated in recent years, the changing climate of sex roles has led to greater consideration of sex differences and similarities in identity.

Sex Differences and Similarities in Identity

Is the identity development of the female the same as that of the male? In the 1960s and through the mid-1970s, researchers were finding sex differences in the development of identity during both the high school and college years. For example, Joe LaVoie (1976) found that vocational identity is central to the identity formation of midadolescent males, while affiliative needs are more important to midadolescent females. Similarly, in college-aged adolescents, ideological choices and vocational orientations provide the core for the identity development of males, while intimacy and interpersonal relationships play a more important role in the identity development of females (Constantinople, 1969; Toder & Marcia, 1973). Furthermore, it has been found that, by the end of the college years, males have been able to resolve an identity crisis more readily than females (Constantinople, 1969).

However, with regard to the nature of sex differences in identity, it is important to consider the domain of identity being evaluated and the historical time period in which identity is being assessed. A review of the identity development literature by Alan Waterman (1982) suggests that there actually are fewer sex differences in identity than some of the earlier studies indicated. Because so much emphasis has been placed on vocational commitment in the assessment of identity, it likely is the case that, as adolescent females have assumed a stronger vocational orientation in the late 1970s and in the 1980s, they no longer differ from males in substantial ways with regard to identity development. Among the domains of identity development sampled in Waterman's review were vocational choice, religious beliefs, political ideology, and sex-role attitudes. Not only is it important to consider sex differences in identity, but as we see next, any account of identity also needs to address the role of family influences.

Are there differences in the identity development of males and females?

Family Influences on the Adolescent's Identity

Parents represent important figures in the adolescent's development of identity. By the time individuals have reached adolescence, they have been exposed to a long history of parental interaction and have learned numerous expectations for their conduct. Have their parents, over the course of 15 to 20 years of interaction with them, provided opportunities for them to explore alternative solutions to problems? Or have the parents handed down decisions in an authoritarian manner? Have they been actively interested and involved with the adolescent, or uninterested, uninvolved, and aloof? Have they encouraged their adolescents to go to college, or have they pushed them into low-income jobs and de-emphasized college? What were your parents like? Which paths did they follow in socializing you? Parental influence on identity development is tremendous—extending to sex roles, vocational choices, and moral, political, and religious ideology.

In particular, the work of Harold Grotevant and Catherine Cooper (e.g., Cooper, Grotevant, & Condon, 1983; Grotevant, 1984; Grotevant & Cooper, 1985) has highlighted the importance of a number of family processes in the development of identity. It is the belief of Grotevant and Cooper that both connectedness to parents and the presence of a family context that promotes individuation are likely to promote identity achievement. **Connectedness** is reflected in mutuality and permeability. Mutuality refers to the adolescent's sensitivity to and respect for the views of others. Permeability indexes openness and responsiveness to the views of others. Mutuality can provide adolescents with support, acknowledgement, and respect for their own beliefs, while permeability allows the adolescent to sense how to manage the boundaries between the self and others. **Individuation** is viewed as having two main parts—separateness and self-assertion. Separateness is seen in the expressions of how distinctive the self is from others. Self-assertion is involved in the adolescent's expression of his or her personal point of view and in taking responsibility for communicating this clearly. Focus on Child Development 14.2 presents more about Grotevant and Cooper's research and the family processes involved in identity development.

Now that we have considered the nature of Erikson's ideas on identity, the four statuses of identity, developmental changes, sex differences and similarities, as well as family influences on identity, it also is important to evaluate how identity is measured.

The Measurement of Identity

Identity is a global construct, and like many such broad concepts, is difficult to measure. The same problems associated with the assessment of self-concept also apply to identity evaluation. How do researchers investigate the development of identity status? Many researchers use either a semistructured individual interview procedure, a survey (questionnaire), or a sentence-completion test. For example, Marcia (1966) has developed a 15- to 30-minute structured interview technique that focuses on crisis and commitment in occupation, religion, and politics. His sentence-completion test is comprised of 23 incomplete sentence stems that are to be completed truthfully and honestly by the adolescent. The sentences are usually scored to indicate to what degree the adolescent has reached identity achievement (e.g., Kacerguis & Adams, 1980).

FOCUS ON CHILD DEVELOPMENT 14.2

INDIVIDUATION AND CONNECTEDNESS IN FAMILIES

Harold Grotevant and Catherine Cooper (1985) studied 84 white, middle-class, two-parent families, each with an adolescent and one or two siblings present. The families were observed in a family interaction situation designed to elicit the expression and coordination of different points of view. The mean age of the adolescents was 15.2 years. The family interaction task involved the family in developing plans together for a fictional two-week vacation for which they had unlimited money. Twenty minutes were allowed for discussion, during which the family members were asked to plan a day-by-day itinerary. The family interaction was audiotaped and then coded according to individuation (separateness and self-assertion) and connectedness (mutuality and permeability)—the factors Grotevant and Cooper believe are important in identity development. An overview of the conceptual dimensions of individuation and connectedness is shown in the table, along with family communication patterns that reflect each of the dimensions.

In addition to the family interaction task, the adolescents were given an extension of the ego identity interview developed by Marcia (1966). This extension focuses on six domains of identity: occupational choice, religion, politics, friendship, dating, and sex roles.

The data suggested somewhat different family interaction patterns for male and female adolescents in terms of their identity exploration. The fathers of adolescent males who were exploring identity seemed to be encouraging or at least tolerant of their sons' assertiveness and directedness. By contrast, the fathers of adolescent daughters who were exploring identity seemed to comment on others' suggestions rather than express their own and tended to disagree with both their wives and their daughters. The mothers of daughters who were exploring identity did not just mirror their husbands' views. Rather, the mothers tended to express their own ideas directly and had a strong role in coordinating family discussion. In sum, then, sons' relationships with their father and daughters' relationships with each parent appeared to provide the context for individuality and connectedness important in identity exploration.

Dimensions of Individuation and Connectedness in the Family Context

Individuation

Separateness:	Expresses distinctiveness of self from others
	1. Requests action
	a. Write that down there.
	b. Wait a minute.
	c. Let's vote on it.
	2. Disagrees/challenges others' idea directly
	a. I don't want to go on a train.
	b. No.
	3. Disagrees/challenges others' idea indirectly
	a. But, two or three months.
	b. We don't have time to do all that.
	c. Why do you want to go there?
	4. Irrelevant comment
	a. I'd like some more tea.
	b. You know, we're missing my favorite show.
Self-Assertion:	Displays awareness of own point of view and responsibility for communicating it clearly
	1. Suggests action or location directly
	Examples:
	a. Something I've always wanted to do—to go up to the northwest part of the country.
	b. I'd like to go to Italy.

Connectedness

Mutuality:	Shows sensitivity and respect for others' views
	1. Suggests action or location indirectly
	a. Let's go to Canada.
	b. Would either of you like to go back to Italy?
	2. Initiates compromise
	a. While Mom's in the antique shop, we can hike for a while.
	b. We can take Cindy to the Bahamas, and then we can go wherever you want to go.
	3. States others' feelings
	a. The kids will love to see Disneyworld.
	b. Your mother has always wanted to go to England.
	4. Answers request for information/validation
	a. A rail you go by train.
	b. It's about 400 miles.

Dimensions of Individuation and Connectedness in the Family Context Continued

Connectedness (cont.)

Permeability: Expresses responsiveness to the views of others
1. Acknowledgement
   a. You said go to Canada.
   b. Oh.
   c. Uh-huh.
   d. Okay.
2. Requests information/validation
   a. In what perspective?
   b. What is a rail?
   c. How far is it from Rome to Athens?
3. Agrees with/incorporates others' ideas
   a. I'd like to go there, too.
   b. Yeah, Yellowstone.
   c. Let's use Jim's idea of Spain and go to Madrid.
4. Relevant comment
   a. So, we have two weeks and unlimited funds.
   b. Spain is next to France.
   c. Rail express. (elaborates response)
5. Complies with request for action
   a. I'll write that down right now.
   b. Okay.

From Grotevant, H. D. and C. R. Cooper, "Patterns of interaction in family relationships and the development of identity exploration in adolescence" in *Child Development, 56,* 415–428, 1985. © 1985 by The Society for Research in Child Development. Reprinted by permission.

Harold Grotevant and his colleagues extended Marcia's identity interview so that it would include several important areas of interpersonal relationships (Grotevant, Thorbecke, & Meyer, 1982). As noted in our discussion of Grotevant and Cooper's research, this extension allows identity to be assessed in six different domains: occupational choice, religion, politics, friendships, dating, and sex roles. The latter three categories provide more information about the adolescent's social relationships. The interview includes 11 questions on occupation, 10 on religion, 9 on politics, 15 on friendship, 17 on dating, and 13 on sex roles. Several questions also have probe cues indicated in the interview protocol. Examples of key questions in the three interpersonal areas are shown in Table 14.2.

Table 14.2   Examples of Key Questions in the Extension of Marcia's Identity-Status Interview into the Interpersonal Domain

Friendship   Would you say that your close friends are similar to you or different from you? In what ways? (Probe: How about the rest of your friends and acquaintances?) If your closest friend changed in some way that you didn't, would you still be friends? (for example . . .) What kinds of friends do your parents think you should have? Have you ever begun a friendship or maintained a friendship with someone of whom your parents disapproved? Was this disagreement resolved in some way? How?

Dating   What are you looking for in the people you date? Has that idea changed since you started dating? How? How does that compare to what you look for in a friend? What standards or unwritten rules do you follow on a date? How do your rules compare to those of your friends? Have you changed your rules or standards since you started dating? If yes, what brought about those changes?

Sex roles   Now I'm interested in finding out how you think married couples should deal with the many tasks involved in the family. Who should take care of the young children (infants or preschoolers)? How should major decisions, such as buying a car or house be made? What if only one person makes the money? How do your parents handle each of the family responsibilities we have been discussing? Do you expect that your ideas about men's and women's roles will stay the same or change over the next few years? Have your ideas changed over the last few years?

From Grotevant, H. D., W. Thorbecke, and M. L. Meyer, "An extension of Marcia's identity-status interview into the interpersonal domain" in *Journal of Youth and Adolescence, 11,* 33–47, 1982. Copyright © 1982 Plenum Press, New York.

Constantinople (1969) has developed a questionnaire that asks the adolescent to respond to a number of items, each of which reflects some aspect of one of Erikson's bipolar conflicts. In Constantinople's scale, trust versus mistrust, autonomy versus shame and doubt, and so on can be assessed along with identity. Adolescents simply check whether each of the items is very much like them, somewhat like them, neutral, usually not like them, or definitely not like them.

Such measures represent means of assessing identity that are very different from the psychoanalytic inquiry Erikson has used so ingeniously. Erikson's procedure is more individualized and requires considerable time—he conducts repeated interviews that probe deeply into the adolescent's life or extensively peruses an individual's life through writings and historical documents.

If you want to evaluate an adolescent's identity development, where do you start? You might follow Erikson's pattern of probing the depths of an individual's personality by conducting a number of extensive open-ended interviews. Or you might decide to develop a questionnaire or survey to give to the adolescent that asks how he or she really feels about himself or herself. But are either of these methods adequate for fully and accurately evaluating the adolescent's development of identity? The problem becomes particularly acute when you are faced with the necessity of having to investigate identity development for a large number of adolescents—in most cases, even 10 to 15 hours of in-depth interviewing and analysis of 80 to 100 adolescents may be too time consuming. Researchers who use a survey or questionnaire hope that their instrument will validly and reliably assess the adolescent's identity. However, many experts on adolescent development, such as David Ausubel (Ausubel, Sullivan, & Eves, 1979), as well as experts on personality, such as Walter Mischel (1976), have criticized the use of the survey or questionnaire as a means of getting information about detailed, complex constructs like identity. Such experts believe that multiple assessments of the adolescent's identity development are necessary and that, if possible, these assessments should include information not only from the adolescent, but from others as well.

We have studied many facets of identity development, but one more provides fascinating insights into the transitions we make in the course of becoming mature social beings—the path through identity and intimacy.

Identity and Intimacy

Erikson believes that there are important links between identity and intimacy in development. And others, including Orlofsky, have described the nature of intimacy.

Erikson's Views of Identity and Intimacy

Erikson (1968) has written extensively about intimacy as well as identity. He believes that intimacy should come after adolescents are well on their way to achieving a stable and successful identity. The development of intimacy, in Erikson's view, is another life crisis—if intimacy is not developed in young adulthood, the person may be left with what Erikson refers to as isolation. Erikson described intimacy versus isolation as the sixth stage in the human life cycle, coming after the identity versus identity confusion (diffusion) issue has been explored.

Erikson refers to intimacy in terms of both sexual relationships and friendships. He comments:

> As the young individual seeks at least tentative forms of playful intimacy in friendship and competition, in sex play and love, in argument and gossip, he is apt to experience a peculiar strain, as if such tentative engagement might turn into an interpersonal fusion amounting to a loss of identity and requiring, therefore, a tense inner reservation, a caution in commitment. Where a youth does not resolve such a commitment, he may isolate himself and enter, at best, only stereotyped and formalized interpersonal relations; or he may, in repeated hectic attempts and dismal failures, seek intimacy with the most improbable of partners. For where an assured sense of identity is missing, even friendships and affairs become desperate attempts at delineating the fuzzy outlines of identity by mutual narcissistic mirroring; to fall in love means to fall in love with one's mirror image, hurting oneself and damaging the mirror. (1968, p. 167)

An inability to develop meaningful relationships with others during adolescence and young adulthood can be harmful to an individual's personality. It may lead the adolescent to repudiate, ignore, or attack those who appear frustrating to him or her. Erikson (1968) asserts that such situations can account for the shallow, almost pathetic, attempts of adolescents to merge themselves with a "leader." Many adolescents want to be apprentices or disciples of leaders and adults who will shelter them from the harm of an "out-group" world. If this fails, and Erikson believes that it must, then sooner or later the adolescent will recoil into a self-search to discover where he or she went wrong. Such introspection sometimes leads to painful feelings of isolation and depression and may contribute to mistrust of others and restrict the adolescent's willingness to act on his or her own initiative.

As we see next, some thinkers have classified intimacy into a number of different categories.

The Five Statuses of Intimacy

Just as Marcia has classified the development of identity into four different statuses, he and his colleagues have also divided the development of intimacy into different levels characterized by intimate, preintimate, stereotyped, pseudointimate, and isolated styles of interaction (Orlofsky, Marcia, & Lesser, 1973). The **intimate** individual forms and maintains one or more deep and long-lasting love relationships. The **preintimate** individual has mixed emotions about commitment—this ambivalence is reflected in his or her strategy of offering love without any obligations or long-lasting bonds. In most instances, the **stereotyped** individual has superficial relationships that tend to be dominated by friendship ties with same-sex rather than opposite-sex individuals. The **pseudointimate** individual appears to be maintaining a long-lasting heterosexual attachment, but the relationship has little or no depth or closeness. Finally, the **isolated** individual withdraws from social encounters and has little or no intimate attachment to same- or opposite-sex individuals. Occasionally, the isolate shows signs of developing interpersonal relations, but usually such interactions are anxiety provoking. One investigation indicated that intimate and preintimate individuals are more sensitive to their partners' needs, as well as more open in their friendships, than individuals characterized by the other three intimacy statuses (Orlofsky, 1976).

How might identity influence intimacy?

Research on Intimacy

Research on intimacy has attempted to establish the importance of identity development as a precursor for intimacy. For example, in one investigation, college males and females who indicated that they had a stable sense of identity were more likely to attain intimacy status based on Orlofsky's classification than their counterparts who were less identity achieved (Kacerguis & Adams, 1980). By contrast, students who were foreclosed, in moratorium, or diffused were more likely to have one of the other four intimacy statuses. This work supports Erikson's belief that identity development is closely linked (and perhaps is even an important precursor) to intimacy.

Other recent research (e.g., Levitz-Jones & Orlofsky, 1985) supports the belief that individuation is an important precursor for mature intimacy. For example, low-intimacy women had a lower capacity for individuation and self-reliance and a higher degree of insecure attachment. And Sally Archer (1985) determined that the lack of a mature identity may be involved in the failure of many adolescent marriages. Archer interviewed divorced women about their expressions of identity and intimacy at the points of high school, marriage, divorce, and the present. Foreclosed identity and romantic intimacy were highest during high school and marriage.

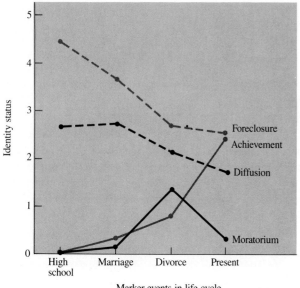

FIGURE 14.1 Identity statuses of divorced women during high school, at the time of marriage, at the time of divorce, and at present.

Identity moratorium was highest at divorce, while identity achievement and friendship intimacy were highest when the divorced women were interviewed in their adult years (see Figure 14.1 for a portrayal of the identity statuses of the divorced women at different points in their lives).

Before we leave the topic of intimacy, a word about the complexity of the path through identity and intimacy is in order.

Complexity of Identity-Intimacy Pathways

We have emphasized that Erikson's belief about identity coming before intimacy seems intuitively correct if optimal development is to occur. However, there are other possibilities, according to John Meacham and Nicholas Santilli (1982). One issue they raise is: What happens when identity foreclosure occurs? One possibility is that the individual progresses to the point of experiencing, but not necessarily resolving, the crisis of intimacy versus isolation. Any of several resolutions is then possible. For

Child Development Concept Table 14.1   Identity

Concept	Processes/Related Ideas	Characteristics/Description
Erikson's ideas on identity	Revisiting the eight stages of the life cycle	Erikson proposed that development through the life cycle occurs in eight stages, with identity versus identity confusion (diffusion) being the fifth stage. This stage corresponds roughly with the adolescent years and is a time when the individual seeks to discover who he or she is as a person.
	Personality and role experimentation	An important aspect of identity development is the opportunity to try out different personalities and roles.
	The complexity of Erikson's theory	Erikson's concept of identity is complex, involving the following components: genetics (including the epigenetic principle), adaptability, structural features, dynamic characteristics, subjective or experiential factors, psychosocial reciprocity, and existential status.
	A contemporary view of identity development	Identity development is a lifelong process, although it is during adolescence that, for the first time in development, physical, cognitive, and social skills are sufficiently advanced to allow serious inquiry and investigation into who an individual is as a person. Although some identity crises may be cataclysmic, the majority involve gradual development over many years.
The four statuses of identity	Crisis and commitment	Marcia described crisis as exploration of alternatives and commitment as the extent to which the person shows a personal investment in what he or she is doing or is going to do.
	Diffusion (confusion), foreclosure, moratorium, and achievement	The adolescent who is identity diffused or confused has not undergone a crisis or made a commitment. The adolescent who is identity foreclosed has made a commitment but has not undergone a crisis. The adolescent in the identity moratorium status is in the midst of a crisis but has not yet made a commitment. The adolescent who is identity achieved has both undergone a crisis and made a commitment.

example, this new crisis may be irresolvable until the individual returns to and successfully resolves the identity crisis. Such a sequence is compatible with Erikson's belief that the crises may be experienced out of order, but must be resolved in a universal order. A second possibility is that the individual may resolve the intimacy crisis and then move forward to the generativity versus stagnation crisis. Finally, a third possibility is that, after resolving the intimacy crisis, the individual may return to the identity crisis. The three possible paths (which at present have not been researched) would then be, respectively: intimacy (unresolved), identity, intimacy, and

generativity; intimacy and generativity; or intimacy, identity, and generativity. Other sequences are possible, but these three provide some indication of the variability in which individuals may experience and/or resolve the identity and intimacy crises. For example, there is some evidence that women experience the crisis of intimacy before identity (e.g., Douvan & Adelson, 1966; Fischer, 1981).

Child Development Concept Table 14.1 summarizes our discussion of identity development. Next, we turn our attention to a number of problems and disturbances that may appear during the adolescent years.

Child Development Concept Table 14.1 Continued

Concept	Processes/Related Ideas	Characteristics/Description
Developmental changes in identity	Early adolescence	Most young adolescents are identity diffused or foreclosed. Confidence in parental support, a self-reflective perspective about the future, and a sense of industry are important early adolescent characteristics that pave the way for the development of more mature identity later in adolescence and early adulthood.
	Late adolescence	During the post-high-school years, the greatest shifts in identity are thought to occur, as many individuals move closer to identity achievement. Some experts believe that college experiences promote identity exploration.
Sex differences and similarities in identity	Vocational and interpersonal identity	Early research indicated that a theme of vocational identity was more characteristic of midadolescent males, while interpersonal interests were more likely to reflect the identity of midadolescent females. However, more recent research has tended to reveal few, if any, sex differences in identity.
Family influences on the adolescent's identity	Their nature	A family context involving individuation and connectedness likely is important in promoting healthy identity exploration and development.
Measuring identity	Problems and prospects	Identity is a global construct, and like many such broad concepts, is very difficult to measure. The same problems associated with the assessment of self-concept apply to identity evaluation as well. Nonetheless, a number of researchers are working on improved assessments of identity—one such measure extends to interpersonal situations.
Identity and intimacy	Erikson's ideas	Erikson describes intimacy versus isolation as the sixth stage in his life-cycle theory, coming after the crisis of identity versus identity confusion (diffusion) has been explored.
	Five statuses of intimacy	Orlofsky describes five statuses of intimacy—intimate, preintimate, stereotyped, pseudointimate, and isolated.
	Research on intimacy	There is some indication that identity exploration prior to the kind of intimacy involved in a deep love relationship is a psychologically healthy developmental path.
	Complexity of identity-intimacy pathways	The link between identity and intimacy, however, is complex, and there often are different developmental paths to maturity.

PROBLEMS AND DISTURBANCES

The problems and disturbances encountered by adolescents are different than those that characterize children. Among the two most pervasive problems of adolescence are drug abuse and delinquency. Suicide and eating disorders also are major concerns, and as we saw in Chapter 11, depression increases in adolescence. School-related problems continue to be a major concern during the adolescent years, just as in the elementary school years. Intriguing questions about disturbances in adolescence focus on whether adolescents experience more problems than children and what steps need to be taken to prevent problems in adolescence.

Drugs

Our focus on drugs investigates the actual incidence of adolescent drug use, with particular emphasis on alcohol and marijuana, and looks at preventive health efforts.

Actual Drug Use by Adolescents

The most extensive data about the use of drugs by adolescents comes from ongoing research by Lloyd Johnston, Jerald Bachman, and Patrick O'Malley at the Institute of Social Research at the University of Michigan. For a number of years, they have been charting the drug habits of very large numbers of randomly selected adolescents across the United States. Among their recent findings for 1984 high school seniors are (Johnston, Bachman, & O'Malley, 1985):

Almost two thirds of all seniors report illicit drug use at some point in their lives. However, a substantial proportion have used only marijuana.

Marijuana is by far the most widely used illicit drug, with 54.9 percent saying that they have used this drug at some point in their lives.

The most widely used class of other drugs is stimulants, with 27.9 percent saying that they have used these at some point in their lives.

Table 14.3   Prevalence (Percent Ever Used) and Recency of Use of 16 Types of Drugs

	Ever Used	Past Month	Past Year, Not Past Month	Not Past Year	Never Used
Marijuana/hashish	54.9	25.2	14.8	14.9	45.1
Inhalants	19.0	2.7	5.2	11.1	81.0
Amyl and butyl Nitrites	8.1	1.4	2.6	4.1	91.9
Hallucinogens	13.3	3.6	4.3	5.4	86.7
LSD	8.0	1.5	3.2	3.3	92.0
PCP	5.0	1.0	1.3	2.7	95.0
Cocaine	16.1	5.8	5.8	4.5	83.9
Heroin	1.3	0.3	0.2	0.8	98.7
Other opiates	9.7	1.8	3.4	4.5	90.3
Stimulants	27.9	8.3	9.4	10.2	72.1
Sedatives	13.3	2.3	1.5	9.5	86.7
Barbiturates	9.9	1.7	3.2	5.0	90.1
Methaqualone	8.3	1.1	2.7	4.5	91.7
Tranquilizers	12.4	2.1	4.0	6.3	87.6
Alcohol	92.6	67.2	18.8	6.6	7.4
Cigarettes	69.7	29.3	(40.4)		30.3

Note: Based on national sample of 15,900 high school seniors in 1984.
Reprinted with permission of Johnston, L. D., O'Malley, P. M., and Bachman, J. G. (1985, January 7). News release on *Use of licit and illicit drugs among America's high school students, 1975, 1984,* through the University of Michigan News and Information Services.

The most widely used licit (legal) drug is alcohol (92.6 percent report having used alcohol at some point in time), with nicotine second in this category (69.7 percent report having smoked cigarettes at some point in their lives).

A summary of these findings for 1984 high school seniors is presented in Table 14.3, along with information pertaining to recency of use of 16 types of drugs.

Now that we have studied current actual drug use, let's see what kinds of trends in drug use have developed over a number of years.

Trends in Drug Use The trends in drug use from 1975 through 1984 indicate that, at some point near the end of the 1970s and the beginning of the 1980s, there was a turning point in adolescents' use of illicit drugs (Johnston, Bachman, & O'Malley, 1985). Since that time, illicit drug use by adolescents overall has gradually declined. Table 14.4 shows the percentage of high school

seniors who used a particular drug in the last 30 days. Note that marijuana use peaked in 1978 and has continued to decline every year thereafter. Also notice that use of hallucinogens peaked in 1979 and has declined each year since that time. With regard to licit drugs, alcohol use peaked in 1980 and has gradually declined thereafter. Cigarette smoking peaked in 1976 and has dropped considerably since that time.

Sex Differences in Drug Use Overall, adolescent males are more involved in drug use than their female counterparts. In the national survey by Johnston, Bachman, & O'Malley (1981), marijuana use at any point in the last 30 days was slightly higher for males, but for daily use, males used marijuana about twice as much as females (9.6 versus 4.2 percent). Adolescent males also take most other illicit drugs more often than females— inhalants, hallucinogens, heroin, cocaine, and barbiturates. For the 1981 data, females were more likely to take stimulants than males at any time during the last

Table 14.4 Trends in 30-Day Prevalence of 15 Types of Drugs

		Percent Who Used in Last 30 Days										
		Class of 1975	Class of 1976	Class of 1977	Class of 1978	Class of 1979	Class of 1980	Class of 1981	Class of 1982	Class of 1983	Class of 1984	1983–1984 Change
	Approx. N =	(9,400)	(15,400)	(17,100)	(17,800)	(15,500)	(15,900)	(17,500)	(17,700)	(16,300)	(15,900)	
Marijuana/hashish		27.1	32.2	35.4	37.1	36.5	33.7	31.6	28.5	27.0	25.2	−1.8
Inhalants		NA	0.9	1.3	1.5	1.7	1.4	1.5	1.5	1.7	1.9	+0.2
Inhalants adjusted[a]		NA	NA	NA	NA	3.1	2.7	2.3	2.5	2.7	2.7	0.0
Amyl and butyl nitrites[b]		NA	NA	NA	NA	2.4	1.8	1.4	1.1	1.4	1.4	0.0
Hallucinogens		4.7	3.4	4.1	3.9	4.0	3.7	3.7	3.4	2.8	3.6	+0.8
LSD		2.3	1.9	2.1	2.1	2.4	2.3	2.5	2.4	1.9	1.5	−0.4
PCP		NA	NA	NA	NA	2.4	1.4	1.4	1.0	1.3	1.0	−0.3
Cocaine		1.9	2.0	2.9	3.9	5.7	5.2	5.8	5.0	4.9	5.8	+0.9
Heroin		0.4	0.2	0.3	0.3	0.2	0.2	0.2	0.2	0.2	0.3	+0.1
Stimulants[c]		8.5	7.7	8.8	8.7	9.9	12.1	15.8	13.7	12.4	NA	NA
Stimulants adjusted[b, c]		NA	NA	NA	NA	NA	NA	NA	10.7	8.9	8.3	−0.6
Sedatives[c]		5.4	4.5	5.1	4.2	4.4	4.8	4.6	3.4	3.0	2.3	−0.7
Barbiturates[c]		4.7	3.9	4.3	3.2	3.2	2.9	2.6	2.0	2.1	1.7	−0.4
Methaqualone[c]		2.1	1.6	2.3	1.9	2.3	3.3	3.1	2.4	1.8	1.1	−0.7
Tranquilizers[c]		4.1	4.0	4.6	3.4	3.7	3.1	2.7	2.4	2.5	2.1	−0.4
Alcohol		68.2	68.3	71.2	72.1	71.8	72.0	70.7	69.7	69.4	67.2	−2.2
Cigarettes		36.7	38.8	38.4	36.7	34.4	30.5	29.4	30.0	30.3	29.3	−1.0

[a]Adjusted for underreporting of amyl and butyl nitrites
[b]Adjusted for overreporting of the nonprescription stimulants
[c]Only drug use which was not under a doctor's orders is included here
Reprinted with permission of Johnston, L. D., O'Malley, P. M., and Bachman, J. G. (1985, January 7). News release on *Use of licit and illicit drugs among America's high school students, 1975, 1984*, through the University of Michigan News and Information Services.

30 days. More recent data reveal how it is important to evaluate stimulants in terms of different classes, such as diet pills versus stay-awake pills. In this regard, females are much more likely than males to have taken diet pills (43.1 percent versus 14.8 percent), while males are somewhat more likely to have taken stay-awake pills in the 30-day period (Johnston, Bachman, & O'Malley, 1985). Also, female adolescents are more likely to have smoked cigarettes than their male counterparts at some point in the last 30 days.

Now that we have studied some trends in the use of a number of drugs, let's look more closely at problems surrounding the widely used drug of alcohol.

Alcohol

Some mornings, Annie, a 15-year-old cheerleader, was too drunk to go to school. Other days, she'd stop for a couple of beers or a screwdriver on the way to school. She was tall and blonde and good-looking, and no one who sold her liquor, even at 8:00 in the morning, questioned her age. Where did she get her money? From baby-sitting and what her mother gave her to buy lunch. Annie no longer is a cheerleader—she was kicked off the squad for missing practice so frequently. Soon, she and several of her peers were drinking almost every morning, and often during and after school. Sometimes, they skipped school and went to the woods to drink. Annie's whole life began to revolve around her drinking. It went on for two years, and during the last summer, anytime anybody saw her she was drunk. After a while, Annie's parents began to suspect her problem. But even when they punished her, it didn't stop her drinking. Finally, this year, Annie started dating a boy she really likes and who wouldn't put up with her drinking. She agreed to go to Alcoholics Anonymous and has just successfully completed treatment. She has stopped drinking for four months now, and hopefully, her abstinence will continue.

Unfortunately, there are hundreds of thousands of adolescents just like Annie. They live in both wealthy suburbs and inner-city housing projects. Annie grew up in a Chicago suburb and said she started drinking when she was 10 because her older brothers always looked like they were having fun when they were doing it. She said it made her feel good and peaceful, and commented that drinking made her feel more sociable, more confident and open. Alcohol abuse often leads to many problems for adolescents, just as it did for Annie.

The Prevalence of Drinking by Adolescents

Alcohol is the most widely used of all drugs by adolescents, according to the national surveys conducted by the Institute of Social Research at the University of Michigan (Johnston, Bachman, & O'Malley, 1981, 1985). There has been concern that, as illicit drug use declines, alcohol use by adolescents would increase. However, since 1979, there has been a slight decrease in alcohol use by adolescents. For example, the proportion of seniors reporting alcohol use in the prior 30-day period was 72 percent in 1979 and 67 percent in 1984 (see Table 14.4). More importantly, the number of seniors drinking daily, or almost daily, fell from 7 percent to 5 percent over the same time period. The number of seniors reporting any occasions of recent "heavy drinking" (defined as five or more drinks in a row during the prior two weeks) still remains alarmingly high, although the percentage did drop from 41 to 39 percent from 1983 to 1984, the first decline since the surveys began.

Personality and Adjustment Factors

Is there a "drinking personality" that characterizes adolescents who drink? That is, is there a type of personality organization that predisposes one adolescent to drink more than another? Most research on the topic of personality/adjustment factors involved in drinking has been carried out with adults, and the results are inconclusive. The only characteristic that shows up consistently in the makeup of adult alcoholics is personal maladjustment, yet most maladjusted people do not become alcoholics. The personality of individuals who drink may result from dependence on alcohol rather than be a contributing factor to drinking.

In a recent study with adolescents, it was found that adolescents at risk for alcohol abuse have stronger expectancies that alcohol will produce "personal effects," such as increased cognitive and motor capabilities, as well as tension reduction (McLaughlin & Chassin, 1985). Such findings also have been revealed with adults (Sher & Levensen, 1982). Adolescents at risk for alcohol abuse may actually experience greater tension reduction benefits from alcohol and therefore come to anticipate that alcohol will bring about this tension reduction. For adolescent males, a strong motive for power also is more evident among the high-risk than low-risk alcohol group.

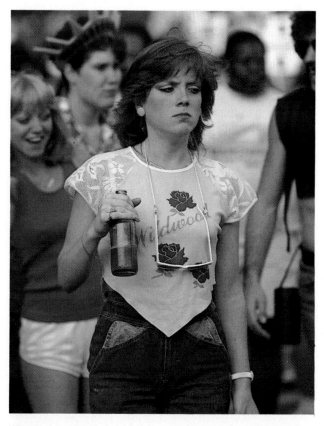

What is the pattern of alcohol consumption among adolescents?

Family and Peer Influences   Grace Barnes has reviewed a number of studies on family relationships and concluded that family socialization is an important factor in adolescent drinking behavior (Barnes, 1977, 1984). A National Institute on Alcohol Abuse and Alcoholism survey of over 13,000 adolescents nationwide (1975) found that heavy adolescent drinkers were more likely to say that their parents sanctioned drinking and had favorable attitudes toward adolescent use of alcohol than those adolescents who were not heavy drinkers. In fact, the survey showed a stronger relation between parental sanctioning of drinking than between peer pressure and drinking. However, there still is a link between adolescent drinking and peer relations (National Institute on Alcohol Abuse and Alcoholism, 1975; Forslund & Gustafson, 1970). It may be, as Barnes (1977) suggests, that the peer group provides the social context for drinking and reinforces adolescent behavior learned as part of the family socialization process.

Other research on adolescent drinking patterns indicates that adolescents who drink heavily often come from unhappy homes in which there is a great deal of tension (e.g., Prendergast & Schaefer, 1974). And in Barnes's (1984) recent research, she found parental nurturance and the ability of the parents to function as a support system for the adolescent to be important factors in preventing heavy drinking by adolescents.

Let's now turn to one final consideration about alcohol use in adolescence—its prevention and programs to help adolescents with a drinking problem.

Prevention and Intervention Programs   One research study investigated the relation of minimum drinking age law changes to adolescents' alcohol-related traffic accidents (Wagenaar, 1983). Increases in automobile crashes were in the 10 to 30 percent range immediately following reductions in the legal drinking age, but when the drinking age was raised, there was a corresponding 10 to 30 percent reduction in such crashes. Despite such findings, agent interventions (such as raising the age at which adolescents can legally drink) alone seem inadequate to curb alcohol abuse.

To evaluate the effectiveness of environmental prevention, Wodarski and Hoffman (1984) developed a school-based program to help students discuss alcohol-related issues in their peer group. It was believed that such peer discussion would help students to become aware of their own drinking problems as well as those of others and to be more likely to seek help for themselves or others once this awareness occurred. At a one-year follow-up, students in the intervention schools reported less alcohol abuse and had more often discouraged one another's drinking than had students in control schools.

Attempts to help the adolescent with a drinking problem vary greatly, as do most intervention efforts to assist adolescents with various disturbances. Therapy may include working with other family members, peer group discussion sessions, and specific behavioral techniques. Unfortunately, there has been little or no concern for identifying different types of alcohol abusers in adolescence and then attempting to match appropriate treatment programs to the particular problems of the adolescent drinker. Most efforts simply assume that adolescents with drinking problems are a homogeneous group and do not take into account the varying developmental patterns and social histories of different adolescents. Some adolescents with drinking problems may be helped more through family therapy, others through peer counseling, and yet others through intensive behavioral strategies, depending on the type of drinking problem and the social agents who have the most influence on the adolescent (Finney & Moos, 1979).

Alcohol is a major problem in adolescence. Another problem that deserves further discussion is the use of marijuana.

Marijuana

Among the questions important to explore about marijuana use by adolescents are: What is marijuana and what are its psychological and behavioral effects? Why do adolescents use marijuana? And what is the nature of parent/peer influences on marijuana use?

Marijuana and Its Psychological and Behavioral Effects

The psychological effects of marijuana use are substantial—relaxation, intensified perception of stimuli, increased self-confidence, a sense of enhanced awareness and creativity, impaired motor coordination, reduced short-term memory, and distorted judgment. This menu of psychological effects suggests that safe driving may be impaired when the adolescent is under the influence of marijuana. The active chemical ingredient in marijuana is delta-9-tetrahydrocannabinol (**THC**). The effects of THC may last for four to eight hours from the time the user feels "high"; by contrast, alcohol becomes metabolized more quickly.

As was just indicated, marijuana use impairs short-term memory. Such effects are particularly relevant for adolescents because marijuana use may be linked to lowered academic performance. In one research investigation, subjects were randomly assigned to a marijuana condition or a placebo condition (a placebo is an inert substance used in place of an active drug) (Miller et al., 1978). Before smoking the real marijuana or the fake marijuana, the subjects were given a list of words and then asked to recall them. Their performance was noted, and no differences were revealed between the two groups. Then they smoked. About an hour later, when the effects of the marijuana should have been at their peak, the subjects were tested again on the words they had seen before

they smoked. The marijuana users did not recall as many of the words as the nonmarijuana users. Most psychologists now concur that marijuana impairs memory, although the precise nature of its effects are still being worked out. For example, some psychologists argue that the influence is greater on short-term memory, or on the transfer of information from short-term to long-term memory, than on long-term memory.

In a massive report issued in 1980, the National Institute on Drug Abuse initiated a campaign to discourage the use of marijuana on a regular basis. This report was not just based on the psychological effects of marijuana. As long ago as 1893, the Indian Hemp Commission found a link between marijuana use and lung disease. Today, researchers have concluded that, when marijuana is used daily in heavy amounts, it also may impair the reproductive system. Marijuana use may produce a significant decline in sperm count, as well as greater abnormalities in sperm produced. Women using marijuana also run the risk of decreased fertility. Although there have been no human studies on the subject, animal studies link marijuana use with an increase in birth defects.

Because of such research conclusions, in 1980 the National Institute on Drug Abuse and in 1982 the National Academy of Sciences issued reports strongly recommending that anyone under the age of 18 not use marijuana on a regular basis. Occasional use by healthy adults seems to have negligible health effects, although there are still unanswered questions about the long-term health effects of marijuana.

Reasons Adolescents Use Marijuana

Why do adolescents use marijuana? In one survey of 26,000 college students, more than two out of every three individuals said that smoking marijuana is fun and enjoyable (Mizner, Barter, & Werme, 1970). More than one out of every two said that the reason they smoked marijuana the first time was because they were curious. Only a very small percentage of the college students said that they smoked marijuana to give them greater insight into their personality. Many adolescents see marijuana as a pleasant alternative to harder drugs and alcohol. Usually, only very heavy users of marijuana progress to the use of hard drugs. Adolescents who smoke marijuana infrequently or moderately are unlikely to take hard drugs

Why do adolescents smoke marijuana?

Note: Refers to mean percentage of total intimacy with youth that is with peers of different ages.

FIGURE 14.2 Adolescent drug use and contact with younger, same-age and older-age youth.

(e.g., Single, Kandel, & Faust, 1974). Many youths take marijuana simply because it produces a pleasurable experience—a type of experience that is not a part of many of their other dealings with the world.

Parent-Peer Influences on Marijuana Use   To what extent do parents and peers influence adolescents to use marijuana? A host of studies have indicated that there are positive correlations between parental drug use (such as using tranquilizers, amphetamines, alcohol, and tobacco) and the use of marijuana by youth (e.g., Shafer et al., 1973). And adolescents whose peers smoke marijuana are also more likely to smoke marijuana than adolescents whose friends do not (e.g., Tec, 1972).

In one investigation of parental and peer influences on marijuana use by adolescents, Denise Kandel (1974) interviewed adolescents, their friends, and their parents about various factors associated with the use of marijuana. Kandel found that associating with friends who use marijuana is more likely to influence an adolescent than parental drug use is. Kandel found that only 15 percent of the adolescents whose friends did not smoke marijuana smoked marijuana themselves. By contrast, 79 percent of the youth whose peers smoked marijuana also smoked it themselves. The highest usage of marijuana occurred when an adolescent's friends smoked marijuana and his or her parents took drugs (barbiturates, alcohol, and so on).

A recent study by Blyth, Durant, and Moosbrugger (1985) investigated more than 2,400 7th- through 10th-graders. Drug-using adolescents reported a larger number of older peers and greater frequency of contact and intimacy with them than nondrug-using adolescents (see Figure 14.2). This suggests differences in the age-appropriateness of particularly intimate peers. Also, drug-using adolescents reported having a higher percentage of older friends and being even more peer- than adult-oriented than nondrug-using adolescents. Finally, parental intimacy was negatively related to drug use.

Let's now turn our attention to some preventive health efforts with drugs.

Preventive Health Efforts

Quite clearly, major efforts are needed to prevent the development of drug problems and disturbances during adolescence. One area where considerable interest has developed in recent years is cigarette smoking. By looking at the manner in which preventive health efforts have been developed with cigarette smoking, we can get a sense for how drug abuse and other problems may possibly be prevented.

Health psychologists are interested in ways to continue the decline in smoking among adolescents. One prevention program designed to help junior high school students resist the urge to smoke focused on pressure from parents and peers (Evans, 1982, 1983). The junior high school students were shown videotapes of individuals their age in situations where they resisted the temptation to smoke when offered a cigarette by a friend. Other tapes dealt with parents who smoked and with the subtle influence of cigarette advertising. Classroom posters also were displayed at the school as reminders, and group discussions continued the negative information about smoking. When compared to a group of control students who did not participate in these experiences, the adolescents in the anti-cigarette program were less likely to smoke in the seventh grade. Focus on Child Development 14.3 presents more information about preventive health efforts with regard to cigarette smoking and explores substance abuse in terms of agent, environment, and host.

Now that we have discussed a number of aspects of drugs during the adolescent years, we turn to another pervasive problem in adolescence—delinquency.

Delinquency

Some important questions to evaluate about juvenile delinquency are: What is juvenile delinquency? Why does it occur? And how do family processes contribute to delinquency?

What Is Juvenile Delinquency?

The label **"juvenile delinquent"** is applied to an adolescent who breaks the law or engages in behavior that is considered illegal. Like other categories of disturbance, juvenile delinquency is a broad concept; legal infractions may range from littering to murder. Because the youth technically becomes a juvenile delinquent only after being judged guilty of a crime by a court of law, official records do not accurately reflect the number of illegal acts committed. Nevertheless, there is still every indication that in the last 10 or 15 years, juvenile delinquency has increased in relation to the number of crimes committed by adults.

Estimates regarding the number of juvenile delinquents in the United States are sketchy, although FBI statistics suggest that at least 2 percent of all youths are involved in juvenile court cases. The number of girls found guilty of juvenile delinquency has increased significantly in recent years. Delinquency rates among blacks, other minority groups, and the lower class are particularly high in relation to the overall populations of these groups. However, such groups have less influence than others over the judicial decision-making process in the United States and thus may be judged delinquent more readily than their white, middle-class counterparts.

What Causes Delinquency?

We have seen that it is difficult to define and measure delinquency; there is also a lack of agreement about the nature of delinquency, or how it should be viewed, what causes it, and what factors are associated with it. Various causes of delinquency have been considered, including those that are based on the beliefs that (1) delinquency is rooted in biological instincts and delinquents are virtually "animals in captivity" (Hall, 1904); (2) delinquency is based on an increased biological drive, not necessarily sexual in nature (McCandless, 1970); (3) delinquency is triggered by the onset of sexual urges that require the adolescent to break away from parents and reestablish bonds with peers, a circumstance that increases the likelihood of acting-out behavior (Blos, 1962); (4) delinquency is one manifestation of the search for identity (Erikson, 1968); and (5) delinquency is caused by blocked opportunities in a culture (Bloch & Niederhoffer, 1958). Let's explore Erikson's ideas on delinquency further.

Recall that the description of Erik Erikson's theory of development that adolescence is the stage when the crisis of identity versus identity confusion (diffusion) should be resolved. Not surprisingly, Erikson's ideas about delinquency are linked to the ability of the adolescent to positively resolve this crisis. Erikson believes that at the time that the biological changes of puberty are occurring, there are concomitant changes in social expectations placed on adolescents by family, peers, and schools. These biological and social changes allow for two kinds of integration to occur in the adolescent's personality—first, the establishment of a sense of consistency in life, and second, the resolution of role identity, a sort of joining of the adolescent's motivation, values, abilities, and styles with the role demands placed on the adolescent.

FOCUS ON CHILD DEVELOPMENT 14.3

AGENT, ENVIRONMENT, AND HOST

It may be helpful to think of preventing substance abuse with adolescents in terms of agent, environment, and host (Schinke & Gilchrist, 1985). **Agent interventions** focus on abused substances per se, such as tobacco and alcohol. **Environment interventions** emphasize the settings where substance abuse originates and where it can be prevented—schools, homes, and communities. And **host interventions** stress those who will use substances—the adolescents themselves.

Agent interventions approach prevention through legal, technological, and social controls of the target substance (e.g., Gordon & McAlister, 1982; Wallack, 1984). Thus, agent prevention might control tobacco through licensing, minimum-age laws, and noncompliance.

Preventive environment interventions in schools, homes, and communities are designed to modify everyday influences on adolescents' substance use (e.g., Bloom, 1983; Perry, 1982). One of the most powerful conduits of intervention is television. One recent study calling on television to prevent adolescent cigarette smoking provided positive results (Flay, in press). Smoking-prevention segments were aired on television to a selected sample of families with young adolescents. A control group did not see the periodic anti-cigarette smoking campaign on television. One year later, the young adolescents who viewed the anti-smoking segments were less likely to have ever smoked cigarettes than the control group.

Host interventions build adolescents' cognitive and behavioral skills so that they will be able to resist substance abuse (e.g., Murray & Perry, 1984; Wills & Shiffman, 1985). One recent host intervention study used a number of strategies to improve the ability of young adolescents to resist smoking cigarettes (Schinke & Gilchrist, 1985). The middle

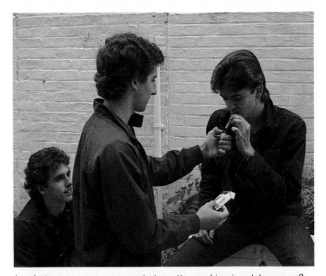

In what ways can we prevent cigarette smoking in adolescence?

school students in the study were shown health-related films regarding smoking, were exposed to peer testimonials on the advantages of nonsmoking, and were shown slides on media glamorization of cigarettes. Also, problem-solving situations were set up in which the adolescents practiced generating, choosing, and applying plans when the temptation to smoke might arise. The group of young adolescents experiencing this skills intervention were less likely to smoke cigarettes at several later measurement dates, one of which was two years later, than a control group of young adolescents who only were given attention.

Erikson believes that delinquency is characterized more by a failure of the adolescent to achieve the second kind of integration, involving the role aspects of identity. He comments that adolescents whose infant, childhood, or adolescent experiences have somehow restricted them from acceptable social roles or made them feel that they can't measure up to the demands placed on them may choose a negative course of identity development. Erikson describes this as "an identity perversely based on all those identifications and roles, which, at critical stages of development, had been presented to them as most undesirable or dangerous and yet also as most real" (1968, p. 197). Some of these adolescents may take on the role of the delinquent, enmeshing themselves in the most negative currents of the youth culture available to them. By organizing their lives around such a negative identity, they establish a continuity of self from one relationship and situation to another, so that they can imagine how they might behave, think, or feel even in encounters that never occur. Not only does their own behavior become predictable to themselves, but they become capable of predicting how others will act toward them. In this manner, the delinquent's self-image and the delinquent's perception of himself or herself in the peer group begin to fuse. As the adolescent finds support for such a delinquent image among peers, who themselves seek reciprocal support, the image is reinforced. Thus, for Erikson, delinquency is an attempt to establish an identity (Gold & Petronio, 1980).

Sociocultural Influences on Delinquency

Among the most important sociocultural influences on delinquency are those involving social class and community and family processes.

Social Class and Community   Although juvenile delinquency is less exclusively a lower-class problem than it was in the past, some characteristics of the lower-class culture are likely to promote delinquency. The norms of many lower-class peer groups and gangs are antisocial, or counterproductive, to the goals and norms of society at large. Getting into and, in some instances, staying out of trouble becomes a prominent feature of the lives of some adolescents from lower-class backgrounds (Miller, 1958). Status in the peer group may be gauged by how often the adolescent can engage in antisocial conduct yet manage to stay out of jail. Since lower-class adolescents have less opportunity to develop skills that are socially desirable, they may sense that they can gain attention and status by performing antisocial actions. Being "tough" and "masculine" are high-status traits for lower-class boys, and these traits are often measured by the adolescent's success in performing delinquent acts and getting away with them.

The nature of a community also may contribute to delinquency. A community with a high crime rate allows the adolescent to observe many models who engage in criminal activities. And adolescents may see these models rewarded for their criminal accomplishments. Such communities often are characterized by poverty, unemployment, and feelings of alienation toward the middle class. The quality of schools, funding for education, and organized neighborhood activities are other community factors that may be related to delinquency. Are there caring adults in the schools and neighborhood who can convince the adolescent with delinquent tendencies that education is the best route to success? When family support becomes inadequate, then such community supports take on added importance in delinquency prevention.

Let's look more closely now at family influences on delinquency.

Family Processes   Even if an adolescent grows up in a high-crime community, his or her peer relationships may influence whether or not he or she becomes a delinquent. In one investigation of 500 delinquents and 500 nondelinquents in Boston, Massachusetts, a much higher percentage of the delinquents had regular associations with delinquent peers (Glueck & Glueck, 1950).

But even more than peers, it has been the influence of family processes on delinquency that has stimulated the most research interest (Glueck & Glueck, 1950; McCord, McCord, & Gudeman, 1960; Rutter, 1971). The most recent focus has been on the nature of family management practices. Disruptions or omissions in the parents' applications of family management practices consistently are linked with antisocial behavior on the part of children and adolescents (e.g., Rutter, Tizrd, & Whitmore, 1970; Forgatch, Chamberlain, & Gabrielson, 1982; Patterson, Reid, Jones, & Conger, 1975; Patterson & Stouthamer-Loeber, 1984). The family management skills in question involve such matters as monitoring the adolescent's whereabouts, using effective discipline for antisocial behavior, calling on effective problem-solving skills, and supporting the development of prosocial skills.

In one recent study, family management practices were related to the delinquency of 7th- and 10th-grade boys (Patterson & Stouthamer-Loeber, 1984). Delinquency was measured both by police contacts and self-report. The measures of family management skills involved monitoring, discipline, problem solving, and reinforcement. Monitoring was assessed through a series of interviews with the parents and the adolescent, basically trying to obtain an accurate account of parental supervision and knowledge of the adolescent's whereabouts. Discipline was assessed in terms of whether the mother followed up on her commands, the father's consistency in discipline style, and the mother's consistency in discipline style. Problem solving was assessed from videotaped observations of the quality of family interaction and problem resolution. Reinforcement was assessed through observation of parent-adolescent interaction, an interview with the adolescent, and interviewers' ratings filled out at the end of sessions with the family.

The results indicated that parental monitoring was much more strongly related to delinquency than discipline, problem solving, or reinforcement. Further, parental monitoring also differentiated moderate offenders from persistent offenders. It seems that parents of delinquents are indifferent trackers of their adolescent's whereabouts, the type of companions they keep, or the kind of activities they engage in. When rule-breaking behavior occurs, such parents are less likely to provide punishment, such as loss of a privilege, work detail, or loss of allowance. If they react to such information at all, it often is in the form of lecturing, scolding, or barking out a threat—abrasive overtures usually not backed up

by effective consequences. The significant association of discipline and delinquency suggests that consistent application of effective punishment, such as time-out, loss of privileges, and the like, is necessary for long-term reduction in adolescents' antisocial behavior. Thus, the Patterson and Stouthamer-Loeber research indicates that both parental monitoring and discipline are key ingredients in determining whether an adolescent will engage in delinquent behavior.

Do family processes cause delinquency? Or are they just correlated with delinquency? And, possibly, are family processes the consequence of delinquency? These questions are explored further in Focus on Child Development 14.4.

Child Development Concept Table 14.2 summarizes our discussion of drugs and delinquency. Next, we look at several additional problems in adolescence.

Suicide

Questions that consistently crop up about adolescent suicide include: Is adolescent suicide increasing? What causes adolescent suicide? And can adolescent suicide be prevented?

Incidence of Suicide

The suicide rate for adolescents has tripled since 1950. Suicide has become the second leading cause of death among adolescents, falling behind only accidents. Approximately 1 out of every 1,000 adolescents attempts suicide, and about 1 out of every 5,100 attempts is successful (Smith, 1980). The prevalence of adolescent suicide is apparent in Figure 14.3, which shows the number of suicides per 100,000 persons 10 to 19 years old in 10 major cities in the United States.

Adolescent males are approximately three times more likely to commit suicide than adolescent females. This sex difference is attributed to the fact that males are more likely to use methods for attempting suicide, such as shooting themselves, that do not allow the adolescent's life to be saved. By contrast, adolescent girls are more likely to use strategies, such as sleeping pills, that do not always produce death (Resnick, 1980).

FOCUS ON CHILD DEVELOPMENT 14.4

DELINQUENCY AND FAMILY PROCESSES—CAUSE, CORRELATE, OR CONSEQUENCE?

Michael Rutter and Norman Garmezy (1983) raised the important question of whether research revealing an association of family experiences with delinquency involves family experiences as a cause, a correlate, or a consequence of delinquency. The associations may simply reflect some third factor, such as genetic influences; they may be a result of the disturbing effect of the child's behavior on family interaction; or they may indicate that family stress may lead to delinquency through some type of environmental effect.

Whether some third factor is involved can be examined by determining whether the association between family experiences and delinquency holds up when other significant variables are controlled for. It has been found that, even when social class and social atmosphere in the neighborhood are controlled for, a link between family experiences and delinquency still holds (McCord, 1980; West & Farrington, 1977; Wilson, 1980). With regard to the possibility that genetic mechanisms are involved in the association between family experience and delinquency, little research is available. However, several studies do suggest that genetic vulnerabilities on the part of the child might render the child more susceptible to environmental stress (Hutchings & Mednick, 1974; Crowe, 1974).

It is not an easy task to test the effects that the child might have on the association between family processes and delinquency. Clearly, socialization is a reciprocal process and one involving mutual regulation. And there is evidence that parental child-rearing practices that seem to be effective with most children are not efficient in controlling delinquents (Patterson, 1982). Nonetheless, while causal influences are likely bidirectional, there probably are a number of circumstances where the predominant influence is from parent to child.

Early family stresses also seem to have long-term effects, mainly because they lead to forms of disturbance in the child that seem to persist, rather than because a delayed or sleeper

What family factors are related to delinquency?

effect has occurred (Robins, 1978; West & Farrington, 1977). Further research also reveals that changes for the better in family relationships are linked with reduced conduct disturbances later in development (Rutter, 1971).

Rutter and Garmezy (1983) concluded that family influences do have some kind of environmental influence on the development of delinquency of other conduct disturbances. The key family factors that seem to be involved in the emergence of conduct disturbances are: family discord, deviant parental (and sibling) models, weak parent-child relationships, and poor discipline and monitoring of the child's activities. An example of research suggesting the importance of such family variables in the emergence of conduct disturbances is the work of Gerald Patterson (1982; Patterson & Stouthamer-Loeber, 1984). As we saw earlier, through careful and systematic observations of children and their families, Patterson concluded that the following two factors were most likely to describe the social world of families with delinquents: (1) inadequate parental supervision and monitoring and (2) inconsistent and inappropriate discipline.

Child Development Concept Table 14.2   Drugs and Delinquency

Concept	Processes/Related Ideas	Characteristics/Description
Drugs	Actual use of drugs by adolescents	Adolescents take a wide range of drugs, from licit drugs such as nicotine to highly illicit drugs like heroin. The most extensive data about drug use come from the Institute of Social Research at the University of Michigan through studies conducted by Johnston, Bachman, and O'Malley. They have been surveying high school seniors on a national basis for a number of years. Almost two thirds of adolescents take an illicit drug at some point in their lives. The most widely used illicit drug is marijuana, while the most widely used licit drug is alcohol. At some point near the end of the 1970s and the beginning of the 1980s, a downward trend in illicit drug use by adolescents began. For the most part, males are more involved in drug use than females, although females take one type of stimulant—diet pills—much more often.
	Alcohol	Alcohol is the most widely used of all drugs by adolescents. There has been a slight decrease in adolescent drinking since 1979, but heavy drinking remains alarmingly high. No specific personality profile has been linked to drinking, although alcoholic individuals do show a pattern of personal maladjustment, and adolescent drinkers seem to have stronger expectancies that alcohol will produce "personal effects." Family procesess in some way likely are involved in adolescent drinking patterns. Prevention programs appear to have some success in discouraging alcohol abuse. Intervention programs have not been very successful, but because adolescents with drinking problems are such a heterogeneous group, it seems important to tailor intervention efforts to the individual adolescent.
	Marijuana	The psychological effects of marijuana include relaxation, increased self-confidence, impaired motor coordination, reduced short-term memory, and distorted judgment. Many adolescents see marijuana as a pleasant alternative to harder drugs and alcohol. Studies reveal positive correlations between parental drug use and the use of marijuana by adolescents. Marijuana use has been declining.
	Preventive health efforts	Preventive health efforts focus on host interventions, environment interventions, and agent interventions.
Delinquency	What is juvenile delinquency?	A "juvenile delinquent" is an adolescent who breaks the law or engages in conduct that is considered illegal. It is a broad concept ranging from littering to murder. Estimates regarding the incidence of delinquency are sketchy, but at least 2 percent of youth are involved in court cases.
	What causes delinquency?	Many different explanations for delinquency have been given, ranging from biological instincts to independence and peer orientation. Erikson's ideas on identity development provide a framework for understanding delinquency.
	Sociocultural influences on delinquency	The norms of many lower-class peer groups and gangs are antisocial. Getting into and, in some instances, staying out of trouble sometimes becomes a prominent feature of adolescent life in some lower-class settings. A community with a high crime rate exposes adolescents to criminal models whose behavior often may be rewarded. A considerable amount of attention has been directed at family influences on delinquency. In particular, Patterson's recent work is important in documenting the importance of parental monitoring and discipline in determining whether an adolescent will engage in delinquent behavior. The question has been raised as to whether family processes cause delinquency, are merely correlated with delinquency, or are possibly a consequence of delinquency. While the evidence is not completely clear, it seems that family processes do play at least some causative role. Also, delinquents tend to associate with delinquent peers.

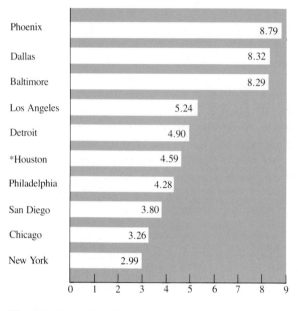

*Houston's rate is estimated

FIGURE 14.3 Number of suicides per 100,000 persons ten to nineteen years old in the ten largest cities in 1981.

Source: U.S. Bureau of the Census. *Population Statistics.* Washington, D.C., 1981.

Causes of Suicide

It may be helpful to think of suicide in terms of long-term experiences and situational, short-term circumstances. In many adolescent suicides, a long-term history of family processes often is involved. Indeed, a number of experts who study suicide feel that depression is involved in suicide (e.g., Jacobs, 1971; Resnick, 1980; Smith, 1980; Weiner, 1980). With regard to the role that childhood experiences and family processes play in depression, a combination of early push for impulse control, achievement emphasis, and a lack of affection and emotional support is implicated. Other research on suicide has found that adolescents who commit suicide have a long history of family instability and unhappiness (e.g., Jacobs, 1971; Weiner, 1980). However, these long-standing family relationships, in themselves, do not alone seem to cause suicide. Rather, more immediate, precipitating factors that occur during adolescence serve as a more proximal trigger for suicide. Such highly stressful circumstances as the loss of a boyfriend/girlfriend,

failure in school, and getting pregnant or fear of getting pregnant may, for some adolescents who come from unstable, unhappy family backgrounds, be sufficient to precipitate a suicide attempt.

There may be a cognitive explanation for why suicide increases dramatically in adolescence (Elkind, 1981; Lipsitz, 1983). Recall from the discussion of cognitive development in Chapter 12 how adolescents often construct a personal fable about themselves in which they tell themselves that they are somehow unique, immune, and even immortal. It is not unusual for adolescents to become locked into their personal fable and thus feel that something like death cannot happen to them. Further, as part of the personal fable, adolescents may think that the stress and pain they feel in life are unique and that no one else can possibly understand how dreadful things are.

In sum, adolescents at greater risk for attempting suicide may have a long history of family relationships that are similar to those promoting depression; may be experiencing precipitating events that trigger a sense of inadequacy, worthlessness, and despair; and may tend to lock themselves in a personal fable.

Prevention of Suicide

The tendency to overdifferentiate oneself in adolescence, which occurs as part of the personal fable, makes suicide prevention difficult. According to Joan Lipsitz (1983), prevention programs with adolescents are more likely to be successful if an adolescent believes that, "It can happen to me," rather than "It can't happen to me—I'm unique." If the adolescent cannot make the cognitive leap from immunity to vulnerability, then suicide prevention efforts often fail.

The fact that adolescent suicide rates have been increasing suggests that prevention efforts have not been very successful. One strategy has been to focus on the precipitating events by setting up telephone hotlines in various communities. While such steps are a positive trend in helping adolescents with suicidal tendencies, there is some indication that they are not highly effective—one investigation found that 98 percent of individuals who commit suicide never call a hotline center (Wilkins, 1970). Table 14.5 provides valuable advice for helping an adolescent who is suspected of contemplating suicide.

Table 14.5   What to Do and What Not to Do When You Suspect an Adolescent Is Likely to Attempt Suicide

What to Do

1. Ask direct, straightforward questions in a calm manner: "Are you thinking about hurting yourself?"
2. Assess the seriousness of the suicidal intent by asking questions about feelings, important relationships, who else the person has talked with, and the amount of thought given to the means to be used. If a gun, pills, rope, or other means has been obtained and a precise plan developed, the situation is clearly dangerous. Stay with the person until some type of help arrives.
3. Be a good listener and be very supportive without being falsely reassuring.
4. Try to persuade the adolescent to obtain professional help and assist him or her in getting this help.

What Not to Do

1. Do not ignore the warning signs.
2. Don't refuse to talk about suicide if an adolescent approaches you about the topic.
3. Do not react with horror, disapproval, or repulsion.
4. Don't give false reassurances by saying things like, "Everything is going to be OK." Also don't give out simple answers or platitudes like, "You have everything to be thankful for."
5. Do not abandon the adolescent after the crisis has passed or after professional help has commenced.

Reprinted from *Living with 10- to 15-Year-Olds: A Parent Education Curriculum.* Copyright by the Center for Early Adolescence, Carrboro, NC, 1982, rev. ed., 1987. Used with permission.

Eating Disorders

Eating disorders have become a major source of concern during the adolescent years. We now examine the incidence of eating disorders and the specific disorders of anorexia nervosa, bulimia, and obesity.

Incidence of Eating Disorders

Two recent Gallup polls (1985) revealed the prevalence of eating disorders among adolescents, particularly adolescent girls. The national poll sampled 502 boys and girls ages 13 to 18 and was the first national look at such eating disorders as anorexia (self-starvation) and bulimia (binge-and-purge syndrome). The poll revealed that 12 percent of the adolescent girls suffered symptoms of eating disorders, while only 4 percent of the boys had such problems. Forty percent of the boys and 34 percent of the girls reported periodic food binges. Clearly, eating problems have become a prevalent aspect of a number of adolescents' lives.

Anorexia Nervosa

The ideal female in our culture today is slender and lithe, particularly in comparison to prior eras, when a more shapely, robust body was the ideal. Because of this standard, many girls constantly worry about their weight. Kim Chernin (1981) described how two facts make this current obsession with weight loss unusual. One is the scope of the trend. Throughout history, there have been dieters, including Roman matrons who willingly starved themselves. But there never has been a period when such large numbers of adolescents and adults have spent so much money, time, and energy on their weight. The second unusual aspect of the current concern about weight loss is the degree to which it involves females rather than males. For example, more than 90 percent of those who are suffering from anorexia nervosa are females.

There are several physical and psychosocial features that characterize **anorexia nervosa** in adolescence (Bruch, 1973). Severe malnutrition and emaciation are accompanied by amenorrhea (the absence of menstrual periods as a result of a decrease in body fat). Often, anorexic adolescents show an obsession with activity, which they feel will peel off fat. Although anorexic adolescents avoid eating, they have an intense interest in food, cook for others, talk about food, and insist on watching others eat. Usually, when they begin dieting, they are average in weight. However, many anorexic adolescents do not feel useful or in control of their lives. They perceive their bodies as something extra—not part of themselves, not their own property. Anorexics complain of feeling full after a few bites of food, which symbolizes a sense of control (by contrast, the obese adolescent feels empty after a full meal and does not feel in control of food). The anorexic adolescent also is excessively preoccupied with body size. A close look at the anorexic adolescent's family often reveals serious problems. The case study presented in Focus on Child Development 14.5 describes some of the family dynamics often experienced by the adolescent with anorexia nervosa.

Bulimia

Bulimia refers to a binge-and-purge syndrome; that is, periods of very heavy eating are followed by self-induced vomiting. Like anorexia nervosa, it, too, is almost exclusively a female disorder.

JANE, A 16-YEAR-OLD ANOREXIC

Sixteen-year-old Jane is the second of three children in a warm, middle-class, Irish Catholic family. She was an "easy" baby who never demanded cuddling. She was also a helpful toddler who learned how to fold clothes at two, a modest child who felt her active siblings deserved more attention than herself, and who, in family snapshots, often stood off to the side as if she were a spectator observing the rest of the family. Her parents are affectionate, but often preoccupied with their own troubles—Mr. Denton has just started a new business and Mrs. Denton is trying to cope with the death of her father. The Denton household has always been well stocked with food, but both parents have broadcast clear messages that thinness is desirable.

When Jane was 15, she felt very threatened by both academic and social aspects of school. She felt she had an ugly face, a dull personality, and too much fat (at 5'8", she weighed 135 pounds). She didn't know how to change her looks or personality, but she felt she could lose weight. Jane went from 135 pounds to 110 pounds and then stopped menstruating. Gradually, she began eliminating more foods; she subsisted by eating *only* applesauce and eggnog.

Jane spent many hours observing her body. She often would wrap her fingers around her wrist to see if it was getting thinner. At the same time, she fantasized that she was going to become a beautiful fashion model who would wear designer bathing suits. But even when she reached 90 pounds, Jane felt she was still too fat. She had disowned her body and even spoke in a whisper so that she would be inaudible as well as invisible. The thought of meeting a boy terrified her. Feelings of incompetence and loss of control overwhelmed Jane. Her parents begged her, and then nagged at her, to eat. They didn't seek clinical help, however, until she totally isolated and emaciated herself.

Anorexia nervosa has become an increasingly frequent problem among adolescent females.

In Jane's case, there were three areas of disordered psychological functions that often characterize anorexic adolescents. First, Jane experienced a disturbance of delusional proportion in her body concept; second, she showed a disturbance in the accuracy of cognitive interpretation of stimuli arising in her body, including failure to recognize hunger and nutritional needs; and third, she demonstrated a paralyzing sense of ineffectiveness that pervaded virtually all of her thinking and activities (Deutsch, 1982).

Bulimia often is a symptom of anorexia nervosa in its final stages, but it is also an eating disorder in its own right. Adolescents who suffer from bulimia frequently repeat a sequence of compulsive dieting, binging, and purging; in other words, they live their life dieting, eating, and throwing up. Like anorexics, bulimics do not feel in control of their lives. Most bulimics are not extremely overweight; they usually weigh between 10 and 30 pounds above average. But even when they reach their desired weight, bulimics feel anxious and out of control (Deutsch, 1982).

What influences obesity in adolescence?

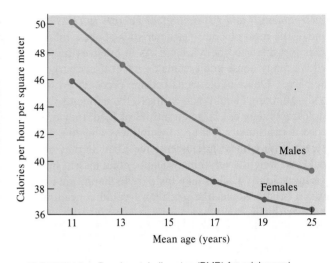

FIGURE 14.4 Basal metabolic rates (BMR) for adolescent females and males.

Obesity

While weight gain in adolescence is associated with the skeletal change in height, many other factors also influence weight. An increase in weight can be due to an increase in the fat content of the adolescent's body. Only about 5 percent of all young adolescents are obese, but by the time they fully reach adolescence, the number increases to 15 percent (Nutrition National Canada Survey, 1973).

Obesity may be defined as weighing more than 20 percent over normal skeletal and physical requirements. For the most part, this is indicated by an excess of fat content in the body. Obesity is influenced by many different factors, among them biological factors and environmental/psychological factors.

Biological Factors in Obesity   Biological factors in obesity include genetic influences, set point theory, and basal metabolism rate. Adolescents may have inherited a tendency to be overweight. In addition, it has been argued that the hypothalamus in the brain acts as a set point for the amount of body weight (Kessey, Boyle, Kemnitz, & Mitchell, 1976). The adolescent's **set point** is the weight he or she maintains when no effort to gain or lose weight is expended. If the adolescent is overweight and loses weight, then body weight goes below the set point. If the adolescent is underweight and gains

weight, body weight goes above the set point. Biologists argue that this set point in the hypothalamus is to some degree genetically transmitted but that it can be influenced by eating patterns.

An additional biological factor involved in obesity is **basal metabolism rate (BMR).** The basal metabolism rate is defined as the minimum amount of energy a person uses in a state of rest. To a considerable extent, BMR is genetically determined (although it can be regulated, within limits, through exercise or drugs). Adolescents with a high basal metabolism rate can eat almost anything and not get fat, while adolescents with a low BMR must constantly monitor their food intake to keep from gaining weight.

As indicated in Figure 14.4, an individual's BMR continuously drops from age 11 to age 20 (from then until old age, it begins to level off). Male adolescents generally have a slightly higher BMR than females. As young adolescents grow older, then, their basal metabolism rate drops, but their food intake does not usually decrease. This explains why there are fewer fat young teenagers than fat older teenagers. But even though BMR exerts powerful control over weight gain and weight loss, energy intake and output still strongly influence weight.

Environmental and Psychological Factors in Obesity

One of the most obvious characteristics of obese adolescents is a distorted body image. As in other eating disorders, many obese adolescents do not feel in charge of their lives. Obese adolescents become preoccupied with food—thinking about it and eating it. Even though obese adolescents may eat large quantities of food, they often sense a continuous feeling of emptiness and low self-esteem. Many obese adolescents feel that, if they only could lose weight, everything would be great in their lives. Losing weight "would make my parents happy, and the kids at school would like me; then I could concentrate on other things."

A typical example is Debby, age 17, who has been obese since she was 12. She comes from a middle-class family in which her parents pressured her to lose weight, repeatedly sending her to reducing centers and taking her to physicians. One summer, Debby was sent to a diet camp, where she went from 200 to 150 pounds. On returning home, she was terribly disappointed that her parents pressured her to reduce more. With increased tension and parental preoccupation with her weight, she gave up all efforts at dieting and her weight rose rapidly. Debby isolated herself and continued her preoccupation with food. Later, clinical help was sought. Fortunately, Debby was able to work through her hostility toward her parents and understand her self-destructive behavior. Eventually, she became willing to reduce for herself and not for her parents or peers.

Behavior modification programs have been developed for overweight adolescents. A typical behavior modification program consists of having the adolescent keep a daily chart of his or her eating patterns, become aware of circumstances that stimulate eating, change the conditions that promote overeating, give himself or herself a reward for good eating habits, and engage in an exercise program. Being involved in such a program for several months often is not that difficult for many individuals, but developing the self-control to maintain the program for one year or longer is very difficult.

One investigation at a Massachusetts girls' camp vividly showed why some people who exercise do not lose weight (Mayer, 1968). The obese girls actually were eating less than the girls of normal weight, but when they exercised, the obese girls exerted far less physical energy than the girls of normal weight. Activity charts suggested that the obese girls were just as likely to participate in sports and other physical activities at the camp as girls of normal weight were. But a critical difference between the physical activity levels of the two groups was that the obese girls did not exercise as vigorously as the normal-weight girls did. The obese girls played tennis, went swimming, and played volleyball, but they moved very lethargically. When a special camera was set up to provide details about their movements, the films indicated that more than 50 percent of the time in all physical activities the obese girls were motionless.

Feedback was given to the obese girls about their inactivity, and they were admonished to "work harder, exercise vigorously, and raise a sweat." The results were encouraging. Not only did the camp counselors get the obese girls to exercise more vigorously, but the girls did not increase their food intake either. Consequently, by creating a negative caloric balance between energy input and energy output, the girls began to lose weight.

In sum, family socialization experiences, a distorted body image, diet, and exercise seem to be among the most important environmental and psychological factors involved in adolescent obesity.

We have considered a number of problems that adolescents can encounter—the popular conception is that adolescents have more disturbances than children. Let's explore whether this is true.

Adolescent Problems Versus Childhood Problems

Are the problems of adolescents more pervasive than those of children? A number of prominent adolescent researchers believe that too much attention has been given to problems and disturbances in adolescence while ignoring the normal course of adolescent development (e.g., Adelson, 1979; Hill, 1983). They argue that most adolescents do not experience the intense turmoil or deep emotional disturbances that the traditional stereotype of storm and stress suggests. Has there been a tendency to overemphasize the degree to which adolescents experience emotional disturbances? Probably so, although there is no overall grand set of data that document the point that adolescents do not experience more emotional problems than children.

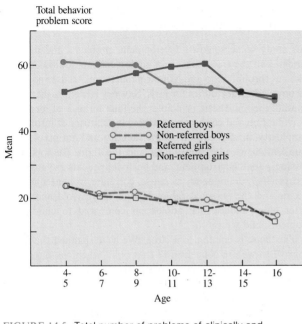

Total behavior
problem score

FIGURE 14.5   Total number of problems of clinically and
nonclinically referred children and adolescents aged 4–16.

One investigation by Thomas Achenbach and Craig
Edelbrock (1981), though, provides at least some support for this position. They investigated 1,300 children
and adolescents who were referred to psychological
clinics for professional help. As indicated in Figure 14.5,
the boys and girls ranged in age from 4 to 16, and the
adolescents who were referred for help did not have a
larger number of problems overall than the younger
children. Thirteen hundred children and adolescents who
were not referred for clinical help also were evaluated.
As indicated in Figure 14.5, the adolescents in the non-
clinical sample, just as in the clinical sample, did not show
a greater number of problems than the children. The
measure used to assess the children's and adolescent's
problems was the Child Behavior Checklist (CBCL),
which consists of 118 problems. In this study, parents
filled out the checklist by checking off which problems
their children had.

While Achenbach and Edelbrock's study did not evaluate the intensity or duration of the problems and was
not based on a national sample (it was conducted in the
Washington, DC area), it casts some gloom over suggestions that there is a dramatic increase in emotional

disturbances during the adolescent years. Indeed, as
noted in Figure 14.5, there actually was a tendency for
behavior problems to decline with age.

THE TRANSITION FROM ADOLESCENCE TO ADULTHOOD

As we move toward the end of our discussion of adolescence, we can look back and realize the complexity of
the path from childhood to adulthood, a path that involves many physical, cognitive, and social changes. In
Chapter 12, we saw that it is not easy to tell when a boy
or girl has entered puberty. Many psychologists, however, believe that the task of determining the beginning
of adolescence is easier than pinpointing its end. In concluding this book, it seems appropriate to think about
what constitutes the end of adolescence and the beginning of adulthood. Although there is no consensus about
when adolescence is left behind and adulthood is entered, the following description provides some ideas that
should be considered as we attempt to understand this
transition in the life cycle.

Faced with a complex world of work, with highly specialized tasks, many postteenagers must spend an extended period of time being trained in technical institutes,
colleges, and postgraduate centers to acquire specialized
skills, educational experiences, and professional training.
For many of them, this creates an extended period of
economic and personal "temporariness." Earning levels
are low and sporadic, and established residences may
change frequently. Marriage and a family often are
shunned. In many instances, this period lasts from two
to four years, although it is not unusual for it to last more
than eight years.

This stage, phase, or transition in development has
been called *youth* by some social scientists. Kenneth
Kenniston (1971) suggests that youth have not settled
the questions whose answers once defined adulthood—
questions of their relationship to the existing society, of
vocation, and of social roles and life-styles. Youth differs
from adolescence in the sense that there is a struggle between developing an autonomous sense of self and becoming socially involved in the case of youth, whereas a
struggle for self-definition represents the core conflict of
adolescence. Kenniston also believes that adolescents are

trying to develop toward an end point—an identity of self-definition—whereas youth already have such a sense of self and continually show an interest in change and development. Youth do not like being in a rut or getting nowhere in life but rather see themselves as on the move.

Two criteria that may signal the end of youth and the beginning of early adulthood are economic independence and autonomous decision making. Probably the most widely recognized marker of entrance into adulthood is the occasion when the young individual takes a more-or-less permanent full-time job. It usually happens when the individual finishes school—high school for some, college for others, and graduate school for still others.

For those who finish high school, move away from home, and assume a career, the transition to adulthood seems to have occurred. However, such a clear-cut pattern is the exception rather than the rule. One out of every four adolescents does not complete high school, and many students who finish college cannot find a job. Furthermore, only a small percentage of graduates settle into jobs that will remain permanent throughout their adult years. Also, attaining economic independence from parents usually is a gradual rather than an abrupt process. It is not unusual to find many college graduates getting a job and continuing to live, or returning to live, with their parents, particularly in the economic climate in which we live today.

The ability to make decisions is another characteristic of early adulthood that does not seem to be fully developed in youth. We refer broadly here to decision making about a career, values, family and relationships, and life-style. During youth, the individual may still be trying out many different roles, exploring alternative careers, thinking about a variety of life-styles, and considering the plurality of relationships available. The individual who enters early adulthood usually has made some of these decisions, especially with regard to a career and life-style.

THINKING BACK, LOOKING AHEAD

Our study of personality development, problems and disturbances, and the transition from adolescence to adulthood has taken us through Sam and Minnie's fourth son; trouser pockets for boys; clitoridectomies for girls; Sawyer, Hitler, Luther, and Gandhi; the epigenetic principle; the four statuses of identity; individuation and connectedness; the five statuses of intimacy; complexity in the path through identity and intimacy; the drunken cheerleader; marijuana and the India Hemp Commission; agent, environment, and host; delinquents as "animals in captivity"; delinquency as cause, correlate, or consequence; suicide and the personal fable; Jane, a 16-year-old anorexic; fatter older adolescents; adolescent compared to childhood problems; and youth.

This book is coming to a close. We have spanned the time from when we are conceived to that point when we make the transition from adolescence to adulthood. Prenatal development is a time Samuel Taylor Coleridge described as when events of greater moment likely occur than all the years that follow it. Conception is a time Jean-Jacques Rousseau portrayed as when we already are capable of learning. Infancy is a period when Erik Erikson says trust and independence are formed. The early childhood years are a time Pablo Picasso says he has spent his whole lifetime trying to return to in his search to be creative, free, and fanciful. Middle and late childhood is a time when Alistair Reed believes we are busy becoming something we do not fully understand. Adolescence is a time when Aristotle said we think we know everything and are very sure of it. And the perplexity of determining when we become an adult is captured in the words of Bob Dylan:

> How many roads must a man walk down
> Before you can call him a man?

SUMMARY

I. Information about identity involves Erik Erikson's theory, the four statuses of identity, developmental changes in identity, sex differences and similarities in identity, family influences on the adolescent's identity, measuring identity, and the relation of identity to intimacy.
   A. To learn more about Erikson's theory of identity, it is necessary to revisit the eight stages of the life cycle, consider personality and role experimentation, examine the complexity of Erikson's theory, and look at a contemporary view of identity development.

1. Erikson proposed that development through the life cycle occurs in eight stages. Identity versus identity confusion (diffusion) is the fifth stage in Erikson's theory, corresponding approximately with the adolescent years. Identity involves the adolescent's search for who he or she is as a person.
2. An important aspect of identity development is the opportunity to try out different personalities and roles.
3. Erikson's concept of identity is complex, involving the following components: genetics (including the epigenetic principle), adaptability, structural features, dynamic characteristics, subjective or experiential factors, psychosocial reciprocity, and existential status.
4. Identity development is a lifelong process, although it is during adolescence that, for the first time in development, physical, cognitive, and social skills are sufficiently advanced to allow serious inquiry and investigation into who an individual is as a person. Although some identity crises may be cataclysmic, the majority involve gradual development over many years.
B. Information about the four statuses of identity focuses on crisis and commitment as well as diffusion (confusion), foreclosure, moratorium, and achievement.
   1. Crisis refers to the exploration of alternatives, while commitment is the extent to which the individual shows a personal investment in what he or she is doing or is going to do.
   2. The adolescent who is identity diffused or confused has not undergone a crisis or made a commitment. The adolescent who is identity foreclosed has made a commitment but has not undergone a crisis. The adolescent in the identity moratorium status is in the midst of a crisis but has not yet made a commitment. The adolescent who is identity achieved has both undergone a crisis and made a commitment.
C. Developmental changes in identity occur in both early and late adolescence.
   1. Most young adolescents are identity diffused or foreclosed. Confidence in parental support, a self-reflective perspective about the future, and a sense of industry are important early adolescent characteristics that pave the way for the development of more mature identity exploration in late adolescence and early adulthood.

2. During the post-high-school years, the greatest shifts in identity are thought to occur as many individuals move closer to identity achievement. Some experts believe that college experiences promote identity exploration.
D. Early research indicated that a theme of vocational identity was more characteristic of midadolescent males, while interpersonal interests were more likely to reflect the identity of midadolescent females. However, more recent research has tended to reveal few, if any, sex differences in identity.
E. A family context involving individuation and connectedness likely is important in promoting healthy identity exploration and development.
F. Identity is a global construct, and like many such broad concepts, is very difficult to measure. The same problems associated with the assessment of self-concept apply to identity evaluation as well. Nonetheless, a number of researchers are working on improved assessments of identity—one such measure extends to interpersonal situations.
G. Ideas about the relation of identity to intimacy focus on Erikson's ideas, the five statuses of intimacy, research on intimacy, and the complexity of identity-intimacy pathways.
   1. Erikson describes intimacy versus isolation as the sixth stage in his life-cycle theory, coming after the crisis of identity versus identity confusion (diffusion) has been explored.
   2. Orlofsky describes five statuses of intimacy—intimate, preintimate, stereotyped, pseudointimate, and isolated.
   3. There is some indication that identity exploration prior to the kind of intimacy involved in a deep love relationship is a psychologically healthy developmental path.
   4. The link between identity and intimacy, however, is complex, and there often are different pathways to developmental maturity.
II. Drugs and delinquency represent two of the most pervasive problems in adolescence.
A. Our discussion of drugs focused on the actual use of drugs by adolescents, alcohol, marijuana, and preventive health efforts.
   1. Adolescents take a wide range of drugs, from licit drugs such as nicotine to highly illicit drugs like heroin. The most extensive data about drug use come from the Institute of Social Research at the University of Michigan through studies conducted by Johnston,

Bachman, and O'Malley. They have been surveying high school seniors on a national basis for a number of years. Almost two thirds of adolescents take an illicit drug at some point in their lives. The most widely used illicit drug is marijuana, while the most widely used licit drug is alcohol. At some point near the end of the 1970s and the beginning of the 1980s, a downward trend in illicit drug use by adolescents began. For the most part, males are more involved in drug use than females, although females take one type of stimulant— diet pills—far more often.

2. Alcohol is the most widely used of all drugs by adolescents. There has been a slight decrease in adolescent drinking since 1979, but heavy drinking remains alarmingly high. No specific personality profile has been linked to drinking, although alcoholic individuals do show a pattern of personal maladjustment, and adolescent drinkers seem to have stronger expectancies that alcohol will produce "personal effects." Family processes in some way likely are involved in adolescent drinking patterns. Prevention programs appear to have some success in discouraging alcohol abuse. Intervention efforts have not been very successful, but because adolescents with drinking problems are such a heterogeneous group, it seems important to tailor intervention programs to the individual adolescent.

3. The psychological effects of marijuana include relaxation, increased self-confidence, impaired motor coordination, reduced short-term memory, and distorted judgment. Many adolescents see marijuana as a pleasant alternative to harder drugs and alcohol. Studies reveal positive correlations between parental drug use and the use of marijuana by adolescents. Marijuana use has been declining.

B. An understanding of delinquency requires knowing what it is, what causes it, and sociocultural influences on delinquency.

1. A "juvenile delinquent" is an adolescent who breaks the law or engages in behavior that is considered illegal. It is a broad concept ranging from littering to murder. Estimates regarding the incidence of delinquency are sketchy, but at least 2 percent of youth are involved in court cases.

2. Many different explanations for delinquency have been given, ranging from biological instincts to independence and peer orientation. Erikson's ideas on identity development provide a framework for understanding delinquency.

3. The norms of many lower-class peer groups and gangs are antisocial. Getting into and, in some instances, staying out of trouble sometimes becomes a prominent feature of adolescent life in some lower-class settings. A community with a high crime rate exposes adolescents to criminal models whose behavior often may be rewarded. A considerable amount of attention has been directed at family influences on delinquency. In particular, Patterson's recent work is important in documenting the importance of parental monitoring and discipline in determining whether an adolescent will engage in delinquent behavior. The question has been raised as to whether family processes cause delinquency, are merely correlated with delinquency, or are possibly a consequence of delinquency. While the evidence is not completely clear, it seems that family processes do play at least some causative role. Also, delinquents tend to associate with delinquent peers.

III. Suicide and eating disorders are two other disturbances that may appear during the adolescent years.

A. Information about suicide focuses on its incidence, its causes, and prevention.

1. The suicide rate for adolescents has tripled since 1950, and suicide now has become the second leading cause of death in adolescence. Boys are more likely to use methods for attempting suicide that do not allow the adolescent's life to be saved, while girls more often use strategies that do not always produce death, which may account for the greater success rate boys have in actually committing suicide.

2. Suicide often is closely related to depression, so the developmental precursors pertaining to depression have implications for understanding suicide as well. Just as with depression, long-standing family socialization patterns likely interact with precipitating events in adolescence to produce a suicide attempt. The dramatic increase in suicide during adolescence likely is

tied to cognitive changes, particularly the adolescent's personal fable.

3. The personal fable makes suicide prevention difficult. Prevention efforts have not been very successful, as evidenced by the increase in suicide. Guidelines for what to do and what not to do when an adolescent is suspected of contemplating suicide have been developed.

B. Eating disorders have become prevalent problems in adolescence, particularly for girls. Anorexia nervosa (self-starvation), bulimia (binge-and-purge syndrome), and obesity are the three main eating disorders of adolescence. Problems that may contribute to anorexia nervosa include an overemphasis on the ideal body build in the culture, disturbances in cognitive interpretation of stimuli arising in the body, a sense that weight is one of the few things in the adolescent's life that can be controlled, and family processes. Like anorexics, bulimics do not feel in control of their lives. Both biological factors, such as genes, set point, and basal metabolism rate, and environmental and psychological factors, such as diet, exercise, family socialization experiences, and a distorted body image are involved in understanding obesity.

IV. Research data suggest that there is no increase in the total number of problems that adolescents encounter when compared with children, although this conclusion does not take into account the intensity or duration of the disturbance. It does appear that the abnormality of adolescence has been overestimated.

V. Defining when an adolescent becomes an adult is not an easy task. Kenniston stresses that a stage called youth exists between adolescence and adulthood. Youth is characterized by a "temporariness" in economic and personal affairs. Two criteria for entering adulthood are economic independence and autonomous decision making. While definite decisions about all alternatives in life may not have been made in early adulthood, the individual who enters early adulthood usually has made some decisions about a career and life-style.

KEY TERMS

agent interventions 607
anorexia nervosa 613

basal metabolism rate (BMR) 615
bulimia 613

connectedness 593
environment interventions 607
epigenetic principle 589
host interventions 607
identity achieved 591
identity crisis 585
identity diffused (confused) 590
identity foreclosure 591

identity moratorium 591
individuation 593
intimate 597
isolated 597
juvenile delinquent 606
obesity 615
preintimate 597
pseudointimate 597
set point 615
stereotyped 597
THC 604

SUGGESTED READINGS

Bruch, H. (1973). *Eating disorders.* New York: Basic Books. An excellent source of information about obese, bulimic, and anorexic adolescents.

Gold, M., & Petronio, R. J. (1980). Delinquent behavior in adolescence. In J. Adelson (Ed.), *Handbook of adolescent psychology.* New York: Wiley. An excellent overview of the nature of delinquency, developmental factors involved in delinquency, and intervention programs.

Journal of Early Adolescence (1983), *3.* This special issue is devoted to identity development, with particular attention given to the neglected topic of identity formation in early adolescence. Includes articles by leading thinkers and researchers, such as Marcia, Grotevant and Cooper, Adams and Montemayor, and Archer and Waterman.

Monitoring the Future (1975–1985). Each year, the Institute of Social Research at the University of Michigan publishes the national results of their survey on drug use by high school seniors. The volumes are edited by Bachman, Johnston, and O'Malley, the order of editorship varying according to the year published.

Weiner, I. B. (1980). Psychopathology in adolescence. In J. Adelson (Ed.), *Handbook of adolescent psychology.* New York: Wiley. Weiner's chapter represents an excellent analysis of some of the major disturbances in adolescence. Included is information about school-related problems, schizophrenia, depression, and suicide.

A

A–B error The infant's inclination to search for an object hidden in a familiar location (A), rather than looking for an object in a new location (B). (p. 173)

ABC method A learning-to-read technique that emphasizes memorization of the names of the letters of the alphabet. (p. 411)

abiding self One of the two facets of the imaginary audience as defined by Elkind; centers on a subject's willingness to reveal characteristics of the self that are believed to be permanent or stable over time; closely related to self-esteem. (p. 530)

accommodation In Piaget's theory of cognitive development, the act of modifying a current mode or structure of thought to deal with new features of the environment. (p. 57)

acquisition or storage components Processes used in learning new information; for example, rehearsing new information to transfer a trace of it into long-term memory. (p. 376)

adolescence The period of transition from childhood to early adulthood, entered at approximately 11 to 13 years of age and ending at age 18 to 21. This period is characterized by the onset of physical, cognitive, and social changes. (p. 16)

adolescent generalization gap The development of widespread generalizations and stereotypes about adolescents that are based on information about a limited set of adolescents due to a weak research base. (p. 505)

adoption studies A strategy of research used to assess the role of heredity in behavior by comparing an adopted child's similarity to his or her biological parents and to his or her adopted parents. (p. 90)

adrenal androgens Hormones secreted by the adrenal gland; associated with the adjustment of adolescent boys. (p. 510)

afterbirth The third birth stage; involves the detachment and expelling of the placenta, fetal membranes, and umbilical cord after delivery. (p. 108)

agent interventions Method of substance abuse prevention that focuses on the target substance itself through legal, technological, and social controls. (p. 607)

alphabetic system One of the three basic writing systems used in the world today; a system in which the visual symbols (letters) correspond roughly to the phonemes of speech. (p. 407)

amenorrhea Abnormal absence or suppression of menstrual discharge. (p. 507)

amniocentesis A procedure by which cells of the fetus are removed from the amniotic sac to test for the presence of certain chromosomal and metabolic disorders. (p. 84)

amnion A sort of bag or envelope of clear fluid in which the developing embryo floats. (p. 96)

amphetamines Synthetic stimulants that are usually available in the form of pills. Amphetamines are often prescribed for hyperactive children. For most people, amphetamines act as a stimulant, but for the hyperactive child, they have a calming effect. (p. 357)

anal stage Freud's second psychosexual stage, lasting from about 18 months of age to three years, during which the child seeks pleasure through exercising the anus and eliminating waste. (p. 47)

androgens Hormones that mature mainly in males and are produced by the sex glands. (p. 508)

androgyny A sex-role orientation consisting of a combination of both masculine and feminine characteristics in the same individual. (p. 467)

animism The belief that inanimate objects have "lifelike" qualities and are capable of action. (p. 274)

anorexia nervosa An eating disorder that leads to self-starvation; primarily found in females. (p. 613)

anoxia Lack of sufficient oxygen to the brain, causing neurological damage or death. (p. 108)

anticonformist Adolescents who react counter to the group's expectations and deliberately move away from the actions or beliefs the group advocates; rebellious. (p. 561)

Apgar scale Method used to assess the health of newborns one and five minutes after birth; evaluates heart rate, respiratory effort, muscle tone, body color, and reflex irritability. (p. 114)

aptitude The academic potential and personality dimensions in which students differ. (p. 455)

aptitude-treatment interaction A field of educational research that determines the best learning conditions for a particular student by considering the interaction between the student's abilities and various teaching methods. (p. 455)

artificial intelligence (AI) The field of inquiry involved with developing computers and robots that perform intellectual tasks that we commonly think of as characterizing human thought. (p. 348)

assimilation In Piaget's theory of cognitive development, the act of incorporating a feature of the environment into an existing mode or structure of thought. (p. 57)

association areas of the cortex Areas of the brain that govern the communication between other brain centers. (p. 134)

associative play A type of play in which there is social interaction with little or no organization. Children engage in play activities similar to those of other children; however, they appear to be more interested in being associated with one another than in the tasks they are involved with. (p. 316)

attachment A relationship between an infant and one or more adult caregivers during the developmental period of birth to two years; characterized by a unique bonding between the two social figures involved. (p. 215)

attribution theory Theory that views individuals as cognitive beings who attempt to understand the causes of their own and others' behavior. (p. 422)

authoritarian parenting A style of parenting that has a restrictive, punitive orientation and places limits and controls on the child with little verbal give-and-take between the child and the parent. This form of parenting is linked with the following social behaviors of the child: an anxiety about social comparison, failure to initiate activity, and ineffective social interaction. (p. 301)

authoritative parenting A style of parenting that encourages the child to be independent, but still places limits, demands, and controls on his or her actions. There is extensive verbal give-and-take, and parents demonstrate a high degree of warmth and nurturance toward the child. This form of parenting is associated with social competency of the child, particularly self-reliance and social responsibility. (p. 301)

autism A severe mental illness of early childhood; characterized by absorption in fantasy, isolation, and extremely defective thinking and language abilities. (p. 246)

automatic processes Processes that are independent of demands on limited attentional capacity, draw minimally on information processing capacity, and are difficult to control once initiated. (p. 63)

autonomy versus shame and doubt The second stage in Erikson's eight-stage theory of development, during which the child may develop either the healthy attitude that he or she is capable of independent control of actions or an unhealthy attitude of shame or doubt in that he or she is incapable of such control. (p. 51)

B

babbling Beginning of vocalization in an infant (three to six months old) that is controlled by biological maturation, not reinforcement or even the ability to hear. (p. 196)

baby talk register A way of speaking to babies, characterized by high pitch, exaggerated intonation, and simple sentences. (p. 194)

basal metabolism rate (BMR) The minimum amount of energy a person uses in a state of rest. (p. 615)

baseline A characteristic level of performance that can be used to assess changes in behavior resulting from experimental conditions. (p. 165)

Bayley Scales of Infant Development Developmental scales developed by Nancy Bayley with three components—a Mental scale, a Motor scale, and an Infant Behavior profile. (p. 179)

behavior genetics The discipline concerned with the degree and nature of the hereditary basis of behavior. (p. 89)

behavior modification The use of learning principles, most often those involving classical and operant conditioning, to change maladaptive or abnormal behavior. (p. 66)

biological processes The influences of evolution, genetics, neurological development, and physical growth on development. These factors contribute to the stability and continuity of the individual. (p. 17)

blastocyst The inner layer of the blastula that later develops into the embryo. (p. 95)

blastula An early embryo form typically having the form of a hollow, fluid-filled, rounded cavity bounded by a single layer of cells. (p. 95)

bonding The forming of a close personal relationship (as between a mother and child) especially through frequent or constant association. (p. 115)

brainstorming Effective technique used to stimulate creativity in which a topic is suggested, ideas are freewheeling, criticism is withheld, and combination of suggested ideas is encouraged. (p. 406)

Brazelton Neonatal Behavioral Assessment Scale A test that detects an infant's neurological integrity; includes an evaluation of the infant's reaction to people along with assessment of 20 reflexes and the infant's reaction to various circumstances. (p. 114)

Brazelton training Involves using the Brazelton scale to show parents how their newborn responds to people. Parents are shown how the neonate can respond positively to people and how such responses can be stimulated. Brazelton training has been shown to improve infants' social skills. (p. 114)

breech position The baby's position in the uterus that would cause the buttocks to be the first part to emerge from the vagina. (p. 111)

Broca's area Area in left hemisphere of the brain; important for speech production. (p. 187)

bulimia A binge-and-purge syndrome that is marked by periods of very heavy eating followed by self-induced vomiting; occurs primarily in females. (p. 613)

C

canalization A genetic principle that refers to the narrow path or track that marks the development of some characteristics. In other words, some human characteristics seem to be immune to vast changes in the environment and stay on track even in the face of drastic environmental inputs. (p. 89)

care perspective An approach to moral development proposed by Gilligan in which people are viewed in terms of their connectedness with other people and the focus is on their communication with others. (p. 483)

cephalocaudal pattern A general pattern of physical growth that suggests that the greatest growth in anatomical differentiation occurs first in the region of the head and later in lower regions. (p. 133)

child-centered education An education program that emphasizes the individual child and provides each child with a number of experiences to make education a fun-filled adventure in exploration. (p. 289)

chorionic villus test A procedure by which a small sample of the placenta is removed during the first trimester, between the ninth and tenth weeks, with the diagnostic results usually requiring two to three weeks. (p. 84)

chromosomes Threadlike structures in each human cell that come in structurally similar pairs (23 pairs in humans). (p. 86)

class inclusion reasoning Comparing the relative number of objects in a subset with the number of objects in the larger set. (p. 280)

classical conditioning Procedure by which a neutral stimulus comes to elicit a response by being paired with a stimulus that regularly evokes the response; also called respondent conditioning. (p. 162)

classical ethological theory The belief that behavior is biologically determined and that many patterns of behavior are transmitted by means of evolution. (p. 70)

Classroom Environment Scale (CES) Measure that attempts to evaluate the social climate of both junior high and high school classrooms through assessment of teacher-student and peer relationships, as well as the organization of the classroom. (p. 453)

cleavage divisions The early process of cell divisions that result in the formation of embryonic cell masses. (p. 94)

clique Peer groups that are smaller in size than a crowd, involve greater member intimacy, and have more group cohesion. Members of a clique are attracted to one another on the basis of similar interests and social ideas. (p. 562)

CMV (cytomegalovirus) An infection that is a member of the herpes simplex family and can be transmitted from the mother to the infant at birth. It infects the genitalia, urinary tract, and breasts and usually does not produce overt symptoms in the woman. The disease is latent and can become reactivated during pregnancy. (p. 102)

cognitive developmental theory Theory that focuses on the rational thinking of the developing individual and stresses that cognitive development unfolds in a stagelike sequence that is ordered and uniform for all individuals. (p. 53)

cognitive processes Mental activities, such as thought, perception, attention, problem solving, and language, that influence development. (p. 18)

cognitive social learning theory Theory associated with Bandura and Mischel stressing that environment-behavior relations are mediated by cognitive factors. (p. 66)

cohort effects Effects that are due to a subject's time of birth or generation, but not actually to his or her age. (p. 34)

compensatory education Programs designed to provide children from low-income families with an opportunity to experience an enriched early environment in an effort to place them on an equal level with other children who are not disadvantaged. (p. 290)

complex stepfamily A family in which both the stepparent and the biological parent have brought children to the newly formed stepfamily. (p. 443)

component An elementary information process that operates on internal representations of objects; a basic concept of componential analysis. (p. 376)

componential analysis Sternberg's information processing view, which attempts to understand the availability, accessibility, and ease of execution of a number of different information processing components. (p. 376)

conception The moment at which a male sperm cell joins or fertilizes a female ovum in the female's fallopian tube, marking the beginning of prenatal development. (p. 92)

concrete operation A reversible mental action on real, concrete objects. (p. 360)

concrete operational stage In Piagetian theory, the stage of thought that follows preoperational thought, lasting from about 7 to 11 years of age and marked primarily by a need to anchor thought to concrete objects and events. This stage reveals conservation skills and is characterized by decentered and reversible thought. (p. 56)

conditioned response (CR) The learned response to a conditioned stimulus. (p. 162)

conditioned stimulus (CS) An environmental event that elicits a response (CR) by being associated repeatedly with an unconditioned stimulus (UCS). (p. 162)

conditioning trials Each individual instance that the conditioning process is used. (p. 165)

conjugate reinforcement technique A technique used to investigate infant memory that has indicated that infants as young as two months old can remember for as long as three days. (p. 176)

connectedness Reflected in mutuality and permeability. Mutuality refers to the adolescent's sensitivity to and respect for the views of others. Permeability indexes openness and responsiveness to the views of others. (p. 593)

conscience Part of the superego that reflects children's moral inhibitions that are the product of their parents' punishments. (p. 44)

constructivist approach The belief that what one experiences is a construction based on sensory input plus information retrieved from memory--a kind of representation of the world one builds up in one's mind. (p. 142)

contact comfort Tactile stimulation believed to serve an important function in attachment. (p. 216)

contagion stage During this stage, concrete operational thought is dominant. The child believes that there is at least temporal or spatial proximity between illness and its source. (p. 264)

contents In Guilford's structure of intellect, the dimension of cognition that is figural (for example, visual or spatial), symbolic (for example, letters, numbers, or words), semantic (word meanings), or behavioral (nonverbal performance). (p. 394)

continuity-discontinuity A complex issue focused on at least three ideas: (1) abruptness/smoothness of stage transition, (2) connectivity of early and later development, and (3) degree to which human development reflects development in lower animals. (p. 20)

control The phase characterized by the emerging ability of infants to show awareness of social or task demands that have been defined by caregivers and to initiate, maintain, modulate, or cease physical acts, communication, and emotional signals accordingly. (p. 241)

control group The group in psychological experiments that is exposed to all experimental conditions except the independent variable; the comparison or baseline group. (p. 31)

control processes Learning and memory strategies that draw heavily on information processing capacities and are under the learner's conscious control. (p. 62)

conventional level The second level in Kohlberg's theory of moral development in which the child's internalization of moral values is intermediate. He or she abides by certain standards of other people, such as parents (stage 3) or the rules of society (stage 4). (p. 476)

convergent thinking A type of thinking wherein attention is directed toward finding a single solution to a problem; contrasts with divergent thinking. (p. 406)

cooperative play Play that is the prototype for the games of middle childhood in which a sense of group identity is present and activity is organized. (p. 316)

coordination of secondary circular reactions During this substage of sensorimotor development, the infant readily combines and recombines previously learned schemes in a coordinated fashion. (p. 170)

coregulation process A gradual transfer of control from parent to child; a transition period between the strong parental control of the preschool years and the increased relinquishment of general supervision that occurs during adolescence. (p. 442)

correlation A mathematical index used to express the degree of association between two variables. (p. 32)

correlation coefficient A measure of the degree of the relationship between two distributions (samples); ranges from +1.00 to −1.00. A positive coefficient means that the distribution increases together; a negative coefficient means that, as one increases, the other decreases; and a zero coefficient means that no correlation exists. (p. 32)

counterconditioning The elimination of a response by conditioning an incompatible response to the same stimulus. (p. 164)

creativity The term used to describe an act or contribution to society that is unique or original. (p. 404)

cretinism A severe form of mental retardation caused by a hormone deficiency in the thyroid gland. (p. 403)

criterion validity The extent to which a measure of a test can be correlated to another measure or can accurately predict another measure or criterion. (p. 394)

critical periods Certain time frames in development that are optimal for the emergence of certain behaviors. Specific forms of stimulation are required during these periods for normal development to proceed. (p. 71)

cross-sectional design A method used to study a large number of representative persons or variables at a given period in time; frequently employed in the establishment of normative data. (p. 33)

crowd The largest and least personal of peer group relationships. Crowd members meet because of their mutual interest in activities, not because of mutual attraction to each other. (p. 562)

crystallized intelligence Intelligence acquired through cultural contact, instruction, and observation; involves skills, abilities, and understanding. (p. 393)

cultural-familial Type of retardation in which there is a family pattern of below-average intellectual capabilities and a family history extending across more than one generation, with others in the family having the same profile. (p. 403)

culture-fair tests Intelligence tests developed in an attempt to eliminate cultural bias. (p. 396)

D

decrement of attention The amount or rate of decay in looking at a repeated or constant stimulus. (p. 181)

deep structure Concerns the syntactic relations among words in a sentence; employs syntactic categories, such as noun phrase, verb phrase, noun, verb, and article. (p. 184)

defense mechanisms Unconscious processes of the ego that keep disturbing and unacceptable impulses from being expressed directly. (p. 44)

delay of gratification Purposefully deferring immediate gratification for delayed but more desired future gratification. (p. 423)

demand feeding When the timing of the feeding as well as the amount is determined by the infant. (p. 131)

dependent variables Variables that are measured and recorded by the experimenter for changes that are presumed to be under the control of the independent or manipulated variables. (p. 30)

deprivation dwarfism Alterations in the release of hormones by the pituitary gland due to lack of affection, thereby causing growth retardation. (p. 259)

development Refers to a pattern of change or movement that begins at conception and continues throughout the entire life span. (p. 19)

developmental lag Term used to describe slow-developing ability in some children. (p. 357)

developmental quotient (DQ) An infant's test scores in four categories of behavior—motor, language, adaptive, and personal-social—combined into one overall developmental score. (p. 179)

developmental scales Intelligence tests that have been created for infants. (p. 179)

direct perception or **ecological view** Based on the hypothesis that we directly perceive information existing in the environment around us; there is no need to build representations of the world within our minds—information about the world is "available" out there. (p. 143)

dishabituation Renewed interest shown by an infant when a new stimulus is presented and distinguished from the old stimulus after habituation has occurred. (p. 174)

displacement The characteristic of language whereby an individual can communicate information about another time and place. (p. 183)

divergent thinking A type of thinking that produces many different answers to a single question. (p. 406)

dizygotic A term that refers to fraternal twins who come from two different eggs and are therefore genetically more different than identical twins. (p. 90)

DNA (deoxyribonucleic acid) A complex molecule running along the length of each chromosome; forms the basis for genetic structure in humans. (p. 86)

dominant-recessive genes In the process of genetic transmission, a dominant gene is one that exerts its full characteristic effect regardless of its gene partner; a recessive gene is one whose code is masked by a dominant gene and is only expressed when paired with another recessive gene. (p. 87)

E

early adolescence Refers to the junior high school years, roughly from 10 to 15 years of age. This period also roughly corresponds to puberty, the time of rapid change to maturity. (p. 17)

early childhood Also called the preschool years; extends from the end of infancy to about five or six years of age, roughly corresponding to the period when the child prepares for formal schooling. (p. 16)

echoing Repetition of what the child says to you, especially if it is an incomplete phrase or sentence. (p. 193)

echolalia A type of speech in which the child echoes rather than responds to what he or she hears. (p. 246)

eclectic orientation An approach that incorporates elements of different theories without strong identification with one particular theoretical model. (p. 74)

ectoderm The outer layer of the blastocyst; eventually becomes the child's hair, skin, nails, and nervous system. (p. 96)

ectomorphic body build Characterized by a thin body shape. (p. 349)

ego Freud's structure of personality that tests reality and mediates between the demands of the id and the superego. (p. 44)

ego ideal Part of the superego that indicates children's standards of perfection that are the result of their parents' reward of good behavior. (p. 44)

ego integrity versus despair The final stage in Erikson's eight-stage theory of development; involves retrospective glances at and evaluations of life. (p. 52)

egocentrism The inability to distinguish between one's own perspective and the perspective of someone else. (p. 270)

egocentrism in adolescence In adolescence, two types of thinking represent the emergence of egocentrism—the imaginary audience and the personal fable. Adolescents' egocentrism involves the belief that others are as interested in them as much as they are, personal uniqueness, and a sense of indestructibility. (p. 529)

elaborative rehearsal A control process that involves extended processing of to-be-remembered material utilizing organizational, elaborative, and imaginative activities. (p. 365)

Electra complex A Freudian conflict involving young girls that is parallel to the Oedipus complex in boys. The girl experiences sexual desire for her father accompanied by hostility toward her mother. (p. 48)

embryonic period A period lasting from about two to eight weeks after conception during which the ectoderm, mesoderm, and endoderm develop and primitive human form takes shape. (p. 96)

empathy The ability to participate in the feelings or ideas of another person. (p. 339)

endoderm The inner layer of the blastocyst; develops into the digestive system, lungs, pancreas, and liver. (p. 96)

endomorphic body build A rounded, somewhat "chubby" body build. (p. 349)

environment interventions Method of substance abuse prevention that focuses on the settings where substance abuse originates and where it can be prevented, such as at school, at home, and in the community. (p. 607)

epigenetic principle States that anything that grows has a ground plan, and out of this ground plan the parts arise, each one having its special time of ascendancy. (p. 589)

equilibration In Piaget's theory, the mechanism by which the child resolves cognitive conflict and reaches a balance of thought. (p. 59)

estradiol Hormone responsible for pubertal development in females; one of the hormones in a complex hormonal system associated with the physical changes of puberty in females. (p. 508)

estrogens Hormones that mature mainly in females and are produced by the sex glands. (p. 508)

executor responses Actions typical of attachment relationships, including clinging, following, sucking, and physical approach. Functionally, the child is the main actor in this type of response. (p. 216)

exosystem Refers to settings in which the child does not participate, although important decisions that affect the individual's life are made in these settings. (p. 208)

expanding Restating what the child has said in a more linguistically sophisticated form. (p. 193)

experiment A carefully controlled method of investigation in which the experimenter manipulates factors (independent variables) believed to be influential on a subject and measures any changes in the subject's behavior (dependent variables) that are presumably due to the influence of the independent variables. (p. 30)

experimental group The group of subjects in an experiment that is exposed to the independent variable. (p. 31)

external locus of control Perception that others have more control over an individual than the individual has over himself or herself. (p. 423)

externality effect   Tendency of infants up to one month of age to fixate on the external parts of a pattern and exclude the internal parts. (p. 175)

extinction   The last phase of a behavioral experiment, following the conditioning trials, in which reinforcements are removed and the conditioned behaviors gradually decrease or become extinct. (p. 163)

extrinsic motivation   Behavior that is influenced by external rewards. (p. 430)

F

family-of-twins design   A strategy of research in which comparisons are made between monozygotic twins, siblings, half-siblings, parents, and offspring to assess the role of heredity in behavior. (p. 90)

fear of failure   Refers to the individual's anxiety about not doing well, which can affect achievement motivation. (p. 420)

fetal alcohol syndrome   A cluster of characteristics identified in children born to mothers who are heavy drinkers. Children may show abnormal behavior, such as hyperactivity or seizures, and the majority of FAS children score below average on intelligence, with a number of them in the mentally retarded range. (p. 104)

fetal period   The period of prenatal development that begins two months after conception and lasts, on the average, for seven months. (p. 97)

fine motor skills   Skills involving more fine-grained movements, such as finger dexterity. (p. 134)

fluid intelligence   The type of intelligence that involves the individual's adaptability and capacity to perceive things and integrate them mentally. This kind of intelligence appears to be intuitive or independent of education and experience. (p. 393)

formal operational stage   The final stage of thought in Piaget's model of cognitive development; appears between 11 and 15 years of age, when the individual is believed to achieve the most advanced form of thought possible. The most important feature characterizing this stage is the development of abstract thought. (p. 57)

G

gametes   The sex cells; the means by which genes are transmitted from parents to offspring. (p. 86)

generativity versus stagnation   The seventh stage in Erikson's eight-stage theory of development; is positively resolved if an adult assists the younger generation in developing and leading useful lives. (p. 52)

genes   Segments of chromosomes; comprised of DNA. (p. 86)

genital stage   Freud's last psychosexual stage, lasting from the beginning of puberty through the rest of the life cycle, during which sexual energy is focused on others and work and love become important themes. (p. 49)

genotype   The unique combination of genes that forms the genetic structure of each individual. (p. 87)

germinal period   The period from conception until about 12 to 14 days later. (p. 95)

gestation   The length of time between conception and birth. (p. 111)

gifted child   An individual with well-above-average intellectual capacity (an IQ of 120 or more, for example) or an individual with a superior talent for something. (p. 403)

global self-concept   The sum total of an individual's feelings and perceptions about himself or herself, including his or her feelings about areas of competence, interests, uniqueness, and so on. This self-knowledge is a key organizing principle of personality, according to humanistic theorists. (p. 327)

gonadal   Refers to the sex glands. (p. 508)

gonadotropin   A hormone released by the pituitary gland that stimulates the gonads (ovaries or testes). (p. 508)

goodness-of-fit model   Theory of evaluation of the nature of pubertal timing; stresses that adolescents may be at risk when the demands of a particular social context and the adolescents' physical and behavioral characteristics are mismatched. (p. 520)

grammar   The formal description of syntactic rules. (p. 184)

gross motor skills   Skills involving large muscle activities, like moving one's arms or walking. (p. 134)

groups   Social structures that carry with them normative expectations about acceptable and unacceptable aspects of behavior and influence both the interactions and relationships of group members. (p. 549)

guilt   The affective state of psychological discomfort arising from a person's feeling of having done something morally wrong. (p. 339)

H

habituation   Technique used to study infants' perceptual world. Repeated presentation of the same stimulus causes a drop in the infant's interest. (p. 124)

heritability   A mathematical estimate of the degree to which a particular characteristic is genetically determined. (p. 90)

holophrase   A single word that implies a whole sentence. (p. 197)

homophobia   Fear of adolescent male that he will be perceived as a homosexual if he does not have sexual intercourse with a female. (p. 516)

hope for success   The equivalent of achievement motivation; the individual's underlying drive for success. (p. 420)

hormones   The secretions of endocrine glands; powerful chemical substances that regulate bodily organs. (p. 508)

host interventions   Method of substance abuse prevention that focuses on who will use the substance. This method builds cognitive and behavioral skills so that the individual will be able to resist substance abuse. (p. 607)

humanism   Psychological tradition that places a strong emphasis on the role of the self and self-concept as central to understanding development. (p. 327)

HVH (herpes virus hominis)   An infection that is mainly transmitted venereally and infects the vagina or cervix. If the virus is active in the mother when a child is born, it may infect the child. (p. 102)

hyperactivity   An increase in purposeless physical activity and a significantly impaired span of focused attention that may generate other conditions, such as disturbed mood and behavior, within the home, at play with peers, or in the schoolroom. (p. 357)

hypothalamic-pituitary-gonadal axis   Aspect of the endocrine system that is important in puberty and involves the interaction of the hypothalamus, the pituitary gland, and the sex glands. (p. 508)

hypothalamus A structure in the higher portion of the brain believed to be important in the regulation of hunger, temperature, emotional control, and other visceral functions. (p. 508)

hypothetical-deductive reasoning Ability to entertain many possibilities and to test many solutions in a planful way when faced with having to solve a problem; an important aspect of logical thought in the formal operational stage. (p. 523)

I

id Freudian part of the personality governed by the pleasure principle; contains all drives present at birth, including sexual and aggressive instincts. (p. 43)

identity achieved Adolescents who have undergone a crisis and made a commitment. To reach the identity achieved status, it is necessary for the adolescent to first experience a crisis and then make an enduring commitment. (p. 591)

identity crisis This term has been applied to anyone of any age who feels a loss of identification or self-image. Erickson believed it optimally occurs during adolescence. (p. 585)

identity diffused (confused) Adolescents who have not experienced any crisis (explored any meaningful alternatives) or made any commitments. (p. 590)

identity foreclosure Adolescents who have made a commitment but not experienced a crisis. (p. 591)

identity moratorium Adolescents in the midst of a crisis, but their commitments are either absent or only vaguely defined. (p. 591)

identity versus identity confusion (diffusion) The fifth stage in Erikson's eight-stage theory of development during which the adolescent may become confident and purposeful or may develop an ill-defined identity. (p. 52)

imaginary audience The egocentric belief that others are as preoccupied with the adolescent's behavior as he or she is with himself or herself. (p. 529)

immanent justice In Piaget's theory of moral development, the naive belief that punishment inevitably follows wrongdoing; part of the early stage of moral realism. (p. 336)

implantation The firm attachment of the zygote to the uterine wall that occurs about 10 days after conception. (p. 95)

implicit personality theory The layperson's conception of personality. (p. 532)

imprinting The process of establishing an attachment on first exposure to an object. (p. 70)

incentives External cues that stimulate motivation; can be positive or negative. (p. 431)

independent variables The factors in an experiment that are manipulated or controlled by the experimenter to determine their impact on the subject's behavior. (p. 30)

individuation The formation of the individual's personal identity, which includes the development of one's sense of self and the forging of a special place for oneself within the social order. Adolescents develop a more distinct view of themselves as unique persons and more readily differentiate themselves from others than they did as children. (p. 593)

industry versus inferiority The fourth stage in Erikson's eight-stage theory of development during which the school-aged child may develop a capacity for work and task-directedness or may view himself or herself as inadequate. (p. 51)

infancy Begins at birth and extends through the 18th to 24th month. A time of extensive dependency on adults. (p. 15)

infantile amnesia Phenomenon that, as children and adults, humans have little or no memory for events experienced before three years of age. (p. 178)

inferences A relationship noted between one event and another that is not directly stated. (p. 370)

infinite generativity Characteristic of language that allows a finite set of rules to generate an infinite number of sentences through sequencing. (p. 183)

information processing perspective Theory of cognition that is concerned with the processing of information; involves such processes as attention, perception, memory, thinking, and problem solving. (p. 60)

information theory An explanation of classical conditioning that stresses the informational value of the conditioned stimulus (CS); that is, the organism sees the CS as a sign of the unconditioned stimulus that follows. (p. 164)

initiative versus guilt The third stage in Erikson's eight-stage theory of development, occurring during the preschool years, during which the child may develop a desire for achievement or he or she may be held back by self-criticism. (p. 51)

innate goodness view Eighteenth-century belief that children are basically and inherently good and should be permitted to grow naturally with little parental monitoring or constraints. (p. 11)

insecure attachment Pattern of attachment behavior characterized by ambivalence of infant to physical contact, heightened separation anxiety, or avoidance of caregiver. (p. 219)

institutionalization The process of placing a person in an institution for corrective or therapeutic purposes. (p. 401)

intention-cue detection Interpretation of social behaviors based on the perceived intent or purpose of the behaviors. (p. 447)

intentionality The separation of means and goals in accomplishing simple feats. (p. 171)

interactions Patterns of communication that occur between persons who may or may not be intimates. (p. 549)

intermodal perception Refers to information that comes through more than one sensory channel; perceiving auditory and visual events in related, unified episodes rather than in unrelated ways. (p. 149)

internal locus of control Individuals' perception that they are in control of their world, that they can cause things to happen if they choose, and that they command their own rewards. (p. 423)

internalization of schemes A substage of Piaget's sensorimotor development in which the 18- to 24-month-old infant develops the ability to use primitive symbols. (p. 171)

interview A method of study in which the researcher asks questions of a person and records that person's responses. (p. 27)

intimacy in friendship Intimate self-disclosure and the sharing of private thoughts; private and personal knowledge about a friend. (p. 450)

intimacy versus isolation The sixth stage in Erikson's eight-stage theory of development during which the young adult may achieve a capacity for honesty and close relationships or may be unable to form these ties, resulting in a feeling of isolation. (p. 52)

intimate An individual who has been able to form and maintain one or more deep and long-lasting love relationships. (p. 597)

intrinsic motivation Behavior that is motivated by an underlying need for competence and self-determination; also referred to as mastery and competence motivation. (p. 430)

intuitive thought A substage of the preoperational stage, during which the child begins to reason about various matters and wants to know the answers to all sorts of questions. (p. 275)

in-vitro fertilization A procedure in which the mother's ovum is removed surgically and fertilized in a laboratory medium with live sperm cells obtained from the father or male donor. Then the fertilized egg is stored in a laboratory solution that substitutes for the uterine environment and is finally implanted in the mother's uterus. (p. 94)

IQ (intelligence quotient) Calculated by using the concept of mental age and comparing it with the child's chronological age. (p. 389)

isolated An individual who withdraws from social encounters and who fails to form an intimate relationship with members of the same or opposite sex. (p. 597)

J

justice perspective An approach to moral development proposed by Gilligan in which people are differentiated and seen as standing alone. The focus is on the rights of the individual (that is, on justice). (p. 483)

juvenile delinquent An adolescent who breaks the law or engages in behavior that is considered illegal. (p. 606)

K

kinship studies A strategy of research used to assess the role of heredity in behavior by comparing the genetic relationship between family members, including uncles, cousins, grandparents, and other more distant relatives. (p. 90)

L

labeling The identification of words associated with objects. (p. 195)

labeling Refers to the assignment of a label, or category, to a child and the effects that label or category may then have. (p. 353)

laboratory A controlled setting in which much of the real world with its complex factors has been removed. (p. 26)

Lamaze method A form of prepared or natural childbirth that involves a way for the pregnant mother to cope with the pain of childbirth in an active way to avoid or reduce medication. (p. 108)

language universals Certain features and consistencies that are shared by all or most languages. (p. 187)

late adolescence Includes the late teenage years and early 20s, roughly from 16 to 21 years of age. (p. 17)

latency stage Freud's fourth psychosexual stage, lasting from about age 6 to age 12 (the elementary school years), during which the child concentrates on such activities as school and getting along in society. Stressful problems of the previous phallic stage are repressed. (p. 49)

lateralization of language A concept referring to the evidence suggesting that language processing in the vast majority of people is controlled by the left hemisphere of the brain. (p. 187)

learned helplessness View of depression proposing that individuals who are exposed to stress, prolonged pain, or loss over which they have no control learn to become helpless. (p. 473)

learning A relatively permanent change in the mind or behavior that occurs through experience and cannot be accounted for by reflexes, instinct, and maturation or the influence of fatigue, injury, disease, or drugs. (p. 161)

learning disabilities Includes children diagnosed as dyslexic, children with minimal brain dysfunction, and children who are hyperactive. (p. 355)

Leboyer method A birth procedure developed to make the birth experience less stressful for the infant; "birth without violence." (p. 108)

logographic Alternative to the alphabetic system. Each visual symbol corresponds to a word. The Chinese writing system is logographic. (p. 407)

longitudinal design A method of study in which the same subject or group of subjects is repeatedly tested over a significant period of time. (p. 33)

low-birth-weight (high-risk) babies Infants born after a regular gestation period of 37 to 40 weeks, but who weigh less than 5½ pounds. (p. 113)

M

macrosystem The most abstract level in Bronfenbrenner's portrayal of culture; refers to the attitudes and ideologies of the culture. (p. 209)

mainstreaming The process in which children in need of special education are placed in regular classrooms rather than special classrooms. (p. 353)

maintenance rehearsal A control process that involves rote restatement or repetition of items. (p. 365)

mean The average score in a distribution of scores. (p. 390)

mean length of utterance (MLU) A measure developed by Roger Brown to chart a child's language development. Morphemes are used as the unit of analysis. (p. 281)

meiosis The process by which gametes reproduce, which allows for the mixing of genetic material. (p. 86)

memory The retention of information over time. (p. 175)

memory span task Task for assessing short-term memory. The individual hears a short list of stimuli, usually digits, presented at a rapid pace and then is asked to repeat the digits. (p. 279)

menarche The first menstruation in pubertal females. (p. 506)

mental age (MA) Concept developed by Binet that describes the general level of a child's intellectual functioning. (p. 389)

mental imagery A control process that involves using the construction of mental pictures or images to aid in memory or recall. (p. 366)

mental retardation Significantly subaverage general intellectual functioning existing concurrently with deficits in adaptive behavior and manifested during the developmental period. (p. 402)

Mental scale This scale, developed by Nancy Bayley, focuses on the following aspects of the infant's development: (1) auditory and visual, (2) manipulation, (3) examiner interaction, (4) relation with toys, (5) memory/awareness of object permanence, (6) goal-directed tasks involving persistence, and (7) the ability to follow directions and knowledge of the names of objects. (p. 179)

mesoderm The middle layer of cells in the embryo; becomes the circulatory system, bones, muscle, excretory system, and reproductive system. (p. 96)

mesomorphic body build Athletic, muscular body build. (p. 349)

mesosystem Refers to linkages between microsystems or connections between contexts; for example, the relation of family experiences to school experiences. (p. 208)

meta-analysis Involves the application of statistical techniques to already existing research studies. (p. 454)

metacomponents High-order control processes used for executive planning and decision making when problem solving is called for. (p. 376)

metamemory Knowledge of one's own memory, including knowledge that learning information is different from simply perceiving information, diagnostic knowledge of the various factors contributing to performance of different memory tasks, and knowledge of how to monitor memory during the course of learning. (p. 368)

metaphor An implied comparison between two ideas that is conveyed by the abstract meaning contained in the words used to make the comparison. (p. 525)

microsystem Refers to contexts in which the child has face-to-face interactions with others who are influential in his or her life. (p. 208)

middle and late childhood Extends from about 6 to 11 years of age and is sometimes called the elementary school years. (p. 16)

molar exchanges Global clusters of responses rather than specific behaviors. (p. 211)

monozygotic A term that refers to identical twins, meaning that they come from the same egg. (p. 90)

Montessori approach A philosophy of education, a psychology of the child, and a group of practical educational exercises that can be used to teach children. Children are permitted considerable

freedom and spontaneity and are encouraged to work independently. (p. 256)

moral autonomy The second stage of moral development in Piaget's theory. The child becomes aware that rules and laws are created by people relative to social systems and that, in judging an action, one should consider the actor's intentions as well as the act's consequences. (p. 336)

moral development The acquisition of rules and conventions about what people should do in their interactions with others. (p. 336)

moral realism The first stage of moral development in Piaget's theory. Justice and rules are conceived of as unchangeable properties of the world, removed from the control of people. (p. 336)

Moro reflex An infantile startle response that is common to all neonates but that disappears by about three to four months of age. When startled, the neonate arches its back and throws its head back, flinging out its arms and legs. The neonate then rapidly closes its arms and legs to the center of the body. (p. 125)

morphemes (morphology) The smallest unit of language that carries meaning. (p. 184)

motherese A characteristic way in which mothers, fathers, and people in general talk to young language learners. Sentences are simple and short with long pauses in between; intonation contours are exaggerated; stress is put on important words; and prompting, echoing, and expanding are used. (p. 193)

motivation The desires, needs, or interests that energize the organism and direct it toward a goal; involves the question of *why* people behave, think, and feel the way they do. (p. 418)

motor cortex Place in the brain that stimulates an action that must be coordinated with environmental information picked up by the five senses. (p. 134)

multiple-factor theory View that a number of specific factors, rather than one general and one specific factor, make up intelligence. (p. 393)

N

n achievement Refers to the need and motivation to achieve and the individual's internal striving for success; viewed as a general property of the individual, remaining consistent across different domains and time. (p. 419)

natural reaction An unlearned action on the part of the infant in response to a stimulus. (p. 124)

natural selection A principle that provides an explanation of the evolutionary process; the belief that humans and other organisms whose characteristics are the most adaptive to the environment are more likely to survive; thus, the more favorable characteristics are perpetuated through reproduction. (p. 85)

naturalistic observations (field studies) Research conducted in real-world or natural settings; for example, observing a child at home, in school, on the playground. (p. 26)

neglected children Children who are not necessarily disliked by their peers but who often do not have many friends. (p. 445)

neo-ethological view A biological view of development that stresses the importance of social relationships, describes sensitive periods of development rather than critical periods, and presents a framework that is beginning to stimulate research with human children. (p. 71)

neo-psychoanalytic theorists Contemporary psychoanalytic theorists who accept a number of Freudian ideas, such as unconscious thought and the developmental unfolding of personality, but place less emphasis on sexuality in development and more emphasis on the importance of culture in determining personality. (p. 50)

neurophysiological modulation Before the child is capable of self-control, the form of control in which arousal states are modulated and reflex patterns become more organized in terms of functional behavior; occurs roughly from birth through two or three months of age. (p. 241)

nonconformists Adolescents who know what people around them expect but do not use these expectations to guide their behavior; independent. (p. 561)

nonnutritive sucking Sucking behavior by the child that is unrelated to the child's feeding. (p. 127)

normal distribution Frequency distribution that is very symmetrical, with a majority of the cases falling in the middle of the possible range of scores and fewer scores appearing toward the ends of the range. (p. 390)

O

obesity Weighing more than 20 percent over normal skeletal and physical requirements. (p. 615)

object permanence Significant sensorimotor accomplishment in which the infant grasps that objects and events continue to exist even though the child is not in direct perceptual contact with them. (p. 172)

observational learning (imitation, modeling, vicarious learning) A form of learning in which new behaviors are acquired by observing others performing the behavior. (p. 166)

Oedipus complex A Freudian conflict beginning in early childhood in which the boy exhibits sexual desire for the mother and hostility and fear of the father. (p. 42)

onlooker play A type of play characterized by the child watching other children playing, but not joining in the activities. (p. 315)

open classroom Classroom climate that offers free choice of activities, space flexibility, varied learning materials, individual instruction, self-responsibility by students, multi-age grouping of children, team teaching, and classrooms without walls; opposite of traditional classroom setting. (p. 453)

operant conditioning (instrumental conditioning) A type of learning described by Skinner in which the individual operates or acts on his or her environment, and what happens to the individual, in turn, controls his or her behavior. That is, the individual's behavior is determined by the consequences of that behavior. Behavior followed by a positive stimulus is likely to recur, while behavior followed by a negative stimulus is not as likely to recur. (p. 65)

operations Internalized sets of actions that allow the child to do mentally what before was done physically. Operations are highly organized and conform to certain rules and principles of logic. In Piaget's theory, operations are mental actions or representations that are reversible. (p. 269)

oral stage The first psychosexual stage in Freud's theory of development, lasting from birth to around one year. This stage centers on the child's pleasure from stimulation of the oral area--mouth, lips, tongue, and gums. (p. 47)

organization The continuous process of refining and integrating every level of thought from sensorimotor to formal operational (Piagetian theory). (p. 59)

organizational processing The active grouping of input items into higher-order units or "chunks" to aid recall. (p. 365)

organogenesis The first two months of prenatal development when the organ systems are being formed; may be adversely influenced by environmental events. (p. 97)

orienting response (OR) Physiological changes that accompany increased attention to a stimulus. (p. 174)

original sin view Middle Ages, Catholic, and Puritan concept of children, reflecting the philosophical perspective that children are basically evil. (p. 10)

overextending The tendency of children to misuse words by extending one word's meaning to include a whole set of objects that are not related to or are inappropriate for the word's meaning. (p. 199)

oxytocin A hormone that stimulates uterine contractions and is widely used to speed up delivery. (p. 111)

P

parallel play A type of play in which the child plays separately from the others, but with toys like those the other children are using or in a manner that mimics the playing behavior of others. (p. 316)

parallel processing The simultaneous consideration of a number of lines of thought at a nonconscious level. (p. 60)

peer sociotherapy A process in which peers are trained to provide support and encouragement to each other in group settings. (p. 440)

peers Refers to children or adolescents who are about the same age or at the same behavioral level. (p. 310)

Perceived Competence Scale for Children Harter's measure emphasizing the assessment of the child's sense of competence across different domains rather than viewing perceived competence as a unitary concept. (p. 462)

perception The interpretation of what is sensed. (p. 141)

perceptual invariant An unchanging reference (from a fixed position) that is perceived by the senses. (p. 143)

performance components Processes used to carry out a problem-solving strategy. A set of performance components involves the actual working through of a problem. (p. 376)

periods Time frames that characterize a particular segment of development. (p. 15)

permissive-indifferent pattern A style of parenting in which the parents are very uninvolved in their children's lives, giving them considerable freedom to regulate their own behavior and taking a nonpunitive stance. These parents are rejecting as well as undemanding, and the result is usually a lack of self-control on the part of the child. (p. 302)

permissive-indulgent pattern A style of parenting in which the parents are highly involved in their children's lives but allow them considerable freedom and do not control their negative behaviors. This type of parenting is associated with children's impulsivity, aggressiveness, lack of independence, and inability to take responsibility. (p. 302)

personal fable Type of adolescent egocentrism that refers to the adolescent's sense of personal uniqueness and indestructibility. (p. 529)

personality processes The influences of aspects of individual personality on development. (p. 18)

perspective taking The ability to understand that other people have feelings and perceptions that are different from one's own. (p. 311)

phallic stage Freud's third psychosexual stage, lasting from about the third to the sixth year, during which the child focuses on the genital area. (p. 47)

phenomenistic stage In this stage, preoperational thought dominates. A child may explain the relation between sources of illness and the body in magiclike terms or believes that the relation is due to mere association. (p. 264)

phenomenological approach A theoretical view that places greater emphasis on understanding the individual's perception of an event than on the behavioral account of the event. (p. 327)

phenotype The observed and measurable characteristics of individuals, including physical characteristics, such as height, weight, eye color, and skin pigmentation, and psychological characteristics, such as intelligence, creativity, personality, and social tendencies. (p. 87)

phobia A strong, persistent, and irrational fear that is elicited by a specific stimulus or situation. (p. 164)

phonemes The basic units of language; single speech sounds. Phonemes are void of meaning. (p. 184)

phonics method Learning-to-read technique that stresses the sounds that letters make when in words. (p. 411)

physical development Involves detectable changes in physical and anatomical features, such as weight gain, overall height changes, growth of head and limbs, gross and fine motor development, and pubertal changes. (p. 18)

pituitary gland A small endocrine gland located at the base of the skull that is responsible for the secretion of hormones that directly affect the activity of glands elsewhere in the body. (p. 508)

placenta A disk-shaped group of tissues in which small blood vessels from the mother and the offspring intertwine but do not join. (p. 96)

play therapy Therapy that allows the child to work off his or her frustrations and serves as a medium through which the therapist can analyze many of the child's conflicts and methods of coping with them. (p. 314)

playing with improbabilities Technique used to encourage creativity that forces children to think about the events that might follow an unlikely occurrence. (p. 406)

pleasure principle Principle governing the id to constantly seek pleasure and avoid pain, regardless of what impact such

pleasure seeking and pain avoiding will have in the real world. (p. 43)

polygenic inheritance A complex form of genetic transmission involving the interaction of many different genes to produce certain traits. (p. 88)

postconventional level The highest level of morality in Kohlberg's theory of moral development, in which moral values are completely internalized and not based on the standards of others. The moral code that is adopted may be among the principles generally accepted by the community (stage 5), or it may be more individualized (stage 6). (p. 476)

pragmatics Rules that pertain to the social context of language and how people use language in conversation. (p. 185)

precipitate A delivery that takes the baby less than 10 minutes to be squeezed through the birth canal. The rapidity of this delivery may disturb the normal flow of blood in the infant, and the pressure on the head may lead to hemorrhaging. (p. 108)

preconventional level The first and lowest level in Kohlberg's theory of moral development. No internalization of morality occurs here. Moral thought follows the belief that morality is determined by the external environment, particularly rewarding and punishing circumstances. (p. 476)

preference The action of repeatedly choosing one object or stimulus over another. (p. 124)

preintimate An individual who has mixed emotions about commitment; reflected in the tendency to offer love without any obligations or long-lasting bonds. (p. 597)

premature birth Babies born before 37 weeks in the womb. This term has lost favor with scientists because it does not sufficiently distinguish early birth from retarded prenatal growth. (The trend now is to refer to babies born after a briefer than regular time period in the womb as short-gestation babies.) (p. 111)

prenatal period Extends from conception to birth. (p. 15)

preoperational stage In Piagetian theory, the stage of thought that lasts from about two to seven years of age and follows the sensorimotor period. Although logical thought is present, there are several "flaws," such as egocentrism, that limit the individual. (p. 55)

pretend play A type of play in which the child transforms the physical environment into a symbol by engaging in make-believe activities and playing out different roles. (p. 317)

primary circular reaction A scheme based upon the one- to four-month-old infant's attempt to reproduce an interesting or pleasurable event that initially occurred by chance. (p. 170)

primary process thinking The thinking of the id that involves the id's efforts to satisfy its wants and needs by simply forming a mental image of the object it desires. (p. 43)

processes The mechanisms that child developmentalists use to explain the nature of change in development. (p. 17)

products In Guilford's structure of intellect, products index the form in which information occurs—units, classes, relations, systems, transformations, or implications. (p. 394)

Project Follow Through A program instituted in 1967 as an adjunct to Project Head Start. Under this program, different kinds of educational programs were devised to see whether specific programs were effective. (p. 290)

Project Head Start Compensatory education program designed to provide the children from low-income families with an opportunity to experience an enriched early environment and to acquire the skills and experiences considered prerequisite for success in school. (p. 290)

projection Perception of one's external world in terms of one's personal conflicts; attributing one's own unacceptable and disturbing impulses or wishes to someone or something else. (p. 45)

prompting Process of rephrasing a sentence you have spoken if it appears not to have been understood. (p. 193)

prospective study A study where data are collected before the assessment of the outcome. (p. 105)

proximodistal pattern A general pattern of physical growth and development that suggests that the pattern of growth starts at the center of the body and moves toward the extremities. (p. 133)

pseudointimate An individual who appears to be maintaining a long-lasting heterosexual attachment, while the relationship actually has little depth or closeness. (p. 597)

psychoanalytic theory A view of personality that emphasizes the private, unconscious aspects of a person's mind. (p. 42)

psychometric The use of measurement to assess a concept of psychology. (p. 389)

psychometricians People who give tests or measures of tests to assess a concept of psychology. (p. 389)

puberty The point in development at which the individual becomes capable of reproduction; usually linked with the onset of adolescence; a period of rapid change to maturation. (p. 507)

punishment Refers to the situation in which a response is followed by an event that reduces the likelihood that the response will occur again. (p. 66)

Q

qualitative change Piaget's view that a child's intelligence is not simply less than an adult's but that it is intelligence of a qualitatively different kind. (p. 19)

quasi experiment An approximation to an experiment in which there is some loss of control over the independent variables due to the real-life manner in which they are defined. (p. 31)

R

reaction formation Freudian defense mechanism that wards off an unacceptable impulse by overemphasizing its opposite in thought and behavior. (p. 45)

reaction range A range of one's potential phenotypical outcomes, given one's genotype and the influences of environmental conditions. The reaction range limits how much environmental change can modify an individual's behavioral characteristics. (p. 89)

reality principle Abiding principle of the ego that finds ways to satisfy the wants and needs of the id within the boundaries of reality. (p. 44)

recasting Responding to a child's utterance by expressing the same or a similar meaning in a different way, perhaps by turning it into a question. (p. 195)

reciprocal determinism The belief that a person's psychological makeup is shaped by the continuous reciprocal interaction between behavior and its controlling conditions. In other words, behavior partly constructs the environment, and the resulting environment, in turn, shapes behavior. (p. 67)

reciprocal socialization A view of the socialization process as a mutual interaction between parents and the child. The child socializes the parent just as the parent socializes the child. (p. 211)

recovery of attention Novelty preference or response to novelty. Greater amounts of looking in the novelty situation are generally thought to reflect more efficient information processing. (p. 181)

reflexive smile A smile that does not occur in response to external stimuli. (p. 127)

register A way of speaking to address a particular category, such as babies, pets, or foreigners. (p. 194)

regression Freudian defense mechanism that occurs when the individual reverts to an earlier stage of development. (p. 45)

rehearsal The extended processing of to-be-remembered material after it has been presented; a control process used to facilitate long-term memory. (p. 365)

reinforcement Stimulation following a response that increases the probability that the same response will occur again in the same situation. (p. 66)

rejected children Children who are overtly disliked by their peers and who often have more long-term maladjustment than neglected children. (p. 445)

relational words Words that specify relationships among objects, events, or people. (p. 286)

relationships Patterns of communication that occur between people with enduring bonds to each other and are often marked by histories of past interactions as well as commitments to the future. (p. 549)

REM sleep Rapid eye movement sleep. (p. 129)

representation A model of the world built up in the mind and based on sensory input plus information retrieved from memory. (p. 142)

repression Freudian defense mechanism in which an anxiety-arousing memory or impulse is prevented from becoming conscious. (p. 45)

reproduction A process that involves the fertilization of a female gamete (ovum) by a male gamete (sperm) to create a single-celled zygote. (p. 86)

retention (or retrieval) components Processes involved in accessing previously stored information. (p. 376)

retrieval A control process that involves the use of certain search strategies to recover items from memory. (p. 366)

rhythmic motor behavior Rapid, repetitious movements of the limbs, torso, and head during the first year of life. These motor behaviors occur frequently and appear to be a source of pleasure for the infant. (p. 137)

rhythmic stereotypes Common rhythmic motor behaviors occurring during the first year of life that seem to represent an important transition between uncoordinated activity and complex, coordinated, voluntary motor control. (p. 138)

ritual Form of spontaneous play that involves controlled repetition. These interchanges are sometimes referred to as "turns" or "rounds." (p. 316)

role-taking or perspective-taking skills The ability to understand the feelings and perceptions that other people may be experiencing. (p. 340)

S

S-S learning The association in classical conditioning of an unconditioned stimulus (UCS) and a conditioned stimulus (CS). (p. 162)

saccadic movements Rapid movements of the eyes occurring three to four times per second; in infants, the method of scanning visual patterns in which the eyes fixate on one part of the pattern, then on another, then another, and so on. (p. 174)

satire A literary work in which irony, derision, or wit in any form is used to expose folly or wickedness. (p. 525)

scheduled feeding When the time and amount of an infant's feeding are determined by a regular daily schedule (for example, four ounces of formula every six hours). (p. 131)

schemata Active organizations of past experiences that provide a structure from which new information can be judged; a frame of reference for recording events or data. (p. 371)

scheme The basic unit for an organized pattern of sensorimotor functioning in Piaget's theory. (p. 168)

scripts Schemata for events. (p. 371)

second-order effects Third-party influences on the nature of dyadic relationships in families. (p. 213)

secondary circular reactions Schemes based upon the four- to eight-month-old infant becoming more object oriented, or focused on the world, and moving beyond preoccupation with the self in sense-action interactions. (p. 170)

secure attachment A positive bond that develops between the infant and the caregiver; promotes the healthy exploration of the world because the caregiver provides a secure base to which the infant can return if stressors are encountered. (p. 219)

self as knower A component of self-awareness that actively organizes and determines the quality of the person's experiences (the "I"). (p. 328)

self-control Differs from control by virtue of the appearance of representational thinking and recall memory. (p. 241)

self-efficacy A term generated by Bandura to index judgments of how well one can execute courses of action required in situations. (p. 433)

semantic elaboration The process by which information is encoded in a form that preserves the meaning of words and sounds. (p. 365)

semantics Language rules that pertain to the meaning of words and sentences. (p. 185)

semiotic function Piagetian belief that pretend play involves an overlay of meaning on sound patterns, images, or gestures. (p. 320)

sensation The detection of the environment through stimulation of receptors in the sense organs. (p. 141)

sensitive period Less rigid interpretation of the critical period that implies that a given effect can be produced more readily during one period than earlier or later. (p. 72)

sensorimotor modulation By the midpoint of the first year, infants actively use their sensorimotor abilities to modulate such matters as attention and social exchanges. (p. 241)

sensorimotor period The earliest stage of thought in Piaget's model of cognitive development, lasting from birth to about two years of age. This stage extends from simple reflexes through the use of primitive symbols as the means of coordinating sensation and action. (p. 55)

sensory cortex Place in the brain where environmental information picked up through the five senses is registered. (p. 134)

separation-individuation The process characterized by the child's emergence from the symbiotic relationship with the mother (separation) and the child's acquisition of individual characteristics in the first three years of life. (p. 238)

sequential designs Those research designs that combine the features of cross-sectional and longitudinal designs in a search for more effective ways to study development. These designs allow researchers to see whether the same pattern of development is produced by each of the research strategies. (p. 33)

set point The weight an individual can maintain when no effort to gain or lose is expended. (p. 615)

sex steroids Hormones, including testosterone and estradiol, that mature differently in males and females. (p. 510)

sex-linked genes Genes carried on the 23rd chromosome pair. (p. 88)

sex-role stereotypes Personality characteristics attributed to people on the basis of their sex without regard for their individuality. (p. 469)

short-gestation babies Refers to babies born before 37 weeks in the womb. (p. 111)

short-term memory A level of memory storage where stimuli are stored and retrieved for up to 30 seconds, assuming that there is no rehearsal. (p. 279)

siblings Brothers and/or sisters. (p. 303)

sign stimuli Naturally occurring stimuli that trigger unlearned behavior. (p. 70)

signalling responses Attachment behavior characterized by smiling, crying, and calling, in which the infant attempts to elicit reciprocal behaviors from the mother. (p. 216)

simple stepfamily A family in which the stepparent has not brought children from a previous marriage to live in the newly formed stepfamily. (p. 443)

social comparison The individual's seeking out of others within a peer group to evaluate his or her reactions, abilities, talents, and characteristics. (p. 562)

social desirability A response set characterized by the individual giving a response that he or she thinks is more socially acceptable than how he or she truly thinks or feels. (p. 27)

social mold theories Socialization process in which children are considered to be the products of their parents' socialization techniques and of their environment, particularly within the family. (p. 211)

social processes A person's interactions with other individuals in the environment and these interactions' effects on development. (p. 18)

social smiling Smile that occurs in response to a face. (p. 127)

societalism View of morality that argues that society is the source of all values, not the individual, and that moral development should be construed as a matter of the individual's accommodation to the values and requirements of society. (p. 484)

solitary play A type of play in which the child plays alone and independently of those around him or her, with little or no concern for anything else that is going on. (p. 315)

SOMPA (System of Multicultural Pluralistic Assessment) Battery of tests that includes information about the child's intellectual functioning in verbal and nonverbal areas, social and economic background, social adjustment, and physical health. (p. 396)

spontaneous recovery In classical conditioning, an increase in the tendency to perform an extinguished response after a time interval in which no additional stimulus or reinforcement is presented. (p. 163)

stages Sequence of qualitative changes in development that are age related. (p. 20)

standard deviation A measure of scatter or dispersion of a distribution. (p. 390)

standardized tests Questionnaires, structured interviews, or behavioral tests that are developed to identify an individual's characteristics or abilities, relative to those of a large group of similar individuals. (p. 27)

state anxiety Anxiety that comes and goes depending upon particular experiences. (p. 421)

stereotyped An individual who has superficial relationships that tend to be dominated by friendship ties with same-sex rather than opposite-sex individuals. (p. 597)

stimulus substitution theory An explanation of classical conditioning that argues that the central nervous system is structured in such a way that the contiguity of the conditioned stimulus (CS) and the unconditioned stimulus (USC) creates a bond between them that eventually allows the CS to substitute for the UCS. (p. 163)

storm and stress view View of adolescence proposed by Hall that sees adolescence as a turbulent time charged with conflict and characterized by contradiction and wide swings in mood and emotion. (p. 503)

structure of intellect A concept referring to Guilford's perspective of intelligence; proposes that an individual's intellect is composed of 120 mental abilities formed by all the possible combinations of five operations, four contents, and six products. (p. 393)

sudden infant death syndrome (SIDS) An as yet unexplained phenomenon in which infants die in their sleep without a known cause; also known as "crib death." (p. 106)

superego Freudian part of the personality that serves as the internal representative of the values of one's parents and society; the moral branch of the personality. (p. 44)

surface structure The actual order of words in a spoken sentence. (p. 184)

survey/questionnaire A highly structured interview in which the individual reads the question and marks his or her answer on a sheet of paper, rather than verbally responding to the interviewer. (p. 27)

syllabic writing system Writing system in which each written symbol corresponds to a spoken syllable. (p. 407)

syllogism A type of reasoning problem, consisting of two premises, or statements, that are assumed to be true, plus a conclusion. (p. 282)

symbol An internalized sensory image or word that represents an event. (p. 171)

symbolic function substage Substage of preoperational thought that exists roughly between the ages of two to four years. The child begins to use symbols (mental representations) to represent objects that are not present. (p. 270)

syntax A set of language rules that involves the combining of words into acceptable phrases and sentences. (p. 184)

systematic observation Method of data collection that is characterized by a well-defined set of objectives, including what is to be observed, where and when the observation will take place, how the observation will be made, and in what form the data are to be reported. (p. 25)

T

tabula rasa **view** Locke's view that children are not innately evil, but instead are like a blank tablet, becoming a particular kind of child or adult because of his or her particular life experiences. (p. 11)

telegraphic speech Speech that includes content words, such as nouns and verbs, but omits the extra words that only serve a grammatical function, such as prepositions and articles. (p. 200)

teratogen Any agent that causes birth defects. (p. 100)

teratology The field of study that investigates the causes of congenital (birth) defects. (p. 100)

tertiary circular reactions Schemes in which the 12- to 18-month-old infant purposefully explores new possibilities with objects, continuously changing what is done to them and exploring the results. (p. 171)

testosterone A male sex hormone important in the development of sexual characteristics and behavior. (p. 508)

thalidomide A sedative and antinausea drug that, if taken by the mother early in pregnancy, is associated with a number of malformations, (many of which involve arm and/or leg deformities). (p. 104)

THC (delta-9-tetrahydrocannabinol) The active chemical ingredient in marijuana that produces a "high." (p. 604)

three mountains task Three mountains of varying sizes are set on a square table, with one chair at each side of the table. The child is seated on one chair, and a doll is placed sequentially on the other chairs. The child is asked to identify what the doll is seeing from each of the three positions. (p. 270)

thyroid gland The gland that interacts with the pituitary to influence growth. (p. 511)

top-dog phenomenon Moving from the top position (in elementary school, as the oldest, biggest, and most powerful students in the school) to the lowest position (in middle or junior high school, as the youngest, smallest, and least powerful group of students). (p. 573)

trait anxiety The more or less stable and permanent tendency to experience a certain level of anxiety across time and circumstances. (p. 421)

transactive discussion Reasoning that operates on the reasoning of another individual. It is of interest to researchers who study the role of communication among peers in moral development. (p. 480)

transfer components Processes used in generalization, such as using information learned on one task to help solve another task. (p. 376)

transient self One of two facets of the imaginary audience as defined by Elkind; characteristics of the individual that vary over a period of time; not permanent fixtures of the self. (p. 530)

treatment Refers to the educational technique (for example, structured class or flexible class) adopted in the classroom. (p. 455)

trophoblast The outer layer of the blastula that provides nutrition and support for the embryo. (p. 95)

trust versus mistrust The first stage in Erikson's eight-stage theory of development, during which infants develop either the comfortable feeling that those around them care for their needs or the worry that their needs will not be taken care of. (p. 50)

twin study A strategy of research that focuses on the genetic relationship between identical twins (monozygotic) and fraternal twins (dizygotic). (p. 90)

two-factor theory A theory of intelligence stressing that intelligence consists of *g* for general intelligence and *s* for specific intelligence. (p. 393)

Type A behavioral pattern The Type A individual is excessively competitive, has an accelerated pace of ordinary activities, is impatient with the rate at which most events occur, and often thinks about doing several things at the same time. (p. 350)

U

umbilical cord   Contains two arteries and one vein and connects the baby to the placenta. (p. 96)

unconditioned response (UCR)   A reflexive and automatic response to an unconditioned stimulus (UCS). (p. 162)

unconditioned stimulus (UCS)   An environmental event that automatically triggers a response (UCR) without learning having to take place. (p. 162)

underextending   A tendency of children to misuse words by not extending one word's meaning to other appropriate contexts for the word. (p. 199)

undifferentiated   Refers to individuals who perceive themselves as neither masculine nor feminine in gender-role orientation. (p. 467)

unoccupied play   A type of play in which the child is not engaged in activities that are normally regarded as play. The child may stand in one spot, look around the room, or perform random movements that seem to have no goal. (p. 315)

V

validity   The extent to which a test evaluates what it purports to evaluate. (p. 394)

visual accommodation   Maintenance of high visual acuity over a range of viewing distances. (p. 144)

visual acuity   Sensitivity to fine visual detail. (p. 144)

W

Wernicke's area   Area of the left hemisphere of the brain heavily involved in speech comprehension. (p. 187)

whole-word method   A learn-to-read technique that focuses on learning direct associations between whole words and their meanings. (p. 411)

Z

zygote   A single-celled fertilized ovum (egg) created in the reproductive process. (p. 94)

zygote period   The early period of conception, cleavage divisions, the journey of the zygote to the uterus, and the development of embryonic cell masses; occurs during approximately the first three to four days after conception. (p. 94)

REFERENCES

A

Abel, E. L. (1981). Behavioral teratology of alcohol. *Psychological Bulletin, 90,* 564–581.

Abramovitch, R., Corter, C., Pepler, D. J., & Stanhope, L. (1986). Sibling and peer interaction: A final follow-up and comparison. *Child Development, 57,* 217–229.

Achenbach, T. M., & Edelbrock, C. S. (1981). Behavioral problems and competencies reported by parents of normal and disturbed children aged four through sixteen. *Monographs of the Society for Research in Child Development, 46* (1, Serial No. 188).

Acredolo, L. P. (1978). Development of spatial orientation in infancy. *Developmental Psychology, 14,* 224–234.

Acredolo, L. P. (1979). Laboratory versus home: The effect of the environment on the nine-month-old infant's choice of spatial reference system. *Developmental Psychology, 15,* 666–667.

Acredolo, L. P., & Evans, D. (1980). Developmental changes in the effects of landmarks on infant spatial behavior. *Developmental Psychology, 16,* 312–318.

Acredolo, L. P., & Hake, J. L. (1982). Infant perception. In B. B. Wolman (Ed.), *Handbook of developmental psychology.* Englewood Cliffs, NJ: Prentice-Hall.

Adams, G., & Fitch, S. A. (1982). Ego state and identity status development: A cross-sequential analysis. *Journal of Personality and Social Psychology, 43,* 574–583.

Adams, G., & Jones, R. (1981). Imaginary audience behavior: A validation study. *Journal of Early Adolescence, 1,* 1–10.

Adams, G. R., & Montemayor, R. (1983). Identity formation during early adolescence. *Journal of Early Adolescence, 3,* 193–202.

Adelson, J. (1979, January). Adolescence and the generalization gap. *Psychology Today,* pp. 33–37.

Adelson, J., & Doehrman, M. J. (1980). The psychodynamic approach to adolescence. In J. Adelson (Ed.), *Handbook of adolescent psychology.* New York: Wiley.

Ainsworth, M. D. S. (1967). *Infancy in Uganda: Infant care and the growth of love.* Baltimore, MD: Johns Hopkins University Press.

Ainsworth, M. D. S. (1973). The development of mother-infant attachment. In B. Caldwell & H. N. Riccuiti (Eds.), *Review of child development research,* Vol. 3. Chicago: University of Chicago Press.

Ainsworth, M. D. S. (1979). Infant-mother attachment. *American Psychologist, 34,* 932–937.

Akiyami, M. M. (1984). Are language-acquisition strategies universal? *Developmental Psychology, 20,* 219–228.

Allen, C. (1965). Photographing the TV audience. *Journal of Advertising Research, 14,* 2–8.

Allen, G. L., Kirasic, K. C., & King, S. (1985, April). *Preschool children's use of spatial frames of reference in seeking, finding, and remembering where.* Paper presented at the biennial meeting of the Society for Research in Child Development, Toronto.

Altus, W. D. (1970). Marriage and order of birth. *Proceedings of the 78th Annual Convention of the American Psychological Association, 5,* 361–362.

Ames, C. (1984). Competitive, cooperative, and individualistic goal structures: A cognitive-motivational analysis. In R. E. Ames & C. Ames (Eds.), *Motivation in education.* New York: Academic Press.

Ames, R. E., & Ames, C. (Eds.). (1984). *Motivation in education.* New York: Academic Press.

Ames, R. E., Ames, C., & Garrison, W. (1977). Children's causal ascriptions for positive and negative interpersonal outcomes. *Psychological Reports, 41,* 595–602.

Amsterdam, B. K. (1968). *Mirror behavior in children under two years of age.* Unpublished doctoral dissertation. University of North Carolina, Chapel Hill.

Anastasi, A. (1976). *Psychological testing* (2nd ed.). New York: Macmillan.

Anders, T. F., & Chalemian, R. J. (1974). The effect of circumcision on sleep-wake states in human neonates. *Psychosomatic Medicine, 36,* 174–179.

Anderson, D., Lorch, E., Smith, R., Bradford, R., & Levin, S. (1981). Effects of peer presence on preschool children's television viewing behavior. *Developmental Psychology, 17,* 446–453.

Anderson, D. R., & Levin, S. R. (1976). Young children's attention to "Sesame Street." *Child Development, 47,* 806–811

Anderson, D. R., & Lorch, E. P. (1983). Looking at television: Action or reaction? In J. Bryant & D. R. Anderson (Eds.), *Children's understanding of television: Research on attention and comprehension.* New York: Academic Press.

Anderson, D. R., Lorch, E. P., Field, D. E., Collins, P. A., & Nathan, J. G. (1985, April). *Television viewing at home: Age trends in visual attention and time with TV.* Paper presented at the biennial meeting of the Society for Research in Child Development, Toronto.

Anderson, J. R. (1976). *Language, memory, and thought.* Hillsdale, NJ: Erlbaum.

Anderson, J. R. (1980). *A theory of language acquisition based on general learning principles.* Unpublished manuscript, Carnegie-Mellon University, Pittsburgh.

Andrews, G. R., & Debus, R. L. (1978). Persistence and causal perception of failure: Modifying cognitive attributions. *Journal of Educational Psychology, 70,* 154–166.

Andrews, S. R., Blumenthal, J. M., Bache, W. L., & Weiner, G. (1975, April). *The New Orleans model: Parents as early childhood educators.* Paper presented at the meeting of the Society for Research in Child Development, Denver.

Anglin, J. M. (1970). *The growth of word meaning.* Cambridge, MA: MIT Press.

Antill, J. K., & Cunningham, J. D. (1979). Self-esteem as a function of masculinity in both sexes. *Journal of Consulting and Clinical Psychology, 47,* 783–785.

Apgar, V. A. (1953). A proposal for a new method of evaluation of a newborn infant. *Anesthesia and Analgesia: Current Research, 32,* 260–267.

Archer, S. L. (1982). The lower age boundaries of identity development. *Child Development, 53,* 1551–1556.

Archer, S. L. (1985, April). *Reflections on earlier life decisions: Implications for adult functioning.* Paper presented at the biennial meeting of the Society for Research in Child Development, Toronto.

Aries, P. (1962). *Centuries of childhood* (R. Baldrick, Trans.). New York: Knopf.

Armsden, G. G., & Greenberg, M. T. (1982). *The inventory of parent and peer attachment: Individual differences and their relationship to psychological well-being.* Unpublished manuscript, University of Washington, Seattle.

Asarnow, J. R., & Callan, J. W. (1985). Boys with peer adjustment problems: Social cognitive processes. *Journal of Consulting and Clinical Psychology, 53,* 80–87.

Asarnow, R. F., & Asarnow, J. R. (1982). Attention-information processing dysfunction and vulnerability to schizophrenia: Implications for prevention. In M. Goldstein & E. Rodnick (Eds.), *Preventive intervention in schizophrenia.* Washington, DC: U.S. Government Printing Office.

Asberg, M., Thoren, P., Traskman, L., Bertilsson, L., & Ringberger, V. (1976). Serotonin depression, a biochemical subgroup within the affective disorders. *Science, 191,* 478–480.

Asher, J., & Garcia, R. (1969). The optimal age to learn a foreign language. *Modern Language Journal, 53,* 334–341.

Asher, S. R., & Dodge, K. A. (1986). Identifying children who are rejected by their peers. *Developmental Psychology, 22,* 444–449.

Asher, S. R., & Renshaw, P. D. (1981). Children without friends: Social knowledge and social skill training. In S. R. Asher & J. M. Gottman (Eds.), *The development of children's friendships.* New York: Cambridge University Press.

Asher, S. R., & Wheeler, V. A. (1985). Children's loneliness: A comparison of rejected and neglected peer status. *Journal of Consulting and Clinical Psychology, 53,* 500–505.

Ashmead, D. H., & Perlmutter, M. (1979, September). *Infant memory in everyday life.* Paper presented at the meeting of the American Psychological Association, New York.

Ashmead, D. H., & Perlmutter, M. (1980). Infant memory in everyday life. In M. Perlmutter (Ed.), *New directions in child development, 10: Childrens' memory.* San Francisco: Jossey-Bass.

Aslin, R. N., Pisoni, D. B., & Jusczyk, P. W. (1983). Auditory development and speech perception in infancy. In P. H. Mussen (Ed.), *Handbook of child psychology* (4th ed.), Vol. 2. New York: Wiley.

Atkinson, J. W., & Feather, N. T. (Eds.). (1966). *A theory of achievement motivation.* New York: Wiley.

Atkinson, J. W., & Raynor, I. O. (1974). *Motivation and achievement.* Washington, DC: Winston & Sons.

Attneave, F., & Farrar, P. (1977). The visual world behind the head. *American Journal of Psychology, 90,* 549–563.

Ausubel, D. P. (1968). *Educational psychology.* New York: Holt, Rinehart & Winston.

Ausubel, D. P., Sullivan, E. V., & Eves, S. W. (1979). *Theory and problems of child development* (3rd ed.). New York: Grune & Stratton.

Axia, G., & Baroni, M. R. (1985). Linguistic politeness at different age levels. *Child Development, 56,* 918–927.

B

Bachman, J. G. (1982, June). *The American high school student: A profile based on national survey data.* Paper presented at a conference entitled, "The American High School Today and Tomorrow," Berkeley, CA.

Bahrick, L. E. (1983). Infants' perception of substance and temporal synchrony in multi-modal events. *Infant Behavior and Development, 6,* 429–451.

Bakeman, R., & Brown, J. V. (1980). Early interaction: Consequences for social and mental development at three years. *Child Development, 51,* 437–447.

Baldwin, A. L. (1946). Differences in parent behavior toward three- and nine-year-old children. *Journal of Personality, 15,* 143–165.

Ball, S. J. (1981). *Beachside comprehensive.* Cambridge, England: Cambridge University Press.

Baltes, P. B. (1973). Prototypical paradigms and questions in life-span research on development and aging. *The Gerontologist, 13,* 458–467.

Baltes, P. B., Reese, H. W., & Lipsitt, L. P. (1980). Life-span developmental psychology. *Annual Review of Psychology, 31,* 65–110.

Bandura, A. (1971). *Social learning theory.* Englewood Cliffs, NJ: Prentice-Hall.

Bandura, A. (1977). *Social learning theory.* Englewood Cliffs, NJ: Prentice-Hall.

Bandura, A. (1981). Self-referent thought: A developmental analysis of self-efficacy. In J. H. Flavell & L. Ross (Eds.), *Social cognitive development.* Cambridge, England: Cambridge University Press.

Bandura, A. (1986). *Social foundations of thought and action: A social cognitive theory.* Englewood Cliffs, NJ: Prentice-Hall.

Bane, M. J. (1978). *HEW policy toward children, youth, and families.* Discussion paper prepared under Order #SA–8139–77 for the Office of the Assistant Secretary for Planning and Evaluation, Cambridge, MA.

Banks, M. S., & Salapatek, P. (1983). Infant visual perception. In P. H. Mussen (Ed.), *Handbook of child psychology* (4th ed.), Vol. 2. New York: Wiley.

Barcus, F. E. (1978). *Commercial children's television on weekends and weekday afternoons.* Newtonville, MA: Action for Children's Television.

Barenboim, C. (1977). Developmental changes in the interpersonal cognitive system from middle childhood to adolescence. *Child Development, 48,* 1467–1474.

Barenboim, C. (1981). The development of person perception in childhood and adolescence: From behavioral comparisons to psychological constructs to psychological comparisons. *Child Development, 52,* 129–144.

Barenboim, C. (1985, April). *Person perception and interpersonal behavior.* Paper presented at the biennial meeting of the Society for Research in Child Development, Toronto.

Barker, R., & Wright, H. F. (1951). *One boy's day.* New York: Harper & Row.

Barker, R. G., & Wright, H. F. (1955). *Midwest and its children.* New York: Harper & Row.

Barnes, G. M. (1977). The development of adolescent drinking behavior: An evaluative review of the impact of the socialization process within the family. *Adolescence, 13,* 571–591.

Barnes, G. M. (1984). Adolescent alcohol abuse and other problem behaviors: Their relationships and common parental influences. *Journal of Youth and Adolescence, 13,* 329–348.

Barnes, K. E. (1971). Preschool play norms: A replication. *Developmental Psychology, 5,* 99–103.

Barrett, D. E., Radke-Yarrow, M., & Klein, R. E. (1982). Chronic malnutrition and child behavior: Effects of caloric supplementation on social and emotional functioning at school age. *Developmental Psychology, 18,* 541–556.

Barron, F. (1985). *Rationality and intelligence.* Cambridge, England: Cambridge University Press.

Bart, W. M. (1971). The factor structure of formal operations. *British Journal of Educational Psychology, 41,* 40–77.

Bartel, N. R., & Guskin, S. L. (1971). A handicap as a social phenomena. In W. M. Cruikshank (Ed.), *Psychology of exceptional children and youth.* Englewood Cliffs, NJ: Prentice-Hall.

Bartlett, F. C. (1932). *Remembering: A study in experimental and social psychology.* Cambridge, MA: Cambridge University Press.

Baskett, L. (1974). *The young child's interactions with parents and siblings: A behavioral analysis.* Unpublished doctoral dissertation, University of Oregon.

Baskett, L. M., & Johnson, S. M. (1982). The young child's interaction with parents versus siblings. *Child Development, 53,* 643–650.

Bates, E. (1979). *The emergence of symbols: Cognition and communication in infancy.* New York: Academic Press.

Bates, E., & MacWhinney, B. (1982). A functionalist approach to grammatical development. In L. Gleitman & H. E. Wanner (Eds.), *Language acquisition: The state of the art.* Cambridge, MA: Cambridge University Press.

Baucom, D. H. (1976). Independent masculinity and femininity scales on the California Psychological Inventory. *Journal of Consulting and Clinical Psychology, 44,* 876.

Baucom, D. H., & Danker-Brown, P. (1979). Influence of sex roles on the development of learned helplessness. *Journal of Consulting and Clinical Psychology, 47,* 928–936.

Baumrind, D. (1971). Current patterns of parental authority. *Developmental Psychology Monographs, 4* (1, Pt. 2).

Baumrind, D. (1972). Socialization and instrumental competence in young children. In W. W. Hartup (Ed.), *The young child,* Vol. 2. Washington, DC: National Association for the Education of Young Children.

Bayley, N. (1969). *Manual for the Bayley Scales of Infant Development.* New York: Psychological Corporation.

Bayley, N. (1970). Development of mental abilities. In P. H. Mussen (Ed.), *Handbook of child psychology* (3rd ed.), Vol. 1. New York: Wiley.

Bechtel, R., Achelpohl, C., & Akers, R. (1972). Correlates between observed behavior and questionnaire responses on television viewing. In Rubenstein, E. A., Comstock, G. A., & J. P. Murray (Eds.), *Television and Social Behavior.* Vol. 4. Washington, DC: U.S. Government Printing Office.

Beck, A. T. (1967). *Depression.* New York: Harper & Row.

Beck, A. T. (1973). *The diagnosis and management of depression.* Philadelphia: University of Pennsylvania Press.

Becker, W. (1971). *Parents are teachers.* Champaign, IL: Research Press.

Bell, D. (Ed.). (1980). *Shades of brown.* New York: Teachers College Press.

Bell, S. M. (1970). The development of the concept of the object as related to mother-infant attachment. *Child Development, 41,* 291–311.

Bell, S. M., & Ainsworth, M. D. S. (1972). Infant crying and maternal responsiveness. *Child Development, 43,* 1171–1190.

Belsky, J. (1981). Early human experience: A family perspective. *Developmental Psychology, 17,* 3–23.

Belsky, J., Gilstrap, B., & Rovine, M. (1984). The Pennsylvania Infant and Family Development Project I: Stability and change in mother-infant and father-infant interaction in a family setting at one, three, and nine months. *Child Development, 55,* 692–705.

Belsky, J., & Most, R. (1981). From exploration to play: A cross-sectional study of infant free play behavior. *Developmental Psychology, 17,* 630–639.

Belsky, J., Rovine, M., & Taylor, D. G. (1984). The Pennsylvania Infant and Family Development Project III: The origins of individual differences in infant-mother attachment: Maternal and infant contributions. *Child Development, 55,* 718–728.

Belsky, J., & Steinberg, L. D. (1978). The effects of day care: A critical review. *Child Development, 49,* 929–949.

Bem, S. L. (1974). The measurement of psychological androgyny. *Journal of Consulting and Clinical Psychology, 42,* 155–162.

Bem, S. L. (1977). On the utility of alternative procedures for assessing psychological androgyny. *Journal of Consulting and Clinical Psychology, 45,* 196–205.

Bender, L. (1968). Neuropsychiatric disturbance in dyslexia. In A. H. Keeney & V. J. Keeney (Eds.), *Dyslexia.* St. Louis, MO: Mosby.

Bereiter, C., & Scardamalia, M. (1982). From conversation to composition: The role of instruction in a developmental process. In R. Glaser (Ed.), *Advances in instructional psychology,* Hillsdale, NJ: Erlbaum.

Berg, C. A., & Sternberg, R. J. (1985, April). *Novelty as a component of intelligence throughout development.* Paper presented at the meeting of the Society for Research in Child Development, Toronto.

Berg, W. K., & Berg, K. M. (1979). Psychophysiological development in infancy: State, sensory function, and attention. In J. D. Osofsky (Ed.), *Handbook of infant development.* New York: Wiley.

Berkeley, G. (1709/1923). An essay toward a new theory of vision. In *Theory of vision and other writings* by Bishop Berkeley. London: Dent.

Berko, J. (1958). The child's learning of English morphology. *Word, 14,* 150–177.

Berkowitz, M. (1981). A critical appraisal of the educational and psychological perspectives on moral discussion. *Journal of Educational Thought, 15,* 20–33.

Berkowitz, M., & Gibbs, J. (1983). Measuring the developmental features of moral discussion. *Merrill-Palmer Quarterly, 29,* 399–410.

Berkowitz, M., Gibbs, J., & Broughton, J. (1980). The relation of moral judgment stage disparity to development effects of peer dialogues. *Merrill-Palmer Quarterly, 26,* 341–357.

Berlyne, D. (1960). *Conflict, arousal, and curiosity.* New York: McGraw-Hill.

Berman, P. W. (1985, April). Discussant, symposium on fathering in the context of varying employment patterns. Biennial meeting of the Society for Research in Child Development, Toronto.

Berndt, T. J. (1979). Developmental changes in conformity to peers and parents. *Developmental Psychology, 15,* 608–616.

Berndt, T. J. (1981). Relations between social cognition, nonsocial cognition, and social behavior: The case of friendship. In J. H. Flavell & L. D. Ross (Eds.), *Social cognitive development.* Cambridge, England: Cambridge University Press.

Berndt, T. J. (1982). The features and effects of friendship in early adolescence. *Child Development, 53,* 1447–1460.

Berscheid, E., & Walster, E. (1974). Physical attractiveness. In L. Berkowitz (Ed.), *Advances in experimental social psychology.* New York: Academic Press.

Bertelsen, A., Harvald, A., & Hauge, M. (1977). A Danish twin study of manic-depressive disorders. *British Journal of Psychiatry, 130,* 330–351.

Berzins, J. I., Wellings, M. A., & Wetter, R. E. (1978). A new measure of psychological androgyny based on the Personality Research Form. *Journal of Consulting and Clinical Psychology, 46,* 126–138.

Berzonsky, M. D., Weiner, A. S., & Raphael, D. (1975). Interdependence of formal reasoning. *Developmental Psychology, 11,* 258.

Best, D. L., Williams, J. E., Cloud, J. M., Davis, S. W., Robertson, L. S., Edwards, J. R., Giles, H., & Fowles, J. (1977). Development of sex-trait stereotypes among young children in the United States, England, and Ireland. *Child Development, 48,* 1375–1384.

Bibace, R., & Walsh, M. E. (1979). Developmental stages in children's conception of illness. In G. C. Stone, F. Cohen, & N. E. Adler (Eds.), *Health psychology.* San Francisco: Jossey-Bass.

Bieglow, B. J., & LaGaipa, J. J. (1980). The development of friendship values and choices. In H. C. Foot, A. J. Chapman, & J. R. Smith (Eds.), *Friendship and social relations in children.* New York: Wiley.

Biehler, R. F., & Snowman, J. (1986). *Psychology applied to teaching* (5th ed.). Boston: Houghton-Mifflin.

Biemer, L. (1975). Female studies: The elective approach. *Social Science Record, 12,* 7–11.

Bijou, S. W. (1976). *The basic stage of early childhood development.* Englewood Cliffs, NJ: Prentice-Hall.

Bindra, I., & Palfai, T. (1967). Nature of positive and negative incentive motivational effects on general activity. *Journal of Comparative and Physiological Psychology, 63,* 288–297.

Birrell, R. G., & Birrell, J. M. W. (1968). The maltreatment syndrome in children: A hospital survey. *Medical Journal of Australia, 3,* 1023–1029.

Blaine, G. B., & McArthur, C. C. (1971). Problems connected with studying. In G. B. Blaine & C. C. McArthur (Eds.), *Emotional problems of the student* (2nd ed.), New York: Appleton-Century-Crofts.

Blanchard, R. J., & Blanchard, D. C. (1969). Crouching as an index of fear. *Journal of Comparative and Physiological Psychology, 67,* 370–375.

Bloch, H. A., & Niederhoffer, A. (1958). *The gang: A study in adolescent behavior.* New York: Philosophical Library.

Block, J. (1973). Conception of sex role: Some cross-cultural and longitudinal perspectives. *American Psychologist, 28,* 512–526.

Block, J. (1976). Issues, problems, and pitfalls in assessing sex differences: A critical review of the psychology of sex differences. *Merrill-Palmer Quarterly, 22,* 283–308.

Bloom, B. S. (1983, April). *The development of exceptional talent.* Paper presented at the meeting of the Society for Research in Child Development, Detroit.

Bloom, L. M. (1973). *One word at a time: The use of single-word utterances before syntax.* The Hague: Mouton.

Bloom, L. M., Hood, L., & Lightbown, P. (1974). Imitation in language development: If, when, and why. *Cognitive Psychology, 6,* 380–420.

Bloom, M. (1983). Prevention/promotion with minorities. *Journal of Primary Prevention, 3,* 224–234.

Blos, P. (1962). *On adolescence.* New York: Free Press.

Blos, P. (1978). Children think about illness: Their concepts and beliefs. In E. Gellert (Ed.), *Psychosocial aspects of pediatric care.* New York: Gruen & Stratton.

Blum, R. W., & Goldhagen, J. (1981). Teenage pregnancy in perspective. *Clinical Pediatrics, 20,* 335–340.

Blumberg, M. L. (1974). Psychopathology of the abusing parent. *American Journal of Psychotherapy, 28,* 1121–1129.

Blyth, D. A., Bulcroft, R., & Simmons, R. G. (1981, August). *The impact of puberty on adolescents: A longitudinal study.* Paper presented at the annual meeting of the American Psychological Association, Los Angeles, CA.

Blyth, D. A., Durant, D., & Moosbrugger, L. (1985, April). *Perceived intimacy in the social relationships of drug- and nondrug-using adolescents.* Paper presented at the biennial meeting of the Society for Research in Child Development, Toronto.

Blyth, D. A., Simmons, R. G., & Bush, D. (1978). The transitions into early adolescence: A longitudinal comparison of youth in two educational contexts. *Sociology of Education, 51,* 149–162.

Blyth, D. A., Simmons, R. G., & Carlton-Ford, S. (1983). The adjustment of early adolescents to school transitions. *Journal of Early Adolescence, 3,* 105–120.

Bobrow, S., & Bower, G. (1969). Comprehension and recall of sentences. *Journal of Experimental Psychology, 80,* 455–461.

Bornstein, M. H. (1976). Infants are trichromats. *Journal of Experimental Child Psychology, 21,* 421–445.

Bornstein, M. H. (1984). Perceptual development. In M. H. Bornstein & M. E. Lamb (Eds.), *Developmental psychology: An advanced textbook.* Hillsdale, NJ: Erlbaum.

Bornstein, M. H. (1985a). Habituation of attention as a measure of visual information processing in infants: Summary, systematization, and synthesis. In G. Gottlieb & N. A. Krasnegor (Eds.), *Measurement of audition and vision in the first year of postnatal life: A methodological overview.* Norwood, NJ: Ablex.

Bornstein, M. H. (1985b). *How infant and mother contribute to developing cognitive competence in the child.* Proceedings of the National Academy of Sciences (USA).

Bornstein, M. H., & Sigman, M. D. (1986). Continuity in mental development from infancy. *Child Development, 57,* 251–274.

Borstelmann, L. J. (1983). Children before psychology: Ideas about children from antiquity to the late 1800s. In P. H. Mussen (Ed.), *Handbook of child psychology* (4th ed.), Vol. 1. New York: Wiley.

Bourne, E. (1978). The state of research on ego identity: A review and appraisal (Part I). *Journal of Youth and Adolescence, 7,* 223–251.

Bower, G. H., Black, J. B., & Turner, T. J. (1979). Scripts in memory for text. *Cognitive Psychology, 11,* 177–220.

Bower, T. G. R. (1974). *Development in infancy.* San Francisco: W. H. Freeman.

Bower, T. G. R. (1982). *Development in infancy* (2nd ed.). San Francisco: W. H. Freeman.

Bowlby, J. (1958). The nature of the child's tie to his mother. *International Journal of Psychoanalysis, 39,* 35.

Bowlby, J. (1969). *Attachment and loss* (Vol. 1). London: Hogarth (New York: Basic Books).

Bowlby, J. (1973). *Attachment and loss* (Vol. 2). London: Hogarth.

Bowlby, J. (1980). *Attachment and loss, Vol. 3: Loss, sadness, and depression.* New York: Basic Books.

Brackbill, V. (1962). *Research and clinical work with children.* Washington, DC: American Psychological Association.

Brackbill, V. (1979). Obstetric medication and infant behavior. In J. D. Osofsky (Ed.), *Handbook of infant development.* New York: Wiley.

Bracken, B. A. (1985). A critical review of the Kaufman assessment battery for children (K-ABC). *School Psychology Review, 14,* 21–36.

Bradley, R. M., & Stearn, I. B. (1977). The development of the human taste bud during the fetal period. *Journal of Anatomy, 101,* 743–752.

Braine, M. D. (1976). Children's first word combinations. *Monographs of the Society for Research in Child Development, 41* (Serial No. 164).

Brainerd, C. J. (1978). The stage question in cognitive-developmental theory. *The Behavioral and Brain Sciences, 1,* 173–182.

Brazelton, T. B. (1956). Sucking in infancy. *Pediatrics, 17,* 400–404.

Brazelton, T. B. (1973). *Neonatal behavioral assessment scale.* London: Heinemann Medical Books.

Brazelton, T. B. (1975). Anticipatory guidance. *The Pediatric Clinics of North America, 22,* 132.

Brazelton, T. B. (1979). Behavioral competence in the newborn infant. *Seminars in Perinatology, 3,* 35–44.

Breitmayer, B. J., & Ramey, C. T. (1983, April). *Biological vulnerability and quality of postnatal environment as co-determinants of intellectual development.* Paper presented at the biennial meeting of the Society for Research in Child Development, Detroit.

Bremnar, J. G. (1985, April). *The role of active movement in the development of search in infancy.* Paper presented at the meeting of the Society for Research in Child Development, Toronto.

Bretherton, I. (1984). Social referencing and the interfacing of minds. *Merrill-Palmer Quarterly, 30,* 419–427.

Bretherton, I., & Beeghly, M. (1982). Talking about internal states: The acquisition of an explicit theory of mind. *Developmental Psychology, 18,* 906–921.

Bretherton, I., Fritz, J., Zahn-Waxler, C., & Ridgeway, D. (1986). Learning to talk about emotions. *Child Development, 57,* 529–548.

Brewster, A. B. (1982). Chronically ill hospitalized children's concepts of illness. *Pediatrics, 69,* 355–362.

Brittain, C. V. (1963). Adolescent choices and parent-peer cross pressures. *American Sociological Review, 13,* 59–68.

Broadbent, D. E. (1958). *Perception and communication.* London: Pergamon Press.

Brody, G. H., Stoneman, Z., & MacKinnon, C. E. (1982). Role asymmetries in interaction between school-age children, their younger siblings, and their friends. *Child Development, 53,* 1364–1370.

Brody, S., & Axelrad, S. (1970). *Anxiety and ego formation in infancy.* New York: International Universities Press.

Broman, S. H., & Nichols, P. L. (1981, August). *Predictors of superior cognitive ability in young children.* Paper presented at the meeting of the American Psychological Association, Los Angeles.

Bronfenbrenner, U. (1970). *Two worlds of childhood: U.S. and U.S.S.R.* New York: Russell Sage Foundation.

Bronfenbrenner, U. (1972). Is 80 percent of intelligence genetically determined? In U. Bronfenbrenner (Ed.), *Influences on human development.* Hinsdale, IL: Dryden Press.

Bronfenbrenner, U. (1979). Contexts of child rearing: Problems and prospects. *American Psychologist, 34,* 844–850.

Bronfenbrenner U., & Crouter, A. C. (1983). The evolution of environmental models in developmental research. In P. H. Mussen (Ed.), *Handbook of child psychology* (4th ed.), Vol. 1. New York: Wiley.

Bronfenbrenner, U., & Garbarino, J. (1976). The socialization of moral judgment and behavior in cross-sectional perspective. In T. Lickona (Ed.), *Moral development and behavior.* New York: Holt, Rinehart & Winston.

Bronson, W. C. (1974). Mother-toddler interaction: A perspective on studying the development of competence. *Merrill-Palmer Quarterly, 20,* 275–281.

Brooks-Gunn, J., Petersen, A. C., & Eichorn, D. (1985). The study of maturational timing effects in adolescence. *Journal of Youth and Adolescence, 14,* 149–161.

Brooks-Gunn, J., Warren, M. P. (1985). The effects of delayed menarche in different contexts: Dance and nondance students. *Journal of Youth and Adolescence, 14,* 285–300.

Brophy, J. (1979). Teacher behavior and its effects. *Journal of Educational Psychology, 71,* 733–750.

Brophy, J., & Everston, C. (1974). *The Texas Teacher Effectiveness Project: Presentation of nonlinear relationships and summary discussion* (Report No. 74–6). Austin: University of Texas Research and Development Center for Teacher Education.

Broughton, J. (1981). Piaget's structural developmental psychology IV. Knowledge without a self and without history. *Human Development, 24,* 320–346.

Brown, A. L. (1976). Semantic integration in children's reconstruction of narrative sequences. *Cognitive Psychology, 8,* 247–262.

Brown, A. L., Bransford, J. D., Ferrara, R. A., & Campione, J. C. (1983). Learning, remembering and understanding. In P. H. Mussen (Ed.), *Handbook of child psychology,* Vol. 3. New York: Wiley.

Brown, A. L., & Smiley, S. S. (1977). Rating the importance of structural units of prose passages: A problem of metacognitive development. *Child Development, 48,* 1–8.

Brown, B. B., Clasen, D. R., & Eicher, S. A. (in press). Perceptions of peer pressure, peer conformity dispositions, and self-reported behavior among adolescents. *Developmental Psychology.*

Brown, B. B., & Lohr, M. J. (in press). Peer group affiliation and adolescent self-esteem: An integration of ego identity and symbolic interaction theories. *Journal of Personality and Social Psychology.*

Brown, F. (1973). *The reform of secondary education: Report of the national commission on the reform of secondary education.* New York: McGraw-Hill.

Brown, J. L. (1964). States in newborn infants. *Merrill-Palmer Quarterly, 10,* 313–327.

Brown, J. V., & Bakeman, R. (1980). Relationships of human mothers with their infants during the first year of life. In R. W. Bell & W. P. Smotherman (Eds.), *Maternal influences and early behavior.* Jamaica, NY: Spectrum.

Brown, R. (1973). *A first language: The early stages.* Cambridge, MA: Harvard University Press.

Brown, R. (1977). Introduction. In C. E. Snow & C. A. Ferguson (Eds.), *Talking to children.* Cambridge, England: Cambridge University Press.

Brown, R. (1986). *Social psychology* (2nd ed.). New York: Free Press.

Brown, R., & Hanlon, C. (1970). Derivational complexity and order of acquisition in child speech. In J. R. Yaeys (Ed.), *Cognition and the development of language.* New York: Wiley.

Brown, R., Cazden, C. B., & Bellugi-Klima, U. (1969). The child's grammar from I to III. In J. P. Hill (Ed.), *Minnesota Symposia on Child Psychology,* Vol. 2. Minneapolis: University of Minnesota Press.

Brownell, C. A., & Brown, E. (1985, April). *Toddler-peer interactions in relation to cognitive development.* Paper presented at the biennial meeting of the Society for Research in Child Development, Toronto.

Bruch, H. (1973). *Eating disorders: Obesity, anorexia nervosa, and the person within.* New York: Basic Books.

Bruner, J. (1966). *Toward a theory of instruction.* Cambridge, MA: Harvard University Press.

Bruner, J. S. (1973). *Beyond the information given.* New York: Norton.

Bryant, B. (1974). Locus of control related to teacher-child interperceptual experiences. *Child Development, 45,* 157–174.

Bryant, B. K. (1985). The Neighborhood Walk: Sources of support in middle childhood. *Monographs of the Society for Research in Child Development, 50* (3, Serial No. 210).

Bryant, P. (1985, April). *Discussion of papers on spatial problem solving and early cognitive development.* Paper presented at the biennial meeting of the Society for Research in Child Development, Toronto.

Bullock, M. (1985). Animism in childhood thinking: A new look at an old question. *Developmental Psychology, 21,* 217–225.

Burkett, C. L. (1985, April). *Child-rearing behaviors and the self-esteem of preschool-age children.* Paper presented at the biennial meeting of the Society for Research in Child Development, Toronto.

Burleson, B. R. (1985, April). *Communicative correlates of peer acceptance in childhood.* Paper presented at the meeting of the Society for Research in Child Development, Toronto.

Butler, L., & Meichenbaum, D. (1981). The assessment of interpersonal problem-solving skills. In P. C. Kendall & S. D. Hollon (Eds.), *Assessment strategies for cognitive-behavioral interventions.* New York: Academic Press.

C

Cairns, R. (1983). The emergence of developmental psychology. In P. H. Mussen (Ed.), *Handbook of child psychology* (4th ed.), Vol. 1. New York: Wiley.

Califano, J. A. (1979). *Healthy people: The surgeon general's report on health promotion and disease prevention.* Washington, D.C.: U.S. Government Printing Office.

Callahan, R. (1962). *Education and the cult of efficiency.* Chicago: University of Chicago Press.

Calvert, S. L., Huston, A. C., Watkins, B. A., & Wright, J. C. (1982). The relation between selective attention to television forms and children's comprehension of content. *Child Development, 53,* 601–610.

Campbell, B. (1985). *Human evolution: An introduction to man's adaptation* (3rd ed.). Hawthorne, NY: Aldine.

Campbell, B. K. (1977). An assessment of early mother-infant interaction and the subsequent development of the infant in the first two years of life. *Dissertation Abstracts International, 38,* 1856–1857.

Campbell, T. A., Wright, J. C., & Huston, A. C. (1983, August). *Format cues and content difficulty as determinants of children's cognitive processing of televised educational messages.* Paper presented at the annual meeting of the American Psychological Association, Anaheim, CA.

Campos, J. J., Barrett, K. C., Lamb, M. E., Goldsmith, H. H., & Stenberg, C. (1983). Socioemotional development. In P. H. Mussen (Ed.), *Handbook of child psychology* (4th ed.), Vol. 2. New York: Wiley.

Campos, J. J., Langer, A., & Krowitz, A. (1970). Cardiac responses on the visual cliff in prelocomotor human infants. *Science, 170,* 196–197.

Caplan, F. (1981). *The first twelve months of life.* New York: Bantam.

Caplan, F., & Caplan, T. (1981). *The second twelve months of life.* New York: Bantam.

Card, J. J., Steele, L., & Abeles, R. P. (1980). Sex differences in realization of potential for achievement. *Journal of Vocational Behavior, 17,* 1–21.

Carey, S. (1977). The child as word learner. In M. Halle, J. Bresman, & G. A. Miller (Eds.), *Linguistic theory and psychological reality.* Cambridge, MA: MIT Press.

Carlson, S. G., Fagerberg, H., Horneman, G., Hwang, C. P., Larsson, K., Rodholm, M., Schaller, J., Danielsson, B., & Gundewall, C. (1979). Effects of various amounts of contact between the mother and child on the mother's nursing behavior. *Developmental Psychobiology, 11,* 143–150.

Carper, L. (1978, April). Sex roles in the nursery. *Harper's.*

Case, R. (1984). The process of stage transition: A neo-Piagetian view. In R. J. Sternberg (Ed.), *Mechanisms of cognitive development.* New York: W. H. Freeman.

Case, R., Kurland, D. M., & Goldberg, J. (1982). Operational efficiency and the growth of short-term memory span. *Journal of Experimental Child Psychology, 33,* 386–404.

Casteñada, A., Ramirez, M., Cortes, C. E., & Barrera, M. (Eds.) (1971). *Mexican-Americans and educational change.* Unpublished manuscript, University of California, Riverside, CA.

Cattell, P. (1940). *The measurement of intelligence in young children.* New York: Psychological Corporation.

Cattell, R. B. (1963). Theory of fluid and crystallized intelligence: A critical experiment. *Journal of Educational Psychology, 54,* 1–22.

Center for Early Adolescence. (1982). *Living with 10- to 15-year-olds, a planning guide for a one-day conference.* Carrboro, NC: Author.

Chaillé, C. (1978). The child's conceptions of play, pretending, and toys: Sequences and structural parallels. *Human Development, 21,* 201–210.

Chall, J. S. (1967). *Learning to read: The great debate.* New York: McGraw-Hill.

Chapin, M., & Dyck, D. G. (1976). Persistence in children's reading behavior as a function of N length and attribution retraining. *Journal of Abnormal Psychology, 85,* 97–111.

Chase, W. G., & Simon, H. A. (1973). Perception in chess. *Cognitive Psychology, 4,* 44–81.

Chernin, K. (1981, November 22). Women and weight consciousness. *New York Times News Service.*

Cherry, L. (1975). The preschool teacher-child dyad: Sex differences in verbal interaction. *Child Development, 46,* 532–535.

Chess, S., & Thomas, A. (1982). Infant bonding: Mystique and reality. *American Journal of Orthopsychiatry, 52,* 213–222.

Chi, M. T. (1978). Knowledge structures and memory development. In R. S. Siegler (Ed.), *Children's thinking: What develops?* Hillsdale, NJ: Erlbaum.

Chilman, C. (1979). *Adolescent sexuality in a changing American society: Social and psychological perspectives.* Washington, DC: Public Health Service, National Institute of Mental Health.

Chomsky, N. (1957). *Syntactic structures.* The Hague: Mouton.

Chomsky, N. (1965). *Aspects of the theory of syntax.* Cambridge, MA: MIT Press.

Cicirelli, V. (1972). The effect of sibling relationships on concept learning of young children taught by child-teachers. *Child Development, 43,* 282–287.

Cicirelli, V. (1977). Family structure and interaction: Sibling effects on socialization. In M. McMillan & M. Sergio (Eds.), *Child psychiatry: Treatment and research.* New York: Brunner/Mazel.

Clark, E. V. (1972). On the child's acquisition of antonyms in two semantic fields. *Journal of Verbal Learning and Verbal Behavior, 11,* 750–758.

Clark, E. V. (1979). Building a vocabulary: Words for objects, actions, and relations. In P. Fletcher & M. Garman (Eds.), *Language acquisition.* Cambridge, England: Cambridge University Press.

Clark, E. V. (1983). Meanings and concepts. In P. H. Mussen (Ed.), *Handbook of child psychology* (4th ed.), Vol. 3. New York: Wiley.

Clark, H. H., & Clark, E. V. (1977). *Psychology and language.* New York: Harcourt, Brace Jovanovich.

Clark, K. (1965). *Dark ghetto.* New York: Harper & Row.

Clarke-Stewart, K. A. (1973). Interactions between mothers and their young children: Characteristics and consequences. *Monographs of the Society for Research in Child Development, 38* (6–7, Serial No. 153).

Clarke-Stewart, K. A. (1978). Recasting the lone stranger. In J. Glick & K. A. Clarke-Stewart (Eds.), *The development of social understanding.* New York: Gardner Press.

Clarke-Stewart, K. A., & Fein, G. G. (1983). Early childhood programs. In P. H. Mussen (Ed.), *Handbook of child psychology* (4th ed.), Vol. 2. New York: Wiley.

Clifford, E. (1959). Discipline in the American home: A controlled observational study of parental practices. *Journal of Genetic Psychology, 5,* 45–82.

Cohen, A. K. (1964). Foreword. In P. Musgrove, *Youth and social order.* Bloomington, IN: Indiana University Press.

Coie, J. D., & Dodge, K. A. (1983). Continuities and changes in children's social status: A five-year longitudinal study. *Merrill-Palmer Quarterly, 29,* 261–281.

Coie, J. D., & Kupersmidt, J. (1983). A behavioral analysis of emerging social status in boys' groups. *Child Development, 54,* 1400–1416.

Colby, A., Kohlberg, L., Gibbs, J., & Lieberman, M. (1980). *A longitudinal study of moral judgment.* Unpublished manuscript, Harvard University, Cambridge, MA.

Cole, S. (1981). *Working kids on working.* New York: Lothrop, Lee, & Shephard.

Coleman, J., Bremner, R., Clark, B., Davis, J., Eichorn, D., Grilliches, Z., Kett, J., Ryder, N., Doering, Z., & Mays, J. (1974). *Youth, transition to adulthood.* Chicago: University of Chicago Press.

Coleman, J. S. (1961). *The adolescent society.* New York: Free Press.

Coles, R. (1970). *Erik H. Erikson: The growth of his work.* Boston: Little, Brown.

Colletta, N. D. (1978). *Divorced mothers at two income levels: Stress, support, and child-rearing practices.* Unpublished thesis, Cornell University.

Collins, W. A. (1985, April). *Cognition, affect, and development in parent-child relationships.* Paper presented at the biennial meeting of the Society for Research in Child Development, Toronto.

Comber, L. C., & Keeves, J. P. (1973). *Scientific achievement in nineteen countries.* New York: Wiley.

Condry, J. C., Simon, M. L., & Bronfenbrenner, U. (1968). *Characteristics of peer- and adult-oriented children.* Unpublished manuscript, Cornell University, Ithaca, NY.

Constantinople, A. (1969). An Eriksonian measure of personality development in college students. *Developmental Psychology, 1,* 357–372.

Cook, T. D., & Campbell, D. T. (1979). *Quasi-experimentation.* Chicago: Rand-McNally.

Cooper, C. R., & Ayers-Lopez, S. (1985). Family and peer systems in early adolescence: New models of the role of relationships in development. *Journal of Early Adolescence, 5,* 9–22.

Cooper, C. R., Grotevant, H. D., Moore, M. S., & Condon, S. M. (1982, August). *Family support and conflict: Both foster adolescent identity and role taking.* Paper presented at the meeting of the American Psychological Association, Washington, DC.

Cooper, H., & Tom, D. Y. H. (1984). Socioeconomic status and ethnic group differences in achievement motivation. In R. E. Ames & C. Ames (Eds.), *Motivation in education.* New York: Academic Press.

Coopersmith, S. (1967). *The antecedents of self-esteem.* San Francisco: W. H. Freeman.

Corrigan, R. (1981). The effects of task and practice on search for invisibly displaced objects. *Developmental Review, 1,* 1–17.

Covington, M. V. (1984). The motive for self-worth. In R. E. Ames & C. Ames (Eds.), *Motivation in education.* New York: Academic Press.

Cowan, C. P., & Cowan, P. (1983, April). *A preventive intervention for couples during family formation.* Paper presented at the biennial meeting of the Society for Research in Child Development, Detroit.

Cowan, C. P., & Cowan, P. A. (1985, April). *Parents' work patterns, couple and parent-child relationships.* Paper presented at the biennial meeting of the Society for Research in Child Development, Toronto.

Cowan, P. (1978). *Piaget with feeling.* New York: Holt, Rinehart & Winston.

Cowen, E. L., Pederson, A., Babigian, H., Izzo, L. D., & Trost, M. A. (1973). Long-term follow-up of early detected vulnerable children. *Journal of Consulting and Clinical Psychology, 41,* 438–446.

Craik, F. I. M., & Lockhart, R. S. (1972). Levels of processing: A framework for memory research. *Journal of Verbal Learning and Verbal Behavior, 11,* 671–684.

Crandall, V. C., & Battle, E. S. (1970). The antecedents and adult correlates of academic and intellectual achievement effort. In J. P. Hill (Ed.), *Minnesota Symposium on Child Psychology,* Vol. 4. Minneapolis, MN: University of Minnesota Press.

Crandall, V. J., & Rabson, A. (1960). Children's repetition choices in an intellectual achievement situation following success and failure. *Journal of Genetic Psychology, 97,* 161–168.

Cratty, B. (1974). *Psychomotor behavior in education and sport.* Springfield, IL: Charles C. Thomas.

Cratty, B. (1978). *Perceptual and motor development in infants and children* (2nd ed.). Englewood Cliffs, NJ: Prentice-Hall.

Crawford, J. W. (1982). Mother-infant interaction in premature and full-term infants. *Child Development, 53,* 957–962.

Cremin, L. (1961). *The transformation of the school.* New York: Knopf.

Crimmings, A. M. (1978). *Female causal attribution for success and failure outcomes as a function of sex-role identity and degree of competitiveness in the achievement situation.* Unpublished doctoral dissertation, Ohio State University, Columbus, OH (University Microfilms No. 7902104).

Critelli, J. W., & Baldwin, A. (1979). Birth order complementarity versus homogamy as determinants of attraction in dating relationships. *Perceptual and Motor Skills, 49,* 467–471.

Cronbach, L. J. (1970). *Essentials of psychological testing.* New York: Harper & Row.

Cronbach, L. J., & Snow, R. E. (1977). *Aptitudes and instructional methods.* New York: Irvington Books.

Crook, C. K., & Lipsitt, L. P. (1976). Neonatal nutritive sucking: Effects of taste stimulation upon sucking rhythm and heart rate. *Child Development, 47,* 518–522.

Cross, K. P. (1984, November). The rising tide of school reform reports. *Phi Delta Kappan,* pp. 167–172.

Crouter, A. C., & Huston, T. L. (1985, April). *Social, psychological, and contextual antecedents of fathering in dual-earner families.* Paper presented at the biennial meeting of the Society for Research in Child Development, Toronto.

Crowder, R. G. (1982). *The psychology of reading.* New York: Oxford University Press.

Crowe, R. R. (1974). An adoption study of antisocial personality. *Archives of General Psychiatry, 31,* 785–791.

Cummings, C. M. (1979). *Psychological androgyny in new fathers and their expectations of the fathering role.* Unpublished doctoral dissertation, Columbia University, New York (University Microfilms No. 8006796).

Curran, J. P. (1975). Social skills training and systematic desensitization in reducing dating anxiety. *Behavior Research and Therapy, 13,* 65–68.

Cushna, B. (1966). *Agency and birth order differences in early childhood.* Paper presented at the meeting of the American Psychological Association, New York.

Cvetkovich, G., & Grote, B. (1975, May). *Psychological factors associated with adolescent premarital coitus.* Paper presented at the National Institute of Child Health and Human Development, Bethesda, MD.

D

Dale, P. S. (1976). *Language development* (2nd ed.). New York: Holt, Rinehart & Winston.

Damon, W., & Hart, D. (1982). The development of self-understanding from infancy through adolescence. *Child Development, 53,* 841–864.

Danner, F. (1986). Personal communication. Quoted in Lapsley, D. K., Enright, R. D., & Serlin, R. C. Moral and social education. In J. Worrell & F. Danner (Eds.), *Adolescent Development: Issues in Education.* New York: Academic Press.

Darling, C. A., Kallen, D. J., & VanDusen, J. E. (1984). Sex in transition, 1900–1984. *Journal of Youth and Adolescence, 13,* 385–399.

Darwin, C. (1859). *On the origin of species.* London: John Murray.

Davids, A., & Hainsworth, P. K. (1967). Maternal attitudes toward family life and child rearing as avowed by mothers and perceived by their underachieving and high-achieving sons. *Journal of Consulting Psychology, 31,* 29–37.

Davis, G. A. (1981). *Creativity is forever.* Cross Plains, WI: Badger Press.

Davison, G. C., & Neale, J. M. (1975). *Abnormal psychology,* New York: Wiley.

de Villiers, J. G., & de Villiers, P. A. (1978). *Language acquisition.* Cambridge, MA: Harvard University Press.

Deci, E. L. (1975). *Intrinsic motivation.* New York: Plenum.

Demorest, A., Meyer, C., Phelps, E., Gardner, H., & Winner, E. (1984). Words speak louder than actions: Understanding deliberately false remarks. *Child Development, 55,* 1527–1534.

Dempster, F. N. (1981). Memory span: Sources of individual and developmental differences. *Psychological Bulletin, 89,* 63–100.

Dempster, F. N. (1985). Short-term memory development in childhood and adolescence. In C. J. Brainerd & M. Pressley (Eds.), *Basic processes in memory development: Progress in cognitive development research.* New York: Springer-Verlag.

DeOreo, K. L. (1976). Unpublished current work on the assessment of the development of gross motor skills. Kent State University, Kent, Ohio.

Deutsch, C., Deutsch, M., Jordan, T., & Grallo, R. (1981, August). *Long-term effects of Project Head Start.* Paper presented at the annual meeting of the American Psychological Association, Los Angeles.

Deutsch, C. J., & Gilbert, L. A. (1976). Sex-role stereotypes: Effect of perceptions of self and others on personal adjustment. *Journal of Counseling Psychology, 23,* 373–379.

Deutsch, G. (1982). *Eating disorders in adolescence.* Unpublished manuscript, University of Texas at Dallas.

Dewey, J. (1933). *How we think: A restatement of the relation of reflective thinking to the educative process.* Lexington, MA: D. C. Heath.

Diamond, A. (1985). Development of the ability to use recall to guide action, as indicated by infants' performance on AB. *Child Development, 56,* 868–883.

Diaz, R. M., & Berndt, T. J. (1982). Children's knowledge of a best friend: Fact or fancy? *Developmental Psychology, 18,* 787–794.

Dickinson, A. (1980). *Contemporary animal learning theory.* Cambridge, England: Cambridge University Press.

Dickinson, G. E. (1975). Dating behavior of black and white adolescents before and after desegregation. *Journal of Marriage and the Family, 37,* 602–608.

Dickstein, E. (1977). Self and self-esteem: Theoretical functions and their implications for research. *Human Development, 20,* 219–240.

Dillon, R. S. (1980). *Diagnosis and management of endocrine and metabolic disorders* (2nd ed.). Philadelphia: Lea & Febiger.

Dion, K., Berscheid, E., & Walster, E. (1972). What is beautiful is good. *Journal of Personality and Social Psychology, 234,* 285–290.

Dion, K. K. (1974). Children's physical attractiveness and sex as determinants of adults' punitiveness. *Developmental Psychology, 10,* 772–778.

Dodge, K. A. (1983). Behavioral antecedents of peer social status. *Child Development, 54,* 1386–1399.

Dodge, K. A., Murphy, R. R., & Buchsbaum, K. (1984). The assessment of intention-cue detection skills: Implications for developmental psychopathology. *Child Development, 55,* 163–173.

Dolgin, K. G., & Behrend, D. A. (1984). Children's knowledge about animates and inanimates. *Child Development, 55,* 1646–1650.

Douvan, E., & Adelson, J. (1966). *The adolescent experience.* New York: Wiley.

Dreyer, P. H. (1982). Sexuality during adolescence. In B. J. Wolman (Ed.), *Handbook of developmental psychology.* Englewood Cliffs, NJ: Prentice-Hall.

Duck, S. W. (1975). Personality similarity and friendship choices by adolescents. *European Journal of Social Psychology, 5,* 351–365.

Dunn, J., & Kendrick, C. (1981). Social behavior of young siblings in the family context: Differences between same-sex and different-sex dyads. *Child Development, 52,* 1265–1273.

Dunn, J., & Kendrick, C. (1982). The speech of two- and three-year-olds to infant siblings: "Baby talk" and the context of communication. *Journal of Child Language, 9,* 579–595.

Dunn, J., & Kendrick, C. (1982). *Siblings.* Cambridge, MA: Harvard University Press.

Dunn, J., & Kendrick, C. (1985). Personal conversation reported in W. W. Hartup & Z. Rubin (Eds.), *Relationships and development.* Hillsdale, NJ: Erlbaum.

Dunphy, D. C. (1963). The social structure of urban adolescent peer groups. *Society, 26,* 230–246.

Durkheim, E. (1961, originally published 1925). *Moral education.* New York: Free Press.

Dweck, C. S. (1975). The role of expectation and attribution in the alleviation of learned helplessness. *Journal of Personality and Social Psychology, 31,* 674–685.

Dweck, C. S., & Bush, E. S. (1976). Sex differences in learned helplessness: I. Differential debilitation with peer and adult evaluators. *Developmental Psychology, 12,* 147–156.

Dweck, C. S., & Eliot, E. S. (1983). Achievement motivation. In P. H. Mussen (Ed.), *Handbook of child psychology* (4th ed.), Vol. 4. New York: Wiley.

Dweck, C. S., & Gilliard, D. (1975). Expectancy statements as determinants of reactions to failure: Sex differences in persistence and expectancy change. *Journal of Personality and Social Psychology, 32,* 1077–1088.

Dweck, C. S., & Reppucci, N. D. (1973). Learned helplessness and reinforcement responsibility in children. *Journal of Personality and Social Psychology, 25,* 109–116.

E

Eagleston, J. R., Kirmil-Gray, K., Thoresen, C. E., Wiedenfeld, S. A., Bracke, P., Heft, L., & Arnow, B. (1986). Physical health correlates of Type A behavior in children and adolescents. *Journal of Behavioral Medicine, 4,* 341–362.

Earley, L. A., Griesler, P. C., & Rovee-Collier, C. (1985, April). *Ontogenetic changes in retention in early infancy.* Paper presented at the meeting of the Society for Research in Child Development, Toronto.

Eckerman, C. O., Whatley, J. L., & Kutz, S. L. (1975). The growth of social play with peers during the second year of life. *Developmental Psychology, 11,* 42–49.

Ehrhardt, A., & Baker, S. W. (1973, March). *Hormonal aberrations and their implications for the understanding of normal sex differentiation.* Paper presented at the meeting of the Society for Research in Child Development, Philadelphia.

Eichorn, D. (1970). Physiological development. In P. H. Mussen (Ed.), *Handbook of child psychology* (3rd ed.), Vol. 1. New York: Wiley.

Eitzen, D. S. (1975). Athletics in the status system of male adolescents: A replication of Coleman's *The Adolescent Society. Adolescence, 10,* 267–276.

Elder, G. H. (1968). Democratic parent-youth relationships in cross-national perspective. *Social Science Quarterly, 40,* 216–228.

Elder, G. H. (1975). Adolescence in the life cycle. In S. E. Dragastin & G. H. Elder (Eds.), *Adolescence in the life cycle: Psychological change and social context.* New York: Wiley.

Elkind, D. (1967). Egocentrism in adolescence. *Child Development, 38,* 1025–1034.

Elkind, D. (1976). *Child development and education.* New York: Oxford University Press.

Elkind, D. (1978). *A sympathetic understanding of the child: Birth to sixteen* (2nd ed.). Boston: Allyn & Bacon.

Elkind, D. (1979, February). Growing up faster. *Psychology Today,* pp. 38–43.

Elkind, D. (1981). *The hurried child.* Reading, MA: Addison-Wesley.

Elkind, D. (in press). Reply to D. Lapsley and M. Murphy's *Developmental Review* paper. *Developmental Review, 5,* 218–226.

Elkind, D., & Bowen, R. (1979). Imaginary audience behavior in children and adolescents. *Developmental Psychology, 15,* 38–44.

Emde, R., Harmon, R., Metcalf, D., Koenig, K., & Wagonfeld, S. (1971). Stress and neonatal sleep. *Psychosomatic Medicine, 33,* 491–497.

Emde, R. N., Gaensbauer, T. G., & Harmon, R. J. (1976). Emotional expression in infancy: A biobehavioral study. *Psychological Issues, Monograph Series, 10* (37).

Emma Willard Task Force on Education. (1971). *Sexism in education.* Minneapolis: Author.

Emmer, E. T., Evertson, C. M., & Anderson, L. M. (1980). Effective classroom management at the beginning of the school year. *Elementary School Journal, 80,* 219–231.

Emmerich, W. (1979, March). *Developmental trends in sex-stereotyped values.* Paper presented at the biennial meeting of the Society for Research in Child Development, San Francisco.

Emmerich, W., Goldman, K. S., & Shore, R. E. (1971). Differentiation and development of social norms. *Journal of Personality and Social Psychology, 18,* 323–353.

Engen, T., & Lipsitt, L. P. (1965). Decrement and recovery of responses to olfactory stability of children's social and play behavior. *Journal of Comparative and Physiological Psychology, 59*, 312–316.

Enright, R., Lapsley, D., & Olson, L. (1984). Moral judgment and the social cognitive developmental research program. In S. Modgil & C. Modgil (Eds.), *Lawrence Kohlberg: Consensus and controversy.* Slough, England: NFER Press.

Enright, R., Shukla, D., & Lapsley, D. (1980). Adolescent egocentrism in early and late adolescence. *Journal of Youth and Adolescence, 9*, 101–11.

Enslein, J., & Fein, G. G. (1981). Temporal and cross-situational stability of children's social and play behavior. *Developmental Psychology, 17*, 760–761.

Entus, A. K. (1975). *Hemispheric asymmetry in processing of dichotically presented speech and nonspeech stimuli by infants.* Paper presented at the biennial meeting of the Society for Research in Child Development, Denver.

Epstein, J. L. (1980). *After the bus arrives: Resegregation in desegrated schools.* Paper presented at the meeting of the American Educational Research Association, Boston.

Epstein, J. L. (in press). Choice of friends over the life span: Developmental and environmental influences. In E. C. Mueller & C. R. Cooper (Eds.), *Process and outcome in peer relations.* New York: Academic Press.

Erikson, E. H. (1950). *Childhood and society.* New York: Norton.

Erikson, E. H. (1962). *Young man Luther.* New York: Norton.

Erikson, E. H. (1968). *Identity: Youth and crisis.* New York: Norton.

Erikson, E. H. (1969). *Gandhi's truth.* New York: Norton.

Evans, R. I. (1982). Training social psychologists in behavioral medicine research. In J. R. Eiser (Ed.), *Social psychology and behavioral medicine.* New York: Wiley.

Evans, R. I. (1983). Deterring smoking in adolescents: Evolution of an applied research program in social psychology. *International Review of Applied Psychology, 32*, 71–83.

F

Fabricius, W. V., & Hagen, J. W. (1984). Use of causal attributions about recall performance to assess metamemory and predict strategic memory behavior in young children. *Developmental Psychology, 20*, 975–987.

Fagan, J. F., III. (1985, April). *Early novelty preferences and later intelligence.* Paper presented at the meeting of the Society for Research in Child Development, Toronto.

Fagen, J. W., Ohr, P. S., & Fleckenstein, L. K. (1985, April). *A recency effect on the reactivation of infant memory.* Paper presented at the meeting of the Society for Research in Child Development, Toronto.

Fagot, B. I. (1973). Influence of teacher behavior in the preschool. *Developmental Psychology, 9*, 198–206.

Fagot, B. I. (1974). Sex differences in toddlers' behavior and parental reaction. *Developmental Psychology, 10*, 554–558.

Fagot, B. I. (1975, April). *Teacher reinforcement of feminine-preferred behavior revisited.* Paper presented at the meeting of the Society for Research in Child Development, Denver.

Fantz, R. L. (1958). Pattern vision in young infants. *Psychological Record, 8*, 43–49.

Fantz, R. L. (1961). The origin of form perception. *Scientific American, 204*, 66–72.

Fantz, R. L. (1966). Pattern discrimination and selective attention as determinants in infancy. In A. H. Kidd & J. L. Rivoire (Eds.), *Perceptual development in children.* New York: International Universities Press.

Fassinger, R. E. (1985). A causal model of college women's career choices. *Journal of Vocational Behavior, 27*, 123–153.

Faust, M. S. (1977). Somatic development of adolescent girls. *Monographs of the Society for Research in Child Development, 42*, (1, Serial No. 169).

Feck, G., Baptiste, M. S., & Tate, C. L. (1978). *An epidemiologic study of burn injuries and strategies of prevention.* Washington, DC.: U.S. Department of Health, Education, and Welfare.

Feigley, D. A., & Spear, N. E. (1970). Effect of age and punishment conditions on long-term retention by the rat in active- and passive-avoidance learning. *Journal of Comparative and Physiological Psychology, 73*, 515–526.

Fein, G. G. (1975). A transformational analysis of pretending. *Developmental Psychology, 1*, 291–296.

Fein, G. G., & Apfel, N. (1979). The development of play: Style, structure, and situation. *Genetic Psychology Monographs, 99*, 231–250.

Feiring, C., & Lewis, M. (1978). The child as a member of the family system. *Behavioral Science, 23*, 225–233.

Feldman-Summers, S., & Kiesler, S. B. (1974). Those who are number two try harder: The effect of sex on attributions of causality. *Journal of Personality and Social Psychology, 30*, 846–855.

Feldstein, M., & Ellwood, D. (1982). Teenage unemployment: What is the problem? In R. Freeman & D. Wise (Eds.), *The youth labor market problem: Its nature, causes, and consequences.* Chicago: University of Chicago Press.

Ferguson, C. A. (1977). Baby talk as a simplified register. In C. E. Snow & C. A. Ferguson (Eds.), *Talking to children.* Cambridge, England: Cambridge University Press.

Fernald, A. (1983). The perceptual and affective salience of mothers' speech to infants. In L. Feagans (Ed.), *The origins and growth of communication.* New Brunswick, NJ: Ablex.

Fernald, A. (1985, April). *Affect and intonation in mothers' speech.* Paper presented at the biennial meeting of the Society for Research in Child Development, Toronto.

Fernald, A., & Simon, T. (1984). Expanded intonation contours in mothers' speech to newborns. *Developmental Psychology, 20*, 104–113.

Festinger, L. (1954). A theory of social comparison processes. *Human Relations, 7*, 117–150.

Field, D., & Anderson, D. (in press). Instruction and modality effects on children's television attention and comprehension. *Journal of Educational Psychology.*

Field, J. (1981). Wither quantitative history? A review of some recent work in the economic and social history of education. *Historical Methods, 14,* 85–95.

Field, T. M. (1977). Effects of early separation, interactive effects, and experimental manipulation on mother-infant face-to-face interaction. *Child Development, 48,* 763–771.

Field, T. M. (1979). Visual and cardiac responses to animate and inanimate faces by young term and preterm infants. *Child Development, 50,* 188–194.

Field, T. M., Woodson, R., Greenberg, R., & Cohen, D. (1982). Discrimination and imitation of facial expressions by neonates. *Science, 218,* 179–181.

Finley, M. I. (1985, 3 February). Review of D. B. Davis. Slavery and human progress. *New York Times Book Review,* p. 26.

Finney, J. W., & Moos, R. H. (1979). Treatment and outcome for empirical subtypes of alcoholic patients. *Journal of Consulting and Clinical Psychology, 47,* 25–38.

Fischer, J. L. (1981). Transitions in relationship style from adolescence to young adulthood. *Journal of Youth and Adolescence, 10,* 11–24.

Fischer, K. W. (1980). A theory of cognitive development: The control and construction of hierarchies of skills. *Psychological Review, 87,* 477–531.

Fischer, K. W., & Jennings, S. (1981). The emergence of representation in search: Understanding the hider as an independent agent. *Quarterly Review of Development, 1,* 18–30.

Fischer, K. W., & Lazerson, A. (1984). *Human development.* San Francisco: W. H. Freeman.

Flavell, J. H. (1979). Metacognition and cognitive monitoring: A new area of psychological inquiry. *American Psychologist, 34,* 906–911.

Flavell, J. H. (1985). *Cognitive development* (2nd ed.). Englewood Cliffs, NJ: Prentice-Hall.

Flavell, J. H., Beach, D. R., & Chinsky, J. M. (1966). Spontaneous verbal rehearsal in a memory task as a function of age. *Child Development, 37,* 283–299.

Flavell, J. H., Botkin, P. T., Fry, C. L., Wright, J. W., & Jarvis, P. E. (1968). *The development of role taking and communication skills in children.* New York: Wiley.

Flavell, J. H., Friedrichs, A. G., & Hoyt, J. D. (1970). Developmental changes in memorization processes. *Cognitive Psychology, 1,* 324–340.

Flavell, J. H., Shipstead, S. G., & Croft, K. (1978). *What young children think you see when their eyes are closed.* Unpublished manuscript, Stanford University, Palo Alto, CA.

Flavell, J. H., & Wellman, H. M. (1977). Metamemory. In R. V. Kail & J. W. Hagen (Eds.), *Perspectives on the development of memory and cognition.* Hillsdale, NJ: Erlbaum.

Flay, B. R. (in press). What do we know about the social influences approach to smoking prevention? In P. McGrath & P. Firestone (Eds.), *Pediatric and adolescent behavioral medicine.* New York: Springer-Verlag.

Ford, M. E. (1986). *Androgyny as self-assertion and integration: Implications for psychological and social competence.* Unpublished manuscript, Stanford University, School of Education, Stanford, CA.

Ford, M. E. (1986). A living systems conceptualization of social intelligence: Outcomes, processes, and developmental change. In R. J. Sternberg (Ed.), *Advances in the psychology of human intelligence,* Vol. 3. Hillsdale, NJ: Erlbaum.

Forehand, G., Ragosta, J., & Rock, D. (1976). *Conditions and processes of effective school desegregation.* (Final report, U.S. Office of Education, Department of Health, Education, and Welfare.) Princeton, NJ: Educational Testing Service.

Forgatch, M. S., Chamberlain, P., & Gabrielson, P. (1982). *Time-out: A video training tape.* Eugene, OR: Castalia.

Forslund, M. A., & Gustafson, T. J. (1970). Influence of peers and parents and sex differences in drinking by high school students. *Quarterly Journal of Studies on Alcohol, 31,* 868–875.

Foulkes, D. (1972). *Children's dreams: Longitudinal studies.* New York: Wiley.

Foulkes, D. (1982). *Children's dreams: Longitudinal studies.* New York: Wiley.

Fowler, W. (1978). *Day care and its effects on early development.* Toronto: Ontario Institute for Studies in Education.

Fowler, W., & Kahn, N. (1974). *The later effects of infant group care: A follow-up study.* Toronto: Ontario Institute for Studies in Education.

Fox, L. H. (1976, September). *Changing behaviors and attitudes of gifted girls.* Paper presented at the meeting of the American Psychological Association, Washington, DC.

Fox, L. H., Brody, L., & Tobin, D. (1979). *Women and mathematics: The impact of early intervention programs on course-taking and attitudes in high school.* Baltimore: Intellectual Gifted Study Group, Johns Hopkins University.

Fox, N., Kagan, J., & Weiskopf, F. (1979). The growth of memory during infancy. *Genetic Psychology Monographs, 99,* 91–130.

Fraiberg, S. (1977). *Insights from the blind: Comparative studies of blind and sighted infants.* New York: Basic Books.

Fraiberg, S. (1977). *Every child's birthright: In defense of mothering.* New York: Basic Books.

Fregly, M. J., & Luttge, W. G. (1982). *Human endocrinology: An interactive text.* New York: Elsevier Science.

Freud, A. (1958). Adolescence. In R. S. Eissler (Ed.), *Psychoanalytic study of the child,* Vol. 13. New York: International Universities Press.

Freud, A. (1966). Instinctual anxiety during puberty. In *The writings of Anna Freud: The ego and its mechanisms of defense.* New York: International Universities Press.

Freud, A., & Dann, S. (1951). An experiment in group upbringing. In R. S. Eissler, A. Freud, H. Hartmann, & E. Kris (Eds.), *The psychoanalytic study of the child,* Vol. 6. New York: International Universities Press.

Freud, S. (1924). *A general introduction to psychoanalysis.* New York: Boni & Liveright.

Freud, S. (1953/1905). Three essays on the theory of sexuality. In J. Strachey (Ed.), *The standard edition of the complete psychological works of Sigmund Freud,* Vol. 7. London: Hogarth.

Friedman, M., & Rosenman, R. M. (1974). *Type A behavior and your heart.* New York: Knopf.

Frieze, I. H. (1975). Women's expectations for and causal attributions of success and failure. In M. T. S. Mednick, S. S. Tangri, & L. W. Hoffman (Eds.), *Women and achievement.* New York: Wiley.

Frisch, R., & Revelle, R. (1970). Height and weight at menarche and a hypothesis of critical body weights and adolescent events. *Science, 169,* 397–399.

Fromkin, V. A., Krashen, S., Curtiss, S., Rigler, D., & Rigler, M. (1974). The development of language in Genie: A case of language acquisition beyond the "critical period." *Brain and Language, 1,* 81–107.

Frommer, E., & O'Shea, G. (1973). Antenatal identification of women liable to have problems in managing their infants. *British Journal of Psychiatry, 123,* 149–156.

Furman, W., Rahe, D. F., & Hartup, W. W. (1979). Rehabilitation of socially withdrawn preschool children through mixed-age and same-age socialization. *Child Development, 50,* 915–922.

Furth, H. G., & Wachs, H. (1975). *Thinking goes to school.* New York: Oxford University Press.

G

Gage, N. L. (1965). Desirable behaviors of teachers. *Urban Education, 1,* 85–96.

Gagne, E. D. (1985). *The cognitive psychology of school learning.* Boston: Little, Brown.

Gagne, E. D., Weidemann, C., Bell, M. S., & Ander, T. D. (in press). Training thirteen-year-olds to elaborate while studying text. *Journal of Human Learning.*

Gallup, G. (1985, November 8). Poll of adolescent eating disorders. Presented in *USA Today.*

Galst, J. P. (1980). Television food commercials and pronutritional public service announcements as determinants of young children's snack choices. *Child Development, 51,* 935–938.

Garbarino, J. (1976). The ecological correlates of child abuse: The impact of socioeconomic stress on mothers. *Child Development, 47,* 178–185.

Gardner, B. T., & Gardner, R. A. (1971). Two-way communication with an infant chimpanzee. In A. Schrier & F. Stollnitz (Eds.), *Behavior of nonhuman primates,* Vol. 4. New York: Academic Press.

Gardner, H. (1983). *Frames of mind.* New York: Basic Books.

Gardner, L. I. (1972). Deprivation dwarfism. *Scientific American, 227,* 76–82.

Garelik, G. (1985, October). Are the progeny prodigies? *Discover, 6,* 45–48.

Garmezy, N. (1981). Children under stress: Perspectives on antecedents and correlates of vulnerability and resistance to psychopathology. In A. I. Rabin, J. Aronoff, A. M. Barclay, & R. A. Zucker (Eds.), *Further explorations in personality.* New York: Wiley.

Garmezy, N., Masten, A. S., & Tellegen, A. (1984). The study of stress and competence in children: A building block for developmental psychopathology. *Child Development, 44,* 97–111.

Garnica, O. K. (1977). Some prosodic and paralinguistic features of speech to young children. In C. E. Snow & C. A. Ferguson (Eds.), *Talking to children.* Cambridge, England: Cambridge University Press.

Garvey, C. (1977). *Play.* Cambridge, MA: Harvard University Press.

Gaskell, J., & Knapp, H. (1976). *Resource guide for women's studies for high school students.* Victoria, BC: Department of Education.

Gearheart, B. R. (1973). *Learning disabilities: Educational strategies.* St. Louis, MO: Mosby.

Gearheart, B. R., & Weishahan, M. W. (1984). *The exceptional student in the regular classroom* (3rd ed.). St. Louis, MO: Times Mirror/Mosby.

Geis, G., & Monahan, J. (1976). The social ecology of violence. In T. Lickona (Ed.), *Moral development and behavior.* New York: Holt, Rinehart & Winston.

Gelman, R. (1969). Conservation acquisition: A problem of learning to attend to relevant attributes. *Journal of Experimental Child Psychology, 7,* 67–87.

Gelman, R. (1972). Logical capacity of very young children: Number invariance rules. *Child Development, 43,* 75–90.

Gelman, R. (1979). Preschool thought. *American Psychologist, 34,* 900–905.

Gelman, R. (1986, August). *First principles for structuring acquisition.* Paper presented at the meeting of the American Psychological Association, Washington, DC.

Gelman, R., & Baillargeon, R. (1983). A review of some Piagetian concepts. In P. H. Mussen (Ed.), *Handbook of child psychology* (4th ed.), Vol. 3. New York: Wiley.

Gelman, R., & Gallistel, C. R. (1978). *The child's understanding of number.* Cambridge, MA: Harvard University Press.

Gelman, R., & Spelke, E. (1981). The development of thoughts about animate and inanimate objects: Implications for research. In J. H. Flavell & L. Ross (Eds.), *Social cognitive development: Frontiers and possible futures.* Cambridge, MA: Cambridge University Press.

Gentner, D. (1975). Evidence for the psychological reality of semantic components: The verbs of possession. In D. A. Norman, D. E. Rumelhart, & LNR Research Group (Eds.), *Explorations in cognition.* San Francisco: W. H. Freeman.

Gergen, K. J. (in press). Theory of the self: Impasse and evolution. In L. Berkowitz (Ed.), *Advances in experimental social psychology.* New York: Academic Press.

Gesell, A. (1954). The ontogenesis of infant behavior. In L. Carmichael (Ed.), *Manual of child psychology.* New York: Wiley.

Gesell, A. et al. (1934). *An atlas of infant behavior.* New Haven, CT: Yale University Press.

Gesell, A., & Amatruda, C. S. (1941). *Developmental diagnosis.* New York: Hoeber.

Gesell, A. L. (1928). Growth potential and infant personality. In *Infancy and human growth.* New York: Macmillan.

Gesell, A. L., & Ilg, F. L. (1949). *Child development.* New York: Harper & Row.

Getzels, J. W., & Dillon, T. J. (1973). The nature of giftedness and the education of the gifted. In R. M. W. Travers (Ed.), *Second handbook of research on teaching.* Chicago: Rand McNally.

Gewirtz, J. L. (1969). Mechanisms of social learning. In D. A. Goslin (Ed.), *Handbook of socialization theory and research.* Chicago: Rand McNally.

Gewirtz, J. L. (1977). Maternal responding and the conditioning of infant crying: Directions of influence within the attachment-acquisition process. In B. C. Etzel, J. M. LeBlanc, & D. M. Baer (Eds.), *New developments in behavioral research*. Hillsdale, NJ: Erlbaum.

Gewirtz, J. L., & Gewirtz, H. B. (1965). Stimulus conditions, infant behaviors, and social learning in four Israeli child-rearing environments: A preliminary report illustrating differences in environment and behavior between the "only" and the "youngest" child. In B. M. Foss (Ed.), *Determinants of infant behavior*, Vol. 3. New York: Wiley.

Giaconia, R. M., & Hedges, L. V. (1982). Identifying features of effective open education. *Review of Educational Research, 52*, 579–602.

Gibbs, J., & Schnell, S. V. (1985, April). *Moral development "versus" socialization: A critique of the controversy*. Paper presented at the meeting of the Society for Research in Child Development, Toronto.

Gibson, E. J. (1969). *The principles of perceptual learning and development*. New York: Appleton-Century-Crofts.

Gibson, E. J., & Spelke, E. S. (1983). The development of perception. In P. H. Mussen (Ed.), *Handbook of child psychology* (4th ed.), Vol. 3. New York: Wiley.

Gibson, E. J., & Walk, R. D. (1960). The "visual cliff." *Scientific American, 202*, 64–71.

Gibson, J. J. (1979). *The ecological approach to visual perception*. Boston: Houghton Mifflin.

Gilligan, C. (1982). *In a different voice: Psychological theory and women's development*. Cambridge, MA: Harvard University Press.

Gilligan, C. (1985a). *Responses to critics*. Unpublished manuscript, Harvard University, Cambridge, MA.

Gilligan, C. (1985b, April). *Remapping development*. Paper presented at the meeting of the Society for Research in Child Development, Toronto.

Glaser, N. (1976). Social and cultural factors in economic growth. In H. Patrick & H. Rosovsky (Eds.), *Asia's new giant*. Washington, DC: Brookings Institution.

Glaser, R. (1982). Instructional psychology: Past, present and future. *American Psychologist, 37*, 292–305.

Glass, D. C., Neulinger, J., & Brim, O. G. (1974). Birth order, verbal intelligence, and educational aspiration. *Child Development, 45*, 807–811.

Glick, P. C. (1977). Updating the life cycle of the family. *Journal of Marriage and the Family, 39*, 5–13.

Glueck, S., & Glueck, E. (1950). *Unraveling juvenile delinquency*. Cambridge, MA: Harvard University Press.

Gold, D., Andres, D., & Glorieux, J. (1979). The development of Francophone nursery-school children with employed and nonemployed mothers. *Child Development, 49*, 75–84.

Gold, M., & Petronio, R. J. (1980). Delinquent behavior in adolescence. In J. Adelson (Ed.), *Handbook of adolescent psychology*. New York: Wiley.

Gold, M., & Yanof, D. S. (1985). Mothers, daughters, and girlfriends. *Journal of Personality and Social Psychology, 49*, 654–659.

Goldberg, S. (1977). Prematurity: Effects on parent-infant interaction. *Merrill-Palmer Quarterly, 23*, 163–177.

Goldberg, S., Brachfield, S., & Divitto, B. (1980). Feeding, fussing, and play. In T. M. Field, S. Goldberg, D. Stern, & A. M. Sostek (Eds.), *High-risk infants and children: Adult and peer interactions*. New York: Academic Press.

Goldman-Rakic, P. S., Isseroff, A., Schwartz, M. L., & Bugbee, N. M. (1983). The neurobiology of cognitive development. In P. H. Mussen (Ed.), *Handbook of child psychology* (4th ed.), Vol. 2. New York: Wiley.

Goodall, J. V. L. (1972). *In the shadow of man*. New York: Dell.

Goodlad, J. I. (1983). *A place called school*. New York: McGraw-Hill.

Goodwin, F. K., & Athanascious, P. Z. (1979). Lithium in the treatment of mania. *Archives of General Psychiatry, 36*, 840–844.

Gordon, N. P., & McAlister, A. L. (1982). Adolescent drinking. In T. J. Coates, A. C. Petersen, & C. Perry (Eds.), *Promoting adolescent health*. New York: Academic Press.

Goren, C. G., Sarty, M., & Wu, P. Y. K. (1975). Visual following and pattern discrimination of facelike stimuli by newborn infants. *Pediatrics, 56*, 544–549.

Gottlieb, D. (1966). Teaching and students: The views of Negro and white teachers. *Sociology of Education, 37*, 345–353.

Gottman, J. H., & Parkhurst, J. T. (1978, October). *A developmental theory of friendship and acquaintanceship processes*. Paper presented at the Minnesota Symposium of Child Psychology, Minneapolis.

Gould, S. J. (1983). *Hen's teeth and horse's toes: Reflections on natural history*. New York: Norton.

Graham, D. (1981). The obstetric and neonatal consequences of adolescent pregnancy. In E. R. McAnarney & G. Stickle (Eds.), *Pregnancy and childbearing during adolescence: Research priorities for the 1980s*. New York: Alan R. Liss.

Granrud, C. E., Arterberry, M., & Yonas, A. (1985, April). *Size constancy in 12-week-old infants*. Paper presented at the biennial meeting of the Society for Research in Child Development, Toronto.

Granrud, C. E., Yonas, A., Smith, I. M., Arterberry, M. E., Glicksman, M. L., & Snorknes, A. C. (1984). Infants' sensitivity to accretion and deletion of texture as information for depth at an edge. *Child Development, 55*, 1630–1636.

Gratch, G. (1977). Review of Piagetian infancy research: Object concept development. In W. F. Overton & J. M. Gallagher (Eds.), *Knowledge and development*, Vol. 1. New York: Plenum.

Gray, W. M., & Hudson, L. M. (1984). Formal operations and the imaginary audience. *Developmental Psychology, 20*, 619–627.

Green, R. (1974). One-hundred-ten feminine and masculine boys: Behavioral contrasts and demographic similarities. *Archives of Sexual Behavior, 5*, 425–446.

Greenberg, B. S., & Domonick, J. R. (1969). *Television behavior among disadvantaged children*. Unpublished manuscript, Michigan State University, East Lansing.

Greenberger, E., & Steinberg, L. (1981). Sex differences in early work experience: Harbinger of things to come? *Social Forces, 62*, 467–486.

Greenwald, A., & Albert, R. (1968). Acceptance and recall of improvised arguments. *Journal of Personality and Social Psychology, 8*, 31–34.

Greenwald, A., & Pratkanis, A. (in press). The self. In R. Wyer & T. Srull (Eds.), *Handbook of social cognition.* Hillsdale, NJ: Erlbaum.

Grimes, J. W., & Allinsmith, W. (1961). Compulsivity, anxiety, and school achievement. *Merrill-Palmer Quarterly, 7*, 247–269.

Grossman, H. J. (Ed.). (1977). *Manual on terminology and classification in mental retardation.* Washington, DC: American Association on Mental Deficiency.

Grossman, K., Thane, K., & Grossman, K. E. (1981). Maternal tactual contact of the newborn after various postpartum conditions of mother-infant contact. *Developmental Psychology, 17*, 158–169.

Grotevant, H. D. (1984, February). *Exploration and negotiation of differences within families during adolescence.* Paper presented at the biennial conference on adolescence, Tucson.

Grotevant, H. D., & Cooper, C. R. (1985). Patterns of interaction in family relationships and the development of identity exploration in adolescence. *Child Development, 56*, 415–428.

Grotevant, H. D., Thorbecke, W., & Meyer, M. L. (1982). An extension of Marcia's identity status interview into the interpersonal domain. *Journal of Youth and Adolescence, 11*, 33–47.

Gruendel, J. (1980). *Scripts and stories: A study of children's event narratives.* Unpublished doctoral dissertation, Yale University.

Guilford, J. P. (1967). *Structure of intellect.* New York: McGraw-Hill.

Gump, P. V. (1980). The school as a social situation. In M. R. Rosenzweig & L. V. Porter (Eds.), *Annual Review of Psychology,* Vol. 31. Palo Alto, CA: Annual Reviews.

Gunnar, M. R., Malone, S., & Fisch, R. O. (in press). The psychobiology of stress and coping in the human neonate: Studies of adrenocortical activity in response to stress in the first week of life. In T. Field, P. McCabe, & N. Schneiderman (Eds.), *Stress and coping.* Hillsdale, NJ: Erlbaum Press.

H

Haas, A. (1979). *Teenage sexuality: A survey of teenage sexual behavior.* New York: MacMillan.

Haeberle, E. (1978). *The sex atlas.* New York: Seaburg Press.

Hahn, C. L. (1975). Eliminating sexism from the schools: Implementing change. *Social Education, 39*, 140–143.

Hall, G. S. (1904). *Adolescence* (Vols. I and II). Englewood Cliffs, NJ: Prentice-Hall.

Hall, J. A., & Halberstadt, A. G. (1980). Masculinity and femininity in children: Development of the Children's Personal Attributes Questionnaire. *Developmental Psychology, 16*, 270–280.

Hallinan, M. T. (1979). Structural effects on children's friendships and cliques. *Social Psychology Quarterly, 42*, 43–54.

Hamburg, B. (1974). Early adolescence: A specific and stressful stage of the life cycle. In G. Coelho, D. A. Hamburg, & J. E. Adams (Eds.), *Coping and adaptation.* New York: Basic Books.

Hamm, C. M. (1977). The content of moral education, or in defense of the "bag of virtues." *School Review, 85*, 218–228.

Hansson, R. O., O'Conner, M. E., Jones, W. H., & Mihelich, M. H. (1980). Role relevant sex typing and opportunity in agentic and communal domains. *Journal of Personality, 48*, 419–434.

Hardy-Brown, K., & Plomin, R. (1985, April). Infant communicative development: Evidence from adoptive biological families for genetic and environmental influences on rate differences. *Developmental Psychology, 21*, 378–385.

Harlap, S., & Shiono, P. H. (1980). Alcohol, smoking, and incidence of spontaneous abortions in the first trimester. *Lancet, 8*, 173–176.

Harlow, H. F., & Zimmerman, R. R. (1959). Affectional responses in the infant monkey. *Science, 130*, 421–432.

Harris, F. R., Wolf, M. M., & Baer, D. M. (1964). Effects of adult social reinforcement on child behavior. *Young Children, 20*, 8–17.

Harris, P. L. (1975). Development of search and object permanence during infancy. *Psychological Bulletin, 82*, 332–344.

Harter, S. (1982). The perceived competence scale for children. *Child Development, 53*, 87–97.

Harter, S. (1983). Developmental perspectives on the self-system. In P. H. Mussen (Ed.), *Handbook of child psychology* (4th ed.), Vol. 4. New York: Wiley.

Harter, S., & Pike, R. (1984). The pictorial scale of perceived competence and social acceptance for young children. *Child Development, 55*, 1969–1982.

Hartley, R. E., Frank, L. K., & Goldenson, R. M. (1952). *Understanding children's play.* New York: Columbia University Press.

Hartup, W. W. (1970). Peer interaction and social organization. In P. H. Mussen (Ed.), *Carmichael's manual of child psychology* (3rd ed.), Vol. 2. New York: Wiley.

Hartup, W. W. (1976). Peer interaction and the development of the individual child. In E. Schopler & R. J. Reichler (Eds.), *Psychopathology and child development.* New York: Plenum.

Hartup, W. W. (1979). The social worlds of childhood. *American Psychologist, 34*, 944–950.

Hartup, W. W. (1983). Peer relations. In P. H. Mussen (Ed.), *Handbook of child psychology* (4th ed.), Vol. 4. New York: Wiley.

Hartup, W. W. (1986). On relationships and development. In W. W. Hartup & Z. Rubin (Eds.), *Relationships and development.* Hillsdale, NJ: Erlbaum.

Hasher, L., & Zacks, R. T. (1979). Automatic and effortful processes in memory. *Journal of Experimental Psychology: General, 108*, 356–388.

Havighurst, R. J. (1976). Choosing a middle path for the use of drugs with hyperactive children. *School Review, 85*, 61–77.

Hawkins, J., Pea, R. D., Glick, J., & Scribner, S. (1984). "Merds that laugh don't like mushrooms": Evidence for deductive reasoning by preschoolers. *Developmental Psychology, 20*, 584–594.

Hawkins, J. A., & Berndt, T. J. (1985, April). *Adjustment following the transition to junior high school.* Paper presented at the biennial meeting of the Society for Research in Child Development, Toronto.

Hay, D. F. (1985). *The search for general principles in social life: Some lessons from young peers.* Paper presented at the biennial meeting of the Society for Research in Child Development, Toronto.

Hayes, K. J., & Hayes, C. (1951). Picture perception in a home-raised chimpanzee. *Journal of Comparative and Physiological Psychology, 46,* 470–474.

Hayne, H., & Rovee-Collier, C. (1985, April). *Contextual determinants of reactivated memories in infants.* Paper presented at the biennial meeting of the Society for Research in Child Development, Toronto.

Hazen, N. L., Lockman, J. J., & Pick, H. L., Jr. (1978). The development of children's representations of large-scale environments. *Child Development, 49,* 623–636.

Heibeck, T. H., & Markman, E. (1985, April). *Word learning in children: An examination of fast mapping.* Paper presented at the meeting of the Society for Research in Child Development, Toronto.

Heider, F. (1958). *The psychology of interpersonal relations.* New York: Wiley.

Heilbrun, A. B. (1976). Measurement of masculine and feminine sex-role identities as independent dimensions. *Journal of Consulting and Clinical Psychology, 44,* 183–190.

Helmreich, R. L., Spence, J. T., & Holahan, C. K. (1979). Psychological androgyny and sex-role flexibility: A test of two hypotheses. *Journal of Personality and Social Psychology, 37,* 1631–1644.

Henderson, N. D. (1982). Human behavior genetics. *Annual Review of Psychology, 33,* 403–440.

Hess, R. D. (1981). Approaches to the measurement and interpretation of parent-child interaction. In R. W. Henderson (Ed.), *Parent-child interaction.* New York: Academic Press.

Hetherington, E. M. (1972). Effects of father-absence on personality development in adolescent daughters. *Developmental Psychology, 7,* 313–326.

Hetherington, E. M. (1977). *My heart belongs to Daddy: A study of the remarriages of daughters of divorcees and widows.* Unpublished manuscript, University of Virginia, Charlottesville, VA.

Hetherington, E. M., Cox, M., & Cox, R. (1978). The aftermath of divorce. In J. H. Stevens & M. Mathews (Eds.), *Mother-child/father-child relations.* Washington, DC: National Association for the Education of Young Children.

Hetherington, E. M., Cox, M., & Cox, R. (1982). Effects of divorce on parents and children. In M. E. Lamb (Ed.), *Nontraditional families.* Hillsdale, NJ: Erlbaum.

Higgens-Trenk, A., & Gaite, A. J. H. (1971). *Elusiveness of formal operational thought in adolescents.* Paper presented at the proceedings of the 79th Annual Convention of the American Psychological Association.

Higgins, A., Power, C., & Kohlberg, L. (1983, April). Moral atmosphere and moral judgment. Paper presented at the biennial meeting of the Society for Research in Child Development, Detroit.

Hill, C. R., & Stafford, F. P. (1980). Parental care of children: Time diary estimate of quantity, predictability, and variety. *Journal of Human Resources, 15,* 219–239.

Hill, J. P. (1980). *Understanding early adolescence: A framework.* Carrboro, NC: Center for Early Adolescence.

Hill, J. P. (1980). The early adolescent and the family. In *The seventy-ninth yearbook of the National Society for the Study of Education.* Chicago: University of Chicago Press.

Hill, J. P. (1983, April). *Adolescent development.* Paper presented at the biennial meeting of the Society for Research in Child Development, Detroit.

Hill, J. P., & Holmbeck, G. N. (in press). Attachment and autonomy during adolescence. *Annals of Child Development.*

Hill, J. P., Holmbeck, G. N., Marlow, L., Green, T. M., & Lynch, M. E. (1985). Pubertal status and parent-child relations in families of seventh-grade boys. *Journal of Early Adolescence, 5,* 31–44.

Hinde, R. A. (1983). Ethology and child development. In P. H. Mussen (Ed.), *Handbook of child psychology* (4th ed.), Vol. 2. New York: Wiley.

Hochberg, J. E. (1978). *Perception* (2nd ed.). Englewood Cliffs, NJ: Prentice-Hall.

Hoffman, L. W. (1974). Effects of maternal employment on the child: A review of the research. *Developmental Psychology, 10,* 204–228.

Hoffman, L. W. (1979). Maternal employment: 1979. *American Psychologist, 34,* 859–865.

Hoffman, M. L. (1975). Developmental synthesis of affect and cognition and its implications for altruistic motivation. *Developmental Psychology, 11,* 607–622.

Holland, J. L., & Richards, J. M. (1965). Academic and nonacademic accomplishments: Correlated or uncorrelated? *Journal of Educational Psychology, 56,* 165–174.

Hollingshead, A. B. (1975). *Elmtown's youth and Elmtown revisited.* New York: Wiley.

Hollis, M. (1975). Logical operations and role-taking abilities in two cultures: Norway and Hungary. *Child Development, 46,* 638–649.

Holman, D. R. (1975). Teaching about women in secondary schools: Springboard for inquiry. *Social Education, 39,* 140–143.

Honzik, M. P., MacFarlane, J. W., & Allen, L. (1948). The stability of mental test performance between two and eighteen years. *Journal of Experimental Education, 17,* 309–324.

Horn, J. M. (1983). The Texas adoption project: Adopted children and their intellectual resemblance to biological and adoptive parents. *Child Development, 54,* 268–275.

Howes, C. (1985, April). *Predicting preschool sociometric status from toddler-peer interaction.* Paper presented at the biennial meeting of the Society for Research in Child Development, Toronto.

Hunt, J. M. (1976). Ordinal scales of infant development and the nature of intelligence. In L. B. Resnick (Ed.), *The nature of intelligence.* Hillsdale, NJ: Erlbaum.

Hunt, K. W. (1970). Syntactic maturity in schoolchildren and adults. *Monographs of the Society for Research in Child Development, 35,* (1, Serial No. 134).

Hunt, M. (1982). *The universe within.* New York: Simon & Schuster.

Hurley, L. S. (1980). *Developmental nutrition.* Englewood Cliffs, NJ: Prentice-Hall.

Huston, A., & Wright, J. (1983). Children's processing of television: The informative functions of formal features. In J. Bryant & D. Anderson (Eds.), *Children's understanding of television.* New York: Academic Press.

Huston, A. C. (1983). Sex typing. In P. H. Mussen (Ed.), *Handbook of child psychology* (4th ed.), Vol. 4. New York: Wiley.

Huston, A. C., Seigle, J., & Bremer, M. (1983, April). *Family environment and television use by preschool children.* Paper presented at the biennial meeting of the Society for Research in Child Development, Detroit.

Huston, T. L., & Burgess, R. L. (1980). Social exchange in developing relationships. An overview. In T. L. Huston & R. L. Burgess (Eds.), *Social exchange in developing relationships.* New York: Academic Press.

Huston-Stein, A., & Higgens-Trenk, A. (1978). Development of females from childhood through adulthood: Career and feminine role orientations. In P. Baltes (Ed.), *Life-span development and behavior,* Vol. 1. New York: Academic Press.

Hutchings, B., & Mednick, S. A. (1974). Registered criminality in the adoptive and biological parents of registered male adoptees. In S. A. Mednick, F. Schulsinger, J. Higgins, & B. Bell (Eds.). *Genetics, environment, and psychopathology.* Amsterdam: North-Holland.

Hyde, J. S. (1984). Children's understanding of sexist language. *Developmental Psychology, 20,* 697–706.

Hyman, H. M. (1959). *Political socialization.* New York: Free Press.

I

Ianotti, R. J. (1978). Effect of role-taking experiences on role taking, empathy, altruism, and aggression. *Developmental Psychology, 14,* 119–124.

Isenberg, P. I., & Schatzberg, A. F. (1978). Psychoanalytic contributions to a theory of depression. In J. O. Cole, A. F. Schatzberg, & S. H. Frazier (Eds.), *Depression.* New York: Plenum.

Izard, C. E. (1978). Emotions as motivations: An evolutionary-developmental perspective. In R. A. Dienstbier (Ed.), *Nebraska Symposium on Motivation.* Lincoln, NE: University of Nebraska Press.

Izard, C. E. (1982). *Measuring emotions in infants and children.* New York: Cambridge University Press.

Izard, C. E., Huebner, R. R., Risser, D., McGinnes, G. C., & Dougherty, L. M. (1980). The young infant's ability to produce discrete emotion expressions. *Developmental Psychology, 16,* 132–140.

J

Jacobs, J. (1971). *Adolescent suicide.* New York: Wiley.

Jacobson, J. L. (1981). The role of inanimate objects in early peer interaction. *Child Development, 52,* 618–626.

Jacoby, L. (1978). On interpreting the effects of repetition: Solving a problem versus remembering a solution. *Journal of Verbal Learning and Verbal Behavior, 17,* 649–667.

James, W. (1950/1890). *The principles of psychology.* New York: Dover.

James, W. (1963). *Psychology.* New York: Fawcett. (Originally published, 1890).

Jay, S. M., & Elliott, C. H. (1984). Psychological intervention for pain in pediatric cancer patients. In G. B. Humphrey, L. P. Dehner, G. G. Grindey, & R. T. Acton (Eds.), *Pediatric oncology,* Vol. 3. Boston: Martinus Nijhoff.

Jeans, P. C., Smith, M. B., & Stearns, G. (1955). Incidence of prematurity in relation to maternal nutrition. *Journal of the American Dietary Association, 31,* 576–581.

Jenkins, J. J. (1969). Language and thought. In J. F. Voss (Ed.), *Approaches to thought.* Columbus, OH: Merrill.

Jensen, A. R. (1969). How much can we boost IQ and scholastic achievement? *Harvard Educational Review, 39,* 1–123.

Johnson, S. B. (1984). Knowledge, attitudes, and behavior: Correlates of health in childhood diabetes. *Clinical Psychology Review, 4,* 503–524.

Johnson, W., Emde, R. N., Pannabecker, B., Stenberg, C., & Davis, M. (1982). Maternal perception of infant emotion from birth through eighteen months. *Infant Behavior and Development, 5,* 313–322.

Johnston, L. D., Bachman, J. G., & O'Malley P. M. (1981). *Student drug use in America, 1975–1981.* Rockville, MD: National Institute of Drug Abuse.

Johnston, L. D., Bachman, J. G., & O'Malley, P. M. (1985, January 4). News and Information Services Release, Institute of Social Research, University of Michigan, Ann Arbor, MI.

Jones, K. L., Smith, D. W., Ulleland, C. N., & Streissguth, A. P. (1973). Patterns of malformation in offspring of chronic alcoholic mothers. *Lancet, 1,* 1267–1271.

Jones, M. C. (1965). Psychological correlates of somatic development. *Child Development, 36,* 899–911.

Jones, W. H., Chernovetz, M. E., & Hansson, R. O. (1978). The enigma of androgyny: Differential implications for males and females? *Journal of Consulting and Clinical Psychology, 46,* 298–313.

Jordaan, J. P. (1963). Exploratory behavior. In D. E. Super, R. Statishersky, N. Mattin, & J. P. Jordaan, (Eds.), *Career development.* New York: College Entrance Examination Board.

Jordaan, J. P., & Heyde, M. B. (1978). *Vocational development during the high school years.* New York: Teachers College Press.

Jose, P. E. (1985, April). *Development of the immanent justice judgment in moral evaluation.* Paper presented at the biennial meeting of the Society for Research in Child Development, Toronto.

Juster, F. T. (in press). A note on recent changes in time use. In F. T. Juster & F. Stafford (Eds.), *Studies in the measurement of time allocation.* Ann Arbor, MI: Institute for Social Research.

K

Kacerguis, M. A., & Adams, G. R. (1980). Erikson stage resolution: The relationship between identity and intimacy. *Journal of Youth and Adolescence, 9,* 117–126.

Kagan, J. (1980). Perspectives on continuity. In O. G. Brim & J. Kagan (Eds.), *Constancy and change in human development.* Cambridge, MA: Harvard University Press.

Kagan, J. (1982). The construct of difficult temperament: A reply to Thomas, Chess, and Korn. *Merrill-Palmer Quarterly, 28,* 21–24.

Kagan, J. (1986). Perspectives on infancy. In J. Osofsky (Ed.), *Handbook of infant development.* New York: Wiley.

Kagan, J. (March, 1986). *The temperament of inhibition.* School of Human Development Colloquium Series, University of Texas at Dallas, Richardson, TX.

Kagan, J., & Moss, H. A. (1962). *Birth to maturity.* New York: Wiley.

Kagan, J., Kearsley, R. B., & Zelazo, P. R. (1978). *Infancy.* Cambridge, MA: Harvard University Press.

Kail, R. (1984). *The development of memory in children.* San Francisco: W. H. Freeman.

Kamin, L. J. (1974). *The science and politics of IQ.* New York: Halsted Press.

Kandel, D., & Lesser, G. S. (1969). Parent-adolescent relationships and adolescent independence in the United States and Denmark. *Journal of Marriage and the Family, 31,* 348–358.

Kandel, D. B. (1974). The role of parents and peers in adolescent marijuana use. *Journal of Social Issues, 30,* 107–135.

Kantner, J., & Zelnick, M. (1973). Contraception and pregnancy: Experience of young unmarried women in the United States. *Family Planning Perspectives, 5,* 21–35.

Katz, P. A. (1968). *No time for youth.* San Francisco: Jossey-Bass.

Kaufman, A. S., & Kaufman, N. L. (1983). *Kaufman assessment battery for children Interpretive manual.* Circle Pines, MN: American Guidance Service.

Keeney, T. J., Cannizzo, S. R., & Flavell, J. H. (1967). Spontaneous and induced verbal rehearsal in a recall task. *Child Development, 38,* 953–966.

Keil, F. C. (1984). Mechanisms in cognitive development and the structure of knowledge. In R. J. Sternberg (Ed.), *Mechanisms of cognitive development.* New York: W. H. Freeman.

Keith, T. Z. (1985). Questioning the K-ABC. What does it measure? *School Psychology Review, 14,* 9–20.

Kellman, P. J., & Spelke, E. S. (1979, March). *Perception of partly occluded objects in infancy.* Paper presented at the biennial meeting of the Society for Research in Child Development, San Francisco.

Kellman, P. J., & Spelke, E. S. (1981, April). *Infant perception of partly occluded objects: Sensitivity to movement and configuration.* Paper presented at the biennial meeting of the Society for Research in Child Development, Boston.

Kellogg, W. N., & Kellogg, C. A. (1933). *The ape and the child.* New York: McGraw-Hill.

Kelly, J. A., & Worrell, J. (1977). New formulations of sex roles and androgyny: A critical view. *Journal of Consulting and Clinical Psychology, 45,* 1101–1115.

Kendell, R. E., Rennie, D., Clarke, J. A., & Dean, C. (1981). The social and obstetric correlates of psychiatric admission in the puerperium. *Psychological Medicine, 11,* 341–350.

Kendrick, C., & Dunn, J. (1980). Caring for the second baby: Effects on interaction between mother and firstborn. *Developmental Psychology, 16,* 303–311.

Kenniston, K. (1971). The tasks of adolescence. In *Developmental Psychology Today.* Del Mar, CA: CRM Books.

Kenworthy, J. A. (1979). Androgyny in psychotherapy: But will it sell in Peoria? *Psychology of Women Quarterly, 3,* 231–240.

Kerr, B. A. (1983). Raising the career aspirations of gifted girls. *Vocational Guidance Quarterly, 32,* 37–43.

Kessen, W. (1965). *The child.* New York: Wiley.

Kessen, W. (1979). The American child and other cultural inventions. *American Psychologist, 34,* 815–820.

Kessen, W., Haith, M. M., & Salapatek, P. (1970). Human infancy. In P. H. Mussen (Ed.), *Handbook of child psychology* (3rd ed.), Vol. 1. New York: Wiley.

Kessey, R. E., Boyle, P. C., Kemnitz, J. W., & Mitchell, J. S. (1976). The role of the lateral hypothalamus in determining the body weight set point. In D. Novin (Ed.), *Hunger.* New York: Raven Press.

Kinsey, A. C., Pomeroy, W. B., & Martin, C. E. (1948). *Sexual behavior in the human male.* Philadelphia: Saunders.

Kintsch, W. (1982). Text representation. In W. Otto & S. White (Eds.), *Reading expository text.* New York: Academic Press.

Kisilevsky, B. S., & Muir, D. W. (1984). Neonatal habituation and dishabituation to tactile stimulation during sleep. *Developmental Psychology, 20,* 367–373.

Kister, M. C., & Patterson, C. J. (1980). Children's conceptions of the causes of illness: Understanding contagion and use of immanent justice. *Child Development, 51,* 839–846.

Klatsky, R. L. (1984). *Memory and awareness.* New York: W. H. Freeman.

Klaus, M. H., & Kennell, J. H. (1976). *Maternal-infant bonding.* St. Louis: Mosby.

Klaus, M. H., Jerauld, R., Kreger, N. C., McAlpine, W., Steffa, M., & Kennell, J. H. (1972). Maternal attachment: Importance of the first postpartum days. *New England Journal of Medicine, 286,* 460–463.

Klein, P. S., Forbes, G. B., & Nadar, P. R. (1976). Letter: Short-term starvation in infancy re subsequent learning disabilities—A proven relationship? *Journal of Pediatrics, 88,* 702–703.

Knox, D., & Wilson, K. (1981). Dating behaviors of university students. *Family Relations, 30,* 255–258.

Kobasigawa, A. (1974). Utilization of retrieval cues by children in recall. *Child Development, 45,* 127–134.

Kohlberg, L. (1958). *The development of modes of moral thinking and choice in the years 10 to 16.* Unpublished doctoral dissertation, University of Chicago, Chicago.

Kohlberg, L. (1966). A cognitive-developmental analysis of children's sex-role concepts and attitudes. In E. E. Maccoby (Ed.), *The development of sex differences.* Stanford, CA: Stanford University Press.

Kohlberg, L. (1969). Stage and sequence: The cognitive-developmental approach to socialization. In D. A. Goslin (Ed.), *Handbook of socialization theory and research.* Chicago: Rand McNally.

Kohlberg, L. (1976). Moral stages and moralization: The cognitive-developmental approach. In T. Lickona (Ed.), *Moral development and behavior.* New York: Holt, Rinehart & Winston.

Kohlberg, L. (1981). *The philosophy of moral development: Moral stages and the idea of justice.* New York: Harper & Row.

Kopp, C. B. (1982). Antecedents of self-regulation: A developmental perspective. *Developmental Psychology, 18,* 199–215.

Kopp, C. B. (1983). Risk factors in development. In P. H. Mussen (Ed.), *Handbook of child psychology* (4th ed.), Vol. 2. New York: Wiley.

Kopp, C. B., & Parmelee, A. H. (1979). Prenatal and perinatal influences on behavior. In J. D. Osofsky (Ed.), *Handbook of infant development.* New York: Wiley.

Korner, A. F., Hutchinson, C. A., Koperski, J. A., Kraemer, H. C., & Schneider, P. A. (1981). Stability of individual differences of neonatal motor and crying patterns. *Child Development, 40,* 137–141.

Kozlowski, L. T., & Bryant, K. J. (1977). Sense of direction, spatial orientation, and cognitive maps. *Journal of Experimental Psychology: Human Perception and Performance, 3,* 590–598.

Kravitz, H., & Boehm, J. (1971). Rhythmic habit patterns in infancy: Their sequences, age of onset, and frequency. *Child Development, 42,* 399–413.

Krogman, W. M. (1970). Growth of head, face, trunk, and limbs in Philadelphia white and Negro children of elementary and high school age. *Monographs of the Society for Research in Child Development, 35* (3, Serial No. 136).

Kruper, J. C. (1985, April). *Fathers' and mothers' speech to infants.* Paper presented at the biennial meeting of the Society for Research in Child Development, Toronto.

Kuczaj, S. A. (1985, April). *On the development of meanings and concepts.* Paper presented at the meeting of the Society for Research in Child Development, Toronto.

Kuczaj, S. A., & Brannick, N. (1979). Children's use of the *Wh* question modal auxiliary placement rule. *Journal of Experimental Child Psychology, 28,* 43–67.

Kuhn, D. (1984). Cognitive development. In M. H. Bornstein & M. E. Lamb (Eds.), *Developmental psychology: An advanced textbook.* Hillsdale, NJ: Erlbaum.

Kupersmidt, J. B. (1983, April). *Assessment and training of isolated children's social skills.* Paper presented at the biennial meeting of the Society for Research in Child Development, Detroit.

L

La Barbera, J. D., Izard, C. E., Vietze, P., & Parisi, S. A. (1976). Four- and six-month old infants' visual responses to joy, anger, and neutral expressions. *Child Development, 47,* 535–538.

Labov, W. (1970). *The study of nonstandard English.* Urbana, IL: National Council of Teachers of English.

Labov, W. (1972). *Language in the inner city.* Philadelphia: University of Pennsylvania Press.

Ladd, G. W., & Emerson, E. S. (1984). Shared knowledge in children's friendships. *Developmental Psychology, 20,* 932–940.

Lahey, B. B., Hammer, D., Crumrine, P. L., & Forehand, R. L. (1980). Birth order × sex interactions in child behavior problems. *Developmental Psychology, 16,* 608–615.

Lally, J. R., & Honig, A. S. (1977). *The family development research program* (Final report No. OCD–CB–100). Syracuse, NY: University of Syracuse.

Lamb, M. E. (1976). *The role of the father in child development.* New York: Wiley.

Lamb, M. E. (1977). The development of mother-infant and father-infant attachments in the second year of life. *Developmental Psychology, 13,* 637–648.

Lamb, M. E. (1981). Fathers and child development: An integrative overview. In M. E. Lamb (Ed.), *The father's role in child development.* New York: Wiley.

Lamb, M. E. (Ed.). (1986). *The father's role: Applied perspectives.* New York: Wiley.

Lamb, M. E., Frodi, A. M., Hwang, C. P., Frodi, M., & Steinberg, J. (1982). Mother- and father-infant interaction involving play and holding in traditional and nontraditional Swedish families. *Developmental Psychology, 18,* 215–221.

Lamb, M. E., Thompson, R. A., Gardner, W. R., Charnov, E. L., and Estes, D. P. (1984). Security of infantile attachment as assessed in the "strange situation": Its study and biological interpretation. *The Behavioral and Brain Sciences, 7,* 121–171.

Landesman-Dwyer, S., & Sackett, G. P. (1983, April). *Prenatal nicotine exposure and sleep-wake patterns in infancy.* Paper presented at the biennial meeting of the Society for Research in Child Development, Detroit.

Lapsley, D. K. (1985). Elkind on egocentrism. *Developmental Review, 5,* 227–236.

Lapsley, D. K., & Murphy, M. N. (in press). Another look at the theoretical assumptions of adolescent egocentrism. *Developmental Review, 5.*

Lapsley, D. K., Enright, R. D., & Serlin, R. C. (1985). Toward a theoretical perspective on the legislation of adolescence. *Journal of Early Adolescence, 5,* 441–466.

Lapsley, D. K., Enright, R. D., & Serlin, R. C. (1986). Moral and social education. In J. Worrell & F. Danner (Eds.), *Adolescent development: Issues in education.* New York: Academic Press.

Lapsley, D. K., & Quintana, S. M. (1985). Integrative themes in social and developmental theories of self. In J. B. Pryor & J. Day (Eds.), *Social and developmental perspectives of social cognition.* New York: Springer-Verlag.

Lapsley, D. K., & Quintana, S. M. (in press). Recent approaches in children's elementary moral and social education. *Elementary School Guidance and Counseling Journal.*

Larson, M. E. (1973). Humbling cases for career counselors. *Phi Delta Kappan, 54,* 374.

Lasater, T. M., Briggs, J., Malone, P., Gilliom, C. F., & Weisburg, P. (1975, April). *The Birmingham model for parent education.* Paper presented at the meeting of the Society for Research in Child Development, Denver.

Lasko, J. K. (1954). Parent behavior toward first- and second-born children. *Genetic Psychological Monographs, 49.*

Lasky, R. E., & Klein, R. E. (1979). The reactions of five-month-old infants to eye contact of the mother and of a stranger. *Merrill-Palmer Quarterly, 25,* 163–170.

LaVoie, J. (1976). Ego identity formation in middle adolescence. *Journal of Youth and Adolescence, 5,* 371–385.

Lazar, I., Darlington, R., & Collaborators. (1982). Lasting effects of early education: A report from the consortium for longitudinal studies. *Monographs of the Society for Research in Child Development, 47,* Nos. 2–3 (Whole Number 195).

Lazarus, R. S. (1974). Cognitive and coping processes in emotion. In B. Weiner (Ed.), *Cognitive views of human motivation.* New York: Academic Press.

Leboyer, F. (1975). *Birth without violence.* New York: Knopf.

Ledger, G. W., & Graoff, R. A. (1985, April). *Working memory, M-space and metacognitive development in skilled and less-skilled readers.* Paper presented at the meeting of the Society for Research in Child Development, Toronto.

Lee, C. L. (1973, August). *Social encounters of infants: The beginnings of popularity.* Paper presented at the International Society for the Study of Behavioral Development, Ann Arbor, MI.

Leifer, A. D. (1973). *Television and the development of social behavior.* Paper presented at the meeting of the International Society for the Study of Behavioral Development, Ann Arbor, MI.

Leifer, A. D., Gordon, N. J., & Graves, S. B. (1974). Children's television: More than entertainment. *Harvard Educational Review, 44,* 213–245.

Leifer, A. D., Leiderman, P. H., Barnett, C. R., & Williams, J. A. (1972). Effects of mother-infant separation on maternal attachment behavior. *Child Development, 43,* 1203–1218.

Leler, H., Johnson, D. L., Kahn, A. J., Hines, R. P., & Torres, M. (1975, April). *The Houston model for parent education.* Paper presented at the meeting of the Society for Research in Child Development, Denver.

Lenneberg, E. H. (1962). *Biological foundations of language.* New York: Wiley.

Lenneberg, E. H. (1967). *Biological foundations of language.* New York: Wiley.

Lenneberg, E. H., Rebelsky, F. G., & Nichols, I. A. (1965). The vocalization of infants born to deaf and hearing parents. *Human Development, 8,* 23–37.

Lepper, M., Greene, D., & Nisbett, R. E. (1973). Undermining children's intrinsic interest with extrinsic rewards. *Journal of Personality and Social Psychology, 28,* 129–137.

Lerner, J. W. (1971). *Children with learning disabilities: Theories, diagnosis, and teaching strategies.* Boston: Houghton Mifflin.

Lerner, R. M., & Karabenick, S. A. (1974). Physical attractiveness, body attitudes, and self-concept in late adolescence. *Journal of Youth and Adolescence, 3,* 307–316.

Lester, B. M., & Brazelton, T. B. (1982). Cross-cultural assessment of neonatal behavior. In D. A. Wagner & H. W. Stevenson (Eds.), *Cultural perspectives on child development.* San Francisco: W. H. Freeman.

Levin, J. (1976). What have we learned about maximizing what children learn? In J. Levin & V. Allen (Eds.), *Cognitive learning in children.* New York: Academic Press.

Levitz-Jones, E. M., & Orlofsky, J. L. (1985). Separation-individuation and intimacy capacity in college women. *Journal of Personality and Social Psychology, 49,* 156–169.

Levy, D. M., & Patrick, H. T. (1928). Relation of infantile convulsions, head-banging, and breath-holding to fainting and headaches (migraine) in the parents. *Archives of Neurology and Psychiatry, 19,* 865–887.

Lewis, M. (1972). State as an infant-environment interaction: An analysis of mother-infant interaction as a function of sex. *Merrill-Palmer Quarterly, 18,* 95–121.

Lewis, M., & Brooks-Gunn, J. (1979). *Social cognition and the acquisition of the self.* New York: Plenum.

Lewis, M., & Rosenblum, L. A. (Eds.) (1975). *Friendship and peer relations,* Vol. 4. New York: Plenum.

Lewis, M., Feiring, C., McGuffog, C., & Jaskir, J. (1984). Predicting psychopathology in six-year-olds from early social relations. *Child Development, 55,* 123–136.

Lewkowicz, D. J. (1985). Bisensory response to temporal frequency in 4-month-old infants. *Developmental Psychology, 21,* 306–317.

Lieberman, A. F. (1977). Preschoolers' competence with a peer: Relations with attachment and peer experience. *Child Development, 48,* 1277–1287.

Lipsitt, L. P. (1979). Critical conditions in infancy: A psychological perspective. *American Psychologist, 34,* 973–980.

Lipsitt, L. P., Engen, T., & Kaye, H. (1963). Developmental changes in the olfactory threshold of the neonate. *Child Development, 34,* 371–376.

Lipsitt, L. P., Reilly, B. M., Butcher, M. J. & Greenwood, M. M. (1976). The stability and interrelationships of newborn sucking and heart rate. *Developmental Psychology, 9,* 305–310.

Lipsitz, J. (1980, March). *Sexual development in young adolescents.* Invited speech given at the American Association of Sex Educators, Counselors, and Therapists.

Lipsitz, J. (1983, October). *Making it the hard way: Adolescents in the 1980s.* Testimony prepared for the Crisis Intervention Task Force, House Select Committee on Children, Youth, and Families, Washington, DC.

Lipsitz, J. (1984). *Successful schools for young adolescents.* New Brunswick, NJ: Transaction Books.

Livesley, W. J., & Bromley, D. B. (1973). *Person perception in childhood and adolescence.* London: Wiley.

Lockhart, R. S. (1984). What do infants remember? In M. Moscovitch (Ed.), *Infant memory: Its relation to normal and pathological memory in humans and other animals.* New York: Plenum Press.

Long, T., & Long, L. (1983). *Latchkey children.* New York: Penguin.

Lorenz, K. Z. (1935). Der Kumpan in der Umwelt des Vogels. *Journal fur Ornithologie, 83,* 137–213.

Lorenz, K. Z. (1965). *Evolution and modification of behavior.* Chicago: University of Chicago Press.

Lowrey, G. H. (1978). *Growth and development of children* (7th ed.). Chicago: Year Book Medical Publishers.

Lucariello, J., & Nelson, J. (1985). Slot-filler categories as memory organizers for young children. *Developmental Psychology, 21,* 272–282.

Lundsteen, S. W., & Bernstein-Tarrow, N. B. (1981). *Guiding young children's learning.* New York: McGraw-Hill.

Luria, Z., & Herzog, E. (1985, April). *Gender segregation across and within settings.* Paper presented at the biennial meeting of the Society for Research in Child Development, Toronto.

Lyle, J., & Hoffman, H. R. (1972). Children's use of television and other media. In E. A. Rubenstein, G. A. Comstock, & J. P. Murray (Eds.), *Television and social behavior,* Vol. 4. Washington, DC: U.S. Government Printing Office.

Lytton, H. (1976). The socialization of two-year-old boys: Ecological findings. *Journal of Child Psychology and Psychiatry, 17,* 287–304.

M

Maccoby, E. E. (1980). *Social development.* New York: Harcourt, Brace Jovanovich.

Maccoby, E. E. (1984). Middle childhood in the context of the family. In *Development during middle childhood.* Washington, DC: National Academy Press.

Maccoby, E. E., & Jacklin, C. N. (1974). *The psychology of sex differences.* Stanford, CA: Stanford University Press.

Maccoby, E. E., & Jacklin, C. N. (1980). Sex differences in aggression: A rejoinder and reprise. *Child Development, 51,* 964–980.

Maccoby, E. E., & Martin, J. A. (1983). Socialization in the context of the family: Parent-child interaction. In P. H. Mussen (Ed.), *Handbook of child psychology* (4th ed.), Vol. 4. New York: Wiley.

Maccoby, E. E., & Masters, J. C. (1970). Attachment and dependency. In P. H. Mussen (Ed.), *Carmichael's manual of child psychology* (3rd ed.), Vol. 2. New York: Wiley.

MacFarlane, J. A. (1975). Olfaction in the development of social preferences in the human neonate. In *Parent-infant interaction, Ciba Foundation Symposium, 33.* Amsterdam: Elsevier.

Mackintosh, N. J. (1983). *Conditioning and associative learning.* New York: Oxford University Press.

Maddux, J. E., Roberts, M. C., Sledden, E. A., & Wright, L. (1986). Developmental issues in child health psychology. *American Psychologist, 41,* 25–34.

Maeher, M. L. (1984). Meaning and motivation: Toward a theory of personal investment. In R. E. Ames & C. Ames (Eds.), *Motivation in education.* New York: Academic Press.

Mahler, M. S. (1979). *Separation-individuation* (Vol. 2). London: Jason Aronson.

Main, M. (1973). *Exploration, play and cognitive functioning as related to child-mother attachment.* Unpublished doctoral dissertation, Johns Hopkins University.

Main, M., Kaplan, N., & Cassidy, J. (1985). Security in infancy, childhood, and adulthood: A move to the level of representation. *Monographs of the Society for Research in Child Development, 50* (Serial No. 209).

Main, M., & Londerville, S. (1977, March). *Compliance and aggression in toddlerhood.* Paper presented at the meeting of the Society for Research in Child Development, New Orleans, LA.

Malatesta, G. Z., & Haviland, J. (1982). Learning display rules: The socialization of emotional expressions in infancy. *Child Development, 55,* 991–1003.

Malatesta, G. Z., & Haviland, J. (1985). Signals, symbols, and socialization. In M. Lewis & C. Saarni (Eds.), *The socialization of emotions.* New York: Plenum.

Mandler, G. (1980). Recognizing the judgment of previous occurrence. *Psychological Review, 87,* 252–271.

Mandler, J. M. (1983). Representation. In P. H. Mussen (Ed.), *Handbook of child psychology* (4th ed.), Vol. 3. New York: Wiley.

Mandler, J. M., & Robinson, C. A. (1977). Developmental changes in picture recognition. *Journal of Experimental Child Psychology, 3,* 386–396.

Mannarino, A. P. (1978). Friendship patterns and self-concept in preadolescent males. *Journal of Genetic Psychology, 133,* 105–110.

Mannarino, A. P. (1979). The relationship between friendship and altruism in preadolescent girls. *Psychiatry, 42,* 280–284.

Maratsos, M. (1983). Some current issues in the study of the acquisition of grammar. In P. H. Mussen (Ed.), *Handbook of child psychology* (4th ed.), Vol. 3. New York: Wiley.

Maratsos, M. P., & Chalkey, M. A. (1980). The internal language of children's syntax: The ontogenesis and representation of syntactic categories. In K. E. Nelson (Ed.), *Children's language,* Vol. 2. New York: Gardner Press.

Marcia, J. (1966). Development and validation of ego identity status. *Journal of Personality and Social Psychology, 3,* 551–558.

Marcia, J. (1976). Identity six years after: A follow-up study. *Journal of Youth and Adolescence, 5,* 145–160.

Marcia, J. (1980). Ego identity development. In J. Adelson (Ed.), *Handbook of adolescent psychology.* New York: Wiley.

Marcia, J. (1983). *Journal of Early Adolescence, 3.*

Marcus, T. L., & Corsini, D. A. (1978). Parental expectation of preschool children as related to gender and socioeconomic status. *Child Development, 29,* 243–246.

Markus, H. (1977). Self-schemata and processing information about the self. *Journal of Personality and Social Psychology, 35,* 63–78.

Marr, D. B., & Sternberg, R. J. (1985, April). *Effects of contextual relevance on attention to novel information.* Paper presented at the meeting of the Society for Research in Child Development, Toronto.

Marshall, H. (1981). Open classroom: Has the term outlived its usefulness? *Review of Educational Research, 51,* 181–192.

Marshall, R. E., Porter, F. L., Rogers, A. G., Moore, J., Anderson, B., & Boxerman, S. B. (1982). Circumcision II: Effects upon mother-infant interaction. *Early Human Development, 7,* 367–374.

Martin, B. (1977). *Abnormal psychology.* New York: Holt, Rinehart & Winston.

Martin, G. B., & Clark, R. D. (1982). Distress crying in neonates: Species and peer specificity. *Developmental Psychology, 18,* 3–9.

Martin, J. (1976). *The education of adolescents.* Washington, DC: U.S. Office of Education.

Marx, G. (1977). *The Groucho Phile.* New York: Pocket Books.

Maslow, A. H. (1970). *Motivation and personality* (2nd ed.). New York: Harper & Row.

Matas, L., Arend, R. A., & Sroufe, L. A. (1978). Continuity in the adaptation in the second year: The relationships between quality of attachment and later competence. *Child Development, 49,* 547–556.

Matthews, K. A. (1982). Psychological perspectives on the Type A behavior pattern. *Psychological Bulletin, 91,* 293–323.

Mauer, D., & Salapatek, P. H. (1976). Developmental changes in the scanning of faces by young infants. *Child Development, 47,* 523–527.

Mayer, J. (1968). *Overweight: Causes, cost, and control.* Englewood Cliffs, NJ: Prentice-Hall.

McCabe, M. P., & Collins, J. K. (1979). Sex role and dating orientation. *Journal of Youth and Adolescence, 8,* 407–425.

McCall, R. B. (1982). A hard look at stimulating and predicting development: The cases of bonding and screening infants. *Pediatrics in Review, 3,* 205–212.

McCall, R. B. (1985, April). *Discussion—Novelty as a source of developmental continuity in intelligence.* Paper presented at the meeting of the Society for Research in Child Development, Toronto.

McCall, R. B., Applebaum, M. I., & Hogarty, P. S. (1973). Developmental changes in mental performance. *Monographs of the Society for Research in Child Development, 38,* (Serial No. 150).

McCandless, B. R. (1970). *Adolescents: Behavior and development.* Hinsdale, IL: Dryden Press.

McCandless, B. R. (1973). *Male caregivers in day care: Demonstration project.* Atlanta, GA: Emory University.

McCandless, B. R., & Evans, E. (1973). *Children and youth.* New York: Holt, Rinehart & Winston.

McClelland, D. C. (1961). *The achieving society.* New York: Van Nostrand.

McClelland, D. C., Atkinson, J. R., Clark, R. A., & Lowell, E. O. (1953). *The achievement motive.* New York: Appleton-Century-Crofts.

McConaghy, M. J. (1979). Gender permanence and the genital basis of gender: Stages in the development of constancy of gender identity. *Child Development, 50,* 1223–1226.

McCord, J. (1980). Antecedents and correlates of vulnerability and resistance to psychopathology. In R. Zucker & A. Rabin (Eds.), *Further explorations in personality.* New York: Wiley.

McCord, W., McCord, J., & Gudeman, J. (1960). *Origins of alcoholism.* Palo Alto, CA: Stanford University Press.

McKean, K. (1985, October). The assault on IQ. *Discover,* pp. 25–44.

McLaughlin, B. (1978). *Second-language acquisition in childhood.* Hillsdale, NJ: Erlbaum.

McLaughlin, L., & Chassin, L. (1985, April). *Adolescents at risk for future alcohol abuse.* Paper presented at the biennial meeting of the Society for Research in Child Development, Toronto.

McNeill, D. (1970). *The acquisition of language.* New York: Harper & Row.

Meacham, J. A., & Santilli, N. R. (1982). Interstage relationships in Erikson's theory: Identity and intimacy. *Child Development, 53,* 1461–1467.

Medrich, E. A., Rosen, J., Rubin, V., & Buckley, S. (1982). *The serious business of growing up.* Berkeley: University of California Press.

Meier, J. H. (1971). Prevalence and characteristics of learning disabilities found in second-grade children. *Journal of Learning Disabilities, 4,* 1–16.

Meilman, P. W. (1979). Cross-sectional age changes in ego identity status during adolescence. *Developmental Psychology, 15,* 230–231.

Meltzoff, A. N., & Borton, R. W. (1979). Intermodal matching in human neonates. *Nature, 282,* 403–404.

Meltzoff, A. N., & Moore, M. K. (1977). Interpreting "imitative" responses in early infancy. *Science, 205,* 217–219.

Mercer, J. R., & Lewis, J. F. (1978). *System of multicultural pluralistic assessment.* New York: Psychological Corporation.

Meredith, H. V. (1978). Research between 1960 and 1970 on the standing height of young children in different parts of the world. In H. W. Reese & L. P. Lipsitt (Eds.), *Advances in child development and behavior,* Vol. 12. New York: Academic Press.

Merrill, D. J. (1986). An update on human evolution. *Contemporary Psychology, 31,* 585.

Michaels, C., & Carello, C. (1981). *Direct perception.* Englewood Cliffs, NJ: Prentice-Hall.

Milham, J., Widmayer, S., Bauer, C. R., & Peterson, L. (1983, April). *Predictory cognitive deficits for preterm, low-birth-weight infants.* Paper presented at the biennial meeting of the Society for Research in Child Development, Detroit.

Mill, J. (1869). *An analysis of the phenomena of the human mind.* London: Longmans, Green, Roeder, & Dyer.

Miller, G. (1981). *Language and speech.* New York: W. H. Freeman.

Miller, L. L. et al. (1978). Marijuana: An analysis of storage and retrieval deficits in memory and the technique of restricted reminding. *Pharmacology, Biochemistry and Behavior, 8,* 327–332.

Miller, N., & Maruyama, G. (1976). Ordinal position and peer popularity. *Journal of Personality and Social Psychology, 33,* 123–131.

Miller, N. B., & Cantwell, D. P. (1976). Siblings as therapists. *American Journal of Psychiatry, 133,* 447–450.

Miller, N. E. (1981). *Language and speech.* San Francisco: W. H. Freeman.

Miller, W. B. (1958). Lower-class culture as a generating milieu of gang delinquency. *Journal of Social Issues, 14,* 5–19.

Minard, J., Coleman, D., Williams, G., & Ingledyne, E. (1968). Cumulative REM of three- to five-day-olds: Effects of normal external noise and maturation. *Psychophysiology, 5,* 232.

Minnett, A. M., Vandell, D. L., & Santrock, J. W. (1983). The effects of sibling status on sibling interaction: Influence of birth order, age spacing, sex of the child, and sex of sibling. *Child Development, 54,* 1064–1072.

Minuchin, P. P., & Shapiro, E. K. (1983). The school as a context for social development. In P. H. Mussen (Ed.), *Handbook of child psychology* (4th ed.), Vol. 4. New York: Wiley.

Mischel, W. (1970). Sex typing and socialization. In P. H. Mussen (Ed.), *Carmichael's manual of child psychology* (3rd ed.), Vol. 2. New York: Wiley.

Mischel, W. (1973). Toward a cognitive social learning reconceptualization of personality. *Psychological Review, 80,* 252–283.

Mischel, W. (1974). Processes in delay of gratification. In L. Berkowitz (Ed.), *Advances in experimental social psychology,* Vol. 7. New York: Academic Press.

Mischel, W. (1976). *Introduction to personality* (2nd ed.). New York: Holt, Rinehart & Winston.

Mischel, W. (1983, August). *Convergences and challenges in the search for the person.* Invited address at the meeting of the American Psychological Association, Los Angeles.

Mischel, W. (1984). Convergences and challenges in the search for consistency. *American Psychologist, 39,* 351–364.

Mischel, W., & Baker, N. (1975). Cognitive transformations of reward objects through instructions. *Journal of Personality and Social Psychology, 31,* 254–261.

Mischel, W., & Patterson, C. J. (1976). Substantive and structural elements of effective plans for self-control. *Journal of Personality and Social Psychology, 34,* 942–950.

Mischel, W., Peake, K., & Zeiss, A. R. (1984). *Longitudinal studies on delay of gratification.* Unpublished manuscript, Stanford University, Palo Alto, CA.

Mistry, J. J., & Lange, G. W. (1985). Children's organization and recall of information in scripted narratives. *Child Development, 56,* 953–961.

Mitchell, R. G., & Etches, P. (1977). Rhythmic habit patterns (stereotypies). *Developmental Medicine and Child Neurology, 19,* 545–550.

Mitteness, L. S., & Nydegger, C. N. (1982, October). *Dimensions of parent-child relations in adulthood.* Paper presented at the meeting of the American Gerontological Association.

Mizner, G. L., Barter, J. T., & Werme, P. H. (1970). Patterns of drug use among college students. *American Journal of Psychiatry, 127,* 15–24.

Moely, B. E., Olson, F. A., Halwes, T. G., & Flavell, J. H. (1969). Production deficiency in young children's clustered recall. *Developmental Psychology, 1,* 26–34.

Moerk, E. L. (1985, April). *The fuzzy set called imitations.* Paper presented at the meeting of the Society for Research in Child Development, Toronto.

Montemayor, R. (1982, October). *Parent-adolescent conflict: A critical review of the literature.* Paper presented at the first Biennial Conference on Adolescent Research, Tucson, Arizona.

Moore, D. (1985, April). *Parent-adolescent separation: The construction of adulthood by late adolescents.* Paper presented at the biennial meeting of the Society for Research in Child Development, Toronto.

Moore, T. (1975). Exclusive mothering and its alternatives: The outcomes to adolescence. *Scandinavian Journal of Psychology, 17,* 255–272.

Moos, R. H., & Moos, B. S. (1978). Classroom social climate and student absences and grades. *Journal of Educational Psychology, 70,* 263–269.

Morgan, G. A., & Ricciuti, H. N. (1969). Infants' responses to strangers during the first year. In B. M. Foss (Ed.), *Determinants of infant behavior,* Vol. 4. London: Methuen.

Morgan, J. L. (1985). *Prosodic encoding of syntactic information in speech to young children.* Paper presented at the biennial meeting of the Society for Research in Child Development, Toronto.

Morris, D. (1967). *The naked ape.* New York: McGraw-Hill.

Mowat, F. (1963). *Never cry wolf.* Boston: Little, Brown.

Mueller, E. (1979). (Toddlers + Toys) = (An autonomous social system). In M. Lewis & L. A. Rosenblum (Eds.), *The child and its family.* New York: Plenum.

Mueller, E. (1985, April). Discussant for *Early peer relations: Ten years of research.* Symposium presented at the biennial meeting of the Society for Research in Child Development, Toronto.

Mueller, E., & Brenner, J. (1977). The origins of social skills, and interaction among playgroup toddlers. *Child Development, 48,* 854–861.

Murray, A. D., Dolby, R. M., Nation, R. L., & Thomas, D. B. (1981). Effects of epidural anesthesia on newborns and their mothers. *Child Development, 52,* 71–82.

Murray, D. M., & Perry, C. L. (1984, August). *The functional meaning of adolescent drug use.* Paper presented at the 92nd annual meeting of the American Psychological Association, Toronto.

Murray, F. B. (1978, August). *Generation of educational practice from developmental theory.* Paper presented at the meeting of the American Psychological Association, Toronto, Canada.

Murray, H. A. (1938). *Explorations in personality.* New York: Oxford.

Mussen, P. H., & Jones, M. C. (1958). The behavior-inferred motivations of late- and early-maturing boys. *Child Development, 29,* 61–67.

Myers, B. J. (1982). Early intervention using the Brazelton training with middle-class mothers and fathers of newborns. *Child Development, 53,* 462–471.

Myles-Worsley, M., Cromer, C. C., & Dodd, D. H. (1986). Children's preschool script reconstruction: Reliance on general knowledge as memory fades. *Developmental Psychology, 22,* 22–30.

N

Naeye, R. L. (1979). Relationship of cigarette smoking to congenital anomalies and perinatal death. *American Journal of Pathology, 90,* 289–293.

National Advisory Committee on Handicapped Children. (1968). *Special education for handicapped children, first annual report.* Washington, DC: U.S. Department of Health, Education, and Welfare. (Conference)

National Assessment of Educational Progress. (1976). *Adult work skills and knowledge* (Report No. 35–COD–01). Denver, CO: National Assessment of Educational Progress.

National Education Association. (1974). *Today's changing roles: An approach to nonsexist teaching.* Minneapolis: Author.

National Institute on Alcohol Abuse and Alcoholism. (1975). *A national study of adolescent drinking behavior, attitudes, and correlates.* Final report prepared by Research Triangle Institute, Research Triangle Park, NC.

Neimark, E. D. (1982). Adolescent thought: Transition to formal operations. In B. B. Wolman (Ed.), *Handbook of developmental psychology.* Englewood Cliffs, NJ: Prentice-Hall.

Nelson, K. (1977). Cognitive development and the acquisition of concepts. In R. C. Anderson, R. J. Spiro, & W. E. Montague (Eds.), *Schooling and the acquisition of knowledge.* Hillsdale, NJ: Erlbaum.

Nelson, K. (1981). Social cognition as a script framework. In J. H. Flavell & L. Ross (Eds.), *Cognitive development: Frontiers and possible futures.* New York: Cambridge University Press.

Nelson, K. E. (1975, April). *Facilitating syntax acquisition.* Paper presented at the Eastern Psychological Association, New York.

Nelson, K. E. (1978). How children represent knowledge of their world in and out of language. In R. S. Siegler (Ed.), *Children's thinking: What develops?* Hillsdale, NJ: Erlbaum.

Nelson, K. E., Carskaddon, G., & Bonvillian, J. D. (1973). Syntax acquisition: Impact of experimental variation in adult verbal communication with the child. *Child Development, 44,* 497–504.

Nelson, W. E., Vaughn, V. C., & McKay, R. J. (1975). *Textbook of pediatrics.* Philadelphia: Saunders.

Neugarten, B., & Datan, N. (1973). Sociological perspectives on the life cycle. In P. B. Baltes & K. W. Schale (Eds.), *Life-span developmental psychology.* New York: Academic Press.

Newcomb, A. F., & Bukowski, W. M. (1984). A longitudinal study of the utility of social preference and social impact sociometric classification schemes. *Child Development, 55,* 1434–1447.

Newell, A., & Simon, H. A. (1972). *Human problem solving.* Englewood Cliffs, NJ: Prentice-Hall.

Newson, J., & Newson, E. (1968). *Four years old in an urban community.* Chicago: Aldine.

Newson, J., & Newson, E. (1976). *Seven years old in the home environment.* New York: Wiley.

Nichols, J. G. (1979). Quality and equality in intellectual development: The role of motivation in education. *American Psychologist, 34,* 1071–1084.

Nichols, J. G. (1984). Conceptions of ability and achievement motivation. In R. E. Ames & C. Ames (Eds.), *Motivation in education.* New York: Academic Press.

Nickerson, E. T. (1975). *Intervention strategies for modifying sex stereotypes.* Paper presented at the annual convention of school psychologists, Atlanta.

Nicolich, L. (1977). Beyond sensorimotor intelligence: Assessment of symbolic maturity through analysis of pretend play. *Merrill-Palmer Quarterly, 23,* 89–99.

Nielson Television Index. (1981). *Child and teenage television viewing* (Special release). New York: NTI.

Norman, D. (1982). Personal conversation. In M. Hunt, *The universe within.* New York: Simon & Schuster.

Nottelman, E. D. (1982). *The interaction of physical maturity and school transition.* Paper presented at the meeting of the American Educational Research Association, New York.

Nottelman, E. D., Susman, E. J., Blue, J. H., Inoff-Germain, G., Dorn, L. D., Loriaux, D. L., Cutler, G. B., & Chrousos, G. P. (in press). Gonadal and adrenal hormone correlates of adjustment in early adolescence. In R. M. Lerner & T. T. Foch (Eds.), *Biological-psychosocial interactions in early adolescence: A life-span perspective.* Hillsdale, NJ: Erlbaum.

Nucci, L. (1982). Conceptual development in the moral and conventional domains: Implications for values education. *Review of Educational Research, 52,* 93–122.

Nutrition Committee of the Canadian Pediatric Society and the Committee on Nutrition of the American Academy of Pediatrics. (1978). Breast-feeding. *Pediatrics, 62,* 591–601.

Nutrition National Canada Survey. (1973). Toronto, Canada: Canadian Government Publications.

Nydegger, C. N. (1975, October). *Age and parental behavior.* Paper presented at the meeting of the Gerontological Society of America, Louisville, KY.

Nydegger, C. N. (1981, October). *The ripple effect of parental timing.* Paper presented at the meeting of the American Gerontological Association.

O'Conner-Francoeur, P. (1983, April). *Children's concepts of health and their health behavior.* Paper presented at the meeting of the Society for Research in Child Development, Detroit.

O'Connor, M. J., Cohen, S., & Parmelee, A. H. (1984). Infant auditory discrimination in preterm and full-term infants as predictor of five-year intelligence. *Child Development, 20,* 159–165.

O'Keefe, E. S. C., & Hyde, J. S. (1983). The development of occupational sex-role stereotypes: The effects of gender stability and age. *Sex Roles, 9,* 481–492.

Oden, S. L., & Asher, S. R. (1975, April). *Coaching children in social skills for friendship making.* Paper presented at the meeting of the Society for Research in Child Development, Denver, CO.

Olds, D. E., & Shaver, P. (1980). Masculinity, femininity, academic performance, and health: Further evidence concerning the androgyny controversy. *Journal of Personality, 48,* 323–341.

Olson, D. R. (1977). From utterance to text: The bias of language in speech and writing. *Harvard Educational Review, 47,* 257–281.

Olson, G. M., & Strauss, M. S. (1984). The development of infant memory. In M. Moscovitch (Ed.), *Infant memory.* New York: Plenum.

Orlofsky, J. (1976). Intimacy status: Relationship to interpersonal perception. *Journal of Youth and Adolescence, 5,* 73–88.

Orlofsky, J., Marcia, J., & Lesser, I., (1973). Ego identity status and the intimacy versus isolation crisis of young adulthood. *Journal of Personality and Social Psychology, 27,* 211–219.

Ottinger, D. R., & Simmons, J. E. (1964). Behavior of human neonates and prenatal maternal anxiety. *Psychological Reports, 14,* 391–394.

Ourselves and our children. (1978). New York: Random House.

Overton, W. F., & Meehan, A. M. (1982). Individual differences in formal operational thought: Sex roles and learned helplessness. *Child Development, 53,* 1536–1543.

Owen, S. V., Froman, R. D., & Moscow, H. (1981). *Educational psychology.* Boston: Little, Brown.

P

Paivio, A. (1971). *Imagery and verbal processes*. New York: Holt, Rinehart & Winston.

Pancake, V. R. (1985, April). *Continuity between mother-infant attachment and ongoing dyadic peer relationships in preschool*. Paper presented at the biennial meeting of the Society for Research in Child Development, Toronto.

Papoušek, H. (1961). Conditioned head rotation reflexes in infants in the first months of life. *Acta Pediatrica, 50*, 565–576.

Papoušek, H. (1976). Experimental studies of appetitional behavior in human newborns and infants. In H. W. Stevenson, E. H. Hess, & H. L. Rheingold (Eds.), *Early behavior: Comparative and developmental approaches*. New York: Wiley.

Parcel, G. S., Tiernan, K., Nadar, P. R., & Gottlob, D. (1979). Health education and kindergarten children. *Journal of School Health, 49*, 129–131.

Paris, S. C., & Lindauer, B. K. (1976). The role of inferences in children's comprehension and memory for sentences. *Cognitive Psychology, 8*, 217–227.

Paris, S. C., & Lindauer, B. K. (1982). The development of cognitive skills during childhood. In B. B. Wolman (Ed.), *Handbook of developmental psychology*. Englewood Cliffs, NJ: Prentice-Hall.

Paris, S. C., Lindauer, B. K., & Cox, G. L. (1977). The development of inferential comprehension. *Child Development, 48*, 1728–1733.

Parke, R. D. (1972). Some effects of punishment on children's behavior. In W. W. Hartup (Ed.), *The young child*, Vol. 2. Washington, DC: NAEYC.

Parke, R. D. (1976, September). *Child abuse: An overview of alternative models*. Paper presented at the meeting of the American Psychological Association, Washington, DC.

Parke, R. D. (1977). Some effects of punishment on children's behavior—revisited. In E. M. Hetherington & R. D. Parke (Eds.), *Contemporary readings in child psychology*. New York: McGraw-Hill.

Parke, R. D., & Lewis, N. G. (1980). The family in context: A multilevel interactional analysis of child abuse. In R. W. Henderson (Ed.), *Parent-child interaction: Theory, research, and prospect*. New York: Academic Press.

Parke, R. D., & Sawin, D. B. (1980). The family in early infancy: Social interactional and attitudinal analyses. In F. Pedersen (Ed.), *The father-infant relationship: Observational studies in a family context*. New York: Praeger.

Parke, R. D., & Suomi, S. (1983). Adult male-infant relationships: Human and nonhuman primate evidence. In K. Immelmann, G. Barlow, M. Main, & L. Petrinovitch (Eds.), *Behavioral development: The Bielefeld interdisciplinary project*. New York: Cambridge University Press.

Parker, J., & Gottman, J. (1985, April). *Making friends with an extraterrestrial: Conversational skills and friendship formation in young children*. Paper presented at the meeting of the Society for Research in Child Development, Toronto.

Parmelee, A. H. (1986). Children's illnesses: Their beneficial effects on behavioral development. *Child Development, 57*, 1–10.

Parmelee, A. H., & Sigman, M. D. (1983). Perinatal brain development and behavior. In P. H. Mussen (Ed.), *Handbook of child psychology* (4th ed.), Vol. 2. New York: Wiley.

Parmelee, A. H., & Stern, E. (1972). Development of states in infants. In C. B. Clemente, D. P. Purura, & F. E. Mayer (Eds.), *Sleep and the maturing of the nervous system*. New York: Academic Press.

Parmelee, A. H., Schulz, H. R., & Disbrow, M. A. (1961). Sleep patterns of the newborn. *Journal of Pediatrics, 48*, 241–250.

Parmelee, A. H., Wenne, W. H., & Schulz, H. R. (1964). Infant sleep patterns from birth to sixteen weeks of age. *Journal of Pediatrics, 65*, 576–582.

Parten, M. (1932). Social play among preschool children. *Journal of Abnormal and Social Psychology, 27*, 243–269.

Pascual-Leone, J. A. (1970). A mathematical model for the transition rule in Piaget's developmental stages. *Acta Psychologica, 32*, 301–345.

Patterson, G. R. (1982). *Coercive family process*. Eugene, OR: Castalia.

Patterson, G. R., Reid, J. B., Jones, R. R., & Conger, R. (1975). *A social learning approach to family intervention: Parent training* (Vol. 1). Eugene, OR: Castalia.

Patterson, G. R., & Stouthamer-Loeber, M. (1984). The correlation of family management practices and delinquency. *Child Development, 55*, 1299–1307.

Pavlov, I. P. (1927). *Conditioned reflexes* (F. V. Anrep, Trans. and Ed.). New York: Dover.

Pawson, M., & Morris, N. (1972). The role of the father in pregnancy and labor. In N. Morris (Ed.), *Psychological medicine in obstetrics and gynecology*. Basel: Karger.

Pedersen, F. A., Anderson, B. J., & Cain, R. L. (1977, March). *An approach to understanding linkages between the parent-infant and spouse relationship*. Paper presented at the meeting of the Society for Research in Child Development. New Orleans, LA.

Pedersen, F. A., Anderson, B. J., & Cain, R. L. (1980). Parent-infant and husband-wife interactions observed at age five months. In F. A. Pedersen (Ed.), *The father-infant relationship: Observational studies in the family setting*. New York: Praeger.

Pepler, D. J., Abramovitch, R., & Corter, C. (1981). Sibling interaction in the home: A longitudinal study. *Child Development, 52*, 1344–1347.

Perlmutter, M. (1980). Development of memory in the preschool years. In R. Green & T. D. Yawkey (Eds.), *Early and middle childhood: Growth, abuse, and delinquency and its effects on individual, family, and community*. Westport, CT: Technomic.

Perry, C. (1982). Adolescent health: An educational-ecological perspective. In T. J. Coates, A. C. Peterson, & C. Peery (Eds.), *Promoting adolescent health*. New York: Academic Press.

Peskin, H. (1967). Pubertal onset and ego functioning. *Journal of Abnormal Psychology, 72*, 1–15.

Petersen, A. C., & Taylor, B. (1980). The biological approach to adolescence. In J. Adelson (Ed.), *Handbook of adolescent psychology.* New York: Wiley.

Peterson, P. L. (1977). Interactive effects of student anxiety, achievement orientation, and teacher behavior on student achievement and attitude. *Journal of Educational Psychology, 69,* 779–792.

Phares, E. J. (1976). *Locus of control in personality.* Morristown, NJ: General Learning Press.

Phares, E. J., & Lamiell, J. T. (1975). Internal-external control, interpersonal judgments of others in need, and attribution of responsibility. *Journal of Personality, 43,* 23–28.

Piaget, J. (1932). *The moral judgment of the child.* New York: Harcourt, Brace Jovanovich.

Piaget, J. (1952). Jean Piaget. In C. A. Murchison (Ed.), *A history of psychology in autobiography,* Vol. 4. Worcester, MA: Clark University Press.

Piaget, J. (1954). *The construction of reality in the child.* New York: Basic Books.

Piaget, J. (1962). *Play, dreams, and imitation in childhood.* New York: Norton.

Piaget, J. (1967). *The child's conception of the world.* Totowa, NJ: Littlefield, Adams & Co.

Piaget, J., & Inhelder, B. (1969). *The child's conception of space* (F. J. Langdon & J. L. Lunzer, Trans.). New York: Norton (originally published 1948).

Piers, E. V., & Harris, D. B. (1964). Age and other correlates of self-concept in children. *Journal of Educational Psychology, 55,* 91–95.

Piontkowski, D., & Calfee, R. (1979). Attention in the classroom. In G. Hale & M. Lewis (Eds.), *Attention and cognitive development.* New York: Plenum.

Piotrkowski, C. S., & Stark, E. (1985, April). *The effects of occupational stress on fathering.* Paper presented at the biennial meeting of the Society for Research in Child Development, Toronto.

Place, D. M. (1975). The dating experience for adolescent girls. *Adolescence, 38,* 157–173.

Pleck, J. (1975). Masculinity-femininity: Current and alternative paradigms. *Sex Roles, 1,* 161–178.

Pleck, J. H. (1984). *Working wives and family well-being.* Beverly Hills, CA: Sage.

Plomin, R., & DeFries, J. C. (1983). The Colorado Adoption Project. *Child Development, 54,* 276–289.

Porteus, A. (1976). *Teacher-centered versus student-centered instruction: Interactions with cognitive and motivational aptitudes.* Unpublished doctoral dissertation, Stanford University, Stanford, CA.

Potter, P. C., & Roberts, M. C. (1984). Children's perceptions of chronic illness: The roles of disease symptoms, cognitive development, and information. *Journal of Pediatric Psychology, 9,* 13–28.

Power, C. (1984). *Moral atmosphere.* Paper presented at the meeting of the American Educational Research Association, New Orleans.

Prechtl, H. F. R. (1965). Problems of behavioral studies in the newborn infant. In D. S. Lehrman, R. A. Hinde, & E. Shaw (Eds.), *Advances in the study of behavior.* New York: Academic Press.

Premack, A. J., & Premack, D. (1972). Teaching language to an ape. *Scientific American, 227,* 92–98.

Prendergast, T. J., & Schaefer, E. S. (1974). Correlates of drinking and drunkenness among high school students. *Quarterly Journal of Studies on Alcohol, 35,* 232–242.

Pressley, M. (1982). Elaboration and memory development. *Child Development, 53,* 296–309.

Pressley, M., & Levin, J. R. (1977). Task parameters affecting the efficacy of a visual imagery learning strategy in younger and older children. *Journal of Experimental Child Psychology, 24,* 53–59.

Pressley, M., & Levin, J. R. (1980). The development of mental imagery retrieval. *Child Development, 51,* 558–560.

Pritscher, C. M. G. (1980). *A study of choices: Expectancy and attribution patterns of psychologically androgynous and sex-role congruent females and males.* Unpublished doctoral dissertation, University of Toledo, Toledo, OH (University Microfilms No. 8110598).

Psathas, G. (1957). Ethnicity, social class, and adolescent independence. *American Sociological Review, 22,* 415–523.

Pulos, E., Teller, D. Y., & Buck, S. (1980). Infant color vision: A search for short wavelength-sensitive mechanisms by means of chromatic adaptation. *Vision Research, 20,* 485–493.

Q

Quadagno, D. M., Briscoe, R., & Quadagno, J. S. (1977). Effect of perinatal gonadal hormones on selected nonsexual behavior patterns: A critical assessment of the nonhuman and human literature. *Psychological Bulletin, 84,* 62–80.

R

Rabinowitz, M., Valentine, K. M., & Mandler, J. M. (1981, September). *A developmental comparison of inferential processing: When adults don't always know best.* Paper presented at the meeting of the American Psychological Association, Los Angeles.

Ramey, C. T., MacPhee, D., & Yeates, K. O. (1982). Preventing developmental retardation: A general systems model. In L. Bond & J. Joffe (Eds.), *Facilitating infant and early childhood development.* Hanover, NH: University Press of New England.

Raven, J. C. (1960). *Guide to using the Standard Progressive Matrices.* London: Lewis.

Rebecca, M., Hefner, R., & Oleshanksy, B. (1976). A model of sex-role transcendence. *Journal of Social Issues, 32,* 197–206.

Rehm, L., & Marston, R. (1968). Reduction of anxiety through modification of self-reinforcement: An instigation therapy technique. *Journal of Consulting and Clinical Psychology, 36,* 556–574.

Reiss, I. F. (1967). *The social context of premarital sexual permissiveness.* New York: Holt, Rinehart & Winston.

Rekers, G. A. (1979). Psychosexual and gender problems. In E. J. Mash & L. G. Terdal (Eds.), *Behavioral assessment of childhood disorders.* New York: Guilford Press.

Rescorla, R. A. (1967). Pavlovian conditioning and its proper control procedures. *Psychological Review, 74,* 71–80.

Resnick, H. L. P. (1980). Suicide. In H. I. Kaplan, A. M. Freedman, & B. J. Sadock (Eds.), *Comprehensive textbook of psychiatry,* Vol. 2. Baltimore: Williams & Wilkins.

Resnick, L. B. (1980). The role of invention in the development of mathematical competence. In R. H. Kluwe & H. Spada (Eds.), *Developmental models of thinking.* New York: Academic Press.

Rest, J., Turiel, E., & Kohlberg, L. (1969). Relations between level of moral judgment and preference and comprehension of the moral judgments of others. *Journal of Personality, 37,* 225–252.

Rest, J. R. (1976). New approaches in the assessment of moral judgment. In T. Lickona (Ed.), *Moral development and behavior.* New York: Holt, Rinehart & Winston.

Rest, J. R. (1977, March). *Development in judging moral issues—A summary of research using the defining issues test.* Paper presented at the meeting of the Society for Research in Child Development, New Orleans.

Rest, J. R. (1983). Morality. In P. H. Mussen (Ed.), *Handbook of child psychology* (4th ed.), Vol. 3. New York: Wiley.

Reynolds, L. G., & Shister, J. (1949). *Job horizons.* New York: Harper.

Rheingold, H. L. (1969). The social and socializing infant. In D. A. Goslin (Ed.), *Handbook of socialization theory and research.* Chicago: Rand McNally.

Rheingold, H. L. (1973). Independent behavior of the human infant. In A. Pick (Ed.), *Minnesota Symposium of Child Psychology* (Vol. 7). Minneapolis: University of Minnesota Press.

Rheingold, H. L., & Eckerman, C. O. (1970). The infant separates himself from his mother. *Science, 168,* 78–83.

Rheingold, H. L., Gewirtz, J. L., & Ross, H. W. (1959). Social conditioning of vocalizations in the infant. *Journal of Comparative and Physiological Psychology, 52,* 68–73.

Rheingold, H. L., & Samuels, H. R. (1969). Mainstreaming the positive behavior of infants by increased stimulation. *Developmental Psychology, 1,* 520–527.

Rholes, W. S., & Ruble, D. N. (1984). Children's understanding of dispositional characteristics of others. *Child Development, 55,* 550–560.

Richards, R. A. (1976). A comparison of selected Guilford and Wallach-Kogan creativity thinking tests in conjunction with measures of intelligence. *Journal of Creative Behavior, 10,* 154–164.

Richardson, J. G., & Simpson, C. H. (1982). Children, gender, and social structure: An analysis of the contents of letters to Santa Claus. *Child Development, 53,* 429–436.

Roberts, G. C., Block, J. H., & Block, J. (1981, April). *Continuity and change in parents' child-rearing practices.* Paper presented at the biennial meeting of the Society for Research in Child Development, Boston.

Roberts, M. C., Elkins, P. D., & Royal, G. P. (1984). Psychological applications to the prevention of accidents and illness. In M. C. Roberts & L. Peterson (Eds.), *Prevention of problems in childhood.* New York: Wiley.

Roberts, M. C., & Wright, L. (1982). Role of the pediatric psychologist as consultant to pediatricians. In J. M. Tuma (Ed.), *Handbook for the practice of pediatric psychology.* New York: Wiley.

Robins, L. N. (1978). Sturdy childhood predictors of adult antisocial behavior: Replications from longitudinal studies. *Psychological Medicine, 8,* 611–622.

Robinson, H. F. (1977). *Exploring teaching in early childhood education.* Boston: Allyn & Bacon.

Rode, S. S., Chang, P., Fisch, R. O., & Sroufe, L. A. (1981). Attachment patterns of infants separated at birth. *Developmental Psychology, 17,* 188–191.

Rodman, H., Pratto, D., & Nelson, R. (1985). Child-care arrangements and children's functioning: A comparison of self-care and adult-care children. *Developmental Psychology, 21,* 413–418.

Roff, M., Sells, S. B., & Golden, M. W. (1972). *Social adjustment and personality development in children.* Minneapolis, MN: University of Minnesota Press.

Roffwarg, H. P., Muzio, J. N., & Dement, W. C. (1966). Ontogenic development of the human sleep-dream cycle. *Science, 152,* 604–619.

Rogers, C. R. (1951). *Client-centered therapy.* Boston: Houghton-Mifflin.

Rogers, T. (1981). A model of the self as an aspect of the human information-processing system. In N. Cantor & J. Kihlstrom (Eds.), *Cognition, social interaction, and personality.* Hillsdale, NJ: Erlbaum.

Rogers, T., Kuiper, N., & Kirker, W. (1977). Self-reference and the encoding of personal information. *Journal of Personality and Social Psychology, 35,* 677–688.

Roper, R., & Hinde, R. A. (1978). Social behavior in a play group: Consistency and complexity. *Child Development, 45,* 920–927.

Rose, S. A., Gottfried, A. W., & Bridger, W. H. (1981). Cross-modal transfer in six-month-old infants. *Developmental Psychology, 17,* 661–669.

Rose, S. A., & Wallace, I. F. (1985). Visual recognition memory: A predictor of later cognitive functioning in preterms. *Child Development, 56,* 843–852.

Rosen, B. C. (1959). Race, ethnicity, and the achievement syndrome. *American Sociological Review, 24,* 47–60.

Rosenbaum, A. (1983). *The young people's Yellow Pages: A national sourcebook for youth.* New York: Putnam.

Rosenberg, M. (1965). *Society and the adolescent self-image.* Princeton, NJ: Princeton University Press.

Rosenblatt, D. (1977). Developmental trends in infant play. In B. Tizard & D. Harvey (Eds.), *The biology of play.* Philadelphia: Lippincott.

Rosenblith, J. F., & Sims-Knight, J. E. (1985). *In the beginning: Development in the first two years.* Monterey, CA: Brooks/Cole.

Rosenkrans, M. A. (1967). Imitation in children as a function of perceived similarity to a social model and vicarious reinforcement. *Journal of Personality and Social Psychology, 7,* 307–315.

Rosenman, R. H., Friedman, M., Straus, R., Jenkins, C. D., Zyzanski, S., Wurm, M., Kositchek, R., Hah, W., & Werthessen, N. T. (1970). Coronary heart disease in the Western collaborative group study: A follow-up experience of 4½ years. *Journal of Chronic Diseases, 23,* 173–190.

Ross, A. O. (1974). *Psychological disorders of children: A behavioral approach to theory, research, and therapy.* New York: McGraw-Hill.

Ross, D. G. (1972). *G. Stanley Hall.* Chicago: University of Chicago Press.

Rotenberg, K. J. (1980). Children's use of intentionality in judgments of character and disposition. *Child Development, 51,* 282–284.

Rothbart, M. L. K. (1967). Birth order and mother-child interaction. *Dissertation Abstracts, 27,* 45–57.

Rovee-Collier, C. K. (1984). The ontogeny of learning and memory in human infancy. In R. Kail & N. E. Spear (Eds.), *Comparative perspectives on the development of memory.* Hillsdale, NJ: Erlbaum.

Rozin, P., & Gleitman, L. R. (1977). The structure and acquisition of reading II: The reading process and the acquisition of the alphabetic principle. In A. S. Reber & D. L. Scarborough (Eds.), *Toward a psychology of reading.* Hillsdale, NJ: Erlbaum.

Rubenstein, J. L., Howes, C., & Boyle, P. (1981). A two-year follow-up of infants in community-based infant day care. *Journal of Child Psychology and Psychiatry, 22,* 209–218.

Rubin, D. C., & Kozin, M. (1984). Vivid memories. *Cognition, 16,* 81–95.

Rubin, K. H. (1977). The social and cognitive value of preschool toys and activities. *Canadian Journal of Behavioural Science, 9,* 382–385.

Rubin, K. H. (1978). Role-taking in childhood: Some methodological considerations. *Child Development, 49,* 428–433.

Rubin, K. H. (1982). Nonsocial play in preschoolers: Necessary evil? *Child Development, 53,* 651–657.

Rubin, K. H., & Pepler, D. J. (1980). The relationship of child's play to social-cognitive development. In H. Foot, T. Chapman, & J. Smith (Eds.), *Friendship and childhood relationships.* London: Wiley.

Rubin, K. H., & Schneider, F. W. (1973). The relationship between moral judgment, egocentrism, and altruistic behavior. *Child Development, 44,* 661–665.

Rubin, K. H., Fein, G. G., & Vandenberg, B. (1983). Play. In P. H. Mussen (Ed.), *Handbook of child psychology* (4th ed.), Vol. 4. New York: Wiley.

Rubin, Z., & Sloman, J. (1984). How parents influence their children's friendships. In M. Lewis (Ed.), *Beyond the dyad.* New York: Plenum.

Ruble, D. N., & Ruble, T. L. (1980). Sex stereotypes. In A. G. Miller (Ed.), *In the eye of the beholder: Contemporary issues in stereotyping.* New York: Holt, Rinehart & Winston.

Ruff, H. A., & Kohler, C. J. (1978). Tactual-visual transfer in six-month-old infants. *Infant Behavior and Development, 1,* 259–264.

Rutter, M. (1971). Parent-child separation: Psychological effects on the children. *Journal of Child Psychology and Psychiatry, 12,* 233–256.

Rutter, M. (1981). Stress, coping and development: Some issues and questions. *Journal of Child Psychology and Psychiatry, 22,* 323–356.

Rutter, M. (1983, April). *Influences from family and school.* Paper presented at the meeting of the Society for Research in Child Development, Detroit.

Rutter, M., & Garmezy, N. (1983). Developmental psychopathology. In P. H. Mussen (Ed.), *Handbook of child psychology* (4th ed.), Vol. 4. New York: Wiley.

Rutter, M., Tizard, J., & Whitmore, K. (1970). *Education, health, and behavior.* New York: Wiley.

S

Sagan, C. (1979). *Broca's brain.* New York: Ballentine.

Sagan, C. (1980). *Cosmos.* New York: Random House.

Sakabe, N., Arayama, T. & Suzuki, T. (1969). Human fetal evoked response to acoustic stimulation. *Acta Oto-laryngologica, 252* (Suppl.), 29–36.

Salapatek, P. (1975). Pattern perception in early infancy. In L. B. Cohen & P. Salapatek (Eds.), *Infant perception: From sensation to cognition,* Vol. 1. Orlando, FL: Academic Press.

Samuels, H. R. (1977, March). *The sibling in the infant's social environment.* Paper presented at the biennial meeting of the Society for Research in Child Development, New Orleans.

Santrock, J. W. (1972). The relations of onset and type of father absence to cognitive development. *Child Development, 43,* 455–469.

Santrock, J. W. (1986). *Psychology: The science of mind and behavior.* Dubuque, IA: Wm. C. Brown Publishers.

Santrock, J. W., Smith, P. C., & Bourbeau, P. (1976). Effects of group social comparison upon aggressive and regressive behavior in children. *Child Development, 47,* 831–837.

Santrock, J. W., & Tracy, R. L. (1978). The effects of children's family structure status on the development of stereotypes by teachers. *Journal of Educational Psychology, 70,* 754–757.

Santrock, J. W., & Warshak, R. A. (1979). Father custody and social development in boys and girls. *Journal of Social Issues, 35,* 112–125.

Santrock, J. W., & Warshak, R. A. (1986). Development, relationships, and legal/clinical considerations in father-custody families. In M. E. Lamb (Ed.), *The father's role: Applied perspectives.* New York: Wiley.

Santrock, J. W., Smith, P. C., & Bourbeau, P. (1976). Effects of group social comparison upon aggressive and regressive behavior in children. *Child Development, 47,* 831–837.

Santrock, J. W., Warshak, R. A., Sitterle, K. A., Dozier, C., & Stephens, M. (1985, August). *The social development of children in stepparent families.* Paper presented at the meeting of the American Psychological Association, Los Angeles.

Santrock, J. W., & Yussen, S. R. (1987). *Child Development* (3rd ed.). Dubuque, IA: Wm. C. Brown Company Publishers.

Sarason, I., & Spielberger, C. D. (Eds.). (1975). *Stress and anxiety.* Washington, DC: Hemisphere.

Scardamalia, M., Bereiter, C., & Goelman, H. (1982). The role of production factors in writing ability. In M. Nystrand (Ed.), *What writers know: The language, process, and structure of written discourse.* New York: Academic Press.

Scarr, S. (1984, May). [Interview]. *Psychology Today,* pp. 59–63.

Scarr, S. S., & Kidd, K. K. (1983). Developmental behavior genetics. In P. H. Mussen (Ed.), *Handbook of child psychology* (4th ed.), Vol. 2. New York: Wiley.

Scarr, S., & Weinberg, R. A. (1976). IQ test performance of black children adopted by white families. *American Psychologist, 31,* 726–739.

Scarr, S., & Weinberg, R. A. (1980). Calling all camps! The war is over. *American Sociological Review, 45,* 859–865.

Scarr, S., & Weinberg, R. A. (1983). The Minnesota adoption studies: Genetic differences and malleability. *Child Development, 54,* 260–267.

Schachter, S. (1963). Birth order, eminence, and higher education. *American Sociological Review, 28,* 757–767.

Schacter, D. L., & Moscovitch, M. (1984). Infants, amnesiacs, and dissociable memory systems. In M. Moscovitch (Ed.), *Infant memory.* New York: Plenum.

Schaffer, H. R. (1977). *Mothering.* Cambridge, MA: Harvard University Press.

Schaffer, H. R., & Emerson, P. E. (1964). The development of social attachments in infancy. *Monographs of the Society for Research in Child Development, 29* (3, Serial No. 94).

Schaie, K. W. (1965). A general model for the study of developmental problems. *Psychological Bulletin, 64,* 92–107.

Schaie, K. W. (1977). Quasi-experimental research designs in the psychology of aging. In J. E. Birren & K. W. Schaie (Eds.), *Handbook of the psychology of aging.* New York: Van Nostrand Reinhold.

Schaller, G. B. (1963). *The mountain gorilla.* Chicago: University of Chicago Press.

Schank, R., & Abelson, R. (1977). *Scripts, plans, goals and understanding.* Hillsdale, NJ: Erlbaum.

Schinke, S. P., & Gilchrist, L. D. (1985). Preventive substance abuse with children and adolescents. *Journal of Consulting and Clinical Psychology, 53,* 596–602.

Schramm, W., Lyle, J., & Parker, E. B. (1961). *Television in the lives of children.* Stanford, CA: Stanford University Press.

Schunk, D. H. (1983). Developing children's self-efficacy and skills: The roles of social comparative information and goal setting. *Contemporary Educational Psychology, 8,* 76–86.

Schwartz, D., & Mayaux, M. J. (1982). Female fecundity as a function of age: Results of artificial insemination in nulliparous women with azoospermic husbands. *New England Journal of Medicine, 306,* 404–406.

Schwartz, K. (1978). Proximity to mother and wariness in infants associated with exploration of an unfamiliar object. *Dissertation Abstracts International, 38* (12B), 6204–6205.

Sears, P. S., & Barbee, A. H. (1975, November). *Career and life satisfaction among Terman's gifted women.* Paper presented at the Terman Memorial Symposium on Intellectual Talent, Johns Hopkins University.

Sears, R. R. (1977). Sources of life satisfactions of the Terman gifted men. *American Psychologist, 32,* 119–128.

Sears, R. R., Maccoby, E. E., & Levin, H. (1957). *Patterns of child rearing.* Evanston, IL: Row, Peterson.

Seligman, M. E. P. (1975). *Learned helplessness.* San Francisco: W. H. Freeman.

Seligman, M. E. P., & Peterson, C. (in press). A learned helplessness perspective on childhood depression. In M. Rutter & C. E. Izard (Eds.), *Depression in childhood.* New York: Guilford Press.

Selman, R. L. (1971). The relation of role-taking ability to the development of moral judgment in children. *Child Development, 42,* 79–81.

Selman, R. L. (1976). Social-cognitive understanding. In T. Lickona (Ed.), *Moral development and behavior.* New York: Holt, Rinehart & Winston.

Selman, R. L., Newberger, C. M., & Jacquette, D. (1977, March). *Observing interpersonal reasoning in a clinic/educational setting: Toward the integration of development and clinical-child psychology.* Paper presented at the meeting of the Society for Research in Child Development, New Orleans.

Serbin, L. A., O'Leary, K. D., Kent, R. N., & Tonick, I. J. (1973). A comparison of teacher response to the preacademic and problem behavior of boys and girls. *Child Development, 44,* 796–804.

Shafer, R. P. et al. (1973). *Drug use in America: Problem in perspective* (Second report of the National Commission on Marijuana and Drug Abuse, No. 5266–00003). Washington, DC: U.S. Government Printing Office.

Shantz, C. U. (1983). Social cognition. In P. H. Mussen (Ed.), *Handbook of child psychology* (4th ed.), Vol. 3. New York: Wiley.

Sharabany, R., Gershoni, R., & Hofman, J. E. (1981). Girlfriend, boyfriend: Age and sex differences in intimate friendship. *Developmental Psychology, 17,* 800–808.

Sharpe, L. W. (1976). The effects of a creative thinking program on intermediate-grade educationally handicapped children. *Journal of Creative Behavior, 10*(2), 138–145.

Shatz, M., & Gelman, R. (1973). The development of communication skills: Modifications in the speech of young children as a function of the listener. *Monographs of the Society for Research in Child Development, 38* (Serial No. 152).

Sheingold, K., & Tenney, Y. J. (1982). Memory for a salient childhood event. In U. Neisser (Ed.), *Memory observed.* San Francisco: W. H. Freeman.

Sher, K. J., & Levenson, R. W. (1982). Risk for alcoholism and individual differences in the stress-response-dampening effect of alcohol. *Journal of Abnormal Psychology, 91,* 350–367.

Sherif, M., Harvey, O. J., White, B. J., Hood, W. R., & Sherif, C. W. (1961). *Intergroup conflict and cooperation: The Robber's Cave experiment.* Norman, OK: Institute of Group Relations, University of Oklahoma.

Shiffrin, R. M., & Schneider, W. (1977). Controlled and automatic human information processing. *Psychological Review, 84,* 127–190.

Short, E. (1985, April). *The relationship between children's memory performance and metacognitive knowledge: A developmental analysis of task-specific and general metamemory.* Paper presented at the meeting of the Society for Research in Child Development, Toronto.

Siegler, R. (1983). Information processing approaches to development. In P. H. Mussen (Ed.), *Handbook of child psychology* (4th ed.), Vol. 3. New York: Wiley.

Sigman, M. (1983). Individual differences in infant attention: Relations to birth status and intelligence at five years. In T. Field & A. Sostek (Eds.), *Infants born at risk: Physiological, perceptual, and cognitive processes.* New York: Grune & Stratton.

Silvern, L. E., & Ryan, V. L. (1979). Self-rated adjustment and sex typing on the Bem Sex-Role Inventory: Is masculinity the primary indicator of adjustment? *Sex Roles, 5*, 739–763.

Simmons, R. G., Rosenberg, F., & Rosenberg, M. (1973). Disturbance in the self-image at adolescence. *American Sociological Review, 38*, 553–568.

Simon, W., & Gagnon, J. H. (1969). On psychosexual development. In D. Goslin (Ed.), *Handbook of socialization theory and research.* Chicago: Rand McNally.

Simpson, E. (1976). A holistic approach to moral development and behavior. In T. Lickona (Ed.), *Moral development and behavior.* New York: Holt, Rinehart & Winston.

Single, E., Kandel, D., & Faust, R. (1974). Patterns of multiple drug use in high school. *Journal of Health and Social Behavior, 15*, 344–357.

Sizer, T. R. (1984). *Horace's compromise: The dilemma of the American high school today.* Boston: Houghton-Mifflin.

Sjolund, A. (1971). *The effect of day-care institutions on children's development: An analysis of international research.* Copenhagen: The Danish National Institute of Social Research.

Skeels, H. (1966). Adult status of children with contrasting early life experiences. *Monographs of the Society for Research in Child Development, 31* (3, Serial No. 105).

Skinner, B. F. (1948). *Walden Two.* New York: Macmillan.

Skinner, B. F. (1953). *Science and human behavior.* New York: Macmillan.

Skipper, J. K., & Nass, G. (1966). Dating behavior: A framework for analysis and an illustration. *Journal of Marriage and the Family, 28*, 412–420.

Slaby, R. G., & Frey, K. S. (1975). Development of gender constancy and selective attention to same-sex models. *Child Development, 47*, 349–356.

Slobin, D. (1972, July). Children and language: They learn the same around the world. *Psychology Today*, pp. 71–76.

Slobin, D. (1973). Cognitive prerequisites for the development of grammar. In C. A. Ferguson & D. I. Slobin (Eds.), *Studies of child language development.* New York: Holt, Rinehart & Winston.

Smetana, J. (1983). Social-cognitive development: Domain distinctions and coordinations. *Developmental Review, 3*, 131–147.

Smetana, J. (1985). Preschool children's conceptions of transgressions: Effects of varying moral and conventional domain-related attributes. *Developmental Psychology, 21*, 18–29.

Smith, D. F. (1980). Adolescent suicide. In R. E. Muuss (Ed.), *Adolescent behavior and society* (3rd ed.). New York: Random House.

Snow, C. E. (1985, April). *Imitation as a cognitive mechanism: A discussion.* Paper presented at the meeting of the Society for Research in Child Development, Toronto.

Snow, R. E. (1977). Individual differences and instructional theory. *Educational Researcher, 6*, 11–15.

Sokolov, E. N. (1976). Learning and memory: Habituation as negative learning. In M. R. Rosenzweig & E. L. Bennett (Eds.), *Neural mechanisms of learning and memory.* Cambridge, MA: MIT Press.

Sophian, C. (1985). Perseveration and infants' search: A comparison of two- and three-location tasks. *Developmental Psychology, 21*, 187–194.

Sorensen, R. C. (1973). *Adolescent sexuality in contemporary America.* New York: World.

Spearman, C. E. (1927). *The abilities of man.* New York: Macmillan.

Spelke, E. S. (1979). Perceiving bimodally specified events in infancy. *Developmental Psychology, 15*, 626–636.

Spelke, E. S., & Born, W. S. (1982). *Perception of visual objects by three-month-old infants.* Unpublished manuscript, University of Pennsylvania, Philadelphia.

Spence, J. T., Helmreich, R., & Stapp, J. (1974). The Personal Attributes Questionnaire: A measure of sex-role stereotypes and masculinity-femininity. *JSAS Catalog of Selected Documents in Psychology, 4*, 127.

Spielberger, C. D. (1966). The effects of anxiety on complex learning and academic achievement. In C. D. Spielberger (Ed.), *Anxiety and behavior.* New York: Academic Press.

Spielberger, C. D., Gorsuch, R. L., & Lushene, R. E. (1970). *Manual for the state-trait anxiety inventory.* Palo Alto, CA: Consulting Psychologists Press.

Spitz, R. A. (1945). Hospitalism: An inquiry into the genesis of psychiatric conditions in early childhood. *Psychoanalytic Study of the Child, 1*, 53–74.

Spivack, G., Platt, J. J., & Shure, M. B. (1976). *The problem-solving approach to adjustment.* San Francisco: Jossey-Bass.

Sporull, N. (1973). Visual attention, modeling behaviors, and other verbal and nonverbal metacommunication of prekindergarten viewing of "Sesame Street." *American Educational Research Journal, 10*, 101–114.

Sprague, R. L., & Gadow, K. D. (1976). The role of the teacher in drug treatment. *School Review, 85*, 109–140.

Sprague, R. L., & Sleator, E. K. (1975). What is the proper dosage of stimulant drugs in children? *International Journal of Mental Health, 4*, 75–104.

Sroufe, L. A. (1979). The coherence of individual development. *American Psychologist, 34*, 834–841.

Sroufe, L. A. (1985). Attachment classification from the perspective of infant-caregiver relationships and infant temperament, *Child Development, 56*, 1–14.

Sroufe, L. A., & Fleeson, J. (1986). Attachment and the construction of relationships. In W. W. Hartup & Z. Rubin (Eds.), *Relationships and development.* Hillsdale, NJ: Erlbaum.

Sroufe, L. A., & Rutter, M. (1984). The domain of developmental psychopathology. *Child Development, 55*, 17–29.

Sroufe, L. A., & Waters, E. (1976). The ontogenesis of smiling and laughter: A perspective on the organization of development in infancy. *Psychological Review, 83*, 173–189.

Sroufe, L. A., & Waters, E. (1982). Issues of temperament and attachment. *American Journal of Orthopsychiatry, 52,* 743–746.

Stagno, S. (1980). Comparative study of diagnostic procedures for congenital cytomegalovirus infection. *Pediatrics, 65,* 251–255.

Stallings, J. (1975). Implementation and child effects of teaching practices in Follow Through classrooms. *Monographs of the Society for Research in Child Development, 40* (Serial No. 163).

Starkey, P., Spelke, E. S., & Gelman, R. (1983). Detection of intermodal numerical correspondences by human infants. *Science, 222,* 179–181.

Stedman, L., & Smith, M. (1983). Recent reform proposals for American education. *Contemporary Education Review, 2,* 85–104.

Stein, A. H. (1972). Mass media and young children's development. In I. J. Gordon (Ed.), *Early childhood education: The seventy-first yearbook of the National Society for the Study of Education* (Part 2). Chicago: University of Chicago Press.

Stein, A. H., & Bailey, M. M. (1973). The socialization of achievement orientation in females. *Psychological Bulletin, 80,* 345–365.

Stein, M. (Ed.). (1972). *Changing sexist practices in the classroom.* Washington, DC: American Federation of Teachers.

Stein, N. L., & Levine, L. J. (in press). Thinking about feelings: The development and organization of emotional knowledge. In R. E. Snow & M. Farr (Eds.), *Aptitude, learning and instruction, Vol. 3.: Cognition, conation, and affect.* Hillsdale, NJ: Erlbaum.

Steinberg, L. D. (1980). *Understanding families with young adolescents.* Carrboro, NC: Center for Early Adolescence.

Steinberg, L. D. (1981). Transformations in family relations at puberty. *Developmental Psychology, 17,* 833–840.

Steinberg, L. D. (1986). Latchkey children and susceptibility to peer pressure: An ecological analysis. *Developmental Psychology, 22,* 433–439.

Steinberg, L. D., & Hill, J. P. (1978). Patterns of family interaction as a function of the onset of puberty, and formal thinking. *Developmental Psychology, 14,* 683–684.

Steiner, J. E. (1979). Human facial expressions in response to taste and smell stimulation. In H. Reese & L. Lipsitt (Eds.), *Advances in child development and behavior,* Vol. 13. New York: Academic Press.

Stephens, M. W., & Delys, P. (1973). External control expectancies among disadvantaged children at preschool age. *Child Development, 44,* 670–674.

Stephenson, B., & Wicklund, R. (1983). Self-directed attention and taking the other's perspective. *Journal of Experimental Social Psychology, 19,* 58–77.

Stern, D. (1985). *The interpersonal world of the infant.* New York: Basic Books.

Stern, D. N. (1974). Mother and infant at play: The dyadic interaction involving facial, vocal, and gaze behaviors. In M. Lewis & L. A. Rosenblum (Eds.), *The effect of the infant on its caregiver.* New York: Wiley.

Stern, D. N., Beebe, B., Jaffe, J., & Bennett, S. L. (1977). The infant's stimulus world during social interaction: A study of caregiver behaviors with particular reference to repetition and timing. In H. R. Schaffer (Ed.), *Studies in mother-infant interaction.* London: Academic Press.

Sternberg, R. J. (1977). *Intelligence, information processing, and analogical reasoning: The componential analysis of human abilities.* Hillsdale, NJ: Erlbaum.

Sternberg, R. J. (Ed.). (1982). *Advances in the psychology of human intelligence.* Hillsdale, NJ: Erlbaum.

Sternberg, R. J. (in press). *Intelligence applied.* San Diego: Harcourt Brace.

Sternberg, R. J., & Davidson, J. E. (1983). Insight in the gifted. *Educational Psychologist, 18,* 52–58.

Steuer, F. B., Applefield, J. M., & Smith, R. (1971). Televised aggression and interpersonal aggression of preschool children. *Journal of Experimental Child Psychology, 11,* 442–447.

Stevenson, H. W. (1972). *Children's learning.* New York: Appleton-Century-Crofts.

Stevenson, H. W. (1974). Reflections on the China visit. *Society for Research in Child Development Newsletter,* Fall, 3.

Stevenson, H. W. (1982). Influences of schooling on cognitive development. In D. A. Wagner & H. W. Stevenson (Eds.), *Cultural perspectives on child development.* San Francisco: W. H. Freeman.

Stevenson, H. W., Hale, G. A., Klein, R. E., & Miller, L. K. (1968). Interrelations and correlates in children's learning and problem solving. *Monographs of the Society for Research in Child Development, 33,* (Serial No. 123).

Stevenson, H. W., Stigler, J. W., & Lee, S. (1986). Achievement in mathematics. In H. W. Stevenson, H. Azuma, & K. Hakuta (Eds.), *Child development and education in Japan.* San Francisco: W. H. Freeman.

Stipak, D. J. (1981). Adolescents—Too young to earn, too old to learn? Compulsory school attendance and intellectual development. *Journal of Youth and Adolescence, 10,* 113–139.

Stipak, D. J., & Hoffman, J. M. (1980). Children's achievement and related experiences as a function of academic performance histories and set. *Journal of Educational Psychology, 72,* 861–865.

Stone, C. A., & Day, M. C. (1980). Competence and performance models and the characterization of formal operational skills. *Human Development, 23,* 323–353.

Stone, G. C. (Ed.). (1983). Proceedings of the National Working Conference on Education and Training in Health Psychology. *Health Psychology, 2* (Supplement).

Stone, G. C., Cohen, F., & Adler, N. E. (1979). *Health psychology—A handbook.* San Francisco: Jossey-Bass.

Stone, N. W., & Chesney, B. H. (1978). Attachment behaviors in handicapped infants. *Mental Retardation, 16,* 8–12.

Storms, M. D. (1980). Theories of sexual orientation. *Journal of Personality and Social Psychology, 38,* 783–792.

Strauss, M. S., & Curtis, L. E. (1982). Infant perception of numerosity. *Child Development, 52,* 1146–1152.

Streissguth, A. P., Barr, H. M., & Martin, D. C. (1983). Maternal alcohol use and neonatal habituation assessed with the Brazelton Scale. *Child Development, 44,* 1109–1118.

Streissguth, A. P., Martin, D. C., Martin, J. C., & Barr, H. M. (1981). The Seattle longitudinal prospective study of alcohol and pregnancy. *Neurobehavioral Toxicology and Teratology, 3,* 223–233.

Streissguth, A. P., Martin, D. C., Sandman, B. M., Kirchner, G. L., & Darby, B. L. (1984). Intra-uterine alcohol and nicotine exposure: Attention and reaction time in four-year-old children. *Developmental Psychology, 20,* 533–541.

Strodtbeck, F. L. (1958). Family interaction, values, and achievement. In D. C. McClelland (Ed.), *Talent and society.* Princeton, NJ: Van Nostrand.

Sullivan, H. S. (1953). *The interpersonal theory of psychiatry.* New York: Norton.

Sullivan, K., & Sullivan, A. (1980). Adolescent-parent separation. *Developmental Psychology, 16,* 93–99.

Suomi, S. J., & Harlow, H. F. (1972). Social rehabilitation of isolate-reared monkeys. *Developmental Psychology, 6,* 487–496.

Suomi, S. J., Harlow, H. F., & Domek, C. J. (1970). Effect of repetitive infant-infant separations of young monkeys. *Journal of Abnormal Psychology, 76,* 161–172.

Super, D. E., & Hall, D. T. (1978). Career development: Exploration and planning. *Annual Review of Psychology, 29,* 333–372.

Super, D. E., Kowalski, R., & Gotkin, E. (1967). *Floundering and trial after high school.* Unpublished manuscript, Columbia University, New York.

Sutton-Smith, B. (1973). *Child psychology.* New York: Appleton-Century-Crofts.

Sutton-Smith, B., & Rosenberg, B. G. (1970). *The sibling.* New York: Holt, Rinehart & Winston.

Swadesh, M. (1971). *The origin and diversification of language.* Chicago: Aldine-Atherton.

Szasz, T. (1970). *The manufacture of madness.* New York: Harper & Row.

T

Talbert, C. M., Kraybill, S. N., & Potter, H. (1976). Adrenal cortisol response to circumcision in the neonate. *Obstetrics and Gynecology, 48,* 208–210.

Tanner, J. M. (1970). Physical growth. In P. H. Mussen (Ed.), *Carmichael's manual of child psychology,* Vol. 1. New York: Wiley.

Tarpy, R. M., & Mayer, R. E. (1978). *Foundations of learning and memory.* Glenview, IL: Scott, Foresman.

Tec, N. (1972). Some aspects of high school status and differential involvement with marijuana. *Adolescence, 7,* 1–28.

Terman, L. M. (1925). *Genetic studies of genius: Mental and physical traits of a thousand gifted children* (Vol. 1). Stanford, CA: Stanford University Press.

Terr, L. C. (1970). A family study of child abuse. *American Journal of Psychiatry, 223,* 102–109.

Terrace, H. (1979). *Nim.* New York: Knopf.

Thelen, E. (1979). Rhythmical stereotypies in normal human infants. *Animal Behavior, 27,* 699–715.

Thelen, E. (1981). Rhythmical behavior in infancy: An ethological perspective. *Developmental Psychology, 17,* 237–257.

Thomas, A., & Chess, S. (1977). *Temperament and development.* New York: Brunner/Mazel.

Thomas, E. A. C., & Martin, J. A. (1976). Analyses of parent-infant interaction. *Psychological Review, 83,* 141–156.

Thompson, G. G. (1944). The social and emotional development of preschool children under two types of educational programs. *Psychological Monographs, 56* (5, Whole No. 258).

Thoresen, C., Eagleston, J., Kirmil-Gray, K., & Bracke, P. (1985, August). *Type A children.* Paper presented at the annual meeting of the American Psychological Association, Los Angeles.

Thorndike, R. L., Hagen, E. P. & Sattler, J. M. (1985). *Stanford-Binet* (4th ed.). Chicago: Riverside Publishing.

Thurstone, L. L. (1938). Primary mental abilities. *Psychometric Monographs* (No. 1).

Tieger, T. (1980). On the biological basis of sex differences in aggression. *Child Development, 51,* 943–963.

Tinbergen, N. (1969). *The study of instinct.* New York: Oxford University Press. (Original work published 1951)

Toder, N., & Marcia, J. (1973). Ego identity status and response to conformity pressure in college women. *Journal of Personality and Social Psychology, 26,* 287–294.

Tolman, E. C. (1932). *Purposive behavior in animals and man.* New York: Appleton-Century-Crofts.

Toman, W. (1971). The duplication theorem of social relationships as tested in the general population. *Psychological Review, 79,* 380–390.

Tomasello, M., & Mannle, S. (1985). Pragmatics of sibling speech to one-year-olds. *Child Development, 56,* 911–917.

Torrance, E. P., & Torrance, P. (1972). Combining creative problem solving with creative expressive activities in the education of disadvantaged young people. *Journal of Creative Behavior, 6*(1), 1–10.

Toth, S. A. (1981). *Blooming.* Boston: Little, Brown.

Trabasso, T. (1977). The role of memory as a system in making transitive inferences. In R. V. Kail, Jr. & J. W. Hagen (Eds.), *Perspectives on the development of memory and cognition.* Hillsdale, NJ: Erlbaum.

Trickett, E., & Moos, R. (1974). Personal correlates of contrasting environments: Student satisfaction in high school classrooms. *American Journal of Community Psychology, 2,* 1–12.

Trotter, R. (1981). Head Start children in young adulthood. *APA Monitor, 15,* 37.

Trupin, T. (1979). *The measurement of psychological androgyny in children.* Unpublished doctoral dissertation, University of Washington, Seattle, WA (University Microfilms No. 7917653).

Tuchman-Duplessis, H. (1975). Drug effects on the fetus. *Monographs on Drugs,* Vol. 2. Sydney: ADIS Press.

Turiel, E. (1966). An experimental test of the sequentiality of developmental stages in the child's moral judgments. *Journal of Personality and Social Psychology, 3,* 611–618.

Turiel, E. (1977). A critical analysis of Kohlberg's contributions to the study of moral thought. *Journal of Social Behavior, 7,* 41–63.

Turiel, E. (1978). Social regulations and domains of social concepts. In W. Damon (Ed.), *New directions for child development, Vol. 1: Social cognition.* San Francisco: Jossey-Bass.

Turnbull, A. P., & Schulz, J. B. (1979). *Mainstreaming handicapped students.* Boston: Allyn & Bacon.

Turnbull, C. M. (1972). *The mountain people.* New York: Simon and Schuster.

Tyack, D. (1976). Ways of seeing: An essay on the history of compulsory schooling. *Harvard Educational Review, 46,* 355–389.

U

U.S. Department of Commerce, Bureau of the Census. (1979, April). *Population profile of the United States: 1978, population characteristics* (Current Population Reports, Series P–20, No. 336). Washington, DC: U.S. Government Printing Office.

Uddenberg, N. (1974). Reproductive adaptation in mother and daughter. *Acta Psychiatrica Scandanavia, 254.*

Underwood, B., & Moore, B. S. (1980). *Perspective taking and altruism.* Unpublished manuscript, University of Texas.

Ungerer, J., Zelazo, P. R., Kearsley, R. B., & O'Leary, K. (1981). Developmental changes in the representation of objects in symbolic play from 18 to 34 months. *Child Development, 52,* 186–195.

Uzgiris, I. C., & Hunt, J. M. (1972). *Toward ordinal scales of psychological development in infancy.* Unpublished manuscript, University of Illinois, Urbana.

Uzgiris, I. C., & Hunt, J. M. (1975). *Assessment in infancy: Ordinal scales of psychological development.* Urbana, IL: University of Illinois Press.

V

Vaillancourt, P. M. (1973). Stability of children's survey responses. *Public Opinion Quarterly, 37,* 373–387.

Vandell, D. L. (1985, April). *Relationship between infant-peer and infant-mother interactions: What we have learned.* Paper presented at the biennial meeting of the Society for Research in Child Development, Toronto.

Vandell, D. L., Wilson, K. S., & Buchanan, N. R. (1980). Peer interaction in the first year of life: An examination of its structure, content, and sensitivity of toys. *Child Development, 51,* 481–488.

Vandiver, R. (1972). *Sources and interrelation of premarital sexual standards and general liberality and conservatism.* Unpublished doctoral dissertation, Southern Illinois University.

Vaughn, B. E., Gove, F. L., & Egeland, B. (1980). The relationship between out-of-home care and the quality of infant-mother attachment in an economically disadvantaged population. *Child Development, 51,* 1203–1214.

Vener, A., & Stewart, C. (1974). Adolescent sexual behavior in middle America revisited: 1970–1973. *Journal of Marriage and the Family, 36,* 728–735.

Visher, E., & Visher, J. (1978). Common problems of stepparents and their spouses. *American Journal of Orthopsychiatry, 48,* 252–262.

Volterra, V., & Taeschner, T. (1978). The acquisition and development of language by bilingual children. *Journal of Child Language, 5,* 311–326.

Vurpillot, E. (1968). The development of scanning strategies and their relation to visual differentiation. *Journal of Experimental Child Psychology, 6,* 632–650.

Vygotsky, L. S. (1978). Play and its role in the mental development of the child. *Soviet Psychology, 12,* 62–76.

W

Waddington, C. H. (1957). *The strategy of the genes.* London: Allen & Sons.

Wagenaar, A. C. (1983). *Alcohol, young drivers, and traffic accidents.* Lexington, MA: Heath.

Wagner, S., Winner, E., Cicchetti, D., & Gardner, H. (1981). Metaphorical mapping in human infants. *Child Development, 52,* 728–731.

Walberg, H. J., Harnisch, D. L., & Tsai, S. L. (1984). *Mathematics productivity in Japan and Illinois.* Unpublished manuscript, University of Illinois at Chicago.

Walker, L. (1980). Cognitive and perspective-taking prerequisites for moral development. *Child Development, 51,* 131–139.

Walker, L. (1982). The sequentiality of Kohlberg's stages of moral development. *Child Development, 53,* 1330–1336.

Walker, L. (1984). Sex differences in the development of moral reasoning: A critical review. *Child Development, 55,* 677–691.

Walker-Andrews, A. S., & Lennon, E. M. (1985). Auditory-visual perception of changing distance by human infants. *Child Development, 56,* 544–548.

Wallach, M. A. (1973). Ideology, evidence, and creative research. *Contemporary Psychology, 18,* 162–164.

Wallack, L. M. (1984). Practical issues, ethical concerns, and future directions in the prevention of alcohol-related problems. *Journal of Primary Prevention, 4,* 199–224.

Wallerstein, J. S. (1982, July). *Children of divorce: Preliminary report of a ten-year follow-up.* Paper presented at the 10th International Congress of the International Association for Child and Adolescent Psychiatry and Allied Professions, Dublin, Ireland.

Wallerstein, J. S., & Kelly, J. B. (1980). *Surviving the breakup: How children actually cope with divorce.* New York: Basic Books.

Warden, D. A. (1976). The influence of context on children's use of identifying expressions and references. *British Journal of Psychology, 67,* 101–112.

Washburn, K. J., & Hakes, D. T. (1985, April). *Changes in children's semantic and syntactic acceptability judgments.* Paper presented at the meeting of the Society for Research in Child Development, Toronto.

Waterman, A. S. (1982). Identity development from adolescence to adulthood: An extension of theory and a review of research. *Developmental Psychology, 21,* 341–358.

Waterman, A. S., Geary, P. S., & Waterman, C. K. (1974). A longitudinal study of changes in ego identity status from the freshman to the senior at college. *Developmental Psychology, 10,* 387–392.

Waterman, A. S., & Waterman, C. K. (1971). A longitudinal study of changes in ego identity status during the freshman year of college. *Developmental Psychology, 5,* 167–173.

Waterman, A. S., & Waterman, C. K. (1972). Relationship between ego identity status and subsequent academic behavior: A test of the predictive validity of Marcia's categorization for identity status. *Developmental Psychology, 6,* 179.

Waters, E. (1978). The reliability and stability of individual differences in infant-mother attachment. *Child Development, 49,* 483–494.

Waters, E., & Sroufe, L. A. (1983). Social competence as a developmental construct. *Developmental Review, 3,* 79–97.

Waters, E., Wippman, J., & Sroufe, L. A. (1979). Attachment, positive affect, and competence in the peer group: Two studies in construct validation. *Child Development, 50,* 821–829.

Watson, J. B. (1924). *Behaviorism.* New York: Norton.

Watson, J. B. (1928). *Psychological care of infant and child.* New York: Norton.

Watson, J. B., & Rayner, R. (1920). Conditioned emotional reactions. *Journal of Experimental Psychology, 3,* 1–4.

Watson, M. W., & Fischer, K. W. (1977). A developmental sequence of agent use in late infancy. *Child Development, 48,* 828–836.

Watson, M. W., & Fischer, K. W. (1980). Development of social roles in elicited and spontaneous behavior during the preschool years. *Developmental Psychology, 16,* 483–494.

Webb, W. B. (1975). *Sleep, the gentle tyrant.* Englewood Cliffs, NJ: Prentice-Hall.

Weber, R. A., Levitt, M. J., & Clark, M. C. (1986). Individual variation in attachment security and strange situation behavior: The role of maternal and infant temperament. *Child Development, 57,* 56–65.

Wechsler, D. (1958). *The measurement and appraisal of adult intelligence* (4th ed.). Baltimore: Williams & Wilkins.

Wechsler, D. (1974). *Manual for the Wechsler Intelligence Scale for Children—Revised.* New York: The Psychological Association.

Weiner, B. (1984). Principles for a theory of student motivation and their application within an attributional framework. In R. E. Ames & C. Ames (Eds.), *Motivation in education.* New York: Academic Press.

Weiner, B., Kun, A., & Benesh-Weiner, M. (1980). The development of mastery, emotion, and morality from an attributional perspective. In W. A. Collins (Ed.), *Minnesota Symposium on Child Psychology,* Vol. 13. Minneapolis: University of Minnesota Press.

Weiner, I. B. (1980). Pschopathology in adolescence. In J. Adelson (Ed.), *Handbook of adolescent psychology.* New York: Wiley.

Wellman, H. M., Ritter, K., & Flavell, J. H. (1975). Deliberate memory behavior in the delayed reactions of very young children. *Developmental Psychology, 11,* 780–787.

Werner, E. E. (1979). *Cross-cultural child development: A view from planet earth.* Monterey, CA: Brooks/Cole.

Werner, E. E., & Smith, R. S. (1982). *Vulnerable but invincible: A longitudinal study of resilient children and youth.* New York: McGraw-Hill.

Werner, H., & Kaplan, B. (1963). *Symbol formation.* New York: Wiley.

Werner, H., & Kaplan, E. (1952). The acquisition of word meanings: A developmental study. *Monographs of the Society for Research in Child Development, 15,* (1, Serial No. 51).

Werner, P. (1982). Playground injuries and voluntary product standards for homes and playgrounds. *Pediatrics, 69,* 18–20.

Wertheimer, M. (1961). Psychomotor coordination of auditory and visual space at birth. *Science, 134,* 1692.

West, D. J., & Farrington, D. P. (1977). *The delinquent way of life.* London: Heinemann Educational.

White House Conference on Children. (1931). Report of the committee on special classes: Gifted children. In *Special education: The handicapped and the gifted. Education and training,* Section 3. New York: Century, pp. 537–550.

White, S. H. (1985, April). *Risings and fallings of developmental psychology.* Paper presented at the biennial meeting of the Society for Research in Child Development, Toronto.

Whitehurst, G. J. (1985, April). *The role of imitation in language learning by children with language delay.* Paper presented at the meeting of the Society for Research in Child Development, Toronto.

Whitehurst, G. J., & Vasta, R. (1975). Is language acquired through imitation? *Journal of Psycholinguistic Research, 4,* 37–58.

Whiting, B. B., & Whiting, J. W. M. (1975). *Children of six cultures: A psychocultural analysis.* Cambridge, MA: Harvard University Press.

Wicklund, R. (1979). The influence of self-awareness on human behavior. *American Scientist, 67,* 187–193.

Widmayer, S., & Field, T. (1980). Effects of Brazelton demonstrations on early patterns of preterm infants and their teenage mothers. *Infant Behavior and Development, 3,* 79–89.

Wilkins, J. (1970). A follow-up study of those who called a suicide prevention center. *American Journal of Psychiatry, 127,* 155–161.

Wilkinson, A. (1976). Counting strategies and semantic analysis as applied to class inclusion. *Cognitive Psychology, 8,* 64–85.

Wilkinson, L. C., Wilkinson, A. C., Spinelli, F., & Chiang, C. P. (1984). Metalinguistic knowledge of pragmatic rules in school-age children. *Child Development, 55,* 2130–2140.

Williams, J. (1979). Reading instruction today. *American Psychologist, 34,* 917–922.

Williams, J. A. (1979). Psychological androgyny and mental health. In O. Hartnet, G. Boden, & M. Fuller (Eds.), *Sex-role stereotyping.* London: Tavistock.

Willis, D. J., Elliott, C. H., & Jay, S. (1982). Psychological effects of physical illness and its psychological concomitants. In J. M. Tuma (Ed.), *Handbook for the practice of pediatric psychology.* New York: Wiley.

Wills, T. A., & Shiffman, S. (1985). Coping and substance use: A conceptual framework. In S. Shiffman & T. A. Wills (Eds.), *Coping and substance use.* New York: Academic Press.

Wilson, H. (1980). Parental supervision: A neglected aspect of delinquency. *British Journal of Criminology, 20,* 203–235.

Windle, W. F. (1940). *Physiology of the fetus.* Philadelphia: Saunders.

Wing, J. W. (1977). *Early childhood autism.* Elmsford, NY: Pergamon Press.

Winner, E. (1986, August). Where pelicans kiss seals. *Psychology Today,* pp. 24–35.

Winterbottem, M. R. (1958). The relation of need for achievement to learning experiences in independence and mastery. In J. W. Atkinson (Ed.), *Motives in fantasy, action, and society.* New York: Van Nostrand.

Wisely, D. W., Masur, F. T., & Morgan, S. B. (1983). Psychological aspects of severe burn injuries in children. *Health Psychology, 2,* 45–72.

Wodarski, J. S., & Hoffman, S. D. (1984). Alcohol education for adolescents. *Social Work in Education, 6*, 69–92.

Wohlwill, J. F. (1973). *The study of behavioral development*. New York: Academic Press.

Wolfe, L. K., & Betz, N. E. (1981). Traditionality of choice and sex-role identification as moderators of the congruence of occupational choice in college women. *Journal of Vocational Behavior, 18*, 43–55.

Wolff, P. H. (1966). The causes, controls, and organization of behavior in the neonate. *Psychological Issues, 5* (1, Whole No. 7).

Wolff, P. H. (1968). Stereotypic behavior and development. *Canadian Psychologist, 9*, 474–483.

Worobey, J., & Belsky, J. (1982). Employing the Brazelton Scale to influence mothering: An experimental comparison of three strategies. *Developmental Psychology, 18*, 736–743.

Worrell, J. (1978). Sex roles and psychological well-being: Perspectives on methodology. *Journal of Consulting and Clinical Psychology, 46*, 777–791.

Wright, J. C., & Huston, A. C. (1985, April). *Developmental changes in children's understanding of form and content*. Paper presented at the biennial meeting of the Society for Research in Child Development, Toronto.

Wylie, R. C. (1974). *The self-concept*. Lincoln, NE: University of Nebraska Press.

Y

Yando, R. M., & Kagan, J. (1968). The effect of teacher tempo on the child. *Child Development, 39*, 27–34.

Yankelovich, D. (1974). *The new morality: A profile of American youth in the 1970s*. New York: McGraw-Hill.

Yarrow, L. J. (1964). Separation from parents during early childhood. In L. W. Hoffman & M. L. Hoffman (Eds.), *Review of child development research*, Vol. 1. New York: Russell Sage Foundation.

Yeaton, W. H., & Bailey, J. S. (1978). Teaching pedestrian safety skills to young children: An analysis and a one-year follow-up. *Journal of Applied Behavior Analysis, 11*, 315–329.

Yonas, A., Granrud, C. E., & Pettersen, L. (1985). Infants' sensitivity to relative size information for distance. *Developmental Psychology, 21*, 161–167.

Yussen, S. R., & Santrock, J. W. (1982). *Child development* (2nd ed.). Dubuque, IA: Wm. C. Brown Company Publishers.

Z

Zahn-Waxler, C., Radke-Yarrow, M., & King, R. M. (1979). Child rearing and children's prosocial initiations toward victims of distress. *Child Development, 50*, 319–330.

Zajonc, R. B., & Markus, G. B. (1975). Birth order and intellectual development. *Psychological Review, 82*, 74–88.

Zakin, D. F., Blyth, D. A., & Simmons, R. G. (1984). Physical attractiveness as a mediator of the impact of early pubertal changes for girls. *Journal of Youth and Adolescence, 13*, 439–450.

Zamenhof, S., van Marthens, E., & Margolis, F. L. (1968). DNA (cell number) and protein in neonatal brain: Alteration by maternal dietary protein restriction. *Science, 160*, 322–323.

Zeldow, P. B. (1976). Psychological androgyny and attitudes toward feminism. *Journal of Consulting and Clinical Psychology, 44*, 150.

Zelnick, M., & Kantner, J. F. (1978a). First pregnancies in women ages fifteen to nineteen: 1976 and 1971. *Family Planning Perspectives, 10*, 11–20.

Zelnick, M., & Kantner, J. F. (1978b). Contraceptive patterns and premarital pregnancy among women aged fifteen to nineteen in 1976. *Family Planning Perspectives, 10*, 135–142.

Zelnicker, T., & Jeffrey, W. E. (1979). Attention and cognitive style in children. In G. Hale & M. Lewis (Eds.), *Attention and cognitive development*. New York: Plenum.

Zembar, M. J., & Naus, M. J. (1985, April). *The combined effects of knowledge base and mnemonic strategies on children's memory*. Paper presented at the meeting of the Society for Research in Child Development, Toronto.

Zeskind, P. S. (1980). Adult responses to cries of low- and high-risk infants. *Infant Behavior and Development, 3*, 167–177.

Zeskind, P. S., Sale, J., Maio, M. L., Huntington, L., & Weiseman, J. R. (1984, April). *Adult perceptions of pain and hunger cries: A synchrony of arousal*. Paper presented at the biennial meeting of the International Conference on Infant Studies, New York.

Zill, N. (1977). *National survey of children: Summary of preliminary results*. Unpublished manuscript, Foundation for Child Development, New York.

CREDITS

PHOTOS

Postnatal Development of the Human Cerebral Cortex. Cambridge: Harvard University Press, Vols. I–VI, 1939–1963; **page 142:** © Yves DeBraine/Black Star; **figure 4.4:** © David Linton; **page 146:** © Marla Murphy; **figure 4.7:** © William Vandivert.

CHAPTER 5

Opener: © Alan Carey/The Image Works; **page 167:** "Figure 2 from": "Discrimination and Imitation of Facial Expressions by Neonates," 1. Field, et al., vol. 218, #4568, pp. 179–181, (figure on page 81), 8 October 1982; **page 170:** © Helena Frost/Frost Publishing Group, Ltd.; **page 171:** © Chip and Rosa Maria Peterson; **page 173:** © James L. Shaffer; **figure 5.7:** courtesy Carolyn Rovee-Collier, Rutgers University; **page 178:** © Suzanne Arms/Jeroboam, Inc.; **figure 5.8:** courtesy Dr. James Bartlett; **page 183:** © Chip and Rosa Maria Peterson; **figure 5.13:** © Robert and Beatrix Gardner; **page 194:** © Chip and Rosa Maria Peterson.

CHAPTER 6

Opener: © Jeff Hunter/The Image Bank; **page 208:** © Howard Dratch/The Image Works; **page 212:** © Alan Carey/The Image Works; **figure 6.3:** courtesy University of Wisconsin, Harlow Primate Lab.; **page 220:** © Howard Dratch/The Image Works; **page 223:** © James L. Shaffer; **page 225:** © Alan Carey/The Image Works; **page 226:** © I.P.A./The Image Works; **page 232:** © Michael Siluk; **figure 6.7:** © James L. Reynolds; **page 233:** © Michael Siluk; **page 244:** © Joe Baker/The Image Bank, Chicago.

CHAPTER 7

Opener: © Gail B. Int Veldt; **page 257:** © James L. Shaffer; **page 261:** © Alan Carey/The Image Works; **page 262:** © James L. Reynolds; **page 265:** © Alan Carey/The Image Works; **page 267:** © Alan Carey/The Image Works; **page 269:** © Alan Carey/The Image Works; **page 276:** © McDonald Photography; **page 287:** © McDonald Photography; **page 290:** © McDonald Photography; **page 292:** © Bill Powers/Frost Publishing Group, Ltd.

CHAPTER 8

Opener: © James L. Shaffer; **page 304:** © Ken Gaghan/Jeroboam, Inc.; **page 308:** © Marla Murphy; **page 313:** © Marla Murphy; **page 318:** © Michael Siluk; **page 322:** © Chip and Rosa Maria Peterson; **page 327:** © Joe Sohm/The Image Works; **page 330:** © Marla Murphy; **page 334:** © James L. Shaffer; **page 338:** © McDonald Photography.

CHAPTER 9

Opener: © Norman Prince; **page 349:** © McDonald Photography; **page 353:** © Joe Sohm/The Image Works; **page 354:** © James L. Shaffer; **page 361:** © James L. Shaffer; **page 363:** © Michael Siluk; **page 367:** Jordan Information Bureau/Frost Publishing Group, Ltd.; **page 372:** courtesy R. J. Sternberg; **page 380:** © James L. Shaffer.

CHAPTER 10

Opener: © McDonald Photography; **page 391:** Culver Pictures; **page 398 left:** © Chip and Rosa Maria Peterson; **page 398 right:** © Helena Frost/Frost Publishing Group, Ltd.; **page 405:** © James L. Shaffer; **page 407:** © Marla Murphy; **page 413:** © James L. Shaffer; **page 419:** © Helena Frost/Frost Publishing Group, Ltd.; **page 423:** © Joe Sohm/The Image Works; **page 426:** © Mark Antman/The Image Works; **page 429:** © James L. Shaffer; **page 433:** © Alan Carey/The Image Works.

CHAPTER 11

Opener: © Alan Carey/The Image Works; **page 441:** © Alan Carey/The Image Works; **page 447:** © James L. Shaffer; **page 452:** © Alan Carey/The Image Works; **page 458:** © Michael Siluk; **page 463:** Delaware State Travel Service/Frost Publishing Group, Ltd.; **page 470:** © Michael Siluk; **page 475:** © Hill Frost/Frost Publishing Group, Ltd.; **page 476:** Harvard University News Office; **page 483:** © Mark Antman/The Image Works; **page 491:** © Gail B. Int Veldt.

CHAPTER 12

Opener: © Yokhi R. Okamoto/Photo Researchers, Inc.; **page 512:** © James L. Shaffer; **page 516:** © James L. Reynolds; **page 517:** © James L. Shaffer; **page 520:** © James L. Shaffer; **page 523:** © Michael Siluk; **page 528:** © James L. Shaffer; **page 531:** © Mark Antman/The Image Works; **page 533:** © James L. Shaffer; **page 536:** © Marla Murphy; **page 537:** © James L. Reynolds.

CHAPTER 13

Opener: © Chip and Rosa Maria Peterson; **page 550:** © James L. Shaffer; **page 551:** © Harriet Gans/The Image Works; **page 558:** © James L. Shaffer; **page 560:** © James L.

Shaffer; **page 564:** © Marla Murphy; **page 568:** © Gail B. Int Veldt; **page 570:** © Marla Murphy; **page 572:** © Michael Siluk; **page 574:** © Alan Carey/The Image Works.

CHAPTER 14

Opener: © Marla Murphy; **page 587:** Bettman Archives; **page 588:** Historical Pictures Service; **page 592:** © Patsy Davidson/The Image Works; **page 593:** © James L. Shaffer; **page 597:** © Harriet Gans/The Image Works; **page 603:** © Alan Carey/The Image Works; **page 605:** © Michael Siluk; **page 607:** © Dave Schaefer/Jeroboam; **page 610:** © James L. Reynolds; **page 614:** © Susan Rosenberg/Photo Researchers, Inc.; **page 615:** © James L. Shaffer.

ILLUSTRATIONS AND TEXT

SECTION OPENER 1

From the Prologue by Carl Sandburg to *The Family of Man,* edited by Edward Steichen. Copyright © 1955, renewed 1983, The Museum of Modern Art. All Rights Reserved. Reprinted by permission of the publisher, The Museum of Modern Art.

CHAPTER 1

Page 6 From E. D. Nottelmann, et al., "Hormone Level and Adjustment and Behavior During Early Adolescence." Paper presented at AAAS meeting, Los Angeles, May 1985. **Figure 1.3** From Santrock, John W., Life-Span Development, 2d ed. © 1983, 1986 Wm. C. Brown Publishers, Dubuque, Iowa. All Rights Reserved. Reprinted by permission. **Figure 1.4** From Santrock, John W., *Child Development,* 3d ed. © 1978, 1982, 1987 Wm. C. Brown Publishers, Dubuque, Iowa. All Rights Reserved. Reprinted by permission.

CHAPTER 2

Figure 2.1 From *Psychology: A Scientific Study of Human Behavior,* Fifth Edition, by L. S. Wrightsman, C. K. Sigelman, and F. H. Sanford. Copyright © 1961, 1965, 1970, 1975, 1979 by Wadsworth Publishing Company, Inc. Reprinted by permission of Brooks/Cole Publishing Company, Monterey, California. **Figure 2.2** From Santrock, John W., *Life-Span Development.* © 1983 Wm. C. Brown Publishers, Dubuque, Iowa. All Rights Reserved. Reprinted by permission. **Figures 2.3 and 2.4** From Bruno, F. J., *Adjustment*

CHAPTER 3

CHAPTER 4

CHAPTER 5

CHAPTER 6

author. **Figure 6.4** Figure 1 from: "Affectional Responses in the Infant Monkey," H. Harlow, et al., *Science,* Vol. 130, #3373, pp. 421–432, (figure on p. 422), 21 August 1959. Copyright © 1959 by the American Association for the Advancement of Science. Reprinted by permission. **Figure 6.5** From Schaffer, H. R. and P. E. Emerson, "The development of social attachments in infancy" in *Monographs of the Society for Research in Child Development, 29.* © by The Society for Research in Child Development. Reprinted by permission. **Figure, page 222** From Matas, L., R. A. Arend, and L. A. Sroufe, "Continuity in adaptation: Quality of attachment and later competence" in *Child Development, 49,* 547–556, 1978. © 1978 by The Society for Research in Child Development. Reprinted by permission. **Figure, page 223** From Lewis, M. C., et al., "Predicting psychopathology in six-year-olds from early social relations" in *Child Development, 55,* 123–126, 1984. © 1984 by The Society for Research in Child Development. Reprinted by permission. **Figure, page 225** From Weber, R. A., et al., "Individual variation in attachment security and strange situation behavior: The role of maternal and infant temperament" in *Child Development, 57,* 56–65, 1986. © 1986 by The Society of Research in Child Development. Reprinted by permission. **Figure 6.6** From Lamb, Michael E., et al., "Mother-and-father-infant interaction involving play and holding in traditional and non-traditional Swedish families" in *Developmental Psychology, 18,* 215–221, 1982. Copyright © 1982 American Psychological Association. Reprinted by permission of the author. **Figure 6.7** From Lewis, M. and J. Brooks-Gunn, *Social Cognition and the Acquisition of the Self.* © 1979 Plenum Publishing Corporation, New York. Reprinted by permission.

CHAPTER 7

Figures 7.1, 7.6, and Table, page 292 From Santrock, John W., *Life-Span Development,* 2d ed. © 1983, 1986 Wm. C. Brown Publishers, Dubuque, Iowa. All Rights Reserved. Reprinted by permission.
Illustrations, Page 271 (right), and page 273 Courtesy Dr. Ellen Winner, Project Zero.
Illustration, page 272 From Golomb, Claire, *The Child's Invention of a Pictorial World: Studies in the Psychology of Child Art.* (in

preparation). **Figures 7.2 and 7.3** From Santrock, John W. and Steven R. Yussen, *Children and Adolescents.* © 1984 Wm. C. Brown Publishers, Dubuque, Iowa. All Rights Reserved. Reprinted by permission. **Figure 7.4** From Vurpillot, Elaine, "The development of scanning strategies and their relation to visual differentiation" in *Journal of Developmental Psychology, 6,* 632–650, 1968. Copyright © 1968 Academic Press, Inc., Orlando, Florida. Reprinted by permission. **Figure 7.5** From Dempster, Frank N., "Memory span: Sources of individual and developmental differences" in *Psychological Bulletin, 89,* 63–100, 1981. © 1981 American Psychological Association. Reprinted by permission of the author. **Figure, page 283** From Hawkins, J., et al., "Merds that laugh don't like mushrooms: Evidence for deductive reasoning by preschoolers" in *Developmental Psychology, 20,* 584–594, 1984. Copyright © American Psychological Association. Reprinted by permission of the author. **Figure 7.7** From R. Brown, et al., *Minnesota Symposium on Child Psychology, Vol. 2,* in J. P. Hill, 1969. Reprinted by permission. **Figure, page 285** From Berko, J., "The child's learning of English morphology" in *Word, 14,* 150–177, 361, 1958. © 1958 International Linguistic Association. Reprinted by permission. **Figures, page 291** From Stallings, J., "Implementation and child effects of teaching practices in follow through classrooms" in *Monographs of The Society for Research in Child Development, 40,* Serial No. 163, 1975. © 1975 by The Society for Research in Child Development. Reprinted by permission. **Page 294** From "To a Child" by Christopher Morley, in *Chimney Smoke.* © 1917 George H. Doran Co.

CHAPTER 8

Child Development Concept Table 8.1, p. 309 From Santrock, John W., *Life-Span Development,* 2d ed. © 1983, 1986 Wm. C. Brown Publishers, Dubuque, Iowa. All Rights Reserved. Reprinted by permission. **Figure 8.1** From Maccoby, E. E. and J. A. Martin, "Socialization in the context of the family: Parent-child interaction" in P. H. Mussen, (Ed.), *Handbook of Child Psychology,* 4th ed, Vol. 4. © 1983 John Wiley & Sons, New York. Reprinted by permission. **Figure 8.2** From Santrock, J. W. and R. L. Tracy, "The effects of children's family structure status on the development of stereotypes by teachers" in *Journal of Educational Psychology, 70,*

754–757, 1978. © 1978 American Psychological Association. Reprinted by permission of the authors. **Figure 8.3** From Santrock, J. W. and R. A. Warshak, "Father custody and social development in boys and girls" in *Journal of Social Issues, 35,* 4, pp. 112–125, 1979. © 1979 Society for the Psychological Study of Social Issues, Ann Arbor, Michigan. Reprinted by permission. **Figure 8.4** From Hollis, M., "Logical operations and role-taking abilities in two cultures: Norway and Hungary" in *Child Development, 46,* 645–646, 1975. © 1975 by The Society for Research in Child Development. Reprinted by permission. **Figure 8.5** From Barnes, K. E., "Preschool play norms: A replication" in *Developmental Psychology, 5,* 99–103, 1971. Copyright © 1971 American Psychological Association. Reprinted by permission of the author. **Figure 8.6** From Chaille, C., "The child's conception of play, pretending, and toys: Sequences and structural parallels" in *Human Development, 21,* 201–210, 1978. © 1978 S. Karger A. G., Basel, Switzerland. Reprinted by permission. **Figure 8.7** From Anderson, Daniel R., et al., "Television viewing at home: Age trends in visual attention and time with TV" from a paper presented at the meeting of The Society for Research in Child Development, Toronto. © 1985 Daniel R. Anderson. Reprinted with permission. **Figure 8.8** From Rogers, T. B., N. Kuiper, and W. Kirker, "Self reference and the encoding of personal information" in *Journal of Personality and Social Psychology, 35,* 677–688, 1977. Copyright © 1977 American Psychological Association. Reprinted by permission of the author. **Figure, page 333** From Hyde, Janet S., "Children's understanding of sexist language" in *Developmental Psychology, 20,* 703, 1984. Copyright © 1984 American Psychological Association. Reprinted by permission of the author.

CHAPTER 9

Figure, page 353 From J. R. Eagleston, et al., "Physical health correlates of Type A behavior in children and adolescents" in *Journal of Behavioral Medicine, 4,* 341–362, 1986. Copyright © 1986 Plenum Publishing Corporation, New York. Reprinted by permission. **Figure 9.1 and 9.2** From Santrock, John W. and Steven R. Yussen, *Children and Adolescents.* © 1984 Wm. C. Brown Publishers, Dubuque, Iowa. All Rights Reserved. Reprinted by permission. **Figure**

Child Development, 55, 152–154, 1984. © 1984 by The Society for Research in Child Development. Reprinted by permission. **Figure, page 531** From Elkind, David and R. Bowen, "Imaginary audience behavior in children and adolescents" in *Developmental Psychology, 15,* 38–44, 1979. Copyright © 1979 American Psychological Association. Reprinted by permission of the author.

CHAPTER 13

Excerpts, pages 544–545 and 572–573 Published by permission of Transaction, Inc., from *Successful Schools for Young Adolescents,* by Joan Lipsitz. Copyright © 1984 by Transaction, Inc. **Figure, page 552** From Steinberg, Laurence, "Latchkey children and susceptibility to peer pressure: An ecological analysis" in *Developmental Psychology, 22,* 438, 1986. © 1986 American Psychological Association. Reprinted by permission of the author. **Figure 13.1** From Hill, J. P., Holmbeck, G. N., Marlow, L., Green, T. M., and Lynch, M. E., "Pubertal status and parent-child relations in families

of seventh-grade boys" in *Journal of Early Adolescence, 5,* 31–44. Reprinted with permission of H.E.L.P. Books, Inc. **Figure, page 563** From Brown, Bradford B. and M. J. Lohr, "Peer group affiliation and adolescent self-esteem: An integration of ego identity and symbolic interaction theories" in *Journal of Personality and Social Psychology,* in press. Copyright © American Psychological Association. Reprinted with permission of the author. **Figure 13.2** From Berndt, Thomas J., "Developmental changes in conformity to peers and parents" in *Developmental Psychology, 15,* 608–616, 1979. Copyright © 1979 American Psychological Association. Reprinted by permission of the author. **Figure 13.3** From Dunphy, D. C., "The social structure of peer groups" in *Sociometry, 26,* fig. 1, p. 263, 1963. © 1963 American Sociological Association. Reprinted by permission.

CHAPTER 14

Excerpts, pages 582–583 From G. Marx, *The GrouchoPhile.* © 1977 Bobbs-Merrill Company, New York. **Figure 14.1** From

Archer, S. L., "The lower age boundaries of identity development" in *Child Development, 53,* 1551–1556, 1982. © 1982 by The Society for Research in Child Development. Reprinted by permission. **Figure 14.2** From Blyth, Dale A., D. Durant, and L. Moosbrugger, "Perceived intimacy in the social relationships of drug and non-drug using adolescents." Paper presented at biennial meeting of The Society for Research in Child Development, Toronto, April 1985. Reprinted by permission of the author. **Figure 14.4** From Langley, Lee L., *Physiology of Man.* © 1971 Van Nostrand Reinhold, New York. Reprinted with permission of the author. **Figure 14.5** From Achenbach, T. M. and C. S. Edelbrock, "Behavioral problems and competencies reported by parents of normal and disturbed children aged four through sixteen" in *Monographs of The Society for Research in Child Development,* Serial No. 188, Vol. 46, No. 1, 1981. © 1981 by The Society for Research in Child Development. Reprinted by permission.

NAME INDEX

A

Abel, E.L., 104
Abeles, R.P., 473
Abelson, R., 371
Achelpohl, C., 322
Achenbach, T., 485, 617
Acredolo, L.P., 148, 149, 152
Adams, G., 531, 592
Adams, G.R., 591, 593, 597
Adelson, J., 46, 450, 505, 561, 566, 573, 599, 616
Adler, N.E., 9
Ainsworth, M., 218, 219, 220, 224
Ainsworth, M.D.S., 127, 229, 230, 231, 237, 465, 548
Akers, R., 322
Akiyami, M., 285
Albert, R., 328
Allen, G.L., 149
Allen, L., 397
Allinsmith, W., 456
Altus, W.D., 567
Amatruda, C.S., 137
Ambramovitch, R., 304, 305
Ames, C., 428, 429, 430, 437
Ames, R.E., 428, 429, 430, 437
Amsterdam, B.K., 238
Anastasi, A., 396
Ander, T.D., 380
Anders, T.F., 153
Anderson, B., 154
Anderson, B.J., 210, 213
Anderson, D.R., 278, 322, 323, 325
Anderson, L.M., 430
Anderson, R.J., 191
Andres, D., 335
Andrews, G.R., 429
Andrews, S.R., 401
Anglin, J.M., 525
Antill, J.K., 469
Apfel, N., 318
Apgar, V., 114, 129
Applebaum, M.I., 37, 397
Applefield, J.M., 323
Arayama, T., 149
Archer, S., 591, 597
Arend, R.A., 222, 314
Aries, P., 9, 14, 35

Armsden, G.G., 548
Arterberry,, 147
Asarnow, J.R., 446
Asberg, M., 490
Asher, J., 188
Asher, S.R., 445, 446
Ashmead, D.H., 177, 362
Aslin, R.N., 149
Athanascious, P.Z., 490
Atkinson, J.R., 419, 420, 421, 427
Attneave, F., 142
Ausubel, D., 404
Ausubel, D.P., 596
Axelrad, S., 137
Axia, G., 287
Ayers-Lopez, S., 549

B

Babigian, H., 446
Bache, W.L., 401
Bachman, J., 600, 601, 602, 611
Bachman, J.G., 536
Baer, D.M., 313
Bahrick, L.E., 153
Bailey, J.S., 263
Bailey, M., 472
Baillargeon, R., 277, 361, 362, 363
Bakeman, R., 117
Baker, N., 424
Baker, S.W., 329
Baldwin, A., 567
Baldwin, A.L., 303
Ball, S.J., 450
Baltes, P.B., 33
Bandura, A., 65, 66, 67, 68, 69, 77, 79, 166, 169, 186, 428, 430, 433, 561
Bane, M.J., 306
Banks, M.S., 145, 157, 175
Baptiste, M.S., 264
Barbee, A.H., 472
Barcus, F.E., 324
Barenboim, C., 532
Barker, R., 445
Barker, R.G., 26
Barnes, G., 603
Barnes, K., 316
Barnett, C.R., 117

Barnstein, M.H., 143, 145, 157, 181
Baroni, M.R., 287
Barr, H.M., 104, 105
Barrera, M., 457
Barrett, D., 21
Barrett, K.C., 116, 224, 235
Barron, F., 381
Bart, W.M., 529
Bartel, N.R., 355
Barter, J.T., 604
Bartlett, F.C., 371
Baskett, L.M., 303
Bates, E., 191, 197
Battle, E.S., 428, 472
Baucom, D.H., 467, 468
Bauer, C.R., 113
Baumrind, D., 301, 472
Bayley, N., 179, 180, 182, 202, 263
Beach, D.R., 328, 365
Bechtel, R., 322
Beck, A., 490
Becker, W., 66, 343
Beebe, B., 211
Beeghley, M., 265, 266
Behrend, D.A., 274
Bell, D., 458
Bell, S.M., 127, 218, 380
Bellugi-Klima, U., 283
Belsky, J., 114, 213, 220, 228, 230, 234, 320
Bem, S.L., 468
Bender, L., 357
Benesh-Weiner, M., 422
Bennett, S.L., 211
Bereiter, C., 524, 525, 526
Berg, C.A., 398
Berg, K.M., 174
Berg, W.K., 174
Berkeley, G., 150
Berko, J., 285
Berkowitz, M., 478, 480, 481
Berlyne, D., 314
Berman, P.W., 306
Berndt, T., 560
Berndt, T.J., 450, 573, 574, 575
Bernstein-Tarrow, N.B., 258, 350
Berscheid, E., 519
Bertelsen, A., 490
Bertilsson, L., 490
Berzins, J.I., 467
Berzonsky, M.D., 529
Best, D.L., 335
Betz, N.E., 468
Bibace, R., 264
Bieglow, B.J., 450
Biehler, R.F., 414
Biemer, L., 335
Bijou, S.W., 165
Bindra, I., 163

Binet, A., 40, 389, 408
Birrell, J.M., 246
Birrell, R.G., 246
Black, J.B., 371
Blaine, G.B., 489
Blanchard, D.C., 163
Blanchard, R.J., 163
Bloch, H.A., 606
Block, J., 330, 331, 442, 468, 471, 472
Block, J.H., 442
Bloom, B.S., 404, 607
Bloom, L.M., 186, 199
Blos, P., 45, 46, 54, 265, 567, 606
Blue, J.H., 6, 508, 509, 510
Blum, R.W., 103
Blumberg, M.L., 245
Blumenthal, J.M., 401
Blyth, D., 519, 520
Blyth, D.A., 517, 573, 605
Bobrow, S., 328
Boehm, J., 137
Bonvillian, J.D., 195
Born, W.S., 146
Borstelmann, L.J., 9, 10, 37
Borton, R.W., 153
Botkin, P.T., 340
Bourbeau, P., 303
Bourne, E., 589
Bowen, R., 530, 531
Bower, G., 328
Bower, G.H., 371
Bower, T.G.R., 143, 146, 157, 173
Bowlby, J., 72, 215, 216, 218, 224, 229, 230, 231, 235, 490, 491, 548
Boxerman, S.B., 154
Boyle, P., 289
Boyle, P.C., 615
Brackbill, Y., 111, 112, 401
Bracke, P., 352
Bracken, B.A., 396
Bradford, R., 322
Bradley, R.M., 152
Braine, M.D., 200
Brainerd, C.J., 281
Brannick, N., 284
Bransford, J.D., 203, 368
Brazelton, T.B., 112, 114, 121, 126, 129, 130, 132, 154, 156, 179, 263
Breitmayer, B.J., 401
Bremer, M., 324
Bremnar, J.G., 149
Bremner, R., 568
Brenner, J., 232
Bretherton, I., 235, 236, 265, 266
Brewster, A.B., 265
Bridger, W.H., 153
Briggs, J., 401
Brim, O.G., 305

Brittain, C.V., 549
Broadbent, D., 60, 61, 77
Brody, G.H., 305
Brody, L., 473
Brody, S., 137
Broman, S.H., 106
Bromley, D.B., 532
Bronfenbrenner, U., 208, 209, 215, 229, 231, 251, 399, 401, 445, 482, 484, 506
Bronson, W.C., 212
Brooks-Gunn, J., 238, 518, 520, 521
Brophy, J., 456
Broughton, J., 328, 480
Brown, A.L., 203, 368, 371, 524, 526
Brown, B.B., 561, 563, 564
Brown, E., 232
Brown, J.L., 128
Brown, J.V., 117
Brown, R., 186, 194, 195, 281, 283, 284, 289, 568
Brownell, C.A., 232
Bruch, H., 613
Bruner, J., 203, 523
Bruner, J.S., 135
Bryant, B., 423
Bryant, B.K., 28, 29
Bryant, K.J., 261
Bryant, P., 149
Buchanan, N.R., 232
Buchsbaum, K., 447
Buck, S., 145
Buckley, S., 445
Bugbee, N.M., 140
Bukatko, D., 296
Bukowski, W.M., 446
Bulcroft, R., 517, 520
Bullock, M., 274
Burgess, R.L., 450
Burkett, C.L., 328
Burleson, B.R., 451
Bush, D., 573
Bush, E.S., 473
Butcher, M.J., 152
Butler, L., 446

C

Cain, R.L., 210, 213
Cairns, R., 9, 70
Calfee, E., 279
Califano, J.A., 263
Callahan, R., 504
Callan, J.W., 446
Calvert, S.L., 324
Campbell, B., 85
Campbell, B.K., 117
Campbell, D.T., 31
Campbell, T.A., 325

Campione, J.C., 203, 368
Campos, J.J., 116, 147, 224, 235
Cannizzo, S.R., 365
Cantwell, D.P., 304
Caplan, F., 126, 136, 137, 157
Caplan, T., 136, 137
Card, J.J., 473
Carello, C., 143
Carey, S., 286
Carleton-Ford, S., 573
Carlson, S.G., 117
Carper, L., 300
Carskaddon, G., 195
Case, R., 280, 362, 363, 364
Cassidy, J., 224
Castenada, A., 457
Cattell, J.M., 389
Cattell, P., 180, 183
Cattell, R., 393, 408
Cavan, P.A., 524
Cazden, C.B., 283
Chaille, C., 320
Chalemian, R.J., 153
Chalkey, M.A., 191
Chall, J.S., 411
Chamberlain, P., 609
Chang, P., 117
Chapin, M., 429
Charnov, E.L., 229
Chase, W.G., 62
Chassin, L., 602
Chernin, K., 613
Chernovetz, M.E., 469
Cherry, L., 334
Chesney, B.H., 218
Chess, S., 224
Chi, M.T., 367, 371
Chiang, C.P., 287
Chilman, C., 514, 515
Chinsky, J.M., 328, 365
Chomsky, N., 184, 187, 191
Cicchetti, D., 153
Cicirelli, V., 303, 305
Clark, B., 568
Clark, E., 286
Clark, E.V., 196, 197, 198, 199, 203
Clark, H.H., 196
Clark, K., 457
Clark, M.C., 224
Clark, R.A., 420
Clark, R.D., 166
Clarke, J.A., 490
Clarke-Stewart, K.A., 218, 220, 221, 234, 289, 296
Clasen, D.R., 561
Clifford, E., 442
Cloud, J.M., 335

Cohen, A.K., 504
Cohen, D., 166
Cohen, F., 9
Cohen, S., 398
Coie, J.D., 445
Colby, A., 477
Cole, S., 536
Coleman, D., 129
Coleman, J., 534, 562, 563, 568, 569
Coleridge, S.T., 85, 618
Coles, R., 41
Colletta, N.D., 307
Collins, A., 554
Collins, J.K., 566
Collins, P.A., 322
Collins, W.A., 555
Comber, L.C., 415
Condon, S.M., 553, 593
Condry, J.C., 445
Conger, R., 609
Constantinople, A., 592, 596
Cook, T.D., 31
Cooper, C., 549, 593, 594, 595
Cooper, H., 428
Cooper, R., 553
Coopersmith, S., 462
Corrigan, R., 171, 173
Corsini, D.A., 335
Corter, C., 304, 305
Cortes, C.E., 457
Covington, M.V., 428
Cowan, C.P., 213, 306
Cowan, P., 79, 213, 529
Cowan, P.A., 306
Cowen, E.L., 446
Cox, G.L., 365
Cox, M., 307, 331, 443
Cox, R., 307, 331, 443
Craik, F.I.M., 365
Crandall, V.C., 428, 472, 473
Cratty, B., 260, 350, 385
Crawford, J.W., 117
Cremin, L., 504
Crimmings, A.M., 468
Critelli, J.W., 567
Croft, K., 6, 329
Cromer, C.C., 373
Cronbach, L., 455
Cronbach, L.J., 394
Crook, C.K., 152
Cross, K.P., 570
Cross, P., 377, 380
Crouter, A.C., 251, 306, 505
Crowder, R., 407, 411
Crumrine, P.L., 305
Cummings, C.M., 468
Cunningham, J.D., 469
Curran, J.P., 566

Curtis, L., 160
Curtiss, S., 188, 189
Cushna, B., 305
Cutler, G.B., 6, 508, 509, 510
Cvetkovich, G., 515

D

Daehler, M.W., 296
Damek, C.J., 310
Damon, W., 531
Danielssan, B., 117
Danker-Brown, P., 468
Dann, S., 310
Danner, F., 480
Darby, B.L., 105
Darling, C.A., 515
Darlington, R., 293
Darwin, C., 11, 14, 17, 35, 85, 93, 118, 503
Daton, N., 520
Davids, A., 491
Davidson, E.S., 343
Davidson, J.E., 405
Davis, G.A., 385, 406
Davis, J., 568
Davis, M., 236
Davis, S.W., 335
Davison, G.C., 403
Day, M.C., 529
de Villiers, J.G., 186, 188, 189, 193, 195, 197, 200, 286
de Villiers, P.A., 186, 188, 189, 193, 195, 197, 200, 286
Dean, C., 490
Debus, R.L., 429
Deci, E.L., 431
DeFries, J.C., 90
Delys, P., 423
Demorest, A., 527
Dement, W.C., 129
Dempster, F.N., 279, 280
DeOreo, K.L., 260
Deutsch, C., 293
Deutsch, C.J., 469
Deutsch, G., 614
Deutsch, M., 293
Dewey, J., 484, 487
Diamond, A., 173
Diaz, R.M., 450
Dickinson, A., 164
Dickinson, G.E., 566
Dickstein, E., 328
Dillon, R.S., 509
Dillon, T.J., 404
Dion, K.K., 246, 519
Disbrow, M.A., 129
Divitto, B.A., 121
Dodd, D.H., 373

Dodge, K.A., 445, 446, 447
Doehrman, M., 46
Doering, Z., 568
Dolby, R.M., 112, 130
Dolgin, K.G., 274
Doman, G., 160
Domonick, J.R., 323
Dorn, L.D., 6, 508, 509, 510
Dougherty, L.M., 236
Douvan, E., 450, 561, 566, 573, 599
Dove, A., 396, 397
Dozier, C., 443
Dreyer, P.H., 514, 515
Duck, S.W., 450
Dunn, J., 194, 231, 242, 251, 304
Dunphy, D., 564, 565, 568
Durant, D., 605
Durkheim, E., 337
Dweck, C.S., 429, 437, 473
Dyck, D.G., 429

E

Eagleston, J., 352
Earley, L.A., 176
Eckerman, C.O., 232, 240, 312
Edelbrock, C., 485, 617
Edwards, J.R., 335
Egeland, B., 233
Ehrhardt, A., 329, 330
Eicher, S.A., 561
Eichorn, D., 258, 518, 568
Eitzen, D.S., 562
Elder, G.H., 504, 547
Eliot, E.S., 437, 473
Elkind, D., 9, 275, 276, 361, 428, 444, 525,
    529, 530, 531, 535, 612
Elliott, C.H., 264, 267
Ellwood, D., 537
Emde, R., 153
Emde, R.N., 127, 236
Emerson, E., 451
Emerson, P.E., 218, 219
Emerson, R.W., 25
Emmer, E.T., 430
Emmerich, W., 312, 335
Engen, T., 152
Enright, R.D., 481, 484, 504, 531
Enslein, J., 319
Entus, A.K., 188
Epstein, J.L., 458, 549
Erikson, E. H., 39, 40, 41, 42, 50, 51, 52, 53,
    54, 74, 75, 76, 77, 79, 92, 216, 237, 239,
    240, 242, 245, 248, 301, 314, 329, 337,
    339, 340, 434, 454, 455, 563, 584, 585,
    586, 587, 588, 589, 592, 593, 596, 597,
    598, 599, 606, 608, 618

Estes, D.P., 229
Etches, P., 137
Evans, D., 148
Evans, E., 461, 462
Evans, R.I., 606
Evertson, C., 456
Evertson, C.M., 430
Eves, S.W., 596

F

Fabricius, W.V., 368
Fagan, J.F., III, 398
Fagen, J.W., 176
Fagerberg, H., 117
Fagot, B., 334
Fagot, B.I., 335
Falkner, F., 121
Fantz, R., 144, 145, 146, 147, 151, 156
Farrar, P., 142
Farrington, D.P., 610
Fassinger, R.E., 475
Faust, M.S., 511, 512
Faust, R., 605
Feather, N.T., 420
Feck, G., 264
Feigley, D.A., 178
Fein, G.G., 234, 289, 296, 317, 318, 319, 320
Feiring, C., 210, 212, 223
Feldman-Summers, S., 472
Feldstein, M., 537
Ferguson, C.A., 194
Fernald, A., 193
Ferrara, R.A., 203, 368
Festinger, L., 563
Field, D.E., 322
Field, J., 504
Field, T., 114, 116
Field, T.M., 117, 166
Finley, M.I., 504
Finney, J.W., 604
Fisch, R.O., 117, 153, 154
Fischer, J.L., 599
Fischer, K.W., 171, 173, 318, 320, 361, 524,
    525, 526
Fitch, S.A., 592
Flavell, J., 533, 534
Flavell, J.H., 6, 19, 20, 62, 172, 176, 177,
    193, 195, 196, 197, 198, 200, 203, 278,
    285, 328, 329, 340, 365, 368, 369
Flay, B.R., 607
Fleckenstein, L.K., 176
Fleeson, J., 214, 224, 251, 548
Forbes, G.B., 103
Ford, M.E., 396, 467, 468, 475
Forehand, G., 458
Forehand, R.L., 305
Forgatch, M.S., 609

Forslund, M.A., 603
Foulkes, D., 8, 59, 129
Fowler, W., 289
Fowles, J., 335
Fox, L.H., 473, 475
Fox, N., 177
Fraiberg, S., 138, 139, 206
Frank, L.K., 317
Fredkin, E., 348
Fregly, M.J., 508, 509
Freud, A., 45, 46, 54, 310
Freud, S., 3, 11, 12, 14, 35, 39, 42, 43, 44,
    45, 47, 48, 49, 50, 51, 52, 54, 58, 59, 75,
    76, 77, 79, 178, 216, 230, 314, 319, 329,
    337, 419
Frey, K.S., 335
Friedman, M., 9, 351
Friedrich, 322
Friedrichs, A.G., 368
Frieze, I.H., 472
Frisch, R., 507
Fritz, J., 235, 236
Frodi, M., 228
Froman, R.D., 403
Fromkin, V.A., 188, 189
Frommer, E., 224
Fry, C.L., 340
Fucigna, C., 271
Furman, W., 310
Furth, H.G., 360, 385

G

Gabrielson, P., 609
Gadow, K.D., 357
Gage, N.L., 454
Gagne, E., 429
Gagne, E.D., 379, 380
Gagnon, J.H., 566
Gaite, A.J.H., 529
Gallistel, C.R., 277
Galst, J., 324
Gandhi, M., 588
Garbarino, J., 246, 482, 484
Garcia, R., 188
Gardner, B.T., 191
Gardner, H., 153, 271, 395, 396, 524, 527
Gardner, L., 259
Gardner, R., 394, 408
Gardner, R.A., 191
Gardner, W.R., 229
Garmezy, N., 246, 491, 492, 496, 610
Garnica, O.K., 194
Garrelik, G., 400
Garrison, W., 429
Garvey, C., 316, 317
Gaskell, J., 335
Gazensbauer, T.G., 127

Gearheart, B.R., 351, 355
Geary, P.S., 592
Gein, G.G., 343
Geis, G., 245
Gelman, R., 153, 193, 274, 277, 287, 288, 358, 361, 362, 363
Gentner, D., 286
Gergen, K.J., 328
Gershoni, R., 450
Gesell, A., 137, 182
Gesell, A.L., 12, 13, 14, 18, 22, 35, 79, 179, 202
Getzels, J.W., 404
Gewirtz, H.B., 127, 305
Gewirtz, J.L., 165, 217, 305
Giaconia, R.M., 453, 454
Gibbs, J., 477, 478, 479, 480, 481, 484
Gibson, E.J., 141, 143, 144, 146, 150, 151, 153, 155, 156, 157, 161
Gibson, J.J., 141, 143, 144, 145, 150, 151, 153, 155, 156, 157, 161
Gilbert, L.A., 469
Gilchrist, L.D., 607
Giles, H., 335
Gilliard, D., 473
Gilligan, C., 433, 481, 482, 483, 496
Gilliom, C.F., 401
Gilstrap, B., 228
Ginsburg, H., 203
Glaser, N., 415
Glaser, R., 377
Glass, D.C., 305
Gleitman, L., 409, 410, 411, 418
Glick, J., 282
Glick, P.C., 443
Glicksman, M.L., 147
Glorieux, J., 335
Glueck, E., 608
Glueck, S., 608
Goelman, H., 526
Gold, D., 335
Gold, M., 550, 608
Goldberg, J., 280
Goldberg, S., 116, 121
Golden, M.W., 446
Goldenson, R.M., 317
Goldhagen, J., 103
Goldman, K.S., 312
Goldman-Rakic, P.S., 140
Goldsmith, H.H., 116, 224, 235
Golomb, C., 272
Goodall, J., 26
Goodlad, J.I., 570, 573
Goodwin, F.K., 490
Gordon, I., 292
Gordon, N.J., 324
Gordon, N.P., 607
Goren, C.G., 146

Gorsuch, R.L., 421
Gotkin, E., 534
Gottfried, A.W., 153
Gottlieb, D., 457
Gottlob, D., 264
Gottman, J., 451
Gould, S., 121
Gould, S.J., 86
Gove, F.L., 233
Gowan, J.C., 437
Graff, R.A., 368
Graham, D., 103
Graham, R., 400
Grallo, R., 293
Granrud, C.E., 147
Gratch, G., 171
Graves, S.B., 324
Gray, W.M., 531
Greatheart, B.R., 385
Green, R., 334
Green, T.M., 554
Greenberg, B.S., 323
Greenberg, M.T., 548
Greenberg, R., 166
Greenberger, E., 536
Greene, D., 431
Greenwald, A., 328
Greenwood, M.M., 152
Griesler, P.C., 176
Grilliches, Z., 568
Grimes, J.W., 456
Grossman, H.J., 402
Grossman, K., 117
Grossman, K.E., 117
Grote, B., 515
Grotevant, H., 593, 594, 595
Grotevant, H.D., 553
Gruendel, J., 371
Gudeman, J., 608
Guilford, J.P., 393, 394, 404, 406, 408
Gump, P.V., 573
Gundewall, C., 117
Gunnar, M.R., 153, 154
Guskin, S.L., 355
Gustafson, T.J., 603

H

Haeberle, E., 514
Hagan, J.W., 368
Hagarty, P.S., 397
Hagen, E.P., 391
Hah, W., 351
Hahn, C.L., 335
Hainsworth, P.K., 491
Haith, M.M., 126
Hake, J.L., 152
Hakes, D.T., 192

Halberstadt, A.G., 467
Hale, G.A., 394
Hall, D., 534
Hall, G.S., 11, 13, 14, 35, 503, 504, 505, 507, 538, 584, 606
Hall, J.A., 467
Hallinan, M.T., 450
Halwes, T.G., 365
Hamburg, B., 516
Hamm, C.M., 485
Hammer, D., 305
Hanlon, C., 186
Hansson, R.O., 469
Hardy-Brown, K., 195
Harlap, S., 104
Harlow, H., 216, 217
Harlow, H.F., 310
Harmon, R., 153
Harmon, R.J., 127
Harnisch, D.L., 415
Harris, D.B., 462, 463
Harris, F.R., 313
Harris, P.L., 173
Hart, D., 531
Harter, S., 27, 239, 327, 328, 462, 463, 466, 486
Hartley, R.E., 317
Hartup, W., 211, 316, 335
Hartup, W.W., 214, 224, 251, 310, 311, 312, 314, 343, 445, 449, 450, 452, 549, 561
Harvald, A., 490
Harvey, O.J., 452
Hasher, L., 63
Hass, A., 514, 515, 516
Hauge, M., 490
Havighurst, R.J., 357
Haviland, J., 236
Hawkins, J., 282
Hawkins, J.A., 573, 574, 575
Hay, D.F., 232
Hayes, C., 190
Hayes, K.J., 190
Hayne, H., 176
Hazen, N.L., 261
Hedges, L.V., 453, 454
Hefner, R., 330
Heibeck, T.H., 286
Heider, F., 422
Heilbrun, A.B., 467
Helmreich, R., 467, 468
Henderson, N., 399
Herzog, E., 333
Hess, R.D., 442
Hetherington, E.M., 307, 331, 443, 557, 558, 559, 567
Heyde, M.B., 534
Higgens-Trenk, A., 472, 529

Hill, C.R., 441
Hill, J.P., 312, 504, 505, 514, 522, 529, 546, 554, 556, 571, 616
Hinde, R., 39, 70, 71, 72, 73, 74, 78, 79, 208, 549
Hinde, R.A., 319
Hines, R.P., 401
Hochberg, J.E., 142
Hoffman, H.R., 321
Hoffman, J.M., 473
Hoffman, L., 306, 444
Hoffman, L.W., 306
Hoffman, M.L., 340
Hoffman, S.D., 603
Holahan, C.K., 468
Holland, J.L., 420
Hollingshead, A.B., 445
Hollis, M., 311, 312
Holman, D.R., 335
Holmbeck, G.N., 546, 554
Honig, A.S., 290
Honzik, M.P., 397
Hood, L., 186
Hood, W.R., 452
Horn, J.M., 90
Horneman, G., 117
Howes, C., 232, 289
Hoyt, J.D., 368
Hudson, L.M., 531
Huebner, R.R., 236
Hume, D., 349
Hunt, J.M., 173, 181, 183, 202, 218
Hunt, K.W., 526
Hunt, M., 60, 79, 385
Huntington, L., 127
Hurley, L.S., 103
Huston, A., 322, 325, 330
Huston, A.C., 324, 331, 334, 335, 466
Huston, T.L., 306, 450
Huston-Stein, A., 472
Hutchings, B., 610
Hutchinson, C.A., 127
Hwang, C.P., 117
Hyde, J., 332
Hyde, J.S., 482, 496
Hyman, H.M., 561

Ianotti, R.J., 340
Ilg, F.L., 12
Ingledyne, E., 129
Inhelder, B., 270, 274
Inoff-Germain, G., 6, 508, 509, 510
Isenberg, P.L., 490
Isseroff, 140
Izard, C.E., 235, 236, 251
Izzo, L.D., 446

J
Jacklin, C., 470, 471, 472, 487
Jacobs, J., 612
Jacobson, J.L., 232
Jacoby, L., 328
Jacquette, D., 440
Jaffe, J., 211
James, W., 141, 144, 151, 156, 327
Jarvis, P.E., 340
Jaskir, J., 223
Jay, S., 264, 267
Jeans, P.C., 103
Jeffrey, W.E., 279
Jenkins, C.D., 351
Jenkins, J.J., 524
Jennings, S., 171, 173
Jensen, A., 399
Jerauld, R., 117
Johnson, D.L., 401
Johnson, S.B., 267
Johnson, S.M., 303
Johnson, W., 236
Johnston, L., 600, 601, 602, 611
Jones, K.L., 104
Jones, M.C., 164, 517
Jones, R., 531
Jones, R.R., 609
Jones, W.H., 469
Jordaan, J.P., 534
Jordan, T., 293
Jose, P.E., 336
Jung, C., 301, 340
Jusczyk, D.W., 149
Juster, F.T., 228

K
Kacerguis, M.A., 593, 597
Kagan, J., 89, 153, 177, 207, 224, 229, 231, 234, 289, 454, 472
Kahn, A.J., 401
Kahn, N., 289
Kail, R., 177, 178, 385
Kallen, D.J., 515
Kamin, L.J., 399
Kandel, D., 547, 561, 605
Kantner, J., 515
Kaplan, B., 320
Kaplan, E., 524
Kaplan, N., 224
Karabenick, S.A., 517
Katz, P.A., 449
Kaufman, A.S., 396
Kaufman, N.L., 396
Kaye, H., 152
Kearsley, R.B., 234, 289, 318
Keeney, T.J., 365
Keeves, J.P., 415

Keil, F., 376
Keith, T.Z., 396
Kelley, J.B., 308
Kellman, P.J., 146
Kellogg, C.A., 190
Kellogg, W.N., 190
Kelly, J., 557
Kelly, J.A., 469
Kemnitz, J.W., 615
Kendell, R.E., 490
Kendrick, C., 194, 231, 242, 304
Kennell, J., 115, 116
Kenniston, K., 591, 617
Kent, R.N., 334
Kenworthy, J.A., 469
Kerr, B., 474
Kessen, W., 9, 11, 37, 126
Kessey, R.E., 615
Kett, J., 568
Khatena, J., 437
Kidd, K., 90, 91, 92
Kiesler, S.B., 472
King, R.M., 339, 340
King, S., 149
Kinsey, A.C., 514
Kintsch, W., 371
Kirasic, K.C., 149
Kirchner, G.L., 105
Kirker, W., 328
Kirmil-Gray, K., 352
Kisilevsky, B.S., 174
Kister, M.C., 265
Klatzky, R., 61, 62, 64, 77
Klaus, M., 115, 117
Klein, P.S., 103
Klein, R., 21
Klein, R.E., 221, 394
Knapp, H., 335
Knox, D., 567
Kobasigawa, A., 366
Koenig, K., 153
Kohlberg, L., 53, 217, 230, 330, 337, 433, 440, 476, 477, 478, 479, 480, 481, 482, 483, 484, 485, 487
Kohler, C.J., 153
Koperski, J.A., 127
Kopp, C.B., 111, 113, 114, 116, 241, 243, 244
Korner, A.F., 127
Kositchek, R., 351
Kowalski, R., 534
Kozin, M., 576
Kozlowski, L.T., 261
Kraemer, H.C., 127
Krashen, S., 188, 189
Kravitz, H., 137
Kraybill, S.N., 154
Kreger, N.C., 117

Krogman, W.M., 259, 349
Krowitz, A., 147
Kruper, J.C., 193
Kuczaj, S.A., 199, 284
Kuhn, D., 361
Kuiper, N., 328
Kun, A., 422
Kupersmidt, J.B., 446
Kurland, D.M., 280
Kutz, S.L., 232, 312

L

La Barbera, J.D., 236
Labov, W., 188, 524
Ladd, G., 451
LaGaipa, J.J., 450
Lahey, B.B., 305
Lally, J.R., 290
Lamaze, F., 108, 109, 113, 117, 119
Lamb, M., 226, 228
Lamb, M.E., 116, 157, 212, 224, 226, 228,
    229, 235, 251, 331
Lamiell, J.T., 423
Landesman-Dwyer, S., 106
Lange, G.W., 372
Langer, A., 147
Lapsley, D., 328, 329, 478, 480, 481, 484,
    504, 531, 532
Larson, M.E., 404
Larsson, K., 117
Lasater, T.M., 401
Lasko, J.K., 303
Lasky, R.E., 221
La Voie, J., 592
Lazar, I., 293
Lazarus, R.S., 235
Lazerson, A., 524, 525, 526
Leboyer, F., 108, 113, 117, 119, 121
Ledger, G.W., 368
Lee, C.L., 232
Lee, S.S., 415
Leiderman, P.H., 117
Leifer, A.D., 117, 324
Leler, H., 401
Lenneberg, E., 186, 188, 196
Lennon, E., 150
Lepper, M., 431
Lerner, R.M., 517, 520
Lesser, G.S., 547, 561
Lesser, I., 597
Lester, B.M., 121, 130
Levensen, R.W., 602
Levin, H., 441
Levin, J., 328
Levin, J.R., 366
Levin, S., 322
Levin, S.R., 278

Levine, L.J., 235
Levitt, M.J., 224
Levitz-Jones, E.M., 597
Levy, D.M., 137
Lewis, J.F., 396
Lewis, M., 210, 212, 223, 230, 238, 310
Lewis, N.G., 245
Lewkowicz, D.J., 150
Lieberman, A.F., 222
Lieberman, M., 477
Liebert, R.M., 343
Lightbown, P., 186
Lindauer, B.K., 278, 365
Lipsitt, L.P., 33, 152, 165
Lipsitz, J., 428, 502, 544, 545, 570, 571, 572,
    573, 575, 576, 612
Livesley, W.J., 532
Locke, J., 11
Lockhart, R.S., 176, 365
Lockman, J.J., 261
Lohr, M.J., 563, 564
Long, L., 444
Long, T., 444
Lorch, E.P., 322, 325
Lorenz, K., 70, 71, 72, 73, 74, 76, 78
Loriaux, D.L., 6, 508, 509, 510
Louderville, S., 222
Lowell, E.O., 420
Lowrey, G.H., 258, 259
Lucariello, J., 372
Lundsteen, S.W., 258, 350
Luria, Z., 333
Lushene, R.E., 421
Luttge, W.G., 508, 509
Lyle, J., 321, 322, 323
Lynch, M.E., 554
Lytton, H., 243

M

McAlister, A.L., 607
McAlpine, W., 117
McArthur, C.C., 489
McCabe, M.P., 566
McCall, R., 397
McCall, R.B., 37, 117, 397, 398
McCandless, B., 334
McCandless, B.R., 461, 462, 606
McClelland, D.C., 419, 420, 427, 464
Maccoby, E.E., 117, 207, 212, 251, 302, 303,
    312, 441, 442, 460, 465, 470, 471, 472,
    487, 555
McConaghy, M.J., 335
McCord, J., 608, 610
McCord, W., 608
MacFarlane, J., 13
MacFarlane, J.A., 152, 397
McGinnes, G.C., 236

McKay, R.J., 263
McKean, K., 388, 395
MacKinnon, C.E., 305
Mackintosh, N.J., 164
McLaughlin, B., 413, 414
McLaughlin, L., 602
McNeill, D., 187, 191
MacPhee, D., 289
MacWhinney, B., 191
Macy, C., 121
Maddux, J.E., 9, 263
Maeher, M.L., 428
Mahler, M., 238, 239, 242
Main, M., 219, 222, 224, 465
Maio, M.L., 127
Malatesta, C., 236
Malone, P., 401
Malone, S., 153, 154
Mandler, J., 148
Mandler, J.M., 177, 361, 362, 363, 367, 371,
    372
Mannarina, A.P., 450
Mannle, S., 287
Maratsos, M.P., 187, 191, 192, 203
Marcia, J., 590, 591, 592, 593, 594, 595, 597
Marcus, T.L., 335
Margolis, F.L., 263
Markman, E., 286
Markus, G.B., 401
Markus, H., 328
Marlow, L., 554
Marr, D.B., 398
Marshall, H., 453
Marshall, R.E., 154
Marston, R., 566
Martin, B., 354
Martin, C.E., 514
Martin, D.C., 104, 105
Martin, G.B., 166
Martin, J., 212, 302, 568
Martin, J.A., 117, 251, 442, 465
Martin, J.C., 104
Maruyama, G., 305
Marx, G., 582, 583, 584
Maslow, A.H., 327
Masten, A.S., 492
Masters, J.C., 312
Masur, F.T., 264
Matas, L., 222, 314
Matthews, K.A., 351
Mauer, D., 175
Mayaux , M.J., 103
Mayer, J., 616
Mayer, R.E., 163
Mays, J., 568
Meacham, J., 598
Mednick, S.A., 610
Medrich, E.A., 445

Meehan, A.M., 529
Meichenbaum, D., 446
Meier, J.H., 355, 356
Meilman, P.W., 591
Meltzoff, A.N., 153, 166
Mendel, G., 87
Mercer, J.R., 396, 397
Meredith, H.V., 259
Merrill, D.J., 86
Metcalf, D., 153
Meyer, C., 527
Meyer, M.L., 595
Michaels, C., 143
Mihelich, M.H., 469
Miler, N.B., 304
Milham, J., 113
Mill, J., 150
Miller, G., 185, 188, 190, 192
Miller, L.K., 394
Miller, L.L., 604
Miller, N., 305
Miller, N.E., 286
Miller, W.B., 608
Minard, J., 129
Minnett, A.M., 304
Minuchin, P.P., 457, 458, 496
Mischel, W., 65, 66, 68, 69, 77, 79, 339, 420, 423, 424, 425, 426, 427, 470, 596
Mistry, J.J., 372
Mitchell, J.S., 615
Mitchell, R.G., 137
Mitteness, L.S., 556
Mizner, G.L., 604
Moely, B.E., 365
Moerk, E.L., 186
Monahan, J., 245
Montemayor, R., 553, 591
Montessori, M., 256, 257
Moore, B.S., 339
Moore, D., 547
Moore, J., 154
Moore, M.K., 166
Moore, M.S., 553
Moore, T., 306
Moos, B.S., 453
Moos, R.H., 453, 604
Moosbrugger, L., 605
Morgan, G.A., 220
Morgan, J., 193
Morgan, S.B., 264
Morris, D., 228
Morris, N., 109
Moscovitch, M., 177
Moscow, H., 403
Moss, H.A., 472
Most, R., 320
Mowat, F., 228

Mueller, E., 232
Muir, D.W., 174
Murphy, M.N., 531, 532
Murphy, R.R., 447
Murray, A.D., 112, 130
Murray, D.M., 607
Murray, F., 360
Murray, H., 419
Mussen, P.H., 37, 517
Muzio, J.N., 129
Myers, B.J., 114
Myles-Worsley, M., 373

N
Nadar, P.R., 103, 264
Naeye, R.L., 106
Nass, G., 566
Nathan, J.G., 322
Nation, R.L., 112, 130
National Institute on Alcohol Abuse and Alcoholism, 603
Naus, M., 368
Naus, M.J., 377
Neale, J.M., 343, 403
Neimark, E.D., 529
Nelson, J., 372
Nelson, K., 371, 372, 446
Nelson, K.E., 195, 197, 371
Nelson, R., 552
Nelson, W.E., 263
Neugarten, B., 520
Neulinger, J., 305
Newberger, C.M., 440
Newcomb, A.F., 446
Newell, A., 376
Newson, E., 441, 442
Newson, J., 441, 442
Nichols, I.A., 196
Nichols, J.G., 428
Nichols, P.L., 106
Nickerson, E.T., 335
Nicolich, L., 320
Niederhoffer, A., 606
Nilsson, L., 121
Nisbett, R.E., 431
Norman, D., 348
Nottelmann, E.D., 508, 509, 510, 511, 573
Nucci, L., 484
Nutrition National Canada Survey, 615
Nydegger, C.N., 556

O
O'Connor, M., 398
O'Connor, M.E., 469
O'Connor-Francoeur, P., 350
Oden, S.L., 445
Ohr, P.S., 176

Olds, D.E., 469
O'Leary, K., 318
O'Leary, K.D., 334
Oleshansky, B., 330
Olson, D.R., 525
Olson, F.A., 365
Olson, G.M., 177
Olson, L., 484
O'Malley, P., 600, 601, 602, 611
Opper, S., 203
Orlofsky, J., 597, 599
O'Shea, G., 224
Ottinger, D.R., 104
Overton, W.F., 529
Owen, S.V., 403

P

Paivo, A., 366
Palfai, T., 163
Pancake, V., 223
Pannabecker, B., 236
Papousek, H., 164, 165
Parcel, G.S., 264
Paris, S.C., 278, 365
Parisi, S.A., 236
Parke, R.D., 228, 245, 246, 338
Parker, E.B., 322, 323
Parker, J., 451
Parkhurst, J., 451
Parmelee, A., 265, 267, 398
Parmelee, A.H., 111, 129, 140
Parten, M., 13, 315, 316
Pascual-Leone, J.A., 362
Patrick, H.T., 137
Patterson, C.J., 265, 339
Patterson, G.R., 609, 610, 613
Pavlov, I., 161, 162, 163, 164, 165, 168, 169
Pawson, M., 109
Pea, R.D., 282
Peake, K., 425
Pedersen, F.A., 210, 213
Pederson, A., 446
Pepler, D.J., 304, 305, 320
Perlmutter, M., 177, 278, 362
Perry, C., 607
Perry, C.L., 607
Peskin, H., 517
Petersen, A.C., 508
Peterson, A., 518
Peterson, C., 490
Peterson, L., 113
Peterson, P.L., 455
Petronio, R.J., 608
Pettersen, L., 147
Phares, E.J., 423
Phares, J., 423
Phelps, E., 527

Piaget, J., 13, 18, 19, 26, 39, 40, 41, 42, 53, 55, 56, 57, 59, 60, 63, 64, 74, 75, 76, 77, 79, 92, 135, 137, 141, 142, 148, 150, 151, 153, 155, 160, 161, 166, 167, 168, 170, 171, 172, 173, 177, 181, 182, 197, 201, 202, 269, 270, 274, 275, 276, 280, 288, 292, 296, 314, 318, 319, 320, 336, 337, 358, 359, 360, 361, 362, 363, 364, 382, 419, 475, 487, 522, 524, 528, 535
Pick, H.L., Jr., 261
Piers, E.V., 462, 463
Pike, R., 463, 466
Piontkowski, D., 279
Piotrkowski, C.S., 306
Pisoni, D.B., 149
Place, D.M., 568
Platt, J.J., 446
Pleck, J., 330, 331
Pleck, J.H., 226
Plomin, R., 90, 195, 251
Pomeroy, W.B., 514
Porter, F.L., 154
Porteus, A., 455
Potter, H., 154
Potter, P.C., 264
Power, C., 485
Pratkanis, A., 328
Pratto, D., 552
Prechtl, H.F.R., 128
Premack, A.J., 189, 191
Premack, D., 189, 191
Prendergast, T.J., 603
Pressley, M., 328, 329, 366
Pritscher, C.M.G., 468
Psathas, G., 546
Pulos, E., 145

Q

Quadagno, J.S., 330
Quintana, S., 328, 329, 478

R

Rabinowitz, M., 371
Rabson, A., 473
Radholm, M., 117
Radke-Yarrow, M., 21, 339, 340
Ragosta, J., 458
Rahe, D.F., 310
Ramey, C.T., 289, 401
Ramirez, M., 457
Raphael, D., 529
Rathbart, M.L.K., 305
Raven, J.C., 396
Rayner, R., 164
Raynor, I.O., 420
Rebecca, M., 330

Rebelsky, F.G., 196
Reese, H.W., 33
Rehm, L., 566
Reid, J.B., 609
Reilly, B.M., 152
Reiss, I.F., 515
Rekers, G.A., 334, 335
Rennie, D., 490
Renshaw, P.D., 446
Reppucci, N.D., 473
Rescorla, R.A., 164
Resnick, H.L.P., 281, 609, 612
Rest, J.R., 478, 479, 496
Revelle, R., 507
Reynolds, L.G., 534
Rheingold, H.L., 165, 220, 240
Rholes, W.S., 532
Ricciuti, H.N., 220
Richards, J.M., 420
Richards, R.A., 394, 404
Richardson, J.G., 466
Ridgeway, D., 235
Rigler, D., 188, 189
Rigler, M., 188, 189
Ringberger, V., 490
Risser, D., 236
Ritter, K., 278
Roberts, G.C., 442
Roberts, M.C., 9, 263, 264
Robertson, L.S., 335
Robins, L.N., 610
Robinson, C.A., 367
Robinson, H.F., 259
Rock, D., 458
Rode, S.S., 117
Rodman, H., 552
Roff, M., 446
Roffwarg, H.P., 129
Rogers, A.G., 154
Rogers, C.R., 327
Rogers, T., 328
Roper, R., 319
Rose, S., 398
Rose, S.A., 153
Rosen, B.C., 427
Rosen, J., 445
Rosenbaum, A., 537
Rosenberg, B.G., 305
Rosenberg, F., 530, 573
Rosenberg, M., 530, 563, 573
Rosenblatt, D., 320
Rosenblith, J.F., 96, 100, 106, 109, 111, 117, 131, 174, 180
Rosenblum, L.A., 310
Rosenkrans, M.A., 561
Rosenman, R.H., 9, 351
Ross, A.O., 402
Ross, D.G., 503

Ross, H.W., 165
Rotenberg, K.J., 532
Rousseau, J.J., 11, 161, 340, 618
Rovee-Collier, C.K., 176
Rovine, M., 220, 228
Rozin, P., 409, 410, 411, 418
Rubenstein, J.L., 289
Rubin, D.C., 576
Rubin, K., 318
Rubin, K.H., 274, 319, 320, 340, 343
Rubin, V., 445
Rubin, Z., 251, 549
Ruble, D.N., 335, 532
Ruble, T.L., 335
Ruff, H.A., 153
Russell, B., 34
Rutter, M., 244, 245, 246, 307, 488, 491, 496, 608, 609, 610
Ryder, N., 568

S

Sackett, G.P., 106
Sagan, C., 7, 80
Sakabe, N., 149
Salapatek, P., 126, 145, 157, 175, 176, 241
Sale, J., 127
Salkind, N., 79
Samuels, H., 305
Samuels, H.R., 220
Sand, G., 25
Sandman, B.M., 105
Santilli, N., 598
Santrock, J.W., 8, 53, 59, 173, 303, 304, 307, 308, 363, 401, 443
Sarason, I., 421
Sarty, M., 146
Sattler, J., 437
Sattler, J.M., 391
Sawin, D.B., 228
Scardamalia, M., 524, 525, 526
Scarr, S., 89, 90, 91, 92, 399
Schachter, S., 305
Schacter, D.L., 177
Schaefer, E.S., 603
Schaffer, H.R., 195, 218, 219
Schaie, K.W., 31, 33
Schaller, J., 117
Schank, R., 371
Schatzberg, A.F., 490
Schinke, S.P., 607
Schneider, F.W., 340
Schneider, P.A., 127
Schneider, W., 63
Schnell, S.V., 479, 484
Schramm, W., 322, 323
Schulz, H.R., 129
Schulz, J.B., 354

Schunk, D.H., 432
Schwartz, D., 103
Schwartz, K., 220
Scott, J.A., 385
Scribner, S., 282
Sears, P.S., 472
Sears, R.R., 404, 441
Seigle, J., 324
Seligman, M.E.P., 473, 490
Sells, S.B., 446
Selman, R.L., 340, 440, 450, 461, 463, 531, 532, 535, 555
Serbin, L.A., 334
Serlin, R.C., 481, 484, 504
Shantz, C.U., 274, 450
Shapiro, E.K., 457, 458, 496
Sharabany, R., 450
Sharpe, L.W., 406
Shatz, M., 193, 287
Shaver, P., 469
Sheingold, K., 178
Sher, K.J., 602
Sherif, C.W., 452
Sherif, M., 452
Shiffman, S., 607
Shiffrin, R.M., 63
Shiono, P.H., 104
Shipstead, S.G., 6, 329
Shister, J., 534
Shockley, W., 400
Shore, R.E., 312
Short, E., 368
Shukla, D., 531
Shure, M.B., 446
Siegel, A.E., 296
Siegler, R., 60, 328, 329
Siggman, M.D., 140
Sigman, M., 181
Simmons, J.E., 104
Simmons, R., 519, 520, 530
Simmons, R.G., 517, 573
Simon, H.A., 62, 376
Simon, M.L., 445
Simon, T., 193, 389
Simon, W., 566
Simpson, C.H., 466
Simpson, E., 479
Sims-Knight, J.E., 96, 100, 106, 109, 111, 117, 131, 174, 180
Singer, P., 121
Single, E., 605
Sitterle, K.A., 443
Sizer, T.R., 570
Skeels, H., 401
Skinner, B.F., 65, 66, 67, 68, 69, 76, 77, 79, 165, 168, 186, 207, 211, 419

Skipper, J.K., 566
Slaby, R.G., 335
Sleator, E.K., 357
Sledden, E.A., 9, 263
Slobin, D., 191, 192
Sloman, J., 549
Smetana, J., 484
Smiley, S.S., 524, 526
Smith, D.F., 609, 612
Smith, D.W., 104
Smith, I.M., 147
Smith, M., 504
Smith, M.B., 103
Smith, P.C., 303
Smith, R., 322, 323
Smith, R.S., 243
Snorknes, A.C., 147
Snow, C.E., 186
Snow, R., 455, 456
Snowman, J., 414
Sokolov, E.N., 174
Sophian, C., 173
Sorenson, R.C., 515, 566
Spear, N.E., 178
Spearman, C.E., 393, 408
Spelke, E., 274
Spelke, E.S., 146, 149, 150, 153, 157
Spence, J.T., 467, 468
Spielberger, C.D., 421
Spinelli, F., 287
Spitz, R.A., 401
Spivack, G., 446
Sporull, N., 322
Sprague, R.L., 357
Sroufe, L.A., 117, 127, 214, 221, 222, 224, 229, 245, 251, 314, 464, 465, 466, 488, 548
Stafford, F.P., 441
Stallings, J., 291
Stanhope, L., 305
Stapp, J., 467
Stark, E., 306
Starkey, P., 153
Stearn, I.B., 152
Stearns, G., 103
Stedman, L., 504
Steele, L., 473
Steffa, M., 117
Stein, 322
Stein, A., 323, 472
Stein, N.L., 235
Steinberg, J., 228
Steinberg, L., 536, 552
Steinberg, L.D., 234, 554, 556
Steiner, J.E., 152
Stenberg, C., 224, 235, 236
Stephens, M., 443
Stephens, M.W., 423

Stephenson, B., 531
Stern, D., 236
Stern, D.N., 211, 241
Stern, E., 129
Sternberg, C., 116
Sternberg, R.J., 372, 376, 378, 382, 385, 389, 394, 396, 398, 402, 404, 405, 408, 409
Steuer, F.B., 323
Stevenson, H., 380
Stevenson, H.W., 245, 278, 296, 394, 415, 417
Stewart, C., 515
Stigler, J.W., 415
Stipak, D.J., 568
Stipek, J.D., 473
Stone, C.A., 529
Stone, G.C., 9, 263
Stone, N.W., 218
Stoneman, Z., 305
Storms, M.D., 468
Stouthamer-Loeber, M., 609, 610, 613
Straus, R., 351
Strauss, M., 160
Strauss, M.S., 177
Streissguth, A.P., 104, 105
Strodtbeck, F.L., 427
Sullivan, E.V., 596
Sullivan, H.S., 449
Suomi, S., 228
Suomi, S.J., 310
Super, D., 534
Susman, E.J., 6, 508, 509, 510
Sutton-Smith, B., 305, 314
Suzuki, T., 149
Swadesh, M., 192
Szasz, T., 353

T

Taeschner, T., 412
Talbert, C.M., 154
Tanner, J.M., 511, 512, 513
Tarpy, R.M., 163
Tate, C.L., 264
Taylor, B., 508
Taylor, D.G., 220
Tellegen, A., 492
Teller, D.Y., 145
Tenney, Y.J., 178
Terman, L., 403, 404
Terr, L.C., 246
Terrace, H., 191
Thane, K., 117
Thelen, E., 137, 138
Thomas, A., 224
Thomas, D.B., 112, 130
Thomas, E.A.C., 212
Thompson, G.G., 454

Thompson, R.A., 229
Thorbecke, W., 595
Thoren, P., 490
Thoresen, C., 352
Thorndike, R.L., 391
Thurstone, L.L., 393
Tieger, T., 471, 472
Tiernan, K., 264
Tinbergen, N., 70, 72, 73, 74, 78
Tizrd, J., 609
Tobin, D., 473
Toder, N., 592
Tolman, E.C., 164
Tom, D.Y.H., 428
Toman, W., 567
Tomasello, M., 287
Tones, M., 401
Tonick, I.J., 334
Torrance, E.P., 406, 437
Torrance, P., 406
Toth, S.A., 562
Trabasso, T., 281, 361
Tracy, R.L., 307
Traskman, L., 490
Tricket, E., 453
Trost, M.A., 446
Trotter, R., 293
Trupin, T., 467
Tsai, S.L., 415
Tuchmann-Duplessis, H., 100
Turiel, E., 478, 484
Turnbull, A.P., 354
Turnbull, C., 23
Turner, T.J., 371
Tyack, D., 504

U
Uddenberg, N., 224
Ulleland, C.N., 104
Underwood, B., 339
Ungerer, J., 318
Uzgirir, I., 173, 180, 181, 183, 202, 218

V
Vaillancourt, 27
Valentine, K.M., 371
Vandell, D.L., 232, 304
Vandenberg, B., 319, 343
Vandiver, R., 561
VanDusen, J.E., 515
van Marthens, E., 263
Vasta, R., 186
Vaughn, B.E., 233
Vaughn, V.C., 263
Vener, A., 515
Vietze, P., 236

Visher, E., 443
Visher, J., 443
Volterra, V., 412
Vurpillot, E., 278
Vygotsky, L.S., 320

W
Wachs, H., 360, 385
Waddington, C.H., 89
Wagenaar, A.C., 603
Wagner, D.A., 130
Wagner, S., 153
Wagonfeld, S., 153
Walberg, H.J., 415
Walk, R., 146
Walk, R.D., 157
Walker, L., 478, 481, 482
Walker-Andrews, A., 150
Wallace, I., 398
Wallach, M., 407
Wallach, M.A., 404
Wallack, L.M., 607
Wallerstein, J., 557
Wallerstein, J.S., 308
Walsh, M.E., 264
Walster, E., 519
Walters, W., 121
Warden, D.A., 287
Warren, M.P., 520, 521
Warshak, R.A., 308, 443
Washburn, K.J., 192
Waterman, A.S., 592
Waterman, C.K., 592
Waters, E., 127, 214, 219, 221, 222, 224,
    464, 465, 466
Watkins, B.A., 324
Watson, J., 12, 13, 14, 18, 22, 35, 127, 131,
    164, 168, 169, 201, 207, 301
Watson, M.W., 318, 320
Webb, W.B., 129
Weber, R.A., 224
Wechsler, D., 370, 391
Weidemann, C., 380
Weikart, D., 292
Weinberg, R.A., 90, 91, 399
Weiner, A.S., 529
Weiner, B., 422, 423
Weiner, G., 401
Weiner, I.B., 489, 491, 612
Weisburg, P., 401
Weiseman, J.R., 127
Weishahan, M.W., 351, 385
Weiskopf, F., 177
Wellings, M.A., 467
Wellman, H.M., 278, 368
Wenne, W.H., 129
Werme, P.H., 604

Werner, E.E., 243
Werner, H., 320, 524
Werner, P., 263
Wertheimer, M., 149
Werthessen, N.T., 351
West, D.J., 610
Wetter, R.E., 467
Whatley, J.L., 232, 312
Wheeler, V.A., 446
White, B.J., 452
White, S.H., 11, 13, 503
Whitehurst, G.J., 186
Whiting, B., 311
Whiting, J., 311
Whitmore, K., 609
Wicklund, R., 531
Widmayer, S., 113, 114
Wilkinson, A., 281
Wilkinson, A.C., 287
Wilkinson, L.C., 287
Willard, E., 335
Williams, J., 411, 469
Williams, J.A., 117
Williams, J.E., 335
Williams, S.G., 129
Willis, D.J., 264, 267
Wills, T.A., 607
Wilson, H., 610
Wilson, K., 567
Wilson, K.S., 232
Windle, W.F., 152
Wing, J.W., 246
Winner, E., 153, 258, 527
Winterbottem, M.R., 420
Wippman, J., 214, 221, 222
Wisely, D.W., 264
Wodarski, J.S., 603
Wohlwill, J.E., 20
Wolf, D., 271
Wolf, M.M., 313
Wolfe, L.K., 468
Wolff, P.H., 128, 138
Woodson, R., 166
Worobey, J., 114
Worrell, J., 468, 469
Wright, H.F., 26, 445
Wright, J., 322
Wright, J.C., 324, 325
Wright, J.W., 340
Wright, L., 9, 263
Wu, P.Y.K., 46
Wurm, M., 351
Wylie, R., 327
Wylie, R.C., 462

Y

Yando, R.M., 454
Yankelovitch, D., 505
Yanof, D., 550
Yarrow, L.J., 401
Yeates, K.O., 289
Yeaton, W.H., 263
Yonas, A., 147
Yussen, S.R., 8, 59, 173 263, 281, 370, 480

Z

Zacks, R.T., 63
Zahn-Waxler, C., 235, 236, 339, 340
Zajonc, R.B., 401
Zakin, D., 519
Zamenhof, S., 263
Zeiss, A.R., 425
Zelazo, P.R., 234, 289, 318
Zeldow, P.B., 468
Zelnick, M., 515
Zelnicker, T., 279
Zembar, M., 368
Zembar, M.J., 377
Zeskind, P.S., 117, 127
Zill, N., 27
Zimmerman, R., 216
Zyzanski, S., 351

A

Abstractness, formal operational thought, 522–23
Accommodation
  Piaget's theory, 57, 59
  visual, 144
Achievement
  anxiety, 421
  attribution theory, 422–23
  cultural standards of, 427
  delay of gratification, 423–24
  fear of failure, 420
  hope for success, 420
  males vs. females, 472–75
    learned helplessness, 473
  motivation, 419–21
  and observational learning, 430
  parental influences, 428
  peer influences, 428
  and reinforcement, 430–31
    incentives, 431
  school influences, 428–29
  teacher influences, 429
Adjective Check List, 467
Adolescence, 16–17, 552
  biology/culture as influences, 505–6
  career/work orientation, 534–37
  childbearing in, 102–3
  cognitive development, 522–29, 554–56
  continuity/discontinuity in development, 506
  defense mechanisms, 46
  disturbances/problems in, 600
    comparison to childhood problems, 616–17
    delinquency, 606–9
    drug use, 600–606
    eating disorders, 613–16
    suicide, 609–13
  egocentrism in, 528, 529, 531–32
  family relationships, 546–59
  historical views, 503–5
    inventionist view, 504–5
    stereotyping, adolescents, 505
    storm/stress view, 503–4, 505
  identity, 582–99
  intimacy, 596–99
  language development, 524–28

  peer relations, 560–68
  perspective taking, 528
  physical development, 506–22, 553
  school influences, 544–45, 568–76
  sex in, 502
  social cognition, 529–34, 556
  transition to adulthood, 617–18
  See also specific topics.
Adoption studies, 90
Adulthood, adolescent's transition to, 617–18
Afterbirth, 108
Aggression
  early childhood, 313
  intention-cue detection, 447
  and television viewing, 323
Alcohol use, 602–4
  family/peer influences, 603
  personality/adjustment factors, 602
  and prenatal development, 104–5
  prevalence of, 602
  prevention/intervention, 603–4
Altruism, 339–40
Amniocentesis, 84
Amnion, 96
Anal stage, 47
Ancient times, view of child, 10
Androgens, 508
Androgyny, 467–69
  and competence, 467–69
  measures of, 467
  self-assertion and, 468–69
Animism, 274–75
Anoxia, 108
Anxiety
  and achievement, 421
  state anxiety, 421
  trait anxiety, 421
Apgar Scale, 114
Aptitude-Treatment Interaction (ATI), 455–56
Artificial intelligence, computers, 348
Assimilation, Piaget's theory, 57
Associative play, 316
Attachment, 214–30, 314
  in adolescence, 548
  and construction of relationships, 221, 224
  and day care, 235
  developmental course of, 218–19

SUBJECT INDEX

691

fathers and, 227–29
individual differences, 219–21
insecure attachment, 219–20, 222, 223
and peer relations, 314
and schizoid tendencies, 223
secure attachment, 219, 220, 222–23
situational influences, 220–21
and temperament, 224–25
theories of
    cognitive developmental theory, 217–18
    ethological theory, 215–16
    evaluation of theories, 218
    psychoanalytic theory, 216
    social learning theory, 216–17
Attention
    decrement of, 181
    and incompetence, 492
    infancy
        externality effect, 175
        habituation/dishabituation, 174, 277
        orienting response, 174
        pattern scanning, 174–75
    preschool child, 277–79
        cognitive control of, 278–79
    recovery of, 181
Attribution theory, 422–23, 432–33
    attributions and school setting, 429–30
    emotional reactions, 422
    internal/external factors, 422, 432
    locus of control, 422–23
        internal/external, 423
    self-efficacy, 433
Auditory perception, 149
    fetus/newborn, 149
    intermodal perception, 149, 150
Authoritarian parenting, 301
Authoritative parenting, 301
Autism, 246–47
Automatic processes, 63
Autonomy
    adolescence, 546–48
        adolescent's view of, 547
        multidimensionality of, 546–47
        parenting styles and, 547–48
    autonomy versus shame and doubt, 51
    infancy, 239–40

B

Babbling, 196
Baby talk, 194
Bayley Scales of Infant Development,
        179–80, 181
    Mental Scale, 179–80
    Motor Scale, 259

Behavioral approach, 65–69
    language acquisition, 185–86
    Skinner's theory, 65–66
    social learning theory, 66–69
Behavior genetics, 89–91
    adoption studies, 90
    kinship studies, 90
    twin studies, 90
Behaviorism, and view of child, 12, 13
Behavior modification, procedure in, 66
Bem Sex-Role Inventory, 467
Bilingualism, 412–14
    acquisition of two languages
        factors for success, 413–14
        simultaneous, 412
        successive, 412–14
Binet test
    IQ, 389
    standardization of, 390
Biological influences
    sex role development, 329–30
    social development, 207–8
Biological processes, 17–18
Birth order, 305
    and dating, 567
Blastocyst, 95
Blastula, 95
Body image
    adolescence, 516–17, 519–20
        attractive/unattractive girls, 519–20
Brain
    infancy, 134, 139–40
    lateralization of language, 187–88, 189
Brainstorming, 406
Brazelton Neonatal Behavioral Assessment
        Scale, 114, 131
Brazelton training, 114
Breech position, 111
Broca's area, 187

C

California Psychological Inventory, 467
Canalization, 89
Career/work orientation
    adolescence, 534–37
        cognitive factors, 534
        effect on grades, 536–37
        part-time work, 536
        unemployment, 537
Care perspective, moral reasoning, 483
Cattell test, 180
Cephalocaudal pattern, 133
Child abuse, 245–46

Childbirth, 106–17
    assessment of newborn, 114
        Apgar Scale, 114
        Brazelton Neonatal Behavioral
            Assessment Scale, 114
    bonding, 115, 117
    complications, 108, 111
        anoxia, 108
        breech position, 111
    drugs, 111, 112
        oxytocin, 111, 112
    father's role, 109
    Lamaze method, 108, 109
    Leboyer method, 108
    preterm infants, 111, 113, 114–15, 116
    stages of, 108
    standard procedure, 106
Child development
    approaches to study
        behavioral approach, 65–69
        cognitive theories, 53–64
        eclectic orientation, 74–76
        ethological theory, 70–73
        psychoanalytic theories, 42–53, 54
    in contemporary society, 7–9
        computers and children, 8
        divorced families, 7–8
        Type A behavior, 8–9
    development, use of term, 19
    historical view, 9–14
        ancient Greece/Rome, 10
        Middle Ages, 10
        19th century, late, 11
        Renaissance, 11
        twentieth century, 11–13
    issues in, 19–23
        continuity-discontinuity, 20
        genetic/biological and environmental/
            social influences, 22–23
        individual differences, 20, 22
        qualitative change, 19
        stages of development, 19–20
    periods of, 15–17
        adolescence, 16–17
        early childhood, 16
        infancy, 15
        late childhood, 16
        middle childhood, 16
        prenatal period, 15
    process of, 17–19
        biological processes, 17–18
        cognitive processes, 18
        personality processes, 18
        social processes, 18
    See also specific topics.
Child development research
    ethical considerations, 34

observation methods, 23–30
  interviews, 26
  standardized tests, 27, 30
  surveys/questionnaires, 27
  systematic observation, 25–26
research strategies, 30–32
  correlational strategy, 32
  cross-sectional designs, 33
  experimental strategy, 30–31
  longitudinal designs, 33
  quasi-experimental strategy, 31
  sequential designs, 33–34
Children's groups, 452
Child Welfare Research Stations, 12
Chimpanzees, nonhuman communication,
  189–91
Chorionic villus test, 84
Chromosomes, 86
Cigarette smoking, prenatal development,
  106
Circumcision, and pain, 153, 154
Classical conditioning
  conditioned response (CR), 162, 163
  conditioned stimulus (CS), 162
  evaluation of, 164–65
  extinction, 163
  in infancy, 164
    newborns, 164
    phobias, 164
  Pavlov's experiment, 161–63
  process of, 163–64
  S-S learning, 162
  unconditioned response (UCR), 162
  unconditioned stimulus (US), 162
Classical ethological theory, 70
Class inclusion reasoning, 280–81
Classroom Environment Scale (CES), 453
Cleavage divisions, 94
Cliques/crowds
  adolescence, 562–64
    research study, 562
    and self-esteem, 563–64
Cognitive development
  adolescence, 522–29, 554–56
    Piaget's theory, 522–29
  early childhood, 269–81
    information processing, 277–81
    Piaget's theory, 269–77
    syllogisms, use in assessment, 282–83
  health and, 264
  middle/late childhood, 358–81
    Piaget's theory, 358–63
  and play, 320
  and sex-role development, 330–31
  See also Piaget's theory.
Cognitive developmental theory, 53, 55–57,
  59–60

attachment, 217–18
  Kohlberg's theory, 53
  Piaget's theory, 53, 55–57, 59–60
Cognitive processes, 18
Cognitive theories, 53–66, 191–93
  cognitive developmental theory, 53, 55–
    57, 59–60
  cognitive social learning theory, 66
  information processing approach, 60–63
  proponents of, 192
  strengths/weaknesses of, 63–64
  See also specific theories.
Cohort effects, 34
Color-blindness, 145
Color perception, 145
Competence
  masculinity/femininity/androgyny,
    467–69
  resilient children, 492
Complications of delivery, 108, 111
Computers
  artificial intelligence, 348
  computers and children, 8
Conception
  cleavage divisions, 94
  in-vitro fertilization, 94–95
  zygote period, 94
Concepts and words, 198–99
Concrete operational stage, 56
Conditioning, 161–65
  classical, 161–65
  conditioned response (CR), 162, 163
  conditioned stimulus (CS), 162
  operant, 165–66
Conflict, parent-adolescent conflict, 551, 553
Conformity
  nonconformist/anticonformist, 561
  peer influences, 560–61
Conjugate reinforcement technique, memory,
  176
Conscience, 44
Conscious memory, 176–77
Contagion stage, 264
Continuity-discontinuity
  in adolescent development, 506
  as research issue, 20
Control group, 31
Control processes, 62
  memory, 365–66
Convergent thinking, 406
Cooperative play, 316
Coregulation process, 442
Correlational strategy, 32
  correlation coefficient, 32
Counterconditioning, 164
Creativity, 404–7

definitional problems, 404
  divergent thinking, 406
  encouragement of, 406–7
    brainstorming, 406
    in classroom, 407
    playing with improbabilities, 406
Cretinism, 403
Critical/sensitive periods, 71, 72
  language acquisition, 188–89
Cross-sectional designs, 33
Crying of infant, 127
  parental reactions to, 127
Crystallized intelligence, 393
Cultural-familial, 403
Culture-fair tests, 395–96

D

Dating, 565–68
  age factors, 566
  functions of, 566
  incidence of, 566
  parental relationships, influence on, 567
  peer relations, influence on, 568
  sex differences/similarities, 566
Day care
  and attachment, 234
  effects on development, 233–34
  scope/nature of, 232–33
  and social development, 233–34
Defense mechanisms
  projection, 45
  reaction formation, 45
  regression, 45
  repression, 45
Defining Issue Test, 479
Delay of gratification, 423–24, 425–26
Delinquency
  causes of, 606
  definition of, 606
  Erikson's view, 608
  family influences, 608–9, 610
  social class influences, 608
Denver Developmental Screening Test, 260
Depression, 488–89, 490–92
  adolescent suicide, 609–12
  age-related aspects, 489
  causes of, 490–91
  developmental view, 488
Depth perception, 146–47
Developmental lag, 357
Developmental tests/scales
  Denver Developmental Screening Test,
    260
  De Oreo Fundamental Motor Skills
    Inventory, 260
  See also Infant testing.

Direct perception, 143
Discipline, parental, middle/late childhood, 442
Divergent thinking, creativity, 406
Divorce, 307–9
    effect on adolescents, 557–59
        distanced teenagers, 557
        girls' behavior, 557–59
    effects of (general)
        age factors, 308
        quality of parenting, 307
        support systems, role of, 307–8
Dominant-recessive genes, 87
Dove Counterbalance General Intelligence Test, 396
Down's syndrome, 84–85, 403
Dreams, content of, and development, 58–59
Drug abuse, use, 600–606
    alcohol use, 602–4
    marijuana use, 604–6
    prevalence of, 600–601
    prevention/intervention, 607
    sex differences in, 601–2
Drugs
    use during childbirth, 111, 112
    use during pregnancy, 104–6
Dwarfism, deprivation dwarfism, 259

E

Early childhood, 16
    aggression, 313
    cognitive development, 269–81
    early childhood education, 289–93
    family relationships, 301–10
    language development, 281–89
    moral development, 336–40
    peer relationships, 310–14
    physical development, 258–68
    play, 314–20
    self-concept, 327–29
    sex role development, 329–36
    television viewing, 320–25
    See also specific topics.
Early childhood education
    child-centered education, 289
    effects of, 289–90
    Project Follow Through, 290–92
    Project Head Start, 290
        long-term effects, 293
Early/late maturation, adolescence, 517–18
Eating behavior (infant)
    breast-feeding, 131
    demand vs. scheduled feeding, 131
Eating disorders
    anorexia nervosa, 613, 614
    bulimia, 613–14

incidence of, 613
    obesity, 615–16
Echoing, language acquisition, 193, 195
Eclectic orientation, 74–76
Ecological view, perceptual/sensory development, 143
Ectomorphic body, 349
Education, effect on intelligence, 401
Educational approaches, Montessori approach, 256–57
Ego, 44
Egocentric frame of reference, and spatial relations, 148–49
Egocentrism
    adolescence, 528, 529, 531–32
        imaginary audience, 529, 531–32
        personal fable, 529, 531
    and perspective taking, 311
    and preoperational thought, 270, 274
    and three mountains task, 270
Ego ideal, 44
Electra complex, 48
Embryonic period, 96–97
Emotional development
    infancy, 234–37
        age factors, 236–37
        communication of emotions, 235
        display of emotions, 236
        functions of emotions, 235
        recognition of emotions, 236
    See also Attachment.
Empathy, 339
Endocrine system, 508–11
    gonadotropin, 508
    hypothalamus, 508, 511
    pituitary gland, 508
    sex hormones, 508–11
        and adjustment, 510–11
        androgens, 508
        estradiol, 508–9
        estrogens, 508
        testosterone, 508, 509
Endomorphic body, 349
Environmental influences, 193, 195
    echoing, 193, 195
    intelligence, 399–402
    labeling, 195
    motherese, 193
    recasting, 195
    sex role development, 331–35
Equilibrium, Piaget's theory, 59
Erikson, E., profile of, 41–42
Erikson's theory, 50–52
    identity in adolescence
        epigenetic principle, 589
        identity crisis, 585–86, 590
        role experimentation, 586, 589

intimacy, 596
    play, role of, 314
    stages in, 50–52
        autonomy versus shame and doubt, 51
        generativity versus stagnation, 52
        identity versus identity confusion, 52
        industry versus inferiority, 51–52
        initiative versus guilt, 51
        intimacy versus isolation, 52
        trust versus mistrust, 50–51
    teacher traits, good teacher, 455
Estrogens, 508
Ethical considerations, child development research, 34
Ethnicity, effect on schooling, 457–58
Ethological theory, 70–73
    attachment, 215–16
    classical ethological theory, 70
    critical period, 71, 72
    imprinting, 70
    issues of interest related to, 72–73
    neo-ethological view, 71
    questions related to child development, 71–72
    sign stimuli, 70
    strengths/weaknesses of, 73
Evolutionary approach, 85–86
    natural selection, 85
Exercise, health and, 267
Exosystem, 208
Experimental strategy, 30–31
    dependent/independent variables, 30–31
    experimental/control group, 31
Externality effect, 175
Extinction, 163
Extrinsic motivation, 430

F

Face perception, 146, 166
Family influences
    effect on intelligence, 401
    social development, 210–14
Family-of-twins design, 90
Family relationships
    adolescence, 546–59
        attachment, 548
        autonomy, 546–48
        conflict, 551, 553
        connectedness related to, 549
        coordinated relationships, 548–49
        dating and, 567–68
        delinquency and, 608–9, 610
        divorce, effects of, 557–59
        drug use, 603, 605
        identity, influence on, 593, 594
        latchkey adolescents, 552
        maturation of adolescents and, 553–56

maturation of parents and, 556–57
  mother/daughter relations, 550
  parenting strategies, 551
in changing society, 306
early childhood, 301–10
  divorce, effects of, 307–9
  parenting styles, 301–3
  sibling relationships, 303–5
  working mothers, 306–7
middle/late childhood, 441–44
  coregulation process, 442
  discipline, 442
  latchkey children, 444
  mutual cognitions, 442–43
  parental attention, 441
  parental maturation, 443
  parent-child issues, 441
  stepfamilies, 443–44
and sex-role development, 331
Fathers
  attachment, 227–29
  engagement/interaction with child,
    226–27
Fear of failure, 420
Fetal alcohol syndrome (FAS), 104
Fetal period, 97–98
Field studies, 26
Fine motor development, infancy, 134–35,
    136
Fluid intelligence, 393
Formal operational stage, 57
Freudian theory
  defense mechanisms, 44–45
    in adolescence, 46
    projection, 45
    reaction formation, 45
    regression, 45
    repression, 45
  neo-psychoanalytic theories, 50
  personality structure, 42–44
    ego, 44
    id, 43–44
    superego, 44
  pleasure principle, 43
  primary process thinking, 43
  psychosexual stages, 45, 47–50
    anal stage, 47
    Electra complex, 48
    genital stage, 49
    latency stage, 49
    Oedipal complex, 42, 46
    oral stage, 47
    phallic stage, 47–48
  reality principle, 44
Friendships, 449–51
  children's groups, 452
  cognitive factors, 449
  conversational skills, 451
  intimacy in friendships, 450

sharing in, 451
similarity in friendship, 450

G

Gametes, 86
Gender-deviance, 334–35
  changing behavior of, 334–35
  characteristics of, 334
Generativity versus stagnation, 52
Genetic influences
  genetic/biological and environmental/
    social influences, as research issue,
    22–23
  intelligence, 399–400, 402
Genetics, 86–92
  amniocentesis, 84
  behavior genetics, 89–91
    adoption studies, 90
    heritability, 90–91
    kinship studies, 90
    twin studies, 90
  canalization, 89
  chorionic villus test, 84
  dominant-recessive genes, 87
  genes
    components of, 86–87
    genotypes/phenotypes, 87
    transmittal of, 86–87
  genetic/environmental interaction, 91–92
  genetic screening, 84–85
  polygenic inheritance, 88
  reaction range, 88–89
  sex-linked genes, 88
Genital stage, 49
Genotypes/phenotypes, 87
Germinal period, 95
Gesell test, 179, 259
Gifted children, 403–4
  stardom, training for, 404
  Terman study, 403–4
Gonadotropin, 508
Goodness-of-fit model, 520
Grammar, 184
  surface/deep structure, 184
Gross motor development
  early childhood, 259–60
  infancy, 134, 136
Growth problems, early childhood, 259
Guilt, 339

H

Habituation, 124
Habituation/dishabituation, 174, 277
Handicapped children, 351–52
  developmental lag, 357
  education of, 352
  hyperactive children, 357

labeling issue, 353–54
  learning disabilities, 355
  mainstreaming, 354–55
  prevalence of, 351
Harter Perceived Competence Scale for
    Children, 27
Health and development
  cognitive development, 264
  exercise, 267
  internal states, 265–66
  middle/late childhood, 350–51
  motor development, 263
  social development, 264, 267
Height/weight changes, adolescence, 511–12
Heritability, 90–91
Herpes simplex virus, prenatal development,
    102
Heterosexual behavior, adolescence, 515–16
Holophrase hypothesis, language
    development, 197
Homophobia, 516
Homosexual behavior, adolescence, 514
Humanistic view, self-concept, 327
Hyperactive children, drug therapy, 357
Hypothalamus, 508, 511
Hypothetical-deductive reasoning, 523–24

I

Id, 43–44
Idealism, formal operational thought, 523
Identity, 582–99
  developmental changes in, 591–92
  Erikson's theory, 584–90
    epigenetic principle, 589
    identity crisis, 585–86, 590
    role experimentation, 586, 589
  family influences, 593, 594
  Groucho Marx, case example, 582–84
  identity versus identity confusion, 52
  and intimacy, 596–99
  measurement of, 593, 595–96
  sex differences/similarities and, 592
  statuses of, 590–91
    identity achieved, 591
    identity diffused (confused), 590–91
    identity foreclosure, 591, 598
    identity moratorium, 591
  See also Intimacy.
Ik of Uganda, 23
Imaginary audience, egocentrism, 529,
    531–32
Imitation/modeling, 68, 166–68
  and achievement, 430
  language acquisition, 186
  and moral development, 476, 480
  peer modeling, 561–62
  Piaget's view, 167

Implantation, zygote, 95
Implicit personality theory, adolescence, 532
Imprinting, 70
Independence, research on, infancy, 240–41
Individual differences
    attachment, 219–21
    infant development, 177–81
    physical development, early childhood, 259
    as research issue, 20, 22
Industry versus inferiority, 51–52
Infancy, 15
    attachment, 214–30
    disturbances/problems in, 243–47
        autism, 246–47
        child abuse, 245–46
        and early experiences, 244–45
        genetic influences, 243–44
    emotional development, 234–37
    language acquisition, 185–95
    language development, 195–200
    learning in, 161–81
    perceptual/sensory development, 141–55
        auditory perception, 149
        constructivist approach, 142
        ecological view, 143
        pain, sense of, 153
        sensory dimensions, relatedness of, 150, 153
        smell, sense of, 152
        taste, sense of, 152
        touch, sense of, 152–53
        visual perception, 141–49
    personality development, 237–43
    physical development, 125–41
    social development, 207–34
    See also specific topics.
Infantile amnesia, 178
Infant testing, 179–81
    Bayley Scales of Infant Development, 179–80, 181
    Cattell test, 180
    evaluation of, 181
    Gesell test, 179
    historical view, 179
    Piagetian test, 181
Inferences (drawing), 370–72
    scripts/schemata, use of, 371–72
Information processing
    and education, 377–81
    infancy
        attention, 174–75
        memory, 175–77
    middle/late childhood, 364–81
        drawing inferences, 370–72
        knowledge versus process views of intelligence, 376–77
        memory, 364

preschool child
    attention, 277–79
    memory, 279–80
    task dimensions and analyses, 280–81
sensory dimensions in infancy, relatedness of, 150, 153
view of intelligence, 372
    components of intelligence, 376
    structure/process dilemma, 376–77
Information processing approach
    Broadbent's model, 60–61
        parallel processing, 60–61
    Klatzky's model, 61–62
    memory in, 60, 62
    processes
        automatic processes, 63
        controlled processes, 62
    questions raised by, 62–63
    See also Attention; Memory.
Information theory, 164
Initiative versus guilt, 51
Insecure attachment, 219–20, 222, 223
Institutionalization, effect on intelligence, 401
Intelligence, 388–407
    creativity, 404–7
    crystallized intelligence, 393
    dual-facet view, 405
    environmental influences, 399–402
        education/social class, 401
        home, 401
        institutionalization, 401
    fluid intelligence, 393
    genetic influences, 399–400, 402
    gifted child, 403–4
    information processing view, 372, 376–77
    mental retardation, 402–3
    multiple-factor theory, 393
    seven intelligences theory, 395
    stability over time, 397–98
    structure of intellect model, 393–94
    two-factor theory, 393
Intelligence measures
    Binet test, 389–91
        IQ, calculation of, 389
        standardization of, 390
    culture-fair tests, 395–96
        Dove Counterbalance General Intelligence Test, 396
        Kaufman Assessment Battery for Children, 396
        Raven Progressive Matrices Test, 396
    social intelligence, 396–97
        SOMPA, 396
    validity, 394
        criterion validity, 394
    Wechsler Scales, 391
Intention-cue detection, 447
Intermodal perception, 149, 150

Internalization of schemes, 171
Internal states, health and, 265–66
Interviews, 26
Intimacy
    adolescence, 596–99
    Erikson's theory, 596
    in friendship, 450
    identity-intimacy pathways, 598–99
    research on, 597–98
    statuses of, 597
        intimate individual, 597
        isolated individual, 597
        preintimate individual, 597
        pseudointimate individual, 597
        stereotyped individual, 597
Intimacy versus isolation, 52
Intrinsic motivation, 430
Intuitive thought, 275–76
Inventionist view, adolescence, 504–5
In-vitro fertilization, 94–95
IQ, calculation of, 389

K

Kaufman Assessment Battery for Children, 396
Kinship studies, 90
Kohlberg's theory
    criticisms of theory, 479–82, 484
    and modeling, 476
    peer relations, 479
    research approach, 477–78

L

Labeling, language acquisition, 195
Labeling issue, handicapped children, 353–54
Laboratory settings, systematic observation, 26
Lamaze method, 108, 109
Language
    grammar, 184
    nature of, 183–84
        displacement, 183
        infinite generativity, 183, 187
    rule systems, 184–85
        morphology, 184
        phonology, 184
        pragmatics, 185
        semantics, 185
        syntax, 184
Language acquisition, 185–200
    behavioral view, 185–86
    cognitive theory, 191–93
    environmental influences, 193, 195
    imitation/modeling, 186
    language acquisition device, 187, 191
    nativist theory, 187–91

shaping/reinforcement, 186
See also specific topics.
Language development
    adolescence, 524–28
        advanced understanding, 524–25
        metaphor, 525
        pragmatics, 526
        sarcasm, 527–28
        satire, 525
        written language, 525–26
    early childhood, 281–89
        mean length of utterance measure,
            281, 283
    infancy, 195–200
        babbling, 196
        cognitive development, 197
        concepts and words, 198–99
        holophrase hypothesis, 197
        one-word utterances, 197, 198
        overextensions/underextensions of
            words, 199–200
        pragmatic communication skills,
            196–97
        preverbal developments, 195–96
        telegraphic speech, 200
        two-word utterances, 200
    and play, 320
    rule systems
        morphology, 284
        phonology, 284
        pragmatics, 286–87
        semantics, 286
        syntax, 284–85
Language universals, 187
Latchkey children, 8, 444
Late childhood, 16
Latency stage, 49
Lateralization of language, 187–88, 189
Learned helplessness, males vs. females, 473
Learning
    and attention, 174–75
    conditioning
        classical, 161–65
        operant, 165–66
    dimensions of, 161
    evaluation of approaches, 168
    imitation, 166–67
    infant testing, 179–81
    and memory, 175–77
    Piaget's theory, 168–73
    See also specific topics.
Learning disabled, 355
    behavioral characteristics, 355–56
Leboyer method, 108
Locus of control, 422–23
    internal/external, 423
Longitudinal designs, 33
Low-birth-weight infants, 113

M
Macrosystem, 209
Mainstreaming, handicapped children,
    354–55
Marijuana use, 604–6
    effects of, 604
    parent/peer influences, 605
    prevention/intervention, 605–6
    reasons for use, 604–5
Masculinity/femininity, middle/late
    childhood, 466–67
Mathematics, 414–18
    achievement
        cross-cultural comparisons, 414–17
        factors for success, 415–17
    educational goals for, 414
Maturation
    early/late maturation, 517–18
    sex differences, 517–18
Maturational theory, and view of child, 12
Meiosis, 86
Memory
    conscious memory, 176–77
        in strict sense, 177
        in wide sense, 177
    control processes, 365–66
        mental imagery, 366
        organizational processing, 365
        rehearsal, 365
        retrieval, 366
        semantic elaboration, 365
    infancy, conjugate reinforcement
        technique, 176
    infantile amnesia, 178
    and information processing approach, 60,
        62
    and learner characteristics, 366–68
    meta memory, 368–69
    preschool child, 279–80
        age factors, 280
        memory span, 279–80
        short-term memory, 279
    and self schema, 328–29
    short-term memory, 362–63
Menarche, 506–7
Mental imagery, memory, 366
Mental retardation, 402–3
    causes of, 403
    definition of, 402
    labeling, 402
Mesomorphic body, 349
Mesosystem, 208
Meta-analysis, 454
Meta memory, 368–69
Metaphor, adolescence, language
    development, 525
Microsystem, 208

Middle Ages, view of child, 10
Middle/late childhood, 16
    cognitive development, 358–81
    disturbances/problems in, 485, 488–92
        depression, 488–89, 490–92
        school-related problems, 489, 492
        scope of, 485, 488
    family relationships, 441–44
    handicapped children, 351–52
    moral development, 475–85
    peer relations, 444–52
    physical development, 349–51
    resilient children, 492
    school influences, 452–60
    self-concept, 460–66
    sex role development, 466–75
Modeling/imitation, 68
    See also Imitation/modeling.
Molar exchanges, 211–12
Moral behavior, 338–39
    resisting temptation, 338–39
    social learning theory, 338, 339
Moral development
    components of, 336
    culture-specific nature, 482, 484
    Defining Issue Test, 479
    early childhood, 336–40
    Kohlberg's theory, 476–82
        cognitive development and, 478
        criticisms of theory, 479–82, 484
        and modeling, 476
        peer relations, 479
        research approach, 477–78
        stages of moral development, 476–77
    moral reasoning
        care perspective, 483
        justice perspective, 483
        social conventional reasoning, 484
    Piaget's theory, 336–38
        imminent justice, 336
        moral autonomy, 336
        moral realism, 336
    sex differences, 481–82, 483
    societalism, 484
    transactive discussion, 480–81
Moral education, 484–85
Moral feelings, 339–40
    altruism, 339–40
    empathy, 339
    guilt, 339
    perspective taking, 340
Moro reflex, 125
Morphology, 184
    development in early childhood, 284
Mother/child interaction
    bonding, 115, 117
    influence on outside relationships of child,
        214
    interconnection of, 212

preterm infants, 116
See also Attachment.
Mother/daughter relations, adolescence, 550
Motherese, language acquisition, 193
Mothers
    working mothers, 306–7
        and father's role, 306
        influencing factors, 306
Motivation
    and achievement, 419–21
        achievement motivation (in achievement), 419–20
        anxiety, effects of, 421
        fear of failure, 420
        hope for success, 420
    compared to learning, 418–19
    extrinsic motivation, 430
    intrinsic motivation, 430
Motor development
    fine motor development, 134–35, 136
    gross motor development
        early childhood, 259–60
        infancy, 134, 136
    health and, 263
Multiple-factor theory, intelligence, 393
Mutual cognitions, 442–43

N

Nativist theory
    brain, lateralization of language, 187–88, 189
    critical/sensitive periods, 188–89
    language acquisition, 187–91
    language universals, 187
    nonhuman communication and, 189–91
Naturalistic observations, 26
Natural reaction, 124
Neglected children, 445–46
Neighborhood Walk experiment, 28
Neo-psychoanalytic theories, 50
Newborn
    assessment of, 114
        Apgar Scale, 114
        Brazelton Neonatal Behavioral Assessment Scale, 114
    bonding, 115, 117
    classical conditioning of, 164

    preterm infants, 111, 113, 114–15, 116
    See also Infancy.
19th century, view of child, 11
Nonhuman communication, chimpanzees, 189–91
Nutrition
    maternal diet and infants, 21
    physical development, early childhood, 263

O

Obesity, 615–16
    biological factors, 615
    environmental factors, 616
Objective frame of reference, spatial relations, 148, 149
Object perception, 145–46
Object permanence
    criticism of concept, 173
    stages of, 172
Observation methods
    interviews, 26
    surveys/questionnaires, 27
    systematic observation, 25–26
Oedipal complex, 42, 46
One-word utterances, 197, 198
Onlooker play, 315
On-time/off-time, 518–21
Open classrooms, 453–54
    assessment measures, 453–54
    and individual differences, 456
    results of, 454
Operant conditioning, 65–66
    of infant behavior, 165
Oral stage, 47
Organization, Piaget's theory, 59
Organizational processing, memory, 365
Organogenesis, 96
Orienting response, 174
Original sin view, 10
Overextensions/underextensions of words, 199–200
Oxytocin, 111, 112

P

Pain, 153
Parallel play, 316
Parallel processing, 60–61
Parental influences, achievement, 428
    See also Family relationships.
Parental maturation, 443
Parenting styles, 301–3
    and adolescent autonomy, 547–48
    age factors, 302–3
    authoritarian parenting, 301
    authoritative parenting, 301
    permissive-indifferent parenting, 302–3
    permissive-indulgent parenting, 302
Pattern scanning, 174–75
Pavlov's experiment, 161–63
Peer relations
    and achievement, 428
    adolescence, 560–68
        children versus adolescent groups, 564–66
        cliques/crowds, 562–64

conformity, 560–61
        dating, 565–68
        drug use, 603, 605
        parental influences, 549
        peer modeling, 561–62
        self-esteem and, 563–64
        social comparison, 562
    early childhood, 310–14
        compared to parent-child relations, 312, 314
        cross-cultural comparisons, 311
        development of, 311–12
        peers, use of term, 310
        and perspective taking, 311
        same age peers, 310
        and social development, 310
    middle/late childhood 444–52
        children's groups, 452
        friendships, 449–51
        and intention-cue detection, 447
        neglected children, 445–46
        popular children, 445
        rejected children, 445–46
        social cognition, 446, 449
        time spent with peers, 445
    moral development, 479
Peer relations
    and sex-role development, 332
    and social development, 232
Peer sociotherapy, 440
Perceived Competence Scale for Children, 462
Perceptual/sensory development
    auditory perception, 149
    constructivist approach, 142
    pain, 153
    perception, meaning of, 141
    sensation, meaning of, 141
    sensory dimensions, 150, 153
    smell, 152
    taste, 152
    touch, 152–53
    visual perception, 141–49
Permissive-indifferent parenting, 302–3
Permissive-indulgent parenting, 302
Personal Attributes Questionnaire, 467
Personal fable, egocentrism, 529, 531
Personality development
    infancy, 237–43
        autonomy, 239–40
        independence, research on, 240–41
        self-control, 241, 243
        sense of self, 237–38
        separation-individuation, 238–39
        trust, 237
Personality processes, 18
Personality Research Form ANDRO Scale, 467

Perspective taking, 340
    adolescence, 528
    middle/late childhood, 461–62
    and peer relations, 311
Phallic stage, 47–48
Phenomenistic stage, 264
Phenomenological view, self-concept, 327
Phenotypes/genotypes, 87
Phenylketonuria (PKU), 92
Phobias, counterconditioning, 164
Phonology, 184
    development in early childhood, 284
Physical attractiveness, self-esteem in
        adolescence, 519–20
Physical development
    adolescence, 506–22, 553
        body image, 516–17, 519–520
        early/late maturation, 517–18
        endocrine system, 508–11
        height/weight changes, 511–12
        on-time/off-time, 518–21
        pubertal process, 506–8
        sexual maturation, 513–16
    early childhood, 258–68
        gross motor development, 259–60
        growth problems, 259
        individual differences, 259
        nutrition, 263
        spatial relations, development of,
            260–61
    health and development, 263–67
        cognitive development, 264
        exercise, 267
        internal states, communication of,
            265–66
        motor development, 263
        social development, 264, 267
    infancy, 125–41
        brain, 134, 139–40
        cephalocaudal pattern, 133
        fine motor development, 134–35, 136
        gross motor development, 134, 136
        proximodistal pattern, 133
        reflexes, 125–27
        rhythmic motor behavior, 137–39
        states, 128–29, 131
    middle/late childhood, 349–51
        body builds, types of, 349
        health and fitness, 350–51
        physical skills, 350
        sensory development, 350
        Type A behavior, 350–51, 352
        Type B behavior, 351
Piaget, J., profile of, 40–41
Piaget's theory, 53, 55–57, 59–60, 168–73
    accommodation in, 57, 59
    assimilation in, 57
    class inclusion reasoning, 280–81

concrete operational thought, 56, 359–60
    classification, 360
    conservation, 359
    constraints on, 360
    operations in, 359–60
and education, 360–61
equilibration in, 59
formal operational thought, 57, 522–29
    abstractness, 522–23
    early/late formal operational thought,
        528–29
    hypothetical-deductive reasoning,
        523–24
    idealism, 523
    individual differences, 529
moral development
    imminent justice, 336
    moral autonomy, 336
    moral realism, 336
neo-Piagetian critiques, 361–63
object permanence, 172–73
    criticism of concept, 173
    stages of, 172
organization in, 59
play, role of, 314, 318
preoperational thought, 55, 269–77
    animism, 274–75
    criticisms of concept, 276–77
    egocentrism, 270, 274
    intuitive thought, 275–76
    operations in, 269–70
    symbolic function substage, 270
schema in, 168
sensorimotor development, 55, 168–71
    internalization of schemes, 171
    primary circular reactions, 170
    secondary circular reactions, 170–71
    simple reflexes, 170
    tertiary circular reactions, 171
symbol in, 171
Pictorial Scale of Perceived Competence and
        Social Acceptance for Young
        Children, 463
Piers-Harris Scale, 462, 463
Pituitary gland, 508
Placenta, 96
Play
    assessment measures and, 319
    and cognition, 320
    developmental changes in, 316, 319
    early childhood, 314–20
    functions of, 314
    and language development, 320
    play behavior, categories of, 318–19
    play therapy, 314
    ritualized interchanges, 316–17

types of, 315–17
    associative play, 316
    cooperative play, 316
    onlooker play, 315
    parallel play, 316
    pretend play, 317, 319
    solitary play, 315
    unoccupied play, 315
Pleasure principle, 43
Polygenic inheritance, 88
Popular children, 445
Pragmatics, 185
    adolescence, 526
    development in early childhood, 286–87
Precipitate, childbirth, 108
Preference, 124
Prenatal development, 15, 92–106
    conception, 92–95
        cleavage divisions, 94
        in-vitro fertilization, 94–95
        zygote period, 94
    effect of drugs, 104–6
        alcohol, 104–5
        cigarette smoking, 106
        thalidomide, 104
    embryonic period, 96–97
        cell layers, development, 96
        organogenesis, 96
        placenta/umbilical cord/amnion, 96
    fetal period, 97–98
    germinal period, 95
    and maternal age, 102–3
        adolescent mothers, 102–3
        thirties and over, 103
    and maternal disease, 102
        herpes simplex virus, 102
        rubella, 102
        syphilis, 102
    and maternal emotions/stress level,
        103–4
    and maternal nutrition, 103
    teratology, 100, 101
    See also Childbirth.
Preoperational thought, 55, 269–77
    animism, 274–75
    criticisms of concept, 276–77
    egocentrism, 270, 274
    intuitive thought, 275–76
    operations in, 269–70
    symbolic function substage, 270
Pretend play, 317, 319
Preterm infants, 111, 113, 114–15, 116
    conclusions related to, 114–15
    differences, mother/child interaction, 116
    time factors, 111, 113

Primary circular reactions, 170
Primary process thinking, 43
Project Head Start, 13
Projection, 45
Prosocial behavior, television viewing, 324
Proximodistal pattern, 133
Psychoanalytic theories, 42–53, 54
　attachment, 216
　Erikson's theory, 50–52
　Freudian theory, 42–50
　strengths/weaknesses of, 52–53
　view of child, 11, 12
　See also specific theories.
Psychosexual stages
　anal stage, 47
　Electra complex, 48
　genital stage, 49
　latency stage, 49
　Oedipal complex, 42, 46
　oral stage, 47
　phallic stage, 47–48
　See also Freudian theory.
Puberty, 506–8
　definition of, 507–8
　menarche, 506–7
　on-time/off-time, 518–21
　See also Physical development,
　　adolescence.
Punishment, Skinner's theory, 66

Q

Qualitative change, as research issue, 19
Quasi-experimental strategy, 31
Questionnaires/surveys, 27

R

Raven Progressive Matrices Test, 396
Reaction formation, 45
Reaction range, 88–89
Reading, 409–11
　ABC method, 411
　phonics method, 411
　stages in learning of, 409–10
　whole-word method, 411
Reality principle, 44
Reasoning, hypothetical-deductive reasoning,
　523–24
Recasting, language acquisition, 5
Reciprocal determinism, 67
Reciprocal socialization, 211
Reflexes (infant), 125–27, 170
　crying, 127
　moro reflex, 125
　smiling, 127
　sucking reflex, 126–27

Regression, 45
Rehearsal, memory, 365
Reinforcement, 66
Rejected children, 445–46
Relationships of child
　and attachment, 221, 224
　and mother/child interaction, 214
　See also Peer relations.
REM sleep, infancy, 129
Renaissance, view of child, 11
Repression, 45
Reproduction, genes, 86–87
Research strategies
　correlational strategy, 32
　cross-sectional designs, 33
　experimental strategy, 30–31
　longitudinal designs, 33
　quasi-experimental strategy, 31
　sequential designs, 33–34
Resilient children, 492
　middle/late childhood, 441–44
Retrieval, memory, 366
Rhythmic motor behavior
　and blind infants, 138–39
　infancy, 137–39
　rhythmic stereotypes, 138
Ritualized interchanges, 316–17
Rubella, prenatal development, 102

S

Sarcasm, adolescence, and language
　development, 527–28
Satire, adolescence, and language
　development, 525
Schema, in Piaget's theory, 168
School influences
　achievement, 428–29
　adolescence, 544–45, 568–76
　　after-school needs, 575–76
　　community context, 573
　　curriculum, 572
　　effective schools, characteristics of,
　　　570–71
　　function of schools controversy, 568–
　　　70
　　leadership, 572
　　organization of schools and, 571, 573
　　school climate, 572
　　transition to middle/junior high
　　　school, 573–75
　middle/late childhood, 452–60
　　Aptitude-Treatment Interaction
　　　(ATI), 455–56
　　ethnicity factors, 457–58
　　open classrooms, 453–54, 456
　　social class considerations, 457
School-related problems
　middle/late childhood, 489, 492
　underachievement, 491–92

Scripts, 371–72, 373–75
　development of, 371–72
Secondary circular reactions, 170–71
Secure attachment, 219, 220, 222–23
Self-assertion, and sex roles, 468–69, 475
Self-concept
　early childhood, 327–29
　　global self-concept, 327
　　humanistic view, 327
　　"I" and "me," 327, 328
　　implications in memory research,
　　　328–29
　　internal state, communication of,
　　　265–66
　　phenomenological view, 327
　　private self, sense of, 329
　　self as knower, 328
　　self-generation, 328
　　self-reference, 328
　infancy, 237–38
　middle/late childhood, 460–66
　　changes in, 460–61
　　measurement of, 462–63
　　perspective taking, 461–62
　　self-esteem, 462
　　social competence, 464–66
　　See also Identity; Sex role development.
Self-control
　delay of gratification, 423–24
　infancy, 241, 243
　　age factors, 241
　　neurophysiological/sensorimotor
　　　modulation, 241
　resisting temptation, 338–39
Self-esteem
　adolescent girls, 519–20
　middle/late childhood, 462
　Self-Esteem Inventory, 462
Self-stimulation, adolescence, 514
Semantic elaboration, memory, 365
Semantics, 185
　development in early childhood, 286
Semiotic function, 320
Sensation
　meaning of, 141
　See also Perceptual/sensory development.
Sensorimotor development, 55, 168–71
　infancy
　　internalization of schemes, 171
　　primary circular reactions, 170
　　secondary circular reactions, 170–71
　　simple reflexes, 170
　　tertiary circular reactions, 171
　middle/late childhood, 350
　See also Perceptual/sensory development.
Sensory dimensions, 150, 153
Separation-individuation, 238–39
Sequential designs, 33–34

Sex differences
  middle/late childhood, 470–72
  moral development, 481–82
Sex hormones, 508–11
Sex-linked genes, 88
Sex role development
  early childhood, 329–36
    age factors, 335
    biological influences, 329–30
    cognitive factors, 330–31
    environmental influences, 331–35
    gender-deviance, 334–35
    language, role of, 331, 332–33
    parent-child relationships and, 331
    peer influences, 332
    teacher influences, 334
  middle/late childhood, 466–75
    and achievement, 472–75
    androgyny, 467–69
    competence and, 467–69
    masculinity/femininity, 466–67
    sex differences, 470–72
    sex-role stereotypes, 469–70
Sex-role stereotypes, middle/late childhood, 469–70
Sexual fantasies, adolescence, 514
Sexual maturation
  in boys, 513–14
  heterosexual behavior, 515–16
  homosexual behavior, 514
  self-stimulation, 514
  sexual fantasies, 514
Shaping/reinforcement, language acquisition, 186
Short-term memory, 362–63
Sibling relationships, 303–5
  birth order, 305
  influence of, 303–4
  sibling rivalry, 304
  siblings as models/teachers, 305
  and social development, 231
Sign stimuli, 70
Simple reflexes, 170
Situational influences, attachment, 220–21
Skinner's theory, 65–66
  behavior modification and, 66
  operant conditioning, 65–66
  punishment, 66
  reinforcement, 66
Sleeping-waking cycle
  REM sleep, 129
  time factors, 128
Smell, 152
Smiling, 127
  reflexive smile, 127
  social smile, 127
Social class
  effect on intelligence, 401
  effect on schooling, 457

Social cognition, 446, 449
  adolescence, 529–34, 556
    egocentrism, 529, 531–32
    implicit personality theory, 532
    social monitoring, 533–34
  social information processing, 446
  social knowledge, 446
Social comparison, adolescence, 562
Social competence, 464–66
  assessment of, 465–66
  definition of, 464–65
Social conventional reasoning, moral reasoning, 484
Social desirability, 27
Social development
  biological influences, 207–8
  day care, 233–34
  and family processes, 210–14
    influences on outside relationships, 214
    marital relationship and, 213
    molar exchanges, 211–12
    reciprocal socialization, 211
    social mold theories, 211
  health and, 264, 267
  peer influences, 232, 310
  sibling influences, 231
  sociocultural influences, 208–9
  See also Attachment.
Social intelligence, 396–97
Social learning theory
  attachment, 216–17
  modeling/imitation, 68
  moral behavior, 338, 339
  reciprocal determinism, 67
Social mold theories, 211
Social monitoring, adolescence, 533–34
Social processes, 18
Social smile, 127
Societalism
  and adolescence, 5–6
  moral development, 484
Sociocultural influences, social development, 208–9
Solitary play, 315, 319
SOMPA, 396
Spatial relations
  development of, physical development, 260–61
  egocentric frame of reference, 148–49
  objective frame of reference, 148, 149
Spontaneous recovery, 163
S-S learning, 162
Stages of development, as research issue, 19–20
Standardized tests, 27, 30
  observation methods, 27, 30
Stanford Binet Intelligence Test, 27
State anxiety, 421

States, 128–29, 131
  Brazelton Neonatal Behavioral Assessment Scale, 131
  classification of, 128
  eating behavior, 131
  sleeping-waking cycle, 128–29
Stepfamilies, 443–44
Stereotyping, adolescents, 505
Stimulus substitution theory, 163
Storm/stress view, adolescence, 503–4, 505
Stress, in pregnancy, 103–4
Structure of intellect model, 393–94
  operations/contents/products in, 394
Sucking reflex, 126–27
  nonnutritive sucking, 127
Sudden infant death syndrome (SIDS), 106
Suicide
  causes of, 612
  prevalence of, 609
  prevention of, 612
  sex differences, 609
Superego, 44
Surveys/questionnaires, 27
Syllogisms, 282
  reasoning, assessment of, 282–83
Symbolic function substage, 270
Symbols, in Piaget's theory, 171
Syntax, 184
  development in early childhood, 284–85
Syphilis, prenatal development, 102
Systematic observation, 25–26
  laboratory settings, 26
  naturalistic observations, 26

T

Tabula rasa, 11
Taste, 152
Teacher influences
  achievement, 429
  middle/late childhood
    Erikson's view, 455
    traits of teacher and, 454, 456
  sex role development, 334
Telegraphic speech, 200
Television viewing
  commercials, 324
  early childhood, 320–25
  exposure of child, statistical information, 322–23
  formal features of, 324–25
  functions of television, 321
  and social behavior, 323–24
    aggression, 323
    prosocial behavior, 324
    social context of viewing, 324

Temperament
    and attachment, 224
    mother/infant patterns, 225
Tertiary circular reactions, 171
Thalidomide, prenatal development, 104
Touch, 152–53
Trait anxiety, 421
Transactive discussion, moral development,
    480–81
Trophoblast, 95
Trust
    infancy, 237
    versus mistrust, 50–51
Twentieth century, view of child, 11–13
Twins, monozygotic/dizygotic, 90
Twin studies, 90
Two-factor theory, intelligence, 393
Two-word utterances, 200
Type A behavior, 350–51, 352
Type B behavior, 351

U

Umbilical cord, 96
Unconditioned response (UCR), 162
Unconditioned stimulus (US), 162
Underachievement, 491–92
Unemployment, adolescence, 537
Unoccupied play, 315

V

Validity, 394
    criterion validity, 394
Vicarious learning, 68
Visual perception, 141–49
    color perception, 145
    depth perception, 146–47
    face perception, 146
    object perception, 145–46
    spatial relations, frames of reference,
      148–49

    visual accommodation, 144
    visual acuity, 144–45
    visual preferences, 144

W

Wechsler Scales, 391
Wernicke's area, 187
Working mothers, 306–7
Writing, 407, 409
    evolution of, 409
    writing systems, 407
Written language, adolescence, language
    development, 525–26

Z

Zygote, 87, 94
    and conception, 92–95
    implantation, 95